GATEWAYS TO
WORLD LITERATURE

VOLUME 2

The Seventeenth Century to Today

DAVID DAMROSCH (Harvard University)

His books include *The Narrative Covenant: Transformations of Genre in the Growth of Biblical Literature* (1987), *Meetings of the Mind* (2000), *What Is World Literature?* (2003), and *How to Read World Literature* (2009). He has been president of the American Comparative Literature Association (2001–2003) and is founding general editor of *The Longman Anthology of British Literature* (1998; fifth edition, 2012).

GATEWAYS TO
WORLD LITERATURE

VOLUME 2

The Seventeenth Century to Today

David Damrosch
General Editor

PEARSON

Boston Columbus Indianapolis New York San Francisco Upper Saddle River
Amsterdam Cape Town Dubai London Madrid Milan Munich Paris Montreal Toronto
Delhi Mexico City São Paulo Sydney Hong Kong Seoul Singapore Taipei Tokyo

Editor-in-Chief: *Joseph Terry*
Development Editor: *Erin Reilly*
Editorial Assistant: *Kelly Carroll*
Executive Marketing Manager: *Joyce Nilsen*
Senior Supplements Editor: *Donna Campion*
Production Manager: *Ellen MacElree*
Project Coordination, Text Design, and Page Makeup: *PreMediaGlobal, Inc.*
Senior Design Manager/Cover Designer: *John Callahan*
Cover Image: *Copyright © Jose Antonio Sanchez/Shutterstock*
Senior Manufacturing Buyer: *Dennis J. Para*
Printer and Binder: *RR Donnelley/Crawfordsville*
Cover Printer: *Lehigh-Phoenix Color/Hagerstown*

For permission to use copyrighted material, grateful acknowledgment is made to the copyright holders on page 1029–1031, which are hereby made part of this copyright page.

Library of Congress Cataloging-in-Publication Data

Gateways to world literature / David Damrosch, general editor.
    p. cm.
  Includes bibliographical references and index.
  ISBN 978-0-205-78711-1 (v. 2)
  1. Literature—Collections.   2. Literature—History and criticism.   I. Damrosch, David.
PN6014.G28 2012
808.8—dc23

                                             2011032685

3 4 5 6 7 8 9 10—DOC—15 14

www.pearsonhighered.com

ISBN–13: 978-0-205-78711-1
ISBN–10:   0-205-78711-8

contents

CONTENTS

list of illustrations

Our world today is both expanding and growing smaller at the same time. Expanding, through a tremendous increase in the range of cultures that actively engage with each other; and yet growing smaller as well, as people and products surge across borders in the process known as globalization. This double movement creates remarkable opportunities for cross-cultural understanding, as well as new kinds of tensions, miscommunications, and uncertainties. Both the opportunities and the uncertainties are amply illustrated in the changing shape of world literature. A generation ago, when the term "world literature" was used in North America, it largely meant masterworks by European writers from Homer onward, together with a few favored North American writers, heirs to the Europeans. Today, however, it is generally recognized that Europe is only part of the story of the world's literatures, and only part of the story of North America's cultural heritage. An extraordinary range of exciting material is now in view, from the earliest Sumerian lyrics inscribed on clay tablets to the latest Kashmiri poetry circulated on the Internet. Many new worlds—and newly visible *older* worlds of classical traditions around the globe—await us today.

How can we best approach such varied materials from so many cultures? Can we deal with this embarrassment of riches without being overwhelmed by it, and without merely giving a glancing regard to less familiar traditions? This anthology has been designed to help readers successfully navigate "the sea of stories"—as Salman Rushdie has described the world's literary heritage. This preface will outline the ways we've gone about this challenging, fascinating task.

Connecting Distinctive Traditions

Works of world literature engage in a double conversation: with their culture of origin and with the varied contexts into which they travel away from home. To look broadly at world literature is therefore to see patterns of difference as well as points of contact and commonality. The world's disparate traditions have developed very distinct kinds of literature, even very different ideas as to what should be called "literature" at all. Beyond our immediate groupings, our overall selections have been made with an eye to fostering connections across time and space. We have worked to create an exceptionally coherent and well-integrated presentation of an extraordinary variety of works from around the globe, from the dawn of writing to the present. Recognizing that different sorts of works have counted as literature in differing times and places, we have taken an inclusive approach, centering on poems, plays, and fictional narratives but also including selections from rich historical, religious, and philosophical texts. We present many complete masterworks, including Molière's *Tartuffe,* Voltaire's *Candide,* Conrad's *Heart of Darkness,* and Kafka's *The Metamorphosis*, and we have extensive, teachable selections from such long works as Cao Xueqin's *Story of the Stone,* Goethe's *Faust,* and Naguib Mahfouz's *Arabian Nights and Days. Gateways to World Literature* retains a global focus while concentrating on the major works that are essential to a single-semester course.

Along with these major selections we continue to present a great array of shorter works, some of which have been known only to specialists and only now are entering into world literature. It is our experience as readers and as teachers that the established classics themselves can best be understood when they're set in a varied literary landscape. Nothing is included here, though, simply to make a point: whether world-renowned or recently rediscovered, these are compelling works to read. Throughout our work on this book, we've tried to be highly inclusive in principle and yet carefully selective in practice, avoiding tokenism and also its inverse, the piling up of an unmanageable array of heterogeneous material. If we've succeeded as we hope, the result will be coherent as well as capacious, substantive as well as stimulating.

Aids to Understanding

A major emphasis of our work has been to introduce each culture and each work to best effect. Each major period and section of the anthology, each grouping of works, and each individual author has an introduction by a member of our editorial team. Our goal has been to write introductions informed by deep knowledge worn lightly. Neither talking down to our readers nor overwhelming them with masses of unassimilable information, our introductions don't seek to "cover" the material but instead try to uncover it, to provide ways in and connections outward. Similarly, our footnotes and glosses are concise and informative, rather than massive or interpretive. Timelines, maps, and pronunciation guides throughout the anthology all aim to foster an informed and pleasurable reading of the works.

Going Further

Gateways to World Literature makes connections beyond its covers as well as within them. Bibliographies at the end of the volume point the way to historical and critical readings for students wishing to go into greater depth for term papers. The website for the text offers practice quizzes, an interactive timeline, a searchable glossary of literary terms, audio pronunciation guides, and many more resources. Finally, an extensive instructor's manual is available to adopters at www.pearsonhighered.com.

We hope that the results of our work on this project will be as enjoyable to use as the book has been to create. We welcome you now inside our pages.

David Damrosch

acknowledgments

In the extended process of planning and preparing this anthology, the editors have been fortunate to have the support, advice, and assistance of many people. Our editor, Joe Terry, and our publisher, Roth Wilkofsky, have supported our project in every possible way and some seemingly impossible ones as well, helping us produce the best possible book despite all challenges to budgets and well-laid plans in a rapidly evolving field. Their associates, Erin Reilly and Kelly Carroll, have shown unwavering enthusiasm in developing the book and its related supplements.

Gateways to World Literature is largely indebted to the editorial team of the *Longman Anthology of World Literature:* April Alliston, Marshall Brown, Page duBois, Sabry Hafez, Ursula K. Heise, Djelal Kadir, David Pike, Sheldon Pollack, Bruce Robbins, Haruo Shirane, Jane Tylus, and Pauline Yu.

We are grateful for the guidance of the many reviewers who advised us on the creation of this first edition of *Gateways* and our other World literature volumes, in their many incarnations: Adetutu Abatan (Floyd College); Roberta Adams (Fitchburg State College); Magda al-Nowaihi (Columbia University); Kyoka Amano (University of Indianapolis); Nancy Applegate (Floyd College); Susan Atefat-Peckham (Georgia College and State University); Evan Balkan (CCBC-Catonsville); Charles Bane (University of Central Arkansas); Michelle Barnett (University of Alabama, Birmingham); Colonel Bedell (Virginia Military Institute); Thomas Beebee (Pennsylvania State University); Paula Berggren (Baruch College); Mark Bernier (Blinn College); Ronald Bogue (University of Georgia); Laurel Bollinger (University of Alabama in Huntsville); Ashley S. Bonds (Copiah-Lincoln Community College); Theodore Bouabre (Jackson State University); Debra Taylor Bourdeau (Kennesaw State University); Terre Burton (Dixie State College); Patricia Cearley (South Plains College); Raj Chekuri (Laredo Community College); Sandra Clark (University of Wyoming); Maren Clegg-Hyer (Valdosta State University); Thomas F. Connolly (Suffolk University); Vilashini Cooppan (Yale University); Bradford Crain (College of the Ozarks); Robert W. Croft (Gainesville College); Patsy J. Daniels (Jackson State University); Frank Day (Clemson University); Michael Delahoyde (Washington State University); Elizabeth Otten Delmonico (Truman State University); Jo Devine (University of Alaska Southeast); Brian Doherty (University of Texas–Austin); Gene Doty (University of Missouri–Rolla); Jennifer Duncan (Chattagnooga State Technical Community College); James Earle (University of Oregon); Ed Eberhart (Troy University); R. Steve Eberly (Western Carolina University); Khalil Elayan (Kennesaw State University); Walter Evans (Augusta State University); Fidel Fajardo-Acosta (Creighton University); Gene C. Fant (Union University); Mike Felker (South Plains College); Kathy Flann (Eastern Kentucky University); Janice Gable (Valley Forge Christian College); Stanley Galloway (Bridgewater College); Doris Gardenshire (Trinity Valley Community College); Diana C. Gingo (Uniersity of Texas–Dallas); Jonathan Glenn (University of Central Arkansas); Kyle Glover (Lindenwood University); Lauri Goodling (Georgia Perimeter College); Michael Grimwood (North Carolina State University); Dean Hall (Kansas State University); Dorothy Hardman (Fort Valley State University); Katona D. Hargrave (Troy University); Joel Henderson (Chattanooga State Technical College); Nainsi J. Houston (Creighton University); Elissa Heil (University of the Ozarks); David Hesla (Emory University); Susan Hillabold (Purdue University North Central); Karen Hodges (Texas Wesleyan); David Hoegberg (Indiana University-Purdue University–Indianapolis); Sheri Hoem (Xavier University); Michael Hutcheson (Landmark College); Mary Anne Hutchinson (Utica College); Raymond Ide (Lancaster Bible College); James Ivory (Appalachian State University); Craig Kallendorf (Texas A & M University); Ernest N. Kaulbach (University of Texas–Austin); Bridget Keegan (Creighton

University); Steven Kellman (University of Texas–San Antonio); Hans Kellner (North Carolina State University); Roxanne Kent-Drury (Northern Kentucky University); Robert M. Kirschen (University of Nevada–Las Vegas); Barry Kitterman (Austin Peay State University); Susan Kroeg (Eastern Kentucky University); Tamara Kuzmenkov (Tacoma Community College); Marta Kvande (Valdosta State University); Jennifer Lawrence (Georgia State University); Heather Levy (University of Texas–Arlington); Patricia Lonchair (University of the Incarnate Word); Robert Lorenzi (Camden County College–Blackwood); David Lowery (Jones County Junior College); Mark Mazzone (Tennessee State University); David McCracken (Coker College); Judith Broome Mesa-Pelly (Austin Peay State University); George Mitrenski (Auburn University); J. Hunter Morgan (Glenville State College); Wayne Narey (Arkansas State University); James Nicholl (Western Carolina University); Roger Osterholm (Embry-Riddle University); James W. Parins (University of Arkansas–Little Rock); Joe Pellegrino (Eastern Kentucky University); Linda Lang-Peralta (Metropolitan State College of Denver); Sandra Petree (University of Arkansas); David E. Phillips (Charleston Southern University);Kevin R. Rahimzadeh (Eastern Kentucky University); Elizabeth L. Rambo (Campbell University); Melissa Rankin (University of Texas–Arlington); Terry Reilly (University of Alaska); Constance Relihan (Auburn University); Nelljean Rice (Coastal Carolina University); Gavin Richardson (Union University); Colleen Richmond (George Fox University); Elizabeth M. Richmond-Garza (University of Texas–Austin); Gretchen Ronnow (Wayne State University); Joseph Rosenblum (University of North Carolina at Greensboro); John Rothfork (West Texas A & M University); Elise Salem-Manganaro (Fairleigh Dickinson University); David P. Schenck (University of South Florida); Daniel Schierenbeck (Central Missouri State University); Asha Sen (University of Wisconsin Eau Claire); Richard Sha (American University); Edward Shaw (University of Central Florida); Jack Shreve (Allegany College of Maryland); Stephen Slimp (University of West Alabama); Jimmy Dean Smith (Union College); Gabriele Ulrike Stauf (Georgia Southwestern State University); Floyd C. Stuart (Norwich University); Barbara Szubinska (Eastern Kentucky University); Eleanor Sumpter-Latham (Central Oregon Community College); Ron Swigger (Albuquerque Technical Vocational Institute); Barry Tharaud (Mesa State College); Theresa Thompson (Valdosta State College); Douglass H. Thomson (Georgia Southern University); Teresa Thonney (Columbia Basin College); Charles Tita (Shaw University); Tomasz Warchol (Georgia Southern University); Scott D. Vander Ploeg (Madisonville Community College); Marian Wernicke (Pensacola Junior College); Sally Wheeler (Georgia Perimeter College); Nancy Wilson (Texas State University); Sallie Wolf (Arapahoe Community College); R. Paul Yoder (University of Arkansas–Little Rock); Racheal Yeatts (University of North Texas); Dede Yow (Kennesaw State University); and Jianqing Zheng (Mississippi Valley State University).

It has been a great pleasure to work with all these colleagues both at Longman and at schools around the country. This book exists for its readers, whose reactions and suggestions we warmly welcome, as *Gateways to World Literature* moves out into the world.

GATEWAYS TO
WORLD LITERATURE

VOLUME 2

The Seventeenth Century to Today

The Age of the Enlightenment

LE ROY DE FRANCE.
l'Homme immortel Chef de la S.te Ligue.

Mon soleil par sa force éclaira l'heretique.
Il chassa tout d'un coup les brouillards de Calvin:
Non pas par un Zele divin,
Mais a fin de cacher ma fine Politique.

Anonymous drawing of Louis XIV as the "Sun King." The verses below the image are a masterpiece of propaganda, describing the French king's conservative Counter-Reformation policy, reversing earlier religious tolerance in the new terms of the Enlightenment: the power of Louis's "sun" will enlighten heretics, evaporating the mists of John Calvin's Protestant teachings—not because of any religious zeal, but to conceal his subtle political strategy.

THE MIDDLE DECADES OF THE 1600s MARKED A TIME OF TRANSITION IN MANY PARTS OF THE WORLD. The Manchu dynasty came to power in China in 1644 and continued to rule the world's most populous country until 1912. In Japan, the Tokugawa clan of warlords, or shoguns, had begun to establish themselves in 1600; they cemented their control over the country in the next few decades. By mid-century they had succeeded in their ambition of closing Japan to outside influence, and after 1641 the sole foreign presence in Japan was a small Dutch trade mission confined to an island in Nagasaki Harbor—a situation that wouldn't change for over two hundred years. Both local and colonial rule began to assume new forms in Africa and the Americas: the great Bambara kingdom was established in midcentury along the upper reaches of the Niger River, and in 1652 Dutch settlers founded a colony at Capetown in what would become the English colony of South Africa. While the Dutch gained in Africa, they lost in the Western hemisphere: in 1654 Portugal took back Brazil from them, and a decade later the English expelled them from their colony of New Amsterdam, renaming it New York.

Europe too saw sweeping changes during these years. A long period of conflict in and around Germany, the Thirty Years War, finally ended in 1648, while in France the "Sun King" Louis XIV ascended the throne at age five in 1643 and began to rule in his own right in 1661; he remained the dominant political figure of his era until his death in 1715, after a record-breaking reign of seventy-two years. Gathering the French nobility into the gilded cage of his lavish palace complex at Versailles, Louis proclaimed absolute authority granted by divine right, asserting "L'état, c'est moi"—"I am the state." The Mughal Empire reached its height under a similarly absolutist monarch, Aurangzeb (r. 1685–1707), who extended his realm to include most of India and what is now Pakistan. Yet neither monarch bequeathed a stable situation to his successors: Louis's unrestrained spending on frequent wars and on lavish palaces left France's treasuries depleted on his death, while his insistence on Catholicism as the sole permitted religion led to the departure of tens of thousands of French Protestants, many of them enterprising small manufacturers and artisans, seriously weakening the French economy. Growing popular discontent in France would lead to revolution by the end of the century. In India, Aurangzeb tried to unify his widened realm by making Islam the state religion and repressing the practice of Hinduism; his restless Hindu subjects repeatedly revolted and his sons fought each other, and the empire declined after his death.

The splendor of courts like Versailles in France, Saint Petersburg in Russia, and Delhi in India was underwritten by the growing economic contributions of traders and manufacturers, who provided new sources of wealth beyond the traditional base of peasant agriculture. A new "middle class" was growing up between the aristocracy and the peasantry, often congregating in towns and known on the Continent as bürger or bourgeois (from the German and French terms for "town"). The new bourgeoisie often favored self-government and flexibility over aristocratic authority, and they increasingly proposed that laws, not monarchs, should have the final say. As the philosopher John Locke wrote in 1690, "Wherever Law ends, Tyranny begins." Or as an antiroyal rebel, Richard Rumbold, declared in 1685, as he stood on the scaffold waiting to be executed: "I never could believe that Providence had sent a few men into the world, ready booted and spurred to ride, and millions ready saddled and bridled to be ridden."

Commerce and Industry

Some small countries, such as Holland and Switzerland, asserted their freedom by abolishing monarchy altogether and becoming republics. In England, the unpopular monarch Charles I was beheaded by Puritan rebels in 1649; though the monarchy was restored in 1660, Charles II and his successors were increasingly subject to parliamentary control. Elsewhere, monarchs such as Russia's Peter the Great prospered by working closely with the bourgeoisie to modernize agriculture and establish the rudiments of modern industry. In Persia, the ruler Karim Khan developed his capital of Shiraz as a commercial center accessible to the Persian Gulf and trade with India. A driving force in the changing expectations of middle-class subjects, in fact, was the opening up of the world through rapidly expanding travel and trade. Though the Dutch East India Company maintained only a tenuous foothold in Japan, it assumed greater and greater influence in Indonesia, while French and British trading companies jostled for influence in India. In 1661 the British East India Company took control of Bombay, and in 1690 the company founded the major city of Calcutta. Gradually the East India Company became the *de facto* ruler of much of the Indian subcontinent. Trade steadily increased as well between Europe and the Americas, which now provided not only gold and silver but also a growing bulk of goods like sugar, cotton, hides, and timber. England and other nations developed a further trade, in human bodies, to support these enterprises: the "triangular trade" of slaves from Africa to the Americas and of slave-produced sugar and cotton from the Americas to Europe, which in turn manufactured finished goods to sell back to Africa and the Americas.

This was a new sort of empire: developed and maintained less by governments and guns than by companies and invoices. As the Scottish economic theorist Adam Smith said in his 1776 book *The Wealth of Nations*: "To found a great empire for the sole purpose of raising up a people of customers, may at first sight appear a project fit for a nation of shopkeepers; but extremely fit for a nation whose Government is influenced by shopkeepers." Elsewhere in the world, too, there was a growing sense of social life as a changing and changeable reality, subject to personal initiative more than to inherited status or direct divine intervention. The writers of this era responded to these new circumstances in realistic accounts of the new social mobility and in fictional or literal travel narratives as well. Voltaire's comic hero Candide ventures from a Europe torn by war to South America, searching for happiness and security in what his teacher Pangloss asserts is "the best of all possible worlds." The great Japanese poet and traveler Matsuo Bashō sees travel as the condition of life itself, shared even by the passing seasons: "The months and days are the travelers of eternity. The years that come and go are also voyagers.... I too for years past have been stirred by the sight of a solitary cloud drifting with the wind to ceaseless thoughts of roaming."

Science and Technology

The growth of commerce and industry was fed by rapid developments in science and technology, and commerce in turn fed the advance of science. The scientific revolution inaugurated during the early modern period took on new force in the late seventeenth century. In a period of three years in the 1660s, for example,

England's Isaac Newton made three major discoveries: he formulated the theory of gravitation; determined that white light is composed of colored rays; and invented calculus. Far from resting on his laurels, Newton continued to press for new understanding. As he famously remarked,

> I do not know what I may appear in the world; but to myself I seem to have been only like a boy playing on the seashore, and diverting myself in now and then finding a smoother pebble or a prettier shell than ordinary, whilst the great ocean of truth lay all undiscovered before me.

Major practical advances in technology followed from the new research. The spinning and weaving of cloth, formerly laborious handwork, became mechanized with the invention of the flying shuttle in 1733 and the spinning jenny in 1764. The first modern factories were built, and their output grew enormously with the invention of the steam engine, perfected by James Watt in 1769. Steam power vastly multiplied the work that an individual could accomplish, and humanity seemed poised to rise above its traditional limits—literally so, when the Montgolfier brothers launched the first hot air balloon in France in 1783.

The rapidly increasing grasp of the laws of nature prompted major shifts in religious understanding. Many scientists—Newton included—saw their discoveries as illuminating God's sublime handiwork; as one early scientist, Sir Thomas Pope Blount, asserted in 1693, "Every flower of the field, every fiber of a plant, every particle of an insect, carries with it the impress of its Maker, and can—if duly considered—read us lectures of ethics or divinity." Others took a more skeptical view, and increasingly began to view religious beliefs as projections of human needs and understanding: as the French philosopher Montesquieu put it in 1721, "If triangles had a god, he would have three sides."

Increasingly the ideals of science and rational planning came to be applied to the social world as well as to the world of nature. In Europe, this broad movement became known as "the Enlightenment." By the late eighteenth century, Enlightenment ideas of political, economic, and intellectual liberty stimulated and shaped the revolutionary movements that led to America's declaration of independence from England and the French Revolution of 1789. The outlines of our modern world were beginning to emerge, along with the increasingly visible figure of the modern artist as a skeptical observer, independent of royal patronage or received ideas, even of received literary forms. Alexander Pope used the mock-epic to satirize English court culture, while Lady Mary Wortley Montagu used sharply pointed couplets to mock Jonathan Swift's own mockery of women. Everywhere the period's writers vanquished their enemies in print if not in fact: as Voltaire wrote to a friend late in life: "I have never made but one prayer to God, a very short one: 'O Lord, make my enemies ridiculous.' And God granted it."

The Enlightenment

France and England were the two primary poles generating the massive charge of intellectual and political energy that spread so much "light" in Europe and beyond. Many other countries contributed to the Enlightenment and experienced its profound influence, but in general all were responding to the social, scientific, industrial, and intellectual revolutions that accompanied the political ones in France and

England, the two most centralized and powerful nations in Europe at the time. What eighteenth-century philosophers themselves baptized as "the Enlightenment" was the continued trend in Europe, after the early modern wars of religion, to question received authority—religious, political, moral, and intellectual. Absolute, received authority was to be tempered or even replaced by the guidance of reason, understood as a faculty common to all humankind. Such questioning brought with it an increasing recognition that reason must also master the passions that drove the wars of religion by fostering religious tolerance alongside free intellectual experimentation and argument.

Many Enlightenment thinkers, from Locke and Leibniz in the late seventeenth century through Voltaire to Jean-Jacques Rousseau and the leaders of the American Revolution toward the end of the eighteenth century, adopted a stance of Christian theism as a solution to the fundamental tension between religious dogma and freethinking. Theism, as Leibniz put it, meant that, "We believe the Scriptures ... but reason controls our interpretation of them." More radical thinkers, such as David Hume, Denis Diderot, and William Godwin, rejected the authority of received religious doctrine altogether. As in the early modern period, religious reformation was tied to political revolution. Rousseau described the "social contract" as a bond willingly built up from below by individuals in need of mutual support, rather than imposed upon them from above. His concept crystallized the long-standing critique of monarchical rule by divine right that went back at least as far as Locke, and prepared the philosophical justification for the French Revolution a century after Locke. Rousseau's rather pessimistic outlook held that humankind had been happiest in a lost state of nature. The German philosopher Immanuel Kant's more optimistic view was more representative of the widespread Enlightenment belief in progress and the infinite perfectibility of mankind. It was the idea of fundamental human equality, most forcefully formulated by Rousseau and Kant, that gave rise to the concept of inalienable political rights upon which both the French and American Revolutions were based, and which still drives the civil rights movement in the United States and human rights activism around the world.

The opening up of the whole world, as it seemed to many Europeans, to the power of reason fostered an encyclopedic approach to knowledge. Diderot and D'Alembert's *Encylclopédie* (1751–1765) was only the most ambitious and influential of a long series of attempts to catalogue systematically the entirety of human knowledge and experience. In Britain, Samuel Johnson added his famous *Dictionary* (1755) to Chambers's *Cyclopaedia* (London, 1728), followed by the *Encyclopedia Britannica* (Edinburgh, 1768–1771). Modern readers may wonder how such sober reference books could once have been so revolutionary as to provoke attacks by the clergy and government censorship. The revolutionary aim of the *Encyclopédie* was the unification of knowledge centered around humankind rather than God. Its anatomical illustrations offended morality. Its description of non-Western cultures called European norms into question. Its explanations of recent scientific discoveries challenged traditional and religious beliefs. Even its detailed descriptions of industrial processes unveiled trade secrets closely guarded by guilds for centuries. But the most revolutionary aspect of encyclopedias and dictionaries was their widespread distribution in print.

If the Enlightenment was an age of revolution, it was so because all this burgeoning progress was not free simply to happen. When control was suddenly released or overcome, decadence, bloodshed, and new abuses of power often ensued. Literature played a crucial role in these revolutionary power struggles, often deployed directly as a weapon through a revival of the classical genre of satire. It is hard for readers of the twenty-first century to appreciate the power of satire in the eighteenth. Writing was dangerous, and therefore important. Royal spies filled court circles, salons, and coffeehouses, and opened private letters, trying to control the circulation of unpublished writings. The theater was such a good medium for Molière's social satire because during his time any material could be staged at least once—before the theater was shut down. A few satirists, such as Lady Mary Wortley Montagu, were aristocrats, but most were not: Molière and Voltaire in France, and in Britain Jonathan Swift and Alexander Pope, "the Wasp of Twickenham." They judged their targets by the measures of virtue and reason, showing shocking disrespect for social hierarchies. The upper classes weren't their only objects of derision; the satirists attacked vice and folly wherever they found it. And they found it so universally that Dr. Johnson wrote of Swift and Pope: "whoever should form his opinion of the age from their representation, would suppose them to have lived amidst ignorance and barbarity, unable to find among their contemporaries either virtue or intelligence, and persecuted by those that could not understand them."

It was during the Enlightenment that women in large numbers began reading and writing secular and imaginative literature in all genres—drama, poetry, letters. Above all, and increasingly as the period wore on, women employed the new experimental and popular genre of plausible prose fiction that came to be called the novel. Paradoxically, the very age that saw unprecedented access by women to literacy and publishing was also one that transformed the conventional European image of femininity from one of barely controlled sexual power and cunning into one of relatively desexualized passivity combined with a new moral rectitude. The long literary career of Eliza Haywood illustrates how rapidly and thoroughly the shift took hold: she began by publishing best-selling novels about dangerously desirous heroines such as "Fantomina" (1724), but then the success of Samuel Richardson's sentimental novels of the 1740s forced her to take a sudden turn to similarly domestic and sentimental fiction about passively virtuous heroines, in order to stay in business as a novelist.

Just as the characteristic concerns of the Enlightenment didn't emerge suddenly with the English Revolution in 1642, neither did they vanish with the French one in 1789. By the end of the Enlightenment period, political liberation was only just beginning in earnest, with the French and American Revolutions—for European men of property at least. It had scarcely begun for women of any class, and for slaves it was only a faint and distant glimmer of hope. Even for European men of the laboring classes, the famous battle cry of "liberty, equality, fraternity" referred to ideals that remained largely abstract. The struggles of all of these groups to realize the best promise of the Enlightenment would continue to gather force over the course of the nineteenth century, with the movements for the abolition of slavery, for women's education and suffrage, and for the liberation of workers from the new capitalist oppression—as analyzed by Karl Marx—that was fast replacing the feudal kind. For better and worse, most of the world is still deeply affected by Enlightenment ideas today. Wherever popular democracy and individual civil liberties are valued, or the scientific method and the technological advances

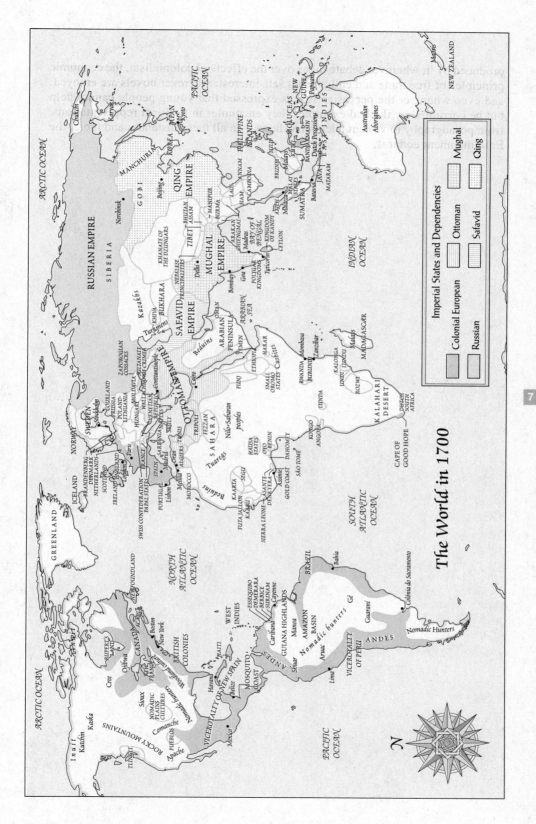

The World in 1700

Imperial States and Dependencies

- Colonial European
- Russian
- Ottoman
- Safavid
- Mughal
- Qing

ARCTIC OCEAN

GREENLAND

ICELAND

NORTH ATLANTIC OCEAN

NEWFOUNDLAND

BRITISH COLONIES

NEW FRANCE

CANADA

RUPERT'S LAND

Cree

Ojibwa

Inuit

Kutchin

Kaska

Tlingit

NOMADIC PLAINS CULTURES

Sioux

Comanche

Apache

ROCKY MOUNTAINS

Woodland Cultures

Boston

New York

Havana

WEST INDIES

HAITI

MOSQUITO COAST

Belize

Mexico

VICEROYALTY OF NEW SPAIN

PACIFIC OCEAN

ANDES

Lima

VICEROYALTY OF PERU

AMAZON BASIN

Nomadic Hunters

Shuar

Arauá

Carib ona

Manoa

GUIANA HIGHLANDS

ESSEQUIBO

DEMERARA

BERBICE

SURINAM

Cayenne

BRAZIL

Bahia

Gé

Guarani

Colônia do Sacramento

Nomadic Hunters

SOUTH ATLANTIC OCEAN

N

ICELAND

NORWAY

SWEDEN

Stockholm

DENMARK

SCOTLAND

IRELAND

ENGLAND

London

NETHERLANDS

BRANDENBURG

PRUSSIA

COURLAND

POLAND-LITHUANIA

Paris

FRANCE

SWISS CONFEDERATION

PAPAL STATES

SPAIN

Madrid

PORTUGAL

Lisbon

MOROCCO

Melilla

Oran

Bedouins

SARDINIA

NAPLES

SICILY

TUNIS

ALGIERS

TRIPOLI

FEZZAN

SAHARA

Tuaregs

KAARTA

Kasyi

SEGU

FUTA JALLON

SIERRA LEONE

ASANTE

DENKYERA

GOLD COAST

Assine

SÃO TOMÉ

OYO

DAHOMEY

BENIN

HAUSA STATES

Nilo-Saharan peoples

KONGO

ANGOLA

CAPE OF GOOD HOPE

CAPE SOUTH AFRICA

KALAHARI DESERT

Desert

HUNGARY

VENETIAN REPUBLIC

WALLACHIA

MOLDAVIA

Constantinople

OTTOMAN EMPIRE

SULTANATE OF CRIMEA

ZAPOROGIAN COSSACKS

Cairo

ARABIAN PENINSULA

OMAN

YEMEN

Bedouins

RED SEA

ETHIOPIA

HARAR

Cushites

SMALL OROMO STATES

FUNJ

RWANDA

BURUNDI

HINDA

Mombasa

Zanzibar

KALONGA

UNDI

Lundu

ROZWI

Malays

MADAGASCAR

INDIAN OCEAN

RUSSIAN EMPIRE

SIBERIA

Nerchinsk

GOBI

MANCHURIA

QING EMPIRE

Beijing

KHANATE OF THE DZUNGARS

Kazakhs

Turkmens

BUKHARA

KHIVA

SAFAVID EMPIRE

Delhi

MUGHAL EMPIRE

NEPALESE PRINCIPALITIES

TIBET

BHUTAN

ASSAM

MANIPUR

BURMA

ARAKAN

CHIENGMAI

Bombay

Goa

POLIGAR KINGDOMS

Madras

BAY OF BENGAL

KINGDOM OF KANDY

CEYLON

Tuticorin

LAOS

SIAM

ANNAM

CAMBODIA

PHILIPPINE ISLANDS

NEW GUINEA

Papuans

MOLUCCAS

CELEBES

BANDA

Batavia

JAVA

SUMATRA

BORNEO

BRUNEI

MALAY STATES

Malacca

Acheh

MATARAM

Dutch Possessions

EAST INDIES

Malays

Amboyna

PACIFIC OCEAN

JAPAN

Kyoto

KOREA

Chukchi

Koryaks

ARCTIC OCEAN

NEW ZEALAND

Maoris

Australian Aborigines

gradual one, in which debate focused on the effects of colonialism, the economic principles of free trade and protectionism, the skill-interested novel-readers and enjoyed and even whether the new ... expressed that young people ... help ... and became fashionable ... and amateur ... regions ... their philosophical ... in all ... Western and ... the Enlightenment could ...

produced by it; wherever debate rages over the effects of colonialism, the economic principles of free trade and enlightened self-interest; wherever novels are enjoyed; and even wherever the pervasive fear is expressed that young people cannot help but be corrupted by the bad examples they encounter in fictional representations, from pornography to violent television shows—in all these instances and more, the Enlightenment endures.

THE SEVENTEENTH AND EIGHTEENTH CENTURIES

YEAR	THE WORLD	LITERATURE
1600		
	1603 Death of Elizabeth I of England, accession of James I	1605, 1615 Cervantes, *Don Quixote*
	1605 Death of Akbar; Jahangir ascends Mughal throne	
	1607 British settlement of Virginia	
	1608–1648 Marquise de Rambouillet's "Blue Room," first important Parisian salon	
	1609 Tokugawa shogunate founded in Japan	
1610		
		1616 Death of Shakespeare
	1618 Bohemian revolt against Habsburgs initiates Thirty Years' War	
	1619 First African slaves taken to Virginia	
1620		
	1620 English Pilgrims begin migration to New England	
		1624 Babur, *Memoirs of Babur*
1630		
	1633 Tokugawa shoguns close Japan to foreigners	
	1634 First official meeting of the Académie Française	
		1637 Maria de Zayas, *Amorous and Exemplary Novellas*
1640		
		1641 René Descartes, *Meditations on First Philosophy;* Banarasidas, *Half a Life*
	1642 English Civil War begins; Tasman discovers New Zealand and Tasmania	
	1643 Shah Jahan rules much of India; Taj Mahal completed	
	1644 Manchu dynasty begins in China (to 1912)	
	1648 The Fronde, civil war in France; Treaty of Westphalia ends Thirty Years' War	
	1649 Execution of Charles I of England, which becomes a republic under Oliver Cromwell and Parliament	
1650		
		1651 Thomas Hobbes, *Leviathan*
	1652 Dutch establish colony in South Africa	
	1653 Louis XIV returns to Paris from exile with his powerful minister Cardinal Mazarin, ending the Fronde rebellion	1654–1660 Madeleine de Scudéry, *Clélie*
	1658 Oliver Cromwell dies	

continued

YEAR	THE WORLD	LITERATURE
1660	1660 Restoration of Charles II to the English throne; Royal Society founded; rise of Bambara kingdom on upper Niger River 1661 Louis XIV, aged 23, assumes the full government of France after the death of his protector Cardinal Mazarin and the arrest of his finance minister, Fouquet 1662 English Royal Society receives its charter from Charles II 1663 Brazil becomes Portuguese Viceroyalty 1664 England seizes New Amsterdam from Dutch, changes name to New York 1665 Last "Great Plague" in England 1666 Great Fire of London destroys the city, which is rebuilt on a neoclassical plan; Isaac Newton formulates the law of gravity	1660 Pierre Corneille, collected plays and discourses on the art of the theater 1662–1663 Molière, *The School for Wives* 1665 Katherine Philips, *Poems*; George Warren, *An Impartial Description of Surinam* 1667 John Milton, *Paradise Lost* 1668 Jean de la Fontaine, *Fables*
1670	1670 Hudson's Bay Company incorporated in London to conduct trade in North America	1678 Comtesse de Lafayette, *The Princess of Clèves*
1680	1683 Ottoman siege of Vienna fails after intervention of the Poles 1685 Death of Charles II of England, accession of James II; Louis XIV revokes the Edict of Nantes, ending tolerance for Protestants in France 1686 The English establish Calcutta as a factory and port settlement in Bengal 1688 "Glorious Revolution" in England: Mary, daughter of James II of England, and her spouse the Dutch Prince William of Orange oust her father in a bloodless coup 1689 Treaty of Nerchinsk between Russian and Qing Empires	1680 Unauthorized posthumous edition of the Earl of Rochester's poems 1686 Ihara Saikaku, *Life of a Sensuous Woman* 1687 Isaac Newton, *Principia Mathematica* 1688 Aphra Behn, *Oroonoko*; Ihara Saikaku, *Japan's Eternal Storehouse*
1690	1698 Omani Arabs capture Mombasa and Zanzibar in Africa	1690 John Locke, *Essay Concerning Human Understanding* 1694 *Dictionary* of the French Academy 1697 Charles Perrault, *Tales of Past Times, with Morals* (*Mother Goose Tales*); Pierre Bayle, *Historical and Critical Dictionary*

YEAR	THE WORLD	LITERATURE
1700	**1700** Charles II of Spain dies, leaving the kingdom to the French duke of Anjou	**1701** Mary Chudleigh, *The Ladies Defence*
	1702 War of Spanish Succession; Holy Roman Emperor Charles XII invades Poland; death of William III of England and accession of Queen Anne	
	1703 St. Petersburg founded by Czar Peter the Great, who has just visited Western Europe and vowed to modernize Russia	
	1704 English capture Gibraltar (in War of the Spanish Succession)	**1704–1717** Galland's French translation of *The Thousand and One Nights,* its first translation into a European language
	1707 United Kingdom links formerly separate kingdoms of England and Scotland; death of Aurangzeb in India, leading to the decline of the Mughal Empire; first pipe organ built by Gottfried Silbermann in Germany	
	1708 Robert Walpole, first to use title of Prime Minister, takes charge of the Whig government in London	
	1709 Technique for making Chinese porcelain first replicated in Europe, Meissen factory established the following year; modern piano invented in Padua by Bartolomeo Cristofori	
1710		**1710** Gottfried Wilhelm von Leibniz, *Theodicy*
	1712 German composer Georg Friedrich Händel moves permanently to London	**1712, 1717** Alexander Pope, *The Rape of the Lock*
	1713 Treaty of Utrecht ends the War of the Spanish Succession for Britain and the Netherlands: France cedes most Canadian holdings to Britain; Pope Clement XI condemns the powerful Jansenist sect as heretical	**1713** Anne Finch, Countess of Winchilsea, *Miscellaneous Poems on Several Occasions, Written by a Lady*
	1714 Death of Queen Anne and accession of George I of Great Britain; Tripoli becomes independent from the Ottoman Empire; France makes peace with Austria, Bavaria, and the Holy Roman Empire; Fahrenheit invents the mercury thermometer	
	1715 Death of Louis XIV; partisans of the exiled Stuart heir (Jacobites) rebel and are suppressed in Britain	
	1716 Ottoman Turks defeated by forces of the Holy Roman Empire at the Battle of Peterwardein	
	1717 France, Britain, and Holland form the Triple Alliance; Walpole resigns as prime minister of Great Britain	

continued

YEAR	THE WORLD	LITERATURE
	1718 Ottoman and Holy Roman Empires sign Treaty of Passarowitz; Triple Alliance becomes Quadruple Alliance when Holy Roman Emperor Charles VI joins it	1718, 1724 Comtesse de Lafayette, *The Countess of Tende* (published posthumously)
1720		
	1720 "South Sea Bubble" bursts in Britain, ruining many; Manchus seize control of Xinjiang	1721 Chikamatsu Mon'zaemon, *Love Suicides at Amijima;* Baron de Montesquieu, *Persian Letters*
	1722 Dutch East India Company founded by Holy Roman Emperor Charles VI	
	1723 French Regency ends with majority of Louis XV; Ottoman Empire attacks Persia	
	1724 Treaty of Constantinople: Russian and Ottoman Empires partition Persia	1724 Eliza Haywood, *Fantomina*
		1725, 1754 Marquise de Sévigné, *Correspondence* (written 1648–1696)
	1727 Oxygen isolated by Stephen Hales in England	1726 Jonathan Swift, *Gulliver's Travels; Dictionary* of the Spanish Academy
	1728 Bering Strait first explored by Europeans	1729 First secular Turkish literature published in Constantinople
1730		
	1730 Ottoman Emperor Achmet III deposed in favor of Mahmud I	
	1731 John Hadley invents the sextant, improving navigation	1732 Swift, "The Lady's Dressing Room"
	1733 War of the Polish Succession	1733–1734 Alexander Pope, *An Essay on Man*
		1734 Lady Mary Wortley Montagu, "The Reasons that Induced Doctor S. to Write a Poem called The Lady's Dressing Room"
		1735 Alexander Pope, *Epistle II: To a Lady (Of the Characters of Women)*
	1736 War between Ottoman, Holy Roman, and Russian Empires	
	1738 War of the Polish Succession ends	
	1739 Nadir Shah of Persia sacks Delhi; slave rebellion in South Carolina	
1740		
	1740 Holy Roman Emperor Charles VI dies; Frederick II the Great crowned king of Prussia; invading Silesia, he begins the War of the Austrian Succession	1740 Samuel Richardson, *Pamela*
	1742 Handel's *Messiah* first performed in Dublin	
	1746 Uprising in western Szechuan province, China; French conquer Madras, India	
	1747 Achmed Khan Abdali establishes kingdom of Afghanistan and invades India	1747 Françoise de Graffigny, *Letters from a Peruvian Woman*

YEAR	THE WORLD	LITERATURE
	1748 War of the Austrian Succession ends, confirming the taking of Silesia from Austria by Prussia, while Britain surrenders Asiento (Italy) to Spain	1748 Baron de Montesquieu, *The Spirit of the Laws*
1750		
	1750s Emergence of Wahhabi movement in Arabia	1750–1760 Cao Xueqin, *The Story of the Stone*
	1751 Chinese invade Tibet; Portugal and Spain divide their South American colonies by treaty	1751 First volume of Diderot's *Encyclopedia* published
	1752 Benjamin Franklin proves that lightning is electricity; start of Konbuang dynasty in Burma	
	1753 British Museum founded; Swedish Academy of Letters founded	
		1754 Etienne Bonnot de Condillac, *Treaty on the senses*
	1755 Lisbon earthquake kills 30,000–40,000 people	1755 Samuel Johnson, *Dictionary of the English Language*
	1756 Seven Years' War begins when Frederick the Great of Prussia invades Saxony; English lose settlement at Calcutta to the nawab of Bengal, suffering great loss of life in the "Black Hole of Calcutta"	
	1757 British regain Calcutta; start of British imperial rule in India	
	1758 Invention of the threshing machine	
		1759 Voltaire, *Candide*
		1759–1767 Laurence Sterne, *Tristram Shandy*
1760		
	1760s Start of Industrial Revolution, inventions of Hargreaves's "spinning jenny" in 1765 and Watt's improved steam engine in 1769 help to mechanize the textile industry	
	1760 George III succeeds George II as King of Great Britain	
	1762 Catherine the Great crowned Empress of Russia	1762 Jean-Jacques Rousseau, *The Social Contract*
	1763 Seven Years' War ends; France is awarded Guadeloupe, Martinique, and parts of Africa and India; Britain takes over Canada and Florida; Spain takes Cuba and the Philippines	1763 Lady Mary Wortley Montagu, *The Turkish Embassy Letters* (written 1716–1718)
	1764 Jesuits expelled from France	1764 Voltaire, *Philosophical Dictionary*; Horace Walpole, *The Castle of Otranto*
	1765 British East India Company wins control of Bengal and Bihar	
	1766 Britain occupies the Falkland Islands; hydrogen discovered by Henry Cavendish	
	1766–1769 Louis Antoine de Bougainville circumnavigates the world	

continued

YEAR	THE WORLD	LITERATURE
	1767 Jesuits expelled from Spain, Parma, and Sicily	
	1768–1771 Captain James Cook explores Australia and New Zealand	
1770	1770 The Boston Massacre; Spain seizes Falklands from Britain; famine in Bengal kills one-third of the population	1771 Louis Antoine de Bougainville, *Voyage around the World*
	1772 War between Russian and Ottoman Empires ends with First Partition of Poland; nitrogen discovered by Daniel Rutherford; Captain James Cook begins a three-year voyage of the South Seas	1772 Gotthold Lessing, *Emilia Galotti*
	1773 Boston Tea Party; Jesuit order abolished by Pope Clement XIV	
	1774 Louis XVI succeeds Louis XV in France; Joseph Priestley isolates oxygen; Karl Scheele identifies chlorine; Nguyen Anh becomes emperor of Vietnam	1774 Johann Wolfgang Goethe, *The Sufferings of Young Werther*
	1775 Start of American Revolution	1775 Pierre de Beaumarchais, *The Barber of Seville*
	1776 Declaration of Independence adopted by the Continental Congress in Philadelphia; first submarine, David Bushnell's *Turtle;* the following year he invents the torpedo	
	1778 War of the Bavarian Succession begins; hypnotism first used by Friedrich Mesmer in Paris	1778 Frances Burney, *Evelina*
	1779 Captain James Cook killed in Hawaii; First Kaffir War between Dutch Boer settlers and the Xhosa of South Africa	
1780	1780 Anti-Catholic "Gordon Riots" in England; waltz invented in Germany and Austria	
	1781 Continental Army defeats British at Yorktown, Virginia; Uranus, first planet discovered since antiquity, identified by William Herschel	1781 First Polish encyclopedia; Sauda, *Satires*
	1782 Irish gain legislative independence	1782 Pierre Choderlos de Laclos, *Les Liaisons dangereuses;* first volume of Jean-Jacques Rousseau's *Confessions*
	1783 Treaty of Versailles ends war between Britain, France, and Spain, recognizes American independence and extends borders of the United States as far as the Mississippi River and the Great Lakes; first demonstrations of the hot air balloon and the steamboat	

YEAR	THE WORLD	LITERATURE
	1784 Ottoman Empire cedes Crimea to Russians	1784 Immanuel Kant, "An Answer to the Question: What Is Enlightenment?"
		1785 Charles Wilkins translates the *Bhagavad Gita* into English (first translation of an important Sanskrit text into a European language); Ann Yearsley, *Poems, on Several Occasions*
	1786 Death of Frederick the Great of Prussia	1786 Robert Burns, *Poems Chiefly in the Scottish Dialect*; Ann Yearsley, *Poems, on Various Subjects*
	1787 Constitution of the United States of America; British begin to settle freed slaves in Sierra Leone	1787 Lorenzo Da Ponte and Wolfgang Amadeus Mozart, *Don Giovanni*
	1788 First British settlement in Australia	1789 Olaudah Equiano, *Interesting Narrative of the Life of Olaudah Equiano*
	1789 Declaration of the Rights of Man and Citizen adopted by the French National Assembly; storming of the Bastille political prison in Paris; Antoine Lavoisier creates first table of elements; start of French Revolution	1789–1792 Benedikte Naubert, *New German Folk Tales*
1790		
	1791 French National Assembly abolishes royal censorship; start of Haitian Revolution	
	1792 France declared a republic; Revolutionary Assembly legalizes divorce; Manchus invade Nepal	1792 Mary Wollstonecraft, *A Vindication of the Rights of Woman*
	1793 Execution of Louis XVI of France; the Louvre palace becomes a public art gallery; France at war against Britain, Holland, Spain, Portugal, Tuscany, and the Holy Roman Empire; Second Kaffir War between Boer settlers and Xhosa of South Africa	
	1794 Fall of Robespierre ends French "Reign of Terror"; Qajar Dynasty founded in Persia (to 1925); Eli Whitney invents the cotton gin in the United States	1794 Ann Radcliffe, *The Mysteries of Udolpho*
	1795 White Lotus Uprising in China; Mungo Park explores West Africa and River Niger	1795 Anna Letitia Barbauld, "The Rights of Woman"; Marquis de Sade, *Philosophy in the Boudoir*
	1796 Death of Russian Empress Catherine the Great; Dr. Edward Jenner introduces smallpox vaccine; first exhibition of paintings by J.M.W. Turner	1796 Denis Diderot, *Supplement to the Voyage of Bougainville* (written 1772)
	1798–1799 Napoleon's expedition to Egypt results in discovery of Rosetta Stone and naval defeat by British	1798 William Wordsworth and Samuel Taylor Coleridge, *Lyrical Ballads*
	1799 War of the Second Coalition (Great Britain, Portugal, and Naples, with the Holy Roman, Russian, and Ottoman Empires) against France, where the Directory Government is overthrown and Napoleon Bonaparte is named First Consul	

PRONUNCIATIONS:

Académie Française: ah-kah-day-MEE frahn-SEZ

l'Age des Lumières: LAHZH day leu-mee-AYR

d'Alembert: da-lahm-BAYR

Candide: kahn-DEED

Pierre Corneille: pee-AYR kohr-NEH

Denis Diderot: duh-NEE DEE-duh-ROH

Don Juan: don HWAHN

Fronde: FROND

François, duc de La Rochefoucauld: frahnh-SWAH deuk duh lah rohsh-foo-KOH

Gottfried Wilhelm von Leibniz: got-freed vil-helm fon LAIB-nits

Mazarin: MA-za-RANH

Molière: moh-LYEHR

philosophe: fee-loh-ZOF

privilège du roi: pree-vee-LEZH deu RWAH

quérelle des femmes: kay-rel day FUM

Marquise de Rambouillet: mahr-KEEZ duh RAHM-boo-YAY

Jean-Jacques Rousseau: zhahnh-ZHAHK roo-SOH

Versailles: vehr-SAI

JEAN-BAPTISTE POQUELIN [MOLIÈRE] ■ (1622–1673)

Molière's great ambition in life was to distinguish himself in the preeminent genre of the golden age of French literature: tragedy. He failed miserably—but just as his stage career seemed to be over for good, he made the king laugh. From that moment, he became one of the greatest French authors of all time by creating a new kind of comedy, which he elevated to the status of high literary art.

Jean-Baptiste Poquelin was born and raised to cover with silk damask the ornate gilded chairs on which the king sat with his court. His father and both grandfathers had amassed such a fortune in upholstery that by 1631 M. Poquelin senior was able to purchase the office of upholsterer-in-ordinary to the King. This meant access to court society and a hereditary monopoly for his eldest son, Jean-Baptiste, who was accordingly groomed to hobnob with the aristocracy through an elite education, including law school. His classical training at a Jesuit college known for freethinking nurtured his independence along with his interest in drama (he is said to have memorized all the Latin comedies of Terence—which owed much to ancient mime show situations that survived in the *commedia dell'arte* so popular in Molière's Paris). Upon graduation at twenty-one he replaced his father in the service of Louis XIII for one year. That was enough. Adopting the stage name "Molière" in 1643, he abandoned the family business to run off to the theater, becoming a founding member of the "Illustre Théâtre." Funded by the Béjart theatrical family and managed by the young actress Madeleine Béjart, this upstart company staged the great neoclassical tragedies in a converted tennis court. The venture failed disastrously. Molière's stutter was no obstacle in *commedia dell'arte* mime, but was a serious one to his ambition as a tragic actor. Within two years, bankrupt, he was thrown into debtor's prison. Released when his father paid off his debts, he fled Paris with other members of the original troupe to tour the southern provinces for the next thirteen years as its star, alongside Madeleine as business manager and female lead. By 1650 he was directing the company, and began writing original plays for it.

Molière's company was at last invited back to Paris in 1658 to perform for the young king Louis XIV at the Louvre. Their production of Corneille's tragedy *Nicomède* did not impress, and Molière was judged a mediocre actor. He snatched victory from the jaws of defeat by persuading the king, in a witty closing speech, to allow his company to close by presenting his original farce *The Doctor in Love,* in which he played the lead. The king couldn't stop laughing, so his courtiers all tittered along with him. The result was that the company was allowed to share a royal theater with an Italian company of *commedia dell'arte* mimes led by the renowned "Scaramouche" (Tiberio Fiorelli), who had been Molière's drama teacher, and who left the space entirely to his former student the following year. That year Molière came through with his first major success, *Les Précieuses ridicules* (1659), in which he satirized ladies who imitated the linguistic and literary pretensions, rarefied manners, and ideals of platonic love cultivated in the salons of such important literary women as the Marquise de Rambouillet, Madeleine de Scudéry, Marie-Madeleine de Lafayette, and the Marquise de Sévigné—known as *précieuses.* No mere farce like his earlier comedies, this play addressed contemporary ideas. So incendiary was it considered that it was temporarily withdrawn, probably under pressure from influential *précieuses* or offended members of their circles. This play was perhaps the first modern comedy of manners, in which Molière's innovation was to employ more recognizably realistic characters, speaking a more straightforward language than was customary in tragedy. His satire of the mannered language of the *précieuses* was also indirectly a satire on the stilted verse of neoclassical tragedy.

A writer who achieves fame by exposing recognizable people to public ridicule is bound to make enemies, and Molière made many powerful ones. The year after his inaugural Parisian success (and its suppression), intriguers against him managed to have his theater demolished. His company moved the following year to the Palais-Royal theater, and followed up with another hit which brought Molière to the peak of his career: *The School for Wives* (1662), about the absurd and futile jealousies of a forty-two-year-old man (rather ancient in those days) who wants to marry a young girl. Molière himself was forty and had just wed nineteen-year-old Armande Béjart, who had replaced Madeleine—probably her mother—as Molière's costar, and the newlyweds played the husband and wife roles in the new piece. His marriage actually was troubled by jealousy and differences in age and temperament. Even during their repeated separations, however, the couple continued to act together on stage. Molière often drew on his personal troubles and vulnerabilities for comic material—making fun not only of jealous husbands but of middle-class men who, like himself, mixed with the aristocracy; playing the hypochondriac in *The Imaginary Invalid* when he was really at death's door; and even making two plays out of the extended controversy that arose in response to *The School for Wives,* which included charges of bad art and bad morals. In March 1663 he published the text of *The School for Wives,* dedicating it to "Madame" (Elizabeth Charlotte, Duchess of Orléans), the king's sister-in-law, which resulted in a generous royal pension, citing Molière as an "excellent comic poet." His company was soon renamed "The King's Company." That December the controversy reached its nadir when a rival actor wrote to the king accusing Molière of having "married the daughter and slept with the mother." This was effectively rebuffed when Louis XIV himself served as godfather in February 1664 to the son Armande had just borne Molière (the baby died soon after).

Tartuffe premiered later in 1664, a satire on religious hypocrisy. Another brilliant success, it added to Molière's roster of powerful enemies the clergy, who now denounced him as a blasphemous libertine. *Dom Juan* (1665), yet another success, was also attacked as impious, so much so that it was withdrawn and never again presented in Molière's lifetime. A daughter, Esprit-Madeleine (his only child to survive), was born the same year. By the next year he was continually ill and estranged from his wife. Yet the several years following saw more than one version of *Tartuffe,* first banned under pressure from the clergy but then revived to acclaim, and another of his greatest plays, *The Bourgeois Gentleman*

(1670). In 1672 Madeleine Béjart died, Molière was reconciled with Armande, and a second son was born, who also died in infancy. He wrote *The Imaginary Invalid* so that he could perform the lead role even with his horrible cough. A theatrical rival, Lully, succeeded in having the play rejected for court performance; nevertheless it was a success at the Palais-Royal. Molière was overcome by coughing in the middle of the fourth performance on February seventeenth, and died soon after. Burial in consecrated ground was at first refused by the Archbishop of Paris, as it would be later to Voltaire, but on the King's petition it was permitted, albeit at night and without ceremony. Lully took over the Palais-Royal theater after Molière's death, but in 1680 his former company, having merged with its rivals, formed the *Comédie Française,* which remains to this day France's leading company for classical theater.

Tartuffe *Tartuffe, or The Impostor* (1664–1669), has been considered Molière's masterpiece by many critics ever since its first publication. Voltaire wrote, *"Tartuffe* is a eulogy of Molière that will last as long as the French language." This play exemplifies the original contributions to drama for which all his best work is known, combining poetic yet plain language with the broad, physical routines of farce and the stock situations of the ancient *commedia dell'arte* theater to create plausible plots about recognizably current character types. Tartuffe, the religious hypocrite, is perhaps the most famous of the major satirical character types featured in Molière's mature work, which also include the jealous husband, the spendthrift, the miser, the snob, the vulgar social climber, the learned lady, and the hypochondriac. The aesthetic norms of the period held that literature should instruct as well as delight, rendering comedy morally suspect, as more frivolous and less instructive than tragedy; but Molière sought to teach through the cautionary character types he created.

Molière's innovative, modern approach to theater was fabulously successful in his time but also caused repeated explosive controversies. *Tartuffe* was not the first of his plays to send shock waves of scandal and bitter aesthetic and moral controversy through Parisian society; for it was not the first of his plays to use the combination of stock comic plot devices with recognizable character types to afford commentary on the contemporary social scene. *The Ridiculous Précieuses* had ruffled feathers as early as 1659, while *The School for Wives* engendered a sustained critical controversy, dubbed by one participant "The Comic War," which exploded theatrical as well as literary rivalries while fueling the antagonisms of literary women and religious prudes. These hostile rivalries had everything to do with the immense popular appeal of Molière's plays. The critic Boileau's response to the controversy, addressed to Molière a mere week after the first performance of *The School for Wives,* reassured him, "If you pleased a bit less, you would not displease so much." For several years thereafter, the play was attacked in a whole series of critical dialogues and satirical one-act plays published by numerous rival writers and actors. Molière replied with his own brief plays, in which he rebuts rivals in the established theater by satirizing the mannered and emphatic tragic delivery then in vogue, using his own more natural acting style. The force and duration of the Comic War, and the repeated controversies in response to his later plays, show how new and how threatening to the social and literary status quo were Molière's innovations in creating serious literary drama with broad popular appeal, his alterations to the conventional styles of language and acting then dominating the established theater, and his attacks on powerful social groups.

No group, however, was more powerful than the Church in Molière's time, and those already offended by what they saw as blasphemous elements in *The School for Wives* (principally in a scene where the husband is made to look absurd as he lectures his wife on the ten rules of marriage, which some saw as a mockery of the Ten Commandments) became implacable when he turned his sights from the character type of the jealous husband to that of the religious hypocrite. The court of Louis XIV, as the letters of his sister-in-law Duchess of Orleans collected in this volume so vividly illustrate, was deeply ambivalent about theatrical spectacle, and the early reception of Tartuffe expresses that ambivalence to a degree that may now appear incomprehensibly contradictory. The theater in general was under severe and sustained attack from this period through that of Rousseau for what was seen as its general fostering of immorality, indecency, and irreligion. Yet Louis XIV was known as the Sun King not only for his splendor but also for his enlightened liberality, his fostering of the arts and sciences, and his love of the pleasure and luxury that he lavished in every form on his court, which could itself be seen as one extended theatrical spectacle. Indeed *Tartuffe* was first performed at one of the Sun King's most lavish court entertainments, which he called "The Enchanted Island," where his courtiers were to forget the outside world in a weeklong round of pleasures in the gardens of Versailles. A first version of Molière's play in three acts, entitled *The Hypocrite,* was presented between a ballet and a jousting tournament on 12 May 1664. Although the king may have commissioned the play for the occasion, and in any case certainly permitted it to be performed there, a few days afterward a newspaper reported that he had deemed it "injurious to religion, and capable of producing very dangerous consequences." Pamphlets were published denouncing Molière as a libertine and calling for him to be burned at the stake. While the king's official report declared the play amusing and did not doubt the author's good intentions, he forbade its public performance until it could be examined by the royal censors.

Molière followed the king to his palace at Fontainebleau that summer to plead his own case with his patron. A nephew of the Pope, Cardinal Chigi, was there on a delegation from Rome, and took up the examination of Molière's play. He approved it, finding nothing offensive to Christianity, upon which Molière wrote a formal petition to the king asking for permission to stage a public performance. Molière's request was refused, and yet the play continued to circulate and to be performed and read privately in the homes of the aristocracy for several years. The Versailles version was performed at the palace of the king's brother, and the complete, five-act play was performed two months later at the palace of his wife, the Duchess of Orleans in honor of the prince de Condé, who thereupon declared himself its staunchest defender and Molière's friend and protector. Although the king continued to ban public performances, he compensated Molière and his company for the resulting loss of revenue by instituting a royal pension of 6,000 livres for him in August 1665, increasing it still more soon after. Meanwhile the grandest of the *précieuses*—the group targeted by Molière's first successful satire of a few years earlier—made it the height of fashion to host dramatic readings of a four-act version of the play in their salons.

With his next play, *Dom Juan* (1665), also banned and denounced on similar charges of libertinism, Molière sought to evade the ban on *Tartuffe* by performing a new and altered version of the play at the Palais-Royal theater, re-entitled *The Impostor,* with five acts, a protagonist named Panulphe who represented a higher social class than the Tartuffe character, and a general softening of the play's language and tone. Nevertheless the very next day, on 6 August 1667, the president of the Parisian parliament banned the play until further notice. Molière again took his case to the king himself, closing his theater and actually sending two of his actors to Flanders, where the king was engaged in the siege of Lille, bearing a second formal petition. Still no favorable answer was forthcoming, and meanwhile the archbishop of Paris banned even the private reading of the play. It is speculated that Molière made the play more complex but also made its acceptance more difficult by satirizing not only Tartuffe, the con man who only pretends to be devout, but also Orgon, the sincerely religious man whose subtler fault is to be too rigid and extreme in his virtue. It is possible at the same time that the king was torn between his own fondness for the playwright and the pleasures he offered, on the one hand, and the rigid Catholicism of his mother, Anne of Austria, on the other. In any event, another year and half would pass before the authorities relented and the play was once again put on at the Palais-Royal, where it went through more than thirty performances in its first season, with Molière himself in the role of Orgon and the Béjart sisters as Mme Pernelle and Dorine. As is so often the case, the very prohibition of the play seems to have contributed to its huge success. Molière published it at his own expense after the first performance in 1669; it was snapped up by a publisher who rapidly produced a second edition. After that it was revived frequently in France, and inspired a number of different English adaptations through the middle of the eighteenth century, by such authors as Congreve and Cibber.

That Molière became such a threat within only five years on the Parisian theater scene—beginning with *The Ridiculous Précieuses* and *The School for Wives* and succeeded swiftly by *Tartuffe* and *Dom Juan*—demonstrates how important was the enthusiastic public response to his new brand of comedy. Crucial as was the king's support to Molière's ability to continue producing plays in Paris in the face of scandal, it never would have been sufficient, alone, to make them survive the centuries.

Tartuffe[1]

Characters[2]

MADAME PERNELLE, *Orgon's mother*

ORGON, *Elmire's husband*

ELMIRE, *Orgon's wife*

DAMIS, *Orgon's son, Elmire's stepson*

MARIANE, *Orgon's daughter, Elmire's stepdaughter, in love with Valère*

VALÈRE, *in love with Mariane*

CLÉANTE, *Orgon's brother-in-law*

TARTUFFE, *a hypocrite*

DORINE, *Mariane's lady's-maid*

M. LOYAL, *a bailiff*

A POLICE OFFICER

FLIPOTE, *Mme. Pernelle's maid*

The scene throughout: Orgon's house in Paris

Act 1

Scene 1[3]

Madame Pernelle and Flipote, her maid, Elmire, Mariane, Dorine, Damis, Cléante

MADAME PERNELLE: Come, come, Flipote; it's time I left this place.

ELMIRE: I can't keep up, you walk at such a pace.

MADAME PERNELLE: Don't trouble, child; no need to show me out.
It's not your manners I'm concerned about.

ELMIRE: We merely pay you the respect we owe.
But, Mother, why this hurry? Must you go?

MADAME PERNELLE: I must. This house appals me. No one in it
Will pay attention for a single minute.
I offer good advice, but you won't hear it.

10   Children, I take my leave much vexed in spirit.

1. Translated by Richard Wilbur.
2. The name Tartuffe has been traced back to an older word associated with liar or charlatan: *truffer*, "to deceive" or "to cheat." Then there was also the Italian actor Tartufo, physically deformed and truffle shaped. Most of the other names are typical of the genre of court comedy and possess rather elegant connotations of pastoral and *bergerie*. Dorine would be a *demoiselle de campagne* and not a mere maid—that is, a female companion to Mariane of roughly the same social status. This in part accounts for the liberties she takes in conversation with Orgon, Madame Pernelle, and others. Her name is short for Théodorine.
3. In French drama, the scene changes every time a character enters or exits.

You all break in and chatter on and on.
It's like a madhouse with the keeper gone.
DORINE: If...
MADAME PERNELLE: Girl, you talk too much, and I'm afraid
You're far too saucy for a lady's-maid.
15   You push in everywhere and have your say.
DAMIS: But...
MADAME PERNELLE: You, boy, grow more foolish every day.
To think my grandson should be such a dunce!
I've said a hundred times, if I've said it once,
That if you keep the course on which you've started,
20   You'll leave your worthy father broken-hearted.
MARIANE: I think...
MADAME PERNELLE: And you, his sister, seem so pure,
So shy, so innocent, and so demure.
But you know what they say about still waters.
I pity parents with secretive daughters.
ELMIRE: Now, Mother...
MADAME PERNELLE: And as for you, child, let me add
That your behavior is extremely bad,
And a poor example for these children, too.
Their dear, dead mother did far better than you.
You're much too free with money, and I'm distressed
30   To see you so elaborately dressed.
When it's one's husband that one aims to please,
One has no need of costly fripperies.
CLÉANTE: Oh, Madam, really...
MADAME PERNELLE: You are her brother, Sir,
And I respect and love you; yet if I were
35   My son, this lady's good and pious spouse,
I wouldn't make you welcome in my house.
You're full of worldly counsels which, I fear,
Aren't suitable for decent folk to hear.
I've spoken bluntly, Sir; but it behooves us
40   Not to mince words when righteous fervor moves us.
DAMIS: Your man Tartuffe is full of holy speeches...
MADAME PERNELLE: And practises precisely what he preaches.
He's a fine man, and should be listened to.
I will not hear him mocked by fools like you.
DAMIS: Good God! Do you expect me to submit
To the tyranny of that carping hypocrite?
Must we forgo all joys and satisfactions
Because that bigot censures all our actions?
DORINE: To hear him talk—and he talks all the time—
50   There's nothing one can do that's not a crime.
He rails at everything, your dear Tartuffe.
MADAME PERNELLE: Whatever he reproves deserves reproof.
He's out to save your souls, and all of you
Must love him, as my son would have you do.

DAMIS: Ah no, Grandmother, I could never take
      To such a rascal, even for my father's sake.
      That's how I feel, and I shall not dissemble.
      His every action makes me seethe and tremble
      With helpless anger, and I have no doubt
60   That he and I will shortly have it out.

DORINE: Surely it is a shame and a disgrace
      To see this man usurp the master's place—
      To see this beggar who, when first he came,
      Had not a shoe or shoestring to his name
65   So far forget himself that he behaves
      As if the house were his, and we his slaves.

MADAME PERNELLE: Well, mark my words, your souls would fare far better
      If you obeyed his precepts to the letter.

DORINE: You see him as a saint. I'm far less awed;
70   In fact, I see right through him. He's a fraud.

MADAME PERNELLE: Nonsense!

DORINE: His man Laurent's the same, or worse;
      I'd not trust either with a penny purse.

MADAME PERNELLE: I can't say what his servant's morals may be;
      His own great goodness I can guarantee.
75   You all regard him with distaste and fear
      Because he tells you what you're loath to hear,
      Condemns your sins, points out your moral flaws,
      And humbly strives to further Heaven's cause.

DORINE: If sin is all that bothers him, why is it
80   He's so upset when folk drop in to visit?
      Is Heaven so outraged by a social call
      That he must prophesy against us all?
      I'll tell you what I think: if you ask me,
      He's jealous of my mistress' company.

MADAME PERNELLE: Rubbish!
85   [*To Elmire.*]   He's not alone, child, in complaining
      Of all your promiscuous entertaining.
      Why, the whole neighborhood's upset, I know,
      By all these carriages that come and go,
      With crowds of guests parading in and out
90   And noisy servants loitering about.
      In all of this, I'm sure there's nothing vicious;
      But why give people cause to be suspicious?

CLÉANTE: They need no cause; they'll talk in any case.
      Madam, this world would be a joyless place
95   If, fearing what malicious tongues might say,
      We locked our doors and turned our friends away.
      And even if one did so dreary a thing,
      D' you think those tongues would cease their chattering?
      One can't fight slander; it's a losing battle;
100   Let us instead ignore their tittle-tattle.
      Let's strive to live by conscience clear decrees,
      And let the gossips gossip as they please.

DORINE: If there is talk against us, I know the source:
It's Daphne and her little husband, of course.
105　Those who have greatest cause for guilt and shame
Are quickest to besmirch a neighbor's name.
When there's a chance for libel, they never miss it;
When something can be made to seem illicit
They're off at once to spread the joyous news,
110　Adding to fact what fantasies they choose.
By talking up their neighbor's indiscretions
They seek to camouflage their own transgressions,
Hoping that others' innocent affairs
Will lend a hue of innocence to theirs,
115　Or that their own black guilt will come to seem
Part of a general shady color-scheme.

MADAME PERNELLE: All that is quite irrelevant. I doubt
That anyone's more virtuous and devout
Than dear Orante; and I'm informed that she
120　Condemns your mode of life most vehemently.

DORINE: Oh, yes, she's strict, devout, and has no taint
Of worldliness; in short, she seems a saint.
But it was time which taught her that disguise;
She's thus because she can't be otherwise.
125　So long as her attractions could enthrall,
She flounced and flirted and enjoyed it all,
But now that they're no longer what they were
She quits a world which fast is quitting her,
And wears a veil of virtue to conceal
130　Her bankrupt beauty and her lost appeal.
That's what becomes of old coquettes today:
Distressed when all their lovers fall away,
They see no recourse but to play the prude,
And so confer a style on solitude.
135　Thereafter, they're severe with everyone,
Condemning all our actions, pardoning none,
And claiming to be pure, austere and zealous
When, if the truth were known, they're merely jealous,
And cannot bear to see another know
140　The pleasures time has forced them to forgo.

MADAME PERNELLE [*Initially to Elmire.*]:
That sort of talk[4] is what you like to hear;
Therefore you'd have us all keep still, my dear,
While Madam rattles on the livelong day.
Nevertheless, I mean to have my say.
145　I tell you that you're blest to have Tartuffe
Dwelling, as my son's guest, beneath this roof;

---

4. In the original, a reference to a collection of novels about chivalry found in *La Bibliothèque bleue* (The blue library), written for children.

That Heaven has sent him to forestall its wrath
By leading you, once more, to the true path;
That all he reprehends is reprehensible,
150 And that you'd better heed him, and be sensible.
These visits, balls, and parties in which you revel
Are nothing but inventions of the Devil.
One never hears a word that's edifying:
Nothing but chaff and foolishness and lying,
155 As well as vicious gossip in which one's neighbor
Is cut to bits with epee, foil, and saber.
People of sense are driven half-insane
At such affairs, where noise and folly reign
And reputations perish thick and fast.
160 As a wise preacher said on Sunday last,
Parties are Towers of Babylon,[5] because
The guests all babble on with never a pause;
And then he told a story, which, I think . . .
(To Cléante.) I heard that laugh, Sir, and I saw that wink!
165 Go find your silly friends and laugh some more!
Enough; I'm going; don't show me to the door.
I leave this household much dismayed and vexed;
I cannot say when I shall see you next.

[Slapping Flipote.]

Wake up, don't stand there gaping into space!
170 I'll slap some sense into that stupid face.
Move, move, you slut.

Scene 2

Cléante, Dorine

CLÉANTE:　　　　　　　I think I'll stay behind;
I want no further pieces of her mind.
How that old lady . . .
DORINE:　　　　　　Oh, what wouldn't she say
If she could hear you speak of her that way!
5 She'd thank you for the *lady,* but I'm sure
She'd find the *old* a little premature.
CLÉANTE:　My, what a scene she made, and what a din!
And how this man Tartuffe has taken her in!
DORINE:　Yes, but her son is even worse deceived;
10 His folly must be seen to be believed.
In the late troubles,[6] he played an able part
And served his king with wise and loyal heart,

5. Tower of Babel, Madame Pernelle's malapropism is the cause of Cléante's laughter.

6. A series of political disturbances, during the minority of Louis XIV. Specifically these consisted of the *Fronde* ("opposition") of the Parlement (1648–1649) and the *Fronde* of the Princes (1650–1653). Orgon is depicted as supporting Louis XIV in these outbreaks and their resolution.

But he's quite lost his senses since he fell
Beneath Tartuffe's infatuating spell.
15 He calls him brother, and loves him as his life,
Preferring him to mother, child, or wife.
In him and him alone will he confide;
He's made him his confessor and his guide;
He pets and pampers him with love more tender
20 Than any pretty mistress could engender,
Gives him the place of honor when they dine,
Delights to see him gorging like a swine,
Stuffs him with dainties till his guts distend,
And when he belches, cries "God bless you, friend!"
25 In short, he's mad; he worships him; he dotes;
His deeds he marvels at, his words he quotes,
Thinking each act a miracle, each word
Oracular as those that Moses heard.
Tartuffe, much pleased to find so easy a victim,
30 Has in a hundred ways beguiled and tricked him,
Milked him of money, and with his permission
Established here a sort of Inquisition.
Even Laurent, his lackey, dares to give
Us arrogant advice on how to live;
35 He sermonizes us in thundering tones
And confiscates our ribbons and colognes.
Last week he tore a kerchief into pieces
Because he found it pressed in a *Life of Jesus:*
He said it was a sin to juxtapose
40 Unholy vanities and holy prose.

Scene 3

Elmire, Mariane, Damis, Cléante, Dorine

ELMIRE [*To Cléante*]: You did well not to follow; she stood in the door
 And said *verbatim* all she'd said before.
 I saw my husband coming. I think I'd best
 Go upstairs now, and take a little rest.
CLÉANTE: I'll wait and greet him here; then I must go.
 I've really only time to say hello.
DAMIS: Sound him about my sister's wedding, please.
 I think Tartuffe's against it, and that he's
 Been urging Father to withdraw his blessing.
10 As you well know, I'd find that most distressing.
 Unless my sister and Valère can marry,
 My hopes to wed *his* sister will miscarry,
 And I'm determined...
DORINE: He's coming.

Scene 4

Orgon, Cléante, Dorine

ORGON: Ah, Brother, good-day.

CLÉANTE: Well, welcome back. I'm sorry I can't stay.
How was the country? Blooming, I trust, and green?

ORGON: Excuse me, Brother; just one moment.
[*To Dorine.*]   Dorine...

5   [*To Cléante.*] To put my mind at rest, I always learn
The household news the moment I return.
[*To Dorine.*] Has all been well, these two days I've been gone?
How are the family? What's been going on?

DORINE: Your wife, two days ago, had a bad fever,
10   And a fierce headache which refused to leave her.

ORGON: Ah. And Tartuffe?

DORINE: Tartuffe? Why, he's round and red,
Bursting with health, and excellently fed.

ORGON: Poor fellow!

DORINE: That night, the mistress was unable
To take a single bite at the dinner-table.
15   Her headache-pains, she said, were simply hellish.

ORGON: Ah. And Tartuffe?

DORINE: He ate his meal with relish,
And zealously devoured in her presence
A leg of mutton and a brace of pheasants.

ORGON: Poor fellow!

DORINE: Well, the pains continued strong.
20   And so she tossed and tossed the whole night long,
Now icy-cold, now burning like a flame.
We sat beside her bed till morning came.

ORGON: Ah. And Tartuffe?

DORINE: Why, having eaten, he rose
And sought his room, already in a doze,
25   Got into his warm bed, and snored away
In perfect peace until the break of day.

ORGON: Poor fellow!

DORINE: After much ado, we talked her
Into dispatching someone for the doctor.
He bled her, and the fever quickly fell.

ORGON: Ah. And Tartuffe?

DORINE: He bore it very well.
To keep his cheerfulness at any cost,
And make up for the blood *Madame* had lost,
He drank, at lunch, four beakers full of port.

ORGON: Poor fellow!

DORINE: Both are doing well, in short.
35   I'll go and tell *Madame* that you've expressed
Keen sympathy and anxious interest.

Scene 5

Orgon, Cléante

CLÉANTE: That girl was laughing in your face, and though
I've no wish to offend you, even so
I'm bound to say that she had some excuse.
How can you possibly be such a goose?
5   Are you so dazed by this man's hocus-pocus
That all the world, save him, is out of focus?
You've given him clothing, shelter, food, and care;
Why must you also...
ORGON: Brother, stop right there.
You do not know the man of whom you speak.
CLÉANTE: I grant you that. But my judgment's not so weak
That I can't tell, by his effect on others...
ORGON: Ah, when you meet him, you two will be like brothers!
There's been no loftier soul since time began.
He is a man who...a man who...an excellent man.
15   To keep his precepts is to be reborn,
And view this dunghill of a world with scorn.
Yes, thanks to him I'm a changed man indeed.
Under his tutelage my soul's been freed
From earthly loves, and every human tie:
20   My mother, children, brother, and wife could die,
And I'd not feel a single moment's pain.
CLÉANTE: That's a fine sentiment, Brother; most humane.
ORGON: Oh, had you seen Tartuffe as I first knew him,
Your heart, like mine, would have surrendered to him.
25   He used to come into our church each day
And humbly kneel nearby, and start to pray.
He'd draw the eyes of everybody there
By the deep fervor of his heartfelt prayer;
He'd sigh and weep, and sometimes with a sound
30   Of rapture he would bend and kiss the ground;
And when I rose to go, he'd run before
To offer me holy-water at the door.
His serving-man, no less devout than he,
Informed me of his master's poverty;
35   I gave him gifts, but in his humbleness
He'd beg me every time to give him less.
"Oh, that's too much," he'd cry, "too much by twice!
I don't deserve it. The half, Sir, would suffice."
And when I wouldn't take it back, he'd share
40   Half of it with the poor, right then and there.
At length, Heaven prompted me to take him in
To dwell with us, and free our souls from sin.
He guides our lives, and to protect my honor
Stays by my wife, and keeps an eye upon her;
45   He tells me whom she sees, and all she does,

And seems more jealous than I ever was!
And how austere he is! Why, he can detect
A mortal sin where you would least suspect;
In smallest trifles, he's extremely strict.
50 Last week, his conscience was severely pricked
Because, while praying, he had caught a flea
And killed it, so he felt, too wrathfully.[7]

CLÉANTE: Good God, man! Have you lost your common sense—
Or is this all some joke at my expense?
55 How can you stand there and in all sobriety...

ORGON: Brother, your language savors of impiety.
Too much free-thinking's made your faith unsteady,
And as I've warned you many times already,
'Twill get you into trouble before you're through.

CLÉANTE: So I've been told before by dupes like you:
Being blind, you'd have all others blind as well;
The clear-eyed man you call an infidel,
And he who sees through humbug and pretense
Is charged, by you, with want of reverence.
65 Spare me your warnings, Brother; I have no fear
Of speaking out, for you and Heaven to hear,
Against affected zeal and pious knavery.
There's true and false in piety, as in bravery,
And just as those whose courage shines the most
70 In battle, are the least inclined to boast,
So those who hearts are truly pure and lowly
Don't make a flashy show of being holy.
There's a vast difference, so it seems to me,
Between true piety and hypocrisy:
75 How do you fail to see it, may I ask?
Is not a face quite different from a mask?
Cannot sincerity and cunning art,
Reality and semblance, be told apart?
Are scarecrows just like men, and do you hold
80 That a false coin is just as good as gold?
Ah, Brother, man's a strangely fashioned creature
Who seldom is content to follow Nature,
But recklessly pursues his inclination
Beyond the narrow bounds of moderation,
85 And often, by transgressing Reason's laws,
Perverts a lofty aim or noble cause.
A passing observation, but it applies.

ORGON: I see, dear Brother, that you're profoundly wise;
You harbor all the insight of the age.
90 You are our one clear mind, our only sage,

---

7. In the *Golden Legend (Legenda sanctorum)*, a popular collection of the lives of the saints written in the 13th century, it is said of St. Marcarius, the Elder (d. 390) that he dwelt naked in the desert for six months, a penance he felt appropriate for having killed a flea.

The era's oracle, its Cato[8] too,
And all mankind are fools compared to you.

CLÉANTE: Brother, I don't pretend to be a sage,
Nor have I all the wisdom of the age.

95   There's just one insight I would dare to claim:
I know that true and false are not the same;
And just as there is nothing I more revere
Than a soul whose faith is steadfast and sincere,
Nothing that I more cherish and admire

100   Than honest zeal and true religious fire,
So there is nothing that I find more base
Than specious piety's dishonest face—
Than these bold mountebanks, these histrios
Whose impious mummeries and hollow shows

105   Exploit our love of Heaven, and make a jest
Of all that men think holiest and best;
These calculating souls who offer prayers
Not to their Maker, but as public wares,
And seek to buy respect and reputation

110   With lifted eyes and sighs of exaltation;
These charlatans, I say, whose pilgrim souls
Proceed, by way of Heaven, toward earthly goals,
Who weep and pray and swindle and extort,
Who preach the monkish life, but haunt the court,

115   Who make their zeal the partner of their vice—
Such men are vengeful, sly, and cold as ice,
And when there is an enemy to defame
They cloak their spite in fair religion's name,
Their private spleen and malice being made

120   To seem a high and virtuous crusade,
Until, to mankind's reverent applause,
They crucify their foe in Heaven's cause.
Such knaves are all too common; yet, for the wise,
True piety isn't hard to recognize,

125   And, happily, these present times provide us
With bright examples to instruct and guide us.
Consider Ariston and Périandre;
Look at Oronte, Alcidamas, Clitandre;[9]
Their virtue is acknowledged; who could doubt it?

130   But you won't hear them beat the drum about it.
They're never ostentatious, never vain,
And their religion's moderate and humane;
It's not their way to criticize and chide:
They think censoriousness a mark of pride,

135   And therefore, letting others preach and rave,

8. Roman statesman (95–46 B.C.E.) with an enduring reputation for honesty and incorruptibility.
9. Vaguely Greek and Roman names derived from the elegant literature of the day.

They show, by deeds, how Christians should behave.
They think no evil of their fellow man,
But judge of him as kindly as they can.
They don't intrigue and wangle and conspire;
140   To lead a good life is their one desire;
The sinner wakes no rancorous hate in them;
It is the sin alone which they condemn;
Nor do they try to show a fiercer zeal
For Heaven's cause than Heaven itself could feel.
145   These men I honor, these men I advocate
As models for us all to emulate.
Your man is not their sort at all, I fear:
And, while your praise of him is quite sincere,
I think that you've been dreadfully deluded.

ORGON: Now then, dear Brother, is your speech concluded?
CLÉANTE: Why, yes.
ORGON: Your servant, Sir.

[*He turns to go.*]

CLÉANTE: No, Brother; wait.
There's one more matter. You agreed of late
That young Valère might have your daughter's hand.
ORGON: I did.
CLÉANTE: And set the date, I understand.
ORGON: Quite so.
CLÉANTE: You've now postponed it; is that true?
ORGON: No doubt.
CLÉANTE: The match no longer pleases you?
ORGON: Who knows?
CLÉANTE: D'you mean to go back on your word?
ORGON: I won't say that.
CLÉANTE: Has anything occurred
Which might entitle you to break your pledge?
ORGON: Perhaps.
CLÉANTE: Why must you hem, and haw, and hedge?
The boy asked me to sound you in this affair...
ORGON: It's been a pleasure.
CLÉANTE: But what shall I tell Valère?
ORGON: Whatever you like.
CLÉANTE: But what have you decided?
What are your plans?
ORGON: I plan, Sir, to be guided
By Heaven's will.
CLÉANTE: Come, Brother, don't talk rot.
You've given Valère your word; will you keep it, or not?
ORGON: Good day.
CLÉANTE: This looks like poor Valère's undoing;
I'll go and warn him that there's trouble brewing.

Act 2

Scene 1

Orgon, Mariane

ORGON: Mariane.

MARIANE: Yes, Father?

ORGON: A word with you; come here.

MARIANE: What are you looking for?

ORGON [*Peering into a small closet*]: Eavesdroppers, dear.
    I'm making sure we shan't be overheard.
    Someone in there could catch our every word.
5   Ah, good, we're safe. Now, Mariane, my child,
    You're a sweet girl who's tractable and mild,
    Whom I hold dear, and think most highly of.

MARIANE: I'm deeply grateful, Father, for your love.

ORGON: That's well said, Daughter; and you can repay me
10   If, in all things, you'll cheerfully obey me.

MARIANE: To please you, Sir, is what delights me best.

ORGON: Good, good. Now, what d'you think of Tartuffe, our guest?

MARIANE: I, Sir?

ORGON: Yes. Weigh your answer; think it through.

MARIANE: Oh, dear. I'll say whatever you wish me to.

ORGON: That's wisely said, my Daughter. Say of him, then,
    That he's the very worthiest of men,
    And that you're fond of him, and would rejoice
    In being his wife, if that should be my choice.
    Well?

MARIANE: What?

ORGON: What's that?

MARIANE: I...

ORGON: Well?

MARIANE: Forgive me, pray.

ORGON: Did you not hear me?

MARIANE: Of *whom*, Sir, must I say
    That I am fond of him, and would rejoice
    In being his wife, if that should be your choice?

ORGON: Why, of Tartuffe.

MARIANE: But, Father, that's false, you know.
    Why would you have me say what isn't so?

ORGON: Because I am resolved it shall be true.
    That it's my wish should be enough for you.

MARIANE: You can't mean, Father...

ORGON: Yes, Tartuffe shall be
    Allied by marriage[1] to this family,

---

1. This assertion is important and more than a mere device in the plot of the day. The second *placet* or petition insists that Tartuffe be costumed as a layman, and Orgon's plan for him to marry again asserts Tartuffe's position in the laity. In the 1664 version of the play Tartuffe had been dressed in a cassock suggestive of the priesthood, and Molière was now anxious to avoid any suggestion of this kind.

And he's to be your husband, is that clear?
30 It's a father's privilege...

Scene 2

Dorine, Orgon, Mariane

ORGON [*To Dorine*]: What are you doing in here?
        Is curiosity so fierce a passion
        With you, that you must eavesdrop in this fashion?
DORINE: There's lately been a rumor going about—
5   Based on some hunch or chance remark, no doubt—
        That you mean Mariane to wed Tartuffe.
        I've laughed it off, of course, as just a spoof.
ORGON: You find it so incredible?
DORINE: Yes, I do.
        I won't accept that story, even from you.
ORGON: Well, you'll believe it when the thing is done.
DORINE: Yes, yes, of course. Go on and have your fun.
ORGON: I've never been more serious in my life.
DORINE: Ha!
ORGON: Daughter, I mean it; you're to be his wife.
DORINE: No, don't believe your father; it's all a hoax.
ORGON: See here, young woman...
DORINE: Come, Sir, no more jokes;
        You can't fool us.
ORGON: How dare you talk that way?
DORINE: All right, then: we believe you, sad to say.
        But how a man like you, who looks so wise
        And wears a moustache of such splendid size,
        Can be so foolish as to...
ORGON: Silence, please!
        My girl, you take too many liberties.
        I'm master here, as you must not forget.
DORINE: Do let's discuss this calmly; don't be upset.
        You can't be serious, Sir, about this plan.
25   What should that bigot want with Mariane?
        Praying and fasting ought to keep him busy.
        And then, in terms of wealth and rank, what is he?
        Why should a man of property like you
        Pick out a beggar son-in-law?
ORGON: That will do.
30   Speak of his poverty with reverence.
        His is a pure and saintly indigence.
        Which far transcends all worldly pride and pelf.
        He lost his fortune, as he says himself,
        Because he cared for Heaven alone, and so
35   Was careless of his interests here below.
        I mean to get him out of his present straits

And help him to recover his estates—
Which, in his part of the world, have no small fame.
Poor though he is, he's a gentleman just the same.

DORINE: Yes, so he tells us; and, Sir, it seems to me
Such pride goes very ill with piety.
A man whose spirit spurns this dungy earth
Ought not to brag of lands and noble birth;
Such worldly arrogance will hardly square

45 With meek devotion and the life of prayer.
...But this approach, I see, has drawn a blank;
Let's speak, then, of his person, not his rank.
Doesn't it seem to you a trifle grim
To give a girl like her to a man like him?

50 When two are so ill-suited, can't you see
What the sad consequence is bound to be?
A young girl's virtue is imperilled, Sir,
When such a marriage is imposed on her;
For if one's bridegroom isn't to one's taste,

55 It's hardly an inducement to be chaste,
And many a man with horns upon his brow
Has made his wife the thing that she is now.
It's hard to be a faithful wife, in short,
To certain husbands of a certain sort,

60 And he who gives his daughter to a man she hates
Must answer for her sins at Heaven's gates.
Think, Sir, before you play so risky a role.

ORGON: This servant-girl presumes to save my soul!

DORINE: You would do well to ponder what I've said.

ORGON: Daughter, we'll disregard this dunderhead.
Just trust your father's judgment. Oh, I'm aware
That I once promised you to young Valère;
But now I hear he gambles, which greatly shocks me;
What's more, I've doubts about his orthodoxy.

70 His visits to church, I note, are very few.

DORINE: Would you have him go at the same hours as you,
And kneel nearby, to be sure of being seen?

ORGON: I can dispense with such remarks, Dorine.
[To Mariane.] Tartuffe, however, is sure of Heaven's blessing,

75 And that's the only treasure worth possessing.
This match will bring you joys beyond all measure;
Your cup will overflow with every pleasure;
You two will interchange your faithful loves
Like two sweet cherubs, or two turtle-doves.

80 No harsh word shall be heard, no frown be seen,
And he shall make you happy as a queen.

DORINE: And she'll make him a cuckold, just wait and see.

ORGON: What language!

DORINE: Oh, he's a man of destiny;

He's *made* for horns, and what the stars demand
85   Your daughter's virtue surely can't withstand.
ORGON: Don't interrupt me further. Why can't you learn
That certain things are none of your concern?
DORINE: It's for your own sake that I interfere.

[*She repeatedly interrupts Orgon just as he is turning to speak to his daughter.*]

ORGON: Most kind of you. Now, hold your tongue, d'you hear?
DORINE: If I didn't love you...
ORGON: Spare me your affection.
DORINE: I'll love you, Sir, in spite of your objection.
ORGON: Blast!
DORINE: I can't bear, Sir, for your honor's sake,
To let you make this ludicrous mistake.
ORGON: You mean to go on talking?
DORINE: If I didn't protest
95   This sinful marriage, my conscience couldn't rest.
ORGON: If you don't hold your tongue, you little shrew...
DORINE: What, lost your temper? A pious man like you?
ORGON: Yes! Yes! You talk and talk. I'm maddened by it.
Once and for all, I tell you to be quiet.
DORINE: Well, I'll be quiet. But I'll be thinking hard.
ORGON: Think all you like, but you had better guard
That saucy tongue of yours, or I'll...
[*Turning back to Mariane.*]   Now, child,
I've weighed this matter fully.
DORINE [*Aside*]:   It drives me wild
That I can't speak.

[*Orgon turns his head, and she is silent.*]

ORGON: Tartuffe is no young dandy,
But, still, his person...
DORINE [*Aside.*]:   Is as sweet as candy.
ORGON: Is such that, even if you shouldn't care
For his other merits...

[*He turns and stands facing Dorine, arms crossed.*]

DORINE [*Aside.*]:   They'll make a lovely pair.
If I were she, no man would marry me
Against my inclination, and go scot-free.
110   He'd learn, before the wedding-day was over,
How readily a wife can find a lover.
ORGON   [*To Dorine*]: It seems you treat my orders as a joke.
DORINE: Why, what's the matter? 'Twas not to you I spoke.
ORGON: What *were* you doing?
DORINE: Talking to myself, that's all.
ORGON: Ah! [*Aside.*] One more bit of impudence and gall,
And I shall give her a good slap in the face.

[*He puts himself in position to slap her; Dorine, whenever he glances at her, stands immobile and silent.*]

    Daughter, you shall accept, and with good grace,
    The husband I've selected... Your wedding-day...
    [*To Dorine.*] Why don't you talk to yourself?

DORINE: I've nothing to say.

ORGON: Come, just one word.

DORINE: No, thank you, Sir. I pass.

ORGON: Come, speak; I'm waiting.

DORINE: I'd not be such an ass.

ORGON: [*Turning to Mariane.*]
    In short, dear Daughter, I mean to be obeyed,
    And you must bow to the sound choice I've made.

DORINE   [*Moving away*]: I'd not wed such a monster, even in jest.

[*Orgon attempts to slap her, but misses.*]

ORGON: Daughter, that maid of yours is a thorough pest;
    She makes me sinfully annoyed and nettled.
    I can't speak further; my nerves are too unsettled.
    She's so upset me by her insolent talk,
    I'll calm myself by going for a walk.

Scene 3

Dorine, Mariane

DORINE   [*Returning*]: Well, have you lost your tongue, girl? Must I play
    Your part, and say the lines you ought to say?
    Faced with a fate so hideous and absurd,
    Can you not utter one dissenting word?

MARIANE: What good would it do? A father's power is great.

DORINE: Resist him now, or it will be too late.

MARIANE: But...

DORINE: Tell him one cannot love at a father's whim;
    That you shall marry for yourself, not him;
10   That since it's you who are to be the bride,
    It's you, not he, who must be satisfied;
    And that if his Tartuffe is so sublime,
    He's free to marry him at any time.

MARIANE: I've bowed so long to Father's strict control,
15   I couldn't oppose him now, to save my soul.

DORINE: Come, come, Mariane. Do listen to reason, won't you?
    Valère has asked your hand. Do you love him, or don't you?

MARIANE: Oh, how unjust of you! What can you mean
    By asking such a question, dear Dorine?
20   You know the depth of my affection for him;
    I've told you a hundred times how I adore him.

DORINE: I don't believe in everything I hear;

Who knows if your professions were sincere?

MARIANE: They were, Dorine, and you do me wrong to doubt it;

25   Heaven knows that I've been all too frank about it.

DORINE: You love him, then?

MARIANE: Oh, more than I can express.

DORINE: And he, I take it, cares for you no less?

MARIANE: I think so.

DORINE: And you both, with equal fire,

        Burn to be married?

MARIANE: That is our one desire.

DORINE: What of Tartuffe, then? What of your father's plan?

MARIANE: I'll kill myself, if I'm forced to wed that man.

DORINE: I hadn't thought of that recourse. How splendid!

        Just die, and all your troubles will be ended!

        A fine solution. Oh, it maddens me

35   To hear you talk in that self-pitying key.

MARIANE: Dorine, how harsh you are! It's most unfair.

        You have no sympathy for my despair.

DORINE: I've none at all for people who talk drivel

        And, faced with difficulties, whine and snivel.

MARIANE: No doubt I'm timid, but it would be wrong . . .

DORINE: True love requires a heart that's firm and strong.

MARIANE: I'm strong in my affection for Valère,

        But coping with my father is his affair.

DORINE: But if your father's brain has grown so cracked

45   Over his dear Tartuffe that he can retract

        His blessing, though your wedding-day was named,

        It's surely not Valère who's to be blamed.

MARIANE: If I defied my father, as you suggest,

        Would it not seem unmaidenly, at best?

50   Shall I defend my love at the expense

        Of brazenness and disobedience?

        Shall I parade my heart's desires, and flaunt . . .

DORINE: No, I ask nothing of you. Clearly you want

        To be Madame Tartuffe, and I feel bound

55   Not to oppose a wish so very sound.

        What right have I to criticize the match?

        Indeed, my dear, the man's a brilliant catch.

        Monsieur Tartuffe! Now, there's a man of weight!

        Yes, yes, Monsieur Tartuffe, I'm bound to state,

60   Is quite a person; that's not to be denied;

        'Twill be no little thing to be his bride.

        The world already rings with his renown;

        He's a great noble—in his native town;

        His ears are red, he has a pink complexion,

65   And all in all, he'll suit you to perfection.

MARIANE: Dear God!

DORINE: Oh, how triumphant you will feel

        At having caught a husband so ideal!

MARIANE: Oh, do stop teasing, and use your cleverness
        To get me out of this appalling mess.
70   Advise me, and I'll do whatever you say.
DORINE: Ah no, a dutiful daughter must obey
        Her father, even if he weds her to an ape.
        You've a bright future; why struggle to escape?
        Tartuffe will take you back where his family lives,
75   To a small town as warm with relatives—
        Uncles and cousins whom you'll be charmed to meet.
        You'll be received at once by the elite,
        Calling upon the bailiff's[2] wife, no less—
        Even, perhaps, upon the mayoress,[3]
80   Who'll sit you down in the *best* kitchen chair.[4]
        Then, once a year, you'll dance at the village fair
        To the drone of bagpipes—two of them, in fact—
        And see a puppet-show, or an animal act.[5]
        Your husband . . .
MARIANE: Oh, you turn my blood to ice!
85   Stop torturing me, and give me your advice.
DORINE   [*Threatening to go*]:
        Your servant, Madam.
MARIANE: Dorine, I beg of you . . .
DORINE: No, you deserve it; this marriage must go through.
MARIANE: Dorine!
DORINE: No.
MARIANE: Not Tartuffe! You know I think him . . .
DORINE: Tartuffe's your cup of tea, and you shall drink him.
MARIANE: I've always told you everything, and relied . . .
DORINE: No. You deserve to be tartuffified.
MARIANE: Well, since you mock me and refuse to care,
        I'll henceforth seek my solace in despair:
        Despair shall be my counsellor and friend,
95   And help me bring my sorrows to an end. [*She starts to leave.*]
DORINE: There now, come back; my anger has subsided.
        You do deserve some pity, I've decided.
MARIANE: Dorine, if Father makes me undergo
        This dreadful martyrdom, I'll die, I know.
DORINE: Don't fret; it won't be difficult to discover
        Some plan of action . . . But here's Valère, your lover.

2. A high-ranking official in the judiciary, not simply a sheriffs deputy as today.

3. The wife of a tax collector (*élue*), an important official controlling imports, elected by the Estates General.

4. In elegant society of Molière's day, there was a hierarchy of seats, and the use of each was determined by rank. The seats descended from *fauteuils* to *chaises, perroquets, tabourets,* and *plints*. Thus Mariane would get the lowest seat in the room.

5. In the original, *fagotin*, literally "a monkey dressed up in a man's clothing."

Valère, Mariane, Dorine

VALÈRE: Madam, I've just received some wondrous news
            Regarding which I'd like to hear your views.
MARIANE: What news?
VALÈRE: You're marrying Tartuffe.
MARIANE: I find
            That Father does have such a match in mind.
VALÈRE: Your father, Madam…
MARIANE: …has just this minute said
            That it's Tartuffe he wishes me to wed.
VALÈRE: Can he be serious?
MARIANE: Oh, indeed he can;
            He's clearly set his heart upon the plan.
VALÈRE: And what position do you propose to take,
            Madam?
MARIANE: Why—I don't know.
VALÈRE: For heaven's sake—
            You don't know?
MARIANE: No.
VALÈRE: Well, well!
MARIANE: Advise me, do.
VALÈRE: Marry the man. That's my advice to you.
MARIANE: That's your advice?
VALÈRE: Yes.
MARIANE: Truly?
VALÈRE: Oh, absolutely.
            You couldn't choose more wisely, more astutely.
MARIANE: Thanks for this counsel; I'll follow it, of course.
VALÈRE: Do, do; I'm sure 'twill cost you no remorse.
MARIANE: To give it didn't cause your heart to break.
VALÈRE: I gave it, Madam, only for your sake.
MARIANE: And it's for your sake that I take it, Sir.
DORINE: [*Withdrawing to the rear of the stage.*]
20   Let's see which fool will prove the stubborner.
VALÈRE: So! I am nothing to you, and it was flat
            Deception when you…
MARIANE: Please, enough of that.
            You've told me plainly that I should agree
            To wed the man my father's chosen for me,
25   And since you've deigned to counsel me so wisely,
            I promise, Sir, to do as you advise me.
VALÈRE: Ah, no, 'twas not by me that you were swayed.
            No, your decision was already made;
            Though now, to save appearances, you protest
30   That you're betraying me at my behest.
MARIANE: Just as you say.
VALÈRE: Quite so. And I now see

That you were never truly in love with me.

MARIANE: Alas, you're free to think so if you choose.

VALÈRE: I choose to think so, and here's a bit of news:

35 You've spurned my hand, but I know where to turn
For kinder treatment, as you shall quickly learn.

MARIANE: I'm sure you do. Your noble qualities
Inspire affection...

VALÈRE: Forget my qualities, please.
They don't inspire you overmuch, I find.

40 But there's another lady I have in mind
Whose sweet and generous nature will not scorn
To compensate me for the loss I've borne.

MARIANE: I'm no great loss, and I'm sure that you'll transfer
Your heart quite painlessly from me to her.

VALÈRE: I'll do my best to take it in my stride.
The pain I feel at being cast aside
Time and forgetfulness may put an end to.
Or if I can't forget, I shall pretend to.
No self-respecting person is expected

50 To go on loving once he's been rejected.

MARIANE: Now, that's a fine, high-minded sentiment.

VALÈRE: One to which any sane man would assent.
Would you prefer it if I pined away
In hopeless passion till my dying day?

55 Am I to yield you to a rival's arms
And not console myself with other charms?

MARIANE: Go then: console yourself; don't hesitate.
I wish you to; indeed, I cannot wait.

VALÈRE: You wish me to?

MARIANE: Yes.

VALÈRE: That's the final straw.

60 Madam, farewell. Your wish shall be my law.

[*He starts to leave, and then returns: this repeatedly.*]

MARIANE: Splendid.

VALÈRE [*Coming back again*]: This breach, remember, is of your making;
It's you who've driven me to the step I'm taking.

MARIANE: Of course.

VALÈRE [*Coming back again*]: Remember, too, that I am merely
Following your example.

MARIANE: I see that clearly.

VALÈRE: Enough. I'll go and do your bidding, then.

MARIANE: Good.

VALÈRE [*Coming back again*]: You shall never see my face again.

MARIANE: Excellent.

VALÈRE [*Walking to the door, then turning about*]:
Yes?

MARIANE: What?

VALÈRE: What's that? What did you say?

MARIANE: Nothing. You're dreaming.

VALÈRE: Ah. Well, I'm on my way.

    Farewell, Madame.

[He moves slowly away.]

MARIANE: Farewell.

DORINE   *[To Mariane]*:   If you ask me,

70   Both of you are as mad as mad can be.
    Do stop this nonsense, now. I've only let you
    Squabble so long to see where it would get you.
    Whoa there, Monsieur Valère!

[She goes and seizes Valère by the arm; he makes a great show of resistance.]

VALÈRE: What's this, Dorine?

DORINE: Come here.

VALÈRE: No, no, my heart's too full of spleen.

75   Don't hold me back; her wish must be obeyed.

DORINE: Stop!

VALÈRE: It's too late now; my decision's made.

DORINE: Oh, pooh!

MARIANE   *[Aside]*: He hates the sight of me, that's plain.
    I'll go, and so deliver him from pain.

DORINE   *[Leaving Valère, running after Mariane]*:
    And now *you* run away! Come back.

MARIANE: No, no.

80   Nothing you say will keep me here. Let go!

VALÈRE   *[Aside]*: She cannot bear my presence, I perceive.
    To spare her further torment, I shall leave.

DORINE   *[Leaving Mariane, running after Valère]*:
    Again! You'll not escape, Sir; don't you try it.
    Come here, you two. Stop fussing, and be quiet.

[She takes Valère by the hand, then Mariane, and draws them together.]

VALÈRE   *[To Dorine]*: What do you want of me?

MARIANE   *[To Dorine]*: What is the point of this?

DORINE: We're going to have a little armistice.
    [To Valère.] Now, weren't you silly to get so overheated?

VALÈRE: Didn't you see how badly I was treated?

DORINE   *[To Mariane]*: Aren't you a simpleton, to have lost your head?

MARIANE: Didn't you hear the hateful things he said?

DORINE   *[To Valère]*: You're both great fools. Her sole desire, Valère,
    Is to be yours in marriage. To that I'll swear.
    [To Mariane.] He loves you only, and he wants no wife

95   But you, Mariane. On that I'll stake my life.

MARIANE   *[To Valère]*: Then why you advised me so, I cannot see.

VALÈRE   *[To Mariane]*: On such a question, why ask advice of *me*?

DORINE: Oh, you're impossible. Give me your hands, you two.
    [To Valère.] Yours first.

VALÈRE   *[Giving Dorine his hand]*: But why?

DORINE [*To Mariane*]: And now a hand from you.

MARIANE   [*Also giving Dorine her hand*]:
What are you doing?

DORINE: There: a perfect fit.
You suit each other better than you'll admit.

[*Valère and Mariane hold hands for some time without looking at each other.*]

VALÈRE   [*Turning toward Mariane*]:
Ah, come, don't be so haughty. Give a man
A look of kindness, won't you, Mariane?

[*Mariane turns toward Valère and smiles.*]

DORINE: I tell you, lovers are completely mad!

VALÈRE   [*To Mariane*]: Now come, confess that you were very bad
To hurt my feelings as you did just now.
I have a just complaint, you must allow.

MARIANE: *You* must allow that you were most unpleasant...

DORINE: Let's table that discussion for the present;
Your father has a plan which must be stopped.

MARIANE: Advise us, then; what means must we adopt?

DORINE: We'll use all manner of means, and all at once.
[*To Mariane.*] Your father's addled; he's acting like a dunce.

115   Therefore you'd better humor the old fossil.
Pretend to yield to him, be sweet and docile,
And then postpone, as often as necessary,
The day on which you have agreed to marry.
You'll thus gain time, and time will turn the trick.

120   Sometimes, for instance, you'll be taken sick,
And that will seem good reason for delay;
Or some bad omen will make you change the day—
You'll dream of muddy water, or you'll pass
A dead man's hearse, or break a looking-glass.

125   If all else fails, no man can marry you
Unless you take his ring and say "I do."
But now, let's separate. If they should find
Us talking here, our plot might be divined.
[*To Valère.*] Go to your friends, and tell them what's occurred,

130   And have them urge her father to keep his word.
Meanwhile, we'll stir her brother into action,
And get Elmire,[6] as well, to join our faction.
Good-bye.

VALÈRE   [*To Mariane*]: Though each of us will do his best,

135   It's your true heart on which my hopes shall rest.

MARIANE   [*To Valère*]: Regardless of what Father may decide,
None but Valère shall claim me as his bride.

6. Orgon's second wife.

VALÈRE: Oh, how those words content me! Come what will...
DORINE: Oh, lovers, lovers! Their tongues are never still.
          Be off, now.
VALÈRE   [*Turning to go, then turning back*]:
          One last word...
DORINE: No time to chat:
          You leave by this door; and *you* leave by that.

[*Dorine pushes them, by the shoulders, toward opposing doors.*]

ACT 3

Scene 1

Damis, Dorine

DAMIS: May lightning strike me even as I speak,
          May all men call me cowardly and weak,
          If any fear or scruple holds me back
          From settling things, at once, with that great quack!
DORINE: Now, don't give way to violent emotion.
          Your father's merely talked about this notion,
          And words and deeds are far from being one.
          Much that is talked about is left undone.
DAMIS: No, I must stop that scoundrel's machinations;
10   I'll go and tell him off; I'm out of patience.
DORINE: Do calm down and be practical. I had rather
          My mistress dealt with him—and with your father.
          She has some influence with Tartuffe, I've noted.
          He hangs upon her words, seems most devoted,
15   And may, indeed, be smitten by her charm.
          Pray Heaven it's true! 'Twould do our cause no harm.
          She sent for him, just now, to sound him out
          On this affair you're so incensed about;
          She'll find out where he stands, and tell him, too,
20   What dreadful strife and trouble will ensue
          If he lends countenance to your father's plan.
          I couldn't get in to see him, but his man
          Says that he's almost finished with his prayers.
          Go, now. I'll catch him when he comes downstairs.
DAMIS: I want to hear this conference, and I will.
DORINE: No, they must be alone.
DAMIS: Oh, I'll keep still.
DORINE: Not you. I know your temper. You'd start a brawl,
          And shout and stamp your foot and spoil it all.
          Go on.
DAMIS: I won't; I have a perfect right...
DORINE: Lord, you're a nuisance! He's coming; get out of sight.

[*Damis conceals himself in a closet at the rear of the stage.*]

Scene 2

Tartuffe, Dorine

TARTUFFE   [*Observing Dorine, and calling to his manservant offstage*]:
        Hang up my hair-shirt, put my scourge in place,
        And pray, Laurent, for Heaven's perpetual grace.
        I'm going to the prison now, to share
        My last few coins with the poor wretches there.

DORINE   [*Aside*]: Dear God, what affectation! What a fake!

TARTUFFE: You wished to see me?

DORINE: Yes...

TARTUFFE   [*Taking a handkerchief from his pocket.*]:
                            For mercy's sake,
        Please take this handkerchief, before you speak.

DORINE: What?

TARTUFFE: Cover that bosom,[1] girl. The flesh is weak,
        And unclean thoughts are difficult to control.
10   Such sights as that can undermine the soul.

DORINE: Your soul, it seems, has very poor defenses,
        And flesh makes quite an impact on your senses.
        It's strange that you're so easily excited;
        My own desires are not so soon ignited,
15   And if I saw you naked as a beast,
        Not all your hide would tempt me in the least.

TARTUFFE: Girl, speak more modestly; unless you do,
        I shall be forced to take my leave of you.

DORINE: Oh, no, it's I who must be on my way;
20   I've just one little message to convey.
        Madame is coming down, and begs you, Sir,
        To wait and have a word or two with her.

TARTUFFE: Gladly.

DORINE   [*Aside*]: *That* had a softening effect!
        I think my guess about him was correct.

TARTUFFE: Will she be long?

DORINE: No: that's her step I hear.
        Ah, here she is, and I shall disappear.

Scene 3

Elmire, Tartuffe

TARTUFFE: May Heaven, whose infinite goodness we adore,
        Preserve your body and soul forevermore,
        And bless your days, and answer thus the plea
        Of one who is its humblest votary.

---

1. The Brotherhood of the Holy Sacrament practiced alms-giving to prisoners and kept a careful censorious check on women's clothing if they deemed it lascivious. Thus Molière's audience would have identified Tartuffe as sympathetic—hypocritically—to the aims of the organization.

ELMIRE: I thank you for that pious wish. But please,
          Do take a chair and let's be more at ease.

[*They sit down.*]

TARTUFFE: I trust that you are once more well and strong?
ELMIRE: Oh, yes: the fever didn't last for long.
TARTUFFE: My prayers are too unworthy, I am sure,
10   To have gained from Heaven this most gracious cure;
          But lately, Madam, my every supplication
          Has had for objects your recuperation.
ELMIRE: You shouldn't have troubled so. I don't deserve it.
TARTUFFE: Your health is priceless, Madam, and to preserve it
15   I'd gladly give my own, in all sincerity.
ELMIRE: Sir, you outdo us all in Christian charity.
          You've been most kind. I count myself your debtor.
TARTUFFE: 'Twas nothing, Madam. I long to serve you better.
ELMIRE: There's a private matter I'm anxious to discuss.
20   I'm glad there's no one here to hinder us.
TARTUFFE: I too am glad; it floods my heart with bliss
          To find myself alone with you like this.
          For just this chance I've prayed with all my power—
          But prayed in vain, until this happy hour.
ELMIRE: This won't take long, Sir, and I hope you'll be
          Entirely frank and unconstrained with me.
TARTUFFE: Indeed, there's nothing I had rather do
          Than bare my inmost heart and soul to you.
          First, let me say that what remarks I've made
30   About the constant visits you are paid
          Were prompted not by any mean emotion,
          But rather by a pure and deep devotion,
          A fervent zeal...
ELMIRE: No need for explanation.
          Your sole concern, I'm sure, was my salvation.
TARTUFFE [*Taking Elmire's hand and pressing her fingertips*]:
35   Quite so; and such great fervor do I feel...
ELMIRE: Ooh! Please! You're pinching!
TARTUFFE: 'Twas from excess of zeal.
          I never meant to cause you pain, I swear.
          I'd rather...

[*He places his hand on Elmire's knee.*]

ELMIRE: What can your hand be doing there?
TARTUFFE: Feeling your gown, what soft, fine-woven stuff.
ELMIRE: Please, I'm extremely ticklish. That's enough.

[*She draws her chair away; Tartuffe pulls his after her.*]

TARTUFFE [*Fondling the lace collar of her gown*]:
          My, my, what lovely lacework on your dress!
          The workmanship's miraculous, no less.

I've not seen anything to equal it.

ELMIRE: Yes, quite. But let's talk business for a bit.
45   You say my husband means to break his word
          And give his daughter to you, Sir. Had you heard?

TARTUFFE: He did once mention it. But I confess
          I dream of quite a different happiness.
          It's elsewhere, Madam, that my eyes discern
50   The promise of that bliss for which I yearn.

ELMIRE: I see: you care for nothing here below.

TARTUFFE: Ah, well—my heart's not made of stone, you know.

ELMIRE: All your desires mount heavenward, I'm sure,
          In scorn of all that's earthly and impure.

TARTUFFE: A love of heavenly beauty does not preclude
          A proper love for earthly pulchritude;
          Our senses are quite rightly captivated
          By perfect works our Maker has created.
          Some glory clings to all that Heaven has made;
60   In you, all Heaven's marvels are displayed.
          On that fair face, such beauties have been lavished,
          The eyes are dazzled and the heart is ravished;
          How could I look on you, O flawless creature,
          And not adore the Author of all Nature,
65   Feeling a love both passionate and pure
          For you, his triumph of self-portraiture?
          At first, I trembled lest that love should be
          A subtle snare that Hell had laid for me;
          I vowed to flee the sight of you, eschewing
70   A rapture that might prove my soul's undoing;
          But soon, fair being, I became aware
          That my deep passion could be made to square
          With rectitude, and with my bounden duty.
          I thereupon surrendered to your beauty.
75   It is, I know, presumptuous on my part
          To bring you this poor offering of my heart,
          And it is not my merit, Heaven knows,
          But your compassion on which my hopes repose.
          You are my peace, my solace, my salvation;
80   On you depends my bliss—or desolation;
          I bide your judgment and, as you think best,
          I shall be either miserable or blest.

ELMIRE: Your declaration is most gallant, Sir,
          But don't you think it's out of character?
85   You'd have done better to restrain your passion
          And think before you spoke in such a fashion.
          It ill becomes a pious man like you . . .

TARTUFFE: I may be pious, but I'm human too:
          With your celestial charms before his eyes,
90   A man has not the power to be wise,

I know such words sound strangely, coming from me,
But I'm no angel, nor was meant to be,
And if you blame my passion, you must needs
Reproach as well the charms on which it feeds.

95   Your loveliness I had no sooner seen
Than you became my soul's unrivalled queen;
Before your seraph glance, divinely sweet,
My heart's defenses crumbled in defeat,
And nothing fasting, prayer, or tears might do

100   Could stay my spirit from adoring you.
My eyes, my sighs have told you in the past
What now my lips make bold to say at last,
And if, in your great goodness, you will deign
To look upon your slave, and ease his pain,—

105   If, in compassion for my soul's distress,
You'll stoop to comfort my unworthiness,
I'll raise to you, in thanks for that sweet manna,
An endless hymn, an infinite hosanna.
With me, of course, there need be no anxiety,

110   No fear of scandal or of notoriety.
These young court gallants, whom all the ladies fancy,
Are vain in speech, in action rash and chancy;
When they succeed in love, the world soon knows it;
No favor's granted them but they disclose it

115   And by the looseness of their tongues profane
The very altar where their hearts have lain.
Men of my sort, however, love discreetly,
And one may trust our reticence completely.
My keen concern for my good name insures

120   The absolute security of yours;
In short, I offer you, my dear Elmire,
Love without scandal, pleasure without fear.

ELMIRE: I've heard your well-turned speeches to the end,
And what you urge I clearly comprehend.

125   Aren't you afraid that I may take a notion
To tell my husband of your warm devotion,
And that, supposing he were duly told,
His feelings toward you might grow rather cold?

TARTUFFE: I know, dear lady, that your exceeding charity

130   Will lead your heart to pardon my temerity;
That you'll excuse my violent affection
As human weakness, human imperfection;
And that—O fairest!—you will bear in mind
That I'm but flesh and blood, and am not blind.

ELMIRE: Some women might do otherwise, perhaps,
But I shall be discreet about your lapse;
I'll tell my husband nothing of what's occurred
If, in return, you'll give your solemn word

To advocate as forcefully as you can
The marriage of Valère and Mariane,
Renouncing all desire to dispossess
Another of his rightful happiness,
And...

Scene 4

Damis, Elmire, Tartuffe

DAMIS [*Emerging from the closet where he has been hiding*]:
No! We'll not hush up this vile affair;
I heard it all inside that closet there,
Where Heaven, in order to confound the pride
Of this great rascal, prompted me to hide.
Ah, now I have my long-awaited chance
To punish his deceit and arrogance,
And give my father clear and shocking proof
Of the black character of his dear Tartuffe.

ELMIRE: Ah no, Damis; I'll be content if he
Will study to deserve my leniency.
I've promised silence—don't make me break my word;
To make a scandal would be too absurd.
Good wives laugh off such trifles, and forget them;
Why should they tell their husbands, and upset them?

DAMIS: You have your reasons for taking such a course,
And I have reasons, too, of equal force.
To spare him now would be insanely wrong.
I've swallowed my just wrath for far too long
And watched this insolent bigot bringing strife
And bitterness into our family life.
Too long he's meddled in my father's affairs,
Thwarting my marriage-hopes, and poor Valère's.
It's high time that my father was undeceived,
And now I've proof that can't be disbelieved—
Proof that was furnished me by Heaven above.
It's too good not to take advantage of.
This is my chance, and I deserve to lose it
If, for one moment, I hesitate to use it.

ELMIRE: Damis...

DAMIS: No, I must do what I think right
Madam, my heart is bursting with delight,
And, say whatever you will, I'll not consent
To lose the sweet revenge on which I'm bent.
I'll settle matters without more ado;
And here, most opportunely, is my cue.[2]

2. In the original stage directions, Tartuffe now reads silently from his breviary—in the Roman Catholic Church, the book containing the Divine Office for each day, which those in holy orders are required to recite.

47

Scene 5

Orgon, Damis, Tartuffe, Elmire

DAMIS: Father, I'm glad you've joined us. Let us advise you
Of some fresh news which doubtless will surprise you.
You've just now been repaid with interest
For all your loving-kindness to our guest.
5   He's proved his warm and grateful feelings toward you;
It's with a pair of horns he would reward you.
Yes, I surprised him with your wife, and heard
His whole adulterous offer, every word.
She, with her all too gentle disposition,
10   Would not have told you of his proposition;
But I shall not make terms with brazen lechery,
And feel that not to tell you would be treachery.

ELMIRE: And I hold that one's husband's peace of mind
Should not be spoilt by tattle of this kind.
15   One's honor doesn't require it: to be proficient
In keeping men at bay is quite sufficient.
These are my sentiments, and I wish, Damis,
That you had heeded me and held your peace.

Scene 6

Orgon, Damis, Tartuffe

ORGON: Can it be true, this dreadful thing I hear?

TARTUFFE: Yes, Brother, I'm a wicked man, I fear:
A wretched sinner, all depraved and twisted,
The greatest villain that has ever existed.
5   My life's one heap of crimes, which grows each minute;
There's naught but foulness and corruption in it;
And I perceive that Heaven, outraged by me,
Has chosen this occasion to mortify me.
Charge me with any deed you wish to name;
10   I'll not defend myself, but take the blame.
Believe what you are told, and drive Tartuffe
Like some base criminal from beneath your roof;
Yes, drive me hence, and with a parting curse:
I shan't protest, for I deserve far worse.

ORGON   [*To Damis*]: Ah, you deceitful boy, how dare you try
To stain his purity with so foul a lie?

DAMIS: What! Are you taken in by such a bluff?
Did you not hear...?

ORGON: Enough, you rogue, enough!

TARTUFFE: Ah, Brother, let him speak: you're being unjust.
20   Believe his story; the boy deserves your trust.
Why, after all, should you have faith in me?
How can you know what I might do, or be?
Is it on my good actions that you base
Your favor? Do you trust my pious face?

25   Ah, no, don't be deceived by hollow shows;
        I'm far, alas, from being what men suppose;
        Though the world takes me for a man of worth,
        I'm truly the most worthless man on earth.
        [*To Damis*] Yes, my dear son, speak out now: call me the chief
30   Of sinners, a wretch, a murderer, a thief;
        Load me with all the names men most abhor;
        I'll not complain; I've earned them all, and more;
        I'll kneel here while you pour them on my head
        As a just punishment for the life I've led.

ORGON [*To Tartuffe*]:
        This is too much, dear Brother.
35   [*To Damis*]   Have you no heart?

DAMIS: Are you so hoodwinked by this rascal's art...?

ORGON: Be still, you monster.
        [*To Tartuffe*]   Brother, I pray you, rise.
        [*To Damis*] Villain!

DAMIS: But...

ORGON: Silence!

DAMIS: Can't you realize...?

ORGON: Just one word more, and I'll tear you limb from limb.

TARTUFFE: In God's name, Brother, don't be harsh with him.
        I'd rather far be tortured at the stake
        Than see him bear one scratch for my poor sake.

ORGON   [*To Damis*]: Ingrate!

TARTUFFE: If I must beg you, on bended knee,
        To pardon him...

ORGON [*Falling to his knees, addressing Tartuffe*]:
                Such goodness cannot be!
        [*To Damis*] Now, *there's* true charity!

DAMIS: What, you...?

ORGON: Villain, be still!
        I know your motives; I know you wish him ill:
        Yes, all of you—wife, children, servants, all—
        Conspire against him and desire his fall,
        Employing every shameful trick you can
50   To alienate me from this saintly man.
        Ah, but the more you seek to drive him away,
        The more I'll do to keep him. Without delay,
        I'll spite this household and confound its pride
        By giving him my daughter as his bride.

DAMIS: You're going to force her to accept his hand?

ORGON: Yes, and this very night, d'you understand?
        I shall defy you all, and make it clear
        That I'm the one who gives the orders here.
        Come, wretch, kneel down and clasp his blessed feet,
60   And ask his pardon for your black deceit.

DAMIS: I ask that swindler's pardon? Why, I'd rather...

ORGON: So! You insult him, and defy your father!

A stick! A stick! [*To Tartuffe.*] No, no—release me, do.
[*To Damis.*] Out of my house this minute! Be off with you,
65   And never dare set foot in it again.

DAMIS: Well, I shall go, but...

ORGON: Well, go quickly, then.
I disinherit you; an empty purse
Is all you'll get from me—except my curse!

Scene 7

Orgon, Tartuffe

ORGON: How he blasphemed your goodness! What a son!

TARTUFFE: Forgive him, Lord, as I've already done.
[*To Orgon.*] You can't know how it hurts when someone tries
To blacken me in my dear Brother's eyes.

ORGON: Ahh!

TARTUFFE: The mere thought of such ingratitude
Plunges my soul into so dark a mood...
Such horror grips my heart... I gasp for breath,
And cannot speak, and feel myself near death.

ORGON: [*He runs, in tears, to the door through which he has just driven his son.*]
You blackguard! Why did I spare you? Why did I not
10   Break you in little pieces on the spot?
Compose yourself, and don't be hurt, dear friend.

TARTUFFE: These scenes, these dreadful quarrels, have got to end.
I've much upset your household, and I perceive
That the best thing will be for me to leave.

ORGON: What are you saying!

TARTUFFE: They're all against me here:
They'd have you think me false and insincere.

ORGON: Ah, what of that? Have I ceased believing in you?

TARTUFFE: Their adverse talk will certainly continue,
And charges which you now repudiate
20   You may find credible at a later date.

ORGON: No, Brother, never.

TARTUFFE: Brother, a wife can sway
Her husband's mind in many a subtle way.

ORGON: No, no.

TARTUFFE: To leave at once is the solution;
Thus only can I end their persecution.

ORGON: No, no, I'll not allow it; you shall remain.

TARTUFFE: Ah, well; 'twill mean much martyrdom and pain,
But if you wish it...

ORGON: Ah!

TARTUFFE: Enough; so be it.
But one thing must be settled, as I see it.
For your dear honor, and for our friendship's sake,
30   There's one precaution I feel bound to take.
I shall avoid your wife, and keep away...

ORGON: No, you shall not, whatever they may say.
          It pleases me to vex them, and for spite
          I'd have them see you with her day and night.
35   What's more, I'm going to drive them to despair
          By making you my only son and heir;
          This very day, I'll give to you alone
          Clear deed and title to everything I own.
          A dear, good friend and son-in-law-to-be
40   Is more than wife, or child, or kin to me.
          Will you accept my offer, dearest son?
TARTUFFE: In all things, let the will of Heaven be done.
ORGON: Poor fellow! Come, we'll go draw up the deed,
          Then let them burst with disappointed greed!

Act 4

Scene 1

Cléante, Tartuffe

CLÉANTE: Yes, all the town's discussing it, and truly,
          Their comments do not flatter you unduly.
          I'm glad we've met, Sir, and I'll give my view
          Of this sad matter in a word or two.
5   As for who's guilty, that I shan't discuss;
          Let's say it was Damis who caused the fuss;
          Assuming, then, that you have been ill-used
          By young Damis, and groundlessly accused,
          Ought not a Christian to forgive, and ought
10   He not to stifle every vengeful thought?
          Should you stand by and watch a father make
          His only son an exile for your sake?
          Again I tell you frankly, be advised:
          The whole town, high and low, is scandalized;
15   This quarrel must be mended, and my advice is
          Not to push matters to a further crisis.
          No, sacrifice your wrath to God above,
          And help Damis regain his father's love.
TARTUFFE: Alas, for my part I should take great joy
20   In doing so. I've nothing against the boy.
          I pardon all, I harbor no resentment;
          To serve him would afford me much contentment.
          But Heaven's interest will not have it so:
          If he comes back, then I shall have to go.
25   After his conduct—so extreme, so vicious—
          Our further intercourse would look suspicious.
          God knows what people would think! Why, they'd describe
          My goodness to him as a sort of bribe;
          They'd say that out of guilt I made pretense
30   Of loving-kindness and benevolence—

That, fearing my accuser's tongue, I strove
To buy his silence with a show of love.
CLÉANTE: Your reasoning is badly warped and stretched,
And these excuses, Sir, are most far-fetched.
35   Why put yourself in charge of Heaven's cause?
Does Heaven need our help to enforce its laws?
Leave vengeance to the Lord, Sir; while we live,
Our duty's not to punish, but forgive;
And what the Lord commands, we should obey
40   Without regard to what the world may say.
What! Shall the fear of being misunderstood
Prevent our doing what is right and good?
No, no; let's simply do what Heaven ordains,
And let no other thoughts perplex our brains.
TARTUFFE: Again, Sir, let me say that I've forgiven
Damis, and thus obeyed the laws of Heaven;
But I am not commanded by the Bible
To live with one who smears my name with libel.
CLÉANTE: Were you commanded, Sir, to indulge the whim
50   Of poor Orgon, and to encourage him
In suddenly transferring to your name
A large estate to which you have no claim?
TARTUFFE: 'Twould never occur to those who know me best
To think I acted from self-interest.
55   The treasures of this world I quite despise;
Their specious glitter does not charm my eyes;
And if I have resigned myself to taking
The gift which my dear Brother insists on making,
I do so only, as he well understands,
60   Lest so much wealth fall into wicked hands,
Lest those to whom it might descend in time
Turn it to purposes of sin and crime,
And not, as I shall do, make use of it
For Heaven's glory and mankind's benefit.
CLÉANTE: Forget these trumped-up fears. Your argument
Is one the rightful heir might well resent;
It *is* a moral burden to inherit
Such wealth, but give Damis a chance to bear it.
And would it not be worse to be accused
70   Of swindling, than to see that wealth misused?
I'm shocked that you allowed Orgon to broach
This matter, and that you feel no self-reproach;
Does true religion teach that lawful heirs
May freely be deprived of what is theirs?
75   And if the Lord has told you in your heart
That you and young Damis must dwell apart,
Would it not be the decent thing to beat
A generous and honorable retreat,
Rather than let the son of the house be sent,

80   For your convenience, into banishment?
      Sir, if you wish to prove the honesty
      Of your intentions...
TARTUFFE: Sir, it is half-past three.
      I've certain pious duties to attend to,
      And hope my prompt departure won't offend you.
CLÉANTE [*Alone*]: Damn.

Scene 2

Elmire, Mariane, Cléante, Dorine

DORINE: Stay, Sir, and help Mariane, for Heaven's sake!
      She's suffering so, I fear her heart will break.
      Her father's plan to marry her off tonight
      Has put the poor child in a desperate plight.
5   I hear him coming. Let's stand together, now,
      And see if we can't change his mind, somehow,
      About this match we all deplore and fear.

Scene 3

Orgon, Elmire, Mariane, Cléante, Dorine

ORGON: Hah! Glad to find you all assembled here.
      [*To Mariane.*] This contract, child, contains your happiness,
      And what it says I think your heart can guess.
MARIANE [*Falling to her knees*]:
      Sir, by that Heaven which sees me here distressed,
5   And by whatever else can move your breast,
      Do not employ a father's power, I pray you,
      To crush my heart and force it to obey you,
      Nor by your harsh commands oppress me so
      That I'll begrudge the duty which I owe—
10   And do not so embitter and enslave me
      That I shall hate the very life you gave me.
      If my sweet hopes must perish, if you refuse
      To give me to the one I've dared to choose,
      Spare me at least—I beg you, I implore—
15   The pain of wedding one whom I abhor;
      And do not, by a heartless use of force,
      Drive me to contemplate some desperate course.
ORGON   [*Feeling himself touched by her*]:
      Be firm, my soul. No human weakness, now.
MARIANE: I don't resent your love for him. Allow
20   Your heart free rein, Sir; give him your property,
      And if that's not enough, take mine from me;
      He's welcome to my money; take it, do,
      But don't, I pray, include my person too.
      Spare me, I beg you; and let me end the tale
25   Of my sad days behind a convent veil.
ORGON: A convent! Hah! When crossed in their amours,

All lovesick girls have the same thought as yours.
Get up! The more you loathe the man, and dread him,
The more ennobling it will be to wed him.

30   Marry Tartuffe, and mortify your flesh!
Enough; don't start that whimpering afresh.

DORINE: But why...?

ORGON: Be still, there. Speak when you're spoken to.
Not one more bit of impudence out of you.

CLÉANTE: If I may offer a word of counsel here...

ORGON: Brother, in counseling you have no peer;
All your advice is forceful, sound, and clever;
I don't propose to follow it, however.

ELMIRE   [*To Orgon*]:
I am amazed, and don't know what to say;
Your blindness simply takes my breath away.

40   You are indeed bewitched, to take no warning
From our account of what occurred this morning.

ORGON: Madam, I know a few plain facts, and one
Is that you're partial to my rascal son;
Hence, when he sought to make Tartuffe the victim

45   Of a base lie, you dared not contradict him.
Ah, but you underplayed your part, my pet;
You should have looked more angry, more upset.

ELMIRE: When men make overtures, must we reply
With righteous anger and a battle-cry?

50   Must we turn back their amorous advances
With sharp reproaches and with fiery glances?
Myself, I find such offers merely amusing,
And make no scenes and fusses in refusing;
My taste is for good-natured rectitude,

55   And I dislike the savage sort of prude
Who guards her virtue with her teeth and claws,
And tears men's eyes out for the slightest cause:
The Lord preserve me from such honor as that,
Which bites and scratches like an alley-cat!

60   I've found that a polite and cool rebuff
Discourages a lover quite enough.

ORGON: I know the facts, and I shall not be shaken.

ELMIRE: I marvel at your power to be mistaken.
Would it, I wonder, carry weight with you

65   If I could *show* you that our tale was true?

ORGON: Show me?

ELMIRE: Yes.

ORGON: Rot.

ELMIRE: Come, what if I found a way
To make you see the facts as plain as day?

ORGON: Nonsense.

ELMIRE: Do answer me; don't be absurd.
I'm not now asking you to trust our word.

70 Suppose that from some hiding-place in here
    You learned the whole sad truth by eye and ear—
    What would you say of your good friend, after that?
ORGON: Why, I'd say…nothing, by Jehoshaphat!
    It can't be true.
ELMIRE: You've been too long deceived,
75 And I'm quite tired of being disbelieved.
    Come now: let's put my statements to the test,
    And you shall see the truth made manifest.
ORGON: I'll take that challenge. Now do your uttermost.
    We'll see how you make good your empty boast.
ELMIRE [*To Dorine*]: Send him to me.
DORINE: He's crafty; it may be hard
    To catch the cunning scoundrel off his guard.
ELMIRE: No, amorous men are gullible. Their conceit
    So blinds them that they're never hard to cheat.
    Have him come down.
    [*To Cléante and Mariane.*] Please leave us, for a bit.

Scene 4

Elmire, Orgon

ELMIRE: Pull up this table, and get under it.
ORGON: What?
ELMIRE: It's essential that you be well-hidden.
ORGON: Why there?
ELMIRE: Oh, Heaven's! Just do as you are bidden.
    I have my plans; we'll soon see how they fare.
5   Under the table, now; and once you're there,
    Take care that you are neither seen nor heard.
ORGON: Well, I'll indulge you, since I gave my word
    To see you through this infantile charade.
ELMIRE: Once it is over, you'll be glad we played.

[*To her husband, who is now under the table.*]

10 I'm going to act quite strangely, now, and you
    Must not be shocked at anything I do.
    Whatever I may say, you must excuse
    As part of that deceit I'm forced to use.
    I shall employ sweet speeches in the task
15 Of making that imposter drop his mask;
    I'll give encouragement to his bold desires,
    And furnish fuel to his amorous fires.
    Since it's for your sake, and for his destruction,
    That I shall seem to yield to his seduction,
20 I'll gladly stop whenever you decide
    That all your doubts are fully satisfied.
    I'll count on you, as soon as you have seen
    What sort of man he is, to intervene,

25   And not expose me to his odious lust
      One moment longer than you feel you must.
      Remember: you're to save me from my plight
      Whenever... He's coming! Hush! Keep out of sight!

Scene 5

Tartuffe, Elmire, Orgon

TARTUFFE: You wish to have a word with me, I'm told.

ELMIRE: Yes. I've a little secret to unfold.
      Before I speak, however, it would be wise
      To close that door, and look about for spies.

[Tartuffe goes to the door, closes it, and returns.]

5   The very last thing that must happen now
      Is a repetition of this morning's row.
      I've never been so badly caught off guard.
      Oh, how I feared for you! You saw how hard
      I tried to make that troublesome Damis
10   Control his dreadful temper, and hold his peace.
      In my confusion, I didn't have the sense
      Simply to contradict his evidence;
      But as it happened, that was for the best,
      And all has worked out in our interest.
15   This storm has only bettered your position;
      My husband doesn't have the least suspicion,
      And now, in mockery of those who do,
      He bids me be continually with you.
      And that is why, quite fearless of reproof,
20   I now can be alone with my Tartuffe,
      And why my heart—perhaps too quick to yield—
      Feels free to let its passion be revealed.

TARTUFFE: Madam, your words confuse me. Not long ago,
      You spoke in quite a different style, you know.

ELMIRE: Ah, Sir, if that refusal made you smart,
      It's little that you know of woman's heart,
      Or what that heart is trying to convey
      When it resists in such a feeble way!
      Always, at first, our modesty prevents
30   The frank avowal of tender sentiments;
      However high the passion which inflames us,
      Still, to confess its power somehow shames us.
      Thus we reluct, at first, yet in a tone
      Which tells you that our heart is overthrown,
35   That what our lips deny, our pulse confesses,
      And that, in time, all noes will turn to yesses.
      I fear my words are all too frank and free,
      And a poor proof of woman's modesty;
      But since I'm started, tell me, if you will—

40   Would I have tried to make Damis be still,
    Would I have listened, calm and unoffended,
    Until your lengthy offer of love was ended,
    And been so very mild in my reaction,
    Had your sweet words not given me satisfaction?
45   And when I tried to force you to undo
    The marriage-plans my husband has in view,
    What did my urgent pleading signify
    If not that I admired you, and that I
    Deplored the thought that someone else might own
50   Part of a heart I wished for mine alone?

TARTUFFE: Madam, no happiness is so complete
    As when, from lips we love, come words so sweet;
    Their nectar floods my every sense, and drains
    In honeyed rivulets through all my veins.
55   To please you is my joy, my only goal;
    Your love is the restorer of my soul;
    And yet I must beg leave, now, to confess
    Some lingering doubts as to my happiness.
    Might this not be a trick? Might not the catch
60   Be that you wish me to break off the match
    With Mariane, and so have feigned to love me?
    I shan't quite trust your fond opinion of me
    Until the feelings you've expressed so sweetly
    Are demonstrated somewhat more concretely,
65   And you have shown, by certain kind concessions,
    That I may put my faith in your professions.

ELMIRE [*She coughs, to warn her husband*]:
    Why be in such a hurry? Must my heart
    Exhaust its bounty at the very start?
    To make that sweet admission cost me dear,
70   But you'll not be content, it would appear,
    Unless my store of favors is disbursed
    To the last farthing, and at the very first.

TARTUFFE: The less we merit, the less we dare to hope,
    And with our doubts, mere words can never cope.
75   We trust no promised bliss till we receive it;
    Not till a joy is ours can we believe it.
    I, who so little merit your esteem,
    Can't credit this fulfillment of my dream,
    And shan't believe it, Madam, until I savor
80   Some palpable assurance of your favor.

ELMIRE: My, how tyrannical your love can be,
    And how it flusters and perplexes me!
    How furiously you take one's heart in hand,
    And make your every wish a fierce command!
85   Come, must you hound and harry me to death?
    Will you not give me time to catch my breath?
    Can it be right to press me with such force,

Give me no quarter, show me no remorse,
And take advantage, by your stern insistence,
90   Of the fond feelings which weaken my resistance?
TARTUFFE: Well, if you look with favor upon my love,
Why, then, begrudge me some clear proof thereof?
ELMIRE: But how can I consent without offense
To Heaven, toward which you feel such reverence?
TARTUFFE: If Heaven is all that holds you back, don't worry.
I can remove that hindrance in a hurry.
Nothing of that sort need obstruct our path.
ELMIRE: Must one not be afraid of Heaven's wrath?
TARTUFFE: Madam, forget such fears, and be my pupil,
100   And I shall teach you how to conquer scruple.
Some joys, it's true, are wrong in Heaven's eyes;
Yet Heaven is not averse to compromise;
There is a science, lately formulated,
Whereby one's conscience may be liberated,[1]
105   And any wrongful act you care to mention
May be redeemed by purity of intention.
I'll teach you, Madam, the secrets of that science;
Meanwhile, just place on me your full reliance.
Assuage my keen desires, and feel no dread:
110   The sin, if any, shall be on my head.

[*Elmire coughs, this time more loudly.*]

You've a bad cough.
ELMIRE: Yes, yes. It's bad indeed.
TARTUFFE   [*Producing a little paper bag*]:
A bit of licorice may be what you need.
ELMIRE: No, I've a stubborn cold, it seems. I'm sure it
Will take much more than licorice to cure it.
TARTUFFE: How aggravating.
ELMIRE: Oh, more than I can say.
TARTUFFE: If you're still troubled, think of things this way:
No one shall know our joys, save us alone,
And there's no evil till the act is known;
It's scandal, Madam, which makes it an offense,
120   And it's no sin to sin in confidence.
ELMIRE   [*Having coughed once more*]:
Well, clearly I must do as you require,
And yield to your importunate desire.
It is apparent, now, that nothing less
Will satisfy you, and so I acquiesce.
125   To go so far is much against my will;
I'm vexed that it should come to this; but still,
Since you are so determined on it, since you

---

1. Molière created his own footnote to this line: "It is a scoundrel who speaks."

Will not allow mere language to convince you,
And since you ask for concrete evidence, I
130   See nothing for it, now, but to comply.
If this is sinful, if I'm wrong to do it,
So much the worse for him who drove me to it.
The fault can surely not be charged to me.
TARTUFFE: Madam, the fault is mine, if fault there be,
And...
ELMIRE: Open the door a little, and peek out;
I wouldn't want my husband poking about.
TARTUFFE: Why worry about the man? Each day he grows
More gullible; one can lead him by the nose.
To find us here would fill him with delight,
140   And if he saw the worst, he'd doubt his sight.
ELMIRE: Nevertheless, do step out for a minute
Into the hall, and see that no one's in it.

Scene 6

Orgon, Elmire

ORGON   [*Coming out from under the table*]:
That man's a perfect monster, I must admit!
I'm simply stunned. I can't get over it.
ELMIRE: What, coming out so soon? How premature!
Get back in hiding, and wait until you're sure.
5   Stay till the end, and be convinced completely;
We mustn't stop till things are proved concretely.
ORGON: Hell never harbored anything so vicious!
ELMIRE: Tut, don't be hasty. Try to be judicious.
Wait, and be certain that there's no mistake.
10   No jumping to conclusions, for Heaven's sake!

[*She places Orgon behind her, as Tartuffe re-enters*]

Scene 7

Tartuffe, Elmire, Orgon

TARTUFFE   [*Not seeing Orgon*]:
Madam, all things have worked out to perfection;
I've given the neighboring rooms a full inspection;
No one's about; and now I may at last...
ORGON   [*Intercepting him*]: Hold, my passionate fellow, not so fast!
5   I should advise a little more restraint.
Well, so you thought you'd fool me, my dear saint!
How soon you wearied of the saintly life—
Wedding my daughter, and coveting my wife!
I've long suspected you, and had a feeling
10   That soon I'd catch you at your double-dealing.

Just now, you've given me evidence galore;
It's quite enough; I have no wish for more.

ELMIRE: [*To Tartuffe*]: I'm sorry to have treated you so slyly,
But circumstances forced me to be wily.

TARTUFFE: Brother, you can't think...

ORGON: No more talk from you;
Just leave this household, without more ado.

TARTUFFE: What I intended...

ORGON: That seems fairly clear.
Spare me your falsehoods and get out of here.

TARTUFFE: No, I'm the master, and you're the one to go!
20   This house belongs to me, I'll have you know,
And I shall show you that you can't hurt *me*
By this contemptible conspiracy,
That those who cross me know not what they do,
And that I've means to expose and punish you,
25   Avenge offended Heaven, and make you grieve
That ever you dared order me to leave.

Scene 8

Elmire, Orgon

ELMIRE: What was the point of all that angry chatter?
ORGON: Dear God, I'm worried. This is no laughing matter.
ELMIRE: How so?
ORGON: I fear I understood his drift.
I'm much disturbed about that deed of gift.
ELMIRE: You gave him...?
ORGON: Yes, it's all been drawn and signed.
But one thing more is weighing on my mind.
ELMIRE: What's that?
ORGON: I'll tell you; but first let's see if there's
A certain strong-box in his room upstairs.

Act 5

Scene 1

Orgon, Cléante

CLÉANTE: Where are you going so fast?
ORGON: God knows!
CLÉANTE: Then wait;
Let's have a conference, and deliberate
On how this situation's to be met.
ORGON: That strong-box has me utterly upset;
5   This is the worst of many, many shocks.
CLÉANTE: Is there some fearful mystery in that box?
ORGON: My poor friend Argas brought that box to me

With his own hands, in utmost secrecy;
'Twas on the very morning of his flight.

10   It's full of papers which, if they came to light,
Would ruin him—or such is my impression.

CLÉANTE: Then why did you let it out of your possession?

ORGON: Those papers vexed my conscience, and it seemed best
To ask the counsel of my pious guest.

15   The cunning scoundrel got me to agree
To leave the strong-box in his custody,
So that, in case of an investigation,
I could employ a slight equivocation
And swear I didn't have it, and thereby,

20   At no expense to conscience, tell a lie.

CLÉANTE: It looks to me as if you're out on a limb.
Trusting him with that box, and offering him
That deed of gift, were actions of a kind
Which scarcely indicate a prudent mind.

25   With two such weapons, he has the upper hand,
And since you're vulnerable, as matters stand,
You erred once more in bringing him to bay.
You should have acted in some subtler way.

ORGON: Just think of it: behind that fervent face,

30   A heart so wicked, and a soul so base!
I took him in, a hungry beggar, and then ...
Enough, by God! I'm through with pious men:
Henceforth I'll hate the whole false brotherhood,
And persecute them worse than Satan could.

CLÉANTE: Ah, there you go—extravagant as ever!
Why can you not be rational? You never
Manage to take the middle course, it seems,
But jump, instead, between absurd extremes.
You've recognized your recent grave mistake

40   In falling victim to a pious fake;
Now, to correct that error, must you embrace
An even greater error in its place,
And judge our worthy neighbors as a whole
By what you've learned of one corrupted soul?

45   Come, just because one rascal made you swallow
A show of zeal which turned out to be hollow,
Shall you conclude that all men are deceivers,
And that, today, there are no true believers?
Let atheists make that foolish inference;

50   Learn to distinguish virtue from pretense,
Be cautious in bestowing admiration,
And cultivate a sober moderation.
Don't humor fraud, but also don't asperse
True piety; the latter fault is worse,

55   And it is best to err, if err one must,
As you have done, upon the side of trust.

Scene 2

Damis, Orgon, Cléante

DAMIS: Father, I hear that scoundrel's uttered threats
Against you; that he pridefully forgets
How, in his need, he was befriended by you,
And means to use your gifts to crucify you.

ORGON: It's true, my boy. I'm too distressed for tears.

DAMIS: Leave it to me, Sir; let me trim his ears.
Faced with such insolence, we must not waver.
I shall rejoice in doing you the favor
Of cutting short his life, and your distress.

CLÉANTE: What a display of young hotheadedness!
Do learn to moderate your fits of rage.
In this just kingdom, this enlightened age,
One does not settle things by violence.

Scene 3

Madame Pernelle, Mariane, Elmire, Dorine, Damis, Orgon, Cléante

MADAME PERNELLE: I hear strange tales of very strange events.

ORGON: Yes, strange events which these two eyes beheld.
The man's ingratitude is unparalleled.
I save a wretched pauper from starvation,
5   House him, and treat him like a blood relation,
Shower him every day with my largesse,
Give him my daughter, and all that I possess;
And meanwhile the unconscionable knave
Tries to induce my wife to misbehave;
10   And not content with such extreme rascality,
Now threatens me with my own liberality,
And aims, by taking base advantage of
The gifts I gave him out of Christian love,
To drive me from my house, a ruined man,
15   And make me end a pauper, as he began.

DORINE: Poor fellow!

MADAME PERNELLE: No, my son, I'll never bring
Myself to think him guilty of such a thing.

ORGON: How's that?

MADAME PERNELLE: The righteous always were maligned.

ORGON: Speak clearly, Mother. Say what's on your mind.

MADAME PERNELLE: I mean that I can smell a rat, my dear.
You know how everybody hates him, here.

ORGON: That has no bearing on the case at all.

MADAME PERNELLE: I told you a hundred times, when you were small,
That virtue in this world is hated ever;
25   Malicious men may die, but malice never.

ORGON: No doubt that's true, but how does it apply?

MADAME PERNELLE: They've turned you against him by a clever lie.

ORGON: I've told you, I was there and saw it done.

MADAME PERNELLE: Ah, slanderers will stop at nothing, Son.

ORGON: Mother, I'll lose my temper… For the last time,
    I tell you I was witness to the crime.

MADAME PERNELLE: The tongues of spite are busy night and noon,
    And to their venom no man is immune.

ORGON: You're talking nonsense. Can't you realize
35   I saw it; saw it; saw it with my eyes?
    Saw, do you understand me? Must I shout it
    Into your ears before you'll cease to doubt it?

MADAME PERNELLE: Appearances can deceive, my son. Dear me,
    We cannot always judge by what we see.

ORGON: Drat! Drat!

MADAME PERNELLE: One often interprets things awry;
    Good can seem evil to a suspicious eye.

ORGON: Was I to see his pawing at Elmire
    As an act of charity?

MADAME PERNELLE: Till his guilt is clear,
    A man deserves the benefits of the doubt.
45   You should have waited, to see how things turned out.

ORGON: Great God in Heaven, what more proof did I need?
    Was I to sit there, watching, until he'd…
    You drive me to the brink of impropriety.

MADAME PERNELLE: No, no, a man of such surpassing piety
50   Could not do such a thing. You cannot shake me.
    I don't believe it, and you shall not make me.

ORGON: You vex me so that, if you weren't my mother,
    I'd say to you… some dreadful thing or other.

DORINE: It's your turn now, Sir, not to be listened to;
55   You'd not trust us, and now she won't trust you.

CLÉANTE: My friends, we're wasting time which should be spent
    In facing up to our predicament.
    I fear that scoundrel's threats weren't made in sport.

DAMIS: Do you think he'd have the nerve to go to court?

ELMIRE: I'm sure he won't: they'd find it all too crude
    A case of swindling and ingratitude.

CLÉANTE: Don't be too sure. He won't be at a loss
    To give his claims a high and righteous gloss;
    And clever rogues with far less valid cause
65   Have trapped their victims in a web of laws.
    I say again that to antagonize
    A man so strongly armed was most unwise.

ORGON: I know it; but the man's appalling cheek
    Outraged me so, I couldn't control my pique.

CLÉANTE: I wish to Heaven that we could devise
    Some truce between you, or some compromise.

ELMIRE: If I had known what cards he held, I'd not
    Have roused his anger by my little plot.

ORGON [To Dorine, as M. Loyal enters]:

What is that fellow looking for? Who is he?
75   Go talk to him—and tell him that I'm busy.

Scene 4

Monsieur Loyal, Madame Pernelle, Orgon, Damis, Mariane, Dorine, Elmire,
Cléante

MONSIEUR LOYAL: Good day, dear sister. Kindly let me see
Your master.
DORINE: He's involved with company,
And cannot be disturbed just now, I fear.
MONSIEUR LOYAL: I hate to intrude; but what has brought me here
5   Will not disturb your master, in any event.
Indeed, my news will make him most content.
DORINE: Your name?
MONSIEUR LOYAL: Just say that I bring greetings from
Monsieur Tartuffe, on whose behalf I've come.
DORINE [*To Orgon*]:
Sir, he's a very gracious man, and bears
10   A message from Tartuffe, which, he declares,
Will make you most content.
CLÉANTE: Upon my word,
I think this man had best be seen, and heard.
ORGON: Perhaps he has some settlement to suggest.
How shall I treat him? What manner would be best?
CLÉANTE: Control your anger, and if he should mention
Some fair adjustment, give him your full attention.
MONSIEUR LOYAL: Good health to you, good Sir. May Heaven confound
Your enemies, and may your joys abound.
ORGON [*Aside, to Cléante*]:
A gentle salutation: it confirms
20   My guess that he is here to offer terms.
MONSIEUR LOYAL: I've always held your family most dear;
I served your father, Sir, for many a year.
ORGON: Sir, I must ask your pardon; to my shame,
I cannot now recall your face or name.
MONSIEUR LOYAL: Loyal's my name; I come from Normandy,
And I'm a bailiff, in all modesty.
For forty years, praise God, it's been my boast
To serve with honor in that vital post,
And I am here, Sir, if you will permit
30   The liberty, to serve you with this writ...
ORGON: To—*what?*
MONSIEUR LOYAL: Now, please, Sir, let us have no friction:
It's nothing but an order of eviction.
You are to move your goods and family out
And make way for new occupants, without
35   Deferment or delay, and give the keys...
ORGON: I? Leave this house?

64

MONSIEUR LOYAL: Why yes, Sir, if you please.
          This house, Sir, from the cellar to the roof,
          Belongs now to the good Monsieur Tartuffe,
          And he is lord and master of your estate
40   By virtue of a deed of present date,
          Drawn in due form, with clearest legal phrasing...
DAMIS: Your insolence is utterly amazing!
MONSIEUR LOYAL: Young man, my business here is not with you,
          But with your wise and temperate father, who,
45   Like every worthy citizen, stands in awe
          Of justice, and would never obstruct the law.
ORGON: But...
MONSIEUR LOYAL: Not for a million, Sir, would you rebel
          Against authority; I know that well.
          You'll not make trouble, Sir, or interfere
50   With the execution of my duties here.
DAMIS: Someone may execute a smart tattoo
          On that black jacket[1] of yours, before you're through.
MONSIEUR LOYAL: Sir, bid your son be silent. I'd much regret
          Having to mention such a nasty threat
55   Of violence, in writing my report.
DORINE   [*Aside*]: This man Loyal's a most disloyal sort!
MONSIEUR LOYAL: I love all men of upright character,
          And when I agreed to serve these papers, Sir,
          It was your feelings that I had in mind.
60   It couldn't bear to see the case assigned
          To someone else, who might esteem you less
          And so subject you to unpleasantness.
ORGON: What's more unpleasant than telling a man to leave
          His house and home?
MONSIEUR LOYAL: You'd like a short reprieve?
65   If you desire it, Sir, I shall not press you,
          But wait until tomorrow to dispossess you.
          Splendid. I'll come and spend the night here, then,
          Most quietly, with half a score of men.
          For form's sake, you might bring me, just before
70   You go to bed, the keys to the front door.
          My men, I promise, will be on their best
          Behavior, and will not disturb your rest.
          But bright and early, Sir, you must be quick
          And move out all your furniture, every stick:
75   The men I've chosen are both young and strong,
          And with their help it shouldn't take you long.
          In short, I'll make things pleasant and convenient,
          And since I'm being so extremely lenient,

---

1. In the original, *justaucorps à longues bargues,* a close-fitting, long black coat with skirts, the customary dress of a bailiff.

Please show me, Sir, a like consideration,
80   And give me your entire cooperation.
ORGON   [Aside]: I may be all but bankrupt, but I vow
I'd give a hundred louis, here and now,
Just for the pleasure of landing one good clout
Right on the end of that complacent snout.
CLÉANTE: Careful; don't make things worse.
DAMIS: My bootsole itches
To give that beggar a good kick in the breeches.
DORINE: Monsieur Loyal, I'd love to hear the whack
Of a stout stick across your fine broad back.
MONSIEUR LOYAL: Take care: a woman too may go to jail if
90   She uses threatening language to a bailiff.
CLÉANTE: Enough, enough, Sir. This must not go on.
Give me that paper, please, and then begone.
MONSIEUR LOYAL: Well, *au revoir.* God give you all good cheer!
ORGON: May God confound you, and him who sent you here!

Scene 5

Orgon, Cléante, Mariane, Elmire, Madame Pernelle, Dorine, Damis

ORGON: Now, Mother, was I right or not? This writ
Should change your notion of Tartuffe a bit.
Do you perceive his villainy at last?
MADAME PERNELLE: I'm thunderstruck. I'm utterly aghast.
DORINE: Oh, come, be fair. You mustn't take offense
At this new proof of his benevolence.
He's acting out of selfless love, I know.
Material things enslave the soul, and so
He kindly has arranged your liberation
10   From all that might endanger your salvation.
ORGON: Will you not ever hold your tongue, you dunce?
CLÉANTE: Come, you must take some action, and at once.
ELMIRE: Go tell the world of the low trick he's tried.
The deed of gift is surely nullified
15   By such behavior, and public rage will not
Permit the wretch to carry out his plot.

Scene 6

Valère, Orgon, Cléante, Elmire, Mariane, Madame Pernelle, Damis, Dorine

VALÈRE: Sir, though I hate to bring you more bad news,
Such is the danger that I cannot choose.
A friend who is extremely close to me
And knows my interest in your family
5   Has, for my sake, presumed to violate
The secrecy that's due to things of state,
And sends me word that you are in a plight
From which your one salvation lies in flight.

That scoundrel who's imposed upon you so
10 Denounced you to the King an hour ago
And, as supporting evidence, displayed
The strong-box of a certain renegade
Whose secret papers, so he testified,
You had disloyally agreed to hide.
15 I don't know just what charges may be pressed,
But there's a warrant out for your arrest;
Tartuffe has been instructed, furthermore,
To guide the arresting officer to your door.

CLÉANTE: He's clearly done this to facilitate
20 His seizure of your house and your estate.

ORGON: That man, I must say, is a vicious beast!

VALÈRE: You can't afford to delay, Sir, in the least.
My carriage is outside, to take you hence;
This thousand louis should cover all expense.
25 Let's lose no time, or you shall be undone;
The sole defense, in this case, is to run.
I shall go with you all the way, and place you
In a safe refuge to which they'll never trace you.

ORGON: Alas, dear boy, I wish that I could show you
30 My gratitude for everything I owe you.
But now is not the time; I pray the Lord
That I may live to give you your reward.
Farewell, my dears; be careful . . .

CLÉANTE: Brother, hurry.
We shall take care of things; you needn't worry.

Scene 7

The Officer, Tartuffe, Valère, Orgon, Elmire, Mariane, Madame Pernelle, Dorine, Cléante, Damis

TARTUFFE: Gently, Sir, gently; stay right where you are.
No need for haste; your lodging isn't far.
You're off to prison, by order of the Prince.

ORGON: This is the crowning blow, you wretch; and since
5 It means my total ruin and defeat,
Your villainy is now at last complete.

TARTUFFE: You needn't try to provoke me; it's no use.
Those who serve Heaven must expect abuse.

CLÉANTE: You are indeed most patient, sweet, and blameless.

DORINE: How he exploits the name of Heaven! It's shameless.

TARTUFFE: Your taunts and mockeries are all for naught;
To do my duty is my only thought.

MARIANE: Your love of duty is most meritorious,
And what you've done is little short of glorious.

TARTUFFE: All deeds are glorious, Madam, which obey
The sovereign prince who sent me here today.

ORGON: I rescued you when you were destitute;

Have you forgotten that, you thankless brute?

TARTUFFE: No, no, I well remember everything;

20 But my first duty is to serve my King.
That obligation is so paramount
That other claims, beside it, do not count;
And for it I would sacrifice my wife,
My family, my friend, or my own life.

ELMIRE: Hypocrite!

DORINE: All that we most revere, he uses
To cloak his plots and camouflage his ruses.

CLÉANTE: If it is true that you are animated
By pure and loyal zeal, as you have stated,
Why was this zeal not roused until you'd sought

30 To make Orgon a cuckold, and been caught?
Why weren't you moved to give your evidence
Until your outraged host had driven you hence?
I shan't say that the gift of all his treasure
Ought to have damped your zeal in any measure;

35 But if he is a traitor, as you declare,
How could you condescend to be his heir?

TARTUFFE: [*To the Officer*]
Sir, spare me all this clamor; it's growing shrill.
Please carry out your orders, if you will.

OFFICER:[2] Yes, I've delayed too long, Sir. Thank you kindly.

40 You're just the proper person to remind me.
Come, you are off to join the other boarders
In the King's prison, according to his orders.

TARTUFFE: Who? I, Sir?

OFFICER: Yes.

TARTUFFE: To prison? This can't be true!

OFFICER: I owe an explanation, but not to you.

45 [*To Orgon.*] Sir, all is well; rest easy, and be grateful.
We serve a Prince to whom all sham is hateful,
A Prince who sees into our inmost hearts,
And can't be fooled by any trickster's arts.
His royal soul, though generous and human,

50 Views all things with discernment and acumen;
His sovereign reason is not lightly swayed,
And all his judgments are discreetly weighed.
He honors righteous men of every kind,
And yet his zeal for virtue is not blind,

55 Nor does his love of piety numb his wits
And make him tolerant of hypocrites.
'Twas hardly likely that this man could cozen
A King who's foiled such liars by the dozen.
With one keen glance, the King perceived the whole

2. In the original, *un exempt*. He would actually have been a gentleman from the king's personal body-guard with the rank of lieutenant colonel or "master of the camp."

60 Perverseness and corruption of his soul,
  And thus high Heaven's justice was displayed:
  Betraying you, the rogue stood self-betrayed.
  The King soon recognized Tartuffe as one
  Notorious by another name, who'd done
65 So many vicious crimes that one could fill
  Ten volumes with them, and be writing still.
  But to be brief: our sovereign was appalled
  By this man's treachery toward you, which he called
  The last, worst villainy of a vile career,
70 And bade me follow the impostor here
  To see how gross his impudence could be,
  And force him to restore your property.
  Your private papers, by the King's command,
  I hereby seize and give into your hand.
75 The King, by royal order, invalidates
  The deed which gave this rascal your estates,
  And pardons, furthermore, your grave offense
  In harboring an exile's documents.
  By these decrees, our Prince rewards you for
80 Your loyal deeds in the late civil war,[3]
  And shows how heartfelt is his satisfaction
  In recompensing any worthy action,
  How much he prizes merit, and how he makes
  More of men's virtues than of their mistakes.

DORINE: Heaven be praised!
MADAME PERNELLE: I breathe again, at last.
ELMIRE: We're safe.
MARIANE: I can't believe the danger's past.
ORGON [*To Tartuffe.*]: Well, traitor, now you see...
CLÉANTE: Ah, Brother, please
  Let's not descend to such indignities.
  Leave the poor wretch to his unhappy fate,
90 And don't say anything to aggravate
  His present woes; but rather hope that he
  Will soon embrace an honest piety,
  And mend his ways, and by a true repentance
  Move our just King to moderate his sentence.
95 Meanwhile, go kneel before your sovereign's throne
  And thank him for the mercies he has shown.

ORGON: Well said: let's go at once and, gladly kneeling,
  Express the gratitude which all are feeling.
  Then, when that first great duty has been done,
100 We'll turn with pleasure to a second one,
  And give Valère, whose love has proven so true,
  The wedded happiness which is his due.

---

3. A reference to Orgon's role in supporting the king during the *Frondes*.

Japanese puppet theater emerged in the early seventeenth century and flourished thereafter as popular entertainment. In contrast to noh—a medieval dramatic genre that continued to be staged but whose audience was largely samurai or merchant elite—puppet theater was aimed at a wide audience. Puppet theater consists of three elements that are closely coordinated: the puppets, the music (played by a banjo-like *shamisen*), and the chanting (*jōruri*) performed by a chanter who sits to the side of the stage and who speaks or sings all the roles of the puppets, including the third-person narration. Puppet theater began with one-man puppets, but by the eighteenth century it had evolved into a complex art with three-man puppets whose handlers are visible to the audience: the head puppeteer controls the head and right hand, the second manipulates the left hand, and the third is in charge of the feet. Of the three elements—puppets, music, and chanting—the chanting is the most important, so much so that the chanter is usually the star performer and the chanting is sometimes performed alone, without the puppets.

Chikamatsu Mon'zaemon was the greatest of the puppet theater playwrights. He came from a relatively well-off samurai (warrior) family and served in the households of royalty and aristocrats in Kyoto in his youth, before going into the theater and moving to Osaka, the city of merchants and urban commoners. One consequence is that Chikamatsu describes the life of townspeople but is deeply interested in samurai values and society. Chikamatsu's earliest play on contemporary social life was the one-act *Love Suicides at Sonezaki* (1703), which depicts an actual incident of the time and which became a model for subsequent contemporary life plays.

Love Suicides at Amijima, first performed at the Takemoto Theater in Osaka in 1721, is widely considered to be Chikamatsu Mon'zaemon's best puppet play concerning contemporary life. The source for the play is unclear, but the incident inspired a number of later plays. In the play, Kamiya (literally, "paper merchant") Jihei, an Osaka paper merchant with a wife and children, falls in love with Koharu, a prostitute under contract to the Kinokuniya House in Sonezaki (a licensed quarter in Osaka). Forced into tragic circumstances, the two of them commit suicide at a temple in Amijima, in Osaka.

About half of Chikamatsu's twenty-four contemporary-life plays focus on an incident concerning an Osaka urban commoner. Almost all the male protagonists are young and of low social station, either an adopted son or a shop clerk, and most of them become involved with a low-level prostitute. In that the lovers have already decided to commit double suicide at the beginning, *The Love Suicides at Amijima* differs from such double-suicide plays as *The Love Suicides at Sonezaki,* which show the tragic chain of events that lead to death. Instead, the focus in *Amijima* is on the desperate efforts of those who attempt to prevent the suicide of the two lovers. Chikamatsu places the tragedy in a tight web of urban commoner social relationships and obligations, particularly the hierarchical relations between master and apprentice, parent and child, and husband and wife, as well as in the context of the new monetary economy and commercial life of Osaka. Jihei and Koharu bear a great social burden, particularly as Jihei is a pillar of the family business, and the tragic result pulls down not only the two lovers but others in the family. Here Chikamatsu develops one of the central themes of his contemporary-life plays: the conflict between those who try to preserve the family *and* the individual, driven by his or her own desires, who works against that social order.

Chikamatsu focuses on *giri*, or sense of social obligation, including that between women, between Koharu and Jihei's wife Osan, whose conflicted relationship develops into a tense mutual understanding. Not only does Chikamatsu create complex conflicts between individual desire and obligation, he focuses on conflicts between competing obligations that result in extreme pathos. Desire and obligation are also reflected in the settings: the first act occurs in the pleasure quarters, a world of desire, passion, and the individual; and the second act takes place in the paper shop, a world of responsibility, reason, and the family, with Jihei caught between the two. The third act focuses on a journey in which the lovers leave behind both places and travel toward death.

In the poetic journey in the third act there is a double movement: a downward movement, the Buddhist cycle of *samsara*, of birth and death, of suffering, which leads to hell; and an upward movement, leading from hell to possible salvation. The fundamental assumption behind the two movements, which is symbolically mapped out, is that awakening is the result of some profound crisis or suffering. Accordingly, the lovers initially pass such places as Tenma Bridge and the River of the Three Fords—which represent places in hell—before they cross over Kyō (Sutra) Bridge and Onari (Becoming a Buddha) Bridge. The final scene has the added function of praying for the spirits of the dead—that is, the play implicitly recalls to this world the spirits or ghosts of the two lovers, who have recently died a gruesome death, and now sends them off again to the world of the dead.

PRONUNCIATIONS:

Chikamatsu Mon'zaemon: chi-ka-mah-tsu mon-ZAH-e-mon
Gozaemon: go-zah-e-mon
Jihei: ji-hay
Koharu: ko-hah-reu
Osan: o-sahn
Tahei: tah-hay

The Love Suicides at Amijima[1]

Characters

JIHEI, *aged twenty-eight, a paper merchant*
MAGOEMON, *his brother, a flour merchant*
GOZAEMON, *Jihei's father-in-law*
TAHEI, *a rival for Koharu*
DENBEI, *proprietor of the Yamato House*
SANGORŌ, *Jihei's servant*
KANTARŌ, *aged six, Jihei's son*

KOHARU, *aged nineteen, a courtesan belonging to the Kinokuni House in Sonezaki, a new licensed quarter in the north part of Ōsaka*
OSAN, *Jihei's wife*
OSAN'S MOTHER (*who is also Jihei's aunt*), *aged fifty-six*
OSUE, *aged four, Jihei's daughter*

Act 1

[*In an opening scene, which is rarely performed and is omitted here, Koharu makes her way to the Kawashō Teahouse in Sonezaki licensed quarter to meet Tahei, a samurai customer. We learn that Koharu is in love with Jihei and that Tahei, a man that she*]

1. Translated by Donald Keene.

dislikes immensely, is trying to buy out her contract. Koharu sees Tahei in the street and flees.]

The Kawashō, a Teahouse in Sonezaki.

CHANTER: Koharu slips away, under cover of the crowd, and hurries into the Kawashō Teahouse.

[PROPRIETRESS]:   Well, well, I hadn't expected you so soon—It's been ages since I've even heard your name mentioned. What a rare visitor you are, Koharu! And what a long time it's been!

CHANTER: The proprietress greets Koharu cheerfully.

[KOHARU]:   Oh—you can be heard as far as the gate. Please don't call me Koharu in such a loud voice. That horrible Ri Tōten[2] is out there. I beg you, keep your voice down.

CHANTER: Were her words overheard? In bursts a party of three men.

[TAHEI]:   I must thank you first of all, dear Koharu, for bestowing a new name on me, Ri Tōten. I never was called *that* before. Well, friends, this is the Koharu I've confided to you about—the good-hearted, good-natured, good-in-bed Koharu. Step up and meet the whore who's started all the rivalry! Will I soon be the lucky man and get Koharu for my wife? Or will Kamiya Jihei ransom her?

CHANTER: He swaggers up.

[KOHARU]:   I don't want to hear another word. If you think it's such an achievement to start unfounded rumors about someone you don't even know, go ahead; say what you please. But I don't want to hear.

CHANTER: She steps away suddenly, but he sidles up again.

[TAHEI]:   You may not want to hear me, but the clink of my gold coins will make you listen! What a lucky girl you are! Just think—of all the many men in Tenma and the rest of Ōsaka, you chose Jihei the paper dealer, the father of two children, with his cousin for his wife and his uncle for his father-in-law! A man whose business is so tight he's at his wits' end every sixty days merely to pay the wholesalers' bills! Do you think he'll be able to fork over nearly ten *kanme* to ransom you? That reminds me of the mantis who picked a fight with an oncoming vehicle![3] But look at me—I don't have a wife, a father-in-law, a father, or even an uncle, for that matter. Tahei the Lone Wolf—that's the name I'm known by. I admit that I'm no match for Jihei when it comes to bragging about myself in the Quarter, but when it comes to money, I'm an easy winner. If I pushed with all the strength of my money, who knows what I might conquer?—How about it, men?—Your customer tonight, I'm sure, is none other than Jihei, but I'm taking over. The Lone Wolf's taking over. Hostess! Bring on the saké! On with the saké!

[PROPRIETRESS]:   What are you saying? Her customer tonight is a samurai, and he'll be here any moment. Please amuse yourself elsewhere.

CHANTER: But Tahei's look is playful.

[TAHEI]:   A customer's a customer, whether he's a samurai or a townsman. The only difference is that one wears swords and the other doesn't. But even if this samurai wears his swords, he won't have five or six—there'll only be two, the broadsword and dirk. I'll take care of the samurai and borrow Koharu afterward.

2. The villain of the play *Battles of Coxinga*.

3. A simile, derived from ancient Chinese texts, for someone who doesn't know his own limitations.

[*To Koharu.*] You may try to avoid me all you please, but some special connection from a former life must have brought us together. I owe everything to that ballad-singing priest—what a wonderful thing the power of prayer is! I think I'll recite a prayer of my own. Here, this ashtray will be my bell, and my pipe the hammer. This is fun.

> *Chan Chan Cha Chan Chan.*
> *Ei Ei Ei Ei Ei.*
> *Jihei the paper dealer—*
> *Too much love for Koharu*
> *Has made him a foolscap,*
> *He wastepapers sheets of gold*
> *Till his fortune's shredded to confetti*
> *And Jihei himself is like scrap paper*
> *You can't even blow your nose on!*
> *Hail, Hail Amida Buddha!*
> *Namaida Namaida Namaida.*

CHANTER: As he prances wildly, roaring his song, a man appears at the gate, so anxious not to be recognized that he wears, even at night, a wicker hat.[4]

[TAHEI]: Well, Toilet Paper's showed up! That's quite a disguise! Why don't you come in, Toilet Paper? If my prayer's frightened you, say a Hail Amida![5] Here, I'll take off your hat!

CHANTER: He drags the man in and examines him: it is the genuine article, a two-sworded samurai, somber in dress and expression, who glares at Tahei through his woven hat, his eyeballs round as gongs. Tahei, unable to utter either a Hail or an Amida, gasps "Haaa!" in dismay, but his face is unflinching.

[TAHEI]: Koharu, I'm a townsman. I've never worn a sword, but I've lots of New Silver[6] at my place, and I think that the glint could twist a mere couple of swords out of joint. Imagine that wretch from the toilet paper shop, with a capital as thin as tissue, trying to compete with the Lone Wolf! That's the height of impertinence! I'll wander down now from Sakura Bridge to Middle Street, and if I meet that Wastepaper along the way, I'll trample him under foot. Come on, men.

CHANTER: Their gestures, at least, have a cavalier assurance as they swagger off, taking up the whole street. The samurai customer patiently endures the fool, indifferent to his remarks because of the surroundings, but every word of gossip about Jihei, whether for good or ill, affects Koharu. She is so depressed that she stands there blankly, unable even to greet her guest. Sugi, the maid from the Kinokuni House, runs up from home, looking annoyed.

[SUGI]: When I left you here a while ago, Miss Koharu, your guest hadn't appeared yet, and they gave me a terrible scolding when I got back for not having checked on him. I'm very sorry, sir, but please excuse me a minute.

---

4. Customers visiting the licensed quarter by day wear these deep wicker hats (which virtually conceal the face) in order to preserve the secrecy of their visits. But this customer wears a hat even at night.

5. A play on words centering on the syllables *ami*, part of the name Amida Buddha, and on *amigasa*, meaning "woven hat."

6. Good-quality coinage of about 1720.

CHANTER: She lifts the woven hat and examines the face.

[SUGI]:   Oh—it's not him! There's nothing to worry about, Koharu. Ask your guest to keep you for the whole night, and show him how sweet you can be. Give him a barrelful of nectar![7] Good-bye, madam, I'll see you later, honey.

CHANTER: She takes her leave with a cloying stream of puns. The extremely hard baked[8] samurai is furious.

[SAMURAI]:   What's the meaning of this? You'd think from the way she appraised my face that I was a tea canister or a porcelain cup! I didn't come here to be trifled with. It's difficult enough for me to leave the residence even by day, and in order to spend the night away I had to ask the senior officer's permission and sign the register. You can see how complicated the regulations make things. But I'm in love, miss, just from hearing about you, and I wanted very badly to spend a night with you. I came here a while ago without an escort and made the arrangements with the teahouse. I had been looking forward to your kind reception, a memory to last me a lifetime, but you haven't so much as smiled at me or said a word of greeting. You keep your head down as if you were counting money in your lap. Aren't you afraid of getting a stiff neck? Madam—I've never heard the like. Here I come to a teahouse, and I must play the part of night nurse in a maternity room!

[PROPRIETRESS]:   You're quite right, sir. Your surprise is entirely justified, considering that you don't know the reasons. This girl is deeply in love with a customer named Kamiji. It's been Kamiji today and Kamiji tomorrow, with nobody else allowed a chance at her. Her other customers have scattered in every direction, like leaves in a storm. When two people get so carried away with each other, it often leads to trouble, for both the customer and the girl. In the first place, it interferes with business, and the owner, whoever he may be, must prevent it. That's why all her guests are examined. Koharu is naturally depressed—it's only to be expected. You are annoyed, which is equally to be expected. But speaking as the proprietress here, it seems to me that the essential thing is for you to meet each other halfway and cheer up. Come, have a drink.—Act a little more lively, Koharu.

CHANTER: Koharu, without answering, lifts her tear-stained face.

[KOHARU]:   Tell me, samurai, they say that if you're going to kill yourself anyway, people who die during the Ten Nights[9] are sure to become Buddhas. Is that really true?

[SAMURAI]:   How should I know? Ask the priest at your family temple.

[KOHARU]:   Yes, that's right. But there's something I'd like to ask a samurai. If you're committing suicide, it'd be a lot more painful, wouldn't it, to cut your throat rather than hang yourself?

[SAMURAI]:   I've never tried cutting my throat to see whether or not it hurt. Please ask more sensible questions.—What an unpleasant girl!

CHANTER: Samurai though he is, he looks nonplussed.

[PROPRIETRESS]:   Koharu, that's a shocking way to treat a guest the first time you meet him. I'll go and get my husband. We'll have some saké together. That ought to liven things up a bit.

---

7. The imagery used by the maid has been altered from puns on saltiness (soy sauce, green vegetables, and so forth) to puns on sweetness.

8. A technical term of pottery making, meaning "hard-fired."

9. A period in the Tenth Month when special Buddhist services were conducted in temples of the Pure Land (Jōdo) sect. It was believed that persons who died during this period immediately became Buddhas.

CHANTER: The gate she leaves is lighted by the evening moon low in the sky; the clouds and the passers in the street have thinned.

For long years there has lived in Tenma, the seat of the mighty god,[1] though not a god himself, Kamiji,[2] a name often bruited by the gongs of worldly gossip, so deeply, hopelessly, is he tied to Koharu by the ropes[3] of an ill-starred love. Now is the tenth moon, the month when no gods will unite them;[4] they are thwarted in their love, unable to meet. They swore in the last letters they exchanged that if only they could meet, that day would be their last. Night after night Jihei, ready for death, trudges to the Quarter, distracted, as though his soul had left a body consumed by the fires of love.

At a roadside eating stand he hears people gossiping about Koharu. "She's at Kawashō with a samurai customer," someone says, and immediately Jihei decides, "It will be tonight!"

He peers through the latticework window and sees a guest in the inside room, his face obscured by a hood. Only the moving chin is visible, and Jihei cannot hear what is said.

[JIHEI]: Poor Koharu! How thin her face is! She keeps it turned away from the lamp. In her heart she's thinking only of me. I'll signal her that I'm here, and we'll run off together. Then which will it be——Umeda or Kitano?[5] Oh——I want to tell her I'm here. I want to call her.

CHANTER: He beckons with his heart, his spirit flies to her; but his body, like a cicada's cast-off shell, clings to the latticework. He weeps with impatience. The guest in the inside room gives a great yawn.

[SAMURAI]: What a bore, playing nursemaid to a prostitute with worries on her mind!——The street seems quiet now. Let's go to the end room. We can at least distract ourselves by looking at the lanterns. Come with me.

CHANTER: They go together to the outer room. Jihei, alarmed, squeezes into the patch of shadow under the lattice window. Inside they do not realize that anyone is eavesdropping.

[SAMURAI]: I've been noticing your behavior and the little things you've said this evening. It's plain to me that you intend a love suicide with Kamiji, or whatever his name is—the man the hostess mentioned. I'm sure I'm right. I realize that no amount of advice or reasoning is likely to penetrate the ears of somebody bewitched by the god of death, but I must say that you're exceedingly foolish. The boy's family won't blame him for his recklessness, but they will blame and hate you. You'll be shamed by the public exposure of your body. Your parents may be dead, for all I know, but if they're alive, you'll be punished in hell as a wicked daughter. Do you think you'll become a buddha? You and your lover won't even be able to fall smoothly into hell together! What a pity—and what a tragedy! This is only our first meeting, but as a samurai, I can't let you die without trying to save you. No doubt money's the problem. I'd like to help, if five or ten *ryō* would be of service.

1. Tenma, one of the principal districts of Ōsaka, was the site of the Tenjin Shrine, for the worship of the deified Sugawara no Michizane (845–903).

2. The word *kami*, for "paper," sounds like *kami*, "god." We have thus "Kami who is not a *kami*"—the paper dealer who isn't a god.

3. The sacred ropes at a Shintō shrine.

4. The Tenth Month was a time when the gods were believed to gather at Izumo; they thus were absent from the rest of Japan.

5. Both places had well-known cemeteries.

I swear by the god Hachiman and by my good fortune as a samurai that I will never reveal to anyone what you tell me. Open your heart without fear.

CHANTER: He whispers these words. She joins her hands and bows.

[KOHARU]: I'm extremely grateful. Thank you for your kind words and for swearing an oath to me, someone you've never had for a lover or even a friend. I'm so grateful that I'm crying.—Yes, it's as they say, when you've something on your mind it shows on your face. You were right. I have promised Kamiji to die with him. But we've been completely prevented from meeting by my master, and Jihei, for various reasons, can't ransom me at once. My contracts with my former master[6] and my present one still have five years to run. If somebody else claimed me during that time, it would be a blow to me, of course, but a worse disgrace to Jihei's honor. He suggested that it would be better if we killed ourselves, and I agreed. I was caught by obligations from which I could not withdraw, and I promised him before I knew what I was doing. I said, "We'll watch for a chance, and I'll slip out when you give the signal." "Yes," he said, "slip out somehow." Ever since then I've been leading a life of uncertainty, never knowing from one day to the next when my last hour will come.

I have a mother living in a back alley south of here. She has no one but me to depend on, and she does piecework to eke out a living. I keep thinking that after I'm dead she'll become a beggar or an outcast, and maybe she'll die of starvation. That's the only sad part about dying. I have just this one life. I'm ashamed that you may think me a coldhearted woman, but I must endure the shame. The most important thing is that I don't want to die. I beg you, please help me stay alive.

CHANTER: As she speaks, the samurai nods thoughtfully. Jihei, crouching outside, hears her words with astonishment; they are so unexpected to his manly heart that he feels like a monkey who has tumbled from a tree. He is frantic with agitation.

[JIHEI, *to himself*]: Then was everything a lie? Ahhh—I'm furious! For two whole years I've been bewitched by that rotten she-fox! Shall I break in and kill her with one blow of my sword? Or shall I satisfy my anger by shaming her to her face?

CHANTER: He gnashes his teeth and weeps in chagrin. Inside the house Koharu speaks through her tears.

[KOHARU]: It's a curious thing to ask, but would you please show the kindness of a samurai and become my customer for the rest of this year and into next spring? Whenever Jihei comes, intent on death, please step in and force him to postpone his plan. In this way our relations can be broken quite naturally. He won't have to kill himself, and my life will also be saved.—What evil connection from a former existence made us promise to die? How I regret it now!

CHANTER: She weeps, leaning on the samurai's knee.

[SAMURAI]: Very well, I'll do as you ask. I think I can help you.—But I feel a breeze. Somebody may be watching.

CHANTER: He slams shut the latticework *shōji*. Jihei, listening outside, is in a frenzy.

[JIHEI]: Exactly what you'd expect from a whore, a cheap whore! I misjudged her foul nature. She robbed the soul from my body, the thieving harlot! Shall I slash her or run her through? What am I to do?

CHANTER: The shadows of two profiles fall on the *shōji*.

6. The master at the bathhouse where Koharu formerly worked.

[JIHEI]: I'd like to give her a taste of my fist and trample her.—What are they chattering about? See how they nod to each other! Now she's bowing to him, whispering and sniveling. I've tried to control myself—I've pressed my chest, I've stroked it—but I can't stand any more. This is too much to endure!

CHANTER: His heart pounds wildly as he unsheathes his dirk, a Magoroku of Seki. "Koharu's side must be here," he judges, and stabs through an opening in the latticework. But Koharu is too far away for his thrust, and although she cries out in terror, she remains unharmed. Her guest instantly leaps at Jihei, grabs his hands, and jerks them through the latticework. With his sword knot he quickly and securely fastens Jihei's hands to the window upright.

[SAMURAI]: Don't scream, Koharu. Don't look at him.

CHANTER: At this moment the proprietor and his wife return. They exclaim in alarm.

[SAMURAI]: This needn't concern you. Some ruffian ran his sword through the *shōji*, and I've tied his arms to the latticework. I have my own way of dealing with him. Don't untie the cord. If you attract a crowd, the place is sure to be thrown in an uproar. Let's all go inside. Come with me, Koharu. We'll go to bed.

CHANTER: Koharu answers yes, but she recognizes the handle of the dirk, and the memory—if not the blade—transfixes her breast.

[KOHARU]: There're always people doing crazy things in the Quarter when they've had too much to drink. Why don't you let him go without making any trouble? I think that's best, don't you?

[SAMURAI]: Out of the question. Do as I say—inside, all of you. Koharu, come along.

CHANTER: Jihei can still see their shadows even after they enter the inner room, but he is bound to the spot, his hands held in fetters that grip him more tightly as he struggles, his body beset by suffering as he tastes a living shame worse than a dog's.[7] More determined than ever to die, he sheds tears of blood, a pitiful sight. Tahei the Lone Wolf returns from his carousing.

[TAHEI]: That's Jihei standing by Kawashō's window. I'll give him a thrashing.

CHANTER: He catches Jihei by the collar and starts to lift him over his back.

[JIHEI]: Owww!

[TAHEI]: Owww? What kind of weakling are you? Oh, I see—you're tied here. You must've been pulling off a robbery. You dirty pickpocket! You rotten pickpocket!

CHANTER: He beats Jihei mercilessly.

[TAHEI]: You burglar! You convict!

CHANTER: He kicks him wildly.

[TAHEI]: Kamiya Jihei's been caught burgling, and they've tied him up!

CHANTER: Passersby and people of the neighborhood, attracted by his shouts, quickly gather. The samurai rushes from the house.

[SAMURAI]: Who's calling him a burglar? You? Tell me what Jihei's stolen! Out with it!

CHANTER: He seizes Tahei and forces him into the dirt. Tahei rises to his feet only for the samurai to kick him down again and again. He grabs Tahei.

[SAMURAI]: Jihei! Kick him to your heart's content!

CHANTER: He pushes Tahei under Jihei's feet. Bound though he is, Jihei stamps furiously on Tahei's face. Tahei, thoroughly kicked and covered with muck, gets to his feet and glares around him.

---

7. A proverb of Buddhist origin: "Suffering follows one like a dog."

[TAHEI, *to bystander*]:   How could you fools just stand there and let him step on me? I know every one of your faces, and I intend to pay you back. Remember that!

CHANTER: He makes his escape, still determined to have the last word. The spectators burst out laughing.

[VOICES]:   Listen to him brag, even after he's been beaten up! Let's throw him from the bridge and give him a drink of water! Don't let him get away!

CHANTER: They chase after him. When the crowd has dispersed, the samurai goes to Jihei and unfastens the knots. He shows his face with his hood removed.

[JIHEI]:   Magoemon! My brother! How shameful!

CHANTER: He sinks to the ground and weeps, prostrating himself in the dirt.

[KOHARU]:   Are you his brother, sir?

CHANTER: Koharu runs to them. Jihei, catching her by the front of the kimono, forces her to the ground.

[JIHEI]:   Beast! She-fox! I'd sooner kick you than Tahei!

CHANTER: He raises his foot, but Magoemon calls out.

[MAGOEMON]:   That's the kind of foolishness that's gotten you into all this trouble. A prostitute's business is to deceive men. Are you just realizing that? I could see to the bottom of her heart the very first time I met her, but you're so scatterbrained that in more than two years of sleeping with this woman you never figured out what she was thinking. Instead of kicking Koharu, why don't you use your feet on your own misguided disposition?—It's deplorable. You may be my younger brother, but you're almost thirty, and you've got a six-year-old boy and a four-year-old girl, Kantarō and Osue. You run a shop with a thirty-six-foot frontage,[8] but you don't seem to realize that your whole fortune's collapsing. You shouldn't have to be lectured to by your brother. Your father-in-law is your aunt's husband, and your mother-in-law is your aunt. They've always been like real parents to you. Your wife Osan is my cousin, too. The ties of marriage are multiplied by those of blood. But when the family has a reunion, the only subject of discussion is our mortification over your incessant visits to Sonezaki. I feel sorry for our poor aunt. You know what a stiff-necked gentleman of the old school her husband Gozaemon is. He's forever flying into a rage and saying, "We've been tricked by your nephew. He's deserted our daughter. I'll take Osan back and ruin Jihei's reputation throughout Tenma." Our aunt, with all the heartache to bear herself, sometimes sides with him and sometimes with you. She's worried herself sick. What an ingrate not to appreciate how she's defended you in your shame! This one offense is enough to make you the target for Heaven's future punishment!

I realized that your marriage couldn't last much longer at this rate. So I decided, in the hopes of relieving our aunt's worries, that I'd see with my own eyes what kind of woman Koharu was and work out some sort of solution afterward. I consulted the proprietor here, then came myself to investigate the cause of your sickness. I see now how easy it was for you to desert your wife and children. What a faithful prostitute you discovered! I congratulate you!

And here I am, Magoemon the Miller,[9] known far and wide for my paragon of a brother, dressed up like a masquerader at a festival or maybe a lunatic! I put

---

8. A large shop.

9. Magoemon is a dealer in flour (for noodles). His shop name Konaya—"the flour merchant"—is used almost as a surname.

on swords for the first time in my life and announced myself, like a bit player in a costume piece, as an officer at a residence. I feel like an absolute idiot with these swords, but there's nowhere I can dispose of them now.—It's so infuriating—and ridiculous—that it's given me a pain in the chest.

CHANTER: He gnashes his teeth and grimaces, attempting to hide his tears. Koharu, choking all the while with emotion, can only say:

[KOHARU]:   Yes, you're entirely right.

CHANTER: The rest is lost in tears. Jihei pounds the ground with his fist.

[JIHEI]:   I was wrong. Forgive me, Magoemon. For three years I've been possessed by that witch. I've neglected my parents, relatives—even my wife and children—and wrecked my fortune, all because I was deceived by Koharu, that sneak thief! I'm utterly mortified. But I'm through with her now, and I'll never set foot here again. Weasel! Vixen! Sneak thief! Here's proof that I've broken with her!

CHANTER: He pulls out the amulet bag that has rested next to his skin.

[JIHEI]:   Here are the written oaths we've exchanged, one at the beginning of each month, twenty-nine in all. I am returning them. This means our love and affection are over. Take them.

CHANTER: He flings the notes at her.

[JIHEI]:   Magoemon, get my pledges from her. Please make sure you get them all. Then burn them with your own hands. [*To Koharu.*] Give them to my brother.

[KOHARU]:   As you wish.

CHANTER: In tears, she surrenders the amulet bag. Magoemon opens it.

[MAGOEMON]:   One, two, three, four...ten...twenty-nine. They're all here. There's also a letter from a woman. What's this?

CHANTER: He starts to unfold it.

[KOHARU]:   That's an important letter. I can't let you see it.

CHANTER: She clings to Magoemon's arm, but he pushes her away. He holds the letter to the lamplight and examines the address, "To Miss Koharu from Kamiya Osan." As soon as he reads the words, he casually thrusts the letter into his kimono.

[MAGOEMON]:   Koharu. A while ago I swore by my good fortune as a samurai, but now Magoemon the Miller swears by his good fortune as a businessman that he will show this letter to no one, not even his wife. I alone will read it, then burn it with the oaths. You can trust me. I will not break this oath.

[KOHARU]:   Thank you. You save my honor.

CHANTER: She bursts into tears again.

[JIHEI *laughs contemptuously*]:   Save your honor! You talk like a human being! [*To Magoemon.*] I don't want to see her cursed face another minute. Let's go. No—I can't hold so much resentment and bitterness! I'll kick her one in the face, a memory to treasure for the rest of my life. Excuse me, please.

CHANTER: He strides up to Koharu and stamps on the ground.

[JIHEI]:   For three years I've loved you, delighted in you, longed for you, adored you; but today my foot will say my only farewells.

CHANTER: He kicks her sharply on the forehead and bursts into tears. The brothers leave, forlorn figures. Koharu, unhappy woman, raises her voice in lament as she watches them go. Is she faithful or unfaithful? Her true feelings are hidden in the words penned by Jihei's wife, a letter that no one has seen. Jihei goes his separate way without learning the truth.

Act 2

Scene 1

Scene: The house and shop of Kamiya Jihei. Time: Ten days later.

CHANTER: The busy street that runs straight to Tenjin Bridge,[1] named for the god of Tenma, bringer of good fortune, is known as the Street Before the Kami,[2] and here a paper shop does business under the name Kamiya Jihei. The paper is honestly sold, and the shop is well situated; it is a long-established firm, and customers come thick as raindrops.

   Outside, crowds pass in the street, on their way to the Ten Nights service, while inside, the husband dozes in the kotatsu,[3] shielded from drafts by a screen at his pillow. His wife Osan keeps solitary, anxious watch over shop and house.

[OSAN]:   The days are so short—it's dinnertime already, but Tama still hasn't returned from her errand to Ichinokawa.[4] I wonder what can be keeping her. That scamp Sangorō isn't back either. The wind is freezing. I'm sure both the children will be cold. He doesn't even realize that it's time for Osue to be nursed. Heaven preserve me from ever becoming such a fool! What an infuriating creature!

CHANTER: She speaks to herself.

[KANTARŌ]:   Mama, I've come back all by myself.

CHANTER: Her son, the older child, runs up to the house.

[OSAN]:   Kantarō—is that you? What's happened to Osue and Sangorō?

[KANTARŌ]:   They're playing by the shrine. Osue wanted her milk, and she was bawling her head off.

[OSAN]:   I was sure she would. Oh—your hands and feet are frozen stiff as nails! Go and warm yourself at the *kotatsu*. Your father's sleeping there.—What am I to do with that idiot?

CHANTER: She runs out impatiently to the shop just as Sangorō shuffles back, alone.

[OSAN]:   Come here, you fool! Where have you left Osue?

[SANGORŌ]:   You know, I must've lost her somewhere. Maybe somebody's picked her up. Should I go back for her?

[OSAN]:   How could you! If any harm has come to my precious child, I'll beat you to death!

CHANTER: But while she is screaming at him, the maid Tama returns with Osue on her back.

[TAMA]:   The poor child—I found her in tears at the corner. Sangorō, when you're supposed to look after the child, do it properly.

[OSAN]:   You poor dear. You must want your milk.

CHANTER: She joins the others by the *kotatsu* and nurses the child.

[OSAN]:   Tama—give that fool a taste of something that he'll remember![5]

CHANTER: Sangorō shakes his head.

[SANGORŌ]:   No, thanks. I gave each of the children two tangerines just a while ago at the shrine, and I tasted five myself.

---

1. The reference is to Tenma Tenjin, a deified form of Sugawara no Michizane.
2. Again, a play on the words *kami* (god) and *kami* (paper).
3. A source of heat in which a charcoal burner is placed under a low, quilt-covered table.
4. The site of a large vegetable market near the north end of Tenjin Bridge.
5. A pun on the two meanings of *kurawasu:* "to cause to eat" and "to beat."

CHANTER: Fool though he is, bad puns come from him nimbly enough, and the others can only smile despite themselves.

[TAMA]:   Oh—I've become so involved with this half-wit that I almost forgot to tell you, ma'am, that Mr. Magoemon and his aunt[6] are on their way here from the west.

[OSAN]:   Oh dear! In that case, I'll have to wake Jihei. [*To Jihei*] Please get up. Mother and Magoemon are coming. They'll be upset again if you let them see you, a businessman, sleeping in the afternoon, with the day as short as it is.

[JIHEI]:   All right.

CHANTER: He struggles to a sitting position and, with his abacus in one hand, pulls his account book to him with the other.

[JIHEI]:   Two into ten goes five, three into nine goes three, three into six goes two, seven times eight is fifty-six.

CHANTER: His fifty-six-year-old aunt enters with Magoemon.

[JIHEI]:   Magoemon, aunt. How good of you. Please come in. I was in the midst of some urgent calculations. Four nines makes thirty-six *monme*. Three sixes make eighteen *fun*. That's two *monme* less two *fun*.[7] Kantarō! Osue! Granny and Uncle have come! Bring the tobacco tray! One times three makes three. Osan, serve the tea.[8]

CHANTER: He jabbers away.

[AUNT]:   We haven't come for tea or tobacco. Osan, you're young, I know, but you're the mother of two children, and your excessive forbearance does you no credit. A man's dissipation can always be traced to his wife's carelessness. Remember, it's not only the man who's disgraced when he goes bankrupt and his marriage breaks up. You'd do well to take notice of what's going on and assert yourself a bit more.

[MAGOEMON]:   It's foolish to hope for any results, aunt. The scoundrel deceives even me, his elder brother. Why should he take to heart criticism from his wife? Jihei—you played me for a fool. After showing me how you returned Koharu's pledges, here you are, not ten days later, redeeming her! What does this mean? I suppose your urgent calculations are of Koharu's debts! I've had enough!

CHANTER: He snatches away the abacus and flings it clattering into the hallway.

[JIHEI]:   You're making an enormous fuss without any cause. I haven't left the house since the last time I saw you, except to go twice to the wholesalers in Imabashi and once to the Tenjin Shrine. I haven't even thought of Koharu, much less redeemed her.

[AUNT]:   None of your evasions! Last evening at the Ten Nights service I heard the people in the congregation gossiping. Everybody was talking about the great patron from Tenma who'd fallen in love with a prostitute named Koharu from the Kinokuni House in Sonezaki. They said he'd driven away her other guests and was going to ransom her in the next couple of days. There was all kinds of gossip about the abundance of money and fools even in these days of high prices.

My husband Gozaemon has been hearing about Koharu constantly, and he's sure that her great patron from Tenma must be you, Jihei. He told me, "He's your nephew, but to me he's a stranger, and my daughter's happiness is my chief

6. Magoemon's (and Jihei's) aunt but Osan's mother.

7. Meaningless calculations. Twenty *fun* made two *monme*.

8. The name Osan echoes the word *san* (three).

concern. Once he ransoms the prostitute he'll no doubt sell his wife to a brothel. I intend to take her back before he starts selling her clothes."

He was halfway out of the house before I could stop him. "Don't get so excited. We can settle this calmly. First we must make sure whether or not the rumors are true."

That's why Magoemon and I are here now. He was telling me a while ago that the Jihei of today was not the Jihei of yesterday—that you'd broken all connections with Sonezaki and completely reformed. But now I hear that you've had a relapse. What disease can this be?

Your father was my brother. When the poor man was on his deathbed, he lifted his head from the pillow and begged me to look after you, as my son-in-law and nephew. I've never forgotten those last words, but your perversity has made a mockery of his request!

CHANTER: She collapses in tears of resentment. Jihei claps his hands in sudden recognition.

[JIHEI]:   I have it! The Koharu everybody's gossiping about is the same Koharu, but the great patron who's to redeem her is a different man. The other day, as my brother can tell you, Tahei—they call him the Lone Wolf because he hasn't any family or relations—started a fight and was beaten up. He gets all the money he needs from his home town, and he's been trying for a long time to redeem Koharu. I've always prevented him, but I'm sure he's decided that now is his chance. I have nothing to do with it.

CHANTER: Osan brightens at his words.

[OSAN]:   No matter how forbearing I might be—even if I were an angel—you don't suppose I'd encourage my husband to redeem a prostitute! In this instance at any rate there's not a word of untruth in what my husband has said. I'll be a witness to that, Mother.

CHANTER: Husband's and wife's words tally perfectly.

[AUNT]:   Then it's true?

CHANTER: The aunt and nephew clap their hands with relief.

[MAGOEMON]:   Well, I'm happy it's over, anyway. To make us feel doubly reassured, will you write an affidavit that will dispel any doubts your stubborn uncle may have?

[JIHEI]:   Certainly. I'll write a thousand if you like.

[MAGOEMON]:   Splendid! I happen to have bought this on the way here.

CHANTER: Magoemon takes from the fold of his kimono a sheet of oath-paper from Kumano, the sacred characters formed by flocks of crows.[9] Instead of vows of eternal love, Jihei now signs under penalty of Heaven's wrath an oath that he will sever all ties and affections with Koharu. "If I should lie, may Bonten and Taishaku above, and the Four Great Kings below, afflict me!"[1] So the text runs and to it is appended the names of many Buddhas and gods. He signs his name, Kamiya Jihei, in bold characters, seals the oath with blood, and hands it over.

[OSAN]:   It's a great relief to me too. Mother, I have you and Magoemon to thank. Jihei and I have had two children, but this is his firmest pledge of affection. I hope you share my joy.

9. The charms issued by the Shintō shrine at Kumano were printed with six Chinese characters, whose strokes were in the shape of crows. The reverse side of these charms was used for writing oaths.

1. A formal oath. Bonten (Brahma) and Taishaku (Indra), though Hindu gods, were considered to be protective deities of the Buddhist law. The four Deva kings served under Indra and were also protectors of Buddhism.

[AUNT]: Indeed we do. I'm sure that Jihei will settle down and his business will improve, now that he's in this frame of mind. It's been entirely for his sake and for love of the grandchildren that we've intervened. Come, Magoemon, let's be on our way. I'm anxious to set my husband's mind at ease.—It's become chilly here. See that the children don't catch cold.—This, too, we owe to the Buddha of the Ten Nights. I'll say a prayer of thanks before I go. Hail, Amida Buddha!

CHANTER: She leaves, her heart innocent as Buddha's. Jihei is perfunctory even about seeing them to the door. Hardly have they crossed the threshold than he slumps down again at the kotatsu. He pulls the checked quilting over his head.

[OSAN]: You still haven't forgotten Sonezaki, have you?

CHANTER: She goes up to him in disgust and tears away the quilting. He is weeping; a waterfall of tears streams along the pillow, deep enough to bear him afloat. She tugs him upright and props his body against the kotatsu frame. She stares into his face.

[OSAN]: You're acting outrageously, Jihei. You shouldn't have signed that oath if you felt so reluctant to leave her. The year before last, on the middle day of the boar of the Tenth Month,[2] we lit the first fire in the kotatsu and celebrated by sleeping here together, pillow to pillow. Ever since then—did some demon or snake creep into my bosom that night?—for two whole years I've been condemned to keep watch over an empty nest. I thought that tonight at least, thanks to Mother and Magoemon, we'd share sweet words in bed as husbands and wives do, but my pleasure didn't last long. How cruel of you, how utterly heartless! Go ahead, cry your eyes out, if you're so attached to her. Your tears will flow into Shijimi River, and Koharu, no doubt, will ladle them out and drink them! You're ignoble, inhuman.

CHANTER: She embraces his knees and throws herself over him, moaning in supplication. Jihei wipes his eyes.

[JIHEI]: If tears of grief flowed from the eyes and tears of anger from the ears, I could show my heart without saying a word. But my tears all pour in the same way from my eyes, and there's no difference in their color. It's not surprising that you can't tell what's in my heart. I have not a shred of attachment left for that vampire in human skin, but I bear a grudge against Tahei. He has all the money he wants and no wife or children. He's schemed again and again to redeem her, but Koharu refused to give in, at least until I broke with her. She told me time and again, "You have nothing to worry about. I'll never let myself be redeemed by Tahei, not even if my ties with you are ended and I can no longer stay by your side. If my master is induced by Tahei's money to deliver me to him, I'll kill myself in a way that'll do you credit!" But think—not ten days have passed since I broke with her, and she's to be redeemed by Tahei! That rotten whore! That animal! No, I haven't a trace of affection left for her, but I can just hear how Tahei will be boasting. He'll spread the word around Ōsaka that my business has come to a standstill and I'm hard pressed for money. I'll meet with contemptuous stares from the wholesalers. I'll be dishonored. My heart is broken, and my body burns with shame. What a disgrace! How maddening! I've passed the stage of shedding hot tears, tears of blood, sticky tears—my tears now are of molten iron!

CHANTER: He collapses, weeping. Osan turns pale with alarm.

[OSAN]: If that's the situation, poor Koharu will surely kill herself.

2. It was customary to light the first fire of the winter on this day.

[JIHEI]: You're too well bred, despite your intelligence, to understand someone like her! What makes you suppose that faithless creature would kill herself? Far from it— she's probably taking moxa treatments and medicine to prolong her life!

[OSAN]: No, that's not true. I was determined never to tell you so long as I lived, but I'm afraid of the crime I'd be committing if I concealed the facts and let her die with my knowledge. I will reveal my great secret. There is not a grain of deceit in Koharu. It was I who schemed to end the relations between you. I could see signs that you were drifting toward suicide. I felt so unhappy that I wrote a letter, begging her as one woman to another to break with you, even though I knew how painful it would be. I asked her to save your life. The letter must have moved her. She answered that she would give you up, even though you were more precious than life itself, because she could not shirk her duty to me. I've kept her letter with me ever since—it's been like a protective charm. Would such a noble-hearted woman break her promise and brazenly marry Tahei? When a woman—I no less than another—has given herself completely to a man, she does not change. I'm sure she'll kill herself. I'm sure of it. Ahhh—what a dreadful thing to have happened! Save her, please.

CHANTER: Her voice rises in agitation. Her husband is thrown into a turmoil.

[JIHEI]: There was a letter in an unknown woman's hand among the written oaths she surrendered to my brother. It must have been from you. If that's the case, Koharu will surely commit suicide.

[OSAN]: Alas! I'd be failing in the obligations I owe her as another woman if I allowed her to die. Please go to her at once. Don't let her kill herself.

CHANTER: Clinging to her husband, she melts in tears.

[JIHEI]: But what can I possibly do? It'd take half the amount of her ransom in earnest money merely to keep her out of Tahei's clutches. I can't save Koharu's life without administering a dose of 750 *monme* in New Silver.[3] How could I raise that much money in my present financial straits? Even if I crush my body to powder, where will the money come from?

[OSAN]: Don't exaggerate the difficulties. If that's all you need, it's simple enough.

CHANTER: She goes to the wardrobe, and opening a small drawer takes out a bag fastened with cords of twisted silk. She unhesitatingly tears it open and throws down a packet which Jihei retrieves.

[JIHEI]: What's this? Money? Four hundred *monme* in New Silver? How in the world—

CHANTER: He stares astonished at this money he never put there.

[OSAN]: I'll tell you later where this money came from. I've scraped it together to pay the bill for Iwakuni paper that falls due the day after tomorrow. We'll have to ask Magoemon to help us keep the business from going bankrupt. But Koharu comes first. The packet contains 400 *monme*. That leaves 350 *monme* to raise.

CHANTER: She unlocks a large drawer. From the wardrobe lightly fly kite-colored Hachijō silks; a Kyōto crepe kimono lined in pale brown, insubstantial as her husband's life, which flickers today and may vanish tomorrow; a padded kimono of Osue's, a flaming scarlet inside and out—Osan flushes with pain to part with it; Kantarō's sleeveless, unlined jacket—if she pawns this, he'll be cold this winter. Next comes a garment of striped Gunnai silk lined in pale blue and never worn, and then her best formal costume—heavy black silk

3. Koharu's plight is described as a sickness. If 750 *me* is half the sum needed to redeem Koharu, the total of 1,500 *me* (or 6,000 *me* in Old Silver) is considerably less than the 10 *kanme,* or 10,000 *me* in Old Silver, mentioned by Tahei.

dyed with her family crest, an ivy leaf in a ring. They say that those joined by marriage ties can even go naked at home, although outside the house clothes make the man: she snatches up even her husband's finery, a silken cloak, making fifteen articles in all.

[OSAN]: The very least the pawnshop can offer is 350 *monme* in New Silver.

CHANTER: Her face glows as though she already held the money she needs; she hides in the one bundle her husband's shame and her own obligation and puts her love in besides.

[OSAN]: It doesn't matter if the children and I have nothing to wear. My husband's reputation concerns me more. Ransom Koharu. Save her. Assert your honor before Tahei.

CHANTER: But Jihei's eyes remain downcast all the while, and he is silently weeping.

[JIHEI]: Yes, I can pay the earnest money and keep her out of Tahei's hands. But once I've redeemed her, I'll either have to maintain her in a separate establishment or bring her here. Then what will become of you?

CHANTER: Osan is at a loss to answer.

[OSAN]: Yes, what shall I do? Shall I become your children's nurse or the cook? Or perhaps the retired mistress of the house?

CHANTER: She falls to the floor with a cry of woe.

[JIHEI]: That would be too selfish. I'd be afraid to accept such generosity. Even if the punishment for my crimes against my parents, against Heaven, against the gods and the Buddhas fails to strike me, the punishment for my crimes against my wife alone will be sufficient to destroy all hope for the future life. Forgive me, I beg you.

CHANTER: He joins his hands in tearful entreaty.

[OSAN]: Why should you bow before me? I don't deserve it. I'd be glad to rip the nails from my fingers and toes, to do anything that might serve my husband. I've been pawning my clothes for some time in order to scrape together the money for the paper wholesalers' bills. My wardrobe is empty, but I don't regret it in the least. But it's too late now to talk of such things. Hurry, change your cloak and go to her with a smile.

CHANTER: He puts on an underkimono of Gunnai silk, a robe of heavy black silk, and a striped cloak. His sash of figured damask holds a dirk of middle length worked in gold: Buddha surely knows that tonight it will be stained with Koharu's blood.

[JIHEI]: Sangorō! Come here!

CHANTER: Jihei loads the bundle on the servant's back, intending to take him along. Then he firmly thrusts the wallet next to his skin and starts toward the gate.

[VOICE]: Is Jihei at home?

CHANTER: A man enters, removing his fur cap. They see—good heavens!—that it is Gozaemon.

[OSAN AND JIHEI]: Ahhh—how fortunate that you should come at this moment!

CHANTER: Husband and wife are upset and confused. Gozaemon snatches away Sangorō's bundle and sits heavily. His voice is sharp.

[GOZAEMON]: Stay where you are, harlot!—My esteemed son-in-law, what a rare pleasure to see you dressed in your finest attire, with a dirk and a silken cloak! Ahhh—that's how a gentleman of means spends his money! No one would take you for a paper dealer. Are you perchance on your way to the New Quarter? What commendable perseverance! You have no need for your wife, I take it.—Give her a divorce. I've come to take her home with me.

CHANTER: He speaks needles and his voice is bitter. Jihei has not a word to reply.

[OSAN]:   How kind of you, Father, to walk here on such a cold day. Do have a cup of tea.

CHANTER: Offering the teacup serves as an excuse for edging closer.

[OSAN]:   Mother and Magoemon came here a while ago, and they told my husband how much they disapproved of his visits to the New Quarter. Jihei was in tears and he wrote out an oath swearing he had reformed. He gave it to Mother. Haven't you seen it yet?

[GOZAEMON]:   His written oath? Do you mean this?

CHANTER: He takes the paper from his kimono.

[GOZAEMON]:   Libertines scatter vows and oaths wherever they go, as if they were monthly statements of accounts. I thought there was something peculiar about this oath, and now that I am here I can see I was right. Do you still swear to Bonten and Taishaku? Instead of such nonsense, write out a bill of divorcement!

CHANTER: He rips the oath to shreds and throws down the pieces. Husband and wife exchange looks of alarm, stunned into silence. Jihei touches his hands to the floor and bows his head.

[JIHEI]:   Your anger is justified. If I were still my former self, I would try to offer explanations, but today I appeal entirely to your generosity. Please let me stay with Osan. I promise that even if I become a beggar or an outcast and must sustain life with the scraps that fall from other people's chopsticks, I will hold Osan in high honor and protect her from every harsh and bitter experience. I feel so deeply indebted to Osan that I cannot divorce her. You will understand that this is true as time passes and I show you how I apply myself to my work and restore my fortune. Until then please shut your eyes and allow us to remain together.

CHANTER: Tears of blood stream from his eyes and his face is pressed to the matting in contrition.

[GOZAEMON]:   The wife of an outcast! That's all the worse. Write the bill of divorcement at once! I will verify and seal the furniture and clothes Osan brought in her dowry.

CHANTER: He goes to the wardrobe. Osan is alarmed.

[OSAN]:   All my clothes are here. There's no need to examine them.

CHANTER: She runs up to stop him, but Gozaemon pushes her aside and jerks open a drawer.

[GOZAEMON]:   What does this mean?

CHANTER: He opens another drawer: it too is empty. He pulls out every last drawer, but not so much as a foot of patchwork cloth is to be seen. He tears open the wicker hampers, long boxes, and clothes chests.

[GOZAEMON]:   Stripped bare, are they?

CHANTER: His eyes set in fury. Jihei and Osan huddle under the striped kotatsu quilts, ready to sink into the fire with humiliation.

[GOZAEMON]:   This bundle looks suspicious.

CHANTER: He unties the knots and dumps out the contents.

[GOZAEMON]:   As I thought! You were sending these to the pawnshop, I take it. Jihei— you'd strip the skin from your wife's and your children's bodies to squander the money on your whore! Dirty thief! You're my wife's nephew, but an utter stranger to me, and I'm under no obligation to suffer for your sake. I'll explain to Magoemon what has happened and ask him to make good on whatever you've already stolen from Osan's belongings. But first, the bill of divorcement!

CHANTER: Even if Jihei could escape through seven padlocked doors, eight layers of chains, and a hundred retention walls, he could not escape so stringent a demand.

[JIHEI]:   I won't use a brush to write the bill of divorcement. Here's what I'll do instead! Good-bye, Osan.

CHANTER: He lays his hand on his dirk, but Osan clings to him.

[OSAN]:   Father—Jihei admits that he's done wrong and he's apologized in every way. You press your advantage too hard. Jihei may be a stranger, but his children are your grandchildren. Have you no affection for them? I will not accept a bill of divorcement.

CHANTER: She embraces her husband and raises her voice in tears.

[GOZAEMON]:   Very well. I won't insist on it. Come with me, woman.

CHANTER: He pulls her to her feet.

[OSAN]:   No, I won't go. What bitterness makes you expose to such shame a man and wife who still love each other? I will not suffer it.

CHANTER: She pleads with him, weeping, but he pays her no heed.

[GOZAEMON]:   Is there some greater shame? I'll shout it through the town!

CHANTER: He pulls her up, but she shakes free. Caught by the wrist she totters forward when—alas!—her toes brush against her sleeping children. They open their eyes.

[CHILDREN]:   Mother dear, why is Grandfather, the bad man, taking you away? Whom will we sleep beside now?

CHANTER: They call out after her.

[OSAN]:   My poor dears! You've never spent a night away from Mother's side since you were born. Sleep tonight beside your father. [To Jihei.] Please don't forget to give the children their tonic before breakfast.—Oh, my heart is broken!

CHANTER: These are her parting words. She leaves her children behind, abandoned as in the woods; the twin-trunked bamboo of conjugal love is sundered forever.

Act 3

Scene 1

In Sonezaki, in front of the Yamato Teahouse.

CHANTER: This is Shijimi River, the haunt of love and affection. Its flowing water and the feet of passersby are stilled now at two in the morning, and the full moon shines clear in the sky. Here in the street a dim doorway lantern is marked "Yamatoya Denbei" in a single scrawl. The night watchman's clappers take on a sleepy cadence as he totters by on uncertain legs. The very thickness of his voice crying, "Beware of fire! Beware of fire!" tells how far advanced the night is. A serving woman from the upper town comes along, followed by a palanquin. "It's terribly late," she remarks to the bearers as she clatters open the side door of the Yamato Teahouse and steps inside.

[SERVANT]:   I've come to take back Koharu of the Kinokuni House.

CHANTER: Her voice is faintly heard outside. A few moments later, after hardly time enough to exchange three or four words of greeting, she emerges.

[SERVANT]:   Koharu is spending the night. Bearers, you may leave now and get some rest. [To proprietress, inside the doorway.] Oh, I forgot to tell you, madam. Please keep an eye on Koharu. Now that the ransom to Tahei has been arranged and the money's been accepted, we're merely her custodians. Please don't let her drink too much saké.

CHANTER: She leaves, having scattered at the doorway the seeds that before morning will turn Jihei and Koharu to dust.

At night between two and four even the teahouse kettle rests; the flame flickering in the low candle stand narrows; and the frost spreads in the cold river-wind of the deepening night. The master's voice breaks the stillness.

[DENBEI, *to Jihei*]: It's still the middle of the night. I'll send somebody with you. [*To the servants.*] Mr. Jihei is leaving. Wake Koharu. Call her here.

CHANTER: Jihei slides open the side door.

[JIHEI]: No, Denbei, not a word to Koharu. I'll be trapped here until dawn if she hears I'm leaving. That's why I'm letting her sleep and slipping off this way. Wake her up after sunrise and send her back then. I'm returning home now and will leave for Kyōto immediately on business. I have so many engagements that I may not be able to return in time for the interim payment.[4] Please use the money I gave you earlier this evening to clear my account. I'd like you also to send 150 *me* of Old Silver to Kawashō for the moon-viewing party last month. Please get a receipt. Give Saietsubō[5] from Fukushima one piece of silver as a contribution to the Buddhist altar he's bought, and tell him to use it for a memorial service. Wasn't there something else? Oh yes—give Isoichi a tip of four silver coins. That's the lot. Now you can close up and get to bed. Good-bye. I'll see you when I return from Kyōto.

CHANTER: Hardly has he taken two or three steps than he turns back.

[JIHEI]: I forgot my dirk. Fetch it for me, won't you?—Yes, Denbei, this is one respect in which it's easier being a townsman. If I were a samurai and forgot my sword, I'd probably commit suicide on the spot!

[DENBEI]: I completely forgot that I was keeping it for you. Yes, here's the knife with it.

CHANTER: He gives the dirk to Jihei, who fastens it firmly into his sash.

[JIHEI]: I feel secure as long as I have this. Good night!

CHANTER: He goes off.

[DENBEI]: Please come back to Ōsaka soon! Thank you for your patronage!

CHANTER: With this hasty farewell Dembei rattles the door bolt shut; then not another sound is heard as the silence deepens. Jihei pretends to leave, only to creep back again with stealthy steps. He clings to the door of the Yamato Teahouse. As he peeps inside he is startled by shadows moving toward him. He takes cover at the house across the way until the figures pass.

Magoemon the Miller, his heart pulverized with anxiety over his younger brother, comes first, followed by the apprentice Sangorō with Jihei's son Kantarō on his back. They hurry along until they see the lantern of the Yamato Teahouse. Magoemon pounds on the door.

[MAGOEMON]: Excuse me. Kamiya Jihei's here, isn't he? I'd like to see him a moment.

CHANTER: Jihei thinks, "It's my brother!" but dares not stir from his place of concealment. From inside a man's sleep-laden voice is heard.

[DENBEI]: Jihei left a while ago saying he was going up to Kyōto. He's not here.

CHANTER: Not another sound is heard. Magoemon's tears fall unchecked.

[MAGOEMON, *to himself.*]: I ought to have met him on the way if he'd been going home. I can't understand what would take him to Kyōto. Ahhh—I'm shivering all over with worry. I wonder whether he took Koharu with him.

CHANTER: The thought pierces his heart; unable to bear the pain, he pounds again on the door.

4. On the last day of the Tenth Month, one of the times during the year for making payments.

5. The name of a male entertainer in the quarter. Fukushima was west of Sonezaki.

[DENBEI]:   Who is it, so late at night? We've gone to bed.

[MAGOEMON]:   I'm sorry to disturb you, but I'd like to ask one more thing. Has Koharu of the Kinokuni House left? I was wondering whether she might have gone with Jihei.

[DENBEI]:   What's that? Koharu's upstairs, sound asleep.

[MAGOEMON]:   That's a relief, anyway. There's no fear of a lovers' suicide. But where is he hiding himself, causing me all this anxiety? He can't imagine the agony of suspense that the whole family is going through on his account. I'm afraid that bitterness toward his father-in-law may make him forget himself and do something rash. I brought Kantarō along, hoping he would help to dissuade Jihei, but the gesture was in vain. I wonder why I never saw him?

CHANTER: He murmurs to himself, his eyes wet with tears. Jihei's hiding place is close enough for him to hear every word. He chokes with emotion but can only swallow his tears.

[MAGOEMON]:   Sangorō! Where does the fool go night after night? Don't you know anywhere else?

CHANTER: Sangorō imagines that he himself is the fool referred to.

[SANGORŌ]:   I know a couple of places, but I'm too embarrassed to mention them.

[MAGOEMON]:   You know them? Where are they? Tell me.

[SANGORŌ]:   Please don't scold me when you've heard. Every night I wander down below the warehouses by the market.

[MAGOEMON]:   Imbecile! Who's asking about that? Come on, let's search the back streets. Don't let Kantarō catch a chill. The poor kid's having a hard time of it, thanks to that useless father of his. Still, if the worst the boy experiences is the cold, I won't complain. I'm afraid that Jihei may cause him much greater pain. The scoundrel!

CHANTER: But beneath the rancor in his heart of hearts is profound pity.

[MAGOEMON]:   Let's look at the back street!

CHANTER: They pass on. As soon as their figures have gone off a distance, Jihei runs from his hiding place. Standing on tiptoes he gazes with yearning after them and cries out in his heart.

[JIHEI]:   He cannot leave me to my death, even though I am the worst of sinners! I remain to the last a burden to him! I'm unworthy of such kindness!

CHANTER: He joins his hands and kneels in prayer.

[JIHEI]:   If I may make one further request of your mercy, look after my children!

CHANTER: These are his only words; for a while he chokes with tears.

[JIHEI]:   At any rate, our decision's been made. Koharu must be waiting.

CHANTER: He peers through a crack in the side door of the Yamato Teahouse and glimpses a figure.

[JIHEI]:   That's Koharu, isn't it? I'll let her know I'm here.

CHANTER: He clears his throat, their signal. "Ahem, ahem"—the sound blends with the clack of wooden clappers as the watchman comes from the upper street, coughing in the night wind. He hurries on his round of fire warning, "Take care! Beware!" Even this cry has a dismal sound to one in hiding. Jihei, concealing himself like the god of Katsuragi,[6] lets the watchman pass. He sees his chance and rushes to the side door, which softly opens from within.

[JIHEI]:   Koharu?

[KOHARU]:   Were you waiting? Jihei—I want to leave quickly.

6. The god was so ashamed of his ugliness that he ventured forth only at night.

CHANTER: She is all impatience, but the more quickly they open the door, the more likely people will be to hear the casters turning. They lift the door; it makes a moaning sound that thunders in their ears and in their hearts. Jihei lends a hand from the outside, but his fingertips tremble with the trembling of his heart. The door opens a quarter of an inch, a half, an inch—an inch ahead are the tortures of hell, but more than hell itself they fear the guardian-demon's eyes. At last the door opens, and with the joy of New Year's morning[7] Koharu slips out. They catch each other's hands. Shall they go north or south, west or east? Their pounding hearts urge them on, though they know not to what destination: turning their backs on the moon reflected in Shijimi River, they hurry eastward as fast as their legs will carry them.

Scene 2

The farewell journey of many bridges.

CHANTER: *The running hand in texts of nō is always Konoe style;*
                      An actor in a woman's part is sure to wear a purple hat.
                      Does some teaching of the Buddha as rigidly decree
                      That men who spend their days in evil haunts must end like this?

Poor creatures, although they would discover today their destiny in the Sutra of Cause and Effect,[8] tomorrow the gossip of the world will scatter like blossoms the scandal of Kamiya Jihei's love suicide, and carved in cherry wood,[9] his story to the last detail will be printed in illustrated sheets.

Jihei, led on by the spirit of death—if such there be among the gods—is resigned to this punishment for neglect of his trade. But at times—who could blame him?—his heart is drawn to those he has left behind, and it is hard to keep walking on. Even in the full moon's light, this fifteenth night of the Tenth Month,[1] he cannot see his way ahead—a sign perhaps of the darkness in his heart? The frost now falling will melt by dawn, but even more quickly than this symbol of human frailty, the lovers themselves will melt away. What will become of the fragrance that lingered when he held her tenderly at night in their bedchamber?

This bridge, Tenjin Bridge, he has crossed every day, morning and night, gazing at Shijimi River to the west. Long ago, when Tenjin, then called Michizane,[2] was exiled to Tsukushi, his plum tree, following its master, flew in one bound to Dazaifu, and here is Plum-Field Bridge.[3] Green Bridge recalls the aged pine that followed later, and Cherry Bridge the tree that withered

---

7. Mention of the new year is connected with Koharu's name, in which *haru* means "spring."

8. A sacred text of Buddhism, which states: "If you wish to know the past cause, look at the present effect; if you wish to know the future effect, look at the present cause."

9. The blocks from which illustrated books were printed were frequently made of cherrywood. The illustrated sheets mentioned here featured current scandals, such as lovers' suicides.

1. November 14, 1720. In the lunar calendar the full moon occurs on the fifteenth of the month.

2. Sugawara no Michizane, unfairly abused at court, was exiled to Dazaifu in Kyūshū. When he was about to depart, he composed a poem of farewell to his favorite plum tree. The tree, moved by this honor, flew after him to Kyūshū. The cherry tree in his garden withered away in grief. Only the pine seemed indifferent, as Michizane complained in another poem. The pine thereupon also flew to Kyūshū.

3. Umeda Bridge. "Green Bridge" is Midori-bashi.

away in grief over parting. Such are the tales still told, demonstrating the power of a single poem.[4]

[JIHEI]:   Though born the parishioner of so holy and mighty a god, I shall kill you and then myself. If you ask the cause, it was that I lacked even the wisdom that might fill a tiny Shell Bridge.[5] Our stay in this world has been short as an autumn day. This evening will be the last of your nineteen, of my twenty-eight years. The time has come to cast away our lives. We promised we'd remain together faithfully until you were an old woman and I an old man, but before we knew each other three full years, we have met this disaster. Look, there is Ōe Bridge. We will follow the river from Little Naniwa Bridge to Funairi Bridge. The farther we journey, the closer we approach the road to death.

CHANTER: He laments. She clings to him.

[KOHARU]:   Is this already the road to death?

CHANTER: Falling tears obscure from each the other's face and threaten to immerse even the Horikawa bridges.

[JIHEI]:   A few steps north and I could glimpse my house, but I will not turn back. I will bury in my breast all thoughts of my children's future, all pity for my wife. We cross southward over the river. Why did they call a place with as many buildings as a bridge has piers "Eight Houses"? Hurry, we want to arrive before the downriver boat from Fushimi comes—with what happy couples sleeping aboard!

Next is Tenma Bridge, a frightening name[6] for us about to depart this world. Here the two streams Yodo and Yamato join in one great river, as fish with water, and as Koharu and I, dying on one blade, will cross together the River of Three Fords.[7] I would like this water for our tomb offering!

[KOHARU]:   What have we to grieve about? Although in this world we could not stay together, in the next and through each successive world to come until the end of time we shall be husband and wife. Every summer for my devotions[8] I have copied the All Compassionate and All Merciful Chapter of the Lotus Sutra, in the hope that we may be reborn on one lotus.

CHANTER: They cross over Sutra Bridge and reach the opposite shore.[9]

[KOHARU]:   If I can save living creatures at will when once I mount a lotus calyx in Paradise and become a Buddha, I want to protect women of my profession, so that never again will there be love suicides.

CHANTER: This unattainable prayer stems from worldly attachment, but it touchingly reveals her heart. They cross Onari Bridge.[1] The waters of Noda Creek are shrouded with morning haze; the mountain tips show faintly white.

---

4. The poem by Michizane bewailing the inconstancy of his pine tree.

5. The lovers' journey takes them along the north bank of Shijimi River ("Shell River") to Shijimi Bridge, where they cross to Dōjima. At Little Naniwa Bridge they cross back again to Sonezaki. Continuing eastward, they cross Horikawa, then cross the Tenma Bridge over the Ōkawa. At "Eight Houses" (Hakkenya) they journey eastward along the south bank of the river as far as Kyō Bridge. They cross this bridge to the tip of land at Katamachi and then take the Onari Bridge to Amijima.

6. The characters used for "Tenma" literally mean "demon."

7. A river in the Buddhist underworld that had to be crossed to reach the world of the dead. This is arithmetic association: one blade plus two people equals three fords.

8. It was customary for Buddhist monks to observe a three-month summer retreat during which they practiced various austerities.

9. Kyōbashi is literally "Sutra Bridge." "Opposite Shore" implies the Buddhist term for nirvana.

1. The name Onari means "to become a Buddha."

[JIHEI]:   Listen—the voices of the temple bells begin to boom. How much farther can we go on this way? We are not fated to live any longer—let us end it quickly. Come this way.

CHANTER: Tears are strung with the 108 beads of the rosaries in their hands. They have come now to Amijima, to the Daichō Temple. The overflowing sluice gate of a little stream beside a bamboo thicket will be their place of death.

Scene 3

Amijima.

[JIHEI]:   No matter how far we walk, there'll never be a spot marked "For Suicides." Let us kill ourselves here.

CHANTER: He takes her hand and sits on the ground.

[KOHARU]:   Yes, that's true. One place is as good as another to die. But I've been thinking on the way that if they find our dead bodies together, people will say that Koharu and Jihei committed a lovers' suicide. Osan will think then that I treated as mere scrap paper the letter I sent promising her, when she asked me not to kill you, that I would not and vowing to break off all relations with you. She will be sure that I lured her precious husband into a lovers' suicide. She will despise me as a one-night prostitute, a false woman with no sense of decency. I fear her contempt more than the slander of a thousand or ten thousand strangers. I can imagine how she will resent and envy me. That is the greatest obstacle to my salvation. Kill me here, then choose another spot, far away, for yourself.

CHANTER: She leans against him. Jihei joins in her tears of pleading.

[JIHEI]:   What foolish worries! Osan has been taken back by my father-in-law. I've divorced her. She and I are strangers now. Why should you feel obliged to a divorced woman? You were saying on the way that you and I will be husband and wife through each successive world until the end of time. Who can criticize us, who can be jealous if we die side by side?

[KOHARU]:   But who is responsible for your divorce? You're even less reasonable than I. Do you suppose that our bodies will accompany us to the afterworld? We may die in different places, our bodies may be pecked by kites and crows, but what does it matter as long as our souls are twined together? Take me with you to heaven or to hell!

CHANTER: She sinks again in tears.

[JIHEI]:   You're right. Our bodies are made of earth, water, fire, and wind, and when we die they revert to emptiness. But our souls will not decay, no matter how often they're reborn. And here's a guarantee that our souls will be married and never part!

CHANTER: He whips out his dirk and slashes off his black locks at the base of the topknot.

[JIHEI]:   Look, Koharu. As long as I had this hair, I was Kamiya Jihei, Osan's husband, but cutting it has made me a monk. I have fled the burning house of the three worlds of delusion; I am a priest, unencumbered by wife, children, or worldly possessions. Now that I no longer have a wife named Osan, you owe her no obligations either.

CHANTER: In tears he flings away the hair.

[KOHARU]:   I am happy.

CHANTER: Koharu takes up the dirk and ruthlessly, unhesitatingly, slices through her flowing Shimada coiffure. She casts aside the tresses she has so often washed and combed and stroked. How heartbreaking to see their locks tangled with the weeds and midnight frost of this desolate field!

[JIHEI]:   We have escaped the inconstant world, a nun and a priest. Our duties as husband and wife belong to our profane past. It would be best to choose quite separate places for our deaths, a mountain for one, the river for the other. We will pretend that the ground above this sluice gate is a mountain. You will die there. I shall hang myself by this stream. The time of our deaths will be the same, but the method and place will differ. In this way we can honor to the end our duty to Osan. Give me your undersash.

CHANTER: Its fresh violet color and fragrance will be lost in the winds of impermanence; the crinkled silk long enough to wind twice round her body will bind two worlds, this and the next. He firmly fastens one end to the crosspiece of the sluice, then twists the other into a noose for his neck. He will hang for love of his wife like the "pheasant in the hunting grounds."[2] Koharu watches Jihei prepare for his death. Her eyes swim with tears, her mind is distraught.

[KOHARU]:   Is that how you're going to kill yourself?—If we are to die apart, I have only a little while longer by your side. Come near me.

CHANTER: They take each other's hands.

[KOHARU]:   It's over in a moment with a sword, but I'm sure you'll suffer. My poor darling!

CHANTER: She cannot stop the silent tears.

[JIHEI]:   Can suicide ever be pleasant, whether by hanging or cutting the throat? You mustn't let worries over trifles disturb the prayers of your last moments. Keep your eyes on the westward-moving moon, and worship it as Amida himself.[3] Concentrate your thoughts on the Western Paradise. If you have any regrets about leaving the world, tell me now, then die.

[KOHARU]:   I have none at all, none at all. But I'm sure you must be worried about your children.

[JIHEI]:   You make me cry all over again by mentioning them. I can almost see their faces, sleeping peacefully, unaware, poor dears, that their father is about to kill himself. They're the one thing I can't forget.

CHANTER: He droops to the ground with weeping. The voices of the crows leaving their nests at dawn rival his sobs. Are the crows mourning his fate? The thought brings more tears.

[JIHEI]:   Listen to them. The crows have come to guide us to the world of the dead. There's an old saying that every time somebody writes an oath on the back of a Kumano charm, three crows of Kumano die on the holy mountain. The first words we've written each New Year have been vows of love, and how often we've made oaths at the beginning of the month! If each oath has killed three crows, what a multitude must have perished! Their cries have always sounded like "beloved, beloved," but hatred for our crime of taking life

2. A reference to a poem by Ōtomo no Yakamochi (718–785): "The pheasant foraging in the fields of spring reveals his whereabouts to man as he cries for his mate."

3. Amida's paradise lies in the west. The moon is often used as a symbol of Buddhist enlightenment.

makes their voices ring tonight "revenge, revenge!"[4] Whose fault is it they demand revenge? Because of me you will die a painful death. Forgive me!

CHANTER: He takes her in his arms.

[KOHARU]:   No, it's my fault!

CHANTER: They cling to each other, face pressed to face; their sidelocks, drenched with tears, freeze in the winds blowing over the fields. Behind them echoes the voice of the Daichō Temple.

[JIHEI]:   Even the long winter night seems as short as our lives.

CHANTER: Dawn is already breaking, and matins can be heard. He draws her to him.

[JIHEI]:   The moment has come for our glorious end. Let there be no tears on your face when they find you later.

[KOHARU]:   There won't be any.

CHANTER: She smiles. His hands, numbed by the frost, tremble before the pale vision of her face, and his eyes are first to cloud. He is weeping so profusely that he cannot control the blade.

[KOHARU]:   Compose yourself—but be quick!

CHANTER: Her encouragement lends him strength; the invocations to Amida carried by the wind urge a final prayer. *Namu Amida Butsu.* He thrusts in the savaging sword.[5] Stabbed, she falls backward, despite his staying hand, and struggles in terrible pain. The point of the blade has missed her windpipe, and these are the final tortures before she can die. He writhes with her in agony, then painfully summons his strength again. He draws her to him and plunges his dirk to the hilt. He twists the blade in the wound, and her life fades away like an unfinished dream at dawning.

He arranges her body with her head to the north, face to the west, lying on her right side,[6] and throws his cloak over her. He turns away at last, unable to exhaust with tears his grief over parting. He pulls the sash to him and fastens the noose around his neck. The service in the temple has reached the closing section, the prayers for the dead. "Believers and unbelievers will equally share in the divine grace," the voices proclaim, and at the final words Jihei jumps from the sluice gate.

[JIHEI]:   May we be reborn on one lotus! Hail Amida Buddha!

CHANTER: For a few moments he writhes like a gourd swinging in the wind, but gradually the passage of his breath is blocked as the stream is dammed by the sluice gate, where his ties with this life are snapped. Fishermen out for the morning catch find the body in their net.[7]

[FISHERMEN]:   A dead man! Look, a dead man! Come here, everybody!

CHANTER: The tale is spread from mouth to mouth. People say that they who were caught in the net of Buddha's vow immediately gained salvation and deliverance, and all who hear the tale of the Love Suicides at Amijima are moved to tears.

---

4. The cries have always sounded like *kawai, kawai* (beloved), but now they sound like *mukui, mukui* (revenge).

5. The invocation of Amida's name freed one from spiritual obstacles, just as a sword freed one from physical obstacles. Here the two images are blended.

6. The dead were arranged in this manner because Shakyamuni Buddha chose this position when he died.

7. "Net" (*ami*) is echoed a few lines later in the name Amijima. The vow of the Buddha to save all living creatures is likened to a net that catches people in its meshes.

After Buddhism was introduced into Tibet following the seventh century, the Himalayan kingdom became a center for monastic culture and religious thought and poetry. Over time, the major priests or lamas came to have wide political influence as well, often supported by Chinese emperors to the east or Mongol khans to the north. In the sixteenth century, the Mongol leader proclaimed the head of a major sect the Dalai Lama, recognizing him as the legitimate successor of the previous chief lama (whose name, Gyatso, means "ocean" in Tibetan; "dalai" was the Mongol equivalent, which came to serve as a formal title). In 1642, the fifth Dalai Lama became the country's effective ruler, presiding over a united and prosperous nation for forty years. Each Dalai Lama was believed to be the reincarnation of his predecessor, and a year after one died, a national search would be launched for a newborn who would be revealed to be his reincarnation. A regent would then rule the country until the new (or newly reborn) lama came of age, a system still used in 1939 to discover the present, fourteenth Dalai Lama, who has been recognized worldwide as a spiritual leader as well as the voice of Tibet's struggle for independence in the decades since its absorption by China in 1950.

Though the fifth Dalai Lama codified this system of selection, it was disrupted upon his own death in 1682, when the ambitious regent took effective power, actually concealing news of the lama's death from the outside world. Tsangyang Gyatso was eventually located, at the age of five, as the reincarnated Dalai Lama, but he was brought up in private; he wasn't publicly proclaimed the Sixth Dalai Lama until 1696, and even then he was kept under the regent's thumb. Deprived of real authority, Tsangyang Gyatso devoted himself to the study of Buddhist scriptures, to archery, and to love affairs. His visits were said to be considered a great honor by the young women in the village of Shol, beneath the walls of the towering Potala monastery where he lived, and families would repaint their white houses yellow in honor of his visits. Farther afield, though, the young Dalai Lama's activities shocked monks who held more strictly to their vows, particularly when Tsangyang Gyatso gained a reputation for writing love songs to his sweethearts. Tibet's neighbors took the opportunity to intervene: with the approval of China's Manchu emperor, the Mongol khan invaded, killed the aging regent, and deposed Tsangyang Gyatso, asserting that he wasn't the true reincarnation of the Fifth Dalai Lama at all. The Mongol ruler attempted to install his own son in his place, and the twenty-three-year-old Tsangyang Gyatso was sent over the mountains toward exile in China. He never reached his destination but disappeared en route, most likely assassinated by his guards—though according to popular tradition, still widely believed by Tibetans, he escaped and lived out his life as a wandering religious mendicant.

Some seventy short poems survive, attributed to him since the eighteenth century, though their authorship can't be proven. Some treat strictly religious themes, but most take erotic love as their subject. The examples given here offer a striking self-portrait of a libertine who chafes under extreme social constraint, yet also playfully exploits the physical and emotional opportunities his exceptional situation offers.

PRONUNCIATION:

Tsangyang Gyatso: TSANG-yang g'YAHT-SO

from Love Poems of the Sixth Dalai Lama[1]

1

I sought my lover at twilight
Snow fell at daybreak.
Secret or not, no matter.
Footprints have been left in the snow.

2

Residing at the Potala
I am Rigdzin Tsangyang Gyatso
But in the back alleys of Shol-town
I am rake and stud.

3

Lover met by chance on the road,
Girl with delicious-smelling body –
Like picking up a small white turquoise
Only to toss it away again.

5

If the one I love gives up everything
to study the teachings,
I'll take the holy path too.
I'll live in a secluded retreat
and forget how young I am.

6

During meditation my lama's face
Will not come forth in my mind;
But my lover's face, unmeditated,
So clear, so clear in my mind.

7

If I could meditate as deeply
on the sacred texts as I do
on you, I would clearly be
enlightened in this lifetime!

8

Pure snow-water from the holy mountain.
Dew of the rare Naga Vajra grass.[2]
These essences make a nectar
which is fermented by one
who has incarnated as a maiden.
Her cup's contents can protect you
from rebirth in lower form,
if it is tasted in the state
of awareness it deserves.

1. Translated by Rick Fields and Brian Cutillo (poems 1–3 and 10); Coleman Barks (poems 5, 7, 8); and Per K. Sorensen (poems 6, 11, 13, 14).
2. A plant growing on the slopes of a holy mountain in southeast Tibet, sacred to "the Sow-headed Goddess." Drinking the elixir made from this herb would bring the adept into symbolic union with the goddess and produce enlightenment.

Wild horses running in the hills
Can be caught with snares or lassoes
But not even magic charms can stop
A lover's heart that's turned away.

11

Rock and wind kept tryst
To abrade the vulture's plumage;
People fraught with deceptive schemes
Fray me to the very bone.[3]

13

Beyond death, in the Realm of Hell,
The karma-mirror of Yama[4] stands:
Judge me, but yield me fairness in the hereafter
Because this life paid me none!

14

In this life's short walk
We have faced up to so much.
Let us now see whether we shall meet again
In the young years of our next life!

MATSUO BASHŌ ■ (1644–1694)

Matsuo Bashō was born in the castle town of Ueno, southeast of Kyōto. Bashō's grand-father and great-grandfather belonged to the samurai class, but by Bashō's generation, the family had fallen so low that they had become farmers with only tenuous ties to the samurai class. Bashō at first served as a domestic employee of the Tōdō house, presumably as a companion to the son of the Tōdō lord. During this time, Bashō began to write linked verse (*haikai*). The linked verse sequence, usually consisting of 36 or 100 linked verses, began with the seventeen-syllable poetic form now known as haiku.

In the spring of 1672, at the age of twenty-nine, Bashō moved to Edo to establish himself as a linked-verse and haiku master who could charge fees for his services. By the mid-1670s Bashō had attracted the nucleus of his disciples and patrons who played a major role in the formation of what came to be known as the Bashō circle. In the winter of 1680, at the age of thirty-seven, Bashō left Edo and retreated to Fukagawa, on the banks of the Sumida River, on the outskirts of Edo. During the next four years he wrote in the so-called Chinese style, creating the persona of the recluse poet who was opposed to the materialism and social ambitions of the new urban culture. One of Bashō's literary achievements was fusing the earlier recluse poet tradition with the new commoner genre of haiku. He took his poetic name from the *bashō* plant, or Japanese plantain, whose large leaves sometimes tear in the wind, thus representing the fragility of the hermit-traveler's life.

In the fall of 1684, Bashō began the first of a series of journeys that occupied much of the remaining ten years of his life. On his first journey, commemorated in his travel diary *Skeleton in the Fields*, Bashō traveled to several western provinces, recruiting followers before returning to Edo in the summer of 1685. In the spring of 1689, Bashō departed

3. This poem has traditionally been read as expressing Tsangyang Gyatso's frustration with the double-dealing of the Regent who kept him from full power.

4. Lord of the Underworld, and holder of the mirror in which one's destiny was reflected.

once again, this time with his disciple Sora, for Michinoku ("Deep North") in the northeast, in an expedition later commemorated in *Narrow Road to the Deep North*. For the next two years, Bashō remained in the Kyōto-Ōsaka area. Together with two disciples in Kyōto, Bashō then edited *Monkey's Straw Coat*, the magnum opus of the Bashō school, which was published in the summer of 1691. Bashō died in 1694 on a journey to Ōsaka.

Bashō and the Art of Haiku   The seventeen-syllable haiku, which is usually translated into English in three lines, requires a cutting word and a seasonal word. The cutting word, often indicated in English translation by a dash, divides the haiku into two parts, which constitute two parts of the same scene while at the same time resonating with each other (often in a contrastive or parallel structure). The seasonal word is a word that, as a result of a long tradition of poetic use, not only indicates a specific season but usually possesses a cluster of associations that the poet draws on to widen the scope and complexity of the poem. For example, the seasonal word "evening in autumn" (*aki no kure*), which can also be translated as "end of autumn," is associated in the Japanese poetic tradition with loneliness. In the following haiku by Bashō, the cutting word, marked by a dash, creates a resonance between the implicit loneliness of the crow(s) on a withered branch and the implicit loneliness of an autumn evening or the end of autumn (also implying the end of life).

> kareeda ni   Crows resting
> karasu no tomarikeri   on a withered branch—
> aki no kure   evening in autumn

In Bashō's time, the spirit of haiku meant taking pleasure in seeing things freshly: both dislocating habitual, conventionalized perceptions *and* also recasting established poetic topics into contemporary language and culture. In the previous haiku, the topic of "evening in autumn," which classical poets from the Heian and medieval periods had composed on, is given new life by juxtaposing it with the surprising image of "crows on a withered branch," which had hitherto appeared only in Chinese ink painting.

Of particular interest here is the complex relationship between haiku and tradition. Bashō looked to classical and medieval poets for poetic and spiritual inspiration. He especially admired Saigyō (1118–1190) and Sōgi (1421–1502)—who were travelers and poet-priests—and he was strongly influenced by Chinese poetry and poetics. At the same time, Bashō was a poet of haiku (called haikai at the time), which, by its very nature, was parodic, oppositional, and immersed in popular culture. One result was the emergence in the seventeenth century of a culture of *mitate* (literally, seeing by comparison), which moved back and forth between the two starkly different worlds, that of the Japanese classics and that of the new popular literature and drama, each providing a lens or filter with which to view the other. Artists such as Hishikawa Moronobu (1618–1694), a pioneer of *ukiyo-e* prints, used the technique of *mitate* in the visual arts, both alluding to and radically transforming the topics and imagery of the classical tradition into a contemporary form.

Bashō's haiku differed from the *mitate* found in Moronobu's *ukiyo-e* woodblock prints in that the popular culture in his poetry and prose was not that of the stylish men and women of the great urban centers but, rather, that of the mundane, everyday lives of farmers and fishermen in the provinces. Bashō himself was a socially marginal figure, and his poetry and prose are pervaded by marginal figures such as the beggar, the old man, the outcast, and the traveler, no doubt reflecting his own provincial origins. Likewise, his

A *haiga* (haikai sketch), on the Chinese painting
theme of cold crows on a withered branch. The
painting is by Morikawa Kyoriki, 1656–1715,
Bashō's disciple and his painting instructor, and the
calligraphy and poem are by Bashō: "On a withered
branch, a crow comes to rest—evening in autumn"
(*Kareeda ni / karasu no tomarikeri / aki no kure*).
Probably done around 1692/1693 while Kyoriki, a
samurai from Hikone, was in Edo. Signed "Bashō
Tōsei." (42.1 in. × 12.2 in.)

allusions were not to famous lovers like the shining Genji but, rather, to medieval traveler poets such as Saigyō and Sōgi.

In the seventeenth century, the popular vernacular genres such as Saikaku's tales frequently parodied their classical predecessors by borrowing the elegant, aristocratic forms of traditional literature and giving them a popular, vulgar, or erotic content. In a reverse movement, Bashō gave a popular, vernacular genre (haiku) a spiritual or refined content, or more accurately, he sought out the spiritual and poetic in commoner culture, giving to contemporary language and provincial subject matter the kind of nuances and sentiments hitherto found only in classical or Chinese poetry. In this way, Bashō was able to raise haiku—which until then had been considered a form of light entertainment—into a serious literary genre and a vehicle for cultural transmission.

Selected Haiku[1]

kareeda ni	On a withered branch
karasu no tomarikeri	a crow comes to rest—
aki no kure	evening in autumn[2]

Going out on the beach while the light is still faint:

akebono ya—	early dawn—
shirauo shiroki	whitefish, an inch
koto issun	of whiteness[3]

Having stayed once more at the residence of Master Tōyō, I was about to leave for the Eastern Provinces.

botan shibe fukaku	From deep within
wakeizuru hachi no—	the peony pistils, withdrawing
nagori kana	regretfully, the bee[4]

Spending a whole day on the beach:

umi kurete	The sea darkening—
kamo no koe	the voice of a wild duck
honoka ni shiroshi	faintly white[5]

1. Translated by Haruo Shirane.

2. Bashō first composed this haiku in the spring of 1681, during his late Chinese-style period. *Aki no kure* can be read as either "end of autumn" or "autumn nightfall." In a 1698 collection of Bashō's haiku, this haiku is preceded by the title "On Evening in Autumn" (*aki no kure to wa*), indicating that the poem was written on a seasonal topic closely associated with Fujiwara Shunzei (d. 1204) and his medieval aesthetics of quiet, meditative loneliness. Crows perched on a withered branch, on the other hand, was a popular subject in Chinese ink painting. In this context, Bashō's haiku juxtaposes a medieval poetic topic with a Chinese painting motif, causing the two to resonate in montage fashion.

3. Bashō composed this haiku in the Eleventh Month of 1684 while visiting the Ise area during the *Skeleton in the Fields* journey. Drawing on the phonic connotations of *shirauo* (literally, white fish), Bashō establishes a connotative correspondence between the semitranslucent "whiteness" (*shiroki koto*) of the tiny fish and the pale, faint light of early dawn (*akebono*). The poem has a melodic rhythm, resulting from the repeated "o" vowel mixed with the consonantal "s."

4. This is a good example of a semiallegorical poetic greeting. Bashō composed the haiku, which appears in *Skeleton in the Fields*, when he left the house of his friend Tōyō in the Fourth Month of 1685. The bee, representing Bashō, is resting peacefully in the peony, an elegant summer flower that symbolizes Tōyō's residence, joyfully imbibing the rich pollen of the pistils, but now, with much reluctance, it must leave. The haiku is an expression of gratitude and a farewell not only to Tōyō but to all the Nagoya-area poets who have hosted him on this journey.

5. The opening verse of a linked-verse sequence composed in Atsuta, in Nagoya, in 1685. The poet looks out toward the voice of the wild duck (*kamo*), which has disappeared with the approaching darkness, and sees only a faint whiteness (*shiroshi* implies a kind of translucency), which may be the waves or the reflection of the sea in the dusk. *Kamo* is a seasonal word for winter.

furuike ya	An old pond—
kawazu tobikomu	a frog leaps in,
mizu no oto	the sound of water[6]

On the road:

kutabirete	Exhausted,
yado karu koro ya	time to find a lodging—
fuji no hana	hanging wisteria[7]

Lodging for the night at Akashi:

takotsubo ya	Octopus traps—
hakanaki yume o	fleeting dreams
natsu no tsuki	under the summer moon[8]

hototogisu	The cuckoo—
kieyuku kata ya	where it disappears
shima hitotsu	a single island[9]

While sleeping in a lodge in the capital and hearing each night the sorrowful chanting of the Kūya pilgrims:

karazake mo	Dried salmon
Kūya no yase mo	the gauntness of a Kūya pilgrim
kan no uchi	in the cold season[1]

---

6. Written in 1686 and collected in *Spring Days*. Since the ancient period, the frog had been admired for its singing and its beautiful voice. In the Heian period it became associated with spring, the *yamabuki*—the bright yellow globeflower—and limpid mountain streams. According to one source, Kikaku, one of Bashō's disciples, suggested that Bashō use *yamabuki* in the opening phrase. Instead, Bashō works against the classical associations of the frog. In place of the plaintive voice of the frog singing in the rapids or calling out for its lover, Bashō evokes the sound of the frog jumping into the water. And instead of the elegant image of a frog in a fresh mountain stream beneath the *yamabuki*, the haiku presents a stagnant pond. At the same time, the haiku offers a fresh twist to the seasonal association of the frog with spring: the sudden movement of the frog, which suggests rebirth and the awakening of life in spring, is contrasted with the implicit winter stillness of the old pond.

7. This haiku, which Bashō composed in 1688, appears in *Backpack Notes*. The wisteria (*fuji no hana*), with its long drooping flowers, is blooming outside the lodge even as it functions as a metaphor for the traveler's heart.

8. Bashō composed this poem, which appears in *Backpack Notes,* in the Fourth Month of 1688. The octopus traps were lowered in the afternoon and raised the next morning, after the octopus had crawled inside. The octopus in the jars implicitly suggest the troops of the Heike clan that were massacred on these shores at the end of the 12th century and whose ghosts subsequently appear before the traveler in *Backpack Notes*. Now these octopi are having "fleeting dreams," not knowing they are about to be harvested. Bashō juxtaposes the "summer moon" (*natsu no tsuki*), which the classical tradition deemed to be as brief as the summer night and thus associated with ephemerality, and the "octopus traps" (*takotsubo*), a vernacular word, giving new life to the theme of impermanence. The poem is intended to be humorous and sad at the same time.

9. Diverging from the classical poetic association of the cuckoo (*hototogisu*), which was its singing, Bashō focuses here on its arrow-like flight. In this poem, which Bashō wrote in 1688 during his *Backpack Notes* journey, the speaker implicitly hears the cuckoo, but by the time he looks up, it has disappeared, replaced by a single island, presumably Awajishima, the small island across the bay from Suma and Akashi, where the speaker stands. The haiku is also parodic, twisting a well-known classical poem in the *Senzaishū* (1188): "When I gaze in the direction of the crying cuckoo, only the moon lingers in the dawn." Another possible pretext is the following poem in the classic collection: "Faintly, in the morning mist on Akashi Bay, it disappears behind an island, the boat I long for." In Bashō's haiku, the flight of the disappearing cuckoo, which the poet implicitly longs to see, becomes the path of the ship, which "disappears behind" (*shimagakureyuku*) Awajishima, the "one island."

1. Bashō composed this haiku while visiting Kyōto in the Twelfth Month of 1690 and later included it in *Monkey's Straw Coat*. Kūya were lay monks or pilgrims who commemorated the anniversary of the death of Priest Kūya by begging and chanting Buddhist songs in the streets of Kyōto for 48 days beginning in the middle of the Eleventh Month. *Kan* (cold season), a roughly 30-day period from the Twelfth Month through the beginning of the First Month (February), was the coldest part of the year. The three parts—dried salmon (*karazake*), the gauntness of the Kūya pilgrim (*Kūya no yase*), and the cold season (*kan no uchi*), each of which is accentuated by a hard beginning "k" consonant and by the repeated *mo* (also)—suggest three different dimensions (material, human, and seasonal) of the loneliness of a traveler on a distant journey.

kogarashi ya	Withering winds—
hohobare itamu	the face of a man
hito no kao	pained by swollen cheeks[2]
mugimeshi ni	A cat's wife—
yatsururu koi ka	grown thin from
neko no tsuma—	love and barley?[3]
hototogisu	A cuckoo—
koe yokotau ya	the voice lies stretched
mizu no ue	over the water[4]
hiyahiya to	Taking a midday nap
kabe o fumaete	feet planted
hirune kana	on a cool wall[5]
kiku no ka ya	Chrysanthemum scent—
Nara ni wa furuki	in Nara ancient statues
hotoketachi	of the Buddha[6]
aki fukaki	Autumn deepening—
tonari wa nani o	my neighbor
suru hito zo	how does he live, I wonder?[7]

2. Composed in the winter of 1691. The two parts of the haiku—separated by the cutting word ya—can be read together as one continuous scene or separately as two parts reverberating against each other. In the first part, a person suffering from mumps (hohobare, literally, swollen cheeks) stands outside, his or her face contorted by the kogarashi, the strong winds that blow the leaves off the trees in the winter. In the second part, the person's face inflamed by and suffering from mumps echoes the cold, stinging wind. The expectations generated by withering winds, a classical seasonal topic associated with cold winter landscapes, are humorously undercut by the haiku phrase hohobare itamu (pained by swollen cheeks), which then leads to a double reversal: after the initial collision, the reader discovers a fusion between the withering winds and the painfully swollen cheeks.

3. "Cat's love for its mate" (neko no tsumagoi), later simply called cat's love (neko no koi), was a haiku seasonal topic that became popular in the Edo period. Bashō composed this haiku in 1691 and included it in Monkey's Straw Coat. Bashō humorously depicts a female cat that has grown emaciated not only from being fed only barley—a situation that suggests a poor farmhouse—but from intense lovemaking. (Yatsururu modifies both mugimeshi and koi, implying "emaciating barley and love.")

4. Bashō apparently wrote this haiku in the Fourth Month of 1693 after being urged by his disciples to compose on the topic of "cuckoos on the water's edge." As the cuckoo flies overhead, it makes a sharp penetrating cry, which "lies sideways" (yokotau), hanging over the quiet surface of the water, probably at dusk or night when it traditionally sings. The cuckoo quickly disappears, but the sound lingers, like an overtone.

5. This haiku appears in Backpack Diary; Bashō composed it in 1694 at the residence of Mokusetsu in Ōtsu (near Lake Biwa). This poem uses hiyahiya (cool) as a seasonal word for autumn. The speaker, cooling the bottoms of his bare feet on the wall, has fallen asleep on a hot afternoon. The implied topic is lingering summer heat (zansho), which is captured from a humorous, haiku angle, in the feet, through which the speaker feels the arrival of autumn.

6. Bashō composed this haiku in 1694, on Chrysanthemum Festival Day (Chōyō), which fell on the ninth day of the Ninth Month, while stopping at Nara on the way to Ōsaka on his last journey. Nara, the capital of Japan in the 8th century, is known for its many temples and buddha statues. The chrysanthemum, considered the aristocrat of flowers in classical poetry and a seasonal word for late autumn, possess a strong but refined fragrance. The many buddhas in the ancient capital of Nara evoke a similar sense of dignity, solemnity, and refinement as well as nostalgia for a bygone era.

7. Bashō composed this haiku, which appears in Backpack Diary, in the autumn of 1694, shortly before he died in Ōsaka. Bashō had been invited to a poem party at the home of one of his close followers, but he didn't feel well enough to go and instead sent a poem which subtly expresses his deep regret at not being able to meet this friends. In highly colloquial language, the poem suggests the loneliness of a traveler implicitly seeking companionship, or the loneliness of those who live together and yet apart in urban society, or the loneliness of life itself, particularly in the face of death—all of which resonate with late autumn (aki fukaki), associated in classical poetry with loneliness and sorrow.

kono michi ya	This road—
yuku hito nashi ni	no one goes down it
aki no kure	autumn's end[8]

Composed while ill:

tabi ni yande	Sick on a journey
yume wa kareno o	dreams roam about
kakemeguru	on a withered moor[9]

Narrow Road to the Deep North   In the spring of 1689, Bashō and his companion Sora departed for Michinoku, or Oku (Interior), the relatively unsettled area of Japan's north-eastern Honshū. Bashō traveled north to present-day Sendai, crossed west over the mountains to the Japan Sea side, then moved south, down the coast, through Kanazawa, and arrived at Ōgaki in Mino Province (Gifu), after a five-month journey (see map on page 106). Although *Narrow Road to the Deep North* is often read as a faithful travel account, it is best regarded as a kind of fiction loosely based on the actual journey. Bashō depicts an ideal world in which the traveler devotes himself to poetic life in a manner that Bashō himself probably aspired to but found impossible in the busy world of a linked-verse and haiku master.

The text consists of fifty or so discrete sections strung together like a linked-verse sequence. They describe a series of interrelated journeys: a search for noted poetic places, especially the traces of ancient poets such as Saigyō, the medieval poet-priest to whom this account pays special homage; a journey into the past to such historical places as the old battlefield at Hiraizumi; an ascetic journey and a pilgrimage to sacred places; and interesting encounters with individuals and poetic partners, with whom he exchanges poetic greetings.

The interest of travel literature, at least in the Anglo-European tradition, generally lies in the unknown, new worlds, new knowledge, new perspectives, and new experiences. But for Japanese medieval poets, the object of travel was to confirm what already existed, to reinforce the roots of cultural memory. By visiting noted poetic locales, the poet-traveler hoped to relive the experience of his or her literary predecessors, to be moved to compose poetry on the same landscape, thereby joining his or her cultural forebears. The travel diary itself became a link in a chain of poetic and literary transmission.

In contrast to medieval Japanese poets, however, who attempted to preserve the classical associations of the poetic topics, Bashō sought out new poetic associations in classic sites and discovered new poetic places. In the passage on Muro-no-yashima, toward the beginning, Bashō suggests that *Narrow Road* will take a new approach, exploring both the local place and its historical and poetic roots in an effort to re-envision the landscape. A contrast can be seen between the places visited in the first

8. Bashō composed this in the late autumn of 1694, at the end of his life, at a large haiku gathering. The poem can be read as an expression of disappointment that, at the end of his life, in the autumn of his career—*aki no kure* can mean either "autumn's end" or "autumn evening"—he is alone, and/or as an expression of disappointment at the lack of sympathetic poetic partners, as an expression of desire for those who can engage in the poetic dialogue necessary to continue on this difficult journey.

9. Bashō's last poem, written four days before his death on the twelfth day of the Tenth Month of 1694, during a journey in Ōsaka.

half of *Narrow Road*, which tend to be major poetic sites and which bear the weight of the classical tradition, and those found along the Japan Sea side in the second half, such as Kisagata, which tend to be lesser poetic locales or even unknown in the classical tradition. In writing *Narrow Road*, Bashō sought a Chinese poetic ideal of "landscape in human emotion, and human emotion in landscape," in which the landscape becomes infused with cultural memory and a wide variety of human emotions and associations, from the sensual to the spiritual.

A number of the early sections imply that the journey also is a form of ascetic practice. The title of *Narrow Road to the Deep North* (*Oku no hosomichi*) implies not only the narrow and difficult roads (*hosomichi*) of Michinoku but the difficulty of the spiritual journey "within" (*oku*). Pilgrimages to sacred places, to temples and shrines, were popular from as early as the medieval Heian period and formed an integral part of travel literature, particularly those written by hermit-priests, a persona that Bashō adopts here. *Narrow Road,* in fact, has far more sections on this topic than usually found in medieval travel diaries. A typical passage begins with a description of the place and a history of the shrine or temple, usually giving some detail about the founder or the name. The climactic haiku, which may be a poetic greeting to the divine spirit or head of the temple/shrine, usually conveys a sense of the sacred quality or efficacy of the place.

Bashō wrote *Narrow Road* a considerable time after the actual journey, probably in 1694 at the end of his life, when he was developing his new ideal of *haibun*, or haiku-prose, in which haiku was embedded in poetic prose. *Narrow Road to the Deep North* is marked by a great variety of prose styles, and it may best be understood as an attempt to reveal the different possibilities of *haibun* in the form of travel literature. The resulting fusion of vernacular Japanese, classical Japanese, and classical Chinese, with its parallel and contrastive couplet-like phrases, had a profound impact on the development of Japanese prose. Of particular interest is the close fusion between the prose and the poetry, in which the prose creates a dramatic context for many of the best haiku that Bashō wrote.

PRONUNCIATIONS:

Hiraizumi: hee-rye-zou-mee
Ise: ee-say
Matsuo Bashō: mah-tsu-oh bah-show
Saigyō: sigh-gyoh

from Narrow Road to the Deep North[1]

The months and days, the travelers of a hundred ages;
the years that come and go, voyagers too.
floating away their lives on boats,
growing old as they lead horses by the bit,
for them, each day a journey, travel their home.
Many, too, are the ancients who perished on the road.

---

1. Translated by Haruo Shirane.

Some years ago, seized by wanderlust, I wandered along the shores of the sea. Then, last autumn, I swept away the old cobwebs in my dilapidated dwelling on the river's edge.

As the year gradually came to an end and spring arrived, filling the sky with mist, I longed to cross the Shirakawa Barrier, the most revered of poetic places. Somehow or other, I became possessed by a spirit, which crazed my soul. Unable to sit still, I accepted the summons of the Deity of the Road. No sooner had I repaired the holes in my trousers, attached a new cord to my rain hat, and cauterized my legs with moxa than my thoughts were on the famous moon at Matsushima. I turned my dwelling over to others and moved to Sanpū's villa.

> kusa no to mo   Time even for the grass hut
> sumikawaru yo zo   to change owners—
> hina no ie   house of dolls[2]

I left a sheet of eight linked verses on the pillar of the hermitage.

I started out on the twenty-seventh day of the Third Month.

The dawn sky was misting over; the moon lingered, giving off a pale light; the peak of Mount Fuji appeared faintly in the distance. I felt uncertain, wondering whether I would see again the cherry blossoms on the boughs at Ueno and Yanaka. My friends had gathered the night before to see me off and joined me on the boat. When I disembarked at a place called Senju, my breast was overwhelmed by thoughts of the "three thousand leagues ahead," and standing at the crossroads of the illusory world, I wept at the parting.

> yuku haru ya   Spring going—
> tori naki uo no   birds crying and tears
> me wa namida   in the eyes of the fish[3]

Making this my first journal entry, we set off but made little progress. People lined the sides of the street, seeing us off, it seemed, as long as they could see our backs.

Was it the second year of Genroku? On a mere whim, I had resolved that I would make a long journey to the Deep North. Although I knew I would probably suffer, my hair growing white under the distant skies of Wu, I wanted to view those places that I had heard of but never seen and placed my faith in an uncertain future, not knowing if I would return alive. We barely managed to reach the Sōka post station that night. The luggage that I carried over my bony shoulders began to cause me pain. I had departed on the journey thinking that I need bring only myself, but I ended up carrying a coat to keep me warm at night, a night robe, rain gear, inkstone, brush, and the like, as well as the farewell presents that I could not refuse. All these became a burden on the road.

We paid our respects to the shrine at Muro-no-yashima, Eight Islands of the Sealed Room. Sora, my travel companion, noted: "This deity is called the Goddess of the Blooming Cherry Tree and is the same as that worshiped at Mount Fuji. Since the goddess entered a sealed hut and burned herself giving birth to Hohodemi, the God of Emitting Fire, and proving her vow, they call the place Eight Islands of the Sealed Room.

2. *Hina* (dolls), a new seasonal word for late spring, meant Hinamatsuri, the girls' festival on the third of the Third Month, when families with daughters displayed dolls in their houses. The time has come for even the recluse hut—symbolized by the "grass door"—to become a domestic, secular dwelling, with family and daughter(s).

3. The birds and fish mourn the passing of spring and, by implication, the departure of the travelers. Some commentators see the fish as the disciples left behind and the birds as the departing travelers (Bashō and Sora); others interpret the departing spring as the traveler. *Yuku*, a key word in *Narrow Road*, means both "to go" and "to pass time," thereby fusing passings in time and in space.

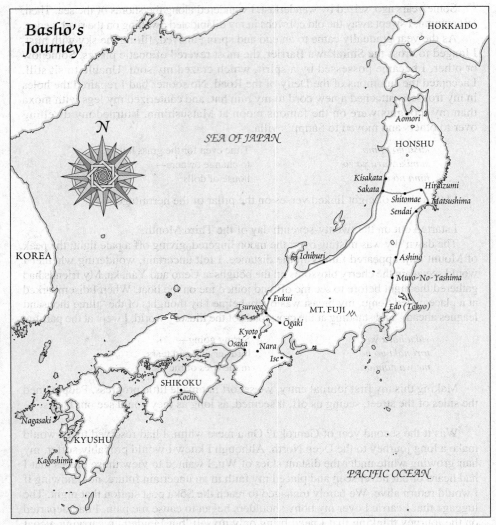

Bashō's Journey

HOKKAIDO

SEA OF JAPAN

HONSHU

Aomori

Kisakata
Sakata
Hiraizumi
Shitomae
Matsushima
Sendai

KOREA

Ichiburi
Ashino
Muro-No-Yashima

Fukui
MT. FUJI
Edo (Tokyo)
Tsuruga
Kyoto
Ōgaki
Osaka
Nara
Ise

SHIKOKU
Kochi

Nagasaki
KYUSHU
Kagoshima

PACIFIC OCEAN

In spring 1687, Bashō and his disciple Sora departed Edo, the capital of Tokagawa Japan, for Michinoku (Deep North). Their five month journey concluded at Ōgaki.

The custom of including smoke in poems on this place also derives from this story. It is forbidden to consume a fish called *konoshiro,* or shad, which is thought to smell like flesh when burned. The essence of this shrine history is already known to the world."[4]

On the thirtieth, stopped at the foot of Nikkō Mountain. The owner said, "My name is Buddha Gozaemon. People have given me this name because I make honesty my first concern in all matters. As a consequence, you can relax for one night on the road. Please stay here." I wondered what kind of buddha had manifested itself in this

4. A typical classical poem on Muro-no-yashima, by Fujiwara Sanekata, reads: "How could I let you know of my longing were it not for the smoke of Muro-no-yashima?" Classical poets believed that the steam from a stream in Muro-no-yashima looked like smoke. However, Sora, who came from a family of Shintō priests, presents here a different explanation, taking a revisionary approach to *utamakura,* or poetic places.

soiled world to help someone like me, traveling like a beggar priest on a pilgrimage. I observed the actions of the innkeeper carefully and saw that he was neither clever nor calculating. He was nothing but honesty—the type of person that Confucius referred to when he said, "Those who are strong in will and without pretension are close to humanity." I had nothing but respect for the purity of his character.

On the first of the Fourth Month, we paid our respects to the holy mountain. In the distant past, the name of this sacred mountain was written with the characters Nikkōzan, Two Rough Mountain, but when Priest Kūkai established a temple here, he changed the name to Nikkō, Light of the Sun. Perhaps he was able to see a thousand years into the future. Now this venerable light shines throughout the land, and its benevolence flows to the eight corners of the earth, and the four classes—warrior, samurai, artisan, and merchant—all live in peace. Out of a sense of reverence and awe, I put my brush down here.

aratōto	Awe inspiring!
aoba wakaba no	on the green leaves, budding leaves
hi no hikari	light of the sun

Black Hair Mountain, enshrouded in mist, the snow still white.

sorisutete	Shaving my head
Kurokamiyama ni	at Black Hair Mountain—
koromogae	time for summer clothes[5]

[Sora]

Sora's family name is Kawai; his personal name is Sōgoro. He lived near me, helping me gather wood and heat water, and was delighted at the thought of sharing with me the sights of Matsushima and Kisagata. At the same time, he wanted to help me overcome the hardships of travel. On the morning of the departure, he shaved his hair, changed to dark black robes, and took on the Buddhist name of Sōgo. That is why he wrote the Black Hair Mountain poem. I thought that the words "time for summer clothes" were particularly effective.

Climbing more than a mile up a mountain, we came to a waterfall. From the top of the cavern, the water flew down a hundred feet, falling into a blue pool of a thousand rocks. I squeezed into a hole in the rocks and entered the cavern: they say that this is called Back-View Falls because you can see the waterfall from the back, from inside the cavern.

shibaraku wa	Secluded for a while
taki ni komoru ya	in a waterfall—
ge no hajime	beginning of summer austerities[6]

There is a mountain-priest temple called Kōmyōji. We were invited there and prayed at the Hall of Gyōja.

natsuyama ni	Summer mountains—
ashida o ogamu	praying to the tall clogs
kadode kana	at journey's start[7]

5. Embarking on a journey becomes synonymous with entering the Buddhist path: both imply a firm resolve and a new life, symbolized here by the seasonal word *koromogae* (change of clothes at the beginning of summer).

6. This line refers both to the beginning of summer and to the Buddhist austerities of summer, in which Buddhist practitioners remained indoors for three months fasting, reciting sutras, and carrying out such ascetic and purification practices as standing under a waterfall. The traveler stands behind the waterfall, which gives him the cool, pure feeling of being cleansed of the dirt of the world.

7. At the beginning of the journey, the traveler bows before the high clogs, a prayer for the foot strength of En no Gyōja, the founder of a mountain priest sect and an "austerity man" (gyōja) believed to have acquired superhuman power from rigorous mountain training.

The willow that was the subject of Saigyō's poem, "Where a Crystal Stream Flows,"[8] still stood in the village of Ashino, on a footpath in a rice field. The lord of the manor of this village had repeatedly said, "I would like to show you this willow," and I had wondered where it was. Today I was able to stand in its very shade.

ta ichimai	Whole field of
uete tachisaru	rice seedlings planted—I part
yanagi kana	from the willow[9]

The days of uncertainty piled one on the other, and when we came upon the Shirakawa Barrier, I finally felt as if I had settled into the journey. I can understand why that poet had written, "Had I a messenger, I would send a missive to the capital!" One of three noted barriers, the Shirakawa Barrier captured the hearts of poets. With the sound of the autumn wind in my ears and the image of the autumn leaves in my mind, I was moved all the more by the tops of the green-leafed trees.[1] The flowering of the wild rose amid the white deutzia clusters made me feel as if I were crossing over snow.

At the Sukagawa post station, we visited a man named Tōkyū. He insisted that we stay for four or five days and asked me how I had found the Shirakawa Barrier. I replied, "My body and spirit were tired from the pain of the long journey; my heart overwhelmed by the landscape. The thoughts of the distant past tore through me, and I couldn't think straight." But feeling it would be a pity to cross the barrier without producing a single verse, I wrote:

fūryū no	Beginnings of poetry—
hajime ya oku no	rice-planting songs
taue uta	of the Deep North[2]

This opening verse was followed by a second verse and then a third; before we knew it, three sequences.

The next day we went to Shinobu Village and visited Shinobu Mottling Rock. The rock was in a small village, half buried, deep in the shade of the mountain. A child from the village came and told us, "In the distant past, the rock was on top of

8. Poem by Saigyō in the *Shinkokinshū* collection (1205): "I thought to pause on the roadside where a crystal stream flows beneath a willow and stood rooted to the spot."

9. The entire passage alludes to *The Wandering Priest and the Willow,* a nō play based on Saigyō's poem just referred to, in which an itinerant priest, retracing the steps of Saigyō through the Deep North, meets an old man who shows him the withered willow about which Saigyō wrote his famous poem. The old man later turns out to be the spirit of that willow. At the end of the play the priest offers prayers to the spirit of the willow, thereby enabling it to achieve salvation. When the district officer offers to introduce Saigyō's willow to the traveler, the passage takes on the atmosphere of a nō dream play in which the traveler encounters the spirit of Saigyō, embodied in the willow. In contrast to Saigyō's classical poem, in which time passes as the traveler rests near a beautiful stream, in Bashō's haiku, time passes as the traveler journeys to meet Saigyō's spirit.

1. The Shirakawa Barrier here exists almost entirely in the traveler's imagination as a circle of poetic associations. Taira Kanemori (d. 990), referred to as "that poet," was the first in a long line of classical poets to compose on the barrier: "Had I a messenger I would send a missive to the capital!" A poem by Priest Nōin, who first traveled to the Deep North in 1025, created the association of the Shirakawa Barrier with autumn wind. At a poetry contest in 1170, Minamoto Yorimasa composed a variation on Nōin's poem that also linked the Shirakawa Barrier with bright autumn leaves: "In the capital the leaves were still green when I saw them, but bright autumn leaves now scatter at the Shirakawa Barrier." Now Bashō follows the traces of Saigyō, Yorimasa, and others who had earlier sought the traces of Nōin, who in turn had followed the traces of Kanemori.

2. This haiku, which Bashō composed in the summer of 1689 and later placed in *Narrow Road*, is a greeting to his friend and host Tōkyū (1638–1715), a station master at Sukagawa, at the entrance to the Deep North (*oku*), the northeast region. Hearing the rice-planting songs in the fields (probably owned by Tōkyū), Bashō composes a poem that compliments the host on the elegance of his home and region. The poem also expresses Bashō's joy and gratitude at being able to compose linked verse for the first time in the Interior.

this mountain, but the villagers, angered by the visitors who had been tearing up the barley grass to test the rock, pushed it down into the valley, where it lies face down." Perhaps that was the way it had to be.

sanae toru	Planting rice seedlings
temoto ya mukashi	the hands—in the distant past pressing
shinobuzuri	the grass of longing[3]

* * *

The Courtyard Inscribed-Stone was in Taga Castle in the Village of Ichikawa. More than six feet tall and about three feet wide; the moss had eaten away the rock, and the letters were faint. On the memorial, which listed the number of miles to the four borders of the province: "This castle was built in 724 by Lord Ōno Azumabito, the Provincial Governor and General of the Barbarian-Subduing Headquarters. In 762, on the first of the Twelfth Month, it was rebuilt by the Councillor and Military Commander of the Eastern Seaboard, Lord Emi Asakari." The memorial belonged to the era of the sovereign Shōmu.[4] Famous places in poetry have been collected and preserved; but mountains crumble, rivers shift, roads change, rock are buried in dirt; trees age, saplings replace them; times change, generations come and go. But here, without a doubt, was a memorial of a thousand years: I was peering into the heart of the ancients. The virtues of travel, the joys of life, forgetting the weariness of travel, I shed only tears.* * *

It was already close to noon when we borrowed a boat and crossed over to Matsushima. The distance was more than two leagues, and we landed on the shore of Ojima. It has been said many times, but Matsushima is the most beautiful place in all of Japan. First of all, it can hold its head up to Dongting Lake or West Lake. Letting in the sea from the southeast, it fills the bay, three leagues wide, with the tide of Zhejiang. Matsushima has gathered countless islands: the high ones point their fingers to heaven; those lying down crawl over the waves. Some are piled two deep; some, three deep. To the left, the islands are separated from one another; to the right, they are linked. Some seem to be carrying islands on their backs; others, to be embracing them like a person caressing a child. The green of the pine is dark and dense, the branches and leaves bent by the salty sea breeze—as if they were deliberately twisted. A soft, tranquil landscape, like a beautiful lady powdering her face. Did the god of the mountain create this long ago, in the age of the gods? Is this the work of the Creator? What words to describe this?

The rocky shore of Ojima extended out from the coast and became an island protruding in the sea. Here were the remains of Priest Ungo's dwelling and the rock on which he meditated. Again, one could see, scattered widely in the shadow of the pines, people who had turned their backs on the world. They lived quietly in grass huts, the smoke from burning rice ears and pinecones rising from the huts. I didn't know what kind of people they were, but I was drawn to them, and

3. Shinobu was the most famous *utamakura*, or poetic place, in the Deep North. Women there would rub ferns onto woven cloth so as to create a wild pattern or design, which became associated with uncontrolled longing. The traveler in *Narrow Road* is disappointed to discover that an *utamakura* that had given birth to countless poems has been neglected and abused, but the powerful memory of that poetic place enables the poet to find new poetry in the mundane, as Bashō sees the women's hands planting seedlings instead of rubbing the famous ferns.

4. Emperor Shōmu, r. 724–748. In actuality, Shōmu wasn't alive at the time of this memorial.

when I approached, the moon was reflected on the sea, and the scenery changed again, different from the afternoon landscape. When we returned to the shore and took lodgings, I opened the window. It was a two-story building, and I felt like a traveler sleeping amid the wind and the clouds: to a strange degree it was a good feeling.

Matsushima ya	Matsushima—
tsuru ni mi kare	borrow the body of a crane
hototogisu	cuckoo!!

[Sora]

I closed my mouth and tried to sleep but couldn't. When I left my old hermitage, Sodō had given me a Chinese poem on Matsushima, and Hara Anteki had sent me a waka on Matsugaurashima. Opening my knapsack, I made those poems my friends for the night. There also were hokku by Sanpū and Jokushi.

On the eleventh, made a pilgrimage to Zuiganji temple. Thirty-two generations ago, Makabe Heishirō took holy vows, went to China, returned, and founded this temple. Owing to his good works, the seven halls of the temple have been splendidly rebuilt, the gold-foiled walls and the grand decorations casting a light on everything. The temple, a realization of the land of the buddha in this world. Wondered where that temple of the famous Kenbutsu sage was.

On the twelfth we headed for Hiraizumi. We had heard of such places as the Pine at Anewa and the Thread-Broken Bridge, but there were few human traces, and finding it difficult to recognize the path normally used by the rabbit hunters and woodcutters, we ended up losing our way and came out at a harbor called Ishi no maki. Across the water we could see Kinkazan, the Golden Flower Mountain, where the "Blooming of the Golden Flower" poem had been composed as an offering to the emperor. Several hundred ferry boats gathered in the inlet; human dwellings fought for space on the shore; and the smoke from the ovens rose high. Never occurred to me I would come across such a prosperous place. Attempted to find a lodging, but no one gave us a place for the night. Finally, spent the night in an impoverished hovel and, at dawn, wandered off again onto an unknown road. Looking afar at Sode no watari, Obuchi no maki, Mano no kayahara, and other famous places, made our way over a dike that extended into the distance. Followed the edge of a lonely and narrow marsh, lodged for the night at a place called Toima and then arrived at Hiraizumi: a distance, I think, of more than twenty leagues.

The glory of three generations of Fujiwara vanished in the space of a dream; the remains of the Great Gate stood two miles in the distance. Hidehira's headquarters had turned into rice paddies and wild fields. Only Kinkeizan, Golden Fowl Hill, remained as it was. First, we climbed Takadachi, Castle-on-the Heights, from where we could see the Kitakami, a broad river that flowed from the south. The Koromo River rounded Izumi Castle, and at a point beneath Castle-on-the-Heights, it dropped into the broad river. The ancient ruins of Yasuhira and others, lying behind Koromo Barrier, appear to close off the southern entrance and guard against the Ainu barbarians. Selecting his loyal retainers, Yoshitsune fortified himself in the castle, but his glory quickly turned to grass. "The state is destroyed; rivers and hills remain. The city walls turn to spring; grasses and trees are green." With these lines from Du Fu in my head, I lay down my bamboo hat, letting the time and tears flow.

natsugusa ya	Summer grasses—
tsuwamonodomo ga	the traces of dreams
yume no ato	of ancient warriors[5]
unohana ni	In the deutzia
Kanefusa miyuru	Kanefusa appears
shiraga kana	white haired[6]

[Sora]

The two halls about which we had heard such wonderful things were open. The Sutra Hall held the statues of the three chieftains, and the Hall of Light contained the coffins of three generations, preserving three sacred images. The seven precious substances were scattered and lost; the doors of jewels, torn by the wind; the pillars of gold, rotted in the snow. The hall should have turned into a mound of empty, abandoned grass, but the four sides were enclosed, covering the roof with shingles, surviving the snow and rain. For a while, it became a memorial to a thousand years.

samidare no	Have the summer rains
furinokoshite	come and gone, sparing
hikaridō	the Hall of Light?

Gazing afar at the road that extended to the south, we stopped at the village of Iwade. We passed Ogurazaki and Mizu no ojima, and from Narugo Hot Springs we proceeded to Passing-Water Barrier and attempted to cross into Dewa Province. Since there were few travelers on this road, we were regarded with suspicion by the barrier guards, and it was only after considerable effort that we were able to cross the barrier. We climbed a large mountain, and since it had already grown dark, we caught sight of a house of a border guard and asked for lodging. For three days, the wind and rain were severe, forcing us to stay in the middle of a boring mountain.

nomi shirami	Fleas, lice—
uma no shito suru	a horse passes water
makuramoto	by my pillow

I visited a person named Seifū at Obanazawa. Though wealthy, he had the spirit of a recluse. Having traveled repeatedly to the capital, he understood the tribulations of travel and gave me shelter for a number of days. He eased the pain of the long journey.

5. The four successive heavy "o" syllables in *tsuwamonodomo* ("warriors") suggest the ponderous march of soldiers or the thunder of battle. This haiku depends on multiple meanings: *ato* can mean "site," "aftermath," "trace," or "track"; and *yume* can mean "dream," "ambition," or "glory." The traveler here takes on the aura of the traveling priest in a nō warrior play who visits the site of a former battlefield and then, as if in a dream, watches the ghost of the slain warrior reenact his most tragic moments on the battlefield. Through the reference to Tang Dynasty poet Du Fu's noted Chinese poem on the impermanence of civilization—"The state is destroyed, rivers and hills remain / The city walls turn to spring, grasses and trees are green"—Bashō transforms these classical associations of eroticism and fertility into those of battle and the larger theme of the ephemerality of human ambitions.

6. The white flowers of the deutzia, a kind of briar, appear in the midst of a field of summer grass, from which the figure of Kanefusa rises like a ghost. According to the *Record of Yoshitsune,* Kanefusa, Yoshitsune's loyal retainer, helped Yoshitsune's wife and children commit suicide; saw his master to his end; set fire to the fort at Takadachi; slew an enemy captain; and then leaped into the flames—a sense of frenzy captured in the image of the white hair.

suzushisa o	Taking coolness
waga yado ni shite	for my lodging
nemaru nari	I relax[7]

In Yamagata there was a mountain temple, the Ryūshakuji, founded by the high priest Jikaku, an especially pure and tranquil place. People had urged us to see this place at least once, so we backtracked from Obanazawa, a distance of about seven leagues. It was still light when we arrived. We borrowed a room at a temple at the mountain foot and climbed to the Buddha hall at the top. Boulders were piled on boulders; the pines and cypress had grown old; the soil and rocks were aged, covered with smooth moss. The doors to the temple buildings at the top were closed, not a sound to be heard. I followed the edge of the cliff, crawling over the boulders, and then prayed at the Buddhist hall. It was a stunning scene wrapped in quiet—I felt my spirit being purified.

shizukasa ya	Stillness—
iwa ni shimiiru	sinking deep into the rocks
semi no koe	cries of the cicada[8]

The Mogami River originates in the Deep North; its upper reaches are in Yamagata. As we descended, we encountered frightening rapids with names like Scattered Go Stones and Flying Eagle. The river skirts the north side of Mount Itajiki and then finally pours into the sea at Sakata. As I descended, passing through the dense foliage, I felt as if the mountains were covering the river on both sides. When filled with rice, these boats are apparently called "rice boats." Through the green leaves, I could see the falling waters of White-Thread Cascade. Sennindō, Hall of the Wizard, stood on the banks, directly facing the water. The river was swollen with rain, making the boat journey perilous.

samidare wo	Gathering the rains
atsumete hayashi	of the wet season—swift
Mogamigawa	the Mogami River[9]

Haguroyama, Gassan, and Yudono are called the Three Mountains of Dewa. At Haguroyama, Feather Black Mountain—which belongs to the Tōeizan Temple in Edo, in Musashi Province—the moon of Tendai concentration and contemplation shines, and the lamp of the Buddhist Law of instant enlightenment glows. The temple quarters stand side by side, and the ascetics devote themselves to their calling. The efficacy of the divine mountain, whose prosperity will last forever, fills people with awe and fear.

On the eighth, we climbed Gassan, Moon Mountain. With purification cords around our necks and white cloth wrapped around our heads, we were led up the mountain by a person called a "strongman." Surrounded by clouds and mist, we walked over ice and snow and climbed for twenty miles. Wondering if we had passed Cloud Barrier, beyond which the sun and moon move back and forth, I ran out of breath, my body frozen. By the time we reached the top, the sun had set and the moon

7. Bashō, exhausted from a difficult journey, finds Seifū's residence and hospitality to be "coolness" itself and "relaxes" (nemaru)—a word in the local dialect—as if he were at home. In an age without air conditioners, the word "cool" (suzushisa), a seasonal word for summer, was the ultimate compliment that could be paid to the host of a summer's lodging.

8. In classical poetry, the cicada was associated with its raucous, unpleasant cries. In a paradoxical twist, the sharp, high-pitched cries of the cicada deepen the stillness by penetrating the rocks on top of the mountain.

9. Here Bashō gives a new "poetic essence," based on personal experience, to the Mogami River, an utamakura (poetic place) long associated with rice-grain boats, which were thought to ply the river.

had come out. We spread bamboo grass on the ground and lay down, waiting for the dawn. When the sun emerged and the clouds cleared away, we descended to Yudono, Bathhouse Mountain.

On the side of the valley were the so-called Blacksmith Huts. Here blacksmiths collect divine water, purify their bodies and minds, forge swords admired by the world, and engrave them with "Moon Mountain." I hear that in China they harden swords in the sacred water at Dragon Spring, and I was reminded of the ancient story of Gan Jiang and Mo Ye, the two Chinese who crafted famous swords. The devotion of these masters to the art was extraordinary. Sitting down on a large rock for a short rest, I saw a cherry tree about three feet high, its buds half open. The tough spirit of the late-blooming cherry tree, buried beneath the accumulated snow, remembering the spring, moved me. It was as if I could smell the "plum blossom in the summer heat," and I remembered the pathos of the poem by Priest Gyōson.[1] Forbidden to speak of the details of this sacred mountain, I put down my brush.

When we returned to the temple quarters, at priest Egaku's behest, we wrote down verses about our pilgrimage to the Three Mountains.

suzushisa ya	Coolness—
hono mikazuki no	faintly a crescent moon over
Haguroyama	Feather Black Mountain[2]
kumo no mine	Cloud peaks
ikutsu kuzurete	crumbling one after another—
tsuki no yama	Moon Mountain[3]
katararenu	Forbidden to speak—
yudono ni nurasu	wetting my sleeves
tamoto kana	at Bathhouse Mountain![4]

Left Haguro and at the castle town of Tsurugaoka were welcomed by the samurai Nagayama Shigeyuki. Composed a round of haikai. Sakichi accompanied us this far. Boarded a boat and went down to the port of Sakata. Stayed at the house of a doctor named En'an Fugyoku.

1. "Plum blossoms in summer heat" is a Zen phrase for the unusual ability to achieve enlightenment. The plum tree blooms in early spring and generally never lasts until the summer. The poem by the priest Gyōson (1055–1135) is "think of us as feeling sympathy for each other! Mountain cherry blossoms! I know of no one beside you here."

2. Greetings to the spirit of the land often employed complex wordplay and associative words, which interweave the place-name into the physical description. Here the prefix *hono* (faintly or barely) and *mikazuki* (third-day moon) create a visual contrast between the thin light of the crescent moon and the blackness of the night, implied in the name Feather Black Mountain. The silver hook of the moon, which casts a thin ray of light through the darkness, brings a sense of "coolness" amid the summer heat, suggesting both the hospitality and the spiritual purity of the sacred mountain.

3. *Kumo no mine* (literally, cloud peak) is a high, cumulus cloud that results from intense moisture and heat. The mountain-shaped clouds, which have gathered during midday at the peak of Gassan, or Moon Mountain, crumble or collapse one another after another until they are finally gone, leaving the moon shining over the mountain (*tsuki no yama*), a Japanese reading for "Gassan." Movement occurs from midday, when the clouds block the view, to night, when the mountain stands unobscured, and from mental obscurity to enlightenment.

4. In contrast to the first two mountains, which never appeared in classical poetry, Yudono (literally, Bathhouse) was often referred to in classical poetry as Koi-no-yama, Mountain of Love. The body of the Yudono deity was a huge red rock that spouted hot water and was said to resemble sexual organs. "Forbidden to speak" refers to the rule that all visitors to Yudono are forbidden to speak about the appearance of the mountain to others. The wetting of the sleeves echoes the erotic association with love and bathing and also suggests the speaker's tears of awe at the holiness of the mountain.

Atsumiyama ya	From Hot Springs Mountain
Fukuura kakete	to the Bay of Breezes,
yusuzumi	the evening cool

atsuki hi o	Pouring the hot day
umi ni iretari	into the sea—
Mogamigawa	Mogami River[5]

Having seen all the beautiful landscapes—rivers, mountains, seas, and coasts—I now prepared my heart for Kisagata. From the port at Sakata moving northeast, we crossed over a mountain, followed the rocky shore, and walked across the sand—all for a distance of ten miles. The sun was on the verge of setting when we arrived. The sea wind blew sand into the air; the rain turned everything to mist, hiding Chōkai Mountain. I groped in the darkness. Having heard that the landscape was exceptional in the rain, I decided that it must also be worth seeing after the rain, too, and squeezed into a fisherman's thatched hut to wait for the rain to pass.

By the next morning the skies had cleared, and with the morning sun shining brightly, we took a boat to Kisagata. Our first stop was Nōin Island, where we visited the place where Nōin had secluded himself for three years. We docked our boat on the far shore and visited the old cherry tree on which Saigyō had written the poem about "a fisherman's boat rowing over the flowers."[6] On the shore of the river was an imperial mausoleum, the gravestone of Empress Jingū. The temple was called Kanmanju Temple. I wondered why I had yet to hear of an imperial procession to this place.

We sat down in the front room of the temple and raised the blinds, taking in the entire landscape at one glance. To the south, Chōkai Mountain held up the heavens, its shadow reflected on the bay of Kisagata; to the west, the road came to an end at Muyamuya Barrier; and to the east, there was a dike. The road to Akita stretched into the distance. To the north was the sea, the waves pounding into the bay at Shiogoshi, Tide-Crossing. The face of the bay, about two and a half miles in width and length, resembled Matsushima but with a different mood. If Matsushima was like someone laughing, Kisagata resembled a resentful person filled with sorrow and loneliness. The land was as if in a state of anguish.

Kisagata ya	Kisagata—
ame ni Seishi ga	Xi Shi asleep in the rain
nebu no hana	flowers of the silk tree[7]

5. The first version was composed by Bashō at the residence of Terajima Hikosuke, a wealthy merchant at Sakata: "Coolness— / pouring into the sea, / Mogami River." The haiku praises the view from Hikosuke's house, which overlooks the great Mogami River where it flows into the Japan Sea. In the revised version, the Mogami River is pouring the *atsuki hi*, "hot sun" or "hot day," suggesting both a setting sun washed by the waves at sea and a hot summer's day coming to a dramatic close in the sea. Bashō drops the word "coolness" and the constraints of the greeting to his host to create a more dramatic image, one that suggests coolness without using the word.

6. The poem attributed to Saigyō is "The cherry trees at Kisakata are buried in waves—a fisherman's boat rowing over the flowers."

7. Kisagata was an *utamakura* (poetic place) associated, particularly as a result of the famous poem by Nōin (d. 1050), with wandering, the thatched huts of fisherfolk, lodgings, and a rocky shore. The traveler relives these classical associations, but in the end, he draws on Chinese poet Su Dongpo's "West Lake," which compares the noted lake to Xi Shi, a legendary Chinese beauty who was forced to debauch an enemy emperor and cause his defeat. She was thought to have a constant frown, her eyes half closed, as a result of her tragic fate. Dampened and shriveled by the rain, the silk tree flower echoes the resentful Chinese consort: both in turn became a metaphor for the rain-enshrouded, emotionally dark bay.

shiogoshi ya	In the shallows—
tsuru hagi nurete	cranes wetting their legs
umi suzushi	coolness of the sea[8]

Reluctant to leave Sakata, the days piled up; now I turn my gaze to the far-off clouds of the northern provinces. Thoughts of the distant road ahead fill me with anxiety; I hear it is more than 325 miles to the castle town in Kaga. After we crossed Nezu-no-seki, Mouse Barrier, we hurried toward Echigo and came to Ichiburi, in Etchū Province. During these nine days, I suffered from the extreme heat, fell ill, and did not record anything.

fumizuki ya	The Seventh Month—
muika mo tsune no	the sixth day, too, is different
yo ni wa nizu	from the usual night[9]

araumi ya	A wild sea—
Sado ni yokotau	stretching to Sado Isle
Amanogawa	the River of Heaven[1]

Today, exhausted from crossing the most dangerous places in the north country—places with names like Children Forget Parents, Parents Forget Children, Dogs Turn Back, Horses Sent Back—I drew up my pillow and lay down to sleep, only to hear in the adjoining room the voices of two young women. An elderly man joined in the conversation, and I gathered that they were women of pleasure from a place called Niigata in Echigo Province. They were on a pilgrimage to Ise Shrine, and the man was seeing them off as far as the barrier here at Ichiburi. They seemed to be writing letters and giving him other trivial messages to take back to Niigata tomorrow. Like "the daughters of the fishermen, passing their lives on the shore where the white waves roll in,"[2] they had fallen low in this world, exchanging vows with every passerby. What terrible lives they must have had in their previous existence for this to occur. I fell asleep as I listened to them talk. The next morning, they came up to us as we departed. "The difficulties of road, not knowing our destination, the uncertainty and sorrow—it makes us want to follow your tracks. We'll be inconspicuous. Please bless us with your robes of compassion, link us to the Buddha," they said tearfully.

"We sympathize with you, but we have many stops on the way. Just follow the others. The gods will make sure that no harm occurs to you." Shaking them off with these remarks, we left, but the pathos of their situation lingered with us.

hitotsu ya ni	Under the same roof
yūjo mo netari	women of pleasure also sleep—
hagi to tsuki	bush clover and moon[3]

I dictated this to Sora, who wrote it down.

8. Bashō here describes Kisagata after the rains, closing out a series of contrasts: between lightness and darkness, laughter and resentment, the dark brooding atmosphere of Kisagata during the rains and the cool, light atmosphere that follows.

9. The seventh night of the Seventh Month was when the legendary constellations, the Herd Boy and Weaver Girl, two separated lovers, cross over the Milky Way for their annual meeting. Even the night before is unusual.

1. Sado, an island across the water from Izumozaki (Izumo Point), was known for its long history of political exiles. Here the island, standing under the vast River of Heaven or Milky Way, comes to embody the feeling of loneliness, both of the exiles and of the traveler himself.

2. From the anonymous *Shinkokinshū* poem "Since I am the daughter of a fisherman, passing my life on the shore where the white waves roll in, I have no home."

3. The haiku suggests Bashō's surprise that two very different parties—the young prostitutes and the male priest-travelers—have something in common, implicitly the uncertainty of life and of travel. The bush clover (*hagi*), the object of love in classical poetry, suggests the prostitutes, while the moon, associated with enlightenment and clarity, may imply Bashō and his priest friend.

We visited Tada Shrine where Sanemori's helmet and a piece of his brocade robe were stored. They say that long ago when Sanemori belonged to the Genji clan, Lord Yoshitomo offered him the helmet. Indeed, it was not the armor of a common soldier. A chrysanthemum and vine carved design inlaid with gold extended from the visor to the ear flaps, and a two-horn frontpiece was attached to the dragon head. After Sanemori died in battle, Kiso Yoshinaka attached a prayer sheet to the helmet and offered it to the shrine. Higuchi Jirō had acted as Kiso's messenger. It was as if the past were appearing before my very eyes.

muzan ya na	"How pitiful!"
kabuto no shita no	beneath the warrior helmet
kirigirisu	cries of a cricket[4]

The sixteenth. The skies had cleared, and we decided to gather little red shells at Iro-no-hama, Color Beach, seven leagues across the water. A man named Ten'ya made elaborate preparations—lunch boxes, wine flasks, and the like—and ordered a number of servants to go with us on the boat. Enjoying a tailwind, we arrived quickly. The beach was dotted with a few fisherman's huts and a dilapidated Lotus Flower temple. We drank tea, warmed up saké, and were overwhelmed by the loneliness of the evening.

sabishisa ya	Loneliness—
Suma ni kachitaru	an autumn beach judged
hama no aki	superior to Suma's[5]

nami no ma ya	Between the waves—
kogai ni majiru	mixed with small shells
hagi no chiri	petals of bush clover

I had Tōsai write down the main events of that day and left it at the temple.

Rotsū came as far as the Tsuruga harbor to greet me, and together we went to Mino Province. With the aid of horses, we traveled to Ōgaki. Sora joined us from Ise. Etsujin galloped in on horseback, and we gathered at the house of Jokō. Zensen-shi, Keiko, Keiko's sons, and other intimate acquaintances visited day and night. For them, it was like meeting someone who had returned from the dead. They were both overjoyed and sympathetic. Although I had not yet recovered from the weariness of the journey, we set off again on the sixth of the Ninth Month. Thinking to pay our respects to the great shrine at Ise, we boarded a boat.

hamaguri no	Autumn going—
futami ni wakare	parting for Futami
yuku aki zo	a clam pried from its shell[6]

4. In *The Tales of Heike*, Saitō Sanemori, not wanting other soldiers to realize his advanced age, dyed his white hair black and fought valiantly before being slain by the retainers of Kiso Yoshinaka (1154–1184). According to legend, Yoshinaka, who had been saved by Sanemori as a child, wept at seeing the washed head of the slain warrior and subsequently made an offering of the helmet and brocade to Tada Shrine. The cricket, a seasonal word for autumn, was associated in classical poetry with pathos and the loneliness that comes from inevitable decline.

5. Suma was closely associated with the poetry of Ariwara no Yukihira (d. 893), who was exiled to Suma, and the hero of *The Tale of Genji*, who was also exiled there, and so it was considered to be the embodiment of loneliness in the classical tradition.

6. Bashō's closing haiku turns on a series of puns: *wakaru* means both "to depart for" and "to tear from," and *futami* refers to a noted place on the coast of Ise Province (the traveler's next destination and a place known for clams) as well as the shell (*futa*) and body (*mi*) of the clam (*hamaguri*). The phrase "autumn going" (*yuku aki*) directly echoes the phrase "spring going" (*yuku haru*) in the poem at the beginning of the narrative.

Voltaire's life and writings embody the philosophy of the Enlightenment—yet his contemporaries in the Age of Reason forced him into a life of exile. Like his fellow *philosophes* Diderot and Rousseau, François-Marie Arouet was born into a middle-class family. Finding an entrée into aristocratic Parisian society—where wit sparkled, ideas were circulated, and connections were made—was therefore a challenge. The Arouets were engaged in farming and trade, but François's father had become a lawyer and minor government official in Paris, and his son was meant to follow in his footsteps. He received a Jesuit education—the best to be had—but soon thereafter abandoned the study of law, pursuing literary satire as a better way to get the attention of Parisian high society. When he was only twenty-two he began unleashing his satirical wit in anti-aristocratic verses and was exiled from Paris on suspicion of having written a satire against Philippe d'Orléans, Regent of France since the death the previous year of Louis XIV. The next year he did it again, and on this second offense the regent, ready to display some wit of his own, wagered that he could show the unruly author something he had never seen before. When young Arouet asked, "What is that?" he received the reply, "The inside of the Bastille." He spent nearly a year studying the interior of this famous dungeon for political prisoners. He was allowed to bring his books with him, however, to dine frequently with the prison governor, and to write his tragedy *Oedipe* there.

Upon his release in 1718, exiled again to the suburbs outside Paris, Arouet adopted the pen name Voltaire, staged the play he had written in prison, and upon its brilliant success received a gold medal and an annuity from the very Regent who had imprisoned him. In 1723 he cemented his literary reputation with the publication of a poem received as both a masterpiece and the first French national epic, *La Henriade,* a work on the theme of religious tolerance centered around Henri IV, the great Protestant king of the previous century. The same year Voltaire almost died of smallpox, a disease that ravaged Europe and the Americas; he claimed to have saved himself by drinking two hundred pints of lemonade. Over the next several years he added wealth to his new fame and social status by shrewd investments in the period's colonial exploitations. Yet in 1726, just at the moment when his speculations in the stock of the Compagnie des Indes were making him a rich man, Voltaire was forced to renew his acquaintance with the inside of the Bastille. The Chevalier de Rohan, insulted by Voltaire in return for having cast aspersions on the celebrated author's humble origins, retorted by ordering his footmen to beat up the young upstart as he watched from his carriage, and then had him thrown once more into prison. This time Voltaire was released only on condition of exile, not just from Paris but from France.

Far from teaching him to keep to his proper station, his time in prison made Voltaire realize that he would forever remain an outsider to French society, grounded as it was in inherited privilege and unquestioned authority. Having begun as something of a social climber, he became a leader in the great Enlightenment battle against *préjugé,* or "prejudice," in the original sense of that word: literally pre-judgment, the blind acceptance of received ideas without having subjected them to the judgment of reason. Like many other thinkers of the period, Voltaire devoted his career to the critique of traditional, received authority, whether intellectual, religious, or political, which culminated in the American and French revolutions toward the end of the century. He adopted the motto *Ecrasez l'infame!* (Crush infamy!) by which he meant the infamous injustices perpetrated in the name of organized religion—whether Roman Catholicism or Calvinist Protestantism—and of absolute power.

Voltaire spent his exile in London, where he found himself welcomed at all levels of society. The English had beheaded their king nearly a century earlier, and although the monarchy had been restored it clung to legitimacy through anxious attempts to square its authority with the principles of individual freedom from tyranny. By the eighteenth century England had an international reputation for religious and political liberty, and especially for freedom of speech. By contrast with France and many other European countries, this reputation was deserved. Voltaire saw literary men like Joseph Addison entrusted with political responsibilities, and Sir Isaac Newton honored for his scientific achievements in Westminster Abbey. He met John Locke, his predecessor among the foremost philosophers of political liberty and human reason, as well as Pope and Swift, who preceded him as the most important satirists of the age. King George I, who had given Voltaire a gold medal and a watch on the success of *Oedipe,* also welcomed him to England.

Allowed to return to France after several years, Voltaire published his *Letters Concerning the English Nation* begun in exile. This book appeared first in England (1733) and the following year in a French version. This time his French publisher was thrown into the Bastille, the books condemned by the Parliament of Paris and burnt. Voltaire himself retreated to the château of the philosopher Madame du Châtelet at Cirey in Champagne, where he spent much of his time over the next fifteen years living in a ménage à trois with her and her husband. In the 1740s he gained the protection of the king's mistress, Madame de Pompadour, and was again received at court—even appointed Historiographer to the King (1745) and elected to the Académie Française (1746), as he had been to the Royal Society in London in 1743. Shortly after Madame du Châtelet's death in childbirth, Voltaire left France again in 1750 to accept an invitation to the court of Prussia's King Frederick the Great. Within a few years he had angered this king too, fleeing Prussia in 1753, but detained for a time in Germany by Frederick's soldiers on his way back to France. After his experiences at royal courts Voltaire bought two houses near the republic of Geneva during the later 1750s, Les Délices (1755) and later Ferney, just over the Swiss border in France (1759). There he held court himself, continuing to disseminate his revolutionary ideas. It was the custom for young men of the upper crust to crown their educations with the Grand Tour of Europe, and many visited Voltaire at Ferney to learn the new ideas of the Enlightenment firsthand from one of its most famous exponents.

Voltaire returned to Paris one last time in 1778 for the production of his final tragedy, *Irène*. He arrived to find himself celebrated by the entire capital; saw the opening of his play, met Benjamin Franklin, and addressed the Académie Française. All this overwhelmed the aged exile, who died shortly thereafter. Back at Ferney he had already made plans for his tomb to be placed half in and half out of the chapel he had built there and engraved with the dedication, "Deo erexit Voltaire" ("Voltaire erected [it] to God")—"a fine word between two great names," as he quipped. He was never to rest there, however, as neither transportation nor embalming were quite what they are now. The Archbishop of Paris refused him Christian burial, as it had been refused to Molière; Voltaire's body was disguised and smuggled under cover of darkness to be buried at an abbey outside the city limits. The itinerary of Voltaire's corpse reflects that of his life: at first seemingly exiled forever, in the end he was brought back to Paris in triumph—where his remains are still enshrined in the Pantheon, a neoclassical secular temple dedicated on its frieze AUX GRANDS HOMMES. Voltaire's status as the original "Great Man" is literally written in stone.

CANDIDE, OR OPTIMISM: TRANSLATED FROM THE GERMAN OF DR. RALPH TOGETHER WITH THE ADDENDA WHICH WERE FOUND IN THE DOCTOR'S POCKET WHEN HE DIED AT MINDEN IN THE YEAR OF GRACE 1759 This is the full title readers found when they opened the first edition of *Candide* in 1759. Even though he at first denied authorship of the work, no one who read it had much trouble guessing that it was written by Voltaire, who was already well known for using pseudonyms. This was a strategy to protect himself while publishing his merciless satires exposing established religious and secular power structures—and even the thought of some of his fellow Enlightenment philosophers—as irrational and absurd. Like his other works, *Candide* champions the cause of reason and freedom against superstition, intolerance, and privilege. When he published *Candide* at the age of sixty-five, Voltaire was perhaps the most famous living author in Europe. He had already distinguished himself in all the most respected literary genres—tragedy, history, and epic—and was renowned also for his satires and philosophical works. In an encyclopedic age he had written a dictionary and contributed to Diderot's *Encyclopédie*. He had even previously invented the philosophical tale with *Zadig* (1748) and *Micromégas* (1750), perfecting this new genre in *Candide*. It was an immediate bestseller, reprinted about forty times during its first year and soon translated into several European languages.

The eighteenth century was fond of tales of simpleton protagonists whose misadventures expose the folly and vice of all they encounter and the absurdities of the philosophical systems they take to heart. Such, for example, are Sarah Fielding's *The Adventures of David Simple* and Henry Mackenzie's *The Man of Feeling*. The type goes back much further, however, the most famous example being Cervantes's *Don Quixote* (1605); even earlier, several of the tales in Boccaccio's *Decameron* relate the adventures of fools in order to poke fun at the corrupt clergy who take advantage of them. Voltaire also mocks the church, but like other eighteenth-century writers, he used the device of the foolish protagonist to expose the dangers of contemporary philosophical systems. *Candide* attacks the widespread idealist system of philosophical optimism, which could be seen as justifying human suffering as a necessary part of a cosmic order beyond human ken, implicitly condoning a passive resistance to the effort required to prevent or alleviate suffering.

The age was also fond of romance, a genre of prose fiction going back to late antiquity, featuring amazing adventures, disguises, enslavements, escapes, and world-wanderings, and often winding up with miraculous reunions under the most unlikely circumstances. Probability is not necessary in a world ordered by Providence. In *Candide* Voltaire exposes the irrationality of this form of narrative, which was beginning to be challenged by the novel, an emerging form of fiction governed by standards of verisimilitude, or plausibility. By putting his tale in romance form, however, he is also taking advantage of its lingering popularity.

The parody of romance in *Candide* also helps Voltaire make a point shared by Cervantes and by the authors of many novels in their attack on romance: an emphasis on firsthand experience, rather than idealism, reading or instruction, as the ultimate means to truth. Romance was the product of an aesthetic that held that art should represent the world as it should be, rather than as it is. Everything Candide's teacher Dr. Pangloss tells him about the "best of all possible worlds" is belied by Candide's own experiences of the world he actually inhabits. This stress on individual experience and judgment as the only true path to knowledge characterizes the Enlightenment's more general challenge to received wisdom and authority, as well as its reliance on the senses, rather than the soul, as the way to truth: a vast shift that gave us, among other things, the scientific method. It also gave us one of the Western world's most enduringly delightful and instructive fictions.

PRONUNCIATIONS:

Abare: ah-BAHRH
François-Marie Arouet: frahnh-SWAH mah-REE ah-roo-AY
Cacambo: kah-KAHM-*boh*
Candide: cahn-DEED
Madame du Châtelet: mah-DAHM deu SHAH-te-LAY
Cunégonde: keu-nay-GOND
Giroflée: zhee-roh-FLAY
Issachar: ee-sah-KAHR
Pangloss: PAN-gloss
Paquette: pah-KET
Pococurante: poh-koh-keu-RAHN-tay
Thunder-ten-tronckh: TUHN-dayr-ten-TROHNK

Candide, or Optimism[1]

Translated from the German of Dr. Ralph Together with the addenda which were found in the Doctor's pocket when he died at Minden in the year of grace 1759

Chapter 1

HOW CANDIDE WAS BROUGHT UP IN A BEAUTIFUL CASTLE, AND HOW
HE WAS KICKED OUT OF THE SAME

Once upon a time in Westphalia,[2] in the castle of Baron Thunder-ten-tronckh, there lived a young boy whom nature had endowed with the gentlest of dispositions. His soul was written upon his countenance. He was quite sound in his judgement, and he had the most straightforward of minds. It is for this reason, I believe, that he was called Candide. The older servants of the household suspected that he was the son of the Baron's sister by a kind and upright gentleman of the neighbourhood, a man whom this lady had consistently refused to marry because he had only ever been able to establish seventy-one heraldic quarterings,[3] the rest of his family tree having been destroyed by the ravages of time.

The Baron was one of the most powerful noblemen in Westphalia, for his castle had a door and windows. His great hall was even adorned with a tapestry. All the dogs in his farmyards would combine, when the need arose, to make up a pack of hounds: his grooms were his whippers-in, and the local vicar his great almoner.[4] They all called him "Your Lordship," and laughed at his jokes.

The Baroness, who weighed approximately 350 pounds, therefore enjoyed a large measure of public esteem; and she performed the honours of the house with a degree of dignified aplomb that rendered her all the more respectable. Her daughter Cunégonde,[5] being seventeen and of a high complexion, looked fresh, chubby, and toothsome. The Baron's son seemed in every way worthy of his father. Pangloss,[6] the

---

1. Translated by Roger Pearson.
2. Region of western Germany.
3. Each quartering or division of a coat of arms represented a separate line of noble ancestry.
4. Grooms care for horses, but here have to double as the beaters who scare small game animals and birds out of the underbrush during a hunt. A truly powerful nobleman would also maintain a separate servant to distribute his alms to the poor.
5. This name puns on the French and Latin words for female genitalia.
6. All tongues (Greek).

tutor, was the oracle of the household, and little Candide would listen to his lessons with all the good faith of his age and character.

Pangloss taught metaphysico-theologico-cosmo-codology. He could prove wonderfully that there is no effect without cause and that, in this best of all possible worlds, His Lordship the Baron's castle was the most beautiful of castles and Madam the best of all possible baronesses.

"It is demonstrably true," he would say, "that things cannot be other than as they are. For, everything having been made for a purpose, everything is necessarily for the best purpose. Observe how noses were made to bear spectacles, and so we have spectacles. Legs are evidently devised to be clad in breeches, and breeches we have. Stones were formed in such a way that they can be hewn and made into castles, and so His Lordship has a very beautiful castle. The greatest baron in the province must be the best lodged. And since pigs were made to be eaten, we eat pork all the year round. Consequently, those who have argued that all is well have been talking nonsense. They should have said that all is for the best."

Candide would listen attentively, and innocently he would believe: for he found Miss Cunégonde extremely beautiful, though he had never made bold to tell her so. His conclusion was that, next to the happiness of being born Baron Thunder-ten-tronckh, the second degree of happiness was being Miss Cunégonde, the third was seeing her every day, and the fourth was listening to Maître Pangloss, the greatest philosopher in the province and therefore in the whole world.

One day, as Cunégonde was taking a stroll near the castle in the little wood they referred to as their "parkland," she caught a glimpse through the bushes of Dr. Pangloss giving a lesson in applied physiology to her mother's maid, a very pretty and very receptive little brunette. As Miss Cunégonde had quite a gift for science, she noted in breathless silence the repeated experiments to which she was witness. She saw clearly the doctor's sufficient reason, the effects and the causes, and returned home all agitated, her thoughts provoked, and filled with desire to be a scientist, musing that she might well be able to be young Candide's sufficient reason, just as he could well be hers.

She met Candide on her return to the castle and blushed. Candide blushed too. She greeted him in a choked voice, and Candide spoke to her without knowing what he was saying. The next day after dinner, as they were leaving the table, Cunégonde and Candide found themselves behind a screen. Cunégonde dropped her handkerchief, Candide picked it up. Innocently she took his hand, innocently the young man kissed the young lady's hand, and with quite singular vivacity, sensibility, and grace. Their mouths met, their eyes shone, their knees trembled, their hands strayed. Baron Thunder-ten-tronckh passed by the screen and, seeing this cause and this effect, chased Candide out of the castle with a number of hefty kicks up the backside. Cunégonde fainted. As soon as she recovered her senses, the Baroness slapped her. And all was consternation in the most beautiful and most agreeable of all possible castles.

Chapter 2

What became of Candide among the Bulgars

Candide, thus expelled from paradise on earth, walked on for a long time, not knowing where he was going, weeping, raising his eyes to heaven, and turning them often in the direction of the most beautiful of castles, which contained the most beautiful of barons' daughters. He went to sleep in the middle of the fields, supperless, in a furrow. The snow fell in large flakes. Next day, soaked to the skin, Candide dragged himself as far as the neighbouring town, which was called Wald-berghoff-trarbk-dikdorff. He had no money, and he was dying of hunger and exhaustion. He stopped wistfully at the door of a small hostelry. Two men dressed in blue spotted him.

"Comrade," said one, "there's a fine figure of a young man, and he's the right height."

They went up to Candide and very civilly invited him to dine with them.

"Gentlemen," said Candide with charming modesty, "you do me great honour, but I have not the means to pay my corner."

"Oh, sir," replied one of the men in blue, "people of your looks and quality[7] never pay. Are you not five feet five inches tall?"

"Yes, gentlemen, that is my height," he said with a bow.

"Oh sir, come, do sit yourself down at the table. Not only will we pay for you, but we will not see a man such as yourself go short either. Man was made that he might help his fellow-man."

"You are right," said Candide. "That's what Mr. Pangloss always told me, and I can see that everything is for the best."

They pressed him to accept a few crowns. He took them and wanted to make out a receipt. It was not required. They all sat down at the table.

"Don't you love...?"

"Oh, yes," he replied. "I love Miss Cunégonde."

"No," said one of the gentlemen, "what we want to know is whether you love the King of the Bulgars[8] or not."

"Not in the least," he said, "for I have never met him."

"What! He is the most charming of kings and we must drink to his health."

"Oh, very willingly, gentlemen," and he drank.

"That will do nicely," he was told. "That makes you a supporter, a defender, a champion, nay a hero of the Bulgars. Your fortune is made and your glory assured."

His feet were promptly clapped in irons and he was taken off to the regiment. They made him do right turns, left turns, draw ramrods, replace ramrods, take aim, fire, quick march, and then they gave him thirty strokes of the birch. Next day he performed the drill a little less badly, and he received only twenty. The next day they gave him only ten, and his comrades thought him a prodigy.

Candide, totally bewildered, could not yet quite make out how he was a hero. One fine day in spring he took it into his head to go for a stroll, simply walking straight ahead, in the belief that it was the privilege of the human, as of the animal species to use its legs how it wanted. He had not gone two leagues when up came four other heroes, each six feet tall, who tied him up and carted him off to a dungeon. They asked him which, juridically speaking, he preferred: whether to run the gauntlet of the entire regiment thirty-six times, or to have twelve lead bullets shot through his brains at one go. It did no good his talking about the freedom of the individual and saying that, personally, he wished for neither: a choice had to be made. He resolved, by virtue of that gift of God called "freedom," to run the gauntlet thirty-six times. He managed two. The regiment numbered two thousand men. For him that meant four thousand birch strokes, which laid bare every muscle and sinew in his body from the nape of his neck right down to his butt. As they were preparing for his third run, Candide, quite done for, implored them to be so kind as to do him the favour of bashing his head in.

7. Social class.
8. An allusion to Frederick the Great, 1712–1786, King of Prussia.

This favour was granted. His eyes were bandaged, he was made to kneel. At that moment the King of the Bulgars passed by and inquired what crime the condemned man had committed. As this King was a great genius, he understood from everything that Candide told him that here was a young metaphysician much in ignorance of the ways of the world: and he pardoned him with a clemency that will be praised in every newspaper and in every century. A splendid surgeon cured Candide in three weeks with the emollients prescribed by Dioscorides.[9] He already had a little skin and could walk when the King of the Bulgars joined battle with the King of the Abars.[1]

Chapter 3

How Candide escaped from the Bulgars and what became of him

Never was there anything so fine, so dashing, so glittering, or so well-regulated as those two armies. The trumpets, the fifes, the oboes, the drums, and the cannon produced a harmony such as was never heard in hell. First the cannon felled about six thousand men on each side. Then the musketry removed from the best of all worlds nine or ten thousand ruffians who were polluting its surface. The bayonet, too, was the sufficient reason for the death of a few thousand. The sum total may well have come to about thirty thousand souls. Candide, who was trembling like a philosopher, hid himself as best he could during this heroic butchery.

At length, while the two Kings were having *Te Deums*[2] sung in their respective camps, he made up his mind to go and think about cause and effect elsewhere. He climbed over the heaps of dead and dying, and came first to a neighbouring village. It was in ashes. This was an Abar village which the Bulgars had burnt to the ground in accordance with international law. In one part, old men riddled with shot looked on as their wives lay dying, their throats slit, and clutching their children to blood-spattered breasts. In another, young girls lay disembowelled, having satisfied the natural urges of a hero or two, breathing their last; others, half burnt to death, cried out for someone to finish them off. Brains lay scattered on the ground beside severed arms and legs.

Candide fled as fast as he could to another village. It belonged to Bulgars, and Abar heroes had given it the same treatment. Candide, continually stepping over quivering limbs or through the midst of ruins, eventually left the battlefield behind, taking with him some few provisions in his bag and with Miss Cunégonde never far from his thoughts. His provisions had run out by the time he reached Holland but, having heard that the people there were all rich and all Christians, he had no doubt that he would be treated as well as he had been in the Baron's castle before he had been turned out on account of Miss Cunégonde's pretty eyes.

He begged alms of several solemn personages, who all replied that if he continued in this occupation, he would be locked up in a house of correction and taught how to earn a living.

He then spoke to a man who, all on his own, had just been addressing a large gathering for a whole hour on the subject of charity. This orator scowled at him and said:

"What are you doing here? Do you support the good cause?"

"There is no effect without a cause," replied Candide humbly. "Everything is connected in a chain of necessity, and has all been arranged for the best. It was necessary

9. Famous ancient Greek doctor.
1. Likely a reference to the Seven Years' War, with the "Bulgars" and the "Abars" representing the Prussians and the French.
2. Hymns of thanks to God.

that I should be separated from Miss Cunégonde and that I should run the gauntlet, and it is necessary that I should beg for my bread until such time as I can earn it. All this could not have been otherwise."

"My friend," said the orator, "do you believe that the Pope is the Antichrist?"

"I've never heard that before," replied Candide. "But whether he is or he isn't, I need bread."

"You don't deserve to eat it," said the other. "Be off with you, you rogue! Away with you, you miserable wretch! And don't you come near me ever again."

The orator's wife, having stuck her head out of the window and set eyes on a man who could doubt that the Pope was the Antichrist, poured a pot full of . . . over his head. Heavens! To what lengths the ladies do carry their religious zeal!

A man who had never been baptized, a worthy Anabaptist named Jacques,[3] saw the cruel and ignominious treatment being meted out in this way to one of his brothers, a living being with two feet, no feathers, and possessed of a soul.[4] He took him home with him, cleaned him up, gave him some bread and beer, presented him with two florins, and even wanted to train him for work in his factories, which produced that "Persian" material[5] that is made in Holland. Candide, almost prostrate before him, exclaimed:

"Maître Pangloss was quite right when he told me that everything in this world is for the best. For I am infinitely more touched by your extreme generosity than by the harshness of that gentleman with the black hat and his lady wife."

The next day, while out walking, he met a beggar all covered in sores. His eyes were glazed, the end of his nose was eaten away, his mouth was askew, his teeth black, and he spoke from the back of his throat. He was racked by a violent cough and spat out a tooth with every spasm.

Chapter 4

How Candide Chanced upon His Old Philosophy Tutor, Dr. Pangloss, and What Came of It

Candide, again more moved by compassion than by disgust, gave this appalling beggar the two florins which he had received from his worthy Anabaptist, Jacques. The phantom stared at him, wept, and fell upon his neck. Candide, startled, recoiled.

"Alas!" said the one unfortunate to the other, "do you no longer recognize your dear Pangloss?"

"What do I hear? You? My dear tutor?! You in this dreadful state?! But what misfortune has befallen you? Why are you no longer in the most beautiful of castles? What has become of Miss Cunégonde, that pearl of a daughter, that masterpiece of nature?"

"I'm famished," said Pangloss.

Whereupon Candide took him to the Anabaptist's stable, where he gave him a little bread to eat and, when Pangloss had recovered, said:

"Well? What about Cunégonde?"

"She is dead," replied the other.

Candide fainted on hearing this. His friend brought him round with some old vinegar that was lying about in the stable. Candide opened his eyes.

3. Anabaptists, known for their peacefulness and charitability, rejected infant baptism and were regarded by Catholics as heretics.
4. Jacques follows Aristotle's definition of common humanity.
5. Silk.

"Cunégonde is dead! Ah, best of all worlds, where are you now? But what did she die of? It wouldn't have been at seeing me kicked out of her father's beautiful castle, would it?"

"No," said Pangloss. "She was eviscerated by Bulgar soldiers after they'd raped her as many times as anyone can be. They smashed the Baron's head in as he tried to protect her, the Baroness was hacked to pieces, my poor pupil received precisely the same treatment as his sister, and as for the castle, not one stone remains standing on another. Not a single barn, or sheep, or duck, or tree is left. But we had our revenge, for the Abars did exactly the same to the neighbouring barony of a Bulgar lord."

At this account Candide fainted again. But having recovered his senses and said everything one should say in such circumstances, he enquired as to the cause and the effect and the sufficient reason which had reduced Pangloss to such a woeful state.

"Alas," said the other, "the answer is love: love, the solace and comfort of the human race, the preserver of the universe, the soul of all sentient beings, tender love."

"Alas," said Candide, "I too have known it, this love of yours, this sovereign ruler of the heart, this soul of our soul. All the good it ever did me was one kiss and a score of kicks up the backside. How can this fine cause have had such an abominable effect on you?"

Pangloss replied in these terms:

"O my dear Candide! You knew Paquette, that pretty lady's maid to our noble Baroness. In her arms I tasted the delights of paradise, and in turn they have led me to these torments of hell by which you see me now devoured. She had the disease,[6] and may have died of it by now. Paquette was made a present of it by a very knowledgeable Franciscan who had traced it back to its source. For he had got it from an old countess, who had contracted it from a captain in the cavalry, who owed it to a marchioness, who had it from a page, who had caught it from a Jesuit, who, during his novitiate, had inherited it in a direct line from one of Christopher Columbus's shipmates. For my part I shall give it to no one, because I'm dying."

"O Pangloss!" cried Candide. "What a strange genealogy! Was it not the devil who began it?"

"Not at all," replied the great man. "It was an indispensable part of the best of all worlds, a necessary ingredient. For if Columbus, on an island in the Americas, had not caught this disease which poisons the spring of procreation, which often even prevents procreation, and which is evidently the opposite of what nature intended, we would have neither chocolate nor cochineal.[7] Moreover one must remember that up till now this disease has been unique to the inhabitants of our continent, like controversy. The Turks, the Indians, the Persians, the Chinese, the Siamese, the Japanese, they have all yet to know it. But there is sufficient reason for them to know it in their turn a few centuries hence. In the mean time it is making spectacular progress among our population, and especially among those great armies of fine, upstanding, well-bred mercenaries who decide the destiny of nations. One can be sure that when thirty thousand soldiers are fighting against a similar number in pitched battle, there are about twenty thousand cases of the pox on either side."

---

6. Syphilis.

7. A scarlet dye, imported, like chocolate, from the Americas.

"Well, isn't that extraordinary," said Candide. "But you must go and get treated."

"And how am I supposed to do that?" said Pangloss. "I haven't a penny, my friend, and in the whole wide world you can't so much as be bled or have an enema without paying for it, or without someone else paying for you."

These last remarks decided Candide. He went and threw himself at the feet of his charitable Anabaptist, Jacques, and painted such a poignant picture of the state to which his friend was reduced that the good fellow did not hesitate to take Dr. Pangloss under his roof: and he had him cured at his own expense. In the process Pangloss lost but one eye and one ear. He could write well and had a perfect grasp of arithmetic. Jacques the Anabaptist made him his bookkeeper. Two months later, having to go to Lisbon on business, he took his two philosophers with him on the ship. Pangloss explained to him how things could not be better. Jacques was not of this opinion.

"Men must surely have corrupted nature a little," he would say, "for they were not born wolves, and yet wolves they have become. God gave them neither twenty-four pounders nor bayonets, and they have made bayonets and twenty-four pounders in order to destroy each other. I could also mention bankruptcies, and the courts who seize the assets of bankrupts and cheat their creditors of them."

"That was all indispensable," was the one-eyed doctor's reply. "Individual misfortunes contribute to the general good with the result that the more individual misfortunes there are, the more all is well."

While he was presenting his argument, the air grew thick, the winds blew from the four corners of the earth, and the ship was assailed by the most terrible storm, within sight of the port of Lisbon.

Chapter 5

Storm, shipwreck, earthquake, and what became of Dr. Pangloss, Candide, and Jacques the Anabaptist

Half the passengers on board, weakened and near dead from those unimaginable spasms that the rolling of a ship can induce in every nerve and humour of the body by tossing them in opposite directions, did not even have the strength to worry about the danger. The other half shrieked and prayed. The sails were rent, the masts were smashed, the ship broke up. Work as they might, no one could make himself understood, and there was no one in charge. The Anabaptist was helping out with the rigging down on the decks. Furious, a sailor came up, gave him a good clout, and laid him flat on the boards. But the force of the blow jerked him so violently that he himself fell head first overboard and ended up suspended in mid-air, hanging from a piece of broken mast. Kind Jacques ran to his rescue, helped him back on board, and in the process was precipitated into the sea in full view of the sailor—who left him to perish without so much as a backward glance. Along came Candide, saw his benefactor momentarily reappear on the surface and then sink without trace, and wanted to jump in after him. Pangloss the philosopher prevented him, arguing that Lisbon harbour had been created expressly so that the Anabaptist would be drowned in it. While he was proving this a priori,[8] the ship foundered and everyone perished, except for Pangloss, Candide, and the brute of a sailor who had drowned the virtuous Anabaptist.

---

8. By logic as opposed to experience.

The blackguard swam safely to the very shore where Pangloss and Candide were also carried on a plank.

When they had recovered a little, they proceeded on foot towards Lisbon. They had some money left and hoped with this to escape hunger, just as they had survived the storm.

Scarcely had they set foot in the city, still weeping over the death of their benefactor, than they felt the earth quake beneath their feet. In the port a boiling sea rose up and smashed the ships lying at anchor. Whirlwinds of flame and ash covered the streets and public squares: houses disintegrated, roofs were upended upon foundations, and foundations crumbled.

Thirty thousand inhabitants of both sexes and all ages were crushed beneath the ruins. The sailor said with a whistle and an oath:

"There'll be some rich pickings here."

"What can be the sufficient reason for this phenomenon?" wondered Pangloss.

"The end of the world is come!" Candide shouted.

The sailor forthwith dashed into the midst of the rubble, braving death in search of money; he duly found some, grabbed it, got drunk and, having slept it off, bought the favours of the first willing girl he met among the remains of the ruined houses, among the dying and the dead.

Pangloss, however, took him aside:

"My friend," he said, "this is not right. You are in breach of universal reason, and this is hardly the moment."

"Hell's teeth!" replied the other. "I'm a sailor and I come from Batavia. Four times I've trampled on the crucifix, on four separate voyages to Japan.[9] You've picked the wrong man, you and your universal reason!"

One or two fragments of stone had injured Candide. He was lying in the street covered in rubble. He kept calling out to Pangloss:

"Help! Get me some wine and oil. I'm dying."

"This earthquake is nothing new," replied Pangloss. "The city of Lima felt the same tremors in America last year. Same causes, same effects. There must be a vein of sulphur running underground from Lima to Lisbon."[1]

"Nothing is more probable," said Candide, "but for God's sake get me some oil and wine."

"What do you mean, probable?" the philosopher retorted. "I maintain that the thing is proven."

Candide lost consciousness, and Pangloss brought him some water from a nearby fountain.

The next day, having located some food by crawling about among the rubble, they recovered their strength a little. Then they worked like everyone else at giving assistance to the inhabitants who had survived. One group of citizens they had helped gave them as good a dinner as was possible in such a disaster. It is true that the meal was a sad one, and the company wept over their bread; but Pangloss consoled them by assuring them that things could not be otherwise:

"For all this is the best there is. If the volcanic activity is in Lisbon, it means it could not have been anywhere else. For it is impossible for things not to be where they are. For all is well."

9. In the 18th century Dutch traders could enter Japan only after renouncing Christianity in this way.
1. Lima was destroyed by an earthquake in 1746, and Lisbon suffered a catastrophic earthquake in 1755.

A little man in black, an agent of the Inquisition,[2] was sitting next to him. He intervened politely and said:

"Apparently sir does not believe in original sin. For if everything is as well as can be, there has been neither Fall nor punishment."

"I most humbly beg Your Excellency's pardon," replied Pangloss even more politely, "but the Fall of man and the curse entered necessarily into the scheme of the best of all possible worlds."

"So sir does not believe in freedom?" said the agent.

"Your Excellency will forgive me," said Pangloss. "Freedom can exist alongside absolute necessity, for it was necessary for us to be free. For ultimately, the will once determined..."

Pangloss was in the middle of his sentence when the agent nodded to his henchman, who was pouring him some port, or rather Oporto, wine.

Chapter 6

HOW THEY HAD A SPLENDID *AUTO-DA-FÉ*[3] TO PREVENT EARTHQUAKES, AND HOW CANDIDE WAS FLOGGED

After the earthquake which had destroyed three quarters of Lisbon, the wise men of the country had not been able to come up with any more effective means of preventing total ruin than to give the people a splendid *auto-da-fé*. It was decided by the University of Coimbra that the spectacle of a few people being ceremonially burnt over a low flame is the infallible secret of preventing earthquakes.

Consequently they had arrested a man from Biscay who had been found guilty of marrying his fellow godparent, and two Portuguese who had removed the bacon when eating a chicken.[4] After dinner men came and tied up Dr. Pangloss and his disciple Candide, one for what he had said, and the other for having listened with an air of approval. Both were led away to separate apartments, which were extremely cool and where the sun was never troublesome. A week later they were both dressed in a *san-benito*,[5] and paper mitres were placed upon their heads. Candide's mitre and *san-benito* were painted with flames that were upside down and with devils which had neither claws nor tails, but Pangloss's devils had claws and tails, and his flames were the right way up. So dressed, they walked in procession and listened to a very moving sermon, followed by a beautiful recital of plainchant. Candide was flogged in time to the singing; the man from Biscay and the two men who had not wanted to eat bacon were burned; and Pangloss was hanged, despite the fact that this was not the custom. The very same day the earth quaked once more: the din was fearful.

Terrified, confounded, thoroughly distraught, all bleeding and trembling, Candide reflected to himself:

"If this is the best of all possible worlds, then what must the others be like? I wouldn't mind if I'd only been flogged. That happened with the Bulgars. But, o my dear Pangloss! You, the greatest of philosophers! Did I have to see you hanged without my knowing why?! O my dear Anabaptist! You, the best of men! Did you have to

2. The tribunal that violently persecuted persons accused of religious heresy.

3. "Act of faith," the public judgment (and often burning) of an accused authorized by the Inquisition.

4. Implying that they were Jewish; chickens were frequently covered with bacon strips to keep the meat moist while roasting.

5. A shirt worn by condemned heretics, usually with painted flames to indicate whether the heretic had confessed (upside down) or remained unrepentant (upright).

drown in the port?! O Miss Cunégonde! You pearl among daughters! Did you have to get your stomach slit open?!"

He was just leaving the scene afterwards, scarcely able to stand up, and having been preached at, flogged, absolved, and blessed, when an old woman came up to him and said:

"Take courage, my son, follow me."

Chapter 7

HOW AN OLD WOMAN TOOK CARE OF CANDIDE, AND HOW HE WAS REUNITED WITH THE ONE HE LOVED

Candide did not take courage, but he did follow the old woman into a hovel. She gave him a pot of ointment to rub on himself, set things out for him to eat and drink, and indicated a small, moderately clean bed, beside which lay a full set of clothes.

"Eat, drink, and sleep," she said, "and may Our Lady of Atocha, His Eminence Saint Anthony of Padua, and His Eminence Saint James of Compostella[6] watch over you. I'll be back tomorrow."

Candide, still astonished at all he had seen and suffered, and even more astonished at the charity of the old woman, wanted to kiss her hand.

"It's not my hand you should be kissing. I'll be back tomorrow. Rub yourself with ointment, eat, and sleep."

Candide, despite so many misfortunes, ate and slept. The next day the old woman brought him breakfast, inspected his back, and rubbed a different ointment on it herself. Then she brought him dinner, and in the evening she returned with supper. The day after that she went through the same ritual again.

"Who are you?" Candide kept asking her. "What has made you so kind? How can I repay you?"

The good woman did not answer. She returned that evening bringing nothing for supper.

"Come with me," she said, "and not a word."

She took him by the arm and walked with him for about a quarter of a mile into the country. They arrived at a house standing on its own, surrounded by gardens and waterways. The old woman knocked at a little door. Someone opened it. She led Candide up a secret staircase into a small gilded room, left him sitting on a brocaded couch, shut the door after her, and departed. Candide thought he was dreaming; his whole life seemed to him like a bad dream, and the present moment a sweet one.

The old woman soon reappeared. She was supporting with some difficulty the trembling figure of a majestic-looking woman, all sparkling with jewels and hidden by a veil.

"Remove this veil," the old woman told Candide.

The young man drew near. With a timid hand he lifted the veil. What a moment! What a surprise! He thought he was looking at Miss Cunégonde. He was indeed looking at her, for it was she. His strength failed him, words failed him, and he fell at her feet. Cunégonde fell on the couch. The old woman showered them with various waters. They came to their senses. They spoke to each other. At first it was all half-finished

6. Patron saints of Portugal and Spain.

sentences, and questions and answers getting crossed, and sighs, and tears, and exclamations. The old woman suggested they make less noise and left them to it.

"What! It is you!" said Candide. "You're alive! To think that I should find you in Portugal! So you weren't raped? So you didn't have your stomach slit open as Pangloss the philosopher assured me you did?"

"I certainly was, and did," said the fair Cunégonde. "But those two particular misfortunes are not always fatal."

"But were your father and mother killed?"

"That is only too true," said Cunégonde tearfully.

"And your brother?"

"My brother was killed, too."

"And why are you in Portugal? And how did you know that I was here? And how on earth did you arrange to have me brought to this house?"

"I will tell you all these things," the young lady replied. "But first you must tell me all that has happened to you since that innocent kiss you gave me and those kicks you got."

With deep respect Candide obeyed her, and although he was at a loss for words, and his voice was weak and quavering, and his spine still hurt a little, he gave her the most artless account of all that had happened to him since the moment of their separation. Cunégonde raised her eyes to heaven, and she shed tears at the deaths of the good Anabaptist and Pangloss; after which she spoke in these terms to Candide, who missed not a word and devoured her with his eyes.

Chapter 8

CUNÉGONDE'S STORY

"I was in bed fast asleep when it pleased heaven to send the Bulgars into our beautiful castle of Thunder-ten-tronckh. They slit the throats of my father and brother, and hacked my mother to pieces. A great big Bulgar, six feet tall, seeing that I had passed out at the sight of all this, began to rape me. That brought me round. I came to, screamed, struggled, bit him, scratched him. I wanted to tear that big Bulgar's eyes out, little realizing that what was taking place in my father's castle was standard practice. The brute knifed me in the left side, and I still have the scar."

"Dear, oh dear! I hope I may see it," said the guileless Candide.

"You shall," said Cunégonde, "but let me continue."

"Go on," said Candide.

She took up the thread of her story thus:

"A Bulgar captain came into the room and saw me all covered in blood. The soldier didn't take any notice. The captain became angry at this lack of respect being shown him by the brute and killed him where he lay on top of me. Then he had me bandaged up and took me to his quarters as a prisoner of war. I used to wash what few shirts he had, and I cooked for him. He found me very pretty, I must admit, and I won't deny he was a good-looking man himself, with skin that was white and soft. Apart from that, not much brain, not much of a thinker. You could tell he hadn't been educated by Dr. Pangloss. Three months later, having lost all his money and grown tired of me, he sold me to a Jew called Don Issacar, who was a dealer in Holland and Portugal, and who was passionately fond of women. This Jew became much attached to my person, but he was unable to get the better of it. I resisted his advances more successfully than I had the Bulgar soldier's. A woman of honour may be raped once, but her virtue is all the stronger for it. In an attempt to win me over, the Jew brought me here to this country house. I had previously thought that there was nothing in the world as beautiful as the castle of Thunder-ten-tronckh. I have been disabused.

"The Grand Inquisitor noticed me one day during Mass. He kept eyeing me, and then sent word that he had to speak to me on a confidential matter. I was taken to his palace. I told him who I was. He pointed out how far beneath my station it was to belong to an Israelite. It was suggested on his behalf to Don Issacar that he should cede me to His Eminence. Don Issacar, who is the Court's banker and a man of some influence, would have none of it. The Inquisitor threatened him with an *auto-da-fé*. In the end, under intimidation, my Jew agreed to a deal whereby the house and I would belong to both of them jointly. The Jew would have Mondays, Wednesdays, and the sabbath, and the Inquisitor would have the other days of the week. This convention has been operating for six months now. It has not been without its quarrels, for it has often been a moot point which sabbath the period from Saturday night to Sunday morning belongs to, the Old Testament one or the New. For my own part I have resisted both men up till now, and I'm sure that's why they still love me.

"Anyway, in order to ward off the scourge of the earthquakes and to intimidate Don Issacar, it pleased my lord and master the Inquisitor to celebrate an *auto-da-fé*. He did me the honour of inviting me. I had a very good seat, and the ladies were served refreshments between the Mass and the execution. I was horrified, it must be said, to see those two Jews being burnt, as well as that nice man from Biscay who had married his fellow godparent. But how surprised, how shocked, how upset I was to see someone that looked like Pangloss in a *san-benito* and wearing a mitre! I rubbed my eyes, stared, saw him hanged, and fainted. I had hardly come to when I saw you standing there stark naked. That was my moment of greatest horror and consternation, the moment of greatest pain and despair. I can tell you truthfully, your skin is even fairer and more perfectly pink than my Bulgar captain's. The sight of it lent added force to all the feelings which were surging through me and devouring me. I screamed, I wanted to shout out: 'Stop, you animals!,' but nothing came out, and anyway my screaming and shouting would have done no good. 'How is it,' I said to myself, when you had been well and truly flogged, 'that nice Candide and wise Pangloss come to be in Lisbon, and that one of them gets a hundred lashes, and the other is hanged by order of His Eminence the Inquisitor, who in turn is in love with me? So Pangloss deceived me cruelly when he told me that all was well with the world.'

"Distressed, agitated, beside myself with anger one minute and ready to faint clean away the next, all I could think about was the massacre of my father and mother and brother, the insolence of my ugly Bulgar soldier, and the knife wound he gave me, my bondage, my menial work as a cook, my Bulgar captain, my ugly Don Issacar, my abominable Inquisitor, the hanging of Dr. Pangloss, that great *Miserere* they sang in plainchant while you were being flogged, and above all that kiss I gave you behind a screen the day I last saw you. I praised God for bringing you back to me after so many trials and tribulations. I instructed my old servant to tend to you and to bring you here as soon as she could. She has carried out my commission most capably. I have had the indescribable pleasure of seeing you again, of hearing you and speaking to you. You must have a terrible hunger, and I have a large appetite. Let's begin with supper."

With which they both sat down to eat. After supper they resumed their positions on the aforementioned beautiful couch. There they were when Señor Don Issacar, one of the masters of the house, arrived. It was the sabbath. He had come to enjoy his rights and press his suit.

Chapter 9

What became of Cunégonde, Candide, the Grand Inquisitor, and a Jew

This Issacar was the most irascible Hebrew in the tribe of Israel since the time of the Captivity in Babylon.[7]

"What!" he said, "you whore of Galilee! So Mr. Inquisitor isn't enough for you then? I've got to share you with this infidel too?"

With these words he drew a long dagger which he always carried with him and, not thinking his adversary would be armed, attacked Candide. But the old woman had given our good Westphalian a fine sword with his suit of clothes. Gentle though his disposition was, he drew his sword, and that was it: one Israelite stone dead on the floor at the feet of the fair Cunégonde.

"Holy Virgin!" cried she. "What is to become of us? A man killed in my house! If the police come, we're lost!"

"If Pangloss had not been hanged," said Candide, "he would have given us some good advice in this predicament, for he was a great philosopher. Since he's not here, let's ask the old woman."

She was a most prudent sort, and was just beginning to give her opinion when another little door opened. It was one hour after midnight: Sunday was beginning. This day belonged to His Eminence the Inquisitor. In he came to find Candide, who had been flogged, now standing sword in hand, with a corpse stretched out on the ground, Cunégonde in a fluster, and the old woman giving advice.

Here is what went through Candide's mind at that moment, and how he reasoned:

"If this holy man calls for help, he will certainly have me burned. He may well do the same to Cunégonde. He has already had me mercilessly whipped. He is my rival. I've already started killing. There's nothing else for it."

This reasoning was clear and quick, and without giving the Inquisitor the time to recover from his surprise, he ran him through and hurled him down beside the Jew.

"Well, here's a fine mess," said Cunégonde. "There's no going back now. That's us excommunicated. Our last hour has come. How is it that someone as soft-hearted as you can have ended up killing a Jew and a prelate in a matter of minutes?"

"My dear girl," replied Candide, "when a man's in love, jealous, and flogged by the Inquisition, there's no knowing what he may do."

The old woman then broke in and said:

"There are three Andalusian horses in the stable, as well as saddles and bridles. Let brave Candide get them ready. Madam has moidores[8] and diamonds. Let us mount quickly—though my seat is but one buttock—and ride to Cadiz.[9] The weather is of the best, and it is always a great pleasure to travel in the cool of the night."

At once Candide saddled up the three horses. Cunégonde, the old woman, and he covered thirty miles without stopping. While they were making their escape, the Holy Hermandad[1] reached the house. They buried His Eminence in a beautiful church, and threw Issacar on to the rubbish-heap.

Candide, Cunégonde, and the old woman had by this time reached the small town of Avacena, in the middle of the Sierra Morena mountains, where they had the following conversation in an inn.

7. The period of Hebrew captivity in the 6th century B.C.E.
8. Portuguese coins.
9. Coastal town in southwestern Spain.
1. The "Holy Brotherhood," agents of the Inquisition.

Chapter 10

In what distress Candide, Cunégonde, and the old woman arrived in Cadiz, and of their embarkation

"But who can possibly have stolen my pistoles[2] and diamonds?" sobbed Cunégonde. "What will we live on? How shall we manage? Where will I find the Inquisitors and the Jews to replace them?"

"Alas!" said the old woman, "I have a strong suspicion it was that Franciscan monk who spent yesterday night in the same inn as us in Badajoz. God preserve me from jumping to conclusions, but he did come into our room twice and he did leave long before us."

"Oh dear!" said Candide. "Good Pangloss often used to argue that the fruits of the earth are common to all and that everyone has an equal right to them. According to his principles, that Franciscan ought to have left us enough money behind to finish our journey. Have you really not got anything left, my fair Cunégonde?"

"Not a maravedi,"[3] said she.

"What shall we do?" said Candide.

"Let's sell one of our horses," said the old woman. "I can ride behind Miss Cunégonde, even though I have only one buttock to sit on, and we'll make it to Cadiz."

There was a Benedictine prior staying in the same hostelry. He bought the horse cheaply. Candide, Cunégonde, and the old woman passed through Lucena, Chillas, and Lebrija, and came at last to Cadiz. There a fleet was being fitted out and troops were being mustered to go and knock some sense into the Jesuit reverend fathers in Paraguay, who were accused of having incited one of their local native hordes to revolt against the Kings of Spain and Portugal near the town of San Sacramento.[4] Candide, having served with the Bulgars, performed the Bulgar drill for the general of this little army with so much grace, speed, skill, agility, and panache that he was given command of a company of foot soldiers. So there he was a captain. He boarded ship with Miss Cunégonde, the old woman, two valets, and the two Andalusian horses which had belonged to the Grand Inquisitor of Portugal.

During the crossing they discussed poor Pangloss's philosophy a great deal.

"We're going to another world," Candide would say. "I expect it must be there that all is well. For you have to admit, one could grumble rather at what goes on in our one, both physically and morally."

"I love you with all my heart," Cunégonde would say, "but my soul is still in something of a state, what with all I've seen and been through."

"All will be well," was Candide's reply. "Already the sea in this new world is better than those we have in Europe. It's calmer, and the winds are more constant. It is assuredly the new world which is the best of all possible worlds."

"God willing!" said Cunégonde. "But I have been so horribly unfortunate in my own that my heart is almost closed to hope."

"*You're* complaining!" said the old woman. "Alas! You haven't had the misfortunes I have."

---

2. Spanish gold coins.

3. Spanish copper coin.

4. Jesuit missionaries who controlled Paraguay resisted Spain's attempt to transfer this territory to Portugal. Spain sent troops from Cadiz to crush the rebellion; Voltaire invested in this expedition as part owner of one of the ships.

Cunégonde almost burst out laughing and found it extremely droll of this little old woman to claim to be more unfortunate than she.

"I'm afraid, my good woman," she said to her, "that unless you have been raped by two Bulgars, stabbed twice in the stomach, had two of your castles demolished, seen two mothers' and two fathers' throats slit before your very eyes, and watched two of your lovers being flogged at an *auto-da-fé,* then I don't see you bettering me. Added to which, I was born a Baroness with seventy-two heraldic quarterings and yet I have been a cook."

"My young lady," replied the old woman, "you do not know who I am by birth, and if I were to show you my bottom, you would not speak as you do, and you would reserve judgement."

This declaration aroused the deepest curiosity in the minds of Cunégonde and Candide. The old woman had this to say to them.

Chapter 11

THE OLD WOMAN'S STORY

"My eyes haven't always been bloodshot and red-rimmed, my nose hasn't always come down to my chin, and I haven't always been a servant. I am the daughter of Pope Urban X[5] and the Princess of Palestrina. Until the age of fourteen I was brought up in a palace, next to which not one of your German barons' castles would even have done as a stable. And any single one of my dresses was worth more than all the treasures of Westphalia put together. As I grew older, so I grew in beauty, grace, and fine accomplishments. I took pleasure in life; I commanded respect; I had prospects. I was already able to inspire love, and my breasts were forming. And what breasts they were! White and firm, just like those of the Medici Venus.[6] And what eyes! What eyelids! What black eyebrows! What fire burned in my pupils and outshone the sparkling of the stars, as the poets in that part of the world used to tell me. The women who dressed and undressed me would go into ecstasies when they saw me, back and front, and all the men would love to have changed places with them.

"I was engaged to be married to a sovereign prince of Massa-Carrara. What a prince! As handsome as I was beautiful, gentle and charming to a fault, brilliant in mind and ardent in love. I loved him as one does love for the first time, I worshipped him with passionate abandon. Arrangements were made for the wedding. The pomp and magnificence of it! No one had seen their like before. It was one continual round of entertainments, tournaments, opera buffa. And all Italy composed sonnets for me, though not one of them was any good. My moment of bliss was at hand when an old marchioness, who had been my prince's mistress, invited him to take chocolate with her. He died less than two hours later after appalling convulsions. But that was a trifle. My mother, being in despair and yet much less grief-stricken than I, wanted to absent herself for a time from so dreadful a scene. She had a very fine property near Gaeta.[7] We took ship on a local galley, which was all covered in gilt like the altar of Saint Peter's in Rome. What happens but a corsair from Salé[8] makes straight for us and boards us. Our soldiers defended themselves as if they were the Pope's own: they all knelt down, cast their weapons aside, and asked the corsair for absolution *in articulo mortis.*[9]

5. A fictional pope (the joke is that popes were of course expected to remain celibate).

6. A famous white marble sculpture.

7. A port in southern Italy.

8. A port in Morocco which was a center of piracy in the 18th century.

9. "At the point of death."

"At once they were stripped as naked as monkeys, as were my mother, and our ladies-in-waiting, and I also. It is a remarkable thing, the eagerness of these gentlemen to undress everybody. But what surprised me more was that they put a finger up all of us in a place where we women ordinarily allow only enema nozzles to enter. This ritual struck me as being most odd. But that's how one judges everything when one's never been abroad. I soon gathered that it was to see if we'd hadn't hidden any diamonds up there. It has been established practice among civilized seafaring nations since time immemorial. I discovered that those religious gentlemen, the Knights of Malta,[1] never fail to do it when they capture any Turks, men or women. It is one article of the law of nations which has never been infringed.

"I needn't tell you how hard it is for a young princess to be taken to Morocco as a slave with her mother. You can well imagine all we had to suffer on the pirate ship. My mother was still very beautiful. Our ladies-in-waiting, even our maids, had more charms than are to be found in the whole of Africa. As for me, I was ravishing. I was beauty, grace itself, and I was a virgin. I wasn't one for long. The flower which had been kept for the handsome prince of Massa-Carrara was ravished by the pirate captain. He was a loathsome Negro, who even thought he was doing me a great honour. Yes indeed, the Princess of Palestrina and I had to be extremely tough to survive everything we went through up until our arrival in Morocco. But enough of this. Such things are so commonplace they're not worth talking about.

"Morocco was bathed in blood when we arrived. The fifty sons of the Emperor Muley-Ismael each had his own followers, which in effect meant fifty civil wars—blacks against blacks, blacks against browns, browns against browns, mulattos against mulattos. It was one long bloodbath from one end of the empire to the other.

"We had scarcely disembarked when some blacks belonging to a faction opposed to that of my pirate appeared on the scene wanting to relieve him of his booty. After the diamonds and the gold, we were the most precious things he had. I was witness to a fight the like of which you in your European climates just never see. The Northern races are simply not hot-blooded enough. They don't have that thirst for women that they have in Africa. It's as if you Europeans had milk in your veins, whereas it is vitriol, fire, that flows in the veins of the inhabitants of Mount Atlas and that part of the world. They fought with the fury of the lions and tigers and serpents of their own country to decide which of them should have us. A Moor grabbed my mother by the right arm, my pirate's lieutenant held on to her left, a Moorish soldier took her by one leg, and one of our other pirates held her by the other. In an instant almost all our ladies-in-waiting found themselves being torn like this between four soldiers. My captain kept me hidden behind him. Scimitar in hand, he was killing anything that stood in the way of his own particular thirst. In the end I saw all our Italian women and my mother torn apart, cut to pieces, massacred by the monsters who were fighting over them. My fellow captives and their captors, soldiers, sailors, blacks, browns, whites, mulattos, and finally my captain, all were killed, and I lay dying on top of a pile of corpses. Similar scenes were taking place, as you know, over an area more than three hundred leagues across: and never once did they fail to say the five daily prayers ordered by Mahomet.

"I extricated myself with great difficulty from the piled heap of all these blood-soaked corpses, and dragged myself over to a tall orange-tree next to a nearby stream.

---

1. An old religious order active in the Crusades.

There I collapsed in shock, exhaustion, horror, hunger, and despair. Soon afterwards my shattered senses gave themselves up to a sleep that was more like unconsciousness than rest. I was in this enfeebled and insensible state, halfway between life and death, when I felt myself being pressed down on by something squirming on my body. I opened my eyes and saw a white man with a friendly face sighing and muttering between his teeth: '*O che sciagura d'essere senza coglioni!*'[2]

Chapter 12

THE CONTINUING STORY OF THE OLD WOMAN'S MISFORTUNES

"Astonished and delighted to hear my native tongue, and no less surprised at the words the man was uttering, I replied that there were greater misfortunes than that of which he complained. I informed him in a few words of the horrors to which I had been subjected, and passed out. He carried me to a house nearby, had me put to bed and given something to eat, waited on me, comforted me, flattered me, told me that he had never seen anything so beautiful, and that never had he so much regretted the loss of that which no one could restore to him.

"'I was born in Naples,' he told me. 'They castrate two or three thousand children every year there. Some die, some develop a voice more beautiful than any woman's, and some go off and govern the Papal States.[3] They carried out this operation most successfully on me, and I sang in the chapel of the Princess of Palestrina.'

"'My mother!' cried I.

"'Your mother!' cried he, with tears in his eyes. 'What! Then you would be that young princess I taught till she was six, and who promised even then to be as beautiful as you are?'

"'I am she. My mother lies not four hundred yards from here, in four pieces, beneath a pile of corpses...'

"I told him everything that had happened to me. He told me his adventures too, and about how one of the Christian powers had sent him as an envoy to sign a treaty with the King of Morocco, whereby this monarch would be supplied with powder, cannon, and ships to assist him in putting an end to the trading of the other Christian powers.

"'My mission is complete,' the worthy eunuch told me. 'I am on my way to board ship at Ceuta, and I will take you back to Italy. *Ma che sciagura d'essere senza coglioni!*'

"I thanked him with tears of tender gratitude: instead of taking me to Italy, he took me to Algiers and sold me to the local dey.[4] Hardly had I been sold than the plague which was going round Africa, Asia, and Europe broke out with a vengeance in Algiers. You have seen earthquakes; but you, my young lady, have you ever had the plague?"

"Never," the Baron's daughter replied.

"If you had," the old woman went on, "you would agree that it comes well above an earthquake. It is extremely rife in Africa, and I caught it. Can you imagine? What a situation for the fifteen-year-old daughter of a pope to be in, and for one who in the

---

2. "O what calamity it is to lack testicles" (editions after 1759 usually abbreviated the last word); many Italian boys were castrated to give them a future as male sopranos.

3. In the 18th century Farinelli, a castrato, became a top adviser to the king of Spain. At this time, much of northern Italy was governed by the Pope and known as the Papal States.

4. A ruling official of the Ottoman Empire.

space of three months had suffered poverty and enslavement, been raped almost daily, seen her mother torn limb from limb, survived starvation and war, and was now dying of the plague in Algiers. Die, however, I did not. But my eunuch and the dey and almost the entire seraglio at Algiers perished.

"When the first wave of this appalling plague had passed, they sold the dey's slaves. A merchant bought me and took me to Tunis. He sold me to another merchant who in turn sold me in Tripoli. After Tripoli I was resold in Alexandria, after Alexandria I was resold in Smyrna, and after Smyrna in Constantinople. In the end I became the property of an aga in the janissaries,[5] who shortly afterwards received orders to go and defend Azov against the Russians, who were laying siege to it.[6]

"This aga, who was quite a ladies' man, took his whole seraglio with him, and housed us in a little fort on the Palus-Meotides under the guard of two black eunuchs and twenty soldiers. An enormous number of Russians were killed, but they gave as good as they got. Azov was put to fire and sword, and no quarter was given either as to sex or to age. All that was left was our little fort. The enemy determined to starve us out. The twenty janissaries had sworn not to surrender. The extremes of hunger to which they were reduced forced them to eat our two eunuchs, for fear of breaking their oath. After a few days they decided to eat the women.

"We had a very pious and very understanding imam,[7] who preached a fine sermon to them persuading them not to kill us outright.

"'Cut off one buttock from each of these ladies,' he said, 'and you will eat well. If you have to come back for more in a few days' time, you'll still be able to have the same again. Heaven will be grateful to you for such a charitable deed, and you will be saved.'

"He was very eloquent: he convinced them. They performed this dreadful operation on us. The imam rubbed on us the ointment they use on children who have just been circumcised. We were all at death's door.

"Hardly had the janissaries finished the meal with which we'd provided them than the Russians turn up in flat-bottomed boats. Not one janissary got away. The Russians paid not a blind bit of notice to the state we were in. There are French surgeons all over the world, and a very skilful one took charge of us and made us better. And I shall never forget how, once my wounds were well and truly healed, he then propositioned me. That apart, he told us all to cheer up and assured us that this sort of thing happened in lots of sieges, and that it was one of the laws of warfare.

"As soon as my companions could walk, they were sent to Moscow. I was part of a boyar's share of the spoils, and he put me to work in his garden and gave me twenty lashes a day. But after this nobleman was broken on the wheel two years later, along with thirty other boyars, because of some trouble or other at court, I took my chance and made my escape. I crossed the whole of Russia. For a long time I served in inns, first in Riga, then in Rostock, Wismar, Leipzig, Kassel, Utrecht, Leiden, The Hague, and Rotterdam. I grew old in poverty and dishonour, having but half a bottom, yet always mindful that I was the daughter of a pope. A hundred times I wanted to kill myself, but still I loved life. This ridiculous weakness for living is perhaps one of our most fatal tendencies. For can anything be sillier than to insist on carrying a burden one would continually much rather throw to the ground? Sillier than to feel disgust at

5. Turkish soldiers; an aga is a commanding officer.
6. In the 17th century the Russians invaded the sea of Azov, the northern arm of the Black Sea, which contained the islands of Palus-Meotides.
7. Leader of a mosque.

one's own existence and yet cling to it? Sillier, in short, than to clasp to our bosom the serpent that devours us until it has gnawed away our heart? In the countries through which it has been my fate to travel and in the inns where I have served, I have seen a huge number of people who felt abhorrence for their own lives. But I've seen only a dozen voluntarily put an end to their wretchedness: three Negroes, four Englishmen, four Genevans, and a German professor called Robeck.[8]

"In the end I finished up as one of the servants in the household of Don Issacar the Jew. He gave me to you, my fair young lady, as your maid. I have become involved in your destiny and been more concerned with your adventures than with my own. Indeed I would never have mentioned my misfortunes if you hadn't provoked me to it a little, and if it were not the custom on board ship to tell stories to pass the time. So there you are, Miss. I have lived, and I know the world. Just for fun, why not get each passenger to tell you the story of his life, and if there is one single one of them who hasn't often cursed the day he was born and hasn't often said to himself that he was the most unfortunate man alive, then you can throw me into the sea head first."

Chapter 13

HOW CANDIDE WAS OBLIGED TO PART FROM FAIR CUNÉGONDE AND THE OLD WOMAN

Fair Cunégonde, having heard the old woman's story, treated her with all the civilities due to a person of her rank and quality. She accepted her suggestion and got all the passengers one after another to tell her their adventures. Candide and she conceded that the old woman was right.

"It's a great pity," said Candide, "that wise Pangloss was hanged, contrary to the usual custom, during an *auto-da-fé*. He would have some remarkable things to tell us about the physical and moral evil that prevails over land and sea—and I would feel able to venture a few respectful objections."

While each person told his story, the ship continued on its way. They docked at Buenos Aires. Cunégonde, Captain Candide, and the old woman went to call on the Governor, Don Fernando d'Ibaraa y Figueora y Mascarenes y Lampourdos y Souza. This grandee had a pride to match his many names. He spoke to people with the most noble disdain, sticking his nose so far in the air, speaking in such a mercilessly loud voice, adopting so high and mighty a tone, and affecting so haughty a gait, that all who greeted him were also tempted to hit him. He loved women to distraction. Cunégonde seemed to him more beautiful than any he had ever seen. The first thing he did was to ask if she were not by any chance the Captain's wife. The air with which he put this question alarmed Candide. He did not dare say she was his wife, because in fact she was not. He did not dare say she was his sister, because she was not that either. And although this white lie had once been very fashionable among the Ancients,[9] and could still come in very useful to the Moderns, his soul was too pure to be unfaithful to the truth.

"Miss Cunégonde," he said, "is to do me the honour of marrying me, and we humbly beseech Your Excellency to condescend to officiate at our wedding."

With a twirl of his moustache Don Fernando d'Ibaraa y Figueora y Mascarenes y Lampourdos y Souza smiled a bitter smile, and ordered Captain Candide to go and review his company. Candide obeyed. The Governor remained with Miss Cunégonde.

---

8. Author of a book promoting suicide who drowned himself in 1739.

9. The patriarchs Abraham and Isaac passed off their wives as their sisters when in hostile territory (Genesis 12 and 26).

He declared his love for her and made protestations that on the morrow he would marry her, in the eyes of the Church or anyone else's, just as it might please her lovely self. Cunégonde asked him for a quarter of an hour in which to collect herself, consult with the old woman, and come to a decision.

The old woman said to Cunégonde:

"Miss, you have seventy-two quarterings, and not a penny to your name. You can be the wife of the greatest nobleman in South America, who also has a very fine moustache. Are you in any position to make a point of unswerving fidelity? You have been raped by the Bulgars. A Jew and an Inquisitor have enjoyed your favours. Misfortune does give people some rights. Frankly, if I were in your position, I would have no scruples about marrying the Governor and making Captain Candide's fortune for him."

While the old woman was speaking with all the prudence of age and experience, a small ship was seen entering the port. On board were an alcalde and some alguazils:[1] what had happened was this.

The old woman had quite rightly guessed that it had been the Cordelier[2] with the loose sleeves who had stolen the money and jewels from Cunégonde in the town of Badajoz, when she was making her rapid escape with Candide. This monk tried to sell some of the stones to a jeweller. The merchant recognized them as belonging to the Grand Inquisitor. The Franciscan, before being hanged, confessed that he had stolen them. He gave a description of the people concerned and the route they were taking. Cunégonde and Candide were already known to have escaped. They were followed to Cadiz. No time was lost in sending a ship after them, and this ship was already in the port of Buenos Aires. Rumour spread that an alcalde was about to come ashore, and that they were after the Grand Inquisitor's murderers. The prudent old woman saw at once what was to be done.

"You cannot run away," she told Cunégonde, "and you have nothing to fear. It wasn't you who killed His Eminence and, anyway, the Governor loves you and won't allow any harm to come to you. Stay here."

Whereupon she rushed off to Candide: "Quick, off you go," she said, "or in an hour you'll be burnt."

There was not a moment to lose. But how could he leave Cunégonde, and where was he to hide?

Chapter 14

How Candide and Cacambo were received by the Jesuits of Paraguay

Candide had brought a manservant with him from Cadiz of the kind frequently found along the coasts of Spain and in the colonies. He was a quarter Spanish, the son of a half-breed in the Tucuman.[3] He had been a choir-boy, sexton, sailor, monk, commercial agent, soldier, and lackey. His name was Cacambo, and he loved his master very much, because his master was a very good man. He saddled up the two Andalusian horses as quickly as he could.

"Come on, master, let's do as the old woman says and be off. Let's ride away, and no looking back."

Candide burst out crying.

1. A Spanish mayor and some officers.
2. A Franciscan friar who typically wore a loose habit as a sign of poverty.
3. Region in Argentina.

"O my darling Cunégonde! Must I abandon you just when the Governor was going to marry us! Cunégonde, what will become of you so far from home?"

"She'll become what she can," said Cacambo. "Women are never stuck. God sees to that. Let's go."

"Where are you taking me? Where are we going? What will we do without Cunégonde?" said Candide.

"By Saint James of Compostella," said Cacambo, "you were going to fight against the Jesuits. Let's go and fight for them instead. I know the roads well enough. I'll take you to their kingdom. They'll be delighted to have a captain who can do drill the Bulgar way. You'll be all the rage. If one doesn't get what one wants in one world, one can always get it in another. It's always a great pleasure to see new places and do different things."

"So you've already been to Paraguay then?" said Candide.

"I've been there all right!" said Cacambo. "I used to be a servant at the College of the Assumption, and I know los Padres' way of running things like I know the streets of Cadiz. It's a wonderful way of governing they have. Their kingdom is already more than three hundred leagues wide, and it's been divided into thirty provinces. Los Padres own everything in it, and the people nothing—a masterpiece of reason and justice. If you ask me, nothing could be more divine than los Padres making war on the Kings of Spain and Portugal over here and being confessors to the very same Kings back in Europe, or than killing Spaniards here and speeding them on their way to heaven back in Madrid. It appeals to me, that does. Come on, let's go. You're about to become the happiest man alive. How pleased los Padres are going to be when they discover there's a captain coming who knows the Bulgar drill!"

The moment they arrived at the first border post, Cacambo told the advance guard that a captain was asking to speak to His Eminence, the commanding officer. The main guard was notified. A Paraguayan officer made haste to go and kneel at the feet of the commanding officer and inform him of the news. Candide and Cacambo were first disarmed, and then their two Andalusian horses were taken from them. Both strangers were ushered between two lines of soldiers. The commanding officer was standing at the far end, with the three-cornered hat on his head, his cassock hitched up, a sword at his side, and a halberd in his hand. He made a sign. Instantly twenty-four soldiers surrounded the two newcomers. A sergeant told them they must wait, that the commanding officer could not speak to them, that the Reverend Father Provincial did not permit Spaniards to open their mouths unless he was present, or to remain in the country for more than three hours.

"And where is the Reverend Father Provincial?" asked Cacambo.

"He has said Mass, and now he's taking parade," replied the sergeant. "And you won't be able to kiss his spurs for another three hours yet."

"But," said Cacambo, "the Captain—who incidentally is dying of hunger, as indeed I am—isn't Spanish. He's German. Couldn't we have lunch while we wait for His Reverence?"

With this the sergeant went off to tell the commanding officer what had been said.

"May God be praised!" said this reverend gentleman. "Since he's German, I can speak to him. Show him to my arbour."

At once Candide was led into a closet of greenery, embellished with a very pretty colonnade of green and gold marble, and trellis-work containing parrots, colibris, humming-birds, guinea-fowl, and all manner of rare birds. An excellent lunch had been laid out in vessels of gold, and while the Paraguayans ate maize from wooden bowls out in the open in the full glare of the sun, the reverend father-in-command entered the arbour.

He was a very handsome young man, rather pale-skinned, with a round, ruddy face, arched eyebrows, a keen gaze, red ears, vermilion lips, and a proud demeanour—though proud in a way quite unlike a Spaniard or a Jesuit. Candide and Cacambo were given back the weapons which had been taken from them, as well as their two Andalusian horses. Cacambo gave the latter their oats near the arbour and kept a watchful eye on them in case of surprise.

First Candide kissed the hem of the commanding officer's cassock, and then they all sat down to table.

"So you're German, you say?" said the Jesuit in that language.

"Yes, reverend father," said Candide.

As they uttered these words, they looked at each other in absolute astonishment and with a degree of emotion which it was beyond them to control.

"And from which part of Germany do you come?" said the Jesuit.

"From the filthy province of Westphalia," said Candide. "I was born in the castle of Thunder-ten-tronckh."

"Good heavens! It's not possible?" exclaimed the commanding officer.

"It's a miracle!" exclaimed Candide.

"Can it really be you?" said the commanding officer.

"It's impossible," said Candide.

They both fell back in amazement, and kissed each other, and wept buckets of tears.

"What! Can it really be you, reverend father? You, the brother of the fair Cunégonde! You who were killed by the Bulgars! You the son of the Baron! You a Jesuit in Paraguay! The world really is a very strange place, I must say. O Pangloss! Pangloss! how pleased you would be now if you hadn't been hanged!"

The commanding officer dismissed the Negro slaves and the Paraguayans who were serving drinks in goblets of rock-crystal. He thanked God and Saint Ignatius[4] a thousand times, and he hugged Candide. Their faces were bathed in tears.

"You will be even more astonished, even more moved, even more beside yourself," said Candide, "when I tell you that Miss Cunégonde, your sister whom you thought disembowelled, is in the best of health."

"Where?"

"Not far from here, with the Governor of Buenos Aires. And I was coming over here to fight against you."

Each word they uttered in this long conversation piled wonder upon wonder. The soul of each took wing upon his tongue, paid careful heed with either ear, and sparkled in his eyes. Being Germans, they sat on at table for a long time; and while they waited for the Reverend Father Provincial, the commanding officer spoke thus to his dear Candide.

Chapter 15

How Candide killed the brother of his dear Cunégonde

"For as long as I live I shall always remember that dreadful day when I saw my father and mother killed and my sister raped. When the Bulgars had gone, my adorable sister was nowhere to be found, and my mother and father and I, together with two servant

4. Ignatius of Loyola (1491–1556), founder of the Jesuit order.

girls and three little boys who'd had their throats slit, were placed on a cart to be taken for burial at a Jesuit chapel two leagues from our ancestral home. A Jesuit threw some holy water over us. It was horribly salty. A few drops of it went in my eyes. The reverend father saw my eyelids quiver. He put his hand on my heart and felt it beating. I was saved, and three weeks later you wouldn't have known there'd been anything the matter. You know how good-looking I was, my dear Candide. I became even more so, with the result that the reverend father Croust,[5] who was Father Superior, developed the most tender affection for me. He initiated me as a novice. Some time later I was sent to Rome. The Father General had need of a batch of young German Jesuit recruits. The rulers of Paraguay admit as few Spanish Jesuits as they can. They prefer foreign ones in the belief that they can control them better. The Father General thought I was just the right sort of person to go and toil in this particular vineyard. So off we went, a Pole, a Tyrolean,[6] and myself. On arrival I had the honour of being made sub-deacon and lieutenant. Today I am colonel and priest. We shall give the King of Spain's troops a warm reception. They will be excommunicated and beaten, I can promise you. Providence has sent you here to help us. But is it really true that my dear sister Cunégonde is not far away, at the Governor's in Buenos Aires?"

Candide swore to him that nothing could be more true. Their tears began once more to flow.

The Baron could not desist from embracing Candide. He called him his brother, his saviour.

"Ah, my dear Candide," he said, "perhaps we can enter the city as victors, the two of us together, and rescue my dear sister Cunégonde."

"There's nothing I'd like better," said Candide, "for I was intending to marry her, and I still hope to."

"You insolent man!" retorted the Baron. "You would have the audacity to marry my sister who has seventy-two quarterings! I consider it great effrontery on your part to dare speak to me of so rash an intention!"

Candide's blood turned to stone at such a statement. He answered him:

"Reverend father, all the quarterings in the world have nothing to do with it. I have rescued your sister from the arms of a Jew and an Inquisitor. She owes me a number of debts, and she intends to marry me. Maître Pangloss always told me that men are equal, and marry her I most assuredly will."

"We'll see about that, you scoundrel!" said the Jesuit Baron of Thunder-ten-tronckh and, so saying, struck him a heavy blow across the face with the flat of his sword.

Candide, quick as a flash, drew his own and plunged it up to the hilt into the Jesuit Baron's gut. But as he withdrew it, all steaming, he began to cry.

"Dear God," he said, "I've killed my former master, my friend, my brother-in-law. I am the best fellow in the world, and already that makes three men I've killed, and two of them priests!"

Cacambo, who had been standing guard at the door of the arbour, came running.

"There's nothing for it but to sell our lives dearly," his master said to him. "They're bound to come into the arbour, so we'll have to die fighting."

---

5. Name of a Jesuit who had helped drive Voltaire from Colmar in 1754.

6. Tyrol: Alpine region in present-day Austria and Italy.

Cacambo, who had seen a thing or two, kept his head. He removed the Baron's Jesuit cassock, put it on Candide, handed him the dead man's biretta,[7] and made him mount his horse. This was all done in a trice.

"Quickly, master, at the gallop. Everyone will take you for a Jesuit dashing off to give orders, and we'll have passed the frontier before they can give chase."

He was already riding like the wind when he said this, shouting out in Spanish:

"Make way, make way for the reverend father colonel."

Chapter 16

WHAT BECAME OF THE TWO TRAVELLERS WITH TWO GIRLS, TWO MONKEYS, AND THE SAVAGES CALLED THE LOBEIROS

Candide and his manservant were past the frontier, and still no one in the camp knew the German Jesuit was dead. The vigilant Cacambo had taken care to fill his bag with bread, chocolate, ham, fruit, and a quantity of wine. They rode their Andalusian horses deep into unknown country where they found no sign of a track. Eventually a beautiful stretch of grassland, criss-crossed with streams, opened up before them. Our two travellers halted to allow their mounts to graze. Cacambo suggested to his master that they eat something and duly set him an example.

"How do you expect me to eat ham," said Candide, "when I have killed the Baron's son and see myself doomed never to see fair Cunégonde again in my life? What's the use of prolonging my miserable existence if I must drag it out, far away from her, in remorse and despair? And what will the *Journal de Trévoux* say?"[8]

So saying, he did not abstain from eating. The sun was setting. The two lost travellers heard one or two faint cries which sounded as though they came from women. They could not tell if they were cries of joy or pain, but they quickly sprang to their feet, full of that apprehension and alarm which anything in a strange land can arouse. The clamour was emanating from two completely naked girls who were scampering along the edge of the meadow pursued by two monkeys who were nibbling at their bottoms. Candide was moved to pity. He had learnt to shoot with the Bulgars, and he could have downed a hazelnut in a thicket without so much as touching a single leaf. He raised his Spanish double-barrelled gun, fired, and killed the two monkeys.

"God be praised, my dear Cacambo! I have delivered those two poor creatures from great peril. If it was a sin to kill an Inquisitor and a Jesuit, I've certainly atoned for it by saving the lives of these two girls. Perhaps the two young ladies are well-to-do and this chance episode will prove to be of great advantage to us hereabouts."

He was about to continue, but he was struck dumb when he saw the two girls throw loving arms around the two monkeys, dissolve into tears over their dead bodies, and rend the air with wails of utmost grief.

"I didn't expect the kindness of their hearts to go that far," Candide said at last to Cacambo, who replied:

"A fine thing you've done there, master. You've just killed those two young ladies' lovers."

"Their lovers! Impossible! You're joking, Cacambo. How can they possibly be?"

---

7. Priest's square hat.

8. This was a Jesuit publication that had been critical of Voltaire.

"My dear master," continued Cacambo, "you're always surprised by everything. Why do you find it so strange that in some countries monkeys should enjoy the favours of the ladies? They're a quarter human, just as I am a quarter Spanish."

"Oh, dear!" replied Candide, "I remember now Maître Pangloss saying that such accidents did use to happen once upon a time, and that these couplings produced centaurs, fauns, and satyrs, and that several of the great names of antiquity had seen them. But I used to think that it only happened in fables."

"Well, you ought to be convinced now that it's true," said Cacambo. "You see how people behave when they haven't had a bit of education. All I hope is that these ladies don't cause us any trouble."

These solid reflections persuaded Candide to leave the meadow and plunge into a wood. There he supped with Cacambo and, having cursed the Inquisitor of Portugal, the Governor of Buenos Aires, and the Baron, they both fell asleep on some moss. When they awoke, they felt unable to move. The reason was that during the night the Lobeiros,[9] who inhabit that country, and to whom the two ladies had denounced them, had pinioned them with rope made of bark. They were surrounded by some fifty naked Lobeiros armed with arrows, cudgels, and hatchets made of flint. Some of them were warming a large cauldron, others were preparing skewers, and they were all chanting:

"It's a Jesuit! It's a Jesuit! We will be avenged, our stomachs will be full. Let's eat Jesuit! Let's eat Jesuit!"

"I told you so, my dear master," cried Cacambo sadly. "I told you those two girls would play us false."

Candide, seeing the cauldron and the skewers, exclaimed:

"We're going to be roasted or boiled, that's for certain. Ah! what would Maître Pangloss say if he could see how human nature is in its pure state? All is well. So it may be. But I must say it's pretty rotten to have lost Miss Cunégonde and be spit-roasted by Lobeiros."

Cacambo was not one to lose his head.

"Don't despair," he said to the disconsolate Candide. "I know these people's lingo a bit. I'll have a word with them."

"Make sure you point out to them," said Candide, "how frightfully inhuman it is to cook people, and how unchristian it is too."

"So, gentlemen," said Cacambo, "you think you're going to have Jesuit today. That's fine by me. Nothing could be fairer than to treat your enemies this way. The laws of nature do indeed tell us to kill our neighbour, and that is the way people behave throughout the world. If we ourselves do not exercise our right to eat our neighbour, that's because we've got better things to eat. But you haven't the same resources as we have. Certainly it is better to eat one's enemies than to leave the fruits of one's victory for the rooks and the crows. But, gentlemen, you would not want to eat your friends. You think you're about to skewer a Jesuit, while in fact it's your defender, the enemy of your enemies, that you'll be roasting. Me, I was born in these parts. This gentleman here is my master and, far from being a Jesuit, he has just killed a Jesuit and is wearing the spoils of combat. That's how you came to be mistaken. If you want to check the truth of what I say, take his cassock to the nearest frontier post of the kingdom of los Padres. Ask them if my master didn't kill a Jesuit officer. It

9. Tribe in Paraguay.

won't take you long, and you'll always be able to eat us anyway if you discover I've lied to you. But if I've told you the truth, you are too well acquainted with the principles, articles, and procedures of international law not to pardon us."

The Lobeiros found this speech very reasonable. They deputed two eminent persons to proceed post-haste to find out the truth. The two deputies carried out their commission like intelligent men and soon returned bearing good tidings. The Lobeiros untied their two prisoners, did them all kinds of honour, offered them girls, gave them refreshments, and escorted them back to the boundary of their lands merrily chanting: "He isn't a Jesuit, he isn't a Jesuit!"

Candide could not get over the manner of his deliverance.

"What a people!" he was saying. "What men! What manners! If I hadn't had the good fortune to run Miss Cunégonde's brother through with a hefty thrust of my sword, I would have been eaten, and without remission of sentence. But human nature in its pure state is good after all, since these people, instead of eating me, were all sweetness and light the minute they knew I wasn't a Jesuit."

Chapter 17

THE ARRIVAL OF CANDIDE AND HIS MANSERVANT IN ELDORADO,[1]
AND WHAT THEY SAW THERE

When they reached the Lobeiro frontier, Cacambo said to Candide:

"You see, this half of the world is no better than the other. Take my advice, let's head back to Europe by the shortest route possible."

"But how?" said Candide, "and where to? If I go back to my own country, I'll find the Bulgars and Abars busy cutting everyone's throats. If I return to Portugal, I'll be burnt at the stake. And if we stay here, we may end up on a spit at any moment. But how can I bring myself to leave the part of the world that contains Miss Cunégonde?"

"Let's make for Cayenne,"[2] said Cacambo. "We'll find the French there. They travel all over the place. They'll be able to help us. Perhaps God will have pity on us."

Getting to Cayenne was no simple matter. They knew roughly which direction to take, but what with mountains, rivers, precipices, brigands, and savages, terrible obstacles presented themselves at every turn. Their horses died of exhaustion, they ran out of provisions, and for a whole month they survived on wild fruits, before they eventually found themselves by a small river lined with coconut palms, which kept both them and their hopes alive.

Cacambo, whose advice was always as good as the old woman's had been, said to Candide:

"We've had it, we've walked as far as we can. I see an empty canoe on the bank. Let's fill it with coconuts, get in and let the current take us. A river always leads to some kind of habitation. If we don't find anything nice, at least we'll find something new,"

"All right," said Candide. "Let's trust in Providence."

They drifted downstream for a few leagues between riverbanks now covered in flowers, now bare of vegetation, now flat, now steep. The river grew wider and wider. At length it ran under a vault of fearsome-looking rocks that reached high into the

1. A rumored city of gold deep in the interior, sought by Sir Walter Raleigh and others. Voltaire's description draws heavily from Garcilaso de la Vega's *History of the Inca.*
2. The capital of French Guiana.

sky. The two travellers had the pluck to let the water carry them under this vault. The river, which narrowed at this point, swept them along with horrifying speed and made a terrifying din. Twenty-four hours later they saw the light of day once more, but their boat was dashed to pieces in the rapids. They had to drag themselves from rock to rock for a whole league. Eventually they came to a vast open space surrounded by impassable peaks. The land had been cultivated as much to give pleasure as to serve a need. Everywhere whatever was useful was also agreeable. The roads were covered, or rather adorned, with conveyances of the most lustrous form and substance, bearing men and women of singular beauty, and drawn at great speed by large red sheep who could outpace the finest horses in Andalusia, Tetuan, or Mequinez.[3]

"This, on the other hand," said Candide, "is something of an improvement on Westphalia."

He and Cacambo stepped ashore at the first village they came to. A few village children, covered in tattered gold brocade, were playing quoits[4] at the entrance to the settlement. Our two men from the other world stopped to watch them. Their quoits were fairly large round objects, some of them yellow, some red, some green, and they gleamed in an odd way. The travellers were prompted to pick some of them up. They were pieces of gold, emerald, and ruby, and the smallest of them would have been the greatest ornament on the Mogul's throne.

"No doubt," said Candide, "these children playing quoits are the sons of the King of this country."

The village schoolmaster appeared at that moment to call them back to the classroom.

"That," said Candide, "must be the royal family's private tutor."

The little urchins stopped their game at once, leaving their quoits and everything else they had been playing with lying on the ground. Candide picked them up, ran to the tutor, and humbly presented him with them, explaining in sign language that their Royal Highnesses had forgotten their gold and their precious stones. The village schoolmaster threw them on the ground with a smile, stared at Candide for a moment in great surprise, and walked off.

The travellers did not fail to gather up the gold, rubies, and emeralds.

"Where can we be?" exclaimed Candide. "The royal children here must be very well brought up if they're taught to turn their noses up at gold and precious stones."

Cacambo was just as surprised as Candide. At length they drew near to the first house in the village. It was built like a European palace. There was a crowd of people at the door, and an even bigger one inside. Some very pleasant music could be heard, and there was a mouth-watering smell of cooking. Cacambo went up to the door and heard Peruvian being spoken. This was his native tongue; for, as everyone knows, Cacambo was born in the Tucuman in a village where this was the only language they knew.

"I'll interpret for you," he told Candide. "Let's go inside. This is an inn."

At once two waiters and two waitresses, dressed in cloth of gold and wearing ribbons in their hair, showed them to a table and offered them the table d'hôte. The meal consisted of four different soups, each garnished with a couple of parrots, then a boiled condor weighing two hundred pounds, two excellent roast monkeys, one platter of three hundred colibris, and another of six hundred humming-birds, some exquisite casseroles, and delicious pastries. Everything was served on dishes made of a

3. These last two are towns in Morocco.
4. A game similar to ring toss.

kind of rock-crystal. The waiters and waitresses poured out a variety of liqueurs made from sugar-cane.

The guests were tradesmen and waggoners for the most part, all of them extremely polite. They asked Cacambo one or two questions with the most scrupulous discretion, and returned full answers to those he put to them.

When the meal was over, Cacambo thought, as Candide did, that he could more than cover the cost of their meal by tossing two of the large pieces of gold he had picked up on to the table. The landlord and his wife burst out laughing and held their sides for a long time. Finally they recovered themselves:

"Gentlemen," said the host, "we can see you're strangers. We're not used to them here. Forgive us if we started laughing when you offered to pay with the stones off our roads. Presumably you don't have any of the local currency, but you don't need any to dine here. All inns set up for the convenience of those engaged in commerce are paid for by the government. The meal wasn't very good here because this is a poor village, but anywhere else you'll get the kind of reception you deserve."

Cacambo interpreted for Candide all that the landlord had said, and Candide was as amazed and bewildered to hear it as Cacambo was to tell it.

"What is this place," said one to the other, "which is unknown to the rest of the world and where the whole nature of things is so different from ours? It's probably the place where all goes well, for there absolutely must be such a place. And whatever Maître Pangloss might have said, I often observed that everything went rather badly in Westphalia."

Chapter 18

WHAT THEY SAW IN THE LAND OF ELDORADO

Cacambo gave the landlord to understand how curious he was to know more. The landlord said:

"I know very little about things, and that suits me well enough. But we have an old man living in the village who used to be at court and who is the most knowledgeable man in the kingdom, as well as the most communicative."

Thereupon he took Cacambo to see the old man. Candide was playing second fiddle now, and it was he who accompanied his servant. They entered a house of a very modest sort, for its front door was only of silver and the panelling of its room merely gold, though the workmanship was in such good taste that more opulent panelling could not have outshone it. It has to be said that the antechamber was studded only with rubies and emeralds, but the pattern in which they had all been arranged more than made up for this extreme simplicity.

The old man received the two strangers on a sofa stuffed with colibri feathers and gave orders for them to be served various liquors in diamond goblets. After which he satisfied their curiosity in the following fashion:

"I am one hundred and seventy-two years old, and I learnt from my late father, who was a crown equerry,[5] of the extraordinary upheavals which he witnessed in Peru. This kingdom we are in now is the former homeland of the Incas, who most imprudently left it to go and conquer another part of the world and ended up being wiped out by the Spanish.

5. Master of the royal horses.

"The princes of their race who remained behind in their native country were wiser. They ordained, with the consent of the nation, that no inhabitant was ever to leave our little kingdom. And that's how we've managed to remain innocent and happy. The Spanish knew vaguely about the place and called it Eldorado, and an English knight called Raleigh even came fairly near it about a hundred years ago. But since we are surrounded by unclimbable rocks and cliffs, we have always hitherto been safe from the rapacity of European nations with their unaccountable fondness for the pebbles and dirt off our land, and who would kill us to the very last man just to lay their hands on the stuff."

Their conversation was a long one and touched on the form of government there, on local customs, on women, public entertainment, and the arts. Eventually Candide, ever one for metaphysics, asked through Cacambo if there was a religion in this country.

The old man flushed a little.

"But how could you suppose there might not be?" he said. "What do you take us for? Ungrateful wretches?"

Cacambo humbly asked what the religion of Eldorado was. The old man flushed again.

"Can there be more than one religion?" he asked. "As far as I know, we have the same religion as everyone else. We worship God from dusk till dawn."

"Do you worship only one God?" asked Cacambo, who was still acting as interpreter to the doubting Candide.

"Obviously," said the old man. "There aren't two Gods, or three, or four. I must say people from your part of the world do ask some very strange questions."

Candide persisted in having further questions put to this genial old man. He wanted to know how they prayed to God in Eldorado.

"We don't pray to God," said the good and worthy sage. "We have nothing to ask him for. He has given us all we need, and we never cease to thank him."

Candide was curious to see the priests. He had Cacambo ask where they were. The kindly old man smiled.

"My friends," he said, "we are all priests. The King and the head of each family sing hymns of thanksgiving solemnly every morning, to the accompaniment of five or six thousand musicians."

"What! You mean you don't have any monks to teach and dispute and govern and intrigue and burn people to death who don't agree with them?"

"We'd be mad to," said the old man. "We're all of like mind here, and we can't see the point of your monks."

Each of these remarks left Candide in raptures, and he kept thinking to himself:

"This is all rather different from Westphalia and His Lordship's castle. If our friend Pangloss had seen Eldorado, he would no longer have said that the castle of Thunder-ten-tronckh was the best place on earth. It just goes to show: travel's the thing."

After this long conversation the kind old man had six sheep harnessed to a carriage and lent the two travellers twelve of his servants to take them to the court.

"Forgive me," he said to them, "if my advancing years deprive me of the honour of accompanying you. You will not be dissatisfied with the way the King receives you, and I am sure you will be tolerant of our customs if any are not to your liking."

Candide and Cacambo stepped into the carriage. The six sheep went like the wind, and in less than four hours they had arrived at the palace of the King, situated at one end of the capital. The main entrance was two hundred and twenty feet high and one hundred wide. There are no words to describe what it was made of, which in itself gives some idea of just how prodigiously superior it was to the sand and pebbles we call "gold" and "precious stones."

Twenty beautiful guardswomen received Candide and Cacambo upon arrival, escorted them to the baths, and dressed them in robes of humming-bird down, after which the Grand Officers and the Grand Dames of the Crown led them to His Majesty's apartments between two lines of musicians each a thousand strong, in accordance with normal protocol. As they approached the throne-room, Cacambo asked one of the Grand Officers what to do when being presented to His Majesty. Should one fall on one's knees or flat on the ground; should one put one's hands on one's head or over one's backside; should one lick the dust off the floor? In a word, what was the done thing?

"It is customary," said the Grand Officer, "to embrace the King and kiss him on both cheeks."

Candide and Cacambo fell upon His Majesty's neck. He welcomed them with all imaginable graciousness and politely asked them to supper.

Before then they were shown round the city, with its public buildings raised (and praised) to the skies, its market-places decorated with a thousand columns, its fountains of spring-water and rose-water and sugar-cane liquors, all playing ceaselessly in the middle of large squares paved with special stones which gave off an aroma similar to that of clove and cinnamon. Candide asked to see the law courts. He was told there weren't any, and that there were never any cases to hear. He asked if there were any prisons, and he was told there weren't. What surprised him most and gave him the greatest pleasure was the Palace of Science, in which he saw a gallery two thousand feet long all full of instruments for the study of mathematics and physics.

Having seen about a thousandth part of the city in the course of the entire afternoon, they were then brought back to the King. Candide sat down to table next to His Majesty, his servant Cacambo, and several ladies. Never did anyone dine better, and never was anyone wittier at supper than His Majesty. Cacambo interpreted the King's "bons mots"[6] for Candide, and even in translation they still seemed "bons." Of all the things that surprised Candide, this was not what surprised him the least.

They spent a month in this hospice. Candide never stopped saying to Cacambo:

"It's true, my friend, and I'll say it again. The castle where I was born is nothing compared to this place. But still, Miss Cunégonde isn't here, and doubtless you have some sweetheart back in Europe. If we stay on here, we'll simply be the same as everyone else, whereas if we return to Europe with even a mere dozen sheep loaded up with Eldorado pebbles, then we'll be richer than all the kings put together, we'll have no more inquisitors to worry about, and we'll easily be able to get Miss Cunégonde back."

Cacambo liked what he heard. Such is the desire to be always on the move, to be somebody, and to show off about what you've seen on your travels, that the two happy men resolved to be happy no longer and to ask leave of His Majesty to depart.

"You're making a great mistake," the King told them. "I know my country isn't up to much, but when one is reasonably content in a place, one ought to stay there. But I certainly have no right to stop strangers from leaving. That is a piece of tyranny which has no part in our customs or our laws. All men are free. Leave when you wish, though getting out is difficult. It is impossible to return up the rapids which, by a miracle, you

6. Witty remarks.

managed to come down: the river runs under vault after vault of rock. The mountains which surround my kingdom are ten thousand feet high and as sheer as a city wall. Each one is about ten leagues thick, and the only way down the other side is one long cliff-face. However, since you are absolutely determined to leave, I shall give orders for the machine intendants to make one which will transport you in comfort. When they've got you to the other side of the mountains, no one will be able to accompany you any further, for my subjects have vowed never to set foot outside these boundaries, and they are too sensible to break their vow. Apart from that you can ask me for whatever you want."

"All we ask of Your Majesty," said Cacambo, "is a few sheep laden with provisions and pebbles and some of the local dirt."

The King laughed.

"I really don't understand this passion you Europeans have for our yellow dirt," said the King, "but take all you want, and much good may it do you."

He immediately ordered his engineers to make a machine to windlass these two extraordinary men out of his kingdom. Three thousand of the best scientists worked on it. It was ready in a fortnight and cost no more than the equivalent of twenty thousand pounds sterling in local currency. Candide and Cacambo were installed on the machine, together with two large red sheep saddled up for them to ride when they had crossed the mountains, twenty pack-sheep laden with provisions, thirty carrying a selection of the best local curios and gifts the country could offer, and fifty loaded up with gold, diamonds, and other precious stones. The King embraced the two wanderers and bid them a fond farewell.

They presented quite a sight as they departed, as did the ingenious way in which they were hoisted, men and sheep together, to the top of the mountains. The scientists took their leave of them once they were safely across, and Candide was left with no other desire or object but to go and present Miss Cunégonde with his sheep.

"We have the wherewithal to pay the Governor of Buenos Aires now," he said, "if a price can be put on Miss Cunégonde, that is. Let's head for Cayenne and take ship there, and then we'll see what kingdom we're going to buy."

Chapter 19

WHAT HAPPENED TO THEM IN SURINAM AND HOW CANDIDE MET MARTIN

For our two travellers the first day's journey passed pleasantly enough. They were spurred on by the prospect of themselves as owners of more treasures than Asia, Europe, and Africa can muster between them. Candide, quite carried away, carved the name of Cunégonde on trees as he passed. On the second day, two of their sheep became bogged down in a swamp and were swallowed up with their entire load. A few days afterwards two more sheep died of exhaustion. Seven or eight then starved to death in a desert. Others fell down some mountain-sides a day or two later. In the end, after a hundred days of journeying, they had only two sheep left.

Said Candide to Cacambo:

"My friend, you see how perishable are the riches of this world. The only sure thing is virtue and the happiness of seeing Miss Cunégonde again."

"I'm sure," said Cacambo. "But we do still have two sheep left and more treasure than the King of Spain will ever have, and in the distance I can see a town which, I suspect, is Surinam, where the Dutch are. Our troubles are over and the good times are just beginning."

As they drew near to the town, they came on a Negro lying on the ground half-naked, which in his case meant in half a pair of short denim breeches. The poor man was missing his left leg and his right hand.

"My God!" said Candide in Dutch, "what are you doing lying here, my friend, in this dreadful state?"

"I'm waiting for my master, Mr. Van der Hartbargin,[7] the well-known trader," replied the Negro.

"And is it Mr. Van der Hartbargin," said Candide, "who has treated you like this?"

"Yes, sir," said the Negro, "it is the custom. We are given one pair of short denim breeches twice a year, and that's all we have to wear. When we're working at the sugar-mill and catch our finger in the grinding-wheel, they cut off our hand. When we try to run away, they cut off a leg. I have been in both these situations. This is the price you pay for the sugar you eat in Europe. However, when my mother sold me for ten Patagonian crowns on the coast of Guinea, she said to me: 'My dear child, bless our fetishes,[8] worship them always, they will bring you a happy life. You have the honour of being a slave to our lords and masters the Whites and, by so being, you are making your father's and mother's fortune.' Alas! I don't know if I made their fortune, but they didn't make mine. Dogs, monkeys, parrots, they're all a thousand times less wretched than we are. The Dutch fetishes who converted me tell me every Sunday that we are all the sons of Adam, Whites and Blacks alike. I'm no genealogist, but if these preachers are right, we are all cousins born of first-cousins. Well, you will grant me that you can't treat a relative much worse than this."

"O Pangloss!" cried Candide, "this is one abomination you never thought of. That does it. I shall finally have to renounce your Optimism."

"What's Optimism?" asked Cacambo.

"I'm afraid to say," said Candide, "that it's a mania for insisting that all is well when things are going badly."

And he began to weep as he gazed at his Negro, and he entered Surinam in tears.

The first thing they enquired about was whether there were a ship in the port which could be sent to Buenos Aires. The person they approached happened to be a Spanish skipper, who offered to name them a fair price himself. He arranged to meet them in an inn. Candide and the faithful Cacambo went to wait for him there along with their two sheep.

Candide, whose heart was always on his lips, told the Spaniard all about his adventures and confessed that he wished to carry off Miss Cunégonde.

"I'm not taking you to Buenos Aires, that's for sure," said the skipper. "I'd be hanged, and so would you. The fair Cunégonde is His Excellency's favourite mistress."

This came as a bolt from the blue to Candide. He wept for a long time. Eventually he took Cacambo to one side:

"Look, my dear friend," he said to him, "this is what you must do. We've each got about five or six million in diamonds in our pockets. You're cleverer than I am. Go and fetch Miss Cunégonde from Buenos Aires. If the Governor makes difficulties about it, give him a million. If he won't budge, give him two. You haven't killed any

---

7. In the original French Voltaire has "Vanderdendur," thought to be a dig at a Dutch bookseller, Van Duren, who had driven a hard bargain with Voltaire over a manuscript.

8. Objects thought to possess magical protective power.

inquisitors, they won't be suspicious of you. I'll have another ship made ready. I'll go and wait for you in Venice. Theirs is a free country where one has nothing to fear from Bulgars or Abars or Jews or Inquisitors."

Cacambo applauded this wise decision. He was in despair at the thought of parting from so good a master, who had become his close friend. But the pleasure of being of use to him outweighed the pain of leaving him. They tearfully embraced each other. Candide told him to make sure and not forget the kind old woman. Cacambo left the same day. He was a very fine fellow, Cacambo.

Candide stayed some while longer in Surinam, waiting to find another skipper who would be prepared to take him and his two remaining sheep to Italy. He engaged servants and bought everything he needed for a long voyage. At last Mr. Van der Hartbargin, the master of a large ship, came and introduced himself.

"How much will you charge," he asked this man, "to take myself, my servants, my baggage, and these two sheep directly to Venice?"

The master asked ten thousand piastres. Candide did not hesitate.

"Hallo," the careful Van der Hartbargin said to himself, "this stranger parts with ten thousand piastres just like that! He must be pretty rich."

He came back at him a moment later and indicated that he could not sail for less than twenty thousand.

"Very well, then, you shall have them," said Candide.

"Blow me!" said the merchant under his breath. "This man parts with twenty thousand piastres as easily as ten."

He came back at him once more and said that he could not take him to Venice for less than thirty thousand piastres.

"Then thirty thousand it is," replied Candide.

"Hallo, indeed!" the Dutch merchant said to himself again. "Thirty thousand piastres are nothing to this man. Those two sheep must be carrying immense treasures. Better not press things any further. Let's get paid the thirty thousand piastres first, and then we'll see."

Candide sold two little diamonds, the smaller of which was worth more than all the money the shipmaster was asking. He paid him in advance. The two sheep were loaded on board. Candide was following behind in a small boat to join the ship moored out in the roads,[9] when the master calmly set his sails and weighed anchor. The wind favoured him. Candide, helpless and quite flabbergasted, soon lost sight of him.

"Alas!" he lamented, "that's just the kind of dirty trick you'd expect from the old world."

He returned to the shore deep in misery, for, after all, he had lost what would have been enough to make the fortune of twenty monarchs.

He took himself off to the Dutch Resident Magistrate and, as he was a little upset, knocked rather peremptorily on the door. In he went, explained what had happened to him, and shouted rather more loudly than was proper. The magistrate began by fining him ten thousand piastres for the noise he had made. Then he listened to him patiently, promised to look into his case as soon as the merchant returned, and charged a further ten thousand piastres for the cost of the hearing.

This treatment was the last straw for Candide in his despair. To be sure, he had suffered misfortunes a thousand times more grievous, but the sang-froid of the magistrate, and of that shipmaster who had robbed him, stirred his bile and plunged him

9. Sheltered water near shore.

into a black melancholy. The wickedness of men struck him in all its ugliness, and his mind fed on images of gloom. Finally, there being a French vessel all ready to sail for Bordeaux, and as he had no more sheep laden with diamonds to place aboard, he paid for a cabin on the ship at the standard price, and made it known in the town that he would pay passage and board for, and give two thousand piastres to, any respectable person who would make the journey with him, on condition that this person was the most disgusted with his lot and the unhappiest man in the province.

A crowd of applicants came forward such as an entire fleet could not have carried. Wanting to choose among the most likely candidates, Candide selected twenty who seemed to him fairly companionable and who all claimed to deserve preference. He got them together in his inn and gave them supper on condition that each would swear to give a faithful version of his story. He undertook to choose the one who would seem to him most to be pitied and to have the greatest reason for being the most dis-satisfied with his lot. To the others he promised a small consideration.

The session lasted until four o'clock in the morning. Candide, as he listened to all their adventures, recalled what the old woman had said to him on their way to Buenos Aires and how she had wagered that not a single person on board would not have suf-fered very great misfortunes. He thought of Pangloss with every story he was told.

"Pangloss," he said, "would be hard put to it to prove his system. I wish he were here. One thing's certain: if all is going well, it's happening in Eldorado and not in the rest of the world."

In the end he decided in favour of a poor scholar who had spent ten years working for the publishing houses of Amsterdam. He took the view that there was no form of employment in the world with which one could possibly be more disgusted.[1]

This man of learning, who was a perfectly decent fellow moreover, had been robbed by his wife, assaulted by his son, and abandoned by his daughter, who had eloped with a Portuguese. He had just been removed from a small post which had pro-vided him with a living, and the preachers of Surinam were persecuting him because they took him for a Socinian.[2] It must be admitted that the other applicants were at least as unhappy as him, but Candide hoped that the scholar would keep him amused on the voyage. All his rivals considered that Candide was doing them a great injus-tice, but he pacified them by giving them a hundred piastres each.

Chapter 20

WHAT HAPPENED TO CANDIDE AND MARTIN AT SEA

So the old scholar, who was called Martin, took ship for Bordeaux with Candide. Both had seen much and suffered much, and even if the ship had had to sail all the way from Surinam to Japan via the Cape of Good Hope, they would still have had matter enough to sustain their discussion of physical and moral evil throughout the entire voyage.

However, Candide had one great advantage over Martin, which was that he was still hoping to see Miss Cunégonde again, while Martin had nothing to hope for. Moreover, he had gold and diamonds, and although he had lost a hundred large sheep laden with the greatest treasure on earth, and although the Dutch master's villainy

---

1. Voltaire had had difficult dealings with Dutch publishers.
2. A sect resembling present-day Unitarians who denied the Trinity and Christ's divinity.

still rankled, nevertheless when he thought about what he had left in his pockets, and when he talked about Cunégonde, especially at the end of a meal, then he would be inclined to favour the philosophical system of Pangloss.

"But you, Mr. Martin," he said to the scholar, "what are your thoughts on all this? How do you see physical and moral evil?"

"Sir," replied Martin, "my priests accused me of being a Socinian, but the fact of the matter is that I am a Manichean."[3]

"You're pulling my leg," said Candide. "There aren't any Manicheans left any more."

"There's me," said Martin. "I can't help it. I just can't see things any other way."

"It's the devil in you," said Candide.

"He's mixed up in the affairs of this world to such an extent," said Martin, "that he may well be in me, just as he's in everything else. But to be frank, when I look about me on this globe, or rather this globule, I begin to think God has abandoned it to some malign being—apart from Eldorado, that is. I've scarcely seen one town that did not wish the ruination of its neighbour, or one family that did not want to see the end of another. Everywhere you look, the weak execrate the strong while they grovel at their feet, and the strong treat them like so many sheep, providing wool and meat to be sold. One million regimented assassins, rushing from one end of Europe to the other, commit murder and brigandage by the rule book in order to earn their daily bread, because there is no more respectable profession; and in the cities, where people appear to live in peace and the arts flourish, men are devoured by more envy, worry, and dissatisfaction than all the scourges of a city under siege. Secret sorrows are more cruel even than public tribulations. In short, I have seen so many of them, and suffered so many, that I am a Manichean."

"Yet there is good," Candide would answer.

"That's as may be," Martin would say, "but I've never met it."

In the middle of this debate, they heard the sound of cannon fire. The noise increased by the moment. Each of them grabbed his telescope. Two ships were to be seen engaging at a distance of about three miles. The wind brought both of these ships so close to the French vessel that they had the pleasure of seeing the engagement in perfect comfort. Eventually one ship let fly a broadside at the other that was so low and so accurate that it sank it. Candide and Martin could distinctly see a hundred men on the deck of the ship which was going down. They were all raising their hands heavenwards and letting out the most appalling screams. In an instant everything disappeared beneath the waves.

"Well, there you are," said Martin. "That's how men treat each other."

"It is true," said Candide. "The devil has had a hand in this business."

So saying, he noticed something bright red swimming near their ship. The ship's launch was lowered to go and see what it could be. It was one of his sheep. There was more joy in Candide at finding this one sheep than there had been sorrow at losing an hundredfold all laden with large Eldorado diamonds.

The French captain soon observed that the captain of the sinker was Spanish, while the captain of the sunk was a Dutch pirate. It was the very man who had robbed Candide. The immense riches with which this villain had absconded had gone down with him, and all that had been saved was one sheep.

---

3. Ancient religious philosophy that posits two equal forces of good and evil governing the world; one of the earliest Christian heresies.

"You see," Candide said to Martin, "crime is sometimes punished. That scoundrel of a Dutch skipper got the fate he deserved."

"Yes," said Martin, "but did the passengers on his ship have to perish also? God punished the rogue: the devil drowned the rest."

Meanwhile the French and Spanish ships resumed their voyages, and Candide and Martin their conversations. They argued for a solid fortnight, and at the end of the fortnight they were as far forward as the day they began. But, well, they talked, and exchanged ideas, and consoled each other. Candide would stroke his sheep and say:

"I have found you, so I may well be able to find Cunégonde."

Chapter 21

CANDIDE AND MARTIN APPROACH THE FRENCH COAST
AND REASON TOGETHER

At last they came in sight of the French coast.

"Have you ever been to France, Mr. Martin?" said Candide.

"Yes," said Martin, "I've travelled through several of its provinces. There are some where half the inhabitants are mad, one or two where they're too clever by half, some where they're generally quite gentle and rather stupid, and others where they try to be witty. And in all of them the principal occupation is love. Next comes slander and gossip, and third comes talking nonsense."

"But, Mr. Martin, have you been to Paris?"

"Yes, I've been to Paris. There they have all of these types. It's chaos there, a throng in which everyone is searching for pleasure and where practically no one finds it, at least not as far as I could see. I haven't spent much time there. When I arrived, I was robbed of everything I had by pickpockets at the Saint-Germain fair. I myself was taken for a thief and spent a week in prison, after which I did some proof-reading to earn enough to be able to return to Holland on foot. I got to know the pen-pushing brigade, and the political intriguers, and the religious convulsions crowd.[4] They say there are some very well-mannered people in that city. I dare say there are."

"Personally I have no desire to see France," said Candide. "As I'm sure you can imagine, when one's spent a month in Eldorado, there's nothing in the world one much wants to see other than Miss Cunégonde. I'm on my way to wait for her in Venice. We will be going through France to get to Italy. Why don't you come with me?"

"Delighted to," said Martin. "They say Venice is only fit to live in if you're a Venetian nobleman, but that foreigners are well looked after none the less, providing they have a lot of money. I haven't, you have; I'll follow you anywhere."

"Incidentally," said Candide, "do you believe the Earth was originally a sea, as they say it was in that big book the captain has?"[5]

"I don't believe anything of the sort," said Martin, "no more than I believe any of the other rubbish they've been coming out with recently."

"But for what purpose was this world created then?" said Candide.

"To drive us mad," replied Martin.

"Don't you find it absolutely amazing," Candide went on, "the way the two girls I told you about, the ones who lived in the land of the Lobeiros, loved those two monkeys?"

---

4. Jansenist extremists, who were known for convulsions and trances, through which they supposedly performed miracles.
5. Probably the Bible, in which God creates the sea before dry land (Genesis 1).

"Not at all," said Martin. "I don't see what's odd about that particular passion. I've seen so many extraordinary things that nothing's extraordinary any more."

"Do you think," said Candide, "that men have always massacred each other the way they do now? that they've always been liars, cheats, traitors, ingrates, brigands? that they've always been feeble, fickle, envious, gluttonous, drunken, avaricious, ambitious, bloodthirsty, slanderous, debauched, fanatical, hypocritical, and stupid?"

"Do you think," said Martin, "that hawks have always eaten pigeons when they find them?"

"Yes, no doubt," said Candide.

"Well, then," said Martin, "if hawks have always had the same character, why do you expect men to have changed theirs?"

"Oh!" said Candide, "there's a big difference, because free will..." Arguing thus the while, they arrived in Bordeaux.

Chapter 22

What happened to Candide and Martin in France

Candide broke his journey in Bordeaux just long enough to sell a few Eldorado pebbles and to procure a good post-chaise with two seats, for he could no longer be without Martin, his philosopher. He was only very sorry to be parted from his sheep, which he left with the Academy of Science at Bordeaux. They set as the subject of that year's prize the question why the wool of this sheep was red, and the prize was awarded to a scientist from the North[6] who proved by A plus B minus C divided by Z that the sheep had necessarily to be red, and to die of sheep-pox.

Meanwhile all the travellers Candide met in the inns along the way told him: "We're off to Paris." In the end this universal eagerness made him want to see that capital city. It would not take him much out of his way on his journey to Venice.

He entered by the Faubourg Saint-Marceau and thought he was in the ugliest village in Westphalia.

Scarce had Candide put up at his inn than he was laid low by a minor indisposition brought on by his exertions. As he had an enormous diamond on his finger, and as an extremely heavy strong box had been noticed among his luggage, he soon had by him two doctors whom he had not sent for, a number of bosom companions who never left his side, and two ladies of good works who were heating up his broth.

Martin said:

"I remember being ill on my first trip to Paris too. I was very poor, so I had no friends or do-gooders or doctors, and I got better."

Meanwhile, by dint of many potions and bloodlettings, Candide's illness became serious. A local priest came and kindly asked him for a confessional note payable to bearer in the other world.[7] Candide would have none of it. The ladies of good works assured him that it was the new fashion. Candide replied that he was not a one for fashion. Martin was for throwing the priest out of the window. The cleric swore that Candide would not be granted burial. Martin swore that he would bury the cleric if he continued to bother them. The quarrel grew more heated. Martin took him by the

---

6. A reference to Maupertuis, the president of Frederick the Great's Berlin Academy of Sciences, who was often ridiculed by Voltaire.

7. In order to receive the last sacraments, Parisians were required to present a note from their confessor indicating they had subscribed to the Papal Bull *Unigenitus,* which condemned the Jansenist heresy.

shoulders and unceremoniously ejected him. This caused a great scandal, which was the subject of an official enquiry.

Candide recovered, and during his convalescence he had some very fine company to supper with him. There was gambling for high stakes. Candide was most surprised never to get a single ace, and Martin was not surprised.

Among those who did him the honours of the city was a little abbé[8] from Périgord, one of those busy little, pushy, fawning, frightfully accommodating types, always on the make, always ready to please, who lie in wait for strangers passing through and give them all the local gossip and scandal and offer them entertainments at all sorts of prices. This one took Candide and Martin to the theatre first. A new tragedy was on. Candide found himself sitting next to some of the intellectual smart set. This did not prevent him from crying at scenes that were played to perfection.

One of these arbiters of taste sitting near him said to him during an interval:

"You are quite wrong to cry. That actress is very bad. The actor playing opposite her is still worse. The play is even worse than the actors. The author doesn't know a word of Arabic, and yet the play is set in Arabia.[9] And what's more, the man doesn't believe in innate ideas. Tomorrow I can bring you twenty pamphlets criticizing him."

"Sir, how many plays do you have in France?" Candide asked the abbé, who replied:

"Five or six thousand."

"That's a lot," said Candide. "How many of them are any good?"

"Fifteen or sixteen," was the answer.

"That's a lot," said Martin.

Candide was much taken with an actress who was playing Queen Elizabeth in a rather dull tragedy which is sometimes put on.

"I do like that actress," he said to Martin. "She looks a bit like Miss Cunégonde. I should be rather pleased to call on her."

The abbé from Périgord offered to effect an introduction. Candide, brought up in Germany, asked what the form was and how queens of England were treated in France.

"We must distinguish," said the abbé. "In the provinces you take them to an inn. In Paris you respect them when they're beautiful, and you throw them on to the rubbish-heap when they're dead."[1]

"Queens on the rubbish-heap!" said Candide.

"Yes, really," said Martin. "The abbé is right. I was in Paris when Mlle Monime passed, as they say, from this life to the next. She was refused what people here call 'the honours of the grave,' that is to say of rotting in a filthy cemetery with all the beggars of the neighbourhood. Unlike the rest of her troupe she was buried alone at the corner of the rue de Bourgogne, which must have pained her exceedingly, for she thought very nobly."

"That's not a very nice way to treat people," said Candide.

"What can you expect?" said Martin. "That's the way they are round here. Take any contradiction or inconsistency you can think of, and you will find it in the government, the courts, the churches, or the theatres of this strange nation."

"Is it true that people in Paris are always laughing?" enquired Candide.

---

8. French clergyman.

9. Voltaire himself had written a play, *Mahomet*, set in Arabia.

1. Actors and actresses were denied Christian burial in France at this time; Voltaire had assisted in the secret burial of an actress in 1730.

"Yes," said the abbé, "but through gritted teeth. For they complain about everything with great gales of laughter, and they laugh even when doing the most detestable things."

"Who," asked Candide, "was the fat pig who was telling me so many bad things about that play I cried such a lot at, and about those actors I liked so much?"

"He is evil incarnate," replied the abbé. "He earns his living by decrying all new plays and books. He hates the up-and-coming writer, just as eunuchs hate the up-and-coming lover. He's one of those vipers of literature that feeds off filth and venom. He's a hack."

"What do you mean by 'hack'?" said Candide.

"I mean," said the abbé, "someone who churns out articles by the dozen, a Fréron."[2]

Such was the discussion between Candide, Martin, and the man from Périgord as they stood on the staircase, watching people pass by on their way out after the play.

"Although I can't wait to see Miss Cunégonde again," said Candide, "nevertheless I would like to have supper with Mlle Clairon,[3] for she did seem quite admirable to me."

The abbé was not the right man for an approach to Mlle Clairon, who moved only in the best circles.

"She has a prior engagement this evening," he said, "but if you will allow me the honour of taking you to a lady of quality, there you will get to meet Paris society as if you'd already been living here for years."

Candide, who was curious by nature, allowed himself to be taken to the lady, at the bottom end of the Faubourg Saint-Honoré.[4] There they were busy playing faro.[5] Twelve sad punters each held a small hand of cards, the dog-eared register of their misfortunes. A profound silence reigned; pallor was upon the punters' brows, anxiety upon that of the banker; and the lady of the house, seated beside this implacable banker, noted with the eyes of a lynx all the doubling up and any illegal antes whenever each player turned down the corner of his card. She would make them turn the corners back with firm but polite insistence, and never lost her temper for fear of losing her clients. This lady called herself the Marchioness of Dubelauchwitz. Her daughter, aged fifteen, was one of the punters and would indicate with a wink any cheating on the part of these poor people endeavouring to repair the cruel blows of fate. The abbé from Périgord, Candide, and Martin walked in. No one got up, or greeted them, or looked at them; they were all deeply engrossed in their cards.

"The Baroness of Thunder-ten-tronckh was more civil," said Candide.

Meanwhile the abbé had a word in the ear of the Marchioness, who half rose and honoured Candide with a gracious smile and Martin with a thoroughly grand tilt of the head. She had Candide given a seat and dealt a hand: he lost fifty thousand francs in two rounds. Afterwards they supped merrily, and everyone was surprised that Candide was not more upset about his losses. The lackeys said to each other in their own lackey language:

"He must be one of your English lords."

The supper was like most suppers in Paris. First, silence; then a cacaphonous welter of words which no one can make out; and then jokes, which mostly fall flat, false

2. Name of one of Voltaire's harshest critics, who had panned his play *Tancrède*.
3. An actress who often performed in Voltaire's plays.
4. A wealthy section of Paris.
5. Popular card game in which "punters" bet against the bank.

rumours, false arguments, a smattering of politics, and a quantity of slander. They even talked about the latest books.

"Have you read," said the abbé from Périgord, "that nonsense by Master Gauchat,[6] doctor of theology?"

"Yes," replied one of the party, "but I couldn't finish it. There's enough irrelevant rubbish in print as it is, but the whole lot put together doesn't come anywhere near the irrelevance of Master Gauchat, doctor of theology. I'm so sick of this great flood of detestable books that I've taken to punting at faro."

"And the *Miscellany* of Archdeacon T...?[7] What do you think of that?" said the abbé.

"Oh," said the Marchioness of Dubelauchwitz, "that crashing bore! The way he tells you with great interest what everybody knows already! The ponderous discussion of points that aren't even worth a passing reference! The witless way he borrows other people's wit! How he ruins what he filches! How he disgusts me! But he won't disgust me any further. One or two pages of the archdeacon are quite enough."

At table there was a man of taste and learning, who agreed with what the Marchioness was saying. Conversation then moved on to tragedies. The lady asked why it was that some tragedies were staged from time to time but were totally unreadable. The man of taste explained very well how a play could be of some interest but of almost no merit. He showed in a few words how it was not enough to contrive one or two of the stock situations which can be found in any novel, and which always captivate the audience, but that one had to be original without being far-fetched; often sublime and always natural; to know the human heart and to make it speak; to be a great poet without any of the characters in the play appearing to be poets themselves; to have perfect command of one's own language, and to use it with fluent euphony, without forcing it, and without ever sacrificing the sense to the rhyme.

"Whoever fails to follow every one of these rules," he added, "may produce one or two tragedies that are applauded in the theatre, but he will never be counted a good writer. There are very few good tragedies. Some are simply idylls in a dialogue that happens to be well-written and well-rhymed; some have political messages, and send you to sleep, while others are so overdone they fail to move; and some are the fantasies of fanatics, written in a barbarous style with broken-off sentences and long speeches to the gods—because they don't know how to communicate with human beings—and full of false maxims and pompous platitudes."

Candide listened attentively to these remarks and formed a high opinion of the speaker. As the Marchioness had taken good care to place Candide next to her, he took the liberty of asking, by means of a whisper in her ear, who this man was who spoke so well.

"He's a man of learning," said the lady, "who doesn't gamble and whom the abbé brings to supper sometimes. He knows all about tragedies and books, and he has himself written a tragedy, which was whistled off the stage, and a book, of which but one copy has ever been seen outside a bookshop, and that was the one he presented to me with a dedication."

"A great man!" said Candide. "He's another Pangloss."

Then, turning to him, he said:

6. Author of a series of refutations of Voltaire's *Encyclopédie*.
7. Trublet, another critic of Voltaire.

"Sir, doubtless you think that everything is for the best in the physical and moral worlds, and that things could not be other than as they are?"

"I, sir?" replied the man of learning. "I don't think anything of the sort. I find that everything in our world is amiss, that nobody knows his place or his responsibility, or what he's doing or what he should do, and that, except for supper parties, which are quite jolly and where people seem to get on reasonably well, the rest of the time is spent in pointless quarrelling: Jansenists with Molinists,[8] parliamentarians with churchmen, men of letters with men of letters, courtiers with courtiers, financiers with the general public, wives with husbands, relatives with relatives. It's one battle after another."

Candide answered him:

"I've seen worse ones. But a wise man, who has since had the misfortune to be hanged, told me that that's all fine. Those are just the shadows in a beautiful painting."

"Your hanged man was having people on," said Martin. "What you call shadows are horrible stains."

"It's human beings who make the stains," said Candide. "They can't help it."

"So it's not their fault," said Martin.

The majority of the punters, who did not understand a word of all this, were drinking. Martin had a discussion with the man of learning; and Candide recounted some of his adventures to the lady of the house.

After supper the Marchioness took Candide to her room and bid him be seated on a couch.

"Well, then," she said to him, "so you're still madly in love with Miss Cunégonde de Thunder-ten-tronckh?"

"Yes, madame."

The Marchioness returned a tender smile:

"You answer like the young man from Westphalia you are. A Frenchman would have said to me: 'It is true that I did once love Miss Cunégonde, but on seeing you, madame, I fear that I love her no longer.'"

"Oh, dear," said Candide. "Madame, I shall answer as you please."

"Your passion for her began," said the Marchioness, "when you picked up her handkerchief. I want you to pick up my garter."

"With all my heart," said Candide, and he picked it up.

"But I want you to put it back for me," said the lady, and Candide put it back for her.

"You see," she said, "you are a foreigner. Sometimes I make my Parisian lovers wait a whole fortnight, but here I am giving myself to you on the very first night, because one must do the honours of one's country to a young man from Westphalia."

The fair lady, having noticed two enormous diamonds on the hands of her young foreigner, enthused about them with such sincerity that from Candide's fingers they passed on to the fingers of the Marchioness.

Candide, as he returned home with his abbé from Périgord, felt some remorse at having been unfaithful to Miss Cunégonde. The abbé commiserated with him; he was only slightly responsible for the fifty thousand francs Candide had lost at cards and the value of the two brilliants which had been half given and half extorted. His object was to profit as much as he possibly could from the advantages that knowing

8. Followers of Luis Molina (1535–1600), a Spanish Jesuit who promoted the doctrine of free will. Jansenists, on the other hand, believed in predestination.

Candide might bring him. He asked him all about Cunégonde, and Candide told him that he would certainly beg that fair lady's pardon for his infidelity when he saw her in Venice.

The man from Périgord became even more courteous and attentive and took a touching interest in everything that Candide said, or did, or wanted to do.

"So you have arranged to meet in Venice then, sir?" he said.

"Yes, Monsieur l'abbé," said Candide. "I really must go and find Miss Cunégonde."

Then, drawn on by the pleasure of talking about the one he loved, he recounted, as was his wont, a part of his adventures with this illustrious Westphalian lady.

"I expect Miss Cunégonde is witty and clever," said the abbé, "and that she writes charming letters?"

"I've never had any from her," said Candide. "The thing is, you see, having been kicked out of the castle for loving her, I couldn't write to her, and then I learnt soon afterwards that she was dead, and then I found her again, and then I lost her, and then I sent an express messenger two thousand five hundred leagues to her, and I am still awaiting a reply."

The abbé listened attentively and seemed somewhat lost in thought. Soon he took his leave of the two strangers, after embracing them warmly. The next day, upon waking, Candide received the following letter:

> My very dear and beloved sir, I have been lying ill in this city for the past week. I discover that you are here too. I would fly to your arms if I could move. I heard in Bordeaux that you had passed through. I left the faithful Cacambo there and the old woman, and they are soon to follow on after me. The Governor of Buenos Aires took everything, but I still have your heart. Come to me. Your presence will restore me to life, or make me die of pleasure.

This charming, this unexpected letter sent Candide into transports of inexpressible joy, while the illness of his dear Cunégonde weighed him down with grief. Torn between these two emotions, he grabbed his gold and diamonds and had someone take him and Martin to the hotel where Miss Cunégonde was staying. He entered the room trembling with emotion, his heart aflutter, his voice choked. He made to open the curtains round the bed and was about to send for a lamp.

"Do no such thing," said the maid, "the light will kill her." And at once she shut the curtains:

"My dear Cunégonde," wept Candide, "How are you? If you cannot look at me, at least speak to me."

"She cannot speak," said the maid. The lady then drew from the bedclothes a chubby little hand, which Candide bathed with his tears for a long time and subsequently filled with diamonds, leaving a pouch full of gold on the chair.

In the midst of his transports an officer of the watch arrived, followed by the abbé from Périgord and a squad of men.

"Are these the two suspicious foreigners then?" he said.

He had them arrested on the spot and ordered his lads to haul them off to prison.

"This is not how they treat travellers in Eldorado," said Candide.

"I feel more Manichean than ever," said Martin.

"But, sir, where are you taking us?" said Candide.

"To the deepest of dark dungeons," said the officer.

Martin, having recovered his sang-froid, judged that the lady claiming to be Cunégonde was a fraud, the abbé from Périgord a scoundrel who had taken advantage of

Candide's innocence at the earliest opportunity, and the officer another scoundrel, whom it would be easy to be rid of.

Rather than be exposed to the process of law, Candide, enlightened by Martin's counsel and, more especially, ever impatient to see the real Miss Cunégonde again, offered the officer three little diamonds worth about three thousand pistoles each.

"Ah, sir," the man with the ivory baton said to him, "had you committed every crime in the book, you'd still be the most honest man alive. Three diamonds! And each worth three thousand pistoles! Sir, I'd sooner die for you than take you to a dungeon. There are orders to arrest all foreigners, but leave it to me. I have a brother in Normandy, in Dieppe, I'll take you there. And if you have a diamond or two to give him, he'll take care of you as if it were myself he was looking after."

"And why are they arresting all foreigners?" says Candide.

The abbé from Périgord intervened:

"It's because a wretch from Atrabatia listened to some silly talk, which was all it took to make him commit parricide—not like the one in May 1610 but like the one in December 1594, and like several others committed in other months and other years by other wretches who had listened to similar silly talk."[9]

The officer then explained what this was all about.

"Ah, the monsters!" exclaimed Candide. "What! Such horrors, and from a people that loves singing and dancing! Can't I leave this very minute? Let me out of this country where monkeys provoke tigers. I have seen bears in my own country; I have seen men only in Eldorado. In the name of God, officer, take me to Venice, where I am to wait for Miss Cunégonde."

"Lower Normandy is the best I can do," said the right arm of the law.

Thereupon he had his irons removed, said he must have made a mistake, dismissed his men, and took Candide and Martin to Dieppe and left them in the hands of his brother. There was a small Dutch ship out in the roads. The Norman, who with the help of three more diamonds had now become the most obliging of men, put Candide and his servants aboard the ship, which was about to set sail for Portsmouth in England. It was not the way to Venice, but Candide felt as though he was being delivered from hell, and he fully intended to rejoin the route to Venice at the first opportunity.

Chapter 23

CANDIDE AND MARTIN PROCEED TO THE SHORES OF ENGLAND; WHAT THEY SEE THERE

"Ah, Pangloss! Pangloss! Ah, Martin! Martin! Ah, my dear Cunégonde! What sort of a world is this?" Candide was asking on board the Dutch ship.

"A rather mad and rather awful one," answered Martin.

"You know England. Are they as mad there as they are in France?"

"It's a different kind of madness," said Martin. "As you know, the two countries are at war over a few acres of snow across in Canada, and they're spending more on this war than the whole of Canada is worth.[1] To tell you exactly if there are more people who should be locked up in one country than in the other is something my

9. Atrabatia is the Latin name for the French province Artois, the birthplace of Damiens, who attempted to assassinate Louis XV in 1757. Châtel attempted to assassinate Henry IV in December 1594, and in May 1610 Ravaillac assassinated Henry IV.

1. This colonial struggle between Britain and France culminated in the French and Indian War. It was resolved in 1763 by the Treaty of Paris, which transferred Canada from French to British control.

feeble lights do not permit. All I know is that, by and large, the people we are going to see are extremely glum."[2]

Thus conversing, they landed at Portsmouth. A multitude of people covered the shore, all gazing intently at a rather stout man who was kneeling blindfold on the deck of one of the naval ships. Four soldiers, posted opposite this man, each fired three shots into his skull, as calmly as you please, and the assembled multitude then dispersed, thoroughly satisfied.

"What is all this?" said Candide. "And what demon is it that holds such universal sway?"

He asked who this stout man was who had just been ceremonially killed.

"He's an admiral," came the answer.[3]

"And why kill this admiral?"

"Because he didn't kill enough people," Candide was told. "He gave battle to a French admiral, and it has been found that he wasn't close enough."

"But," said Candide, "the French admiral was just as far away from the English admiral as he was from him!"

"Unquestionably," came the reply. "But in this country it is considered a good thing to kill an admiral from time to time so as to encourage the others."

Candide was so dumbfounded and so shocked by what he was seeing and hearing that he refused even to set foot ashore, and he negotiated with the Dutch master of the ship (it was just too bad if he fleeced him like the one in Surinam) to take him to Venice as soon as possible.

The master was ready in two days. They sailed down the French coast. They passed within sight of Lisbon, and Candide shuddered. They entered the straits and the Mediterranean. At last they put in at Venice.

"God be praised!" said Candide, embracing Martin. "This is where I shall see fair Cunégonde again. I trust Cacambo as I would myself. All is well, all is going well, all is going as well as it possibly can."

Chapter 24

Of Paquette and Brother Giroflée

As soon as he reached Venice, he instigated a search for Cacambo in every inn and coffee house, and in all the brothels. He was nowhere to be found. Each day he had enquiries made of every new ship or boat that came in. No sign of Cacambo.

"I don't know," he was saying to Martin. "I have had time to cross from Surinam to Bordeaux, to go from Bordeaux to Paris, from Paris to Dieppe, from Dieppe to Portsmouth, to sail the length of Portugal and Spain, to cross the entire Mediterranean, to spend several months in Venice, and fair Cunégonde has still not got here! All I've encountered instead is some hussy and an abbé from Périgord. Cunégonde is probably dead, so I may as well die too. Ah! it would have been better to remain in the paradise of Eldorado than come back to this accursed Europe. How right you are, my dear Martin! All is but illusion and calamity."

2. The British were thought to be characteristically melancholic.

3. Admiral Byng, who had been in charge of British naval forces during their defeat by the French in a battle off Minorca, was court-martialed and tried for cowardice. He was executed by firing squad on his own quarterdeck in 1757; Voltaire had unsuccessfully attempted to intercede on Byng's behalf.

He sank into a dark melancholy and took no part in the opera *alla moda* or in any of the other carnival entertainments. Not a single lady caused him a moment's temptation.

Martin said to him:

"You really are rather simple to imagine that a half-caste[4] manservant with five or six millions in his pocket will go and look for your lady-love on the other side of the world and bring her to you in Venice. He'll take her for himself if he finds her. If he doesn't find her, he'll take somebody else. My advice to you is to forget your manservant Cacambo and your beloved Cunégonde."

Martin was not consoling. Candide's melancholy deepened, and Martin kept on proving to him that there was little virtue and little happiness in this world—except perhaps in Eldorado, where no one could ever go.

While they disputed this important subject and waited for Cunégonde, Candide noticed a young Theatine[5] monk in Saint Mark's Square, who was walking with a girl on his arm. The Theatine had a fresh, chubby, robust appearance. His eyes shone, and there was an air of assurance about him. His expression was haughty, his gait proud. The girl, who was very pretty, was singing. She gazed lovingly at her Theatine, and tweaked his pudgy cheeks from time to time.

"You'll grant me at least," Candide said to Martin, "that those two are happy. So far, throughout the inhabited world, I have encountered only unfortunates—except in Eldorado, that is. But as for that girl and her Theatine, I bet they are very happy creatures."

"I bet they're not," said Martin.

"All we have to do is to invite them to dinner," said Candide, "and you'll see if I'm wrong."

Thereupon he went up to them, presented his compliments, and invited them back to his hostelry for some macaroni, Lombardy partridge, and caviar, washed down with Montepulciano, lachryma Christi,[6] and some of the wines of Cyprus and Samos. The young lady blushed, the Theatine accepted the invitation, and the girl followed him, glancing at Candide with eyes wide in surprise and embarrassment and clouded with tears.

Scarcely had she entered Candide's room than she said to him:

"Well? Doesn't Master Candide recognize Paquette any more?"

At these words Candide, who had not looked at her closely until then (because he had thoughts only for Cunégonde), said to her:

"Oh dear, my poor girl, so you are the one who got Dr. Pangloss into the fine state I saw him in?"

"Alas, sir, I am indeed," said Paquette. "I see you know all about it. I heard about the dreadful misfortunes that befell Her Ladyship's household and the fair Miss Cunégonde. I swear to you, my own fate has hardly been less wretched. I was utterly innocent when last you saw me. A Franciscan monk who was my confessor had no difficulty in seducing me. The consequences were terrible. I was obliged to leave the castle not long after His Lordship kicked you up the backside and sent you packing. If a famous doctor had not taken pity on me, I'd have had it. For a time I became the doctor's mistress, as a way of showing my gratitude. His wife, who was madly

4. Mixed-race.
5. An order founded in 1524.
6. Fine Italian wines.

jealous, beat me every day without mercy. She was a fury. This doctor was the ugliest of men, and I the unhappiest of creatures to be continually beaten for a man I did not love. As you know, sir, it's very dangerous for a shrewish woman to have a doctor for a husband. One day, sick and tired of the way his wife was behaving, he treated her for a slight cold by giving her some medicine, which proved so effective that within two hours she was dead, having had some horrible convulsions. The mistress's family brought an action against the master. He upped and fled, and I was put in prison. My innocence would not have saved me had I not been reasonably pretty. The judge let me go on condition that he would succeed the doctor. I was soon supplanted by a rival, dismissed without a penny, and obliged to continue in this unspeakable profession which seems so harmless to you men, and which for us is nothing but a vale of tears. I chose Venice to practise my profession in. Oh, sir, if you could imagine what it's like having to caress just anybody, an old merchant, a lawyer, a monk, a gondolier, an abbé; to be exposed to all manner of insult and degradation; to be reduced often to having to borrow a skirt, only then to go and have it lifted up by some disgusting man or other; to be robbed by one of what one's earned with another; to be held to ransom by officers of the law, and to have nothing to look forward to but a gruesome old age, the workhouse, and the rubbish-heap; then you would agree that I am one of the unhappiest and most unfortunate creatures alive."

This was how, in a private room in the hostelry, Paquette opened her heart to good Candide in the presence of Martin, who said to Candide:

"You see, I've already won half my bet."

Brother Giroflée had remained in the dining-room, and was having a drink as he waited for dinner.

"But," Candide said to Paquette, "you were looking so gay, so happy, when I ran into you. You were singing, you were fondling the Theatine quite naturally and willingly. You seemed to me every bit as happy as you say you are unhappy."

"Ah, sir," replied Paquette, "that's another of the awful things about our profession. Yesterday I was robbed and beaten by an officer, and today I have to appear to be in a good mood just to please a monk."

That was enough for Candide; he admitted that Martin was right. They sat down to dinner with Paquette and the Theatine. The meal was quite good-humoured, and at the end they were all talking to each other with some degree of freedom.

"Father," Candide said to the monk, "you seem to me to be enjoying the kind of life everyone must envy. You are the picture of health, you have a happy face, you have a very pretty girl to keep you amused, and you seem perfectly content with your monastic condition."

"By my faith, sir," said Brother Giroflée, "I wish all Theatines were at the bottom of the sea. I've been tempted a hundred times to set fire to the monastery and to go and turn Turk.[7] My parents forced me to don this detestable habit at the age of fifteen so that I would leave a bigger fortune for my damned elder brother, may God confound him! The monastery is rife with jealousy, and backbiting, and bad feeling. It's true that I have preached a few miserable sermons that have brought me in some money, half of which the Prior steals—the rest I use for keeping girls. But when I get back to the monastery in the evening, I'm ready to beat my head in on the dormitory walls. And all the brothers feel the same way."

---

7. A common expression signifying the ultimate infidelity or treachery.

Martin turned to Candide with his usual sang-froid:

"Well?" he said. "Have I not won the whole bet?"

Candide gave Paquette two thousand piastres, and Brother Giroflée a thousand.

"I guarantee you," he said, "that with this money they'll be happy."

"I shouldn't think so for a minute," said Martin. "With these piastres you may make them even more unhappy still."

"Whatever shall be, shall be," said Candide. "But one thing consoles me. I see that people one never thought to see again often do turn up. It may well turn out that, having run into my red sheep and Paquette, I will also run into Cunégonde."

"I wish," said Martin, "that she may one day make you happy. But I very much doubt she will."

"You are a bit hard," said Candide.

"That's because I've lived," said Martin.

"But look at those gondoliers," said Candide. "They're always singing, aren't they?"

"You don't see them at home with their wives and screaming children," said Martin. "The doge[8] has his problems, the gondoliers have theirs. It is true that, all things considered, the life of a gondolier is preferable to that of a doge, but I think there's so little in it that it's not worth arguing about."

"I've heard people talk," said Candide, "about a Senator Pococurante[9] who lives in that beautiful palace on the Brenta, and who's very hospitable to visiting foreigners. They say he's a man who's never had any troubles."

"I'd like to meet such a rare breed," said Martin.

Candide at once sent someone to ask the noble Signor Pococurante's permission to call on him the following day.

Chapter 25

The visit to Signor Pococurante, a Venetian nobleman

Candide and Martin proceeded down the Brenta by gondola and came to the palace of the noble Pococurante. The gardens were well laid out and embellished with beautiful marble statues, while the palace itself was a fine piece of architecture. The master of the house, a man of sixty, and very rich, received the two curious visitors most politely but with very little fuss, which disconcerted Candide and did not displease Martin.

First, two pretty and neatly dressed girls poured out some chocolate, managing to give it a good frothy top. Candide could not help but compliment them on their beauty, their kindness, and their skill.

"They're not bad creatures," said Senator Pococurante. "I have them sleep with me sometimes, because I'm rather tired of the society ladies here with all their flirting, and their jealousy, and their quarrelling, and their moods, and their petty-mindedness, and their arrogance, and their silliness, not to mention the sonnets you have to compose, or have composed, for them. But, well, in the end I'm beginning to find these two girls exceedingly boring too."

Candide, walking in a long gallery after lunch, was surprised at the beauty of the paintings. He asked which master had painted the first two.

"They're by Raphael,"[1] said the Senator. "I bought them out of vanity some years ago for a considerable amount of money. They are said to be the finest in Italy, but I

8. Chief magistrate of Venice.

9. "Caring little."

1. Famous Renaissance painter whose works were known for their clarity of form and subtle gravity.

don't like them at all. The colouring is very dark, the faces aren't sufficiently rounded and don't stand out enough, and the draperies don't bear the slightest resemblance to any real cloth. Basically, whatever anyone may say, I don't consider they're a true imitation of nature. You'll only get me to like a picture when I think I'm looking at nature itself—and there aren't any like that. I have lots of paintings, but I don't look at them any more."

As they waited for dinner, Pococurante gave orders for a concerto to be played. Candide found the music delightful.

"This sort of noise helps pass the odd half-hour," said Pococurante, "but if it goes on any longer, everybody finds it tedious, though no one dares say so. Nowadays music is simply nothing more than the art of playing difficult pieces, and that which is merely difficult gives no pleasure in the end.

"Perhaps I'd prefer opera, if they hadn't found a way of turning it into a monstrous hybrid which I find quite repugnant. Let anyone who wishes go and see bad tragedies set to music, with all those scenes that have been put together simply as pretexts—and pretty poor ones at that—for two or three ridiculous songs which allow an actress to show off her vocal cords. Let anyone that wants to—and that can—go and swoon away with ecstasy at the sight of a *castrato* humming the roles of Caesar and Cato[2] and strutting about the stage in that ungainly fashion. For my part I have long since given up going to these paltry affairs, even though nowadays they are the glory of Italy and put its ruling princes to so much expense."

Candide demurred somewhat, though with tact. Martin was entirely of the Senator's opinion.

They sat down to eat, and after an excellent dinner, they went into the library. Candide, on seeing a magnificently bound edition of Homer, complimented his most illustrious host on his good taste.

"This book," he said, "used to delight the great Pangloss, the finest philosopher in Germany."

"It doesn't delight me," said Pococurante coolly. "They did once have me believe that I took pleasure in reading it. But that endless repetition of combats which all seem the same, those gods who are always doing things but never getting anywhere, that Helen who causes the war and then plays scarcely any part in the thing, that Troy they besiege and never take, I found all that deadly boring. I've sometimes asked men of learning if they found reading it as boring as I did. The honest ones admitted that the book used to drop from their hands, but said that you had to have it in your library, like an ancient monument, or like those rusty medals that have no commercial value."

"Your Excellency doesn't think the same about Virgil?" said Candide.

"I agree that the second, fourth, and sixth books of the *Aeneid* are excellent," said Pococurante. "But as for his pious Aeneas, and valiant Cloanthus, and faithful Achates, and little Ascanius, not to mention half-witted King Latinus, and parochial Amata, and insipid Lavinia, I can think of nothing more disagreeable or more likely to leave one absolutely cold. I prefer Tasso and those improbable tales of Ariosto."[3]

"Dare I ask, sir," said Candide, "whether Horace does not afford you considerable pleasure?"

2. Caesar and Cato are the two principal roles in Vivaldi's 1735 opera *Catone in Utica;* such serious heroic roles were commonly sung by castrati. The joke is that Roman statesmen are represented by eunuchs.

3. Voltaire faithfully traces the history of the epic here. Homer's *Iliad* (which recounts the Trojan War) and *Odyssey* were imitated by Virgil's *Aeneid*. Ariosto's *Orlando Furioso* and Tasso's *Gerusalemme Liberata* in turn were partly modeled on the *Aeneid.*

"There are one or two maxims," said Pococurante, "which a man of the world may profit by, and which fix themselves more readily in the memory for being compressed in powerful verse. But I care very little for his journey to Brindisi, or the description of that poor dinner he had, or that foulmouthed quarrel between someone or other called Pupilus, whose language, he says, 'was full of pus,' and someone else whose language 'was like vinegar.' It was only with extreme distaste that I read his crude verses against old women and witches, and I cannot see what merit there can be in telling his friend Maecenas that if he were to place him among the ranks of the lyric poets, he would bang his sublime forehead on the stars in the heavens.[4] Fools admire everything in a respected author. I read only for myself. I like only what may be of use to me."

Candide, who had been brought up never to judge things for himself, was much astonished by what he heard; and Martin found Pococurante's way of thinking rather sensible.

"Oh, look! Here's a copy of Cicero," said Candide. "I'm sure when it comes to this great man, you never tire of reading him?"

"I never read him," replied the Venetian. "What does it matter to me whether he defended Rabirius or Cluentius?[5] What with the cases I try myself, I have quite enough of all that as it is. I might have got on better with his philosophical works, but when I saw that he doubted everything, I decided that I knew as much as he did, and that I didn't need anyone else's help if I was going to be ignorant."

"Ah, look, eighty volumes of the proceedings of an Academy of Science," exclaimed Martin. "There may be something worthwhile there."

"There would be," said Pococurante, "if but one of the authors of all that rubbish had so much as invented the art of making pins. But in every one of those books there's nothing but pointless theorizing, and not a single thing that's useful."

"What a lot of plays there are!" said Candide; "in Italian, in Spanish, in French!"

"Yes," said the Senator, "there are three thousand of them, and not three dozen good ones. As for the collected sermons, which between them aren't worth one page of Seneca, and all those fat tomes on theology, well, you can be sure I never open them, not I, not anyone."

Martin noticed some shelves full of English books.

"I imagine," he said, "that a republican[6] must find most of these enjoyable to read, given how free the authors were to write them?"

"Yes," answered Pococurante, "it is a fine thing to write what one thinks. It is man's privilege. Throughout this Italy of ours, people write only what they do not think. Those who live in the land of the Caesars and the Antonines dare not have an idea without obtaining permission from a Dominican friar. I would be content with the freedom which inspires these English men of genius if their passion for the party interest didn't spoil all the estimable things that would otherwise flow from this precious freedom."

Candide, catching sight of a copy of Milton, asked him if he did not regard this author as a great man.

"Who?" said Pococurante, "that barbarian with his long commentary on the first book of *Genesis* in ten books of difficult verse?[7] That crude imitator of the Greeks who

---

4. These refer to passages in Horace's *Satires* 1.5, 2.8, 1.7 (Voltaire changes Rupilius to Pupilus), *Epodes* 5, 8, 12, and *Odes* 1.1.

5. Referring to orations by Ciceros.

6. A citizen of a free republic like Venice.

7. *Paradise Lost,* the first edition of which was in ten books, and later in twelve books. As Pococurante implies, Milton's poem at points imitates the epics of Tasso and Ariosto (as well as those of Homer and Virgil). Voltaire criticized Milton along similar lines in his *Essay on Epic Poetry* and *Age of Louis XIV.*

gives such a distorted view of the Creation and, where Moses shows the Eternal Being producing the world with the spoken word, has the Messiah take a great big compass out of a tool-chest in heaven and start drawing a plan? Me, admire the man who ruined Tasso's vision of hell and the devil; who has Lucifer appear disguised variously as a toad or a pygmy; who makes him say the same things over and over again; who makes him discuss theological points; who takes Ariosto's bit of comic invention about the fire-arms seriously and has the devils firing the cannon into heaven? Neither I nor anyone else in Italy has ever been able to enjoy all these extravagant absurdities. The marriage of Sin and Death, and the adders to which Sin gives birth, are enough to make anyone with a delicate stomach vomit. And his long description of a hospital is fit only for a grave-digger. That obscure, bizarre, disgusting poem was spurned at birth. Now I treat it the way it was treated in its own time by the readers in its own country. Anyway, I say what I think, and I couldn't care less whether anyone thinks the way I do or not."

Candide was distressed to hear all this. He admired Homer, and he had a sneaking fondness for Milton.

"Oh, dear!" he said to Martin under his breath, "I'm very much afraid that this man may have a sovereign disregard for our German poets."

"There would be no great harm in that," said Martin.

"Oh, what a great man!" Candide continued to mutter to himself. "What a great genius this Pococurante is! There is no pleasing him."

Having thus inspected all the books, they went down into the garden. Candide praised all its finer features.

"I know of nothing that could be in worse possible taste," said the master of the house. "All you see here are just pretty bits and pieces. But, as from tomorrow, I'm going to have a new one planted along much nobler lines."

When the two curious visitors had taken their leave of His Excellency, Candide turned to Martin:

"Well, there you are," he said. "You will agree that there is the happiest of men, for he is above all that he owns."

"Don't you see," said Martin, "that he's sated on everything he owns? Plato said a long time ago that the best stomachs are not those which reject all foods."

"But," said Candide, "isn't there pleasure in criticizing everything, in finding fault where other men think they find beauty?"

"Which is to say," rejoined Martin, "that there's pleasure in not having pleasure?"

"Oh, all right. Have it your way then," said Candide. "So the only one who's happy is me, when I see Miss Cunégonde again."

"One does well to hope," said Martin.

Meanwhile the days, the weeks went by. Still Cacambo did not return, and Candide was so sunk in misery that it did not even occur to him that Paquette and Brother Giroflée had not so much as come to thank him.

Chapter 26

OF A SUPPER THAT CANDIDE AND MARTIN ATE IN THE COMPANY OF SIX STRANGERS, AND WHO THEY WERE

One evening as Candide, accompanied by Martin, was about to sit down to table with the other passing strangers staying in the same hostelry, a man with a face the colour of soot came up behind him and, taking him by the arm, said:

"Be ready to leave when we do, and do not fail."

He turned round: it was Cacambo. Only the sight of Cunégonde could have surprised and pleased him more. He went nearly mad with joy. He embraced his dear friend.

"Cunégonde must be here, then. Where is she? Take me to her. Let me die of joy with her."

"Cunégonde is not here," said Cacambo. "She's in Constantinople."

"Ah, heavens! In Constantinople! But were she in China, I should fly to her! Let's go!"

"We will leave after supper," replied Cacambo. "I can't say any more. I'm a slave and my master's waiting for me. I've got to go and wait on him at table. Don't breathe a word. Have supper, and then be ready and waiting."

Candide, torn between joy and pain, absolutely delighted to have seen his faithful agent again, surprised to see him now a slave, full of the idea of being reunited with his beloved, his heart in tumult and his mind in a spin, sat down to eat in the company of Martin, who was watching all these goings-on with equanimity, and of the six strangers who had come to spend carnival in Venice.

Cacambo, who was filling the glass of one of these strangers, drew near to his master's ear at the end of the meal and said to him:

"Sire, Your Majesty may depart when he wishes. The ship is ready."

Having said this, he left the room. Astonished, the supper guests were exchanging silent glances, when another servant came up to his master and said:

"Sire, Your Majesty's carriage is at Padua, and the boat is ready."

His master made a sign, and the servant left. All the guests stared at each other again, and the general amazement increased. A third servant, coming up to a third stranger, said to him:

"Believe me, Sire, Your Majesty must not stay here a moment longer. I shall go and get everything ready."

And he disappeared at once.

Candide and Martin now had no doubt that this was some masquerade to do with the carnival. A fourth servant said to a fourth master:

"Your Majesty may depart at his convenience," and left the room like the others.

The fifth servant said the same to the fifth master. But the sixth servant spoke differently to the sixth stranger, who was sitting next to Candide.

He said to him:

"Lor me, Sire, they're refusing to let Your Majesty have any more credit, nor me neither, and the pair of us'll as like be carted off to the clink this very night. I'm off to look after number one, thank you very much. Good-bye."

The servants having all vanished, the six strangers, Candide and Martin remained deep in silence. Finally Candide broke it:

"Gentlemen," he said, "this is some strange joke. How is it that you are all Kings? For my part I must tell you that neither I nor Martin are anything of the sort."

Cacambo's master then intervened gravely and said in Italian:

"I am no joke, my name is Achmed III.[8] I was Grand Sultan for several years; I dethroned my brother; my nephew has dethroned me; my viziers have had their heads cut off; I am spending the rest of my days in the old seraglio; my nephew the

---

8. Sultan of the Ottoman Empire from 1703 until 1730, when he was deposed by a military coup.

Grand Sultan Mahmood occasionally allows me to travel for my health, and I have come to spend carnival in Venice."

A young man who was next to Achmed spoke after him and said:

"My name is Ivan, I was Emperor of all the Russias.[9] I was dethroned in my cradle; my father and mother were locked up; I was brought up in prison; I occasionally get permission to travel, accompanied by my guards, and I have come to spend carnival in Venice."

The third said:

"I am Charles Edward, King of England.[1] My father renounced his claim to the throne in my favour; I have fought many battles to make good my claim; eight hundred of my supporters had their hearts ripped out and their cheeks slapped with them; I was put in prison; I am on my way to Rome to visit my father the King, dethroned like me and my grandfather, and I have come to spend carnival in Venice."

The fourth then spoke up and said:

"I am the King of Poland.[2] The fortunes of war have dispossessed me of my ancestral domains; my father suffered the same reverses; I am resigned to Providence like Sultan Achmed, Emperor Ivan, and King Charles Edward, whom God preserve, and I have come to spend carnival in Venice."

The fifth said: "I too am the King of Poland.[3] I have lost my kingdom twice; but Providence has given me another domain, in which I have done more good than all the Kings of Sarmatia put together have ever been able to manage on the banks of the Vistula. I too am resigned to Providence, and I have come to spend carnival in Venice."

It remained for the sixth monarch to speak.

"Gentlemen," he said, "I am not so great a lord as any of you but, well, I have been a King just like everyone else. I am Theodore;[4] I was elected King in Corsica; they called me "Your Majesty", and now they hardly call me "Sir"; once I minted money, and now I haven't a penny; once I had two secretaries of state, and now I have scarcely a valet; I once sat on a throne, and I have spent a long time in prison in London, with straw for a bed. I am much afraid I shall be treated in the same way here, although I came like Your Majesties to spend carnival in Venice."

The other five Kings listened to this speech with a noble compassion. Each of them gave King Theodore twenty sequins[5] to buy coats and shirts, and Candide made him a present of a diamond worth two thousand sequins.

"Who can this be then," said the five Kings, "a mere private individual who is in a position to give a hundred times as much as each of us, and who gives it?"

Just as they were leaving the table, there arrived in the same hostelry four Serene Highnesses who had also lost their domains through the fortunes of war, and who were coming to spend what was left of the carnival in Venice. But Candide did not even notice these new arrivals. All he could think about was going to find his dear Cunégonde in Constantinople.

---

9. Ivan VI, whom Catherine the Great imprisoned and ultimately put to death in 1764.

1. The "Young Pretender" (1720–1788), son of James Stuart (the "Old Pretender") and grandson of King James II of England; called "Bonnie Prince Charlie" by the Scots supporters of the uprising he led against the English crown, disastrously defeated at the Battle of Culloden in 1746.

2. Augustus III, Elector of Saxony and King of Poland, was driven from Saxony by Frederick the Great in 1756. His father Augustus II had similarly been dispossessed by Charles XII of Sweden.

3. Stanislas Lesczinski, King of Poland from 1704 to 1709, when he was driven out by the Russians. He unsuccessfully attempted to regain the Polish throne in 1733 and was made Duke of Lorraine in 1735.

4. The representative of Holy Roman Emperor Charles VI, who led a revolt in Corsica against the Genoese in the 1730s.

5. Venetian coins.

Chapter 27

CANDIDE'S JOURNEY TO CONSTANTINOPLE

Faithful Cacambo had already obtained permission from the Turkish captain who was to take Sultan Achmed back to Constantinople for Candide and Martin to join them on board. Together they made their way to the ship, having prostrated themselves before His unhappy Highness.

On the way Candide was saying to Martin:

"There you are, you see. That was six dethroned Kings we had supper with. And that's not all. Among those six Kings there was one I could give alms to. Perhaps there are lots more princes who are even more unfortunate. Whereas me, all I've lost is a hundred sheep, and I'm flying to the arms of Cunégonde. My dear Martin, once more, Pangloss was right: all is well."

"I certainly hope so," said Martin.

"But," said Candide, "that was a pretty unlikely adventure we had in Venice. Who ever saw or heard tell of six dethroned kings having supper together in a tavern."

"It's no more extraordinary," said Martin, "than most of the things that have happened to us. It's very common for kings to be dethroned, and as for the honour of having supper with them, there's nothing special about that."

Scarce was Candide aboard than he fell upon the neck of his former manservant, his friend Cacambo.

"Well, then," said Candide, "what's Cunégonde doing? Is she still a paragon of beauty? Does she still love me? How is she? Presumably you bought her a palace in Constantinople?"

"My dear master," replied Cacambo, "Cunégonde is washing dishes on the shores of the Sea of Marmara for a prince who has very few dishes. She's a slave in the household of an ex-ruler called Ragotsky,[6] to whom in his exile the Grand Turk gives three crowns a day. But, worse than that, she has lost her beauty and become horribly ugly."

"Ah, beautiful or ugly," said Candide, "I'm a man of honour, and my duty is to love her always. But how can she possibly have fallen so low with the five or six millions you took her?"

"Look here," said Cacambo. "Didn't I have to give two million to Señor don Fernando d'Ibaraa y Figueora y Mascarenes y Lampourdos y Souza, Governor of Buenos Aires, for permission to take Miss Cunégonde back? And didn't a pirate very kindly relieve us of the rest? And didn't the same pirate take us to Cape Matapan, Milo, Nicaria, Samos, Petra, the Dardanelles, Marmara, and Scutari? Cunégonde and the old woman are now working as servants to the prince I told you about, and I am a slave of the dethroned sultan."

"What a chain of appalling calamities one after another," said Candide. "But after all, I do still have some diamonds left. I will easily secure Cunégonde's release. It really is a pity that she has become so ugly."

Then, turning to Martin:

"Who do you think one should feel most sorry for," he said, "Emperor Achmed, Emperor Ivan, King Charles Edward, or me?"

"I've no idea," said Martin. "I'd have to see inside all your hearts to know the answer to that."

6. Rákóczy (1676–1735), prince of Transylvania, led an unsuccessful uprising against Joseph I in Hungary in the early 1700s and subsequently fled to the Sea of Marmara.

"Ah!" said Candide, "if Pangloss were here, he would know, he would tell us the answer."

"I don't know what sort of scales your Pangloss could have used to weigh the misfortunes of men and calculate their sufferings," said Martin. "All I presume is that there are millions of people on this earth one might feel a hundred times sorrier for than King Charles Edward, Emperor Ivan, and Sultan Achmed."

"That may well be so," said Candide.

In a few days they reached the channel leading to the Black Sea. The first thing Candide did was to buy Cacambo back at a very high price, and then without delay he and his companions quickly boarded a galley and made for the shores of the Sea of Marmara in search of Cunégonde, ugly though she might be.

Amongst the galley-slaves were two prisoners who rowed extremely badly, and to whose naked shoulders the Levantine captain would periodically apply a few lashes of his bull's pizzle. Candide's natural reaction was to pay more attention to them than to the other galley-slaves, and he drew near them with compassion. One or two features on their disfigured faces seemed to him to bear some resemblance to those of Pangloss and that unfortunate Jesuit, Miss Cunégonde's brother, the Baron. The thought touched and saddened him. He watched them even more closely.

"Quite honestly," he said to Cacambo, "if I hadn't seen Maître Pangloss hanged and if I hadn't had the misfortune to kill the Baron, I could swear it was them rowing on this galley."

On hearing the names of the Baron and Pangloss, the two galley-slaves gave a great shout, stopped still on their bench, and dropped their oars. The Levantine captain rushed up to them, and the lashes from his bull's pizzle rained down anew.

"Stop, stop, good sir," screamed Candide. "I will give you all the money you want."

"Why, it's Candide!" said one of the two galley-slaves.

"Why, it's Candide!" said the other.

"Am I dreaming all this?" said Candide. "Am I awake? Am I really here on this galley? Is that the Baron I killed? Is that the Maître Pangloss I saw hanged?"

"It is we, it is we," they replied.

"What, so that's the great philosopher?" said Martin.

"Look here, Mr. Levantine captain," said Candide, "how much ransom do you want for Mr. von Thunder-ten-tronckh, one of the foremost barons of the Empire, and for Mr. Pangloss, the profoundest metaphysician in Germany?"

"You Christian cur," replied the Levantine slave-driver. "Since these two Christian slave dogs are barons and metaphysicians, which is no doubt a great honour where they come from, you can give me fifty thousand sequins."

"You shall have them, sir. Get me to Constantinople as fast as you possibly can, and you will be paid on the spot. On second thought, take me to Miss Cunégonde."

The Levantine captain, at Candide's first offer, had already altered course for the city, and he bid the crew row faster than a bird may cleave the air.

Candide embraced the Baron and Pangloss a hundred times.

"And how did I not kill you, my dear Baron? And you, my dear Pangloss, how is it that you are alive after being hanged? And what are you both doing on a galley in Turkey?"

"Is it really true that my dear sister is here in this country?" said the Baron.

"Yes," replied Cacambo.

"So here is my dear Candide again," exclaimed Pangloss.

Candide introduced them to Martin and Cacambo. They all embraced; everybody talked at once. The galley was flying along; they were already in port. A Jew was summoned, to whom Candide sold a diamond worth a hundred thousand sequins for fifty thousand, and who swore by Abraham that he could offer not a sequin more. Thereupon Candide paid the ransom for the Baron and Pangloss. The latter threw himself at the feet of his liberator and bathed them in tears; the other thanked him with a nod of his head and promised to reimburse him at the earliest opportunity.

"But can it really be that my sister is in Turkey?" he said.

"It really can," retorted Cacambo, "seeing as how she's washing dishes for a Prince of Transylvania."

At once two Jews were sent for. Candide sold some more diamonds, and they all left by another galley to go and deliver Cunégonde from bondage.

Chapter 28

WHAT HAPPENED TO CANDIDE, CUNÉGONDE, PANGLOSS, MARTIN, AND CO.

"Once more, forgive me," Candide said to the Baron. "Forgive me, reverend father, for running you through with my sword like that."

"We'll say no more about it," said the Baron. "I did speak rather sharply, I admit. But since you want to know how you came to find me on a galley, I will tell you that after being cured of my wounds by the college's apothecary monk, I was set upon and abducted by a group of Spaniards. I was put in prison in Buenos Aires just after my sister left there. I asked to be allowed to return to Rome to be with the Father General: I was appointed almoner to His Excellency the ambassador of France in Constantinople. I hadn't been in post more than a week when one evening I ran into a young icoglan,[7] who was very good-looking. It was extremely hot: the young man wanted to go for a swim; I took the opportunity to go swimming too. I did not know that it was a capital offence for a Christian to be found stark naked with a young Muslim. A cadi[8] had me birched a hundred times on the soles of the feet and sent me to the galleys. I don't believe there's ever been a more ghastly miscarriage of justice. But what I'd like to know is why my sister is working in the kitchens of a Transylvanian ruler in exile among the Turks."

"But you, my dear Pangloss," said Candide, "how is it that we meet again?"

"It is true that you did see me hanged," said Pangloss. "I was, of course, to have been burned but, as you will remember, it poured with rain just as they were about to roast me. The storm was so violent that they gave up trying to light the fire, and I was hanged for want of a better alternative. A surgeon bought my body, took me home with him, and dissected me. First he made a cruciform incision in me from my navel to my collar-bone. One can't have a worse hanging than I'd had. The executive arm of the high works of the Holy Inquisition, namely a sub-deacon, certainly did a splendid job when it came to burning people, but he wasn't used to hanging. The rope was wet and wouldn't slip through properly, and it got caught. So I was still breathing. The crucial incision made me give such an enormous shriek that my surgeon fell over backwards and, thinking it was the devil himself he was dissecting, rushed away, nearly dying of fright, and then, to cap it all, fell down the

7. A page of the Sultan, often employed in the seraglio.
8. A ranking Muslim official.

stairs in his flight. His wife came running from the next room at the noise, saw me stretched out on the table with my crucial incision, took even greater fright than her husband, fled, and fell over him.

"When they had collected their wits a little, I heard the surgeon's wife say to her husband: 'My dear, what on earth were you thinking of, dissecting a heretic like that? Don't you know those sort of people always have the devil in them? I'm going to fetch a priest this minute to exorcize him.' I shuddered to hear this, and I mustered what little strength I had left and cried out: 'Have mercy on me!' In the end the Portuguese barber plucked up courage.[9] He sewed me up again, and his wife even nursed me. I was up and about again in a fortnight. The barber found me a position and made me lackey to a Knight of Malta who was going to Venice. But since my master had not the means to pay me, I entered service with a merchant of Venice and followed him to Constantinople.

"One day I happened to enter a mosque. There was no one in there apart from an old imam and a very pretty young worshipper, who was saying her paternosters. Her bosom was uncovered for all to see, and in her cleavage was a lovely posy of tulips, roses, anemones, buttercups, hyacinths, and auriculas. She dropped her posy; I picked it up and replaced it for her with respectful zeal. I took so long about replacing it that the imam became angry and, seeing I was a Christian, called for help. I was taken to the cadi, who sentenced me to a hundred strokes of the lath on the soles of my feet and sent me to the galleys. I was chained up in precisely the same galley and on precisely the same bench as His Lordship the Baron. On the galley were four young men from Marseilles, five Neapolitan priests, and two monks from Corfu, who all told us that this sort of thing happened every day. His Lordship claimed he'd been more unjustly treated than I had. I maintained for my part that it was much more permissible putting a posy back on a woman's bosom than being stark naked with an icoglan. We used to argue the whole time, and were getting twenty lashes a day with the bull's pizzle when, by a turn in the chain of events that governs this universe, you were led to our galley and bought us back."

"Now then, my dear Pangloss!" Candide said to him. "When you were being hanged, and dissected, and beaten, and made to row in a galley, did you continue to think that things were turning out for the best?"

"I still feel now as I did at the outset," replied Pangloss. "I am a philosopher after all. It wouldn't do for me to go back on what I said before, what with Leibniz not being able to be wrong, and pre-established harmony being the finest thing in the world, not to mention the *plenum* and *materia subtilis*."[1]

Chapter 29

How Candide was reunited with Cunégonde
AND THE OLD WOMAN

While Candide, the Baron, Pangloss, Martin, and Cacambo were recounting their adventures, and philosophizing about which events in the universe are contingent and which not contingent, and arguing about effects and causes, moral and physical evil,

9. Barbers often did minor surgery.

1. Leibniz posited the idea of a preestablished harmony to describe the correspondence between the physical and spiritual realms. Leibniz and Descartes argued that the universe was a *plenum* ("fullness"), meaning there is no empty space in the universe, and that the space between planets was filled by an ethereal *materia subtilis* ("fine matter"). This philosophy was discredited by Newton.

freedom and necessity, and about what consolations are to be had on board a Turkish galley, they landed on the shores of the Sea of Marmara at the house of the Prince of Transylvania. The first thing they saw was Cunégonde and the old woman hanging towels out on a line to dry.

The Baron went pale at the sight. Candide, the tender-hearted lover, on seeing his fair Cunégonde all brown, with her eyes bloodshot, her bosom shrivelled, her cheeks wrinkled, and her arms red and peeling, recoiled three paces in horror, and then went forward out of sheer good manners. She embraced Candide and her brother. They embraced the old woman. Candide bought them both free.

There was a small farm in the vicinity. The old woman suggested to Candide that it would do them nicely while they waited for the whole company to fall on better times. Cunégonde did not know that she had become ugly; no one had told her. She reminded Candide of his promises in such a firm tone that good Candide did not dare refuse her. He intimated to the Baron, therefore, that he was going to marry his sister.

"I will not tolerate such a demeaning act on her part," he said, "nor such insolence from you. Never shall it be said that I allowed such infamy: my wife's children would never be able to mix in Germany's noble chapters.[2] No, my sister will marry no one but a baron of the Empire."

Cunégonde threw herself at his feet and bathed them with her tears; he was inflexible.

"You great numskull," said Candide, "I've saved you from the galleys, I've paid your ransom, and I've paid your sister's. She was washing dishes here, she's ugly, I have the goodness to make her my wife, and you still think you're going to stand in our way! I'd kill you all over again if I let my anger have its way."

"You can kill me all over again if you want," said the Baron, "but you won't marry my sister so long as I live."

Chapter 30

CONCLUSION

Candide, in his heart of hearts, had no desire to marry Cunégonde. But the extreme impertinence of the Baron made him decide to go through with the marriage, and Cunégonde was pressing him so keenly that he could not go back on his word. He consulted Pangloss, Martin, and the faithful Cacambo. Pangloss wrote a fine dissertation in which he proved that the Baron had no rights over his sister, and that it was open to her, under all the laws of the Empire, to marry Candide with the left hand.[3] Martin was for throwing the Baron into the sea. Cacambo decided they should return him to the Levantine captain and have him put back in the galleys, after which he was to be packed off to the Father General in Rome on the first available ship. This view of the matter was thought to be very sound. The old woman approved, nothing was said to his sister, the thing was done with the help of a little money, and they had the pleasure of bettering a Jesuit and punishing the arrogance of a German baron.

2. Assemblies of the nobility.

3. A marriage between persons of different rank in which the inferior's status is not raised.

It was quite natural to imagine that, after so many disasters, Candide, now married to his sweetheart and living with the philosophical Pangloss, the philosophical Martin, the prudent Cacambo and the old woman and, moreover, having brought back so many diamonds from the land of the ancient Incas, would be leading the most agreeable of all possible lives. But he was swindled so many times by the Jews that all he had left in the end was his little farm; his wife, who grew uglier with every day that passed, became shrewish and impossible to live with; the old woman was infirm and even more bad-tempered than Cunégonde; Cacambo, who worked in the garden and travelled to Constantinople to sell vegetables, was worn out with work and cursed his fate; Pangloss was in despair at not being a luminary in some German university. As for Martin, he was firmly persuaded that one is just as badly off wherever one is; he put up with things as they were. Candide, Martin, and Pangloss would argue sometimes about metaphysics and ethics. They would often see boats passing beneath the windows of the farm-house laden with effendis, pashas, and cadis,[4] who were being exiled to Lemnos or Mytilene or Erzerum. They would see more cadis, more pashas, and more effendis coming to take the place of those who had been expelled, and being themselves in their turn expelled. They would see heads duly stuffed with straw being taken for display before the Sublime Porte.[5] Such sights would give rise to yet further disquisitions, and when they were not arguing, the boredom was so excessive that the old woman made bold to say to them one day:

"I would like to know which is worse: being raped a hundred times by negro pirates, having a buttock chopped off, running the gauntlet of the Bulgars, being flogged and hanged in an *auto-da-fé,* being dissected, rowing in a galley, in short, suffering all the misfortunes we've all suffered, or simply being stuck here doing nothing?"

"That is a good question," said Candide.

This speech gave rise to renewed speculation, and Martin in particular came to the conclusion that man was born to spend his life alternately a prey to the throes of anxiety and the lethargy of boredom. Candide did not agree, but asserted nothing. Pangloss admitted that he had always suffered horribly; but having once maintained that everything was going marvellously, he still maintained it, and believed nothing of the sort.

One thing finally confirmed Martin in his detestable principles, gave Candide more than ever pause, and embarrassed Pangloss. This was the sight one day of Paquette and Brother Giroflée arriving at their farm in a state of extreme wretchedness. They had very quickly gone through their three thousand piastres, left each other, patched things up, quarrelled again, been put in prison, escaped; and in the end Brother Giroflée had turned Turk. Paquette still pursued her profession, and no longer earned any money at it.

"I told you so," Martin said to Candide. "I knew what you gave them would soon be gone and would only make them even more wretched. You had more piastres than you knew what to do with, you and Cacambo, and you are no happier than Brother Giroflée and Paquette."

4. Men of high rank.
5. The gate of the Turkish court.

"Aha!" said Pangloss to Paquette, "so heaven brings you back here among us, my poor child! Do you know, you've cost me the tip of my nose, an eye and an ear? And you, just look at the state you're in! What a world we live in!"

This new turn of events led them to philosophize more than ever.

There lived in the neighbourhood a very famous dervish,[6] who passed for the greatest philosopher in Turkey. They went to consult him. Pangloss acted as their spokesman and said to him:

"Master, we have come to ask you to tell us why such a strange animal as man was created."

"What's that to you?" said the dervish. "Is it any of your business?"

"But, reverend father," said Candide, "there's an awful lot of evil in the world."

"What does it matter whether there's evil or there's good," said the dervish. "When His Highness sends a ship to Egypt, does he worry whether the mice on board are comfortable or not?"

"So what must we do then?" said Pangloss.

"Be silent," said the dervish.

"I had flattered myself," said Pangloss, "that we might have a talk about effects and causes, the best of all possible worlds, the origin of evil, the nature of the soul, and pre-established harmony."

The dervish, at these words, slammed the door in their faces.

During this conversation news had spread that two viziers of the bench and the mufti[7] had been strangled in Constantinople, and several of their friends impaled. This catastrophe made a great stir everywhere for some hours. On their way back to the farm Pangloss, Candide, and Martin met a kindly old man who was taking the air at his door beneath an arbour of orange-trees. Pangloss, who was as curious as he was prone to philosophizing, asked him the name of the mufti who had just been strangled.

"I have no idea," replied the fellow, "and I never have known what any mufti or vizier was called. What you have just told me means absolutely nothing to me. I have no doubt that in general those who get involved in public affairs do sometimes come to a sad end and that they deserve it. But I never enquire what's going on in Constantinople. I am content to send my fruit for sale there from the garden I cultivate."

Having said this, he invited the strangers into his house. His two daughters and two sons offered them several kinds of sorbet which they made themselves, some *kaïmak*[8] sharpened with the zest of candied citron, some oranges, lemons, limes, pineapple, and pistachio nuts, and some Mocha coffee which had not been blended with that awful coffee from Batavia and the islands. After which the two daughters of this good Muslim perfumed the beards of Candide, Pangloss, and Martin.

"You must have a vast and magnificent property," said Candide to the Turk.

"I have but twenty acres," replied the Turk. "I cultivate them with my children. Work keeps us from three great evils: boredom, vice, and need."

Candide, on his way back to his farm, thought long and hard about what the Turk had said, and commented to Pangloss and Martin:

"That kind old man seems to me to have made a life for himself which is much preferable to that of those six Kings with whom we had the honour of having supper."

---

6. Muslim holy man.
7. Judge.
8. Sweet cream.

"High rank can be very dangerous," said Pangloss; "all the philosophers say so. For the fact is, Eglon, King of the Moabites, was slain by Ehud; Absalom was hanged by the hair on his head and had three darts thrust through his heart; King Nadab, son of Jeroboam, was smitten by Baasha; King Elah by Zimri; Joram by Jehu; Athaliah by Jehoiada; and Kings Jehoiakim, Jehoiachin, and Zedekiah entered into captivity.[9] You know what sort of deaths befell Croesus, Astyages, Darius, Dionysius of Syracuse, Pyrrhus, Perseus, Hannibal, Jugurtha, Ariovistus, Caesar, Pompey, Nero, Otho, Vitellius, Domitian, Richard II of England, Edward II, Henry VI, Richard III, Mary Stuart, Charles I, France's three Henris, and the Emperor Henri IV? You know..."

"I also know," said Candide, "that we must cultivate our garden."

"You're right," said Pangloss; "for when man was placed in the garden of Eden, he was placed there *ut operaretur eum*—that he might work[1]—which proves that man was not born to rest."

"Let's get down to work and stop all this philosophizing," said Martin. "It's the only way to make life bearable."

The little society all fell in with this laudable plan. Each began to exercise his talents. Their small amount of land produced a great deal. Cunégonde was in truth very ugly, but she became an excellent pastry-cook. Paquette embroidered. The old woman took care of the linen. Everyone made himself useful, including Brother Giroflée; he was a very fine carpenter, and even became quite the gentleman. And sometimes Pangloss would say to Candide:

"All events form a chain in the best of all possible worlds. For in the end, if you had not been given a good kick up the backside and chased out of a beautiful castle for loving Miss Cunégonde, and if you hadn't been subjected to the Inquisition, and if you hadn't wandered about America on foot, and if you hadn't dealt the Baron a good blow with your sword, and if you hadn't lost all your sheep from that fine country of Eldorado, you wouldn't be here now eating candied citron and pistachio nuts."

"That is well put," replied Candide, "but we must cultivate our garden."

ELIZA HAYWOOD ■ (c. 1693–1756)

Eliza Haywood was possibly the most prolific of all the verbose writers of the eighteenth century, and also one of the most famous and widely read. She was so good at constructing fictional personae, however, and masking her private identity—much like her character, "Fantomina"—that virtually nothing is known for certain about her life. That she was born, married, and divorced or separated in England in the early part of the century are uncontested, but where and to whom, and whether she had children, are matters of debate. Like many women novelists of her century, she began her public career as an actress, first in Dublin at the Smock Alley Theatre and then in London. She soon tried her hand at fiction, and her first novel, *Love in Excess* (1719), was one of three major bestsellers published in English within the next few years, alongside Defoe's *Robinson Crusoe* (1719) and Swift's *Gulliver's Travels* (1726). Over the next forty years she published more than sixty titles in many genres: novels, short fiction, plays, poetry, translations, political tracts, and entire periodical series that she wrote and edited herself.

---

9. Having given a string of biblical examples, Pangloss next turns to classical and then modern cases.
1. Genesis 2:15.

Haywood became so successful during the 1720s as a writer of "scandalous" narratives that she was mocked by fellow novelist Henry Fielding as "Mrs. Novel," and viciously lampooned by Pope in his *Dunciad* (1728). These attacks had their effect on Haywood, and she temporarily stopped publishing novels. Moreover, the general tone of British fiction changed markedly in the direction of moralizing prudishness after the success of Samuel Richardson's sentimental novels of the 1740s, which Haywood first satirized (as did Fielding), and then imitated. "Fantomina" (1724) characterizes Haywood's best early fiction, with its open expression of female sexual desire—which, nevertheless, must always be masked, and finally punished.

PRONUNCIATIONS:
   Beauplaisir: BOH-play-ZEER
   Fantomina: fan-to-MAI-nah

Fantomina: Or, Love in a Maze

Being a Secret History of an Amour Between Two Persons of Condition[1]

> In love the victors from the vanquished fly.
> They fly that wound, and they pursue that die.
>
> —Waller[2]

A young lady of distinguished birth, beauty, wit, and spirit, happened to be in a box one night at the playhouse; where, though there were a great number of celebrated toasts,[3] she perceived several gentlemen extremely pleased themselves with entertaining a woman who sat in a corner of the pit,[4] and, by her air and manner of receiving them, might easily be known to be one of those who come there for no other purpose than to create acquaintance with as many as seem desirous of it. She could not help testifying her contempt of men who, regardless either of the play or circle, threw away their time in such a manner, to some ladies that sat by her: but they, either less surprised by being more accustomed to such sights than she who had been bred for the most part in the country, or not of a disposition to consider anything very deeply, took but little notice of it. She still thought of it, however; and the longer she reflected on it, the greater was her wonder that men, some of whom she knew were accounted to have wit,[5] should have tastes so very depraved.—This excited a curiosity in her to know in what manner these creatures were addressed:[6]—she was young, a stranger to the world, and consequently to the dangers of it; and having nobody in town at that time to whom she was obliged to be accountable for her actions, did in everything as her inclinations or humors rendered most agreeable to her: therefore thought it not in the least a fault to put in practice a little whim which came immediately into her head, to dress herself as near as she could in the fashion of those women who make sale of their favors, and set herself in the way of

1. Upper-class rank.

2. The final lines of Edmund Waller's "To a Friend, on the different success of their loves" (1645), in which a man describes how his infatuation with a proud woman named Celia met with her rejection, while his subsequent loss of interest turned the tables and made her solicitous of him. "To die" here also means "to experience orgasm."

3. Belles, fine young ladies (whose health was commonly drunk by gentlemen in toasts).

4. The area below the stage generally occupied by gentlemen, law students, professional or literary types, and (in this case) prostitutes. Aristocracy generally sat in the boxes above.

5. Intelligence, good taste, judgment.

6. Creatures: common term of disrespect for women of low birth or reputation. Addressed: approached, solicited.

being accosted as such a one, having at that time no other aim, than the gratification of an innocent curiosity.—She no sooner designed this frolic than she put it in execution; and muffling her hoods over her face, went the next night into the gallery-box, and practicing as much as she had observed at that distance the behavior of that woman, was not long before she found her disguise had answered the ends she wore it for.—A crowd of purchasers of all degrees and capacities were in a moment gathered about her, each endeavoring to outbid the other in offering her a price for her embraces.—She listened to 'em all, and was not a little diverted in her mind at the disappointment she should give to so many, each of which thought himself secure of gaining her.—She was told by 'em all that she was the most lovely woman in the world; and some cried, *Gad, she is mighty like my fine Lady Such-a-one*—naming her own name. She was naturally vain, and received no small pleasure in hearing herself praised, though in the person of another, and a supposed prostitute; but she dispatched as soon as she could all that had hitherto attacked her, when she saw the accomplished *Beauplaisir*[7] was making his way through the crowd as fast as he was able, to reach the bench she sat on. She had often seen him in the drawing-room, had talked with him; but then her quality[8] and reputed virtue kept him from using her with that freedom she now expected he would do, and had discovered something in him which had made her often think she should not be displeased, if he would abate some part of his reserve.—Now was the time to have her wishes answered:—he looked in her face, and fancied, as many others had done, that she very much resembled that lady whom she really was; but the vast disparity there appeared between their characters prevented him from entertaining even the most distant thought that they could be the same.—He addressed her at first with the usual salutations of her pretended profession, as, *Are you engaged, Madam?—Will you permit me to wait on you home after the play?—By Heaven, you are a fine girl!—How long have you used this house?*—and such like questions; but perceiving she had a turn of wit, and a genteel manner in her raillery, beyond what is frequently to be found among those wretches, who are for the most part gentlewomen but by necessity, few of 'em having had an education suitable to what they affect to appear, he changed the form of his conversation, and showed her it was not because he understood no better that he had made use of expressions so little polite.—In fine, they were infinitely charmed with each other: he was transported to find so much beauty and wit in a woman, who he doubted not but on very easy terms he might enjoy; and she found a vast deal of pleasure in conversing with him in this free and unrestrained manner. They passed their time all the play with an equal satisfaction; but when it was over, she found herself involved in a difficulty, which before never entered into her head, but which she knew not well how to get over.—The passion he professed for her, was not of that humble nature which can be content with distant adorations:—he resolved not to part from her without the gratifications of those desires she had inspired; and presuming on the liberties which her supposed function allowed of, told her she must either go with him to some convenient house of his procuring, or permit him to wait on her to her own lodgings.—Never had she been in such a *dilemma:* three or four times did she open her mouth to confess her real quality; but the influence of her ill stars prevented it, by putting an excuse into her head, which did the business as well, and at the same time did not take from her the power of seeing and entertaining him a second time with the same freedom she had done this.—She told him, she was under obligations to a man who maintained her, and whom she durst not disappoint, having promised to meet him that night at a house hard by.[9]—This story so

7. Lovely pleasure (French).
8. High social station.
9. Nearby.

like what those ladies sometimes tell was not at all suspected by *Beauplaisir;* and assuring her he would be far from doing her a prejudice,[1] desired that in return for the pain he should suffer in being deprived of her company that night, that she would order her affairs, so as not to render him unhappy the next. She gave a solemn promise to be in the same box on the morrow evening; and they took leave of each other; he to the tavern to drown the remembrance of his disappointment; she in a hackney-chair[2] hurried home to indulge contemplation on the frolic she had taken, designing nothing less on her first reflections than to keep the promise she had made him, and hugging herself with joy, that she had the good luck to come off undiscovered.

But these cogitations were but of a short continuance; they vanished with the hurry of her spirits, and were succeeded by others vastly different and ruinous:—all the charms of *Beauplaisir* came fresh into her mind; she languished, she almost died for another opportunity of conversing with him; and not all the admonitions of her discretion were effectual to oblige her to deny laying hold of that which offered itself the next night.—She depended on the strength of her virtue, to bear her fate through trials more dangerous than she apprehended this to be, and never having been addressed by him as Lady —— was resolved to receive his devoirs[3] as a town-mistress, imagining a world of satisfaction to herself in engaging him in the character of such a one, observing the surprise he would be in to find himself refused by a woman, who he supposed granted her favors without exception.—Strange and unaccountable were the whimsies she was possessed of—wild and incoherent her desires—unfixed and undetermined her resolutions, but in that of seeing *Beauplaisir* in the manner she had lately done. As for her proceedings with him, or how a second time to escape him, without discovering who she was, she could neither assure herself, nor whether or not in the last extremity she would do so.—Bent, however, on meeting him, whatever should be the consequence, she went out some hours before the time of going to the playhouse, and took lodgings in a house not very far from it, intending, that if he should insist on passing some part of the night with her, to carry him there, thinking she might with more security to her honor entertain him at a place where she was mistress, than at any of his own choosing.

The appointed hour being arrived, she had the satisfaction to find his love in his assiduity: he was there before her; and nothing could be more tender than the manner in which he accosted her: but from the first moment she came in, to that of the play being done, he continued to assure her no consideration should prevail with him to part from her again, as she had done the night before; and she rejoiced to think she had taken that precaution of providing herself with a lodging, to which she thought she might invite him, without running any risk, either of her virtue or reputation.—Having told him she would admit of his accompanying her home, he seemed perfectly satisfied; and leading her to the place, which was not above twenty houses distant, would have ordered a collation[4] to be brought after them. But she would not permit it, telling him she was not one of those who suffered themselves to be treated at their own lodgings; and as soon she was come in, sent a servant, belonging to the house, to provide a very handsome supper, and wine, and everything was served to table in a manner which showed the director neither wanted money, nor was ignorant how it should be laid out.

1. Injury.
2. Hired sedan chair carried by two men.
3. Respects.
4. Light meal.

This proceeding, though it did not take from him the opinion that she was what she appeared to be, yet it gave him thoughts of her, which he had not before.—He believed her a *mistress,* but believed her to be one of a superior rank, and began to imagine the possession of her would be much more expensive than at first he had expected: but not being of a humor to grudge anything for his pleasures, he gave himself no farther trouble than what were occasioned by fears of not having money enough to reach her price, about him.

Supper being over, which was intermixed with a vast deal of amorous conversation, he began to explain himself more than he had done; and both by his words and behavior let her know he would not be denied that happiness the freedoms she allowed had made him hope.—It was in vain; she would have retracted the encouragement she had given:—in vain she endeavored to delay, till the next meeting, the fulfilling of his wishes:—she had now gone too far to retreat:—*he* was bold;—he was resolute: *she* fearful—confused, altogether unprepared to resist in such encounters, and rendered more so, by the extreme liking she had to him.—Shocked, however, at the apprehension of really losing her honor, she struggled all she could, and was just going to reveal the whole secret of her name and quality, when the thoughts of the liberty he had taken with her, and those he still continued to prosecute, prevented her, with representing[5] the danger of being exposed, and the whole affair made a theme for public ridicule.—Thus much, indeed, she told him, that she was a virgin, and had assumed this manner of behavior only to engage him. But that he little regarded, or if he had, would have been far from obliging him to desist;—nay, in the present burning eagerness of desire, 'tis probable, that had he been acquainted both with who and what she really was, the knowledge of her birth would not have influenced him with respect sufficient to have curbed the wild exuberance of his luxurious wishes, or made him in that longing—that impatient moment, change the form of his addresses. In fine, she was undone; and he gained a victory, so highly rapturous, that had he known over whom, scarce could he have triumphed more. Her tears, however, and the distraction she appeared in, after the ruinous ecstasy was past, as it heightened his wonder, so it abated his satisfaction:—he could not imagine for what reason a woman, who, if she intended not to be a *mistress,* had counterfeited the part of one, and taken so much pains to engage him, should lament a consequence which she could not but expect, and till the last test, seemed inclinable to grant; and was both surprised and troubled at the mystery.—He omitted nothing that he thought might make her easy; and still retaining an opinion that the hope of interest had been the chief motive which had led her to act in the manner she had done, and believing that she might know so little of him, as to suppose, now she had nothing left to give, he might not make that recompense she expected for her favors: to put her out of that pain, he pulled out of his pocket a purse of gold, entreating her to accept of that as an earnest of what he intended to do for her; assuring her, with ten thousand protestations, that he would spare nothing, which his whole estate could purchase, to procure her content and happiness. This treatment made her quite forget the part she had assumed, and throwing it from her with an air of disdain, Is this a reward (*said she*) for condescensions,[6] such as I have yielded to?—Can all the wealth you are possessed of make a reparation for my loss of honor?—Oh! no, I am undone beyond the power of heaven itself to help me!—She uttered many more such exclamations; which the

---

5. By calling to mind.
6. Unworthiness, vice.

amazed *Beauplaisir* heard without being able to reply to, till by degrees sinking from that rage of temper, her eyes resumed their softening glances, and guessing at the consternation he was in, No, my dear *Beauplaisir, (added she)* your love alone can compensate for the shame you have involved me in; be you sincere and constant, and I hereafter shall, perhaps, be satisfied with my fate, and forgive myself the folly that betrayed me to you.

Beauplaisir thought he could not have a better opportunity than these words gave him of inquiring who she was, and wherefore she had feigned herself to be of a profession which he was now convinced she was not; and after he had made her a thousand vows of an affection, as inviolable and ardent as she could wish to find in him, entreated she would inform him by what means his happiness had been brought about, and also to whom he was indebted for the bliss he had enjoyed.—Some remains of yet unextinguished modesty, and sense of shame, made her blush exceedingly at this demand; but recollecting herself in a little time, she told him so much of the truth, as to what related to the frolic she had taken of satisfying her curiosity in what manner *mistresses,* of the sort she appeared to be were treated by those who addressed them; but forbore discovering her true name and quality, for the reasons she had done before, resolving, if he boasted of this affair, he should not have it in his power to touch her character: she therefore said she was the daughter of a country gentleman, who was come to town to buy clothes, and that she was called *Fantomina.* He had no reason to distrust the truth of this story, and was therefore satisfied with it; but did not doubt by the beginning of her conduct, but that in the end she would be in reality, the thing she so artfully had counterfeited; and had good nature enough to pity the misfortunes he imagined would be her lot: but to tell her so, or offer his advice in that point, was not his business, at least, as yet.

They parted not till towards morning; and she obliged him to a willing vow of visiting her the next day at three in the afternoon. It was too late for her to go home that night, therefore contented herself with lying there. In the morning she sent for the woman of the house to come up to her; and easily perceiving, by her manner, that she was a woman who might be influenced by gifts, made her a present of a couple of broad pieces,[7] and desired her, that if the gentleman, who had been there the night before, should ask any questions concerning her, that he should be told, she was lately come out of the country, had lodged there about a fortnight, and that her name was *Fantomina.* I shall (*also added she*) lie but seldom here; nor, indeed, ever come but in those times when I expect to meet him: I would, therefore, have you order it so, that he may think I am but just gone out, if he should happen by any accident to call when I am not here; for I would not, for the world, have him imagine I do not constantly lodge here. The landlady assured her she would do everything as she desired, and gave her to understand she wanted not the gift of secrecy.

Everything being ordered at this home for the security of her reputation, she repaired to the other, where she easily excused to an unsuspecting aunt, with whom she boarded, her having been abroad all night, saying, she went with a gentleman and his lady in a barge, to a little country seat of theirs up the river, all of them designing to return the same evening; but that one of the bargemen happening to be taken ill on the sudden, and no other waterman to be got that night, they were obliged to tarry till morning. Thus did this lady's wit and vivacity assist her in all, but where it was most needed.—She had discernment to foresee, and avoid all those ills which might attend

7. Gold coins.

the loss of her *reputation*, but was wholly blind to those of the ruin of her *virtue;* and having managed her affairs so as to secure the *one,* grew perfectly easy with the remembrance she had forfeited the *other.*—The more she reflected on the merits of *Beauplaisir,* the more she excused herself for what she had done; and the prospect of that continued bliss she expected to share with him took from her all remorse for having engaged in an affair which promised her so much satisfaction, and in which she found not the least danger of misfortune.—If he is really (*said she, to herself*) the faithful, the constant lover he has sworn to be, how charming will be our amor?—And if he should be false, grow satiated, like other men, I shall but, at the worst, have the private vexation of knowing I have lost him;—the intrigue being a secret, my disgrace will be so too:—I shall hear no whispers as I pass—She is forsaken:—the odious word *forsaken* will never wound my ears; nor will my wrongs excite either the mirth or pity of the talking world:—it would not be even in the power of my undoer himself to triumph over me; and while he laughs at, and perhaps despises the fond, the yielding *Fantomina,* he will revere and esteem the virtuous, the reserved lady.—In this manner did she applaud her own conduct, and exult with the imagination that she had more prudence than all her sex beside. And it must be confessed, indeed, that she preserved an economy in the management of this intrigue beyond what almost any woman but herself ever did: in the first place, by making no person in the world a confidant in it; and in the next, in concealing from *Beauplaisir* himself the knowledge who she was; for though she met him three or four days in a week, at that lodging she had taken for that purpose, yet as much as he employed her time and thoughts, she was never missed from any assembly she had been accustomed to frequent.—The business of her love has engrossed her till six in the evening, and before seven she has been dressed in a different habit, and in another place.—Slippers, and a night-gown loosely flowing, has been the garb in which he has left the languishing *Fantomina;*— laced and adorned with all the blaze of jewels has he, in less than an hour after, beheld at the royal chapel, the palace gardens, drawing-room, opera, or play, the haughty awe-inspiring lady—a thousand times has he stood amazed at the prodigious likeness between his little mistress and this court beauty; but was still as far from imagining they were the same as he was the first hour he had accosted her in the playhouse, though it is not impossible but that her resemblance to this celebrated lady might keep his inclination alive something longer than otherwise they would have been; and that it was to the thoughts of this (as he supposed) unenjoyed charmer she owed in great measure the vigor of his latter caresses.

But he varied not so much from his sex as to be able to prolong desire to any great length after possession: the rifled charms of *Fantomina* soon lost their potency, and grew tasteless and insipid; and when the season of the year inviting the company to the *Bath*,[8] she offered to accompany him, he made an excuse to go without her. She easily perceived his coldness, and the reason why he pretended her going would be inconvenient, and endured as much from the discovery as any of her sex could do: she dissembled it, however, before him, and took her leave of him with the show of no other concern than his absence occasioned: but this she did to take from him all suspicion of her following him, as she intended, and had already laid a scheme for.—From her first finding out that he designed to leave her behind, she plainly saw it was for no other reason, than that being tired of her conversation, he was willing to be at liberty to pursue new conquests; and wisely considering that complaints, tears, swoonings,

8. Town in southwestern England, popular as a resort because of its hot springs.

and all the extravagancies which women make use of in such cases, have little preva-
lence over a heart inclined to rove, and only serve to render those who practice them
more contemptible, by robbing them of that beauty which alone can bring back the
fugitive lover, she resolved to take another course; and remembering the height of
transport she enjoyed when the agreeable *Beauplaisir* kneeled at her feet, imploring
her first favors, she longed to prove the same again. Not but a woman of her beauty
and accomplishments might have beheld a thousand in that condition *Beauplaisir* had
been; but with her sex's modesty, she had not also thrown off another virtue equally
valuable, though generally unfortunate, *constancy:* she loved *Beauplaisir;* it was only
he whose solicitations could give her pleasure; and had she seen the whole species
despairing, dying for her sake, it might, perhaps, have been a satisfaction to her pride,
but none to her more tender inclination.—Her design was once more to engage him,
to hear him sigh, to see him languish, to feel the strenuous pressures of his eager
arms, to be compelled, to be sweetly forced to what she wished with equal ardor, was
what she wanted, and what she had formed a stratagem to obtain, in which she promised herself success.

She no sooner heard he had left the town, than making a pretense to her aunt,
that she was going to visit a relation in the country, went towards *Bath*, attended but
by two servants, who she found reasons to quarrel with on the road and discharged:
clothing herself in a habit she had brought with her, she forsook the coach, and went
into a wagon, in which equipage she arrived at *Bath*. The dress she was in was a
round-eared cap,[9] a short red petticoat, and a little jacket of gray stuff;[1] all the rest of
her accoutrements were answerable to these, and joined with a broad country dialect,
a rude unpolished air, which she, having been bred in these parts, knew very well
how to imitate, with her hair and eye-brows blacked, made it impossible for her to
be known, or taken for any other than what she seemed. Thus disguised did she offer
herself to service in the house where *Beauplaisir* lodged, having made it her business
to find out immediately where he was. Notwithstanding this metamorphosis she was
still extremely pretty; and the mistress of the house happening at that time to want a
maid was very glad of the opportunity of taking her. She was presently received into
the family; and had a post in it (such as she would have chose, had she been left at
her liberty), that of making the gentlemen's beds, getting them their breakfasts, and
waiting on them in their chambers. Fortune in this exploit was extremely on her side;
there were no others of the male-sex in the house than an old gentleman, who had lost
the use of his limbs with the rheumatism, and had come thither for the benefit of the
waters, and her beloved *Beauplaisir;* so that she was in no apprehensions of any amorous violence, but where she wished to find it. Nor were her designs disappointed: He
was fired with the first sight of her; and though he did not presently take any farther
notice of her, than giving her two or three hearty kisses, yet she, who now understood that language but too well, easily saw they were the prelude to more substantial
joys.—Coming the next morning to bring his chocolate, as he had ordered, he catched
her by the pretty leg, which the shortness of her petticoat did not in the least oppose;
then pulling her gently to him, asked her, how long she had been at service?—How
many sweethearts she had? If she had ever been in love? and many other such questions, befitting one of the degree she appeared to be: all which she answered with
such seeming innocence, as more enflamed the amorous heart of him who talked to

9. Style of cap associated with country women.
1. Coarse wool fabric.

her. He compelled her to sit in his lap; and gazing on her blushing beauties, which, if possible, received addition from her plain and rural dress, he soon lost the power of containing himself.—His wild desires burst out in all his words and actions: he called her little angel, cherubim, swore he must enjoy her, though death were to be the consequence, devoured her lips, her breasts with greedy kisses, held to his burning bosom her half-yielding, half-reluctant body, nor suffered her to get loose, till he had ravaged all, and glutted each rapacious sense with the sweet beauties of the pretty *Celia*,[2] for that was the name she bore in this second expedition.—Generous as liberality itself to all who gave him joy this way, he gave her a handsome sum of gold, which she durst not now refuse, for fear of creating some mistrust, and losing the heart she so lately had regained; therefore taking it with an humble courtesy, and a well counterfeited show of surprise and joy, cried, O law, Sir! what must I do for all this? He laughed at her simplicity, and kissing her again, though less fervently than he had done before, bad her not be out of the way when he came home at night. She promised she would not, and very obediently kept her word.

His stay at *Bath* exceeded not a month; but in that time his supposed country lass had persecuted him so much with her fondness, that in spite of the eagerness with which he first enjoyed her, he was at last grown more weary of her, than he had been of *Fantomina;* which she perceiving, would not be troublesome, but quitting her service, remained privately in the town till she heard he was on his return; and in that time provided herself of another disguise to carry on a third plot, which her inventing brain had furnished her with, once more to renew his twice-decayed ardors. The dress she had ordered to be made, was such as widows wear in their first mourning, which, together with the most afflicted and penitential countenance that ever was seen, was no small alteration to her who used to seem all gaiety.—To add to this, her hair, which she was accustomed to wear very loose, both when *Fantomina* and *Celia,* was now tied back so straight, and her pinners[3] coming so very forward, that there was none of it to be seen. In fine, her habit and her air were so much changed, that she was not more difficult to be known in the rude country *girl,* than she was now in the sorrowful *widow.*

She knew that *Beauplaisir* came alone in his chariot to the *Bath,* and in the time of her being servant in the house where he lodged, heard nothing of any body that was to accompany him to *London,* and hoped he would return in the same manner he had gone: She therefore hired horses and a man to attend her to an inn about ten miles on this side of *Bath,* where having discharged them, she waited till the chariot should come by; which when it did, and she saw that he was alone in it, she called to him that drove it to stop a moment, and going to the door saluted the master with these words:

The distressed and wretched, Sir (*said she*), never fail to excite compassion in a generous mind; and I hope I am not deceived in my opinion that yours is such:—You have the appearance of a gentleman, and cannot, when you hear my story, refuse that assistance which is in your power to give to an unhappy woman, who without it, may be rendered the most miserable of all created beings.

It would not be very easy to represent the surprise, so odd an address created in the mind of him to whom it was made.—She had not the appearance of one who wanted

---

2. In Renaissance literature the name Celia is frequently associated with vanity or pride, as in Lyly's *Love's Metamorphosis* as well as Waller's "To Phyllis" and "To a Friend" (quoted in the epigraph).

3. The side flaps of a close-fitting hat, usually worn by women of higher rank.

charity; and what other favor she required he could not conceive: but telling her she might command any thing in his power gave her encouragement to declare herself in this manner: You may judge (*resumed she*), by the melancholy garb I am in, that I have lately lost all that ought to be valuable to womankind; but it is impossible for you to guess the greatness of my misfortune, unless you had known my husband, who was master of every perfection to endear him to a wife's affections.—But, notwithstanding, I look on myself as the most unhappy of my sex in out-living him, I must so far obey the dictates of my discretion, as to take care of the little fortune he left behind him, which being in the hands of a brother of his in *London,* will be all carried off to *Holland,*[4] where he is going to settle; if I reach not the town before he leaves it, I am undone for ever.—To which end I left *Bristol,* the place where we lived, hoping to get a place in the stage at *Bath,* but they were all taken up before I came; and being, by a hurt I got in a fall, rendered incapable of traveling any long journey on horseback, I have no way to go to *London,* and must be inevitably ruined in the loss of all I have on earth, without you have good nature enough to admit me to take part of your chariot.

Here the feigned widow ended her sorrowful tale, which had been several times interrupted by a parenthesis of sighs and groans; and *Beauplaisir,* with a complaisant and tender air, assured her of his readiness to serve her in things of much greater consequence than what she desired of him; and told her it would be an impossibility of denying a place in his chariot to a lady who he could not behold without yielding one in his heart. She answered the compliments he made her but with tears, which seemed to stream in such abundance from her eyes, that she could not keep her handkerchief from her face one moment. Being come into the chariot, *Beauplaisir* said a thousand handsome things to persuade her from giving way to so violent a grief; which, he told her, would not only be destructive to her beauty, but likewise her health. But all his endeavors for consolement appeared ineffectual, and he began to think he should have but a dull journey, in the company of one who seemed so obstinately devoted to the memory of her dead husband, that there was no getting a word from her on any other theme:—but bethinking himself of the celebrated story of the *Ephesian* matron,[5] it came into his head to make trial, she who seemed equally susceptible of *sorrow,* might not also be so too of *love:* and having began a discourse on almost every other topic, and finding her still incapable of answering, resolved to put it to the proof, if this would have no more effect to rouse her sleeping spirits:—with a gay air, therefore, though accompanied with the greatest modesty and respect, he turned the conversation, as though without design, on that joy-giving passion, and soon discovered that was indeed the subject she was best pleased to be entertained with; for on his giving her a hint to begin upon, never any tongue run more voluble than hers, on the prodigious power it had to influence the souls of those possessed of it, to actions even the most distant from their intentions, principles, or humors.—From that she passed to a description of the happiness of mutual affection;—the unspeakable ecstasy of those who meet with equal ardency; and represented it in colors so lively, and disclosed by the gestures with which her words were accompanied, and the accent of her voice so true a feeling of what she said, that *Beauplaisir,* without being as stupid, as he was really the contrary, could not avoid perceiving there were seeds of fire, not yet extinguished, in this fair widow's soul, which wanted but the kindling breath of tender sighs to light into a blaze.—He now thought himself as fortunate, as some moments before he had the

4. Holland had been a frequent destination for English religious dissenters in exile.

5. In Petronius's *Satyricon,* the Ephesian matron is a faithful wife who stays by her dead husband's burial vault day and night until she is seduced by a soldier who guards the nearby bodies of crucified criminals. When one of the bodies is stolen, the matron gives her own husband's body to the soldier to save him from punishment.

reverse; and doubted not, but, that before they parted, he should find a way to dry the tears of this lovely mourner, to the satisfaction of them both. He did not, however, offer, as he had done to *Fantomina* and *Celia,* to urge his passion directly to her, but by a thousand little softening artifices, which he well knew how to use, gave her leave to guess he was enamored. When they came to the inn where they were to lie, he declared himself somewhat more freely, and perceiving she did not resent it past forgiveness, grew more encroaching still:—he now took the liberty of kissing away her tears, and catching the sighs as they issued from her lips; telling her if grief was infectious, he was resolved to have his share; protesting he would gladly exchange passions with her, and be content to bear her load of *sorrow,* if she would as willingly ease the burden of his *love.*—She said little in answer to the strenuous pressures with which at last he ventured to enfold her, but not thinking it decent, for the character she had assumed, to yield so suddenly, and unable to deny both his and her own inclinations, she counterfeited a fainting, and fell motionless upon his breast.—He had no great notion that she was in a real fit, and the room they supped in happening to have a bed in it, he took her in his arms and laid her on it, believing, that whatever her distemper was, that was the most proper place to convey her to.—He laid himself down by her, and endeavored to bring her to herself; and she was too grateful to her kind physician at her returning sense, to remove from the posture he had put her in, without his leave.

It may, perhaps, seem strange that *Beauplaisir* should in such near intimacies continue still deceived: I know there are men who will swear it is an impossibility, and that no disguise could hinder them from knowing a woman they had once enjoyed. In answer to these scruples, I can only say, that besides the alteration which the change of dress made in her, she was so admirably skilled in the art of feigning, that she had the power of putting on almost what face she pleased, and knew so exactly how to form her behavior to the character she represented, that all the comedians at both playhouses[6] are infinitely short of her performances: she could vary her very glances, tune her voice to accents the most different imaginable from those in which she spoke when she appeared herself.—These aids from nature, joined to the wiles of art, and the distance between the places where the imagined *Fantomina* and *Celia* were, might very well prevent his having any thought that they were the same, or that the fair *widow* was either of them: it never so much as entered his head, and though he did fancy he observed in the face of the latter, features which were not altogether unknown to him, yet he could not recollect when or where he had known them;—and being told by her, that from her birth, she had never removed from *Bristol,* a place where he never was, he rejected the belief of having seen her, and supposed his mind had been deluded by an idea of some other, whom she might have a resemblance of.

They passed the time of their journey in as much happiness as the most luxurious gratification of wild desires could make them; and when they came to the end of it, parted not without a mutual promise of seeing each other often.—He told her to what place she should direct a letter to him; and she assured him she would send to let him know where to come to her, as soon as she was fixed in lodgings.

She kept her promise; and charmed with the continuance of his eager fondness, went not home, but into private lodgings, whence she wrote to him to visit her the first opportunity, and inquire for the Widow *Bloomer.*—She had no sooner dispatched this billet,[7] than she repaired to the house where she had lodged as *Fantomina,* charging

---

6. Comedians are actors. There were only two public playhouses in London, established by royal decree in 1660.
7. Note, brief letter.

the people if *Beauplaisir* should come there, not to let him know she had been out of town. From thence she wrote to him, in a different hand, a long letter of complaint, that he had been so cruel in not sending one letter to her all the time he had been absent, entreated to see him, and concluded with subscribing herself his unalterably affectionate *Fantomina*. She received in one day answers to both these. The first contained these lines:

To the Charming Mrs. Bloomer,

It would be impossible, my Angel! for me to express the thousandth part of that infinity of transport, the sight of your dear letter gave me.—Never was woman formed to charm like you: never did any look like you,—write like you,—bless like you;—nor did ever man adore as I do.—Since yesterday we parted, I have seemed a body without a soul; and had you not by this inspiring billet, gave me new life, I know not what by tomorrow I should have been.—I will be with you this evening about five:—O, 'tis an age till then!—But the cursed formalities of duty oblige me to dine with my lord —— who never rises from table till that hour;—therefore adieu till then sweet lovely mistress of the soul and all the faculties of

Your most faithful,
BEAUPLAISIR.

The other was in this manner:

To the Lovely Fantomina,

If you were half so sensible as you ought of your own power of charming, you would be assured, that to be unfaithful or unkind to you, would be among the things that are in their very natures impossibilities.—It was my misfortune, not my fault, that you were not persecuted every post with a declaration of my unchanging passion; but I had unluckily forgot the name of the woman at whose house you are, and knew not how to form a direction that it might come safe to your hands.—And, indeed, the reflection how you might misconstrue my silence, brought me to town some weeks sooner than I intended—If you knew how I have languished to renew those blessings I am permitted to enjoy in your society, you would rather pity than condemn

Your ever faithful,
BEAUPLAISIR.

P.S. *I fear I cannot see you till tomorrow; some business has unluckily fallen out that will engross my hours till then.—Once more, my dear, Adieu.*

Traitor! (*cried she*) as soon as she had read them, 'tis thus our silly, fond, believing sex are served when they put faith in man: so had I been deceived and cheated, had I like the rest believed, and sat down mourning in absence, and vainly waiting recovered tendernesses.—How do some women (*continued she*) make their life a hell, burning in fruitless expectations, and dreaming out their days in hopes and fears, then wake at last to all the horror of despair?—But I have outwitted even the most subtle of the deceiving kind, and while he thinks to fool me, is himself the only beguiled person.

She made herself, most certainly, extremely happy in the reflection on the success of her stratagems; and while the knowledge of his inconstancy and levity of nature kept her from having that real tenderness for him she would else have had, she found the means of gratifying the inclination she had for his agreeable person, in as full a manner as she could wish. She had all the sweets of love, but as yet had tasted none of the gall, and was in a state of contentment, which might be envied by the more delicate.

When the expected hour arrived, she found that her lover had lost no part of the fervency with which he had parted from her; but when the next day she received him as *Fantomina,* she perceived a prodigious difference; which led her again into reflections on the unaccountableness of men's fancies, who still prefer the last conquest, only because it is the last.—Here was an evident proof of it; for there could not be a difference in merit, because they were the same person; but the Widow *Bloomer* was a more new acquaintance than *Fantomina,* and therefore esteemed more valuable. This, indeed, must be said of *Beauplaisir,* that he had a greater share of good nature than most of his sex, who, for the most part, when they are weary of an intrigue, break it entirely off, without any regard to the despair of the abandoned nymph. Though he retained no more than a bare pity and complaisance for *Fantomina,* yet believing she loved him to an excess, would not entirely forsake her, though the continuance of his visits was now become rather a penance than a pleasure.

The Widow *Bloomer* triumphed some time longer over the heart of this inconstant, but at length her sway was at an end, and she sunk in this character, to the same degree of tastelessness, as she had done before in that of *Fantomina* and *Celia.*—She presently perceived it, but bore it as she had always done; it being but what she expected, she had prepared herself for it, and had another project in embryo, which she soon ripened into action. She did not, indeed, complete it altogether so suddenly as she had done the others, by reason there must be persons employed in it; and the aversion she had to any confidants in her affairs, and the caution with which she had hitherto acted, and which she was still determined to continue, made it very difficult for her to find a way without breaking through that resolution to compass what she wished.—She got over the difficulty at last, however, by proceeding in a manner, if possible, more extraordinary than all her former behavior:—muffling herself up in her hood one day, she went into the park about the hour when there are a great many necessitous gentlemen,[8] who think themselves above doing what they call little things for a maintenance, walking in the *Mall,*[9] to take a *Camelion* Treat,[1] and fill their stomachs with air instead of meat. Two of those, who by their physiognomy she thought most proper for her purpose, she beckoned to come to her; and taking them into a walk more remote from company, began to communicate the business she had with them in these words: I am sensible, gentlemen (*said she*), that, through the blindness of fortune, and partiality of the world, merit frequently goes unrewarded, and that those of the best pretentions meet with the least encouragement:—I ask your pardon (*continued she*), perceiving they seemed surprised, if I am mistaken in the notion, that you two may, perhaps, be of the number of those who have reason to complain of the injustice of

---

8. Poor men.
9. A popular walk in St. James's Park.
1. Chameleons were thought to subsist on air.

fate; but if you are such as I take you for, I have a proposal to make you, which may be of some little advantage to you. Neither of them made any immediate answer, but appeared buried in consideration for some moments. At length, we should, doubtless, madam (*said one of them*), willingly come into any measures to oblige you, provided they are such as may bring us into no danger, either as to our persons or reputations. That which I require of you (*resumed she*), has nothing in it criminal: All that I desire is *secrecy* in what you are entrusted, and to disguise yourselves in such a manner as you cannot be known, if hereafter seen by the person on whom you are to impose.— In fine, the business is only an innocent frolic, but if blazed abroad, might be taken for too great a freedom in me:—Therefore, if you resolve to assist me, here are five pieces to drink my health, and assure you, that I have not discoursed you[2] on an affair, I design not to proceed in; and when it is accomplished fifty more lie ready for your acceptance. These words, and, above all, the money, which was a sum which, 'tis probable, they had not seen of a long time, made them immediately assent to all she desired, and press for the beginning of their employment: but things were not yet ripe for execution; and she told them, that the next day they should be let into the secret, charging them to meet her in the same place at an hour she appointed. 'Tis hard to say, which of these parties went away best pleased; *they*, that fortune had sent them so unexpected a windfall; or *she*, that she had found persons, who appeared so well qualified to serve her.

Indefatigable in the pursuit of whatsoever her humor was bent upon, she had no sooner left her new-engaged emissaries, than she went in search of a house for the completing of her project.—She pitched on one very large, and magnificently furnished, which she hired by the week, giving them the money beforehand, to prevent any inquiries. The next day she repaired to the park, where she met the punctual 'squires of low degree; and ordering them to follow her to the house she had taken, told them they must condescend to appear like servants, and gave each of them a very rich livery. Then writing a letter to *Beauplaisir,* in a character vastly different from either of those she had made use of, as *Fantomina,* or the fair Widow *Bloomer,* ordered one of them to deliver it into his own hands, to bring back an answer, and to be careful that he sifted out nothing of the truth.—I do not fear (*said she*), that you should discover to him who I am, because that is a secret, of which you yourselves are ignorant; but I would have you be so careful in your replies, that he may not think the concealment springs from any other reasons than your great integrity to your trust.— Seem therefore to know my whole affairs; and let your refusing to make him partaker in the secret, appear to be only the effect of your zeal for my interest and reputation. Promises of entire fidelity on the one side, and reward on the other, being past, the messenger made what haste he could to the house of *Beauplaisir;* and being there told where he might find him, performed exactly the injunction that had been given him. But never astonishment exceeded that which *Beauplaisir* felt at the reading this billet, in which he found these lines:

To the All-conquering Beauplaisir:

I imagine not that 'tis a new thing to you, to be told, you are the greatest charm in nature to our sex: I shall therefore, not to fill up my letter with any impertinent praises on your wit or person, only tell you, that I am infinite in love with both, and if you have a heart not too deeply engaged, should think myself the happiest

2. Talked to you.

*of my sex in being capable of inspiring it with some tenderness.—There is but
one thing in my power to refuse you, which is the knowledge of my name, which
believing the sight of my face will render no secret, you must not take it ill that I
conceal from you.—The bearer of this is a person I can trust; send by him your
answer; but endeavor not to dive into the meaning of this mystery, which will be
impossible for you to unravel, and at the same time very much disoblige me:—
But that you may be in no apprehensions of being imposed on by a woman unworthy of your regard, I will venture to assure you, the first and greatest men in
the kingdom would think themselves blessed to have that influence over me you
have, though unknown to yourself, acquired.—But I need not go about to raise
your curiosity, by giving you any idea of what my person is; if you think fit to be
satisfied, resolve to visit me tomorrow about three in the afternoon; and though
my face is hid, you shall not want sufficient demonstration, that she who takes
these unusual measures to commence a friendship with you, is neither old, nor
deformed. Till then I am,*

Yours,
INCOGNITA.[3]

He had scarce come to the conclusion, before he asked the person who brought
it, from what place he came;—the name of the lady he served;—if she were a wife,
or widow, and several other questions directly opposite to the directions of the
letter; but silence would have availed him as much as did all those testimonies of
curiosity: no *Italian Bravo,*[4] employed in a business of the like nature, performed
his office with more artifice; and the impatient inquirer was convinced, that nothing but doing as he was desired, could give him any light into the character of the
woman who declared so violent a passion for him; and little fearing any consequence which could ensue from such an encounter, resolved to rest satisfied till
he was informed of everything from herself, not imagining this *Incognita* varied
so much from the generality of her sex, as to be able to refuse the knowledge of
anything to the man she loved with that transcendency of passion she professed,
and which his many successes with the ladies gave him encouragement enough to
believe. He therefore took pen and paper, and answered her letter in terms tender
enough for a man who had never seen the person to whom he wrote. The words
were as follows:

To the Obliging and Witty Incognita.

*Though to tell me I am happy enough to be liked by a woman, such, as by your
manner of writing, I imagine you to be, is an honor which I can never sufficiently
acknowledge, yet I know not how I am able to content myself with admiring the
wonders of your wit alone: I am certain, a soul like yours must shine in your eyes
with a vivacity, which must bless all they look on.—I shall, however, endeavor to
restrain myself in those bounds you are pleased to set me, till by the knowledge of
my inviolable fidelity, I may be thought worthy of gazing on that heaven I am now
but to enjoy in contemplation.—You need not doubt my glad compliance with your
obliging summons: there is a charm in your lines, which gives too sweet an idea*

3. Unknown woman (Latin); i.e., a woman in disguise.
4. Hired assassin.

of their lovely author to be resisted.—I am all impatient for the blissful moment, which is to throw me at your feet, and give me an opportunity of convincing you that I am,

Your everlasting slave,
BEAUPLAISIR.

Nothing could be more pleased than she, to whom it was directed, at the receipt of this letter; but when she was told how inquisitive he had been concerning her character and circumstances, she could not forbear laughing heartily to think of the tricks she had played him, and applauding her own strength of genius, and force of resolution, which by such unthought-of ways could triumph over her lover's inconstancy, and render that very temper, which to other women is the greatest curse, a means to make herself more blessed.—Had he been faithful to me (*said she, to herself*), either as *Fantomina,* or *Celia,* or the Widow *Bloomer,* the most violent passion, if it does not change its object, in time will wither: possession naturally abates the vigor of desire, and I should have had, at best, but a cold, insipid, husband-like lover in my arms; but by these arts of passing on him as a new mistress whenever the ardor, which alone makes love a blessing, begins to diminish, for the former one, I have him always raving, wild, impatient, longing, dying.—O that all neglected wives, and fond abandoned nymphs would take this method!—Men would be caught in their own snare, and have no cause to scorn our easy, weeping, wailing sex! Thus did she pride herself as if secure she never should have any reason to repent the present gaiety of her humor. The hour drawing near in which he was to come, she dressed herself in as magnificent a manner, as if she were to be that night at a ball at court, endeavoring to repair the want of those beauties which the vizard[5] should conceal, by setting forth the others with the greatest care and exactness. Her fine shape, and air, and neck appeared to great advantage; and by that which was to be seen of her, one might believe the rest to be perfectly agreeable. *Beauplaisir* was prodigiously charmed, as well with her appearance, as with the manner she entertained him: but though he was wild with impatience for the sight of a face which belonged to so exquisite a body, yet he would not immediately press for it, believing before he left her he should easily obtain that satisfaction.—A noble collation being over, he began to sue for the performance of her promise of granting everything he could ask, excepting the sight of her face, and knowledge of her name. It would have been a ridiculous piece of affectation in her to have seemed coy in complying with what she herself had been the first in desiring: she yielded without even a show of reluctance: and if there be any true felicity in an amour such as theirs, both here enjoyed it to the full. But not in the height of all their mutual raptures, could he prevail on her to satisfy his curiosity with the sight of her face: she told him that she hoped he knew so much of her, as might serve to convince him, she was not unworthy of his tenderest regard; and if he could not content himself with that which she was willing to reveal, and which was the conditions of their meeting, dear as he was to her, she would rather part with him for ever, than consent to gratify an inquisitiveness, which, in her opinion, had no business with his love. It was in vain that he endeavored to make her sensible of her mistake; and that this restraint was the greatest enemy imaginable to the happiness of them both: she was not to be persuaded, and he was obliged to desist his solicitations, though determined in his

5. Mask or veil.

mind to compass what he so ardently desired, before he left the house. He then turned the discourse wholly on the violence of the passion he had for her; and expressed the greatest discontent in the world at the apprehensions of being separated;—swore he could dwell for ever in her arms, and with such an undeniable earnestness pressed to be permitted to tarry with her the whole night, that had she been less charmed with his renewed eagerness of desire, she scarce would have had the power of resisting him; but in granting this request, she was not without a thought that he had another reason for making it besides the extremity of his passion, and had it immediately in her head how to disappoint him.

The hours of repose being arrived, he begged she would retire to her chamber, to which she consented, but obliged him to go to bed first; which he did not much oppose, because he supposed she would not lie in her mask, and doubted not but the morning's dawn would bring the wished discovery.—The two imagined servants ushered him to his new lodging; where he lay some moments in all the perplexity imaginable at the oddness of this adventure. But she suffered not these cogitations to be of any long continuance: she came, but came in the dark; which being no more than he expected by the former part of her proceedings, he said nothing of; but as much satisfaction as he found in her embraces, nothing ever longed for the approach of day with more impatience than he did. At last it came; but how great was his disappointment, when by the noises he heard in the street, the hurry of the coaches, and the cries of penny-merchants,[6] he was convinced it was night nowhere but with him? He was still in the same darkness as before; for she had taken care to blind the windows in such a manner, that not the least chink was left to let in day.—He complained of her behavior in terms that she would not have been able to resist yielding to, if she had not been certain it would have been the ruin of her passion:—she, therefore, answered him only as she had done before; and getting out of the bed from him, flew out of the room with too much swiftness for him to have overtaken her, if he had attempted it. The moment she left him, the two attendants entered the chamber, and plucking down the implements which had screened him from the knowledge of that which he so much desired to find out, restored his eyes once more to day:—they attended to assist him in dressing, brought him tea, and by their obsequiousness, let him see there was but one thing which the mistress of them would not gladly oblige him in.—He was so much out of humor, however, at the disappointment of his curiosity, that he resolved never to make a second visit.—Finding her in an outer room, he made no scruple of expressing the sense he had of the little trust she reposed in him, and at last plainly told her, he could not submit to receive obligations from a lady, who thought him uncapable of keeping a secret, which she made no difficulty of letting her servants into.—He resented—he once more entreated—he said all that man could do, to prevail on her to unfold the mystery; but all his adjurations were fruitless; and he went out of the house determined never to re-enter it, till she should pay the price of his company with the discovery of her face and circumstances.—She suffered him to go with this resolution, and doubted not but he would recede from it, when he reflected on the happy moments they had passed together; but if he did not, she comforted herself with the design of forming some other stratagem, with which to impose on him a fourth time.

6. Street vendors of cheap wares.

She kept the house, and her gentlemen-equipage[7] for about a fortnight, in which time she continued to write to him as *Fantomina* and the Widow *Bloomer,* and received the visits he sometimes made to each; but his behavior to both was grown so cold, that she began to grow as weary of receiving his now insipid caresses as he was of offering them: she was beginning to think in what manner she should drop these two characters, when the sudden arrival of her mother, who had been some time in a foreign country, obliged her to put an immediate stop to the course of her whimsical adventures.—That lady, who was severely virtuous, did not approve of many things she had been told of the conduct of her daughter; and though it was not in the power of any person in the world to inform her of the truth of what she had been guilty of, yet she heard enough to make her keep her afterwards in a restraint, little agreeable to her humor, and the liberties to which she had been accustomed.

But this confinement was not the greatest part of the trouble of this now afflicted lady: she found the consequences of her amorous follies would be, without almost a miracle, impossible to be concealed:—she was with child; and though she would easily have found means to have screened even this from the knowledge of the world, had she been at liberty to have acted with the same unquestionable authority over herself, as she did before the coming of her mother, yet now all her invention was at a loss for a stratagem to impose on a woman of her penetration:—by eating little, lacing prodigious straight, and the advantage of a great hoop-petticoat, however, her bigness was not taken notice of, and, perhaps, she would not have been suspected till the time of her going into the country, where her mother designed to send her, and from whence she intended to make her escape to some place where she might be delivered with secrecy, if the time of it had not happened much sooner than she expected.—A ball being at court, the good old lady was willing she should partake of the diversion of it as a farewell to the town.—It was there she was seized with those pangs, which none in her condition are exempt from:—she could not conceal the sudden rack which all at once invaded her; or had her tongue been mute, her wildly rolling eyes, the distortion of her features, and the convulsions which shook her whole frame, in spite of her, would have revealed she labored under some terrible shock of nature.— Everybody was surprised, everybody was concerned, but few guessed at the occasion.— Her mother grieved beyond expression, doubted not but she was struck with the hand of death; and ordered her to be carried home in a chair, while herself followed in another.—A physician was immediately sent for: but he presently perceiving what was her distemper, called the old lady aside, and told her, it was not a doctor of his sex, but one of her own, her daughter stood in need of.—Never was astonishment and horror greater than that which seized the soul of this afflicted parent at these words: she could not for a time believe the truth of what she heard; but he insisting on it, and conjuring her to send for a midwife, she was at length convinced of it.—All the pity and tenderness she had been for some moment before possessed of now vanished, and were succeeded by an adequate[8] shame and indignation:—she flew to the bed where her daughter was lying, and telling her what she had been informed of, and which she was now far from doubting, commanded her to reveal the name of the person whose insinuations had drawn her to this dishonor.—It was a great while before she could be brought to confess anything, and much longer before she could be prevailed on to name the man whom she so fatally had loved; but the rack of nature growing more

7. Retinue of footmen.
8. Equal.

fierce, and the enraged old lady protesting no help should be afforded her while she persisted in her obstinacy, she, with great difficulty and hesitation in her speech, at last pronounced the name of *Beauplaisir.* She had no sooner satisfied her weeping mother, than that sorrowful lady sent messengers at the same time, for a midwife, and for that gentleman who had occasioned the other's being wanted.—He happened by accident to be at home, and immediately obeyed the summons, though prodigiously surprised what business a lady so much a stranger to him could have to impart.—But how much greater was his amazement, when taking him into her closet, she there acquainted him with her daughter's misfortune, of the discovery she had made, and how far he was concerned in it?—All the idea one can form of wild astonishment, was mean to what he felt:—he assured her, that the young lady her daughter was a person whom he had never, more than at a distance, admired:—that he had indeed, spoke to her in public company, but that he never had a thought which tended to her dishonor.—His denials, if possible, added to the indignation she was before enflamed with:—she had no longer patience; and carrying him into the chamber, where she was just delivered of a fine girl, cried out, I will not be imposed on: the truth by one of you shall be revealed.—*Beauplaisir* being brought to the bedside, was beginning to address himself to the lady in it, to beg she could clear the mistake her mother was involved in; when she, covering herself with the cloths, and ready to die a second time with the inward agitations of her soul, shrieked out, Oh, I am undone!—I cannot live, and bear this shame!—But the old lady believing that now or never was the time to dive into the bottom of this mystery, forcing her to rear her head, told her, she should not hope to escape the scrutiny of a parent she had dishonored in such a manner, and pointing to *Beauplaisir,* Is this the gentleman (*said she*), to whom you owe your ruin? or have you deceived me by a fictitious tale? Oh! no (*resumed the trembling creature*), he is, indeed, the innocent cause of my undoing:—Promise me your pardon (*continued she*), and I will relate the means. Here she ceased, expecting what she would reply, which, on hearing *Beauplaisir* cry out, What mean you, madam? I your undoing, who never harbored the least design on you in my life, she did in these words, Though the injury you have done your family (*said she*), is of a nature which cannot justly hope forgiveness, yet be assured, I shall much sooner excuse you when satisfied of the truth, than while I am kept in a suspense, if possible, as vexatious as the crime itself is to me. Encouraged by this she related the whole truth. And 'tis difficult to determine, if *Beauplaisir,* or the lady, were most surprised at what they heard; he, that he should have been blinded so often by her artifices; or she, that so young a creature should have the skill to make use of them. Both sat for some time in a profound reverie; till at length she broke it first in these words: Pardon, sir (*said she*),[9] the trouble I have given you: I must confess it was with a design to oblige you to repair the supposed injury you had done this unfortunate girl, by marrying her, but now I know not what to say:—The blame is wholly hers, and I have nothing to request further of you, than that you will not divulge the distracted folly she has been guilty of.—He answered her in terms perfectly polite; but made no offer of that which, perhaps, she expected, though could not, now informed of her daughter's proceedings, demand. He assured her, however, that if she would commit the newborn lady to his care, he would discharge it faithfully. But neither of them would consent to that; and he took his leave, full of cogitations,[1] more confused than ever he had known in his

9. I.e., the elder lady.
1. Anxious thoughts.

whole life. He continued to visit there, to inquire after her health every day; but the old lady perceiving there was nothing likely to ensue from these civilities, but, perhaps, a renewing of the crime, she entreated him to refrain; and as soon as her daughter was in a condition, sent her to a monastery in *France,* the abbess of which had been her particular friend. And thus ended an intrigue, which, considering the time it lasted, was as full of variety as any, perhaps, that many ages have produced.

CAO XUEQIN ▪ (c. 1715–1763)

Scholars and readers alike have agreed that *The Story of the Stone* is the greatest Chinese novel, but about the nature of its greatness lively differences of opinion have swirled from its first appearance. Uncertainty and controversy surround its very authorship. Of its 120 chapters, only the first eighty were written by its supposed author, Cao Xueqin, the descendant of a family of distinguished generals and government officials whose fortunes had recently drastically declined. Copies of the unfinished manuscript circulated among the author's circle of friends for decades, augmented by a running commentary penned by someone clearly familiar with details of his life and identified only as Red Inkstone, along with additional remarks by several other readers. When the novel was finally published in 1791, long after Cao's death, it was accompanied by the prefaces of two other individuals who also claimed to have found a fragmentary conclusion that they edited and completed. These additional forty chapters recount a dizzying set of events whose correspondence to the author's original intention was almost immediately debated. Even the title of the novel has been subject to discussion. Cao refers to it as *The Story of the Stone* in his first chapter, but it has been more commonly known in China by another title drawn from a list of alternatives he also provides there, *Dream of the Red Chamber.*

Subsequent generations of amateurs and scholars have generated a cottage industry of *"Red* studies" arguing about the facts and the merits of the novel's authorship and its themes. Early readers assumed a close connection to Cao Xueqin's own life, about which surprisingly little is known for certain, given the prominence of his family. Even before the conquest of China by the Manchus, his forefathers had been captured by the future rulers of the Qing Empire (1644–1911) and entered into their service. Cao's grandfather held the relatively powerful post of Imperial Textile Commissioner in Nanjing and was succeeded by his son. The family's fortunes shifted, however, when a struggle for the throne after the emperor's death found it allied with the losing side. Its considerable estate was confiscated, and it was forced to live largely off the kindness of relatives in Beijing. Cao's pampered childhood thus became a distant memory. He worked as a clerk in the imperial school, may have passed a low-level civil service examination and held minor office, and appears to have also supported himself by selling his own paintings (although not well enough to pay off rather hefty drinking debts). *The Story of the Stone,* which he drafted between 1740 and 1750 and revised five times, was clearly his major accomplishment and appears to have drawn heavily upon his family's experiences.

The novel has successfully resisted the dogged efforts of generations of Chinese critics to establish precise correspondences between its characters and events and those of the author's own life. Cao Xueqin was the first major author to base his novel on personal history, but he was also clearly fascinated by the many possibilities for manipulating illusion and reality opened up by fiction. An often-cited couplet from the novel proclaims that "Truth becomes fiction when the fiction's true; / Real becomes not-real where the unreal's real," and the work plays with both language and plot to test the patience of would-be literary detectives. The surname of its main family, for example,

Jia, is a homophone for "false," and a second family introduced late in the novel is surnamed Zhen, which sounds like the word "true"; their fortunes mirror in reverse those of the protagonists. Two minor characters are named Zhen Shiyin and Jia Yucun, puns on phrases meaning "true things hidden" and "false words preserved."

The opening chapter of *The Story of the Stone* literally contains the novel in its entirety. A stone rejected by a goddess who was repairing the sky is picked up by a Buddhist monk and a Daoist priest and taken into the world of mortals, to be found eons later in the same place by another Daoist, with the long story of its worldly experiences inscribed upon it. The story of the stone, then, is on the stone itself. In addition to situating the novel's origins within the realm of myth, perhaps seeking to deflect in some measure the suspicions of some readers who might want to discern political allegory or critique within it, this first chapter provides an opportunity for Cao to foreground his interest in the nature of fiction, which is the topic of a conversation between the second Daoist and the inscribed stone itself. It also explains the dynamic of the novel's most important relationship, for before going into the world the stone tenderly waters with sweet dew a lovely flower, who thus incurs a karmic debt of a lifetime of tears. As it turns out, this will be repaid in the rest of the novel by the young Lin Dai-yu, whose love for her cousin Jia Bao-yu ("Precious Jade"), the protagonist born with a jade stone in his mouth, is cause for constant weeping throughout the story. Other elements of this narrative envelope, like the Buddhist and Daoist priests, appear at crucial moments of the boy's life as well.

Vanitas (*Kongkong daoren,* or the Daoist of Emptiness) is the name of the second Daoist, suggesting the importance of understanding *The Story of the Stone* within a religious or philosophical framework that would insist on the vain and transitory nature of the material world. Curious nonetheless about the human world of sentiments and attachments, the stone is given the opportunity to be reincarnated as the adolescent Bao-yu, whose nine years of embroilment in a panoply of pleasures and sorrows are a necessary prerequisite to eventual detachment, enlightenment and return from that world. Yet the vivid and loving detail of his experiences recorded in this five-volume novel belies such an unequivocal commitment to disengagement from it.

Indeed, no other traditional Chinese novel provides such a richly depicted account of both the emotions and the contexts of human interaction. Jia Bao-yu is the scion of an extended family that occupies two large and complex households in some unspecified city with characteristics of both Nanjing and Beijing. His father is a rising official and his older sister an honored imperial concubine, but the family's position and wealth decline, first gradually and then precipitously, over the course of the novel. His early "golden" days are spent cavorting with cousins and friends, mostly girls, in a vast garden constructed by the family to honor a rare visit home by his sister and in which the children have afterward been given permission to reside. Parties, opera performances and poetry contests punctuate the leisurely daily rhythms of rich meals, sexual experimentation, and intrigues between and among the children and their personal servants. As the years go by Bao-yu, with the frequent protection of his doting grandmother, must resist two pressures to abandon these carefree pursuits: his father's stern, rigidly Confucian injunctions to study hard for the civil service examinations and a successful career as a bureaucrat, and his mother's concern that he find an appropriate match for his own sake and that of the family line. Bao-yu's affection for his cousin Dai-yu feels predetermined to him (as indeed it is), but worries about her frail health lead the adults to focus on another differently attractive cousin, both sturdier and less temperamental, Xue Bao-chai. Having been given a gold locket at her birth by a strange monk, with the instruction to seek a mate of jade, she seems equally destined for Bao-yu. The charged and complicated interactions within this triangle, captured with unprecedented psychological depth and animation, have captivated the attention and allegiances of readers for generations.

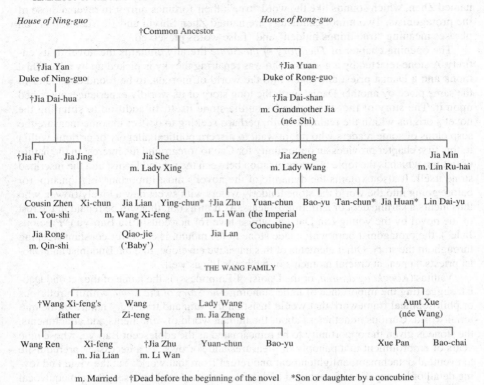

GENEALOGY OF THE NING-GUO AND RONG-GUO HOUSES OF THE JIA CLAN

House of Ning-guo   *House of Rong-guo*

†Common Ancestor

†Jia Yan
Duke of Ning-guo

†Jia Yuan
Duke of Rong-guo

†Jia Dai-hua

†Jia Dai-shan
m. Grandmother Jia
(née Shi)

†Jia Fu   Jia Jing

Jia She
m. Lady Xing

Jia Zheng
m. Lady Wang

Jia Min
m. Lin Ru-hai

Cousin Zhen   Xi-chun   Jia Lian   Ying-chun*   †Jia Zhu   Yuan-chun   Bao-yu   Tan-chun*   Jia Huan*   Lin Dai-yu
m. You-shi   m. Wang Xi-feng   m. Li Wan   (the Imperial

Jia Rong   Qiao-jie   Jia Lan   Concubine)
m. Qin-shi   ('Baby')

THE WANG FAMILY

†Wang Xi-feng's
father

Wang
Zi-teng

Lady Wang
m. Jia Zheng

Aunt Xue
(née Wang)

Wang Ren   Xi-feng   †Jia Zhu   Yuan-chun   Bao-yu   Xue Pan   Bao-chai
m. Jia Lian   m. Li Wan

m. Married   †Dead before the beginning of the novel   *Son or daughter by a concubine

The Story of the Stone also serves as a veritable encyclopedia of late imperial Chinese society and culture. Over four hundred characters enter its pages, hailing from all walks of life and involved in subplots of often considerable intricacy. Detailed descriptions of buildings, gardens, furniture, medicines, food, and drink are matched by exquisitely described clothing, jewelry, makeup, and coiffures. There is a wealth of information regarding family structure, rituals, etiquette, games, performances, and other pastimes of the aristocracy, as well as the extraordinary complexity of running such vast domains. With the exception of Bao-yu himself, the novel focuses on the fate of the family's numerous young women. They are both the most talented and capable characters of the lot and the most vulnerable; indeed, the lives of most end miserably, in unhappy marriages, nunneries, suicides, or painful deaths.

The fate of the Jia family as a whole unfolds inexorably over the first eighty chapters, its decline attributable to a number of factors such as overindulgence, corruption, and Bao-yu's own weakness, not to mention the narrative frame that requires it. During the last third of the novel, the pace of events quickens markedly as the family's fortune and position are lost and its property confiscated, before the novel finally ends in the renunciation provided for in the beginning of *The Story of the Stone*. Only a small portion of this vast work could be included here, but the process of excerpting does less damage than might be expected, since the work is shaped as much by sequences of vignettes as it is by the forward movement of plot. If Cao Xueqin wants the reader to take heed of the risks of attachment to this world, he provides at the same time lessons worth lingering over.

PRONUNCIATIONS:
   Cao Xueqin: TSAO shweh-CHIN
   Jia Bao-yu: GEE-ah BOW-yü
   Lin Dai-yu: LIN DIE-yü
   Xue Bao-chai: SHWEH BOW-chai

from The Story of the Stone[1]

Chapter 1

> *Zhen Shi-yin makes the Stone's acquaintance in a dream*
> *And Jia Yu-cun finds that poverty is not incompatible with romantic feelings*

GENTLE READER,

What, you may ask, was the origin of this book?

Though the answer to this question may at first seem to border on the absurd, reflection will show that there is a good deal more in it than meets the eye.

Long ago, when the goddess Nü-wa was repairing the sky, she melted down a great quantity of rock and, on the Incredible Crags of the Great Fable Mountains, moulded the amalgam into thirty-six thousand, five hundred and one large building blocks, each measuring seventy-two feet by a hundred and forty-four feet square. She used thirty-six thousand five hundred of these blocks in the course of her building operations, leaving a single odd block unused, which lay, all on its own, at the foot of Greensickness Peak in the aforementioned mountains.

Now this block of stone, having undergone the melting and moulding of a goddess, possessed magic powers. It could move about at will and could grow or shrink to any size it wanted. Observing that all the other blocks had been used for celestial repairs and that it was the only one to have been rejected as unworthy, it became filled with shame and resentment and passed its days in sorrow and lamentation.

One day, in the midst of its lamentings, it saw a monk and a Taoist approaching from a great distance, each of them remarkable for certain eccentricities of manner and appearance. When they arrived at the foot of Greensickness Peak, they sat down on the ground and began to talk. The monk, catching sight of a lustrous, translucent stone—it was in fact the rejected building block which had now shrunk itself to the size of a fan-pendant and looked very attractive in its new shape—took it up on the palm of his hand and addressed it with a smile:

"Ha, I see you have magical properties! But nothing to recommend you. I shall have to cut a few words on you so that anyone seeing you will know at once that you are something special. After that I shall take you to a certain

brilliant
successful
poetical

1. Translated by David Hawkes.

cultivated

aristocratic

elegant

delectable

luxurious

opulent

locality on a little trip."

The stone was delighted.

"What words will you cut? Where is this place you will take me to? I beg to be enlightened."

"Do not ask," replied the monk with a laugh. "You will know soon enough when the time comes."

And with that he slipped the stone into his sleeve and set off at a great pace with the Taoist. But where they both went to I have no idea.

Countless aeons went by and a certain Taoist called Vanitas in quest of the secret of immortality chanced to be passing below that same Greensickness Peak in the Incredible Crags of the Great Fable Mountains when he caught sight of a large stone standing there, on which the characters of a long inscription were clearly discernible.

Vanitas read the inscription through from beginning to end and learned that this was a once lifeless stone block which had been found unworthy to repair the sky, but which had magically transformed its shape and been taken down by the Buddhist mahāsattva Impervioso and the Taoist illuminate Mysterioso into the world of mortals, where it had lived out the life of a man before finally attaining nirvana and returning to the other shore. The inscription named the country where it had been born, and went into considerable detail about its domestic life, youthful amours, and even the verses, mottoes and riddles it had written. All it lacked was the authentication of a dynasty and date. On the back of the stone was inscribed the following quatrain:

> Found unfit to repair the azure sky
> Long years a foolish mortal man was I.
> My life in both worlds on this stone is writ:
> Pray who will copy out and publish it?

From his reading of the inscription Vanitas realized that this was a stone of some consequence. Accordingly he addressed himself to it in the following manner:

"Brother Stone, according to what you yourself seem to imply in these verses, this story of yours contains matter of sufficient interest to merit publication and has been carved here with that end in view. But as far as I can see (a) it has no discoverable dynastic period, and (b) it contains no examples of moral grandeur among its characters—no statesmanship, no social message of any kind. All I can find in it, in fact, are a number of females, conspicuous, if at all, only for their passion or folly or for some trifling talent or insignificant virtue. Even if I were to copy all this out, I cannot see that it would make a very remarkable book."

"Come, your reverence," said the stone (for Vanitas had been correct in assuming that it could speak) "must you be so obtuse? All the romances ever written have an artificial period setting—Han or Tang for the most part. In refusing to make use of that stale old convention and telling my *Story of the Stone* exactly as it occurred, it seems to me that, far from *depriving* it of anything, I have given it a freshness these other books do not have.

"Your so-called 'historical romances,' consisting, as they do, of scandalous anecdotes about statesmen and emperors of bygone days and scabrous attacks on the reputations of long-dead gentlewomen, contain more wickedness and immorality than I care to mention. Still worse is the 'erotic novel,' by whose filthy obscenities our young folk are all too easily corrupted. And the 'boudoir romances,' those dreary stereotypes with their volume after volume all pitched on the same note and their different characters undistinguishable except by name (all those ideally beautiful young ladies and ideally eligible young bachelors)—even they seem unable to avoid descending sooner or later into indecency.

"The trouble with this last kind of romance is that it only gets written in the first place because the author requires a framework in which to show off his love-poems. He goes about constructing this framework quite mechanically, beginning with the names of his pair of young lovers and invariably adding a third character, a servant or the like, to make mischief between them, like the *chou*[2] in a comedy.

"What makes these romances even more detestable is the stilted, bombastic language—inanities dressed in pompous rhetoric, remote alike from nature and common sense and teeming with the grossest absurdities.

"Surely my 'number of females,' whom I spent half a lifetime studying with my own eyes and ears, are preferable to this kind of stuff? I do not claim that they are better people than the ones who appear in books written before my time; I am only saying that the contemplation of their actions and motives may prove a more effective antidote to boredom and melancholy. And even the inelegant verses with which my story is interlarded could serve to entertain and amuse on those convivial occasions when rhymes and riddles are in demand.

"All that my story narrates, the meetings and partings, the joys and sorrows, the ups and downs of fortune, are recorded exactly as they happened. I have not dared to add the tiniest bit of touching-up, for fear of losing the true picture.

"My only wish is that men in the world below may sometimes pick up this tale when they are recovering from sleep or drunkenness, or when they wish to escape from business worries or a fit of the dumps, and in doing so find not only mental refreshment but even perhaps, if they will heed its lesson and abandon their vain and frivolous pursuits, some small arrest in the deterioration of their vital forces. What does your reverence say to that?"

For a long time Vanitas stood lost in thought, pondering this speech. He then subjected the *Story of the Stone* to a careful second reading. He could see that its main theme was love; that it consisted quite simply of a true record of real events; and that it was entirely free from any tendency to deprave and corrupt. He therefore copied it all out from beginning to end and took it back with him to look for a publisher.

As a consequence of all this, Vanitas, starting off in the Void (which is Truth) came to the contemplation of Form (which is Illusion); and from Form engendered Passion; and by communicating Passion, entered again into Form; and from Form awoke to the Void (which is Truth). He therefore changed his name from Vanitas to Brother Amor, or the Passionate Monk (because he had approached Truth by way of Passion), and changed the title of the book from *The Story of the Stone* to *The Tale of Brother Amor.*

2. A buffoon.

Old Kong Mei-xi from the homeland of Confucius called the book *A Mirror for the Romantic*. Wu Yu-feng called it *A Dream of Golden Days*. Cao Xueqin in his Nostalgia Studio worked on it for ten years, in the course of which he rewrote it no less than five times, dividing it into chapters, composing chapter headings, renaming it *The Twelve Beauties of Jinling,* and adding an introductory quatrain. Red Inkstone restored the original title when he recopied the book and added his second set of annotations to it.

This, then, is a true account of how *The Story of the Stone* came to be written.

> Pages full of idle words
> Penned with hot and bitter tears:
> All men call the author fool;
> None his secret message hears.

The origin of *The Story of the Stone* has now been made clear. The same cannot, however, be said of the characters and events which it recorded. Gentle reader, have patience! This is how the inscription began:

Long, long ago the world was tilted downwards towards the south-east; and in that lower-lying south-easterly part of the earth there is a city called Soochow; and in Soochow the district around the Chang-men Gate is reckoned one of the two or three wealthiest and most fashionable quarters in the world of men. Outside the Chang-men Gate is a wide thoroughfare called Worldly Way; and somewhere off Worldly Way is an area called Carnal Lane. There is an old temple in the Carnal Lane area which, because of the way it is bottled up inside a narrow *cul-de-sac,* is referred to locally as Bottle-gourd Temple. Next door to Bottle-gourd Temple lived a gentleman of private means called Zhen Shi-yin and his wife Feng-shi, a kind, good woman with a profound sense of decency and decorum. The household was not a particularly wealthy one, but they were nevertheless looked up to by all and sundry as the leading family in the neighbourhood.

Zhen Shi-yin himself was by nature a quiet and totally unambitious person. He devoted his time to his garden and to the pleasures of wine and poetry. Except for a single flaw, his existence could, indeed, have been described as an idyllic one. The flaw was that, although already past fifty, he had no son, only a little girl, just two years old, whose name was Ying-lian.

Once, during the tedium of a burning summer's day, Shi-yin was sitting idly in his study. The book had slipped from his nerveless grasp and his head had nodded down onto the desk in a doze. While in this drowsy state he seemed to drift off to some place he could not identify, where he became aware of a monk and a Taoist walking along and talking as they went.

"Where do you intend to take that thing you are carrying?" the Taoist was asking.

"Don't you worry about him!" replied the monk with a laugh. "There is a batch of lovesick souls awaiting incarnation in the world below whose fate is due to be decided this very day. I intend to take advantage of this opportunity to slip our little friend in amongst them and let him have a taste of human life along with the rest."

"Well, well, so another lot of these amorous wretches is about to enter the vale of tears," said the Taoist. "How did all this begin? And where are the souls to be reborn?"

"You will laugh when I tell you," said the monk. "When this stone was left unused by the goddess, he found himself at a loose end and took to wandering about all over the place for want of better to do, until one day his wanderings took him to the place where the fairy Disenchantment lives.

"Now Disenchantment could tell that there was something unusual about this stone, so she kept him there in her Sunset Glow Palace and gave him the honorary title of Divine Luminescent Stone-in-Waiting in the Court of Sunset Glow.

"But most of his time he spent west of Sunset Glow exploring the banks of the Magic River. There, by the Rock of Rebirth, he found the beautiful Crimson Pearl Flower, for which he conceived such a fancy that he took to watering her every day with sweet dew, thereby conferring on her the gift of life.

"Crimson Pearl's substance was composed of the purest cosmic essences, so she was already half-divine; and now, thanks to the vitalizing effect of the sweet dew, she was able to shed her vegetable shape and assume the form of a girl.

"This fairy girl wandered about outside the Realm of Separation, eating the Secret Passion Fruit when she was hungry and drinking from the Pool of Sadness when she was thirsty. The consciousness that she owed the stone something for his kindness in watering her began to prey on her mind and ended by becoming an obsession.

"'I have no sweet dew here that I can repay him with,' she would say to herself. 'The only way in which I could perhaps repay him would be with the tears shed during the whole of a mortal lifetime if he and I were ever to be reborn as humans in the world below.'

"Because of this strange affair, Disenchantment has got together a group of amorous young souls, of which Crimson Pearl is one, and intends to send them down into the world to take part in the great illusion of human life. And as today happens to be the day on which this stone is fated to go into the world too, I am taking him with me to Disenchantment's tribunal for the purpose of getting him registered and sent down to earth with the rest of these romantic creatures."

"How very amusing!" said the Taoist. "I have certainly never heard of a debt of tears before. Why shouldn't the two of us take advantage of this opportunity to go down into the world ourselves and save a few souls? It would be a work of merit."

"That is exactly what I was thinking," said the monk. "Come with me to Disenchantment's palace to get this absurd creature cleared. Then, when this last batch of romantic idiots goes down, you and I can go down with them. At present about half have already been born. They await this last batch to make up the number."

"Very good, I will go with you then," said the Taoist. Shi-yin heard all this conversation quite clearly, and curiosity impelled him to go forward and greet the two reverend gentlemen. They returned his greeting and asked him what he wanted.

"It is not often that one has the opportunity of listening to a discussion of the operations of *karma* such as the one I have just been privileged to overhear," said Shi-yin. "Unfortunately I am a man of very limited understanding and have not been able to derive the full benefit from your conversation. If you would have the very great kindness to enlighten my benighted understanding with a somewhat fuller account of what you were discussing, I can promise you the most devout attention. I feel sure that your teaching would have a salutary effect on me and—who knows—might save me from the pains of hell."

The reverend gentlemen laughed. "These are heavenly mysteries and may not be divulged. But if you wish to escape from the fiery pit, you have only to remember us when the time comes, and all will be well."

Shi-yin saw that it would be useless to press them. "Heavenly mysteries must not, of course, be revealed. But might one perhaps inquire what the 'absurd creature' is that you were talking about? Is it possible that I might be allowed to see it?"

"Oh, as for that," said the monk: "I think it is on the cards for you to have a look at *him,*" and he took the object from his sleeve and handed it to Shi-yin.

Shi-yin took the object from him and saw that it was a clear, beautiful jade on one side of which were carved the words "Magic Jade." There were several columns of smaller characters on the back, which Shi-yin was just going to examine more closely when the monk, with a cry of "Here we are, at the frontier of Illusion," snatched the stone from him and disappeared, with the Taoist, through a big stone archway above which

THE LAND OF ILLUSION

was written in large characters. A couplet in smaller characters was inscribed vertically on either side of the arch:

> Truth becomes fiction when the fiction's true;
> Real becomes not-real where the unreal's real.

Shi-yin was on the point of following them through the archway when suddenly a great clap of thunder seemed to shake the earth to its very foundations, making him cry out in alarm.

And there he was sitting in his study, the contents of his dream already half forgotten, with the sun still blazing on the ever-rustling plantains outside, and the wet-nurse at the door with his little daughter Ying-lian in her arms. Her delicate little pink-and-white face seemed dearer to him than ever at that moment, and he stretched out his arms to take her and hugged her to him.

After playing with her for a while at his desk, he carried her out to the front of the house to watch the bustle in the street. He was about to go in again when he saw a monk and a Taoist approaching, the monk scabby-headed and barefoot, the Taoist tousle-haired and limping. They were behaving like madmen, shouting with laughter and gesticulating wildly as they walked along.

When this strange pair reached Shi-yin's door and saw him standing there holding Ying-lian, the monk burst into loud sobs. "Patron," he said, addressing Shi-yin, "what are you doing, holding in your arms that ill-fated creature who is destined to involve both her parents in her own misfortune?"

Shi-yin realized that he was listening to the words of a madman and took no notice. But the monk persisted:

"Give her to me! Give her to me!"

Shi-yin was beginning to lose patience and, clasping his little girl more tightly to him, turned on his heel and was about to re-enter the house when the monk pointed his finger at him, roared with laughter, and then proceeded to intone the following verses:

> "Fond man, your pampered child to cherish so—
> That caltrop-glass which shines on melting snow!
> Beware the high feast of the fifteenth day,
> When all in smoke and fire shall pass away!"

Shi-yin heard all this quite plainly and was a little worried by it. He was thinking of asking the monk what lay behind these puzzling words when he heard the Taoist say, "We don't need to stay together. Why don't we part company here and each go about his own business? Three *kalpas* from now I shall wait for you on Bei-mang Hill. Having joined forces again there, we can go together to the Land of Illusion to sign off."

"Excellent!" said the other. And the two of them went off and soon were both lost to sight.

"There must have been something behind all this," thought Shi-yin to himself. "I really ought to have asked him what he meant, but now it is too late."

* * *

One day a desire to savour country sights and sounds led him[3] outside the city walls, and as he walked along with no fixed destination in mind, he presently found himself in a place ringed with hills and full of murmuring brooks and tall stands of bamboo where a temple stood half-hidden among the trees. The walled approach to the gateway had fallen in and parts of the surrounding wall were in ruins. A board above the gate announced the temple's name:

THE TEMPLE OF PERFECT KNOWLEDGE

while two cracked and worn uprights at the sides of the gate were inscribed with the following couplet:

> (on the right-hand side)
> As long as there is a sufficiency behind you, you press greedily forward.

> (on the left-hand side)
> It is only when there is no road in front of you that you think of turning back.

"The wording is commonplace to a degree," Yu-cun reflected, "yet the sentiment is quite profound. In all the famous temples and monasteries I have visited, I cannot recollect having ever seen anything quite like it. I shouldn't be surprised to find that some story of spectacular downfall and dramatic conversion lay behind this inscription. It might be worth going in and inquiring."

But when he went inside and looked around, he saw only an ancient, wizened monk cooking some gruel who paid no attention whatsoever to his greetings and who proved, when Yu-cun went up to him and asked him a few questions, to be both deaf and partially blind. His toothless replies were all but unintelligible, and in any case bore no relation to the questions.

Yu-cun walked out again in disgust. He now thought that in order to give the full rural flavour to his outing he would treat himself to a few cups of wine in a little country inn and accordingly directed his steps towards the near-by village. He had scarcely set foot inside the door of the village inn when one of the men drinking at separate tables inside rose up and advanced to meet him with a broad smile.

"Fancy meeting you!"

It was an antique dealer called Leng Zi-xing whom Yu-cun had got to know some years previously when he was staying in the capital. Yu-cun had a great admiration for Zi-xing as a practical man of business, whilst Zi-xing for his part was tickled to claim acquaintanceship with a man of Yu-cun's great learning and culture. On the basis of this mutual admiration the two of them had got on wonderfully well, and Yu-cun now returned the other's greeting with a pleased smile.

"My dear fellow! How long have you been here? I really had no idea you were in these parts. It was quite an accident that I came here today at all. What an extraordinary coincidence!"

"I went home at the end of last year to spend New Year with the family," said Zi-xing. "On my way back to the capital I thought I would stop off and have a few words with a friend of mine who lives hereabouts, and he very kindly invited me to spend

---

3. Zhen Shi-yin's neighbor, a student named Jia Yu-cun.

a few days with him. I hadn't got any urgent business waiting for me, so I thought I might as well stay on a bit and leave at the middle of the month. I came out here on my own because my friend has an engagement today. I certainly didn't expect to run into *you* here."

Zi-xing conducted Yu-cun to his table as he spoke and ordered more wine and some fresh dishes to be brought. The two men then proceeded, between leisurely sips of wine, to relate what each had been doing in the years that had elapsed since their last meeting.

Presently Yu-cun asked Zi-xing if anything of interest had happened recently in the capital.

"I can't think of anything particularly deserving of mention," said Zi-xing. "Except, perhaps, for a very small but very unusual event that took place in your own clan there."

"What makes you say that?" said Yu-cun, "I have no family connections in the capital."

"Well, it's the same name," said Zi-xing. "They must be the same clan."

Yu-cun asked him what family he could be referring to.

"I fancy you wouldn't disown the Jias of the Rong-guo mansion as unworthy of you."

"Oh, you mean them," said Yu-cun. "There are so many members of my clan, it's hard to keep up with them all. Since the time of Jia Fu of the Eastern Han dynasty there have been branches of the Jia clan in every province of the empire. The Rong-guo branch is, as a matter of fact, on the same clan register as my own; but since they are exalted so far above us socially, we don't normally claim the connection, and nowadays we are completely out of touch with them."

Zi-xing sighed. "You shouldn't speak about them in that way, you know. Nowadays both the Rong and Ning mansions are in a greatly reduced state compared with what they used to be."

"When I was last that way the Rong and Ning mansions both seemed to be fairly humming with life. Surely nothing could have happened to reduce their prosperity in so short a time?"

"Ah, you may well ask. But it's a long story."

"Last time I was in Jinling," went on Yu-cun, "I passed by their two houses one day on my way to Shi-tou-cheng to visit the ruins. The Ning-guo mansion along the eastern half of the road and the Rong-guo mansion along the western half must between them have occupied the greater part of the north side frontage of that street. It's true that there wasn't much activity outside the main entrances, but looking up over the outer walls I had a glimpse of the most magnificent and imposing halls and pavilions, and even the rocks and trees of the gardens beyond seemed to have a sleekness and luxuriance that were certainly not suggestive of a family whose fortunes were in a state of decline."

"Well! For a Palace Graduate Second Class, you ought to know better than that! Haven't you ever heard the old saying, 'The beast with a hundred legs is a long time dying'? Although I say they are not as prosperous as they used to be in years past, of course I don't mean to say that there is not still a world of difference between *their* circumstances and those you would expect to find in the household of your average government official. At the moment the numbers of their establishment and the activities they engage in are, if anything, on the increase. Both masters and servants all lead lives of luxury and magnificence. And they still have plenty of plans and projects under way. But they can't bring themselves to economize or make any adjustment in their accustomed style of living. Consequently, though outwardly they still manage to keep up appearances, inwardly they are beginning to feel the pinch. But that's a small matter. There's something much more seriously wrong with them than that. They are not able to turn out good sons, those stately houses, for all their pomp and show. The males in the family get more degenerate from one generation to the next."

"Surely," said Yu-cun with surprise, "it is inconceivable that such highly cultured households should not give their children the best education possible? I say nothing of other families, but the Jias of the Ning and Rong households used to be famous for the way in which they brought up their sons. How could they come to be as you describe?"

"I assure you, it is precisely those families I am speaking of. Let me tell you something of their history. The Duke of Ning-guo and the Duke of Rong-guo were two brothers by the same mother. Ning-guo was the elder of the two. When he died, his eldest son, Jia Dai-hua, inherited his post. Dai-hua had two sons. The elder, Jia Fu, died at the age of eight or nine, leaving only the second son, Jia Jing, to inherit. Nowadays Jia Jing's only interest in life is Taoism. He spends all his time over retorts and crucibles concocting elixirs, and refuses to be bothered with anything else.

"Fortunately he had already provided himself with a son, Jia Zhen, long before he took up this hobby. So, having set his mind on turning himself into an immortal, he has given up his post in favour of this son. And what's more he refuses outright to live at home and spends his time fooling around with a pack of Taoists somewhere outside the city walls.

"This Jia Zhen has got a son of his own, a lad called Jia Rong, just turned sixteen. With old Jia Jing out of the way and refusing to exercise any authority, Jia Zhen has thrown his responsibilities to the winds and given himself up to a life of pleasure. He has turned that Ning-guo mansion upside down, but there is no one around who dares gainsay him.

"Now I come to the Rong household—it was there that this strange event occurred that I was telling you about. When the old Duke of Rong-guo died, his eldest son, Jia Dai-shan, inherited his emoluments. He married a girl from a very old Nanking family, the daughter of Marquis Shi, who bore him two sons, Jia She and Jia Zheng.

"Dai-shan has been dead this many a year, but the old lady is still alive. The elder son, Jia She, inherited; but he's only a very middling sort of person and doesn't play much part in running the family. The second son, though, Jia Zheng, has been mad keen on study ever since he was a lad. He is a very upright sort of person, straight as a die. He was his grandfather's favourite. He would have sat for the examinations, but when the emperor saw Dai-shan's testamentary memorial that he wrote on his death bed, he was so moved, thinking what a faithful servant the old man had been, that he not only ordered the elder son to inherit his father's position, but also gave instructions that any other sons of his were to be presented to him at once, and on seeing Jia Zheng he gave him the post of Supernumerary Executive Officer, brevet rank, with instructions to continue his studies while on the Ministry's payroll. From there he has now risen to the post of Under Secretary.

"Sir Zheng's lady was formerly a Miss Wang. Her first child was a boy called Jia Zhu. He was already a Licensed Scholar at the age of fourteen. Then he married and had a son. But he died of an illness before he was twenty. The second child she bore him was a little girl, rather remarkable because she was born on New Year's day. Then after an interval of twelve years or more she suddenly had another son. He was even more remarkable, because at the moment of his birth he had a piece of beautiful, clear, coloured jade in his mouth with a lot of writing on it. They gave him the name 'Bao-yu' as a consequence. Now tell me if you don't think that is an extraordinary thing."

"It certainly is," Yu-cun agreed. "I should not be at all surprised to find that there was something very unusual in the heredity of that child."

"Humph," said Zi-xing. "A great many people have said that. That is the reason why his old grandmother thinks him such a treasure. But when they celebrated the First Twelve-month and Sir Zheng tested his disposition by putting a lot of objects in front of him and seeing which he would take hold of, he stretched out his little hand and started playing with some women's things—combs, bracelets, pots of rouge and powder and the like—completely ignoring all the other objects. Sir Zheng was very displeased. He said he would grow up to be a rake, and ever since then he hasn't felt much affection for the child. But to the old lady he's the very apple of her eye.

"But there's more that's unusual about him than that. He's now rising ten and unusually mischievous, yet his mind is as sharp as a needle. You wouldn't find one in a hundred to match him. Some of the childish things he says are most extraordinary. He'll say, 'Girls are made of water and boys are made of mud. When I am with girls I feel fresh and clean, but when I am with boys I feel stupid and nasty.' Now isn't that priceless! He'll be a lady-killer when he grows up, no question of that."

***

Everyone's attention now centred on Dai-yu.[4] They observed that although she was still young, her speech and manner already showed unusual refinement. They also noticed the frail body which seemed scarcely strong enough to bear the weight of its clothes, but which yet had an inexpressible grace about it, and realizing that she must be suffering from some deficiency, asked her what medicine she took for it and why it was still not better.

"I have always been like this," said Dai-yu. "I have been taking medicine ever since I could eat and been looked at by ever so many well-known doctors, but it has never done me any good. Once, when I was only three, I can remember a scabby-headed old monk came and said he wanted to take me away and have me brought up as a nun; but of course, Mother and Father wouldn't hear of it. So he said, 'Since you are not prepared to give her up, I am afraid her illness will never get better as long as she lives. The only way it might get better would be if she were never to hear the sound of weeping from this day onwards and never to see any relations other than her own mother and father. Only in those conditions could she get through her life without trouble.' Of course, he was quite crazy, and no one took any notice of the things he said. I'm still taking Ginseng Tonic Pills."

"Well, that's handy," said Grandmother Jia. "I take the Pills myself. We can easily tell them to make up a few more each time."

She had scarcely finished speaking when someone could be heard talking and laughing in a very loud voice in the inner courtyard behind them.

"Oh dear! I'm late," said the voice. "I've missed the arrival of our guest."

"Everyone else around here seems to go about with bated breath," thought Dai-yu. "Who can this new arrival be who is so brash and unmannerly?"

Even as she wondered, a beautiful young woman entered from the room behind the one they were sitting in, surrounded by a bevy of serving women and maids. She was dressed quite differently from the others present, gleaming like some fairy princess with sparkling jewels and gay embroideries.

4. Lin Dai-yu, a young girl whom Jia Yu-cun tutored. After her mother's death she has been sent to live with her maternal grandmother Jia, whose family has just been described.

Her chignon was enclosed in a circlet of gold filigree and clustered pearls. It was fastened with a pin embellished with flying phoenixes, from whose beaks pearls were suspended on tiny chains.

Her necklet was of red gold in the form of a coiling dragon.

Her dress had a fitted bodice and was made of dark red silk damask with a pattern of flowers and butterflies in raised gold thread.

Her jacket was lined with ermine. It was of a slate-blue stuff with woven insets in coloured silks.

Her under-skirt was of a turquoise-coloured imported silk crêpe embroidered with flowers.

She had, moreover,

> eyes like a painted phoenix,
> eyebrows like willow-leaves,
> a slender form,
> seductive grace;
> the ever-smiling summer face
> of hidden thunders showed no trace;
> the ever-bubbling laughter started
> almost before the lips were parted.

"You don't know her," said Grandmother Jia merrily. "She's a holy terror this one. What we used to call in Nanking a 'peppercorn.' You just call her 'Peppercorn Feng.' She'll know who you mean!"

Dai-yu was at a loss to know how she was to address this Peppercorn Feng until one of the cousins whispered that it was "Cousin Lian's wife," and she remembered having heard her mother say that her elder uncle, Uncle She, had a son called Jia Lian who was married to the niece of her Uncle Zheng's wife, Lady Wang. She had been brought up from earliest childhood just like a boy, and had acquired in the school-room the somewhat boyish-sounding name of Wang Xi-feng. Dai-yu accordingly smiled and curtseyed, greeting her by her correct name as she did so.

Xi-feng took Dai-yu by the hand and for a few moments scrutinized her carefully from top to toe before conducting her back to her seat beside Grandmother Jia.

"She's a beauty, Grannie dear! If I hadn't set eyes on her today, I shouldn't have believed that such a beautiful creature could exist! And everything about her so *distingué!* She doesn't take after your side of the family, Grannie. She's more like a Jia. I don't blame you for having gone on so about her during the past few days—but poor little thing! What a cruel fate to have lost Auntie like that!" and she dabbed at her eyes with a handkerchief.

"I've only just recovered," laughed Grandmother Jia. "Don't you go trying to start me off again! Besides, your little cousin is not very strong, and we've only just managed to get *her* cheered up. So let's have no more of this!" ∗∗∗

Dai-yu had long ago been told by her mother that she had a boy cousin who was born with a piece of jade in his mouth and who was exceptionally wild and naughty. He hated study and liked to spend all his time in the women's apartments with the girls; but because Grandmother Jia doted on him so much, no one ever dared to correct him. She realized that it must be this cousin her aunt was now referring to.

"Do you mean the boy born with the jade, Aunt?" she asked. "Mother often told me about him at home. She told me that he was one year older than me and that his name was Bao-yu. But she said that though he was very wilful, he always behaved very nicely to girls. Now that I am here, I suppose I shall be spending all my time with my girl cousins and not in the same part of the house as the boys. Surely there will be no danger of *my* provoking him?"

Lady Wang gave a rueful smile. "You little know how things are here! Bao-yu is a law unto himself. Because your grandmother is so fond of him she has thoroughly spoiled him. When he was little he lived with the girls, so with the girls he remains now. As long as they take no notice of him, things run quietly enough. But if they give him the least encouragement, he at once becomes excitable, and then there is no end to the mischief he may get up to. That is why I counsel you to ignore him. He can be all honey-sweet words one minute and ranting and raving like a lunatic the next. So don't believe anything he says."

Dai-yu promised to follow her aunt's advice. ✳✳✳

Lady Wang now led Dai-yu along a gallery, running from east to west, which brought them out into the courtyard behind Grandmother Jia's apartments. Entering these by a back entrance, they found a number of servants waiting there who, as soon as they saw Lady Wang, began to arrange the table and chairs for dinner. The ladies of the house themselves took part in the service. Li Wan brought in the cups, Xi-feng laid out the chopsticks, and Lady Wang brought in the soup.

The table at which Grandmother Jia presided, seated alone on a couch, had two empty chairs on either side. Xi-feng tried to seat Dai-yu in the one on the left nearer to her grandmother—an honour which she strenuously resisted until her grandmother explained that her aunt and her elder cousins' wives would not be eating with them, so that, since she was a guest, the place was properly hers. Only then did she ask permission to sit, as etiquette prescribed. Grandmother Jia then ordered Lady Wang to be seated. This was the cue for the three girls to ask permission to sit. Ying-chun sat in the first place on the right opposite Dai-yu, Tan-chun sat second on the left, and Xi-chun sat second on the right.

While Li Wan and Xi-feng stood by the table helping to distribute food from the dishes, maids holding fly-whisks, spittoons, and napkins ranged themselves on either side. In addition to these, there were numerous other maids and serving-women in attendance in the outer room, yet not so much as a cough was heard throughout the whole of the meal.

When they had finished eating, a maid served each diner with tea on a little tray. Dai-yu's parents had brought their daughter up to believe that good health was founded on careful habits, and in pursuance of this principle, had always insisted that after a meal one should allow a certain interval to elapse before taking tea in order to avoid indigestion. However, she could see that many of the rules in this household were different from the ones she had been used to at home; so, being anxious to conform as much as possible, she accepted the tea. But as she did so, another maid proferred a spittoon, from which she inferred that the tea was for rinsing her mouth with. And it was not, in fact, until they had all rinsed out their mouths and washed their hands that another lot of tea was served, this time for drinking.

Grandmother Jia now dismissed her lady servers, observing that she wished to enjoy a little chat with her young grand-children without the restraint of their grownup presence.

Lady Wang obediently rose to her feet and, after exchanging a few pleasantries, went out, taking Li Wan and Wang Xi-feng with her.

Grandmother Jia asked Dai-yu what books she was studying.

"*The Four Books*"[5] said Dai-yu, and inquired in turn what books her cousins were currently engaged on.

"Gracious, child, they don't study books," said her grandmother; "they can barely read and write!"

While they were speaking, a flurry of footsteps could be heard outside and a maid came in to say that Bao-yu was back.

"I wonder," thought Dai-yu, "just what sort of graceless creature this Bao-yu is going to be!"

The young gentleman who entered in answer to her unspoken question had a small jewel-encrusted gold coronet on the top of his head and a golden headband low down over his brow in the form of two dragons playing with a large pearl.

He was wearing a narrow-sleeved, full-skirted robe of dark red material with a pattern of flowers and butterflies in two shades of gold. It was confined at the waist with a court girdle of coloured silks braided at regular intervals into elaborate clusters of knotwork and terminating in long tassels.

Over the upper part of his robe he wore a jacket of slate-blue Japanese silk damask with a raised pattern of eight large medallions on the front and with tas-selled borders.

On his feet he had half-length dress boots of black satin with thick white soles.

> As to his person, he had:
> a face like the moon of Mid-Autumn,
> a complexion like flowers at dawn,
> a hairline straight as a knife-cut,
> eyebrows that might have been painted by an artist's brush,
> a shapely nose, and
> eyes clear as limpid pools,
> that even in anger seemed to smile,
> and, as they glared, beamed tenderness the while.

Around his neck he wore a golden torque in the likeness of a dragon and a woven cord of coloured silks to which the famous jade was attached.

Dai-yu looked at him with astonishment. How strange! How very strange! It was as though she had seen him somewhere before, he was so extraordinarily familiar. Bao-yu went straight past her and saluted his grandmother, who told him to come after he had seen his mother, whereupon he turned round and walked straight out again.

Quite soon he was back once more, this time dressed in a completely different outfit.

The crown and circlet had gone. She could now see that his side hair was dressed in a number of small braids plaited with red silk, which were drawn round to join the long hair at the back in a single large queue of glistening jet black, fastened at intervals from the nape downwards with four enormous pearls and ending in a jewelled gold clasp. He had changed his robe and jacket for a rather more worn-looking rose-coloured gown, sprigged with flowers. He wore the gold torque and his jade as before, and she observed that the collection of objects round his neck had been further augmented by a padlock-shaped amulet and a lucky charm. A pair of ivy-coloured embroidered silk trousers were partially visible beneath his gown, thrust into black and white socks trimmed with brocade. In place of the formal boots he was wearing thick-soled crimson slippers. ✳✳✳

5. Four texts central to Confucianism: *Analects, Mencius, Doctrine of the Mean,* and *The Great Learning.*

"Fancy changing your clothes before you have welcomed the visitor!" Grandmother Jia chided indulgently on seeing Bao-yu back again. "Aren't you going to pay your respects to your cousin?"

Bao-yu had already caught sight of a slender, delicate girl whom he surmised to be his Aunt Lin's daughter and quickly went over to greet her. Then, returning to his place and taking a seat, he studied her attentively. How different she seemed from the other girls he knew!

Her mist-wreathed brows at first seemed to frown, yet were not frowning;

> Her passionate eyes at first seemed to smile, yet were not merry.
> Habit had given a melancholy cast to her tender face;
> Nature had bestowed a sickly constitution on her delicate frame.
> Often the eyes swam with glistening tears;
> Often the breath came in gentle gasps.
> In stillness she made one think of a graceful flower reflected in the water;
> In motion she called to mind tender willow shoots caressed by the wind.
> She had more chambers in her heart than the martyred Bi Gan;[6]
> And suffered a tithe more pain in it than the beautiful Xi Shi.[7]

Having completed his survey, Bao-yu gave a laugh.

"I have seen this cousin before."

"Nonsense!" said Grandmother Jia. "How could you possibly have done?"

"Well, perhaps not," said Bao-yu, "but her face seems so familiar that I have the impression of meeting her again after a long separation."

"All the better," said Grandmother Jia. "That means that you should get on well together."

Bao-yu moved over again and, drawing a chair up beside Dai-yu, recommenced his scrutiny.

Presently: "Do you study books yet, cousin?"

"No," said Dai-yu. "I have only been taking lessons for a year or so. I can barely read and write."

"What's your name?"

Dai-yu told him.

"What's your school-name?"

"I haven't got one."

Bao-yu laughed. "I'll give you one, cousin. I think 'Frowner' would suit you perfectly."

"Where's your reference?" said Tan-chun.

"In the *Encyclopedia of Men and Objects Ancient and Modern* it says that somewhere in the West there is a mineral called 'dai' which can be used instead of eye-black for painting the eye-brows with. She has this 'dai' in her name and she knits her brows together in a little frown. I think it's a splendid name for her!"

"I expect you made it up," said Tan-chun scornfully.

"What if I did?" said Bao-yu. "There are lots of made-up things in books—apart from the *Four Books,* of course."

He returned to his interrogation of Dai-yu.

---

6. When Bi Gan scolded his nephew, the tyrannical last ruler of the Shang dynasty, for his barbarous behavior, the king responded that people said that a sage had a heart with seven openings, and that he would have to tear his uncle's heart out to see if he qualified.

7. A legendary beauty known for a slight frown.

"Have you got a jade?"

The rest of the company were puzzled, but Dai-yu at once divined that he was asking her if she too had a jade like the one he was born with.

"No," said Dai-yu. "That jade of yours is a very rare object. You can't expect everybody to have one."

This sent Bao-yu off instantly into one of his mad fits. Snatching the jade from his neck he hurled it violently on the floor as if to smash it and began abusing it passionately.

"Rare object! Rare object! What's so lucky about a stone that can't even tell which people are better than others? Beastly thing! I don't want it!"

The maids all seemed terrified and rushed forward to pick it up, while Grandmother Jia clung to Bao-yu in alarm.

"Naughty, naughty boy! Shout at someone or strike them if you like when you are in a nasty temper, but why go smashing that precious thing that your very life depends on?"

"None of the girls has got one," said Bao-yu, his face streaming with tears and sobbing hysterically. "Only I have got one. It always upsets me. And now this new cousin comes here who is as beautiful as an angel and she hasn't got one either, so I *know* it can't be any good."

"Your cousin did have a jade once," said Grandmother Jia, coaxing him like a little child, "but because when Auntie died she couldn't bear to leave her little girl behind, they had to let her take the jade with her instead. In that way your cousin could show her mamma how much she loved her by letting the jade be buried with her; and at the same time, whenever Auntie's spirit looked at the jade, it would be just like looking at her own little girl again.

"So when your cousin said she hadn't got one, it was only because she didn't want to boast about the good, kind thing she did when she gave it to her mamma. Now you put yours on again like a good boy, and mind your mother doesn't find out how naughty you have been."

So saying, she took the jade from the hands of one of the maids and hung it round his neck for him. And Bao-yu, after reflecting for a moment or two on what she had said, offered no further resistance. * * *

Chapter 5

Jia Bao-yu visits the Land of Illusion
And the fairy Disenchantment performs the "Dream of Golden Days"

From the moment Lin Dai-yu entered the Rong mansion, Grandmother Jia's solicitude for her had manifested itself in a hundred different ways. The arrangements made for her meals and accommodation were exactly the same as for Bao-yu. The other three granddaughters, Ying-chun, Tan-chun and Xi-chun, were relegated to a secondary place in the old lady's affections, and the objects of her partiality themselves began to feel an affection for each other which far exceeded what they felt for any of the rest. Sharing each other's company every minute of the day and sleeping in the same room at night, they developed an understanding so intense that it was almost as if they had grown into a single person.

And now suddenly this Xue Bao-chai[8] had appeared on the scene—a young lady who, though very little older than Dai-yu, possessed a grown-up beauty and aplomb

8. Another of Bao-yu's cousins, the daughter of his mother's sister.

in which all agreed Dai-yu was her inferior. Moreover, in contrast to Dai-yu with her air of lofty self-sufficiency and total obliviousness to all who did not move on the same exalted level as herself, Bao-chai had a generous, accommodating disposition which greatly endeared her to subordinates, so that even the tiniest maid looked on Miss Bao-chai as a familiar friend. Dai-yu could not but feel somewhat put out by this—a fact of which Bao-chai herself, however, was totally unaware.

As for Bao-yu, he was still only a child—a child, moreover, whom nature had endowed with the eccentric obtuseness of a simpleton. Brothers, sisters, cousins, were all one to him. In his relationships with people he made no distinction between one person and another. If his relationship with Dai-yu was exceptional, it was because greater proximity—since she was living with him in his grandmother's quarters—made her more familiar to him than the rest; and greater familiarity bred greater intimacy.

And of course, with greater intimacy came the occasional tiffs and misunderstandings that are usual with people who have a great deal to do with each other.

One day the two of them had fallen out over something or other and the argument had ended with Dai-yu crying alone in her room and Bao-yu feeling remorsefully that perhaps he had spoken too roughly. Presently he went in to make his peace with her and gradually, very gradually, Dai-yu's equanimity was restored.

The winter plum in the gardens of the Ning Mansion was now at its best, and this particular day Cousin Zhen's wife, You-shi, had some wine taken into the gardens and came over in person, bringing her son Jia Rong and his young wife with her, to invite Grandmother Jia, Lady Xing and Lady Wang to a flower-viewing party.

Grandmother Jia and the rest went round as soon as they had finished their breakfast. The party was in the All-scents Garden. It began with tea and continued with wine, and as it was a family gathering confined to the ladies of the Ning and Rong households, nothing particularly worth recording took place.

At one point in the party Bao-yu was overcome with tiredness and heaviness and expressed a desire to take an afternoon nap. Grandmother Jia ordered some of the servants to go back to the house with him and get him comfortably settled, adding that they might return with him later when he was rested; but Qin-shi, the little wife of Jia Rong, smilingly proposed an alternative.

"We have got just the room here for Uncle Bao. Leave him to me, Grannie dear! He will be quite safe in my hands."

She turned to address the nurses and maidservants who were in attendance on Bao-yu.

"Come, my dears! Tell Uncle Bao to follow me."

Grandmother Jia had always had a high opinion of Qin-shi's trustworthiness—she was such a charming, delightful little creature, the favourite among her great-granddaughters-in-law—and was quite content to leave the arrangements to her.

Qin-shi conducted Bao-yu and his little knot of attendants to an inner room in the main building. As they entered, Bao-yu glanced up and saw a painting hanging above them on the opposite wall. The figures in it were very finely executed. They represented Scholarly Diligence in the person of the Han philosopher Liu Xiang at his book, obligingly illuminated for him by a supernatural being holding a large flaming torch. Bao-yu found the painting—or rather its subject—distasteful. But the pair of mottoes which flanked it proved the last straw:

> True learning implies a clear insight into human activities.
> Genuine culture involves the skilful manipulation of human relationships.

In vain the elegant beauty and splendid furnishings of the room! Qin-shi was given to understand in no uncertain terms that her uncle Bao-yu wished to be out of it *at once*.

"If this is not good enough for you," said Qin-shi with a laugh, "where *are* we going to put you?—unless you would like to have your rest in my bedroom."

A little smile played over Bao-yu's face and he nodded. The nurses were shocked.

"An uncle sleep in the bedroom of his nephew's wife! Who ever heard of such a thing!"

Qin-shi laughed again.

"He won't misbehave. Good gracious, he's only a little boy! We don't have to worry about that sort of thing yet! You know my little brother who came last month: he's the same age as Uncle Bao, but if you stood them side by side I shouldn't be a bit surprised if he wasn't the taller of the two."

"Why haven't I seen your brother yet?" Bao-yu demanded. "Bring him in and let me have a look at him!"

The servants all laughed.

"Bring him in? Why, he's ten or twenty miles away! But I expect you'll meet him one of these days."

In the course of this exchange the party had made its way to Qin-shi's bedroom. As Bao-yu entered, a subtle whiff of the most delicious perfume assailed his nostrils, making a sweet stickiness inside his drooping eyelids and causing all the joints in his body to dissolve.

"What a lovely smell!"

He repeated the words several times over.

Inside the room there was a painting by Tang Yin[9] entitled "Spring Slumber" depicting a beautiful woman asleep under a crab-apple tree, whose buds had not yet opened. The painting was flanked on either side by a pair of calligraphic scrolls inscribed with a couplet from the brush of the Song poet Qin Guan:[1]

> (on one side)
> The coldness of spring has imprisoned the soft buds in a wintry dream;

> (on the other side)
> The fragrance of wine has intoxicated the beholder with imagined flower-scents.

On a table stood an antique mirror that had once graced the tiring-room of the lascivious empress Wu Ze-tian.[2] Beside it stood the golden platter on which Flying Swallow[3] once danced for her emperor's delight. And on the platter was that very quince which the villainous An Lu-shan threw at beautiful Yang Gui-fei,[4] bruising her plump white breast. At the far end of the room stood the priceless bed on which Princess Shou-yang was sleeping out of doors under the eaves of the Han-zhang Palace when the plum-flower lighted on her forehead and set a new fashion for coloured patches. Over it hung a canopy commissioned by Princess Tong-chang entirely fashioned out of ropes of pearls.

"I like it here," said Bao-yu happily.

"My room," said Qin-shi with a proud smile, "is fit for an immortal to sleep in." And she unfolded a quilted coverlet, whose silk had been laundered by the fabulous

9. A well-known Ming dynasty painter (1470–1523).

1. A major composer of song lyrics (1049–1100).

2. A Tang imperial consort who managed to gain control of the government through her son and rule China from 684 to 705.

3. A consort of a Han dynasty emperor, said to be so light she could dance on a platter.

4. Yang Gui-fei, the beloved consort of the Tang emperor Xuanzong, was blamed for distracting him from his proper job, which allowed the general An Lu-shan to mount a successful rebellion in 755.

Xi Shi, and arranged the double head-rest that Hong-niang[5] once carried for her amorous mistress.

The nurses now helped Bao-yu into bed and then tiptoed out, leaving him attended only by his four young maids: Aroma, Skybright, Musk, and Ripple. Qin-shi told them to go outside and stop the cats from fighting on the eaves.

As soon as Bao-yu closed his eyes he sank into a confused sleep in which Qin-shi was still there yet at the same time seemed to be drifting along weightlessly in front of him. He followed her until they came to a place of marble terraces and vermilion balustrades where there were green trees and crystal streams. Everything in this place was so clean and so pure that it seemed as if no human foot could ever have trodden there or floating speck of dust ever blown into it. Bao-yu's dreaming self rejoiced. "What a delightful place!" he thought. "If only I could spend all my life here! How much nicer it would be than living under the daily restraint of my parents and teachers!"

These idle reflections were interrupted by someone singing a song on the other side of a hill:

> "Spring's dream-time will like drifting clouds disperse,
> Its flowers snatched by a flood none can reverse.
> Then tell each nymph and swain
> 'Tis folly to invite love's pain!"

It was the voice of a girl. Before its last echoes had died away, a beautiful woman appeared in the quarter from which the voice had come, approaching him with a floating, fluttering motion.

Observing delightedly that the lady was a fairy, Bao-yu hurried forward and saluted her with a smile.

"Madam Fairy, I don't know where you have come from or where you are going to, but as I am quite lost in this place, will you please take me with you and be my guide?"

"I am the fairy Disenchantment," the fairy woman replied. "I live beyond the Realm of Separation, in the Sea of Sadness. There is a Mountain of Spring Awakening which rises from the midst of that sea, and on that mountain is the Paradise of the Full-blown Flower, and in that paradise is the Land of Illusion, which is my home. My business is with the romantic passions, love-debts, girlish heartbreaks and male philanderings of your dust-stained, human world. The reason I have come here today is that recently there has been a heavy concentration of love-*karma* in this area, and I hope to be able to find an opportunity of distributing a quantity of amorous thoughts by implanting them in the appropriate breasts. My meeting you here today is no accident but a part of the same project.

"This place where we are now is not so very far from my home. I have not much to offer you, but would you like to come back with me and let me try to entertain you? I have some fairy tea, which I picked myself. You could have a cup of that. And I have a few jars of choice new wine of my own brewing. I have also been rehearsing a fairy choir and a troupe of fairy dancers in a twelve-part suite which I recently composed called 'A Dream of Golden Days.' I could get them to perform it for you. What do you think?"

---

5. The maid Crimson, who facilitated a tryst between her mistress Yingying and a young student Zhang in *The Story of the Western Wing*, a well-known Yuan dynasty romantic comedy.

CAO XUEQIN

218

Bao-yu was so excited by this invitation that he quite forgot to wonder what had become of Qin-shi in his eagerness to accompany the fairy. As he followed her, a big stone archway suddenly loomed up in front of them on which

THE LAND OF ILLUSION

was written in large characters. A couplet in smaller characters was inscribed on either side of the arch:

> Truth becomes fiction when the fiction's true;
> Real becomes not-real when the unreal's real.

Having negotiated the archway, they presently came to the gateway of a palace. The following words were inscribed horizontally above the lintel:

SEAS OF PAIN AND SKIES OF PASSION

whilst the following words were inscribed vertically on the two sides:

> Ancient earth and sky
> Marvel that love's passion should outlast all time,
> Star-crossed men and maids
> Groan that love's debts should be so hard to pay.

"I see," said Bao-yu to himself. "I wonder what the meaning of 'passion that outlasts all time' can be. And what are 'love's debts'? From now on I must make an effort to understand these things."

He could not, of course, have known it, but merely by thinking this he had invited the attentions of the demon Lust, and at that very moment a little of the demon's evil poison had entered Bao-yu's body and lodged itself in the innermost recesses of his heart.

Wholly unconscious of his mortal peril, Bao-yu continued to follow the fairy woman. They passed through a second gateway, and Bao-yu saw a range of palace buildings ahead of them on either hand. The entrance to each building had a board above it proclaiming its name, and there were couplets on either side of the doorways. Bao-yu did not have time to read all of the names, but he managed to make out a few, viz.:

DEPARTMENT OF FOND INFATUATION

DEPARTMENT OF CRUEL REJECTION

DEPARTMENT OF EARLY MORNING WEEPING

DEPARTMENT OF LATE NIGHT SOBBING

DEPARTMENT OF SPRING FEVER

DEPARTMENT OF AUTUMN GRIEF

"Madam Fairy," said Bao-yu, whose interest had been whetted by what he had managed to read, "couldn't you take me inside these offices to have a look around?"

"In these offices," said the fairy woman, "are kept registers in which are recorded the past, present and future of girls from all over the world. It is not permitted that your earthly eyes should look on things that are yet to come."

Bao-yu was most unwilling to accept this answer, and begged and pleaded so persistently that at last Disenchantment gave in.

"Very well. You may make a very brief inspection of this office here."

Delighted beyond measure, Bao-yu raised his head and read the notice above the doorway:

DEPARTMENT OF THE ILL-FATED FAIR

The couplet inscribed vertically on either side of the doorway was as follows:

> Spring griefs and autumn sorrows were by yourselves provoked.
> Flower faces, moonlike beauty were to what end disclosed?

Bao-yu grasped enough of the meaning to be affected by its melancholy.

* * *

At once she ordered the remains of the feast to be removed and conducted Bao-yu to a dainty bedroom. The furnishings and hangings of the bed were more sumptuous and beautiful than anything he had ever seen. To his intense surprise there was a fairy girl sitting in the middle of it. Her rose-fresh beauty reminded him strongly of Bao-chai, but there was also something about her of Dai-yu's delicate charm. As he was pondering the meaning of this apparition, he suddenly became aware that Disenchantment was addressing him.

"In the rich and noble households of your mortal world, too many of those bowers and boudoirs where innocent tenderness and sweet girlish fantasy should reign are injuriously defiled by coarse young voluptuaries and loose, wanton girls. And what is even more detestable, there are always any number of worthless philanderers to protest that it is woman's beauty alone that inspires them, or loving feelings alone, unsullied by any taint of lust. They lie in their teeth! To be moved by woman's beauty is itself a kind of lust. To experience loving feelings is, even more assuredly, a kind of lust. Every act of love, every carnal congress of the sexes is brought about precisely because sensual delight in beauty has kindled the feeling of love.

"The reason I like you so much is because you are full of lust. You are the most lustful person I have ever known in the whole world!"

Bao-yu was scared by the vehemence of her words.

"Madam Fairy, you are wrong! Because I am lazy over my lessons, Mother and Father still have to scold me quite often; but surely that doesn't make me *lustful?* I'm still too young to know what they do, the people they use that word about."

"Ah, but you *are* lustful!" said Disenchantment. "In principle, of course, all lust is the same. But the word has many different meanings. For example, the typically lustful man in the common sense of the word is a man who likes a pretty face, who is fond of singing and dancing, who is inordinately given to flirtation; one who makes love in season and out of season, and who, if he could, would like to have every pretty girl in the world at his disposal, to gratify his desires whenever he felt like it. Such a person is a mere brute. His is a shallow, promiscuous kind of lust.

"But your kind of lust is different. That blind, defenceless love with which nature has filled your being is what we call here 'lust of the mind.' 'Lust of the mind' cannot be explained in words, nor, if it could, would you be able to grasp their meaning. Either you know what it means or you don't.

"Because of this 'lust of the mind' women will find you a kind and understanding friend; but in the eyes of the world I am afraid it is going to make you seem unpractical and eccentric. It is going to earn you the jeers of many and the angry looks of many more.

"Today I received a most touching request on your behalf from your ancestors the Duke of Ning-guo and the Duke of Rong-guo. And as I cannot bear the idea of

220

your being rejected by the world for the greater glory of us women, I have brought you here. I have made you drunk with fairy wine. I have drenched you with fairy tea. I have admonished you with fairy songs. And now I am going to give you my little sister Two-in-one—'Ke-qing' to her friends—to be your bride.

"The time is propitious. You may consummate the marriage this very night. My motive in arranging this is to help you grasp the fact that, since even in these immortal precincts love is an illusion, the love of your dust-stained, mortal world must be doubly an illusion. It is my earnest hope that, knowing this, you will henceforth be able to shake yourself free of its entanglements and change your previous way of thinking, devoting your mind seriously to the teachings of Confucius and Mencius and your person wholeheartedly to the betterment of society."

Disenchantment then proceeded to give him secret instructions in the art of love; then, pushing him gently inside the room, she closed the door after him and went away.

Dazed and confused, Bao-yu nevertheless proceeded to follow out the instructions that Disenchantment had given him, which led him by predictable stages to that act which boys and girls perform together—and which it is not my intention to give a full account of here.

Next morning he lay for a long time locked in blissful tenderness with Ke-qing, murmuring sweet endearments in her ear and unable to tear himself away from her. Eventually they emerged from the bedroom hand in hand to walk together out-of-doors.

Their walk seemed to take them quite suddenly to a place where only thorn-trees grew and wolves and tigers prowled around in pairs. Ahead of them the road ended at the edge of a dark ravine. No bridge connected it with the other side. As they hesitated, wondering what to do, they suddenly became aware that Disenchantment was running up behind them.

"Stop! Stop!" she was shouting. "Turn back at once! Turn back!"

Bao-yu stood still in alarm and asked her what place this was.

"This is the Ford of Error," said Disenchantment. "It is ten thousand fathoms deep and extends hundreds of miles in either direction. No boat can ever cross it; only a raft manned by a lay-brother called Numb and an acolyte called Dumb. Numb holds the steering-paddle and Dumb wields the pole. They won't ferry anyone across for money, but only take those who are fated to cross over.

"If you had gone on walking just now and had fallen in, all the good advice I was at such pains to give you would have been wasted!"

Chapter 17

The inspection of the new garden becomes a test of talent
And Rong-guo House makes itself ready for an important visitor[6]

One day Cousin Zhen came to Jia Zheng with his team of helpers to report that work on the new garden had been completed.

"Uncle She has already had a look," said Cousin Zhen. "Now we are only waiting for you to look round it to tell us if there is anything you think will need altering and also to decide what inscriptions ought to be used on the boards everywhere."

Jia Zheng reflected a while in silence.

6. Bao-yu's sister Yuan-chun, who has become an Imperial Concubine, is returning home for a visit, in honor of which the family is constructing a magnificent garden complete with dwellings of all sorts.

"These inscriptions are going to be difficult," he said eventually. "By rights, of course, Her Grace should have the privilege of doing them herself; but she can scarcely be expected to make them up out of her head without having seen any of the views which they are to describe. On the other hand, if we wait until she has already visited the garden before asking her, half the pleasure of the visit will be lost. All those prospects and pavilions—even the rocks and trees and flowers will seem somehow incomplete without that touch of poetry which only the written word can lend a scene."

"My dear patron, you are so right," said one of the literary gentlemen who sat with him. "But we have had an idea. The inscriptions for the various parts of the garden obviously cannot be dispensed with; nor, equally obviously, can they be decided in advance. Our suggestion is that we should compose provisional names and couplets to suit the places where inscriptions are required, and have them painted on rectangular paper lanterns which can be hung up temporarily—either horizontally or vertically as the case may be—when Her Grace comes to visit. We can ask her to decide on the permanent names after she has inspected the garden. Is not this a solution of the dilemma?"

"It is indeed," said Jia Zheng. "When we look round the garden presently, we must all try to think of words that can be used. If they seem suitable, we can keep them for the lanterns. If not, we can call for Yu-cun to come and help us out."

"Your own suggestions are sure to be admirable, Sir Zheng," said the literary gentlemen ingratiatingly. "There will be no need to call in Yu-cun."

Jia Zheng smiled deprecatingly.

"I am afraid it is not as you imagine. In my youth I had at best only indifferent skill in the art of writing verses about natural objects—birds and flowers and scenery and the like; and now that I am older and have to devote all my energies to official documents and government papers, I am even more out of touch with this sort of thing than I was then; so that even if I were to try my hand at it, I fear that my efforts would be rather dull and pedantic ones. Instead of enhancing the interest and beauty of the garden, they would probably have a deadening effect upon both."

"That doesn't matter," the literary gentlemen replied. "We can *all* try our hands at composing. If each of us contributes what he is best at, and if we then select the better attempts and reject the ones that are not so good, we should be able to manage all right."

"That seems to me a very good suggestion," said Jia Zheng. "As the weather today is so warm and pleasant, let us all go and take a turn round the garden now!"

So saying he rose to his feet and conducted his little retinue of literary luminaries towards the garden. Cousin Zhen hurried on ahead to warn those in charge that they were coming.

As Bao-yu was still in very low spirits these days because of his grief for Qin Zhong, Grandmother Jia had hit on the idea of sending him into the newly made garden to play. By unlucky chance she had selected this very day on which to try out her antidote. He had in fact only just entered the garden when Cousin Zhen came hurrying towards him.

"Better get out of here!" said Cousin Zhen with an amused smile. "Your father will be here directly!"

Bao-yu streaked back towards the gate, a string of nurses and pages hurrying at his heels. But he had only just turned the corner on coming out of it when he almost ran into the arms of Jia Zheng and his party coming from the opposite direction. Escape was impossible. He simply had to stand meekly to one side and await instructions.

Jia Zheng had recently received a favourable report on Bao-yu from his teacher Jia Dai-ru in which mention had been made of his skill in composing couplets. Although the boy showed no aptitude for serious study, Dai-ru had said, he nevertheless possessed a certain meretricious talent for versification not undeserving of commendation. Because of this report, Jia Zheng ordered Bao-yu to accompany him into the garden, intending to put his aptitude to the test. Bao-yu, who knew nothing either of Dai-ru's report or of his father's intentions, followed with trepidation.

As soon as they reached the gate they found Cousin Zhen at the head of a group of overseers waiting to learn Jia Zheng's wishes.

"I want you to close the gate," said Jia Zheng, "so that we can see what it looks like from outside before we go in."

Cousin Zhen ordered the gate to be closed, and Jia Zheng stood back and studied it gravely.

It was a five-frame gate-building with a hump-backed roof of half-cylinder tiles. The wooden lattice-work of the doors and windows was finely carved and ingeniously patterned. The whole gatehouse was quite unadorned by colour or gilding, yet all was of the most exquisite workmanship. Its walls stood on a terrace of white marble carved with a pattern of passion-flowers in relief, and the garden's whitewashed circumference wall to left and right of it had a footing made of black-and-white striped stone blocks arranged so that the stripes formed a simple pattern. Jia Zheng found the unostentatious simplicity of this entrance greatly to his liking, and after ordering the gates to be opened, passed on inside.

A cry of admiration escaped them as they entered, for there, immediately in front of them, screening everything else from their view, rose a steep, verdure-clad hill.

"Without this hill," Jia Zheng somewhat otiosely observed, "the whole garden would be visible as one entered, and all its mystery would be lost."

The literary gentlemen concurred. "Only a master of the art of landscape could have conceived so bold a stroke," said one of them.

As they gazed at this miniature mountain, they observed a great number of large white rocks in all kinds of grotesque and monstrous shapes, rising course above course up one of its sides, some recumbent, some upright or leaning at angles, their surfaces streaked and spotted with moss and lichen or half concealed by creepers, and with a narrow, zig-zag path only barely discernible to the eye winding up between them.

"Let us begin our tour by following this path," said Jia Zheng. "If we work our way round towards the other side of the hill on our way back, we shall have made a complete circuit of the garden."

He ordered Cousin Zhen to lead the way, and leaning on Bao-yu's shoulder, began the winding ascent of the little mountain. Suddenly on the mountainside above his head, he noticed a white rock whose surface had been polished to mirror smoothness and realized that this must be one of the places which had been prepared for an inscription.

"Aha, gentlemen!" said Jia Zheng, turning back to address the others who were climbing up behind him. "What name are we going to choose for this mountain?"

"Emerald Heights," said one.

"Embroidery Hill," said another.

Another proposed that they should call it "Little Censer" after the famous Censer Peak in Kiangsi. Another proposed "Little Zhong-nan." Altogether some twenty or thirty names were suggested—none of them very seriously, since the literary gentlemen were aware that Jia Zheng intended to test Bao-yu and were anxious not to make the boy's task too difficult. Bao-yu understood and was duly grateful.

When no more names were forthcoming Jia Zheng turned to Bao-yu and asked him to propose something himself.

"I remember reading in some old book," said Bao-yu, "that 'to recall old things is better than to invent new ones; and to recut an ancient text is better than to engrave a modern.' We ought, then, to choose something old. But as this is not the garden's principal 'mountain' or its chief vista, strictly speaking there is no justification for having an inscription here at all—unless it is to be something which implies that this is merely a first step towards more important things ahead. I suggest we should call it 'Pathway to Mysteries' after the line in Chang Jian's[7] poem about the mountain temple:

> A path winds upwards to mysterious places.

A name like that would be more distinguished."

There was a chorus of praise from the literary gentlemen:

"Exactly right! Wonderful! Our young friend with his natural talent and youthful imagination succeeds immediately where we old pedants fail!"

Jia Zheng gave a deprecatory laugh:

"You mustn't flatter the boy! People of his age are adept at making a little knowledge go a long way. I only asked him as a joke, to see what he would say. We shall have to think of a better name later on."

As he spoke, they passed through a tunnel of rock in the mountain's shoulder into an artificial ravine ablaze with the vari-coloured flowers and foliage of many varieties of tree and shrub which grew there in great profusion. Down below, where the trees were thickest, a clear stream gushed between the rocks. After they had advanced a few paces in a somewhat northerly direction, the ravine broadened into a little flat-bottomed valley and the stream widened out to form a pool. Gaily painted and carved pavilions rose from the slopes on either side, their lower halves concealed amidst the trees, their tops reaching into the blue. In the midst of the prospect below them was a handsome bridge:

> In a green ravine
> A jade stream sped.
> A stair of stone
> Plunged to the brink.
> Where the water widened
> To a placid pool,
> A marble baluster
> Ran round about.
> A marble bridge crossed it
> With triple span,
> And a marble lion's maw
> Crowned each of the arches.

Over the centre of the bridge there was a little pavilion, which Jia Zheng and the others entered and sat down in.

"Well, gentlemen!" said Jia Zheng. "What are we going to call it?"

CAO XUEQIN

7. A Tang dynasty poet of the 8th century.

"Ou-yang Xiu[8] in his *Pavilion of the Old Drunkard* speaks of 'a pavilion poised above the water,'" said one of them. "What about 'Poised Pavilion'?"

"'Poised Pavilion' is good," said Jia Zheng, "but *this* pavilion was put here in order to dominate the water it stands over, and I think there ought to be some reference to water in its name. I seem to recollect that in that same essay you mention Ou-yang Xiu speaks of the water 'gushing between twin peaks.' Could we not use the word 'gushing' in some way?"

"Yes, yes!" said one of the literary gentlemen. "'Gushing Jade' would do splendidly."

Jia Zheng fondled his beard meditatively, then turned to Bao-yu and asked him for *his* suggestion.

"I agreed with what you said just now, Father," said Bao-yu, "but on second thought it seems to me that though it may have been all right for Ou-yang Xiu to use the word 'gushing' in describing the source of the river Rang, it doesn't really suit the water round this pavilion. Then again, as this is a Separate Residence specially designed for the reception of a royal personage, it seems to me that something rather formal is called for, and that an expression taken from the *Drunkard's Pavilion* might seem a bit improper. I think we should try to find a rather more imaginative, less obvious sort of name."

"I hope you gentlemen are all taking this in!" said Jia Zheng sarcastically. "You will observe that when we suggest something original we are recommended to prefer the old to the new, but that when we *do* make use of an old text we are 'improper' and 'unimaginative'!—Well, carry on then! Let's have your suggestion!"

"I think 'Drenched Blossoms' would be more original and more tasteful than 'Gushing Jade.'"

Jia Zheng stroked his beard and nodded silently. The literary gentlemen could see that he was pleased and hastened to commend Bao-yu's remarkable ability.

"That's the two words for the framed board on top," said Jia Zheng. "*Not* a very difficult task. But what about the seven-word lines for the sides?"

Bao-yu glanced quickly round, seeking inspiration from the scene, and presently came up with the following couplet:

> "Three pole-thrust lengths of bankside willows green,
> One fragrant breath of bankside flowers sweet."

Jia Zheng nodded and a barely perceptible smile played over his features. The literary gentlemen redoubled their praises.

They now left the pavilion and crossed to the other side of the pool. For a while they walked on, stopping from time to time to admire the various rocks and flowers and trees which they passed on their way, until suddenly they found themselves at the foot of a range of whitewashed walls enclosing a small retreat almost hidden among the hundreds and hundreds of green bamboos which grew in a dense thicket behind them. With cries of admiration they went inside. A cloister-like covered walk ran round the walls from the entrance to the back of the forecourt and a cobbled pathway led up to the steps of the terrace. The house was a tiny three-frame one, two parts latticed, the third part windowless. The tables, chairs and couches which furnished it seemed to have been specially made to fit the interior. A door in the rear wall opened

8. Song dynasty scholar and statesman (1007–1072).

onto a garden of broad-leaved plantains dominated by a large flowering pear-tree and overlooked on either side by two diminutive lodges built at right angles to the back of the house. A stream gushed through an opening at the foot of the garden wall into a channel barely a foot wide which ran to the foot of the rear terrace and thence round the side of the house to the front, where it meandered through the bamboos of the forecourt before finally disappearing through another opening in the surrounding wall.

"This must be a pleasant enough place at any time," said Jia Zheng with a smile. "But just imagine what it would be like to sit studying beside the window here on a moonlight night! It is pleasures like that which make a man feel he has not lived in vain!"

As he spoke, his glance happened to fall on Bao-yu, who instantly became so embarrassed that he hung his head in shame. He was rescued by the timely intervention of the literary gentlemen who changed the subject from that of study to a less dangerous topic. Two of them suggested that the name given to this retreat should be a four-word one. Jia Zheng asked them what four words they proposed.

"'Where Bends the Qi'" said one of them, no doubt having in mind the song in the *Poetry Classic* which begins with the words

> See in that nook where bends the Qi,
> The green bamboos, how graceful grown![9]

"No," said Jia Zheng. "Too obvious!"

"'North of the Sui,'" said the other, evidently thinking of the ancient Rabbit Garden of the Prince of Liang in Suiyang—also famous for its bamboos and running water.

"No," said Jia Zheng. "Still too obvious!"

"You'd better ask Cousin Bao again," said Cousin Zhen, who stood by listening.

"He always insists on criticizing everyone else's suggestions before he will deign to make one of his own," said Jia Zheng. "He is a worthless creature." * * *

They had been moving on meanwhile, and he now led them into the largest of the little thatched buildings, from whose simple interior with its paper windows and plain deal furniture all hint of urban refinement had been banished. Jia Zheng was inwardly pleased. He stared hard at Bao-yu:

"How do you like *this* place, then?"

With secret winks and nods the literary gentlemen urged Bao-yu to make a favourable reply, but he wilfully ignored their promptings.

"Not nearly as much as 'The Phoenix Dance.'"

His father snorted disgustedly.

"Ignoramus! You have eyes only for painted halls and gaudy pavilions— the rubbishy trappings of wealth. What can *you* know of the beauty that lies in quietness and natural simplicity? This is a consequence of your refusal to study properly."

"Your rebuke is, of course, justified, Father," Bao-yu replied promptly, "but then I have never really understood what it was the ancients *meant* by 'natural.'"

The literary gentlemen, who had observed a vein of mulishness in Bao-yu which boded trouble, were surprised by the seeming naïveté of this reply.

9. From *The Book of Songs,* poem 55.

"Why, fancy not knowing what 'natural' means—you who have such a good understanding of so much else! 'Natural' is that which is *of nature,* that is to say, that which is produced by nature as opposed to that which is produced by human artifice."

"There you are, you see!" said Bao-yu. "A farm set down in the middle of a place like this is obviously the product of human artifice. There are no neighbouring villages, no distant prospects of city walls; the mountain at the back doesn't belong to any system; there is no pagoda rising from some tree-hid monastery in the hills above; there is no bridge below leading to a near-by market town. It sticks up out of nowhere, in total isolation from everything else. It isn't even a particularly remarkable view—not nearly so 'natural' in either form or spirit as those other places we have seen. The bamboos in those other places may have been planted by human hand and the streams diverted out of their natural courses, but there was no *appearance* of artifice. That's why, when the ancients use the term 'natural' I have my doubts about what they really meant. For example, when they speak of a 'natural painting,' I can't help wondering if they are not referring to precisely that forcible interference with the landscape to which I object: putting hills where they are not meant to be, and that sort of thing. However great the skill with which this is done, the results are never quite..."

His discourse was cut short by an outburst of rage from Jia Zheng.

"Take that boy out of here!"

Bao-yu fled.

"Come back!"

He returned.

"You still have to make a couplet on this place. If it isn't satisfactory, you will find yourself reciting it to the tune of a slapped face!"

Bao-yu stood quivering with fright and for some moments was unable to say anything. At last he recited the following couplet:

> "Emergent buds swell where the washerwoman soaks her cloth.
> A fresh tang rises where the cress-gatherer fills his pannier."

Jia Zheng shook his head: "Worse and worse."

***

Leaving the place of many fragrances behind them, they had not advanced much further when they could see ahead of them a building of great magnificence which Jia Zheng at once identified as the main reception hall of the Residence.

> Roof above roof soared,
> Eye up-compelling,
> Of richly-wrought chambers
> And high winding galleries.
> Green rafts of dark pine
> Brushed the eaves' edges.
> Milky magnolias
> Bordered the buildings.
> Gold-glinting cat-faces,
> Rainbow-hued serpents' snouts
> Peered out or snarled down
> From cornice and finial.

"It is rather a showy building," said Jia Zheng. But the literary gentlemen reassured him:

"Although Her Grace is a person of simple and abstemious tastes, the exalted position she now occupies makes it only right and proper that there should be a certain amount of pomp in her reception. This building is in no way excessive."

Still advancing in the same direction, they presently found themselves at the foot of the white marble memorial arch which framed the approach to the hall. The pattern of writhing dragons protectively crouched over its uppermost horizontal was so pierced and fretted by the sculptor's artistry as to resemble lacework rather than solid stone.

"What inscription do we want on this arch?" Jia Zheng inquired.

"'Peng-lai's Fairy Precincts' is the only name that would do it justice," said the literary gentlemen.

Jia Zheng shook his head and said nothing.

The sight of this building and its arch had inspired a strange and unaccountable stir of emotion in Bao-yu which on reflection he interpreted as a sign that he must have known a building somewhat like this before—though where or when he could not for the life of him remember. He was still racking his brains to recall what it reminded him of, when Jia Zheng ordered him to produce a name and couplet for the arch, and he was quite unable to give his mind to the task of composition. The literary gentlemen, not knowing the nature of his preoccupation, supposed that his father's incessant bullying had worn him out and that he had finally come to the end of his inspiration. They feared that further bullying might once more bring out the mulish streak in him, thereby provoking an explosion which would be distasteful for everybody. Accordingly they urged Jia Zheng to allow him a day's grace in which to produce something suitable. Jia Zheng, who was secretly beginning to be apprehensive about the possible conquences of Grandmother Jia's anxiety for her darling grandson, yielded, albeit with a bad grace:

"Jackanapes! So even you have your off moments it seems. Well, I'll give you a day to do it in. But woe betide you if you can't produce something tomorrow! And it had better be something good, too, because this is the most important building in the garden."

After they had seen over the building and come out again, they stopped for a while on the terrace to look at a general view of the whole garden and attempted to make out the places they had already visited. They were surprised to find that even now they had covered little more than half of the whole area. Just at that moment a servant came up to report that someone had arrived with a message from Yu-cun.

"I can see that we shan't be able to finish today," said Jia Zheng. "However, if we go out by the way I said, we should at least be able to get some idea of the general layout."

He conducted them to a large bridge above a crystal curtain of rushing water. It was the weir through which the water from the little river which fed all the pools and watercourses of the garden ran into it from outside. Jia Zheng invited them to name it.

"This is the source of the 'Drenched Blossoms' stream we looked at earlier on," said Bao-yu. "We should call it "Drenched Blossoms Weir.'"

"Rubbish!" said Jia Zheng. "You may as well forget about your 'Drenched Blossoms,' because we are not going to use that name!"

Their progress continued past many unexplored features of the garden, viz.:

a summer lodge
a straw-thatched cot
a dry-stone wall
a flowering arch
a tiny temple nestling beneath a hill
a nun's retreat hidden in a little wood
a straight gallery

      a crooked cave
      a square pavilion
      and a round belvedere.

But Jia Zheng hurried past every one of them without entering. However, he had now been walking for a very long time without a rest and was beginning to feel somewhat footsore; and so, when the next building appeared through the trees ahead, he proposed that they should go in and sit down, and led his party towards it by the quickest route possible. They had to walk round a stand of double-flowering ornamental peach-trees and through a circular opening in a flower-covered bamboo trellis. This brought them in sight of the building's whitewashed enclosing wall and the contrasting green of the weeping willows which surrounded it. A roofed gallery ran from each side of the gate round the inner wall of the forecourt, in which a few rocks were scattered. On one side of it some green plantains were growing and on the other a weeping variety of Szechwan crab, whose pendant clusters of double-flowering carmine blossoms hung by stems as delicate as golden wires on the umbrella-shaped canopy of its boughs. ***

He led them inside the building. Its interior turned out to be all corridors and alcoves and galleries, so that properly speaking it could hardly have been said to have *rooms* at all. The partition walls which made these divisions were of wooden panelling exquisitely carved in a wide variety of motifs: bats in clouds, the "three friends of winter"—pine, plum and bamboo, little figures in landscapes, birds and flowers, scrollwork, antique bronze shapes, "good luck" and "long life" characters, and many others. The carvings, all of them the work of master craftsmen, were beautified with inlays of gold, mother-o'-pearl and semi-precious stones. In addition to being panelled, the partitions were pierced by numerous apertures, some round, some square, some sunflower-shaped, some shaped like a fleur-de-lis, some cusped, some fan-shaped. Shelving was concealed in the double thickness of the partition at the base of these apertures, making it possible to use them for storing books and writing materials and for the display of antique bronzes, vases of flowers, miniature tray-gardens and the like. The overall effect was at once richly colourful and, because of the many apertures, airy and graceful.

The *trompe-l'œil* effect of these ingenious partitions had been further enhanced by inserting false windows and doors in them, the former covered in various pastel shades of gauze, the latter hung with richly-patterned damask portières. The main walls were pierced with window-like perforations in the shape of zithers, swords, vases and other objects of virtù.

The literary gentlemen were rapturous:

"Exquisite!" they cried. "What marvellous workmanship!"

Jia Zheng, after taking no more than a couple of turns inside this confusing interior, was already lost. To the left of him was what appeared to be a door. To the right was a wall with a window in it. But on raising its portière he discovered the door to be a bookcase; and when, looking back, he observed—what he had not noticed before—that the light coming in through the silk gauze of the window illuminated a passageway leading to an open doorway, and began walking towards it, a party of gentlemen similar to his own came advancing to meet him, and he realized that he was walking towards a large mirror. They were able to circumvent the mirror, but only to find an even more bewildering choice of doorways on the other side.

"Come!" said Cousin Zhen with a laugh. "Let me show you the way! If we go out here we shall be in the back courtyard. We can reach the gate of the garden much more easily from the back courtyard than from the front."

He led them round the gauze hangings of a summer-bed, then through a door into a garden full of rambler roses. Behind the rose-trellis was a stream running between green banks. The literary gentlemen were intrigued to know where the water came from. Cousin Zhen pointed in the direction of the weir they had visited earlier:

"The water comes in over that weir, then through the grotto, then under the lea of the north-east 'mountain' to the little farm. There a channel is led off it which runs into the southeast corner of the garden. Then it runs round and rejoins the main stream here. And from here the water flows out again underneath that wall."

"How very ingenious!"

They moved on again, but soon found themselves at the foot of a tall "mountain."

"Follow me!" said Cousin Zhen, amused at the bewilderment of the others, who were now completely at sea as to their whereabouts. He led them round the foot of the "mountain"—and there, miraculously, was a broad, flat path and the gate by which they had entered, rising majestically in front of them.

"Well!" exclaimed the literary gentlemen. "This beats everything! The skill with which this has all been designed is quite out of this world!"

Whereupon they all went out of the garden.[1]

from Chapter 23

One day after lunch—it was round about the Midwash of the third month, as our forefathers, who measured the passage of time by their infrequent ablutions, were wont to say—Bao-yu set off for Drenched Blossoms Weir with the volumes of *Western Chamber*[2] under his arm, and sitting down on a rock underneath the peach-tree which grew there beside the bridge, he took up the first volume and began, very attentively, to read the play. He had just reached the line

> The red flowers in their hosts are falling

when a little gust of wind blew over and a shower of petals suddenly rained down from the tree above, covering his clothes, his book and all the ground about him. He did not like to shake them off for fear they got trodden underfoot, so collecting as many of them as he could in the lap of his gown, he carried them to the water's edge and shook them in. The petals bobbed and circled for a while on the surface of the water before finally disappearing over the weir. When he got back he found that a lot more of them had fallen while he was away. As he hesitated, a voice behind him said,

"What are you doing here?"

He looked round and saw that it was Dai-yu. She was carrying a garden hoe with a muslin bag hanging from the end of it on her shoulder and a garden broom in her hand.

"You've come just at the right moment," said Bao-yu, smiling at her. "Here, sweep these petals up and tip them in the water for me! I've just tipped one lot in myself."

"It isn't a good idea to tip them in the water," said Dai-yu. "The water you see here is clean, but farther on beyond the weir, where it flows past people's houses, there are all sorts of muck and impurity, and in the end they get spoiled just the same. In that corner over there I've got a grave for the flowers, and what I'm doing now is sweeping them up and putting them in this silk bag to bury them there, so that they can gradually turn back into earth. Isn't that a cleaner way of disposing of them?"

---

1. After the Imperial Concubine's visit, Bao-yu and his young female relatives are allowed to move into the garden's dwellings.

2. The comic play also known as *The Story of the Western Wing.*

Bao-yu was full of admiration for this idea.

"Just let me put this book somewhere and I'll give you a hand."

"What book?" said Dai-yu.

"Oh . . . The *Doctrine of the Mean* and *The Greater Learning*,"[3] he said, hastily concealing it.

"Don't try to fool *me!*" said Dai-yu. "You would have done much better to let me look at it in the first place, instead of hiding it so guiltily."

"In your case, coz, I have nothing to be afraid of," said Bao-yu; "but if I do let you look, you must promise not to tell anyone. It's marvellous stuff. Once you start reading it, you'll even stop wanting to eat!"

He handed the book to her, and Dai-yu put down her things and looked. The more she read, the more she liked it, and before very long she had read several acts. She felt the power of the words and their lingering fragrance. Long after she had finished reading, when she had laid down the book and was sitting there rapt and silent, the lines continued to ring on in her head.

"Well," said Bao-yu, "is it good?"

Dai-yu smiled and nodded.

Bao-yu laughed:

> "How can I, full of sickness and of woe,
> Withstand that face which kingdoms could o'erthrow?"

Dai-yu reddened to the tips of her ears. The eyebrows that seemed to frown yet somehow didn't were raised now in anger and the lovely eyes flashed. There was rage in her crimson cheeks and resentment in all her looks.

"You're *hateful!*"—she pointed a finger at him in angry accusal—"deliberately using that horrid play to take advantage of me. I'm going straight off to tell Uncle and Aunt!"

At the words "take advantage of me" her eyes filled with tears, and as she finished speaking she turned from him and began to go. Bao-yu rushed after her and held her back:

"Please, *please* forgive me! Dearest coz! If I had the slightest intention of taking advantage of you, may I fall into the water and be eaten up by an old bald-headed turtle! When you have become a great lady and gone at last to your final resting-place, I shall become the stone turtle that stands in front of your grave and spend the rest of eternity carrying your tombstone on my back as a punishment!"

His ridiculous declamation provoked a sudden explosion of mirth. She laughed and simultaneously wiped the tears away with her knuckles:

"Look at you—the same as ever! Scared as anything, but you still have to go on talking nonsense. Well, I know you now for what you are:

> "Of silver spear the leaden counterfeit!"

"Well! *You* can talk!" said Bao-yu laughing. "Listen to *you!* Now *I'm* going off to tell on *you!*"

"You needn't imagine you're the only one with a good memory," said Dai-yu haughtily. "I suppose I'm allowed to remember lines too if I like."

Bao-yu took back the book from her with a good-natured laugh:

3. Two of what were known as the Four Books, important Confucian texts.

"Never mind about all that now! Let's get on with this flower-burying!"

And the two of them set about sweeping together the fallen flower-petals and putting them into the bag. They had just finished burying it when Aroma came hurrying up to them:

"So there you are! I've been looking for you everywhere. Your Uncle She isn't well and the young ladies have all gone over to visit him. Her Old Ladyship says you are to go as well. You'd better come back straight away and get changed!"

Bao-yu picked up his book, took leave of Dai-yu, and accompanied Aroma back to his room.

And there, for the moment, we shall leave him.

Chapter 27

We now return to Dai-yu, who, having slept so little the night before, was very late getting up on the morning of the festival.[4] Hearing that the other girls were all out in the garden 'speeding the fairies' and fearing to be teased by them for her lazy habits, she hurried over her toilet and went out as soon as it was completed. A smiling Bao-yu appeared in the gateway as she was stepping down into the courtyard.

"Well, coz," he said, "I hope you *didn't* tell on me yesterday. You had me worrying about it all last night."

Dai-yu turned back, ignoring him, to address Nightingale inside:

"When you do the room, leave one of the casements open so that the parent swallows can get in. And put the lion doorstop on the bottom of the blind to stop it flapping. And don't forget to put the cover back on the burner after you've lighted the incense."

She made her way across the courtyard, still ignoring him.

Bao-yu, who knew nothing of the little drama that had taken place outside his gate the night before, assumed that she was still angry about his unfortunate lapse earlier on that same day, when he had offended her susceptibilities with a somewhat risqué quotation from *The Western Chamber*. He offered her now, with energetic bowing and hand-pumping, the apologies that the previous day's emergency had caused him to neglect. But Dai-yu walked straight past him and out of the gate, not deigning so much as a glance in his direction, and stalked off in search of the others.

Bao-yu was nonplussed. He began to suspect that something more than he had first imagined must be wrong.

"Surely it can't only be because of yesterday lunchtime that she's carrying on in this fashion? There must be something else. On the other hand, I didn't get back until late and I didn't see her again last night, so how *could* I have offended her?"

Preoccupied with these reflections, he followed her at some distance behind.

Not far ahead Bao-chai and Tan-chun were watching the ungainly courtship dance of some storks. When they saw Dai-yu coming, they invited her to join them, and the three girls stood together and chatted. Then Bao-yu arrived. Tan-chun greeted him with sisterly concern:

"How have you been keeping, Bao? It's three whole days since I saw you last."

Bao-yu smiled back at her.

CAO XUEQIN

---

4. The festival of Grain in Ear marked the beginning of summer, which young girls would celebrate by fashioning miniature coaches and banners of twigs and brocade to speed the flower fairies on their way.

"How have *you* been keeping, sis? I was asking Cousin Wan about you the day before yesterday."

"Come over here a minute," said Tan-chun. "I want to talk to you."

He followed her into the shade of a pomegranate tree a little way apart from the other two.

"Has Father asked to see you at all during this last day or two?" Tan-chun began.

"No."

"I thought I heard someone say yesterday that he had been asking for you."

"No," said Bao-yu, smiling at her concern. "Whoever it was was mistaken. He certainly hasn't asked for *me*."

Tan-chun smiled and changed the subject.

"During the past few months," she said, "I've managed to save up another ten strings or so of cash. I'd like you to take it again like you did last time, and next time you go out, if you see a nice painting or calligraphic scroll or some amusing little thing that would do for my room, I'd like you to buy it for me."

"Well, I don't know," said Bao-yu. "In the trips I make to bazaars and temple fairs, whether it's inside the city or round about, I can't say that I ever see anything *really* nice or out of the ordinary. It's all bronzes and jades and porcelain and that sort of stuff. Apart from that it's mostly dress-making materials and clothes and things to eat."

"Now what would I want things like that for?" said Tan-chun. "No, I mean something like that little wickerwork basket you bought me last time, or the little box carved out of bamboo root, or the little clay burner. I thought they were sweet. Unfortunately the others took such a fancy to them that they carried them off as loot and wouldn't give them back to me again."

"Oh, if *those* are the sort of things you want," said Bao-yu laughing, "it's very simple. Just give a few strings of cash to one of the boys and he'll bring you back a whole cartload of them."

"What do the boys know about it?" said Tan-chun. "I need someone who can pick out the interesting things and the ones that are in good taste. You get me lots of nice little things, and I'll embroider a pair of slippers for you like the ones I made for you last time—only this time I'll do them more carefully."

"Talking of those slippers reminds me," said Bao-yu. "I happened to run into Father once when I was wearing them. He was Most Displeased. When he asked me who made them, I naturally didn't dare to tell him that *you* had, so I said that Aunt Wang had given them to me as a birthday present a few days before. There wasn't much he could do about it when he heard that they came from Aunt Wang; so after a very long pause he just said, 'What a pointless waste of human effort and valuable material, to produce things like that!' I told this to Aroma when I got back, and she said, 'Oh, that's nothing! You should have heard your Aunt Zhao complaining about those slippers. She was *furious* when she heard about them: "Her own natural brother so down at heel he scarcely dares show his face to people, and she spends her time making things like that!"'"

Tan-chun's smile had vanished:

"How *can* she talk such nonsense? Why should *I* be the one to make shoes for him? Huan gets a clothing allowance, doesn't he? He gets his clothing and footwear provided for the same as all the rest of us. And fancy saying a thing like that in front of a roomful of servants! For whose benefit was this remark made, I wonder? I make an occasional pair of slippers just for something to do in my spare time; and if I give a pair to someone I particularly like, that's my own affair. Surely no one else has any business to start telling me who I should give them to? Oh, she's so petty!"

Bao-yu shook his head:

"Perhaps you're being a bit hard on her. She's probably got her reasons."

This made Tan-chun really angry. Her chin went up defiantly:

"Now you're being as stupid as her. Of *course* she's got her reasons; but they are ignorant, stupid reasons. But she can think what she likes: as far as *I* am concerned, Sir Jia is my father and Lady Wang is my mother, and who was born in whose room doesn't interest me—the way I choose my friends inside the family has nothing to do with that. Oh, I know I shouldn't talk about her like this; but she is *so* idiotic about these things. As a matter of fact I can give you an even better example than your story of the slippers. That last time I gave you my savings to get something for me, she saw me a few days afterwards and started telling me how short of money she was and how difficult things were for her. I took no notice, of course. But later, when the maids were out of the room, she began attacking me for giving the money I'd saved to other people instead of giving it to Huan. Really! I didn't know whether to laugh or get angry with her. In the end I just walked out of the room and went round to see Mother."

There was an amused interruption at this point from Bao-chai, who was still standing where they had left her a few minutes before:

"Do finish your talking and come back soon! It's easy to see that you two are brother and sister. As soon as you see each other, you get into a huddle and start talking about family secrets. Would it *really* be such a disaster if anything you are saying were to be overheard?"

Tan-chun and Bao-yu rejoined her, laughing.

Not seeing Dai-yu, Bao-yu realized that she must have slipped off elsewhere while he was talking.

"Better leave it a day or two," he told himself on reflection. "Wait until her anger has calmed down a bit."

While he was looking downwards and meditating, he noticed that the ground where they were standing was carpeted with a bright profusion of wind-blown flowers— pomegranate and balsam for the most part.

"You can see she's upset," he thought ruefully. "She's neglecting her flowers. I'll bury this lot for her and remind her about it next time I see her."

He became aware that Bao-chai was arranging for him and Tan-chun to go with her outside.

"I'll join you two presently," he said, and waited until they were a little way off before stooping down to gather the fallen blossoms into the skirt of his gown. It was quite a way from where he was to the place where Dai-yu had buried the peach-blossom on that previous occasion, but he made his way towards it, over rocks and bridges and through plantations of trees and flowers. When he had almost reached his destination and there was only the spur of a miniature "mountain" between him and the burial-place of the flowers, he heard the sound of a voice, coming from the other side of the rock, whose continuous, gentle chiding was occasionally broken by the most pitiable and heart-rending sobs.

"It must be a maid from one of the apartments," thought Bao-yu. "Someone has been ill-treating her, and she has run here to cry on her own."

He stood still and endeavoured to catch what the weeping girl was saying. She appeared to be reciting something:

The blossoms fade and falling fill the air,
Of fragrance and bright hues bereft and bare.
Floss drifts and flutters round the Maiden's bower,
Or softly strikes against her curtained door.

The Maid, grieved by these signs of spring's decease,
Seeking some means her sorrow to express,
Has rake in hand into the garden gone,
Before the fallen flowers are trampled on.

Elm-pods and willow-floss are fragrant too;
Why care, Maid, where the fallen flowers blew?
Next year, when peach and plum-tree bloom again,
Which of your sweet companions will remain?

This spring the heartless swallow built his nest
Beneath the eaves of mud with flowers compressed.
Next year the flowers will blossom as before,
But swallow, nest, and Maid will be no more.

Three hundred and three-score the year's full tale:
From swords of frost and from the slaughtering gale
How can the lovely flowers long stay intact,
Or, once loosed, from their drifting fate draw back?

Blooming so steadfast, fallen so hard to find!
Beside the flowers' grave, with sorrowing mind,
The solitary Maid sheds many a tear,
Which on the boughs as bloody drops appear.

At twilight, when the cuckoo sings no more,
The Maiden with her rake goes in at door
And lays her down between the lamplit walls,
While a chill rain against the window falls.

I know not why my heart's so strangely sad,
Half grieving for the spring and yet half glad:
Glad that it came, grieved it so soon was spent.
So soft it came, so silently it went!

Last night, outside, a mournful sound was heard:
The spirits of the flowers and of the bird.
But neither bird nor flowers would long delay,
Bird lacking speech, and flowers too shy to stay.

And then I wished that I had wings to fly
After the drifting flowers across the sky:
Across the sky to the world's farthest end,
The flowers' last fragrant resting-place to find.

But better their remains in silk to lay
And bury underneath the wholesome clay,
Pure substances the pure earth to enrich,
Than leave to soak and stink in some foul ditch.

Can I, that these flowers' obsequies attend,
Divine how soon or late *my* life will end?

Let others laugh flower-burial to see:
Another year who will be burying me?

As petals drop and spring begins to fail,
The bloom of youth, too, sickens and turns pale.
One day, when spring has gone and youth has fled,
The Maiden and the flowers will both be dead.

All this was uttered in a voice half-choked with sobs; for the words recited seemed only to inflame the grief of the reciter—indeed, Bao-yu, listening on the other side of the rock, was so overcome by them that he had already flung himself weeping upon the ground.

But the sequel to this painful scene will be told in the following chapter.

Chapter 28

A crimson cummerbund becomes a pledge of friendship
And a chaplet of medicine-beads becomes a source of embarrassment

On the night before the festival, it may be remembered, Lin Dai-yu had mistakenly supposed Bao-yu responsible for Sky-bright's refusal to open the gate for her. The ceremonial farewell to the flowers of the following morning had transformed her pent-up and still smouldering resentment into a more generalized and seasonable sorrow. This had finally found its expression in a violent outburst of grief as she was burying the latest collection of fallen blossoms in her flower-grave. Meditation on the fate of flowers had led her to a contemplation of her own sad and orphaned lot; she had burst into tears, and soon after had begun a recitation of the poem whose words we recorded in the preceding chapter.

Unknown to her, Bao-yu was listening to this recitation from the slope of the near-by rockery. At first he merely nodded and sighed sympathetically; but when he heard the words

"Can I, that these flowers' obsequies attend,
Divine how soon or late *my* life will end?"

and, a little later,

"One day when spring has gone and youth has fled,
The Maiden and the flowers will both be dead."

he flung himself on the ground in a fit of weeping, scattering the earth all about him with the flowers he had been carrying in the skirt of his gown.

Lin Dai-yu dead! A world from which that delicate, flower-like countenance had irrevocably departed! It was unutterable anguish to think of it. Yet his sensitized imagination *did* now consider it—went on, indeed, to consider a world from which the others, too—Bao-chai, Caltrop, Aroma and the rest—had also irrevocably departed. Where would *he* be then? What would have become of him? And what of the Garden, the rocks, the flowers, the trees? To whom would they belong when he and the girls were no longer there to enjoy them? Passing from loss to loss in his imagination, he plunged deeper and deeper into a grief that seemed inconsolable. As the poet says:

Flowers in my eyes and bird-song in my ears
Augment my loss and mock my bitter tears.

Dai-yu, then, as she stood plunged in her own private sorrowing, suddenly heard the sound of another person crying bitterly on the rocks above her.

"The others are always telling me I'm a 'case,'" she thought. "Surely there can't be another 'case' up there?"

But on looking up she saw that it was Bao-yu.

"Pshaw!" she said crossly to herself. "I thought it was another girl, but all the time it was that cruel, hate—"

"Hateful" she had been going to say, but clapped her mouth shut before uttering it. She sighed instead and began to walk away.

By the time Bao-yu's weeping was over, Dai-yu was no longer there. He realized that she must have seen him and have gone away in order to avoid him. Feeling suddenly rather foolish, he rose to his feet and brushed the earth from his clothes. Then he descended from the rockery and began to retrace his steps in the direction of Green Delights. Quite by coincidence Dai-yu was walking along the same path a little way ahead.

"Stop a minute!" he cried, hurrying forward to catch up with her. "I know you are not taking any notice of me, but I only want to ask you one simple question, and then you need never have anything more to do with me."

Dai-yu had turned back to see who it was. When she saw that it was Bao-yu still, she was going to ignore him again; but hearing him say that he only wanted to ask her one question, she told him that he might do so.

Bao-yu could not resist teasing her a little.

"How about *two* questions? Would you wait for two?"

Dai-yu set her face forwards and began walking on again.

Bao-yu sighed.

"If it has to be like this now," he said, as if to himself, "it's a pity it was ever like it was in the beginning."

Dai-yu's curiosity got the better of her. She stopped walking and turned once more towards him.

"Like *what* in the beginning?" she asked. "And like what now?"

"Oh, the *beginning!*" said Bao-yu. "In the *beginning,* when you first came here, I was your faithful companion in all your games. Anything I had, even the thing most dear to me, was yours for the asking. If there was something to eat that I specially liked, I had only to hear that you were fond of it too and I would religiously hoard it away to share with you when you got back, not daring even to touch it until you came. We ate at the same table. We slept in the same bed. I used to think that because we were so close then, there would be something special about our relationship when we grew up—that even if we weren't particularly affectionate, we should at least have more understanding and forbearance for each other than the rest. But how wrong I was! Now that you *have* grown up, you seem only to have grown more touchy. You don't seem to care about *me* any more at all. You spend all your time brooding about outsiders like Feng and Chai. I haven't got any *real* brothers and sisters left here now. There are Huan and Tan, of course; but as you know, they're only my half-brother and half-sister: they aren't my mother's children. I'm on my own, like you. I should have thought we had so much in common—But what's the use? I try and try, but it gets me nowhere; and nobody knows or cares."

At this point—in spite of himself—he burst into tears.

The palpable evidence of her own eyes and ears had by now wrought a considerable softening on Dai-yu's heart. A sympathetic tear stole down her own cheek, and she hung her head and said nothing. Bao-yu could see that he had moved her.

"I know I'm not much use nowadays," he continued, "but however bad you may think me, I would never wittingly do anything in your presence to offend you. If I *do* ever slip up in some way, you ought to tell me off about it and warn me not to do it again, or shout at me—hit me, even, if you feel like it; I shouldn't mind. But you don't do that. You just ignore me. You leave me utterly at a loss to know what I'm supposed to have done wrong, so that I'm driven half frantic wondering what I ought to do to make up for it. If I were to die now, I should die with a grievance, and all the masses and exorcisms in the world wouldn't lay my ghost. Only when you explained what your reason was for ignoring me should I cease from haunting you and be reborn into another life."

Dai-yu's resentment for the gate incident had by now completely evaporated. She merely said:

"Oh well, in that case why did you tell your maids not to let me in when I came to call on you?"

"I honestly don't know what you are referring to," said Bao-yu in surprise. "Strike me dead if I ever did any such thing!"

"Hush!" said Dai-yu. "Talking about death at this time of the morning! You should be more careful what you say. If you did, you did. If you didn't, you didn't. There's no need for these horrible oaths."

"I really and truly didn't know you had called," said Bao-yu. "Cousin Bao came and sat with me a few minutes last night and then went away again. That's the only call I know about."

Dai-yu reflected for a moment or two, then smiled.

"Yes, it must have been the maids being lazy. Certainly they can be very disagreeable at such times."

"Yes, I'm sure that's what it was," said Bao-yu. "When I get back, I'll find out who it was and give her a good talking-to."

"I think some of your young ladies could *do* with a good talking-to," said Dai-yu, "—though it's not really for me to say so. It's a good job it was only me they were rude to. If Miss Bao or Miss Cow were to call and they behaved like that to *her,* that would be really serious."

She giggled mischievously. Bao-yu didn't know whether to laugh with her or grind his teeth. But just at that moment a maid came up to ask them both to lunch and the two of them went together out of the Garden and through into the front part of the mansion, calling in at Lady Wang's on the way.

"How did you get on with that medicine of Dr Bao's," Lady Wang asked Dai-yu as soon as she saw her, "—the Court Physician? Do you think you are any better for it?"

"It didn't seem to make very much difference," said Dai-yu. "Grandmother has put me back on Dr Wang's prescription."

"Cousin Lin has got a naturally weak constitution, Mother," said Bao-yu. "She takes cold very easily. These strong decoctions are all very well provided she only takes one or two to dispel the cold. For regular treatment it's probably best if she sticks to pills."

"The doctor was telling me about some pills for her the other day," said Lady Wang, "but I just can't remember the name."

"I know the names of most of those pills," said Bao-yu. "I expect he wanted her to take Ginseng Tonic Pills."

"No, that wasn't it," said Lady Wang.

"Eight Gem Motherwort Pills?" said Bao-yu. "Zhang's Dextrals? Zhang's Sinistrals? If it wasn't any of them, it was probably Dr Cui's Adenophora Kidney Pills."

"No," said Lady Wang, "it was none of those. All I can remember is that there was a 'Vajra' in it."

Bao-yu gave a hoot and clapped his hands:

"I've never heard of 'Vajra Pills.' If there are 'Vajra Pills,' I suppose there must be 'Buddha Boluses!'"

The others all laughed. Bao-chai looked at him mockingly.

"I should think it was probably 'The Deva-king Cardiac Elixir Pills,'" she said.

"Yes, yes, that's it!" said Lady Wang. "Of course! How stupid of me!"

"No, Mother, not stupid," said Bao-yu. "It's the strain. All those Vajra-kings and Bodhisattvas have been overworking you!"

"You're a naughty boy to make fun of your poor mother," said Lady Wang. "A good whipping from your Pa is what you need."

"Oh, Father doesn't whip me for that sort of thing nowadays," said Bao-yu.

"Now that we know the name of the pills, we must get them to buy some for your Cousin Lin," said Lady Wang.

"None of those things are any good," said Bao-yu. "You give me three hundred and sixty taels of silver and I'll make up some pills for Cousin Lin that I guarantee will have her completely cured before she has finished the first boxful."

"Stuff!" said Lady Wang. "Whoever heard of a medicine that cost so much?"

"No, honestly!" said Bao-yu. "This prescription is a very unusual one with very special ingredients. I can't remember all of them, but I know they include

> the caul of a first-born child;
> a ginseng root shaped like a man, with the leaves still on it;
> a turtle-sized polygonum root;

and

> lycoperdon from the stump of a thousand-year-old pine-tree.

—Actually, though, there's nothing so *very* special about those ingredients. They're all in the standard pharmacopoeia. For 'sovereign remedies' they use ingredients that would *really* make you jump. I once gave the prescription for one to Cousin Xue. He was more than a year begging me for it before I would give it to him, and it took him another two or three years and nearly a thousand taels of silver to get all the ingredients together. Ask Bao-chai if you don't believe me, Mother."

"I know nothing about it," said Bao-chai. "I've never heard it mentioned. It's no good telling Aunt to ask *me*."

"You see! Bao-chai is a *good* girl. *She* doesn't tell lies," said Lady Wang.

Bao-yu was standing in the middle of the floor below the kang.[5] He clapped his hands at this and turned to the others appealingly.

"But it's the *truth* I'm telling you. This is no lie."

As he turned, he happened to catch sight of Dai-yu, who was sitting behind Bao-chai, smiling mockingly and stroking her cheek with her finger—which in sign-language means, "You are a great big liar and you ought to be ashamed of yourself."

But Xi-feng, who happened to be in the inner room supervising the laying of the table and had overheard the preceding remarks, now emerged into the outer room to corroborate:

"It's quite true, what Bao says. I don't think he *is* making it up," she said. "Not so long ago Cousin Xue came to me asking for some pearls, and when I asked him what

5. A brick platform, often carpeted, that could be sat and slept on.

he wanted them for, he said, 'To make medicine with.' Then he started grumbling about the trouble he was having in getting the right ingredients and how he had half a mind not to make this medicine up after all. I said, 'What medicine?' and he told me that it was a prescription that Cousin Bao had given him and reeled off a lot of ingredients—I can't remember them now. 'Of course,' he said, 'I could easily enough *buy* a few pearls; only these have to be ones that have been worn. That's why I'm asking *you* for them. If you haven't got any loose ones,' he said, 'a few pearls broken off a bit of jewellery would do. I'd get you something nice to replace it with.' He was so insistent that in the end I had to break up two of my ornaments for him. Then he wanted a yard of Imperial red gauze. That was to put over the mortar to pound the pearls through. He said they had to be ground until they were as fine as flour."

"You see!" "You see!" Bao-yu kept interjecting throughout this recital.

"Incidentally, Mother," he said, when it was ended, "even *that* was only a sub-stitute. According to the prescription, the pearls ought really to have come from an ancient grave. They should really have been pearls taken from jewellery on the corpse of a long-buried noblewoman. But as one can't very well go digging up graves and rifling tombs every time one wants to make this medicine, the prescription allows pearls worn by the living as a second-best."

"Blessed name of the Lord!" said Lady Wang. "What a *dreadful* idea! Even if you *did* get them from a grave, I can't believe that a medicine made from pearls that had been come by so wickedly—desecrating people's bones that had been lying peace-fully in the ground all those hundreds of years—could possibly do you any good."

Bao-yu turned to Dai-yu.

"Did you hear what Feng said?" he asked her. "I hope you're not going to say that *she* was lying."

Although the remark was addressed to Dai-yu, he winked at Bao-chai as he made it.

Dai-yu clung to Lady Wang.

"Listen to him, Aunt!" she wailed. "Bao-chai won't be a party to his lies, but he still expects *me* to be."

"Bao-yu, you are very unkind to your cousin," said Lady Wang.

Bao-yu only laughed.

"You don't know the reason, Mother. Bao-chai didn't know a half of what Cousin Xue got up to, even when she was living with her mother outside; and now that she's moved into the Garden, she knows even less. When she said she didn't know, she *really* didn't know: she wasn't giving me the lie. What you don't realize is that Cousin Lin was all the time sitting behind her making signs to show that she didn't believe me."

Just then a maid came from Grandmother Jia's apartment to fetch Bao-yu and Dai-yu to lunch.

Without saying a word to Bao-yu, Dai-yu got up and, taking the maid's hand, be-gan to go. But the maid was reluctant.

"Let's wait for Master Bao and we can go together."

"He's not eating lunch today," said Dai-yu. "Come on, let's go!"

"Whether he's eating lunch or not," said the maid, "he'd better come with us, so that he can explain to Her Old Ladyship about it when she asks."

"All right, you wait for him then," said Dai-yu. "I'm going on ahead."

And off she went.

"I think I'd rather eat with *you* today, Mother," said Bao-yu.

"No, no, you can't," said Lady Wang. "Today is one of my fast-days: I shall only be eating vegetables. You go and have a proper meal with your Grandma."

"I shall share your vegetables," said Bao-yu. "Go on, you can go," he said, dismissing the maid; and rushing up to the table, he sat himself down at it in readiness.

"You others had better get on with your own lunch," Lady Wang said to Bao-chai and the girls. "Let him do as he likes."

"You really ought to go," Bao-chai said to Bao-yu. "Whether you have lunch there or not, you ought to keep Cousin Lin company. She is very upset, you know. Why don't you?"

"Oh, leave her alone!" said Bao-yu. "She'll be all right presently."

Soon they had finished eating, and Bao-yu, afraid that Grandmother Jia might be worrying and at the same time anxious to rejoin Dai-yu, hurriedly demanded tea to rinse his mouth with. Tan-chun and Xi-chun were much amused.

"Why are you always in such a hurry, Bao?" they asked him. "Even your eating and drinking all seems to be done in a rush."

"You should let him finish quickly, so that he can get back to his Dai-yu," said Bao-chai blandly. "Don't make him waste time here with us."

Bao-yu left as soon as he had drunk his tea, and made straight for the west courtyard where his Grandmother Jia's apartment was. But as he was passing by the gateway of Xi-feng's courtyard, it happened that Xi-feng herself was standing in her doorway with one foot on the threshold, grooming her teeth with an ear-cleaner and keeping a watchful eye on nine or ten pages who were moving potted plants about under her direction.

"Ah, just the person I wanted to see!" she said, as soon as she caught sight of Bao-yu. "Come inside. I want you to write something down for me."

Bao-yu was obliged to follow her indoors. Xi-feng called for some paper, an inkstone and a brush, and at once began dictating:

"Crimson lining-damask forty lengths, dragonet figured satin forty lengths, miscellaneous Imperial gauze one hundred lengths, gold necklets four,—"

"Here, what *is* this?" said Bao-yu. "It isn't an invoice and it isn't a presentation list. How am I supposed to write it?"

"Never you mind about that," said Xi-feng. "As long as I know what it is, that's all that matters. Just put it down anyhow."

Bao-yu wrote down the four items. As soon as he had done so, Xi-feng took up the paper and folded it away.

"Now," she said, smiling pleasantly, "there's something I want to talk to you about. I don't know whether you'll agree to this or not, but there's a girl in your room called 'Crimson' whom I'd like to work for me. If I find you someone to replace her with, will you let me have her?"

"There are so many girls in my room," said Bao-yu. "Please take any you have a fancy to. You really don't need to ask me about it."

"In that case," said Xi-feng, "I'll send for her straight away."

"Please do," said Bao-yu, and started to go.

"Hey, come back!" said Xi-feng. "I haven't finished with you yet."

"I've got to see Grandma now," said Bao-yu. "If you've got anything else to say, you can tell me on my way back."

When he got to Grandmother Jia's apartment, they had all just finished lunch. Grandmother Jia asked him if he had had anything nice to eat with his mother.

"There wasn't anything nice," he said. "But I had an extra bowl of rice."

Then, after the briefest pause:

"Where's Cousin Lin?"

"In the inner room," said Grandmother Jia.

In the inner room a maid stood below the kang blowing on a flat-iron. Up on the kang two maids were marking some material with a chalked string, while Dai-yu, her head bent low over her work, was engaged in cutting something from it with her shears.

"What are you making?" he asked her. "You'll give yourself a headache, stooping down like that immediately after your lunch."

Dai-yu took no notice and went on cutting.

"That corner looks a bit creased still," said one of the maids. "It will have to be ironed again."

"*Leave it alone!*" said Dai-yu, laying down her shears. "*It will be all right presently.*"

Bao-yu found her reply puzzling.

Bao-chai, Tan-chun and the rest had now arrived in the outer room and were talking to Grandmother Jia. Presently Bao-chai drifted inside and asked Dai-yu what she was doing; then, when she saw that she was cutting material, she exclaimed admiringly.

"What a lot of things you can do, Dai! Fancy, even dressmaking now!"

Dai-yu smiled malignantly.

"Oh, it's all lies, really. I just do it to fool people."

"I've got something to tell you that I think will amuse you, Dai," said Bao-chai pleasantly. "When our cousin was holding forth about that medicine just now and I said I didn't know about it, I believe actually he was rather wounded."

"*Oh, leave him alone!*" said Dai-yu. "*He will be all right presently.*"

"Grandma wants someone to play dominoes with," said Bao-yu to Bao-chai. "Why don't you go and play dominoes?"

"Oh, is *that* what I came for?" said Bao-chai; but she went, notwithstanding.

"Why don't *you* go?" said Dai-yu. "There's a tiger in this room. You might get eaten."

She said this still bending over her cutting, which she continued to work away at without looking up at him.

Finding himself once more ignored, Bao-yu nevertheless attempted to remain jovial.

"Why don't you come out for a bit too? You can do this cutting later."

Dai-yu continued to take no notice.

Failing to get a response from her, he tried the maids:

"Who told her to do this dress-making?"

"Whoever told her to do it," said Dai-yu, "it has nothing whatever to do with Master Bao."

Bao-yu was about to retort, but just at that moment someone came in to say that he was wanted outside, and he was obliged to hurry off.

Dai-yu leaned forward and shouted after him:

"Holy name! By the time you get back, I shall be dead."

***

She[6] ordered a little maid to get out Bao-yu's share of the things sent. There were two Palace fans of exquisite workmanship, two strings of red musk-scented medicine-beads, two lengths of maidenhair chiffon and a grass-woven "lotus" mat to lie on in the hot weather.

6. Aroma, Bao-yu's personal maid. The Imperial Concubine has sent gifts to mark the Double Fifth festival, a celebration of the summer solstice on the fifth day of the fifth lunar month.

CAO XUEQIN

"Did the others all get the same?" he asked.

"Her Old Ladyship's presents were the same as yours with the addition of a perfume-sceptre and an agate head-rest, and Sir Zheng's, Lady Wang's and Mrs Xue's were the same as Her Old Ladyship's but without the head-rest; Miss Bao's were exactly the same as yours; Miss Lin, Miss Ying-chun, Miss Tan-chun and Miss Xi-chun got only the fans and the beads; and Mrs Zhu and Mrs Lian both got two lengths of gauze, two lengths of chiffon, two perfume sachets and two moulded medicine-cakes."

"Funny!" said Bao-yu. "I wonder why Miss Lin didn't get the same as me and why only Miss Bao's and mine were the same. There must have been some mistake, surely?"

"When they unpacked them yesterday, the separate lots were all labelled," said Aroma. "I don't see how there could have been any mistake. Your share was in Her Old Ladyship's room and I went round there to get it for you. Her Old Ladyship says she wants you to go to Court at four o'clock tomorrow morning to give thanks."

"Yes, of course," said Bao-yu inattentively, and gave Ripple instructions to take his presents round to Dai-yu:

"Tell Miss Lin that I got these things yesterday and that if there's anything there she fancies, I should like her to keep it."

Ripple went off with the presents. She was back in a very short time, however.

"Miss Lin says she got some yesterday too, and will you please keep these for yourself."

Bao-yu told her to put them away. As soon as he had washed, he left to pay his morning call on Grandmother Jia; but just as he was going out he saw Dai-yu coming towards him and hurried forward to meet her.

"Why didn't you choose anything from the things I sent you?"

Yesterday's resentments were now quite forgotten; today Dai-yu had fresh matter to occupy her mind.

"I'm not equal to the honour," she said. "You forget, I'm not in the gold and jade class like you and your Cousin Bao. I'm only a common little wall-flower!"

The reference to gold and jade immediately aroused Bao-yu's suspicions.

"I don't know what anyone else may have been saying on the subject," he said, "but if any such thought ever so much as crossed *my* mind, may Heaven strike me dead, and may I never be reborn as a human being!"

Seeing him genuinely bewildered, Dai-yu smiled in what was meant to be a reassuring manner.

"I wish you wouldn't make these horrible oaths. It's so disagreeable. Who *cares* about your silly old 'gold and jade,' anyway?"

"It's hard to make you *see* what is in my heart," said Bao-yu. "One day perhaps you will know. But I can tell you this. My heart has room for four people only. Grannie and my parents are three of them and Cousin Dai is the fourth. I swear to you there isn't a fifth."

"There's no need for you to swear," said Dai-yu. "I know very well that Cousin Dai has a place in your heart. The trouble is that as soon as Cousin Chai comes along, Cousin Dai gets forgotten."

"You imagine these things," said Bao-yu. "It really isn't as you say."

"Yesterday when Little Miss Bao wouldn't tell lies for you, why did you turn to *me* and expect *me* to? How would you like it if I did that sort of thing to you?"

Bao-chai happened to come along while they were still talking and the two of them moved aside to avoid her. Bao-chai saw this clearly, but pretended not to notice and hurried by with lowered eyes. She went and sat with Lady Wang for a while and from there went on to Grandmother Jia's. Bao-yu was already at his grandmother's when she got there.

Bao-chai had on more than one occasion heard her mother telling Lady Wang and other people that the golden locket she wore had been given her by a monk, who had insisted that when she grew up the person she married must be someone who had "a jade to match the gold." This was one of the reasons why she tended to keep aloof from Bao-yu. The slight embarrassment she always felt as a result of her mother's chatter had yesterday been greatly intensified when Yuan-chun singled her out as the only girl to receive the same selection of presents as Bao-yu. She was relieved to think that Bao-yu, so wrapped up in Dai-yu that his thoughts were only of her, was unaware of her embarrassment.

But now here was Bao-yu smiling at her with sudden interest.

"Cousin Bao, may I have a look at your medicine-beads?"

She happened to be wearing one of the little chaplets on her left wrist and began to pull it off now in obedience to his request. But Bao-chai was inclined to plumpness and perspired easily, and for a moment or two it would not come off. While she was struggling with it, Bao-yu had ample opportunity to observe her snow-white arm, and a feeling rather warmer than admiration was kindled inside him.

"If that arm were growing on Cousin Lin's body," he speculated, "I might hope one day to touch it. What a pity it's hers! Now I shall never have that good fortune."

Suddenly he thought of the curious coincidence of the gold and jade talismans and their matching inscriptions, which Dai-yu's remark had reminded him of. He looked again at Bao-chai—

> that face like the full moon's argent bowl;
> those eyes like sloes;
> those lips whose carmine hue no Art contrived;
> and brows by none but Nature's pencil lined.

This was beauty of quite a different order from Dai-yu's. Fascinated by it, he continued to stare at her with a somewhat dazed expression, so that when she handed him the chaplet, which she had now succeeded in getting off her wrist, he failed to take it from her.

Seeing that he had gone off into one of his trances, Bao-chai threw down the chaplet in embarrassment and turned to go. But Dai-yu was standing on the threshold, biting a corner of her handkerchief, convulsed with silent laughter.

"I thought you were so delicate," said Bao-chai. "What are you standing there in the draught for?"

"I've been in the room all the time," said Dai-yu. "I just this moment went to have a look outside because I heard the sound of something in the sky. It was a gawping goose."

"Where?" said Bao-chai. "Let me have a look."

"Oh," said Dai-yu, "as soon as I went outside he flew away with a *whir-r-r*—"

She flicked her long handkerchief as she said this in the direction of Bao-yu's face.

"Ow!" he exclaimed—She had flicked him in the eye.

***

from **Chapter 29**

Cousin Zhen was aware that, though Abbot Zhang[7] had started life a poor boy and entered the Taoist church as "proxy novice" of Grandmother Jia's late husband, a former Emperor had with his own Imperial lips conferred on him the title "Doctor Mysticus," and he now held the seals of the Board of Commissioners of the Taoist Church, had been awarded the title "Doctor Serenissimus" by the reigning sovereign, and was addressed as "Holiness" by princes, dukes and governors of provinces. He was therefore not a man to be trifled with. Moreover he was constantly in and out of the two mansions and on familiar terms with most of the Jia ladies. Cousin Zhen at once became affable.

"Oh, *you're* one of the family, Papa Zhang, so let's have no more of that kind of talk, or I'll take you by that old beard of yours and give it a good pull. Come on, follow me!"

Abbot Zhang followed him inside, laughing delightedly.

Having found Grandmother Jia, Cousin Zhen ducked and smiled deferentially.

"Papa Zhang has come to pay his respects, Grannie."

"Help him, then!" said Grandmother Jia; and Cousin Zhen hurried back to where Abbot Zhang was waiting a few yards behind him and supported him by an elbow into her presence. The abbot prefaced his greeting with a good deal of jovial laughter.

"Blessed Buddha of Boundless Life! And how has Your Old Ladyship been all this while? In rude good health, I trust? And Their Ladyships, and all the younger ladies?—also flourishing? It's quite a while since I was at the mansion to call on Your Old Ladyship, but I declare you look more blooming than ever!"

"And how are *you,* old Holy One?" Grandmother Jia asked him with a pleased smile.

"Thank Your Old Ladyship for asking. I still keep pretty fit. But never mind about that. What *I* want to know is, how's our young hero been keeping, eh? We were celebrating the blessed Nativity of the Veiled King here on the twenty-sixth. Very select little gathering. Tasteful offerings. I thought our young friend might have enjoyed it; but when I sent round to invite him, they told me he was out."

"He really *was* out," said Grandmother Jia, and turned aside to summon the "young hero"; but Bao-yu had gone to the lavatory. He came hurrying forward presently.

"Hallo, Papa Zhang! How are you?"

The old Taoist embraced him affectionately and returned his greeting.

"He's beginning to fill out," he said, addressing Grandmother Jia.

"He looks well enough on the outside," said Grandmother Jia, "but underneath he's delicate. And his Pa doesn't improve matters by forcing him to study all the time. I'm afraid he'll end up by *making* the child ill."

"Lately I've been seeing calligraphy and poems of his in all kinds of places," said Abbot Zhang, "—all quite remarkably good. I really can't understand why Sir Zheng is concerned that the boy doesn't study enough. If you ask me, I think he's all right as he is." He sighed. "Of course, you know who this young man reminds me of, don't you? Whether it's his looks or the way he talks or the way he moves, to me he's the spit and image of Old Sir Jia."

The old man's eyes grew moist, and Grandmother Jia herself showed a disposition to be tearful.

"It's quite true," she said. "None of our children or our children's children turned out like him, except my Bao. Only my little Jade Boy is like his grandfather."

7. An old acquaintance of the family who has stopped by for a visit.

"Of course, your generation wouldn't remember Old Sir Jia," Abbot Zhang said, turning to Cousin Zhen. "It's before your time. In fact, I don't suppose even Sir She and Sir Zheng can have a very clear recollection of what their father was like in his prime."

He brightened as another topic occurred to him and once more quaked with laughter.

"I saw a most attractive young lady when I was out visiting the other day. Fourteen this year. Seeing her put me in mind of our young friend here. It must be about time we started thinking about a match for him, surely? In looks, intelligence, breeding, background this girl was ideally suited. What does Your Old Ladyship feel? I didn't want to rush matters. I thought I'd better first wait and see what Your Old Ladyship thought before saying anything to the family."

"A monk who once told the boy's fortune said that he was not to marry young," said Grandmother Jia; "so I think we had better wait until he is a little older before we arrange anything definite. But do by all means go on inquiring for us. It doesn't matter whether the family is wealthy or not; as long as the girl *looks* all right, you can let me know. Even if it's a poor family, we can always help out over the expenses. Money is no problem. It's looks and character that count."

"Now come on, Papa Zhang!" said Xi-feng when this exchange had ended. "Where's that new amulet for my little girl? You had the nerve to send someone round the other day for gosling satin, and of course, as we didn't want to embarrass the old man by refusing, we had to send you some. So now what about that amulet?"

Abbot Zhang once more quaked with laughter.

"Ho! ho! ho! You can tell how bad my eyes are getting; I didn't even see you there, dear lady, or I should have thanked you for the satin. Yes, the amulet has been ready for some time. I was going to send it to you two days ago, but then Her Grace unexpectedly asked us for this *Pro Viventibus* and I stupidly forgot all about it. It's still on the high altar being sanctified. I'll go and get it for you."

He went off, surprisingly nimbly, to the main hall of the temple and returned after a short while carrying the amulet on a little tea-tray, using a red satin book-wrap as a tray-cloth. Baby's nurse took the amulet from him, and he was just about to receive the little girl from her arms when he caught sight of Xi-feng laughing at him mockingly.

"Why didn't you bring it in your hand?" she asked him.

"The hands get so sweaty in this weather," he said. "I thought a tray would be more hygienic."

"You gave me quite a fright when I saw you coming in with that tray," said Xi-feng. "I thought for one moment you were going to take up a collection!"

There was a loud burst of laughter from the assembled company. Even Cousin Zhen was unable to restrain himself.

"Monkey! Monkey!" said Grandmother Jia. "Aren't you afraid of going to the Hell of Scoffers when you die and having your tongue cut out?"

"Oh, Papa and I say what we like to each other," said Xi-feng. *"He's* always telling *me* I must 'acquire merit' and threatening me with a short life if I don't pay up quickly. That's right, isn't it Papa?"

"As a matter of fact I *did* have an ulterior motive in bringing this tray," said Abbot Zhang, laughing, "but it wasn't in order to make a collection, I assure you. I wanted to ask this young gentleman here if he would be so very kind as to lend me the famous jade for a few minutes. The tray is for carrying it outside on, so that my Taoist friends, some of whom have travelled long distances to be here, and my old students, and *their* students, all of whom are gathered here today, may have the privilege of examining it."

"My dear good man, in that case let the boy go with it round his neck and show it to them himself!" said Grandmother Jia. "No need for all this running to and fro with trays—at your age, too!"

"Most kind! Most considerate!—But Your Old Ladyship is deceived," said the abbot. "I may look my eighty years, but I'm still hale and hearty. No, the point is that with so many of them here today and the weather so hot, the smell is sure to be somewhat overpowering. Our young friend here is certainly not used to it. We shouldn't want him to be overcome by the—ah—effluvia, should we?"

Hearing this, Grandmother Jia told Bao-yu to take off the Magic Jade and put it on the tray. Abbot Zhang draped the crimson cloth over his hands, grasped the tray between satin-covered thumbs and fingers, and, holding it like a sacred relic at eye level in front of him, conveyed it reverently from the courtyard.

Grandmother Jia and the others now continued their sightseeing. They had finished with everything at ground level and were about to mount the stairs into the galleries when Cousin Zhen came up to report that Abbot Zhang had returned with the jade. He was followed by the smiling figure of the abbot, holding the tray in the same reverential manner as before.

"Well, they've all seen the jade now," he said, "—and very grateful they were. They agreed that it really is a most remarkable object, and they regretted that they had nothing of value to show their appreciation with. Here you are!—this is the best they could do. These are all little Taoist trinkets they happened to have about them. Nothing very special, I'm afraid; but they'd like our young friend to keep them, either to amuse himself with or to give away to his friends."

Grandmother Jia looked at the tray. It was covered with jewellery. There were golden crescents, jade thumb-rings and a lot of "motto" jewellery—a tiny sceptre and persimmons with the rebus-meaning "success in all things," a little quail and a vase with corn-stalks meaning "peace throughout the years," and many other designs—all in gold- or jade-work, and much of it inlaid with pearls and precious stones. Altogether there must have been about forty pieces.

"What have you been up to, you naughty old man?" she said. "Those men are all poor priests—they can't afford to give things like *this* away. You really shouldn't have done this. We can't possibly accept them."

"It was their own idea, I do assure you," said the abbot. "There was nothing I could do to stop them. If you refuse to take these things, I am afraid you will destroy my credit with these people. They will say that I cannot really have the connection with your honoured family that I have always claimed to have."

After this Grandmother Jia could no longer decline. She told one of the servants to receive the tray.

"We obviously can't refuse, Grannie, after what Papa Zhang has just said," said Bao-yu; 'but I really have no use for this stuff. Why not let one of the boys carry it outside for me and I'll distribute it to the poor?"

"I think that's a very good idea," said Grandmother Jia.

But Abbot Zhang thought otherwise and hastily intervened:

"I'm sure it does our young friend credit, this charitable impulse. However, although these things are, as I said, of no especial value, they are—what shall I say—objects of *virtù,* and if you give them to the poor, in the first place the poor won't have much use for them, and in the second place the objects themselves will get spoiled. If you want to give something to the poor, a largesse of money would, I suggest, be far more appropriate."

"Very well, look after this stuff for me, then," said Bao-yu to the servant, "and this evening you will distribute a largesse." ***

For Bao-yu the whole of the previous day had been spoilt by Abbot Zhang's proposal to Grandmother Jia to arrange a match for him. He came home in a thoroughly bad temper and kept telling everyone that he would "never see Abbot Zhang again as long as he lived." Not associating his ill-humour with the abbot's proposal, the others were mystified.

Grandmother Jia's unwillingness was further reinforced by the fact that Dai-yu, since her return home yesterday, had been suffering from mild sunstroke. What with one thing and another, the old lady declined absolutely to go again, and Xi-feng had to make up her own party and go by herself.

But Xi-feng's play-going does not concern us.

Bao-yu, believing that Dai-yu's sunstroke was serious and that she might even be in danger of her life, was so worried that he could not eat, and rushed round in the middle of the lunch-hour to see how she was. He found her neither as ill as he had feared nor as responsive as he might have hoped.

"Why don't you go and watch your plays?" she asked him. "What are you mooning about at home for?"

Abbot Zhang's recent attempt at match-making had profoundly distressed Bao-yu and he was shocked by her seeming indifference.

"I can forgive the others for not understanding what has upset me," he thought; "but that *she* should want to trifle with me at a time like this . . . !"

The sense that she had failed him made the annoyance he now felt with her a hundred times greater than it had been on any previous occasion. Never could any other person have stirred him to such depths of atrabilious rage. Coming from other lips, her words would scarcely have touched him. Coming from hers, they put him in a passion. His face darkened.

"It's all along been a mistake, then," he said. "You're not what I took you for."

Dai-yu gave an unnatural little laugh.

"Not what you took me for? That's hardly surprising, is it? I haven't got that *little something* which would have made me worthy of you."

Bao-yu came right up to her and held his face close to hers:

"You do realize, don't you, that you are deliberately willing my death?"

Dai-yu could not for the moment understand what he was talking about.

"I swore an oath to you yesterday," he went on. "I said that I hoped Heaven might strike me dead if this 'gold and jade' business meant anything to me. Since you have now brought it up again, it's clear to me that you *want* me to die. Though what you hope to gain by my death I find it hard to imagine."

Dai-yu now remembered what had passed between them on the previous day. She knew that she was wrong to have spoken as she did, and felt both ashamed and a little frightened. Her shoulders started shaking and she began to cry.

"May Heaven strike *me* dead if I ever willed your death!" she said. "But I don't see what you have to get so worked up about. It's only because of what Abbot Zhang said about arranging a match for you. You're afraid he might interfere with your precious 'gold and jade' plans; and because you're angry about that, you have to come along and take it out on me—That's all it is, isn't it?"

Bao-yu had from early childhood manifested a streak of morbid sensibility, which being brought up in close proximity with a nature so closely in harmony with his own

248

had done little to improve. Now that he had reached an age when both his experience and the reading of forbidden books had taught him something about "worldly matters," he had begun to take a rather more grown-up interest in girls. But although there were plenty of young ladies of outstanding beauty and breeding among the Jia family's numerous acquaintance, none of them, in his view, could remotely compare with Dai-yu. For some time now his feeling for her had been a very special one; but precisely because of this same morbid sensibility, he had shrunk from telling her about it. Instead, whenever he was feeling particularly happy or particularly cross, he would invent all sorts of ways of probing her to find out if this feeling for her was reciprocated. It was unfortunate for him that Dai-yu herself possessed a similar streak of morbid sensibility and disguised her real feelings, as he did his, while attempting to discover what *he* felt about *her*.

Here was a situation, then, in which both parties concealed their real emotions and assumed counterfeit ones in an endeavour to find out what the real feelings of the other party were. And because

> When false meets false the truth will oft-times out,

there was the constant possibility that the innumerable little frustrations that were engendered by all this concealment would eventually erupt into a quarrel.

Take the present instance. What Bao-yu was actually thinking at this moment was something like this:

"In my eyes and in my thoughts there is no one else but you. I can forgive the others for not knowing this, but surely *you* ought to realize? If at a time like this you can't share my anxiety—if you can think of nothing better to do than provoke me with that sort of silly talk, it shows that the concern I feel for you every waking minute of the day is wasted: that you just don't care about me at all."

This was what he *thought;* but of course he didn't *say* it. On her side Dai-yu's thoughts were somewhat as follows:

"I know you must care for me a little bit, and I'm sure you don't take this ridiculous 'gold and jade' talk seriously. But if you cared *only* for me and had absolutely no inclination at all in another direction, then every time I mentioned 'gold and jade' you would behave quite naturally and let it pass almost as if you hadn't noticed. How is it, then, that when I do refer to it you get so excited? It shows that it must be on your mind. You *pretend* to be upset in order to allay my suspicions."

Meanwhile a quite different thought was running through Bao-yu's mind:

"I would do anything—absolutely *anything*," he was thinking, "if only you would be nice to me. If you would be nice to me, I would gladly die for you this moment. It doesn't really matter whether you know what I feel for you or not. Just be nice to me, then at least we shall be a little closer to each other, instead of so horribly far apart."

At the same time Dai-yu was thinking:

"Never mind me. Just be your own natural self. If *you* were all right, *I* should be all right too. All these manoeuverings to try and anticipate my feelings don't bring us any closer together; they merely draw us farther apart."

The percipient reader will no doubt observe that these two young people were already of one mind, but that the complicated procedures by which they sought to draw together were in fact having precisely the opposite effect. Complacent reader! Permit us to remind you that your correct understanding of the situation is due solely to the fact that we have been revealing to you the secret, innermost thoughts of those two young persons, which neither of them had so far ever felt able to express.

Let us now return from the contemplation of inner thoughts to the recording of outward appearances.

When Dai-yu, far from saying something nice to him, once more made reference to the "gold and jade," Bao-yu became so choked with rage that for a moment he was quite literally bereft of speech. Frenziedly snatching the "Magic Jade" from his neck and holding it by the end of its silken cord he gritted his teeth and dashed it against the floor with all the strength in his body.

"*Beastly* thing!" he shouted. "I'll smash you to pieces and put an end to this once and for all."

But the jade, being exceptionally hard and resistant, was not the tiniest bit damaged. Seeing that he had not broken it, Bao-yu began to look around for something to smash it with. Dai-yu, still crying, saw what he was going to do.

"Why smash a dumb, lifeless object?" she said. "If you want to smash something, let it be me."

The sound of their quarrelling brought Nightingale and Snowgoose hurrying in to keep the peace. They found Bao-yu apparently bent on destroying his jade and tried to wrest it from him. Failing to do so, and sensing that the quarrel was of more than usual dimensions, they went off to fetch Aroma. Aroma came back with them as fast as she could run and eventually succeeded in prising the jade from his hand. He glared at her scornfully.

"It's my own thing I'm smashing," he said. "What business is it of yours to interfere?"

Aroma saw that his face was white with anger and his eyes wild and dangerous. Never had she seen him in so terrible a rage. She took him gently by the hand:

"You shouldn't smash the jade just because of a disagreement with your cousin," she said. "What do you think she would feel like and what sort of position would it put her in if you really *were* to break it?"

Dai-yu heard these words through her sobs. They struck a responsive chord in her breast, and she wept all the harder to think that even Aroma seemed to understand her better than Bao-yu did. So much emotion was too much for her weak stomach. Suddenly there was a horrible retching noise and up came the tisane of elsholtzia leaves she had taken only a short while before. Nightingale quickly held out her handkerchief to receive it and, while Snowgoose rubbed and pounded her back, Dai-yu continued to retch up wave upon wave of watery vomit, until the whole handkerchief was soaked with it.

"However cross you may be, Miss, you ought to have more regard for your health," said Nightingale. "You'd only just taken that medicine and you were beginning to feel a little bit better for it, and now because of your argument with Master Bao you've gone and brought it all up again. Suppose you were to be *really* ill as a consequence. How do you think Master Bao would feel?"

When Bao-yu heard these words they struck a responsive chord in *his* breast, and he reflected bitterly that even Nightingale seemed to understand him better than Dai-yu. But then he looked again at Dai-yu, who was sobbing and panting by turns, and whose red and swollen face was wet with perspiration and tears, and seeing how pitiably frail and ill she looked, his heart misgave him.

"I shouldn't have taken her up on that 'gold and jade' business," he thought. "I've got her into this state and now there's no way in which I can relieve her by sharing what she suffers." As he thought this, he, too, began to cry.

Now that Bao-yu and Dai-yu were both crying, Aroma instinctively drew towards her master to comfort him. A pang of pity for him passed through her and she squeezed his hand sympathetically. It was as cold as ice. She would have liked to tell him not to cry but hesitated, partly from the consideration that he might be suffering from some deep-concealed hurt which crying would do something to relieve, and partly from the fear that to do so in Dai-yu's presence might seem presumptuous. Torn between a desire to speak and fear of the possible consequences of speaking, she did what girls of her type often do when faced with a difficult decision: she avoided the necessity of making one by bursting into tears.

As for Nightingale, who had disposed of the handkerchief of vomited tisane and was now gently fanning her mistress with her fan, seeing the other three all standing there as quiet as mice with the tears streaming down their faces, she was so affected by the sight that she too started crying and was obliged to have recourse to a second handkerchief.

There the four of them stood, then, facing each other; all of them crying; none of them saying a word. It was Aroma who broke the silence with a strained and nervous laugh.

"You ought not to quarrel with Miss Lin," she said to Bao-yu, "if only for the sake of this pretty cord she made you."

At these words Dai-yu, ill as she was, darted forward, grabbed the jade from Aroma's hand, and snatching up a pair of scissors that were lying nearby, began feverishly cutting at its silken cord with them. Before Aroma and Nightingale could stop her, she had already cut it into several pieces.

"It was a waste of time making it," she sobbed. "He doesn't really care for it. And there's someone else who'll no doubt make him a better one!"

"What a shame!" said Aroma, retrieving the jade. "It's all my silly fault. I should have kept my mouth shut."

"Go on! Cut away!" said Bao-yu. "I shan't be wearing the wretched thing again anyway, so it doesn't matter."

Preoccupied with the quarrel, the four of them had failed to notice several old women, who had been drawn by the sound of it to investigate. Apprehensive, when they saw Dai-yu hysterically weeping and vomiting and Bao-yu trying to smash his jade, of the dire consequences to be expected from a scene of such desperate passion, they had hurried off in a body to the front of the mansion to report the matter to Grandmother Jia and Lady Wang, hoping in this way to establish in advance that whatever the consequences might be, *they* were not responsible for them. From their precipitate entry and the grave tone of their announcement Grandmother Jia and Lady Wang assumed that some major catastrophe had befallen and hurried with them into the Garden to find out what it was.

Their arrival filled Aroma with alarm. "What did Nightingale want to go troubling Their Ladyships for?" she thought crossly, supposing that the talebearer had been sent to them by Nightingale; while Nightingale for her part was angry with Aroma, thinking that the talebearer must have been one of Aroma's minions.

Grandmother Jia and Lady Wang entered the room to find a silent Bao-yu and a silent Dai-yu, neither of whom, when questioned, would admit that anything at all was the matter. They therefore visited their wrath on the heads of the two unfortunate maids, insisting that it was entirely owing to their negligence that matters had got so much out of hand. Unable to defend themselves, the girls were obliged to endure a long and abusive dressing-down, after which Grandmother Jia concluded the affair by carrying Bao-yu off to her own apartment.

Next day, the third of the fifth month, was Xue Pan's birthday and there was a family party with plays, to which the Jias were all invited. Bao-yu, who had still not seen Dai-yu since his outburst—which he now deeply regretted—was feeling far too dispirited to care about seeing plays, and declined to go on the ground that he was feeling unwell.

Dai-yu, though somewhat overcome on the day previous to this by the sultry weather, had by no means been seriously ill. Arguing that if *she* was not ill, it was impossible that *he* should be, she felt sure, when she heard of Bao-yu's excuse, that it must be a false one.

"He usually enjoys drinking and watching plays," she thought. "If he's not going, it must be because he is still angry about yesterday; or if it isn't that, it must be because he's heard that I'm not going and doesn't want to go without me. Oh! I should *never* have cut that cord! Now he won't ever wear his jade again—unless I make him another cord to wear it on."

So she, too, regretted the quarrel.

Grandmother Jia knew that Bao-yu and Dai-yu were angry with each other, but she had been assuming that they would see each other at the Xues' party and make it up there. When neither of them turned up at it, she became seriously upset.

"I'm a miserable old sinner," she grumbled. "It must be my punishment for something I did wrong in a past life to have to live with a pair of such obstinate, addle-headed little geese! I'm sure there isn't a day goes by without their giving me some fresh cause for anxiety. It must be fate. That's what it says in the proverb, after all:

> 'Tis Fate brings foes and lo'es tegither.

I'll be glad when I've drawn my last breath and closed my old eyes for the last time; then the two of them can snap and snarl at each other to their hearts' content, for *I* shan't be there to see it, and 'what the eye doesn't see, the heart doesn't grieve.' The Lord knows, it's not *my* wish to drag on this wearisome life any longer!"

Amidst these muttered grumblings the old lady began to cry.

In due course her words were transmitted to Bao-yu and Dai-yu. It happened that neither of them had ever heard the saying

> 'Tis Fate brings foes and lo'es tegither,

and its impact on them, hearing it for the first time, was like that of a Zen "perception": something to be meditated on with bowed head and savoured with a gush of tears. Though they had still not made it up since their quarrel, the difference between them had now vanished completely:

> In Naiad's House one to the wind made moan,
> In Green Delights one to the moon complained,

to parody the well-known lines. Or, in homelier verses:

> Though each was in a different place,
> Their hearts in friendship beat as one.

On the second day after their quarrel Aroma deemed that the time was now ripe for urging a settlement.

"Whatever the rights and wrongs of all this may be," she said to Bao-yu, "*you* are certainly the one who is *most* to blame. Whenever in the past you've heard about a quarrel between one of the pages and one of the girls, you've always said that the boy was a brute for not understanding the girl's feelings better—yet here you are behaving in exactly the same way yourself! Tomorrow will be the Double Fifth. Her Old Lady-ship will be really angry if the two of you are still at daggers drawn on the day of the festival, and that will make life difficult for *all* of us. Why not put your pride in your pocket and go and say you are sorry, so that we can all get back to normal again?" ***

from **Chapter 30**

Dai-yu, as we have shown, regretted her quarrel with Bao-yu almost as soon as it was over; but since there were no conceivable grounds on which she could run after him and tell him so, she continued, both day and night, in a state of unrelieved depression that made her feel almost as if a part of her was lost. Nightingale had a shrewd idea how it was with her and resolved at last to tackle her:

"I think the day before yesterday you were too hasty, Miss. *We* ought to know what things Master Bao is touchy about, if no one else does. Look at all the quarrels we've had with him in the past on account of that jade!"

"Poh!" said Dai-yu scornfully. "You are trying to make out that it was my fault because you have taken his side against me. Of course I wasn't too hasty."

Nightingale gave her a quizzical smile.

"No? Then why did you cut that cord up? If three parts of the blame was Bao-yu's, I'm sure at least seven parts of it was yours. From what I've seen of it, he's all right with you when you allow him to be; it's because you're so prickly with him and always trying to put him in the wrong that he gets worked up."

Dai-yu was about to retort when they heard someone at the courtyard gate calling to be let in. Nightingale turned to listen:

"That's Bao-yu's voice," she said. "I expect he has come to apologize."

"I forbid you to let him in," said Dai-yu.

"There you go again!" said Nightingale. "You're going to keep him standing out-side in the blazing sun on a day like this. Surely *that's* wrong, if nothing else is?"

She was moving outside, even as she said this, regardless of her mistress's injunc-tion. Sure enough, it *was* Bao-yu. She unfastened the gate and welcomed him in with a friendly smile.

"Master Bao! I was beginning to think you weren't coming to see us any more. I certainly didn't expect to see you here again so soon."

"Oh, you've been making a mountain out of a molehill," said Bao-yu, returning her smile. "Why ever shouldn't I come? Even if I died, my *ghost* would be round here a hundred times a day. How is my cousin? Quite better now?"

"Physically she's better," said Nightingale, "but she's still in very poor spirits."

"Ah yes—I know she's upset."

This exchange took place as they were crossing the forecourt. He now entered the room. Dai-yu was sitting on the bed crying. She had not been crying to start with, but the bittersweet pang she experienced when she heard his arrival had started the tears rolling. Bao-yu went up to the bed and smiled down at her.

"How are you, coz? Quite better now?"

As Dai-yu seemed to be too busy wiping her eyes to make a reply, he sat down close beside her on the edge of the bed:

"I know you're not *really* angry with me," he said. "It's just that if the others noticed I wasn't coming here, they would think we had been quarrelling; and if we waited for them to interfere, we should be allowing other people to come between us. It would be better to hit me and shout at me now and get it over with, if you still bear any hard feelings, than to go on ignoring me. Coz dear! Coz dear!—"

He must have repeated those same two words in the same tone of passionate entreaty upwards of twenty times. Dai-yu had been meaning to ignore him, but what he had just been saying about other people "coming between" them seemed to prove that he must in *some* way feel closer to her than the rest, and she was unable to maintain her silence.

"You don't have to treat me like a child," she blurted out tearfully. "From now on I shall make no further claims on you. You can behave exactly as if I had gone away."

"Gone away?" said Bao-yu laughingly. "Where would you go to?"

"Back home."

"I'd follow you."

"As if I were dead then."

"If you died," he said, "I should become a monk."

Dai-yu's face darkened immediately:

"What an utterly idiotic thing to say! Suppose your own sisters were to die? Just how many times can one person become a monk? I think I had better see what the others think about that remark."

Bao-yu had realized at once that she would be offended; but the words were already out of his mouth before he could stop them. He turned very red and hung his head in silence. It was a good thing that no one else was in the room at that moment to see him. Dai-yu glared at him for some seconds—evidently too enraged to speak, for she made a sound somewhere between a snort and a sigh, but said nothing—then, seeing him almost purple in the face with suppressed emotion, she clenched her teeth, pointed her finger at him, and, with an indignant "Hmn!", stabbed the air quite savagely a few inches away from his forehead:

"You—!"

But whatever it was she had been going to call him never got said. She merely gave a sigh and began wiping her eyes again with her handkerchief.

Bao-yu had been in a highly emotional state when he came to see Dai-yu and it had further upset him to have inadvertently offended her so soon after his arrival. This angry gesture and the unsuccessful struggle, ending in sighs and tears, to say what she wanted to say now affected him so deeply that he, too, began to weep. In need of a handkerchief but finding that he had come out without one, he wiped his eyes on his sleeve.

Although Dai-yu was crying, the spectacle of Bao-yu using the sleeve of his brand-new lilac-coloured summer gown as a handkerchief had not escaped her, and while continuing to wipe her own eyes with one hand, she leaned over and reached with the other for the square of silk that was draped over the head-rest at the end of the bed. She lifted it off and threw it at him—all without uttering a word—then, once more burying her face in her own handkerchief, resumed her weeping. Bao-yu picked up the handkerchief she had thrown him and hurriedly wiped his eyes with it. When he had dried them, he drew up close to her again and took one of her hands in his own, smiling at her gently.

"I don't know why you go on crying," he said. "I feel as if all my insides were shattered. Come! Let's go and see Grandmother together."

Dai-yu flung off his hand.

"Take your hands off me! We're not children any more. You really can't go on mauling me about like this all the time. Don't you understand *anything—?*"

"Bravo!"

The shouted interruption startled them both. They spun round to look just as Xi-feng, full of smiles, came bustling into the room.

"Grandmother has been grumbling away something *awful*," she said. "She insisted that I should come over and see if you were both all right. 'Oh' I said, 'there's no need to go and look, Grannie; they'll have made it up by now without any interference from *us*." So she told me I was lazy. Well, here I am—and of course it's *exactly* as I said it would be. *I* don't know. I don't understand you two. What is it you find to argue about? For every three days that you're friends you must spend at least two days quarrelling. You really are a couple of babies. And the older you get, the worse you get. Look at you *now*—holding hands crying! And a couple of days ago you were glaring at each other like fighting-cocks. Come on! Come with me to see Grandmother. Let's put the old lady's mind at rest."

from **Chapter 34**

Bao-yu kept thinking about Dai-yu and wanted to send someone over to see her, but he was afraid that Aroma would disapprove, so, as a means of getting her out of the way, he sent her over to Bao-chai's place to borrow a book. As soon as she had gone, he summoned Skybright.

"I want you to go to Miss Lin's for me," he said, "Just see what she's doing, and if she asks about me, tell her I'm all right."

"I can't go rushing in there bald-headed without a reason," said Skybright. "You'd better give me *some* kind of a message, just to give me an excuse for going there."

"I have none to give," said Bao-yu.

"Well, give me something to take, then," said Skybright, "or think of something I can ask her for. Otherwise it will look so silly."

Bao-yu thought for a bit and then, reaching out and picking up two of his old handkerchiefs, he tossed them towards her with a smile.

"All right. Tell her I said you were to give her these."

"That's an odd sort of present!" said Skybright. "What's she going to do with a pair of your old handkerchiefs? Most likely she'll think you're making fun of her and get upset again."

"No she won't," said Bao-yu. "She'll understand."

Skybright deemed it pointless to argue, so she picked up the handkerchiefs and went off to the Naiad's House. Little Delicate, who was hanging some towels out to dry on the verandah railings, saw her enter the courtyard and attempted to wave her away.

"She's gone to bed."

Skybright ignored her and went on inside. The lamps had not been lit and the room was in almost total darkness. The voice of Dai-yu, lying awake in bed, spoke to her out of the shadows.

"Who is it?"

"Skybright."

"What do you want?"

"Master Bao has sent me with some handkerchiefs, Miss."

Dai-yu seemed to hesitate. She found the gift puzzling and was wondering what it could mean.

"I suppose they must be very good ones," she said. "Probably someone gave them to him. Tell him to keep them and give them to somebody else. I have no use for them just now myself."

Skybright laughed.

"They're not new ones, Miss. They're two of his old, everyday ones."

This was even more puzzling. Dai-yu thought very hard for some moments. Then suddenly, in a flash, she understood.

"Put them down. You may go now."

Skybright did as she was bid and withdrew. All the way back to Green Delights she tried to make sense of what had happened, but it continued to mystify her.

Meanwhile the message that eluded Skybright had thrown Dai-yu into a turmoil of conflicting emotions.

"I feel so happy," she thought, "that in the midst of his own affliction he has been able to grasp the cause of all *my* trouble.

"And yet at the same time I am sad," she thought; "because how do I know that my trouble will end in the way I want it to?

"Actually, I feel rather amused," she thought. "Fancy his sending a pair of old handkerchiefs like that! Suppose I hadn't understood what he was getting at?

"But I feel alarmed that he should be sending presents to me in secret.

"Oh, and I feel so ashamed when I think how I am forever crying and quarrelling," she thought, "and all the time he has understood!..."

And her thoughts carried her this way and that, until the ferment of excitement within her cried out to be expressed. Careless of what the maids might think, she called for a lamp, sat herself down at her desk, ground some ink, softened her brush, and proceeded to compose the following quatrains, using the handkerchiefs themselves to write on:

1

Seeing my idle tears, you ask me why
These foolish drops fall from my teeming eye:
Then know, your gift, being by the merfolk made,
In merman's currency must be repaid.

2

Jewelled drops by day in secret sorrow shed
Or, in the night-time, in my wakeful bed,
Lest sleeve or pillow they should spot or stain,
Shall on these gifts shower down their salty rain.

3

Yet silk preserves but ill the Naiad's tears:
Each salty trace of them fast disappears.
Only the speckled bamboo stems that grow
Outside the window still her tear-marks show.

She had only half-filled the second handkerchief and was preparing to write another quatrain, when she became aware that her whole body was burning hot all over and her cheeks were afire. Going over to the dressing-table, she removed the brocade cover from the mirror and peered into it.

"Hmn! 'Brighter than the peach-flower's hue,'" she murmured complacently to the flushed face that stared out at her from the glass, and, little imagining that what she had been witnessing was the first symptom of a serious illness, went back to bed, her mind full of handkerchiefs.[8]

8. The next 60 chapters recount daily activities of Bao-yu and his relatives, while intrigue, scandal, and financial troubles—and now an unusual natural occurrence—disturb the Jia household.

When Dai-yu heard that Grandmother Jia was coming, she got up to change and sent Snowgoose on ahead, telling her to report back the moment Her Old Ladyship arrived. She soon came running back.

"Her Old Ladyship and Her Ladyship and a lot of the other ladies have all arrived! Hurry, Miss!"

Dai-yu took a brief look in the mirror, passed a comb quickly through her hair and set off with Nightingale in the direction of Green Delights. She arrived to find Grandmother Jia installed on Bao-yu's day-couch, and after greeting her and Lady Xing and Lady Wang went on to say hello to Li Wan, Tan-chun, Xi-chun and Xing Xiu-yan. She noticed that several people were absent: Xi-feng was ill in bed, Shi Xi-ang-yun had gone home to see her uncle who was in the capital on transfer, while Bao-qin had stayed at home with Bao-chai, and the two Li sisters, Wen and Qi, had been taken to live elsewhere by their mother, whom recent events had convinced that Prospect Garden was a rather unsuitable environment for her daughters.

They were all chatting away, each propounding a different interpretation of the strange phenomenon of the winter-flowering crab-trees.

"They usually flower in the third month, I know," Grandmother Jia was saying. "And we are in the eleventh month now. But then the movable terms in the calendar are rather late this year, so we could say this is more like the tenth month, which is after all sometimes called 'Little Spring.' With the exceptionally warm weather we have been having, a little blossom is only to be expected."

"You are quite right, Mother," agreed Lady Wang. "We need someone of your experience to show us that this is really nothing out of the ordinary."

Lady Xing however was not so easily convinced.

"I heard that these trees had already been struck by the blight for almost a year... How do you explain the fact that half-dead trees should start flowering now, at such an odd time of the year?"

Li Wan spoke next.

"I think you are both right," she said with a smile. "My own humble suggestion is that they have flowered specially to tell us of some happy event that is about to take place in Bao-yu's life."

Tan-chun, although she remained silent, was secretly thinking to herself:

"This must be an ill-omen. Everything that is in harmony with nature prospers, and things out of season, out of time, fade and die. Plants and trees obey a natural cycle. If a tree flowers out of season, it must be an ill-omen."

She kept all this to herself, however. It was Dai-yu who spoke next. She had been struck by Li Wan's mention of a happy event, and said with some excitement:

"There was once a family of farmers who had a thornbush. There were three sons in the family, and one day these three sons decided to leave home and go their separate ways. No sooner had they gone than the thornbush began to fade away and die. But some time later the brothers began to yearn for each other's company, returned home and were reunited. And at once the thornbush began to flourish again. So you see plants follow closely the fortunes of the people to whom they are attached. Now Cousin Bao is devoting himself seriously to his studies, which pleases Uncle Zheng, which pleases the crab-trees, which is why they are flowering!"

This went down very well with Grandmother Jia and Lady Wang.

"What a well-chosen story! Such an interesting idea!"

Jia She and Jia Zheng now arrived to view the flowers, accompanied by Jia Huan and Jia Lan. Jia She spoke first.

"Cut them down. That's what I say. There's evil work afoot here."

"On the contrary," said Jia Zheng. "Leave them alone. Evil manifestations thrive on such superstition. Ignore them and they disappear."

"What's all this?" interrupted Grandmother Jia testily. "We're all gathered here to witness a happy event. Why do you have to start talking about manifestations and what-have-you? When there's good luck then enjoy it while you can. I'll take care of any bad luck. I forbid you to utter another word of such gloomy nonsense."

This silenced Jia Zheng, and he and Jia She effected an awkward departure. Grandmother Jia was unperturbed and determined to enjoy herself.

"Send someone to the kitchen," she said. "We want wine and some nice things to eat. We'll have a little party. I should like you, Bao-yu, Huan and Lan, each to write a poem to celebrate the occasion. Miss Lin has been unwell so she can be excused. If she feels up to it she can help you boys polish yours."

Turning to Li Wan she continued:

"You and the others come up and have some wine with me."

"Yes Grannie," said Li Wan, then turning to Tan-chun she laughed and said:

"This is all your fault, Tan!"

"What do you mean?" protested Tan-chun. "We've been let off the poetry-writing—my fault for what?"

"Aren't you the founder of the Crab-flower Club?" replied Li Wan. "I know *that* crab was an Autumn Crab—but can't you see? Now the *real* crab-blossom wants to join in too…"

Everyone laughed at the idea.

Food and wine were now served, and they all drank and did their best to humour the old lady with light-hearted conversation. Bao-yu came up to pour himself some wine, and standing there thought up a quatrain which he then wrote out and recited for his grandmother.

> I asked the crab-tree why at blossom-time it failed,
> Yet now profusely bloomed so long before the spring?
> The tree replied: "Midwinter marks the birth of light.
> Glad tidings to the Mistress of this House I bring."

It was Huan's turn next. He wrote his out and began to recite:

> Plants should put out buds in spring:
> Our crab tree's timing's topsy-turvy.
> Of all the wonders of the world
> Ours is the only winter-flowering tree.

Then Jia Lan made a careful copy of his poem, in immaculate *kai-shu* calligraphy, and presented it to his great-grandmother, who asked Li Wan to read it out for her.

> Your mist-congealed beauty blighted in the spring,
> Your frosted petals blush now in the snow.
> Hail Tree of Wisdom! Whose Rebirth
> Adds lustre to our Family Hearth.

When she reached the end, Grandmother Jia commented:

"I don't know much about poetry, but I should judge Lan's good, while I should say that Huan's was poor. Come on now, everybody come and have something to eat."

* * *

Earlier that day, Bao-yu had been lounging around indoors, casually dressed in a fur-lined gown with slits at the sides. When he caught sight of the flowering crab-trees through the window, he went out to look at them. The more he gazed at the blossom the more lovely and poignant it seemed, the more strangely it seemed to reflect the mysterious vagaries of destiny, the joy and pathos of life. It was the embodiment of his own thoughts and feelings. Then, when he heard that Grandmother Jia was coming over, he hurried in to change into more formal attire, choosing a pale fox-lined robe with cut-away archer's sleeves and a darker jacket, also fox-lined, to go with it. He emerged again properly dressed to receive his grandmother, and in his hurry quite forgot to put on his Magic Jade.

When Grandmother Jia left he went in again to change back into his comfortable clothes, and it was then that Aroma detected the absence of the jade and asked him where it was.

"I was in such a rush when I came in to change," he replied. "I took it off and left it on the kang-table. Then I forgot to put it on again."

Aroma looked but it was not on the table. She searched everywhere but could see no sign of it. She began to feel frightened, and broke into a cold sweat.

"Please don't worry," Bao-yu begged her. "It must be somewhere in the room. It's bound to turn up. Ask the others—they might know."

It occurred to Aroma that Musk or one of the other maids might have hidden it somewhere as a practical joke and she bore down on them with an expression of playful accusation:

"You mean lot! Can't you think of a better way of amusing yourselves? Come on, where have you hidden it? Don't take this too far! If it really did get lost we'd be in real trouble, all of us!"

But Musk replied with a straight face:

"What on earth do you mean? We'd know better than to play a trick like that. We're not that silly. You're the one who should stop and think a minute. Try to remember where you put it, instead of laying the blame on us!"

Aroma could tell that Musk was in earnest and cried out in alarm:

"Heaven save us then! Oh little ancestor, where *can* you have put it? You must try to remember!"

"I do," replied Bao-yu, "I remember quite clearly putting it on the kang-table. Have another look for it."

The maids were too scared to tell anyone else, and joined together in a furtive search. This went on for most of the day but there was still no sign of the jade. They emptied every box, and rummaged in every trunk, until there simply was nowhere left to look and they began to wonder if perhaps one of the visitors might have picked it up earlier in the day.

"How would anyone dare do such a thing?" said Aroma. "Everyone knows how important it is, and that Master Bao's very life hinges on it. Ask about it, but be very discreet. If you find out that one of the maids has taken it and is playing a trick on us, kowtow to her and beg for it back. If it's a junior maid who's stolen it, don't tell a soul, just do whatever is necessary to get it back. Give her whatever you like in exchange.

This is very serious. It would be terrible if we lost the jade, worse even than losing Master Bao himself!"[9]

from Chapter 96

The time had come round for the triennial review of civil servants stationed in the capital. Jia Zheng's Board gave him a high commendation, and in the second month the Board of Civil Office presented him for an audience with the Emperor. His Majesty, in view of Jia Zheng's record as a "diligent, frugal, conscientious and prudent servant of the Throne," appointed him immediately to the post of Grain Intendant for the province of Kiangsi. The same day, Jia Zheng offered his humble acceptance and gratitude for the honour, and suggested a day for his departure. Friends and relatives were all eager to celebrate, but he was not in festive mood. He was loath to leave the capital at a time when things were so unsettled at home, although at the same time he knew that he could not delay his departure.

He was pondering this dilemma, when a message came to summon him to Grandmother Jia's presence. He made his way promptly to her apartment, where he found Lady Wang also present, despite her illness. He paid his respects to Grandmother Jia, who told him to be seated and then began:

"In a few days, you will be leaving us to take up your post. There is something I should like to discuss with you, if you are willing."

The old lady's eyes were wet with tears. Jia Zheng rose swiftly to his feet, and said:

"Whatever you have to say, Mother, please speak: your word is my command."

"I shall be eighty-one this year," said Grandmother Jia, sobbing as she spoke. "You are going away to a post in the provinces, and with your elder brother still at home, you will not be able to apply for early retirement to come and look after me. When you are gone, of the ones closest to my heart I shall only have Bao-yu left to me. And he, poor darling, is in such a wretched state, I don't know what we can do for him! The other day I sent out Lai Sheng's wife to have the boy's fortune told. The man's reading was uncanny. What he said was: 'This person must marry a lady with a destiny of gold, to help him and support him. He must be given a marriage as soon as possible to turn his luck. If not, he may not live.' Now I know you don't believe in such things, which is why I sent for you, to talk it over with you. You and his mother must discuss it among yourselves. Are we to save him, or are we to do nothing and watch him fade away?"

Jia Zheng smiled anxiously.

"Could I, who as a child received such tender love and care from you, Mother, not have fatherly feelings myself? It is just that I have been exasperated by his repeated failure to make progress in his studies, and have perhaps been too ambitious for him. You are perfectly right in wanting to see him married. How could I possibly wish to oppose you? I am concerned for the boy, and his recent illness has caused me great anxiety. But as you have kept him from me, I have not ventured to say anything. I should like to see him now for myself, and form my own impression of his condition."

Lady Wang saw that his eyes were moist, and knew that he was genuinely concerned. She told Aroma to fetch Bao-yu and help him into the room. He walked in, and when Aroma told him to pay his respects to his father, did exactly as she said. Jia

---

9. Having lost his jade, Bao-yu has lost his wits as well and become seriously ill.

Zheng saw how emaciated his face had grown, how lifeless his eyes were. His son was like some pathetic simpleton. He told them to take him back to his room.

"I shall soon be sixty myself," he mused. "With this provincial posting, it is difficult to tell how many years it will be before I return. If anything were to happen to Bao-yu, I should be left without an heir in my old age. I have a grandson, but that is not the same. And then Bao-yu is the old lady's favourite. If anything untoward occurred, I should be still more deeply at fault."

He glanced at Lady Wang. Her face was wet with tears. He thought of the sorrow it would cause her too, and stood up again to speak.

"If, from your wealth of experience, you have thought of a way to help him, Mother, then how could I possibly raise any objection? We should do whatever you think is best. But has Mrs. Xue been informed?"

"My sister has already expressed her agreement," replied Lady Wang. "We have only been biding our time because Pan's court-case has still not been settled."

"Yes, that is certainly the first obstacle," commented Jia Zheng. "How can a girl be given in marriage while her elder brother is in jail? And besides there is Her Grace's death. Although that does not strictly entail any such prohibition, Bao-yu should at least abide by the set term of mourning for a deceased elder sister, which would mean a period of nine months during which marriage would be highly irregular. And then, my own date of departure has already been reported to the throne, and I cannot postpone it now. That only leaves us a few days. There is not enough time."

Grandmother Jia pondered her son's words. "What he says is true," she thought to herself. "If we wait for all of these conditions to be fulfilled, his father will have left, and who knows to what state the boy's health may deteriorate. And then it may be too late. We shall have to put aside the rules for once. There is no other way."

Having reached this conclusion in her own mind, she spoke to Jia Zheng again.

"If you will agree to this for him, I shall take care of any problems that may arise. There is nothing that cannot be ironed out, of that I am confident. His mother and I shall go over and put the matter personally to Mrs. Xue. As for Pan, I shall ask young Ke to go to him and explain that we are doing this to save Bao-yu's life. When he knows the reason, I am sure he will agree. As for marrying during a period of mourning, strictly speaking one shouldn't, I know. And besides, it is not right for him to marry while he is so ill. But it's a question of turning his luck. Both families are willing, and as the children have the bond of gold and jade to justify their union, we can dispense with the usual reading of horoscopes. We just need to choose an auspicious day to exchange presents in proper style, and then set a date for the wedding itself, possibly afterwards. No music during the wedding itself, but otherwise we can follow court practice: twelve pairs of long-handled lanterns and an eight-man palanquin for the bride. We shall have the ceremony in our southern form, and keep our old customs of throwing dried fruit onto the bridal bed and so forth. That will be enough to make it quite a proper wedding. Bao-chai is a sensible girl. We need not worry on her account. And Aroma is a very reliable person. We can count on her to have a calming influence on Bao-yu. She gets on well with Bao-chai too.

"One other thing: Mrs. Xue once told us that a monk said Bao-chai should only marry someone with a jade to match her golden locket. Perhaps when she comes to live as Bao-yu's wife, her locket will draw the jade back. Once they are married, things will look up and the whole family will benefit. So, we must prepare a courtyard and decorate it nicely—I should like you to choose it. We shan't be inviting any friends or relations to the wedding, and we can have the party later, when

Bao-yu is better and the mourning period is over. This way, everything will be done in time, and you will be able to see the young people married and set off with an easy mind."

Jia Zheng had grave doubts about the proposal. But as it was Grandmother Jia's, he knew he could not go against it. He smiled dutifully, and hastened to reply:

"You have thought it all out very well, Mother, and have taken everything into account. We must tell the servants not to go talking about this to everyone they meet. It would hardly redound to our credit if people knew. And personally I doubt if Mrs. Xue will agree to the idea. But if she does, then I suppose we should do as you suggest."

"You need not worry about Mrs. Xue," said the old lady. "I can explain things to her. Off you go then."

Jia Zheng took his leave. He felt extremely uneasy about the whole idea. Official business soon engulfed him, however—acceptance of his new papers of appointment, recommendations of staff from friends and relatives, an endless round of social gatherings of one sort or another—and he delegated all responsibility for the marriage plans to Grandmother Jia, who in turn left the arrangements to Lady Wang and Xifeng. Jia Zheng's only contribution was to designate a twenty-frame building in a courtyard behind the Hall of Exalted Felicity, to the side of Lady Wang's private apartment, as Bao-yu's new home. Grandmother Jia's mind was now quite made up, and when she sent someone to communicate this to Jia Zheng he just replied: "Very well." But of this, more later.

Bao-yu, after his brief interview with his father, was escorted back by Aroma to his kang in the inner room. Intimidated by the Master's presence in the next room, none of the maids dared speak to him and he soon fell into a deep sleep. As a consequence he did not hear a word of the conversation between his father and Grandmother Jia. Aroma and the others did, however, and stood in complete silence taking it all in. Aroma had heard rumours of this marriage-plan, rumours whose likelihood, it is true, had been strengthened by Bao-chai's repeated absence from family gatherings. Now that she knew it for a fact, all became crystal clear. She was glad.

"They've shown some sense at last!" she thought to herself. "Those two will make by far the better match. And I shall be better off too. With Miss Chai here I'll be able to unload a lot of my responsibilities. The only trouble is, Master Bao still thinks of no one but Miss Lin . . . It's a good thing he didn't hear just now. If he knew what they are planning, I dread to think what trouble we'd have."

This cast a shadow over her previous optimism. "What's to be done?" she continued to brood to herself. "Her Old Ladyship and Her Ladyship obviously don't know about the secret feelings Master Bao and Miss Lin have for each other, and in their enthusiasm they could tell him their plan, to try and cure him. But if he still feels as he did—when he first saw Miss Lin, for instance, and hurled his jade to the ground and wanted to smash it to pieces; or last summer in the Garden, when he mistook me for her and poured his heart out to me; or when Nightingale teased him by saying that Miss Lin was going away, and had him in such floods of tears—and if they go and tell him now that he's betrothed to Miss Chai and will have to give Miss Lin up for ever, so far from turning his luck they'll probably kill him! (Unless of course he's going through one of his deaf-and-dumb spells, in which case he probably won't even notice.) I'd better tell them what I know, or three people may suffer!"

Aroma's mind was made up. As soon as Jia Zheng had taken his leave of the ladies, she left Ripple to look after Bao-yu, and went into the outer room. She walked over to Lady Wang and whispered that she would like a word with her privately in the room to the rear of Grandmother Jia's apartment. Grandmother Jia imagined it to be some message from Bao-yu and did not pay much attention, but continued to engross herself in the wedding arrangements. Lady Wang rose to leave, and Aroma followed her into the rear chamber, where she at once fell on her knees and began crying. Lady Wang had no idea what it was all about, and taking her by the hand, said:

"Come now! What is all this? Has someone done you wrong? If so, stand up, and tell me."

"It is something I shouldn't really say, but in the circumstances I feel I must."

"Well, tell me then. And take your time."

"You and Her Old Ladyship have made an excellent decision, in choosing Miss Bao-chai as Bao-yu's future bride…" began Aroma. "But, I wonder, ma'am, if you have noticed which of the two young ladies Bao-yu is more closely attached to, Miss Chai, or Miss Lin?"

"As they have lived together since they were children," replied Lady Wang, "I suppose he would be a little closer to Miss Lin."

"More than a little!" protested Aroma, and went on to give Lady Wang a detailed history of how things had always stood between Bao-yu and Dai-yu, and of the various incidents that had occurred between them.

"These are all things that you would have seen for yourself, ma'am," she added, "with the exception of his outburst during the summer, which I have not mentioned to a soul until now."

Lady Wang drew Aroma toward her.

"Yes, most of what you have told me I have been able to deduce for myself. What you have said simply bears out my own observations. But you must all have heard the Master's words. Tell me, how did Bao-yu react?"

"As things are at present, ma'am, Bao-yu smiles if someone talks to him, but otherwise he just sleeps. He heard nothing."

"In that case, what are we to do?"

"It is not my place to say," replied Aroma. "Your Ladyship should inform Her Old Ladyship of what I have said, and think of a suitable way of solving the problem."

"Then you had better go," said Lady Wang, "and leave it to me. Now would not be a good moment to bring it up; there are too many people in the room. I shall wait for an opportunity to tell Her Old Ladyship, and we will discuss what to do."

Lady Wang returned to Grandmother Jia's apartment. The old lady was talking to Xi-feng, and when she saw Lady Wang come in, asked:

"What did Aroma want? What was all that mysterious whispering about?"

Lady Wang answered her directly, and told the whole story of Bao-yu's love for Dai-yu, as Aroma had told it her. When she had finished, Grandmother Jia was silent for a long while. Neither Lady Wang nor Xi-feng dared say a word. At last, Grandmother Jia sighed and said:

"Everything else seemed somehow soluble. It does not matter so much about Dai-yu. But if Bao-yu really feels this way about her, it seems we have run into an insoluble problem."

Xi-feng looked very thoughtful for a minute, then said:

"Not insoluble. I think I can see a solution. But I am not sure if you would agree to it or not, Aunt."

"Whatever your idea is," said Lady Wang, "speak up and let Mother know. Then we can all discuss it together."

"There is only one solution that I can think of," said Xi-feng. "It involves two things: a white lie, and a piece of discreet substitution."

"Substitution? What do you mean?" asked Grandmother Jia.

"First of all," replied Xi-feng, "whether Bao-yu knows anything yet or not, we let it be known that Sir Zheng proposes to betroth him to Miss Lin. We must watch for his reaction. If he is quite unaffected, then there is no need to bother with my plan. But if he does seem at all pleased at the news, it will make things rather more complicated."

"Supposing he is pleased?" asked Lady Wang. "What then?"

Xi-feng went over and whispered at some length in Lady Wang's ear. Lady Wang nodded, smiled and said:

"Well, well... An ingenious idea, I must say!"

"Come on, you two!" exclaimed Grandmother Jia. "Let me in on the secret: what are you whispering about?"

Xi-feng was afraid that Grandmother Jia might not grasp her idea at once, and might inadvertently give the game away. She leant across and whispered in the old lady's ear. Grandmother Jia did seem rather puzzled at first. Xi-feng smiled, and added a few more words of explanation. Grandmother Jia finally said with a smile:

"Why not? But isn't it rather hard on Bao-chai? And what about Miss Lin? What if she gets to hear of it?"

"We shall only tell Bao-yu," replied Xi-feng. "No one else will be allowed to mention it. That way no one need know."

***

A day or two after these events, Dai-yu, having eaten her breakfast, decided to take Nightingale with her to visit Grandmother Jia. She wanted to pay her respects, and also thought the visit might provide some sort of distraction for herself. She had hardly left the Naiad's House, when she remembered that she had left her handkerchief at home, and sent Nightingale back to fetch it, saying that she would walk ahead slowly and wait for her to catch up. She had just reached the corner behind the rockery at Drenched Blossoms Bridge—the very spot where she had once buried the flowers with Bao-yu—when all of a sudden she heard the sound of sobbing. She stopped at once and listened. She could not tell whose voice it was, nor could she distinguish what it was that the voice was complaining of, so tearfully and at such length. It really was most puzzling. She moved forward again cautiously and as she turned the corner, saw before her the source of the sobbing, a maid with large eyes and thick-set eyebrows.

Before setting eyes on this girl, Dai-yu had guessed that one of the many maids in the Jia household must have had an unhappy love-affair, and had come here to cry her heart out in secret. But now she laughed at the very idea. "How could such an ungainly creature as this know the meaning of love?" she thought to herself. "This must be one of the odd-job girls, who has probably been scolded by one of the senior maids." She looked more closely, but still could not place the girl. Seeing Dai-yu, the maid ceased her weeping, wiped her cheeks, and rose to her feet.

"Come now, what are you so upset about?" inquired Dai-yu.

"Oh Miss Lin!" replied the maid, amid fresh tears. "Tell me if you think it fair. *They* were talking about it, and how was I to know better? Just because I say one thing wrong, is that a reason for sister to start hitting me?"

Dai-yu did not know what she was talking about. She smiled, and asked again:

"Who is your sister?"

"Pearl," answered the maid.

From this, Dai-yu concluded that she must work in Grandmother Jia's apartment.

"And what is your name?"

"Simple."

Dai-yu laughed. Then:

"Why did she hit you? What did you say that was so wrong?"

"That's what I'd like to know! It was only to do with Master Bao marrying Miss Chai!"

The words struck Dai-yu's ears like a clap of thunder. Her heart started thumping fiercely. She tried to calm herself for a moment, and told the maid to come with her. The maid followed her to the secluded corner of the garden, where the Flower Burial Mound was situated. Here Dai-yu asked her:

"Why should she hit you for mentioning Master Bao's marriage to Miss Chai?"

"Her Old Ladyship, Her Ladyship and Mrs Lian," replied Simple, "have decided that as the Master is leaving soon, they are going to arrange with Mrs. Xue to marry Master Bao and Miss Chai as quickly as possible. They want the wedding to turn his luck, and then..."

Her voice tailed off. She stared at Dai-yu, laughed and continued:

"Then, as soon as those two are married, they are going to find a husband for you, Miss Lin."

Dai-yu was speechless with horror. The maid went on regardless:

"But how was I to know that they'd decided to keep it quiet, for fear of embarrassing Miss Chai? All I did was say to Aroma, that serves in Master Bao's room: 'Won't it be a fine to-do here soon, when Miss Chai comes over, or Mrs. Bao... what *will* we have to call her?' That's all I said. What was there in that to hurt sister Pearl? Can *you* see, Miss Lin? She came across and hit me straight in the face and said I was talking rubbish and disobeying orders, and would be dismissed from service! How was I to know their Ladyships didn't want us to mention it? Nobody told me, and she just hit me!"

She started sobbing again. Dai-yu's heart felt as though oil, soy-sauce, sugar and vinegar had all been poured into it at once. She could not tell which flavour predominated, the sweet, the sour, the bitter or the salty. After a few moments' silence, she said in a trembling voice:

"Don't talk such rubbish. Any more of that, and you'll be beaten again. Off you go!"

She herself turned back in the direction of the Naiad's House. Her body felt as though it weighed a hundred tons, her feet were as wobbly as if she were walking on cotton-floss. She could only manage one step at a time. After an age, she still had not reached the bank by Drenched Blossoms Bridge. She was going so slowly, with her feet about to collapse beneath her, and in her giddiness and confusion had wandered off course and increased the distance by about a hundred yards. She reached Drenched Blossoms Bridge only to start drifting back again along the bank in the direction she had just come from, quite unaware of what she was doing.

Nightingale had by now returned with the handkerchief, but could not find Dai-yu anywhere. She finally saw her, pale as snow, tottering along, her eyes staring straight in front of her, meandering in circles. Nightingale also caught sight of a maid disappearing in the distance beyond Dai-yu, but could not make out who it was. She was most bewildered, and quickened her step.

"Why are you turning back again, Miss?" she asked softly. "Where are you heading for?"

Dai-yu only heard the blurred outline of this question. She replied:

"I want to ask Bao-yu something."

Nightingale could not fathom what was going on, and could only try to guide her on her way to Grandmother Jia's apartment. When they came to the entrance, Dai-yu seemed to feel clearer in mind. She turned, saw Nightingale supporting her, stopped for a moment, and asked:

"What are you doing here?"

"I went to fetch your handkerchief," replied Nightingale, smiling anxiously. "I saw you over by the bridge and hurried across. I asked you where you were going, but you took no notice."

"Oh!" said Dai-yu with a smile. "I thought you had come to see Bao-yu. What else did we come here for?"

Nightingale could see that her mind was utterly confused. She guessed that it was something that the maid had said in the garden, and only nodded with a faint smile in reply to Dai-yu's question. But to herself she was trying to imagine what sort of an encounter this was going to be, between the young master who had already lost his wits, and her young mistress who was now herself a little touched. Despite her apprehensions, she dared not prevent the meeting, and helped Dai-yu into the room. The funny thing was that Dai-yu now seemed to have recovered her strength. She did not wait for Nightingale but raised the portière herself, and walked into the room. It was very quiet inside. Grandmother Jia had retired for her afternoon nap. Some of the maids had sneaked off to play, some were having forty winks themselves and others had gone to wait on Grandmother Jia in her bedroom. It was Aroma who came out to see who was there, when she heard the swish of the portière. Seeing that it was Dai-yu, she greeted her politely:

"Please come in and sit down, Miss."

"Is Master Bao at home?" asked Dai-yu with a smile.

Aroma did not know that anything was amiss, and was about to answer, when she saw Nightingale make an urgent movement with her lips from behind Dai-yu's back, pointing to her mistress and making a warning gesture with her hand. Aroma had no idea what she meant and dared not ask. Undeterred, Dai-yu walked on into Bao-yu's room. He was sitting up in bed, and when she came in made no move to get up or welcome her, but remained where he was, staring at her and giving a series of silly laughs. Dai-yu sat down uninvited, and she too began to smile and stare back at Bao-yu. There were no greetings exchanged, no courtesies, in fact no words of any kind. They just sat there staring into each other's faces and smiling like a pair of half-wits. Aroma stood watching, completely at a loss.

Suddenly Dai-yu said:

"Bao-yu, why are you sick?"

Bao-yu laughed.

"I'm sick because of Miss Lin."

Aroma and Nightingale grew pale with fright. They tried to change the subject, but their efforts only met with silence and more senseless smiles. By now it was clear to Aroma that Dai-yu's mind was as disturbed as Bao-yu's.

"Miss Lin has only just recovered from her illness," she whispered to Nightingale. "I'll ask Ripple to help you take her back. She should go home and lie down." Turning to Ripple, she said: "Go with Nightingale and accompany Miss Lin home. And no stupid chattering on the way, mind."

Ripple smiled, and without a word came over to help Nightingale. The two of them began to help Dai-yu to her feet. Dai-yu stood up at once, unassisted, still staring fixedly at Bao-yu, smiling and nodding her head.

"Come on, Miss!" urged Nightingale. "It's time to go home and rest."

"Of course!" exclaimed Dai-yu. "It's time!"

She turned to go. Still smiling and refusing any assistance from the maids, she strode out at twice her normal speed. Ripple and Nightingale hurried after her. On leaving Grandmother Jia's apartment, Dai-yu kept on walking, in quite the wrong direction. Nightingale hurried up to her and took her by the hand.

"This is the way, Miss."

Still smiling, Dai-yu allowed herself to be led, and followed Nightingale towards the Naiad's House. When they were nearly there, Nightingale exclaimed:

"Lord Buddha be praised! Home at last!"

She had no sooner uttered these words when she saw Dai-yu stumble forwards onto the ground, and give a loud cry. A stream of blood came gushing from her mouth.

from **Chapter 97**

Next day, Xi-feng came over after breakfast. Wishing to sound out Bao-yu according to her plan, she advanced into his room and said:

"Congratulations, Cousin Bao! Uncle Zheng has already chosen a lucky day for your wedding! Isn't that good news?"

Bao-yu stared at her with a blank smile, and nodded his head faintly.

"He is marrying you," went on Xi-feng, with a studied smile, "to your cousin Lin. Are you happy?"

Bao-yu burst out laughing. Xi-feng watched him carefully, but could not make out whether he had understood her, or was simply raving. She went on:

"Uncle Zheng says, you are to marry Miss Lin, *if* you get better. But not if you carry on behaving like a half-wit."

Bao-yu's expression suddenly changed to one of utter seriousness, as he said:

"I'm not a half-wit. You're the half-wit."

He stood up.

"I am going to see Cousin Lin, to set her mind at rest."

Xi-feng quickly put out a hand to stop him.

"She knows already. And, as your bride-to-be, she would be much too embarrassed to receive you now."

"What about when we're married? Will she see me then?"

Xi-feng found this both comic and somewhat disturbing.

"Aroma was right," she thought to herself. "Mention Dai-yu, and while he still talks like an idiot, he at least seems to understand what's going on. I can see we shall be in real trouble, if he sees through our scheme and finds out that his bride is not to be Dai-yu after all."

In reply to his question, she said, suppressing a smile:

"If you behave, she will see you. But not if you continue to act like an imbecile."

To which Bao-yu replied:

"I have given my heart to Cousin Lin. If she marries me, she will bring it with her and put it back in its proper place."

Now this was madman's talk if ever, thought Xi-feng. She left him, and walked back into the outer room, glancing with a smile in Grandmother Jia's direction. The old lady too found Bao-yu's words both funny and distressing.

"I heard you both myself," she said to Xi-feng. "For the present, we must ignore it. Tell Aroma to do her best to calm him down. Come, let us go."

***

Dai-yu meanwhile, for all the medicine she took, continued to grow iller with every day that passed. Nightingale did her utmost to raise her spirits. Our story finds her standing once more by Dai-yu's bedside, earnestly beseeching her:

"Miss, now that things have come to this pass, I simply must speak my mind. We know what it is that's eating your heart out. But can't you see that your fears are groundless? Why, look at the state Bao-yu is in! How can he possibly get married, when he's so ill? You must ignore these silly rumours, stop fretting and let yourself get better."

Dai-yu gave a wraithlike smile, but said nothing. She started coughing again and brought up a lot more blood. Nightingale and Snowgoose came closer and watched her feebly struggling for breath. They knew that any further attempt to rally her would be to no avail, and could do nothing but stand there watching and weeping. Each day Nightingale went over three or four times to tell Grandmother Jia, but Faithful, judging the old lady's attitude towards Dai-yu to have hardened of late, intercepted her reports and hardly mentioned Dai-yu to her mistress. Grandmother Jia was preoccupied with the wedding arrangements, and in the absence of any particular news of Dai-yu, did not show a great deal of interest in the girl's fate, considering it sufficient that she should be receiving medical attention.

Previously, when she had been ill, Dai-yu had always received frequent visits from everyone in the household, from Grandmother Jia down to the humblest maidservant. But now not a single person came to see her. The only face she saw looking down at her was that of Nightingale. She began to feel her end drawing near, and struggled to say a few words to her:

"Dear Nightingale! Dear sister! Closest friend! Though you were Grandmother's maid before you came to serve me, over the years you have become as a sister to me…"

She had to stop for breath. Nightingale felt a pang of pity, was reduced to tears and could say nothing. After a long silence, Dai-yu began to speak again, searching for breath between words:

"Dear sister! I am so uncomfortable lying down like this. Please help me up and sit next to me."

"I don't think you should sit up, Miss, in your condition. You might get cold in the draught."

Dai-yu closed her eyes in silence. A little later she asked to sit up again. Nightingale and Snowgoose felt they could no longer deny her request. They propped her up on both sides with soft pillows, while Nightingale sat by her on the bed to give further support. Dai-yu was not equal to the effort. The bed where she sat on it seemed to dig into her, and she struggled with all her remaining strength to lift herself up and ease the pain. She told Snowgoose to come closer.

"My poems…"

Her voice failed, and she fought for breath again. Snowgoose guessed that she meant the manuscripts she had been revising a few days previously, went to fetch them and laid them on Dai-yu's lap. Dai-yu nodded, then raised her eyes and gazed in the direction of a chest that stood on a stand close by. Snowgoose did not know how to interpret this and stood there at a loss. Dai-yu stared at her now with feverish impatience. She began to cough again and brought up another mouthful of blood. Snowgoose went to fetch some water, and Dai-yu rinsed her mouth and spat into the spittoon. Nightingale wiped her lips with a handkerchief. Dai-yu took the handkerchief from her and pointed to the chest. She tried to speak, but was again seized with an attack of breathlessness and closed her eyes.

"Lie down, Miss," said Nightingale. Dai-yu shook her head. Nightingale thought she must want one of her hand-kerchiefs, and told Snowgoose to open the chest and bring her a plain white silk one. Dai-yu looked at it, and dropped it on the bed. Making a supreme effort, she gasped out:

"The ones with the writing on..."

Nightingale finally realized that she meant the handkerchiefs Bao-yu had sent her, the ones she had inscribed with her own poems. She told Snowgoose to fetch them, and herself handed them to Dai-yu, with these words of advice:

"You must lie down and rest, Miss. Don't start wearing yourself out. You can look at these another time, when you are feeling better."

Dai-yu took the handkerchiefs in one hand and without even looking at them, brought round her other hand (which cost her a great effort) and tried with all her might to tear them in two. But she was so weak that all she could achieve was a pathetic trembling motion. Nightingale knew that Bao-yu was the object of all this bitterness but dared not mention his name, saying instead:

"Miss, there is no sense in working yourself up again."

Dai-yu nodded faintly, and slipped the handkerchiefs into her sleeve.

"Light the lamp," she ordered.

Snowgoose promptly obeyed. Dai-yu looked into the lamp, then closed her eyes and sat in silence. Another fit of breathlessness. Then:

"Make up the fire in the brazier."

Thinking she wanted it for the extra warmth, Nightingale protested:

"You should lie down, Miss, and have another cover on. And the fumes from the brazier might be bad for you."

Dai-yu shook her head, and Snowgoose reluctantly made up the brazier, placing it on its stand on the floor. Dai-yu made a motion with her hand, indicating that she wanted it moved up onto the kang. Snowgoose lifted it and placed it there, temporarily using the floor-stand, while she went out to fetch the special stand they used on the kang. Dai-yu, far from resting back in the warmth, now inclined her body slightly forward—Nightingale had to support her with both hands as she did so. Dai-yu took the handkerchiefs in one hand. Staring into the flames and nodding thoughtfully to herself, she dropped them into the brazier. Nightingale was horrified, but much as she would have liked to snatch them from the flames, she did not dare move her hands and leave Dai-yu unsupported. Snowgoose was out of the room, fetching the brazier-stand, and by now the handkerchiefs were all ablaze.

"Miss!" cried Nightingale. "What are you doing?"

As if she had not heard, Dai-yu reached over for her manuscripts, glanced at them and let them fall again onto the kang. Nightingale, anxious lest she burn these too, leaned up against Dai-yu and freeing one hand, reached out with it to take hold of them. But before she could do so, Dai-yu had picked them up again and dropped them in the flames. The brazier was out of Nightingale's reach, and there was nothing she could do but look on helplessly.

Just at that moment Snowgoose came in with the stand. She saw Dai-yu drop something into the fire, and without knowing what it was, rushed forward to try and save it. The manuscripts had caught at once and were already ablaze. Heedless of the danger to her hands, Snowgoose reached into the flames and pulled out what she could, throwing the paper on the floor and stamping frantically on it. But the fire had done its work, and only a few charred fragments remained.

His brief access of clarity enabled Bao-yu to understand the gravity of his illness. When the others had gone and he was left alone with Aroma, he called her over to his side and taking her by the hand said tearfully:

"Please tell me how Cousin Chai came to be here? I remember Father marrying me to Cousin Lin.[1] Why has *she* been made to go? Why has Cousin Chai taken her place? She has no right to be here! I'd like to tell her so, but I don't want to offend her. How has Cousin Lin taken it? Is she very upset?'

Aroma did not dare tell him the truth, but merely said:

"Miss Lin is ill."

"I must go and see her," insisted Bao-yu. He wanted to get up, but days of going without food and drink had so sapped his strength that he could no longer move, but could only weep bitterly and say:

"I know I am going to die! There's something on my mind, something very important, that I want you to tell Grannie for me. Cousin Lin and I are both ill. We are both dying. It will be too late to help us when we are dead; but if they prepare a room for us now and if we are taken there before it is too late, we can at least be cared for together while we are still alive, and be laid out together when we die. Do this for me, for friendship's sake!"

Aroma found this plea at once disturbing, comical and moving. Bao-chai, who happened to be passing with Oriole, heard every word and took him to task straight away.

"Instead of resting and trying to get well, you make yourself iller with all this gloomy talk! Grandmother has scarcely stopped worrying about you for a moment, and here you are causing more trouble for her. She is over eighty now and may not live to acquire a title because of your achievements; but at least, by leading a good life, you can repay her a little for all that she has suffered for your sake. And I hardly need mention the agonies Mother has endured in bringing you up. You are the only son she has left. If you were to die, think how she would suffer! As for me, I am wretched enough as it is; you don't need to make a widow of me. Three good reasons why even if you want to die, the powers above will not let you and you will not be able to. After four or five days of proper rest and care, your illness will pass, your strength will be restored and you will be yourself again."

For a while Bao-yu could think of no reply to this homily. Finally he gave a silly laugh and said:

"After not speaking to me for so long, here you are lecturing me. You are wasting your breath."

Encouraged by this response to go a step further, Bao-chai said:

"Let me tell you the plain truth, then. Some days ago, while you were unconscious, Cousin Lin passed away."

With a sudden movement, Bao-yu sat up and cried out in horror:

"It can't be true!"

"It is. Would I lie about such a thing? Grandmother and Mother knew how fond you were of each other, and wouldn't tell you because they were afraid that if they did, you would die too."

---

1. The marriage has taken place during the previous chapter, thanks to Xi-feng's idea of disguising Bao-chai as Dai-yu.

Bao-yu began howling unrestrainedly and slumped back in his bed. Suddenly all was pitch black before his eyes. He could not tell where he was and was beginning to feel very lost, when he thought he saw a man walking towards him and asked in a bewildered tone of voice:

"Would you be so kind as to tell me where I am?"

"This," replied the stranger, "is the road to the Springs of the Nether World. Your time is not yet come. What brings you here?"

"I have just learned of the death of a friend and have come to find her. But I seem to have lost my way."

"Who is this friend of yours?"

"Lin Dai-yu of Soochow."

The man gave a chilling smile:

"In life Lin Dai-yu was no ordinary mortal, and in death she has become no ordinary shade. An ordinary mortal has two souls which coalesce at birth to vitalize the physical frame, and disperse at death to rejoin the cosmic flux. If you consider the impossibility of tracing even such ordinary human entities in the Nether World, you will realize what a futile task it is to look for Lin Dai-yu. You had better return at once."

After standing for a moment lost in thought, Bao-yu asked again:

"But if as you say, death is a dispersion, how can there be such a place as the Nether World?"

"There is," replied the man with a superior smile, "and yet there is not, such a place. It is a teaching, devised to warn mankind in its blind attachment to the idea of life and death. The Supreme Wrath is aroused by human folly in all forms—whether it be excessive ambition, premature death self-sought, or futile self-destruction through debauchery and a life of overweening violence. Hell is the place where souls such as these are imprisoned and made to suffer countless torments in expiation of their sins. This search of yours for Lin Dai-yu is a case of futile self-delusion. Dai-yu has already returned to the Land of Illusion and if you really want to find her you must cultivate your mind and strengthen your spiritual nature. Then one day you will see her again. But if you throw your life away, you will be guilty of premature death self-sought and will be confined to Hell. And then, although you may be allowed to see your parents, you will certainly never see Dai-yu again."

When he had finished speaking, the man took a stone from within his sleeve and threw it at Bao-yu's chest. The words he had spoken and the impact of the stone as it landed on his chest combined to give Bao-yu such a fright that he would have returned home at once, if he had only know which way to turn. In his confusion he suddenly heard a voice, and turning, saw the figures of Grandmother Jia, Lady Wang, Bao-chai, Aroma and his other maids standing in a circle around him, weeping and calling his name. He was lying on his own bed. The red lamp was on the table. The moon was shining brilliantly through the window. He was back among the elegant comforts of his own home. A moment's reflection told him that what he had just experienced had been a dream. He was in a cold sweat. Though his mind felt strangely lucid, thinking only intensified his feeling of helpless desolation, and he uttered several profound sighs.

Bao-chai had known of Dai-yu's death for several days. While Grandmother Jia had forbidden the maids to tell him for fear of further complicating his illness, she felt she knew better. Aware that it was Dai-yu who lay at the root of his illness and that the loss of his jade was only a secondary factor, she took the opportunity of breaking the news of her death to him in this abrupt manner, hoping that by severing his attachment once and for all she would enable his sanity and health to be restored. Grandmother Jia, Lady Wang and company were not aware of her intentions and at first reproached her for her lack of caution. But when they saw Bao-yu regain consciousness, they were all greatly relieved and went at once to the library to ask doctor Bi to come in and examine his patient again. The doctor carefully took his pulses.

"How odd!" he exclaimed. "His pulses are deep and still, his spirit calm, the oppression quite dispersed. Tomorrow he must take a regulative draught, which I shall prescribe, and he should make a prompt and complete recovery."

The doctor left and the ladies all returned to their apartments in much improved spirits.

Although at first Aroma greatly resented the way in which Bao-chai had broken the news, she did not dare say so. Oriole, on the other hand, reproved her mistress in private for having been, as she put it, too hasty.

"What do you know about such things?" retorted Bao-chai. "Leave this to me. I take full responsibility."

Bao-chai ignored the opinions and criticisms of those around her and continued to keep a close watch on Bao-yu's progress, probing him judiciously, like an acupuncturist with a needle.

A day or two later, he began to feel a slight improvement in himself, though his mental equilibrium was still easily disturbed by the least thought of Dai-yu. Aroma was constantly at his side, with such words of consolation as:

"The Master chose Miss Chai as your bride for her more dependable nature. He thought Miss Lin too difficult and temperamental for you, and besides there was always the fear that she would not live long. Then later Her Old Ladyship thought you were not in a fit state to know what was best for you and would only be upset and make yourself iller if you knew the truth, so she made Snowgoose come over, to try and make things easier for you."

This did nothing to lessen his grief, and he often wept inconsolably. But each time he thought of putting an end to his life, he remembered the words of the stranger in his dream; and then he thought of the distress his death would cause his mother and grandmother and knew that he could not tear himself away from them. He also reflected that Dai-yu was dead, and that Bao-chai was a fine lady in her own right; there must after all have been some truth in the bond of gold and jade. This thought eased his mind a little. Bao-chai could see that things were improving, and herself felt calmer as a result. Every day she scrupulously performed her duties towards Grandmother Jia and Lady Wang, and when these were completed, did all she could to cure Bao-yu of his grief. He was still not able to sit up for long periods, but often when he saw her sitting by his bedside he would succumb to his old weakness for the fairer sex. She tried to rally him in an earnest manner, saying:

"The important thing is to take care of your health. Now that we are married, we have a whole lifetime ahead of us."

He was reluctant to listen to her advice. But since his grandmother, his mother, Aunt Xue and all the others took it in turns to watch over him during the day, and since Bao-chai slept on her own in an adjoining room, and he was waited on at night by one or two maids of Grandmother Jia's, he found himself left with little choice but to rest and get well again. And as time went by and Bao-chai proved herself a gentle and devoted companion, he found that a small part of his love for Dai-yu began to transfer itself to her. But this belongs to a later part of our story.

The Nineteenth Century

The Pilgrim's Vision. Frontispiece to Mark Twain, *The Innocents Abroad,* 1869.

TOWARD THE END OF THE EIGHTEENTH CENTURY THINGS HEATED UP IN AND AROUND EUROPE. Not the climate—cold weather and bad harvests in the 1780s and 1790s contributed to the anguish of the French Revolution—but socially and politically. After the many political and religious upheavals of the seventeenth century, the century that followed saw long, stable reigns in eighteenth-century England, France, the rapidly westernizing Russia, and the self-isolated Spain, punctuated by relatively local, short-lived conflicts and accompanied by fairly steady economic progress. Under the surface, however, discontent grew as early industrial development increased the gap between the rich and the working poor and as increasing literacy, especially among craftsmen and laborers, raised expectations and hopes. The ringing words that open Rousseau's *Social Contract* fired a flame that spread across the continents and through the century: "Man is born free, and everywhere he is in chains."

The term *revolution* itself originally means rotation. It first came to mean rebellion in 1688 when the "Glorious Revolution" drove the crypto-Catholic James II off the English throne. After that there were no comparable events until the Americans revolted in 1776. The century that followed was strongly marked by turmoil and warfare around Europe, lasting from the fall of the Bastille in 1789 through the definitive fall of Napoleon in 1815, the Greek War of Independence (1821–1828), the Revolution of 1830 in France that replaced the restored Bourbon monarchy with the "Citizen King" Louis-Philippe, the continent-wide revolutions of 1848 that mostly failed but left strong democratic and even communist movements in their wake while overthrowing the French monarchy for good, and the blitzkrieg Franco-Prussian War of 1870, an early salvo in nearly a century of German expansionism.

Meanwhile, the New World was struggling to shake off the yoke of the old, with Haiti rising up soon after the United States, followed by all the major mainland Spanish possessions and, late in the century, trailed peacefully by Canada and violently by Cuba. There had never before been a mass war such as Napoleon led, but then the American Civil War of 1861–1865 and the Paris Commune of 1871 broke out with unprecedented internecine violence. Clearly a whole new kind of energy was on the loose, accompanied and symbolized by the power of steam and the speed of railroads, and reflected, steered, and resisted by the influential and imaginative writers of the era.

Romanticism

"The three great tendencies of the age are the French Revolution, Fichte's *Doctrine of Knowledge*, and Wilhelm Meister." So wrote Friedrich Schlegel in 1798 (in a collection of so-called "Fragments" in his journal *Athenaeum*), one of the cluster of incandescent intellectuals who drove German culture to unprecedented heights around 1800. Schlegel is as responsible as any individual for the label that we attach to the culture and writing of the early decades of the century, and unpacking his utterances can give us a way to organize the multifariousness of the period. Willfully, Schlegel aligns the mass political outburst in France with the latest philosophical blockbuster and the title figure of a massive new novel by Goethe. In the middle of things it was hard to see what was really happening, and indeed modern scholars continue to differ radically about the thrust of the French Revolution, its chronological limits, and even its outcome. Schlegel's brilliance was to see the revolution not as a thing—whether a political event or a social manifestation—but as a "tendency," an ongoing process, escaping definition. And, as Schlegel suggests, books can work on us as powerfully as external actions, if not as dramatically. Johann Gottlieb Fichte was the first great successor to Immanuel Kant's "Copernican revolution" in philosophy; in abstract treatises and fiery moral and political lectures Fichte preached a doctrine of the absolute primacy of the self which must, however, strive for self-fulfillment through the most demanding individual and community discipline. "Tendency" is just the term to capture the perpetual unrest driving a philosopher whose emotions radiated through Thomas Carlyle and Ralph Waldo Emerson into the Victorian soul and through Ludwig Feuerbach and Karl Marx into the social thought of central and eastern Europe.

Schlegel's third "tendency" refers to Goethe's novel *Wilhelm Meister's Apprenticeship*. The title is ironic, since "Meister" means "master," while Wilhelm is in fact just an overprotected bourgeois adolescent. Goethe's novel reflects a focus on individual development; it begins with childhood infatuations as few novels before Rousseau had (but many later ones by Dickens, Flaubert, Joyce, and countless others would), and it proceeds to tell of Wilhelm's unfinished development toward becoming a functioning member of a far-flung society. Individual psychology is thus discovered to be as crucial as mass movements to the destinies of civilization. Like most educated German speakers in subsequent generations, Sigmund Freud was a passionate admirer of Goethe, and his studies in infantile sexuality and his writings on culture stand at the end of tendencies originating in the romantic period. Schlegel's aphorism implies a recognition that mass movements and individual ideals are inseparably connected.

Romantic striving took many forms, all of them intense but not all noisy. "Near is / And hard to grasp / The god," wrote the great German mythic poet Friedrich Hölderlin at the start of his ode "Patmos" (1803), using the simplest words in typically contorted grammar to express everyman's struggle toward comprehension. John Keats and Percy Bysshe Shelley wrote poems to nightingale and skylark, dreaming of flying in the age that invented balloons: "Hail to thee, blithe spirit, / Bird thou never wert," as Shelley wrote in "To a Sky-Lark," with exuberant disrespect for his addressee's identity. Wordsworth counseled humane alertness to the quietest signs of life—the hermit's smoke of "Tintern Abbey," or the quiet play of lights in the late sonnet, "Mark the Concent'red Hazels." William Blake, meanwhile, wrote massive epics of social and sexual struggle, confronting private and public demons such as those imaged in the fearful symmetry of his "tyger."

Parallels can be found in the other arts. Beethoven was composing some of the loudest music yet heard on the face of the earth, to be performed by huge orchestras and choruses in front of vast publics, and explicitly preaching heroism (*Eroica* Symphony), liberation from tyranny (the opera *Fidelio*) and brotherhood (the choral setting of Friedrich Schiller's "Ode to Joy" in the Ninth Symphony). At the same time, romantic exaltation finds quiet expression in Franz Schubert's many hundreds of art-songs (a new musical form), in William Constable's many paintings of the heaven-directed, pastorally sited spire of Salisbury Cathedral and in the natural cathedrals of Caspar David Friedrich's sublime landscapes. Some modern readers complain of too much self-assertion in one kind of Romanticism, others of too much complacency in alternative kinds. But the various moods are best considered to be a dialogue reflecting different attempts to confront the spirit of the age—its vital forces, its electricity (another newly discovered phenomenon). "Spirit of the age" is itself a Romantic idea, the notion that a hidden inner force rather than a rational ideal or external guide permeates and motivates individuals and groups. They share an innovative awareness even where they may disagree about responses.

In another pithy formula, Schlegel called Romanticism "a progressive universal poetry." What did he mean by this? Colonial expansion had been in progress for centuries by then, and not even Goethe's *Faust* could be more cosmic than Dante's *Divine Comedy,* Shakespeare's *King Lear,* or Milton's *Paradise Lost.* But universal doesn't mean overwhelming—an ambition that would be inconsistent with the open-ended striving of Romanticism. Goethe's Faust is a highly educated old man; unlike Renaissance versions of the legend, he wants to know and experience everything, not to have ultimate power, and he dies after a fit of blind philanthropy. Even in the demonic forms of the French Revolution at its worst, universality implies an ideal of brotherhood—a universal embrace rather than a world-order.

The word *Romanticism* itself has universal overtones in this sense. In its derivation from Rome it evokes the grand world-empire of the classical past, and more broadly the glories of thought and imagination of the classical world. But romances (as then conceived) were medieval tales of knighthood and adventure and ballads of the common people. Romance in this sense evokes national histories and traditions, preserved in unschooled writings and obsolete dialects, and in the rural folktales and folk songs that were collected starting gradually from the mid-eighteenth century. Romances suggest the aura of mystery and magic that is part of the transhuman universality of Romanticism, and they also suggest the nation mystically rooted not in political and military history but in the essence of a popular spirit. Then, at an individual level, romance means love. To the eighteenth century, physical love tended to seem irrational (in novels of uncontrolled passion) or ridiculous (as in Lemuel Gulliver's scornful horror at the different kinds of affection he encounters in his various voyages), if not straightforwardly animalistic, as in the many casual marriages of Daniel Defoe's *Moll Flanders.* To the nineteenth century, love was a magical and spiritual passion like that of Wagner's Tristan and Isolde, edifying or terrifying (or both at once, as in much of Baudelaire's poetry), but always a force implicated in moral good or evil, at times even transcending both. Finally, in German as in French, Italian, and Russian, "Roman" or its near equivalent is the term for what English and Spanish call a "novel." Hence the quintessentially "romantic" form of progressive universal poetry is the novel as the story of the new. The great Russian writer Pushkin subtitled *Eugene Onegin* a "Novel in Verse," while Gogol subtitled his comic novel *Dead Souls* a "Poem." Novels are detailed stories based in the everyday world, and romantic writers prepared the way for the great realistic novels that dominated literary production in the second half of the century. Often drawing their inspiration from the comprehensive social vision of Shakespeare, who was just then being rediscovered and translated on the Continent, Romantic writers wanted to bring all things to all people, linking the past with the present, the individual with the nation, Europe with the rest of humanity, the soul with the body, nature with culture.

A World Within the World

Another typical genius in this age of geniuses was Wilhelm von Humboldt—brother of the great explorer and naturalist Alexander von Humboldt. Wilhelm wrote on aesthetics, politics, anthropology, and classical civilization, composed and translated

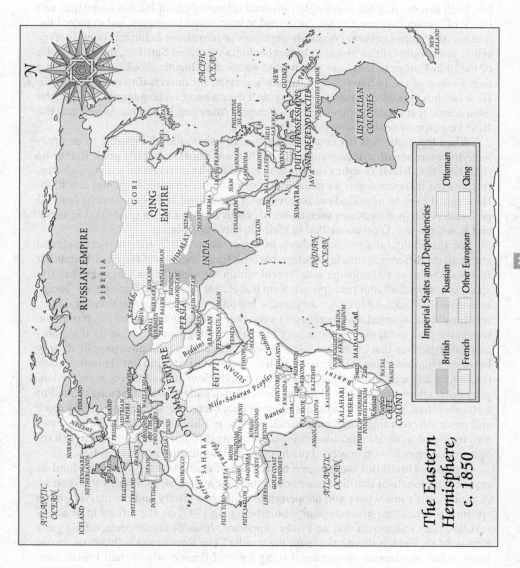

The Eastern Hemisphere, c. 1850

Imperial States and Dependencies
British	Ottoman
Russian	Qing
French	Other European

ATLANTIC OCEAN

ICELAND

NORWAY

SWEDEN

FINLAND

DENMARK

NETHERLANDS

BRITAIN

BELGIUM

SWITZERLAND

FRANCE

SPAIN

PORTUGAL

PRUSSIA

POLAND

AUSTRIAN EMPIRE

KINGDOM OF THE TWO SICILIES

SERBIA

WALLACHIA

MOLDAVIA

RUSSIAN EMPIRE

SIBERIA

GOBI

QING EMPIRE

KOREA

JAPAN

PACIFIC OCEAN

NEW GUINEA

Papua

DUTCH POSSESSIONS AND DEPENDENCIES

PORTUGUESE TIMOR

BORNEO

SARAWAK

BRUNEI

PHILIPPINE ISLANDS

SULU

CELEBES

SUMATRA

JAVA

BALI

MALAY STATES

AUEH

SIAM

CAMBODIA

ANNAM

LUANG PRABANG

BURMA

TENASSERIM

MANIPUR

NEPAL

HIMALAY

INDIA

CEYLON

TIBET

KOKAND

BADAKHSHAN

KUNDUZ

AFGHANISTAN

BALUCHISTAN

KASHMIR

SMALL STATES BALKH

BUKHARA

KHIVA

Kazakhs

PERSIA

OMAN

BAHRAIN

ARABIAN PENINSULA

YEMEN

HADAR

Beduins

TUNIS

ALGERIA

MOROCCO

SAHARA

Berbers

EGYPT

SUDAN

Nilo-Saharan Peoples

ETHIOPIA

Cushites

BUGANDA

BUNYORO

RWANDA

UBHA

BURUNDI

KIKONJA

KAZEMBE

LUBA

KANIOK

LUNDA

ANGOLA

KALUNDE

Bantus

PORTUGUESE EAST AFRICA

MERINA KINGDOM

MADAGASCAR

OTTOMAN EMPIRE

ATLANTIC OCEAN

LIBERIA

GOLD COAST

DAHOMEY

ASANTE

BENIN

BORGU

OYO

KONG

NUPE

SEGU

DAGOMBA

MOSSI

KAARTA

Tuaregs

FUTA TORO

FUTA JALON

KALAHARI DESERT

REPUBLIC OF WINBURG-POTCHEFSTROOM

Khoisan Peoples

CAPE COLONY

BASUTO

NATAL

Zulu

Swazi

INDIAN OCEAN

AUSTRALIAN COLONIES

NEW ZEALAND

N

poetry, served as Prussian ambassador to Rome, and founded the University of Berlin that now bears his name and that established the model for university education to the present day. Of course, every age has its universal intellects. But Wilhelm von Humboldt's greatest passion was distinctive to his age, for he made himself into the founder of modern linguistic study. Linguists from the later eighteenth century had been discovering the seemingly universal relationships of human languages and hence of human cultures. Goethe (who read at least seven languages and explored the literatures of many others) coined the term *world literature*; Schlegel (poet, literary critic, philosopher, historian of culture, theologian) studied Sanskrit, the oldest relic of the Indo-European language family, and wrote an influential book on the language and wisdom of the Indians. But Humboldt's striving for universality outdid them all. He went into unrelated territory, learning well over a hundred languages including the most exotic that could be investigated—Basque, American Indian languages, and the Kavi language of what is now Indonesia.

When the globe was opened on this scale, it was no longer possible to comprehend the commonality of humankind, and that was not Humboldt's goal. Rather he (like his close friend Goethe) sought to understand the differences among cultures. Respect for difference was as much a part of romantic striving as global ambition. It extended even to new kinds of reverence for the animal and plant worlds, familial pets, and ecological treasures such as Wordsworth and Dickinson celebrated in verse, and Rousseau and Thoreau studied in their intensive botanizing.

For Humboldt, as for many others, however, social difference was crucial, and above all the difference among societies that arise from linguistic difference. Humboldt famously referred to language as a "world within the world": the language that you speak governs all of your perceptions. Kant had earlier argued that there are no "things in themselves" accessible to our awareness, but only subjective perceptions of things, and Humboldt asserted that there aren't even perceptions in themselves, but only the words we give to them, and these vary radically among languages, as do the grammatical structures that create meaning. Modern linguistics continues to split sharply between Humboldtians who believe in linguistic relativity and anti-Humboldtians (including artificial intelligence specialists) who believe in a common basis for language that allows for an ideal of perfect equivalence and translation among them. For a Humboldtian, progress then comes to mean either learning and understanding more and more different linguistic and cultural worlds, or else, as in some of the more notorious projects for colonial education, suppressing difference in favor of English (or Spanish or French) as a universal medium of communication and civilization.

Through Humboldt we can see how Romanticism develops into the kind of mystical nationalism that first emerged in the later stages of the French Revolution. A country isn't just where you happen to live, not just family and community, but a spiritual essence that grounds your whole being. In 1847, on the threshold of a new revolutionary movement that he avidly supported, Jules Michelet prefaced his great history of the French Revolution with the words: "The Revolution is inside us, in our souls; it has no external monument. Living spirit of France, where shall I seize thee, if not within myself?" Such a spirit can seem noble, or it can seem tyrannical. The first great English historian of the French Revolution, the "Victorian sage" Thomas Carlyle, imagines that, "as a thing *without* order, . . . it must work and welter, not as a Regularity but as a Chaos; destructive and self-destructive."

Thus the great writers of the nineteenth century are united only in confronting a problem. The electric tendencies of self, nature, language, and national culture no longer seemed masterable in a comprehensive formula such as many had imagined in the eighteenth-century Age of Enlightenment. Karl Marx's greatness as an economic theorist, for instance, was to understand economic relations as mysteriously spiritual forces—describing prices, for example, as "wooing glances cast at money by commodities." By tying national and individual destinies to national and idiosyncratic languages, Walter Scott's novels determined how nineteenth-century Europeans conceived of cooperation or dissension in constructing their polities. Americans explored similar issues via James Fenimore Cooper's fascination with Indian speech. The stirring choruses of Verdi's operas *Nabucco* and *Il Trovatore* caught the pulse of a people and stirred them to action toward Italian independence. Hopeful visionaries like Emerson or Nietzsche looked forward to a reconstructed humanity; pessimists like Leopardi and (sometimes) Melville looked down a tunnel into darkness. Meanwhile, rapid material progress in a century that opened with horse-drawn coaches and ended with telephones and automobiles put the question of what was real to its inhabitants with ever-increasing urgency.

Realism

It has been argued that realism came into being when Walter Scott wrote his novels of historical ambivalence about the downfall of feudalism in the Scottish Highlands and its replacement by the humdrum commercial civilization of the Lowlands and of England. Scott's loyalties were divided between the generously heroic, doomed figures of the old aristocratic order and the rational but mean-spirited representatives of modernity, which promised both greater democracy and a lower, narrowly self-interested view of human motives and aspirations. Realism did not result, as one might think, from a sudden and unprecedented desire to see the world clearly and accurately. Nor did it represent a major break with Romanticism. Rather, it emerged from a conviction (shared with the Romantics) that the social world itself had been set irrevocably in motion. Realists saw that historical change was powered by social contradictions such as those between feudalism and capitalism, and they understood that these contradictions did not just affect society's leaders, but worked themselves out in everyday feelings and relationships. Unlike previous stories of the rise and fall of kings, history now reached down deep into the lives of ordinary people. Thus the ethical meaning of ordinary lives—increasingly the subject literature took for itself—was now increasingly hard to agree upon.

Honoré de Balzac, who sought to understand the passage from an aristocratic to a bourgeois order in France after the fall of Napoleon, was one of many writers inspired by Scott's example. Examining the moral and emotional meaning of this immense transformation, Balzac gave his own loyalty to the reactionaries calling for a return to the old monarchy and its tried-and-true values. But as Friedrich Engels wrote in a famous letter, Balzac's distaste for the direction history was taking did not stop him from becoming a brilliant chronicler of its contradictions—far more useful, Engels went on, than the well-intentioned but tendentious socialism of his successor Émile Zola. Like many other observers, Engels disliked Zola's dark determinism. The coal miners of Zola's *Germinal* were innocent victims, but they were also passive victims, caught up and inevitably destroyed by huge, obscure forces that seemed beyond anyone's control. Naturalism, the more pessimistic variant of realism that was gaining force in the second half of the nineteenth century, was in part an accommodation to the rising authority of natural science, in part a delayed reaction to the general sense of helplessness that followed the failure of the 1848 revolutions.

Revolutions had indeed broken out in 1848 all across Europe and beyond, a "springtime of peoples" seeming to promise that the world could at last be remade in the name of the democratic ideals of 1789. But they also expressed the specific discontent of the new industrial working class, and that is why in early 1848 Alexis de Tocqueville told the Chamber of Deputies in Paris, "We are sleeping on a volcano." Both the sense of hope and the threat to private property that made so many property-holders draw back from this eruption are captured in Marx and Engels's *Communist Manifesto,* which came out the same year. This was a key moment for Gustave Flaubert, who narrates the Paris street fighting in his *Sentimental Education,* as well as for Elizabeth Gaskell, whose novel *Mary Barton* (1848) describes industrial conflict with serious and unprecedented sympathy for the workers. More indirectly, in Charles Dickens's *Bleak House* (1851–1852) a revolution that doesn't happen is displaced onto plague, murder, and "spontaneous combustion."

Science and Technology

The political upheavals of midcentury were matched by a revolutionary ferment in natural science. The period of Charles Darwin's treatise *On the Origin of Species by Means of Natural Selection* (1859) also saw the development of antiseptics by Lister and pasteurization by Pasteur as well as Clerk Maxwell's electromagnetic theory of light (1862), Mendeleyev's presentation of the periodic table of the elements in 1869, and many other breakthroughs of almost incalculable importance. It was perhaps inevitable that such advances would generate a certain overconfidence. The celebrated physicist Lord Kelvin announced, somewhat prematurely, that all the basic problems of physics had been solved. Though scientific advances and their technological applications were gradually responsible for improving the lives of ordinary people in numerous ways, especially in health, transportation, and communication, Antonio Machado de Assis's "The Psychiatrist" and Charlotte Gilman's "The Yellow Wallpaper" testify to a growing awareness of the danger that the authority attributed to science might easily be abused. Though Darwin himself was cautiously modest about the social implications of his discovery, others like Herbert Spencer (1820–1903) hastened to seize his authority on behalf of so-called "Social Darwinism," the belief that competition for survival was as natural in human society as it was among animal species and that, if not meddled with by governments, it would lead to the evolutionary progress of humankind. This political philosophy preexisted Darwin—it had inspired British authorities to let the victims of the Irish famine starve in the 1840s—but with new support from the theory of evolution it became a widespread tool of imperial expansion, generating convenient contempt for peoples held to be below or behind on the evolutionary ladder.

An Age of Empire

A period of relative European stability followed the crushing of the 1848 revolutions, felt by many artists and writers as the defeat of creativity by conformity and philistinism. This calm at home coincided with, and was perhaps made possible by, an enormous expansion of European control over the non-European world. More and more, the social disparities and conflicts that had led to 1848 could in effect be exported to the colonies. Algeria, the first Arabic-speaking country to be conquered, fell to France in 1847. The rest of Africa was swiftly divided up by the various powers, and soon Ethiopia was the only African country that remained unconquered. Colonialism extended across the Pacific as well, and after the Opium War of 1840–1842 (the result of China's refusal to buy English opium imported from India), China was forced to cede Hong Kong to England and to open itself to European traders. Britain took over official control of India after the so-called Mutiny of 1857–1859, better described perhaps as the first Indian war of independence. By the end of the century, Britain alone controlled one quarter of the earth's land area. Between 1804 and 1827, Russia defeated Iran in three wars, thus annexing Georgia and Azerbaijan, and Russian troops were still fighting for control over the mountain tribes of the Caucasus in the late 1830s when the novelist Lermontov's unit was posted there. Russia expanded eastward through Central Asia toward the Pacific, which was soon all that separated it from the westward-expanding United States. In the 1860s, slavery ended in the United States and serfdom ended in Russia, but neither society worried too much about the racially different natives it was subjugating or exterminating. Meanwhile, the settler colonies of Latin America, which had won their independence in the first half of the century, likewise continued their campaigns to seize land from their remaining indigenous populations and make it commercially profitable. From a global perspective, the most striking fact about the nineteenth century is not its proud technological achievements or real if uneven lurches toward domestic democracy, but the fact that it made most of the surface of the earth into colonies, protectorates, and spheres of influence for European states or European settlers. It was, and was seen to be, an age of empire.

The consolidation and clashing of nations and empires came at a high cost even for the Europeans themselves. In the Crimean War (1854–1856), Russia's territorial aspirations ran up against British interests in India and the Middle East, leading to its confrontation with an alliance of British, French, and Ottoman armies in the Crimea—to nineteenth-century Russians, a zone of the mysterious Orient. The war is best known to students of English literature for Alfred Lord Tennyson's poem "The Charge of the Light Brigade," a poem about military courage in the face of mismanagement and, perhaps, the meaninglessness of one's own cause—"Theirs not to reason why, / Theirs but to do and die." On the Russian side, the combatants included Count Leo Tolstoy. In the midst of the war, the great poet and patriot Adam Mickiewicz traveled to Istanbul to organize Polish and Jewish troops to fight with the Ottomans on behalf of his fellow Poles, who remained subject to Russia. Mickiewicz died there of cholera in 1855. As soldiers in the Crimea died like flies, more from disease than from enemy fire, the nurse Florence Nightingale became famous for her struggles on behalf of rational sanitation, thus striking a blow on behalf of professional careers for middle-class women. This brief and inconclusive war resulted in approximately 600,000 casualties, about the same as the American Civil War and many more than the fierce battles for the unification of Germany and Italy that were happening during the same period.

A journey around the world in eighty days, as imagined by Jules Verne, would have been impossible in 1848. With so few railways in operation, it would have taken at least eleven months. By 1872, however, railways had connected huge tracts of territory, and a round-the-world journey in eleven weeks had become quite feasible. Yet the cultural consequences of this new global interconnectedness are complex and often difficult to ascertain with any certainty. Better informed about other regions than they had ever been, thanks to such inventions as the steamship, the telegraph, and the camera, European readers nevertheless had little difficulty embracing Rudyard Kipling's assertion of the absolute difference between civilizations: "East is East and West is West." Imperialist enjoyment of the exotic became an increasing part of everyday European consciousness via the mass market success of boys' adventure novels such as those of the Englishman H. Rider Haggard and the German Karl May, Oriental stereotypes such as Sax Rohmer's Dr. Fu Manchu, and Buffalo Bill's Wild West Show.

On the other hand, some British writers identified with aspirations to national independence even at the expense of Britain's allies. Tennyson's sonnet "Montenegro" (1877)— repeatedly translated into Serbian—glorified the struggles of the Montenegrins, friends of the Russians and enemies of the Ottomans. English became the official language of instruction of India in 1835, replacing Sanskrit, Arabic, and Persian. The intention was to form an English-educated native class through whom much of the administration could be handled. But the results would include an extraordinary cultural flowering, as for example in the bilingual and multicultural writing of Rabindranath Tagore.

Even as nation-states unified themselves, their literary cultures were becoming more and more varied, and writers took inspiration across regions and borders alike. Emerson and his fellow American Transcendentalists were inspired by the new interpretations of Hinduism coming out of British-occupied India; in Paris, Adam Mickiewicz lent his copy of Emerson's *Nature* to his fellow republican Edgar Quinet; Parisian modernism revealed itself to Rubén Darío when he was given Lautréamont's poetry to read on a visit to El Salvador. Industrialization in Britain and political revolutions in France were world-historical events. Unprecedented anywhere in the world, they were extraordinarily and inevitably influential almost everywhere in the world. And so were their cultural sequels.

But it would be a mistake to think of literary schools and fashions as simply emanating out from a center in Europe. Many South American countries became independent before some of the European states that carried out the project of imperialism, and their literatures are thus on a different timetable. There was also a Latin American turn to the folk—including a celebration of the same natives the colonizers were still in the process of subduing and assimilating—in order to define a positive national identity distinct from the European motherland. We find as well a Latin-American tendency (for example, in the Argentine writers Esteban Echevarría and Domingo Sarmiento) to be more enthusiastic about modernizing thought like the positivism of Auguste Comte (1798–1857). The same might be said about the energetic upsurge of thinking in the nineteenth-century Arab world, pondering both its Ottoman and its European masters in relation to its Muslim heritage, and in Asia, particularly in China, though there much of the new thought came through Japan. Warnings against the Romantic illusions of national continuity came from the Frenchman Renan and the German Nietzsche but also (later) the Martiniquan Frantz Fanon. When Mahatma Gandhi read the Victorian art critic John Ruskin, he assimilated him to Hindu thought, which went back centuries and was undergoing a recent renaissance. The self-educated Brazilian writer Machado de Assis quoted many and various European authors but dug deep into Brazilian popular culture for the prime resources of his fiction.

Cities, Women, Artists

Among the common threads that do run through the world literature of the nineteenth century, one of the foremost is the tension between the country and the city. On every continent, an abyss opened up between the modernizing tendencies of the

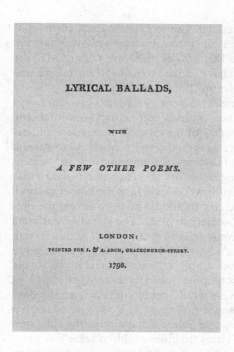

LYRICAL BALLADS,

WITH

A FEW OTHER POEMS.

LONDON:

PRINTED FOR J. & A. ARCH, GRACECHURCH-STREET.

1798.

SENSE AND SENSIBILITY,

A NOVEL,

BY

JANE AUSTEN.

Marianne, suddenly awakened by some accidental noise in the house, started hastily up, and with feverish wildness, cried out "Is mamma coming?"

LONDON:
RICHARD BENTLEY,
NEW BURLINGTON STREET.
BELL AND BRADFUTE, EDINBURGH.

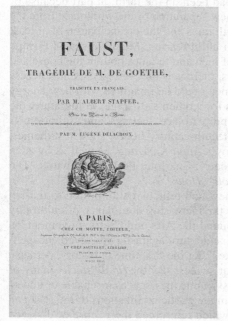

FAUST,

TRAGÉDIE DE M. DE GOETHE,

TRADUITE EN FRANÇAIS.

PAR M. ALBERT STAPFER.

Orné d'un Portrait de l'Auteur.

PAR M. EUGÈNE DELACROIX.

A PARIS,

CHEZ CH. MOTTE, ÉDITEUR,

ET CHEZ SAUTELET, LIBRAIRE,

M DCCC XXVIII.

WALDEN;

OR,

LIFE IN THE WOODS.

BY HENRY D. THOREAU,
AUTHOR OF "A WEEK ON THE CONCORD AND MERRIMACK RIVERS."

I do not propose to write an ode to dejection, but to brag as lustily as chanticleer in the morning, standing on his roost, if only to wake my neighbors up.— Page 92.

BOSTON:
TICKNOR AND FIELDS.
M DCCC LIV.

Like book jackets today, title pages promoted and advertised older books, which were sold unbound. Earlier title pages were typically illustrated and typographically lavish, often containing epigraphs and lengthy descriptions of their contents. Spare title pages like that reproduced on the upper left give only the title, author's name (and not even always that), genre, and publisher. They illustrate how books had become ordinary objects of commerce rather than valuable possessions and were intended for private reading of the contents more than for fashion or display. *Sense and Sensibility* and *Walden,* typical of a later day, illustrate a simple, rather bourgeois nostalgia for earlier modes of book production.

capital and the traditional culture of the hinterland. The sparkling coastal cosmopolitanism of cities like Alexandria and Beirut did not always resonate with small farmers in the interior. The Petersburg of Gogol and Dostoevsky, the New York of Melville and Whitman, the Paris of Baudelaire would have seemed to many of their compatriots as foreign as European cities seemed to the Muslim travelers of the time.

In trying to make sense of urban life, nineteenth-century writers were also trying to make sense of their writerly vocation. The century's second half sees Romantic nature poetry succeeded in part by a new poetry of the city. To Baudelaire and his successors, Paris is as mysterious, inviting, dangerous, and sublime as Romantic nature. Yet its buildings and crowds, its novel rhythms of companionship and perception, also remind the poet of ways of shaping his or her art. The same insight made a home for itself in fiction. "Oh for a good spirit who would take the housetops off," Dickens appealed in *Dombey and Son*. The city should be made to reveal the hidden, often sordid interconnections that held society in place. The spiritlike narrators and complicated plots of Dickens's novels could be seen as an answer to this appeal, especially when they anticipate Conan Doyle's Sherlock Holmes and the urban genre of the detective story. As urbanization inches closer to being a social norm for the first time in history, the poet and the novelist become two of its heroic figures.

As does the new independent woman. One would never guess it from the novels of Emily and Charlotte Brontë, set as they are on the wild Yorkshire heath, but the distinct nineteenth-century rise in literary and political attention to the condition of women has much to do with the rise of cities. In cities children were less of an economic asset to their families than they had been on the farm, in part because of compulsory schooling, in part because of a new separation of the workplace from the place of residence. One result was lower birth rates and the emancipation of at least some women from the burdensome tasks of child rearing. Most women in Europe and elsewhere remained subject to the will of men and to labor both in the house and in the workplace, but for increasing numbers, there was new leisure and new access to education. Thus the emancipation of women could be imagined with new energy and, increasingly, acted upon in movements for women's suffrage. In literature, the questioning of assumptions about women's proper place, feelings, and aspirations is expressed in stories of adultery, one of nineteenth-century fiction's greatest themes, as in Flaubert's *Madame Bovary* and Tolstoy's *Anna Karenina*, as well as by such revolutionary texts as Emily Dickinson's poetry, Charlotte Perkins Gilman's "The Yellow Wallpaper," and Henrik Ibsen's *A Doll's House*.

It was also in the city that the artist's new and reluctant submission to market forces was most visible. Angry reactions to the increasing dominance of culture by mass production and the profit-motive included the Arts and Crafts movement, as represented for example by William Morris, and a turn against a perceived cheapening of art in the direction of "art for art's sake." For the first time in history, perhaps, artists began to boast of their *lack* of popular success. By the *fin de siècle,* many of Europe's artists, increasingly hostile to a mass public they saw as incapable of understanding them, were increasingly interested in the exotic civilizations of the East and the "primitive" art of Africa and Oceania, which reinforced their sense of distance from the status quo at home and its empty claims of progress. The global awareness that Goethe foresaw when he coined the term "world literature" in 1832 was becoming a marked feature of literature at the century's end.

YEAR	THE WORLD	LITERATURE
1770		1774, 1786 Goethe, *Werther*
1780		1781, 1788, 1790 Immanuel Kant, *Critique of Pure Reason, Critique of Practical Reason, Critique of Judgment*
	1783 First balloon flight	1782, 1789 J. J. Rousseau, *Confessions, Reveries*
	1789 Fall of the Bastille (beginning of the French Revolution)	1789, 1794 William Blake, *Songs of Innocence, Songs of Experience*
1790	1792 Discovery of electromagetism 1793 Execution of the king and queen of France	
		1795–1796 Goethe, *Wilhelm Meister's Apprenticeship* 1796 Ludwig Tieck, "Fair Eckbert" 1798–1799 Friedrich Schiller, *Wallenstein* (translated by Coleridge in 1800) 1798 Wordsworth and Coleridge, *Lyrical Ballads*
1800	1800 Volta's invention of the electric battery 1803 Louisiana Purchase 1804 Haitian declaration of independence 1806 Mungo Park expedition to the Niger River 1806 Dissolution of the Holy Roman Empire 1807 Fulton sails a steamboat on the Hudson River 1809–1825 Independence movements in South America	1805 Wordsworth, first version of *Prelude* completed (published, much revised, in 1850) 1807 G. W. F. Hegel, *Phenomenology of Mind* 1808 Goethe, *Faust, Part 1*
1810		1810 Madame de Staël, *On Germany* 1812, 1815 J. and W. Grimm, *Fairy Tales* 1813–1822 E. T. A. Hoffmann's tales published in various collections
	1815 Final defeat of Napoleon; restoration of the Bourbon monarchy in France	1814 Walter Scott, *Waverley* 1819–1824 Lord Byron, *Don Juan*
1820		1820 John Keats, *Lamia, Isabella, The Eve of St. Agnes, and Other Poems*
	1825 Failed "Decembrist" Revolution in Russia 1825 First scheduled railroad	

continued

YEAR	THE WORLD	LITERATURE
1830	1830 Revolution of 1830 in France; Louis-Philippe becomes the "Citizen King" 1830 France seizes Algiers: beginning of French colonization of North Africa	
		1831 Stendhal (Henri Beyle), *The Red and the Black: A Chronicle of 1830* 1831 Honoré de Balzac, *The Wild Ass's Skin* (first work designed as part of the collective *Human Comedy*)
	1832 Death of Goethe; death of Scott; English Reform Bill 1832 Greek Independence achieved after war of 1821–1828 1833 Abolition of slavery in Britain's colonies 1838 Slave mutiny aboard the *Amistad* 1839–1842 Opium War in China	1832 Goethe, *Faust, Part 2* 1833 Alexander Pushkin, *Eugene Onegin* 1836 Ralph Waldo Emerson, *Nature*
1840		1840 Mikhail Lermontov, *A Hero of Our Time* 1842 Nikolai Gogol, "The Overcoat" 1845 Edgar Allan Poe, "The Raven"
	1848 Revolutions throughout Europe, mostly suppressed, but leading to the end of the French monarchy 1848 War between United States and Mexico	
1850	1850–1864 Taiping Uprising in China, eventually put down with Western intervention 1851 Sojourner Truth delivers her "And Ain't I a Woman Speech" at the Woman's Rights Convention in Akron, Ohio 1853–1856 Crimean War	1851 Herman Melville, *Moby Dick;* first issue of *New York Times* 1852 Harriet Beecher Stowe, *Uncle Tom's Cabin* 1854 Alfred Tennyson, "The Charge of the Light Brigade" 1854 Henry David Thoreau, *Walden* 1855 Walt Whitman, *Leaves of Grass*
	1856–1857 British-Persian War 1857 Indian revolt known as "Mutiny" 1858 Chinese ports opened to Western trade 1859–1861 Wars of national unification in Italy	1856 Elizabeth Barrett Browning, *Aurora Leigh* 1857 Gustave Flaubert, *Madame Bovary* 1859 Charles Darwin, *On the Origin of Species by Natural Selection*
1860	1860 Anglo-French troops occupy Beijing and burn Summer Palace 1861 Emancipation of serfs in Russia; outbreak of Civil War in United States 1862 Richard Gatling patents machine-gun	

YEAR	THE WORLD	LITERATURE
	1863 French troops occupy Mexico City	1864 Leo Tolstoy, *War and Peace*
	1868 Meiji restoration in Japan, abolition of Shogunate	1866 Fyodor Dostoevsky, *Crime and Punishment*
		1867 Marx, *Das Kapital*, Volume 1
1870		
	1870–1871 Franco-Prussian War, Paris Commune	1871–1872 George Eliot, *Middlemarch*
	1873 Ashanti tribes fight British in West Africa	1872 Jules Verne, *Around the World in 80 Days*
	1874 Iceland becomes independent from Denmark	
	1875 Korea becomes independent from China	
	1876 Schliemann excavates Mycenae in Greece; massacre of Bulgarians by Turkish troops; General Custer defeated by Sioux at Little Big Horn	1876 George Sand, *Marianne*
	1877 Samurai revolt suppressed in Japan	
	1879 Edison invents electric lightbulb; Britain invades Afghanistan; Chile defeats Bolivia and Peru in "Nitrate War"	
1880		
	1880 France annexes Tahiti	1882 Henrik Ibsen, *An Enemy of the People*
		1883 Friedrich Nietzsche, *Thus Spake Zarathustra*
		1884 Mark Twain, *Huckleberry Finn*
		1885 Emile Zola, *Germinal*
	1886 First meeting of Indian National Congress	
1890		
	1890 New Zealand is the first nation to give women suffrage	1890 Knut Hamsun, *Hunger*
	1894–1895 War between China and Japan; China loses Formosa and Port Arthur	
	1895 Cuban revolution against Spanish rule	1895 Oscar Wilde, *The Importance of Being Earnest*
	1896 Italy is defeated in war with Abyssinia and withdraws	1896 Anton Chekhov, *The Seagull*
	1897 First Zionist congress, Basel, Switzerland	
	1898 Spanish-American War	
1900		
		1899 Joseph Conrad, *Heart of Darkness*
		1900 Sigmund Freud, *The Interpretation of Dreams*

Johann Wolfgang Goethe was an amazing figure by anyone's standards. Not only did he write *Faust,* the epic drama of the scholar's pact with the devil that has come to embody the West and its fatal love affair with knowledge and technology, but he wrote seven other major plays and innumerable smaller ones. He wrote the most popular novel of the eighteenth century (*The Sorrows of Young Werther*), one of the most influential novels of the nineteenth century (*Wilhelm Meister's Apprenticeship*), and a profoundly modern novel of adultery (*Elective Affinities*) that has been widely influential in the twentieth century. He wrote more than a thousand pages of odes, ballads, songs, sonnets, bawdy love elegies, didactic poems, satires, short epics, and other verse. The standard edition of his works and letters runs to 144 volumes.

Goethe was born in 1749 but didn't settle down to literature as his real vocation until he was fifty years old, and he continued to pursue many other interests until his death in 1832. He drew, painted, sculpted, and collected art; he directed the Weimar court theater and personally trained the actors; he published contributions in geology, botany, comparative anatomy, chemistry, meteorology, and especially optics; he was a government official in the small duchy of Saxe-Weimar-Eisenach in central Germany, responsible at different times for mines, roads, finances, the university and all libraries and museums. And from age twenty-five until his death he was Germany's most famous personality and most visited cultural attraction. In his day the French Revolution brought an end to the old feudal order of Europe and ushered in the earliest version of the modern mass society in which we live today: as the greatest European writer of his age he is the cultural figure who embodies for us most clearly the beginning of the modern world.

Goethe was educated at home by his wealthy father, who intended his son to be a lawyer and eventually an influential member of the government in the free city of Frankfurt am Main, where Goethe's maternal grandfather had been the mayor. The son had other ideas. He did finally earn a law degree, but spent most of his time at the universities of Leipzig and Strasbourg studying drawing and medicine, as well as socializing and writing poetry. Under the influence of his friend Johann Gottfried Herder (1744–1803), who coined the term "folk song," Goethe scoured the countryside collecting songs—and pursuing his love life. From the combination of his superb schooling and the language of the people, he forged a poetry previously unheard in European culture, in which an individual voice spoke its most personal feelings without constraint in simple song or even in the apparent spontaneity of free verse. Already a quarter of a century before Wordsworth his poetry seemed to express human experience directly, and for the next two hundred years his example convinced scholars and general readers that true poetry was autobiographical.

In 1775 Goethe took advantage of his status as Germany's most famous writer (he was twenty-six!) to leave Frankfurt and settle in Weimar, long an artistic and cultural center, where the young Duke soon invited him to join the government. He threw himself into governing and practical activity and, gradually, science. In 1782 he was ennobled, adding "von" to his name. By 1786, tired of governing and of his platonic relationship with the difficult (and married) lady-in-waiting Charlotte von Stein, he fled to Italy, where for eighteen months he studied the art, the geology, and the people. He returned from Italy a changed man: he resigned his political responsibilities (but kept his salary), and he also entered into a common-law marriage with Christiane Vulpius, a young woman from the lower middle class. Goethe lived in Weimar for the remainder of his life. Milestones were the 1792 military campaign against France in which he accompanied the Duke and which he chronicled movingly; a profound friendship established in 1794 with the great dramatist Friedrich Schiller (1759–1804); the German defeat of 1806 by Napoleon at Jena, the neighboring city in the Duchy, followed immediately by formalizing his relationship with

Christiane. He began a vast autobiography, *Poetry and Truth* (published in installments beginning in 1810), and devoted himself to his longest book, the thousand-page *Treatise on Optics* (1810). Christiane died in 1816. The major books published in his last years were the *West-Easterly Divan* (1819), a volume of verse written in the manner of the great fourteenth-century Persian poet Hafiz, and an experimental antinovel (*Wilhelm Meister's Journeyman Years,* 1832). The second part of *Faust,* last retouched only weeks before his death, was reserved for posthumous publication.

Assessments of Goethe as a person vary. To some he has seemed aloof, "Olympian," conservative in an era of change; to others he has appeared broadly tolerant, concerned for the welfare of citizens, supportive of countless rival and younger artists even if he did not share their tastes, a nation-builder who was at the same time a committed internationalist. The fifth act of *Faust II* displays his compassionate insight into the ravages of industrialization; earlier, anti-Napoleonic works were powerful pleas for peace in a time of war-mongering. He was an advocate for authentic cultural artifacts worldwide, inventing the term "world literature" and taking an active interest in poetic production from beyond Europe. Religious readers used to consider him immoral, while some recent biographers have suspected frigidity. He has been blamed for condescension toward Christiane and praised for insisting that she be accepted among his friends; he married her late and mourned her death less than that of his close friend Friedrich Schiller, but then few ministers of state married their lower-class mistresses at all. All seem to agree on his commitment to the famous last lines of *Faust,* "Eternal Womanhood / Draws us on high."

Faust   What remains beyond question is the power of Goethe's literary achievement, which is embodied above all in *Faust,* the epic drama to which he kept returning from age twenty-three until his death. Georg Faust was a wandering charlatan who lived from about 1480 to 1540. An anonymous chapbook—a cheap pamphlet for popular consumption—appeared in 1587 recounting his pact with the devil, adventures, and eventual death and damnation. In England the playwright Christopher Marlowe wrote his famous version, *The Tragical History of Dr. Faustus,* about 1590, though Goethe probably didn't read it until 1818, decades after he took up the theme. In Germany the Faust legend lived on in numerous versions of the chapbook and in street theater and puppet plays, the form in which Goethe first became acquainted with the story. Along with other contemporaries, he imagined it as the vehicle for a grand work, though unlike them he treated it as a European legend more than as a strictly Germanic one. He began work on it in 1773. Scenes amounting to about half of the eventual first part were published in 1790 as *Faust: A Fragment.* The entire first part appeared in print in 1808, though it was staged only in 1829. Around the turn of the century he began work on the second part, which he worked on at intervals for the rest of his life, putting the final touches to the manuscript just weeks before he died in 1832. It was published shortly after his death. The first and only complete theatrical performance, a two-day, twenty-two-hour spectacle, ran successively in three cities (Hannover, Berlin, and Vienna) between 1999 and 2001.

Faust is incredibly varied, yet consistent in its intense human sympathies. Goethe didn't hesitate to juxtapose the individual tragedy of Margareta, the heroine of Part I, with the ribald humor of the apes of Witch's Kitchen. He strove to integrate both normal and eccentric people into social and natural totalities. His devil is humane, his god tolerant. From Shakespeare he learned to portray the interactions of all different social classes on stage. Whereas Marlowe had presented Faust's story as high tragedy in his play *Dr. Faustus,* Goethe transforms the scholar's pact with the devil into a sporting bet, endorsed by the Lord in person. Marlowe's Faustus sells his soul for twenty-four years of service leading to wealth and power, but Goethe's Faust will receive from the devil access to all of human experience—its joys and woes—and only when he ceases to desire more experience will he die. And far from embodying a grim vision of degradation, the devil Mephistopheles is urbane and witty as well as immoral, and is often referred to by the almost friendly nickname "Mephisto." In this radically secular revision of the traditional myth, human experience is all.

Unique to Goethe's sense for the human is the way he always foregrounds ordinary people against larger contexts of nature, culture, and history. Nature is not only the object of veneration, as for Rousseau, or the eternal ground of human existence, as for Wordsworth, but the essential creative force that makes all things exist in time. It embraces the entry of all things into life, their departure from it, and all their developmental transformations in between. Thus does Faust's opening monologue express his greatest desire:

> I ought rather to ask,
> To grant me a vision of Nature's forces
> That bind the world, all its seeds and sources
> And innermost life.

Nature encompasses all being from the inanimate, the geological and elemental up the entire chain of being. All manifestations of nature are connected by a web of analogies that can be described with the same basic spiral of development: the forces that Goethe names polarity and enhancement govern phenomena as diverse as the polarization of light, the development of plants, and the weaving of damask linen. All around us, nature is nevertheless ineffable, not fully accessible to human understanding. In the human sphere its force is often represented by love. Animal spirits, sexual attraction, the desire for knowledge, the mystique of childhood, and above all the eternal feminine—these are all forms of the teeming life of nature. Nature's creative power, in turn, finds a conscious equivalent in culture; as a result art becomes an object worthy of the same attention as nature. Through art, as through nature, Goethe's characters, and by implication his readers, learn to know their essential humanity, their place in nature and in the cosmos. The philosopher Immanuel Kant (whose works Goethe studied carefully) argued that the world in which we live is the world constructed through our faculties of perception; just so, Faust discovers that he must learn about nature through representations of it, mostly plays-within-plays, that he himself constructs, and that are preceded by the elaborately stagy Prelude on the Stage and the Prologue in Heaven that follows.

Since nature is constantly changing, it can be comprehended only as a historical phenomenon. *Poetry and Truth* is the first autobiography to explain the development of the author's identity through generous analysis of the history—political, social, cultural—of his times. Nature itself has a history of change; Goethe's concern with the history of the earth and with what came to be called evolution was widely recognized, by Darwin among many others. History not only enters the details of plot but pervades Goethe's style at every point. His works are so varied precisely because they explore so many different historical modes. In *Faust* Goethe evokes and often parodies a vast range of styles: the Bible, Greek tragedy and comedy, medieval troubadour lyric, Dante, Shakespeare, sixteenth-century German comedy, folk song, Renaissance masque, Spanish Golden Age drama, French neoclassicism, the sentimentalism of eighteenth-century Germany and England all the way up to Lord Byron, for whose death in 1824 he set a eulogy at the end of the third act of Part II. That every age and society is a distinct culture with its own value was one of the great insights of the late eighteenth century. Goethe's friend Herder was one of the great early proponents of this "historicism" that refused to judge different societies by a uniform yardstick, while Goethe gave it its most memorable poetic incarnation.

Goethe's concerns thus extend from the depths of the human psyche to the limits of the universe, from the most profound kind of interiority to the most patient and attentive external observation. All objects of knowledge for Goethe are at once external and internal, objective and subjective. Like all the Romantics, Goethe grappled unceasingly with the division between self and world opened up by Kant's metaphysics, and he reflects the dominant philosophy constantly in the opposed pairs that people *Faust*. A work that stretches (as the Prelude says) "from heaven, through the world, right down to hell," that ranges from the mythic origins of classical antiquity to modern industrial society, that mixes popular and ritual forms with the latest in theatrical fashion and technical advances, is the prototype of what has come to be known, not surprisingly, as cosmic drama.

PRONUNCIATIONS:

Altmayer: ALT-mai-er
Baucis: BOW-tsis
Brander: BRAHN-der
Faust: fowst
Goethe: GER-te
Gretchen: GRAYT-shen
Lieschen: LEEZ-shen
Lynceus: LINK-oys
Mephistopheles: me-fis-TO-fe-leez
Mignon: MIN-yohn
Philemon: phi-LAY-mohn
Siebel: ZEE-bel
Wagner: VAG-ner

from Faust[1]

Part I

Dedication[2]

> Uncertain shapes, visitors from the past
> At whom I darkly gazed so long ago,
> My heart's mad fleeting visions—now at last
> Shall I embrace you, must I let you go?
> 5 Again you haunt me: come then, hold me fast!
> Out of the mist and murk you rise, who so
> Besiege me, and with magic breath restore,
> Stirring my soul, lost youth to me once more.
>
> You bring back memories of happier days
> 10 And many a well-loved ghost again I greet;
> As when some old half-faded legend plays
> About our ears, lamenting strains repeat

---

1. Translated by David Luke.
2. Written in 1797, when Goethe was contemplating finishing Part 1 of *Faust,* about eight years after the most recently composed sections. Early portions had been written in the 1770s, with other scenes at intervals through the 1780s. He subsequently continued working on the first part, finally completing it in 1806.

My journey through life's labyrinthine maze,
Old griefs revive, old friends, old loves I meet,
15   Those dear companions, by their fate's unkind
Decree cut short, who left me here behind.

They cannot hear my present music, those
Few souls who listened to my early song;
They are far from me now who were so close,
20   And their first answering echo has so long
Been silent. Now my voice is heard, who knows
By whom? I shudder as the nameless throng
Applauds it. Are they living still, those friends
Whom once it moved, scattered to the world's ends?

25   And I am seized by long unwonted yearning
For that still, solemn spirit-realm which then
Was mine: these hovering lisping tones returning
Sigh as from some Aeolian harp,[3] as when
I sang them first: I tremble, and my burning
30   Tears flow, my stern heart melts to love again.
All that I now possess seems far away
And vanished worlds are real to me today.

Prelude on the Stage

[*The Director. The Poet. The Clown*[4]]

DIRECTOR: Well, here we are on German soil,
My friends. Tell me, you two have stood
35   By me in bad times and in good:
How shall we prosper now? My toil,
Indeed my pleasure, is to please the mob;
And they're a tolerant public, I'll admit.
The posts and boards are up, and it's our job
40   To give them all a merry time of it.
They're in their seats, relaxed, eyes opened wide,
Waiting already to be mystified.
I know how to content popular taste;
But I've a problem here, it must be said:
45   Their customary fare's not of the best—
And yet they are appallingly well-read.
How shall we give them something fresh and new,
That's entertaining and instructive too?
I like to see them all throng through the gate
50   Into our wooden paradise, to watch
Them push and shove and labor up that straight
And narrow way, like babes about to hatch!

3. A wind harp, frequently associated with poetic inspiration.
4. Actor. Frequently played by the same actor as Mephistopheles. Similarly, Faust and the Lord often play the Poet and the Director, respectively.

Our box-office, while it's still broad daylight,
Is under siege; before it's even four
55 They want their tickets. Tooth and nail they fight,
Like some half-famished crowd outside a baker's door.
Only the poet's magic so holds sway
Over them all: make it, my friend, today!

POET: Do not remind me of that motley throng,
60 Spare me the sight of them! Our spirits fail
And flounder in that stream, we are swept along,
Against the unruly flood what can prevail?
Give me the quietness where I belong,
The poet's place, the stillness never stale,
65 The love and friendship! Only there our art
Thrives on the blessed nurture of the heart.
Deep in the soul an impulse there can flow,
An early song still lisping and unclear;
Well-formed or ill, its momentary show
70 Too soon from Time's wild crest will disappear.
Often unseen and darkly it must grow,
Reaching its ripeness after many a year.
What glisters is the moment's, born to be
Soon lost; true gold lives for posterity.

CLOWN: Must we bring in posterity? Suppose
Posterity were all I thought about,
Who'd keep the present public's boredom out?
They must be entertained, it's what one owes
To them. And with a lad like me
80 Performing, they're enjoying what they see!
Communicate and please! You'll not retire
Then into semi-solitude,
Resentful of the public's fickle mood;
The wider circle's easier to inspire.
85 So do what's needed, be a model poet!
Let Fancy's choirs all sing, and interweave
Reason, sense, feeling, passion—but, by your leave,
Let a good vein of folly still run through it!

DIRECTOR: And let's have enough action, above all!
90 They come to look, they want a spectacle.
Let many things unfold before their eyes,
Let the crowd stare and be amazed, for then
You'll win their hearts, and that's to win the prize;
You'll join the ranks of famous men.
95 Mass alone charms the masses; each man finds
Something to suit him, something to take home.
Give much, and you'll have given to many minds;
They'll all leave here contented to have come.
And let your piece be all in pieces too!
100 You'll not go wrong if you compose a stew:
It's quick to make and easy to present.

Why offer them a whole? They'll just fragment
It anyway, the public always do.

POET: I note you don't despise such a *métier*,[5]
105   And have no sense of how it ill beseems
       True art. If I were to do things your way,
       I'd join the bungling amateurs, it seems.

DIRECTOR: Such a reproach offends me not a whit.
       My aim is our success: I must adopt
110   The proper method of achieving it.
       What tool's best, when there's soft wood to be chopped?
       Consider who you're writing for! They come,
       Some of them, from sheer boredom; some
       Arrive here fully sated after feeding;
115   Others again have just been reading
       The newspapers, God help us all.
       They come with absent thoughts, as if to a masked ball;
       Mere curiosity brings them. As for the display
       Of ladies and their finery, why, they
120   Eke out the show, and ask me for no pay!
       Why do you dream your lofty dreams of art?
       Why do full houses flatter you as well?
       Take a look at our patrons: you can tell
       Half of them have no taste, and half no heart.
125   One will be looking forward to a game
       Of cards after the play, another to a night
       In some girl's arms. Poor foolish poet, why invite
       Your Muse to toil for this? Make it your aim
       Merely to give them more—give them excess!
130   It's such a hard job to amuse them
       That your best plan is to confuse them:
       Do that, and you'll be certain of success—
       Now what's the matter? Pain, or ecstasy?

POET: Leave me, and find some other willing slave!
135   Must the poet forgo what Nature gave
       Him as his birthright, forfeit wantonly
       For you that noble gift? How else does he
       Move all men's hearts, what power but his invents
       The conquest of the elements?
140   Song bursts forth from him, a harmonious whole
       Engulfs the world and draws it back into his soul.
       Nature spins out her thread, endlessly long,
       At random on her careless spindle wound;[6]
       All individual lives in chaos throng
145   Together, mixed like harsh discordant sound.
       Who divides up this dull monotonous drift
       Into a living rhythm? Who can lift

5. Job, trade.
6. In contrast to the classical Fates, who measured out people's destiny on their spindles.

Particular things into a general sense
Of some great music's sacred congruence?
150 When passions rage, who makes the tempest sing,
The sunset glow when solemn thought prevails?
Who scatters all the blossoms of the spring
On his beloved's path? Who makes a crown
Of mere green leaves the symbol of renown
155 For high distinction? What is this that fills
Olympus, joins the gods in unity?—
The power of Man, revealed in Poetry!

CLOWN: Use them then, these delightful powers,
And do your poet's work, rather as when
160 One falls in love to pass the amorous hours.
One meets by chance, one lingers, one is smitten,
And one's involvement gradually increases;
Happiness grows, but soon enough it ceases;
Joy ends in tears. And somehow then
165 It all becomes a novel, ready written.
Let's give them that, let's make that kind of show!
Use real life and its rich variety!
They're living it, but unreflectingly;
They'll notice this or that they didn't know.
170 Colorful changing scenes and little sense,
Much error, mixed with just a grain of truth—
That's the best drink for such an audience;
They'll be refreshed and edified. That way
It will attract the flower of our youth:
175 They'll hear your words, and think them revelation,
And every tender soul suck from your play
A sustenance of melancholy sensation.
Each will find something in it to excite him
For what he'll see's already there inside him.
180 They're young yet, ready still to laugh or cry;
Fancy still pleases, rhetoric lifts them high.
The old and hardened are a thankless brood,
But growing minds can still show gratitude.

POET: Ah, give me back those years when I
185 Myself was still developing,
When songs poured forth unceasingly
And thick and fast as from a spring!
Then still my world was misty-veiled,
Then promised wonders were in bud;
190 I picked the myriad flowers that filled
Those valleys in such plenitude.
My poverty was rich profusion;
I longed for truth and loved illusion.
Give unchecked passion back to me,
195 Those deep delights I suffered then,
Love's power, and hatred's energy—

Give back my youth to me again!

CLOWN: My friend, youth's what one needs, of course, when one
    Is in the thick of battle with the foe,
200   Or when sweet girls are hanging on
    One's neck and simply won't let go,
    Or when the finish of a race
    Beckons far off to victory,
    Or when one's danced at furious pace
205   Then spends the night in revelry:
    But boldly, gracefully to play
    Upon the lyre, choose one's own goal
    And reach it by some charming way
    On random motions of the soul—
210   Such is the older poet's task; and we
    Respect you none the less. The proverb's wrong, you see:
    Age is no second childhood—age makes plain,
    Children we were, true children we remain.

DIRECTOR: Come, that's enough of words! What I
215   Want now is deeds. While you, my friends,
    Exchange these well-turned compliments,
    The time for useful work slips by.
    Why all this talk of the right mood?
    It won't just come by dithering.
220   Command your Muses, and they'll sing
    To order, if you're any good!
    You know what we expect of you:
    We're thirsty for a potent brew.
    Prepare it now! What's not begun
225   Today will still be left undone
    Tomorrow. Never miss a day,
    But boldly and with resolution
    Seize Chance's forelock and waylay
    The possible before it slips away;
230   A started task compels completion.

    On German stages, as you know no doubt,
    Producers like to try things out;
    So make sure now we have machines
    And plenty of spectacular scenes!
235   Use the sunshine and moonshine lights,
    Use starlight—we have stars galore,
    Water and fire and rocky heights,
    And birds and animals by the score!
    Thus on these narrow boards[7] you'll seem
240   To explore the entire creation's scheme—
    And with swift steps, yet wise and slow
    From heaven, through the world, right down to hell you'll go!

7. The stage.

Prologue in Heaven

[*The Lord. The Heavenly Hosts, then Mephistopheles. The three Archangels advance.*]

RAPHAEL: The sun proclaims its old devotion
       In rival song with brother spheres,
245   And still completes in thunderous motion
       The circuits of its destined years.
       Angelic powers, uncomprehending.
       Are strengthened as they gaze their fill;
       Thy works, unfathomed and unending,
250   Retain the first day's splendor still.
GABRIEL: The glorious earth, with mind-appalling
       Swiftness, upon itself rotates,
       And with the deep night's dreadful falling
       Its primal radiance alternates.
255   High cliffs stand deep in ocean weather,
       Wide foaming waves flood out and in,
       And cliffs and seas rush on together
       Caught in the globe's unceasing spin.
MICHAEL: And turn by turn the tempests raging
260   From sea to land, from land to sea,
       Build up, in passion unassuaging,[8]
       Their chain of furious energy.
       The thunder strikes, its flash is faster,
       It spreads destruction on its way—
265   But we, thy messengers,[9] O master,
       Revere thy gently circling day.
THE THREE IN CHORUS: And each of us, uncomprehending,
       Is strengthened as we gaze our fill;
       For all thy works, sublime, unending,
270   Retain their first day's splendor still.
MEPHISTOPHELES: Your Grace, since you have called on us again
       To see how things are going, and since you
       Have been quite pleased to meet me now and then,
       I thought I'd come and join your retinue.
275   Forgive me, but grand words are not my trick;
       I cut a sorry figure here, I know,
       But you would laugh at my high rhetoric
       If you'd not left off laughing long ago.
       The solar system I must leave unsung,
280   And to mankind's woes lend my humbler tongue.
       The little earth-god still persists in his old ways,
       Ridiculous as ever, as in his first days.
       He'd have improved if you'd not given

8. Uncalmable.
9. "Angel" comes from the Greek word for "messenger."

Him a mere glimmer of the light of heaven;
285   He calls it Reason, and it only has increased
His power to be beastlier than a beast.
He is—if I may say so, sir—
A little like the long-legged grasshopper,
Which hops and flies, and sings its silly songs
290   And flies, and drops straight back to grass where it belongs.
Indeed, if only he would stick to grass!
He pokes his nose in all the filth he finds, alas.

THE LORD: And that is all you have to say?
Must you complain each time you come my way?
295   Is nothing right on your terrestrial scene?

MEPHISTOPHELES: No, sir! The earth's as bad as it has always been.
I really feel quite sorry for mankind;
Tormenting them myself's no fun, I find.

THE LORD: Do you know Faust?

MEPHISTOPHELES: The doctor? Do you mean—

THE LORD: My servant.

MEPHISTOPHELES: Ah, he serves you well, indeed!
He scorns earth's fare and drinks celestial mead.
Poor fool, his ferment drives him far!
He half knows his own madness, I'll be bound.
He'd pillage heaven for its brightest star,
305   And earth for every last delight that's to be found;
Not all that's near nor all that's far
Can satisfy a heart so restless and profound.

THE LORD: He serves me, but still serves me in confusion;
I will soon lead him into clarity.
310   A gardener knows, one day this young green tree
Will blossom and bear fruit in rich profusion.

MEPHISTOPHELES: If I may be his guide, you'll lose him yet;
I'll subtly lead him my way, if you'll let
Me do so; shall we have a bet?

THE LORD: He lives on earth, and while he is alive
You have my leave for the attempt;
Man errs, till he has ceased to strive.

MEPHISTOPHELES: I thank your Grace; for dead men never tempt
Me greatly, I confess. In this connection
320   I like to see a full and fresh complexion;
A corpse is an unwelcome visitor.
The cat-and-mouse game is what I prefer.

THE LORD: Well, go and try what you can do!
Entice that spirit from its primal source,
325   And lead him, if he's not too hard for you
To grasp, on your own downward course—
And then, when you have failed, with shame confess:
A good man, in his dark, bewildered stress,
Well knows the path from which he should not stray.

MEPHISTOPHELES: No doubt; it's a short journey anyway.

I'll win my wager without much delay.
And when I do, then, if I may,
I'll come back here and boast of my success.
I'll make him greedy for the dust, the way
335   The serpent was, my famous ancestress![1]

THE LORD: Indeed, you may feel free to come and call.
You are a type I never learnt to hate;
Among the spirits who negate,
The ironic scold offends me least of all.
340   Man is too apt to sink into mere satisfaction,
A total standstill is his constant wish:
Therefore your company, busily devilish,
Serves well to stimulate him into action.
But you, the authentic sons of God, enfold
345   With praise the abundant beauty of the world;
Love, as you do, the eternal Process, which
Is ever living and forever rich;
Its vanishing phenomena will last,
By your angelic thoughts made firm and fast.

[*The heavens close, the Archangels disperse.*]

MEPHISTOPHELES: I like to see him sometimes, and take care
Not to fall out with him. It's civil
Of the old fellow, such a *grand seigneur*,°   noble lord
To have these man-to-man talks with the Devil!

The First Part of the Tragedy

Night

[*A high-vaulted, narrow Gothic room.*]

FAUST [*sitting restlessly at his desk*]:
    Well, that's Philosophy I've read,
355   And Law and Medicine, and I fear
Theology too, from A to Z;
Hard studies all, that have cost me dear.
And so I sit, poor silly man,
No wiser now than when I began.
360   They call me Professor and Doctor, forsooth.
For misleading many an innocent youth
These last ten years now, I suppose,
Pulling them to and fro by the nose;
And I see all our search for knowledge is vain,
365   And this burns my heart with bitter pain.
I've more sense, to be sure, than the learned fools,

---

1. In Genesis 3.14 God punishes the serpent for tempting Eve by condemning him to crawl forever on his belly: "and dust you shall eat, all the days of your life."

The masters and pastors, the scribes from the schools;
No scruples to plague me, no irksome doubt,
No hell-fire or devil to worry about—
370   Yet I take no pleasure in anything now;
For I know I know nothing, I wonder how
I can still keep up the pretense of teaching
Or bettering mankind with my empty preaching.
Can I even boast any worldly success?
375   What fame or riches do I possess?
No dog would put up with such an existence!
And so I am seeking magic's assistance,
Calling on spirits and their might
To show me many a secret sight,
380   To relieve me of the wretched task
Of telling things I ought rather to ask,
To grant me a vision of Nature's forces
That bind the world, all its seeds and sources
And innermost life—all this I shall see,
385   And stop peddling in words that mean nothing to me.
Oh sad full moon, my friend, why must
You see me suffer? Look your last!
Here at this desk so many a night
I've watched and waited for your light
390   To visit me again and shine
Over this paper world of mine.
Oh, take me to the hilltops, there
To wander in the sweet moonlit air,
By mountain caves, through fields to roam,
395   Hovering with spirits in your gloam,
Cleansed of book-learning's fog and stew
And healed by bathing in your dew!

God, how these walls still cramp my soul,
This cursèd, stifling prison-hole
400   Where even heaven's dear light must pass
Dimly through panes of painted glass!
Hemmed in by books to left and right
Which worms have gnawed, which dust-layers choke,
And round them all, to ceiling-height,
405   This paper stained by candle-smoke,
These glasses, boxes, instruments,
All stuffed and cluttered anyhow,
Ancestral junk—look at it now,
Your world, this world your brain invents!

410   And can you still ask why your heart
Is pent and pining in your breast,
Why you obscurely ache and smart.
Robbed of all energy and zest?
For here you sit, surrounded not

415   By living Nature, not as when
     God made us, but by reek and rot
     And mouldering bones of beasts and men.

     Come, flee into the open land!
     And this great book of magic lore,
420   By Nostradamus'[2] very hand,
     Shall be my guide, I'll need no more;
     By it I'll see the stars in course,
     And as great Nature rules my mind
     Discover the inner psychic force,
425   The spirit speaking to its kind!
     This arid speculation's vain,
     The sacred diagrams are clear:
     Spirits, you hover close—be plain
     And answer me, if you can hear!

[He throws open the book and sees the Sign of the Macrocosm.[3]]

430   Ha! as I look, what sudden ecstasy
     Floods all my senses, how I feel it flowing
     Through every vein, through every nerve in me,
     Life's sacred joy and youth's renewal glowing!
     Did not some god write these mysterious
435   Signs, by whose might my soul is filled
     With peace again, my poor heart healed,
     And by whose secret impetus
     The powers of Nature all about me are revealed?
     Am I a god? Light fills my mind;
440   In these pure lines and forms appear
     All Nature's workings, to my inner sense made clear.
     That sage's words at last I understand:
     "The spirit-world is open wide,
     Only your heart has closed and died;
445   Come, earth-disciple, boldly lave
     Your bosom in the dawn's red wave!"

[He gazes at the sign.]

     How it all lives and moves and weaves
     Into a whole! Each part gives and receives,
     Angelic powers ascend and redescend
450   And each to each their golden vessels lend;
     Fragrant with blessing, as on wings
     From heaven through the earth and through all things
     Their movement thrusts, and all in harmony it sings!
     How great a spectacle! But that, I fear,
455   Is all it is. Oh, endless Nature, where
     Shall I embrace you? Where, you breasts that flow

2. Author of a 16th-century collection of prophecies.
3. A mystical diagram in a book of alchemy, showing the solar system.

With life's whole life? All earth and heaven hangs
On you, who slake the thirsty pangs
Of every heart—and must I languish vainly so?

[*He turns impatiently to another page of the book and sees the Sign of the Earth Spirit.*[4]]

460   How differently this sign affects me! You,
    Spirit of Earth, are closer to me,
    Fresh strength already pulses through me,
    I glow already from wine so new!
    Now, to go out into the world and bear
465   The earth's whole pain and joy, all this I dare;
    To fight with tempests anywhere,
    And in the grinding shipwreck stand and not despair!
    Clouds gather over me—
    The full moon hides its face—
470   My lamp burns low!
    Mist rises—red fire flashes round
    My head, and from the vaulted roof
    A chill breathes down and strikes
    A shudder into me!
475   Spirit I long to summon, now I feel
    You hovering round me, oh reveal
    Yourself! Ha, this pain tears my heart!
    A new sensation
    Stirs all my senses into perturbation!
480   I am committed: you shall come, you must
    Appear to me, though you may strike me into dust!

[*He seizes the book and secretly pronounces the spirit's sign. A red flame flashes, the spirit appears in the flame.*]

THE SPIRIT: Who is calling me?
FAUST [*turning away*]:   Ah, you are too terrible!
THE SPIRIT: You have drawn me to you with mighty power,
    Sucked at my sphere for many an hour,
    And now—
FAUST: Alas, this sight's unbearable!
THE SPIRIT: You groan and sigh to have me appear,
    To hear my voice, to behold my face:
    Your soul's great plea compels me to this place
    And I have come! What pitiable fear
490   Seizes you, Faust the superman! Where is the call
    Of your creative heart, that carried all
    The world and gave it birth, that shook with ecstasy,
    Swelling, upsurging to the heights where we,
    The spirits, live? Where are you, you whose song
495   I heard besieging me so loud and strong?

4. The Earth Spirit is Goethe's invention.

Can this be you? Now that my breath blows round you,
In the depths of terror I have found you,
Shrinking and writhing like a worm!
FAUST: Am I to quail before you, shape of flame?
500   It is I, Faust! you and I are the same!
THE SPIRIT: In life like a flood, in deeds like a storm
         I surge to and fro,
         Up and down I flow!
         Birth and the grave
505   An eternal wave,
         Turning, returning,
         A life ever burning:
         At Time's whirring loom I work and play
         God's living garment I weave and display.
FAUST: Oh busy spirit! from end to end
         Of the world you roam: how close you are to me!
THE SPIRIT: You match the spirit you can comprehend:
         I am not he. [*It vanishes.*]
FAUST [*collapsing*]:   Not you!
515   Who is he then?
         I, made in God's image
         And not even like you!

[*There is a knock at the door.*]

         Oh, devil take him, it's that dry-as-dust
         Toady, my famulus![5] Why must
520   He interrupt me and destroy
         This supreme hour of visionary joy?

[*Enter Wagner in a nightgown and nightcap, carrying a lamp. Faust turns to him impatiently.*]

WAGNER: Excuse me, sir! I heard your declamation:
         You were reading a Greek tragedy, no doubt?
         That art is one of powerful persuasion
525   These days; I'd like to learn what it's about.
         I've often heard it said an actor might
         Give lessons to a parson.
FAUST: You are right,
         If the parson himself's an actor too;
         As sometimes is the case.
WAGNER: Oh dear, what can one do,
530   Sitting day after day among one's books!
         The world's so distant, and one never looks
         Even through a spyglass at it; so how can
         One learn to bring about the betterment of man?
FAUST: Give up pursuing eloquence, unless
535   You can speak as you feel! One's very heart

5. Assistant.

Must pour it out, with primal power address
One's hearers and compel them with an art
Deeper than words. Clip and compile, and brew
From the leavings of others your ragoût
540   Of rhetoric, pump from your embers
A few poor sparks that nobody remembers!
Children will gape and fools admire,
If that's the audience to which you aspire.
But what can blend all hearts into a whole?
545   Only the language of the soul.

WAGNER: But one must know how to deliver a tirade.[6]
And I fear my training still is uncompleted.

FAUST: Why don't you learn to ply an honest trade?
Why be a fool with tinkling bells?
550   Stick to right thinking and sound sense, it tells
Its own tale, little artifice is needed;
If you have something serious to say,
Drop the pursuit of words! This play
Of dazzling oratory, this paper decoration
555   You fiddle with and offer to the world—
Why, the dry leaves in autumn, whirled
About by foggy winds, carry more inspiration!

WAGNER: Alas, our life is short,
And art is long, they say!
560   My scholarly pursuits, how sore they weigh
Upon my heart and mind! One ought
To learn the means of mounting to the sources,
Yet even this task almost passes my resources;
For we poor devils, by the time we've got
565   Less than halfway, we die, as like as not.

FAUST: A manuscript—is that the sacred spring
That stills one's thirst for evermore?
Refreshment! It's your own soul that must pour
It through you, if it's to be anything.

WAGNER: Excuse me, but it's very pleasant
Studying epochs other than the present,
Entering their spirit, reading what they say,
And seeing how much wiser we have grown today.

FAUST: Oh yes indeed, a wisdom most sublime!—
575   My friend, the spirit of an earlier time,
To us it is a seven-sealed mystery;
And what you learned gentlemen would call
Its spirit, is its image, that is all,
Reflected in your own mind's history.
580   And what a sight it often is! Enough
To run a mile from at first glance. A vast
Old rubbish-dump, an attic of the past,

6. A speech in a play.

At best a royal tragedy—bombastic stuff
Full of old saws, most edifying for us,
585   The strutting speeches of a puppet-chorus!
WAGNER: But the great world! The heart and mind of man!
We all seek what enlightenment we can.
FAUST: Ah yes, we say "enlightenment," forsooth!
Which of us dares to call things by their names?
590   Those few who had some knowledge of the truth,
Whose full heart's rashness drove them to disclose
Their passion and their vision to the mob, all those
Died nailed to crosses or consigned to flames.
You must excuse me, friend, the night's half through.
595   We shall speak further on the next occasion.
WAGNER: I'd stay awake all night, and gladly too,
Enjoying such a learned conversation.
Tomorrow morning, being Easter Day,
I'll ask you some more questions, if I may.
600   I've studied now for years with zeal and zest;
Already I know much I must know all the rest. [*Exit.*]
FAUST: Why does he not despair? A mind so void
And blinkered, so benighted and earthbound!
Greedy for gold, he scratches in the ground,
605   And when he finds some worms he's overjoyed.

Why, when those spirit-voices filled the air
About me, must the speech of such a man
Intrude? And yet for once I can
Thank you, poor mortal wretch: for when despair
610   Was close to me and madness had assailed
My mind, when like a dwarf I seemed to shrink
Before that giant vision, and I quailed,
Dwindling to nothingness—you snatched me from the brink.

I, God's own image! Ah, how close it shone,
615   The mirror of eternal verity!
I fed upon its light and clarity
Within myself, all mortal limits gone,
And with presumption too extreme
Of free, superangelic strength, divine
620   Creative life, thought even now to stream
Through Nature's veins—what sudden shame was mine!
A voice of thunder dashed me from that dream.

Not close to you, not like you; this I dare
No longer claim to be. I had the power
625   To summon you, but could not hold you there.
I felt in that ecstatic hour
So small, and yet so great: and then
You hurled me back so cruelly
Into the changeful common state of men.
630   What must I do now? who shall counsel me?

What urge claims my obedience?
Alas, not only pain, even activity
Itself can stop our life's advance.

The spirit's noblest moments, rare and high,
635   Are choked by matter's alien obtrusion,
And rich with this world's goods, we cry
Scorn on those better things as mere illusion.
Life-giving intuitions of great worth
Are stifled in the muddle of the earth.

640   Imagination, once a flight sublime
That soared in hope beyond the swirl of time,
Now, as each joy is drowned beyond redress,
Sinks down inside us into pettiness:
Care makes its nest in the heart's deepest hole
645   And secretly torments the soul;
Its restless rocking motion mars our mind's content.
Its masks are ever-changing, it appears
As house and home, as wife and child, it will invent
Wounds, poisons, fires and floods—from all
650   These blows we flinch before they ever fall,
And for imagined losses shed continual tears.

I am not like a god! Too deeply now I feel
This truth. I am a worm stuck in the dust,
Burrowing and feeding, where at last I must
655   Be crushed and buried by some rambler's heel.

Is this not dust, filling a hundred shelves
On these high walls that hem me in?
These thousand useless toys that thrust themselves
At me in this moth-mumbled rubbish-bin?
660   How shall I find fulfillment in this jail,
Reading the thousand-times-reprinted tale
Of man's perpetual strife and stress
And rare occasional happiness?—
You hollow skull, what does your grinning say?
665   That brain, in the confusion of its youth,
Like mine, once sought the ethereal dawn of truth
But in the heavy dusk went piteously astray.
And you old instruments, how you too mock,
What scorn your wheels, cogs, pulleys pour on me!
670   I reached the gate, you were to be the key:
Your bit's a well-curled beard, but it won't fit the lock.
We snatch in vain at Nature's veil,
She is mysterious in broad daylight,
No screws or levers can compel her to reveal
675   The secrets she has hidden from our sight.
Useless mechanical contrivances, retained
Because my father used them, old smoke-stained

Parchments that have lain here, untouched by toil,
Since my dull lamp first burnt its midnight oil!
680   I should have squandered all my poor inheritance,
Not sat here sweating while it weighed me down.
What we are born with, we must make our own
Or it remains a mere appurtenance
And is not ours: a load of unused things,
685   Not the live moment's need, raised on the moment's wings.

But what is this? My eyes, magnetically drawn,
Are fixed on that one spot, where I can see
That little flask: why does sweet light break over me,
As when in a dark wood the gentle moonbeams dawn?

690   Unique alembic![7] Reverently I lift
You down and greet you. Now, most subtle gift
Compounded of the wit and art of man,
Distillment of all drowsy syrups, kind
Quintessence of all deadly and refined
695   Elixirs, come, and serve your master as you can!
I see you, and am healed as with a balm,
I seize you, and my striving soul grows calm;
And borne upon my spirit's ebbing tide,
Little by little drifting out to sea,
700   I tread on its bright mirror—far and wide
As new dawn breaks, new shores are beckoning me!

A fiery chariot[8] on light wings descends
And hovers by me! I will set forth here
On a new journey to the heaven's ends,
705   To pure activity in a new sphere!
O sublime life, o godlike joy! And how
Do I, the erstwhile worm, deserve it now?
I will be resolute, and turn away
For ever from the earth's sweet day.
710   Dread doors, though all men sneak and shuffle past
You, I'll confront you, tear you open wide!
Here it is time for me to prove at last
That by his noble deeds a man is deified;
Time not to shrink from the dark cavern where
715   Our fancy damns itself to its own tortured fate;
Time to approach the narrow gate
Ringed by the eternal flames of hell's despair;
Time to step gladly over this great brink,
And if it is the void, into the void to sink!

7. Distilling apparatus.

8. The sunrise is here described using an image that is both classical (Apollo, god of light and reason, drives the sun across the sky) and biblical (a fiery chariot takes the prophet Elijah up to heaven, 2 Kings 2.11).

720   Old goblet of pure crystal, come, now let
            Me take you from your shelf and sheath. Long years
            Have passed since last I thought of you; and yet
            At bygone feasts you were the cup that cheers
            The solemn guests, the gleaming beaker
725   Raised to the toast by many a speaker!
            Your rich engraved pictorial decorations,
            The drinker's task, his rhyming explanations
            Before in one long draught he drained you down—
            These I recall, from revels long ago;
730   I passed you round, I praised your art to show
            My wit. Now I shall not do so.
            I have a potion here whose work's soon done;
            Its dizzying liquid fills you, dark and brown.
            I made and mixed it well, as I know how.
735   And so, with all my heart, I raise it now:
            With this last festive drink I greet the rising sun!

[*He sets the cup to his lips. There is a peal of bells and a sound of choral singing.*]

CHORUS OF ANGELS: Christ is ris'n from the dead!
            Hail to all mortal men,
            From sin's insidious bane,
740   From their inherited
            Bondage set free again!
FAUST: What lilting tones are these, what notes profound
            Cry to me: Do not drink! Have they such power?
            And do these bells with their dull booming sound
745   Announce the Easter festival's first hour?
            Is this already the angelic song
            Of solace, heard above the grave that night so long
            Ago, when the new covenant was sealed and bound?
CHORUS OF WOMEN: Spices we brought and myrrh,
750   We who befriended him,
            Faithfully laid him here,
            Lovingly tended him;
            Clean linen, swaddling-bands,
            We wound with our own hands.
755   Who can have come today
            Taking our Lord away?
CHORUS OF ANGELS: Christ is raised, Christ is blest!
            He bore mankind's ordeal,
            Loving their joys to feel,
760   Suffering the stripes that heal:
            He passed the test!
FAUST: You gentle, puissant choirs of heaven, why
            Do you come seeking me? The dust is stronger!
            Go, chant elsewhere to tenderer souls! For I

765 Can hear the message, but believe no longer.
Wonders are dear to faith, by it they live and die.
I cannot venture to those far-off spheres,
Their sweet evangel[9] is not for my ears.
And yet—these strains, so long familiar, still
770 They call me back to life. There was a time
Of quiet, solemn sabbaths when heaven's kiss would fill
Me with its love's descent, when a bell's chime
Was deep mysterious music, and to pray
Was fervent ecstasy. I could not understand
775 The sweet desire that drove me far away
Out through the woods, over the meadowland:
There I would weep a thousand tears and feel
A whole world come to birth, my own yet real.
Those hymns would herald youthful games we played
780 To celebrate the spring. As I recall
That childhood, I am moved, my hand is stayed,
I cannot take this last and gravest step of all.
Oh sing, dear heaven-voices, as before!
Now my tears flow, I love the earth once more!

CHORUS OF DISCIPLES: Now from his burial
Christ has gone up on high,
Living, no more to die,
Glorious, imperial;
He in creative zest
790 Into the heavens has grown.
On the earth-mother's breast
We still must weep alone;
Yet though we here endure
Exile and anguish,
795 Master, it is in your
Joy that we languish!

CHORUS OF ANGELS: Christ is raised from the tomb,
Snatched from corruption's womb!
Rise and be joyful, all
800 You whom earth's bonds enthrall!
Brothers, o blessed few,
Sharers of love's food, who
Praise him in deeds you do,
Pilgrims whose words renew
805 Man's hope of glory: you
Know that your Lord is near,
See, he is here!

9. Gospel, good news.

from Outside the Town Wall[1]

AN OLD PEASANT: Why, Doctor, now that's very kind
          To join us for your Easter walk,
          Being such a learned gentleman,
          And not look down on us poor folk!
985   Now, here's a jug of finest ale;
          You are the man we've filled it for,
          And in your honor this we wish,
          That it may quench your thirst, and more:
          There's many a drop in this cup I raise—
990   May their number be added to your days!
FAUST: I thank you all; this drink refreshes,
          And I return your kind good wishes.

     [*The people gather round.*]

THE OLD PEASANT: Yes, sir, indeed! we all are glad
          To see you on this day of cheer,
995   For long ago, when times were bad,
          You wished us well for many a year.
          There's many of us might now be dead
          Who've lived on to a healthy age
          Because your father stopped the spread
1000   Of plague, and cooled the fever's rage.
          You were young then, you went about
          Visiting every hospital:
          So many corpses they brought out,
          But you came out alive and well;
1005   Though many a hard time you had too.
          You helped us, and the Lord helped you.
ALL: Long life to our good doctor! May
          He help us yet for many a day.
FAUST: Give thanks to Him who gave these skills
1010   And helps mankind in all its ills.

     [*He walks on with Wagner.*]

WAGNER: Ah, what a sense of your own greatness must
          You have as all these people honor you!
          Happy the man whose gifts bring him such true
          Advantage, as is only just!
1015   They all ask questions, fathers point you out
          To sons, they all rush up to see
          You pass, the fiddling stops, they stand about
          To stare instead of dancing, and the sky
          Is full of cheers and caps thrown high;
1020   They very nearly drop on bended knee
          As if the Sacred Host were being carried by!

1. Faust and Wagner walk out among the peasants celebrating the spring and Easter.

FAUST: A few steps further, to that rock up there;
Now let us rest here from our walk. This place is one
Where I would often sit and meditate alone,
1025 Keeping strict fast, in anguished prayer.
Here, full of hope, firm in belief,
I sought to alter heaven's will;
I groaned, I wrung my hands in grief—
The pestilence continued still.
1030 Now I feel mocked by this mob's adulation.
If only you could read my mind and know
How little we did, so long ago,
I and my father, to deserve such commendation!
My father was a man respected, yet obscure,
1035 Who labored honestly with never a pause,
Though by his own eccentric methods to be sure,
Studying Nature's sacred cyclic laws.
With the initiated few
He practiced in the Black Laboratory,[2]
1040 Mixing, by this or that strange recipe,
Elements in an ill-assorted brew.
Thus in tepid immersion he would wed
The Lily to the Lion bold and red;
Then with intenser heat he forced this bridal pair
1045 From one glass chamber to the other—by and by
The Young Queen was engendered there,
The rainbow-hued precipitate: this, then,
Was our specific. Still the sick would die,
But no one asked why none got well again.
1050 So in these valleys and these villages,
With those hell-syrups as our remedies,
We, worse than any plague, raged far and wide.
I myself poisoned thousands, I saw how
They all wasted away and perished—now
1055 Men praise that cynical mass-homicide.
WAGNER: Sir, do not let that trouble you!
To practice a transmitted skill
With a good conscience and good will
Is all an honest man need do.
1060 If one respects one's father in one's youth,
One will have learnt from him with pleasure;
If as a man one then adds to our store of truth,
One's own son will do this in even greater measure.
FAUST: Happy are they who still hope this is so,
1065 While ignorance surrounds us like an ocean!
The very thing one needs one does not know,

2. Faust here describes chemical operations in the language of alchemy. In his laboratory Faust's father produced his failed "specific" (medication: the precipitate called the Young Queen) by marrying (combining) the Red Lion (mercuric oxide) with the Lily (hydrochloric acid).

And what one knows is needless information.
But let us put these gloomy thoughts away
And let the precious present hour confound them!
1070 Look how they gleam in the last light of day,
Those little huts with green all round them!
Evening has come, our sun is westering now——
But it speeds on to bring new life elsewhere.
Oh if some wings would raise me, if somehow
1075 I could follow its circuit through the air!
For then as I strove onwards I should see
A silent sunset world for ever under me,
The hills aglow, the valleys lost in dreams,
The silver brooks poured into golden streams;
1080 No mountain-range would stop me, not with all
Its rugged chasms; at divine speed I fly,
The sea already greets my wondering eye
With its warm gulfs where now the sun's rays fall.
Now the god seems at last to sink and set,
1085 But a new impulse drives me yet:
I hasten on to drink his endless light,
The day ahead, behind my back the night,
The sky above me and the waves below . . .
A pleasing dream; but the sun vanishes
1090 And it is over. Wings, alas, may grow
Upon our soul, but still our body is
Earthbound. And yet, by inborn instinct given
To each of us, our hearts rise up and soar
For ever onwards, when we hear the lark outpour
1095 Its warbling song, lost in the blue of heaven,
Or when we see the wing-spread eagle hover
Above wild cliffs which pine-trees cover,
Or across marsh and lakeland watch the crane
Fly homeward to its native haunts again.

WAGNER: I too have known fanciful states of mind,
But to such moods as yours I never was inclined.
One soon grows tired of forests and of fields;
I never envied any bird its wings.
But the pursuit of intellectual things
1105 From book to book, from page to page—what joys that yields!
How fine and snug the winter nights become,
What sweet life courses through one's veins!
Is an old parchment not a whole compendium
Of paradise itself, rewarding all our pains?

FAUST: Only one of our needs is known to you;
You must not learn the other, oh beware!
In me there are two souls, alas, and their
Division tears my life in two.
One loves the world, it clutches her, it binds
1115 Itself to her, clinging with furious lust:

	The other longs to soar beyond the dust
	Into the realm of high ancestral minds.
	Are there no spirits moving in the air,
	Ruling the region between earth and sky?
1120	Come down then to me from your golden mists on high,
	And to new, many-colored life, oh take me there!
	Give me a magic cloak to carry me
	Away to some far place, some land untold,
	And I'd not part with it for silk or gold
1125	Or a king's crown, so precious it would be!

WAGNER: Oh do not call the dreaded host that swarms
And streams abroad throughout the atmosphere![3]
They bring men danger in a thousand forms,
From the earth's ends they come to plague us here.

1130   Out of the north the sharp-toothed demons fly,
Attacking us with arrow-pointed tongues:
On the east wind they ride to drain us dry
And slake their hunger on our lungs;
The southern desert sends them to beat down

1135   Upon our heads with fiery beams;
The west will bring refreshment, as it seems,
Till in their flooding rains we and the fields must drown.
Their spiteful ears are open to obey
Our summons, for they love to harm and cheat;

1140   They pose as heaven's angels, and though all they say
Is false, their lisping voice is sweet.
But come, the air grows chill, the world is gray
With dusk and mist already; come away!
When evening falls, indoors is best.—

1145   Why do you stand and stare with such surprise?
What twilight thing has seized your interest?

FAUST: There—in the corn and stubble, do you see
That black dog?

WAGNER: Why, of course; of what account is he?

FAUST: What do you take him for? Come, use your eyes!

WAGNER: A poodle, acting as a dog will do
When it has lost its master, I suppose.

FAUST: He's getting closer; round and round he goes
In a narrowing spiral; no, there's no mistake!
And as he comes—look, can't you see it too?—

1155   A streak of fire follows in his wake!

WAGNER: An ordinary black poodle is all I
Can see; no doubt some trick of light deceives your eye.

FAUST: It is some magic he is weaving, so
Subtly about our feet, some future knot!

WAGNER: He's nervous, jumping round us, since we're not
His master, but two men he doesn't know.

---

3. True to his pedantic nature, Wagner misunderstands Faust's mystical nature spirits as mere weather demons.

FAUST: The circle shrinks; now he is on our ground.

WAGNER: You see! he's not a phantom, just a hound.
He's doubtful still, he growls, he lies down flat,
1165   He wags his tail. All dogs do that.

FAUST: Come to us! Come to heel! Come here!

WAGNER: He's just a foolish poodle-beast, I fear.
Stand still, and he will dance attendance on you;
Speak to him, and he'll put his forepaws on you;
1170   Drop something, and he'll find it, that's his trick—
He'll jump into the water for your stick.

FAUST: No doubt you're right; no spirit after all,
But merely a conditioned animal.

WAGNER: A well-trained dog is one who can
1175   Find favor even with a learned man.
Our students taught him to behave this way;
He far excels his teachers, I must say.

[They pass through the gate into the town.]

Faust's Study (1)

FAUST [*entering with the poodle*]:
Now I have left the fields and hills
Where now the night's dark veil is spread;
1180   Night wakes our better part, and fills
Our prescient soul with holy dread.
The active turmoil leaves my mind,
All wilder passions sleep and cease;
Now I am moved to love mankind,
1185   To love God too, and am at peace.
Stop running about, you poodle-clown!
Why are you snuffling there by the door?
Go behind the stove! Keep still, lie down!
You have my best cushion, I can't do more.
1190   On that path down the hill you jumped and ran
For our delectation, and that was fun;
I will entertain you now if I can,
As a welcome guest, but a silent one.
Back in our little narrow cell
1195   We sit, the lamp glows soft and bright,
And in our heart and mind as well
Self-knowledge sheds its kindly light.
Reason once more begins to speak,
And hope once more is blossoming;
1200   We long to find life's source, to seek
Life's fountainhead, to taste life's spring.
Poodle, stop growling! It does not agree
With my high tone, and my soul's sacred joys
Are interrupted by your animal noise.
1205   We know what scorn and mockery

Uncomprehending man will pour
On anything he has not heard before—
The good, the beautiful, the true;
Must dogs start muttering at it too?

1210   But now, that deep contentment in my breast,
        Alas, wells up no more, in spite of all my best
        Endeavors. Oh, how soon the stream runs dry,
        And in what parching thirst again we lie!
        How often this has happened to me!
1215   And yet, there is a remedy:
        We learn to seek a higher inspiration,
        A supernatural revelation—
        And where does this shine in its fullest glory.
        If not in that old Gospel story?
1220   Here is the Greek text; I am moved to read
        Its sacred words, I feel the need
        Now to translate them true and clear
        Into the German tongue I hold so dear.

    [*He opens a volume and prepares to write.*]

        "In the beginning was the Word":[4] why, now
1225   I'm stuck already! I must change that; how?
        Is then "the word" so great and high a thing?
        There is some other rendering,
        Which with the spirit's guidance I must find.
        We read: "In the beginning was the Mind."
1230   Before you write this first phrase, think again;
        Good sense eludes the overhasty pen.
        Does "mind" set worlds on their creative course?
        It means: "In the beginning was the Force."
        So it should be—but as I write this too,
1235   Some instinct warns me that it will not do.
        The spirit speaks! I see how it must read,
        And boldly write: "In the beginning was the Deed!"

        If we are to share this room in peace,
        Poodle, this noise has got to cease,
1240   This howling and barking has got to end!
        My invitation did not extend
        To so cacophonous a friend.
        In my study I won't put up with it.
        One of us two will have to quit.
1245   I am sorry that we must part so;
        The door stands open, you may go.
        But what is this I see?
        Can it be happening naturally?

---

4. The opening line of John's Gospel.

Is it real? Is it a dream or not?

1250   How long and broad my poodle has got!
He heaves himself upright:
This is no dog, if I trust my sight!
What hobgoblin have I brought home somehow?
He looks like a hippopotamus now,

1255   With fearsome jaws and fiery eyes.
Aha! you'll get a surprise!
With this hybrid half-brood of hell
King Solomon's Key[5] works very well.

SPIRITS [*outside in the passage*]:
He's caught! There's one caught in there!

1260   Don't follow him, don't go in!
Like a fox in a gin
An old hell-lynx is trapped; beware!
But now wait and see!
Hover round, hover

1265   Up and down, he'll recover,
He'll set himself free;
We'll lend a hand to him,
We'll not abandon him;
He's been polite to us,

1270   Always done right by us!

FAUST: First, to defeat this beast,
I need the Spell of the Four,[6] at least.
Salamander, burn!
Water-nymph, twist and turn!

1275   Sylph of the air, dissolve!
Goblin, dig and delve!
When the elements are known,
Each in its own
Qualities and powers,

1280   The mastery is ours
Over all and each,
By this knowledge and speech.
Salamander, in flame
Vanish as you came!

1285   Murmur and mingle,
Nymph of the sea-dingle![7]
Blaze like a meteor,
Sylph-creature!
Serve in the house for us,

1290   Incubus, incubus!
Come out of him, show yourself thus or thus!
None of those four

---

5. A magic book popular from the 16th to the 18th century.
6. The four elements: fire (salamander), water (nymph), air (sylph), and earth (goblin or incubus).
7. Dell or hollow.

316

Rembrandt van Rijn, *The Scholar in His Study*, c. 1652, often known as *Faust in His Study*, was used as the frontispiece to *Faust: A Fragment* (1790), Goethe's first publication of scenes from Part 1.

Has passed through my door.
The beast just lies there grinning at me.
1295   I've not yet hurt him, evidently.
Wait! I can sing
A more powerful spell!
Are you from hell,
You fugitive thing?
1300   Then behold this Sign
Which they fear and know,
The black hosts below!
Now he swells up with bristling spine.
Vile reprobate!
1305   Do you read this name?
He who is nameless,
Uncreated, timeless,
In all worlds the same,
Pierced in impious hate?
1310   Behind the stove he shrinks from my spells;
Like an elephant he swells.

The whole room is filled by this devil-dog.
He wants to dissolve into a fog.
Do not rise to the ceiling, I forbid you!
1315 Lie down at your master's feet, I bid you!
You will see that I utter no idle warning;
With sacred fire I shall set you burning!
Do not dare the might
Of the Thrice-Effulgent Light![8]
1320 Do not dare the might
Of my strongest magic of all!

MEPHISTOPHELES [*stepping out from behind the stove as the mist disperses, dressed as a medieval wandering student*]:
Why all this fuss? How can I serve you, sir?

FAUST: So that was the quintessence of the cur!
A student-tramp! How very comical.

MEPHISTOPHELES: Sir, I salute your learning and your wit!
You made me sweat, I must admit.

FAUST: What is your name?

MEPHISTOPHELES: The question is absurd,
Surely, in one who seeks to know
The inmost essence, not the outward show,
1330 And has such deep contempt for the mere word.

FAUST: Ah, with such gentlemen as you
The name often conveys the essence too,
Clearly enough; we say Lord of the Flies,[9]
Destroyer, Liar—each most fittingly applies.
1335 Well then, who are you?

MEPHISTOPHELES: Part of that Power which would
Do evil constantly, and constantly does good.

FAUST: This riddle has, no doubt, some explanation.

MEPHISTOPHELES: I am the spirit of perpetual negation;
And rightly so, for all things that exist
1340 Deserve to perish, and would not be missed—
Much better it would be if nothing were
Brought into being. Thus, what you men call
Destruction, sin, evil in short, is all
My sphere, the element I most prefer.

FAUST: You seem complete and whole, yet say you are a part?

MEPHISTOPHELES: I speak the modest truth, I use no art.
Let foolish little human souls
Delude themselves that they are wholes.
I am part of that part which once, when all began,
1350 Was all there was; part of the Darkness before man
Whence light was born, proud light, which now makes futile war
To wrest from Night, its mother, what before
Was hers, her ancient place and space. For light depends

8. The sign of the Trinity.
9. Translates Beelzebub, a biblical name for the devil.

On the corporeal worlds—matter that sends
1355   Visible light out, stops light in its stride
And by reflected light is beautified.
So, light will not last long, I fear;
Matter shall be destroyed, and light shall disappear.

FAUST: Well! now I know your high vocation:
1360   Failing that grand annihilation
You try it on a smaller scale.

MEPHISTOPHELES: And frankly, I must own, here too I fail.
The Something, this coarse world, this mess,
Stands in the way of Nothingness,
1365   And despite all I've undertaken,
This solid lump cannot be shaken—
Storms, earthquakes, fire and flood assail the land
And sea, yet firmly as before they stand!
And as for that damned stuff, the brood of beasts and men,
1370   That too is indestructible, I've found;
I've buried millions—they're no sooner underground
Than new fresh blood will circulate again.
So it goes on; it drives me mad. The earth,
The air, the water, all give birth:
1375   It germinates a thousandfold,
In dry or wet, in hot or cold!
Fire is still mine, that element alone—
Without it, I could call no place my own.

FAUST: And so the ever-stirring, wholesome energy
1380   Of life is your arch-enemy;
So in cold rage you raise in vain
Your clenched satanic fist. Why, you
Strange son of chaos! think again,
And look for something else to do!

MEPHISTOPHELES: On such a point there's much to say;
We'll talk again another day.
This time I'll take my leave—if, by your leave, I may.

FAUST: Why not? We are acquainted now,
And you are welcome to come back
1390   And visit me some time, somehow.
Here is the window, there's the door;
I even have a chimney-stack.

MEPHISTOPHELES: I must confess that on the floor,
Across your threshold, you have put
1395   A certain obstacle—a witch's foot—

FAUST: You mean, that pentagram[1] I drew
Hinders a gentleman from hell?
Then how did you get in? Well, well!
How did I fool a sprite like you?

---

1. A five-pointed star.

MEPHISTOPHELES: It's not well drawn; look closely, sir!
                       One of the outside angles—there,
                       You see? the lines do not quite meet.

FAUST: How curious! how very neat!
              And so you are my prisoner.
1405   A lucky chance, I do declare!

MEPHISTOPHELES: The poodle skipped in without noticing,
                       But now it's quite another thing:
                       The Devil can't skip out again.

FAUST: Why don't you use the window, then?

MEPHISTOPHELES: Devils and spirits have a law, as you may know:
                       They must use the same route to come and go.
                       We enter as we please; leaving, we have no choice.

FAUST: So even hell has laws? Good; in that case
              One might conclude a pact with you
1415   Gentlemen, and a guaranteed one too?

MEPHISTOPHELES: Whatever is promised, you shall have your due,
                       There'll be no quibbling, no tergiversation.
                       But that all needs mature consideration;
                       We shall discuss it by and by.
1420   Meanwhile I must most earnestly
                       Repeat my plea to be released.

FAUST: Come, stay a little while at least,
              To edify me with your conversation.

MEPHISTOPHELES: Excuse me now: I soon will reappear
1425   And tell you anything you wish to hear.

FAUST: I did not pursue you, you know;
              You put your own head in the noose.
              Don't catch the Devil and let go,
              They say—it's harder when he's on the loose.

MEPHISTOPHELES: Very well, if you wish, I will remain
                       And help you while the time away;
                       But I insist you let me entertain
                       You with my arts in a befitting way.

FAUST: Certainly, you are welcome to do so;
1435   But you must make it an amusing show.

MEPHISTOPHELES: My friend, you shall in this one night,
                       In this one hour, know greater sensuous delight
                       Than in a whole monotonous year!
                       Delicate spirits now will bring
1440   You visions, and will charm your ear
                       With song; theirs is no empty conjuring.
                       Your palate also shall be sated,
                       Your nostrils sweetly stimulated,
                       Your sense of touch exhilarated.
1445   We are all ready, all are in
                       Our places—come, at once, begin!

SPIRITS:
          Vanish, you darkling

Vaults there above us!
Now let the sweeter
1450 Blue of the ether
Gaze in and love us!
Are not the darkling
Clouds disappearing?
Starlight is sparkling,
1455 Suns of a gentler
Brightness appearing.
Children of light dance
Past in their radiance,
Swaying, inclining,
1460 Hovering, shining:
Passionate yearning
Follows them burning.
And their long vesture
Streams out and flutters,
1465 Streams out and covers
Arbor and pasture,
Where lovers ponder
As they surrender
Each to each other.
1470 Arbor and bower,
Full fruit and flower!
Vines shed their burden
Into the winepress
Rich with their ripeness;
1475 Wines foam unending
In streams descending,
Through precious gleaming
Stones they are streaming,
Leaving behind them
1480 Heights that confined them,
Pleasantly winding
Round the surrounding
Hills and their verdure,
To lakes expanding.
1485 Birds drink their pleasure,
Soaring to sunlight,
Flying to far bright
Islands that shimmer,
Trembling, enticing,
1490 Where the waves glimmer,
Where echo answers
Songs of rejoicing
Shouted in chorus,
Where we see dancers
1495 Leaping before us
Out over green fields;

Over the green hills
Some of them climbing,
Some of them over
1500 Lake-waters swimming,
Some of them hover;
All seeking life, each
Seeking a distant star
Where love and beauty are
1505 Far beyond speech.

MEPHISTOPHELES: He sleeps! Well done, my airy cherubim!
How soon your lullaby enchanted him!
This concert puts me in your debt.
Faust, you are not the man to hold the Devil yet!
1510 Go on deluding him with sweet dream-shapes,
Plunge him into a sea where he escapes
Reality. As for this threshold, I know how
To split the spell: I need a rat's tooth now.
No need to conjure in this place for long!
1515 I hear them scuttling, soon they'll hear my song.

The master of all rats and mice,
All flies and frogs and bugs and lice,
Commands you to poke forth your snout
And gnaw this floor to let me out!
1520 I'll smear it for you with some drops
Of oil. Aha! see, out he hops!
Now set to work. The point where I was stuck
Is at the front here. What a piece of luck!
One little bite more and it's done.[2]—
1525 Now, Faust, until we meet again, dream on!

FAUST [*waking*]: Have I been twice deluded in one day?
The spirit-orgy vanishes: it seems
I merely saw the Devil in my dreams,
And had a dog that ran away!

from Faust's Study (2)

FAUST: A knock? Come in!—Who is this bothering me
Again?
MEPHISTOPHELES: I'm back!
FAUST: Come in!
MEPHISTOPHELES: You must say it three
Times over.
FAUST: Well, come in!
MEPHISTOPHELES [*entering*]: Well done!
I think we're going to get on
Together, you and I. To cheer

---

2. At Mephisto's command the rat gnaws a large enough hole in the pentagram for him to wiggle past.

1535   You up, I've come dressed as a cavalier:
In scarlet, with gold trimmings, cloak
Of good stiff silk, and in my hat
The usual cock's feather; take
A fine long pointed rapier,
1540   And one's complete. So, my dear sir,
Be ruled by me and do just that:
Wear clothes like mine, strike out, be free,
And learn what the good life can be.

FAUST: The earth's a prison—one can't get away
1545   From it, whatever clothes one wears.
I'm still too young to lack desires,
Not young enough now for mere play.
What satisfaction can life hold?
Do without, do without! That old
1550   Command pursues us down the years
Endlessly echoing in our ears—
The same old hoarse repeated song
Heard hour by hour our whole life long!
With each new dawn I wake aghast,
1555   My eyes with bitter tears are filled
To think that when this day has passed
I'll not have had one single wish fulfilled,
That even my presentiments of joy
Will die of nagging scruples, and life's mess
1560   Of trivial impediments destroy
My active soul's creativeness.
When the night falls, I seek my bed
With anxious fears, with many a sigh,
But find no peace: with sights of dread
1565   Wild dreams torment me as I lie.
And though a god lives in my heart,
Though all my powers waken at his word,
Though he can move my every inmost part—
Yet nothing in the outer world is stirred.
1570   Thus by existence tortured and oppressed
I crave for death, I long for rest.

MEPHISTOPHELES: And yet death never is a wholly welcome guest.

FAUST: Happy the man whom glorious death has crowned
With bloodstained victor's laurels, happy he
1575   Whose sudden sweet surcease is found
In some girl's arms, after wild revelry!
And I, who saw that mighty Spirit's power,
Why did I not expire with joy in that same hour!

MEPHISTOPHELES: And yet, in that same night, someone who mixed a brown
1580   Elixir did not drink it down.

FAUST: You seem to like eavesdropping.

MEPHISTOPHELES: I am not
Omniscient, but I know a lot.

FAUST: In that great turmoil and distress
        Sweet well-known echoing notes deceived
1585   My ear, old childhood joys relieved
        My homesick heart—this I confess.
        But now I curse all flattering spells
        That tempt our souls with consolation,
        All that beguilingly compels
1590   Us to endure earth's tribulation!
        A curse first on the high pretences
        Of our own intellectual pride!
        A curse on our deluded senses
        That keep life's surface beautified!
1595   A curse upon our dreams of fame,
        Of honor and a lasting name!
        A curse upon vain property,
        On wife and child and husbandry!
        A curse on Mammon,[3] when his gold
1600   Lures us to rash heroic deeds,
        Or when his easeful arms enfold
        Us softly, pampering all our needs!
        I curse the nectar of the grape,
        I curse love's sweet transcendent call,
1605   My curse on faith! My curse on hope!
        My curse on patience above all!

CHORUS OF INVISIBLE SPIRITS: Alas, alas,
        You have destroyed
        The beautiful world!
1610   At a blow of your clenched fist
        It falls, struck down
        By a demigod, it disappears.[4]

        Into the void
        We carry its fragments, with our tears
1615   We mourn
        The beauty that is lost.
        Mightiest
        Of the sons of earth,
        Let it be built anew
1620   More splendidly, let it come to birth
        Again, within you:
        Begin new
        Ways of living,
        With your mind clear,
1625   New light receiving,
        New music to hear.

---

3. The god of evil wealth.

4. Not a literal destruction (such as the baboon imagines at line 2406), but a metaphorical destruction of beauty through Faust's curse. The name Faust derives from the Latin for "blessed" (*faustus*); Goethe here puns on "Faust," the German word for fist.

MEPHISTOPHELES: My little sprites
        Are performing their rites:
        Full of wise exhortations
1630   And invitations
        To worlds unknown
        Of living and doing.
        Why sit here alone,
        They say, stifling and stewing?
1635   Stop playing with your misery,
        That gnaws your vitals like some carrion-bird!
        Even the worst human society
        Where you feel human, is to be preferred!
        I don't of course propose that we
1640   Should merely mingle with the common herd;
        I'm not exactly a grandee,
        But if you'd fancy getting through
        Your life in partnership with me,
        I shall with pleasure, without more ado,
1645   Wholly devote myself to you.
        You shall have my company,
        And if you are satisfied,
        I shall be your servant, always at your side!
FAUST: And what is your reward for this to be?
MEPHISTOPHELES: Long years will pass till we need think of that.
FAUST: No, no! The Devil has his tit-for-tat;
        He is an egoist, he'll not work for free,
        Merely to benefit humanity.
        State your conditions, make them plain and clear!
1655   Servants like you can cost one dear.
MEPHISTOPHELES: In this world I will bind myself to cater
        For all your whims, to serve and wait on you;
        When we meet in the next world, some time later,
        Wages in the same kind will then fall due.
FAUST: The next world? Well, that's no great matter;
        Here is a world for you to shatter—
        Smash this one first, then let the next be born!
        Out of this earth all my contentment springs,
        This sun shines on my sufferings;
1665   First wean me from all earthly things—
        What happens then's not my concern.
        That's something I've no wish to hear:
        Whether there's hatred still or love
        In that remote supernal sphere,
1670   And who's below and who's above.
MEPHISTOPHELES: Why, in that case, be bold and dare!
        Bind yourself to me, begin life anew:
        You soon will see what I can do.
        No man has ever known a spectacle so rare.
FAUST: Poor devil! What can you offer to me?

A mind like yours, how can it comprehend
A human spirit's high activity?
But have you food that leaves one still unsatisfied,
Quicksilver-gold that breaks up in
1680   One's very hands? Can you provide
A game that I can never win,
Procure a girl whose roving eye
Invites the next man even as I lie
In her embrace? A meteoric fame
1685   That fades as quickly as it came?
Show me the fruit that rots before it's plucked
And trees that change their foliage every day!

MEPHISTOPHELES: I shall perform as you instruct;
All these delights I can purvey.
1690   But there are times in life, my friend,
When one enjoys mere quiet satisfaction.

FAUST: If ever I lie down in sloth and base inaction,
Then let that moment be my end!
If by your false cajolery
1695   You lull me into self-sufficiency,
If any pleasure you can give
Deludes me, let me cease to live!
I offer you this wager!

MEPHISTOPHELES: Done!

FAUST: And done again!
If ever to the moment I shall say:
1700   Beautiful moment, do not pass away!
Then you may forge your chains to bind me,
Then I will put my life behind me,
Then let them hear my death-knell toll,
Then from your labors you'll be free,
1705   The clock may stop, the clock-hands fall,
And time come to an end for me!

MEPHISTOPHELES: We shall remember this; think well what you are doing.

FAUST: That is your right. This bet, which I may lose,
Is no bravado. I must be pursuing
1710   My purpose: once I stand still, I shall be
A slave—yours or no matter whose.

MEPHISTOPHELES: At the doctoral feast I shall display
My willing servitude to you this very day.
One small request—I am sure you'll understand;
1715   It's just in case—I'd like a line or two in your own hand.

FAUST: Poor pedant! Must it be in writing too?
Is a man's plighted word a thing unknown to you?
My spoken word must rule my life's whole course
For ever: is this not enough?
1720   The world streams on with headlong force,
And a promise arrests me. What strange stuff
Of dreams composes us! A pledge that binds

Is a thing rooted in our minds,
And we accept this. Happy is the man

1725 Of pure and constant heart, who can
Regret no choice, no loss! But parchments signed and sealed
Are ghosts that haunt and daunt us; the word dies
Upon the very pen we wield,
And wax and leather tyrannize

1730 Our lives. Well, devil, which is it to be:
Bronze, marble, parchment, paper? Answer me:
What pen, what tool, what chisel shall I use?
The medium is yours to choose!

MEPHISTOPHELES: Come, come, sir, this excited flood

1735 Of rhetoric's quite out of place.
The merest scrap of paper meets the case.
And—for your signature, a drop of blood.

FAUST: If that is all you want, I'll willingly go through
With such a farce to humor you.

MEPHISTOPHELES: Blood is a juice with curious properties.

FAUST: But you need have no fear that I will break
This bond. To strive with all my energies—
Just that is what I undertake.
I have been too puffed up with pride:

1745 I see now I belong beside
Merely the likes of you. With scorn
That mighty Spirit spurned me, Nature's door
Is closed, the thread of thought is torn,
Books sicken me, I'll learn no more.

1750 Now let us slake hot passions in
The depths of sweet and sensual sin!
Make me your magics—I'll not care to know
What lies behind their outward show.
Let us plunge into the rush of things,

1755 Of time and all its happenings!
And then let pleasure and distress,
Disappointment and success,
Succeed each other as they will;
Man cannot act if he is standing still.

MEPHISTOPHELES: Nothing shall limit you; if you wish, sir,
To sample every possible delight,
To snatch your pleasures in full flight,
Then let it be as you prefer.
Enjoy them boldly, grasp at what you want!

FAUST: I tell you, the mere pleasure's not the point!
To dizzying, painful joy I dedicate
Myself, to refreshing frustration, loving hate!
I've purged the lust for knowledge from my soul;
Now the full range of suffering it shall face,

1770 And in my inner self I will embrace
The experience allotted to the whole

Race of mankind; my mind shall grasp the heights
And depths, my heart know all their sorrows and delights.
Thus I'll expand myself, and their self I shall be,
1775 And perish in the end, like all humanity.

MEPHISTOPHELES: Oh, take my word for it, I who have chewed
For centuries on this stale food—
From birth to death a man may do his best,
But this old leavened lump he'll not digest!
1780 We do assure you, such totality
Is only for a god; perpetual light
Is God's alone, me and my kind
He has banished to darkness, and you'll find
You men must live with day and night.

FAUST: Yet I swear I'll achieve it!

MEPHISTOPHELES: Bravely said!
But there's a problem, I'm afraid;
For time is short, and art is long.[5]
Might I suggest you take along
With you some well-known poet? He will teach
1790 You many things: his thoughts will reach
Out far and wide, all sorts of virtues crown
Your noble head at his behest:
The courage of the lion,
The stag's velocity,
1795 The Italian's fiery zest,
The north's tenacity!
He'll find out for you how to mingle guile
With magnanimity, and while
You're still a young warm-blooded man,
1800 How to fall in love by a prearranged plan.
The result, I'm sure, would be well worth meeting;
"Mr. Microcosm!" shall be my respectful greeting.

FAUST: What am I then, if it's impossible
To win that crown of our humanity,
1805 To be what all my senses ache to be?

MEPHISTOPHELES: You are just what you are. Do what you will;
Wear wigs, full-bottomed, each with a million locks,
Stand up yards high on stilts or actor's socks—
You're what you are, you'll be the same man still.

FAUST: How uselessly I've laboured to collect
The treasures of the human intellect,
And now I sit and wonder what I've done.
I feel no new strength surging in my soul
I'm not a hairsbreadth taller, I'm not one
1815 Step nearer to the infinite goal.

5. The Christian devil Mephistopheles here quotes a classical adage.

MEPHISTOPHELES: My dear good sir, I fear your view
　　　　　　Of things is all too common in our day.
　　　　　　Revise it; and let's see what we can do
　　　　　　Before life's pleasures fleet away.
1820　　　　Confound it, man, one's hands and feet of course
　　　　　　Belong to one, so do one's head and arse!
　　　　　　But all the things that give me pleasure,
　　　　　　Are they not mine too, for good measure?
　　　　　　Suppose I keep six stallions, don't you see
1825　　　　The strength of each of them's a part of me?
　　　　　　What a fine fellow I have grown,
　　　　　　Trotting with twenty-four feet of my own!
　　　　　　So come, drop all this cogitation, stir
　　　　　　Yourself, explore the world with me. I say
1830　　　　A philosophic ponderer
　　　　　　Is like a poor beast led astray
　　　　　　By some malignant sprite, to graze on desert ground
　　　　　　When fine green grass is growing all around!
FAUST: How do we start?
MEPHISTOPHELES:　　　　　First we get out of here!
1835　　　　What sort of prison-hole is this? What mere
　　　　　　Shadow of life you live, when all you do
　　　　　　Just bores your pupils and bores you!
　　　　　　Let your fat colleagues take the strain!
　　　　　　Stop threshing empty straw! Why, even when
1840　　　　There's really something you could teach the poor lads, then
　　　　　　It's something you're forbidden to explain.
　　　　　　Ah, I hear one of them outside your door!
FAUST: I can't see any students now.
MEPHISTOPHELES: He's waited a long time, poor chap,
1845　　　　We'll have to comfort him somehow.
　　　　　　Come, let me have your gown and cap.
　　　　　　What a disguise! I'll look my best in it.

　　　[*He dresses up as Faust.*]

　　　　　　Now leave all this to me and to my native wit.
　　　　　　I'll only need a quarter of an hour.
1850　　　　Meanwhile, make ready for our great Grand Tour!

　　　[*Exit Faust.*]

MEPHISTOPHELES [*in Faust's long gown*]:
　　　　　　Scorn reason, despise learning, man's supreme
　　　　　　Powers and faculties; let your vain dream
　　　　　　Of magic arts be fortified with sweet
　　　　　　Flatteries by the Spirit of Deceit,
1855　　　　And you're mine, signature or none!—
　　　　　　Fate has endowed him with the blind
　　　　　　Impatience of an ever-striving mind;
　　　　　　In headlong haste it drives him on,

He skips the earth and leaves its joys behind.

1860 I'll drag him through life's wastes, through every kind
Of meaningless banality;
He'll struggle like a bird stuck fast, I'll bind
Him hand and foot; in his voracity
He'll cry in vain for food and drink, he'll find

1865 Them dangling out of reach—ah, yes!
Even without this devil's bond that he has signed
He's doomed to perish nonetheless![6]

* * *

A Witch's Kitchen

[*A low hearth with a large cauldron hanging over the fire. In the steam that rises
from it various apparitions are seen. A female baboon is sitting by the cauldron
skimming it, taking care not to let it run over. The male baboon with their young sits
nearby warming himself. The walls and ceiling are decorated with strange witch-
paraphernalia. Faust and Mephistopheles enter.*]

FAUST: I'm sick of all this crazy magic stuff!
Is this your vaunted therapy,
This mess of raving mad absurdity?

2340 Advice from an old witch! Am I to slough
Off thirty years, become as good as new,
By swallowing her stinking brew?
God help me now, if that's the best
Hope you can offer! Has man's mind

2345 Devised no other method, can we find
No nobler balm in Nature's treasure-chest?

MEPHISTOPHELES: You're talking sense again now, my dear sir!
There is another means to your rejuvenation,
But it's a very different operation;

2350 I doubt if it's what you'd prefer.

FAUST: I wish to know it.

MEPHISTOPHELES: Very well;
You'll need no fee, no doctor and no spell.
Go out onto the land at once, begin
To dig and delve, be primitive

2355 In body and mind, be bound within
Some altogether narrower sphere;
Eat food that's plain and simple, live
Like cattle with the cattle, humbly reap
The fields you have manured with your own dung;

2360 Believe me, that will make you young
And keep you young until your eightieth year!

6. In the omitted scenes Mephistopheles, impersonating Faust, makes fun of a newly arrived student, then sets out with
Faust on their adventures. They begin with the raucous low life of a Leipzig tavern, where Mephisto scares the drunken
patrons with fire, then deludes them with visions of happiness while he escapes with Faust, bringing him to visit a witch.

FAUST: I'm not used to all that; it's no good now
             Trying to learn the simple life. A spade
             Is something I could never use.
MEPHISTOPHELES: Then I'm afraid
2365   The witch will have to show us how.
FAUST: Why do we need this hag? Can't you
             Prepare the necessary brew?
MEPHISTOPHELES: The Devil's busy, sir! Why, I could build
             A thousand bridges by the time that stuff's distilled!
2370   I have the secret art, indeed,
             But not the patience I should need.
             Quiet laborious years must run their course;
             Time alone can ferment that subtle force.
             And there's a deal of ceremony
2375   To go with it—too weird for me.
             The Devil taught the witch her tricks,
             But she makes potions he can't mix.

         [*Seeing the animals.*]

             Why, look! what charming kith and kin!
             This is her manservant, that's her maid.

         [*To the animals.*]

2380   It seems your mistress is not in?
THE ANIMALS: Dining out!
             Up the chimney-spout!
             She's been delayed!
MEPHISTOPHELES: How long do her trips last, if I may be told?
THE ANIMALS: Till we leave the fire, till our paws get cold.
MEPHISTOPHELES [*to Faust*]:   Delightful creatures, don't you agree?
FAUST: I think they're dreary disgusting brutes.
MEPHISTOPHELES: Not at all; their conversation suits
             Me very well, as you can see.

         [*To the animals.*]

2390   So, what are you stirring there in that pot,
             You damnable apes? What mess have you got?
THE ANIMALS: It's charity soup, very light to digest.
MEPHISTOPHELES: I'm sure your public will be impressed.
THE MALE BABOON [*bounding up to Mephistopheles and coaxing him*]:
             O please, throw the dice!
2395   To be rich is so nice,
             It's so nice to be winning!
             Being poor isn't funny,
             And if I had money
             My head would stop spinning!
MEPHISTOPHELES: This monkey thinks a lucky thing to do
             Would be to play the lottery too!

[*Meanwhile the young baboons have been playing with a large globe, which they roll forward.*]

THE MALE BABOON: The world is this ball:
　　　　　　See it rise and fall
　　　　　　And roll round and round!
2405　　　　It's glass, it will break,
　　　　　　It's an empty fake—
　　　　　　Hear the hollow sound!
　　　　　　See it glow here and shine,
　　　　　　See it glitter so fine!
2410　　　　"I'm alive!" it sings.
　　　　　　O my son, beware of it,
　　　　　　Keep clear of it:
　　　　　　You must die, like all things!
　　　　　　It's made of clay;
2415　　　　Clay gets broken, they say.

MEPHISTOPHELES: What's the use of that sieve?

THE MALE BABOON [*lifting it down*]:   If you were a thief
　　　　　　I could tell straight away![7]

[*He scampers across to the female and makes her look through it.*]

　　　　　　Look through the sieve!
2420　　　　You can name the thief,
　　　　　　And you mustn't say.

MEPHISTOPHELES [*approaching the fire*]:   And what's this pot?

THE BABOONS: Poor ignorant sot!
　　　　　　Doesn't know why the pot,
2425　　　　Why the cauldron's there!

MEPHISTOPHELES: You insolent beast!

THE MALE BABOON: Take this whisk, at least,
　　　　　　And sit down in the chair!

[*He makes Mephistopheles sit down.*]

FAUST [*who in the meantime has been standing in front of a mirror, alternately moving towards it and backing away from it*]:
　　　　　　Oh, heavenly image! What is this I see
2430　　　　Appearing to me in this magic glass?
　　　　　　Love, carry me to where she dwells, alas,
　　　　　　Oh, lend the swiftest of your wings to me!
　　　　　　If I so much as move from this one spot,
　　　　　　If I dare to approach her, then she seems
2435　　　　To fade, I see her as in misty dreams!
　　　　　　The loveliest image of a woman! Is this not
　　　　　　Impossible, can woman be so fair?

7. A folk belief.

I see in that sweet body lying there
The quintessence of paradise! How can one
2440 Believe such things exist beneath the sun?
MEPHISTOPHELES: Well, if a god has worked hard for six days
And on the seventh gives himself high praise,
You'd think it would be reasonably well done!—
Look your fill at her now. I'll find
2445 A little darling for you of that kind;
Then you can try your luck. If you succeed
In winning her, you'll be a happy man indeed!

[*Faust keeps gazing into the mirror. Mephistopheles, lolling in the chair and playing with the whisk, goes on talking.*]

Well, here I sit, a king enthroned in state;
My sceptre's in my hand, my crown I still await.
THE ANIMALS [*who have been scampering about with each other in a bizarre fashion and now bring a crown for Mephistopheles, offering it to him with loud screeches*]:
Oh sir, be so good
As to mend this old crown
With sweat and with blood!

[*They handle the crown clumsily and break it into two pieces, which they then scamper about with.*]

Now it's done! It falls down!—
We can talk, see and hear,
2455 We can rhyme loud and clear!
FAUST [*gazing at the mirror*]:
Oh God! have I gone mad? I'm quite distraught!
MEPHISTOPHELES [*indicating the animals*]:
I think I'm going a bit crazy too.
THE ANIMALS: And when our rhymes fit
We're in luck: that's the thought,
2460 That's the meaning of it!
FAUST [*as above*]:   My heart's on fire, what shall I do?
Quick, let's leave now, let's get away!
MEPHISTOPHELES [*remaining seated, as above*]:
Well, one must certainly admit
These apes are honest poets, in their way!

[*The cauldron, which the female baboon has been neglecting, begins to boil over, and a great tongue of flame blazes up into the chimney. The witch comes down through the flame, screaming hideously.*]

THE WITCH: Ow! ow! ow! ow!
You damned brute, you damned filthy sow!
Not minding the pot! You've burnt me now,
You filthy brute!

[*Seeing Faust and Mephistopheles.*]

What's this here? Who
2470   The hell are you?
        Who let you in?
        What does this mean?
        May hell's hot pains
        Burn in your bones!

[*She plunges the skimming-ladle into the cauldron and splashes flames at Faust,
Mephistopheles, and the animals. The animals whine.*]

MEPHISTOPHELES [*reversing the whisk in his hand and striking out with the handle
        at the glasses and pots*]:
        Split! Split in two!
        That's spilt your stew!
        That's spoilt your cooking!
        I'm only joking,
        Hell-hag! You croon,
2480   I beat the tune!

[*The witch recoils in rage and terror.*]

        Do you know me now? Skinny, cadaverous bitch,
        Do you know your lord and master? Why don't I
        Smash you to pieces, tell me why,
        You and your ape-familiars? Must I teach
2485   You some respect for my red doublet? What
        Is this cock's feather, eh? My face,
        Have I been hiding it? You learn your place,
        Old hag! Am I to name myself or not?
THE WITCH: Oh master, pardon my rude greeting!
2490   But where's your cloven hoof, your horse's leg?
        And your two ravens? Sir, I beg
        To be excused!
MEPHISTOPHELES: Well, well, and so
        You are for once; it's true, I know,
        Some time has passed since our last meeting.
2495   Besides, civilization, which now licks
        Us all so smooth, has taught even the Devil tricks;
        The northern fiend's becoming a lost cause—
        Where are his horns these days, his tail, his claws?
        As for my foot, which I can't do without,
2500   People would think me odd to go about
        With that; and so, like some young gentlemen,
        I've worn false calves since God knows when.
THE WITCH [*capering about*]:   I'm crazy with excitement now I see
        Our young Lord Satan's back again!
MEPHISTOPHELES: Woman, don't use that name to me!
THE WITCH: Why, sir, what harm's it ever done?
MEPHISTOPHELES: The name has been a myth too long.
        Not that man's any better off—the Evil One
        They're rid of, evil is still going strong.

2510   Please call me "Baron," that will do.
         I'm just a gentleman, like others of my kind.
         My blood's entirely noble, you will find;
         My coat of arms may be inspected too.

    [*He makes an indecent gesture.*]

THE WITCH [*shrieking with laughter*]:   Ha! ha! You haven't changed a bit!
2515   Still the same bad lad, by the looks of it!
MEPHISTOPHELES [*to Faust*]:   Mark well, my dear sir! This is how
         One deals with witches.
THE WITCH: Tell me now,
         Gentlemen, what might be your pleasure?
MEPHISTOPHELES: A good glass of the you-know-what;
2520   But please, the oldest vintage you have got—
         Years give it strength in double measure.
THE WITCH: Certainly! I've a bottle on this shelf,
         I sometimes take a swig from it myself;
         By now it's even quite stopped stinking.
2525   A glass for you can well be spared.
         [*Aside.*] But as you know, it's not for casual drinking—
         This man will die of it unless he's been prepared.
MEPHISTOPHELES: No, it will do him good—he's a good friend
         Of ours, and I can safely recommend
2530   Your kitchen to him. Draw your circle, say
         Your spells, pour him a cup without delay!

    [*The witch, with strange gestures, draws a circle and places magic objects in it; as she does so the glasses and pots begin to ring and hum and make music. Finally she fetches a massive tome and puts the baboons in the circle, where they are made to act as a reading-desk for her and hold the torch. She beckons Faust to approach her.*]

FAUST [*to Mephistopheles*]:   Look, what use is all this to me?
         These crazy antics, all that stupid stuff,
         The woman's vulgar trickery—
2535   I know and hate them well enough!
MEPHISTOPHELES: Rubbish, man! Can't you see a joke?
         Don't be pedantic! You must understand,
         As a doctor she's got to hoke and poke
         If her medicine's to take effect as planned.

    [*He makes Faust step into the circle.*]

THE WITCH [*beginning to declaim from the book with great emphasis*]:

         Now hear and see!
         From one make ten,
         Take two, and then
         At once take three,
         And you are rich!
2545   Four doesn't score.
         But, says the witch,

From five and six
Make seven and eight;
That puts it straight.
2550 And nine is one,
And ten is none.
The witch's twice-times-table's done.
FAUST: She's obviously raving mad.
MEPHISTOPHELES: Oh, she has still much more to say!
2555 I know it well, the whole book reads that way.
It's cost me more time than I had.
A complete paradox, you see,
Fills fools and wise men with a sense of mystery.
My friend, the art's both new and old:
2560 Let error, not the truth be told—
Make one of three and three of one;
That's how it always has been done.
Thus to their heart's content they dogmatize,
Plague take the silly chattering crew!
2565 Men hear mere words, yet commonly surmise
Words must have intellectual content too.
THE WITCH [continuing]:
The lofty might
Of wisdom's light,
Hid from the vulgar throng:
2570 It costs no thought,
It's freely taught,
We know it all along!
FAUST: What rubbish is the crone repeating?
My head's half split by this entire
2575 Performance; it's like some massed choir
Of fifty thousand idiots bleating.
MEPHISTOPHELES: Enough, enough, excellent sibyl! Bring
Your cocktail, pour it, fill the cup
Right to the brim, quick, fill it up!
2580 This drink won't harm my friend, he knows a thing
Or two already; many a strong potation
He's swallowed during his initiation!

[The witch, with great ceremony, pours the potion into a cup; as Faust raises it to his lips it flames up a little.]

Come, down with it! Don't dither so!
Soon it will warm the cockles of your heart.
2585 You're practically the Devil's bedfellow,
And fire still makes you flinch and start!

[The witch opens the circle. Faust steps out of it.]

Let's go! You must keep moving now.
THE WITCH: I hope my potion whets your appetite!
MEPHISTOPHELES [to the Witch]: And if I can do you a good turn somehow,

2590   Just tell me on Walpurgis Night.[8]

THE WITCH: Here is a song, sir, you might like to sing;
      You'll find it has a special virtue in it.

MEPHISTOPHELES [*to Faust*]:   Do as I say, come, let's be off this minute;
      You must let yourself sweat, this thing
2595   Must soak right through your guts. Then you shall learn
      How to appreciate your noble leisure,
      And soon, to your consummate pleasure,
      Cupid[9] will stir in you, you'll feel him dance and burn.

FAUST: Let me look once more in the glass before we go—
2600   That woman's lovely shape entrances me.

MEPHISTOPHELES: No, no!
      Before you in the flesh you soon will see
      The very paragon of femininity.

      [*Aside.*] With that elixir coursing through him,
      Soon any woman will be Helen[1] to him.

***[2]

Evening

    [*A small well-kept room.*]

MARGARETA [*plaiting and binding up her hair*]:
      I'd like to find out, I must say,
      Who that gentleman was today.
2680   A handsome man, I do admit,
      And a nobleman by the looks of it.
      I could tell by something in his eyes.
      And he wouldn't have had the cheek otherwise.

    [*Exit. Mephistopheles and Faust enter.*]

MEPHISTOPHELES: Come in, keep quiet! Come, don't delay!

FAUST [*after a pause*]:   Leave me alone, please go away.

MEPHISTOPHELES [*taking a look round the room*]:
      Very neat and tidy, I must say. [*Exit.*]

FAUST [*gazing up and about him*]:
      Welcome, sweet twilight, shining dim all through
      This sanctuary! Now let love's sweet pain
      That lives on hope's refreshing dew
2690   Seize and consume my heart again!
      How this whole place breathes deep content
      And order and tranquillity!
      What riches in this poverty,
      What happiness in this imprisonment!

    [*He sinks into the leather armchair by the bed.*]

8. The night of April 30, when witches were supposed to engage in Satanic rituals on the Brocken, the highest peak of the Harz Mountains.

9. God of love.

1. Helen of Troy, famous for her fatal beauty.

2. Faust, transformed into a dashing youth, meets Margareta, a lower-class girl, and demands that Mephisto seduce her for him. (Later she is also called by her nickname Gretchen.)

2695 Oh let me rest here: long ago, among
Their joys and sorrows, others sat on you,
Embraced and welcomed! Ah, how often too
Round this, their grandsire's throne, the children clung!
My love herself, at Christmas time, a young
2700 Rosy-cheeked child, glad at some gift, knelt here
Perhaps, and kissed his wrinkled hand so dear!
What order, what completeness I am made
To sense in these surroundings! It is yours,
Dear girl, your native spirit that ensures
2705 Maternal daily care, the table neatly laid,
The crisp white sand strewn on the floors!
Oh godlike hand, by whose dear skill and love
This little hut matches the heavens above!
And here!

[*He draws aside a curtain from the bed.*]

What fierce joy seizes me! I could
2710 Stand gazing here for ever. Nature, you
Worked this sweet wonder, here the inborn angel grew
Through gentle dreams to womanhood.
Here the child lay, her tender heart
Full of warm life, here the pure love
2715 Of God's creative forces wove
His likeness by their sacred art!

And I! What purpose brings me? What
Profound emotion stirs me! What did I
Come here to do? Why do I sigh?
2720 Poor wretch! Am I now Faust or not?

Is there some magic hovering round me here?
I was resolved, my lust brooked no delay—
And now in dreams of love I wilt and melt away!
Are we mere playthings of the atmosphere?

2725 If she came in this instant, ah, my sweet,
How she would punish me! How small
The great Don Juan would feel, how he would fall
In tears of languor at her feet!

MEPHISTOPHELES [*entering*]:   Quick, she's down there, she'll be here any minute.

FAUST: Take me away! I'll never come again!

MEPHISTOPHELES: Here's quite a heavy box with nice things in it;
I got it—somewhere else. Now then,
Into her cupboard with it, quick, before we're seen.
I tell you, when she finds that stuff
2735 She'll go out of her mind; I've put enough
Jewelry in there to seduce a queen.
A child's a child, of course, and play's just play.

FAUST: I don't know if I should—

MEPHISTOPHELES: Now what's the fuss about?
You'd like to keep it for yourself, no doubt?
2740   Let me advise you then, Sir Lecher-Lust,
Stop wasting the fine time of day,
And spare me further tasks! I trust
You're not a miser too? I scratch my pate
And bite my nails and calculate—

[*He puts the jewel-case in the cupboard and locks it up again.*]

2745   Quick, we must go!—
How I'm to please your sweetheart for you
And make her want you and adore you;
And now you hesitate
As if this were your lecture-room
2750   Where in gray professorial gloom
Physics and metaphysics wait!
We must go! [*They leave.*]
MARGARETA [*coming in with a lamp*]:
It's so hot and sultry in here somehow,

[*She opens the window.*]

And yet it's quite cool outside just now.
2755   I've got a feeling something's wrong—
I hope my mother won't be long.
It's a sort of scare coming over me—
What a silly baby I must be!

[*She begins singing as she undresses.*]

There once was a king of Thule.[3]
2760   Of the far north land of old:
His dying lady he loved so truly
She gave him a cup of gold.

There was no thing so dear to the king,
And every time he wept
2765   As he drained that cup at each banqueting,
So truly his faith he kept.

And at last, they say, on his dying day
His kingdom was willed and told,
And his son and heir got all his share—
2770   But the king kept the cup of gold.

They feasted long with wine and song,
And there with his knights sat he,
In the ancestral hall, in his castle tall
On the cliffs high over the sea.

---

3. Ultima Thule was the ancient name for the far north.

2775 The old man still drank as his life's flame sank,
Then above the waves he stood,
And the sacred cup he raised it up,
Threw it down to the raging flood.

He watched it fall to the distant shore
2780 And sink in the waters deep;
And never a drop that king drank more,
For he'd closed his eyes to sleep.

[*She opens the cupboard to put her clothes in, and sees the jewel case.*]

However did this pretty box get here?
I left the cupboard locked; how very queer!
2785 Whatever can be in it? Perhaps my mother lent
Some money on it, and it's meant
As a security. Oh dear!
It's got a ribbon with a little key—
I think I'll open it, just to see!
2790 What's this? Oh God in heaven, just look!
I've never seen such things before!
These jewels would be what a princess wore
At the highest feast in the feast-day book!
I wonder how that necklace would suit me?
2795 Whose can these wonderful things be?

[*She puts on some of the jewelry and looks at herself in the glass.*]

If even the earrings were only mine!
My, what a difference it makes!
We young girls have to learn, it takes
More than just beauty; that's all very fine,
2800 But everyone just says "she's pretty,"
And they seem to say it out of pity.
Gold's all they care
About, gold's wanted everywhere;
For us poor folk there's none to spare.

A Promenade

[*Faust walking up and down deep in thought. Enter Mephistopheles.*]

MEPHISTOPHELES: By the pangs of despised love! By the fires of hell!
I wish I knew something worse, to curse it as well!
FAUST: Whatever's the matter? You do look odd
What a sour face for a fine day!
MEPHISTOPHELES: May the devil take me, I would say,
2810 If I weren't the Devil myself, by God.
FAUST: Are you right in the head? Excuse me if I smile;
These rages aren't your usual style.
MEPHISTOPHELES: Just think: those jewels for Gretchen that I got,
A priest has been and swiped the lot!—

FAUST, I. A PROMENADE

2815   Her mother took one look, and hey!
        She had the horrors straight away.
        That woman's got a good nose all right,
        Snuffling her prayer-book day and night,
        With any commodity she can tell
2820   Profane from sacred by the smell:
        And as for those jewels, she knew soon enough
        There was something unholy about that stuff.
        "My child," she exclaimed, ill-gotten wealth
        Poisons one's spiritual health.
2825   To God's blessed Mother it must be given,
        And she will reward us with manna from heaven!
        How Meg's face fell, poor little minx!
        It's a gift-horse after all, she thinks,
        And whoever so kindly brought it—how can
2830   There be anything godless about such a man?
        Ma sends for the priest, and he, by glory!
        Has no sooner heard their little story
        And studied the spoils with great delight,
        Than he says: "Dear ladies, you are quite right!
2835   Who resists the tempter shall gain a crown.
        The Church can digest all manner of meat,
        It's never been known to over-eat
        Although it has gulped whole empires down;
        Holy Church's stomach alone can take
2840   Ill-gotten goods without stomach-ache!"
FAUST: It's common; many a king and Jew
        Has a well-filled belly of that kind too.
MEPHISTOPHELES: So he sweeps every ring and chain and brooch,
        As if they were peanuts, into his pouch:
2845   Takes it no less for granted, indeed,
        Than if it were all just chickenfeed—
        Promises them celestial reward
        And leaves them thanking the blessed Lord.
FAUST: And Gretchen?
MEPHISTOPHELES: Sitting there all of a dither,
2850   Doesn't know what to do or why or whether.
        Can't get the jewels out of her mind—
        Or the gentleman who had been so kind.
FAUST: I can't bear my darling to be sad.
        Get another lot for her! The ones she had
2855   Weren't all that remarkable anyway.
MEPHISTOPHELES: Oh indeed, for my lord it's mere child's play!
FAUST: Do as I tell you!—And one thing more:
        Get to know that friend of hers next door!
        Do something, devil, stir your feet!
2860   And get some more jewels for my sweet!
MEPHISTOPHELES: With pleasure, sir, whatever you say.

341

[Exit Faust.]

> He's just like all the lovesick fools I know;
> To please their darlings they would blow
> The sun and moon and stars out at one go. *[Exit.]*

The Neighbor's House

MARTHA [*alone*]:   My husband, may God pardon him!
> He didn't treat me right. For shame!
> Just went off into the world one day.
> Left me a grass widow, as they say.
> Yet I've never done him any wrong;
2870 I loved him truly all along. [*She weeps.*]
> He may even be dead. Oh, my poor heart bleeds!
> —A death certificate's what one needs.

[Enter Margareta]

MARGARETA: Martha!
MARTHA: Gretchen dear! What a face!
MARGARETA: Martha, I feel quite faint! There's been
2875 This second box—I found it in
> My cupboard there—an ebony case
> Of the grandest jewels you ever saw;
> Much richer than the one before!
MARTHA: Now this time you mustn't tell your mother,
2880 Or the priest'll get it, just like the other.
MARGARETA: Oh, look at this! Just look at this!
MARTHA [*trying out some of the jewels on her*]:
> Aren't you a lucky little miss!
MARGARETA: But I can't wear them in the street, or go
> To church and be seen in them, you know.[4]
MARTHA: Just come whenever you can to me,
> And put on your jewels secretly—
> Walk about in front of the looking-glass here,
> And we'll enjoy them together, my dear.
> Then when there's a feast-day or some occasion,
2890 Let people see one little thing, then another,
> A necklace at first, a pearl earring; your mother
> May not notice, or we'll make up some explanation.
MARGARETA: But all this jewelry—who can have brought it?
> I think there's something funny about it.

[There is a knock at the door.]

2895 Oh God, perhaps that's my mother!
MARTHA [*looking through the peep-hole*]:   No!

---

4. Clothing and ornamentation were regulated by law, according to the social rank of the wearer.

342

It's some gentleman I don't know—

Come in!

[*Enter Mephistopheles*]

MEPHISTOPHELES:　If I may make so bold!
　　　　　　　Forgive me, ladies; I'm looking for
　　　　　　　Frau Martha Schwertlein,[5] who lives here, I'm told.

[*He steps back respectfully on seeing Margareta*]

MARTHA:　That's me; how can I oblige you, sir?
MEPHISTOPHELES [*aside to her*]:　Now that I know you, that will do;
　　　　　　　You have a fine lady visiting you.
　　　　　　　Excuse my taking the liberty;
　　　　　　　I'll call again later when you're free.
MARTHA [*aloud*]:　Do you hear that, child! What a rigmarole!
　　　　　　　He takes you for a lady, bless your soul!
MARGARETA:　Oh sir, you're much too kind to me;
　　　　　　　I'm a poor young woman—this jewelry
　　　　　　　I'm trying on, it isn't mine.
MEPHISTOPHELES:　Why, it's not just the jewels that are fine;
　　　　　　　You have a manner, a look in your eyes.
　　　　　　　Then I may stay? What a pleasant surprise.
MARTHA:　Now, I'm sure your business is interesting—
MEPHISTOPHELES:　I hope you'll pardon the news I bring;
2915　　　I'm sorry to grieve you at our first meeting.
　　　　　　　Your husband is dead, and sends his greeting.
MARTHA:　What, dead? My true love! Alas the day!
　　　　　　　My husband's dead! I shall pass away!
MARGARETA:　Oh, don't despair, Frau Martha dear!
MEPHISTOPHELES:　Well, it's a sad tale you shall hear.
MARGARETA:　I hope I shall never love; I know
　　　　　　　It would kill me with grief to lose someone so.
MEPHISTOPHELES:　Joy and grief need each other, they can't be parted.
MARTHA:　Good sir, pray tell me how he died.
MEPHISTOPHELES:　In Padua, by St. Anthony's[6] side,
　　　　　　　There they interred your late departed,
　　　　　　　In a spot well suited, by God's grace,
　　　　　　　To be his last cool resting-place.
MARTHA:　And have you brought nothing else for me?
MEPHISTOPHELES:　Ah, yes: he requests you solemnly
　　　　　　　To have three hundred masses sung for his repose.
　　　　　　　For the rest, my hands are empty, I fear.
MARTHA:　What! No old medal, not a souvenir
　　　　　　　Or trinket any poor apprentice will lay by,
2935　　　Stuffed in his satchel, and would rather die
　　　　　　　In penury than sell or lose?

---

5. "Schwertlein" means "little sword," an off-color joke.
6. St. Anthony of Padua, the patron saint of brides and wives.

MEPHISTOPHELES: I much regret it, ma'am; but truthfully,
          Your husband wasn't one to waste his property.
          And he rued his faults, but his luck he cursed—
2940   The second more bitterly than the first.
MARGARETA: Oh, why have people such ill luck! I'm sad for them.
          I promise to pray for him with many a requiem.
MEPHISTOPHELES: What a charming child you are! I'd say
          You deserve to be married straight away.
MARGARETA: Oh, I'm still too young, that wouldn't be right.
MEPHISTOPHELES: If a husband won't do, then a lover might.
          Why not? It's life's greatest blessing and pleasure
          To lie in the arms of so sweet a treasure.
MARGARETA: That's not the custom in this country, sir.
MEPHISTOPHELES: Custom or not, it does occur.
MARTHA: Tell me the rest!
MEPHISTOPHELES: I stood by his deathbed;
          It was pretty filthy, it must be said.
          But he died as a Christian, on half-rotten straw.
          His sins were absolved, though he felt he had many more.
2955   "I hate myself," he cried, "for what I've done;
          Away from my trade, away from my wife to run.
          I'm tormented by that memory.
          If only she could forgive me in this life!—"
MARTHA [weeping]:   Oh, he's long been forgiven by his loving wife!
MEPHISTOPHELES: "—But God knows, she was more to blame than me."
MARTHA: Why, that's a lie! What, lie at the point of death!
MEPHISTOPHELES: He was delirious at his last breath,
          If I am any judge of such events.
          "I had my time cut out," he said,
2965   "Providing her with children, then with bread—
          Which meant bread in the very widest sense.
          And then I got no peace to eat my share."
MARTHA: Had he forgotten all my faithful loving care,
          Slaving for him all day and night?
MEPHISTOPHELES: Why no, he had remembered that all right.
          He told me: "When we sailed away from Malta,
          For my wife and brats I said a fervent prayer,
          And by heaven's will, our luck began to alter:
          We took a Turkish ship and boarded her—
2975   The mighty Sultan's treasure-ship! We fought
          Them bravely and deserved our prize.
          And as for me, this bold adventure brought
          Me in a dividend of some size."
MARTHA: What's that? Where is it? Has he buried it?
MEPHISTOPHELES: Who knows now where the four winds carried it!
          He fell in with a lovely lady-friend
          In Naples, visiting the place for fun;
          And fun he got—the kindnesses she'd done,

They left their mark on him till his life's end.[7]

MARTHA: The scoundrel! Stealing his own children's bread!
    Not even want and poverty
    Could stop his vices and debauchery!

MEPHISTOPHELES: Well, there you are, you see; so now he's dead.
    If I were in your place, you know,
2990   I'd mourn him for a decent twelvemonth, then,
    Having looked round a little, choose another beau.

MARTHA: Oh dear, after my first, it will be hard
    To find a second man like him again!
    He was a jolly fellow—everyone enjoyed him;
2995   He just was far too fond of wandering abroad,
    And foreign women, foreign wine,
    And it was that damned gambling that destroyed him.

MEPHISTOPHELES: Well, I daresay it was a fine
    Arrangement, if for his part he
3000   Allowed you equal liberty.
    On such terms, I would hardly hesitate
    Myself to be your second mate.

MARTHA: Oh, sir, you like to have your little joke with me!

MEPHISTOPHELES [aside]:   While there's still time I'd best get out of here;
3005   She'd hold the Devil to his word, that's clear.

    [To Gretchen.]

    And you, my child, are you still fancy-free?

MARGARETA: I don't quite understand.

MEPHISTOPHELES [aside]:   Now there's sweet innocence!
    [Aloud.] Ladies, good day to you!

MARGARETA: Good day!

MARTHA: Sir, one more thing:
    I'd like to have some proper evidence—
3010   The details of my husband's death and burying.
    I've always liked things orderly and neat;
    I want to read it in the weekly notice-sheet.

MEPHISTOPHELES: Indeed, ma'am; when two witnesses agree,
    The truth's revealed infallibly.
3015   I have a companion; he and I
    Can go before the judge to testify.
    I'll bring him here.

MARTHA: Oh by all means do!

MEPHISTOPHELES: And this young miss will be here too?—
    He's a fine lad; seen the world all right;
3020   Very nice to ladies, very polite.

MARGARETA: I shall blush with shame to meet him, I fear.

MEPHISTOPHELES: You need blush before no king, my dear.

7. Syphilis was known as "the Naples disease."

MARTHA: I've a garden at the back; so, gentlemen.
          Please come this evening, we'll expect you then.

A Street

FAUST: Well, what news now? Is it going ahead?
MEPHISTOPHELES: Ah, bravo! So you're well alight!
          Gretchen will soon be in your bed.
          We're to meet her at her neighbour's house tonight.
          That Martha's a proper witch, good Lord,
3030   I couldn't have picked you a better bawd.
FAUST: Good.
MEPHISTOPHELES: But she asks a service of us too.
FAUST: That's fair enough; what do we have to do?
MEPHISTOPHELES: We swear a deposition, warranting
          That her late husband's bones now are
3035   Buried in hallowed ground in Padua.
FAUST: Brilliant; so first we have to travel there.
MEPHISTOPHELES: *Sancta simplicitas!*[8] Why should we care?
          Just testify; no need to make the visit.
FAUST: If that's your scheme, then I'll do no such thing.
MEPHISTOPHELES: Oh, holy Willie! That's your scruple, is it?
          So this is the first time in your career
          That you'll have borne false witness? Have you not
          Laid down authoritative definitions
          Of God and of the world, of all that's there and here,
3045   Man's mind and heart, his motives and conditions,
          With brazen confidence, with all the pride you've got?
          But pause to think—confess, as you draw breath:
          Of all those matters you knew not a jot
          More than of Martha Schwertlein's husband's death!
FAUST: You are, and always were, a sophist[9] and a liar.
MEPHISTOPHELES: And your standards of truth, I know, are so much higher.
          In all good faith, tomorrow, we shall find
          You turning little Gretchen's mind
          With vows of love, and nonsense of that kind.
FAUST: It will come from my heart.
MEPHISTOPHELES: A splendid vow!
          Eternal love, faithfulness to the end,
          Unique all-powerful passion—yes, my friend,
          That will come from the heart too, will it now?
FAUST: Yes! Let me be! It shall!—This deep commotion
3060   And turmoil in me, I would speak
          Its name, find words for this emotion—
          Through the whole world my soul and senses seek

---

8. Holy simplicity!
9. False reasoner.

The loftiest words for it: this flame
That burns me, it must have a name!
3065 And so I say: eternal, endless, endless—why,
You devil, do you call all that a lie?
MEPHISTOPHELES: I am right nonetheless.
FAUST: Listen to me—
And understand, before I burst a lung:
Insist on being right, and merely have a tongue,
3070 And right you'll be.
But now let's go, I'm sick of all this chatter.
And you are right; I've no choice in the matter.

A Garden

[*Margareta walking up and down with Faust, Martha with Mephistopheles.*]

MARGARETA: I'm quite ashamed, I feel you're being so kind
And condescending, just to spare
3075 My feelings, sir! A traveler
Must be polite, and take what he can find.
I know quite well that my poor conversation
Can't entertain a man of education.
FAUST: One look, one word from you—that entertains
3080 Me more than any this wise world contains.

[*He kisses her hand.*]

MARGARETA: Sir, you put yourself out! How can you kiss my hand?
It's so nasty and rough; I have to do
Such a lot of housework with it. If you knew
How fussy Mother is, you'd understand!

[*They pass on.*]

MARTHA: So, sir, you're always traveling, I believe?
MEPHISTOPHELES: Alas, constraints of duty and vocation!
Sometimes a place is very hard to leave—
But it's just not one's destination.
MARTHA: I dare say, when one's young and strong,
3090 It's good to roam the world and to be free;
But there are bad times coming before long,
And creeping to one's grave alone—oh, you'd be wrong
To be a bachelor then, sir, believe me!
MEPHISTOPHELES: I view with horror that approaching fate.
MARTHA: Then think again, while it's not yet too late!

[*They pass on.*]

MARGARETA: Yes, out of sight out of mind it will be!
And though you talk politely—after all,
You've many friends, and I'm sure they are all
More intellectual than me.

FAUST: My sweet, believe me, what's called intellect
Is often shallowness and vanity.

MARGARETA: How so?

FAUST: Oh, why can simple innocence not know
Itself, or humble lowliness respect
Its own great value, feel the awe that's due

3105   To generous Nature's dearest, greatest boon—

MARGARETA: You'll sometimes think of me, and then forget me soon;
But I'll have time enough to think of you.

FAUST: So you're alone a lot?

MARGARETA: Oh yes, you see, our household's not

3110   Big, but one has to see to it;
And we've no maid. I cook and sweep and knit
And sew, all day I'm on my feet.
And my mother insists everything's got
To be so neat!

3115   Not that she's really poor in any way,
In fact, we're better off than most folk, I should say.
We got some money when my father died,
A little house and garden just outside
The town. But mine's a quiet life now, that's true.

3120   My brother's a soldier, he's not here.
My little sister, she died too.
I had such trouble with her, the poor little dear,
And yet I'd gladly have it all again to do,
I loved her so.

FAUST: A darling, just like you.

MARGARETA: I brought her up: she got so fond of me.
She was born after Father's death, you see,
And Mother was so desperately ill then
We thought she never would be well again,
And she got better slowly, very gradually.

3130   She couldn't possibly, you know,
Give the baby her breast; and so
I had to feed her, all alone,
With milk and water; she became my own,
And in my arms and on my breast

3135   She smiled and wriggled and grew and grew.

FAUST: That must have been great happiness for you.

MARGARETA: But very hard as well, although I did my best.
At night she had her little cradle by
My bed; she'd hardly need to move, and I

3140   Was wide awake.
Then I would have to feed her, or else take
Her into bed with me, or if she went
On crying, I'd get up and jog her to and fro.
And then, the washing started at cock-crow;

3145   Then I would shop and cook. That's how I spent
The whole of every blessed day.

So you see, sir, it's not all play!
But you eat well, and you sleep well that way.

[*They pass on.*]

MARTHA: We women do have an unlucky fate!
3150   A confirmed bachelor's hard to educate.
MEPHISTOPHELES: I'm sure it takes a lady of your kind,
Madam, to make one change one's mind.
MARTHA: But tell me truly now, sir: have you never
Lost your hard heart to any woman ever?
MEPHISTOPHELES: One's own fireside, we are so often told,
And a good wife, are worth silver and gold.[1]
MARTHA: I'm asking: have you never felt the inclination—?
MEPHISTOPHELES: I've always been treated with great consideration.
MARTHA: I meant: have things not been serious at any time?
MEPHISTOPHELES: Trifling with ladies is a very serious crime.
MARTHA: Oh, you don't understand!
MEPHISTOPHELES: That grieves me, I confess!
But I do understand—your great obligingness.

[*They pass on.*]

FAUST: You knew me again, sweetheart, immediately,
Here in the garden? Is it really true?
MARGARETA: You saw me cast my eyes down, didn't you.
FAUST: And you've forgiven the liberty
I took outside the church, the insulting way
I spoke to you the other day?
MARGARETA: It was a shock—you see, it never had
3170   Happened before. No one ever says bad
Things of me, and I thought: did I somehow
Seem lacking in modesty to him just now?
He suddenly just thinks, quite without shame:
"I'll pick this girl up;" maybe I'm to blame?
3175   I must confess that something in my heart,
I don't know what, began quite soon to take your part;
In fact I got quite cross with myself, too,
For not being quite cross enough with you.
FAUST: Oh my sweet!
MARGARETA: Wait!

[*She picks a daisy and begins pulling off the petals one by one.*]

FAUST: What's this for? A bouquet?
MARGARETA: No!
FAUST: What?
MARGARETA: You'll laugh at me; it's just a game we play.

[*She murmurs as she picks off the petals.*]

1. Mephisto's proverbial wisdom partly derives from the Bible: "Who can find a virtuous woman? For her price is far above rubies" (Proverbs 31.10).

FAUST: What's this you're murmuring?
MARGARETA [half aloud]:   He loves me—loves me not
FAUST: You dear beloved little thing!
MARGARETA [continuing]:   Loves me—not—loves me—not—

[Pulling off the last petal and exclaiming with joy.]

He loves me!
FAUST: Yes, my love! The flower speaks,
3185   And let it be your oracle! He loves you:
           Do you know what that means? He loves you!

[He clasps both her hands in his.]

MARGARETA: I'm trembling all over!
FAUST: Don't be afraid! Oh, let my eyes,
           My hands on your hands tell you what
3190   No words can say:
           To give oneself entirely and to feel
           Ecstasy that must last for ever!
           For ever!—For its end would be despair.
           No, never-ending! Never-ending!

[Margareta presses his hands, frees herself and runs away. He stands lost in thought for a moment, then follows her. Martha enters with Mephistopheles]

MARTHA: It's getting dark.
MEPHISTOPHELES: Yes, and we must be gone.
MARTHA: I would gladly invite you to stay on,
           But this place has sharp eyes, and sharp tongues too.
           It's as if they all had nothing else to do,
           Day in, day out,
3200   But try to sniff their neighbors' business out.
           It's wicked! But one can't escape their talk.
           And our young pair?
MEPHISTOPHELES: Gone fluttering up that garden walk;
           Wild wayward butterflies!
MARTHA: He seems to have found
           His true love.
MEPHISTOPHELES: So has she. That's how the world goes round!

A Summerhouse

[Margareta runs in, hides behind the door, puts a fingertip to her lips and peeps through a crack.]

MARGARETA: He's coming!
FAUST [entering]:   Little rogue! I've caught you now,
           You tease! [He kisses her.]
MARGARETA [throwing her arms round him and returning his kiss]:
           Darling, I love you so. I can't say how!

[Mephistopheles knocks at the door.]

FAUST [stamping his foot]:   Who's there?

MEPHISTOPHELES:	A friend!
FAUST:	A beast!
MEPHISTOPHELES:	It's time to leave, I fear.

MARTHA [*entering*]:   Yes, sir, it's getting late.

FAUST: May I not escort you, then?

MARGARETA: My mother would—Goodbye!

FAUST: Then I must go, my dear?
          Goodbye!

MARTHA: Adieu!

MARGARETA: Till we soon meet again!

[*Faust and Mephistopheles leave.*]

      Oh goodness gracious, what a lot
      Of clever thoughts in his head he's got!
      I'm so ashamed, I just agree
      With all he says, poor silly me.
3215   I'm just a child and don't know a thing,
      How can he find me so interesting?

from A Forest Cavern

FAUST [*alone*]:   Oh sublime Spirit![2] You have given me,
      Given me all I asked for. From the fire
      You turned your face to me, and not in vain.
3220   You gave me Nature's splendor for my kingdom,
      And strength to grasp it with my heart. No mere
      Cold curious inspection was the privilege
      You granted me, but to gaze deep, as into
      The heart of a dear friend. Before my eyes,
3225   Opened by you, all living creatures move
      In sequence: in the quiet woods, the air,
      The water, now I recognize my brothers.
      And when the storm-struck forest roars and jars,
      When giant pines crash down, whose crushing fall
3230   Tears neighboring branches, neighboring tree-trunks with them,
      And drones like hollow thunder through the hills:
      Then in this cavern's refuge, where you lead me,
      You show me to myself, and my own heart's
      Profound mysterious wonders are disclosed.
3235   And when the pure moon lifts its soothing light
      As I look skywards, then from rocky cliffs
      And dewy thickets the ensilvered shapes
      Of a lost world, hovering there before me,
      Assuage the austere joy of my contemplation.
3240   Oh now I feel this truth, that for mankind
      No boon is perfect. To such happiness,

---

2. The Earth Spirit (lines 460–513).

Which brings me ever nearer to the gods,
You added a companion, who already
Is indispensable to me, although
3245   With one cold mocking breath he can degrade me
In my own eyes, and turn your gifts to nothing.
He stirs my heart into a burning fire
Of passion for that lovely woman's image.
Thus from my lust I stumble to fulfilment,
3250   And in fulfilment for more lust I languish.

                                        ***[3]

Gretchen's Room

[*Gretchen at her spinning-wheel, alone.*]

GRETCHEN: My heart's so heavy,
3375   My heart's so sore,
How can ever my heart
Be at peace any more?

How dead the whole world is,
How dark the day,
3380   How bitter my life is
Now he's away!

My poor head's troubled,
Oh what shall I do?
My poor mind's broken
3385   And torn in two.

My heart's so heavy,
My heart's so sore,
How can ever my heart
Be at peace any more?

3390   When I look from my window
It's him I must see;
I walk out wondering
Where can he be?

Oh his step so proud
3395   And his head so high
And the smile on his lips
And the spell of his eye,

And his voice, like a stream
Of magic it is,
3400   And his hand pressing mine
And his kiss, his kiss!

My heart's so heavy,
My heart's so sore,

---

3. In the omitted lines Faust complains to Mephisto that he is torn by pity for Gretchen.

3405 How can ever my heart
Be at peace any more?

My body's on fire
With wanting him so;
Oh when shall I hold him
And never let go

3410 And kiss him at last
As I long to do,
And swoon on his kisses
And die there too!

Martha's Garden

[*Margareta. Faust.*]

MARGARETA: Promise me, Heinrich.
FAUST: Whatever I can!
MARGARETA: Then tell me what you think about religion.
        I know you are a dear good man,
        But it means little to you, I imagine.
FAUST: My darling, let's not talk of that. You know
        I'd give my life for you, I love you so:
3420   I wouldn't want to take anyone's faith away.
MARGARETA: One must believe! That's not right what you say!
FAUST: Ah, must one?
MARGARETA: Oh, if only I could show you!
        You don't respect the holy Sacraments, do you?
FAUST: I do.
MARGARETA: But you don't want them! You don't go
3425   To Mass or to confession, that I know.
        Do you believe in God?
FAUST: My dear, how can
        Anyone dare to say: I believe in Him?
        Ask a priest how, ask a learned man,
        And all their answers merely seem
3430   To mock the questioner.
MARGARETA: Then you don't believe?
FAUST: My sweet beloved child, don't misconceive
        My meaning! Who dare say God's name?
        Who dares to claim
        That he believes in God?
3435   And whose heart is so dead
        That he has ever boldly said:
        No, I do not believe?
        Embracing all things,
        Holding all things in being,
3440   Does He not hold and keep
        You, me, even Himself?
        Is not the heavens' great vault up there on high,

And here below, does not the earth stand fast?
Do everlasting stars, gleaming with love,
3445 Not rise above us through the sky?
Are we not here and gazing eye to eye?
Does all this not besiege
Your mind and heart,
And weave in unseen visibility
3450 All round you its eternal mystery?
Oh, fill your heart right up with all of this,
And when you're brimming over with the bliss
Of such a feeling, call it what you like!
Call it joy, or your heart, or love, or God!
3455 I have no name for it. The feeling's all there is:
The name's mere noise and smoke—what does it do
But cloud the heavenly radiance?

MARGARETA: Well, I suppose all that makes sense;
I think the priest says something like that too—
3460 Just in the wording there's a difference.

FAUST: It is what all men say,
All human hearts under the blessed day
Speak the same message, each
In its own speech:
3465 May I not speak in mine?

MARGARETA: It sounds all very well, all very fine
But there's still something wrong about it,
For you're not a Christian, I truly doubt it!

FAUST: Sweetheart!

MARGARETA: It's always worried me
3470 To see you keep such company.

FAUST: What do you mean?

MARGARETA: That man you have with you—
I hate him, upon my soul I do!
It pierces me to the heart like a knife.
I've seen nothing so dreadful in all my life
3475 As that man's face and its ugly sneer.

FAUST: My poor child, why, there's nothing to fear!

MARGARETA: It's just that his presence offends me so!
I don't usually dislike people, you know!
And I'd gaze at you just as long as I can,
3480 But it makes my blood freeze to see that man—
And I think he's a scoundrel, anyway.
If I wrong him, God pardon what I say!

FAUST: Well, you know, some people just are rather odd.

MARGARETA: I wouldn't live with a man like that!
3485 As soon as he steps through the door, you can tell
You're being looked so mockingly at
And half fiercely as well;
And he cares for nothing, not man nor God.
It's as if he'd a mark on his brow that said

| 3490 | That he never has loved, that his heart is dead. |

That he never has loved, that his heart is dead.
Each time you put your arms round me
I'm yours so completely, so warm, so free!
But I close up inside at the sight of him.

FAUST: Dear fancy, sweet foreboding whim!

MARGARETA: It upsets me so much, each time I see
Him coming, that I even doubt
If I still love you, when he's about.
Besides, when he's there, I never could pray,
And that's what's eating my heart away.

3500 Dear Heinrich, tell me you feel the same way!

FAUST: You've just taken against him, and that's all.

MARGARETA: I must go home now.

FAUST: Oh, tell me whether
We can have some peaceful hour together,
Lie breast to breast and mingle soul with soul!

MARGARETA: Oh, if only I slept alone it would be all right,
I'd leave you my door unbolted tonight.
But my mother sleeps lightly, and if she
Were to wake up and catch us, oh goodness me,
I'd drop down dead on the very spot!

FAUST: My darling, there need be no such surprise.
Look, take this little flask I've got:
You must put just three drops in her drink
And into a sweet, sound sleep she'll sink.

MARGARETA: What would I not do for your sake!

3515 But she'll be all right again, she'll wake?

FAUST: Would I suggest it otherwise?

MARGARETA: I look at you, dear Heinrich, and somehow
My will is yours, it's not my own will now.
Already I've done so many things for you,

3520 There's—almost nothing left to do.

[*Exit. Enter Mephistopheles*]

MEPHISTOPHELES: Pert monkey! Has she gone?

FAUST: Still eavesdropping and spying?

MEPHISTOPHELES: I listened to it all most carefully.
The learned Doctor was catechized![4]
I hope he will find it edifying.

3525 Girls always check up, if they're well-advised,
On one's simple old-world piety;
Their theory is, if he swallows all
That stuff, he'll be at our beck and call.

FAUST: To your vile mind, of course, it's merely quaint

3530 That that dear loving soul, filled with her faith,
The only road to heaven that she knows,

---

4. Quizzed concerning his faith.

Should so torment herself, poor saint,
Thinking her lover's damned to everlasting death!

MEPHISTOPHELES: You supersensual sensual wooer,
3535   A pretty maid has led you by the nose.

FAUST: You misborn monster, spawn of fire and shit!

MEPHISTOPHELES: And physiognomy,[5] how well she's mastered it!
When I'm around she feels—just what, she's not quite sure;
My face, forsooth! conceals some runic spell;
3540   She guesses I'm a genius certainly,
Perhaps indeed the Devil as well.
So, it's to be tonight—?

FAUST: What's that to you?

MEPHISTOPHELES: I take a certain pleasure in it too!

At the Well

[Gretchen and Lieschen with water jugs.]

LIESCHEN: You've heard about Barbara, haven't you?

GRETCHEN: No; I hardly see anyone.

LIESCHEN: Well, it's true!
She's done it at last; Sybil told me today.
Made a fool of herself. That's always the way
With those airs and graces.

GRETCHEN: But what?

LIESCHEN: It stinks!
There's two to feed now when she eats and drinks!

GRETCHEN: Oh! . . .

LIESCHEN: And serve her right at last, I say.
Throwing herself at the lad for so long!
Always on his arm, always walking along,
Off to the villages, off to the dance;
3555   Oh, she had an eye to the main chance!
Such a beauty, of course, she must lead the way!
He courts her with pastries and wine every day;
She's even so shameless, the little minx,
That she can accept presents from him, she thinks!
3560   Cuddling and petting hour by hour—
Well, now she's lost her little flower!

GRETCHEN: Poor thing!

LIESCHEN: Don't tell me you're sorry for her!
Why, all the rest of us, there we were,
Spinning, our mothers not letting us out
3565   In the evenings, while she's sitting about
In dark doorways with her fancy man,
Lingering in alleys as long as they can!
Well, now she'll have her church penance to do,

---

5. The "science" of discerning character from the face.

And sit in her smock on the sinner's pew!

GRETCHEN: But surely he'll marry her now!

LIESCHEN: Not he!
    A smart boy like that, there are fish in the sea
    In plenty for him; he's not such a fool!
    Anyway, he's left.

GRETCHEN: That's wrong of him!

LIESCHEN: Well,
    If she gets him, she'll get the rest of it too.

3575   The boys'll snatch the flowers from her head,
    And we'll throw her none, just chopped straw instead![6] [*Exit.*]

GRETCHEN [*as she walks home*]:   What angry things I used to say
    When some poor girl had gone astray!
    I used to rack my brains to find
3580   Words to condemn sins of that kind;
    Blacker than black they seemed to be,
    And were still not black enough for me,
    And I crossed myself and made such a to-do—
    Now that sin of others is my sin too!
3585   Oh God! but all that made me do it
    Was good, such dear love drove me to it!

By a Shrine Inside the Town Wall

    [*An icon of the Mater Dolorosa stands in the above with vases of flowers in front of it. Gretchen puts fresh flowers into the vases, then prays.*]

GRETCHEN:
    O Virgin Mother, thou
    Who art full of sorrows, bow
    Thy face in mercy to my anguish now!

3590   O Lady standing by
    Thy Son to watch Him die,
    Thy heart is pierced to hear His bitter cry.

    Seeking the Father there
    Thy sighs rise through the air
3595   From his death-agony, from thy despair.

    Who else can know
    The pain that so
    Burns in my bones like fire from hell?
    How my wretched heart is bleeding,
3600   What it's dreading, what it's needing,
    Lady, only you can tell!

6. Traditional behavior when an unwed mother married.

Wherever I go, wherever,
It never stops, just never;
Oh how it hurts and aches!
3605 When I'm alone, I'm crying,
I cry as if I'm dying,
I cry as my heart breaks.

The flower-pots by my window
I watered with tears like dew
3610 When in the early morning
I picked these flowers for you.

The early sun was gleaming,
I sat up in my bed
My eyes already streaming
3615 As the new dawn turned red.
Help! Save me from shame and death!—O thou
Who art full of sorrows, thou
Most holy Virgin, bow
Thy face in mercy to my anguish now!

Night. The Street Outside Gretchen's Door

VALENTINE [*a soldier, Gretchen's brother*]:
I used to drink with the other chaps;
That's when one likes to boast. Perhaps
They'd start to sing their girl-friends' praises—
All lovely girls, like a ring of roses;
And round and round the full toasts went.
3625 I'd sit there calm and confident,
With my elbows on the table-top;
Sit there and stroke my beard meanwhile,
Wait for their blethering to stop,
Then fill my glass and with a smile
3630 I'd say: All honor where honor's due!
But in this whole land is there one girl who
Can compare with Meg, my sister so sweet,
One worthy to fasten the shoes to her feet?
Then clink! The toasts went round again,
3635 And some of the fellows exclaimed: he's right!
She's the pride of her sex, she's the heart's delight!
And the boasters and praisers sat silent then.
And now—what now?—Shall I tear my hair,
Shall I run up the walls?—I could despair.
3640 Every one of those blackguards now is free
To sneer and wrinkle his nose at me;
I must sweat, like a debtor who can't pay,
At each chance remark that drops my way!
Oh, yes! I could knock out their brains! But why?

3645   I still couldn't tell them they're telling a lie!
       Who's there? Who's sneaking to her door?
       There are two of them, if I know the score.
       If it's him, I'll take him while I can—
       He'll not leave here a living man!

   [*Enter Faust and Mephistopheles.*]

FAUST: Look, through the window of the sacristy
         The sanctuary lamp gleams up and glows,
         Yet to each side, how dim, how weak it shows,
         As darkness clusters round it! So in me
         Night falls and thickens in my heart.
MEPHISTOPHELES: Well, I could act a tom-cat's part,
         Slinking the streets to find a way
         Up to the rooftops where I'll play!
         I feel a healthy appetite
         For some thieving, some lechery tonight.
3660   Walpurgis, Night of the Wild Witching,[7]
         Is coming soon; already I'm twitching
         With expectation. Just you wait!
         One doesn't sleep through that fine date.
FAUST: Is that your buried gold that's rising now,[8]
3665   Back there? It blooms, it shines at us somehow!
MEPHISTOPHELES: Quite so; you soon will have the pleasure
         Of lifting out the pot of treasure.
         I took a squint into it too;
         Fine silver coins I've raised for you.
FAUST: Was there no jewelry you could find?
         My mistress loves those golden toys.
MEPHISTOPHELES: I did see something of the kind;
         A necklace. Pearls that are her eyes.[9]
FAUST: That's good; it makes me sad to go
3675   Without a gift to her, you know.
MEPHISTOPHELES: Come now, you should get used to ladies;
         Sometimes one enjoys their favors gratis.
         But look! The stars are in the sky,
         And being a gifted artist, I
3680   Will now sing her a moral song,
         To confuse her sense of right and wrong.

   [*He sings, accompanying himself on a zither.*]

         Who stands before
         Her sweetheart's door
         Once more, once more,

---

7. See note to line 2590.

8. In lines 2675–77 (omitted from our selection) Mephisto has implied that he will locate buried treasure to seduce Gretchen. There was a folk belief that buried treasure would shine at night.

9. This allusion to a famous song in Shakespeare's *Tempest* does not originate with Goethe but was added by the translator, in the spirit of the many other Shakespeare allusions in *Faust*.

3685 With early morning starting?
Poor Kate, beware!
You'll enter there
A maid so fair—
No maid you'll be departing!

3690 Men must have fun,
But when it's done
They'll up and run—
They're thieves, why should they linger?
Poor darlings all,
3695 Beware your fall:
Do nothing at all
Till you've got the ring on your finger!

VALENTINE: Who are you serenading here?
Damned ratcatcher![1] The devil take
3700 Your zither first; God's blood! I'll make
Him take the singer next, d'you hear?

MEPHISTOPHELES: The instrument's a write-off, I'm afraid.

VALENTINE: Now draw, and there'll be corpses made!

MEPHISTOPHELES: Doctor, don't back away! Now, quick!
3705 Keep close to me, move as I do.
Come on, out with your tickle-stick!
Now lunge! I'll parry him for you.

VALENTINE: Well, parry this one!

MEPHISTOPHELES: Certainly!

VALENTINE: And that!

MEPHISTOPHELES: Why not?

VALENTINE: The devil it must be!
3710 What fencing's this? I think my hand's gone lame.

MEPHISTOPHELES [*to Faust*]:   Strike now!

VALENTINE [*falling*]:   Oh God!

MEPHISTOPHELES: Now the poor lout is tame!
But now let's go! We must get out of here;
They'll start a hue and cry, and all that chatter.
The police I can deal with, but I fear
3715 The High Assize is quite another matter.[2]

[*Exit with Faust.*]

MARTHA [*at her window*]:   Come out! Come out!

GRETCHEN [*at her window*]:   Please, fetch a light!

MARTHA: They're cursing and shouting! There's a fight!

THE CROWD [*gathering*]:   There's someone dead, there's one!

MARTHA [*coming out of her house*]:   Where did the murderers run?

GRETCHEN [*coming out of her house*]:   Who's lying here?

THE CROWD: Your mother's son.

1. A triple allusion: (1) to Mephisto's self-description as a "tomcat" a few lines earlier, though Valentine cannot actually hear the conversation between Mephisto and Faust; (2) to the Pied Piper of Hamelin, subject of a ballad by Goethe; (3) to a line in Shakespeare's *Midsummer Night's Dream* (3.1.75) leading up to a deadly duel: "Tybalt, you ratcatcher, will you walk?"
2. The high court pronounced sentence in God's name, causing problems for Mephisto.

GRETCHEN: Oh God in heaven! What have they done!
VALENTINE: I'm dying; it's a thing soon said,
        And even sooner the thing's real.
        You women-folk, why weep and wail?
3725   Just hear me speak before I'm dead.

[*They all gather round him.*]

        Meg, listen: you're still a poor young chit,
        You've not yet got the hang of it,
        You're bungling things, d'you see?
        Just let me tell you in confidence:
3730   Since you're a whore now, have some sense
        And do it properly!
GRETCHEN: My brother! God! What do you mean?
VALENTINE: Leave God out of this little scene!
        What's done is done, I'm sorry to say,
3735   And things must go their usual way.
        You started in secret with one man;
        Soon others will come where he began,
        And when a dozen have joined the queue
        The whole town will be having you!

3740   Let me tell you about disgrace:
        It enters the world as a secret shame,
        Born in the dark without a name,
        With the hood of night about its face.
        It's something that you'll long to kill.
3745   But as it grows, it makes its way
        Even into the light of day;
        It's bigger, but it's ugly still!
        The filthier its face has grown,
        The more it must be seen and shown.

3750   There'll come a time, and this I know,
        All decent folk will abhor you so,
        You slut! That like a plague-infected
        Corpse you'll be shunned, you'll be rejected,
        They'll look at you and your heart will quail,
3755   Their eyes will all tell the same tale!
        You'll have no gold chains or jewelry then,
        Never stand in church by the altar again,
        Never have any pretty lace to wear
        At the dance, for you'll not be dancing there!
3760   Into some dark corner may you creep
        Among beggars and cripples to hide and weep;
        And let God forgive you as he may—
        But on earth be cursed till your dying day!
MARTHA: Commend your soul to God's mercy too!
3765   Will you die with blasphemy on you?
VALENTINE: Vile hag, vile bawd! If I could take

You by the skinny throat and shake
The life out of you, that alone,
For all my sins it would atone.

GRETCHEN: Oh, brother—how can I bear it—how—

VALENTINE: I tell you, tears won't mend things now.
When you and your honor came to part,
That's when you stabbed me to the heart.
I'll meet my Maker presently—
3775   As the soldier I'm still proud to be.

[*He dies.*]

A Cathedral

[*A Mass for the Dead. Organ and choral singing. Gretchen in a large congregation. An Evil Spirit behind Gretchen.*]

THE EVIL SPIRIT: How different things were for you, Gretchen,
When you were still all innocence,
Approaching that altar,
Lisping prayers from your little
3780   Worn prayer-book;
Your heart had nothing in it
But God and child's play!
Gretchen!
What are you thinking?
3785   What misdeed burdens
Your heart now? Are you praying
For your mother's soul, who by your doing
Overslept into long, long purgatorial pains?
Whose blood stains your doorstep?
3790   —And under your heart is there not
Something stirring, welling up already,
A foreboding presence,
Feared by you and by itself?

GRETCHEN: Oh God! Oh God!
3795   If I could get rid of these thoughts
That move across me and through me,
Against my will!

THE CHOIR: *Dies irae, dies illa*
Solvet saeclum in favilla.[3]

[*Organ.*]

THE EVIL SPIRIT: God's wrath seizes you!
The Last Trumpet scatters its sound!
The graves shudder open!
And your heart
That was at rest in its ashes
3805   Is resurrected in fear,

---

3. A Latin hymn, part of the Requiem Mass for the dead: "Day of wrath, that day / Shall dissolve the world into cinders."

Fanned again to the flames
Of its torment!

GRETCHEN: Let me get away from here!
It's as if the organ
3810 Were choking me
And the singing melting
The heart deep down in me!

THE CHOIR: *Judex ergo cum sedebit,*
Quidquid latet adparebit,
3815 *Nil inultum remanebit.*[4]

GRETCHEN: I can't breathe!
The great pillars
Are stifling me,
The vaulted roof
3820 Crushes me!—Give me air!

THE EVIL SPIRIT: Hide yourself! Sin and shame
Cannot be hidden,
Air? Light?
Woe on you!

THE CHOIR: *Quid sum miser tunc dicturus?*
Quem patronum rogaturus,
Cum vix justus sit securus?[5]

THE EVIL SPIRIT: Souls in bliss
Have turned their faces from you.
3830 They shrink from touching you,
For they are pure!
Woe!

THE CHOIR:
Quid sum miser tunc dicturus?

GRETCHEN: Neighbor! Your smelling-salts!

[*She faints.*]

***[6]

A Gloomy Day. Open Country.

[*Faust and Mephistopheles.*]

FAUST: In misery! In despair! Pitiably wandering about the country for so long, and
now a prisoner! Locked up in prison as a criminal and suffering such torment, the
sweet hapless creature! So this is what it has come to! This!—Vile treacherous
demon, and you told me nothing!—Yes, stand there, stand there and roll your
devilish eyes in fury! Stand and affront me by your unendurable presence! A
prisoner! In utter ruin, delivered over to evil spirits and the judgment of cold
heartless mankind! And meanwhile you lull me with vulgar diversions, hide
her growing plight from me and leave her helpless to her fate!

MEPHISTOPHELES: She is not the first.

4. "Thus when the judge sits, / everything hidden will be manifest / and nothing will remain unavenged."
5. "What am I, miserable, then to say? / What patron shall I call on? / When scarcely the just man is secure?"
6. Mephisto next leads Faust to the orgy at the Walpurgis Night (see note to line 2590). Faust is caught up in the wild
dancing until distracted by a vision of Gretchen.

FAUST: You dog! You repulsive monster! Oh infinite Spirit, change him back, change this reptile back into the form of a dog, the shape he used so often when it amused him to trot along ahead of me at night, suddenly rolling at the feet of innocent wayfarers and leaping on their backs as they fell! Change him back into his favorite shape, let him crawl before me in the sand on his belly, let me trample this reprobate under my feet!—Not the first!—Oh grief, grief that no human soul can grasp, to think that more than one creature has sunk to such depths of wretchedness, that the sins of all the others were not expiated even by the first, as it writhed in its death-agony before the eyes of the eternally merciful God! I am stricken to my life's very marrow by the misery of this one girl—and you calmly sneer at the fate of thousands!

MEPHISTOPHELES: Well, here we are again at the end of our wit's tether, the point where your poor human brains always snap! Why do you make common cause with us, if you can't stand the pace? Why try to fly if you've no head for heights? Did we force ourselves on you, or you on us?

FAUST: Stop baring your greedy fangs at me, it makes me sick!—Oh you great splendid Spirit, who deigned to appear to me, who know my heart and my soul, why did you chain me to this vile companion, who gorges his appetite on ruin and drinks refreshment from destruction?

MEPHISTOPHELES: Have you done talking?

FAUST: Save her! Or woe betide you! May the most hideous curse lie upon you for thousands of years!

MEPHISTOPHELES: I cannot loose the Avenger's bonds or open his bolts!—Save her!—Who was it who ruined her? I, or you?

[*Faust glares about him in speechless rage.*]

Are you snatching for the thunder? A good thing it was not given to you wretched mortals, to blast your adversary when he makes an innocent reply! That's the way of tyrants, venting their spleen when they're in an embarrassing pass.

FAUST: Take me to her! I'll have her set free!

MEPHISTOPHELES: And what of the risk you'll run? I tell you, on that town there lies blood-guilt by your hand. Over the grave of the man you killed there hover avenging spirits, waiting for the murderer to return.

FAUST: Must I hear that from you too? May the murder and death of a world come upon you, you monster! Take me to her, I tell you, and free her!

MEPHISTOPHELES: I will take you, and I will tell you what I can do. Have I all the power in heaven and earth? I will bemuse the jailer's senses, you can take his keys and bring her out with your own human hand! I'll keep watch, the magic horses will be ready, and I'll carry you both to safety. That I can do.

FAUST: Let's go at once!

Night. In Open Country.

[*Faust and Mephistopheles storming past on black horses.*]

FAUST: What's that moving around on the gallows-mound?

MEPHISTOPHELES: I don't know what they're doing and stewing.

FAUST: Up and down they hover, they stoop, they swoop.

MEPHISTOPHELES: A guild of witches!

FAUST: They're scattering something, it's a ritual deed.

MEPHISTOPHELES: Ride on! Ride on!

A Prison

FAUST [*with a bundle of keys and a lamp, by a small iron door*]:
　　That shudder comes again—how long a time
　　Since last I felt this grief for all man's woe!
　　She lies behind this cold, damp wall, I know;
　　And her loving heart's illusion was her crime.
　　Do I pause as I enter this place?
4410　Am I afraid to see her face?
　　Quick! She must die if I keep hesitating so.

[*He grasps the lock. Margareta's voice sings from inside.*]

MARGARETA:　Who killed me dead?
　　My mother, the whore!
　　Who ate my flesh?
4415　My father, for sure!
　　Little sister gathered
　　The bones he scattered;
　　In a cool, cool place they lie.
　　And then I became a birdie so fine,
4420　And away I fly—away I fly.
FAUST [*unlocking the door*]:
　　She doesn't know her lover's listening at the door,
　　Hearing the clank of chains, straw rustling on the floor.

[*He enters the cell.*]

MARGARETA [*hiding her face on her straw mattress*]:
　　Oh! Oh! They're coming! Bitter death!
FAUST [*softly*]:　Quiet! Quiet! I've come to set you free.
MARGARETA [*crawling towards his feet*]:　If you are human, then have pity on me!
FAUST:　You'll waken the jailers, speak under your breath!

[*He takes up her chains to unlock them.*]

MARGARETA [*on her knees*]:　Oh, hangman, who gave you this power
　　Over me? Who said
　　You could fetch me at this midnight hour?
4430　Have pity! Tomorrow morning I'll be dead,
　　Isn't that soon enough for you?

[*She stands up.*]

　　I'm still so young, still so young too!
　　And already I must die!
　　I was pretty too, and that's the reason why.
4435　My lover was with me, now he's far away.
　　They tore my garland off, and threw the flowers away.
　　Why are you clutching at me like this?
　　Oh spare me! What have I done amiss?
　　Let me live! Must I beg you, must I implore
4440　You in vain? I've never even seen you before!
FAUST:　How can I bear this any more!

MARGARETA: I'm in your power now, I'm ready to go.
          Just let me feed my baby first.
          I was cuddling it all last night, you know.
4445   They took it from me; that was just
          To hurt me. I killed it, is what they say.
          Now things will never be the same.
          They're wicked people: they sing songs against me!
          There's an old tale that ends that way—
4450   Who told them it meant me?

FAUST [*throwing himself at her feet*]:
          It's your lover, I'm here at your feet, I came
          To free you from this dreadful place!

MARGARETA [*kneeling down beside him*]:
          Oh, let's kneel, and call on the saints for grace!
          Look, under that stair,
4455   Under the door,
          Hell's boiling there!
          You can hear the voice
          Of his angry roar!

FAUST [*aloud*]:   Gretchen! Gretchen!

MARGARETA [*hearing her name*]:   That was my lover's voice!

          [*She jumps to her feet. Her chains fall off.*]

          Where is he? I heard him call to me.
          No one shall stop me, I am free!
          To his arms I'll fly,
          On his breast I'll lie!
4465   He stood and called "Gretchen"! I recognized him!
          Through the wailing and gnashing of Hell so grim,
          Through the Devil's rage, through his scorn and sneer,
          I knew it was his voice, so loving and dear!

FAUST: I am here!

MARGARETA: It is you! Oh, tell me once again!
          [*Embracing him.*] It's him! It's him! Where's all my suffering, then?
          Where are my chains, my prison and my fear?
          It's you! You've come to rescue me from here
          And I am saved!—
          I think it's here again, that street
4475   Where I first saw you; and by and by
          We're waiting again, Martha and I,
          In that lovely garden where we used to meet.

FAUST [*trying to leave with her*]:   Come! Come with me!

MARGARETA: Oh stay!
          I love being anywhere when you're not away!

          [*Caressing him.*]

FAUST: No, don't delay!
          Or we shall have to pay
          Most bitterly for this!

MARGARETA: What, you've forgotten so soon how to kiss?
              We're together again, my sweetest friend,
4485   And our kissing's come to an end?
              In your arms, why do I tremble so?
              A whole heaven used to close in on me,
              You spoke and you looked so lovingly;
              I was stifled with kisses, you'd never let go.
4490   Oh kiss me now!
              Or I'll show you how!

[*She embraces him.*]

              Oh! Your lips are dumb,
              They've nothing to say!
              Why has your love gone cold?
4495   Who can have come
              Between us to take it away?

[*She turns away from him.*]

FAUST: Come! Follow me! Darling, you must be bold!
          I'll hug you later on ten-thousandfold,
          Just follow me now! It's all I ask of you!
MARGARETA [*turning to him*]:   But is it you, can it be really true?
FAUST: It's me! Come!
MARGARETA: You undid my chains, they fell apart,
          And you will take me back to your heart.
          How is it you don't find me a vile thing?
          Do you really know, my dear, who you are rescuing?
FAUST: Come! Come! The deep night's giving way to dawn!
MARGARETA: My mother's dead; I poisoned her, you see.
          I drowned my child when it was born.
          Hadn't it been God's gift to you and me?
          To you as well—It is you! Can I trust
4510   This not to be a dream?
          Your hand! Your dear hand!—Ugh, but it's wet! You must
          Wipe off the blood! To me there seem
          To be bloodstains on it. Oh my God,
          What did you do!
4515   Put away your sword,
          I beg of you!
FAUST: Forget what happened, let it be!
          You are killing me.
MARGARETA: Oh no, you must survive!
          I'll tell you about the graves now, I'll describe
          Them to you. You must arrange all this,
          Tomorrow as ever is.
          You must choose the places. Mother must have the best,
          And my brother right next to her with his,
4525   And me a little further off—
          But not too far! Just far enough.

And my little baby at my right breast.
There'll be no one else to lie with me!—
When I clung to your side so tenderly,
4530 Oh, that was so blessed, a joy so sweet!
But I can't seem to do it now as I could;
When I come, I seem to be dragging my feet,
And you seem to be pushing me back somehow.
Yet it's still you, you're still gentle and good!

FAUST: If you feel that it's me, come with me now!

MARGARETA: Out there?

FAUST: Into freedom!

MARGARETA: If my grave's out there,
If death is waiting, come with me! No,
From here to my everlasting tomb
4540 And not one step further I'll go!—
You're leaving? Oh Heinrich, if only I could come!

FAUST: You can! Just want to! I've opened the door!

MARGARETA: I can't leave; for me there's no hope any more.
What's the use of escaping? They'll be watching for me.
4545 It's so wretched to have to beg one's way
Through life, and with a bad conscience too,
And to wander abroad; and if I do,
In the end they'll catch me anyway!

FAUST: I'll stay with you always!

MARGARETA: Quick, oh, quick!
Save your poor baby!
Just follow the path
Up the stream, uphill,
Over the bridge,
4555 The wood's just beyond;
In there, on the left, by the fence—
He's in the pond!
Oh, catch hold of him!
He's struggling still,
4560 He's trying to swim!
Save him! Save him!

FAUST: Oh, stop, stop! Think what it is you say!
Just one step, and we're on our way.

MARGARETA: Oh, quick, let's get to the other side
Of the hill! My mother sits on a stone
Up there—oh it's cold, I'm so terrified!—
My mother's sitting up there on a stone,
She's wagging her head, she's all alone,
Not beckoning, not nodding her poor heavy head;
4570 She slept so long that she'll never wake.
She slept so that we could be happy in bed!
Oh, those were good times, and no mistake.

FAUST: If persuasion's no use, if that's how it must be,
I'll have to carry you off with me.

MARGARETA: Don't touch me! Put me down! No, no!
              I'll not be compelled! Don't clutch me so!
              I was always willing, as well you know.
FAUST: The day's dawning! Oh sweetheart! Sweetheart!
MARGARETA: The day! Yes, it's day! The last day dawning!
              I thought it would be my wedding morning.
              Now you've been with Gretchen, don't tell anyone.
              Oh, my garland's spoilt!
              What's done is done!
              We'll meet later on;
4585   But I shan't be dancing.
              I can't hear them, but the crowd's advancing.
              There are so many there,
              The streets and the square
              Are all full; the bell tolls; they break the white rod.[7]
4590   Oh how they bind me and seize me, oh God!
              Now I'm on the execution-chair,
              And at every neck in this whole great throng
              The blade strikes when that sword is swung.
              The world lies silent as the grave.
FAUST: Oh why was I born, at such a cost!
MEPHISTOPHELES [*appearing outside the door*]:
              Come! One more moment and you're lost!
              What's all this dallying, parleying and dithering!
              My night-steeds are quivering,
              The sun's nearly risen.
MARGARETA: What's that? It came out of the floor of my prison!
              It's him! It's him! Send him away!
              He can't come! This place is sacred today!
              He wants me!
FAUST: You're to live!
MARGARETA: Oh my God, I await
4605   Your righteous judgment!
MEPHISTOPHELES [*to Faust*]:
              Come! Come! Or I'll leave
              You both to your fate!
MARGARETA: Oh Father, save me, do not reject me,
              I am yours! Oh holy angels, receive
              Me under your wings, surround me, protect me!—
              Heinrich! You frighten me.
MEPHISTOPHELES: She is condemned!
A VOICE [*from above*]:   She is redeemed!
MEPHISTOPHELES [*to Faust*]:   Come to me!

        [*He vanishes with Faust.*]

    [*Margareta's*] **VOICE** [*from the cell, dying away*]: Heinrich! Heinrich!

___

7. Sign of final condemnation.

For nearly two centuries, Nguyen Du has been seen as the greatest national poet in the modern history of Vietnam—a country that has repeatedly had to struggle to have an independent national existence at all. Ruled by China for a thousand years until the tenth century, Vietnam had been largely independent until Nguyen Du's time, but the old order was changing. A single dynasty, the Le, had ruled Vietnam for 350 years, but then a popular rebellion known as the Tay-son movement began in southern Vietnam in the early 1770s, and by 1789 the monarchy had fallen. Much as in France during the same years, a period of social upheaval followed—including modest redistribution of wealth from rich to poor. These upheavals ended in 1802 with the establishment of a new royal line, the Nguyen house. Not related to this new household, Nguyen Du was a loyalist of the deposed older dynasty, but like many other former Le officials, he reluctantly supported the new dynasty as an improvement over near anarchy. He served the new government in various capacities, including briefly as an ambassador to China.

His primary vocation, though, was as a lyric and narrative poet. Verse novels had become popular in Vietnam, often loosely based on Chinese prose narratives, and in the troubled years of revolution and dynastic struggle, Nguyen Du turned to a sixteenth-century novel called *The Tale of Chin, Yün, and Ch'iao.* Its author, Hsü Wei, had taken part in a campaign in China to suppress a revolt by a populist rebel named Tu Hai. Tu Hai proved too powerful for the Ming emperor to defeat directly, but Tu Hai had a favorite concubine named Wang Ts'ui-ch'iao (Vuong Thuy Kieu in the Chinese-inflected literary Vietnamese of Nguyen Du's day). She persuaded Tu Hai to surrender, whereupon the emperor had him murdered; Kieu then threw herself into a river. In the original version of the novel, she drowned, but Hsü Wei revised the story in a sequel and had her rescued and reunited with her family.

Nguyen Du took up this material and remade it into an extraordinary tale, focusing not on the rebel leader but on Kieu, whom he made into a picaresque heroine, a consummate survivor in a chaotic world. Sudden death and political violence first deprive Kieu of her betrothed and then force her into prostitution, followed by a series of abrupt reversals in fortune. All too trusting of the various shady characters who promise to help her, mourning her lost love yet also quite ready to fall in love again—and again—Kieu rises to every challenge and does what she must, aware that her sufferings play out faults in past lives recorded in the underworld Book of the Damned. Among her many talents, Kieu is presented as a superb poet, and her poetry gets her out of more than one tight situation. Kieu has long been understood as a stand-in for Nguyen Du himself, struggling to stay afloat—and to express himself—in a swiftly changing political situation. In this, Kieu can be compared to Byron's Don Juan and Pushkin's Eugene Onegin, poets' alter egos whose romantic misadventures provide the basis for a broad-based, tragicomic survey of European social and political upheavals in these same years.

Both Nguyen Du and his heroine came to symbolize Vietnam as a whole, though depending on the political needs of the moment, Kieu and her creator could be praised as survivors or excoriated as immoral and disloyal. The relevance of their story only increased as Vietnam lost its independence to France, becoming absorbed in the 1880s into colonial French Indochina, at which point the Vietnamese elite had to face the choice of cooperation or ostracism. Recurrent efforts for national liberation gained momentum during and after World War II. Drawn-out conflicts ensued, first with France and then between the Chinese-supported north and the American-supported south in the Vietnam War of 1965–1973. After a further period of civil conflict, an independent, united Vietnam was established by the communist government of Ho Chi Minh—himself a poet and someone who could quote long stretches of *The Tale of Kieu* from memory.

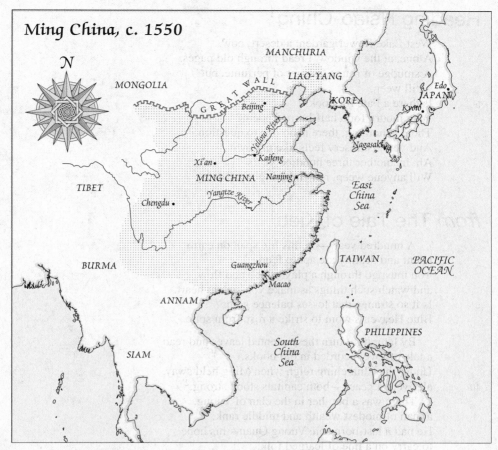

Ming China, c. 1550

N

MONGOLIA

MANCHURIA

LIAO-YANG

GREAT WALL

Beijing

KOREA

Edo
JAPAN

Kyoto

Yellow River

Nagasaki

Xi'an

Kaifeng

MING CHINA

Nanjing

TIBET

Yangtze River

Chengdu

East
China
Sea

BURMA

Guangzhou

Macao

TAIWAN

PACIFIC
OCEAN

ANNAM

South
China
Sea

PHILIPPINES

SIAM

Chinese characters in a Vietnamese fiction, Kieu's family lived in the capital, Beijing.

Nguyen Du's masterpiece continues to resonate on many levels. In addition to the direct political implications that can be drawn from the story, it has long served more generally as a model of the adaptation of classical themes to a modern context. Nguyen Du repeatedly refers to the Confucian classics and China's great T'ang dynasty poets, yet the old images and techniques serve decidedly new purposes, as Kieu fashions a path for herself from the dramatic beginning of the story to its surprising end, bending to circumstances without betraying her highest values, always refusing to take the expected way out. Nguyen Du gives rich and psychologically nuanced portrayals of Kieu, her family, friends, lovers, and her many scheming enemies, in a swift-paced and often humorous narrative that carries heroine and reader alike through shocking events in a disintegrating world.

PRONUNCIATIONS:

Nguyen Du: NWEN DOO
Hsian-Ching: SHAO-JING
Kieu: K'YOU
Ky Thuc: KEY TOOK
Tu Hai: TOO HIGH
Vuong Quan: VWONG KWAHN
Van: VAHN

Reading Hsiao-Ching[1]

West Lake flower garden: a desert, now.
Alone, at the window, I read through old pages.
A smudge of rouge, a scent of perfume, but
I still weep.
5   Is there a Fate for books?
Why mourn for a half-burned poem?
There is nothing, there is no one to question,
And yet this misery feels like my own.
Ah, in another three hundred years
10   Will anyone weep, remembering my Fate?

from The Tale of Kieu[1]

A hundred years—in this life span on earth
talent and destiny are apt to feud.
You must go through a play of ebb and flow
and watch such things as make you sick at heart.
5   Is it so strange that losses balance gains?
Blue Heaven's wont to strike a rose from spite.

By lamplight turn these scented leaves and read
a tale of love recorded in old books.
Under the Chia-ching reign when Ming held sway,
10   all lived at peace—both capitals stood strong.[2]
There was a burgher in the clan of Vuong.
a man of modest wealth and middle rank.
He had a last-born son, Vuong Quan—his hope
to carry on a line of learned folk.
15   Two daughters, beauties both, had come before:
Thúy Kieu was oldest, younger was Thuy Van.
Bodies like slim plum branches, snow-pure souls:
each her own self, each perfect in her way.
In quiet grace Van was beyond compare:
20   her face a moon, her eyebrows two full curves;
her smile a flower, her voice the song of jade;
her hair the sheen of clouds, her skin white snow.
Yet Kieu possessed a keener, deeper charm,
surpassing Van in talents and in looks.
25   Her eyes were autumn streams, her brows spring hills.
Flowers grudged her glamour, willows her fresh hue.
A glance or two from her, and kingdoms rocked!

---

1. Translated by Nguyen Ngoc Bich and Burton Raffel. A talented woman poet at the turn of the 17th century, Feng Hsiao-Ching was forced to become a concubine to a man whose primary wife isolated her. Hsiao-Ching died of grief, whereupon the vengeful first wife burned her manuscript; only a few poems survived.

1. Translated by Huynh Sanh Thong, from whom the following footnotes are adapted.

2. There were two capitals in Ming Dynasty China: Peking in the north (where Kieu's family lived) and Nanking in the south. The emperor Chia-ch'ing ruled from 1522–1566.

Supreme in looks, she had few peers in gifts.
By Heaven blessed with wit, she knew all skills:
30 she could write verse and paint, could sing and chant.
Of music she had mastered all five tones
and played the lute far better than Ai Chang.[3]
She had composed a song called *Cruel Fate*
to mourn all women in soul-rending strains.
35 A paragon of grace for womanhood,
she neared that time when maidens pinned their hair.[4]
She calmly lived behind drawn shades and drapes,
as wooers swarmed, unheeded, by the wall.

Swift swallows and spring days were shuttling by—
40 of ninety radiant ones three score had fled.
Young grass spread all its green to heaven's rim;
some blossoms marked pear branches with white dots.
Now came the Feast of Light in the third month[5]
with graveyard rites and junkets on the green.
45 As merry pilgrims flocked from near and far,
the sisters and their brother went for a stroll.
Fine men and beauteous women on parade:
a crush of clothes, a rush of wheels and steeds.
Folks clambered burial knolls to strew and burn
50 sham gold or paper coins, and ashes swirled.
Now, as the sun was dipping toward the west,
the youngsters started homeward, hand in hand.
With leisured steps they walked along a brook,
admiring here and there a pretty view.
55 The rivulet, babbling, curled and wound its course
under a bridge that spanned it farther down.
Beside the road a mound of earth loomed up
where withered weeds, half yellow and half green.
Kieu asked: "Now that the Feast of Light is on,
60 why is no incense burning for this grave?"
Vuong Quan told her this tale from first to last:
"She was a famous singer once, Dam Tien.
Renowned for looks and talents in her day,
she lacked not lovers jostling at her door.
65 But fate makes roses fragile—in mid-spring
off broke the flower that breathed forth heaven's scents.
From overseas a stranger came to woo
and win a girl whose name spread far and wide.
But when the lover's boat sailed into port,
70 he found the pin had snapped, the vase had crashed.[6]
A death-still silence filled the void, her room;

---

3. A famous classical lutist. The traditional Chinese scale has five tones.
4. Chinese girls would pin up their hair at age 15 as they reached marriageable age.
5. Spring festival when people visit graves and make offerings to the dead.
6. Chinese metaphors for the death of one's beloved.

all tracks of horse or wheels had blurred to moss.
He wept, full of a grief no words could tell:
'Harsh is the fate that has kept us apart!

75   Since in this life we are not meant to meet,
let me pledge you my troth for our next life.'
He purchased both a coffin and a hearse
and rested her in dust beneath this mound,
among the grass and flowers. For many moons,

80   who's come to tend a grave that no one claims?"
        A well of pity lay within Kieu's heart:
as soon as she had heard her tears burst forth.
"How sorrowful is women's lot!" she cried.
"We all partake of woe, our common fate.

85   Creator, why are you so mean and cruel,
blighting green days and fading rose-fresh cheeks?
Alive, she played the wife to all the world,
alas, to end down there without a man!
Where are they now who shared in her embrace?

90   Where are they now who lusted for her charms?
Since no one else gives her a glance, a thought,
I'll light some incense candles while I'm here.
I'll mark our chance encounter on the road—
perhaps, down by the Yellow Springs,[7] she'll know."

95   She prayed in mumbled tones, then she knelt down
to make a few low bows before the tomb.
Dusk gathered on a patch of wilted weeds—
reed tassels swayed as gently blew the breeze.
She pulled a pin out of her hair and graved

100   four lines of stop-short verse on a tree's bark.
Deeper and deeper sank her soul in trance—
all hushed, she tarried there and would not leave.
The cloud on her fair face grew darker yet:
as sorrow ebbed or flowed, tears dropped or streamed.

105   Van said: "My sister, you should be laughed at,
lavishing tears on one long dead and gone!"
"Since ages out of mind," retorted Kieu,
"harsh fate has cursed all women, sparing none.
As I see her lie there, it hurts to think

110   what will become of me in later days."
        "A fine speech you just made!" protested Quan.
"It jars the ears to hear you speak of her
and mean yourself. Dank air hangs heavy here—
day's failing, and there's still a long way home."

115   Kieu said: "When one who shines in talent dies,
the body passes on, the soul remains.
In her, perhaps, I've found a kindred heart:

7. The underworld.

let's wait and soon enough she may appear."
       Before they could respond to what Kieu said,
120   a whirlwind rose from nowhere, raged and raved.
It blustered, strewing buds and shaking trees
and scattering whiffs of perfume in the air.
They strode along the path the whirlwind took
and plainly saw fresh footprints on the moss.
125   They stared at one another, terror-struck.
"You've heard the prayer of my pure faith!" Kieu cried.
"As kindred hearts, we've joined each other here—
transcending life and death, soul sisters meet."
       Dam Tien had cared to manifest herself:
130   to what she'd written Kieu now added thanks.
A poet's feelings, rife with anguish, flowed:
she carved an old-style poem on the tree.[8]

       To leave or stay—they all were wavering still
when nearby rang the sound of harness bells.
135   They saw a youthful scholar come their way
astride a colt he rode with slackened rein.
He carried poems packing half his bag,
and tagging at his heels were some page boys.
His frisky horse's coat was dyed with snow.
140   His gown blent tints of grass and pale blue sky.
He spied them from afar, at once alit
and walked toward them to pay them his respects.
His figured slippers trod the green—the field
now sparkled like some jade-and-ruby grove.
145   Young Vuong stepped forth and greeted him he knew
while two shy maidens hid behind the flowers.
       He came from somewhere not so far away,
Kim Trong, a scion of the noblest stock.
Born into wealth and talent, he'd received
150   his wit from heaven, a scholar's trade from men.
Manner and mien set him above the crowd:
he studied books indoors, lived high abroad.
Since birth he'd always called this region home—
he and young Vuong were classmates at their school.
155   His neighbors' fame had spread and reached his ear:
two beauties locked in their Bronze Sparrow Tower![9]
But, as if hills and streams had barred the way,
he had long sighed and dreamt of them, in vain.
How lucky, in this season of new leaves,
160   to roam about and find his yearned-for flowers!
He caught a fleeting glimpse of both afar:
spring orchid, autumn mum—a gorgeous pair!

---

8. A free-form poem, better suited than the short quatrain to express a flood of feelings.
9. Two sisters over whom rival warlords fought in the third century.

Beautiful girl and talented young man—
what stirred their hearts their eyes still dared not say.
165   They hovered, rapture-bound, 'tween wake and dream:
they could not stay, nor would they soon depart.
The dusk of sunset prompted thoughts of gloom—
he left, and longingly she watched him go.
Below a stream flowed clear, and by the bridge
170   a twilit willow rustled threads of silk.

When Kieu got back behind her flowered drapes,
the sun had set, the curfew gong had rung.
Outside the window, squinting, peeped the moon—
gold spilled on waves, trees shadowed all the yard.
175   East drooped a red camellia, toward the next house:
as dewdrops fell, the spring branch bent and bowed.
Alone, in silence, she beheld the moon,
her heart a raveled coil of hopes and fears:
"Lower than that no person could be brought!
180   It's just a bauble then, the glittering life.
And who is he? Why did we chance to meet?
Does fate intend some tie between us two?"
Her bosom heaved in turmoil—she poured forth
a wondrous lyric fraught with all she felt.
185   The moonlight through the blinds was falling slant.
Leaning against the window, she drowsed off.
Now out of nowhere there appeared a girl
of worldly glamour joined to virgin grace:
face washed with dewdrops, body clad in snow,
190   and hovering feet, two golden lotus blooms.
With joy Kieu hailed the stranger, asking her:
"Did you stray here from that Peach Blossom Spring?"[1]
"We two are sister souls," the other said.
"Have you forgotten? We just met today!
195   My cold abode lies west of here, out there,
above a running brook, below a bridge.
By pity moved, you stooped to notice me
and strew on me poetic pearls and gems.
I showed them to our League Chief[2] and was told
200   your name is marked in the Book of the Damned.
We both reap what we sowed in our past lives:
of the same League, we ride the selfsame boat.
Well, ten new subjects our League Chief just set:
again please work your magic with a brush."
205   Kieu did as asked and wrote—with nymphic grace
her hand dashed off ten lyrics at one stroke.
Dam Tien read them and marveled to herself:

1. A hidden earthly paradise described in a famous prose-poem by the Chinese poet-recluse T'ao Ch'ien.
2. An underworld immortal, head of the League of Sorrow.

NGUYEN DU

376

"Rich-wrought embroidery from a heart of gold!
Included in the Book of Sorrow Songs,
210   they'll yield the palm to none but win first prize."
       The caller crossed the doorsill, turned to leave,
but Kieu would hold her back and talk some more.
A sudden gust of wind disturbed the blinds,
and Kieu awakened, knowing she had dreamed.
215   She looked, but nowhere could she see the girl,
though hints of perfume lingered here and there.

* * *

       How strange, the race of lovers! Try as you will,
you can't unsnarl their hearts' entangled threads.
245   Since Kim was back inside his book-lined walls,
he could not drive her from his haunted mind.
He drained the cup of gloom: it filled anew—
one day without her seemed three autumns long.
Silk curtains veiled her windows like dense clouds,
250   and toward the rose within he'd dream his way.
The moon kept waning, oil kept burning low:
his face yearned for her face, his heart her heart.
The study-room turned icy, metal-cold—
brushes lay dry, lute strings hung loose on frets.
255   Hsiang bamboo blinds stirred rustling in the wind—
incense roused longing, tea lacked love's sweet taste.
If fate did not mean them to join as mates,
why had the temptress come and teased his eyes?
Forlorn, he missed the scene, he missed the girl:
260   he rushed back where by chance the two had met.
A tract of land with grasses lush and green,
with waters crystal-clear he saw naught else.
The breeze at twilight stirred a mood of grief—
the reeds waved back and forth as if to taunt.

[*The love-smitten Kim rents a house next to Kieu's, and they talk across the wall between their gardens. When Kieu's parents go off to a family gathering, she throws caution to the wind and steals away to Kim's house, where she admires his paintings and he admires her poetry. Reluctantly, Kieu returns home at day's end.*]

       News of her folks she learned when she reached home:
430   her feasting parents would not soon be back.
She dropped silk curtains at the entrance door,
then crossed the garden in dark night, alone.
The moon through branches cast shapes bright or dark—
through curtains glimmered flickers of a lamp.
435   The student at his desk had nodded off,
reclining half awake and half asleep.
The girl's soft footsteps woke him from his drowse:
the moon was setting as she hovered near.

He wondered—was this Wu-hsia the fairy hill,[3]
440   where he was dreaming now a spring night's dream?
       "Along a lonesome, darkened path," she said,
"for love of you I found my way to you.
Now we stand face to face—but who can tell
we shan't wake up and learn it was a dream?"
445   He bowed and welcomed her, then he replaced
the candle and refilled the incense urn.
Both wrote a pledge of troth, and with a knife
they cut in two a lock of her long hair.
The stark bright moon was gazing from the skies
450   as with one voice both mouths pronounced the oath.
Their hearts' recesses they explored and probed,
etching their vow of union in their bones.
       Both sipped a nectar wine from cups of jade—
silks breathed their scents, the mirror glassed their selves.
455   "The breeze blows cool, the moon shines clear," he said,
"but in my heart still burns a thirst unquenched.
The pestle's yet to pound on the Blue Bridge[4]—
I fear my bold request might give offense."
She said: "By the red leaf, the crimson thread,
460   we're bound for life—our oath proves mutual faith.
Of love make not a sport, a dalliance,
and what would I begrudge you otherwise?"
He said: "You've won wide fame as lutanist:
like Chung Tzu-ch'i I've longed to hear you play."[5]
465   "It's no great art, my luting," answered she,
"but if you so command, I must submit."
In the back porch there hung his moon-shaped lute:
he hastened to present it in both hands,
at eyebrow's height. "My petty skill," she cried,
470   "is causing you more bother than it's worth!"
       By turns she touched the strings, both high and low,
to tune all four to five tones, then she played.
An air, *The Battlefield of Han and Ch'u,*
made one hear bronze and iron clash and clang.
475   The Ssu-ma tune, *A Phoenix Seeks His Mate,*[6]
sounded so sad, the moan of grief itself.
Here was Chi K'ang's famed masterpiece, *Kuang-ling*—
was it a stream that flowed, a cloud that roamed?
Crossing the Border-gate—here was Chao-chun,
480   half lonesome for her lord, half sick for home.

---

3. Home of a nymph who visited a Chinese king in a dream and made love to him.

4. In a folktale, a task that needed to be accomplished before a marriage would be allowed.

5. The only person who could fully appreciate the playing of the famed lute player Po Ya; when Chung died, Po cut the strings of his lute and played no more.

6. The ancient writer Ssu-ma Hsiang-ju won the heart of his beloved by playing this tune, leading her to elope with him against her father's wishes. Kieu next plays a tune by a famous recluse, then a song associated with a classical beauty, Wang Chao-chin, forced to marry a Tartar Khan against her wishes.

Clear notes like cries of egrets flying past;
dark tones like torrents tumbling in mid-course.
Andantes languid as a wafting breeze;
allegros rushing like a pouring rain.

485   The lamp now flared, now dimmed—and there he sat
hovering between sheer rapture and deep gloom.
He'd hug his knees or he'd hang down his head—
he'd feel his entrails wrenching, knit his brows.
"Indeed, a master's touch," he said at last,

490   "but it betrays such bitterness within!
Why do you choose to play those plaintive strains
which grieve your heart and sorrow other souls?"
"I'm settled in my nature," she replied.
"Who knows why Heaven makes one sad or gay?

495   But I shall mark your golden words, their truth,
and by degrees my temper may yet mend."

      A fragrant rose, she sparkled in full bloom,
bemused his eyes, and kindled his desire.
When waves of lust had seemed to sweep him off,

500   his wooing turned to wanton liberties.
      She said: "Treat not our love as just a game—
please stay away from me and let me speak.
What is a mere peach blossom that one should
fence off the garden, thwart the bluebird's quest?

505   But you've named me your bride—to serve her man,
she must place chastity above all else.
They play in mulberry groves along the P'u,[7]
but who would care for wenches of that ilk?
Are we to snatch the moment, pluck the fruit,

510   and in one sole day wreck a lifelong trust?
Let's ponder those love stories old and new—
what well-matched pair could equal Ts'ui and Chang?[8]
Yet passion's storms did topple stone and bronze:
she cloyed her lover humoring all his whims.

515   As wing to wing and limb to limb they lay,
contempt already lurked beside their hearts.
Under the western roof the two burned out
the incense of their vow, and love turned shame.
If I don't cast the shuttle in defense,[9]

520   we'll later blush for it—who'll bear the guilt?
Why force your wish on your shy flower so soon?
While I'm alive, you'll sometime get your due."
      The voice of sober reason gained his ear,
and tenfold his regard for her increased.

525   As silver paled along the eaves, they heard

7. The mulberry groves were favored for illicit meetings between lovers.
8. The most famous lovers in Chinese literature, from a semiautobiographical story by the T'ang poet Yuan Chen (779–831).
9. A girl hurled a shuttle at an unwanted suitor, breaking his teeth.

an urgent call from outside his front gate.
She ran back toward her chamber while young Kim
rushed out and crossed the yard where peaches bloomed.

530   The brushwood gate unbolted, there came in
a houseboy with a missive fresh from home.
It said Kim's uncle while abroad had died,
whose poor remains were now to be brought back.
To far Liao-yang, beyond the hills and streams,[1]
he'd go and lead the cortege, Father bade.

535   What he'd just learned astounded Kim—at once
he hurried to her house and broke the news.
In full detail he told her how a death,
striking his clan, would send him far away:
"We've scarcely seen each other—now we part.

540   We've had no chance to tie the marriage tie.
But it's still there, the moon that we swore by:
not face to face, we shall stay heart to heart.
A day will last three winters far from you:
my tangled knot of grief won't soon unknit.

545   Care for yourself, my gold, my jade, that I,
at the world's ends, may know some peace of mind."
       She heard him speak, her feelings in a snarl.
With broken words, she uttered what she thought:
"Why does he hate us so who spins silk threads?

550   Before we've joined in joy we part in grief.
Together we did swear a sacred oath:
my hair shall gray and wither, not my love.
What matter if I must wait months and years?
I'll think of my wayfaring man and grieve.

555   We've pledged to wed our hearts—I'll never leave
and play my lute aboard another's boat.
As long as hills and streams endure, come back,
remembering her who is with you today."
       They lingered hand in hand and could not part,

560   but now the sun stood plumb above the roof.
Step by slow step he tore himself away—
at each farewell their tears would fall in streams.
Horse saddled and bags tied in haste, he left:
they split their grief in half and parted ways.

565   Strange landscapes met his mournful eyes—on trees
cuckoos galore, at heaven's edge some geese.
Grieve for him who must bear through wind and rain
a heart more loaded down with love each day.

       There she remained, her back against the porch,

570   her feelings snarled like raveled skeins of silk.
Through window bars she gazed at mists beyond—

---

1. A region in Manchuria, several hundred miles away.

a washed-out rose, a willow gaunt and pale.
　　Distraught, she tarried walking back and forth
when from the birthday feast her folks returned.
575　Before they could trade news of health and such,
in burst a mob of bailiffs on all sides.
　　With cudgels under arm and swords in hand,
those fiends and monsters rushed around, berserk.
They cangued them both,[2] the old man, his young son—
580　one cruel rope trussed two dear beings up.
Then, like bluebottles buzzing through the house,
they smashed workbaskets, shattered looms to bits.
They grabbed all jewels, fineries, personal things,
scooping the household clean to fill greed's bag.
585　　From nowhere woe had struck—who'd caused it all?
Who'd somehow set the snare and sprung the trap?
Upon inquiry it was later learned
some knave who sold raw silk had brought a charge.
Fear gripped the household—cries of innocence
590　shook up the earth, injustice dimmed the clouds.
All day they groveled, begged, and prayed—deaf ears
would hear no plea, harsh hands would spare no blow.
A rope hung each from girders, by his heels—
rocks would have broken, let alone mere men.
595　Their faces spoke sheer pain and fright—this wrong
could they appeal to Heaven far away?
Lawmen behaved that day as is their wont,
wreaking dire havoc just for money's sake.

　　By what means could she save her flesh and blood?
600　When evil strikes, you bow to circumstance.
As you must weigh and choose between your love
and filial duty, which will turn the scale?
She put aside all vows of love and troth—
a child first pays the debts of birth and care.
605　Resolved on what to do, she said: "Hands off—
I'll sell myself and Father I'll redeem."
　　There was an elderly scrivener surnamed Chung,
a bureaucrat who somehow had a heart.
He witnessed how a daughter proved her love
610　and felt some secret pity for her plight.
Planning to pave this way and clear that path,
he reckoned they would need three hundred liang.
He'd have her kinsmen freed for now, bade her
provide the sum within two days or three.
615　　Pity the child, so young and so naïve—
misfortune, like a storm, swooped down on her.
To part from Kim meant sorrow, death in life—

2. A cangue is a wooden yoke, fastened around the neck of a criminal as a punishment.

would she still care for life, much less for love?
A raindrop does not brood on its poor fate;
620   a leaf of grass repays three months of spring.
         Matchmakers were advised of her intent—
brisk rumor spread the tidings near and far.

[*Kieu agrees to a hasty marriage to a middle-aged man named Scholar Ma, who pays off her debt to Chung. Before the wedding, Kieu instructs her younger sister, Van, to marry her beloved Kim in her place once he finally returns. Kieu then leaves, in tears, with Ma.*]

         A carriage, flower-decked, arrived outside
780   with flutes and lutes to bid dear kin part ways.
She grieved to go, they grieved to stay behind:
tears soaked stone steps as parting tugged their hearts.
         Across a twilit sky dragged sullen clouds—
grasses and branches drooped, all drenched with dew.
785   He led her to an inn and left her there
within four walls, a maiden in her spring.
The girl felt torn between dire dread and shame—
she'd sadly brood, her heart would ache and ache.
A rose divine lay fallen in vile hands,
790   once kept from sun or rain for someone's sake:
"If only I had known I'd sink so low,
I should have let my true love pluck my bud.
Because I fenced it well from the east wind,
I failed him then and make him suffer now.
795   When we're to meet again, what will be left
of my poor body here to give much hope?
If I indeed was born to float and drift,
how can a woman live with such a fate?"
         Upon the table lay a knife at hand—
800   she grabbed it, hid it wrapped inside her scarf:
"Yes, if and when the flood should reach my feet,
this knife may later help decide my life."
         The autumn night wore on, hour after hour—
alone, she mused, half wakeful, half asleep.
805   She did not know that Scholar Ma, the rogue,
had always patronized the haunts of lust.
The rake had hit a run of blackest luck:
in whoredom our whoremaster sought his bread.
         Now, in a brothel, languished one Dame Tu
810   whose wealth of charms was taxed by creeping age.
Mere hazard, undesigned, can bring things off:
sawdust and bitter melon met and merged.[3]
They pooled resources, opening a shop

---

3. Proverbial phrase for mutual cheating by two swindlers.

to sell their painted dolls all through the year.
815 Country and town they scoured for "concubines"
whom they would teach the trade of play and love.
  With Heaven lies your fortune, good or ill,
and woe will pick you if you're marked for woe.
Pity a small, frail bit of womankind,
820 a flower sold to board a peddler's boat.
She now was caught in all his bag of tricks:
a paltry bridal gift, some slapdash rites.
  He crowed within: "The flag has come to hand!
I view rare jade—it stirs my heart of gold!
825 The kingdom's queen of beauty! Heaven's scent!
One smile of hers is worth pure gold—it's true.
When she gets there, to pluck the maiden bud,
princes and gentlefolk will push and shove.
She'll bring at least three hundred liang, about
830 what I have paid—net profit after that.
A morsel dangles at my mouth—what God
serves up I crave, yet money hate to lose.
A heavenly peach within a mortal's grasp:
I'll bend the branch, pick it, and quench my thirst.
835 How many flower-fanciers on earth
can really tell one flower from the next?
Juice from pomegranate skin and cockscomb blood
will heal it up and lend the virgin look.
In dim half-light some yokel will be fooled:
840 she'll fetch that much, and not one penny less.
If my old broad finds out and makes a scene,
I'll take it like a man, down on my knees!
Besides, it's still a long, long way from home:
if I don't touch her, later she'll suspect."
845   Oh, shame! A pure camellia had to let
the bee explore and probe all ins and outs.
A storm of lust broke forth—it would not spare
the flawless jade, respect the pristine scent.
All this spring night was one bad dream—she woke
850 to lie alone beneath the nuptial torch.
Her tears of silent grief poured down like rain—
she hated him, she loathed herself as much:
"What breed is he, a creature foul and vile?
My body's now a blot on womanhood.
855 What hope is left to cherish after this?
A life that's come to this is life no more."
  By turns she cursed her fate, she moaned her lot.
She grabbed the knife and thought to kill herself.
She mulled it over: "If I were alone,
860 it wouldn't matter—I've two loved ones, though.
If trouble should develop afterwards,
an inquest might ensue and work their doom.

Perhaps my plight will ease with passing time.
Sooner or later, I'm to die just once."
865   While she kept tossing reasons back and forth,
a rooster shrilly crowed outside the wall.
The watchtower horn soon blared through morning mists,
so Ma gave orders, making haste to leave.
Oh, how it rends the heart, the parting hour,
870   when horse begins to trot and wheels to jolt!

She traveled far, far into the unknown.
Bridges stark white with frost, woods dark with clouds.
Reeds huddling close while blew the cold north wind:
an autumn sky for her and her alone.

[*Taken to a brothel in a distant town, Kieu stabs herself, but survives. She tries to escape but is caught and beaten, then forced to work as a prostitute. She does so for several months, with no hope of release.*]

1275   Now, as a brothel patron, came a man:
Ky Tam of the Thuc clan, a well-read breed.
He'd followed Father leaving Hsi in Ch'ang
to open at Lin-tzu a trading shop.
Kieu's fame as queen of beauty had reached him—
1280   he called and left his card in her boudoir.
Behind the tasseled drapes he faced the flower:
his fancy relished each of all her charms.
The young camellia, shimmering on its stem,
would glow still brighter with each fresh spring shower!
1285   Man and girl, girl and man in fevered clasp:
on a spring night, how can one quell the heart?
Of course, when two kin spirits meet, one tie
soon binds them in a knot none can yank loose.
They'd tryst and cling together night or day.
1290   What had begun as lust soon turned to love.
It chanced that, by a stroke of timely luck,
his father went away to journey home.
And more bewitched than ever, our young man
would often see his darling these spring days.
1295   On wind-swept balconies, in moon-washed yards,
they'd sip rare liquor, improvise linked verse.
With incense burned at dawn, with tea at noon,
they'd play chess games, perform duets on lutes.
One dizzy round of pleasures caught them both—
1300   they knew each other's moods, grew more attached.

[*Kieu has misgivings—young Thuc is married back home—but she agrees to let him ransom her from the brothel, and they begin living together. Kieu urges young Thuc to openly make her his concubine and tell his wife, but he fears his wife's jealousy and keeps putting it off.*]

As lovers joined their lives beneath one roof,
their love grew deeper, deeper than the sea.
Like fire and incense, mutual passion burned—
her jade-and-lotus beauty gleamed and glowed.

1385   For half a year they lived as intimates.
Now, in the courtyard, planes mixed gold with jade.
Along the hedge, frost-hardy mums peeped out.
And lo, the father came a-riding back.
He stormed and thundered in his towering wrath—
1390   filled with concern, he thought to split the pair.
Determined, he passed judgment straightaway:
in her old whorehouse he'd put back the whore.
The father's verdict was clear-cut, forthright—
yet, making bold, the son entreated him:
1395   "I know my many crimes—if thunderbolts
or hatchet blows strike me, I'll die content.
But now my hand has dipped in indigo:[4]
a fool grown wise still can't undo what's done.
Even if I had her for just one day,
1400   who'd hold a lute and then rip off its strings?
If you will not relent and grant me grace,
I'd rather lose my life than play her false."
Those stubborn words aroused the old man's bile,
so at the hall of law he lodged complaint.
1405   Over a peaceful earth the waves now surged—
the prefect sent a warrant for the pair.
They walked behind the sheriff, then at court
they fell upon their knees, still side by side.
They raised their eyes and saw an iron mask—
1410   the prefect, strutting power, spoke harsh words:
"Young wastrel, you have had your foolish fling—
and she, that slut, is nothing but a cheat.
A cast-off rose with all its scent gone stale,
she's put on rouge and powder, duping boors.
1415   To judge the state of things from his complaint,
it's out of joint with either one of you.
I shall uphold the law and try the case.
There are two paths—you're free to opt for which:
either I'll mete out punishment by the book
1420   or to the whorehouse I'll remand the whore."
"Once and for all my mind's made up!" she cried.
"The spider's web shall not catch me again.
Muddy or clear, it's still my life to live.
I shall endure the thunder of the law!"
1425   The judge declared: "The law be carried out!"
A peony in shackles, cuffs, and cangue.

4. An indelible dye.

Resigned, she dared not cry her innocence—
tears stained her cheeks and pain knit tight her brows.
Down on a floor of dust and mud, her face
1430   a tarnished glass, her frame a thin plum branch.
       Oh, poor young Thuc! Consider his sad plight:
he watched her from afar, his entrails torn.
"She suffers so because of me!" he moaned.
"Had I but listened, she'd be spared this wrong.
1435   How ever can a shallow mind think deep?
So now I've caused her all this grief and shame."
       The judge had overheard young Thuc's lament—
by pity moved, he asked for more details.
At once the lover sobbed his story out,
1440   recounting all she'd said when he proposed:
"She pondered what might happen, soon or late,
aware that she herself could come to this.
Because I chose to take it all in hand,
I've brought this woe on her—it's my own fault."
1445   The judge felt sorry when he heard those words—
he smoothed his brow and figured some way out.
"If what you've told me is the truth," he said,
"this harlot, after all, knows right from wrong."
"Though just a lowly woman," Thuc went on,
1450   "she's learned to ply the brush and scribble verse."
"But she must be perfection!" laughed the judge.
"Well, write a piece, The Cangue, and strut your art."
The girl complied—she raised the brush and wrote,
then laid the sheet of paper on his desk.
1455   "It tops the height of T'ang!" he cried in praise.[5]
"All gold on earth can't buy her gifts and charms.
The man of parts has met the woman fair:
a finer match could Chou and Ch'en have bred?
Let's put an end to all this fight and feud:
1460   why sow discord and break a love duet?
When people come before a court of law,
inside the rules of justice mercy dwells.
Your son's own mate belongs within your clan:
forget your own displeasure and forgive."
1465   A wedding he decreed—wind-borne, took off
the bridal carriage, torches raced the stars.
A band of piping flutes and throbbing drums
led bride and groom to their connubial niche.
Old Thuc admired her virtues, prized her gifts—
1470   from him no more harsh word or stormy scene.
Lilies and orchids bathed their home in scents
as bitter sorrow turned to sweeter love.

---

5. The T'ang dynasty (618–906) was the peak period of Chinese poetry.

Time flew amidst delights of wine or chess:
peach red had waned, now lotus green would wax.
1475 Behind their curtains, on a silent night,
she felt misgivings, told him what she felt:
"Since this frail girl found her support in you,
geese followed swallows—almost gone, a year.
Yet not a day's brought news from your own home.
1480 With your new bride, you've cooled toward your old mate.
It seems, upon reflection, rather odd:
from talk and gossip who could have saved us?
The mistress of your household—so I've heard—
does what is proper, says what is correct.
1485 Oh, how I dread all such uncommon souls!
It's hard to plumb the ocean's pits and depths.
We've lived together for these full twelve months—
from her we could not have concealed the fact.
If for so long you've got no news of her,
1490 then something must be brewing in that hush.
Now go back home immediately, I beg you:
you'll please her and we'll know what's in her mind.
If you drag out this game of hide-and-seek
and put off telling her, it just won't work."
1495 He heard those words of counsel, said with calm,
and braced himself to think of going home.
Next day he spoke to Father of his plans—
the old man, too, urged him to make the trip.

* * *

Why tell what our wayfaring man went through?
Let's talk about the mistress of his hearth.
Known as Miss Hoan, she wore a great clan name:
1530 her father ruled the Civil Office Board.
On happy winds of chance Thuc had met her,
and they had tied the nuptial knot long since.
Living above reproach, Miss Hoan could wield
the surest hand in catching one at fault.
1535 His garden boasted now a fresh-blown rose—
so she had heard from every mouth but his.
The fire of wrath kept smoldering in her breast
against the knave whose fickle heart had roamed:
"If only he'd confessed, told me the truth,
1540 I might have favored her with my good grace.
I'd be a fool to lose my stately calm
and gain the stigma of a jealous shrew.
But he's thought fit to pull his boyish prank
and hide his open secret—what a farce!
1545 He's fancied distance keeps me unaware.
Let's hide and seek—I too shall play his game.
I entertain no worry on this score:
the ant's inside the cup—where can it crawl?

1550   I'll make them loathe and shun each other's sight.
I'll crush her so she cannot rear her head.
I'll rub the spectacle in his bare face
and make the traitor feel my iron hand."
    She locked her anger deep inside her heart
and let all rumors breeze right past her ears.

[*While Thuc is visiting Miss Hoan, she sends men to Lin-tzu to kidnap Kieu; they
make it appear that she has died in a fire. Kieu is taken to Miss Hoan's family's home
and forced to work under the new name of Flower the Slave. Thuc returns to Lin-tzu
to find her supposedly dead; while he stays there in mourning, Miss Hoan has Kieu
brought to work in her own household. Kieu still doesn't know who her employer is.*]

    While months reeled on, with worries close at hand,
1790   could Thuc suspect what happened far away?
Since from Lin-tzu his lovebird had flown off,
an empty chamber kept a lonesome man.
He saw her eyebrow in the crescent moon,
breathed hints of old perfume and ached for her.
1795   Just as the lotus wilts, the mums bloom forth—
time softens grief, and winter turns to spring.
Where could he find her he had once so loved?
He called it fate and duller throbbed his pain.
    Nostalgia woke some yearning in his breast
1800   and, sick for home, he made his long way back.[6]
She met him at the gate, she gushed with joy.
Once they had traded news of health and such,
she had all drapes rolled up; then she bade Kieu
appear and greet the lord on his return.
1805   As Kieu came out, she faltered at each step,
for from a distance she perceived the truth:
"Unless the sun and lights have tricked my eyes,
who else but my own Thuc is sitting there?
So now I must confront the blatant fact:
1810   beyond all doubt, she's caught me in her trap.
Could such a hellish plot be hatched on earth?
Why has mankind so erred and bred a fiend?
As bride and groom we two were duly joined—
she splits us into slave and master now.
1815   The face displays sweet smiles, but deep inside
the heart will scheme to kill without a knife.
We stand as far apart as sky and earth:
alas, what now to say, what now to do?"
    She grew bewildered gazing at his face,
1820   her heart a raveled knot of silken threads.
Too awed to disobey, she bowed her head

---

6. To his wife, Miss Hoan.

and prostrated herself upon the floor.
The husband was dismayed, at his wits' end:
"Woe's me! But isn't she right here, my Kieu?

1825   What cause or reason led her to this plight?
Alas, we're caught—and I know by whose hands!"
     Lest he'd betray himself, he'd breathe no word
but could not stop his tears from spilling out.
His lady fixed him with a glare and asked:

1830   "You just came home—why look so woebegone?"
"I just took off my mourning," answered he.
"I think of my lost mother and still grieve."
She sang his praises: "What a loving son!
Let's drink to your return, drown autumn gloom."

1835   Husband and wife exchanged repeated toasts
while Kieu stood by and from the bottle poured.
The lady would berate her, finding fault,
would make her kneel and offer up each drink.
He'd act like one demented more and more

1840   as tears kept flowing while the liquor ebbed.
Averting eyes, he'd talk and laugh by fits;
then, pleading drunk, he'd try a safe retreat.
"You slave," the lady snapped, "persuade the lord
to drain his cup or I shall have you thrashed."

1845   Grief bruised his vitals, panic struck his soul—
he took the proffered cup and quaffed the gall.
The lady talked and laughed as though half drunk—
to crown the evening, she devised a sport.
She said: "That slave has mastered all the arts—

1850   she'll play the lute, treat you to some good piece."
     All dizzied, in a daze, Kieu bowed and sat
before the thin gauze screen to tune the lute.
Four strings together seemed to cry and moan
in tones that wrenched him who was feasting there.

1855   Both heard the selfsame voice of silk and wood—
she smiled and gloated while he wept within.
When he could check his welling tears no more,
he stooped his head and tried to wipe them off.
Again the mistress shouted at the slave:

1860   "Why play that doleful tune and kill our joy?
Don't you give thought to anything you do?
I'll punish you if you distress the lord."
He waxed more frantic still—to lay the storm,
he'd hurriedly attempt a laugh, a grin.

1865   The waterclock now marked the night's third watch—
the lady eyed their faces, looking pleased.
She gloried in her soul: "This sweet revenge
makes up for grief that festered in my breast."
But shrunk with shame and choked with rage inside,

1870   he nursed a wound that rankled more and more.

To share one pillow they regained their niche—
Kieu huddled by her lamp, awake all night
"So now she has unveiled her own true face.
How weird, that jealous humor in her blood!
1875   To split two lovebirds, she contrived it all—
she'd part and tear us from each other's eyes.
Now we're a gulf, a world apart—she's all,
I'm nothing now; she's always right, I'm wrong.
So gently it holds us, her iron hand!
1880   How can we struggle free and save our love?
Frail woman that I was, I tripped and fell:
shall I be rescued whole from furious waves?"
Alone, she brooded far into the night—
as ebbed the lampion's oil, her tears still flowed.

1885   Kieu served there day and night. Once, face to face,
the mistress asked the servant how she fared.
She chose her words with care, gave this reply:
"I sometimes sorrow for my lot in life."
The lady turned to Thuc, requesting him:
1890   "Please grill the slave, pry loose the facts from her."
He felt all torn and rent within his heart,
for he could not confess nor bear the scene.
Afraid he'd draw more outrage on her head,
he ventured, in soft tones, to question her.
1895   Head bowed, the girl knelt down upon the floor
and of her past wrote out a brief account.
Submitted to the lady, it was read—
it seemed to touch some chord inside her heart.
Forthwith she handed it to him and said:
1900   "We should admire her gifts, deplore her woes.
Had fortune favored her with wealth and rank,
she could have graced a palace cast in gold.
A woman bobs upon the sea of life:
so blessed with talent, yet so cursed by fate!"
1905   "Indeed, you speak the utter truth," he said.
"Misfortune's never spared a single rose.
The rule has held since ages out of mind:
show mercy, treat her with a gentler hand."
The lady said: "In her report she begged
1910   to make her home within the Void's great gate.[7]
Well, I'll be pleased to grant her that one wish
and help her break the cycle of her woes.
There in our garden is the Kuan-yin shrine,
with everblooming lotus, tall bo tree,[8]
1915   with many plants and flowers, rocks and pools:

7. The door to nirvana, a general name for Buddhism.
8. The lotus and bo tree are central symbols of Buddhist enlightenment. Kuan-yin is the Buddhist Goddess of Mercy, Listener to the World's Cries.

let her go there to tend the shrine and pray."

The dawn's first glow was glimmering in the skies—
they bore five offerings, incense, flowers, and such,
led Kieu to Buddha's temple: there she pledged
1920 to live by all three vows and five commands.[9]
For a cassock she doffed the slave's blue smock,
and as a nun she now was called Pure Spring.
She was to light the temple morn and eve,
while Spring and Autumn served as altar maids.
1925 So Kieu took refuge in the garden, near
the Purple Grove, far from the world's red dust.
What could she still expect of human ties?

[*Thuc makes a secret visit to Kieu, and they admit their mutual grief. To their shock, Miss Hoan is nearby and overhears them. Sure that some new revenge is brewing, Kieu flees. She ends up with a supposedly compassionate man, but he hands her over to another brothel, where she once again becomes a sought-after beauty.*]

2165 Cool breeze, clear moon—her nights were going round
when from the far frontier a guest turned up.
A tiger's beard, a swallow's jaw, and brows
as thick as silkworms—he stood broad and tall.
A towering hero, he outfought all foes
2170 with club or fist and knew all arts of war.
Between the earth and heaven he lived free:
he was Tu Hai, a native of Yueh-tung.
Plying his oar, he roved the streams and lakes
with sword and lute upon his shoulders slung.
2175 In town for fun, he heard loud praise of Kieu—
love for a woman bent a hero's will.
He brought his calling card to her boudoir—
thus eyes met eyes and heart encountered heart.
"Two kindred souls have joined," Tu said to Kieu.
2180 "We're not those giddy fools who play at love.
For long I've heard them rave about your charms,
but none's won favor yet in your clear eyes.
How often have you lucked upon a *man*?
Why bother with caged birds or fish in pots?"
2185 She said: "My lord, you're overpraising me.
For who am I to slight this man or that?
Within I crave the touchstone for the gold—
but whom can I turn to and give my heart?
As for all those who come and go through here,
2190 am I allowed to sift real gold from brass?"
"What lovely words you utter!" Tu exclaimed.
"They call to mind the tale of Prince P'ing-yuan.[1]
Come here and take a good, close look at me

9. She is taking the vows of a nun and vowing to keep the commandments against killing, stealing, lewdness, lying, and the drinking of alcohol.
1. Kieu's appeal makes Tu Hai think of the prince P'ing-yüan, who found great loyalty in a low-born subordinate.

to see if I deserve a bit of trust."

2195   "It's large, your heart," she said. "One of these days,
Chin-yang² shall see a dragon in the clouds.
If you care for this weed, this lowly flower,
tomorrow may I count on your good grace?"
    Well pleased, he nodded saying with a laugh:
2200 "Through life how many know what moves one's soul?
Those eyes be praised that, keen and worldly-wise,
can see the hero hid in common dust!
Your words prove you discern me from the rest—
we'll sit together when I sit on high."
2205 Two minds as one, two hearts in unison—
unbidden, love will seek those meant for love.
    Now he approached a go-between—through her
he paid some hundred liang for Kieu's release.
They picked a quiet spot, built their love nest:
2210 a sumptuous bed and curtains decked with gods.
The hero chose a phoenix as his mate;
the beauty found a dragon for her mount.

[*Tu Hai embarks on a series of battles, emerging in control of a wide region, then
makes Kieu his formal bride. Once they are married, Kieu tells him her full life story,
and he summons the people who have dealt with her, to receive her judgment. Kieu
pardons the weak Thuc and even his (now contrite) wife Miss Hoan, but has Scholar
Ma and the other pimps and bawds executed. Tu Hai then resumes his wars of conquest.*]

    Bamboos split fast; tiles slip, soon fall apart:
2440 his martial might now thundered far and wide.
In his own corner he installed his court
for peace or war and cut the realm in two.
Time after time he stormed across the land
and trampled down five strongholds in the South.
2445 He fought and honed his sword on wind and dust,
scorning those racks for coats, those sacks for rice.
He stalked and swaggered through his border fief,
with no less stature than a prince, a king.
Who dared oppose his flag, dispute his sway?
2450 For five years, by the sea, he reigned sole lord.

    There was an eminent province governor,
Lord Ho Ton Hien, who plied a statesman's craft.
The emperor sent him off with special powers
to quell revolt and rule the borderland.
2455 He knew Tu Hai would prove a gallant foe—
but then, in all his plans, Kieu had a voice.
He camped his troops and feigned to seek a truce,
sending an envoy with rich gifts for Tu.
For Kieu some presents, too: two waiting maids,

NGUYEN DU

2. Location where the founder of the T'ang dynasty ascended the throne.

2460   a thousand pounds of finest jade and gold.
        When his headquarters got the plea for peace,
     Lord Tu himself felt gnawing doubts and thought,
     "My own two hands have built this realm—at will,
     I've roamed the sea of Ch'u, the streams of Wu.
2465   If I turn up at court, bound hand and foot,
     what will become of me, surrendered man?
     Why let them swaddle me in robes and skirts?
     Why play a duke so as to cringe and crawl?
     Had I not better rule my march domain?
2470   For what can they all do against my might?
     At pleasure I stir heaven and shake earth—
     I come and go, I bow my head to none."
        But trust in people moved Kieu's guileless heart:
     sweet words and lavish gifts could make her yield.
2475   "A fern that floats on water," she now thought,
     "I've wandered long enough, endured enough.
     Let's swear allegiance to the emperor's throne—
     we'll travel far up fortune's royal road.
     Public and private ends will both be met,
2480   and soon I may arrange to go back home.
     A lord's own consort, head erect, I'll walk
     and make my parents glow with pride and joy.
     Then, both the state above, my home below,
     I'll have well served as liege and daughter both.
2485   Is that not better than to float and drift,
     a skiff the waves and waters hurl about?"
        When they discussed the wisest course to take,
     she sought to win him over to her views:
     "The emperor's munificence," she would say,
2490   "has showered on the world like drenching rain.
     His virtues and good works have kept the peace,
     placing each subject deeply in his debt.
     Since you rose up in arms, dead men's white bones
     have piled head-high along the Wayward Stream.[3]
2495   Why should you leave an ill repute behind?
     For ages who has ever praised Huang Ch'ao?[4]
     Why not accept high post and princely purse?
     Is there some surer avenue to success?"
        Her words struck home: he listened, giving ground.
2500   He dropped all schemes for war and sued for peace.
     The envoy he received with pomp and rites—
     he pledged to lay down arms, disband his troops.
        Trusting the truce they'd sworn below the walls,
     Lord Tu let flags hang loose, watch-drums go dead.
2505   He slackened all defense—imperial spies
     observed his camp and learned of its true state.

---

3. River with a shifting riverbed, scene of bloody battles between the Chinese and the Tartars.

4. A failed scholar, whose unsuccessful rebellion in 884 seriously weakened the T'ang dynasty.

Lord Ho conceived a ruse to snatch this chance:
behind a screen of gifts he'd poise his troops.
The flying flag of friendship led the van,
2510   with gifts in front and weapons hid behind.
        Lord Tu suspected nothing, caught off guard—
in cap and gown, he waited at the gate.
Afield, Lord Ho now gave the secret cue:
flags on all sides unfurled and guns fired off.
2515   The fiercest tiger, taken unawares,
will lick the dust and meet an abject end.
Now doomed, Tu fought his one last fight on earth
to show them all a soldier's dauntless heart.
When his brave soul left him to join the gods,
2520   he still stood on his feet amidst his foes.
His body, firm as rock and hard as bronze,
who in the whole wide world could shake or move?

* * *

2565   The troops proclaimed their victory with a feast.
Strings twanged, flutes piped—all reveled and caroused.
The lord forced Kieu to wait on him—half drunk,
he bade her play the lute she'd daily played.
        It moaned like wind and rain—five fingertips
2570   dripped blood upon four strings. When gibbons howl,
cicadas wail, they cannot match such grief.
Ho listened, knitting brows and shedding tears.
He asked: "What are you playing there? It sounds
like all the world's dark sorrows rolled in one."
2575   "My lord, this tune's called *Cruel Fate*," she said.
"I wrote it for the lute when I was young,
in days long gone. But now, of cruel fate
you have a victim under your own eyes."
        Entranced, he heard her; spellbound, he watched her.
2580   O miracle, love disturbed an iron mask!
"We're destined for each other," said the lord.
"Let me restring your lute and make it whole."
"I am a fallen woman," answered she.
"My conscience bears a person's wrongful death.
2585   And what's there left of me, a faded flower?
My heartstrings broke just like Hsiao-lin's lute strings.[5]
Pity a woman—I'll bless my fortune if
I see the elms back home before I die."
        Flushed with success, Lord Ho had drunk too much—
2590   but he regained his senses as light dawned.
He thought, "I am a noble of the realm,
whom both my betters and the rabble watch.
Does it become a lord to toy with love?

5. Hsiao Lin was a concubine of an ancient king of Ch'i; forced to wed another man against her will, she wrote a poem comparing her broken heart to the broken strings of her lute.

Now, how should I untangle this affair?"
2595　　So at the morning levee, he resolved
to carry his expedient out forthwith.
Who dare protest the word a mandarin speaks?
Kieu was compelled to wed a tribal chief.
　　How wayward you can be, O Marriage God,
2600　　at random tying couples with your threads!
The bridal carriage took her to his boat—
curtains came down, the nuptial lamp lit up.

　　Willow all withered, peach blossom all seared—
her freshness was all gone, not one spark left.
2605　　Let waves and sands entomb her self, annul
her parents' love and care, her gifts of mind.
Mere flotsam seaborne toward the world's far bounds,
where could she find a grave and rest her bones?

[*Distraught at having advised Tu Hai to his betrayal, Kieu throws herself into a river to drown. Carried far downstream, she is found by fishermen, who leave her at the hermitage of an old nun, Giac Duyen, who had met her before and had a premonition they would meet again. Kieu now embraces a nun's life with joy. The scene shifts to the home of Kieu's first beloved, Kim, who has followed her wishes and married her sister, Van. Years have passed with no news of Kieu, but then Van—now a prominent government official—is posted to the region of Lin-tzu, where Kieu now is. Van has a dream in which Kieu appears to her. Sure that she must be nearby, they make inquiries, and are told she has drowned. As they set up a memorial stone at the river, Giac Duyen happens by and reveals that Kieu is living with her. Kim, Van, and her aged parents eagerly make their way along the overgrown path to the old nun's hermitage.*]

　　All knelt and bowed their thanks to old Giac Duyen,
then in a group they followed on her heels.
They cut and cleared their way through reed and rush,
their loving hearts half doubting yet her word.
3005　　By twists and turns they edged along the shore,
pushed past that jungle, reached the Buddha's shrine.
In a loud voice, the nun Giac Duyen called Kieu,
and from an inner room she hurried out.
　　She glanced and saw her folks—they all were here:
3010　　Father looked still quite strong, and Mother spry;
both sister Van and brother Quan grown up;
and over there was Kim, her love of yore.
Could she believe this moment, what it seemed?
Was she now dreaming open-eyed, awake?
3015　　Tear-pearls dropped one by one and damped her smock—
she felt such joy and grief, such grief and joy.
　　She cast herself upon her mother's knees
and, weeping, told of all she had endured.
"Since I set out to wander through strange lands,
3020　　a wave-tossed fern, some fifteen years have passed.
I sought to end it in the river's mud—

who could have hoped to see you all on earth?"
The parents held her hands, admired her face:
that face had not much changed since she left home.

3025 The moon, the flower, lashed by wind and rain
for all that time, had lost some of its glow.
What scale could ever weigh their happiness?
Present and past, so much they talked about!
The two young ones kept asking this or that

3030 while Kim looked on, his sorrow turned to joy.
Before the Buddha's altar all knelt down
and for Kieu's resurrection offered thanks.
At once they ordered sedans decked with flowers—
old Vuong bade Kieu be carried home with them.

3035 "I'm nothing but a fallen flower," she said.
"I drank of gall and wormwood half my life.
I thought to die on waves beneath the clouds—
how could my heart nurse hopes to see this day?
Yet I've survived and met you all again,

3040 and slaked the thirst that long has parched my soul.
This cloister's now my refuge in the wilds—
to live with grass and trees befits my age.
I'm used to salt and greens in Dhyana fare;[6]
I've grown to love the drab of Dhyana garb.

3045 Within my heart the fire of lust is quenched—
why should I roll again in worldly dust?
What good is that, a purpose half achieved?
To nunhood vowed, I'll stay here till the end.
I owe to her who saved me sea-deep debts—

3050 how can I cut my bonds with her and leave?"
Old Vuong exclaimed: "Other times, other tides!
Even a saint must bow to circumstance.
You worship gods and Buddhas—who'll discharge
a daughter's duties, keep a lover's vows?

3055 High Heaven saved your life—we'll build a shrine
and have our Reverend come; live there near us."
Heeding her father's word, Kieu had to yield:
she took her leave of cloister and old nun.
The group returned to Kim's own yamen[7] where,

3060 for their reunion, they all held a feast.
After mum wine instilled a mellow mood,
Van rose and begged to air a thought or two;
"It's Heaven's own design that lovers meet,
so Kim and Kieu did meet and swear their troth.

3065 Then, over peaceful earth wild billows swept,
and in my sister's place I wedded him.
Amber and mustard seed, lodestone and pin!

6. The simple fare of monks and nuns.
7. A government official's residence.

Besides, 'when blood is spilt, the gut turns soft.'[8]
Day after day, we hoped and prayed for Kieu

3070   with so much love and grief these fifteen years.
But now the mirror cracked is whole again:
wise Heaven's put her back where she belongs.
She still loves him and, luckily, still has him—
still shines the same old moon both once swore by.

3075   The tree still bears some three or seven plums,
the peach stays fresh—it's time to tie the knot!"
        Kieu brushed her sister's speech aside and said:
"Why now retell a tale of long ago?
We once did pledge our troth, but since those days,

3080   my life has been exposed to wind and rain.
I'd die of shame discussing what's now past—
let those things flow downstream and out to sea!"
        "A curious way to put it!" Kim cut in.
"Whatever you may feel, your oath remains.

3085   A vow of troth is witnessed by the world,
by earth below and heaven far above.
Though things may change and stars may shift their course,
sworn pledges must be kept in life or death.
Does fate, which brought you back, oppose our love?

3090   We two are one—why split us in two halves?"
        "A home where love and concord reign," Kieu said,
"whose heart won't yearn for it? But I believe
that to her man a bride should bring the scent
of a close bud, the shape of a full moon.

3095   It's priceless, chastity—by nuptial torch,
am I to blush for what I'll offer you?
Misfortune struck me—since that day the flower
fell prey to bees and butterflies, ate shame.
For so long lashed by rain and swept by wind,

3100   a flower's bound to fade, a moon to wane.
My cheeks were once two roses—what's now left?
My life is done—how can it be remade?
How dare I, boldfaced, soil with worldly filth
the homespun costume of a virtuous wife?

3105   You bear a constant love for me, I know—
but where to hide my shame by bridal light?
From this day on I'll shut my chamber door:
though I will take no vows, I'll live a nun.
If you still care for what we both once felt,

3110   let's turn it into friendship—let's be friends.
Why speak of marriage with its red silk thread?
It pains my heart and further stains my life."
        "How skilled you are in spinning words!" Kim said.
"You have your reasons—others have their own.

3115   Among those duties falling to her lot,

8. Linked by blood, family members share each other's pain; they had been drawn together as inevitably as an iron pin is drawn to a magnet or a mustard seed to a piece of amber.

a woman's chastity means many things.
For there are times of ease and times of stress:
in crisis, must one rigid rule apply?
True daughter, you upheld a woman's role:
3120   what dust or dirt could ever sully you?
Heaven grants us this hour: now from our gate
all mists have cleared; on high, clouds roll away.
The faded flower's blooming forth afresh,
the waning moon shines more than at its full.
3125   What is there left to doubt? Why treat me like
another Hsiao, a passerby ignored?"[9]
     He argued, pleaded, begged—she heard him through.
Her parents also settled on his plans.
Outtalked, she could no longer disagree:
3130   she hung her head and yielded, stifling sighs.
     They held a wedding-feast—bright candles lit
all flowers, set aglow the red silk rug.
Before their elders groom and bride bowed low—
all rites observed, they now were man and wife.
3135   In their own room they traded toasts, still shy
of their new bond, yet moved by their old love.
Since he, a lotus sprout, first met with her,
a fresh peach bud, fifteen full years had fled.
To fall in love, to part, to reunite—
3140   both felt mixed grief and joy as rose the moon.
     The hour was late—the curtain dropped its fringe:
under the light gleamed her peach-blossom cheeks.
Two lovers met again—out of the past,
a bee, a flower constant in their love.
3145   "I've made my peace with my own fate," she said.
"What can this cast-off body be good for?
I thought of your devotion to our past—
to please you, I went through those wedding rites.
But how ashamed I felt in my own heart,
3150   lending a brazen front to all that show!
Don't go beyond the outward marks of love—
perhaps, I might then look you in the face.
But if you want to get what they all want,
glean scent from dirt, or pluck a wilting flower,
3155   then we'll flaunt filth, put on a foul display,
and only hate, not love, will then remain.
When you make love and I feel only shame,
then rank betrayal's better than such love.
If you must give your clan a rightful heir,
3160   you have my sister—there's need for me.
What little chastity I may have saved,
am I to fling it under trampling feet?
More tender feelings pour from both our hearts—

---

9. After the wife of a commoner named Hsiao was abducted and married to a powerful official, she refused to acknowledge her former husband in the street.

why toy and crumple up a faded flower?"

3165   "An oath bound us together," he replied.
"We split, like fish to sea and bird to sky.
Through your long exile how I grieved for you!
Breaking your troth, you must have suffered so.
We loved each other, risked our lives, braved death—

3170 now we two meet again, still deep in love.
The willow in mid-spring still has green leaves—
I thought you still attached to human love.
But no more dust stains your clear mirror now:
your vow can't but increase my high regard.

3175 If I long searched the sea for my lost pin,
it was true love, not lust, that urged me on.
We're back together now, beneath one roof:
to live in concord, need two share one bed?"
     Kieu pinned her hair and straightened up her gown,

3180 then knelt to touch her head in gratitude:
"If ever my soiled body's cleansed of stains,
I'll thank a gentleman, a noble soul.
The words you spoke came from a kindred heart:
no truer empathy between two souls.

3185 A home, a refuge—what won't you give me?
My honor lives again as of tonight."
     Their hands unclasped, then clasped and clasped again—
now he esteemed her, loved her all the more.
They lit another candle up, refilled

3190 the incense urn, then drank to their new joy.
His old desire for her came flooding back—
he softly asked about her luting skill.
     "Those strings of silk entangled me," she said,
"in sundry woes which haven't ceased till now.

3195 Alas, what's done regrets cannot undo—
but I'll obey your wish just one more time."
     Her elfin fingers danced and swept the strings—
sweet strains made waves with curls of scentwood smoke.
Who sang this hymn to life and peace on earth?

3200 Was it a butterfly or Master Chuang?[1]
And who poured forth this rhapsody of love?
The king of Shu or just a cuckoo-bird?[2]
Clear notes like pearls dropped in a moon-lit bay.
Warm notes like crystals of new Lan-t'ien jade.

3205 His ears drank in all five tones of the scale—
all sounds which stirred his heart and thrilled his soul.
"Whose hand is playing that old tune?" he asked.
"What sounded once so sad now sounds so gay!
It's from within that joy or sorrow comes—

---

1. In the Daoist classic *Chuang Tzu*, Chuang dreams he is a butterfly but then wonders whether in fact a butterfly is dreaming it is a man.

2. Wang-ti, King of Shu, carried on an adulterous affair with the wife of his minister, then fled in disgrace and turned into a cuckoo.

3210 have bitter days now set and sweet ones dawned?"
"This pleasant little pastime," answered she,
"once earned me grief and woe for many years.
For you my lute just sang its one last song—
henceforth, I'll roll its strings and play no more."

3215 The secrets of their hearts were flowing still
when cocks crowed up the morning in the east.
Kim spoke, told all about their private pact.
All marveled at her wish and lauded her—
a woman of high mind, not some coquette

3220 who'd with her favors skip from man to man.
Of love and friendship they fulfilled both claims—
they shared no bed but joys of lute and verse.
Now they sipped wine, now played a game of chess,
admiring flowers, waiting for the moon.

3225 Their wishes all came true since fate so willed,
and of two lovers marriage made two friends.
As pledged, they built a temple on a hill,
then sent a trusted man to fetch the nun.
When he got there, he found doors shut and barred—

3230 he saw a weed-grown rooftop, moss-filled cracks.
She'd gone to gather simples,° he was told: herbs
the cloud had flown, the crane had fled—but where?
For old times' sake, Kieu kept the temple lit,
its incense candles burning night and day.

3235 The twice-blessed home enjoyed both weal and wealth.
Kim climbed the office ladder year by year.
Van gave him many heirs: a stooping tree,
a yardful of sophoras and cassia shrubs.[3]
In rank or riches who could rival them?

3240 Their garden throve, won glory for all times.

This we have learned: with Heaven rest all things.
Heaven appoints each human to a place.
If doomed to roll in dust, we'll roll in dust;
we'll sit on high when destined for high seats.

3245 Does Heaven ever favor anyone,
bestowing both rare talent and good luck?
In talent take no overweening pride,
for talent and disaster form a pair.[4]
Our karma[5] we must carry as our lot—

3250 let's stop decrying Heaven's whims and quirks.
Inside ourselves there lies the root of good:
the heart outweighs all talents on this earth.

May these crude words, culled one by one and strung,
beguile an hour or two of your long night.

3. A "stooping tree" is a first-ranked wife; the ornamental shrubs are her children.
4. The word for "talent" (*tai*) sounds like "misfortune" (*tai*).
5. Destiny across successive lives.

Russia wanted a national poet, and Pushkin filled the bill to perfection. In the previous century Catherine the Great, who ruled from 1762–1796, had worked to westernize and modernize the country, importing leading French and German intellectuals. The upper classes were culturally French. But the failed Napoleonic invasion of 1812 led the once liberal tsar Alexander I to retreat into reaction, leaving the country at Nicholas's accession with much ferment and little direction. There were plenty of writers in Western European modes, but none to capture the popular imagination until Pushkin came along. He wrote with equal success lyric poems, Byronic narratives with native themes, plays, and prose narratives, the longest of which, "The Captain's Daughter," is a historical fiction in Scott's panoramic manner concerning a Cossack rebel against Catherine the Great. He became the founding figure of Russian national literature, as well as the inspiration for the Russian musical school; operas based on his works were composed by Glinka (*Russlan and Ludmilla,* 1842), Mussorgsky (*Boris Godunov,* 1870, rev. 1872), Tchaikovsky (*Eugene Onegin,* 1877; *Queen of Spades,* 1890), Rimsky-Korsakov (*Mozart and Salieri,* 1897), Stravinsky (*Mavra,* 1922), and others.

With his French education and his facility in English and Italian, his deep Russian pedigree, and his "Oriental" ancestry, Pushkin was the perfect figure to represent imperial aspirations. He was fiercely liberal at times, yet ultimately compliant. He wrote in polished Western forms such as the couplets of "The Bronze Horseman." His lyrics show a responsiveness to a nature sensibility resembling Wordsworth's; his story "The Queen of Spades" plays into the fashion for the fantastic tale. At the same time, his Russian themes elevate his native country to all the beauty, sublimity, and dignity of the long-established realms of Europe. All these elements can be found in perfection in his last and most eloquent verse tale, "The Bronze Horseman."

PRONUNCIATIONS:
Pushkin: PUSH-kin
Onegin: ahn-YAY-gin
Nevá: nye-VAH

The Bronze Horseman[1]

A Petersburg Tale

Introduction[2]

> Upon the brink of the wild stream
> *He*[3] stood, and dreamt a mighty dream.
> He gazed far off. Near him the spreading
> river poured by; with flood abeam,
> 5   alone, a flimsy skiff was treading.
> Scattered along those shores of bog

---

1. Translated by Charles Johnston.

2. "The Bronze Horseman" tells a story founded on a real flood in November 1824. The grand modern city of Saint Petersburg was built on swampland on the Baltic Sea, looking out toward Finland and the then powerful kingdom of Sweden.

3. Peter the Great, who founded Saint Petersburg in 1703.

and moss were huts of blackened log,
the wretched fisher's squalid dwelling;
forests, impervious in the fog
10   to hidden suns, all round were telling
their whispered tale.
               And so thought He:
"From here, proud Sweden will get warning;
just here is where a city'll be
founded to stop our foes from scorning;
15   here Nature destines us to throw
out over Europe a window;
to stand steadfast beside the waters;
across waves unknown to the West,
all flags will come, to be our guest—
20   and we shall feast in spacious quarters."

A century went by—a young
city, of Northern lands the glory
and pride, from marsh and overhung
forest arose, story on story:
25   where, earlier, Finland's fisher sank—
of Nature's brood the most downhearted—
alone on the low-lying bank,
his ropy net in the uncharted
current, today, on brinks that hum
30   with life and movement, there have come
enormous mansions that are justling
with graceful towers; and vessels here
from earth's extremities will steer
until the rich quayside is bustling.
35   Nevá[4] now sports a granite face;
bridges are strung across her waters;
in darkly verdant garden-quarters
her isles have vanished without trace;
old Moscow's paled before this other
40   metropolis; it's just the same
as when a widowed Empress-Mother
bows to a young Tsaritsa's° claim.   *Princess's*

I love you, Peter's own creation;
I love your stern, your stately air,
45   Nevá's majestical pulsation,
the granite that her quaysides wear,
your railings with their iron shimmer,
your pensive nights in the half-gloom,

4. The river along which the city is built.

translucent twilight, moonless glimmer,
50 when, sitting lampless in my room,
I write and read; when, faintly shining,
the streets in their immense outlining
are empty, given up to dreams;
when Admiralty's needle gleams;
55 when not admitting shades infernal
into the golden sky, one glow
succeeds another, and nocturnal
tenure has one half-hour to go;
I love your brutal winter, freezing
60 the air to so much windless space;
by broad Nevá the sledges breezing;
brighter than roses each girl's face;
the ball, its brilliance, din, and malice;
bachelor banquets and the due
65 hiss of the overflowing chalice,
and punch's radiance burning blue.
I love it when some warlike duty
livens the Field of Mars, and horse
and foot impose on that concourse
70 their monolithic brand of beauty;
above the smooth-swaying vanguard
victorious, tattered flags are streaming,
on brazen helmets light is gleaming,
helmets that war has pierced and scarred.
75 I love the martial detonation,
the citadel in smoke and roar,
when the North's Empress to the nation
has given a son for empire, or
when there's some new triumph in war
80 victorious Russia's celebrating;
or when Nevá breaks the blue ice,
sweeps it to seaward, slice on slice,
and smells that days of spring are waiting.

Metropolis of Peter, stand,
85 steadfast as Russia, stand in splendor!
Even the elements by your hand
have been subdued and made surrender;
let Finland's waves forget the band
of hate and bondage down the ages,
90 nor trouble with their fruitless rages
Peter the Great's eternal sleep!

A fearful time there was: I keep
its memory fresh in retrospection . . .
My friends, let me turn up for you
95 the dossiers of recollection.
Grievous the tale will be, it's true . . .

Part One

On Petrograd,° the darkened city,   *Saint Petersburg*
November, chill and without pity,
blasted; against its noble brink
Nevá was splashing noisy billows;
5   its restless mood would make one think
of sufferers tossing on their pillows.
The hour was late and dark; the rain
angrily lashed the window-pane,
the wind blew, pitifully shrieking.
10   From house of friends, about this time,
young Evgeny came home . . .
                   My rhyme
selects this name to use in speaking
of our young hero. It's a sound
I like; my pen has long been bound
15   in some way with it; further naming
is not required, though lustre flaming
in years gone by might have lit on
his forebears, and perhaps their story
under Karamzin's[5] pen had shone,
20   resounding to the nation's glory;
but now by all, both high and low,
it's quite forgotten. Our hero
lives in Kolomna,[6] has employment
in some bureau, tastes no enjoyment
25   of wealth or fashion's world, and no
regret for tales of long ago.

So Evgeny came home and, shaking
his greatcoat, got undressed for bed—
but lay long hours awake, his head
30   with various thoughts disturbed and aching.
What did he think about? The fact
that he was penniless; that packed
mountains of work must be surmounted
to earn him freedom, fame, and ease;
35   that wit and money might be counted
to him from God; and that one sees
fellows on permanent vacation,
dull-witted, idle, in whose station
life runs as smooth as in a dream;
40   that he'd served two years altogether . . .
And he thought also that the weather
had got no gentler; that the stream

5. Nikolai Mikhailovich Karamzin (1766–1826), prose writer.
6. A part of Saint Petersburg.

was rising, ever higher lifting;
that soon the bridges might be shifting;
45   that maybe from Parasha° he   *his beloved*
would be cut off, two days or three.

These were his dreams. And a great sadness
came over him that night; he wished
the raindrops with less raging madness
50   would lash the glass, that the wind swished
less drearily . . .

           At last his failing
eyes closed in sleep. But look, the gloom
of that foul-weather night is paling,
and a weak daylight fills the room . . .
55   A dreadful day it was!

               All night
Nevá against the gales to seaward
had battled, but been blown to leeward
by their ungovernable might . . .
That morning, on the quayside, fountains
60   of spray held an admiring crowd,
that pressed to watch the watery mountains,
the foaming waves that roared so loud.
But now, blocked by the headwinds blowing
in from the Gulf, Nevá turned back,
65   in sullen, thunderous fury flowing,
and flooded all the islands; black,
still blacker grew the day; still swelling,
Nevá exploded, raging, yelling,
in kettle-like outbursts of steam—
70   until, mad as a beast, the stream
pounced on the city. From its path
everyone fled, and all around
was sudden desert . . . At a bound
cellars were under inundation,
75   canals leapt rails, forgot their station—
and Triton-Petropol[7] surfaced
with waters lapping round his waist.

Siege and assault! The waves, malicious,
like thieves, burst in through windows; vicious
80   rowboats, careering, smash the panes;
stalls are engulfed; piteous remains,
débris of cabins, roofing, boarding,
wares that a thrifty trade's been hoarding,
poor household goods, dashed all astray,

---

7. Triton is a Greek sea god who rides the waves on sea horses. Petropol is a Greek form of the name Petersburg.

85   bridges the storm has snatched away,
and scooped-up coffins, helter-skelter
swim down the streets!
               All sense alike
God's wrath, and wait for doom to strike.
Everything's ruined: bread and shelter!
90   and where to find them?
              That deathlike,
that frightful year, Tsar Alexander[8]
still ruled in glory. He came out
on the balcony, in grief, in doubt,
and said: "A Tsar is no commander
95   against God's elements." Deep in thought
he gazed with sorrow and confusion,
gazed at the wreck the floods had wrought.
The city squares gave the illusion
of lakes kept brimming to profusion
100   by torrent-streets. The palace stood
sad as an island in the ocean.
And then the Tsar spoke out, for good
or evil set in farflung motion
his generals on their dangerous way
105   along those streets of boisterous waters
to save the people in their quarters,
drowning, unhinged by terror's sway.

And then in Peter's square, where lately
a corner-mansion rose, and stately
110   from its high porch, on either side,
caught as in life, with paws suspended,
two lions,[9] sentry-like, attended—
perched up on one, as if to ride,
arms folded, motionless, astride,
115   hatless, and pale with apprehension,
Evgeny sat. His fear's intention
not for himself, he never knew
just how the greedy waters grew,
how at his boots the waves were sucking,
120   how in his face the raindrops flew;
or how the stormwind, howling, bucking,
had snatched his hat away. His view
was fixed in darkest desperation,
immobile, on a single spot.
125   Mountainous, from the perturbation
down in the depths, the waves had got
on their high horses, raging, pouncing;

8. Alexander I (1777–1825).
9. Statues at the entrance to the War Ministry.

the gale blew up, and, with it, bouncing
wreckage . . . Oh, God, oh God! for there—
130   close to the seashore—almost where
the Gulf ran in, right on the billow—
a fence, untouched by paint, a willow,
a flimsy cottage; *there* were they,
a widow and his dream, her daughter,
135   Parasha . . . or perhaps he may
have dreamt it all? Fickle as water,
our life is as dreamlike as smoke—
at our expense, fate's private joke.
As if by sorcery enchanted,
140   high on the marble fixed and planted,
he can't dismount! And all about
is only water. Looking out,
with back turned to him, on the retching
waves of Nevá in their wild course
145   from his fast summit, arm outstretching,
the Giant rides on his bronze horse.[1]

Part Two

But by now, tired of helter-skelter
ruin and sheer rampaging, back
Nevá was flowing, in its track
admiring its own hideous welter;
5   its booty, as it made for shelter,
it slung away. With his grim crew
so any robber chief will do;
bursting his way into a village,
he'll hack and thrust and snatch and pillage;
10   rape, havoc, terror, howl and wail!
Then, loaded down with loot, and weary—
fear of pursuers makes them leery—
the robbers take the homeward trail
and as they flee they scatter plunder.

15   So, while the water fell asunder,
the road came up. And fainting, pale,
in hope and yearning, fear and wonder,
Evgeny hurries at full steam
down to the scarcely falling stream.
20   And yet, still proud, and still exulting,
the waves, still furious and insulting,
boiled as if over flames alight;
they still were lathered, foaming, seething
and deeply the Nevá was breathing

---

1. Monument to Peter the Great.

25   just like a horse flown from a fight.
Evgeny looks: a skiff is waiting—
Godsent—he rushes, invocating
the ferryman, who without a care
for just a few copecks quite gladly
30   agrees to take him, though still madly
the floods are boiling everywhere.
The boatman fought the agonizing
billows like an experienced hand;
the cockboat with its enterprising
35   crew was quite ready for capsizing
at any moment—but dry land
at last it gained.
             Evgeny, tearful,
rushes along the well-known ways
towards the well-known scene. His gaze
40   finds nothing it can grasp: too fearful
the sight! before him all is drowned,
or swept away, or tossed around;
cottages are askew, some crumbled
to sheer destruction, others tumbled
45   off by the waves; and all about,
as on a field of martial rout,
bodies lie weltered. Blankly staring,
Evgeny, uncomprehending, flies,
faint from a torment past all bearing,
50   runs to where fate will meet his eyes,
fate whose unknown adjudication
still waits as under seal of wax.
And now he's near his destination
and here's the Gulf, here . . . in his tracks
55   Evgeny halts . . . the house . . . where ever?
he goes back, he returns. He'd never . . .
he looks . . . he walks . . . he looks again:
here's where their cottage stood; and then
here was the willow. Gates were standing
60   just here—swept off, for sure. But where's
the cottage gone? Not understanding,
he walked round, full of boding cares,
he talked to himself loud and gruffly,
and then he struck his forehead roughly
65   and laughed and laughed.
                In deepest night
the city trembled at its plight;
long time that day's events were keeping
the citizenry all unsleeping
as they rehearsed them.
                Daylight's ray
70   fell out of tired, pale clouds to play

over a scene of calm—at dawning
yesterday's hell had left no trace.
The purple radiance of the morning
had covered up the dire event.

75   All in its previous order went.
Upon highways no longer flowing,
people as everyday were going
in cold indifference, and the clerk
left where he'd sheltered in the dark

80   and went to work. The daring bosses
of commerce, unperturbed, explore
Nevá's inroads upon their store,
and plan to take their heavy losses
out on their neighbor. From backyards

85   boats are removed.
                        That bard of bards,
Count Khvostov,[2] great poetic master,
begins to sing Nevá's disaster
in unforgettable ballades.

But spare, I pray you, spare some pity

90   for my poor, poor Evgeny, who
by the sad happenings in the city
had wits unhinged. Still the halloo
of tempest and Nevá was shrieking
into his ear; pierced through and through

95   by frightful thoughts, he roamed unspeaking;
some nightmare held him in its thrall.
A week went by, a month—and all
the time he never once was seeking
his home. That small deserted nook,

100   its lease expired, his landlord took
for a poor poet. His possessions
Evgeny never went to claim.
Soon to the world and its professions
a stranger, all day long he came

105   and went on foot, slept by the water;
scraps thrown from windows of the quarter
his only food; always the same,
his clothes wore out to shreds. Malicious
children would stone him; he received

110   from time to time the coachman's vicious
whiplash, for he no more perceived
which way was which, or what direction
led where; he never seemed to know
where he was going, he was so

115   plunged in tumult of introspection.

2. Count D. I. Khvostov (1757–1835), a minor poet.

And so his life's unhappy span
he eked out—neither beast nor man—
not this, nor that—not really living
nor yet a ghost . . .
                          He slept one night
120   by the Nevá. Summer was giving
its place to autumn. Full of spite,
a bad wind blew. In mournful fight
against the embankment, waves were splashing,
their crests on the smooth steps were smashing
125   for all the world like suppliant poor
at some hard-hearted judge's door.
Evgeny woke. Raindrops were falling
in midnight gloom; the wind was calling
piteously—on it, far off, hark,
130   the cry of sentries in the dark . . .
Evgeny rose, and recollection
brought up past horrors for inspection;
he stood in haste, walked off from there,
then halted, and began to stare
135   in silence, with an insensately
wild look of terror on his face.
He was beside the pillared, stately
front of a mansion. In their place,
caught as in life, with paws suspended,
140   two lions, sentry-like, attended,
and there, above the river's course,
atop his rock, fenced-off, defended
on his dark summit, arm extended,
the Idol rode on his bronze horse.

145   Evgeny shuddered. Thoughts were hatching
in frightful clarity. He knew
that spot, where floods ran raging through—
where waves had massed, voracious, snatching,
a riot-mob, vindictive, grim—
150   the lions, and the square, and him
who, motionless and without pity,
lifted his bronze head in the gloom,
whose will, implacable as doom,
had chosen seashore for his city.
155   Fearful he looked in that half-light!
Upon his forehead, what a might
of thought, what strength of concentration!
what fire, what passion, and what force
are all compact in that proud horse!
160   He gallops—to what destination?
On the cliff-edge, O lord of fate,
was it not you, O giant idol,

who, pulling on your iron bridle,
checked Russia, made her rear up straight?

165 Around the hero's plinth of granite
wretched Evgeny, in a daze,
wandered, and turned a savage gaze
on the autocrat of half the planet.
A steely pressure gripped his chest.
170 His brow on the cold railing pressed,
over his eyes a mist was lowering,
and through his heart there ran a flame;
his blood was seething; so he came
to stand before the overpowering
175 image, with teeth and fists again
clenched as if some dark force possessed him.
"Take care," he whisperingly addressed him,
"you marvel-working builder, when . . ."
He shivered with bitter fury, then
180 took headlong flight. He had the impression
that the grim Tsar, in sudden race
of blazing anger, turned his face
quietly and without expression . . .
and through the empty square he runs,
185 but hears behind him, loud as guns
or thunderclap's reverberation,
ponderous hooves in detonation
along the shuddering roadway—
as, lighted by the pale moon-ray,
190 one arm stretched up, on headlong course,
after him gallops the Bronze Rider,
after him clatters the Bronze Horse.
So all night long, demented strider,
wherever he might turn his head—
195 everywhere gallops the Bronze Rider
pursuing him with thunderous tread.

And from then on, if he was chancing
at any time to cross that square,
a look of wild distress came glancing
200 across his features; he would there
press hand to heart, in tearing hurry,
as if to chase away a worry;
take his worn cap off; never raise
up from the ground his distraught gaze,
205 but sidle off.

                        A small isle rises
close to the foreshore. Now and then,
a fisher moors alongside, when
late from his catch, with nets and prizes,

	and cooks his poor meal on the sand;
210	or some official comes to land,
	out for a Sunday's pleasure-boating,
	on the wild islet. Not a blade
	of grass is seen. There, gaily floating,
	the floods had washed up as they played
215	a flimsy cottage. Above water
	it showed up like a bush, quite black—
	last spring they moved it. The small quarter,
	empty, was shipped away, all rack
	and ruin. Near it, my dim-witted
220	my mad Evgeny there they found . . .
	His cold corpse in that self-same ground
	to God's good mercy they committed.

GHALIB ■ (1797–1869)

One of the greatest poets of modern times in two different languages, Persian and Urdu, Ghalib was a religious skeptic whose verses are filled with echoes of the Qur'an. A court poet with little reverence for power, Ghalib was a writer of passionate love poetry and an ironic observer of his own passion. He was born in Agra, in Muslim northern India, as Mirza Asadullah Beg Khan, a descendant of Turkish aristocrats who had come to India seeking to improve their fortunes. His father was killed in battle when he was four years old; his mother and her children then moved in with a wealthy brother, who soon died as well. The children received the education of aristocrats, but they had little wealth of their own. At age thirteen, Ghalib was married into a noble family in Delhi, then the capital of the Mughal Empire. He wrote much of his most famous Urdu poetry over the next several years, shifting to Persian at around age twenty. Though the young poet took the lofty pen name of Ghalib ("Victorious"), he was financially dependent on inconsistent patrons, and his own love of wine and gambling left him often in debt. In a capital of lavish homes, Ghalib never owned a home himself, and even possessed few books, often borrowing from friends and storing his own poems in their libraries.

Ghalib's patrons didn't really know what to make of him, in part because of his unorthodox personal habits and his skeptical, tolerant religious beliefs, and in part for the mysterious beauty of his poems. By the age of eleven he had begun composing poetry in both Persian and Urdu (the common speech of much of north India, derived from Hindi and written in the Arabic alphabet). By his late teens he was already writing many of his most striking and original poems, particularly in the verse form of the *ghazal* or "conversation with the beloved." Such poems could be addressed either to an earthly beloved or to God; in Ghalib's verse, it is often difficult to say which is the case, or whether the poem is addressed to both at once. (In the translations below, the translators use the term "the Great One" to keep these possibilities open.) The *ghazal* is a highly structured poetic form, with strict rules of rhyme and repetition of a key phrase in each of its couplets. In lesser hands, the rhymes can drive the meaning, and the imagery may remain simple or even hackneyed, but Ghalib fashioned his couplets into individual gems, linked together in ways that can be hard to sort out but that cumulatively create powerful images of desire and loss. Ghalib was well aware that his poems weren't generally easy to grasp on a first hearing, and he wrote a *ghazal*—pointedly brief and direct—about this very problem:

> I agree, O heart, that my ghazals are not easy to take in.
> When they hear my work, experienced poets
>
> Tell me I should write something easier to understand.
> I have to write what's difficult, otherwise it is difficult to write.

Like Byron, his contemporary, Ghalib was an aristocratic rebel, a self-styled outsider who sought and enjoyed the admiration of the more conventional readers who read him despite their discomfort with his free-living and free-thinking ways. Like Byron as well, Ghalib made himself a leading figure within his own poems. *Ghazals* had traditionally ended with a coda mentioning the poet's name, often in relatively impersonal fashion, but Ghalib's poems build up a powerful persona of a witty, sophisticated, melancholy commentator on his own life and on life in general. Ghalib is typically indirect in his social and political references, but his verses reflect his ambivalent skepticism toward secular power and religious orthodoxy. Seen in the context of his times, his poems become a personal mirror (a recurrent image in his lyrics) of the declining decades of the Mughal Empire, at a time when British involvement in India was rapidly increasing.

Ghalib was deeply critical of the harshness of British rule, yet he also admired the city planning and prosperity they had introduced in Calcutta. He didn't support the 1857 revolt (or as the British called it, the "Mutiny") against colonial rule, and was shocked at the extent of British reprisals, in which many of his friends were hanged or exiled. An added personal loss was the destruction of the homes and libraries of two friends where many of his poems were housed. Hundreds survived, though, scattered about on paper and in people's memories; one poem was said to have been preserved when a beggar, seeking alms, came to his door and recited it.

Though he wrote for the Mughal emperor and other aristocrats, Ghalib was never a model court poet, and he didn't conceal his lack of admiration for the emperor's own poetry. For the middle decades of his life he enjoyed less royal favor than the emperor's less talented poetry teacher, Zauq; finally, upon Zauq's death in 1847, the emperor rather reluctantly appointed Ghalib his court poet. Ghalib wrote Persian poems in praise of the king, while once again turning to writing *ghazals* in Urdu, until his death in 1869 at the age of seventy-two. Since then, Ghalib has been regarded as the greatest writer of Urdu *ghazals* of any era.

In a classic *ghazal,* both lines of the poem's opening couplet must end with the same word or phrase, which then serves as a refrain at the end of each succeeding couplet. A rhyming word or phrase must appear just before this refrain, and the same rhyme must be carried through the entire poem. The *ghazal* has no set length and no fixed meter, but all the lines in a given *ghazal* have to be of the same length.

The translations below strive to convey the condensed, revelatory beauty of Ghalib's verse rather than the formal patterning of rhymes, but this patterning can be experienced directly in *ghazals* written in English by the contemporary Kashmiri-American poet Agha Shahid Ali (1949–2001), as in these lines from "Ghazal," from his posthumous collection *Call Me Ishmael Tonight: A Book of Ghazals*:

> Where are you now? Who lies beneath your spell tonight
> before you agonize him in farewell tonight?
>
> Pale hands that once loved me beside the Shalimar:
> Whom else from rapture's road will you expel tonight?
>
> Those "fabrics of Cashmere—" "to make Me beautiful—"
> "Trinket"—to gem—"Me to adorn—How—tell"—tonight?
>
> I beg for haven: Prisons, let open your gates—
> A refugee from Belief seeks a cell tonight.

I'm neither the loosening of song[1]

I'm neither the loosening of song nor the close-drawn tent of music;
I'm the sound, simply, of my own breaking.[2]

You were meant to sit in the shade of your rippling hair;
I was made to look further, into a blacker tangle.

5   All my self-possession is self-delusion;
what violent effort, to maintain this nonchalance!

Now that you've come, let me touch you in greeting
as the forehead of the beggar touches the ground.

No wonder you came looking for me, you
10   who care for the grieving, and I the sound of grief.

GHALIB

414

Come now: I want you: my only peace[1]

Come now: I want you: my only peace.
I've passed the age of fencing and teasing.

This life: a night of drinking and poetry.
Paradise: a long hangover.

5   Tears sting my eyes; I'm leaving
lest the other guests see my weakness.

I is another, the rose no rose this year;
without a meaning to perceive, what is perception?

Ghalib: no hangover will cure a man like you
10   knowing as you do the aftertaste of all sweetness.

When I look out, I see no hope for change[1]

When I look out, I see no hope for change.
I don't see how anything in my life can end well.

Their funeral date is already decided, but still
People complain that they can't sleep.

5   When young, my love-disasters made me burst out laughing.
Now even funny things seem sober to me.

1. Translated by Adrienne Rich.
2. The term used, *shikast*, means defeat or breaking; it is also used for a note out of tune.
1. Translated by Adrienne Rich.
1. Translated by Robert Bly and Sunil Dutta, as are the rest of the Ghalib poems.

I know the answer—that's what keeps me quiet.
Beyond that it's clear I know how to speak.

Why shouldn't I scream? I can stop. Perhaps
10   The Great One notices Ghalib only when he stops screaming.

This is the spiritual state I am in:
About myself, there isn't any news.

I do die; the longing for death is so strong it's killing me.
Such a death comes, but the other death doesn't come.

15   What face will you wear when you visit the Kaaba?[2]
Ghalib, you are shameless even to think of that.

If King Jamshid's diamond cup breaks that's it

If King Jamshid's diamond cup breaks, that's it.[1]
But my clay cup I can easily replace, so it's better.

The delight of giving is deeper when the gift hasn't been demanded.
I like the God-seeker who doesn't make a profession of begging.

5   When I see God, color comes into my cheeks.
God thinks—this is a bad mistake—that I'm in good shape.

When a drop falls in the river, it becomes the river.
When a deed is done well, it becomes the future.

I know that Heaven doesn't exist, but the idea
10   Is one of Ghalib's favorite fantasies.

One can sigh, but a lifetime is needed to finish it

One can sigh, but a lifetime is needed to finish it.
We'll die before we see the tangles in your hair loosened.

There are dangers in waves, in all those crocodiles with their jaws open.
The drop of water goes through many difficulties before it becomes a pearl.

5   Love requires waiting, but desire doesn't want to wait.
The heart has no patience; it would rather bleed to death.

I know you will respond when you understand the state of my soul,
But I'll probably become earth before all that is clear to you.

When the sun arrives the dew on the petal passes through existence.
10   I am also me until your kind eye catches sight of me.

How long is our life? How long does an eyelash flutter?
The warmth of a poetry gathering is like a single spark.[1]

2. Sacred shrine in Mecca, which every Muslim hopes to visit at least once.
1. The legendary Persian king Jamshid could see the future inside his jeweled cup.
1. Poets and their friends would gather for long evenings of poetry and feasting.

Oh Ghalib, the sorrows of existence, what can cure them but death?
There are so many colors in the candle flame, and then the day comes.

When the Great One gestures to me

When the Great One gestures to me, the message does not become clear.
When love words are spoken, I get six or seven meanings.

I must tell you, God, this woman doesn't grasp my meaning.
Give her a second heart, please, if you don't give me a second tongue.

5   Her eyebrows do make a bow, but the rest is unclear.
What are her eyes? An arrow or something else?

You come into town, and I still grieve. Of course I can go
To the market and buy another heart and another life.

I'm good at smashing rocks with my head, but it looks as if
10   Someone on this street has been strewing boulders.

My soul is full and it would be good to drain the blood.
The problem is limits; I have only two eyes.

Even though my head flies off, I love to hear her voice
As she remarks to the executioner: "You're doing well."

15   People get a real sense of what the sun is like
When I let the light reflect off one of my scars.

I could have had some peace, had I not fallen in love with you.
If I hadn't died, I could have done a lot more crying and sighing.

A river keeps rising when its bed is not available.
20   When my nature becomes dammed, it just keeps moving.

We know there is more than one good poet in the world,
But the experts say that Ghalib's little jests are great.

For tomorrow's sake, don't skimp with me on wine today

For tomorrow's sake, don't skimp with me on wine today.
A stingy portion implies a suspicion of heaven's abundance.

The horse of life is galloping; we'll never know the stopping place.
Our hands are not touching the reins, nor our feet the stirrups.

5   I keep a certain distance from the reality of things.
It's the same distance between me and utter confusion.

The scene, the one looking, and the ability to see are all the same.
If that is so, why am I confused about what is in front of me?

10   The greatness of a river depends on its magnificent face.
    If we break it into bubbles and drops and waves, we are lost.

    She is not free from her ways to increase her beauty.
    The mirror she sees is on the inside of her veil.

    What we think is obvious is so far beyond our comprehension.
    We are still dreaming even when we dream we are awake.

15   From the smell of my friend's friend I get the smell of my friend.
    Listen, Ghalib, you are busy worshiping God's friend.

I am confused: should I cry over my heart, or slap my chest?

    I am confused: should I cry over my heart, or slap my chest?
    If I could afford it, I'd have a man paid to cry.

    My jealousy is so strong that I refuse to name the street where you live.
    In view of that, "How do I get there?" doesn't make much sense.

5   I was forced to walk to his house a thousand times.
    I wish I'd never known about that path you like so much.

    It's clear to her that my fate is nothing and nobody.
    If I had known that, I would not have thrown away my house.

    Fools typically mistake simple desire for a form of worship.
10   Do I desire a hard woman or do I worship a stone?[1]

    I walk for a short distance with each fast-moving stream.
    But that's because I don't know who the guide is.

    I was so carefree I forgot the roads to my friend's house.
    Now how can I discover who I am?

15   I judge the whole world on the basis of my imagination.
    I think that every person loves a true work of art.

She has a habit of torture, but doesn't mean to end the love

    She has a habit of torture, but doesn't mean to end the love.
    Such oppression is only teasing; we don't imagine it as a test.

    Which of my mouths shall I use to thank her for this delight?
    I know she inquires about me even though no word is exchanged.

5   The one who tortures likes us, and we like the torturers.
    So if she's not kind, we have to say she's not unkind.

1. Perhaps alluding to the Black Stone enshrined at Mecca, which Muslim pilgrims kiss to obtain forgiveness of sin; it is said to have been given to Adam on his expulsion from Paradise.

If you don't give me a kiss, at least curse at me.
That means you have a tongue if you don't have a mouth.

If your heart is still in one piece, cut your chest with a dagger.
10   If eyelashes are not soaked with blood, put a knife in your heart.

The heart is an embarrassment to the chest if it's not on fire.
Releasing a breath brings shame if it's not a fountain of flame.

Well, it's not a loss for me if my madness has destroyed our house.
Giving up a large house for a wilderness is a good bargain.

15   You ask me what is written on my forehead? It shows marks
From being rubbed on the stone floor before some god.

Gabriel[1] sends praise to me for my poems;
That happens even though Gabriel speaks a different language.

For the price of one kiss she sets my whole life—
20   Because she knows Ghalib is only about half alive.

For my weak heart this living in the sorrow house

For my weak heart this living in the sorrow house is more than enough.
The shortage of rose-colored wine is also more than enough.

I'm embarrassed, otherwise I'd tell the wine-server
That even the leftovers in the cup are, for me, enough.

5   No arrow comes flying in; I am safe from hunters.
The comfort level I experience in this cage is more than enough.

I don't see why the so-called elite people are so proud
When the ropes of custom that tie them down are clear enough.

It's hard for me to distinguish sacrifice from hypocrisy,
10   When the greed for reward in pious actions is obvious enough.

Leave me alone at the Zam Zam Well; I won't circle the Kaaba.[1]
The wine stains on my robe are already numerous enough.

If we can't resolve this, it will be a great injustice.
She is not unwilling and my desire is more than strong enough.

15   The blood of my heart has not completely exited through my eyes.
O death, let me stay a while, the work we have to do is abundant enough.

It's difficult to find a person who has no opinion about Ghalib.
He is a good poet, but the dark rumors about him are more than enough.

---

1. Archangel who brought divine revelations to Muhammad, "guidance and glad tidings for those who believe" (Qur'an 2:97).
1. The poet will remain at an oasis short of the pilgrim's destination of the Kaaba, the sacred shrine at Mecca.

Religious people are always praising the Garden of Paradise

Religious people are always praising the Garden of Paradise.
To us ecstatics it's a bouquet left on the bedstand of forgetfulness.

Her eyelashes are so sharp it's hard to describe the pain.
Each drop of eye blood is like a necklace made of coral.

5 If this world gave me free time, I could show you fireworks.
My heart has many scars; each scar signifies a tree all on fire.

You know what the reflected sunlight does to dewdrops.
Your beauty has the same effect on the house of mirrors.

In my beginning there was already the essence of my end.
10 Lightning doesn't care about the crop, it wants the farmer.

In my silence there are thousands of blood-soaked desires.
I am like a candle that has gone out on the grave of a poor man.

I think you must be making love today with that man I hate.
Otherwise why would you smile so mischievously in my dream?

15 Ghalib, I think we have caught sight of the road to death now.
Death is a string that binds together the scattered beads of the universe.

Only a few faces show up as roses

Only a few faces show up as roses; where are the rest?
This dust must be concealing so many poets and saints.

The Seven Pleiades hid behind a veil all day.[1]
At night they changed their minds, and became naked.

5 During the night of separation red tears flow from my eyes.
I will imagine my eyes as two burning candles.

We'll seek revenge in heaven from these hard-hearted beauties.
Of course that presupposes that their destination is heaven.

That man on whose arm your hair is spread out
10 Owns three things: sleep, a quiet mind, and night.

When I visited the Garden, it was as if I started a school.
Even the birds gave poetry readings after hearing me cry.

O God, why do these glances of hers keep invading my heart?
What luck do I have? When I look, I see her lids.

15 All the good words I could remember I gave to the doorman.
How can I change her painful jibes now into blessings?

---

1. The translators use the Pleiades as an equivalent to a cluster of three stars called "Daughters of the Bier" in Urdu.

Whenever a man's hand closes around a cup of wine,
That energy-enhancer, he believes the lines in his palm are life's rivers.

20 I believe in one God only, and my religion is breaking rules:
When all sects go to pieces, they'll become part of the true religion.

When a human being becomes used to sorrow, then sorrow disappears;
Obstacle after obstacle fell on me, and the road was easy.

If Ghalib keeps pouring out the salt of his tears,
Dear people, I say the whole world will become a ruin.

I agree that I'm in a cage, and I'm crying

I agree that I'm in a cage, and I'm crying.
But my crying doesn't affect the happy birds in the garden.

The wound I have in my chest did not bring one tear from you.
But that wound made even the eye of the needle weep.

5 When people began to talk about chains for my ankles,
The gold under the ground began to twist, pushing the iron away.

The essence of faith is loyalty and devotion.
It's all right to bury in the Kaaba the Brahman who died worshiping in the temple.[1]

My destiny was always to have my head cut off.
10 Whenever I see a sword, my neck bends by habit.

I can sleep well at night because I was robbed during the day.
I have to thank the robber for providing such a relaxed sleep.

Why should we bother about diamonds if we can write poems?
We have our own chests to dig in; why bother traveling to the mines?

Each time I open my mouth, the Great One says

Each time I open my mouth, the Great One says: "You—you, who are you?"
Help me, how would you describe the style of such a conversation?

A spark is lacking in awe. Lightning lacks playfulness.
Neither has the Great One's adroit fierceness.

5 My jealousy arises because my rival gets to speak to you;
Otherwise it's okay if he ruins my reputation.

Blood makes my whole shirt stick to my body.
The good thing is I don't have to repair my collar.

1. A Brahman is a member of the Hindu priestly caste, who would never ordinarily be admitted to the precincts of the Muslim shrine at Mecca.

With the whole body cindered, the heart was clearly burnt.
10   Digging into the ashes, what's the point of that?

Blood flowing along through the veins doesn't impress us.
If blood doesn't drop from the eyes, it's not real blood.

My main attraction to Heaven has always been its wine—
That musky, fuschia-colored wine we've been promised.

15   If it's drinking time, I need large containers.
Let's put away these mingy cups and flagons.

My gift of speech is gone but even if I still had it
What reason would I have to put desire into words?

Since he's a friend of the Emperor, he oozes arrogance.[1]
20   How else can Ghalib gain any respect?

My heart is becoming restless again

My heart is becoming restless again;
And my fingernails start looking for my chest.

My fingernails are clawing down toward my heart again.
It must be the right time for planting red tulips.

5   The eyes that are filled with desire have a goal—
The curtained hoodah[1] where the elegant rider sits.

The eye's habit is to buy and sell disreputable goods.
The heart is an enthusiastic purchaser of humiliation.

I'm still giving out the same hundred colorful complaints.
10   Tears are falling now, but a hundred times more.

Because my heart wants so much to look at my lover's beautiful feet,
It has become a scene of great unrest like the paintings of the Last Day.

Beauty is passing by once more and showing her style
So we know that someone will shortly die in the public square.

15   We die over and over for the same unfaithful person.
Our life has fallen back into the old familiar ways.

The whole world is sinking into darkness and corruption
Because she has just thrown back her beautiful hair.

Once more the mashed pieces of the heart send in their petitions
20   Asking why the pain in this world is so repetitive.

The amount of ecstasy has to make some sense, Ghalib.
There must be something hiding behind the curtain.

1. Said to be an allusion to the favored court poet Zauq.
1. A canopied seat for nobility riding on an elephant.

Charles Baudelaire was the consummate modern city-dweller, a bohemian slummer who devoted himself to sex, drugs, alcohol, art, and poetry. His background was typical for an upper-middle-class child in nineteenth-century France: the young second wife adored by her son, the father an ancient civil servant (and poet and painter) dead before his son was ten, the detested and disciplinarian stepfather who sent the boy away to various schools from which he was quickly expelled for bad behavior, the inheritance squandered on a dandy's finery and on every debauchery the city could offer, the enforced South Seas voyage to straighten him out, and the return to Paris more determined than ever to live to the fullest the life of the penniless artist. Baudelaire fell tumultuously in love with the mulatta actress Jeanne Duval, among others; he drank to excess while experimenting with hashish and other intoxicants; he accumulated enormous debts, and contracted syphilis in the bargain while exploring the low life of Paris. He also wrote, constantly.

In the mid-1840s, Baudelaire began publishing reviews of the annual *Salons* (art exhibitions), and composing the poems that he would eventually collect in *Les Fleurs du Mal* (*The Flowers of Evil*). He was involved briefly in radical politics, manning the barricades during the Revolution of 1848, where his primary contribution was to exhort the Republicans to shoot down his stepfather, the General Aupick. He achieved his first literary celebrity with a series of translations of the American writer Edgar Allan Poe. When the first edition of *Les Fleurs du Mal* was finally published in 1857, it was immediately prosecuted for obscenity, the author was fined, and six of the poems were ordered to be excised from further editions. Over the last ten years of his life, as his health deteriorated, Baudelaire revised *Les Fleurs du Mal,* continued publishing criticism, including an influential manifesto of modernism, *The Painter of Modern Life,* and began work on a series of prose poems, *Paris Spleen,* which were published posthumously. By the last years of his life, syphilis had rendered him mute and partially paralyzed; he died an invalid at age forty-six, his mother by his side.

The subject matter of Baudelaire's poetry has retained much of its capacity to shock: the necrophilia of "A Martyr," the rotting corpse of "Carrion," the sheer cruelty of "Ragpicker's Wine." But the key to its power is the decorous language and melodic rhythms with which the poems describe the depravity of modern life. In "Carrion," for example, the poet begins with the familiar theme of a lover remembering a walk in a park alongside his beloved, before bringing his reader face-to-face with a different sort of nature:

> Remember, my soul, the thing we saw
> that lovely summer day?
> On a pile of stones where the path turned off,
> that hideous carrion.

Baudelaire favored regular and often intricate rhyme schemes, short and highly structured verse forms such as the sonnet, and the classically French twelve-syllable line called the alexandrine. In the quatrain quoted above, the narrative alexandrines (1 and 3) alternate with the singsong counterpoint of the brief eight-syllable lines (2 and 4):

> Rappelez-vous l'objet que nous vîmes, mon âme,
> Ce beau matin d'été si doux:
> Au détour d'un sentier une charogne infame
> Sur un lit semé de cailloux.

Just as modern life hid unpleasant surprises behind pleasing exteriors, just as the industrial city brought stark contrasts of experience into close proximity, so the *Fleurs du Mal* wrapped cruel and cynical insights inside perfect poetic artifacts of great beauty.

Although the desire to shock the middle class was a fundamental tenet of Baudelaire's bohemianism, his poetry extended that rebellious impulse into a profound expression of despair. Baudelaire is one of the great love poets of the French language, and yet his poetry is more about the impossibility of love in Paris than about its wonders and delights. The poet appears rooted to Paris, but can conceive of love only outside of its bounds, in an exotic place he will never actually see but where he can hope to escape in his imagination: "All is order there, and elegance, / pleasure, peace, and opulence" ("Invitation to the Voyage"). By contrast, love in reality takes place in the fallen world of Paris, sullied by money and spoiled by boredom, a world where "Man is tired of writing, Woman of love" ("Twilight: Daybreak"). The only joy offered by love in the city lies in a momentary glance or a dream of what might have been, as in the sonnet, "In Passing." Once tasted, passion turns to boredom, and novelty gives way to spleen, the bile of someone who yearns for genuine experience but is convinced he will never find it.

Among the citydwellers who inhabit the world of these poems there is scarcely a glimpse of the figures of elegance, wealth, and beauty for which mid-nineteenth-century Paris was renowned; instead, the poet turns his caustic eye to society's exiles, throwing into the face of his bourgeois readers what they would have seen around them every day but never actually registered: the ragpicking beggars, the prostitutes, the drunkards, and the rundown slums. Whatever his society defined as evil or excluded as diseased, Baudelaire placed in his poetry as a figure of warped beauty. Not for the bohemian the easy pleasures of the summer day and the innocent sweetheart of the traditional lyric; the only response to the cruelty of modern life was a crueler beauty and a fiercely ironic gaze on the world.

Baudelaire brought lyric poetry into the modern world; he invented the persona of the *poète maudit,* the cursed artist who transforms despair into a tool for stripping away the hypocrisies of existence, and who trades in the niceties of society for the grit of the slums. And he perfected another hallmark of modern culture—irony—for he never forgot the fundamentally ridiculous fact that his audience, the "hypocrite reader" of the opening poem of the *Fleurs du Mal,* was not the downtrodden marginals and perverse bohemians of whom he wrote, but the respectable bourgeoisie whom he wanted so desperately to shock. The mythic persona and ironic gaze of Baudelaire's writing resonates through modern poetry from Symbolist admirers such as Rimbaud and Mallarmé to modernist poets such as Pound and Eliot through the American Beat poets of the 1950s all the way to such martyrs to rock music as Jim Morrison, Janis Joplin, and Kurt Cobain.

from the Flowers of Evil[1]

To the Reader

Stupidity, delusion, selfishness and lust
torment our bodies and possess our minds,
and we sustain our affable remorse
the way a beggar nourishes his lice.

5   Our sins are stubborn, our contrition lame;
we want our scruples to be worth our while—
how cheerfully we crawl back to the mire:
a few cheap tears will wash our stains away!

---

1. Translated by Richard Howard.

Satan Trismegistus[2] subtly rocks
10   our ravished spirits on his wicked bed
until the precious metal of our will
is leached out° by this cunning alchemist:[3]   *filtered out*

the Devil's hand directs our every move—
the things we loathed become the things we love;
15   day by day we drop through stinking shades
quite undeterred on our descent to Hell.

Like a poor profligate who sucks and bites
the withered breast of some well-seasoned trull,°   *prostitute*
we snatch in passing at clandestine joys
20   and squeeze the oldest orange harder yet.

Wriggling in our brains like a million worms,
a demon demos° holds its revels there,   *populace*
and when we breathe, the Lethe[4] in our lungs
trickles sighing on its secret course.

25   If rape and arson, poison and the knife
have not yet stitched their ludicrous designs
onto the banal buckram° of our fates,   *coarse linen*
it is because our souls lack enterprise!

But here among the scorpions and the hounds,
30   the jackals, apes and vultures, snakes and wolves,
monsters that howl and growl and squeal and crawl
in all the squalid zoo of vices, one

is even uglier and fouler than the rest,
although the least flamboyant of the lot;
35   this beast would gladly undermine the earth
and swallow all creation in a yawn;

I speak of Boredom[5] which with ready tears
dreams of hangings as it puffs its pipe.
Reader, you know this squeamish monster well,
40   —hypocrite reader,—my alias,—my twin!

The Albatross[1]

Often, to pass the time on board, the crew
will catch an albatross, one of those big birds
which nonchalantly chaperone a ship
across the bitter fathoms of the sea.

2. Meaning "triply great," the term was usually applied to Hermes Trismegistus, legendary author of the Hermetic writings of Egypt and inventor of alchemy.

3. Alchemy manipulates base metals with corrosive acids and water preparations to yield precious metals such as gold and silver.

4. The river of forgetting in the classical underworld.

5. Here as elsewhere in *The Flowers of Evil*, Baudelaire personifies states of mind and other abstractions as active forces or characters.

1. Large seabirds with a wingspan reaching over ten feet, albatrosses spend nearly their entire lives at sea. In sailors' lore, to cause the death of an albatross was considered extremely bad luck.

5   Tied to the deck, this sovereign of space,
    as if embarrassed by its clumsiness,
    pitiably lets its great white wings
    drag at its sides like a pair of unshipped oars.

    How weak and awkward, even comical
10 this traveller but lately so adroit—
    one deckhand sticks a pipestem in its beak,
    another mocks the cripple that once flew!

    The Poet is like this monarch of the clouds
    riding the storm above the marksman's range;
15 exiled on the ground, hooted and jeered,
    he cannot walk because of his great wings.

Correspondences

    The pillars of Nature's temple are alive
    and sometimes yield perplexing messages;
    forests of symbols between us and the shrine
    remark our passage with accustomed eyes.

5   Like long-held echoes, blending somewhere else
    into one deep and shadowy unison
    as limitless as darkness and as day,
    the sounds, the scents, the colors correspond.[1]

    There are odors succulent as young flesh,
10 sweet as flutes, and green as any grass,
    while others—rich, corrupt and masterful—

    possess the power of such infinite things
    as incense, amber, benjamin[2] and musk,
    to praise the senses' raptures and the mind's.

The Head of Hair

    Ecstatic fleece that ripples to your nape
    and reeks of negligence in every curl!
    To people my dim cubicle tonight
    with memories shrouded in that head of hair,
5   I'd have it flutter like a handkerchief!

    For torpid Asia, torrid Africa
    —the wilderness I thought a world away—
    survive at the heart of this dark continent...

---

1. The theory of a universal analogy between sounds, scents, and colors was frequently voiced in mid-19th-century literary circles; among its proponents were the German writer of fantastic stories, E. T. A. Hoffmann, the French novelist Honoré de Balzac, the eccentric poet Alphonse Esquiros, and Alphonse-Louis Constant, who published occult works under the pseudonym Eliphas Levi.

2. Gum benjamin, the resin of the benzoin tree of Southeast Asia, is used as an aromatic in perfumes.

As other souls set sail to music, mine,
10   O my love! embarks on your redolent hair.

Take me, tousled current, to where men
as mighty as the trees they live among
submit like them to the sun's long tyranny;
ebony sea, you bear a brilliant dream
15   of sails and pennants, mariners and masts,

a harbor where my soul can slake its thirst
for color, sound and smell—where ships that glide
among the seas of golden silk throw wide
their yardarms to embrace a glorious sky
20   palpitating in eternal heat.

Drunk, and in love with drunkenness, I'll dive
into this ocean where the other lurks,
and solaced by these waves, my restlessness
will find a fruitful lethargy at last,
25   rocking forever at aromatic ease.

Blue hair, vault of shadows, be for me
the canopy of overarching sky;
here at the downy roots of every strand
I stupefy myself on the mingled scent
30   of musk and tar and coconut oil for hours . . .

For hours? Forever! Into that splendid mane
let me braid rubies, ropes of pearls to bind
you indissolubly to my desire—
you the oasis where I dream, the gourd
35   from which I gulp the wine of memory.

Carrion

Remember, my soul, the thing we saw
    that lovely summer day?
On a pile of stones where the path turned off,
    the hideous carrion—

5   legs in the air, like a whore—displayed,
      indifferent to the last,
a belly slick with lethal sweat
    and swollen with foul gas.

The sun lit up that rottenness
10   as though to roast it through,
restoring to Nature a hundredfold
    what she had here made one.

And heaven watched the splendid corpse
    like a flower open wide—

15 you nearly fainted dead away
  at the perfume it gave off.

Flies kept humming over the guts
  from which a gleaming clot
of maggots poured to finish off
20 what scraps of flesh remained.

The tide of trembling vermin sank,
  then bubbled up afresh
as if the carcass, drawing breath,
  by *their* lives lived again

25 and made a curious music there—
  like running water, or wind,
or the rattle of chaff the winnower
  loosens in his fan.[1]

Shapeless—nothing was left but a dream
30 the artist had sketched in,
forgotten, and only later on
  finished from memory.

Behind the rocks an anxious bitch
  eyed us reproachfully,
35 waiting for the chance to resume
  her interrupted feast.

—Yet you will come to this offence,
  this horrible decay,
you, the light of my life, the sun
40 and moon and stars of my love!

Yes, you will come to this, my queen,
  after the sacraments,°   *funeral rites*
when you rot underground among
  the bones already there.

45 But as their kisses eat you up,
  my Beauty, tell the worms
I've kept the sacred essence, saved
  the form of my rotted loves!

Invitation to the Voyage

 Imagine the magic
  of living together
there, with all the time in the world
  for loving each other,

---

1. A winnower uses a special fan to toss corn or wheat into the air to separate the lighter husks, the chaff, from the edible grain.

5   for loving and dying
where even the landscape resembles you:
    the suns dissolved
    in overcast skies
have the same mysterious charm for me
10   as your wayward eyes
    through crystal tears,
       my sister, my child!

All is order there, and elegance,
    pleasure, peace, and opulence.

15   Furniture gleaming
    with the patina
of time itself in the room we would share;
    the rarest flowers
    mingling aromas
20   with amber's uncertain redolence;
    encrusted ceilings
    echoed in mirrors
and Eastern splendor on the walls—
    here all would whisper
25   to the soul in secret
      her sweet mother tongue.

All is order there, and elegance,
    pleasure, peace, and opulence.

    On these still canals
30   the freighters doze
fitfully: their mood is for roving,
    and only to flatter
    a lover's fancy
have they put in from the ends of the earth.
35   By late afternoon
    the canals catch fire
as sunset glorifies the town;
    the world turns to gold
    as it falls asleep
40   in a fervent light.

All is order there, and elegance,
    pleasure, peace, and opulence.

Spleen (II)[1]

Souvenirs?
More than if I had lived a thousand years!

---

1. In medieval medicine, the spleen was associated with the black bile said to cause melancholy. Baudelaire adapted the English word to express the feeling of bitterness and boredom ("ennui") he considered to be characteristic of modern life.

No chest of drawers crammed with documents,
love-letters, wedding-invitations, wills,
5   a lock of someone's hair rolled up in a deed,
hides so many secrets as my brain.
This branching catacombs, this pyramid
contains more corpses than the potter's field:[2]
I am a graveyard that the moon abhors,
10 where long worms like regrets come out to feed
most ravenously on my dearest dead.
I am an old boudoir where a rack of gowns,
perfumed by withered roses, rots to dust;
where only faint pastels and pale Bouchers[3]
15 inhale the scent of long-unstoppered flasks.

Nothing is slower than the limping days
when under the heavy weather of the years
Boredom, the fruit of glum indifference,
gains the dimension of eternity...
20 Hereafter, mortal clay, you are no more
than a rock encircled by a nameless dread,
an ancient sphinx omitted from the map,
forgotten by the world, and whose fierce moods
sing only to the rays of setting suns.

The Swan

to Victor Hugo[1]

1

Andromache, I think of you! That stream,
the sometime witness to your widowhood's
enormous majesty of mourning—that
mimic Simoïs salted by your tears[2]

5   suddenly inundates my memory
as I cross the new Place du Carrousel.[3]
Old Paris is gone (no human heart
changes half so fast as a city's face)[4]

2. In French *fosse commune,* a burial ground for the poor and for strangers.

3. The French painter François Boucher (1703–1770) was famous for his delicate colors, easy style, and frivolous subjects, and especially for his female nudes.

1. Celebrated French Romantic poet, novelist and dramatist (1802–1885). Baudelaire sent a manuscript copy of the poem to Hugo, who was in political exile at the time on the Channel Islands.

2. The wife of Hector of Troy, Andromache was claimed as prize of war by Achilles's son Pyrrhus. Abandoned by him, she eventually came to settle in Epirus, where Aeneas visits her in Book 3 of Virgil's *Aeneid.* She and her new husband, Hector's brother Helenus, have built a miniature Troy, complete with a replica of its river, Simois, at the shores of which she weeps over the empty grave of her dead husband.

3. The bohemian artists' quarter where Baudelaire and others of his circle had lived had been demolished in 1849 in order to connect the Louvre with the Tuileries Palace. The Place du Carrousel was established in its place.

4. The loss of *vieux Paris,* the narrow winding streets and old buildings dating back to the medieval city, to the demolitions of 19th-century speculation and improvements, was a refrain through most of the century, especially the second half.

and only in my mind's eye can I see
10   The junk laid out to glitter in the booths
among the weeds and splintered capitals,°   *columns*
blocks of marble blackened by the mud;

there used to be a poultry-market here,
and one cold morning—with the sky swept clean,
15   the ground, too, swept by garbage-men who raised
clouds of soot in the icy air—I saw

a swan that had broken out of its cage,
webbed feet clumsy on the cobblestones,
white feathers dragging in the uneven ruts,
20   and obstinately pecking at the drains,

drenching its enormous wings in the filth
as if in its own lovely lake, crying
"Where is the thunder, when will it rain?"
I see it still, inevitable myth,

25   like Daedalus dead-set against the sky[5]—
the sky quite blue and blank and unconcerned—
that straining neck and that voracious beak,
as if the swan were castigating God!

          2

Paris changes...But in sadness like mine
30   nothing stirs—new buildings, old
neighborhoods turn to allegory,
and memories weigh more than stone.

One image, near the Louvre, will not dissolve:
I think of that great swan in its torment,
35   silly, like all exiles, and sublime,
endlessly longing...And again I think

of you, Andromache, dragged off
to be the booty of Achilles' son,
Hector's widow now the wife of Helenus,
40   crouching blindly over an empty grave!

I think of some black woman, starving
and consumptive in the muddy streets,
peering through a wall of fog for those
missing palms of splendid Africa;

45   I think of orphans withering like flowers;
of those who lose what never can be found
again—never! swallowing their tears
and nursing at the she-wolf Sorrow's dugs;

---

5. According to legend, the Greek inventor Daedalus had escaped with his son Icarus from imprisonment in Crete with the help of artificial wings stuck with wax.

50　and in the forest of my mind's exile
　　a merciless memory winds its horn:
　　I hear it and I think of prisoners,
　　of the shipwrecked, the beaten—and so many more!

In Passing

　　The traffic roared around me, deafening!
　　Tall, slender, in mourning—noble grief—
　　a woman passed, and with a jewelled hand
　　gathered up her black embroidered hem;

5　stately yet lithe, as if a statue walked...
　　And trembling like a fool, I drank from eyes
　　as ashen as the clouds before a gale
　　the grace that beckons and the joy that kills.

　　Lightning...then darkness! Lovely fugitive
10　whose glance has brought me back to life! But where
　　is life—not this side of eternity?

　　Elsewhere! Too far, too late, or never at all!
　　Of me you know nothing, I nothing of you—you
　　whom I might have loved and who knew that too!

Twilight: Evening

　　It comes as an accomplice, stealthily,
　　the lovely hour that is the felon's friend;
　　the sky, like curtains round a bed, draws close,
　　and man prepares to become a beast of prey.

5　Longed for by those whose aching arms confess:
　　we earned our daily bread, at last it comes,
　　evening and the anodyne° it brings　　　　　*relief*
　　to workmen free to sleep and dream of sleep,
　　to stubborn scholars puzzling over texts,
10　to minds consumed by one tormenting pain...
　　Meantime, foul demons in the atmosphere
　　dutifully waken—they have work to do—
　　rattling shutters as they take the sky.
　　Under the gaslamps shaken by that wind
15　whoredom invades and everywhere at once
　　debouches° on invisible thoroughfares,　　*pours out*
　　as if the enemy had launched a raid;
　　it fidgets like a worm in the city's filth,
　　filching its portion of Man's daily bread.

20　Listen! Now you can hear the kitchens hiss,
　　the stages yelp, the music drown it all!
　　The dens that specialize in gambling fill
　　with trollops and their vague confederates,

25 and thieves untroubled by a second thought
will soon be hard at work (they also serve)
softly forcing doors and secret drawers
to dress their sluts and live a few days more.

This is the hour to compose yourself, my soul;
ignore the noise they make; avert your eyes.
30 Now comes the time when invalids grow worse
and darkness takes them by the throat; they end
their fate in the usual way, and all their sighs
turn hospitals into a cave of the winds.
More than one will not come back for broth
35 warmed at the fireside by devoted hands.

Most of them, in fact, have never known
a hearth to come to, and have never lived.

Twilight: Daybreak

The morning wind rattles the windowpanes
and over the barracks reveille rings out.

Dreams come now, bad dreams, and teen-age boys
burrow into their pillows. Now the lamp
5 that glowed at midnight seems, like a bloodshot eye,
to throb and throw a red stain on the room;
balked by the stubborn body's weight, the soul
mimics the lamplight's struggles with the dawn.
Like a face in tears—the tears effaced by wind—
10 the air is tremulous with escaping things,
and Man is tired of writing, Woman of love.

Here and there, chimneys begin to smoke.
Whores, mouths gaping, eyelids gray as ash,
sleep on their feet, leaning against the walls,
15 and beggar-women, hunched over sagging breasts,
blow on burning sticks, then on their hands.
Now, the hungry feel the cold the worst,
and women in labor suffer the sharpest pains;
now, like a sob cut short by a clot of blood,
20 a rooster crows somewhere; a sea of mist
swirls around the buildings; in the Hôtel-Dieu[1]
the dying breathe their last, while the debauched,
spent by their exertions, sleep alone.

Shivering dawn, in a wisp of pink and green,
25 totters slowly across the empty Seine,

---

1. A municipal hospital; the one in Paris dates back to the very early Middle Ages, and was demolished in the late 19th century. It stood on the south side of the Ile de la Cité, catercornered to the Notre Dame Cathedral.

and dingy Paris—old drudge rubbing its eyes—
picks up its tools to begin another day.

Ragpickers' Wine[1]

Look—there! in the streetlamp's dingy glow
—wind rattling the glass, lashing the flame—
out of the muddy labyrinth of streets
teeming with unruly, sordid types,

5   a ragpicker stumbles past, wagging his head
and bumping into walls with a poet's grace,
pouring out his heartfelt schemes to one
and all, including spies of the police.[2]

He swears to wonders, lays down noble laws,
10   reforms the wicked, raises up their prey,
and under the lowering canopy of heaven
intoxicates himself on his own boasts.

More such creatures—who knows where they live?—
wracked by drudgery, ruined by the years,
15   staggering under enormous sacks of junk
—the vomit of surfeited Paris—now appear,

whole armies of them, reeking of sour wine,
comrades in arms, whitened by their wars,
whiskers dropping like surrendered flags...
20   Before them wave the banners and the palms—

as if by magic, arches of triumph rise
and in the chaos of exploding flares,
bugle-calls and battle-cries and drums,
they march in glory past a cheering mob!

25   So it is, through frivolous mankind,
that wine like a bright Pactolus pours its gold;[3]
with human tongues it glorifies its deeds
and rules by what it gives, as true kings do.

To drown the spleen and pacify the sloth
30   of these old wrecks who die without a word,
God, taking pity, created Sleep; to which
Man added Wine, the sun's anointed son!

---

1. Ragpickers, or *chiffonniers,* lived off what they scavenged at night from the rags and the garbage of the city.
The *chiffonnier* was an important figure for many writers of the many marginal occupations of the nocturnal city, both
positive and negative, including poetry.

2. *Mouchards,* or police and government spies, were omnipresent under the July Monarchy of Louis-Philippe (1830–1848)
and the Second Empire of Napoleon III (1852–1870). *Chiffonniers* were frequently identified with radical politics.

3. According to Greek myth, King Midas was released from the enchantment that caused whatever he touched to become
gold by bathing in the river Pactolus, filling it with gold.

A Martyr

Drawing by an Unknown Master[1]

Among decanters, ivories and gems,
    sumptuous divans[2]
with gold-brocaded silks and fragrant gowns
    trailing languid folds,

5 where lilies sorrowing in crystal urns
    exhale their final sigh
and where, as if the room were under glass,
    the air is pestilent,

a headless corpse emits a stream of blood
10   the sopping pillows shed
onto thirsty sheets which drink it up
    as greedily as sand.

Pale as the visions which our captive eyes
    discover in the dark,
15 the head, enveloped in its sombre mane,
    emeralds still in its ears,

watches from a stool, a thing apart,
    and from the eyes rolled back
to whiteness blank as daybreak emanates
20   an alabaster stare.[3]

The carcass sprawling naked on the bed
    displays without a qualm
the splendid cynosure[4] which prodigal
    Nature bestowed—betrayed;

25 pink with gold clocks, one stocking clings—
    a souvenir, it seems;
the garter, gleaming like a secret eye,
    darts a jewelled glance.

Doubled by a full-length portrait drawn
30   in the same provocative pose,
the strange demeanor of this solitude
    reveals love's darker side—

profligate practices and guilty joys,
    embraces bound to please

---

1. Rather than referring to a particular work of art, the subtitle emphasizes the visual focus of the poem. The style is of the exotic Romanticism of artists such as Eugène Delacroix, about whose works Baudelaire wrote regularly as an art critic.

2. A decanter is a glass bottle with a stopper in its top; wine is stored in it after it has been decanted, or poured off slowly to eliminate sediment. A divan is a low couch or bed without back or ends; the word comes from the Persian, and the divan was associated with the Orient.

3. Alabaster is a translucent form of gypsum, usually white, used for carving. The adjective is used as a poetic term to describe something white and smooth, such as skin, or, here, in a more symbolic way, the gaze of a dead eye.

4. A brilliant or beautiful focus of attraction or of admiration.

35   the swarm of naughty angels frolicking
            in the curtains overhead;

        yet judging from the narrow elegance
            of her shoulders sloping down
        past the serpentine curve of her waist
40   to the almost bony hips,

        she still is young!—What torment in her soul,
            what tedium that stung
        her senses gave this body to the throng
            of wandering, lost desires?[5]
45   In spite of so much love, did the vengeful man
            she could not, living, sate
        assuage on her inert and docile flesh
            the measure of his lust?

        And did he, gripping her blood-stiffened hair
50   lift up that dripping head
        and press on her cold teeth one final kiss?
            The sullied corpse is still.

        —Far from a scornful world of jeering crowds
            and peering magistrates,
55   sleep in peace, lovely enigma, sleep
            in your mysterious tomb:

        your bridegroom roves, and your immortal form
            keeps vigil when he sleeps;
        like you, no doubt, he will be constant too,
60   and faithful unto death.

GUSTAVE FLAUBERT ▪ (1821–1880)

Gustave Flaubert was almost twenty-eight when he left France for what was then called
"the Orient," a journey that was to last from November 1849 to June 1851. Journeys
to the Middle East were in fashion. This was partly because Napoleon's expedition to
Egypt (1798–1801) and France's strong continuing influence had opened the region to
tourism, which increased after France conquered Algeria in 1847. In part, too, people
had become full of disgust with the sordid money- and title-grubbing and the social
inertia that had followed the epoch of Napoleonic glory. Many of the alienated escaped
into exoticism. But in the profundity of his personal alienation, Flaubert had few if any
competitors.

    Born in 1821 in Rouen, the son of a doctor, Flaubert abandoned the study of law after
a brief and not very successful experience. Supported by a private income, he devoted
himself with an almost theological intensity to writing. He never married or had an ordinary job, and it was largely writing (including voluminous letters to lovers who were

---

5. Opinion at the time had it that the real-life model was a singer, Rosine Stoltz, of whom Baudelaire was enamored, and
whose profile evidently matched this description.

also talented writers) that gave shape to the rest of his life. A perfectionist who worked to discipline his romantic flamboyance, he tried to achieve perfect sentences and perfect detachment. His most famous novel, *Madame Bovary* (1857), scandalized and confused its readers, who couldn't tell whether its author condemned the hungrily misguided aspirations of its adulterous heroine, or secretly identified with them. Prosecuted for "offense to public and religious morality," Flaubert was acquitted but given a severe reprimand and forced to pay the costs of the trial. Subsequent novels added to the sense of public incomprehension, for Flaubert remained absent from his work, refusing to give directions as to how readers were supposed to feel. About *Salammbô* (1862), which fled from the banality of contemporary France into the archaeologically precise strangeness of ancient Carthage, Flaubert famously remarked that few would ever guess how sad he had to be in order to resuscitate this lost kingdom.

Sentimental Education (1869) is set in Paris in the 1840s (the period of Flaubert's own beginnings as a writer) and roughly follows his early passion for an older married woman. But it, too, is distinguished by an apparent disaffection from nearly everything the characters say and do. Franz Kafka, who sets the twentieth-century standard for disaffection, once said that each time he opened Flaubert's book, he felt perfectly at home. *Three Tales* (1877), which includes "A Simple Heart," was a success with the public, but it is simpler only in appearance. Readers have never decided whether Flaubert is or isn't ironic about the servant protagonist of "A Simple Heart," whose life seems empty and who worships a stuffed parrot. Convinced that it was style rather than content that should be decisive, Flaubert once expressed the desire to write a text about "nothing." His extreme horror of cliché and sense of the nothingness lurking behind everyday life are exemplified in two further works, *Bouvard and Pécuchet* and the *Dictionary of Received Ideas,* which were published after his death in 1880.

In 1876, at the funeral of George Sand, a pioneer feminist writer and one of the most famous figures of her generation, Flaubert wept for the loss of his dear friend and long-time correspondent—and for the bad timing that took her away just as he was writing something "exclusively" for her. Sand, who couldn't understand Flaubert's unwillingness to take a moral stand in his fiction, had urged him to write "something down to earth that everybody can enjoy." "A Simple Heart" was his attempt to fulfill her wish. Flaubert insisted that the story was not ironic but intended "to move tender hearts to pity and tears"—just as Sand would have desired. Flaubert would no doubt have appreciated the further irony that we don't know whether or not to trust his own opinion of his story.

PRONUNCIATIONS:
Aubain: oh-BAHNG
Félicité: fay-lee-cee-TAY
Gustave Flaubert: gous-TAHV flow-BARE

A Simple Heart[1]

1

Madame Aubain's servant Félicité was the envy of the ladies of Pont-l'Évêque for half a century.

---

1. Translated by Arthur McDowall.

She received four pounds a year. For that she was cook and general servant, and did the sewing, washing, and ironing; she could bridle a horse, fatten poultry, and churn butter—and she remained faithful to her mistress, unamiable as the latter was.

Mme. Aubain had married a gay bachelor without money who died at the beginning of 1809, leaving her with two small children and a quantity of debts. She then sold all her property except the farms of Toucques and Geffosses, which brought in two hundred pounds a year at most, and left her house in Saint-Melaine for a less expensive one that had belonged to her family and was situated behind the market.

This house had a slate roof and stood between an alley and a lane that went down to the river. There was an unevenness in the levels of the rooms which made you stumble. A narrow hall divided the kitchen from the "parlour" where Mme. Aubain spent her day, sitting in a wicker easy chair by the window. Against the panels, which were painted white, was a row of eight mahogany chairs. On an old piano under the barometer a heap of wooden and cardboard boxes rose like a pyramid. A stuffed arm-chair stood on either side of the Louis-Quinze chimney-piece, which was in yellow marble with a clock in the middle of it modelled like a temple of Vesta.[2] The whole room was a little musty, as the floor was lower than the garden.

The first floor began with "Madame's" room: very large, with a pale-flowered wall-paper and a portrait of "Monsieur" as a dandy of the period. It led to a smaller room, where there were two children's cots without mattresses. Next came the drawing-room, which was always shut up and full of furniture covered with sheets. Then there was a corridor leading to a study. The shelves of a large bookcase were respectably lined with books and papers, and its three wings surrounded a broad writing-table in darkwood. The two panels at the end of the room were covered with pen-drawings, water-colour landscapes, and engravings by Audran, all relics of better days and vanished splendour. Félicité's room on the top floor got its light from a dormer-window, which looked over the meadows.

She rose at daybreak to be in time for Mass, and worked till evening without stopping. Then, when dinner was over, the plates and dishes in order, and the door shut fast, she thrust the log under the ashes and went to sleep in front of the hearth with her rosary in her hand. Félicité was the stubbornest of all bargainers; and as for cleanness, the polish on her saucepans was the despair of other servants. Thrifty in all things, she ate slowly, gathering off the table in her fingers the crumbs of her loaf—a twelve-pound loaf expressly baked for her, which lasted for three weeks.

At all times of year she wore a print hand-kerchief fastened with a pin behind, a bonnet that covered her hair, grey stockings, a red skirt, and a bibbed apron—such as hospital nurses wear—over her jacket.

Her face was thin and her voice sharp. At twenty-five she looked like forty. From fifty onwards she seemed of no particular age; and with her silence, straight figure, and precise movements she was like a woman made of wood, and going by clockwork.

2

She had had her love-story like another.

Her father, a mason, had been killed by falling off some scaffolding. Then her mother died, her sisters scattered, and a farmer took her in and employed her, while

2. Roman goddess of hearth and home.

she was still quite little, to herd the cows at pasture. She shivered in rags and would lie flat on the ground to drink water from the ponds; she was beaten for nothing, and finally turned out for the theft of a shilling which she did not steal. She went to another farm, where she became dairy-maid; and as she was liked by her employers her companions were jealous of her.

One evening in August (she was then eighteen) they took her to the assembly at Colleville. She was dazed and stupefied in an instant by the noise of the fiddlers, the lights in the trees, the gay medley of dresses, the lace, the gold crosses, and the throng of people jigging all together. While she kept shyly apart a young man with a well-to-do air, who was leaning on the shaft of a cart and smoking his pipe, came up to ask her to dance. He treated her to cider, coffee, and cake, and bought her a silk handkerchief; and then, imagining she had guessed his meaning, offered to see her home. At the edge of a field of oats he pushed her roughly down. She was frightened and began to cry out; and he went off.

One evening later she was on the Beaumont road. A big hay-wagon was moving slowly along; she wanted to get in front of it, and as she brushed past the wheels she recognized Theodore. He greeted her quite calmly, saying she must excuse it all because it was "the fault of the drink." She could not think of any answer and wanted to run away.

He began at once to talk about the harvest and the worthies of the commune, for his father had left Colleville for the farm at Les Écots, so that now he and she were neighbours. "Ah!" she said. He added that they thought of settling him in life. Well, he was in no hurry; he was waiting for a wife to his fancy. She dropped her head; and then he asked her if she thought of marrying. She answered with a smile that it was mean to make fun of her.

"But I am not, I swear!"—and he passed his left hand round her waist. She walked in the support of his embrace; their steps grew slower. The wind was soft, the stars glittered, the huge wagon-load of hay swayed in front of them, and dust rose from the dragging steps of the four horses. Then, without a word of command, they turned to the right. He clasped her once more in his arms, and she disappeared into the shadow.

The week after Theodore secured some assignations with her.

They met at the end of farmyards, behind a wall, or under a solitary tree. She was not innocent as young ladies are—she had learned knowledge from the animals—but her reason and the instinct of her honour would not let her fall. Her resistance exasperated Theodore's passion; so much so that to satisfy it—or perhaps quite artlessly—he made her an offer of marriage. She was in doubt whether to trust him, but he swore great oaths of fidelity.

Soon he confessed to something troublesome; the year before his parents had bought him a substitute for the army, but any day he might be taken again, and the idea of serving was a terror to him. Félicité took this cowardice of his as a sign of affection, and it redoubled hers. She stole away at night to see him, and when she reached their meeting-place Theodore racked her with his anxieties and urgings.

At last he declared that he would go himself to the prefecture for information, and would tell her the result on the following Sunday, between eleven and midnight.

When the moment came she sped towards her lover. Instead of him she found one of his friends.

He told her that she would not see Theodore any more. To ensure himself against conscription he had married an old woman, Madame Lehoussais, of Toucques, who was very rich.

There was an uncontrollable burst of grief. She threw herself on the ground, screamed, called to the God of mercy, and moaned by herself in the fields till daylight came. Then she came back to the farm and announced that she was going to leave; and at the end of the month she received her wages, tied all her small belongings with a handkerchief, and went to Pont-l'Évêque.

In front of the inn there she made inquiries of a woman in a widow's cap, who, as it happened, was just looking for a cook. The girl did not know much, but her willingness seemed so great and her demands so small that Mme. Aubain ended by saying:

"Very well, then, I will take you."

A quarter of an hour afterwards Félicité was installed in her house.

She lived there at first in a tremble, as it were, at "the style of the house" and the memory of "Monsieur" floating over it all. Paul and Virginie, the first aged seven and the other hardly four, seemed to her beings of a precious substance; she carried them on her back like a horse; it was a sorrow to her that Mme. Aubain would not let her kiss them every minute. And yet she was happy there. Her grief had melted in the pleasantness of things all round.

Every Thursday regular visitors came in for a game of boston,[3] and Félicité got the cards and foot-warmers ready beforehand. They arrived punctually at eight and left before the stroke of eleven.

On Monday mornings the dealer who lodged in the covered passage spread out all his old iron on the ground. Then a hum of voices began to fill the town, mingled with the neighing of horses, bleating of lambs, grunting of pigs, and the sharp rattle of carts along the street. About noon, when the market was at its height, you might see a tall, hook-nosed old countryman with his cap pushed back making his appearance at the door. It was Robelin, the farmer of Geffosses. A little later came Liébard, the farmer from Toucques—short, red, and corpulent—in a grey jacket and gaiters shod with spurs.

Both had poultry or cheese to offer their landlord. Félicité was invariably a match for their cunning, and they went away filled with respect for her.

At vague intervals Mme. Aubain had a visit from the Marquis de Gremanville, one of her uncles, who had ruined himself by debauchery and now lived at Falaise on his last remaining morsel of land. He invariably came at the luncheon hour, with a dreadful poodle whose paws left all the furniture in a mess. In spite of efforts to show his breeding, which he carried to the point of raising his hat every time he mentioned "my late father," habit was too strong for him; he poured himself out glass after glass and fired off improper remarks. Félicité edged him politely out of the house—"You have had enough, Monsieur de Gremanville! Another time!"—and she shut the door on him.

She opened it with pleasure to M. Bourais, who had been a lawyer. His baldness, his white stock, frilled shirt, and roomy brown coat, his way of rounding the arm as he took snuff—his whole person, in fact, created that disturbance of mind which overtakes us at the sight of extraordinary men.

As he looked after the property of "Madame" he remained shut up with her for hours in "Monsieur's" study, though all the time he was afraid of compromising himself. He respected the magistracy immensely, and had some pretensions to Latin.

To combine instruction and amusement he gave the children a geography book made up of a series of prints. They represented scenes in different parts of the world: cannibals

3. A fashionable card game.

with feathers on their heads, a monkey carrying off a young lady, Bedouins in the desert, the harpooning of a whale, and so on. Paul explained these engravings to Félicité; and that, in fact, was the whole of her literary education. The children's education was undertaken by Guyot, a poor creature employed at the town hall, who was famous for his beautiful hand and sharpened his penknife on his boots.

When the weather was bright the household set off early for a day at Geffosses Farm.

Its courtyard is on a slope, with the farmhouse in the middle, and the sea looks like a grey streak in the distance.

Félicité brought slices of cold meat out of her basket, and they breakfasted in a room adjoining the dairy. It was the only surviving fragment of a country house which was now no more. The wall-paper hung in tatters, and quivered in the draughts. Mme. Aubain sat with bowed head, overcome by her memories; the children became afraid to speak. "Why don't you play, then?" she would say, and off they went.

Paul climbed into the barn, caught birds, played at ducks and drakes over the pond, or hammered with his stick on the big casks which boomed like drums. Virginie fed the rabbits or dashed off to pick cornflowers, her quick legs showing their embroidered little drawers.

One autumn evening they went home by the fields. The moon was in its first quarter, lighting part of the sky; and mist floated like a scarf over the windings of the Toucques. Cattle, lying out in the middle of the grass, looked quietly at the four people as they passed. In the third meadow some of them got up and made a half-circle in front of the walkers. "There's nothing to be afraid of," said Félicité, as she stroked the nearest on the back with a kind of crooning song; he wheeled round and the others did the same. But when they crossed the next pasture there was a formidable bellow. It was a bull, hidden by the mist. Mme. Aubain was about to run. "No! no! don't go so fast!" They mended their pace, however, and heard a loud breathing behind them which came nearer. His hoofs thudded on the meadow grass like hammers; why, he was galloping now! Félicité turned round, and tore up clods of earth with both hands and threw them in his eyes. He lowered his muzzle, waved his horns, and quivered with fury, bellowing terribly. Mme. Aubain, now at the end of the pasture with her two little ones, was looking wildly for a place to get over the high bank. Félicité was retreating, still with her face to the bull, keeping up a shower of clods which blinded him, and crying all the time, "Be quick! be quick!"

Mme. Aubain went down into the ditch, pushed Virginie first and then Paul, fell several times as she tried to climb the bank, and managed it at last by dint of courage.

The bull had driven Félicité to bay against a rail-fence; his slaver was streaming into her face; another second, and he would have gored her. She had just time to slip between two of the rails, and the big animal stopped short in amazement.

This adventure was talked of at Pont-l'Évêque for many a year. Félicité did not pride herself on it in the least, not having the barest suspicion that she had done anything heroic.

Virginie was the sole object of her thoughts, for the child developed a nervous complaint as a result of her fright, and M. Poupart, the doctor, advised sea-bathing at Trouville. It was not a frequented place then. Mme. Aubain collected information, consulted Bourais, and made preparations as though for a long journey.

Her luggage started a day in advance, in Liébard's cart. The next day he brought round two horses, one of which had a lady's saddle with a velvet back to it, while a cloak was rolled up to make a kind of seat on the crupper of the other. Mme. Aubain rode on that, behind the farmer. Félicité took charge of Virginie, and Paul mounted M. Lechaptois' donkey, lent on condition that great care was taken of it.

The road was so bad that its five miles took two hours. The horses sank in the mud up to their pasterns, and their haunches jerked abruptly in the effort to get out; or else they stumbled in the ruts, and at other moments had to jump. In some places Liébard's mare came suddenly to a halt. He waited patiently until she went on again, talking about the people who had properties along the road, and adding moral reflections to their history. So it was that as they were in the middle of Toucques, and passed under some windows bowered with nasturtiums, he shrugged his shoulders and said: "There's a Mme. Lehoussais lives there; instead of taking a young man she…" Félicité did not hear the rest; the horses were trotting and the donkey galloping. They all turned down a bypath; a gate swung open and two boys appeared; and the party dismounted in front of a manure-heap at the very threshold of the farmhouse door.

When Mme. Liébard saw her mistress she gave lavish signs of joy. She served her a luncheon with a sirloin of beef, tripe, black-pudding, a fricassee of chicken, sparkling cider, a fruit tart, and brandied plums; seasoning it all with compliments to Madame, who seemed in better health; Mademoiselle, who was "splendid" now; and Monsieur Paul, who had "filled out" wonderfully. Nor did she forget their deceased grandparents, whom the Liébards had known, as they had been in the service of the family for several generations. The farm, like them, had the stamp of antiquity. The beams on the ceiling were worm-eaten, the walls blackened with smoke, and the window-panes grey with dust. There was an oak dresser laden with every sort of useful article—jugs, plates, pewter bowls, wolf-traps, and sheep-shears; and a huge syringe made the children laugh. There was not a tree in the three courtyards without mushrooms growing at the bottom of it or a tuft of mistletoe on its boughs. Several of them had been thrown down by the wind. They had taken root again at the middle; and all were bending under their wealth of apples. The thatched roofs, like brown velvet and of varying thickness, withstood the heaviest squalls. The cart-shed, however, was falling into ruin. Mme. Aubain said she would see about it, and ordered the animals to be saddled again.

It was another half-hour before they reached Trouville. The little caravan dismounted to pass Écores—it was an overhanging cliff with boats below it—and three minutes later they were at the end of the quay and entered the courtyard of the Golden Lamb, kept by good Mme. David.

From the first days of their stay Virginie began to feel less weak, thanks to the change of air and the effect of the sea-baths. These, for want of a bathing-dress, she took in her chemise; and her nurse dressed her afterwards in a coastguard's cabin which was used by the bathers.

In the afternoons they took the donkey and went off beyond the Black Rocks, in the direction of Hennequeville. The path climbed at first through ground with dells in it like the green sward of a park, and then reached a plateau where grass fields and arable lay side by side. Hollies rose stiffly out of the briary tangle at the edge of the road; and here and there a great withered tree made zigzags in the blue air with its branches.

They nearly always rested in a meadow, with Deauville on their left, Havre on their right, and the open sea in front. It glittered in the sunshine, smooth as a mirror and so quiet that its murmur was scarcely to be heard; sparrows chirped in hiding and the immense sky arched over it all. Mme. Aubain sat doing her needlework; Virginie plaited rushes by her side; Félicité pulled up lavender, and Paul was bored and anxious to start home.

Other days they crossed the Toucques in a boat and looked for shells. When the tide went out sea-urchins, starfish, and jelly-fish were left exposed; and the children ran in pursuit of the foam-flakes which scudded in the wind. The sleepy waves broke on the sand and unrolled all along the beach; it stretched away out of sight, bounded on the land-side by the dunes which parted it from the Marsh, a wide meadow shaped like an arena. As they came home that way, Trouville, on the hill-slope in the background, grew bigger at every step, and its miscellaneous throng of houses seemed to break into a gay disorder.

On days when it was too hot they did not leave their room. From the dazzling brilliance outside light fell in streaks between the laths of the blinds. There were no sounds in the village; and on the pavement below not a soul. This silence round them deepened the quietness of things. In the distance, where men were caulking, there was a tap of hammers as they plugged the hulls, and a sluggish breeze wafted up the smell of tar.

The chief amusement was the return of the fishing-boats. They began to tack as soon as they had passed the buoys. The sails came down on two of the three masts; and they drew on with the foresail swelling like a balloon, glided through the splash of the waves, and when they had reached the middle of the harbour suddenly dropped anchor. Then the boats drew up against the quay. The sailors threw quivering fish over the side; a row of carts was waiting, and women in cotton bonnets darted out to take the baskets and give their men a kiss.

One of them came up to Félicité one day, and she entered the lodgings a little later in a state of delight. She had found a sister again—and then Nastasie Barette, "wife of Leroux," appeared, holding an infant at her breast and another child with her right hand, while on her left was a little cabin boy with his hands on his hips and a cap over his ear.

After a quarter of an hour Mme. Aubain sent them off; but they were always to be found hanging about the kitchen, or encountered in the course of a walk. The husband never appeared.

Félicité was seized with affection for them. She bought them a blanket, some shirts, and a stove; it was clear that they were making a good thing out of her. Mme. Aubain was annoyed by this weakness of hers, and she did not like the liberties taken by the nephew, who said "thee" and "thou" to Paul. So as Virginie was coughing and the fine weather gone, she returned to Pont-l'Évêque.

There M. Bourais enlightened her on the choice of a boys' school. The one at Caen was reputed to be the best, and Paul was sent to it. He said his good-byes bravely, content enough at going to live in a house where he would have companions.

Mme. Aubain resigned herself to her son's absence as a thing that had to be. Virginie thought about it less and less. Félicité missed the noise he made. But she found an occupation to distract her; from Christmas onward she took the little girl to catechism every day.

3

After making a genuflexion at the door she walked up between the double row of chairs under the lofty nave, opened Mme. Aubain's pew, sat down, and began to look about her. The choir stalls were filled with the boys on the right and the girls on the left, and the curé stood by the lectern. On a painted window in the apse the Holy Ghost looked down upon the Virgin. Another window showed her on her knees before the child Jesus, and a group carved in wood behind the altarshrine represented St. Michael overthrowing the dragon.

The priest began with a sketch of sacred history. The Garden, the Flood, the Tower of Babel, cities in flames, dying nations, and overturned idols passed like a dream before her eyes; and the dizzying vision left her with reverence for the Most High and fear of his wrath. Then she wept at the story of the Passion. Why had they crucified Him, when He loved the children, fed the multitudes, healed the blind, and had willed, in His meekness, to be born among the poor, on the dungheap of a stable? The sowings, harvests, wine-presses, all the familiar things the Gospel speaks of, were a part of her life. They had been made holy by God's passing; and she loved the lambs more tenderly for her love of the Lamb, and the doves because of the Holy Ghost.

She found it hard to imagine Him in person, for He was not merely a bird, but a flame as well, and a breath at other times. It may be His light, she thought, which flits at night about the edge of the marshes, His breathing which drives on the clouds, His voice which gives harmony to the bells; and she would sit rapt in adoration, enjoying the cool walls and the quiet of the church.

Of doctrines she understood nothing—did not even try to understand. The curé discoursed, the children repeated their lesson, and finally she went to sleep, waking up with a start when their wooden shoes clattered on the flagstones as they went away.

It was thus that Félicité, whose religious education had been neglected in her youth, learned the catechism by dint of hearing it; and from that time she copied all Virginie's observances, fasting as she did and confessing with her. On Corpus Christi Day they made a festal altar together.

The first communion loomed distractingly ahead. She fussed over the shoes, the rosary, the book and gloves; and how she trembled as she helped Virginie's mother to dress her!

All through the mass she was racked with anxiety. She could not see one side of the choir because of M. Bourais; but straight in front of her was the flock of maidens, with white crowns above their hanging veils, making the impression of a field of snow; and she knew her dear child at a distance by her dainty neck and thoughtful air. The bell tinkled. The heads bowed, and there was silence. As the organ pealed, singers and congregation took up the "Agnus Dei"; then the procession of the boys began, and after them the girls rose. Step by step, with their hands joined in prayer, they went towards the lighted altar, knelt on the first step, received the sacrament in turn, and came back in the same order to their places. When Virginie's turn came Félicité leaned forward to see her; and with the imaginativeness of deep and tender feeling it seemed to her that she actually was the child; Virginie's face became hers, she was dressed in her clothes, it was her heart beating in her breast. As the moment came to open her mouth she closed her eyes and nearly fainted.

She appeared early in the sacristy next morning for Monsieur the curé to give her the communion. She took it with devotion, but it did not give her the same exquisite delight.

Mme. Aubain wanted to make her daughter into an accomplished person; and as Guyot could not teach her music or English she decided to place her in the Ursuline Convent at Honfleur as a boarder. The child made no objection. Félicité sighed and thought that Madame lacked feeling. Then she reflected that her mistress might be right; matters of this kind were beyond her.

So one day an old spring-van drew up at the door, and out of it stepped a nun to fetch the young lady. Félicité hoisted the luggage on to the top, admonished the driver, and put six pots of preserves, a dozen pears, and a bunch of violets under the seat.

At the last moment Virginie broke into a fit of sobbing; she threw her arms round her mother, who kissed her on the forehead, saying over and over "Come, be brave! be brave!" The step was raised, and the carriage drove off.

Then Mme. Aubain's strength gave way; and in the evening all her friends—the Lormeau family, Mme. Lechaptois, the Rochefeuille ladies, M. de Houppeville, and Bourais—came in to console her.

To be without her daughter was very painful for her at first. But she heard from Virginie three times a week, wrote to her on the other days, walked in the garden, and so filled up the empty hours.

From sheer habit Félicité went into Virginie's room in the mornings and gazed at the walls. It was boredom to her not to have to comb the child's hair now, lace up her boots, tuck her into bed—and not to see her charming face perpetually and hold her hand when they went out together. In this idle condition she tried making lace. But her fingers were too heavy and broke the threads; she could not attend to anything, she had lost her sleep, and was, in her own words, "destroyed."

To "divert herself" she asked leave to have visits from her nephew Victor.

He arrived on Sundays after mass, rosy-cheeked, bare-chested, with the scent of the country he had walked through still about him. She laid her table promptly and they had lunch, sitting opposite each other. She ate as little as possible herself to save expense, but stuffed him with food so generously that at last he went to sleep. At the first stroke of vespers she woke him up, brushed his trousers, fastened his tie, and went to church, leaning on his arm with maternal pride.

Victor was always instructed by his parents to get something out of her—a packet of moist sugar, it might be, a cake of soap, spirits, or even money at times. He brought his things for her to mend and she took over the task, only too glad to have a reason for making him come back.

In August his father took him off on a coasting voyage. It was holiday time, and she was consoled by the arrival of the children. Paul, however, was getting selfish, and Virginie was too old to be called "thou" any longer; this put a constraint and barrier between them.

Victor went to Morlaix, Dunkirk, and Brighton in succession and made Félicité a present on his return from each voyage. It was a box made of shells the first time, a coffee cup the next, and on the third occasion a large gingerbread man. Victor was growing handsome. He was well made, had a hint of a moustache, good honest eyes, and a small leather hat pushed backwards like a pilot's. He entertained her by telling stories embroidered with nautical terms.

On a Monday, July 14, 1819 (she never forgot the date), he told her that he had signed on for the big voyage and next night but one he would take the Honfleur boat and join his schooner, which was to weigh anchor from Havre before long. Perhaps he would be gone two years.

The prospect of this long absence threw Félicité into deep distress; one more good-bye she must have, and on the Wednesday evening, when Madame's dinner was finished, she put on her clogs and made short work of the twelve miles between Pont-l'Évêque and Honfleur.

When she arrived in front of the Calvary she took the turn to the right instead of the left, got lost in the timber-yards, and retraced her steps; some people to whom she spoke advised her to be quick. She went all round the harbour basin, full of ships, and knocked against hawsers; then the ground fell away, lights flashed across each other, and she thought her wits had left her, for she saw horses up in the sky.

Others were neighing by the quay-side, frightened at the sea. They were lifted by a tackle and deposited in a boat, where passengers jostled each other among cider casks, cheese baskets, and sacks of grain; fowls could be heard clucking, the captain swore; and a cabin-boy stood leaning over the bows, indifferent to it all. Félicité, who had not recognized him, called "Victor!" and he raised his head; all at once, as she was darting forwards, the gangway was drawn back.

The Honfleur packet, women singing as they hauled it, passed out of harbour. Its framework creaked and the heavy waves whipped its bows. The canvas had swung round, no one could be seen on board now; and on the moonsilvered sea the boat made a black speck which paled gradually, dipped, and vanished.

As Félicité passed by the Calvary she had a wish to commend to God what she cherished most, and she stood there praying a long time with her face bathed in tears and her eyes towards the clouds. The town was asleep, coastguards were walking to and fro; and water poured without cessation through the holes in the sluice, with the noise of a torrent. The clocks struck two.

The convent parlour would not be open before day. If Félicité were late Madame would most certainly be annoyed; and in spite of her desire to kiss the other child she turned home. The maids at the inn were waking up as she came in to Pont-l'Évêque.

So the poor slip of a boy was going to toss for months and months at sea! She had not been frightened by his previous voyages. From England or Brittany you came back safe enough; but America, the colonies, the islands—these were lost in a dim region at the other end of the world.

Félicité's thoughts from that moment ran entirely on her nephew. On sunny days she was harassed by the idea of thirst; when there was a storm she was afraid of the lightning on his account. As she listened to the wind growling in the chimney or carrying off the slates she pictured him lashed by that same tempest, at the top of a shattered mast, with his body thrown backwards under a sheet of foam; or else (with a reminiscence of the illustrated geography) he was being eaten by savages, captured in a wood by monkeys, or dying on a desert shore. And never did she mention her anxieties.

Mme. Aubain had anxieties of her own, about her daughter. The good sisters found her an affectionate but delicate child. The slightest emotion unnerved her. She had to give up the piano.

Her mother stipulated for regular letters from the convent. She lost patience one morning when the postman did not come, and walked to and fro in the parlour from her armchair to the window. It was really amazing; not a word for four days!

To console Mme. Aubain by her own example Félicité remarked:

"As for me, Madame, it's six months since I heard…"

"From whom, pray?"

"Why…from my nephew," the servant answered gently.

"Oh! your nephew!" And Mme. Aubain resumed her walk with a shrug of the shoulders, as much as to say: "I was not thinking of him! And what is more, it's absurd! A scamp of a cabin-boy—what does he matter?…whereas my daughter… why, just think!"

Félicité, though she had been brought up on harshness, felt indignant with Madame—and then forgot. It seemed the simplest thing in the world to her to lose one's head over the little girl. For her the two children were equally important; a bond in her heart made them one, and their destinies must be the same.

She heard from the chemist that Victor's ship had arrived at Havana. He had read this piece of news in a gazette.

Cigars—they made her imagine Havana as a place where no one does anything but smoke, and there was Victor moving among the negroes in a cloud of tobacco. Could you, she wondered, "in case you needed," return by land? What was the distance from Pont-l'Évêque? She questioned M. Bourais to find out.

He reached for his atlas and began explaining the longitudes; Félicité's consternation provoked a fine pedantic smile. Finally he marked with his pencil a black, imperceptible point in the indentations of an oval spot, and said as he did so, "Here it is." She bent over the map; the maze of coloured lines wearied her eyes without conveying anything; and on an invitation from Bourais to tell him her difficulty she begged him to show her the house where Victor was living. Bourais threw up his arms, sneezed, and laughed immensely: a simplicity like hers was a positive joy. And Félicité did not understand the reason; how could she when she expected, very likely, to see the actual image of her nephew—so stunted was her mind!

A fortnight afterwards Liébard came into the kitchen at market-time as usual and handed her a letter from her brother-in-law. As neither of them could read she took it to her mistress.

Mme. Aubain, who was counting the stitches in her knitting, put the work down by her side, broke the seal of the letter, started, and said in a low voice, with a look of meaning:

"It is bad news...that they have to tell you. Your nephew..."

He was dead. The letter said no more.

Félicité fell on to a chair, leaning her head against the wainscot; and she closed her eyelids, which suddenly flushed pink. Then with bent forehead, hands hanging, and fixed eyes, she said at intervals:

"Poor little lad! poor little lad!"

Liébard watched her and heaved sighs. Mme. Aubain trembled a little.

She suggested that Félicité should go to see her sister at Trouville. Félicité answered by a gesture that she had no need.

There was a silence. The worthy Liébard thought it was time for them to withdraw. Then Félicité said:

"They don't care, not they!"

Her head dropped again; and she took up mechanically, from time to time, the long needles on her work-table.

Women passed in the yard with a barrow of dripping linen.

As she saw them through the window-panes she remembered her washing; she had put it to soak the day before, to-day she must wring it out; and she left the room.

Her plank and tub were at the edge of the Toucques. She threw a pile of linen on the bank, rolled up her sleeves, and taking her wooden beater dealt lusty blows whose sound carried to the neighbouring gardens. The meadows were empty, the river stirred in the wind; and down below long grasses wavered, like the hair of corpses floating in the water. She kept her grief down and was very brave until the evening; but once in her room she surrendered to it utterly, lying stretched on the mattress with her face in the pillow and her hands clenched against her temples.

Much later she heard, from the captain himself, the circumstances of Victor's end. They had bled him too much at the hospital for yellow fever. Four doctors held him at once. He had died instantly, and the chief had said:

"Bah! there goes another!"

His parents had always been brutal to him. She preferred not to see them again; and they made no advances, either because they forgot her or from the callousness of the wretchedly poor.

Virginie began to grow weaker.

Tightness in her chest, coughing, continual fever, and veinings on her cheek-bones betrayed some deep-seated complaint. M. Poupart had advised a stay in Provence. Mme. Aubain determined on it, and would have brought her daughter home at once but for the climate of Pont-l'Évêque.

She made an arrangement with a job-master, and he drove her to the convent every Tuesday. There is a terrace in the garden, with a view over the Seine. Virginie took walks there over the fallen vine-leaves, on her mother's arm. A shaft of sunlight through the clouds made her blink sometimes, as she gazed at the sails in the distance and the whole horizon from the castle of Tancarville to the lighthouses at Havre. Afterwards they rested in the arbour. Her mother had secured a little cask of excellent Malaga; and Virginie, laughing at the idea of getting tipsy, drank a thimble-full of it, no more.

Her strength came back visibly. The autumn glided gently away. Félicité reassured Mme. Aubain. But one evening, when she had been out on a commission in the neighbourhood, she found M. Poupart's gig at the door. He was in the hall, and Mme. Aubain was tying her bonnet.

"Give me my foot-warmer, purse, gloves! Quicker, come!"

Virginie had inflammation of the lungs; perhaps it was hopeless.

"Not yet!" said the doctor, and they both got into the carriage under whirling flakes of snow. Night was coming on and it was very cold.

Félicité rushed into the church to light a taper. Then she ran after the gig, came up with it in an hour, and jumped lightly in behind. As she hung on by the fringes a thought came into her mind: "The courtyard has not been shut up; supposing burglars got in!" And she jumped down.

At dawn next day she presented herself at the doctor's. He had come in and started for the country again. Then she waited in the inn, thinking that a letter would come by some hand or other. Finally, when it was twilight, she took the Lisieux coach.

The convent was at the end of a steep lane. When she was about half-way up it she heard strange sounds—a death-bell tolling. "It is for someone else," thought Félicité, and she pulled the knocker violently.

After some minutes there was a sound of trailing slippers, the door opened ajar, and a nun appeared.

The good sister, with an air of compunction, said that "she had just passed away." On the instant the bell of St. Leonard's tolled twice as fast.

Félicité went up to the second floor.

From the doorway she saw Virginie stretched on her back, with her hands joined, her mouth open, and head thrown back under a black crucifix that leaned towards her, between curtains that hung stiffly, less pale than was her face. Mme. Aubain, at the foot of the bed which she clasped with her arms, was choking with sobs of agony. The mother superior stood on the right. Three candlesticks on the chest of drawers made spots of red, and the mist came whitely through the windows. Nuns came and took Mme. Aubain away.

For two nights Félicité never left the dead child. She repeated the same prayers, sprinkled holy water over the sheets, came and sat down again, and watched her. At the end of the first vigil she noticed that the face had grown yellow, the lips turned blue, the nose was sharper, and the eyes sunk in. She kissed them several times, and would not have been immensely surprised if Virginie had opened them again; to minds like hers the supernatural is quite simple. She made the girl's toilette, wrapped her in her shroud, lifted her down into her bier, put a garland on her head, and spread out her hair. It was fair, and extraordinarily long for her age. Félicité cut off a big lock and slipped half of it into her bosom, determined that she should never part with it.

The body was brought back to Pont-l'Évêque, as Mme. Aubain intended; she followed the hearse in a closed carriage.

It took another three-quarters of an hour after the mass to reach the cemetery. Paul walked in front, sobbing. M. Bourais was behind, and then came the chief residents, the women shrouded in black mantles, and Félicité. She thought of her nephew; and because she had not been able to pay these honours to him her grief was doubled, as though the one were being buried with the other.

Mme. Aubain's despair was boundless. It was against God that she first rebelled, thinking it unjust of Him to have taken her daughter from her—she had never done evil and her conscience was so clear! Ah, no!—she ought to have taken Virginie off to the south. Other doctors would have saved her. She accused herself now, wanted to join her child, and broke into cries of distress in the middle of her dreams. One dream haunted her above all. Her husband, dressed as a sailor, was returning from a long voyage, and shedding tears he told her that he had been ordered to take Virginie away. Then they consulted how to hide her somewhere.

She came in once from the garden quite upset. A moment ago—and she pointed out the place—the father and daughter had appeared to her, standing side by side, and they did nothing, but they looked at her.

For several months after this she stayed inertly in her room. Félicité lectured her gently; she must live for her son's sake, and for the other, in remembrance of "her."

"Her?" answered Mme. Aubain, as though she were just waking up. "Ah, yes!... yes!... You do not forget her!" This was an allusion to the cemetery, where she was strictly forbidden to go.

Félicité went there every day.

Precisely at four she skirted the houses, climbed the hill, opened the gate, and came to Virginie's grave. It was a little column of pink marble with a stone underneath and a garden plot enclosed by chains. The beds were hidden under a coverlet of flowers. She watered their leaves, freshened the gravel, and knelt down to break up the earth better. When Mme. Aubain was able to come there she felt a relief and a sort of consolation.

Then years slipped away, one like another, and their only episodes were the great festivals as they recurred—Easter, the Assumption, All Saints' Day. Household occurrences marked dates that were referred to after-wards. In 1825, for instance, two glaziers whitewashed the hall; in 1827 a piece of the roof fell into the courtyard and nearly killed a man. In the summer of 1828 it was Madame's turn to offer the consecrated bread; Bourais, about this time, mysteriously absented himself; and one by one the old acquaintances passed away: Guyot, Liébard, Mme. Lechaptois, Robelin, and Uncle Gremanville, who had been paralysed for a long time.

One night the driver of the mail-coach announced the Revolution of July in Pont-l'Évêque.[4] A new sub-prefect was appointed a few days later—Baron de Larsonnière, who had been consul in America, and brought with him, besides his wife, a sister-in-law and three young ladies, already growing up. They were to be seen about on

4. The July Revolution overthrew King Charles X, marking the ascendancy of the middle class, who installed a king (Louis-Philippe) more to their liking.

their lawn, in loose blouses, and they had a negro and a parrot. They paid a call on Mme. Aubain which she did not fail to return. The moment they were seen in the distance Félicité ran to let her mistress know. But only one thing could really move her feelings—the letters from her son.

He was swallowed up in a tavern life and could follow no career. She paid his debts, he made new ones; and the sighs that Mme. Aubain uttered as she sat knitting by the window reached Félicité at her spinning-wheel in the kitchen.

They took walks together along the espaliered wall, always talking of Virginie and wondering if such and such a thing would have pleased her and what, on some occasion, she would have been likely to say.

All her small belongings filled a cupboard in the two-bedded room. Mme. Aubain inspected them as seldom as she could. One summer day she made up her mind to it—and some moths flew out of the wardrobe.

Virginie's dresses were in a row underneath a shelf, on which there were three dolls, some hoops, a set of toy pots and pans, and the basin that she used. They took out her petticoats as well, and the stockings and handkerchiefs, and laid them out on the two beds before folding them up again. The sunshine lit up these poor things, bringing out their stains and the creases made by the body's movements. The air was warm and blue, a blackbird warbled, life seemed bathed in a deep sweetness. They found a little plush hat with thick, chestnut-coloured pile; but it was eaten all over by moth. Félicité begged it for her own. Their eyes met fixedly and filled with tears; at last the mistress opened her arms, the servant threw herself into them, and they embraced each other, satisfying their grief in a kiss that made them equal.

It was the first time in their lives, Mme. Aubain's nature not being expansive. Félicité was as grateful as though she had received a favour, and cherished her mistress from that moment with the devotion of an animal and a religious worship.

The kindness of her heart unfolded.

When she heard the drums of a marching regiment in the street she posted herself at the door with a pitcher of cider and asked the soldiers to drink. She nursed cholera patients and protected the Polish refugees; one of these even declared that he wished to marry her. They quarrelled, however; for when she came back from the Angelus one morning she found that he had got into her kitchen and made himself a vinegar salad which he was quietly eating.

After the Poles came father Colmiche, an old man who was supposed to have committed atrocities in '93.[5] He lived by the side of the river in the ruins of a pigsty. The little boys watched him through the cracks in the wall, and threw pebbles at him which fell on the pallet where he lay constantly shaken by a catarrh;[6] his hair was very long, his eyes inflamed, and there was a tumour on his arm bigger than his head. She got him some linen and tried to clean up his miserable hole; her dream was to establish him in the bakehouse, without letting him annoy Madame. When the tumour burst she dressed it every day; sometimes she brought him cake, and would put him in the sunshine on a truss of straw. The poor old man, slobbering and trembling, thanked her in his worn-out voice, was terrified that he might lose her, and stretched out his hands when he saw her go away. He died; and she had a mass said for the repose of his soul.

That very day a great happiness befell her; just at dinner-time appeared Mme. de Larsonnière's negro, carrying the parrot in its cage, with perch, chain, and padlock.

5. During the Reign of Terror at the height of the French Revolution.
6. Racking cough.

A note from the baroness informed Mme. Aubain that her husband had been raised to a prefecture and they were starting that evening; she begged her to accept the bird as a memento and mark of her regard.

For a long time he had absorbed Félicité's imagination, because he came from America; and that name reminded her of Victor, so much so that she made inquiries of the negro. She had once gone so far as to say "How Madame would enjoy having him!"

The negro repeated the remark to his mistress; and as she could not take the bird away with her she chose this way of getting rid of him.

4

His name was Loulou. His body was green and the tips of his wings rose-pink; his fore-head was blue and his throat golden.

But he had the tiresome habits of biting his perch, tearing out his feathers, sprinkling his dirt about, and spattering the water of his tub. He annoyed Mme. Aubain, and she gave him to Félicité for good.

She endeavoured to train him; soon he could repeat "Nice boy! Your servant, sir! Good morning, Marie!" He was placed by the side of the door, and astonished several people by not answering to the name Jacquot, for all parrots are called Jacquot. People compared him to a turkey and a log of wood, and stabbed Félicité to the heart each time. Strange obstinacy on Loulou's part!—directly you looked at him he refused to speak.

None the less he was eager for society; for on Sundays, while the Rochefeuille ladies, M. de Houppeville, and new familiars—Onfroy the apothecary, Monsieur Varin, and Captain Mathieu—were playing their game of cards, he beat the windows with his wings and threw himself about so frantically that they could not hear each other speak.

Bourais' face, undoubtedly, struck him as extremely droll. Directly he saw it he began to laugh—and laugh with all his might. His peals rang through the courtyard and were repeated by the echo; the neighbours came to their windows and laughed too; while M. Bourais, gliding along under the wall to escape the parrot's eye, and hiding his profile with his hat, got to the river and then entered by the garden gate. There was a lack of tenderness in the looks which he darted at the bird.

Loulou had been slapped by the butcher-boy for making so free as to plunge his head into his basket; and since then he was always trying to nip him through his shirt. Fabu threatened to wring his neck, although he was not cruel, for all his tattooed arms and large whiskers. Far from it; he really rather liked the parrot, and in a jovial humour even wanted to teach him to swear. Félicité, who was alarmed by such proceedings, put the bird in the kitchen. His little chain was taken off and he roamed about the house.

His way of going downstairs was to lean on each step with the curve of his beak, raise the right foot, and then the left; and Félicité was afraid that these gymnastics brought on fits of giddiness. He fell ill and could not talk or eat any longer. There was a growth under his tongue, such as fowls have sometimes. She cured him by tearing the pellicle off with her finger-nails. Mr. Paul was thoughtless enough one day to blow some cigar smoke into his nostrils, and another time when Mme. Lormeau was teasing him with the end of her umbrella he snapped at the ferrule. Finally he got lost.

Félicité had put him on the grass to refresh him, and gone away for a minute, and when she came back—no sign of the parrot! She began by looking for him in the shrubs, by the waterside, and over the roofs, without listening to her mistress's cries of "Take care, do! You are out of your wits!" Then she investigated all the gardens in Pont-l'Évêque, and stopped the passers-by. "You don't ever happen to have seen my parrot, by any chance, do you?" And she gave a description of the parrot to those who did not know him. Suddenly, behind the mills at the foot of the hill she thought she could make out something green that fluttered. But on the top of the hill there was nothing. A hawker assured her that he had come across the parrot just before, at Saint-Melaine, in Mère Simon's shop. She rushed there; they had no idea of what she meant. At last she came home exhausted, with her slippers in shreds and despair in her soul; and as she was sitting in the middle of the garden-seat at Madame's side, telling the whole story of her efforts, a light weight dropped on to her shoulder—it was Loulou! What on earth had he been doing? Taking a walk in the neighbourhood, perhaps!

She had some trouble in recovering from this, or rather never did recover. As the result of a chill she had an attack of quinsy,[7] and soon afterwards an earache. Three years later she was deaf; and she spoke very loud, even in church. Though Félicité's sins might have been published in every corner of the diocese without dishonour to her or scandal to anybody, his Reverence the priest thought it right now to hear her confession in the sacristy only.

Imaginary noises in the head completed her upset. Her mistress often said to her, "Heavens! how stupid you are!" "Yes, Madame," she replied, and looked about for something.

Her little circle of ideas grew still narrower; the peal of church-bells and the lowing of cattle ceased to exist for her. All living beings moved as silently as ghosts. One sound only reached her ears now—the parrot's voice.

Loulou, as though to amuse her, reproduced the click-clack of the turn-spit, the shrill call of a man selling fish, and the noise of the saw in the joiner's house opposite; when the bell rang he imitated Mme. Aubain's "Félicité! the door! the door!"

They carried on conversations, he endlessly reciting the three phrases in his repertory, to which she replied with words that were just as disconnected but uttered what was in her heart. Loulou was almost a son and a lover to her in her isolated state. He climbed up her fingers, nibbled at her lips, and clung to her kerchief; and when she bent her forehead and shook her head gently to and fro, as nurses do, the great wings of her bonnet and the bird's wings quivered together.

When the clouds massed and the thunder rumbled Loulou broke into cries, perhaps remembering the downpours in his native forests. The streaming rain made him absolutely mad; he fluttered wildly about, dashed up to the ceiling, upset everything, and went out through the window to dabble in the garden; but he was back quickly to perch on one of the fire-dogs and hopped about to dry himself, exhibiting his tail and his beak in turn.

One morning in the terrible winter of 1837 she had put him in front of the fire-place because of the cold. She found him dead, in the middle of his cage: head downwards, with his claws in the wires. He had died from congestion, no doubt. But Félicité thought he had been poisoned with parsley, and though there was no proof of any kind her suspicions inclined to Fabu.

She wept so piteously that her mistress said to her, "Well, then, have him stuffed!"

She asked advice from the chemist, who had always been kind to the parrot. He wrote to Havre, and a person called Fellacher undertook the business. But as parcels sometimes got lost in the coach she decided to take the parrot as far as Honfleur herself.

Along the sides of the road were leafless apple-trees, one after the other. Ice covered the ditches. Dogs barked about the farms; and Félicité, with her hands under her cloak, her little black sabots and her basket, walked briskly in the middle of the road.

She crossed the forest, passed High Oak, and reached St. Gatien.

7. Tonsillitis.

A cloud of dust rose behind her, and in it a mail-coach, carried away by the steep hill, rushed down at full gallop like a hurricane. Seeing this woman who would not get out of the way, the driver stood up in front and the positilion shouted too. He could not hold in his four horses, which increased their pace, and the two leaders were grazing her when he threw them to one side with a jerk of the reins. But he was wild with rage, and lifting his arm as he passed at full speed, gave her such a lash from waist to neck with his big whip that she fell on her back.

Her first act, when she recovered consciousness, was to open her basket. Loulou was happily none the worse. She felt a burn in her right cheek, and when she put her hands against it they were red; the blood was flowing.

She sat down on a heap of stones and bound up her face with her handkerchief. Then she ate a crust of bread which she had put in the basket as a precaution, and found a consolation for her wound in gazing at the bird.

When she reached the crest of Ecquemauville she saw the Honfleur lights sparkling in the night sky like a company of stars; beyond, the sea stretched dimly. Then a faintness overtook her and she stopped; her wretched childhood, the disillusion of her first love, her nephew's going away, and Virginie's death all came back to her at once like the waves of an oncoming tide, rose to her throat, and choked her.

Afterwards, at the boat, she made a point of speaking to the captain, begging him to take care of the parcel, though she did not tell him what was in it.

Fellacher kept the parrot a long time. He was always promising it for the following week. After six months he announced that a packing-case had started, and then nothing more was heard of it. It really seemed as though Loulou was never coming back. "Ah, they have stolen him!" she thought.

He arrived at last, and looked superb. There he was, erect upon a branch which screwed into a mahogany socket, with a foot in the air and his head on one side, biting a nut which the bird-stuffer—with a taste for impressiveness—had gilded.

Félicité shut him up in her room. It was a place to which few people were admitted, and held so many religious objects and miscellaneous things that it looked like a chapel and bazaar in one.

A big cupboard impeded you as you opened the door. Opposite the window commanding the garden a little round one looked into the court; there was a table by the folding-bed with a water-jug, two combs, and a cube of blue soap in a chipped plate. On the walls hung rosaries, medals, several benign Virgins, and a holy water vessel made out of cocoa-nut; on the chest of drawers, which was covered with a cloth like an altar, was the shell box that Victor had given her, and after that a watering-can, a toy-balloon, exercise-books, the illustrated geography, and a pair of young lady's boots; and, fastened by its ribbons to the nail of the looking-glass, hung the little plush hat! Félicité carried observances of this kind so far as to keep one of Monsieur's frock-coats. All the old rubbish which Mme. Aubain did not want any longer she laid hands on for her room. That was why there were artificial flowers along the edge of the chest of drawers and a portrait of the Comte d'Artois[8] in the little window recess.

With the aid of a bracket Loulou was established over the chimney, which jutted into the room. Every morning when she woke up she saw him there in the dawning light, and recalled old days and the smallest details of insignificant acts in a deep quietness which knew no pain.

8. The deposed king Charles X.

Holding, as she did, no communication with anyone, Félicité lived as insensibly as if she were walking in her sleep. The Corpus Christi processions roused her to life again. Then she went round begging mats and candlesticks from the neighbours to decorate the altar they put up in the street.

In church she was always gazing at the Holy Ghost in the window, and observed that there was something of the parrot in him. The likeness was still clearer, she thought, on a crude colour-print representing the baptism of Our Lord. With his purple wings and emerald body he was the very image of Loulou.

She bought him, and hung him up instead of the Comte d'Artois, so that she could see them both together in one glance. They were linked in her thoughts; and the parrot was consecrated by his association with the Holy Ghost, which became more vivid to her eye and more intelligible. The Father could not have chosen to express Himself through a dove, for such creatures cannot speak; it must have been one of Loulou's ancestors, surely. And though Félicité looked at the picture while she said her prayers she swerved a little from time to time towards the parrot.

She wanted to join the Ladies of the Virgin, but Mme. Aubain dissuaded her.

And then a great event loomed up before them—Paul's marriage.

He had been a solicitor's clerk to begin with, and then tried business, the Customs, the Inland Revenue, and made efforts, even, to get into the Rivers and Forests. By an inspiration from heaven he had suddenly, at thirty-six, discovered his real line—the Registrar's Office. And there he showed such marked capacity that an inspector had offered him his daughter's hand and promised him his influence.

So Paul, grown serious, brought the lady to see his mother.

She sniffed at the ways of Pont-l'Évêque, gave herself great airs, and wounded Félicité's feelings. Mme. Aubain was relieved at her departure.

The week after came news of M. Bourais' death in an inn in Lower Brittany. The rumour of suicide was confirmed, and doubts arose as to his honesty. Mme. Aubain studied his accounts, and soon found out the whole tale of his misdoings—embezzled arrears, secret sales of wood, forged receipts, etc. Besides that he had an illegitimate child, and "relations with a person at Dozulé."

These shameful facts distressed her greatly. In March 1853 she was seized with a pain in the chest; her tongue seemed to be covered with film, and leeches did not ease the difficult breathing. On the ninth evening of her illness she died, just at seventy-two.

She passed as being younger, owing to the bands of brown hair which framed her pale, pock-marked face. There were few friends to regret her, for she had a stiffness of manner which kept people at a distance.

But Félicité mourned for her as one seldom mourns for a master. It upset her ideas and seemed contrary to the order of things, impossible and monstrous, that Madame should die before her.

Ten days afterwards, which was the time it took to hurry there from Besançon, the heirs arrived. The daughter-in-law ransacked the drawers, chose some furniture, and sold the rest; and then they went back to their registering.

Madame's armchair, her small round table, her foot-warmer, and the eight chairs were gone! Yellow patches in the middle of the panels showed where the engravings had hung. They had carried off the two little beds and the mattresses, and all Virginie's belongings had disappeared from the cupboard. Félicité went from floor to floor dazed with sorrow.

The next day there was a notice on the door, and the apothecary shouted in her ear that the house was for sale.

She tottered, and was obliged to sit down. What distressed her most of all was to give up her room, so suitable as it was for poor Loulou. She enveloped him with a look of anguish when she was imploring the Holy Ghost, and formed the idolatrous habit of kneeling in front of the parrot to say her prayers. Sometimes the sun shone in at the attic window and caught his glass eye, and a great luminous ray shot out of it and put her in an ecstasy.

She had a pension of fifteen pounds a year which her mistress had left her. The garden gave her a supply of vegetables. As for clothes, she had enough to last her to the end of her days, and she economized in candles by going to bed at dusk.

She hardly ever went out, as she did not like passing the dealer's shop, where some of the old furniture was exposed for sale. Since her fit of giddiness she dragged one leg; and as her strength was failing Mère Simon, whose grocery business had collapsed, came every morning to split the wood and pump water for her.

Her eyes grew feeble. The shutters ceased to be thrown open. Years and years passed, and the house was neither let nor sold.

Félicité never asked for repairs because she was afraid of being sent away. The boards on the roof rotted; her bolster was wet for a whole winter. After Easter she spat blood.

Then Mère Simon called in a doctor. Félicité wanted to know what was the matter with her. But she was too deaf to hear, and the only word which reached her was "pneumonia." It was a word she knew, and she answered softly "Ah! like Madame," thinking it natural that she should follow her mistress.

The time for the festal shrines was coming near. The first one was always at the bottom of the hill, the second in front of the post-office, and the third towards the middle of the street. There was some rivalry in the matter of this one, and the women of the parish ended by choosing Mme. Aubain's courtyard.

The hard breathing and fever increased. Félicité was vexed at doing nothing for the altar. If only she could at least have put something there! Then she thought of the parrot. The neighbours objected that it would not be decent. But the priest gave her permission, which so intensely delighted her that she begged him to accept Loulou, her sole possession, when she died.

From Tuesday to Saturday, the eve of the festival, she coughed more often. By the evening her face had shrivelled, her lips stuck to her gums, and she had vomitings; and at twilight next morning, feeling herself very low, she sent for a priest.

Three kindly women were round her during the extreme unction. Then she announced that she must speak to Fabu. He arrived in his Sunday clothes, by no means at his ease in the funereal atmosphere.

"Forgive me," she said, with an effort to stretch out her arm; "I thought it was you who had killed him."

What did she mean by such stories? She suspected him of murder—a man like him! He waxed indignant, and was on the point of making a row.

"There," said the women, "she is no longer in her senses, you can see it well enough!"

Félicité spoke to shadows of her own from time to time. The women went away, and Mère Simon had breakfast. A little later she took Loulou and brought him close to Félicité with the words:

"Come, now, say good-bye to him!"

Loulou was not a corpse, but the worms devoured him; one of his wings was broken, and the tow was coming out of his stomach. But she was blind now; she kissed him on the forehead and kept him close against her cheek. Mère Simon took him back from her to put him on the altar.

5

Summer scents came up from the meadows; flies buzzed; the sun made the river glitter and heated the slates. Mère Simon came back into the room and fell softly asleep.

She woke at the noise of bells; the people were coming out from vespers. Félicité's delirium subsided. She thought of the procession and saw it as if she had been there.

All the school children, the church-singers, and the firemen walked on the pavement, while in the middle of the road the verger armed with his hallebard and the beadle with a large cross advanced in front. Then came the schoolmaster, with an eye on the boys, and the sister, anxious about her little girls; three of the daintiest, with angelic curls, scattered rose petals in the air; the deacon controlled the band with outstretched arms; and two censerbearers turned back at every step towards the Holy Sacrament, which was borne by Monsieur the curé, wearing his beautiful chasuble, under a canopy of dark-red velvet held up by four churchwardens. A crowd of people pressed behind, between the white cloths covering the house walls, and they reached the bottom of the hill.

A cold sweat moistened Félicité's temples. Mère Simon sponged her with a piece of linen, saying to herself that one day she would have to go that way.

The hum of the crowd increased, was very loud for an instant, and then went further away.

A fusillade shook the window-panes. It was the postilions saluting the monstrance.[9] Félicité rolled her eyes and said as audibly as she could: "Does he look well?" The parrot was weighing on her mind.

Her agony began. A death-rattle that grew more and more convulsed made her sides heave. Bubbles of froth came at the corners of her mouth and her whole body trembled.

Soon the booming of the ophicleides,[1] the high voices of the children, and the deep voices of the men were distinguishable. At intervals all was silent, and the tread of feet, deadened by the flowers they walked on, sounded like a flock pattering on grass.

The clergy appeared in the courtyard. Mère Simon clambered on to a chair to reach the attic window, and so looked down straight upon the shrine. Green garlands hung over the altar, which was decked with a flounce of English lace. In the middle was a small frame with relics in it; there were two orange-trees at the corners, and all along stood silver candlesticks and china vases, with sunflowers, lilies, peonies, foxgloves, and tufts of hortensia. This heap of blazing colour slanted from the level of the altar to the carpet which went on over the pavement; and some rare objects caught the eye. There was a silver-gilt sugar-basin with a crown of violets; pendants of Alençon stone glittered on the moss, and two Chinese screens displayed their landscapes. Loulou was hidden under roses, and showed nothing but his blue forehead, like a plaque of lapis lazuli.

The churchwardens, singers, and children took their places round the three sides of the court. The priest went slowly up the steps, and placed his great, radiant golden sun upon the lace. Everyone knelt down. There was a deep silence; and the censers glided to and fro on the full swing of their chains.

An azure vapour rose up into Félicité's room. Her nostrils met it; she inhaled it sensuously, mystically; and then closed her eyes. Her lips smiled. The beats of her heart lessened one by one, vaguer each time and softer, as a fountain sinks, an echo disappears; and when she sighed her last breath she thought she saw an opening in the heavens, and a gigantic parrot hovering above her head.

---

9. Golden container displaying the consecrated communion bread.
1. Brass wind instruments.

Count Leo Tolstoy was born and raised at Yasnaya Polyana, his family's estate located near Moscow. After an early and unsuccessful attempt to reform the estate, he volunteered for the army. He served first with Russian forces seeking to conquer what were called "mountain tribesmen" in the Caucasus, and then in the Crimean War (1853–1856), in which Russian expansion southward into Orthodox areas of the Ottoman Empire was defeated at great cost by combined Turkish and British armies. Already a published author before beginning his military career, Tolstoy achieved solid success by making use of his military experience to tell realistic, unglamorous tales of the war. He left the army in 1856, traveled around Europe, and before reaching the age of thirty had retired to his estate; its revenues made it possible for him to spend the rest of his life writing. It was there that he wrote his masterpieces, the novels *War and Peace* (1863–1869) and *Anna Karenina* (1875–1877). After a personal crisis (described in *Confession* [1879]), he formulated a philosophy involving nonviolence, the renunciation of wealth, and the value of physical labor. The philosophy was an inspiration to such world figures as Mahatma Gandhi. In *What Is Art?* (1897) Tolstoy renounced much of his earlier fiction on moral grounds. But some of his last works are among his greatest, including "The Death of Ivan Ilych" (1886) and "The Kreutzer Sonata" (1890). In "Hadji Murad" (1896–1904), he returned to the subject of Russia's war of conquest in the Caucasus, but chose a Caucasian protagonist. By the end of Tolstoy's long life, Yasnaya Polyana had become a place of pilgrimage. After a violent quarrel with his wife, Sofia, he left the estate in October 1910, fell ill, and died at a nearby town.

Tolstoy's great counterpart, Dostoevsky, once described Russian literature as "a literature of landowners." He was announcing his desire to write fiction about Russia's urban poor. But the remark also helps explain why, like classical Greece, nineteenth-century Russia sometimes seems to set an unmatchable standard for literary greatness. Russian landowners turned to literature with such passionate seriousness because they could see that their way of life was doomed. The most prophetic, like Tolstoy, could even see that they deserved no better. Their power, based on their ownership of serfs and supporting in turn the increasingly antiquated bureaucratic empire headed by the Czar, appeared to almost everyone as a sign of Russia's backwardness by comparison with Europe. Unless there was some fundamental change, Russia seemed condemned to ongoing feebleness and disrespect, and more humiliations like the Crimean War. Yet what kind of change should there be? Slavophiles, supporters of native Russian traditions, fell back with nationalist fervor on the certainties of the Russian Orthodox tradition or romanticized views of the Russian peasant. But even devout Westernizers joined with them in being critical of the West's version of industrial modernity. There were more questions than answers. Russian writers could see, as their more complacent European contemporaries often did not, that their society had ceased to function, that revolution of some sort was on the horizon, that everything was up in the air. Blocked at the level of political action by the Czarist autocracy, the energy of criticizing the status quo and imagining alternatives went into literature, which took as its ambitious task the largest and most tantalizing mysteries of human existence.

Tolstoy's celebration of peasantlike simplicity and hard work—evident in the character of Gerasim in "The Death of Ivan Ilych"—shares something with Slavophile primitivism, but this story shows that Tolstoy's disaffection was both deeper and more complex, as his dying hero belatedly reflects on the world he is about to leave.

The Death of Ivan Ilych[1]

I

During an interval in the Melvinski trial in the large building of the Law Courts the members and public prosecutor met in Ivan Egorovich Shebek's private room, where the conversation turned on the celebrated Krasovski case. Fedor Vasilievich warmly maintained that it was not subject to their jurisdiction, Ivan Egorovich maintained the contrary, while Peter Ivanovich, not having entered into the discussion at the start, took no part in it but looked through the *Gazette* which had just been handed in.

"Gentlemen," he said, "Ivan Ilych has died!"

"You don't say so!"

"Here, read it yourself," replied Peter Ivanovich, handing Fedor Vasilievich the paper still damp from the press. Surrounded by a black border were the words: "Praskovya Fedorovna Golovina, with profound sorrow, informs relatives and friends of the demise of her beloved husband Ivan Ilych Golovin, Member of the Court of Justice, which occurred on February the 4th of this year 1882. The funeral will take place on Friday at one o'clock in the afternoon."

Ivan Ilych had been a colleague of the gentlemen present and was liked by them all. He had been ill for some weeks with an illness said to be incurable. His post had been kept open for him, but there had been conjectures that in case of his death Alexeev might receive his appointment, and that either Vinnikov or Shtabel would succeed Alexeev. So on receiving the news of Ivan Ilych's death the first thought of each of the gentlemen in that private room was of the changes and promotions it might occasion among themselves or their acquaintances.

"I shall be sure to get Shtabel's place or Vinnikov's," thought Fedor Vasilievich. "I was promised that long ago, and the promotion means an extra eight hundred rubles a year for me besides the allowance."

"Now I must apply for my brother-in-law's transfer from Kaluga,"[2] thought Peter Ivanovich. "My wife will be very glad, and then she won't be able to say that I never do anything for her relations."

"I thought he would never leave his bed again," said Peter Ivanovich aloud. "It's very sad."

"But what really was the matter with him?"

"The doctors couldn't say—at least they could, but each of them said something different. When last I saw him I thought he was getting better."

"And I haven't been to see him since the holidays. I always meant to go."

"Had he any property?"

"I think his wife had a little—but something quiet trifling."

"We shall have to go to see her, but they live so terribly far away."

"Far away from you, you mean. Everything's far away from your place."

1. Translated by Louise Maude and Aylmer Maude.
2. A city in central Russia, about 90 miles southwest of Moscow.

"You see, he never can forgive my living on the other side of the river," said Peter Ivanovich, smiling at Shebek. Then, still talking of the distances between different parts of the city, they returned to the Court.

Besides considerations as to the possible transfers and promotions likely to result from Ivan Ilych's death, the mere fact of the death of a near acquaintance aroused, as usual, in all who heard of it the complacent feeling that, "It is he who is dead and not I." Each one thought or felt, "Well, he's dead but I'm alive!" But the more intimate of Ivan Ilych's acquaintances, his so-called friends, could not help thinking also that they would now have to fulfil the very tiresome demands of propriety by attending the funeral service and paying a visit of condolence to the widow.

Fedor Vasilievich and Peter Ivanovich had been his nearest acquaintances. Peter Ivanovich had studied law with Ivan Ilych and had considered himself to be under obligations to him.

Having told his wife at dinner-time of Ivan Ilych's death, and of his conjecture that it might be possible to get her brother transferred to their circuit, Peter Ivanovich sacrificed his usual nap, put on his evening clothes and drove to Ivan Ilych's house.

At the entrance stood a carriage and two cabs. Leaning against the wall in the hall downstairs near the cloakstand was a coffin-lid covered with cloth of gold, ornamented with gold cord and tassels, that had been polished up with metal powder. Two ladies in black were taking off their fur cloaks. Peter Ivanovich recognized one of them as Ivan Ilych's sister, but the other was a stranger to him. His colleague Schwartz was just coming downstairs, but on seeing Peter Ivanovich enter he stopped and winked at him, as if to say: "Ivan Ilych has made a mess of things—not like you and me."

Schwartz's face with his Piccadilly whiskers, and his slim figure in evening dress, had as usual an air of elegant solemnity which contrasted with the playfulness of his character and had a special piquancy here, or so it seemed to Peter Ivanovich.

Peter Ivanovich allowed the ladies to precede him and slowly followed them upstairs. Schwartz did not come down but remained where he was, and Peter Ivanovich understood that he wanted to arrange where they should play bridge that evening. The ladies went upstairs to the widow's room, and Schwartz with seriously compressed lips but a playful look in his eyes, indicated by a twist of his eyebrows the room to the right where the body lay.

Peter Ivanovich, like everyone else on such occasions, entered feeling uncertain what he would have to do. All he knew was that at such times it is always safe to cross oneself. But he was not quite sure whether one should make obeisances while doing so. He therefore adopted a middle course. On entering the room he began crossing himself and made a slight movement resembling a bow. At the same time, as far as the motion of his head and arm allowed, he surveyed the room. Two young men—apparently nephews, one of whom was a high-school pupil—were leaving the room, crossing themselves as they did so. An old woman was standing motionless, and a lady with strangely arched eyebrows was saying something to her in a whisper. A vigorous, resolute Church Reader, in a frock-coat, was reading something in a loud voice with an expression that precluded any contradiction. The butler's assistant, Gerasim, stepping lightly in front of Peter Ivanovich, was strewing something on the floor.

Noticing this, Peter Ivanovich was immediately aware of a faint odour of a decomposing body.

The last time he had called on Ivan Ilych, Peter Ivanovich had seen Gerasim in the study. Ivan Ilych had been particularly fond of him and he was performing the duty of a sick nurse.

Peter Ivanovich continued to make the sign of the cross slightly inclining his head in an intermediate direction between the coffin, the Reader, and the icons on the table in a corner of the room. Afterwards, when it seemed to him that this movement of his arm in crossing himself had gone on too long, he stopped and began to look at the corpse.

The dead man lay, as dead men always lie, in a specially heavy way, his rigid limbs sunk in the soft cushions of the coffin, with the head forever bowed on the pillow. His yellow waxen brow with bald patches over his sunken temples was thrust up in the way peculiar to the dead, the protruding nose seeming to press on the upper lip. He was much changed and grown even thinner since Peter Ivanovich had last seen him, but, as is always the case with the dead, his face was handsomer and above all more dignified than when he was alive. The expression on the face said that what was necessary had been accomplished, and accomplished rightly. Besides this there was in that expression a reproach and a warning to the living. This warning seemed to Peter Ivanovich out of place, or at least not applicable to him. He felt a certain discomfort and so he hurriedly crossed himself once more and turned and went out of the door—too hurriedly and too regardless of propriety, as he himself was aware.

Schwartz was waiting for him in the adjoining room with legs spread wide apart and both hands toying with his top-hat behind his back. The mere sight of that playful, well-groomed, and elegant figure refreshed Peter Ivanovich. He felt that Schwartz was above all these happenings and would not surrender to any depressing influences. His very look said that this incident of a church service for Ivan Ilych could not be a sufficient reason for infringing the order of the session—in other words, that it would certainly not prevent his unwrapping a new pack of cards and shuffling them that evening while a footman placed fresh candles on the table: in fact, that there was no reason for supposing that this incident would hinder their spending the evening agreeably. Indeed he said this in a whisper as Peter Ivanovich passed him, proposing that they should meet for a game at Fedor Vasilievich's. But apparently Peter Ivanovich was not destined to play bridge that evening. Praskovya Fedorovna (a short, fat woman who despite all efforts to the contrary had continued to broaden steadily from her shoulders downwards and who had the same extraordinarily arched eyebrows as the lady who had been standing by the coffin), dressed all in black, her head covered with lace, came out of her own room with some other ladies, conducted them to the room where the dead body lay, and said: "The service will begin immediately. Please go in."

Schwartz, making an indefinite bow, stood still, evidently neither accepting nor declining this invitation. Praskovya Fedorovna recognizing Peter Ivanovich, sighed, went close up to him, took his hand, and said: "I know you were a true friend to Ivan Ilych..." and looked at him awaiting some suitable response. And Peter Ivanovich knew that, just as it had been the right thing to cross himself in that room, so what he had to do here was to press her hand, sigh, and say, "Believe me..." So he did all this and as he did it felt that the desired result had been achieved: that both he and she were touched.

"Come with me. I want to speak to you before it begins," said the widow. "Give me your arm."

Peter Ivanovich gave her his arm and they went to the inner rooms, passing Schwartz who winked at Peter Ivanovich compassionately.

"That does for our bridge! Don't object if we find another player. Perhaps you can cut in when you do escape," said his playful look.

Peter Ivanovich sighed still more deeply and despondently, and Praskovya Fedorovna pressed his arm gratefully. When they reached the drawing-room, upholstered in pink cretonne and lighted by a dim lamp, they sat down at the table—she on a sofa and Peter Ivanovich on a low pouffe, the springs of which yielded spasmodically under his weight. Praskovya Fedorovna had been on the point of warning him to take another seat, but felt that such a warning was out of keeping with her present condition and so changed her mind. As he sat down on the pouffe Peter Ivanovich recalled how Ivan Ilych had arranged this room and had consulted him regarding this pink cretonne with green leaves. The whole room was full of furniture and knick-knacks, and on her way to the sofa the lace of the widow's black shawl caught on the edge of the table. Peter Ivanovich rose to detach it, and the springs of the pouffe, relieved of his weight, rose also and gave him a push. The widow began detaching her shawl herself, and Peter Ivanovich again sat down, suppressing the rebellious springs of the pouffe under him. But the widow had not quite freed herself and Peter Ivanovich got up again, and again the pouffe rebelled and even creaked. When this was all over she took out a clean cambric handkerchief and began to weep. The episode with the shawl and the struggle with the pouffe had cooled Peter Ivanovich's emotions and he sat there with a sullen look on his face. This awkward situation was interrupted by Sokolov, Ivan Ilych's butler, who came to report that the plot in the cemetery that Praskovya Fedorovna had chosen would cost two hundred rubles. She stopped weeping and, looking at Peter Ivanovich with the air of a victim, remarked in French that it was very hard for her. Peter Ivanovich made a silent gesture signifying his full conviction that it must indeed be so.

"Please smoke," she said in a magnanimous yet crushed voice, and turned to discuss with Sokolov the price of the plot for the grave.

Peter Ivanovich while lighting his cigarette heard her inquiring very circumstantially into the prices of different plots in the cemetery and finally decide which she would take. When that was done she gave instructions about engaging the choir. Sokolov then left the room.

"I look after everything myself," she told Peter Ivanovich, shifting the albums that lay on the table; and noticing that the table was endangered by his cigarette-ash, she immediately passed him an ash-tray, saying as she did so: "I consider it an affectation to say that my grief prevents my attending to practical affairs. On the contrary, if anything can—I won't say console me, but—distract me, it is seeing to everything concerning him." She again took out her handkerchief as if preparing to cry, but suddenly, as if mastering her feeling, she shook herself and began to speak calmly. "But there is something I want to talk to you about."

Peter Ivanovich bowed, keeping control of the springs of the pouffe, which immediately began quivering under him.

"He suffered terribly the last few days."

"Did he?" said Peter Ivanovich.

"Oh, terribly! He screamed unceasingly, not for minutes but for hours. For the last three days he screamed incessantly. It was unendurable. I cannot understand how I bore it; you could hear him three rooms off. Oh, what I have suffered!"

"Is it possible that he was conscious all that time?" asked Peter Ivanovich.

"Yes," she whispered. "To the last moment. He took leave of us a quarter of an hour before he died, and asked us to take Volodya away."

The thought of the suffering of this man he had known so intimately, first as a merry little boy, then as a schoolmate, and later as a grown-up colleague, suddenly struck Peter Ivanovich with horror, despite an unpleasant consciousness of his own and this woman's dissimulation. He again saw that brow, and that nose pressing down on the lip, and felt afraid for himself.

"Three days of frightful suffering and the death! Why, that might suddenly, at any time, happen to me," he thought, and for a moment felt terrified. But—he did not himself know how—the customary reflection at once occurred to him that this had happened to Ivan Ilych and not to him, and that it should not and could not happen to him, and that to think that it could would be yielding to depression which he ought not to do, as Schwartz's expression plainly showed. After which reflection Peter Ivanovich felt reassured, and began to ask with interest about the details of Ivan Ilych's death, as though death was an accident natural to Ivan Ilych but certainly not to himself.

After many details of the really dreadful physical sufferings Ivan Ilych had endured (which details he learnt only from the effect those sufferings had produced on Praskovya Fedorovna's nerves) the widow apparently found it necessary to get to business.

"Oh, Peter Ivanovich, how hard it is! How terribly, terribly hard!" and she again began to weep.

Peter Ivanovich sighed and waited for her to finish blowing her nose. When she had done so he said, "Believe me . . ." and she again began talking and brought out what was evidently her chief concern with him—namely, to question him as to how she could obtain a grant of money from the government on the occasion of her husband's death. She made it appear that she was asking Peter Ivanovich's advice about her pension, but he soon saw that she already knew about that to the minutest detail, more even than he did himself. She knew how much could be got out of the government in consequence of her husband's death, but wanted to find out whether she could not possibly extract something more. Peter Ivanovich tried to think of some means of doing so, but after reflecting for a while and, out of propriety, condemning the government for its niggardliness, he said he thought that nothing more could be got. Then she sighed and evidently began to devise means of getting rid of her visitor. Noticing this, he put out his cigarette, rose, pressed her hand, and went out into the anteroom.

In the dining-room where the clock stood that Ivan Ilych had liked so much and had bought at an antique shop, Peter Ivanovich met a priest and a few acquaintances who had come to attend the service, and he recognized Ivan Ilych's daughter, a handsome young woman. She was in black and her slim figure appeared slimmer than ever. She had a gloomy, determined, almost angry expression, and bowed to Peter Ivanovich as though he were in some way to blame. Behind her, with the same offended look, stood a wealthy young man, and examining magistrate, whom Peter Ivanovich also knew and who was her fiance, as he had heard. He bowed mournfully to them and was about to pass into the death-chamber, when from under the stairs appeared the figure of Ivan Ilych's schoolboy son, who was extremely like his father. He seemed a little Ivan Ilych, such as Peter Ivanovich remembered when they studied law together. His tear-stained eyes had in them the look that is seen in the eyes of boys of thirteen or fourteen who are not pure-minded. When he saw Peter Ivanovich he scowled morosely and shamefacedly. Peter Ivanovich nodded to him and entered the death-chamber. The service began: candles, groans, incense, tears, and sobs. Peter Ivanovich stood looking gloomily down at his feet. He did not look once at the dead man, did not yield to any depressing influence, and was one of the first to leave the room. There was no one in the anteroom, but Gerasim darted out of the dead man's room, rummaged with his strong hands among the fur coats to find Peter Ivanovich's and helped him on with it.

"Well, friend Gerasim," said Peter Ivanovich, so as to say something. "It's a sad affair, isn't it?"

"It's God will. We shall all come to it some day," said Gerasim, displaying his teeth—the even white teeth of a healthy peasant—and, like a man in the thick of urgent work, he briskly opened the front door, called the coachman, helped Peter Ivanovich into the sledge, and sprang back to the porch as if in readiness for what he had to do next. Peter Ivanovich found the fresh air particularly pleasant after the smell of incense, the dead body, and carbolic acid.

"Where to sir?" asked the coachman.

"It's not too late even now....I'll call round on Fedor Vasilievich."

He accordingly drove there and found them just finishing the first rubber, so that it was quite convenient for him to cut in.

II

Ivan Ilych's life had been most simple and most ordinary and therefore most terrible. He had been a member of the Court of Justice, and died at the age of forty-five. His father had been an official who after serving in various ministries and departments in Petersburg had made the sort of career which brings men to positions from which by reason of their long service they cannot be dismissed, though they are obviously unfit to hold any responsible position, and for whom therefore posts are specially created, which though fictitious carry salaries of from six to ten thousand rubles that are not fictitious, and in receipt of which they live on to a great age.

Such was the Privy Councillor and superfluous member of various superfluous institutions, Ilya Epimovich Golovin.

He had three sons, of whom Ivan Ilych was the second. The eldest son was following in his father's footsteps only in another department, and was already approaching that stage in the service at which a similar sinecure would be reached. The third son was a failure. He had ruined his prospects in a number of positions and was not serving in the railway department. His father and brothers, and still more their wives, not merely disliked meeting him, but avoided remembering his existence unless compelled to do so. His sister had married Baron Greff, a Petersburg official of her father's type. Ivan Ilych was *le phenix de la famille*[3]

___
3. The pride of the family (French).

as people said. He was neither as cold and formal as his elder brother nor as wild as the younger, but was a happy mean between them—an intelligent polished, lively and agreeable man. He had studied with his younger brother at the School of Law, but the latter had failed to complete the course and was expelled when he was in the fifth class. Ivan Ilych finished the course well. Even when he was at the School of Law he was just what he remained for the rest of his life: a capable, cheerful, good-natured, and sociable man, though strict in the fulfillment of what he considered to be his duty: and he considered his duty to be what was so considered by those in authority. Neither as a boy nor as a man was he a toady, but from early youth was by nature attracted to people of high station as a fly is drawn to the light, assimilating their ways and views of life and establishing friendly relations with them. All the enthusiasms of childhood and youth passed without leaving much trace on him; he succumbed to sensuality, to vanity, and latterly among the highest classes to liberalism, but always within limits which his instinct unfailingly indicated to him as correct.

At school he had done things which had formerly seemed to him very horrid and made him feel disgusted with himself when he did them; but when later on he saw that such actions were done by people of good position and that they did not regard them as wrong, he was able not exactly to regard them as right, but to forget about them entirely or not be at all troubled at remembering them.

Having graduated from the School of Law and qualified for the tenth rank of the civil service, and having received money from his father for his equipment, Ivan Ilych ordered himself clothes at Scharmer's, the fashionable tailor, hung a medallion inscribed *respice finem*[4] on his watch-chain, took leave of his professor and the prince who was patron of the school, had a farewell dinner with his comrades at Donon's first-class restaurant, and with his new and fashionable portmanteau, linen, clothes, shaving and other toilet appliances, and a travelling rug, all purchased at the best shops, he set off for one of the provinces where through his father's influence, he had been attached to the governor as an official for special service.

In the province Ivan Ilych soon arranged as easy and agreeable a position for himself as he had had at the School of Law. He performed his official task, made his career, and at the same time amused himself pleasantly and decorously. Occasionally he paid official visits to country districts where he behaved with dignity both to his superiors and inferiors, and performed the duties entrusted to him, which related chiefly to the sectarians,[5] with an exactness and incorruptible honesty of which he could not but feel proud.

In official matters, despite his youth and taste for frivolous gaiety, he was exceedingly reserved, punctilious, and even severe; but in society he was often amusing and witty, and always good-natured, correct in his manner, and *bon enfant*,[6] as the governor and his wife—with whom he was like one of the family—used to say of him. In the province he had an affair with a lady who made advances to the elegant young lawyer, and there was also a milliner; and there were carousals with aides-decamp who visited the district, and after-supper visits to a certain outlying street of doubtful reputation; and there was too some obsequiousness to his chief

4. Look to the end (Latin).
5. Christians who had repudiated the Orthodox church.
6. Easygoing, a good citizen; literally, a "good child" (French).

and even to his chief's wife, but all this was done with such a tone of good breeding that no hard names could be applied to it. It all came under the heading of the French saying: "*Il faut que jeunesse se passe.*"[7] It was all done with clean hands, in clean linen, with French phrases, and above all among people of the best society and consequently with the approval of people of rank.

So Ivan Ilych served for five years and then came a change in his official life. The new and reformed judicial institutions were introduced, and new men were needed. Ivan Ilych became such a new man. He was offered the post of examining magistrate, and he accepted it though the post was in another province and obliged him to give up the connexions he had formed and to make new ones. His friends met to give him a send-off; they had a group photograph taken and presented him with a silver cigarette-case, and he set off to his new post.

As examining magistrate Ivan Ilych was just as *comme il faut* and decorous a man, inspiring general respect and capable of separating his official duties from his private life, as he had been when acting as an official on special service. His duties now as examining magistrate were far more interesting and attractive than before. In his former position it had been pleasant to wear an undress uniform made by Scharmer, and to pass through the crowd of petitioners and officials who were timorously awaiting an audience with the governor, and who envied him as with free and easy gait he went straight into his chief's private room to have a cup of tea and a cigarette with him. But not many people had then been directly dependent on him—only police officials and the sectarians when he went on special missions—and he liked to treat them politely, almost as comrades, as if he were letting them feel that he who had the power to crush them was treating them in this simple, friendly way. There were then but few such people. But now, as an examining magistrate, Ivan Ilych felt that everyone without exception, even the most important and self-satisfied, was in his power, and that he need only write a few words on a sheet of paper with a certain heading, and this or that important, self-satisfied person would be brought before him in the role of an accused person or a witness, and if he did not choose to allow him to sit down, would have to stand before him and answer his questions. Ivan Ilych never abused his power; he tried on the contrary to soften its expression, but the consciousness of it and the possibility of softening its effect, supplied the chief interest and attraction of his office. In his work itself, especially in his examinations, he very soon acquired a method of eliminating all considerations irrelevant to the legal aspect of the case, and reducing even the most complicated case to a form in which it would be presented on paper only in its externals, completely excluding his personal opinion of the matter, while above all observing every prescribed formality. The work was new and Ivan Ilych was one of the first men to apply the new Code of 1864.[8]

On taking up the post of examining magistrate in a new town, he made new acquaintances and connexions, placed himself on a new footing and assumed a somewhat different tone. He took up an attitude of rather dignified aloofness towards the provincial authorities, but picked out the best circle of legal gentlemen and wealthy gentry living in the town and assumed a tone of slight dissatisfaction with the government,

7. "Youth must have its day" (French).
8. A legal reform.

of moderate liberalism, and of enlightened citizenship. At the same time, without at all altering the elegance of his toilet, he ceased shaving his chin and allowed his beard to grow as it pleased.

Ivan Ilych settled down very pleasantly in this new town. The society there, which inclined towards opposition to the governor was friendly, his salary was larger, and he began to play vint,[9] which he found added not a little to the pleasure of life, for he had a capacity for cards, played good-humouredly, and calculated rapidly and astutely, so that he usually won.

After living there for two years he met his future wife, Praskovya Fedorovna Mikhel, who was the most attractive, clever, and brilliant girl of the set in which he moved, and among other amusements and relaxations from his labours as examining magistrate, Ivan Ilych established light and playful relations with her.

While he had been an official on special service he had been accustomed to dance, but now as an examining magistrate it was exceptional for him to do so. If he danced now, he did it as if to show that though he served under the reformed order of things, and had reached the fifth official rank, yet when it came to dancing he could do it better than most people. So at the end of an evening he sometimes danced with Praskovya Fedorovna, and it was chiefly during these dances that he captivated her. She fell in love with him. Ivan Ilych had at first no definite intention of marrying, but when the girl fell in love with him he said to himself: "Really, why shouldn't I marry?"

Praskovya Fedorovna came of a good family, was not bad looking, and had some little property. Ivan Ilych might have aspired to a more brilliant match, but even this was good. He had his salary, and she, he hoped, would have an equal income. She was well connected, and was a sweet, pretty, and thoroughly correct young woman. To say that Ivan Ilych married because he fell in love with Praskovya Fedorovna and found that she sympathized with his views of life would be as incorrect as to say that he married because his social circle approved of the match. He was swayed by both these considerations: the marriage gave him personal satisfaction, and at the same time it was considered the right thing by the most highly placed of his associates.

So Ivan Ilych got married.

The preparations for marriage and the beginning of married life, with its conjugal caresses, the new furniture, new crockery, and new linen, were very pleasant until his wife became pregnant—so that Ivan Ilych had begun to think that marriage would not impair the easy, agreeable, gay and always decorous character of his life, approved of by society and regarded by himself as natural, but would even improve it. But from the first months of his wife's pregnancy, something new, unpleasant, depressing, and unseemly, and from which there was no way of escape, unexpectedly showed itself.

His wife, without any reason—*de gaieté de coeur*[1] as Ivan Ilych expressed it to himself—began to disturb the pleasure and propriety of their life. She began to be jealous without any cause, expected him to devote his whole attention to her, found fault with everything, and made coarse and ill-mannered scenes.

At first Ivan Ilych hoped to escape from the unpleasantness of this state of affairs by the same easy and decorous relation to life that had served him heretofore: he tried to ignore his wife's disagreeable moods, continued to live in his usual easy and pleasant way, invited friends to his house for a game of cards, and also tried going out to

9. A form of bridge.
1. Out of sheer exuberance (French).

his club or spending his evenings with friends. But one day his wife began upbraiding him so vigorously, using such coarse words, and continued to abuse him every time he did not fulfil her demands, so resolutely and with such evident determination not to give way till he submitted—that is, till he stayed at home and was bored just as she was—that he became alarmed. He now realized that matrimony—at any rate with Praskovya Fedorovna—was not always conducive to the pleasures and amenities of life, but on the contrary often infringed both comfort and propriety, and that he must therefore entrench himself against such infringement. And Ivan Ilych began to seek for means of doing so. His official duties were the one thing that imposed upon Praskovya Fedorovna, and by means of his official work and the duties attached to it he began struggling with his wife to secure his own independence.

With the birth of their child, the attempts to feed it and the various failures in doing so, and with the real and imaginary illnesses of mother and child, in which Ivan Ilych's sympathy was demanded but about which he understood nothing, the need of securing for himself an existence outside his family life became still more imperative. As his wife grew more irritable and exacting and Ivan Ilych transferred the center of gravity of his life more and more to his official work, so did he grow to like his work better and became more ambitious than before.

Very soon, within a year of his wedding, Ivan Ilych had realized that marriage, though it may add some comforts to life, is in fact a very intricate and difficult affair towards which in order to perform one's duty, that is, to lead a decorous life approved of by society, one must adopt a definite attitude just as towards one's official duties.

And Ivan Ilych evolved such an attitude towards married life. He only required of it those conveniences—dinner at home, housewife, and bed—which it could give him, and above all that propriety of external forms required by public opinion. For the rest he looked for lighthearted pleasure and propriety, and was very thankful when he found them, but if he met with antagonism and querulousness he at once retired into his separate fenced-off world of official duties, where he found satisfaction.

Ivan Ilych was esteemed a good official, and after three years was made Assistant Public Prosecutor. His new duties, their importance, the possibility of indicting and imprisoning anyone he chose, the publicity his speeches received, and the success he had in all these things, made his work still more attractive.

More children came. His wife became more and more querulous and ill-tempered, but the attitude Ivan Ilych had adopted towards his home life rendered him almost impervious to her grumbling.

After seven years' service in that town he was transferred to another province as Public Prosecutor. They moved, but were short of money and his wife did not like the place they moved to. Though the salary was higher the cost of living was greater, besides which two of their children died and family life became still more unpleasant for him. Praskovya Fedorovna blamed her husband for every inconvenience they encountered in their new home. Most of the conversations between husband and wife, especially as to the children's education, led to topics which recalled former disputes, and these disputes were apt to flare up again at any moment. There remained only those rare periods of amorousness which still came to them at times but did not last long. These were islets at which they anchored for a while and then again set out upon that ocean of veiled hostility which showed itself in their aloofness from one another. This aloofness might have grieved Ivan Ilych had he considered that it ought not to exist, but he now regarded the position as normal, and even made it the goal at which he aimed in family life. His aim was to free himself more and more from those unpleasantnesses and to give them a semblance of harmlessness and propriety. He attained this by spending less and less time with his family, and when obliged to be at home he tried to safeguard his position by the presence of outsiders. The chief thing however was that he had his official duties. The whole interest of his life now centered in the official world and that interest absorbed him. The consciousness of his power, being able to ruin anybody he wished to ruin, the importance, even the external dignity of his entry into court, or meetings with his subordinates, his success with superiors and inferiors, and above all his masterly handling of cases, of which he was conscious—all this gave him pleasure and filled his life, together with chats with his colleagues, dinners, and bridge. So that on the whole Ivan Ilych's life continued to flow as he considered it should do—pleasantly and properly.

So things continued for another seven years. His eldest daughter was already sixteen, another child had died, and only one son was left, a schoolboy and a subject of dissension. Ivan Ilych wanted to put him in the School of Law, but to spite him Praskovya Fedorovna entered him at the High School. The daughter had been educated at home and had turned out well: the boy did not learn badly either.

III

So Ivan Ilych lived for seventeen years after his marriage. He was already a Public Prosecutor of long standing, and had declined several proposed transfers while awaiting a more desirable post, when an unanticipated and unpleasant occurrence quite upset the peaceful course of his life. He was expecting to be offered the post of presiding judge in a University town, but Happe somehow came to the front and obtained the appointment instead. Ivan Ilych became irritable, reproached Happe, and quarrelled both with him and with his immediate superiors—who became colder to him and again passed him over when other appointments were made.

This was in 1880, the hardest year of Ivan Ilych's life. It was then that it became evident on the one hand that his salary was insufficient for them to live on, and on the other that he had been forgotten, and not only this, but that what was for him the greatest and most cruel injustice appeared to others a quite ordinary occurrence. Even his father did not consider it his duty to help him. Ivan Ilych felt himself abandoned by everyone, and that they regarded his position with a salary of 3,500 rubles as quite normal and even fortunate. He alone knew that with the consciousness of the injustices done him, with his wife's incessant nagging, and with the debts he had contracted by living beyond his means, his position was far from normal.

In order to save money that summer he obtained leave of absence and went with his wife to live in the country at her brother's place.

In the country, without his work, he experienced *ennui* for the first time in his life, and not only *ennui* but intolerable depression, and he decided that it was impossible to go on living like that, and that it was necessary to take energetic measures.

Having passed a sleepless night pacing up and down the veranda, he decided to go to Petersburg and bestir himself, in order to punish those who had failed to appreciate him and to get transferred to another ministry.

Next day, despite many protests from his wife and her brother, he started for Petersburg with the sole object of obtaining a post with a salary of five thousand rubles a year. He was no longer bent on any particular department, or tendency, or kind of activity. All he now wanted was an appointment to another post with a salary of five thousand rubles, either in the administration, in the banks, with the railways in one of the Empress Marya's Institutions,[2] or even in the customs—but it had to carry with it a salary of five thousand rubles and be in a ministry other than that in which they had failed to appreciate him.

And this quest of Ivan Ilych's was crowned with remarkable and unexpected success. At Kursk[3] an acquaintance of his, F. I. Ilyin, got into the first-class carriage, sat down beside Ivan Ilych, and told him of a telegram just received by the governor of Kursk announcing that a change was about to take place in the ministry: Peter Ivanovich was to be superseded by Ivan Semonovich.

The proposed change, apart from its significance for Russia, had a special significance for Ivan Ilych, because by bringing forward a new man, Peter Petrovich, and consequently his friend Zachar Ivanovich, it was highly favourable for Ivan Ilych, since Sachar Ivanovich was a friend and colleague of his.

In Moscow this news was confirmed, and on reaching Petersburg Ivan Ilych found Zachar Ivanovich and received a definite promise of an appointment in his former Department of Justice.

A week later he telegraphed to his wife: "Zachar in Miller's place. I shall receive appointment on presentation of report."

Thanks to this change of personnel, Ivan Ilych had unexpectedly obtained an appointment in his former ministry which placed him two states above his former colleagues besides giving him five thousand rubles salary and three thousand five hundred rubles for expenses connected with his removal. All his ill humour towards his former enemies and the whole department vanished, and Ivan Ilych was completely happy.

He returned to the country more cheerful and contented than he had been for a long time. Praskovya Fedorovna also cheered up and a truce was arranged between them. Ivan Ilych told of how he had been feted by everybody in Petersburg, how all those who had been his enemies were put to shame and now fawned on him, how envious they were of his appointment, and how much everybody in Petersburg had liked him.

Praskovya Fedorovna listened to all this and appeared to believe it. She did not contradict anything, but only made plans for their life in the town to which they were going. Ivan Ilych saw with delight that these plans were his plans, that he and his wife agreed, and that, after a stumble, his life was regaining its due and natural character of pleasant lightheartedness and decorum.

Ivan Ilych had come back for a short time only, for he had to take up his new duties on the 10th of September. Moreover, he needed time to settle into the new place, to move all his belongings from the province, and to buy and order many additional things: in a word, to make such arrangements as he had resolved on, which were almost exactly what Praskovya Fedorovna too had decided on.

Now that everything had happened so fortunately, and that he and his wife were at one in their aims and moreover saw so little of one another, they got on together better than they had done since the first years of marriage. Ivan Ilych had thought of taking his family away with him at once, but the insistence of his wife's brother and her sister-in-law, who had suddenly become particularly amiable and friendly to him and his family, induced him to depart alone.

So he departed, and the cheerful state of mind induced by his success and by the harmony between his wife and himself, the one intensifying the other, did not leave

2. Marya Fyodorovna (1759–1828), second wife of Tsar Paul I, founded a number of orphanages.
3. An administrative center and railway hub in central Russia.

him. He found a delightful house, just the thing both he and his wife had dreamt of. Spacious, lofty reception rooms in the old style, a convenient and dignified study, rooms for his wife and daughter, a study for his son—it might have been specially built for them. Ivan Ilych himself superintended the arrangements, chose the wallpapers, supplemented the furniture (preferably with antiques which he considered particularly *comme il faut*), and supervised the upholstering. Everything progressed and progressed and approached the ideal he had set himself: even when things were only half completed they exceeded his expectations. He saw what a refined and elegant character, free from vulgarity, it would all have when it was ready. On falling asleep he pictured to himself how the reception room would look. Looking at the yet unfinished drawing room he could see the fireplace, the screen, the what-not, the little chairs dotted here and there, the dishes and plates on the walls, and the bronzes, as they would be when everything was in place. He was pleased by the thought of how his wife and daughter, who shared his taste in this matter, would be impressed by it. They were certainly not expecting as much. He had been particularly successful in finding, and buying cheaply, antiques which gave a particularly aristocratic character to the whole place. But in his letters he intentionally understated everything in order to be able to surprise them. All this so absorbed him that his new duties—though he liked his official work—interested him less than he had expected. Sometimes he even had moments of absent-mindedness during the court sessions and would consider whether he should have straight or curved cornices for his curtains. He was so interested in it all that he often did things himself, rearranging the furniture, or rehanging the curtains. Once when mounting a step-ladder to show the upholsterer, who did not understand, how he wanted the hangings draped, he made a false step and slipped, but being a strong and agile man he clung on and only knocked his side against the knob of the window frame. The bruised place was painful but the pain soon passed, and he felt particularly bright and well just then. He wrote: "I feel fifteen years younger." He thought he would have everything ready by September, but it dragged on till mid-October. But the result was charming not only in his eyes but to everyone who saw it.

In reality it was just what is usually seen in the houses of people of moderate means who want to appear rich, and therefore succeed only in resembling others like themselves: there are damasks, dark wood, plants, rugs, and dull and polished bronzes—all the things people of a certain class have in order to resemble other people of that class. His house was so like the others that it would never have been noticed, but to him it all seemed to be quite exceptional. He was very happy when he met his family at the station and brought them to the newly furnished house all lit up, where a footman in a white tie opened the door into the hall decorated with plants, and when they went on into the drawing-room and the study uttering exclamations of delight. He conducted them everywhere, drank in their praises eagerly, and beamed with pleasure. At tea that evening, when Praskovya Fedorovna among others things asked him about his fall, he laughed, and showed them how he had gone flying and had frightened the upholsterer.

"It's a good thing I'm a bit of an athlete. Another man might have been killed, but I merely knocked myself, just here; it hurts when it's touched, but it's passing off already—it's only a bruise."

So they began living in their new home—in which, as always happens, when they got thoroughly settled in they found they were just one room short—and with the increased income, which as always was just a little (some five hundred rubles) too little, but it was all very nice.

Things went particularly well at first, before everything was finally arranged and while something had still to be done: this thing bought, that thing ordered, another thing moved, and something else adjusted. Though there were some disputes between husband and wife, they were both so well satisfied and had so much to do that it all passed off without any serious quarrels. When nothing was left to arrange it became rather dull and something seemed to be lacking, but they were then making acquaintances, forming habits, and life was growing fuller.

Ivan Ilych spent his mornings at the law court and came home to dinner, and at first he was generally in a good humour, though he occasionally became irritable just on account of his house. (Every spot on the tablecloth or the upholstery, and every broken window-blind string, irritated him. He had devoted so much trouble to arranging it all that every disturbance of it distressed him.) But on the whole his life ran its course as he believed life should do: easily, pleasantly, and decorously.

He got up at nine, drank his coffee, read the paper, and then put on his undress uniform and went to the law courts. There the harness in which he worked had already been stretched to fit him and he donned it without a hitch: petitioners, inquiries at the chancery, the chancery itself, and the sittings public and administrative. In all this the thing was to exclude everything fresh and vital, which always disturbs the regular course of official business, and to admit only official relations with people, and then only on official grounds. A man would come, for instance, wanting some information. Ivan Ilych, as one in whose sphere the matter did not lie, would have nothing to do with him: but if the man had some business with him in his official capacity, something that could be expressed on officially stamped paper, he would do everything, positively everything he could within the limits of such relations, and in doing so would maintain the semblance of friendly human relations, that is, would observe the courtesies of life. As soon as the official relations ended, so did everything else. Ivan Ilych possessed this capacity to separate his real life from the official side of affairs and not mix the two, in the highest degree, and by long practice and natural aptitude had brought it to such a pitch that sometimes, in the manner of a virtuoso, he would even allow himself to let the human and official relations mingle. He let himself do this just because he felt that he could at any time he chose resume the strictly official attitude again and drop the human relation. And he did it all easily, pleasantly, correctly, and even artistically. In the intervals between the sessions he smoked, drank tea, chatted a little about politics, a little about general topics, a little about cards, but most of all about official appointments. Tired, but with the feelings of a virtuoso—one of the first violins who has played his part in an orchestra with precision—he would return home to find that his wife and daughter had been out paying calls, or had a visitor, and that his son had been to school, had done his homework with his tutor, and was surely learning what is taught at High Schools.

Everything was as it should be. After dinner, if they had no visitors, Ivan Ilych sometimes read a book that was being much discussed at the time, and in the evening settled down to work, that is, read official papers, compared the depositions of witnesses, and noted paragraphs of the Code applying to them. This was neither dull nor amusing. It was dull when he might have been playing bridge, but if no bridge was available it was at any rate better than doing nothing or sitting with his wife. Ivan Ilych's chief pleasure was giving little dinners to which he invited men and women of good social position, and just as his drawing-room resembled all other drawing-rooms so did his enjoyable little parties resemble all other such parties.

Once they even gave a dance. Ivan Ilych enjoyed it and everything went off well, except that it led to a violent quarrel with his wife about the cakes and sweets. Praskovya Fedorovna had made her own plans, but Ivan Ilych insisted on getting everything from an expensive confectioner and ordered too many cakes, and the quarrel occurred because some of those cakes were left over and the confectioner's bill came to forty-five rubles. It was a great and disagreeable quarrel. Praskovya Fedorovna called him "a fool and an imbecile," and he clutched at his head and made angry allusions to divorce.

But the dance itself had been enjoyable. The best people were there, and Ivan Ilych had danced with Princess Trufonova, a sister of the distinguished founder of the Society "Bear My Burden."

The pleasures connected with his work were pleasures of ambition; his social pleasures were those of vanity; but Ivan Ilych's greatest pleasure was playing bridge. He acknowledged that whatever disagreeable incident happened in his life, the pleasure that beamed like a ray of light above everything else was to sit down to bridge with good players, not noisy partners, and of course to four-handed bridge (with five players it was annoying to have to stand out, though one pretended not to mind), to play a clever and serious game (when the cards allowed it) and then to have supper and drink a glass of wine. After a game of bridge, especially if he had won a little (to win a large sum was unpleasant), Ivan Ilych went to bed in a specially good humour.

So they lived. They formed a circle of acquaintances among the best people and were visited by people of importance and by young folk. In their views as to their acquaintances, husband, wife and daughter were entirely agreed, and tacitly and unanimously kept at arm's length and shook off the various shabby friends and relations who, with much show of affection, gushed into the drawing-room with its Japanese plates on the walls. Soon these shabby friends ceased to obtrude themselves and only the best people remained in the Golovins' set.

Young men made up to Lisa, and Petrishchev, an examining magistrate and Dmitri Ivanovich Petrishchev's son and sole heir, began to be so attentive to her that Ivan Ilych had already spoken to Praskovya Fedorovna about it, and considered whether they should not arrange a party for them, or get up some private theatricals.

So they lived, and all went well, without change, and life flowed pleasantly.

IV

They were all in good health. It could not be called ill health if Ivan Ilych sometimes said that he had a queer taste in his mouth and felt some discomfort in his left side.

But this discomfort increased and, though not exactly painful, grew into a sense of pressure in his side accompanied by ill humour. And his irritability became worse and worse and began to mar the agreeable, easy, and correct life that had established itself in the Golovin family. Quarrels between husband and wife became more and more frequent, and soon the ease and amenity disappeared and even the decorum was barely maintained. Scenes again became frequent, and very few of those islets remained on which husband and wife could meet without an explosion. Praskovya Fedorovna now had good reason to say that her husband's temper was trying. With characteristic exaggeration she said he had always had a dreadful temper, and that it had needed all her good nature to put up with it for twenty years. It was true that now the quarrels were started by him. His bursts of temper always came just before dinner, often just as he began to eat his soup. Sometimes he noticed that a plate or dish was chipped, or the food was not right, or his son put his elbow on the table, or his daughter's hair was not done as he liked it, and for all this he blamed Praskovya Fedorovna. At first she retorted and said disagreeable things to him, but once or twice he fell into such a rage at the beginning of dinner that she realized it was due to some physical derangement brought on by taking food, and so she restrained herself and did not answer, but only hurried to get the dinner over. She regarded this self-restraint as highly praiseworthy. Having come to the conclusion that her husband had a dreadful temper and made her life miserable, she began to feel sorry for herself, and the more she pitied herself the more she hated her husband. She began to wish he would die; yet she did not want him to die because then his salary would cease. And this irritated her against him still more. She considered herself dreadfully unhappy just because not even his death could save her, and though she concealed her exasperation, that hidden exasperation of hers increased his irritation also.

After one scene in which Ivan Ilych had been particularly unfair and after which he had said in explanation that he certainly was irritable but that it was due to his not being well, she said that if he was ill it should be attended to, and insisted on his going to see a celebrated doctor.

He went. Everything took place as he had expected and as it always does. There was the usual waiting and the important air assumed by the doctor, with which he was so familiar (resembling that which he himself assumed in court), and the sounding and listening, and the questions which called for answers that were foregone conclusions and were evidently unnecessary, and the look of importance which implied that "if only you put yourself in our hands we will arrange everything—we know indubitably how it has to be done, always in the same way for everybody alike." It was all just as it was in the law courts. The doctor put on just the same air towards him as he himself put on towards an accused person.

The doctor said that so-and-so indicated that there was so-and-so inside the patient, but if the investigation of so-and-so did not confirm this, then he must assume that and that. If he assumed that and that, then . . . and so on. To Ivan Ilych only one question was important: was his case serious or not? But the doctor ignored that inappropriate question. From his point of view it was not the one under consideration, the real question was to decide between a floating kidney, chronic catarrh, or appendicitis. It was a question the doctor solved brilliantly, as it seemed to Ivan Ilych, in favour of the appendix, with the reservation that should an examination of the urine give fresh indications the matter would be reconsidered. All this was just what Ivan Ilych had himself brilliantly accomplished a thousand times in dealing with men on trial. The doctor summed up just as brilliantly, looking over his spectacles triumphantly and even gaily at the accused. From the doctor's summing up Ivan Ilych concluded that things were bad, but that for the doctor, and perhaps for everybody else, it was a matter of indifference, though for him it was bad. And this conclusion struck him painfully, arousing in him a great feeling of pity for himself and of bitterness towards the doctor's indifference to a matter of such importance.

He said nothing of this, but rose, placed the doctor's fee on the table, and remarked with a sigh: "We sick people probably often put inappropriate questions. But tell me, in general, is this complaint dangerous, or not? . . ."

The doctor looked at him sternly over his spectacles with one eye, as if to say: "Prisoner, if you will not keep to the questions put to you, I shall be obliged to have you removed from the court."

"I have already told you what I consider necessary and proper. The analysis may show something more." And the doctor bowed.

Ivan Ilych went out slowly, seated himself disconsolately in his sledge, and drove home. All the way home he was going over what the doctor had said, trying to translate those complicated, obscure, scientific phrases into plain language and find in them an answer to the question: "Is my condition bad? Is it very bad? Or is there as yet nothing much wrong?" And it seemed to him that the meaning of what the doctor had said was that it was very bad. Everything in the streets seemed depressing. The cabmen, the houses, the passers-by, and the shops, were dismal. His ache, this dull gnawing ache that never ceased for a moment, seemed to have acquired a new and more serious significance from the doctor's dubious remarks. Ivan Ilych now watched it with a new and oppressive feeling.

He reached home and began to tell his wife about it. She listened, but in the middle of his account his daughter came in with her hat on, ready to go out with her mother. She sat down reluctantly to listen to this tedious story, but could not stand it long, and her mother too did not hear him to the end.

"Well, I am very glad," she said. "Mind now to take your medicine regularly. Give me the prescription and I'll send Gerasim to the chemist's." And she went to get ready to go out.

While she was in the room Ivan Ilych had hardly taken time to breathe, but he sighed deeply when she left it.

"Well," he thought, "perhaps it isn't so bad after all."

He began taking his medicine and following the doctor's directions, which had been altered after the examination of the urine. But then it happened that there was a contradiction between the indications drawn from the examination of the urine and the symptoms that showed themselves. It turned out that what was happening differed from what the doctor had told him, and that he had either forgotten or blundered, or hidden something from him. He could not, however, be blamed for that, and Ivan Ilych still obeyed his orders implicitly and at first derived some comfort from doing so.

From the time of his visit to the doctor, Ivan Ilych's chief occupation was the exact fulfillment of the doctor's instructions regarding hygiene and the taking of medicine, and the observation of his pain and his excretions. His chief interest came to be people's ailments and people's health. When sickness, deaths, or recoveries were mentioned in his presence, especially when the illness resembled his own, he listened with agitation which he tried to hide, asked questions, and applied what he heard to his own case.

The pain did not grow less, but Ivan Ilych made efforts to force himself to think that he was better. And he could do this so long as nothing agitated him. But as soon as he had any unpleasantness with his wife, any lack of success in his official work, or held bad cards at bridge, he was at once acutely sensible of his disease. He had formerly borne such mischances, hoping soon to adjust what was wrong, to master it and attain success, or make a grand slam. But now every mischance upset him and plunged him into despair. He would say to himself: "there now, just as I was beginning to get better and the medicine had begun to take effect, comes this accursed misfortune, or unpleasantness...." And he was furious with the mishap, or with the people who were causing the unpleasantness and killing him, for he felt that this fury was killing him but he could not restrain it. One would have thought that it should have been clear to him that this exasperation with circumstances and people aggravated his illness, and that he ought therefore to ignore unpleasant occurrences. But he drew the very opposite conclusion: he said that he needed peace, and he watched for everything that might disturb it and became irritable at the slightest infringement of it. His condition was rendered worse by the fact that he read medical books and consulted doctors. The progress of his disease was so gradual that he could deceive himself when comparing one day with another—the difference was so slight. But when he consulted the doctors it seemed to him that he was getting worse, and even very rapidly. Yet despite this he was continually consulting them.

That month he went to see another celebrity, who told him almost the same as the first had done but put his questions rather differently, and the interview with this celebrity only increased Ivan Ilych's doubts and fears. A friend of a friend of his, a very good doctor, diagnosed his illness again quite differently from the others, and though he predicted recovery, his questions and suppositions bewildered Ivan Ilych still more and increased his doubts. A homeopathist diagnosed the disease in yet another way, and prescribed medicine which Ivan Ilych took secretly for a week. But after a week, not feeling any improvement and having lost confidence both in the former doctor's treatment and in this one's, he became still more despondent. One day a lady acquaintance mentioned a cure effected by a wonder-working icon. Ivan Ilych caught himself listening attentively and beginning to believe that it had occurred. This incident alarmed him. "Has my mind really weakened to such an extent?" he asked himself. "Nonsense! It's all rubbish. I mustn't give way to nervous fears but having chosen a doctor must keep strictly to his treatment. That is what I will do. Now it's all settled. I won't think about it, but will follow the treatment seriously till summer, and then we shall see. From now there must be no more of this wavering!" This was easy to say but impossible to carry out. The pain in his side oppressed him and seemed to grow worse and more incessant, while the taste in his mouth grew stranger and stranger. It seemed to him that his breath had a disgusting smell, and he was conscious of a loss of appetite and strength. There was no deceiving himself: something terrible, new, and more important than anything before in his life, was taking place within him of which he alone was aware. Those about him did not understand or would not understand it, but thought everything in the world was going on as usual. That tormented Ivan Ilych more than anything. He saw that his household, especially his wife and daughter who were in a perfect whirl of visiting, did not understand anything of it and were annoyed that he was so depressed and so exacting, as if he were to blame for it. Though they tried to disguise it he saw that he was an obstacle in their path, and that his wife had adopted a definite line in regard to his illness and kept to it regardless of anything he said or did. Her attitude was this: "You know," she would say to her friends, "Ivan Ilych can't do as other people do, and keep to the treatment prescribed for him. One day he'll take his drops and keep strictly to his diet and go to bed in good time, but the next day unless I watch him he'll suddenly forget his medicine, eat sturgeon—which is forbidden—and sit up playing cards till one o'clock in the morning."

"Oh, come, when was that?" Ivan Ilych would ask in vexation. "Only once at Peter Ivanovich's."

"And yesterday with Shebek."

"Well, even if I hadn't stayed up, this pain would have kept me awake."

"Be that as it may you'll never get well like that, but will always make us wretched."

Praskovya Fedorovna's attitude to Ivan Ilych's illness, as she expressed it both to others and to him, was that it was his own fault and was another of the annoyances he caused her. Ivan Ilych felt that this opinion escaped her involuntarily—but that did not make it easier for him.

At the law courts too, Ivan Ilych noticed, or thought he noticed, a strange attitude towards himself. It sometimes seemed to him that people were watching him inquisitively as a man whose place might soon be vacant. Then again, his friends would suddenly begin to chaff him in a friendly way about his low spirits, as if the awful, horrible, and unheard-of thing that was going on within him, incessantly gnawing at him and irresistibly drawing him away, was a very agreeable subject for jests. Schwartz in particular irritated him by his jocularity, vivacity, and *savoir-faire*, which reminded him of what he himself had been ten years ago.

Friends came to make up a set and they sat down to cards. They dealt, bending the new cards to soften them, and he sorted the diamonds in his hand and found he had seven. His partner said "No trumps" and supported him with two diamonds. What more could be wished for? It ought to be jolly and lively. They would make a grand slam. But suddenly Ivan Ilych was conscious of that gnawing pain, that taste in his mouth, and it seemed ridiculous that in such circumstances he should be pleased to make a grand slam.

He looked at his partner Mikhail Mikhaylovich, who rapped the table with his strong hand and instead of snatching up the tricks pushed the cards courteously and indulgently towards Ivan Ilych that he might have the pleasure of gathering them up without the trouble of stretching out his hand for them. "Does he think I am too weak to stretch out my arm?" thought Ivan Ilych, and forgetting what he was doing he over-trumped his partner, missing the grand slam by three tricks. And what was most awful of all was that he saw how upset Mikhail Mikhaylovich was about it but did not himself care. And it was dreadful to realize why he did not care.

They all saw that he was suffering, and said: "We can stop if you are tired. Take a rest." Lie down? No, he was not at all tired, and he finished the rubber. All were gloomy and silent. Ivan Ilych felt that he had diffused this gloom over them and could not dispel it. They had supper and went away, and Ivan Ilych was left alone with the consciousness that his life was poisoned and was poisoning the lives of others, and that this poison did not weaken but penetrated more and more deeply into his whole being.

With this consciousness, and with physical pain besides the terror, he must go to bed, often to lie awake the greater part of the night. Next morning he had to get up again, dress, go to the law courts, speak, and write; or if he did not go out, spend at home those twenty-four hours a day each of which was a torture. And he had to live thus all alone on the brink of an abyss, with no one who understood or pitied him.

V

So one month passed and then another. Just before the New Year his brother-in-law came to town and stayed at their house. Ivan Ilych was at the law courts and Praskovya Fedorovna had gone shopping. When Ivan Ilych came home and entered his study he found his brother-in-law there—a healthy, florid man—unpacking his portmanteau himself. He raised his head on hearing Ivan Ilych's footsteps and looked up at him for a moment without a word. That stare told Ivan Ilych everything. His brother-in-law opened his mouth to utter an exclamation of surprise but checked himself, and that action confirmed it all.

"I have changed, eh?"

"Yes, there is a change."

And after that, try as he would to get his brother-in-law to return to the subject of his looks, the latter would say nothing about it. Praskovya Fedorovna came home and her brother went out to her. Ivan Ilych locked the door and began to examine himself in the glass, first full face, then in profile. He took up a portrait of himself taken with his wife, and compared it with what he saw in the glass. The change in him was immense. Then he bared his arms to the elbow, looked at them, drew the sleeves down again, sat down on an ottoman, and grew blacker than night.

"No, no, this won't do!" he said to himself, and jumped up, went to the table, took up some law papers and began to read them, but could not continue. He unlocked the door and went into the reception-room. The door leading to the drawing-room was shut. He approached it on tiptoe and listened.

"No, you are exaggerating!" Praskovya Fedorovna was saying.

"Exaggerating! Don't you see it? Why, he's a dead man! Look at his eyes—there's no life in them. But what is it that is wrong with him?"

"No one knows. Nikolaevich said something, but I don't know what. And Seshchetitsky said quite the contrary..."

Ivan Ilych walked away, went to his own room, lay down, and began musing; "The kidney, a floating kidney." He recalled all the doctors had told him of how it detached itself and swayed about. And by an effort of imagination he tried to catch that kidney and arrest it and support it. So little was needed for this, it seemed to him. "No, I'll go to see Peter Ivanovich again." He rang, ordered the carriage, and got ready to go.

"Where are you going, Jean?" asked his wife with a specially sad and exceptionally kind look.

This exceptionally kind look irritated him. He looked morosely at her.

"I must go to see Peter Ivanovich."

He went to see Peter Ivanovich, and together they went to see his friend, the doctor. He was in, and Ivan Ilych had a long talk with him.

Reviewing the anatomical and physiological details of what in the doctor's opinion was going on inside him, he understood it all.

There was something, a small thing, in the vermiform appendix. It might all come right. Only stimulate the energy of one organ and check the activity of another, then absorption would take place and everything would come right. He got home rather late for dinner, ate his dinner, and conversed cheerfully, but could not for a long time bring himself to go back to work in his room. At last, however, he went to his study and did what was necessary, but the consciousness that he had put something aside—an important, intimate matter which he would revert to when his work was done—never left him. When he had finished his work he remembered that this intimate matter was the thought of his vermiform appendix. But he did not give himself up to it, and went to the drawing-room for tea. There were callers there, including the examining magistrate who was a desirable match for his daughter, and they were conversing, playing the piano, and singing. Ivan Ilych, as Praskovya Fedorovna remarked, spent that evening more cheerfully than usual, but he never for a moment forgot that he had postponed the important matter of the appendix. At eleven o'clock he said goodnight and went to his bedroom. Since his illness he had slept alone in a small room next to his study. He undressed and took up a novel by Zola,[4] but instead of reading it he fell into thought, and in his imagination that desired improvement in the vermiform appendix occurred. There was the absorption and evacuation and the re-establishment of normal activity. "Yes, that's it!" he said to himself. "One need only assist nature, that's all." He remembered his medicine, rose, took it, and lay down on his back watching for the beneficent action of the medicine and for it to lessen the pain. "I need only take it regularly and avoid all injurious influences. I am already feeling better, much better." He began touching his side: it was not painful to the touch. "There, I really don't feel it. It's much better already." He put out the light and turned on his side . . . "The appendix is getting better, absorption is occurring." Suddenly he felt the old, familiar, dull, gnawing pain, stubborn and serious. There was the same familiar loathsome taste in his mouth. His heart sank and he felt dazed. "My God! My God!" he muttered. "Again, again! And it will never cease." And suddenly the matter presented itself in a quite different aspect. "Vermiform appendix! Kidney!" he said to himself. "It's not a question of appendix or kidney, but of life and . . . death. Yes, life was there and now it is going, going and I cannot stop it. Yes. Why deceive myself? Isn't it obvious to everyone but me that I'm dying, and that it's only a question of weeks, days . . . it may happen this moment. There was light and now there is darkness. I was here and now I'm going there! Where?" A chill came over him, his breathing ceased, and he felt only the throbbing of his heart.

"When I am not, what will there be? There will be nothing. Then where shall I be when I am no more? Can this be dying? No, I don't want to!" He jumped up and tried to light the candle, felt for it with trembling hands, dropped candle and candlestick on the floor, and fell back on his pillow.

"What's the use? It makes no difference," he said to himself, staring with wide-open eyes into the darkness. "Death. Yes, death. And none of them knows or wishes to know it, and they have no pity for me. Now they are playing." (He heard through the door the distant sound of a song and its accompaniment.) "It's all the same to them, but they will die too! Fools! I first, and they later, but it will be the same for them. And now they are merry . . . the beasts!"

Anger choked him and he was agonizingly, unbearably miserable. "It is impossible that all men have been doomed to suffer this awful horror!" He raised himself.

"Something must be wrong. I must calm myself—must think it all over from the beginning." And he again began thinking. "Yes, the beginning of my illness: I knocked my side, but I was still quite well that day and the next. It hurt a little, then rather more. I saw the doctors, then followed despondency and anguish, more doctors, and I drew nearer to the abyss. My strength grew less and I kept coming nearer and nearer, and now I have wasted away and there is no light in my eyes. I think of the appendix—but this is death! I think of mending the appendix, and all the while here is death! Can it really be death?" Again terror seized him and he gasped for breath. He leant down and began feeling for the matches, pressing with his elbow on the stand beside the bed. It was in his way and hurt him, he grew furious with it, pressed on it still harder, and upset it. Breathless and in despair he fell on his back, expecting death to come immediately.

Meanwhile the visitors were leaving. Praskovya Fedorovna was seeing them off. She heard something fall and came in.

"What has happened?"

"Nothing. I knocked it over accidentally."

4. The French novelist Emile Zola (1840–1902) was a proponent of the school of naturalism and a virtuoso portraitist of gruesome death from disease.

She went out and returned with a candle. He lay there panting heavily, like a man who has run a thousand yards, and stared upwards at her with a fixed look.

"What is it, Jean?"

"No...o...thing. I upset it." ("Why speak of it? She won't understand," he thought.)

And in truth she did not understand. She picked up the stand, lit his candle, and hurried away to see another visitor off. When she came back he still lay on his back, looking upwards.

"What is it? Do you feel worse?"

"Yes."

She shook her head and sat down.

"Do you know, Jean, I think we must ask Leshchetitsky to come and see you here."

This meant calling in the famous specialist, regardless of expense. He smiled malignantly and said "No." She remained a little longer and then went up to him and kissed his forehead.

While she was kissing him he hated her from the bottom of his soul and with difficulty refrained from pushing her away.

"Good night. Please God you'll sleep."

"Yes."

VI

Ivan Ilych saw that he was dying, and he was in continual despair.

In the depth of his heart he knew he was dying, but not only was he not accustomed to the thought, he simply did not and could not grasp it.

The syllogism he had learnt from Kiesewetter's Logic: "Caius is a man, men are mortal, therefore Caius is mortal," had always seemed to him correct as applied to Caius, but certainly not as applied to himself. That Caius—man in the abstract—was mortal, was perfectly correct, but he was not Caius, not an abstract man, but a creature quite, quite separate from all others. He had been little Vanya, with a mamma and a papa, with Mitya and Volodya, with the toys, a coachman and a nurse, afterwards with Katenka and with all the joys, griefs, and delights of childhood, boyhood, and youth. What did Caius know of the smell of that striped leather ball Vanya had been so fond of? Had Caius kissed his mother's hand like that, and did the silk of her dress rustle so for Caius? Had he rioted like that at school when the pastry was bad? Had Caius been in love like that? Could Caius preside at a session as he did? "Caius really was mortal, and it was right for him to die; but for me, little Vanya, Ivan Ilych, with all my thoughts and emotions, it's altogether a different matter. It cannot be that I ought to die. That would be too terrible." Such was his feeling.

"If I had to die like Caius I would have known it was so. An inner voice would have told me so, but there was nothing of the sort in me and I and all my friends felt that our case was quite different from that of Caius. And now here it is!" he said to himself. "It can't be. It's impossible! But here it is. How is this? How is one to understand it?" He could not understand it, and tried to drive this false, incorrect, morbid thought away and to replace it by other proper and healthy thoughts. But that thought, and not the thought only but the reality itself, seemed to come and confront him.

And to replace that thought he called up a succession of others, hoping to find in them some support. He tried to get back into the former current of thoughts that had once screened the thought of death from him. But strange to say, all that had formerly shut off, hidden, and destroyed his consciousness of death, no longer had that effect. Ivan Ilych now spent most of his time in attempting to re-establish that old current. He would say to himself: "I will take up my duties again—after all I used to live by them." And banishing all doubts he would go to the law courts, enter into conversation with his colleagues, and sit carelessly as was his wont, scanning the crowd with a thoughtful look and leaning both his emaciated arms on the arms of his oak chair; bending over as usual to a colleague and drawing his papers nearer he would interchange whispers with him, and then suddenly raising his eyes and sitting erect would pronounce certain words and open the proceedings. But suddenly in the midst of those proceedings the pain in his side, regardless of the stage the proceedings had reached, would begin its own gnawing work. Ivan Ilych would turn his attention to it and try to drive the thought of it away, but without success. *It* would come and stand before him and look at him, and he would be petrified and the light would die out of his eyes, and he would again begin asking himself whether *It* alone was true. And his colleagues and subordinates would see with surprise and distress that he, the brilliant and subtle judge, was becoming confused and making mistakes. He would shake himself, try to pull himself together, manage somehow to bring the sitting to a close, and return home with the sorrowful consciousness that his judicial labours could not as formerly hide from him what he wanted them to hide, and could not deliver him from *It*. And what was worst of all was that *It* drew his attention to itself not in order to make him take some action but only that he should look at *It*, look it straight in the face: look at it and without doing anything, suffer inexpressibly.

And to save himself from this condition Ivan Ilych looked for consolations—new screens—and new screens were found and for a while seemed to save him, but then they immediately fell to pieces or rather became transparent, as if *It* penetrated them and nothing could veil *It*.

In these latter days he would go into the drawing-room he had arranged—that drawing-room where he had fallen and for the sake of which (how bitterly ridiculous it seemed) he had sacrificed his life—for he knew that his illness originated with that knock. He would enter and see that something had scratched the polished table. He would look for the cause of this and find that it was the bronze ornamentation of an album, that had got bent. He would take up the expensive album which he had lovingly arranged, and feel vexed with his daughter and her friends for their untidiness—for the album was torn here and there and some of the photographs turned upside down. He would put it carefully in order and bend the ornamentation back into position. Then it would occur to him to place all those things in another corner of the room, near the plants. He would call the footman, but his daughter or wife would come to help him. They would not agree, and his wife would contradict him, and he would dispute and grow angry. But that was all right, for then he did not think about *It*. *It* was invisible.

But then, when he was moving something himself, his wife would say: "Let the servants do it. You will hurt yourself again." And suddenly *It* would flash through the screen and he would see it. It was just a flash, and he hoped it would disappear, but he would involuntarily pay attention to his side. "It sits there as before, gnawing just the same!" And he could no longer forget *It*, but could distinctly see it looking at him from behind the flowers. "What is it all for?"

"It really is so! I lost my life over that curtain as I might have done when storming a fort. Is that possible? How terrible and how stupid. It can't be true! It can't, but it is." He would go to his study, lie down, and again be alone with *It*: face to face with *It*. And nothing could be done with *It* except to look at it and shudder.

VII

How it happened it is impossible to say because it came about step by step, unnoticed, but in the third month of Ivan Ilych's illness, his wife, his daughter, his son, his acquaintances, the doctors, the servants, and above all he himself, were aware that the whole interest he had for other people was whether he would soon vacate his place, and at last release the living from the discomfort caused by his presence and be himself released from his sufferings.

He slept less and less. He was given opium and hypodermic injections of morphine, but this did not relieve him. The dull depression he experienced in a somnolent condition at first gave him a little relief, but only as something new, afterwards it became as distressing as the pain itself or even more so.

Special foods were prepared for him by the doctors' orders, but all those foods became increasingly distasteful and disgusting to him.

For his excretions also special arrangements had to be made, and this was a torment to him every time—a torment from the uncleanliness, the unseemliness, and the smell, and from knowing that another person had to take part in it.

But just through his most unpleasant matter, Ivan Ilych obtained comfort. Gerasim, the butler's young assistant, always came in to carry the things out. Gerasim was a clean, fresh peasant lad, grown stout on town food and always cheerful and bright. At first the sight of him, in his clean Russian peasant costume, engaged on that disgusting task embarrassed Ivan Ilych.

Once when he got up from the commode too weak to draw up his trousers, he dropped into a soft armchair and looked with horror at his bare, enfeebled thighs with the muscles so sharply marked on them.

Gerasim with a firm light tread, his heavy boots emitting a pleasant smell of tar and fresh winter air, came in wearing a clean Hessian apron, the sleeves of his print shirt tucked up over his strong bare young arms; and refraining from looking at his sick master out of consideration for his feelings, and restraining the joy of life that beamed from his face, he went up to the commode.

"Gerasim!" said Ivan Ilych in a weak voice.

Gerasim started, evidently afraid he might have committed some blunder, and with a rapid movement turned his fresh, kind, simple young face which just showed the first downy signs of a beard.

"Yes, sir?"

"That must be very unpleasant for you. You must forgive me. I am helpless."

"Oh, why, sir," and Gerasim's eyes beamed and he showed his glistening white teeth, "what's a little trouble? It's a case of illness with you, sir."

And his deft strong hands did their accustomed task, and he went out of the room stepping lightly. Five minutes later he as lightly returned.

Ivan Ilych was still sitting in the same position in the armchair.

"Gerasim," he said when the latter had replaced the freshly-washed utensil. "Please come here and help me." Gerasim went up to him. "Lift me up. It is hard for me to get up, and I have sent Dmitri away."

Gerasim went up to him, grasped his master with his strong arms deftly but gently, in the same way that he stepped—lifted him, supported him with one hand, and with the other drew up his trousers and would have set him down again, but Ivan Ilych asked to be led to the sofa. Gerasim, without an effort and without apparent pressure, led him, almost lifting him, to the sofa and placed him on it.

"Thank you. How easily and well you do it all!"

Gerasim smiled again and turned to leave the room. But Ivan Ilych felt his presence such a comfort that he did not want to let him go.

"One thing more, please move up that chair. No, the other one—under my feet. It is easier for me when my feet are raised."

Gerasim brought the chair, set it down gently in place, and raised Ivan Ilych's legs on it. It seemed to Ivan Ilych that he felt better while Gerasim was holding up his legs.

"It's better when my legs are higher," he said. "Place that cushion under them."

Gerasim did so. He again lifted the legs and placed them, and again Ivan Ilych felt better while Gerasim held his legs. When he set them down Ivan Ilych fancied he felt worse.

"Gerasim," he said. "Are you busy now?"

"Not at all, sir," said Gerasim, who had learnt from the townsfolk how to speak to gentlefolk.

"What have you still to do?"

"What have I to do? I've done everything except chopping the logs for tomorrow."

"Then hold my legs up a bit higher, can you?"

"Of course I can. Why not?" and Gerasim raised his master's legs higher and Ivan Ilych thought that in that position he did not feel any pain at all.

"And how about the logs?"

"Don't trouble about that, sir. There's plenty of time."

Ivan Ilych told Gerasim to sit down and hold his legs, and began to talk to him. And strange to say it seemed to him that he felt better while Gerasim held his legs up.

After that Ivan Ilych would sometimes call Gerasim and get him to hold his legs on his shoulders, and he liked talking to him. Gerasim did it all easily, willingly, simply, and with a good nature that touched Ivan Ilych. Health, strength, and vitality in other people were offensive to him, but Gerasim's strength and vitality did not mortify but soothed him.

What tormented Ivan Ilych most was the deception, the lie, which for some reason they all accepted, that he was not dying but was simply ill, and that he only need keep quiet and undergo a treatment and then something very good would result. He however knew that do what they would nothing would come of it, only still more agonizing suffering and death. This deception tortured him—their not wishing to admit what they all knew and what he knew, but wanting to lie to him concerning his terrible condition, and wishing and forcing him to participate in that lie. Those lies—lies enacted over him on the eve of his death and destined to degrade this awful, solemn act to the level of their visitings, their curtains, their sturgeon for dinner—were a terrible agony for Ivan Ilych. And strangely enough, many times when they were going through their antics over him he had been within a hairbreadth of calling out to them: "Stop lying! You know and I know that I am dying. Then at least stop lying about it!" But he had never had the spirit to do it. The awful, terrible act of his dying was, he could see, reduced by those about him to the level of a casual, unpleasant, and almost indecorous incident (as if someone entered a drawing room defusing an unpleasant odour) and this was done by that very decorum which he had served all his life long. He saw that no one felt for him, because no one even wished to grasp his position. Only Gerasim recognized it and pitied him. And so Ivan Ilych felt at ease only with him. He felt comforted when Gerasim supported his legs (sometimes all night long) and refused to go to bed, saying: "Don't you worry, Ivan Ilych. I'll get sleep enough later on," or when he suddenly became familiar and exclaimed: "If you weren't sick it would be another matter, but as it is, why should I grudge a little trouble?" Gerasim alone did not lie; everything showed that he alone understood the facts of the case and did not consider it necessary to disguise them, but simply felt sorry for his emaciated and enfeebled master. Once when Ivan Ilych was sending him away he even said straight out: "We shall all of us die, so why should I grudge a little trouble?"—expressing the fact that he did not think his work burdensome, because he was doing it for a dying man and hoped someone would do the same for him when his time came.

Apart from this lying, or because of it, what most tormented Ivan Ilych was that no one pitied him as he wished to be pitied. At certain moments after prolonged suffering he wished most of all (though he would have been ashamed to confess it) for someone to pity him as a sick child is pitied. He longed to be petted and comforted. He knew he was an important functionary, that he had a beard turning grey, and that therefore what he longed for was impossible, but still he longed for it. And in Gerasim's attitude towards him there was something akin to what he wished for, and so that attitude comforted him. Ivan Ilych wanted to weep, wanted to be petted and cried over, and then his colleague Shebek would come, and instead of weeping and being petted, Ivan Ilych would assume a serious, severe, and profound air, and by force of habit would express his opinion on a decision of the Court of Cassation and would stubbornly insist on that view. This falsity around him and within him did more than anything else to poison his last days.

VIII

It was morning. He knew it was morning because Gerasim had gone, and Peter the footman had come and put out the candles, drawn back one of the curtains, and begun quietly to tidy up. Whether it was morning or evening, Friday or Sunday, made no difference, it was all just the same: the gnawing, unmitigated, agonizing pain, never ceasing for an instant, the consciousness of life inexorably waning but not yet extinguished, the approach of that ever dreaded and hateful Death which was the only reality, and always the same falsity. What were days, weeks, hours, in such a case?

"Will you have some tea, sir?"

"He wants things to be regular, and wishes the gentlefolk to drink tea in the morning," thought Ivan Ilych, and only said "No."

"Wouldn't you like to move onto the sofa, sir?"

"He wants to tidy up the room, and I'm in the way. I am uncleanliness and disorder," he thought, and said only:

"No, leave me alone."

The man went on bustling about. Ivan Ilych stretched out his hand. Peter came up, ready to help.

"What is it, sir?"

"My watch."

Peter took the watch which was close at hand and gave it to his master.

"Half-past eight. Are they up?"

"No sir, except Vladimir Ivanovich" (the son) "who has gone to school. Praskovya Fedorovna ordered me to wake her if you asked for her. Shall I do so?"

"No, there's no need to." "Perhaps I'd better have some tea," he thought, and added aloud: "Yes, bring me some tea."

Peter went to the door, but Ivan Ilych dreaded being left alone. "How can I keep him here? Oh yes, my medicine." "Peter, give me my medicine." "Why not? Perhaps it may still do some good." He took a spoonful and swallowed it. "No, it won't help. It's all tomfoolery, all deception," he decided as soon as he became aware of the familiar, sickly, hopeless taste. "No, I can't believe in it any longer. But the pain, why this pain? If it would only cease just for a moment!" And he moaned. Peter turned towards him. "It's all right. Go and fetch me some tea."

Peter went out. Left alone Ivan Ilych groaned not so much with pain, terrible though that was, as from mental anguish. Always and forever the same, always these endless days and nights. If only it would come quicker! If only *what* would come quicker? Death, darkness?...No, no! anything rather than death!

When Peter returned with the tea on a tray, Ivan Ilych stared at him for a time in perplexity, not realizing who and what he was. Peter was disconcerted by that look and his embarrassment brought Ivan Ilych to himself.

"Oh, tea! All right, put it down. Only help me to wash and put on a clean shirt."

And Ivan Ilych began to wash. With pauses for rest, he washed his hands and then his face, cleaned his teeth, brushed his hair, looked in the glass. He was terrified by what he saw, especially by the limp way in which his hair clung to his pallid forehead.

While his shirt was being changed he knew that he would be still more frightened at the sight of his body, so he avoided looking at it. Finally he was ready. He drew on a dressing-gown, wrapped himself in a plaid, and sat down in the armchair to take his tea. For a moment he felt refreshed, but as soon as he began to drink the tea he was again aware of the same taste, and the pain also returned. He finished it with an effort, and then lay down stretching out his legs, and dismissed Peter.

Always the same. Now a spark of hope flashes up, then a sea of despair rages, and always pain; always pain, always despair, and always the same. When alone he had a dreadful and distressing desire to call someone, but he knew beforehand that with others present it would be still worse. "Another dose of morphine—to lose consciousness. I will tell him, the doctor, that he must think of something else. It's impossible, impossible, to go on like this."

An hour and another pass like that. But now there is a ring at the door bell. Perhaps it's the doctor? It is. He comes in fresh, hearty, plump, and cheerful, with that look on his face that seems to say: "There now, you're in a panic about something, but we'll arrange it all for you directly!" The doctor knows this expression is out of place here, but he has put it on once for all and can't take it off—like a man who has put on a frock-coat in the morning to pay a round of calls.

The doctor rubs his hands vigorously and reassuringly.

"Brr! How cold it is! There's such a sharp frost; just let me warm myself!" he says, as if it were only a matter of waiting till he was warm, and then he would put everything right.

"Well now, how are you?"

Ivan Ilych feels that the doctor would like to say: "Well, how are our affairs?" but that even he feels that this would not do, and says instead: "What sort of a night have you had?"

Ivan Ilych looks at him as much as to say: "Are you really never ashamed of lying?" But the doctor does not wish to understand this question, and Ivan Ilych says: "Just as terrible as ever. The pain never leaves me and never subsides. If only something..."

"Yes, you sick people are always like that....There, now I think I am warm enough. Even Praskovya Fedorovna, who is so particular, could find no fault with my temperature. Well, now I can say good-morning," and the doctor presses his patient's hand.

Then dropping his former playfulness, he begins with a most serious face to examine the patient, feeling his pulse and taking his temperature, and then begins the sounding and auscultation.

Ivan Ilych knows quite well and definitely that all this is nonsense and pure deception, but when the doctor, getting down on his knee, leans over him, putting his ear first higher then lower, and performs various gymnastic movements over him with a significant expression on his face, Ivan Ilych submits to it all as he used to submit to the speeches of the lawyers, though he knew very well that they were all lying and why they were lying.

The doctor, kneeling on the sofa, is still sounding him when Praskovya Fedorovna's silk dress rustles at the door and she is heard scolding Peter for not having let her know of the doctor's arrival.

She comes in, kisses her husband, and at once proceeds to prove that she has been up a long time already, and only owing to a misunderstanding failed to be there when the doctor arrived.

Ivan Ilych looks at her, scans her all over, sets against her the whiteness and plumpness and cleanness of her hands and neck, the gloss of her hair, and the sparkle of her vivacious eyes. He hates her with his whole soul. And the thrill of hatred he feels for her makes him suffer from her touch.

Her attitude towards him and his diseases is still the same. Just as the doctor had adopted a certain relation to his patient which he could not abandon, so had she formed one towards him—that he was not doing something he ought to do and was himself to blame, and that she reproached him lovingly for this—and she could not now change that attitude.

"You see he doesn't listen to me and doesn't take his medicine at the proper time. And above all he lies in a position that is no doubt bad for him—with his legs up."

She described how he made Gerasim hold his legs up.

The doctor smiled with a contemptuous affability that said: "What's to be done? These sick people do have foolish fancies of that kind, but we must forgive them."

When the examination was over the doctor looked at his watch, and then Praskovya Fedorovna announced to Ivan Ilych that it was of course as he pleased, but she had sent today for a celebrated specialist who would examine him and have a consultation with Michael Danilovich (their regular doctor).

"Please don't raise any objections. I am doing this for my own sake," she said ironically, letting it be felt that she was doing it all for his sake and only said this to leave him no right to refuse. He remained silent, knitting his brows. He felt that he was surrounded and involved in a mesh of falsity that it was hard to unravel anything. Everything she did for him was entirely for her own sake, and she told him she was doing for herself what she actually was doing for herself, as if that was so incredible that he must understand the opposite.

At half-past eleven the celebrated specialist arrived. Again the sounding began and the significant conversations in his presence and in another room, about the kidneys and the appendix, and the questions and answers, with such an air of importance that again, instead of the real question of life and death which now alone confronted him, the question arose of the kidney and appendix which were not behaving as they ought to and would now be attacked by Michael Danilovich and the specialist and forced to amend their ways.

The celebrated specialist took leave of him with a serious though not hopeless look, and in reply to the timid question Ivan Ilych, with eyes glistening with fear and hope, put to him as to whether there was a chance of recovery, said that he could not vouch for it but there was a possibility. The look of hope with which Ivan Ilych watched the doctor out was so pathetic that Praskovya Fedorovna, seeing it, even wept as she left the room to hand the doctor his fee.

The gleam of hope kindled by the doctor's encouragement did not last long. The same room, the same pictures, curtains, wallpaper, medicine bottles, were all there, and the same aching suffering body, and Ivan Ilych began to moan. They gave him a subcutaneous injection and he sank into oblivion.

It was twilight when he came to. They brought him his dinner and he swallowed some beef tea with difficulty, and then everything was the same again and night was coming on.

After dinner, at seven o'clock, Praskovya Fedorovna came into the room in evening dress, her full bosom pushed up by her corset, and with traces of powder on her face. She had reminded him in the morning that they were going to the theatre. Sarah Bernhardt[5] was visiting the town and they had a box, which he had insisted on their taking. Now he had forgotten about it and her toilet offended him, but he concealed his vexation when he remembered that he had himself insisted on their securing a box and going because it would be an instructive and aesthetic pleasure for the children.

Praskovya Fedorovna came in, self-satisfied but yet with a rather guilty air. She sat down and asked how he was, but, as he saw, only for the sake of asking and not in order to learn about it, knowing that there was nothing to learn—and then went on to what she really wanted to say: that she would not on any account have gone but that the box had been taken and Helen and their daughter were going, as well as Petrishchev (the examining magistrate, their daughter's fiancé) and that it was out of the question to let them go alone; but that she would have much preferred to sit with him for a while; and he must be sure to follow the doctor's orders while she was away.

"Oh, and Fedor Petrovich" (the fiancé) "would like to come in. May he? And Lisa?"

"All right."

5. "The Divine Sarah" was the most celebrated actress of her century.

Their daughter came in in full evening dress, her fresh young flesh exposed (making a show of that very flesh which in his own case caused so much suffering), strong, healthy, evidently in love, and impatient with illness, suffering, and death, because they interfered with her happiness.

Fedor Petrovich came in too, in evening dress, his hair curled *a la Capoul*,[6] a tight stiff collar round his long sinewy neck, an enormous white shirt-front and narrow black trousers tightly stretched over his strong thighs. He had one white glove tightly drawn on, and was holding his opera hat in his hand.

Following him the schoolboy crept in unnoticed, in a new uniform, poor little fellow, and wearing gloves. Terribly dark shadows showed under his eyes, the meaning of which Ivan Ilych knew well.

His son had always seemed pathetic to him, and now it was dreadful to see the boy's frightened look of pity. It seemed to Ivan Ilych that Vasya was the only one besides Gerasim who understood and pitied him.

They all sat down and again asked how he was. A silence followed. Lisa asked her mother about the opera glasses, and there was an altercation between mother and daughter as to who had taken them and where they had been put. This occasioned some unpleasantness.

Fedor Petrovich inquired of Ivan Ilych whether he had ever seen Sarah Bernhardt. Ivan Ilych did not at first catch the question, but then replied: "No, have you seen her before?"

"Yes, in *Adrienne Lecouvreur*."[7]

Praskovya Fedorovna mentioned some roles in which Sarah Bernhardt was particularly good. Her daughter disagreed. Conversation sprang up as to the elegance and realism of her acting—the sort of conversation that is always repeated and is always the same.

In the midst of the conversation Fedor Petrovich glanced at Ivan Ilych and became silent. The others also looked at him and grew silent. Ivan Ilych was staring with glittering eyes straight before him, evidently indignant with them. This had to be rectified, but it was impossible to do so. The silence had to be broken, but for a time no one dared to break it and they all became afraid that the conventional deception would suddenly become obvious and the truth become plain to all. Lisa was the first to pluck up courage and break that silence, but by trying to hide what everybody was feeling, she betrayed it.

"Well, if we are going it's time to start," she said, looking at her watch, a present from her father, and with a faint and significant smile at Fedor Petrovich relating to something known only to them. She got up with a rustle of her dress.

They all rose, said good-night, and went away.

When they had gone it seemed to Ivan Ilych that he felt better; the falsity had gone with them. But the pain remained—that same pain and that same fear that made everything monotonously alike, nothing harder and nothing easier. Everything was worse.

Again minute followed minute and hour followed hour. Everything remained the same and there was no cessation. And the inevitable end of it all became more and more terrible.

"Yes, send Gerasim here," he replied to a question Peter asked.

6. An elaborate style named after a French singer.
7. A tragic drama based on the life and early death of an eighteenth-century actress.

IX

His wife returned late at night. She came in on tiptoe, but he heard her, opened his eyes, and made haste to close them again. She wished to send Gerasim away and to sit with him herself, but he opened his eyes and said: "No, go away."

"Are you in great pain?"

"Always the same."

"Take some opium."

He agreed and took some. She went away.

Till about three in the morning he was in a state of stupefied misery. It seemed to him that he and his pain were being thrust into a narrow, deep black sack, but though they were pushed further and further in they could not be pushed to the bottom. And this, terrible enough in itself, was accompanied by suffering. He was frightened yet wanted to fall through the sack, he struggled but yet cooperated. And suddenly he broke through, fell, and regained consciousness. Gerasim was sitting at the foot of the bed dozing quietly and patiently, while he himself lay with his emaciated stockinged legs resting on Gerasim's shoulders; the same shaded candle was there and the same unceasing pain.

"Go away, Gerasim," he whispered.

"It's all right, sir. I'll stay a while."

"No. Go away."

He removed his legs from Gerasim's shoulders, turned sideways onto his arm, and felt sorry for himself. He only waited till Gerasim had gone into the next room and then restrained himself no longer but wept like a child. He wept on account of his helplessness, his terrible loneliness, the cruelty of man, the cruelty of God, and the absence of God.

"Why hast Thou done all this? Why hast Thou brought me here? Why, why dost Thou torment me so terribly?"

He did not expect an answer and yet wept because there was no answer and could be none. The pain again grew more acute, but he did not stir and did not call. He said to himself: "Go on! Strike me! But what is it for? What have I done to Thee? What is it for?"

Then he grew quiet and not only ceased weeping but even held his breath and became all attention. It was as though he were listening not to an audible voice but to the voice of his soul, to the current of thoughts arising within him.

"What is it you want?" was the first clear conception capable of expression in words, that he heard.

"What do you want? What do you want?" he repeated to himself.

"What do I want? To live and not to suffer," he answered.

And again he listened with such concentrated attention that even his pain did not distract him.

"To live? How?" asked his inner voice.

"Why, to live as I used to—well and pleasantly."

"As you lived before, well and pleasantly?" the voice repeated.

And in imagination he began to recall the best moments of his pleasant life. But strange to say none of those best moments of his pleasant life now seemed at all what they had then seemed—none of them except the first recollections of childhood. There, in childhood, there had been something really pleasant with which it would be possible to live if it could return. But the child who had experienced that happiness existed no longer, it was like a reminiscence of somebody else.

As soon as the period began which had produced the present Ivan Ilych, all that had then seemed joys now melted before his sight and turned into something trivial and often nasty.

And the further he departed from childhood and the nearer he came to the present the more worthless and doubtful were the joys. This began with the School of Law. A little that was really good was still found there—there was light-heartedness, friendship, and hope. But in the upper classes there had already been fewer of such good moments. Then during the first years of his official career, when he was in the service of the governor, some pleasant moments again occurred: they were the memories of love for a woman. Then all became confused and there was still less of what was good; later on again there was still less that was good, and the further he went the less there was. His marriage, a mere accident, then the disenchantment that followed it, his wife's bad breath and the sensuality and hypocrisy: then that deadly official life and those preoccupations about money, a year of it, and two, and ten, and twenty, and always the same thing. And the longer it lasted the more deadly it became. "It is as if I had been going downhill while I imagined I was going up. And that is really what it was. I was going up in public opinion, but to the same extent life was ebbing away from me. And now it is all done and there is only death.

"Then what does it mean? Why? It can't be that life is so senseless and horrible. But if it really has been so horrible and senseless, why must I die and die in agony? There is something wrong!

"Maybe I did not live as I ought to have done," it suddenly occurred to him. "But how could that be, when I did everything properly?" he replied, and immediately dismissed from his mind this, the sole solution of all the riddles of life and death, as something quite impossible.

"Then what do you want now? To live? Live how? Live as you lived in the law courts when the usher proclaimed 'The judge is coming!' The judge is coming, the judge!" he repeated to himself. "Here he is, the judge. But I am not guilty!" he exclaimed angrily. "What is it for?" And he ceased crying, but turning his face to the wall continued to ponder on the same question: Why, and for what purpose, is there all this horror? But however much he pondered he found no answer. And whenever the thought occurred to him, as it often did, that it all resulted from his not having lived as he ought to have done, he at once recalled the correctness of his whole life and dismissed so strange an idea.

X

Another fortnight passed. Ivan Ilych now no longer left his sofa. He would not lie in bed but lay on the sofa, facing the wall nearly all the time. He suffered ever the same unceasing agonies and in his loneliness pondered always on the same insoluble question: "What is this? Can it be that it is Death?" And the inner voice answered: "Yes, it is Death."

"Why these sufferings?" And the voice answered, "For no reason—they just are so." Beyond and besides this there was nothing.

From the very beginning of his illness, ever since he had first been to see the doctor, Ivan Ilych's life had been divided between two contrary and alternating moods: now it was despair and the expectation of this uncomprehended and terrible death, and now hope and an intently interested observation of the functioning of his organs.

Now before his eyes there was only a kidney or an intestine that temporarily evaded its duty, and now only that incomprehensible and dreadful death from which it was impossible to escape.

These two states of mind had alternated from the very beginning of his illness, but the further it progressed the more doubtful and fantastic became the conception of the kidney, and the more real the sense of impending death.

He had but to call to mind what he had been three months before and what he was now, to call to mind with what regularity he had been going downhill, for every possibility of hope to be shattered.

Latterly during the loneliness in which he found himself as he lay facing the back of the sofa, a loneliness in the midst of a populous town and surrounded by numerous acquaintances and relations but that yet could not have been more complete anywhere—either at the bottom of the sea or under the earth—during that terrible loneliness Ivan Ilych had lived only in memories of the past. Pictures of his past rose before him one after another. They always began with what was nearest in time and then went back to what was most remote—to his childhood—and rested there. If he thought of the stewed prunes that had been offered him that day, his mind went back to the raw shrivelled French plums of his childhood, their peculiar flavour and the flow of saliva when he sucked their stones, and along with the memory of that taste came a whole series of memories of those days: his nurse, his brother, and their toys. "No, I mustn't think of that.... It is too painful," Ivan Ilych said to himself, and brought himself back to the present—to the button on the back of the sofa and the creases in its morocco. "Morocco is expensive, but it does not wear well: there had been a quarrel about it. It was a different kind of quarrel and a different kind of morocco that time when we tore father's portfolio and were punished, and mamma brought us some tarts...." And again his thoughts dwelt on his childhood, and again it was painful and he tried to banish them and fix his mind on something else.

Then again together with that chain of memories another series passed through his mind—of how his illness had progressed and grown worse. There also the further back he looked the more life there had been. There had been more of what was good in life and more of life itself. The two merged together. "Just as the pain went on getting worse and worse, so my life grew worse and worse," he thought. "There is one bright spot there at the back, at the beginning of life, and afterwards all becomes blacker and blacker and proceeds more and more rapidly—in inverse ratio to the square of the distance from death," thought Ivan Ilych. And the example of a stone falling downwards with increasing velocity entered his mind. Life, a series of increasing sufferings, flies further and further towards its end—the most terrible suffering. "I am flying...." He shuddered, shifted himself, and tried to resist, but was already aware that resistance was impossible, and again with eyes weary of gazing but unable to cease seeing what was before them, he stared at the back of the sofa and waited— awaiting that dreadful fall and shock and destruction.

"Resistance is impossible!" he said to himself. "If I could only understand what it is all for! But that too is impossible. An explanation would be possible if it could be said that I have not lived as I ought to. But it is impossible to say that," and he remembered all the legality, correctitude, and propriety of his life. "That at any rate can certainly not be admitted," he thought, and his lips smiled ironically as if someone could see that smile and be taken in by it. "There is no explanation! Agony, death.... What for?"

XI

Another two weeks went by in this way and during that fortnight an event occurred that Ivan Ilych and his wife had desired. Petrishchev formally proposed. It happened in the evening. The next day Praskovya Fedorovna came into her husband's room considering how best to inform him of it, but that very night there had been a fresh change for the worse in his condition. She found him still lying on the sofa but in a different position. He lay on his back, groaning and staring fixedly straight in front of him.

She began to remind him of his medicines, but he turned his eyes towards her with such a look that she did not finish what she was saying; so great an animosity, to her in particular, did that look express.

"For Christ's sake let me die in peace!" he said.

She would have gone away, but just then their daughter came in and went up to say good morning. He looked at her as he had done at his wife, and in reply to her inquiry about his health said dryly that he would soon free them all of himself. They were both silent and after sitting with him for a while went away.

"Is it our fault?" Lisa said to her mother. "It's as if we were to blame! I am sorry for papa, but why should we be tortured?"

The doctor came at his usual time. Ivan Ilych answered "Yes" and "No," never taking his angry eyes from him, and at last said: "You know you can do nothing for me, so leave me alone."

"We can ease your sufferings."

"You can't even do that. Let me be."

The doctor went into the drawing room and told Praskovya Fedorovna that the case was very serious and that the only resource left was opium to allay her husband's sufferings, which must be terrible.

It was true, as the doctor said, that Ivan Ilych's physical sufferings were terrible, but worse than the physical sufferings were his mental sufferings which were his chief torture.

His mental sufferings were due to the fact that that night, as he looked at Gerasim's sleepy, good-natured face with its prominent cheek-bones, the question suddenly occurred to him: "What if my whole life has been wrong?"

It occurred to him that what had appeared perfectly impossible before, namely that he had not spent his life as he should have done, might after all be true. It occurred to him that his scarcely perceptible attempts to struggle against what was considered good by the most highly placed people, those scarcely noticeable impulses which he had immediately suppressed, might have been the real thing, and all the rest false. And his professional duties and the whole arrangement of his life and of his family, and all his social and official interests, might all have been false. He tried to defend all those things to himself and suddenly felt the weakness of what he was defending. There was nothing to defend.

"But if that is so," he said to himself, "and I am leaving this life with the consciousness that I have lost all that was given me and it is impossible to rectify it—what then?"

He lay on his back and began to pass his life in review in quite a new way. In the morning when he saw first his footman, then his wife, then his daughter, and then the doctor, their every word and movement confirmed to him the awful truth that had been revealed to him during the night. In them he saw himself—all that for which he had lived—and saw clearly that it was not real at all, but a terrible and huge deception which had hidden both life and death. This consciousness intensified his physical suffering tenfold. He groaned and tossed about, and pulled at his clothing which choked and stifled him. And he hated them on that account.

He was given a large dose of opium and became unconscious, but at noon his sufferings began again. He drove everybody away and tossed from side to side. His wife came to him and said:

"Jean, my dear, do this for me. It can't do any harm and often helps. Healthy people often do it."

He opened his eyes wide.

"What? Take communion? Why? It's unnecessary! However...."

She began to cry.

"Yes, do, my dear. I'll send for our priest. He is such a nice man."

"All right. Very well," he muttered.

When the priest came and heard his confession, Ivan Ilych was softened and seemed to feel a relief from his doubts and consequently from his sufferings, and for a moment there came a ray of hope. He again began to think of the vermiform appendix and the possibility of correcting it. He received the sacrament with tears in his eyes.

When they laid him down again afterwards he felt a moment's ease, and the hope that he might live awoke in him again. He began to think of the operation that had been suggested to him. "To live! I want to live!" he said to himself.

His wife came in to congratulate him after his communion, and when uttering the usual conventional words she added:

"You feel better, don't you?"

Without looking at her he said "Yes."

Her dress, her figure, the expression of her face, the tone of her voice, all revealed the same thing. "This is wrong, it is not as it should be. All you have lived for and still live for is falsehood and deception, hiding life and death from you." And as soon as he admitted that thought, his hatred and his agonizing physical suffering again sprang up, and with that suffering a consciousness of the unavoidable, approaching end. And to this was added a new sensation of grinding shooting pain and a feeling of suffocation.

The expression of his face when he uttered that "Yes" was dreadful. Having uttered it, he looked her straight in the eyes, turned on his face with a rapidity extraordinary in his weak state and shouted:

"Go away! Go away and leave me alone!"

XII

From that moment the screaming began that continued for three days, and was so terrible that one could not hear it through two closed doors without horror. At the moment he answered his wife realized that he was lost, that there was no return, that the end had come, the very end, and his doubts were still unsolved and remained doubts.

"Oh! Oh! Oh!" he cried in various intonations. He had begun by screaming "I won't!" and continued screaming on the letter "O."

For three whole days, during which time did not exist for him, he struggled in that black sack into which he was being thrust by an invisible, resistless force. He struggled as a man condemned to death struggles in the hands of the executioner, knowing that he cannot save himself. And every moment he felt that despite all his efforts he was drawing nearer and nearer to what terrified him. He felt that his agony was due to his being thrust into that black hole and still more to his not being able to get right into it. He was hindered from getting into it by his conviction that his life had been a good one. That very justification of his life held him fast and prevented his moving forward, and it caused him most torment of all.

Suddenly some force struck him in the chest and side, making it still harder to breathe, and he fell through the hole and there at the bottom was a light. What had happened to him was like the sensation one sometimes experiences in a railway carriage when one thinks one is going backwards while one is really going forwards and suddenly becomes aware of the real direction.

"Yes, it was not the right thing," he said to himself, "but that's no matter. It can be done. But what *is* the right thing?" He asked himself, and suddenly grew quiet.

This occurred at the end of the third day, two hours before his death. Just then his schoolboy son had crept softly in and gone up to the bedside. The dying man was still screaming desperately and waving his arms. His hand fell on the boy's head, and the boy caught it, pressed it to his lips, and began to cry.

At that very moment Ivan Ilych fell through and caught sight of the light, and it was revealed to him that though his life had not been what it should have been, this could still be rectified. He asked himself, "What *is* the right thing?" and grew still, listening. Then he felt that someone was kissing his hand. He opened his eyes, looked at his son, and felt sorry for him. His wife came up to him and he glanced at her. She was gazing at him open-mouthed, with undried tears on her nose and cheek and a despairing look on her face. He felt sorry for her too.

"Yes, I am making them wretched," he thought. "They are sorry, but it will be better for them when I die." He wished to say this but had not the strength to utter it. "Besides, why speak? I must act," he thought. With a look at his wife he indicated his son and said: "Take him away...sorry for him...sorry for you too...." He tried to add, "Forgive me," but said "Forego" and waved his hand, knowing that He whose understanding mattered would understand.

And suddenly it grew clear to him that what had been oppressing him and would not leave him was all dropping away at once from two sides, from ten sides, and from all sides. He was sorry for them, he must act so as not to hurt them: release them and free himself from these sufferings. "How good and how simple!" he thought. "And the pain?" he asked himself. "What has become of it? Where are you, pain?"

He turned his attention to it.

"Yes, here it is. Well, what of it? Let the pain be."

"And death...where is it?"

He sought his former accustomed fear of death and did not find it. "Where is it? What death?" There was no fear because there was no death.

In place of death there was light.

"So that's what it is!" he suddenly exclaimed aloud. "What joy!"

To him all this happened in a single instant, and the meaning of that instant did not change. For those present his agony continued for another two hours. Something rattled in his throat, his emaciated body twitched, then the gasping and rattle became less and less frequent.

"It is finished!" said someone near him.

He heard these words and repeated them in his soul.

"Death is finished," he said to himself. "It is no more!"

He drew in a breath, stopped in the midst of a sigh, stretched out, and died.

Born in Rio de Janeiro to a Portuguese mother and a Brazilian mulatto father, Machado de Assis was raised in extreme poverty and doesn't seem to have had any education beyond elementary school. His rise to literary greatness is the stuff of Brazilian legend. Between the ages of fifteen and thirty he seems to have worked as typesetter, proofreader, editor, staff writer, and possibly a clerk in a stationery store. In the same years, he also wrote some six thousand lines of poetry, nineteen plays and opera librettos, twenty-four short stories, and numerous articles and translations. These writings are pervaded by allusions to Portuguese, Greek, Latin, French, and English literature. Self-educated as well as self-made, he had to overcome the disadvantages of epilepsy and stuttering as well as racial prejudice and destitution. By the end of his life, he had become a high-level civil servant while being universally recognized as Brazil's foremost prose writer.

A private man, Machado de Assis did everything in his power to discourage people from explaining his fiction on the basis of his biography. His novels, for which he is best known, are elliptical, ironic, and understated, surprisingly modern in their refusal to give the reader any secure and comfortable perspective on Brazilian society. Along with radical social critique and Swiftian satire, he has a taste for the unreliable narrator. Perhaps the most important advice we get from his fiction is that it can be dangerous not to read attentively. In *Dom Casmurro* (1899), which has been obligatory reading in Brazilian schools for decades, he writes, "Not everything is clear in life or in books." Though he was a big winner himself in the game of life, he knew that society's rules were not fair and that chance played a large role. In *Epitaph of a Small Winner* (1881) he declared that, like Stendhal, he could be content with few readers. But despite his uncompromising high principles and constitutional pessimism, he also knew how to draw with bemused detachment on popular genres like melodrama and farce, and his work has always been extremely well received. His satiric story "The Psychiatrist" can read as a straightforward satire on scientific arrogance and its potential collusion in tyranny—compare with Charlotte Perkins Gilman's "The Yellow Wallaper," which follows. Yet "The Psychiatrist" also pokes fun at the doctor's victims and leaves us with anything but a reassuring vision of "normal" society.

PRONUNCIATIONS:

Machado de Assis: mah-SHA-doh day ah-CEASE
Itaguai: EE-tah-GUAI

The Psychiatrist[1]

1. How Itaguai Acquired a Madhouse

The chronicles of Itaguai relate that in remote times a certain physician of noble birth, Simão Bacamarte, lived there and that he was one of the greatest doctors in all Brazil, Portugal, and the Spains.[2] He had studied for many years in both Padua and Coimbra. When, at the age of thirty-four, he announced his decision to return to Brazil and his home town of Itaguai, the King of Portugal tried to dissuade him; he offered Bacamarte his choice between the Presidency of Coimbra University and the office of Chief Expediter of Government Affairs. The doctor politely declined.

"Science," he told His Majesty, "is my only office; Itaguai, my universe."

1. Translated by William L. Grossman.
2. The union of the Spanish crowns of Aragon and Castile.

He took up residence there and dedicated himself to the theory and practice of medicine. He alternated therapy with study and research; he demonstrated theorems with poultices.

In his fortieth year Bacamarte married the widow of a circuit judge. Her name was Dona Evarista da Costa e Mascarenhas, and she was neither beautiful nor charming. One of his uncles, an outspoken man, asked him why he had not selected a more attractive woman. The doctor replied that Dona Evarista enjoyed perfect digestion, excellent eyesight, and normal blood pressure; she had had no serious illnesses and her urinalysis was negative. It was likely she would give him healthy, robust children. If, in addition to her physiological accomplishments, Dona Evarista possessed a face composed of features neither individually pretty nor mutually compatible, he thanked God for it, for he would not be tempted to sacrifice his scientific pursuits to the contemplation of his wife's attractions.

But Dona Evarista failed to satisfy her husband's expectations. She produced no robust children and, for that matter, no puny ones either. The scientific temperament is by nature patient; Bacamarte waited three, four, five years. At the end of this period he began an exhaustive study of sterility. He reread the works of all the authorities (including the Arabian), sent inquiries to the Italian and German universities, and finally recommended a special diet. But Dona Evarista, nourished almost exclusively on succulent Itaguai pork, paid no heed; and to this lack of wifely submissiveness—understandable but regrettable—we owe the total extinction of the Bacamartian dynasty.

The pursuit of science is sometimes itself therapeutic. Dr. Bacamarte cured himself of his disappointment by plunging even deeper into his work. It was at this time that one of the byways of medicine attracted his attention: psychopathology. The entire colony and, for that matter, the kingdom itself could not boast one authority on the subject. It was a field, indeed, in which little responsible work had been done anywhere in the world. Simão Bacamarte saw an opportunity for Lusitanian[3] and, more specifically, Brazilian science to cover itself with "imperishable laurels"—an expression he himself used, but only in a moment of ecstasy and within the confines of his home; to the outside world he was always modest and restrained, as befits a man of learning.

"The health of the soul!" he exclaimed. "The loftiest possible goal for a doctor."

"For a great doctor like yourself, yes." This emendation came from Crispim Soares, the town druggist and one of Bacamarte's most intimate friends.

The chroniclers chide the Itaguai Town Council for its neglect of the mentally ill. Violent madmen were locked up at home; peaceable lunatics were simply left at large; and none, violent or peaceable, received care of any sort. Simão Bacamarte proposed to change all this. He decided to build an asylum and he asked the Council for authority to receive and treat all the mentally ill of Itaguai and the surrounding area. He would be paid by the patient's family or, if the family was very poor, by the Council. The proposal aroused excitement and curiosity throughout the town. There was considerable opposition, for it is always difficult to uproot the established way of doing things, however absurd or evil it may be. The idea of having madmen live together in the same house seemed itself to be a symptom of madness, as many intimated even to the doctor's wife.

"Look, Dona Evarista," said Father Lopes, the local vicar, "see if you can't get your husband to take a little holiday. In Rio de Janeiro, maybe. All this intensive study, a man can take just so much of it and then his mind..."

3. Portuguese.

494

Dona Evarista was terrified. She went to her husband and said that she had a consuming desire to take a trip with him to Rio de Janeiro. There, she said, she would eat whatever he thought necessary for the attainment of a certain objective. But the astute doctor immediately perceived what was on his wife's mind and replied that she need have no fear. He then went to the town hall, where the Council was debating his proposal, which he supported with such eloquence that it was approved without amendment on the first ballot. The Council also adopted a tax designed to pay for the lodging, sustenance, and treatment of the indigent mad. This involved a bit of a problem, for everything in Itaguai was already being taxed. After considerable study the Council authorized the use of two plumes on the horses drawing a funeral coach. Anyone wishing to take advantage of this privilege would pay a tax of a stated amount for each hour from the time of death to the termination of the rites at the grave. The town clerk was asked to determine the probable revenue from the new tax, but he got lost in arithmetical calculations, and one of the Councilmen, who was opposed to the doctor's undertaking, suggested that the clerk be relieved of a useless task.

"The calculations are unnecessary," he said, "because Dr. Bacamarte's project will never be executed. Who ever heard of putting a lot of crazy people together in one house?"

But the worthy Councilman was wrong. Bacamarte built his madhouse on New Street, the finest thoroughfare in Itaguai. The building had a courtyard in the center and two hundred cubicles, each with one window. The doctor, an ardent student of Arabian lore, found a passage in the Koran in which Mohammed declared that the insane were holy, for Allah had deprived them of their judgment in order to keep them from sinning. Bacamarte found the idea at once beautiful and profound, and he had the passage engraved on the façade of the house. But he feared that this might offend the Vicar and, through him, the Bishop. Accordingly, he attributed the quotation to Benedict VIII.

The asylum was called the Green House, for its windows were the first of that color ever seen in Itaguai. The formal opening was celebrated magnificently. People came from the entire region, some even from Rio de Janeiro, to witness the ceremonies, which lasted seven days. Some patients had already been admitted, and their relatives took advantage of this opportunity to observe the paternal care and Christian charity with which they were treated. Dona Evarista, delighted by her husband's glory, covered herself with silks, jewels, and flowers. She was a real queen during those memorable days. Everyone came to visit her two or three times. People not only paid court to her but praised her, for—and this fact does great honor to the society of the time—they thought of Dona Evarista in terms of the lofty spirit and prestige of her husband; they envied her, to be sure, but with the noble and blessed envy of admiration.

2. A Torrent of Madmen

Three days later, talking in an expansive mood with the druggist Crispim Soares, the psychiatrist revealed his inmost thoughts.

"Charity, Soares, definitely enters into my method. It is the seasoning in the recipe, for thus I interpret the words of St. Paul to the Corinthians: 'Though I understand all mysteries and all knowledge . . . and have not charity, I am nothing.' But the main thing in my work at the Green House is to study insanity in depth, to learn its various gradations, to classify the various cases, and finally to discover the cause of the phenomenon and its remedy. This is my heart's desire. I believe that in this way I can render a valuable service to humanity."

"A great service," said Crispim Soares.

"Without this asylum," continued the psychiatrist, "I might conceivably accomplish a little. But it provides far greater scope and opportunity for my studies than I would otherwise have."

"Far greater," agreed the druggist.

And he was right. From all the towns and villages in the vicinity came the violent, the depressed, the monomaniacal—the mentally ill of every type and variety. At the end of four months the Green House was a little community in itself. A gallery with thirty-seven more cubicles had to be added. Father Lopes confessed that he had not imagined there were so many madmen in the world nor that such strange cases of madness existed. One of the patients, a coarse, ignorant young man, gave a speech every day after lunch. It was an academic discourse, with metaphors, antitheses, and apostrophes, ornamented with Greek words and quotations from Cicero, Apuleius, and Tertullian.[4] The Vicar could hardly believe his ears. What, a fellow he had seen only three months ago hanging around street corners!

"Quite so," replied the psychiatrist. "But Your Reverence has observed for himself. This happens every day."

"The only explanation I can think of," said the priest, "is the confusion of languages on the Tower of Babel. They were so completely mixed together that now, probably, when a man loses his reason, he easily slips from one into another."

"That may well be the divine explanation," agreed the psychiatrist after a moment's reflection, "but I'm looking for a purely scientific, human explanation—and I believe there is one."

"Maybe so, but I really can't imagine what it could be."

Several of the patients had been driven mad by love. One of these spent all his time wandering through the building and courtyard in search of his wife, whom he had killed in a fit of jealousy that marked the beginning of his insanity. Another thought he was the morning star. He had repeatedly proposed marriage to a certain young lady, and she had continually put him off. He knew why: she thought him dreadfully dull and was waiting to see if she could catch a more interesting husband. So he became a brilliant star, standing with feet and arms outspread like rays. He would remain in this position for hours, waiting to be supplanted by the rising sun.

There were some noteworthy cases of megalomania. One patient, the son of a cheap tailor, invented a genealogy in which he traced his ancestry back to members of royalty and, through them, ultimately to Jehovah. He would recite the entire list of his male progenitors, with a "begat" to link each father and son. Then he would slap his forehead, snap his fingers, and say it all over again. Another patient had a somewhat similar idea but developed it with more rigorous logic. Beginning with the proposition that he was a child of God, which even the Vicar would not have denied, he reasoned that, as the species of the child is the same as that of the parent, he himself must be a god. This conclusion, derived from two irrefutable premises—one Biblical, the other scientific—placed him far above the lunatics who identified themselves with Caesar, Alexander, or other mere mortals.

More remarkable even than the manias and delusions of the madmen was the patience of the psychiatrist. He began by engaging two administrative assistants—an

4. Three Latin authors; Tertullian was an early Christian theologian.

idea that he accepted from Crispim Soares along with the druggist's two nephews. He gave these young men the task of enforcing the rules and regulations that the Town Council had approved for the asylum. They also kept the records and were in charge of the distribution of food and clothing. Thus, the doctor was free to devote all his time to psychiatry.

"The Green House," he told the Vicar, "now has its temporal government and its spiritual government."

Father Lopes laughed. "What a delightful novelty," he said, "to find a society in which the spiritual dominates."

Relieved of administrative burdens, Dr. Bacamarte began an exhaustive study of each patient: his personal and family history, his habits, his likes and dislikes, his hobbies, his attitudes toward others, and so on. He also spent long hours studying, inventing, and experimenting with psychotherapeutic methods. He slept little and ate little; and while he ate he was still working, for at the dinner table he would read an old text or ponder a difficult problem. Often he sat through an entire dinner without saying a word to Dona Evarista.

3. God Knows What He Is Doing

By the end of two months the psychiatrist's wife was the most wretched of women. She did not reproach her husband but suffered in silence. She declined into a state of deep melancholy, became thin and yellowish, ate little, and sighed continually. One day, at dinner, he asked what was wrong with her. She sadly replied that it was nothing. Then she ventured for the first time to complain a little, saying she considered herself as much a widow now as before she married him.

"Who would ever have thought that a bunch of lunatics..."

She did not complete the sentence. Or, rather, she completed it by raising her eyes to the ceiling. Dona Evarista's eyes were her most attractive feature—large, black, and bathed in a vaporous light like the dawn. She had used them in much the same way when trying to get Simão Bacamarte to propose. Now she was brandishing her weapon again, this time for the apparent purpose of cutting science's throat. But the psychiatrist was not perturbed. His eyes remained steady, calm, enduring. No wrinkle disturbed his brow, as serene as the waters of Botafogo Bay. Perhaps a slight smile played on his lips as he said:

"You may go to Rio de Janeiro."

Dona Evarista felt as if the floor had vanished and she were floating on air. She had never been to Rio, which, although hardly a shadow of what it is today, was, by comparison with Itaguai, a great and fascinating metropolis. Ever since childhood she had dreamed of going there. She longed for Rio as a Hebrew in the captivity must have longed for Jerusalem, but with her husband settled so definitively in Itaguai she had lost hope. And now, of a sudden, he was permitting her to realize her dream. Dona Evarista could not hide her elation. Simão Bacamarte took her by the hand and smiled in a manner at once conjugal and philosophical.

"How strange is the therapy of the soul!" he thought. "This lady is wasting away because she thinks I do not love her. I give her Rio de Janeiro and she is well again." And he made a note of the phenomenon.

A sudden misgiving pierced Dona Evarista's heart. She concealed her anxiety, however, and merely told her husband that, if he did not go, neither would she, for of course she could not travel alone.

"Your aunt will go with you," replied the psychiatrist.

It should be noted that this expedient had occurred to Dona Evarista. She had not suggested it, for it would impose great expense on her husband. Besides, it was better for the suggestion to come from him.

"Oh, but the money it will cost!" she sighed.

"It doesn't matter," he replied. "Have you any idea of our income?"

He brought her the books of account. Dona Evarista, although impressed by the quantity of the figures, was not quite sure what they signified, so her husband took her to the chest where the money was kept.

Good heavens! There were mountains of gold, thousands upon thousands of cruzados and doubloons. A fortune! While she was drinking it in with her black eyes, the psychiatrist placed his mouth close to her and whispered mischievously:

"Who would ever have thought that a bunch of lunatics..."

Dona Evarista understood, smiled, and replied with infinite resignation:

"God knows what he is doing."

Three months later she left for Rio in the company of her aunt, the druggist's wife, one of the druggist's cousins, a priest whom Bacamarte had known in Lisbon and who happened to be in Itaguai, four maidservants, and five or six male attendants. A small crowd had come to see them off. The farewells were sad for everyone but the psychiatrist, for he was troubled by nothing outside the realm of science. Even Dona Evarista's tears, sincere and abundant as they were, did not affect him. If anything concerned him on that occasion, if he cast a restless and police-like eye over the crowd, it was only because he suspected the presence of one or two candidates for commitment to the Green House.

After the departure the druggist and the psychiatrist mounted their horses and rode homeward. Crispim Soares stared at the road, between the ears of his roan. Simão Bacamarte swept the horizon with his eyes, surveyed the distant mountains, and let his horse find the way home. Perfect symbols of the common man and of the genius! One fixes his gaze upon the present with all its tears and privations; the other looks beyond to the glorious dawns of a future that he himself will shape.

4. A New Theory

As his horse jogged along, a new and daring hypothesis occurred to Simão Bacamarte. It was so daring, indeed, that, if substantiated, it would revolutionize the bases of psychopathology. During the next few days he mulled it over. Then, in his spare time, he began to go from house to house, talking with the townspeople about a thousand and one things and punctuating the conversations with a penetrating look that terrified even the bravest.

One morning, after this had been going on for about three weeks, Crispim Soares received a message that the psychiatrist wished to see him.

"He says it's important," added the messenger.

The druggist turned pale. Something must have happened to his wife! The chroniclers of Itaguai, it should be noted, dwell upon Crispim's love for his Cesaria and point out that they had never been separated in their thirty years of marriage. Only against this background can one explain the monologue, often overheard by the servants, with which the druggist reviled himself: "You miss your wife, do you? You're going crazy without her? It serves you right! Always truckling to Dr. Bacamarte! Who told you to let Cesaria go traveling? Dr. Bacamarte, that's who. Anything he says, you say amen. So now see what you get for it, you vile, miserable, groveling little lackey! Lickspittle! Flunky!" And he added many other ugly names that a man ought not call his enemies, much less himself. The effect of the message on him, in this state of mind, can be readily imagined. He dropped the drugs he had been mixing and fairly flew to the Green House. Simão Bacamarte greeted him joyfully, but he wore his joy as a wise man should—buttoned up to the neck with circumspection.

"I am very happy," he said.

"Some news of our wives?" asked the druggist in a tremulous voice.

The psychiatrist made a magnificent gesture and replied:

"It is something much more important—a scientific experiment. I say 'experiment,' for I do not yet venture to affirm the correctness of my theory. Indeed, this is the very nature of science, Soares: unending inquiry. But, although only an experiment as yet, it may change the face of the earth. Till now, madness has been thought a small island in an ocean of sanity. I am beginning to suspect that it is not an island at all but a continent."

He fell silent for a while, enjoying the druggist's amazement. Then he explained his theory at length. The number of persons suffering from insanity, he believed, was far greater than commonly supposed; and he developed this idea with an abundance of reasons, texts, and examples. He found many of these examples in Itaguai, but he recognized the fallacy of confining his data to one time and place and he therefore resorted to history. He pointed in particular to certain historical celebrities: Socrates, who thought he had a personal demon; Pascal, who sewed a report of an hallucination into the lining of his coat; Mohammed, Caracalla, Domitian, Caligula, and others. The druggist's surprise at Bacamarte's mingling of the vicious and the merely ridiculous moved the psychiatrist to explain that these apparently inconsistent attributes were really different aspects of the same thing.

"The grotesque, my friend, is simply ferocity in disguise."

"Clever, very clever!" exclaimed Crispim Soares.

As for the basic idea of enlarging the realm of insanity, the druggist found it a little far-fetched; but modesty, his chief virtue, kept him from stating his opinion. Instead, he expressed a noble enthusiasm. He declared the idea sublime and added that it was "something for the noisemaker." This expression requires explanation. Like the other towns, villages, and settlements in the colony at that time, Itaguai had no newspaper. It used two media for the publication of news: handwritten posters nailed to the doors of the town hall and of the main church, and the noisemaker.

This is how the latter medium worked: a man was hired for one or more days to go through the streets rattling a noisemaker. A crowd would gather and the man would announce whatever he had been paid to announce: a cure for malaria, a gift to the Church, some farm land for sale, and the like. He might even be engaged to read a sonnet to the people. The system continually disturbed the peace of the community, but it survived a long time because of its almost miraculous effectiveness. Incredible as it may seem, the noisemaker actually enabled merchants to sell inferior goods at superior prices and third-rate authors to pass as geniuses. Yes, indeed, not all the institutions of the old regime deserve our century's contempt.

"No, I won't announce my theory to the public," replied the psychiatrist. "I'll do something better: I'll act on it."

The druggist agreed that it might be best to begin that way. "There'll be plenty of time for the noisemaker afterwards," he concluded.

But Simão Bacamarte was not listening. He seemed lost in meditation. When he finally spoke, it was with great deliberation.

"Think of humanity," he said, "as a great oyster shell. Our first task, Soares, is to extract the pearl—that is, reason. In other words, we must determine the nature and boundaries of reason. Madness is simply all that lies beyond those limits. But what is reason if not the equilibrium of the mental faculties? An individual, therefore, who lacks this equilibrium in any particular is, to that extent, insane."

Father Lopes, to whom he also confided his theory, replied that he was not quite sure he understood it but that it sounded a little dangerous and, in any case, would involve more work than one doctor could possibly handle.

"Under the present definition of insanity, which has always been accepted," he added, "the fence around the area is perfectly clear and satisfactory. Why not stay within it?"

The vague suggestion of a smile played on the fine and discreet lips of the psychiatrist, a smile in which disdain blended with pity. But he said nothing. Science merely extended its hand to theology—with such assurance that theology was undecided whether to believe in itself or in science. Itaguai and the entire world were on the brink of a revolution.

5. The Terror

Four days later the population of Itaguai was dismayed to hear that a certain Mr. Costa had been committed to the Green House.

"Impossible!"

"What do you mean, impossible! They took him away this morning."

Costa was one of the most highly esteemed citizens of Itaguai. He had inherited 400,000 cruzados in the good coin of King João V. As his uncle said in the will, the interest on this capital would have been enough to support him "till the end of the world." But as soon as he received the inheritance he began to make loans to people without interest: a thousand cruzados to one, two thousand to another, three hundred to another, eight hundred to another, until, at the end of five years, there was nothing left. If poverty had come to him all at once, the shock to the good people of Itaguai would have been enormous. But it came gradually. He went from opulence to wealth, from wealth to comfort, from comfort to indigence, and from indigence to poverty. People who, five years earlier, had always doffed their hats and bowed deeply to him as soon as they saw him a block away, now clapped him on the shoulder, flicked him on the nose, and made coarse remarks. But Costa remained affable, smiling, sublimely resigned. He was untroubled even by the fact that the least courteous were the very ones who owed him money; on the contrary, he seemed to greet them with especial pleasure.

Once, when one of these eternal debtors jeered at him and Costa merely smiled, someone said to him: "You're nice to this fellow because you still hope you can get him to pay what he owes you." Costa did not hesitate an instant. He went to the debtor and forgave the debt. "Sure," said the man who had made the unkind remark, "Costa canceled the debt because he knew he couldn't collect it anyway." Costa was no fool; he had anticipated this reaction. Inventive and jealous of his honor, he found a way two hours later to prove the slur unmerited: he took a few coins and loaned them to the same debtor.

"Now I hope...," he thought.

This act of Costa's convinced the credulous and incredulous alike. Thereafter no one doubted the nobility of spirit of that worthy citizen. All the needy, no matter how timid, came in their patched cloaks and knocked on his door. The words of the man who had impugned his motive continued, however, to gnaw like worms at his soul. But this also ended, for three months later the man asked him for one hundred and twenty cruzados, promising to repay it in two days. This was all that remained of the inheritance, but Costa made the loan immediately, without hesitation or interest. It was a means of noble redress for the stain on his honor. In time the debt might have been paid; unfortunately, Costa could not wait, for five months later he was committed to the Green House.

The consternation in Itaguai, when the matter became known, can readily be imagined. No one spoke of anything else. Some said that Costa had gone mad during lunch, others said it had happened early in the morning. They told of the mental attacks he had suffered, described by some as violent and frightening, by others as mild and even amusing. Many people hurried to the Green House. There they found poor Costa calm if somewhat surprised, speaking with great lucidity and asking why he had been brought there. Some went and talked with the psychiatrist. Bacamarte approved of their esteem and compassion for the patient, but he explained that science was science and that he could not permit a madman to remain at large. The last person to intercede (for, after what I am about to relate, no one dared go to see the dreadful psychiatrist) was a lady cousin of the patient. The doctor told her that Costa must certainly be insane, for otherwise he would not have thrown away all the money that...

"No! Now there you are wrong!" interrupted the good woman energetically. "He was not to blame for what he did."

"No?"

"No, Doctor. I'll tell you exactly what happened. My uncle was not ordinarily a bad man, but when he became angry he was so fierce that he would not even take off his hat to a religious procession. Well, one day, a short time before he died, he discovered that a slave had stolen an ox from him. His face became as red as a pepper; he shook from head to foot; he foamed at the mouth. Then an ugly, shaggy-haired man came up to him and asked for a drink of water. My uncle (may God show him the light!) told the man to go drink in the river—or in hell, for all he cared. The man glared at him, raised his hand threateningly, and uttered this curse: 'Your money will not last more than seven years and a day, as surely as this is the star of David!' And he showed a star of David tattooed on his arm. That was the cause of it all, Doctor—the hex put on the money by that evil man."

Bacamarte's eyes pierced the poor woman like daggers. When she had finished, he extended his hand as courteously as if she had been the wife of the Viceroy and invited her to go and talk with her cousin. The miserable woman believed him. He took her to the Green House and locked her up in the ward for those suffering from delusions or hallucinations.

When this duplicity on the part of the illustrious Bacamarte became known, the townspeople were terrified. No one could believe that, for no reason at all, the psychiatrist would lock up a perfectly sane woman whose only offense had been to intercede on behalf of an unfortunate relative. The case was gossiped about on street corners and in barber shops. Within a short time it developed into a full-scale novel, with amorous overtures by the psychiatrist to Costa's cousin, Costa's indignation, the cousin's scorn, and finally the psychiatrist's vengeance on them both. It was all very obvious. But did not the doctor's austerity and his life of devotion to science give the lie to such a story? Not at all! This was merely a cloak by which he concealed his treachery. And one of the more credulous of the townspeople even whispered that he knew certain other things—he would not say what, for he lacked complete proof—but he knew they were true, he could almost swear to them.

"You who are his intimate friend," they asked the druggist, "can't you tell us what's going on, what happened, what reason...?"

Crispim Soares was delighted. This questioning by his puzzled friends, and by the uneasy and curious in general, amounted to public recognition of his importance. There was no doubt about it, the entire population knew that he, Crispim the druggist, was the psychiatrist's confidant, the great man's collaborator. That is why they all came running to the pharmacy. All this could be read in the druggist's jocund expression and discreet smile—and in his silence, for he made no reply. One, two, perhaps three dry monosyllables at the most, cloaked in a loyal, constant half-smile and full of scientific mysteries which he could reveal to no human being without danger and dishonor.

"There's something very strange going on," thought the townspeople.

But one of them merely shrugged his shoulders and went on his way. He had more important interests. He had just built a magnificent house, with a garden that was a masterpiece of art and taste. His furniture, imported from Hungary and Holland, was visible from the street, for the windows were always open. This man, who had become rich in the manufacture of packsaddles, had always dreamed of owning a sumptuous house, an elaborate garden, and rare furniture. Now he had acquired all these things and, in semi-retirement, was devoting most of his time to the enjoyment of them. His house was undoubtedly the finest in Itaguai, more grandiose than the Green House, nobler than the town hall. There was wailing and gnashing of teeth among Itaguai's social elite whenever they heard it praised or even mentioned—indeed, when they even thought about it. Owned by a mere manufacturer of packsaddles, good God!

"There he is, staring at his own house," the passers-by would say. For it was his custom to station himself every morning in the middle of his garden and gaze lovingly at the house. He would keep this up for a good hour, until called in to lunch.

Although his neighbors always greeted him respectfully enough, they would laugh behind his back. One of them observed that Mateus could make a lot more money manufacturing packsaddles to put on himself—a somewhat unintelligible remark, which nevertheless sent the listeners into ecstasies of laughter.

Every afternoon, when the families went out for their after-dinner walks (people dined early in those days), Mateus would station himself at the center window, elegantly clothed in white against a dark background. He would remain there in a majestic pose for three or four hours, until it was dark. One may reasonably infer an intention on Mateus's part to be admired and envied, although he confessed no such purpose to anyone, not even to Father Lopes. His good friend the druggist nevertheless drew the inference and communicated it to Bacamarte. The psychiatrist suggested that, as the saddler's house was of stone, he might have been suffering from petrophilia, an illness that the doctor had discovered and had been studying for some time. This continual gazing at the house...

"No, Doctor," interrupted Crispim Soares vigorously.

"No?"

"Pardon me, but perhaps you don't know..." And he told the psychiatrist what the saddler did every afternoon.

Simão Bacamarte's eyes lighted up with scientific voluptuousness. He questioned Crispim at some length, and the answers he received were apparently satisfactory, even pleasant, to him. But there was no suggestion of a sinister intent in the psychiatrist's face or manner—quite the contrary—as he asked the druggist's arm for a little stroll in the afternoon sun. It was the first time he had bestowed this honor on his confidant. Crispim, stunned and trembling, accepted the invitation. Just then, two or three people came to see the doctor. Crispim silently consigned them to all the devils. They were delaying the walk; Bacamarte might even take it into his head to invite one of them in Crispim's stead. What impatience! What anxiety! Finally the visitors left and the two men set out on their walk. The psychiatrist chose the direction of Mateus's house. He strolled by the window five or six times, slowly, stopping now and then and observing the saddler's physical attitude and facial expression. Poor Mateus noticed only that he was an object of the curiosity or admiration of the most important figure in Itaguai. He intensified the nobility of his expression, the stateliness of his pose....Alas! he was merely helping to condemn himself. The next day he was committed.

"The Green House is a private prison," said an unsuccessful doctor.

Never had an opinion caught on and spread so rapidly. "A private prison"—the words were repeated from one end of Itaguai to the other. Fearfully, to be sure, for during the week following the Mateus episode twenty-odd persons, including two or three of the town's prominent citizens, had been committed to the Green House. The psychiatrist said that only the mentally ill were admitted, but few believed him. Then came the popular explanations of the matter: revenge, greed, a punishment from God, a monomania afflicting the doctor himself, a secret plan on the part of Rio de Janeiro to destroy the budding prosperity of Itaguai and ultimately to impoverish this rival municipality, and a thousand other products of the public imagination.

At this time the party of travelers returned from their visit of several weeks to Rio de Janeiro. The psychiatrist, the druggist, Father Lopes, the Councilmen, and several other officials went to greet them. The moment when Dona Evarista laid eyes again on her husband is regarded by the chroniclers of the time as one of the most sublime instants in the moral history of man, because of the contrast between these two extreme (although both commendable) natures. Dona Evarista uttered a cry, stammered a word or two, and threw herself at her husband in a way that suggested at once the fierceness of a wildcat and the gentle affection of a dove. Not so the noble Bacamarte. With diagnostic objectivity, without disturbing for a moment his scientific austerity, he extended his arms to the lady, who fell into them and fainted. The incident was brief; two minutes later Dona Evarista's friends were greeting her and the homeward procession began.

The psychiatrist's wife was Itaguai's great hope. Everyone counted on her to alleviate the scourge. Hence the public acclamation, the crowds in the streets, the pennants, and the flowers in the windows. The eminent Bacamarte, having entrusted her to the arm of Father Lopes, walked contemplatively with measured step. Dona Evarista, on the contrary, turned her head animatedly from side to side, observing with curiosity the unexpectedly warm reception. The priest asked about Rio de Janeiro, which he had not seen since the previous viceroyalty, and Dona Evarista replied that it was the most beautiful sight there could possibly be in the entire world. The Public Gardens, now completed, were a paradise in which she had often strolled—and the Street of Beautiful Nights, the Fountain of Ducks...Ah! the Fountain of Ducks. There really were ducks there, made of metal and spouting water through their mouths. A gorgeous thing. The priest said that Rio de Janeiro had been lovely even in his time there and must be much lovelier now. Small wonder, for it was so much larger than Itaguai and was, moreover, the capital....But one could not call Itaguai ugly; it had some beautiful buildings, such as Mateus's mansion, the Green House...

"And apropos the Green House," said Father Lopes, gliding skillfully into the subject, "you will find it full of patients."

"Really?"

"Yes, Mateus is there...."

"The saddler?"

"Costa is there too. So is Costa's cousin, and So-and-so, and What's-his-name, and..."

"All insane?"

"Apparently," replied the priest.

"But how? Why?"

Father Lopes drew down the corners of his mouth as if to say that he did not know or did not wish to tell what he knew—a vague reply, which could not be repeated to anyone. Dona Evarista found it strange indeed that all those people should have gone mad. It might easily happen to one or another—but to *all* of them? Yet she could hardly doubt the fact. Her husband was a learned man, a scientist; he would not commit anyone to the Green House without clear proof of insanity.

The priest punctuated her observations with an intermittent "undoubtedly... undoubtedly..."

A few hours later about fifty guests were seated at Simão Bacamarte's table for the home-coming dinner. Dona Evarista was the obligatory subject of toasts, speeches, and verses, all of them highly metaphorical. She was the wife of the new Hippocrates, the muse of science, an angel, the dawn, charity, consolation, life itself. Her eyes were two stars, according to Crispim Soares, and two suns, by a Councilman's less modest figure. The psychiatrist found all this a bit tiresome but showed no signs of impatience. He merely leaned toward his wife and told her that such flights of fancy, although permissible in rhetoric, were unsubstantiated in fact. Dona Evarista tried to accept this opinion; but, even if she discounted three fourths of the flattery, there was enough left to inflate her considerably. One of the orators, for example—Martim Brito, twenty-five, a pretentious fop, much addicted to women—declaimed that the birth of Dona Evarista had come about in this manner: "After God gave the universe to man and to woman, who are the diamond and the pearl of the divine crown" (and the orator dragged this phrase triumphantly from one end of the table to the other), "God decided to outdo God and so he created Dona Evarista."

The psychiatrist's wife lowered her eyes with exemplary modesty. Two other ladies, who thought Martim Brito's expression of adulation excessive and audacious, turned to observe its effect on Dona Evarista's husband. They found his face clouded with misgivings, threats, and possibly blood. The provocation was great indeed, thought the two ladies. They prayed God to prevent any tragic occurrence—or, better yet, to postpone it until the next day. The more charitable of the two admitted (to herself) that Dona Evarista was above suspicion, for she was so very unattractive. And yet not all tastes were alike. Maybe some men... This idea caused her to tremble again, although less violently than before; less violently, for the psychiatrist was now smiling at Martim Brito.

When everyone had risen from the table, Bacamarte walked over to him and complimented him on his eulogy of Dona Evarista. He said it was a brilliant improvisation, full of magnificent figures of speech. Had Brito himself originated the thought about Dona Evarista's birth or had he taken it from something he had read? No, it was entirely original; it had come to him as he was speaking and he had considered it suitable for use as a rhetorical climax. As a matter of fact, he always leaned toward the bold and daring rather than the tender or jocose. He favored the epic style. Once, for example, he had composed an ode on the fall of the Marquis of Pombal in which he had said that "the foul dragon of Nihility is crushed in the vengeful claws of the All." And he had invented many other powerful figures of speech. He liked sublime concepts, great and noble images....

"Poor fellow!" thought the psychiatrist. "He's probably suffering from a cerebral lesion. Not a very serious case but worthy of study."

Three days later Dona Evarista learned, to her amazement, that Martim Brito was now living at the Green House. A young man with such beautiful thoughts! The two other ladies attributed his commitment to jealousy on the part of the psychiatrist, for the young man's words had been provocatively bold.

Jealousy? But how, then, can one explain the commitment a short time afterwards of persons of whom the doctor could not possibly have been jealous: innocuous, fun-loving Chico, Fabrício the notary, and many others. The terror grew in intensity. One no longer knew who was sane and who was insane. When their husbands went out in the street, the women of Itaguaí lit candles to Our Lady. And some of the men hired bodyguards to go around with them.

Everyone who could possibly get out of town, did so. One of the fugitives, however, was seized just as he was leaving. He was Gil Bernardes, a friendly, polite young man; so polite, indeed, that he never said hello to anyone without doffing his hat and bowing to the ground. In the street he would sometimes run forty yards to shake the hand of a gentleman or lady—or even of a child, such as the Circuit Judge's little boy. He had a special talent for affability. He owed his acceptance by society not only to his personal charm but also to the noble tenacity with which he withstood any number of refusals, rejections, cold shoulders, and the like, without becoming discouraged. And, once he gained entry to a house, he never left it—nor did its occupants wish him to leave, for he was a delightful guest. Despite his popularity and the self-confidence it engendered, Gil Bernardes turned pale when he heard one day that the psychiatrist was watching him. The following morning he started to leave town but was apprehended and taken to the Green House.

"This must not be permitted to continue."

"Down with tyranny!"

"Despot! Outlaw! Goliath!"

At first such things were said softly and indoors. Later they were shouted in the streets. Rebellion was raising its ugly head. The thought of a petition to the government for the arrest and deportation of Simão Bacamarte occurred to many people even before Porfírio, with eloquent gestures of indignation expounded it in his barber shop. Let it be noted—and this is one of the finest pages of a somber history—that as soon as the population of the Green House began to grow so rapidly, Porfírio's profits also increased, for many of his customers now asked to be bled; but private interests, said the barber, have to yield to the public welfare. "The tyrant must be overthrown!" So great was his dedication to the cause that he uttered this cry shortly after he heard of the commitment of a man named Coelho who was bringing a lawsuit against him.

"How can anyone call Coelho crazy?" shouted Porfírio.

And no one answered. Everybody said he was perfectly sane. The legal action against the barber, involving some real estate, grew not out of hatred or spite but out of the obscure wording of a deed. Coelho had an excellent reputation. A few individuals, to be sure, avoided him; as soon as they saw him approaching in the distance they ran around corners, ducked into stores. The fact is, he loved conversation—long conversation, drunk down in large draughts. Consequently he was almost never alone. He preferred those who also liked to talk, but he would compromise, if necessary, for a unilateral conversation with the more taciturn. Whenever Father Lopes, who disliked Coelho, saw him taking his leave of someone, he quoted Dante, with a minor change of his own:

> La bocca sollevò dal fiero pasto
> Quel seccatore...[5]

But the priest's remark did not affect the general esteem in which Coelho was held, for some attributed the remark to mere personal animosity and others thought it was a prayer in Latin.

6. The Rebellion

About thirty people allied themselves with the barber. They prepared a formal complaint and took it to the Town Council, which rejected it on the ground that scientific research must be tempered neither by hostile legislation nor by the misconceptions and prejudices of the mob.

"My advice to you," said the President of the Council, "is to disband and go back to work."

The group could hardly contain its anger. The barber declared that the people would march to the Green House and destroy it; that Itaguai must no longer be used as a corpse for dissection in the experiments of a medical despot; that several esteemed and even distinguished individuals, not to mention many humble but estimable persons, lay confined in the cubicles of the Green House; that the psychiatrist was clearly motivated by greed, for its compensation varied directly with the number of alleged madmen in his care—

"That's not true," interrupted the President.

"Not true?"

"About two weeks ago we received a communication from the illustrious doctor in which he stated that, in view of the great value, to him as a scientist, of his observations and experiments, he would no longer accept payment from the Council or from the patients' families."

In view of this noble act of self-denial, how could the rebels persist in their attitude? The psychiatrist might, indeed, make mistakes, but obviously he was not motivated by any interest alien to science; and to establish error on his part, something more would be needed than disorderly crowds in the street. So spoke the President, and the entire Council applauded.

The barber meditated for a few moments and then declared that he was invested with a public mandate; he would give Itaguai no peace until the final destruction of the Green House, that "Bastille of human reason"—an expression he had heard a local poet use and which he now repeated with great vigor. Having spoken, he gave his cohorts a signal and led them out.

The Council was faced with an emergency. It must, at all costs, prevent rebellion and bloodshed. To make matters worse, one of the Councilmen who had supported

5. Father Lopes quotes the Italian of Dante's *Inferno* 33.1–2: "That sinner raised his mouth from his fierce meal." The "minor change" is from "peccator" ("sinner") to "seccatore" ("nuisance").

the President was so impressed by the figure of speech, "Bastille of the human reason," that he changed his mind. He advocated adoption of a measure to liquidate the Green House. After the President had expressed his amazement and indignation, the dissenter observed:

"I know nothing about science, but if so many men whom we considered sane are locked up as madmen, how do we know that the real madman is not the psychiatrist himself?"

This Councilman, a highly articulate fellow named Sebastião Freitas, spoke at some length. He presented the case against the Green House with restraint but with firm conviction. His colleagues were dumbfounded. The President begged him at least to help preserve law and order by not expressing his opinions in the street, where they might give body and soul to what was so far merely a whirlwind of uncoordinated atoms. This figure of speech counterbalanced to some extent the one about the Bastille. Sebastião Freitas promised to take no action for the present but reserved the right to seek the elimination of the Green House by legal means. And he murmured to himself lovingly: "That Bastille of the human reason!"

Nevertheless, the crowd grew. Not thirty but three hundred now followed the barber, whose nickname ought to be mentioned at this point because it gave the rebellion its name: he was called Stewed Corn, and the movement was therefore known as the Revolt of the Stewed Corners. Storming through the streets toward the Green House, they might well have been compared to the mob that stormed the Bastille, with due allowance, of course, for the difference between Paris and Itaguai.

A young child attached to the household ran in from the street and told Dona Evarista the news. The psychiatrist's wife was trying on a silk dress (one of the thirty-seven she had bought in Rio).

"It's probably just a bunch of drunks," she said as she changed the location of a pin. "Benedita, is the hem all right?"

"Yes, ma'am," replied the slave, who was squatting on the floor, "it looks fine. Just turn a little bit. Like that. It's perfect, ma'am."

"They're not a bunch of drunks, Dona Evarista," said the child in fear. "They're shouting: 'Death to Dr. Bacamarte the tyrant.'"

"Be quiet! Benedita, look over here on the left side. Don't you think the seam is a little crooked? We'll have to rip it and sew it again. Try to make it nice and even this time."

"Death to Dr. Bacamarte! Death to the tyrant!" howled three hundred voices in the street.

The blood left Dona Evarista's face. She stood there like a statue, petrified with terror. The slave ran instinctively to the back door. The child, whom Dona Evarista had refused to believe, enjoyed a moment of unexpressed but profound satisfaction.

"Death to the psychiatrist!" shouted the voices, now closer than before.

Dona Evarista, although an easy prey to emotions of pleasure, was reasonably steadfast in adversity. She did not faint. She ran to the inside room where her husband was studying. At the moment of her precipitate entrance, the doctor was examining a passage in Averroës.[6] His eyes, blind to external reality but highly perceptive in the realm of the inner life, rose from the book to the ceiling and returned to the book. Twice, Dona Evarista called him loudly by name without his paying her the least attention. The third time, he heard and asked what was troubling her.

6. Averroës (1126–1198) was a major Islamic philosopher of the Middle Ages, known for his synthesis of Islam with ancient Greek thinkers.

"Can't you hear the shouting?"

The psychiatrist listened. The shouts were coming closer and closer, threatening, terrifying. He understood. Rising from the armchair, he shut the book and, with firm, calm step, walked over to the bookcase and put the volume back in its place. The insertion of the volume caused the books on either side of it to be slightly out of line. Simão Bacamarte carefully straightened them. Then he asked his wife to go to her room.

"No, no," begged his worthy helpmeet. "I want to die at your side where I belong."

Simão Bacamarte insisted that she go. He assured her that it was not a matter of life and death and told her that, even if it were, it would be her duty to remain alive. The unhappy lady bowed her head, tearful and obedient.

"Down with the Green House!" shouted the Stewed Corners.

The psychiatrist went out on the front balcony and faced the rebel mob, whose three hundred heads were radiant with civism and somber with fury. When they saw him they shouted: "Die! Die!" Simão Bacamarte indicated that he wished to speak, but they only shouted the louder. Then the barber waved his hat as a signal to his followers to be silent and told the psychiatrist that he might speak, provided his words did not abuse the patience of the people.

"I shall say little and, if possible, nothing at all. It depends on what it is that you have come to request."

"We aren't requesting anything," replied the barber, trembling with rage. "We are demanding that the Green House be destroyed or at least that all the prisoners in it be freed."

"I don't understand."

"You understand all right, tyrant. We want you to release the victims of your hatred, your whims, your greed...."

The psychiatrist smiled, but the smile of this great man was not perceptible to the eyes of the multitude: it was a slight contraction of two or three muscles, nothing more.

"Gentlemen," he said, "science is a serious thing and it must be treated seriously. For my professional decisions I account to no one but God and the authorities in my special field. If you wish to suggest changes in the administration of the Green House, I am ready to listen to you; but if you wish me to be untrue to myself, further talk would be futile. I could invite you to appoint a committee to come and study the way I treat the madmen who have been committed to my care, but I shall not, for to do so would be to account to you for my methods and this I shall never do to a group of rebels or, for that matter, to laymen of any description."

So spoke the psychiatrist, and the people were astounded at his words. Obviously they had not expected such imperturbability and such resoluteness. Their amazement was even greater when the psychiatrist bowed gravely to them, turned his back, and walked slowly back into the house. The barber soon regained his self-possession and, waving his hat, urged the mob to demolish the Green House. The voices that took up the cry were few and weak. At this decisive moment the barber felt a surging ambition to rule. If he succeeded in overthrowing the psychiatrist and destroying the Green House, he might well take over the Town Council, dominate the other municipal authorities, and make himself the master of Itaguai. For some years now he had striven to have his name included in the ballots from which the Councilmen were selected by lot, but his petitions were denied because his position in society was considered incompatible with such a responsibility. It was a case of now or never. Besides, he had carried the street riot to such a point that defeat would mean prison and perhaps banishment or even the scaffold. Unfortunately, the psychiatrist's reply had taken most of the steam out of the Stewed Corners. When the barber perceived this, he felt like shouting: "Wretches! Cowards!" But he contained himself and merely said:

"My friends, let us fight to the end! The salvation of Itaguai is in your worthy and heroic hands. Let us destroy the foul prison that confines or threatens your children and parents, your mothers and sisters, your relatives and friends, and you yourselves. Do you want to be thrown into a dungeon and starved on bread and water or maybe whipped to death?"

The mob bestirred itself, murmured, shouted, and gathered round the barber. The revolt was emerging from its stupor and threatening to demolish the Green House.

"Come on!" shouted Porfírio, waving his hat.

"Come on!" echoed his followers.

At that moment a corps of dragoons turned the corner and came marching toward the mob.

7. The Unexpected

The mob appeared stupefied by the arrival of the dragoons; the Stewed Corners could hardly believe that the force of the law was being exerted against them. The dragoons halted and their captain ordered the crowd to disperse. Some of the rebels felt inclined to obey, but others rallied around the barber, who boldly replied to the captain:

"We shall not disperse. If you wish, you may take our lives, but nothing else: we will not yield our honor or our rights, for on them depends the salvation of Itaguai."

Nothing could have been more imprudent or more natural than this reply. It reflected the ecstasy inspired by great crises. Perhaps it reflected also an excess of confidence in the captain's forbearance, a confidence soon dispelled by the captain's order to charge. What followed is indescribable. The mob howled its fury. Some managed to escape by climbing into windows or running down the street, but the majority, inspired by the barber's words, snorted with anger and stood their ground. The defeat of the Stewed Corners appeared imminent, when suddenly one third of the dragoons, for reasons not set forth in the chronicles, went over to the side of the rebels. This unexpected reenforcement naturally heartened the Stewed Corners and discouraged the ranks of legality. The loyal soldiers refused to attack their comrades and, one by one, joined them, with the result that in a few minutes the entire aspect of the struggle had changed. The captain, defended by only a handful of his men against a compact mass of rebels and soldiers, gave up and surrendered his sword to the barber.

The triumphant rebels did not lose an instant. They carried the wounded into the nearest houses and headed for the town hall. The people and the troops fraternized. They shouted *vivas* for the King, the Viceroy, Itaguai, and "our great leader, Porfírio." The barber marched at their head, wielding the sword as dexterously as if it had been merely an unusually long razor. Victory hovered like a halo above him, and the dignity of government informed his every movement.

The Councilmen, watching from the windows, thought that the troops had captured the Stewed Corners. The Council formally resolved to send a petition to the Viceroy asking him to give an extra month's pay to the dragoons, "whose high devotion to duty has saved Itaguai from the chaos of rebellion and mob rule." This phrase was proposed by Sebastião Freitas, whose defense of the rebels had so scandalized his colleagues. But the legislators were soon disillusioned. They could now clearly hear the *vivas* for the barber and the shouts of "death to the Councilmen" and "death to the psychiatrist." The President held his head high and said: "Whatever may be our fate, let us never forget that we are the servants of His Majesty and of the people of

Itaguaí." Sebastião suggested that perhaps they could best serve the Crown and the town by sneaking out the back door and going to the Circuit Judge's office for advice and help, but all the other members of the Council rejected this suggestion.

A few seconds later the barber and some of his lieutenants entered the chamber and told the Town Council that it had been deposed. The Councilmen surrendered and were put in jail. Then the barber's friends urged him to assume the dictatorship of Itaguaí in the name of His Majesty. Porfírio accepted this responsibility, although, as he told them, he was fully aware of its weight and of the thorny problems it entailed. He said also that he would be unable to rule without their coöperation, which they promptly promised him. The barber then went to the window and told the people what had happened; they shouted their approval. He chose the title, "Town Protector in the Name of His Majesty and of the People." He immediately issued several important orders, official communications from the new government, a detailed statement to the Viceroy with many protestations of obedience to His Majesty, and finally the follow-ing short but forceful proclamation to the people:

Fellow Itaguaians:

A corrupt and irresponsible Town Council was conspiring ignominiously against His Majesty and against the people. Public opinion had condemned it, and now a handful of citizens, with the help of His Majesty's brave dragoons, have dissolved it. By unanimous consent I am empowered to rule until His Majesty chooses to take formal action in the premises. Itaguaians, I ask only for your trust and for your help in restoring peace and the public funds, recklessly squandered by the Council. You may count on me to make every personal sacrifice for the common good, and you may rest assured that we shall have the full support of the Crown.

Porfírio Caetano das Neves

TOWN PROTECTOR IN THE NAME OF HIS MAJESTY AND OF THE PEOPLE

Everyone remarked that the proclamation said nothing whatever about the Green House, and some considered this ominous. The danger seemed all the greater when, in the midst of the important changes that were taking place, the psychiatrist commit-ted to the Green House some seven or eight new patients, including a relative of the Protector. Everybody erroneously interpreted Bacamarte's action as a challenge to the barber and thought it likely that within twenty-four hours the terrible prison would be destroyed and the psychiatrist would be in chains.

The day ended happily. While the crier with the noisemaker went from corner to corner reading the proclamation, the people walked about the streets and swore they would be willing to die for the Protector. There were very few shouts of opposition to the Green House, for the people were confident that the government would soon liq-uidate it. Porfírio declared the day an official holiday and, to promote an alliance be-tween the temporal power and the spiritual power, he asked Father Lopes to celebrate the occasion with a Te Deum. The Vicar issued a public refusal.

"May I at least assume," asked the barber with a threatening frown, "that you will not ally yourself with the enemies of the government?"

"How can I ally myself with your enemies," replied Father Lopes (if one can call it a reply), "when you have no enemies? You say in your proclamation that you are ruling by unanimous consent."

The barber could not help smiling. He really had almost no opposition. Apart from the captain of dragoons, the Council, and some of the town bigwigs, everybody acclaimed him; and even the bigwigs did not actually oppose him. Indeed, the people blessed the name of the man who would finally free Itaguai from the Green House and from the terrible Simão Bacamarte.

8. The Druggist's Dilemma

The next day Porfírio and two of his aides-de-camp left the government palace (the new name of the town hall) and set out for the residence of Simão Bacamarte. The barber knew that it would have been more fitting for him to have ordered Bacamarte to come to the palace, but he was afraid the psychiatrist would refuse and so he decided to exercise forbearance in the use of his powers.

Crispim Soares was in bed at the time. The druggist was undergoing continual mental torture these days. His intimacy with Simão Bacamarte called him to the doctor's defense, and Porfírio's victory called him to the barber's side. This victory, together with the intensity of the hatred for Bacamarte, made it unprofitable and perhaps dangerous for Crispim to continue to associate with the doctor. But the druggist's wife, a masculine woman who was very close to Dona Evarista, told him that he owed the psychiatrist an obligation of loyalty. The dilemma appeared insoluble, so Crispim avoided it by the only means he could devise: he said he was sick, and went to bed.

The next day his wife told him that Porfírio and some other men were headed for Simão Bacamarte's house.

"They're going to arrest him," thought the druggist.

One idea led to another. He imagined that their next step would be to arrest him, Crispim Soares, as an accessory. The therapeutic effect of this thought was remarkable. The druggist jumped out of bed and, despite his wife's protests, dressed and went out. The chroniclers all agree that Mrs. Soares found great comfort in the nobility of her husband, who, she assumed, was going to the defense of his friend, and they note with perspicacity the immense power of a thought, even if untrue; for the druggist walked not to the house of the psychiatrist but straight to the government palace. When he got there he expressed disappointment that the barber was out; he had wanted to assure him of his loyalty and support. Indeed, he had intended to do this the day before but had been prevented by illness—an illness that he now evidenced by a forced cough. The high officials to whom he spoke knew of his intimacy with the psychiatrist and therefore appreciated the significance of this declaration of loyalty. They treated the druggist with the greatest respect. They told him that the protector had gone to the Green House on important business but would soon return. They offered him a chair, refreshments, and flattery. They told him that the cause of the illustrious Porfírio was the cause of every true patriot—a proposition with which Crispim Soares heartily agreed and which he proposed to affirm in a vigorous communication to the Viceroy.

9. Two Beautiful Cases

The psychiatrist received the barber immediately. He told him that he had no means of resistance and was therefore prepared to submit to the new government. He asked only that they not force him to be present at the destruction of the Green House.

"The doctor is under a misapprehension," said Porfírio after pause. "We are not vandals. Rightly or wrongly, everybody thinks that most of the people locked up here are perfectly sane. But the government recognizes that the question is purely scientific and that scientific issues cannot be resolved by legislation. Moreover, the Green House is now an established municipal institution. We must therefore find a compromise that will both permit its continued operation and placate the public."

The psychiatrist could not conceal his amazement. He confessed that he had expected not only destruction of the Green House but also his own arrest and banishment. The last thing in the world he would have expected was—

"That is because you don't appreciate the grave responsibility of government," interrupted the barber. "The people, in their blindness, may feel righteous indignation about something that they do not understand; they have a right, then, to ask the government to act along certain lines. The government, however, must remember its duty to promote the public interest, whether or not this interest is in full accord with the demands made by the public itself. The revolution, which yesterday overthrew a corrupt and despicable Town Council, screams for destruction of the Green House. But the government must remain calm and objective. It knows that elimination of the Green House would not eliminate insanity. It knows that the mentally ill must receive treatment. It knows also that it cannot itself provide this treatment and that it even lacks the ability to distinguish the sane from the insane. These are matters for science, not for politics. They are matters requiring the sort of delicate, trained judgment that you, not we, are fitted to exercise. All I ask is that you help me give some degree of satisfaction to the people of Itaguai. If you and the government present a united front and propose a compromise of some sort, the people will accept it. Let me suggest, unless you have something better to propose, that we free those patients who are practically cured and those whose illnesses are relatively mild. In this way we can show how benign and generous we are without seriously handicapping your work."

Simão Bacamarte remained silent for about three minutes and then asked: "How many casualties were there in the fighting yesterday?"

The barber thought the question a little odd, but quickly replied that eleven had been killed and twenty-five wounded.

"Eleven dead, twenty-five wounded," repeated the psychiatrist two or three times.

Then he said that he did not like the barber's suggestion and that he would try to devise a better compromise, which he would communicate to the government within a few days. He asked a number of questions about the events of the day before: the attack by the dragoons, the defense, the change of sides by the dragoons, the Council's resistance, and so on. The barber replied in detail, with emphasis on the discredit into which the Council had fallen. He admitted that the government did not yet have the support of the most important men in the community and added that the psychiatrist might be very helpful in this connection. The government would be pleased, indeed, if it could count among its friends the loftiest spirit in Itaguai and, doubtless, in the entire kingdom. Nothing that the barber said, however, changed the expression on the doctor's austere face. Bacamarte evidenced neither vanity nor modesty; he listened in silence, as impassive as a stone god.

"Eleven dead, twenty-five wounded," repeated the psychiatrist after the visitors had left. "Two beautiful cases. This barber shows unmistakable symptoms of psychopathic duplicity. As for proof of the insanity of the people who acclaim him, what more could one ask than the fact that eleven were killed and twenty-five wounded? Two beautiful cases!"

"Long live our glorious Protector!" shouted thirty-odd people who had been awaiting the barber in front of the house.

The psychiatrist went to the window and heard part of the barber's speech:

"... for my main concern, day and night, is to execute faithfully the will of the people. Trust in me and you will not be disappointed. I ask of you only one thing: be peaceful, maintain order. For order, my friends, is the foundation on which government must rest."

"Long live Porfírio!" shouted the people, waving their hats.

"Two beautiful cases," murmured the psychiatrist.

Within a week there were fifty additional patients in the Green House, all of them strong supporters of the new government. The people felt outraged. The government was stunned; it did not know how to react. João Pina, another barber, said openly that Porfírio had "sold his birthright to Simão Bacamarte for a pot of gold"—a phrase that attracted some of the more indignant citizens to Pina's side. Porfírio, seeing his competitor at the head of a potential insurrection, knew that he would be overthrown if he did not immediately change his course. He therefore issued two decrees, one abolishing the Green House and the other banishing the psychiatrist from Itaguai.

João Pina, however, explained clearly and eloquently that these decrees were a hoax, a mere face-saving gesture. Two hours later Porfírio was deposed and João Pina assumed the heavy burden of government. Pina found copies of the proclamation to the people, the explanatory statement to the Viceroy, and other documents issued by his predecessor. He had new originals made and sent them out over his own name and signature. The chronicles note that the wording of the new documents was a little different. For example, where the other barber had spoken of "a corrupt and irresponsible Town Council," João Pina spoke of "a body contaminated by French doctrines wholly contrary to the sacrosanct interests of His Majesty."

The new dictator barely had time to dispatch the documents when a military force sent by the Viceroy entered the town and restored order. At the psychiatrist's request, the troops immediately handed over to him Porfírio and some fifty other persons, and promised to deliver seventeen more of the barber's followers as soon as they had sufficiently recovered from their wounds.

This period in the crisis of Itaguai represents the culmination of Simão Bacamarte's influence. He got whatever he wanted. For example, the Town Council, now reestablished, promptly consented to have Sebastião Freitas committed to the asylum. The psychiatrist had requested this in view of the extraordinary inconsistency of the Councilman's opinions, which Bacamarte considered a clear sign of mental illness. Subsequently the same thing happened to Crispim Soares. When the psychiatrist learned that his close friend and staunch supporter had suddenly gone over to the side of the Stewed Corners, he ordered him to be seized and taken to the Green House. The druggist did not deny his switch of allegiance but explained that he had been motivated by an overwhelming fear of the new government. Simão Bacamarte accepted the explanation as true; he pointed out, however, that fear is a common symptom of mental abnormality.

Perhaps the most striking proof of the psychiatrist's influence was the docility with which the Town Council surrendered to him its own President. This worthy official had declared that the affront to the Council could be washed away only by the blood of the Stewed Corners. Bacamarte learned of this through the Secretary of the Council, who repeated the President's words with immense enthusiasm. The psychiatrist first committed the Secretary to the Green House and then proceeded to the town hall. He told the Council that its President was suffering from hemoferal mania, an illness that he planned to study in depth, with, he hoped, immense benefit to the world. The Council hesitated for a moment and then acquiesced.

From that day on, the population of the asylum increased even more rapidly than before. A person could not utter the most commonplace lie, even a lie that clearly benefited him, without being immediately committed to the Green House. Scandalmongers, dandies, people who spent hours at puzzles, people who habitually inquired into the private lives of others, officials puffed up with authority—the psychiatrist's agents brought them all in. He spared sweethearts but not flirts, for he maintained that the former obeyed a healthful impulse, but that the latter yielded to a morbid desire for conquest. He discriminated against neither the avaricious nor the prodigal: both were committed to the asylum; this led people to say that the psychiatrist's concept of madness included practically everybody.

Some of the chroniclers express doubts about Simão Bacamarte's integrity. They note that, at his instigation, the Town Council authorized all persons who boasted of noble blood to wear a silver ring on the thumb of the left hand. These chroniclers point out that, as a consequence of the ordinance, a jeweler who was a close friend of Bacamarte became rich. Another consequence, however, was the commitment of the ring-wearers to the Green House; and the treatment of these unfortunate people, rather than the enrichment of his friend, may well have been the objective of the illustrious physician. Nobody was sure what conduct on the part of the ring-wearers had betrayed their illness. Some thought it was their tendency to gesticulate a great deal, especially with the left hand, no matter where they were—at home, in the street, even in church. Everybody knows that madmen gesticulate a great deal.

"Where will this man stop?" said the important people of the town. "Ah, if only we had supported the Stewed Corners!"

One day, when preparations were being made for a ball to be held that evening in the town hall, Itaguai was shocked to hear that Simão Bacarmarte had sent his own wife to the asylum. At first everyone thought it was a gag of some sort. But it was the absolute truth. Dona Evarista had been committed at two o'clock in the morning.

"I had long suspected that she was a sick woman," said the psychiatrist in response to a question from Father Lopes. "Her moderation in all other matters was hard to reconcile with her mania for silks, velvets, laces, and jewelry, a mania that began immediately after her return from Rio de Janeiro. It was then that I started to observe her closely. Her conversation was always about these objects. If I talked to her about the royal courts of earlier times, she wanted to know what kind of clothes the women wore. If a lady visited her while I was out, the first thing my wife told me, even before mentioning the purpose of the visit, was how the woman was dressed and which jewels or articles of clothing were pretty and which were ugly. Once (I think Your Reverence will remember this) she said she was going to make a new dress every year for Our Lady of the Mother Church. All these symptoms indicated a serious condition. Tonight, however, the full gravity of her illness became manifest. She had selected the entire outfit she would wear to the ball and had it all fixed and ready. All except one thing: she couldn't decide between a garnet necklace and a sapphire necklace. The day before yesterday she asked me which she should wear. I told her it didn't matter, that they both were very becoming. Yesterday at lunch she repeated the question. After dinner she was silent and pensive. I asked her what was the matter. 'I want to wear my beautiful garnet necklace, but my sapphire one is so lovely.' 'Then wear the sapphire necklace.' 'But then I can't wear the garnet necklace.' In the middle of the night, about half-past one, I awoke. She was not in bed. I got up and went to the dressing-room. There she sat with the two necklaces, in front of the mirror, trying on first one and then the other. An obvious case of dementia. I had her put away immediately."

Father Lopes said nothing. The explanation did not wholly satisfy him. Perceiving this, the psychiatrist told him that the specific illness of Dona Evarista was vestimania; it was by no means incurable.

"I hope to have her well within two weeks and, in any event, I expect to learn a great deal from the study of her case," said the psychiatrist in conclusion.

This personal sacrifice greatly enhanced the public image of the illustrious doctor. Suspicion, distrust, accusations were all negated by the commitment of his own wife

514

whom he loved with all his heart. No one could ever again charge him with motives other than those of science itself. He was beyond doubt a man of integrity and profound objectivity, a combination of Cato and Hippocrates.

11. Release and Joy

And now let the reader share with the people of Itaguai their amazement on learning one day that the madmen of the Green House had been released.

"All of them?"

"All of them."

"Impossible. Some, maybe. But all?"

"All. He said so himself in a communique that he sent today to the Town Council."

The psychiatrist informed the Council, first, that he had checked the statistics and had found that four-fifths of the population of Itaguai was in the Green House; second, that this disproportionately large number of patients had led him to reexamine his fundamental theory of mental illness, a theory that classified as sick all people who were mentally unbalanced; third, that as a consequence of this reexamination in the light of the statistics, he had concluded not only that his theory was unsound but also that the exactly contrary doctrine was true—that is, that normality lay in a lack of equilibrium and that the abnormal, the really sick, were the well balanced, the thoroughly rational; fourth, that in view of the foregoing he would release the persons now confined and would commit to the Green House all persons found to be mentally ill under the new theory; fifth, that he would continue to devote himself to the pursuit of scientific truth and trusted that the Council would continue to give him its support; and sixth, that he would give back the funds he had received for the board and lodging of the patients, less the amounts already expended, which could be verified by examination of his records and accounts.

The amazement of Itaguai was no greater than the joy of the relatives and friends of the former patients. Dinners, dances, Chinese lanterns, music, everything to celebrate the happy occasion. I shall not describe the festivities, for they are merely peripheral to this history; suffice it to say that they were elaborate, long, and memorable.

In the midst of all this rejoicing, nobody noticed the last part of the fourth item in the psychiatrist's communique.

12. The Last Part of the Fourth Item

The lanterns were taken down, the ex-patients resumed their former lives, everything appeared normal. Councilman Freitas and the President returned to their accustomed places, and the Council governed Itaguai without external interference. Porfírio the barber had "experienced everything," as the poet said of Napoleon; indeed, Porfírio had experienced more than Napoleon, for Napoleon was never committed to the Green House. The barber now found the obscure security of his trade preferable to the brilliant calamities of power. He was tried for his crimes and convicted, but the people begged His Majesty to pardon their ex-Protector, and His Majesty did so. The authorities decided not to prosecute João Pina, for he had overthrown an unlawful ruler. The chroniclers maintain that Pina's absolution inspired our adage:

> A judge will never throw the book
> At crook who steals from other crook.

An immoral adage, but immensely useful.

There were no more complaints against the psychiatrist. There was not even resentment for his past acts. Indeed, the former patients were grateful because he had declared them sane; they gave a ball in his honor. The chroniclers relate that Dona Evarista decided at first to leave her husband but changed her mind when she contemplated the emptiness of a life without him. Her devotion to this high-minded man overcame her wounded vanity, and they lived together more happily than ever before.

On the basis of the new psychiatric doctrine set forth in the communiqué, Crispim Soares concluded that his prudence in allying himself with the revolution had been a manifestation of mental health. He was deeply touched by Bacamarte's magnanimity: the psychiatrist had extended his hand to his old friend upon releasing him from the Green House.

"A great man," said the druggist to his wife.

We need not specifically note the release of Costa, Coelho, and the other patients named in this history. Each was now free to resume his previous way of life. Martim Brito, for example, who had been committed because of a speech in excessive praise of Dona Evarista, now made another in honor of the doctor, "whose exalted genius lifted its wings and flew far above the common herd until it rivaled the sun in altitude and in brilliance."

"Thank you," said the psychiatrist. "Obviously I was right to set you free."

Meanwhile, the Town Council passed, without debate, an ordinance to take care of the last part of the fourth item in Bacamarte's communiqué. The ordinance authorized the psychiatrist to commit to the Green House all persons whom he found to be mentally well balanced. But, remembering its painful experience in connection with public reaction to the asylum, the Council added a proviso in which it stated that, since the purpose of the ordinance was to provide an opportunity for the doctor to test his new theory, the authorization would remain in effect for only one year, and the Council reserved the right to close the asylum at any time if the maintenance of public order so required.

Sebastião Freitas proposed an amendment to the effect that under no circumstances were members of the Council to be committed to the Green House. The amendment was adopted almost unanimously. The only dissenting vote was cast by Councilman Galvão. He argued calmly that, in authorizing a scientific experiment on the people of Itaguai, the Council would itself be unscientific if it exempted its members or any other segment of the population from subjection to the experiment. "Our public office," he said, "does not exclude us from the human race." But he was shouted down.

Simão Bacamarte accepted the ordinance with all its restrictions. As for the exemption of the Councilmen, he declared that they were in no danger whatever of being committed, for their votes in favor of the amendment showed clearly that they were mentally unbalanced. He asked only that Galvão be delivered to him, for this Councilman had exhibited exceptional mental equilibrium, not only in his objection to the amendment but even more in the calm that he had maintained in the face of unreasonable opposition and abuse on the part of his colleagues. The Council immediately granted the request.

Under the new theory a few acts or statements by a person could not establish his abnormality: a long examination and a thorough study of his history were necessary. Father Lopes, for example, was not taken to the Green House until thirty days after the passage of the ordinance. In the case of the druggist's wife fifty days of study were required. Crispim Soares raged about the streets, telling everybody that he would tear the tyrant's ears off. One of the men to whom he spoke—a fellow who, as everyone knew, had an aversion for Bacamarte—ran and warned the psychiatrist. Bacamarte thanked him warmly and locked him up in recognition of his rectitude and his good will even toward someone he disliked, signs of perfect mental equilibrium.

"This is a very unusual case," said the doctor to Dona Evarista.

By the time Crispim Soares arrived at the psychiatrist's house, sorrow had overcome his anger. He did not tear Bacamarte's ears off. The psychiatrist tried to comfort his old friend. He told him that his wife might be suffering from a cerebral lesion, that there was a fair chance of recovery, and that meanwhile he must of course keep her confined. The psychiatrist considered it desirable, however, for Soares to spend a good deal of time with her, for the druggist's guile and intellectual dishonesty might help to overcome the moral superiority that the doctor found in his patient.

"There is no reason," he said, "why you and your wife should not eat lunch and dinner together every day at the Green House. You may even stay with her at night."

Simão Bacamarte's words placed the druggist in a new dilemma. He wanted to be with his wife, but at the same time he dreaded returning to the Green House. He remained undecided for several minutes. Then Dona Evarista released him from the dilemma: she promised to visit his wife frequently and to bear messages between the two. Crispim Soares kissed her hands in gratitude. His pusillanimous egoism struck the psychiatrist as almost sublime.

Although it took Bacamarte almost half a year to find eighteen patients for the Green House, he did not relax his efforts to discover the insane. He went from street to street, from house to house, observing, inquiring, taking notes. And when he committed someone to the asylum, it was with the same sense of accomplishment with which he had formerly committed dozens at a time. This very disproportion confirmed his new theory. At last the truth about mental illness was definitely known. One day Bacamarte committed the Circuit Judge to the Green House, after weeks of detailed study of the man's acts and thorough interrogation of his friends, who included all the important people of Itaguai.

More than once the psychiatrist was on the point of sending someone to the Green House, only to discover a serious shortcoming at the last moment. In the case of the lawyer Salustiano, for example, he thought he had found so perfect a combination of intellectual and moral qualities that it would be dangerous to leave the man at large. He told one of his agents to bring the man in, but the agent, who had known many lawyers, suspected that he might really be sane and persuaded Bacamarte to authorize a little experiment. The agent had a close friend who was charged with having falsified a will. He advised this friend to engage Salustiano as his lawyer.

"Do you really think he'll take the case?"

"Sure he will. Confess everything to him. He'll get you off."

The agent's friend went to the lawyer, admitted that he had falsified the will, and begged him to accept the case. Salustiano did not turn the man away. He studied the charges and supporting evidence. In court he argued at great length, proving conclusively that the will was genuine. After a verdict of acquittal the defendant received the estate under the terms of the will. To this experiment both he and the learned counselor owed their freedom.

Very little escapes the comprehension of a man of genuine insight. For some time Simão Bacamarte had noted the wisdom, patience, and dedication of the agent who devised the experiment. Consequently he determined to commit him to the Green House, in which he gave him one of the choicest cubicles.

The patients were segregated into classes. In one gallery lived only those whose outstanding moral quality was modesty. The notably tolerant occupied another gallery, and still others were set aside for the truthful, the guileless, the loyal, the magnanimous, the wise. Naturally, the friends and relatives of the madmen railed against the new theory. Some even tried to persuade the Town Council to cancel the authorization it had given Bacamarte. The Councilmen, however, remembered with bitterness the word of their former colleague Galvão; they did not wish to see him back in their midst, and so they refused. Simão Bacamarte sent a message to the Council, not thanking it but congratulating it on this act of personal spite.

Some of the important people of Itaguai then went secretly to the barber Porfírio. They promised to support him with men, money, and influence if he would lead another movement against the psychiatrist and the Town Council. He replied that ambition had once led him to violent transgression of the law but that he now recognized the folly of such conduct; that the Council, in its wisdom, had authorized the psychiatrist to conduct his new experiment for a year; that anybody who objected should wait till the end of the year and then, if the Council insisted on renewing the authorization, should petition the Viceroy; that he would not recommend recourse again to a method that had done no good and had caused several deaths and other casualties, which would be an eternal burden on his conscience.

The psychiatrist listened with immense interest when one of his secret agents told him what Porfírio had said. Two days later the barber was locked up in the Green House. "You're damned if you do and you're damned if you don't," observed the new patient.

At the end of the year allowed for verification of the new theory, the Town Council authorized the psychiatrist to continue his work for another six months in order to experiment with methods of therapy. The result of this additional experimentation is so significant that it merits ten chapters, but I shall content myself with one. It will provide the reader with an inspiring example of scientific objectivity and selflessness.

13. Plus Ultra

However diligent and perceptive he may have been in the discovery of madmen, Simão Bacamarte outdid himself when he undertook to cure them. All the chroniclers agree that he brought about the most amazing recoveries.

It is indeed hard to imagine a more rational system of therapy. Having divided the patients into classes according to their predominant moral qualities, the doctor now proceeded to break down those qualities. He applied a remedy in each case to inculcate exactly the opposite characteristic, selecting the specific medicine and dose best suited to the patient's age, personality, and social position.

The cases of modesty may serve as examples. In some, a wig, a fine coat, or a cane would suffice to restore reason to the madman. In more difficult cases the psychiatrist resorted to diamonds, honorary degrees, and the like. The illness of one modest lunatic, a poet, resisted every sort of therapy. Bacamarte had almost given up, when an idea occurred to him: he would have the crier with the noisemaker proclaim the patient to be as great as Garção or Pindar.

"It was like a miracle," said the poet's mother to one of her friends. "My boy is entirely well now. A miracle..."

Another patient, also in the modest class, seemed incurable. The specific remedy used for the poet would not work, for this patient was not a writer; indeed, he could barely sign his name. But Dr. Bacamarte proved equal to the challenge. He decided to have the patient made Secretary to the Itaguai branch of the Royal Academy. The Secretary and the President of each branch were appointed by the Crown. They enjoyed the privileges of being addressed as Excellency and of wearing a gold medallion. The government at Lisbon refused Bacamarte's request at first; but after the psychiatrist explained that he did not ask the appointment as a real honor for his patient but merely as a therapeutic device to cure a difficult case, and after the Minister of Overseas Possessions (a cousin of the patient) intervened, the government finally granted the request. The consequent cure was hailed as another miracle.

"Wonderful, really wonderful!" said everybody upon seeing the healthy, prideful expression on the faces of the two ex-madmen.

Bacamarte's method was ultimately successful in every case, although in a few the patient's dominant quality proved impregnable. In these cases the psychiatrist won out by attacking at another point, like a good military strategist.

By the end of five months all the patients had been cured. The Green House was empty. Councilman Galvão, so cruelly afflicted with fairness and moderation, had the good fortune to lose an uncle; I say good fortune, for the uncle's will was ambiguous and Galvão obtained a favorable interpretation of it by bribing two judges. With customary integrity, the doctor admitted that the cure had been effected not by him but by nature's *vis medicatrix.* It was quite otherwise in the case of Father Lopes. Bacamarte knew that the priest was utterly ignorant of Greek, and therefore asked him to make a critical analysis of the Septuagint.[7] Father Lopes accepted the task. In two months he had written a book on the subject and was released from the Green House. As for the druggist's wife, she remained there only a short time.

"Why doesn't Crispim come to visit me?" she asked every day.

They gave her various answers and finally told her the plain truth. The worthy matron could not contain her shame and indignation. Her explosions of wrath included such expressions as "rat," "coward," and "he even cheats on prescriptions." Simão Bacamarte remarked that, whether or not these characterizations of her husband were true, they clearly established the lady's return to sanity. He promptly released her.

If you think the psychiatrist was radiant with happiness on seeing the last guest leave the Green House, you apparently do not yet understand the man. *Plus ultra*[8] was his motto. For him the discovery of the true theory of mental illness was not enough, nor was the establishment in Itaguai of the reign of reason with the total elimination of psychological abnormality. *Plus ultra!* Something told him that his new theory bore within itself a better, newer theory.

"Let us see," he said to himself, "if I can discover the ultimate, underlying truth."

He paced the length of the immense room, past bookcase after bookcase—the largest library in His Majesty's overseas possessions. A gold-embroidered, damask dressing-gown (a gift from a university) enveloped the regal and austere body of the illustrious physician. The extensive top of his head, which the incessant cogitations of the scientist had rendered bald, was covered by a wig. His feet, neither dainty nor gross but perfectly proportioned to his body, were encased in a pair of ordinary shoes with plain brass buckles. Note the distinction: only those elements that bore some relationship to his work as a scientist were in any sense luxurious; the rest was simple and temperate.

And so the psychiatrist walked up and down his vast library, lost in thought, alien to everything but the dark problem of psychopathology. Suddenly he stopped. Standing before a window, with his left elbow resting on his open right hand and his chin on his closed left hand, he asked himself:

"Were they all really insane? Did I really cure them? Or is not mental imbalance so natural and inherent that it was bound to assert itself with or without my help?"

He soon arrived at this conclusion: the apparently well-balanced minds that he had just "cured" had really been unbalanced all the time, just like the obviously sane minds of the rest of the people. Their apparent illness was superficial and transient.

7. Greek translation of the Hebrew Bible undertaken in the last centuries B.C.E. in Alexandria, Egypt; the Bible quoted by Jesus and the Apostles in the New Testament.
8. Further beyond, to an extreme (Latin).

The psychiatrist contemplated his new doctrine with mixed feelings. He was happy because, after such long study, experimentation, and struggle, he could at last affirm the ultimate truth: there never were and never would be any madmen in Itaguai or anywhere else. But he was unhappy because a doubt assailed him. In the field of psychiatry a generalization so broad, so absolute, was almost inevitably erroneous. If he could find just one undeniably well balanced, virtuous, insane man, the new theory would be acceptable—not as an absolute, exceptionless principle, which was inadmissible, but as a general rule applicable to all but the most extraordinary cases.

According to the chroniclers, this difficulty constituted the most dreadful of the spiritual tempests through which the courageous Bacamarte passed in the course of his stormy professional life. But tempests terrify only the weak. After twenty minutes a gentle but radiant dawn dispelled the darkness from the face of the psychiatrist.

"Of course. That's it, of course."

What Simão Bacamarte meant was that he had found in himself the perfect, undeniable case of insanity. He possessed wisdom, patience, tolerance, truthfulness, loyalty, and moral fortitude—all the qualities that go to make an utter madman.

But then he questioned his own self-observation. Surely he must be imperfect in some way. To ascertain the truth about himself he convoked a gathering of his friends and questioned them. He begged them to answer with absolute frankness. They all agreed that he had not been mistaken.

"No defects?"

"None at all," they replied in chorus.

"No vices?"

"None."

"Perfect in every respect?"

"In every respect."

"No, impossible!" cried the psychiatrist. "I cannot believe that I am so far superior to my fellow men. You are letting yourselves be influenced by your affection for me."

His friends insisted. The psychiatrist hesitated, but Father Lopes made it difficult for him not to accept their judgment.

"Do you know why you are reluctant to recognize in yourself the lofty qualities which we all see so clearly?" said the priest. "It is because you have an additional quality that enhances all the others: modesty."

Simão Bacamarte bowed his head. He was both sad and happy, but more happy than sad. He immediately committed himself to the Green House. His wife and his friends begged him not to. They told him he was perfectly sane. They wept, they pleaded. All in vain.

"This is a matter of science, of a new doctrine," he said, "and I am the first instance of its application. I embody both theory and practice."

"Simão! Simão, my love!" cried his wife. Her face was bathed in tears.

But the doctor, his eyes alight with scientific conviction, gently pushed her away. He entered the Green House, shut the door behind him, and set about the business of curing himself. The chroniclers state, however, that he died seventeen months later as insane as ever. Some even venture the opinion that he was the only madman (in the vulgar or non-Bacamartian sense) ever committed to the asylum. But this opinion should not be taken seriously. It was based on remarks attributed to Father Lopes—doubtless erroneously, for, as everybody knew, the priest liked and admired the psychiatrist. In any case, the people of Itaguai buried the mortal remains of Simão Bacamarte with great pomp and solemnity.

One of the leading intellectuals of the early American women's movement, Charlotte Perkins Gilman was forgotten for several decades in the mid-twentieth century, then rediscovered in the 1970s by feminists who found virtues in her fiction that had been less obvious to earlier readers. Thus *Herland* (1915), one of Gilman's three utopian novels, has become a landmark in the imagining of alternative sexual relationships. "The Yellow Wallpaper" (1892), with its extraordinary analysis of "normal" marriage and the pathologizing of feminine emotion as "hysterical," has acquired the status of an unquestioned literary classic.

Born in 1860 in Connecticut, Gilman was raised by her mother at the edge of poverty after her father abandoned the family. As soon as she was old enough, she began contributing to the family finances. She studied art and in 1884 married a fellow artist. The birth of a daughter one year later left her in a state of severe depression. Gilman consulted the prominent Dr. S. Weir Mitchell, mentioned by name in "The Yellow Wallpaper," and underwent his so-called "rest cure," which involved total bed rest, confinement, and isolation. Echoing much of the (male) medical opinion of the day, Mitchell advised Gilman after the cure to devote herself entirely to her child and domestic duties—in his view, the proper role for a woman—and avoid all intellectual and artistic work. Unable to follow this advice, Gilman chose instead a trial separation from her husband and a trip to California. Her health was restored, and she and her husband were amicably divorced. A second marriage in 1900 endured until her husband died in 1934, a year before her own death.

During this period, Gilman worked happily and productively as a writer and lecturer on behalf of both women's rights and the political reforms advocated by Edward Bellamy, whose influential Utopian novel *Looking Backward* had appeared in 1888. In 1898 Gilman won international fame with *Women and Economics;* inspired in part by the newly developing social sciences, this pioneering work of what is now called interdisciplinary research explored the historical reasons for women's subordination. Her emphasis on the economic dimension of sexual inequality, or how women's status is determined by the fact that their labor inside the family is unpaid, led her to propose a radical solution: cooking, cleaning, and child care should henceforth be managed by paid professionals, thus leaving women free to choose if they desired to work outside the home. Gilman's sympathy for professionalism sheds an interesting light on the critique of professional medicine that many readers have found in "The Yellow Wallpaper." She elaborated and championed this analysis in a series of further books and in seven years of work on a periodical called *The Forerunner,* which she founded and for which she did virtually all the work of writing and editing.

While suggesting that even loving marriage is too often a punishing form of solitary confinement for women, that every husband in a sense plays the role of doctor, "The Yellow Wallpaper" is also an allegory of the situation of the woman writer. The protagonist is forbidden to exercise her craft on the grounds that it is harmful for her, and she finds allegories of her own situation in what she has access to, the furnishings of the room. But Gilman's premise of the narrator-as-mad(wo)man, shared with such rough contemporaries as Tolstoy and Lu Xun, lends itself to a multiplicity of interpretations.

The Yellow Wallpaper

It is very seldom that mere ordinary people like John and myself secure ancestral halls for the summer.

A colonial mansion, a hereditary estate, I would say a haunted house, and reach the height of romantic felicity—but that would be asking too much of fate!

Still I will proudly declare that there is something queer about it.

Else, why should it be let so cheaply? And why have stood so long untenanted?

John laughs at me, of course, but one expects that in marriage.

John is practical in the extreme. He has no patience with faith, an intense horror of superstition, and he scoffs openly at any talk of things not to be felt and seen and put down in figures.

John is a physician, and *perhaps*—(I would not say it to a living soul, of course, but this is dead paper and a great relief to my mind)—*perhaps* that is one reason I do not get well faster.

You see he does not believe I am sick!

And what can one do?

If a physician of high standing, and one's own husband, assures friends and relatives that there is really nothing the matter with one but temporary nervous depression—a slight hysterical tendency—what is one to do?

My brother is also a physician, and also of high standing, and he says the same thing.

So I take phosphates or phosphites—whichever it is, and tonics, and journeys, and air, and exercise, and am absolutely forbidden to "work" until I am well again.

Personally, I disagree with their ideas.

Personally, I believe that congenial work, with excitement and change, would do me good.

But what is one to do?

I did write for a while in spite of them; but it *does* exhaust me a good deal—having to be so sly about it, or else meet with heavy opposition.

I sometimes fancy that in my condition if I had less opposition and more society and stimulus—but John says the very worst thing I can do is to think about my condition, and I confess it always makes me feel bad.

So I will let it alone and talk about the house.

The most beautiful place! It is quite alone, standing well back from the road, quite three miles from the village. It makes me think of English places that you read about, for there are hedges and walls and gates that lock, and lots of separate little houses for the gardeners and people.

There is a *delicious* garden! I never saw such a garden—large and shady, full of box-bordered paths, and lined with long grape-covered arbors with seats under them.

There were greenhouses, too, but they are all broken now.

There was some legal trouble, I believe, something about the heirs and coheirs; anyhow, the place has been empty for years.

That spoils my ghostliness, I am afraid, but I don't care—there is something strange about the house—I can feel it.

I even said so to John one moonlight evening, but he said what I felt was a *draught,* and shut the window.

I get unreasonably angry with John sometimes. I'm sure I never used to be so sensitive. I think it is due to this nervous condition.

But John says if I feel so, I shall neglect proper self-control; so I take pains to control myself—before him, at least, and that makes me very tired.

I don't like our room a bit. I wanted one downstairs that opened on the piazza and had roses all over the window, and such pretty old-fashioned chintz hangings! but John would not hear of it.

He said there was only one window and not room for two beds, and no near room for him if he took another.

He is very careful and loving, and hardly lets me stir without special direction.

I have a schedule prescription for each hour in the day; he takes all care from me, and so I feel basely ungrateful not to value it more.

He said we came here solely on my account, that I was to have perfect rest and all the air I could get. "Your exercise depends on your strength, my dear," said he, "and your food somewhat on your appetite; but air you can absorb all the time." So we took the nursery at the top of the house.

It is a big, airy room, the whole floor nearly, with windows that look all ways, and air and sunshine galore. It was nursery first and then playroom and gymnasium, I should judge; for the windows are barred for little children, and there are rings and things in the walls.

The paint and paper look as if a boys' school had used it. It is stripped off—the paper—in great patches all around the head of my bed, about as far as I can reach, and in a great place on the other side of the room low down. I never saw a worse paper in my life.

One of those sprawling flamboyant patterns committing every artistic sin.

It is dull enough to confuse the eye in following, pronounced enough to constantly irritate and provoke study, and when you follow the lame uncertain curves for a little distance they suddenly commit suicide—plunge off at outrageous angles, destroy themselves in unheard of contradictions.

The color is repellent, almost revolting; a smouldering unclean yellow, strangely faded by the slow-turning sunlight.

It is a dull yet lurid orange in some places, a sickly sulphur tint in others.

No wonder the children hated it! I should hate it myself if I had to live in this room long.

There comes John, and I must put this away,—he hates to have me write a word.

We have been here two weeks, and I haven't felt like writing before, since that first day.

I am sitting by the window now, up in this atrocious nursery, and there is nothing to hinder my writing as much as I please, save lack of strength.

John is away all day, and even some nights when his cases are serious.

I am glad my case is not serious!

But these nervous troubles are dreadfully depressing.

John does not know how much I really suffer. He knows there is no *reason* to suffer, and that satisfies him.

Of course it is only nervousness. It does weigh on me so not to do my duty in any way!

I meant to be such a help to John, such a real rest and comfort, and here I am a comparative burden already!

Nobody would believe what an effort it is to do what little I am able,—to dress and entertain, and order things.

It is fortunate Mary is so good with the baby. Such a dear baby!

And yet I *cannot* be with him, it makes me so nervous.

I suppose John never was nervous in his life. He laughs at me so about this wallpaper!

At first he meant to repaper the room, but afterwards he said that I was letting it get the better of me, and that nothing was worse for a nervous patient than to give way to such fancies.

He said that after the wallpaper was changed it would be the heavy bedstead, and then the barred windows, and then that gate at the head of the stairs, and so on.

"You know the place is doing you good," he said, "and really, dear, I don't care to renovate the house just for a three months' rental."

"Then do let us go downstairs," I said, "there are such pretty rooms there."

Then he took me in his arms and called me a blessed little goose, and said he would go down to the cellar, if I wished, and have it whitewashed into the bargain.

But he is right enough about the beds and windows and things.

It is an airy and comfortable room as any one need wish, and, of course, I would not be so silly as to make him uncomfortable just for a whim.

I'm really getting quite fond of the big room, all but that horrid paper.

Out of one window I can see the garden, those mysterious deepshaded arbors, the riotous old-fashioned flowers, and bushes and gnarly trees.

Out of another I get a lovely view of the bay and a little private wharf belonging to the estate. There is a beautiful shaded lane that runs down there from the house. I always fancy I see people walking in these numerous paths and arbors, but John has cautioned me not to give way to fancy in the least. He says that with my imaginative power and habit of story-making, a nervous weakness like mine is sure to lead to all manner of excited fancies, and that I ought to use my will and good sense to check the tendency. So I try.

I think sometimes that if I were only well enough to write a little it would relieve the press of ideas and rest me.

But I find I get pretty tired when I try.

It is so discouraging not to have any advice and companionship about my work. When I get really well, John says we will ask Cousin Henry and Julia down for a long visit; but he says he would as soon put fireworks in my pillow-case as to let me have those stimulating people about now.

I wish I could get well faster.

But I must not think about that. This paper looks to me as if it *knew* what a vicious influence it had!

There is a recurrent spot where the pattern lolls like a broken neck and two bulbous eyes stare at you upside down.

I get positively angry with the impertinence of it and the everlastingness. Up and down and sideways they crawl, and those absurd, unblinking eyes are everywhere. There is one place where two breadths didn't match, and the eyes go all up and down the line, one a little higher than the other.

I never saw so much expression in an inanimate thing before, and we all know how much expression they have! I used to lie awake as a child and get more entertainment and terror out of blank walls and plain furniture than most children could find in a toy-store.

I remember what a kindly wink the knobs of our big, old bureau used to have, and there was one chair that always seemed like a strong friend.

I used to feel that if any of the other things looked too fierce I could always hop into that chair and be safe.

The furniture in this room is no worse than inharmonious, however, for we had to bring it all from downstairs. I suppose when this was used as a playroom they had to take the nursery things out, and no wonder! I never saw such ravages as the children have made here.

The wallpaper, as I said before, is torn off in spots, and it sticketh closer than a brother—they must have had perseverance as well as hatred.

Then the floor is scratched and gouged and splintered, the plaster itself is dug out here and there, and this great heavy bed which is all we found in the room, looks as if it had been through the wars.

But I don't mind it a bit—only the paper.

There comes John's sister. Such a dear girl as she is, and so careful of me! I must not let her find me writing.

She is a perfect and enthusiastic housekeeper, and hopes for no better profession. I verily believe she thinks it is the writing which made me sick!

But I can write when she is out, and see her a long way off from these windows.

There is one that commands the road, a lovely shaded winding road, and one that just looks off over the country. A lovely country, too, full of great elms and velvet meadows.

This wallpaper has a kind of sub-pattern in a different shade, a particularly irritating one, for you can only see it in certain lights, and not clearly then.

But in the places where it isn't faded and where the sun is just so—I can see a strange, provoking, formless sort of figure, that seems to skulk about behind that silly and conspicuous front design.

There's sister on the stairs!

Well, the Fourth of July is over! The people are all gone and I am tired out. John thought it might do me good to see a little company, so we just had Mother and Nellie and the children down for a week.

Of course I didn't do a thing. Jennie sees to everything now.

But it tired me all the same.

John says if I don't pick up faster he shall send me to Weir Mitchell in the fall.

But I don't want to go there at all. I had a friend who was in his hands once, and she says he is just like John and my brother, only more so!

Besides, it is such an undertaking to go so far.

I don't feel as if it was worthwhile to turn my hand over for anything, and I'm getting dreadfully fretful and querulous.

I cry at nothing, and cry most of the time.

Of course I don't when John is here, or anybody else, but when I am alone.

And I am alone a good deal just now. John is kept in town very often by serious cases, and Jennie is good and lets me alone when I want her to.

So I walk a little in the garden or down that lovely lane, sit on the porch under the roses, and lie down up here a good deal.

I'm getting really fond of the room in spite of the wallpaper. Perhaps *because* of the wallpaper.

It dwells in my mind so!

I lie here on this great immovable bed—it is nailed down, I believe—and follow that pattern about by the hour. It is as good as gymnastics, I assure you. I start, we'll say, at the bottom, down in the corner over there where it has not been touched, and I determine for the thousandth time that I *will* follow that pointless pattern to some sort of a conclusion.

I know a little of the principle of design, and I know this thing was not arranged on any laws of radiation, or alternation, or repetition, or symmetry, or anything else that I ever heard of.

It is repeated, of course, by the breadths, but not otherwise.

Looked at in one way each breadth stands alone, the bloated curves and flourishes— a kind of "debased Romanesque" with *delirium tremens*—go waddling up and down in isolated columns of fatuity.

But, on the other hand, they connect diagonally, and the sprawling outlines run off in great slanting waves of optic horror, like a lot of wallowing seaweeds in full chase.

The whole thing goes horizontally, too, at least it seems so, and I exhaust myself in trying to distinguish the order of its going in that direction.

They have used a horizontal breadth for a frieze, and that adds wonderfully to the confusion.

There is one end of the room where it is almost intact, and there, when the cross-lights fade and the low sun shines directly upon it, I can almost fancy radiation after all,—the interminable grotesques seem to form around a common centre and rush off in headlong plunges of equal distraction.

It makes me tired to follow it. I will take a nap I guess.

I don't know why I should write this.

I don't want to.

I don't feel able.

And I know John would think it absurd. But I *must* say what I feel and think in some way—it is such a relief!

But the effort is getting to be greater than the relief.

Half the time now I am awfully lazy, and lie down ever so much.

John says I mustn't lose my strength, and has me take cod liver oil and lots of tonics and things, to say nothing of ale and wine and rare meat.

Dear John! He loves me very dearly, and hates to have me sick. I tried to have a real earnest reasonable talk with him the other day, and tell him how I wish he would let me go and make a visit to Cousin Henry and Julia.

But he said I wasn't able to go, nor able to stand it after I got there; and I did not make out a very good case for myself, for I was crying before I had finished.

It is getting to be a great effort for me to think straight. Just this nervous weakness I suppose.

And dear John gathered me up in his arms, and just carried me upstairs and laid me on the bed, and sat by me and read to me till it tired my head.

He said I was his darling and his comfort and all he had, and that I must take care of myself for his sake, and keep well.

He says no one but myself can help me out of it, that I must use my will and self-control and not let any silly fancies run away with me.

There's one comfort, the baby is well and happy, and does not have to occupy this nursery with the horrid wallpaper.

If we had not used it, that blessed child would have! What a fortunate escape! Why, I wouldn't have a child of mine, an impressionable little thing, live in such a room for worlds.

I never thought of it before, but it is lucky that John kept me here after all, I can stand it so much easier than a baby, you see.

Of course I never mention it to them any more—I am too wise,—but I keep watch of it all the same.

There are things in that paper that nobody knows but me, or ever will.

Behind that outside pattern the dim shapes get clearer every day.

It is always the same shape, only very numerous.

And it is like a woman stooping down and creeping about behind that pattern. I don't like it a bit. I wonder—I begin to think—I wish John would take me away from here!

It is so hard to talk with John about my case, because he is so wise, and because he loves me so.

But I tried it last night.

It was moonlight. The moon shines in all around just as the sun does.

I hate to see it sometimes, it creeps so slowly, and always comes in by one window or another.

John was asleep and I hated to waken him, so I kept still and watched the moonlight on that undulating wallpaper till I felt creepy.

The faint figure behind seemed to shake the pattern, just as if she wanted to get out.

I got up softly and went to feel and see if the paper *did* move, and when I came back John was awake.

"What is it, little girl?" he said. "Don't go walking about like that—you'll get cold."

I thought it was a good time to talk, so I told him that I really was not gaining here, and that I wished he would take me away.

"Why darling!" said he, "our lease will be up in three weeks, and I can't see how to leave before.

"The repairs are not done at home, and I cannot possibly leave town just now. Of course if you were in any danger, I could and would, but you really are better, dear, whether you can see it or not. I am a doctor, dear, and I know. You are gaining flesh and color, your appetite is better, I feel really much easier about you."

"I don't weigh a bit more," said I, "nor as much; and my appetite may be better in the evening when you are here, but it is worse in the morning when you are away!"

"Bless her little heart!" said he with a big hug, "she shall be as sick as she pleases! But now let's improve the shining hours by going to sleep, and talk about it in the morning!"

"And you won't go away?" I asked gloomily.

"Why, how can I, dear? It is only three weeks more and then we will take a nice little trip of a few days while Jennie is getting the house ready. Really dear you are better!"

"Better in body perhaps—" I began, and stopped short, for he sat up straight and looked at me with such a stern, reproachful look that I could not say another word.

"My darling," said he, "I beg of you, for my sake and for our child's sake, as well as for your own, that you will never for one instant let that idea enter your mind! There is nothing so dangerous, so fascinating, to a temperament like yours. It is a false and foolish fancy. Can you not trust me as a physician when I tell you so?"

So of course I said no more on that score, and we went to sleep before long. He thought I was asleep first, but I wasn't, and lay there for hours trying to decide whether that front pattern and the back pattern really did move together or separately.

On a pattern like this, by daylight, there is a lack of sequence, a defiance of law, that is a constant irritant to a normal mind.

The color is hideous enough, and unreliable enough, and infuriating enough, but the pattern is torturing.

You think you have mastered it, but just as you get well underway in following, it turns a back-somersault and there you are. It slaps you in the face, knocks you down, and tramples upon you. It is like a bad dream.

The outside pattern is a florid arabesque, reminding one of a fungus. If you can imagine a toadstool in joints, an interminable string of toadstools, budding and sprouting in endless convolutions—why, that is something like it.

That is, sometimes!

There is one marked peculiarity about this paper, a thing nobody seems to notice but myself, and that is that it changes as the light changes.

When the sun shoots in through the east window—I always watch for that first long, straight ray—it changes so quickly that I never can quite believe it.

That is why I watch it always.

By moonlight—the moon shines in all night when there is a moon—I wouldn't know it was the same paper.

At night in any kind of light, in twilight, candle light, lamplight, and worst of all by moonlight, it becomes bars! The outside pattern I mean, and the woman behind it is as plain as can be.

I didn't realize for a long time what the thing was that showed behind, that dim sub-pattern, but now I am quite sure it is a woman.

By daylight she is subdued, quiet. I fancy it is the pattern that keeps her so still. It is so puzzling. It keeps me quiet by the hour.

I lie down ever so much now. John says it is good for me, and to sleep all I can.

Indeed he started the habit by making me lie down for an hour after each meal.

It is a very bad habit I am convinced, for you see I don't sleep.

And that cultivates deceit, for I don't tell them I'm awake—O no!

The fact is I am getting a little afraid of John.

He seems very queer sometimes, and even Jennie has an inexplicable look.

It strikes me occasionally, just as a scientific hypothesis,—that perhaps it is the paper!

I have watched John when he did not know I was looking, and come into the room suddenly on the most innocent excuses, and I've caught him several times *looking at the paper!* And Jennie too. I caught Jennie with her hand on it once.

She didn't know I was in the room, and when I asked her in a quiet, a very quiet voice, with the most restrained manner possible, what she was doing with the paper—she turned around as if she had been caught stealing, and looked quite angry—asked me why I should frighten her so!

Then she said that the paper stained everything it touched, that she had found yellow smooches on all my clothes and John's, and she wished we would be more careful!

Did not that sound innocent? But I know she was studying that pattern, and I am determined that nobody shall find it out but myself!

Life is very much more exciting now than it used to be. You see I have something more to expect, to look forward to, to watch. I really do eat better, and am more quiet than I was.

John is so pleased to see me improve! He laughed a little the other day, and said I seemed to be flourishing in spite of my wallpaper.

I turned it off with a laugh. I had no intention of telling him it was *because* of the wallpaper—he would make fun of me. He might even want to take me away.

I don't want to leave now until I have found it out. There is a week more, and I think that will be enough.

I'm feeling ever so much better! I don't sleep much at night, for it is so interesting to watch developments; but I sleep a good deal in the daytime.

In the daytime it is tiresome and perplexing.

There are always new shoots on the fungus, and new shades of yellow all over it. I cannot keep count of them, though I have tried conscientiously.

It is the strangest yellow, that wallpaper! It makes me think of all the yellow things I ever saw—not beautiful ones like buttercups, but old foul, bad yellow things.

But there is something else about that paper—the smell! I noticed it the moment we came into the room, but with so much air and sun it was not bad. Now we have had a week of fog and rain, and whether the windows are open or not, the smell is here.

It creeps all over the house.

I find it hovering in the dining-room, skulking in the parlor, hiding in the hall, lying in wait for me on the stairs.

It gets into my hair.

Even when I go to ride, if I turn my head suddenly and surprise it—there is that smell!

Such a peculiar odor, too! I have spent hours in trying to analyze it, to find what it smelled like.

It is not bad—at first, and very gentle, but quite the subtlest, most enduring odor I ever met.

In this damp weather it is awful, I wake up in the night and find it hanging over me.

It used to disturb me at first. I thought seriously of burning the house—to reach the smell.

But now I am used to it. The only thing I can think of that it is like is the *color* of the paper! A yellow smell.

There is a very funny mark on this wall, low down, near the mopboard. A streak that runs round the room. It goes behind every piece of furniture, except the bed, a long, straight, even *smooch,* as if it had been rubbed over and over.

I wonder how it was done and who did it, and what they did it for. Round and round and round—round and round and round—it makes me dizzy!

I really have discovered something at last.

Through watching so much at night, when it changes so, I have finally found out.

The front pattern *does* move—and no wonder! The woman behind shakes it!

Sometimes I think there are a great many women behind, and sometimes only one, and she crawls around fast, and her crawling shakes it all over.

Then in the very bright spots she keeps still, and in the very shady spots she just takes hold of the bars and shakes them hard.

And she is all the time trying to climb through. But nobody could climb through that pattern—it strangles so; I think that is why it has so many heads.

They get through, and then the pattern strangles them off and turns them upside down, and makes their eyes white!

If those heads were covered or taken off it would not be half so bad.

I think that woman gets out in the daytime!

And I'll tell you why—privately—I've seen her!

I can see her out of every one of my windows!

It is the same woman, I know, for she is always creeping, and most women do not creep by daylight.

I see her on that long road under the trees, creeping along, and when a carriage comes she hides under the blackberry vines.

I don't blame her a bit. It must be very humiliating to be caught creeping by daylight!

I always lock the door when I creep by daylight. I can't do it at night, for I know John would suspect something at once.

And John is so queer now, that I don't want to irritate him. I wish he would take another room! Besides, I don't want anybody to get that woman out at night but myself.

I often wonder if I could see her out of all the windows at once.

But, turn as fast as I can, I can only see out of one at one time.

And though I always see her, she *may* be able to creep faster than I can turn!

I have watched her sometimes away off in the open country, creeping as fast as a cloud shadow in a high wind.

If only that top pattern could be gotten off from the under one! I mean to try it, little by little.

I have found out another funny thing, but I shan't tell it this time! It does not do to trust people too much.

There are only two more days to get this paper off, and I believe John is beginning to notice. I don't like the look in his eyes.

And I heard him ask Jennie a lot of professional questions about me. She had a very good report to give.

She said I slept a good deal in the daytime.

John knows I don't sleep very well at night, for all I'm so quiet!

He asked me all sorts of questions, too, and pretended to be very loving and kind.

As if I couldn't see through him!

Still, I don't wonder he acts so, sleeping under this paper for three months.

It only interests me, but I feel sure John and Jennie are secretly affected by it.

Hurrah! This is the last day, but it is enough. John is to stay in town over night, and won't be out until this evening.

Jennie wanted to sleep with me—the sly thing! but I told her I should undoubtedly rest better for a night all alone.

That was clever, for really I wasn't alone a bit! As soon as it was moonlight and that poor thing began to crawl and shake the pattern, I got up and ran to help her.

I pulled and she shook, I shook and she pulled, and before morning we had peeled off yards of that paper.

A strip about as high as my head and half around the room.

And then when the sun came and that awful pattern began to laugh at me, I declared I would finish it to-day!

We go away to-morrow, and they are moving all my furniture down again to leave things as they were before.

Jennie looked at the wall in amazement, but I told her merrily that I did it out of pure spite at the vicious thing.

She laughed and said she wouldn't mind doing it herself, but I must not get tired.

How she betrayed herself that time!

But I am here, and no person touches this paper but me,—not *alive!*

She tried to get me out of the room—it was too patent! But I said it was so quiet and empty and clean now that I believed I would lie down again and sleep all I could; and not to wake me even for dinner—I would call when I woke.

So now she is gone, and the servants are gone, and the things are gone, and there is nothing left but that great bedstead nailed down, with the canvas mattress we found on it.

We shall sleep downstairs to-night, and take the boat home to-morrow.

I quite enjoy the room, now it is bare again.

How those children did tear about here!

This bedstead is fairly gnawed!

But I must get to work.

I have locked the door and thrown the key down into the front path.

I don't want to go out, and I don't want to have anybody come in, till John comes.

I want to astonish him.

I've got a rope up here that even Jennie did not find. If that woman does get out, and tries to get away, I can tie her!

But I forgot I could not reach far without anything to stand on!

This bed will *not* move!

I tried to lift and push it until I was lame, and then I got so angry I bit off a little piece at one corner—but it hurt my teeth.

Then I peeled off all the paper I could reach standing on the floor. It sticks horribly and the pattern just enjoys it! All those strangled heads and bulbous eyes and waddling fungus growths just shriek with derision!

I am getting angry enough to do something desperate. To jump out of the window would be admirable exercise, but the bars are too strong even to try.

Besides I wouldn't do it. Of course not. I know well enough that a step like that is improper and might be misconstrued.

I don't like to *look* out of the windows even—there are so many of those creeping women, and they creep so fast.

I wonder if they all come out of that wallpaper as I did?

But I am securely fastened now by my well-hidden rope—you don't get *me* out in the road there!

I suppose I shall have to get back behind the pattern when it comes night, and that is hard!

It is so pleasant to be out in this great room and creep around as I please!

I don't want to go outside. I won't, even if Jennie asks me to.

For outside you have to creep on the ground, and everything is green instead of yellow.

But here I can creep smoothly on the floor, and my shoulder just fits in that long smooch around the wall, so I cannot lose my way.

Why there's John at the door!

It is no use, young man, you can't open it!

How he does call and pound!

Now he's crying for an axe.

It would be a shame to break down that beautiful door!

"John dear!" said I in the gentlest voice, "the key is down by the front steps, under a plantain leaf!"

That silenced him for a few moments.

Then he said—very quietly indeed, "Open the door, my darling!"

"I can't," said I. "The key is down by the front door under a plantain leaf!"

And then I said it again, several times, very gently and slowly, and said it so often that he had to go and see, and he got it of course, and came in. He stopped short by the door.

"What is the matter?" he cried. "For God's sake, what are you doing!"

I kept on creeping just the same, but I looked at him over my shoulder.

"I've got out at last," said I, "in spite of you and Jane. And I've pulled off most of the paper, so you can't put me back!"

Now why should that man have fainted? But he did, and right across my path by the wall, so that I had to creep over him every time!

HENRIK IBSEN ■ (1828–1906)

In 1850, when Henrik Ibsen began writing, theater was largely a form of entertainment, a sort of doll's house where stock figures and neatly contrived plots were expected to provide an evening's innocent amusement. By 1899, when his last play was published, it had become an adult art form comparable to poetry and the novel, shocking and disorienting, giving more strenuous and instructive kinds of pleasure. With the twenty-five plays he wrote in that half century, Ibsen did more than any other single dramatist to bring about this upheaval. The transformation we see in Nora in *A Doll's House* bears a family resemblance to the transformation Ibsen brought to the theater itself.

Born in a small Norwegian town in 1828, Ibsen grew up (like many other nineteenth-century writers, including Dickens and Melville) facing a failure of paternal authority. His father, who had been a prosperous merchant, went bankrupt when Ibsen was a small child, leaving his eldest son to fend for himself in a state of poverty made more bitter by the memory of better days. Ibsen's sense of injustice expressed itself in poems to the European revolutionaries of 1848. Apprenticed to a pharmacist in a small town fifty miles from home, he became involved with a local servant ten years older than himself, got her pregnant, and spent fourteen years paying child support. He had dreams of becoming a doctor, but while studying at night to enter the university in Christiania (now Oslo), he gave them up to join a small theater in Bergen. There he contributed to a radical journal that was suppressed, learned the dramatist's craft, and collected local ballads and legends. Romantic nationalism was in fashion, and for good reason. Norway, which had won its independence from Denmark in 1814, was now united with the more powerful Sweden (it would not become fully independent until 1905), and it still had no national theater. Nor did it have national agreement on its language; it was during these same years that the philologist Ivar Aasen, traveling around the rural west of the country to collect dialects, fashioned a *landsmål* or "national language" to compete with the Dano-Norwegian, or *bokmål*, spoken by eastern urbanites. Of the 145 plays produced in Bergen during Ibsen's years of apprenticeship there, over half were translated from French. What was demanded was a generic, blandly international "well-made play," with a complicated plot involving confidential documents, babies identified by birthmarks, poisoned goblets quaffed by the wrong party, and other devices that had little to do with everyday Norwegian life.

Ibsen married Susannah Thoresen, the daughter of a pastor, in 1858. The couple traveled to Rome on a scholarship in 1864, and it was there that Ibsen wrote *Brand* (1866) and *Peer Gynt* (1867), a play inhabited by trolls and other materials of Nordic legend. These plays established his reputation as his country's first national dramatist. Apart from two short visits to Norway, however, Ibsen spent the next quarter century living in Italy and Germany. Like his admirer James Joyce (who learned Norwegian in order to read his hero in the original), Ibsen was that strange sort of exile, a national poet who felt obliged to examine his homeland from a distance. He became friends with the Danish critic Georg Brandes, author of *Main Currents of Nineteenth-Century Literature* (1872) and translator of John Stuart Mill's *On the Subjection of Women* (in 1869, the same year it came out in English), and Brandes helped turn Ibsen away from verse and toward the realistic wrestling with modern topics for which he was soon to become famous. It's been said that all the poetry Ibsen wrote after 1875 could be put on a single sheet of paper.

Ibsen's treatment of the emancipation of women in *A Doll's House* (1879) marks his full mastery of this new realistic mode. First performed in Copenhagen, Denmark, *A Doll's House* created an immediate sensation. Many found it almost unthinkable that Ibsen should endorse a woman who pays so little heed to her sacred duty as a wife and mother and so much to her own development as an individual. Ten years later, when the play was first presented in London, mainstream reviewers found it morally loathsome; one compared it to a view of an open sewer.

Plays like *A Doll's House*, *Ghosts* (1881), and *An Enemy of the People* (1882) are sometimes described as "naturalist" rather than realist, perhaps because they set their characters in the midst of the large historical processes that define the modern moment and fatally determine the outcome. It was this topical or "problem-play" side of Ibsen that George Bernard Shaw defended in *The Quintessence of Ibsenism* (1891). But *Hedda Gabler* (1890), *The Master Builder* (1892), and *When We Dead Awaken* (1899) returned to a less realistic mode, refashioning the theatrical parable so as to explore high individual aspiration, outside the conventions of society, as Ibsen had already done in *Peer Gynt*. These plays were taken by many to herald the new literary tendency of Symbolism. Older than the other major playwrights of the 1880s and 1890s, the Swedish August Strindberg and the Russian Anton Chekhov, Ibsen nonetheless continued to keep pace with them, and at times to set the pace for them. His last plays were written in Norway, to which he had returned in 1891, and he died there in 1906.

Shocking as *A Doll's House* was to its first audiences, it had an ambiguous relation to the feminism of the time. From the perspective of the two women who had the most direct influence on *A Doll's House,* what is striking is Ibsen's complex and contradictory relations to their cause. Camilla Collett, a pioneering Norwegian novelist and campaigner for women's rights, visited the Ibsens in Germany in the 1870s and, though Ibsen later acknowledged his debt to her, was unimpressed with the playwright's views on the woman question. Laura Kieler wrote a fictional sequel to Ibsen's *Brand* called *Brand's Daughters* (1869) when she was only twenty. It was Kieler's own life story that Ibsen retold in *A Doll's House,* though with changes. When Kieler was attacked as a result of Ibsen's stage portrait of her, she begged him to declare in public that she had acted honorably. He refused. One of his greatest virtues as a dramatist was his ability to separate himself off from unattractive aspects of his personality and put them into his characters.

A Doll's House is after all a well-made play. Like the romantic melodramas Ibsen helped put on in Bergen, it has stock characters (the flighty woman, the heavy insensitive husband, the faithful friend), guilty secrets, sealed lips, and fateful documents. But all these familiar stereotypes are reversed and revalued. After learning to see Nora as a stereotype of silly, childish, thoughtless femininity, we are suddenly asked to reinterpret this stereotype as a piece of theater that for various reasons Nora herself has been staging. In the person of Dr. Rank, we are offered tantalizing hints of the convention by which a rich old gentleman leaves money to the needy heroine and magically resolves all difficulties. Yet instead of the magical denouement that audiences had come to expect, Ibsen offers us, of all things, a serious discussion. We are asked to find the same emotional intensity in ideas about marriage and freedom that we had learned to expect from the discovery of long-lost brothers and sudden inheritances.

Freedom was, of course, more than an issue of sexual justice to Ibsen. Given his mixed feelings about the women's movement, it seems probable that he could make such a strong theatrical statement on Nora's behalf only because in his eyes she was not just a woman, but a figure for his own aspirations as an individual and an artist. Nora's story stood for the artist's defiance of conventional morality and the wishes of those around them, the sacrifice of children in exchange for individual self-realization. It was a defiance and a sacrifice about which he remained ambivalent. In his original notes for the play, Ibsen described it as "a tragedy of modern times." The notes suggest that he knew Nora would have to pay a large price for her liberation, that the story did not end (though this is perhaps the most famous ending in the history of the modern theater) with the slamming of the door.

A Doll's House[1]

Act 1

Characters

TORVALD HELMER
NORA, *his wife*
DOCTOR RANK
MRS. LINDEN
NILS KROGSTAD
THE HELMERS' THREE CHILDREN
ANNA, *their nurse*
A MAID-SERVANT (Ellen)
A PORTER

The action passes in Helmer's house (an apartment) in Christiania.

A room, comfortably and tastefully, but not expensively, furnished. In the back, on the right, a door leads to the hall; on the left another door leads to Helmer's study. Between the two doors a pianoforte. In the middle of the left wall a door, and nearer the front a window. Near the window a round table with arm-chairs and a small sofa. In the right wall, somewhat to the back, a door, and against the same wall, further forward, a procelain stove; in front of it a couple of arm-chairs and a rocking-chair. Between the stove and the side-door a small table. Engravings on the walls. A what-not with china and bric-à-brac. A small bookcase filled with handsomely bound books. Carpet. A fire in the stove. It is a winter day.

A bell rings in the hall outside. Presently the outer door of the flat is heard to open. Then Nora enters, humming gaily. She is in outdoor dress, and carries several parcels, which she lays on the right-hand table. She leaves the door into the hall open, and a Porter is seen outside, carrying a Christmas-tree and a basket, which he gives to the Maid-servant who has opened the door.

NORA: Hide the Christmas-tree carefully, Ellen; the children must on no account see it before this evening, when it's lighted up. [*To the Porter, taking out her purse.*] How much?
PORTER: Fifty öre.[2]
NORA: There is a crown. No, keep the change.

    [*The Porter thanks her and goes. Nora shuts the door. She continues smiling in quiet glee as she takes off her outdoor things. Taking from her pocket a bag of macaroons, she eats one or two. Then she goes on tip-toe to her husband's door and listens.*]

---

1. Translated by William Archer.
2. A hundred öre equal one crown (*krone*), equivalent to a few dollars today.

NORA: Yes; he is at home.

[*She begins humming again, crossing to the table on the right.*]

HELMER [*in his room*]: Is that my lark twittering there?
NORA [*busy opening some of her parcels*]: Yes, it is.
HELMER: Is it the squirrel frisking around?
NORA: Yes!
HELMER: When did the squirrel get home?
NORA: Just this minute. [*Hides the bag of macaroons in her pocket and wipes her mouth.*] Come here, Torvald, and see what I've been buying.
HELMER: Don't interrupt me. [*A little later he opens the door and looks in, pen in hand.*] Buying, did you say? What! All that? Has my little spend-thrift been making the money fly again?
NORA: Why, Torvald, surely we can afford to launch out a little now. It's the first Christmas we haven't had to pinch.
HELMER: Come come; we can't afford to squander money.
NORA: Oh yes, Torvald, do let us squander a little, now—just the least little bit! You know you'll soon be earning heaps of money.
HELMER: Yes, from New Year's Day. But there's a whole quarter before my first salary is due.
NORA: Never mind; we can borrow in the meantime.
HELMER: Nora! [*He goes up to her and takes her playfully by the ear.*] Still my little featherbrain! Supposing I borrowed a thousand crowns to-day, and you made ducks and drakes of them during Christmas week, and then on New Year's Eve a tile blew off the roof and knocked my brains out—
NORA [*laying her hand on his mouth*]: Hush! How can you talk so horridly?
HELMER: But supposing it were to happen—what then?
NORA: If anything so dreadful happened, it would be all the same to me whether I was in debt or not.
HELMER: But what about the creditors?
NORA: They! Who cares for them? They're only strangers.
HELMER: Nora, Nora! What a woman you are! But seriously, Nora, you know my principles on these points. No debts! No borrowing! Home life ceases to be free and beautiful as soon as it is founded on borrowing and debt. We two have held out bravely till now, and we are not going to give in at the last.
NORA [*going to the fireplace*]: Very well—as you please, Torvald.
HELMER [*following her*]: Come come; my little lark mustn't droop her wings like that. What? Is my squirrel in the sulks? [*Takes out his purse.*] Nora, what do you think I have here?
NORA [*turning round quickly*]: Money!
HELMER: There! [*Gives her some notes.*] Of course, I know all sorts of things are wanted at Christmas.
NORA [*counting*]: Ten, twenty, thirty, forty. Oh, thank you, thank you, Torvald! This will go a long way.
HELMER: I should hope so.
NORA: Yes, indeed; a long way! But come here, and let me show you all I've been buying. And so cheap! Look, here's a new suit for Ivar, and a little sword. Here are a horse and a trumpet for Bob. And here are a doll and a cradle for Emmy. They're only common; but they're good enough for her to pull to

pieces. And dress-stuffs and kerchiefs for the servants. I ought to have got something better for old Anna.

HELMER: And what's in that other parcel?

NORA [*crying out*]: No, Torvald, you're not to see that until this evening!

HELMER: Oh! Ah! But now tell me, you little spendthrift, have you thought of anything for yourself?

NORA: For myself! Oh, I don't want anything.

HELMER: Nonsense! Just tell me something sensible you would like to have.

NORA: No, really I don't know of anything—Well, listen, Torvald—

HELMER: Well?

NORA [*playing with his coat-buttons, without looking him in the face*]: If you really want to give me something, you might, you know—you might—

HELMER: Well? Out with it!

NORA [*quickly*]: You might give me money, Torvald. Only just what you think you can spare; then I can buy something with it later on.

HELMER: But, Nora—

NORA: Oh, please do, dear Torvald, please do! I should hang the money in lovely gilt paper on the Christmas-tree. Wouldn't that be fun?

HELMER: What do they call the birds that are always making the money fly?

NORA: Yes, I know—spendthrifts, of course. But please do as I ask you, Torvald. Then I shall have time to think what I want most. Isn't that very sensible, now?

HELMER [*smiling*]: Certainly; that is to say, if you really kept the money I gave you, and really spent it on something for yourself. But it all goes in housekeeping, and for all manner of useless things, and then I have to pay up again.

NORA: But, Torvald—

HELMER: Can you deny it, Nora dear? [*He puts his arm round her.*] It's a sweet little lark, but it gets through a lot of money. No one would believe how much it costs a man to keep such a little bird as you.

NORA: For shame! How can you say so? Why, I save as much as ever I can.

HELMER [*laughing*]: Very true—as much as you can—but that's precisely nothing.

NORA [*hums and smiles with covert glee*]: H'm! If you only knew, Torvald, what expenses we larks and squirrels have.

HELMER: You're a strange little being! Just like your father—always on the look-out for all the money you can lay your hands on; but the moment you have it, it seems to slip through your fingers; you never know what becomes of it. Well, one must take you as you are. It's in the blood. Yes, Nora, that sort of thing is hereditary.

NORA: I wish I had inherited many of papa's qualities.

HELMER: And I don't wish you anything but just what you are—my own, sweet little song-bird. But I say—it strikes me you look so—so—what shall I call it?—so suspicious to-day—

NORA: Do I?

HELMER: You do, indeed. Look me full in the face.

NORA [*looking at him*]: Well?

HELMER [*threatening with his finger*]: Hasn't the little sweet-tooth been playing pranks to-day?

NORA: No; how can you think such a thing!

HELMER: Didn't she just look in at the confectioner's?

NORA: No, Torvald; really—

HELMER: Not to sip a little jelly?

NORA: No; certainly not.

HELMER: Hasn't she even nibbled a macaroon or two?

NORA: No, Torvald, indeed, indeed!

HELMER: Well, well, well; of course I'm only joking.

NORA [goes to the table on the right]: I shouldn't think of doing what you disapprove of.

HELMER: No, I'm sure of that; and, besides, you've given me your word—[Going towards her.] Well, keep your little Christmas secrets to yourself, Nora darling. The Christmas-tree will bring them all to light, I daresay.

NORA: Have you remembered to invite Doctor Rank?

HELMER: No. But it's not necessary; he'll come as a matter of course. Besides, I shall ask him when he looks in to-day. I've ordered some capital wine. Nora, you can't think how I look forward to this evening.

NORA: And I too. How the children will enjoy themselves, Torvald!

HELMER: Ah, it's glorious to feel that one has an assured position and ample means. Isn't it delightful to think of?

NORA: Oh, it's wonderful!

HELMER: Do you remember last Christmas? For three whole weeks beforehand you shut yourself up every evening till long past midnight to make flowers for the Christmas-tree, and all sorts of other marvels that were to have astonished us. I was never so bored in my life.

NORA: I didn't bore myself at all.

HELMER [smiling]: But it came to little enough in the end, Nora.

NORA: Oh, are you going to tease me about that again? How could I help the cat getting in and pulling it all to pieces?

HELMER: To be sure you couldn't, my poor little Nora. You did your best to give us all pleasure, and that's the main point. But, all the same, it's a good thing the hard times are over.

NORA: Oh, isn't it wonderful?

HELMER: Now I needn't sit here boring myself all alone; and you needn't tire your blessed eyes and your delicate little fingers—

NORA [clapping her hands]: No, I needn't, need I, Torvald? Oh, how wonderful it is to think of? [takes his arm] And now I'll tell you how I think we ought to manage, Torvald. As soon as Christmas is over—[The hall-door bell rings.] Oh, there's a ring! [Arranging the room.] That's somebody come to call. How tiresome!

HELMER: I'm "not at home" to callers; remember that.

ELLEN [in the doorway]: A lady to see you, ma'am.

NORA: Show her in.

ELLEN [to Helmer]: And the doctor has just come, sir.

HELMER: Has he gone into my study?

ELLEN: Yes, sir.

[Helmer goes into his study. Ellen ushers in Mrs. Linden, in travelling costume, and goes out, closing the door.]

MRS. LINDEN [embarrassed and hesitating]: How do you do, Nora?

NORA [doubtfully]: How do you do?

MRS. LINDEN: I see you don't recognise me.

NORA: No, I don't think—oh yes!—I believe—[*Suddenly brightening.*] What, Christina! Is it really you?

MRS. LINDEN: Yes; really I!

NORA: Christina! And to think I didn't know you! But how could I—[*More softly.*] How changed you are, Christina!

MRS. LINDEN: Yes, no doubt. In nine or ten years—

NORA: Is it really so long since we met? Yes, so it is. Oh, the last eight years have been a happy time, I can tell you. And now you have come to town? All that long journey in mid-winter! How brave of you!

MRS. LINDEN: I arrived by this morning's steamer.

NORA: To have a merry Christmas, of course. Oh, how delightful! Yes, we will have a merry Christmas. Do take your things off. Aren't you frozen? [*Helping her.*] There; now we'll sit cosily by the fire. No, you take the arm-chair; I shall sit in this rocking-chair. [*Seizes her hands.*] Yes, now I can see the dear old face again. It was only at the first glance—But you're a little paler, Christina— and perhaps a little thinner.

MRS. LINDEN: And much, much older, Nora.

NORA: Yes, perhaps a little older—not much—ever so little. [*She suddenly checks herself; seriously.*] Oh, what a thoughtless wretch I am! Here I sit chattering on, and—Dear, dear Christina, can you forgive me!

MRS. LINDEN: What do you mean, Nora?

NORA [*softly*]: Poor Christina! I forgot; you are a widow.

MRS. LINDEN: Yes; my husband died three years ago.

NORA: I know, I know; I saw it in the papers. Oh, believe me, Christina, I did mean to write to you; but I kept putting it off, and something always came in the way.

MRS. LINDEN: I can quite understand that, Nora, dear.

NORA: No, Christina; it was horrid of me. Oh, you poor darling! how much you must have gone through!—And he left you nothing?

MRS. LINDEN: Nothing.

NORA: And no children?

MRS. LINDEN: None.

NORA: Nothing, nothing at all?

MRS. LINDEN: Not even a sorrow or a longing to dwell upon.

NORA [*looking at her incredulously*]: My dear Christina, how is that possible?

MRS. LINDEN [*smiling sadly and stroking her hair*]: Oh, it happens so sometimes, Nora.

NORA: So utterly alone! How dreadful that must be! I have three of the loveliest children. I can't show them to you just now; they're out with their nurse. But now you must tell me everything.

MRS. LINDEN: No, no; I want you to tell me—

NORA: No, you must begin; I won't be egotistical to-day. To-day I'll think only of you. Oh! but I must tell you one thing—perhaps you've heard of our great stroke of fortune?

MRS. LINDEN: No. What is it?

NORA: Only think! my husband has been made manager of the Joint Stock Bank.

MRS. LINDEN: Your husband! Oh, how fortunate!

NORA: Yes; isn't it? A lawyer's position is so uncertain, you see, especially when he won't touch any business that's the least bit—shady, as of course Torvald never would; and there I quite agree with him. Oh! you can imagine how glad we are. He is to enter on his new position at the New Year, and then he'll have a large salary, and percentages. In future we shall be able to live quite differently— just as we please, in fact. Oh, Christina, I feel so lighthearted and happy! It's delightful to have lots of money, and no need to worry about things, isn't it?

MRS. LINDEN: Yes; at any rate it must be delightful to have what you need.

NORA: No, not only what you need, but heaps of money—heaps!

MRS. LINDEN [*smiling*]:   Nora, Nora, haven't you learnt reason yet? In our school-days you were a shocking little spendthrift.

NORA [*quietly smiling*]:   Yes; that's what Torvald says I am still. [*Holding up her forefinger.*] But "Nora, Nora" is not so silly as you all think. Oh! I haven't had the chance to be much of a spendthrift. We have both had to work.

MRS. LINDEN: You, too?

NORA: Yes, light fancy work: crochet, and embroidery, and things of that sort; [*Carelessly*] and other work too. You know, of course, that Torvald left the Government service when we were married. He had little chance of promo-tion, and of course he required to make more money. But in the first year after our marriage he overworked himself terribly. He had to undertake all sorts of extra work, you know, and to slave early and late. He couldn't stand it, and fell dangerously ill. Then the doctors declared he must go to the South.

MRS. LINDEN: You spent a whole year in Italy, didn't you?

NORA: Yes, we did. It wasn't easy to manage, I can tell you. It was just after Ivar's birth. But of course we had to go. Oh, it was a wonderful, delicious journey! And it saved Torvald's life. But it cost a frightful lot of money, Christina.

MRS. LINDEN: So I should think.

NORA: Twelve hundred dollars! Four thousand eight hundred crowns! Isn't that a lot of money?

MRS. LINDEN: How lucky you had the money to spend.

NORA: We got it from father, you must know.

MRS. LINDEN: Ah, I see. He died just about that time, didn't he?

NORA: Yes, Christina, just then. And only think! I couldn't go and nurse him! I was expecting little Ivar's birth daily; and then I had my poor sick Torvald to attend to. Dear, kind old father! I never saw him again, Christina. Oh! that's the hardest thing I have had to bear since my marriage.

MRS. LINDEN: I know how fond you were of him. But then you went to Italy?

NORA: Yes; you see, we had the money, and the doctors said we must lose no time. We started a month later.

MRS. LINDEN: And your husband came back completely cured.

NORA: Sound as a bell.

MRS. LINDEN: But—the doctor?

NORA: What do you mean?

MRS. LINDEN: I thought as I came in your servant announced the doctor—

NORA: Oh, yes; Doctor Rank. But he doesn't come professionally. He is our best friend, and never lets a day pass without looking in. No, Torvald hasn't had an hour's illness since that time. And the children are so healthy and well, and so am I. [*Jumps up and claps her hands.*] Oh, Christina, Christina, what a wonderful thing it is to live and to be happy!—Oh, but it's really too horrid of me! Here am I talking about nothing but my own concerns. [*Seats herself upon a footstool close to Christina, and lays her arms on her friend's lap.*] Oh, don't be angry with me! Now tell me, is it really true that you didn't love your husband? What made you marry him, then?

MRS. LINDEN: My mother was still alive, you see, bedridden and helpless; and then I had my two younger brothers to think of. I didn't think it would be right for me to refuse him.

NORA: Perhaps it wouldn't have been. I suppose he was rich then?

MRS. LINDEN: Very well off, I believe. But his business was uncertain. It fell to pieces at his death, and there was nothing left.

NORA: And then—?

MRS. LINDEN: Then I had to fight my way by keeping a shop, a little school, any-thing I could turn my hand to. The last three years have been one long strug-gle for me. But now it is over, Nora. My poor mother no longer needs me; she is at rest. And the boys are in business, and can look after themselves.

NORA: How free your life must feel!

MRS. LINDEN: No, Nora; only inexpressibly empty. No one to live for! [*Stands up rest-lessly.*] That's why I could not bear to stay any longer in that out-of-the-way corner. Here it must be easier to find something to take one up—to occupy one's thoughts. If I could only get some settled employment—some office work.

NORA: But, Christina, that's such drudgery, and you look worn out already. It would be ever so much better for you to go to some watering-place and rest.

MRS. LINDEN [*going to the window*]:   I have no father to give me the money, Nora.

NORA [*rising*]:   Oh, don't be vexed with me.

MRS. LINDEN [*going to her*]:   My dear Nora, don't you be vexed with me. The worst of a position like mine is that it makes one so bitter. You have no one to work for, yet you have to be always on the strain. You must live; and so you be-come selfish. When I heard of the happy change in your fortunes—can you believe it?—I was glad for my own sake more than for yours.

NORA: How do you mean? Ah, I see! You think Torvald can perhaps do something for you.

MRS. LINDEN: Yes; I thought so.

NORA: And so he shall, Christina. Just you leave it all to me. I shall lead up to it beautifully!—I shall think of some delightful plan to put him in a good humour! Oh, I should so love to help you.

MRS. LINDEN: How good of you, Nora, to stand by me so warmly! Doubly good in you, who know so little of the troubles and burdens of life.

NORA: I? I know so little of—?

MRS. LINDEN [*smiling*]:   Oh, well—a little fancy-work, and so forth.—You're a child, Nora.

NORA [*tosses her head and paces the room*]:   Oh, come, you mustn't be so patronising!

MRS. LINDEN: No?

NORA: You're like the rest. You all think I'm fit for nothing really serious—

MRS. LINDEN: Well, well—

NORA: You think I've had no troubles in this weary world.

MRS. LINDEN: My dear Nora, you've just told me all your troubles.

NORA: Pooh—those trifles! [*Softly.*] I haven't told you the great thing.

MRS. LINDEN: The great thing? What do you mean?

NORA: I know you look down upon me, Christina; but you have no right to. You are proud of having worked so hard and so long for your mother.

MRS. LINDEN: I am sure I don't look down upon any one; but it's true I am both proud and glad when I remember that I was able to keep my mother's last days free from care.

NORA: And you're proud to think of what you have done for your brothers, too.

MRS. LINDEN: Have I not the right to be?

NORA: Yes, indeed. But now let me tell you, Christina—I, too, have something to be proud and glad of.

MRS. LINDEN: I don't doubt it. But what do you mean?

NORA: Hush! Not so loud. Only think, if Torvald were to hear! He mustn't—not for worlds! No one must know about it, Christina—no one but you.

MRS. LINDEN: Why, what can it be?

NORA: Come over here. [*Draws her down beside her on the sofa.*] Yes, Christina— I, too, have something to be proud and glad of. I saved Torvald's life.

MRS. LINDEN: Saved his life? How?

NORA: I told you about our going to Italy. Torvald would have died but for that.

MRS. LINDEN: Well—and your father gave you the money.

NORA [*smiling*]:   Yes, so Torvald and every one believes; but—

MRS. LINDEN: But—?

NORA: Papa didn't give us one penny. It was *I* that found the money.

MRS. LINDEN: You? All that money?

NORA: Twelve hundred dollars. Four thousand eight hundred crowns. What do you say to that?

MRS. LINDEN: My dear Nora, how did you manage it? Did you win it in the lottery?

NORA [*contemptuously*]:   In the lottery? Pooh! Any one could have done that!

MRS. LINDEN: Then wherever did you get it from?

NORA [*hums and smiles mysteriously*]:   H'm; tra-la-la-la.

MRS. LINDEN: Of course you couldn't borrow it.

NORA: No? Why not?

MRS. LINDEN: Why, a wife can't borrow without her husband's consent.

NORA [*tossing her head*]:   Oh! when the wife has some idea of business, and knows how to set about things—

MRS. LINDEN: But, Nora, I don't understand—

NORA: Well, you needn't. I never said I borrowed the money. There are many ways I may have got it. [*Throws herself back on the sofa.*] I may have got it from some admirer. When one is so—attractive as I am—

MRS. LINDEN: You're too silly, Nora.

NORA: Now I'm sure you're dying of curiosity, Christina—

MRS. LINDEN: Listen to me, Nora dear: haven't you been a little rash?

NORA [*sitting upright again*]:   Is it rash to save one's husband's life?

MRS. LINDEN: I think it was rash of you, without his knowledge—

NORA: But it would have been fatal for him to know! Can't you understand that? He wasn't even to suspect how ill he was. The doctors came to me privately and told me his life was in danger—that nothing could save him but a winter in the South. Do you think I didn't try diplomacy first? I told him how I longed to have a trip abroad, like other young wives; I wept and prayed; I said he ought to think of my condition, and not to thwart me; and then I hinted that he could borrow the money. But then, Christina, he got almost angry. He said I was frivolous, and that it was his duty as a husband not to yield to my whims and fancies—so he called them. Very well, thought I, but saved you must be; and then I found the way to do it.

MRS. LINDEN: And did your husband never learn from your father that the money was not from him?

NORA: No; never. Papa died at that very time. I meant to have told him all about it, and begged him to say nothing. But he was so ill—unhappily, it wasn't necessary.

MRS. LINDEN: And you have never confessed to your husband?

NORA: Good heavens! What can you be thinking of? Tell him, when he has such a loathing of debt! And besides—how painful and humiliating it would be for Torvald, with his manly self-respect, to know that he owed anything to me! It would utterly upset the relation between us; our beautiful, happy home would never again be what it is.

MRS. LINDEN: Will you never tell him?

NORA [*thoughtfully, half-smiling*]:   Yes, some time, perhaps—many, many years hence, when I'm—not so pretty. You mustn't laugh at me! Of course I mean when Torvald is not so much in love with me as he is now; when it doesn't amuse him any longer to see me dancing about, and dressing up and acting. Then it might be well to have something in reserve. [*Breaking off.*] Nonsense! nonsense! That time will never come. Now, what do you say to my grand secret, Christina? Am I fit for nothing now? You may believe it has cost me a lot of anxiety. It has been no joke to meet my engagements punctually. You must know, Christina, that in business there are things called instalments, and quarterly interest, that are terribly hard to provide for. So I've had to pinch a little here and there, wherever I could. I couldn't save much out of the housekeeping, for, of course. Torvald had to live well. And I couldn't let the children go about badly dressed; all I got for them, I spent on them, the blessed darlings!

MRS. LINDEN: Poor Nora! So it had to come out of your own pocket-money.

NORA: Yes, of course. After all, the whole thing was my doing. When Torvald gave me money for clothes, and so on, I never spent more than half of it; I always bought the simplest and cheapest things. It's a mercy that everything suits me so well—Torvald never had any suspicions. But it was often very hard, Christina dear. For it's nice to be beautifully dressed—now, isn't it?

MRS. LINDEN: Indeed it is.

NORA: Well, and besides that, I made money in other ways. Last winter I was so lucky—I got a heap of copying to do. I shut myself up every evening and wrote far into the night. Oh, sometimes I was so tired, so tired. And yet it was splendid to work in that way and earn money. I almost felt as if I was a man.

MRS. LINDEN: Then how much have you been able to pay off?

NORA: Well, I can't precisely say. It's difficult to keep that sort of business clear. I only know that I've paid everything I could scrape together. Sometimes I really didn't know where to turn. [*Smiles.*] Then I used to sit here and pretend that a rich old gentleman was in love with me—

MRS. LINDEN: What! What gentleman?

NORA: Oh, nobody!—that he was dead now, and that when his will was opened, there stood in large letters: "Pay over at once everything of which I die possessed to that charming person, Mrs. Nora Helmer."

MRS. LINDEN: But, my dear Nora—what gentleman do you mean?

NORA: Oh, dear, can't you understand? There wasn't any old gentleman: it was only what I used to dream and dream when I was at my wits' end for money. But it doesn't matter now—the tiresome old creature may stay where he is for me. I care nothing for him or his will; for now my troubles are over. [*Springing up.*] Oh, Christina, how glorious it is to think of! Free from all anxiety! Free, quite free. To be able to play and romp about with the children; to have things tasteful and pretty in the house, exactly as Torvald likes it! And then the spring will soon be here, with the great blue sky. Perhaps then we shall have a little holiday. Perhaps I shall see the sea again. Oh, what a wonderful thing it is to live and to be happy!

[*The hall-door bell rings.*]

MRS. LINDEN [*rising*]:   There's a ring. Perhaps I had better go.

NORA: No; do stay. No one will come here. It's sure to be some one for Torvald.

ELLEN [*in the doorway*]:   If you please, ma'am, there's a gentleman to speak to Mr. Helmer.

NORA: Who is the gentleman?

KROGSTAD [*in the doorway*]:   It is I, Mrs. Helmer.

[*Mrs. Linden starts and turns away to the window.*]

NORA [*goes a step towards him, anxiously, speaking low*]:   You? What is it? What do you want with my husband?

KROGSTAD: Bank business—in a way. I hold a small post in the Joint Stock Bank, and your husband is to be our new chief, I hear.

NORA: Then it is—?

KROGSTAD: Only tiresome business, Mrs. Helmer; nothing more.

NORA: Then will you please go to his study.

[*Krogstad goes. She bows indifferently while she closes the door into the hall. Then she goes to the stove and looks to the fire.*]

MRS. LINDEN: Nora—who was that man?

NORA: A Mr. Krogstad—a lawyer.

MRS. LINDEN: Then it was really he?

NORA: Do you know him?

MRS. LINDEN: I used to know him—many years ago. He was in a lawyer's office in our town.

NORA: Yes, so he was.

MRS. LINDEN: How he has changed!

NORA: I believe his marriage was unhappy.

MRS. LINDEN: And he is a widower now?

NORA: With a lot of children. There! Now it will burn up.

[*She closes the stove, and pushes the rocking-chair a little aside.*]

MRS. LINDEN: His business is not of the most creditable, they say?

NORA: Isn't it? I daresay not. I don't know. But don't let us think of business—it's so tiresome.

[*Dr. Rank comes out of Helmer's room.*]

RANK [*still in the doorway*]:   No, no; I'm in your way. I shall go and have a chat with your wife. [*Shuts the door and sees Mrs. Linden.*] Oh, I beg your pardon. I'm in the way here too.

NORA: No, not in the least. [*Introduces them.*] Doctor Rank—Mrs. Linden.

RANK: Oh, indeed; I've often heard Mrs. Linden's name; I think I passed you on the stairs as I came up.

MRS. LINDEN: Yes; I go so very slowly. Stairs try me so much.

RANK: Ah—you are not very strong?

MRS. LINDEN: Only overworked.

RANK: Nothing more? Then no doubt you've come to town to find rest in a round of dissipation?

MRS. LINDEN: I have come to look for employment.

RANK: Is that an approved remedy for overwork?

MRS. LINDEN: One must live, Doctor Rank.

RANK: Yes, that seems to be the general opinion.

NORA: Come, Doctor Rank—you want to live yourself.

RANK: To be sure I do. However wretched I may be, I want to drag on as long as possible. All my patients, too, have the same mania. And it's the same with people whose complaint is moral. At this very moment Helmer is talking to just such a moral incurable—

MRS. LINDEN [*softly*]:   Ah!

NORA: Whom do you mean?

RANK: Oh, a fellow named Krogstad, a man you know nothing about—corrupt to the very core of his character. But even he began by announcing, as a matter of vast importance, that he must live.

NORA: Indeed? And what did he want with Torvald?

RANK: I haven't an idea; I only gathered that it was some bank business.

NORA: I didn't know that Krog—that this Mr. Krogstad had anything to do with the Bank?

RANK: Yes. He has got some sort of place there. [*To Mrs. Linden.*] I don't know whether, in your part of the country, you have people who go grubbing and sniffing around in search of moral rottenness—and then, when they have found a "case," don't rest till they have got their man into some good position, where they can keep a watch upon him. Men with a clean bill of health they leave out in the cold.

MRS. LINDEN: Well, I suppose the—delicate characters require most care.

RANK [*shrugs his shoulders*]:   There we have it! It's that notion that makes society a hospital.

[*Nora. deep in her own thoughts, breaks into half-stifled laughter and claps her hands.*]

RANK: Why do you laugh at that? Have you any idea what "society" is?

NORA: What do I care for your tiresome society? I was laughing at something else— something excessively amusing. Tell me, Doctor Rank, are all the employees at the Bank dependent on Torvald now?

RANK: Is that what strikes you as excessively amusing?

NORA [*smiles and hums*]:   Never mind, never mind! [*Walks about the room.*] Yes, it is funny to think that we—that Torvald has such power over so many people. [*Takes the bag from her pocket.*] Doctor Rank, will you have a macaroon?

RANK: What!—macaroons! I thought they were contraband here.

NORA: Yes; but Christina brought me these.

MRS. LINDEN: What! I—?

NORA: Oh, well! Don't be frightened. You couldn't possibly know that Torvald had forbidden them. The fact is, he's afraid of me spoiling my teeth. But, oh bother, just for once!—That's for you, Doctor Rank! [*Puts a macaroon into his mouth.*] And you too, Christina. And I'll have one while we're about it— only a tiny one, or at most two. [*Walks about again.*] Oh dear, I am happy! There's only one thing in the world I really want.

RANK: Well; what's that?

NORA: There's something I should so like to say—in Torvald's hearing.

RANK: Then why don't you say it?

NORA: Because I daren't, it's so ugly.

MRS. LINDEN: Ugly?

RANK: In that case you'd better not. But to us you might—What is it you would so like to say in Helmer's hearing?

NORA: I should so love to say "Damn it all!"

RANK: Are you out of your mind?

MRS. LINDEN: Good gracious, Nora—!

RANK: Say it—there he is!

NORA [*hides the macaroons*]:   Hush—sh—sh

[*Helmer comes out of his room, hat in hand, with his overcoat on his arm.*]

NORA [*going to him*]:   Well, Torvald dear, have you got rid of him?

HELMER: Yes; he has just gone.

NORA: Let me introduce you—this is Christina, who has come to town—

HELMER: Christina? Pardon me, I don't know—

NORA: Mrs. Linden, Torvald dear—Christina Linden.

HELMER [*to Mrs. Linden*]:   Indeed! A school-friend of my wife's, no doubt?

MRS. LINDEN: Yes; we knew each other as girls.

NORA: And only think! she has taken this long journey on purpose to speak to you.

HELMER: To speak to me!

MRS. LINDEN: Well, not quite—

NORA: You see, Christina is tremendously clever at office work, and she's so anxious to work under a first-rate man of business in order to learn still more—

HELMER [*to Mrs. Linden*]:   Very sensible indeed.

NORA: And when she heard you were appointed manager—it was telegraphed, you know—she started off at once, and—Torvald, dear, for my sake, you must do something for Christina. Now, can't you?

HELMER: It's not impossible. I presume Mrs. Linden is a widow?

MRS. LINDEN: Yes.

HELMER: And you have already had some experience of business?

MRS. LINDEN: A good deal.

HELMER: Well, then, it's very likely I may be able to find a place for you.

NORA [*clapping her hands*]:   There now! There now!

HELMER: You have come at a fortunate moment, Mrs. Linden.

MRS. LINDEN: Oh, how can I thank you—?

HELMER [*smiling*]:   There is no occasion. [*Puts on his overcoat.*] But for the present you must excuse me—

RANK: Wait; I am going with you.

[*Fetches his fur coat from the hall and warms it at the fire.*]

NORA: Don't be long, Torvald dear.

HELMER: Only an hour; not more.

NORA: Are you going too, Christina?

MRS. LINDEN [*putting on her walking things*]:   Yes; I must set about looking for lodgings.

HELMER: Then perhaps we can go together?

NORA [*helping her*]:   What a pity we haven't a spare room for you; but it's impossible—

MRS. LINDEN: I shouldn't think of troubling you. Goodbye, dear Nora, and thank you for all your kindness.

NORA: Good-bye for the present. Of course, you'll come back this evening. And you, too, Doctor Rank. What! If you're well enough? Of course you'll be well enough. Only wrap up warmly. [*They go out, talking, into the hall. Outside on the stairs are heard children's voices.*] There they are! There they are! [*She runs to the outer door and opens it. The nurse, Anna, enters the hall with the children.*] Come in! Come in! [*Stoops down and kisses the children.*] Oh, my sweet darlings! Do you see them, Christina? Aren't they lovely?

RANK: Don't let us stand here chattering in the draught.

HELMER: Come, Mrs. Linden; only mothers can stand such a temperature.

[*Dr. Rank, Helmer, and Mrs. Linden go down the stairs; Anna enters the room with the children; Nora also, shutting the door.*]

NORA: How fresh and bright you look! And what red cheeks you've got! Like apples and roses. [*The children chatter to her during what follows.*] Have you had great fun? That's splendid! Oh, really! You've been giving Emmy and Bob a ride on your sledge!—both at once, only think! Why, you're quite a man, Ivar. Oh, give her to me a little, Anna. My sweet little dolly! [*Takes the smallest from the nurse and dances with her.*] Yes, yes; mother will dance with Bob too. What! Did you have a game of snowballs? Oh, I wish I'd been there. No; leave them, Anna; I'll take their things off. Oh, yes, let me do it; it's such fun. Go to the nursery; you look frozen. You'll find some hot coffee on the stove.

[*The Nurse goes into the room on the left. Nora takes off the children's things and throws them down anywhere, while the children talk all together.*]

Really! A big dog ran after you? But he didn't bite you? No; dogs don't bite dear little dolly children. Don't peep into those parcels, Ivar. What is it? Wouldn't you like to know? Take care—it'll bite! What? Shall we have a game? What shall we play at? Hide-and-seek? Yes, let's play hide-and-seek. Bob shall hide first. Am I to? Yes, let me hide first.

[*She and the children play, with laughter and shouting, in the room and the adjacent one to the right. At last Nora hides under the table; the children come rushing in, look for her, but cannot find her, hear her half-choked laughter, rush to the table, lift up the cover and see her. Loud shouts. She creeps out, as though to frighten them. Fresh shouts. Meanwhile there has been a knock at the door leading into the hall. No one has heard it. Now the door is half opened and Krogstad appears. He waits a little; the game is renewed.*]

KROGSTAD: I beg your pardon, Mrs. Helmer—

NORA [*with a suppressed cry, turns round and half jumps up*]: Ah! What do you want?

KROGSTAD: Excuse me; the outer door was ajar—somebody must have forgotten to shut it—

NORA [*standing up*]: My husband is not at home, Mr. Krogstad.

KROGSTAD: I know it.

NORA: Then what do you want here?

KROGSTAD: To say a few words to you.

NORA: To me? [*To the children, softly.*] Go in to Anna. What? No, the strange man won't hurt mamma. When he's gone we'll go on playing. [*She leads the children into the left-hand room, and shuts the door behind them. Uneasy, in suspense.*] It is to me you wish to speak?

KROGSTAD: Yes, to you.

NORA: To-day? But it's not the first yet—

KROGSTAD: No, to-day is Christmas Eve. It will depend upon yourself whether you have a merry Christmas.

NORA: What do you want? I'm not ready to-day—

KROGSTAD: Never mind that just now. I have come about another matter. You have a minute to spare?

NORA: Oh, yes, I suppose so; although—

KROGSTAD: Good. I was sitting in the restaurant opposite, and I saw your husband go down the street—

NORA: Well?

KROGSTAD: —with a lady.

NORA: What then?

KROGSTAD: May I ask if the lady was a Mrs. Linden?

NORA: Yes.

KROGSTAD: Who has just come to town?

NORA: Yes. To-day.

KROGSTAD: I believe she is an intimate friend of yours.

NORA: Certainly. But I don't understand—

KROGSTAD: I used to know her too.

NORA: I know you did.

KROGSTAD: Ah! You know all about it. I thought as much. Now, frankly, is Mrs. Linden to have a place in the Bank?

NORA: How dare you catechise me in this way, Mr. Krogstad—you, a subordinate of my husband's? But since you ask, you shall know. Yes, Mrs. Linden is to be employed. And it is I who recommended her, Mr. Krogstad. Now you know.

KROGSTAD: Then my guess was right.

NORA [*walking up and down*]: You see one has a wee bit of influence, after all. It doesn't follow because one's only a woman—When people are in a subordinate position, Mr. Krogstad, they ought really to be careful how they offend anybody who—h'm—

KROGSTAD: —who has influence?

NORA: Exactly.

KROGSTAD [*taking another tone*]: Mrs. Helmer, will you have the kindness to employ your influence on my behalf?

NORA: What? How do you mean?

KROGSTAD: Will you be so good as to see that I retain my subordinate position in the Bank?

NORA: What do you mean? Who wants to take it from you?

KROGSTAD: Oh, you needn't pretend ignorance. I can very well understand that it cannot be pleasant for your friend to meet me; and I can also understand now for whose sake I am to be hounded out.

NORA: But I assure you—

KROGSTAD: Come, come, now, once for all: there is time yet, and I advise you to use your influence to prevent it.

NORA: But, Mr. Krogstad, I have no influence—absolutely none.

KROGSTAD: None? I thought you said a moment ago—

NORA: Of course, not in that sense. I! How can you imagine that I should have any such influence over my husband?

KROGSTAD: Oh, I know your husband from our college days. I don't think he is any more inflexible than other husbands.

NORA: If you talk disrespectfully of my husband, I must request you to leave the house.

KROGSTAD: You are bold, madam.

NORA: I am afraid of you no longer. When New Year's Day is over, I shall soon be out of the whole business.

KROGSTAD [*controlling himself*]: Listen to me, Mrs. Helmer. If need be, I shall fight as though for my life to keep my little place in the Bank.

NORA: Yes, so it seems.

KROGSTAD: It's not only for the salary: that is what I care least about. It's something else—Well, I had better make a clean breast of it. Of course, you know, like every one else, that some years ago I—got into trouble.

NORA: I think I've heard something of the sort.

KROGSTAD: The matter never came into court; but from that moment all paths were barred to me. Then I took up the business you know about. I had to turn my hand to something; and I don't think I've been one of the worst. But now I must get clear of it all. My sons are growing up; for their sake I must try to recover my character as well as I can. This place in the Bank was the first step; and now your husband wants to kick me off the ladder, back into the mire.

NORA: But I assure you, Mr. Krogstad, I haven't the least power to help you.

KROGSTAD: That is because you have not the will; but I can compel you.

NORA: You won't tell my husband that I owe you money?

KROGSTAD: H'm; suppose I were to?

NORA: It would be shameful of you. [*With tears in her voice.*] The secret that is my joy and my pride—that he should learn it in such an ugly, coarse way—and from you. It would involve me in all sorts of unpleasantness—

KROGSTAD: Only unpleasantness?

NORA [*hotly*]: But just do it. It's you that will come off worst, for then my husband will see what a bad man you are, and then you certainly won't keep your place.

KROGSTAD: I asked whether it was only domestic unpleasantness you feared?

NORA: If my husband gets to know about it, he will, of course pay you off at once, and then we shall have nothing more to do with you.

KROGSTAD [*coming a pace nearer*]: Listen, Mrs. Helmer: either your memory is defective, or you don't know much about business. I must make the position a little clearer to you.

NORA: How so?

KROGSTAD: When your husband was ill, you came to me to borrow twelve hundred dollars.

NORA: I knew of nobody else.

KROGSTAD: I promised to find you the money—

NORA: And you did find it.

KROGSTAD: I promised to find you the money, on certain conditions. You were so much taken up at the time about your husband's illness, and so eager to have the wherewithal for your journey, that you probably did not give much thought to the details. Allow me to remind you of them. I promised to find you the amount in exchange for a note of hand, which I drew up.

NORA: Yes, and I signed it.

KROGSTAD: Quite right. But then I added a few lines, making your father security for the debt. Your father was to sign this.

NORA: Was to——? He did sign it!

KROGSTAD: I had left the date blank. That is to say, your father was himself to date his signature. Do you recollect that?

NORA: Yes, I believe——

KROGSTAD: Then I gave you the paper to send to your father, by post. Is not that so?

NORA: Yes.

KROGSTAD: And of course you did so at once; for within five or six days you brought me back the document with your father's signature; and I handed you the money.

NORA: Well? Have I not made my payments punctually?

KROGSTAD: Fairly—yes. But to return to the point: You were in great trouble at the time, Mrs. Helmer.

NORA: I was indeed!

KROGSTAD: Your father was very ill, I believe?

NORA: He was on his death-bed.

KROGSTAD: And died soon after?

NORA: Yes.

KROGSTAD: Tell me, Mrs. Helmer: do you happen to recollect the day of his death? The day of the month, I mean?

NORA: Father died on the 29th of September.

KROGSTAD: Quite correct. I have made inquiries. And here comes in the remarkable point—[*produces a paper*] which I cannot explain.

NORA: What remarkable point? I don't know——

KROGSTAD: The remarkable point, madam, that your father signed this paper three days after his death!

NORA: What! I don't understand——

KROGSTAD: Your father died on the 29th of September. But look here: he has dated his signature October 2nd! Is not that remarkable, Mrs. Helmer? [*Nora is silent.*] Can you explain it? [*Nora continues silent.*] It is noteworthy, too, that the words "October 2nd" and the year are not in your father's handwriting, but in one which I believe I know. Well, this may be explained; your father may have forgotten to date his signature, and somebody may have added the date at random, before the fact of your father's death was known. There is nothing wrong in that. Everything depends on the signature. Of course it is genuine, Mrs. Helmer? It was really your father himself who wrote his name here?

NORA [*after a short silence, throws her head back and looks defiantly at him*]: No, it was not. *I* wrote father's name.

KROGSTAD: Ah!—Are you aware, madam, that that is a dangerous admission?

NORA: How so? You will soon get your money.

KROGSTAD: May I ask you one more question? Why did you not send the paper to your father?

NORA: It was impossible. Father was ill. If I had asked him for his signature, I should have had to tell him why I wanted the money; but he was so ill I really could not tell him that my husband's life was in danger. It was impossible.

KROGSTAD: Then it would have been better to have given up your tour.

NORA: No, I couldn't do that; my husband's life depended on that journey. I couldn't give it up.

KROGSTAD: And did it never occur to you that you were playing me false?

NORA: That was nothing to me. I didn't care in the least about you. I couldn't endure you for all the cruel difficulties you made, although you knew how ill my husband was.

KROGSTAD: Mrs. Helmer, you evidently do not realise what you have been guilty of. But I can assure you it was nothing more and nothing worse that made me an outcast from society.

NORA: You! You want me to believe that you did a brave thing to save your wife's life?

KROGSTAD: The law takes no account of motives.

NORA: Then it must be a very bad law.

KROGSTAD: Bad or not, if I produce this document in court, you will be condemned according to law.

NORA: I don't believe that. Do you mean to tell me that a daughter has no right to spare her dying father trouble and anxiety?—that a wife has no right to save her husband's life? I don't know much about the law, but I'm sure you'll find, somewhere or another, that that is allowed. And you don't know that— you, a lawyer! You must be a bad one, Mr. Krogstad.

KROGSTAD: Possibly. But business—such business as ours—I do understand. You believe that? Very well; now, do as you please. But this I may tell you, that if I am flung into the gutter a second time, you shall keep me company.

[*Bows and goes out through hall.*]

NORA [*stands a while thinking, then tosses her head*]: Oh nonsense! He wants to frighten me. I'm not so foolish as that. [*Begins folding the children's clothes. Pauses.*] But—? No, it's impossible! Why, I did it for love!

CHILDREN [*at the door, left*]: Mamma, the strange man has gone now.

NORA: Yes, yes, I know. But don't tell anyone about the strange man. Do you hear? Not even papa!

CHILDREN: No, mamma; and now will you play with us again?

NORA: No, no; not now.

CHILDREN: Oh, do, mamma; you know you promised.

NORA: Yes, but I can't just now. Run to the nursery; I have so much to do. Run along, run along, and be good, my darlings! [*She pushes them gently into the inner room, and closes the door behind them. Sits on the sofa, embroiders a few stitches, but soon pauses.*] No! [*Throws down the work, rises, goes to the hall door and calls out.*] Ellen, bring in the Christmas-tree! [*Goes to table, left, and opens the drawer; again pauses.*] No, it's quite impossible!

ELLEN [*with Christmas-tree*]: Where shall I stand it, ma'am?

NORA: There, in the middle of the room.

ELLEN: Shall I bring in anything else?

NORA: No, thank you, I have all I want.

[*Ellen, having put down the tree, goes out.*]

NORA [*busy dressing the tree*]: There must be a candle here—and flowers there.— That horrible man! Nonsense, nonsense! there's nothing to be afraid of. The Christmas-tree shall be beautiful. I'll do everything to please you, Torvald; I'll sing and dance, and—

[*Enter Helmer by the hall door, with a bundle of documents.*]

NORA: Oh! You're back already?

HELMER: Yes. Has anybody been here?

NORA: Here? No.

HELMER: That's odd. I saw Krogstad come out of the house.

NORA: Did you? Oh, yes, by-the-bye, he was here for a minute.

HELMER: Nora, I can see by your manner that he has been begging you to put in a good word for him.

NORA: Yes.

HELMER: And you were to do it as if of your own accord? You were to say nothing to me of his having been here. Didn't he suggest that, too?

NORA: Yes, Torvald; but—

HELMER: Nora, Nora! And you could condescend to that! To speak to such a man, to make him a promise! And then to tell me an untruth about it!

NORA: An untruth!

HELMER: Didn't you say that nobody had been here? [*Threatens with his finger.*] My little bird must never do that again! A song-bird must sing clear and true; no false notes. [*Puts his arm round her.*] That's so, isn't it? Yes, I was sure of it. [*Lets her go.*] And now we'll say no more about it. [*Sits down before the fire.*] Oh, how cosy and quiet it is here!

[*Glances into his documents.*]

NORA [*busy with the tree, after a short silence*]: Torvald!

HELMER: Yes.

NORA: I'm looking forward so much to the Stenborgs' fancy ball the day after tomorrow.

HELMER: And I'm on tenterhooks to see what surprise you have in store for me.

NORA: Oh, it's too tiresome!

HELMER: What is?

NORA: I can't think of anything good. Everything seems so foolish and meaningless.

HELMER: Has little Nora made that discovery?

NORA [*behind his chair, with her arms on the back*]: Are you very busy, Torvald?

HELMER: Well—

NORA: What papers are those?

HELMER: Bank business.

NORA: Already!

HELMER: I have got the retiring manager to let me make some necessary changes in the staff and the organization. I can do this during Christmas week. I want to have everything straight by the New Year.

NORA: Then that's why that poor Krogstad—

HELMER: H'm.

NORA [*still leaning over the chair-back and slowly stroking his hair*]: If you hadn't been so very busy, I should have asked you a great, great favour, Torvald.

HELMER: What can it be? Out with it.

NORA: Nobody has such perfect taste as you; and I should so love to look well at the fancy ball. Torvald, dear, couldn't you take me in hand, and settle what I'm to be, and arrange my costume for me?

HELMER: Aha! So my willful little woman is at a loss, and making signals of distress.

NORA: Yes, please, Torvald. I can't get on without your help.

HELMER: Well, well, I'll think it over, and we'll soon hit upon something.

NORA: Oh, how good that is of you! [*Goes to the tree again; pause.*] How well the red flowers show.—Tell me, was it anything so very dreadful this Krogstad got into trouble about?

HELMER: Forgery, that's all. Don't you know what that means?

NORA: Mayn't he have been driven to it by need?

HELMER: Yes; or, like so many others, he may have done it in pure heedlessness. I am not so hard-hearted as to condemn a man absolutely for a single fault.

NORA: No, surely not, Torvald!

HELMER: Many a man can retrieve his character, if he owns his crime and takes the punishment.

NORA: Punishment—?

HELMER: But Krogstad didn't do that. He evaded the law by means of tricks and subterfuges; and that is what has morally ruined him.

NORA: Do you think that—?

HELMER: Just think how a man with a thing of that sort on his conscience must be always lying and canting and shamming. Think of the mask he must wear even towards those who stand nearest him—towards his own wife and children. The effect on the children—that's the most terrible part of it, Nora.

NORA: Why?

HELMER: Because in such an atmosphere of lies home life is poisoned and contaminated in every fibre. Every breath the children draw contains some germ of evil.

NORA [closer behind him]:   Are you sure of that?

HELMER: As a lawyer, my dear, I have seen it often enough. Nearly all cases of early corruption may be traced to lying mothers.

NORA: Why—mothers?

HELMER: It generally comes from the mother's side; but of course the father's influence may act in the same way. Every lawyer knows it too well. And here has this Krogstad been poisoning his own children for years past by a life of lies and hypocrisy—that is why I call him morally ruined. [Holds out both hands to her.] So my sweet little Nora must promise not to plead his cause. Shake hands upon it. Come, come, what's this? Give me your hand. That's right. Then it's a bargain. I assure you it would have been impossible for me to work with him. It gives me a positive sense of physical discomfort to come in contact with such people.

[Nora draws her hand away, and moves to the other side of the Christmas-tree.]

NORA: How warm it is here. And I have so much to do.

HELMER [rises and gathers up his papers]:   Yes, and I must try to get some of these papers looked through before dinner. And I shall think over your costume too. Perhaps I may even find something to hang in gilt paper on the Christmas-tree. [Lays his hand on her head.] My precious little song-bird!

[He goes into his room and shuts the door.]

NORA [softly, after a pause]:   It can't be. It's impossible. It must be impossible!

ANNA [at the door, left]:   The little ones are begging so prettily to come to mamma.

NORA: No, no, no; don't let them come to me! Keep them with you, Anna.

ANNA: Very well, ma'am.

[Shuts the door.]

NORA [pale with terror]:   Corrupt my children!—Poison my home! [Short pause. She throws back her head.] It's not true! It can never, never be true!

Act 2

The same room. In the corner, beside the piano, stands the Christmas-tree, stripped, and with the candles burnt out. Nora's outdoor things lie on the sofa.

Nora, alone, is walking about restlessly. At last she stops by the sofa, and takes up her cloak.

NORA [*dropping the cloak*]:   There's somebody coming! [*Goes to the hall door and listens.*] Nobody; of course nobody will come to-day, Christmas-day; nor to-morrow either. But perhaps——[*Opens the door and looks out.*]—No, nothing in the letter box; quite empty. [*Comes forward.*] Stuff and nonsense! Of course he won't really do anything. Such a thing couldn't happen. It's impossible! Why, I have three little children.

[*Anna enters from the left, with a large cardboard box.*]

ANNA: I've found the box with the fancy dress at last.
NORA: Thanks; put it down on the table.
ANNA [*does so*]:   But I'm afraid it's very much out of order.
NORA: Oh, I wish I could tear it into a hundred thousand pieces!
ANNA: Oh, no. It can easily be put to rights—just a little patience.
NORA: I shall go and get Mrs. Linden to help me.
ANNA: Going out again? In such weather as this! You'll catch cold, ma'am, and be ill.
NORA: Worse things might happen.—What are the children doing?
ANNA: They're playing with their Christmas presents, poor little dears; but—
NORA: Do they often ask for me?
ANNA: You see they've been so used to having their mamma with them.
NORA: Yes; but, Anna, I can't have them so much with me in future.
ANNA: Well, little children get used to anything.
NORA: Do you think they do? Do you believe they would forget their mother if she went quite away?
ANNA: Gracious me! Quite away?
NORA: Tell me, Anna—I've so often wondered about it—how could you bring yourself to give your child up to strangers?
ANNA: I had to when I came to nurse my little Miss Nora.
NORA: But how could you make up your mind to it?
ANNA: When I had the chance of such a good place? A poor girl who's been in trouble must take what comes. That wicked man did nothing for me.
NORA: But your daughter must have forgotten you.
ANNA: Oh, no, ma'am, that she hasn't. She wrote to me both when she was confirmed and when she was married.
NORA [*embracing her*]:   Dear old Anna—you were a good mother to me when I was little.
ANNA: My poor little Nora had no mother but me.
NORA: And if my little ones had nobody else, I'm sure you would—Nonsense, nonsense! [*Opens the box.*] Go in to the children. Now I must—You'll see how lovely I shall be to-morrow.
ANNA: I'm sure there will be no one at the ball so lovely as my Miss Nora.

[*She goes into the room on the left.*]

NORA [*takes the costume out of the box, but soon throws it down again*]:   Oh, if I dared go out. If only nobody would come. If only nothing would happen here in the meantime. Rubbish; nobody is coming. Only not to think. What a delicious muff! Beautiful gloves, beautiful gloves! To forget—to forget! One, two, three, four, five, six—[*With a scream.*] Ah, there they come.

[*Goes towards the door, then stands irresolute.*]

[*Mrs. Linden enters from the hall, where she has taken off her things.*]

NORA: Oh, it's you, Christina. There's nobody else there? I'm so glad you have come.

MRS. LINDEN: I hear you called at my lodgings.

NORA: Yes, I was just passing. There's something you must help me with. Let us sit here on the sofa—so. To-morrow evening there's to be a fancy ball at Consul Stenborg's overhead, and Torvald wants me to appear as a Neapolitan fisher-girl, and dance the tarantella; I learned it at Capri.

MRS. LINDEN: I see—quite a performance.

NORA: Yes, Torvald wishes it. Look, this is the costume; Torvald had it made for me in Italy. But now it's all so torn, I don't know—

MRS. LINDEN: Oh, we shall soon set that to rights. It's only the trimming that has come loose here and there. Have you a needle and thread? Ah, here's the very thing.

NORA: Oh, how kind of you.

MRS. LINDEN [*sewing*]:   So you're to be in costume to-morrow, Nora? I'll tell you what—I shall come in for a moment to see you in all your glory. But I've quite forgotten to thank you for the pleasant evening yesterday.

NORA [*rises and walks across the room*]:   Oh, yesterday, it didn't seem so pleasant as usual.—You should have come to town a little sooner, Christina.—Torvald has certainly the art of making home bright and beautiful.

MRS. LINDEN: You, too, I should think, or you wouldn't be your father's daughter. But tell me—is Doctor Rank always so depressed as he was last evening?

NORA: No, yesterday it was particularly noticeable. You see, he suffers from a dreadful illness. He has spinal consumption, poor fellow. They say his father was a horrible man, who kept mistresses and all sorts of things—so the son has been sickly from his childhood, you understand.

MRS. LINDEN [*lets her sewing fall into her lap*]:   Why, my darling Nora, how do you come to know such things?

NORA [*moving about the room*]:   Oh, when one has three children, one sometimes has visits from women who are half—half doctors—and they talk of one thing and another.

MRS. LINDEN [*goes on sewing; a short pause*]:   Does Doctor Rank come here every day?

NORA: Every day of his life. He has been Torvald's most intimate friend from boyhood, and he's a good friend of mine, too. Doctor Rank is quite one of the family.

MRS. LINDEN: But tell me—is he quite sincere? I mean, isn't he rather given to flattering people?

NORA: No, quite the contrary. Why should you think so?

MRS. LINDEN: When you introduced us yesterday he said he had often heard my name; but I noticed afterwards that your husband had no notion who I was. How could Doctor Rank—?

NORA: He was quite right, Christina. You see, Torvald loves me so indescribably, he wants to have me all to himself, as he says. When we were first married, he was almost jealous if I even mentioned any of my old friends at home; so naturally I gave up doing it. But I often talk of the old times to Doctor Rank, for he likes to hear about them.

MRS. LINDEN: Listen to me, Nora! You are still a child in many ways. I am older than you, and have had more experience. I'll tell you something? You ought to get clear of all this with Doctor Rank.

NORA: Get clear of what?

MRS. LINDEN: The whole affair, I should say. You were talking yesterday of a rich admirer who was to find you money—

NORA: Yes, one who never existed, worse luck. What then?

MRS. LINDEN: Has Doctor Rank money?

NORA: Yes, he has.

MRS. LINDEN: And nobody to provide for?

NORA: Nobody. But—?

MRS. LINDEN: And he comes here every day?

NORA: Yes, I told you so.

MRS. LINDEN: I should have thought he would have had better taste.

NORA: I don't understand you a bit.

MRS. LINDEN: Don't pretend, Nora. Do you suppose I can't guess who lent you the twelve hundred dollars?

NORA: Are you out of your senses? How can you think such a thing? A friend who comes here every day! Why, the position would be unbearable!

MRS. LINDEN: Then it really is not he?

NORA: No, I assure you. It never for a moment occurred to me—Besides, at that time he had nothing to lend; he came into his property afterwards.

MRS. LINDEN: Well, I believe that was lucky for you, Nora, dear.

NORA: No, really, it would never have struck me to ask Doctor Rank—And yet, I'm certain that if I did—

MRS. LINDEN: But of course you never would.

NORA: Of course not. It's inconceivable that it should ever be necessary. But I'm quite sure that if I spoke to Doctor Rank—

MRS. LINDEN: Behind your husband's back?

NORA: I must get clear of the other thing; that's behind his back too. I must get clear of that.

MRS. LINDEN: Yes, yes, I told you so yesterday; but—

NORA [walking up and down]: A man can manage these things much better than a woman.

MRS. LINDEN: One's own husband, yes.

NORA: Nonsense. [Stands still.] When everything is paid, one gets back the paper.

MRS. LINDEN: Of course.

NORA: And can tear it into a hundred thousand pieces, and burn it up, the nasty, filthy thing!

MRS. LINDEN [looks at her fixedly, lays down her work, and rises slowly]: Nora, you are hiding something from me.

NORA: Can you see it in my face?

MRS. LINDEN: Something has happened since yesterday morning. Nora, what is it?

NORA [*going towards her*]:   Christina—! [*Listens.*] Hush! There's Torvald coming home. Do you mind going into the nursery for the present? Torvald can't bear to see dressmaking going on. Get Anna to help you.

MRS. LINDEN [*gathers some of the things together*]:   Very well; but I shan't go away until you have told me all about it.

[*She goes out to the left, as Helmer enters from the hall.*]

NORA [*runs to meet him*]:   Oh, how I've been longing for you to come, Torvald, dear!

HELMER: Was that the dressmaker—?

NORA: No, Christina. She's helping me with my costume. You'll see how nice I shall look.

HELMER: Yes, wasn't that a happy thought of mine?

NORA: Splendid! But isn't it good of me, too, to have given in to you about the tarantella?

HELMER [*takes her under the chin*]:   Good of you! To give in to your own husband? Well, well, you little madcap, I know you don't mean it. But I won't disturb you. I daresay you want to be "trying on."

NORA: And you are going to work, I suppose?

HELMER: Yes. [*Shows her a bundle of papers.*] Look here. I've just come from the Bank—

[*Goes towards his room.*]

NORA: Torvald.

HELMER [*stopping*]:   Yes?

NORA: If your little squirrel were to beg you for something so prettily—

HELMER: Well?

NORA: Would you do it?

HELMER: I must know first what it is.

NORA: The squirrel would skip about and play all sorts of tricks if you would only be nice and kind.

HELMER: Come, then, out with it.

NORA: Your lark would twitter from morning till night—

HELMER: Oh, that she does in any case.

NORA: I'll be an elf and dance in the moonlight for you, Torvald.

HELMER: Nora—you can't mean what you were hinting at this morning?

NORA [*coming nearer*]:   Yes, Torvald, I beg and implore you!

HELMER: Have you really the courage to begin that again?

NORA: Yes, yes; for my sake, you must let Krogstad keep his place in the Bank.

HELMER: My dear Nora, it's his place I intend for Mrs. Linden.

NORA: Yes, that's so good of you. But instead of Krogstad, you could dismiss some other clerk.

HELMER: Why, this is incredible obstinacy! Because you have thoughtlessly promised to put in a word for him, I am to—!

NORA: It's not that, Torvald. It's for your own sake. This man writes for the most scurrilous newspapers; you said so yourself. He can do you no end of harm. I'm so terribly afraid of him—

HELMER: Ah, I understand; it's old recollections that are frightening you.

NORA: What do you mean?

HELMER: Of course you're thinking of your father.

NORA: Yes—yes, of course. Only think of the shameful slanders wicked people used to write about father. I believe they would have got him dismissed if you hadn't been sent to look into the thing, and been kind to him, and helped him.

HELMER: My little Nora, between your father and me there is all the difference in the world. Your father was not altogether unimpeachable. I am; and I hope to remain so.

NORA: Oh, no one knows what wicked men may hit upon. We could live so quietly and happily now, in our cosy, peaceful home, you and I and the children, Torvald! That's why I beg and implore you—

HELMER: And it is just by pleading his cause that you make it impossible for me to keep him. It's already known at the Bank that I intend to dismiss Krogstad. If it were now reported that the new manager let himself be turned round his wife's little finger—

NORA: What then?

HELMER: Oh, nothing, so long as a wilful woman can have her way—! I am to make myself a laughing-stock to the whole staff, and set people saying that I am open to all sorts of outside influence? Take my word for it, I should soon feel the consequences. And besides—there is one thing that makes Krogstad impossible for me to work with—

NORA: What thing?

HELMER: I could perhaps have overlooked his moral failings at a pinch—

NORA: Yes, couldn't you, Torvald?

HELMER: And I hear he is good at his work. But the fact is, he was a college chum of mine—there was one of those rash friendships between us that one so often repents of later. I may as well confess it at once—he calls me by my Christian name; and he is tactless enough to do it even when others are present. He delights in putting on airs of familiarity—Torvald here, Torvald there! I assure you it's most painful to me. He would make my position at the Bank perfectly unendurable.

NORA: Torvald, surely you're not serious?

HELMER: No? Why not?

NORA: That's such a petty reason.

HELMER: What! Petty! Do you consider me petty!

NORA: No, on the contrary, Torvald, dear; and that's just why—

HELMER: Never mind; you call my motives petty; then I must be petty too. Petty! Very well!—Now we'll put an end to this, once for all. [*Goes to the door into the hall and calls.*] Ellen!

NORA: What do you want?

HELMER [*searching among his papers*]: To settle the thing. [*Ellen enters.*] Here; take this letter; give it to a messenger. See that he takes it at once. The address is on it. Here's the money.

ELLEN: Very well, sir. [*Goes with the letter.*]

HELMER [*putting his papers together*]: There, Madam Obstinacy.

NORA [*breathless*]: Torvald—what was in the letter?

HELMER: Krogstad's dismissal.

NORA: Call it back again, Torvald! There's still time. Oh, Torvald, call it back again! For my sake, for your own, for the children's sake! Do you hear, Torvald? Do it! You don't know what that letter may bring upon us all.

HELMER: Too late.

NORA: Yes, too late.

HELMER: My dear Nora, I forgive your anxiety, though it's anything but flattering to me. Why should you suppose that *I* would be afraid of a wretched scribbler's spite? But I forgive you all the same, for it's a proof of your great love for me. [*Takes her in his arms.*] That's as it should be, my own dear Nora. Let what will happen—when it comes to the pinch, I shall have strength and courage enough. You shall see: my shoulders are broad enough to bear the whole burden.

NORA [*terror-struck*]: What do you mean by that?

HELMER: The whole burden, I say—

NORA [*with decision*]: That you shall never, never do!

HELMER: Very well; then we'll share it, Nora, as man and wife. That is how it should be. [*Petting her.*] Are you satisfied now? Come, come, come, don't look like a scared dove. It's all nothing—foolish fancies.—Now you ought to play the tarantella through and practise with the tambourine. I shall sit in my inner room and shut both doors, so that I shall hear nothing. You can make as much noise as you please. [*Turns round in doorway.*] And when Rank comes, just tell him where I'm to be found.

[*He nods to her, and goes with his papers into his room, closing the door.*]

NORA [*bewildered with terror, stands as though rooted to the ground, and whispers*]: He would do it. Yes, he would do it. He would do it, in spite of all the world.— No, never that, never, never! Anything rather than that! Oh, for some way of escape! What shall I do—! [*Hall bell rings.*] Doctor Rank—! —Anything, anything, rather than—!

[*Nora draws her hands over her face, pulls herself together, goes to the door and opens it. Rank stands outside hanging up his fur coat. During what follows it begins to grow dark.*]

NORA: Good-afternoon, Doctor Rank. I knew you by your ring. But you mustn't go to Torvald now. I believe he's busy.

RANK: And you? [*Enters and closes the door.*]

NORA: Oh, you know very well, I have always time for you.

RANK: Thank you. I shall avail myself of your kindness as long as I can.

NORA: What do you mean? As long as you can?

RANK: Yes. Does that frighten you?

NORA: I think it's an odd expression. Do you expect anything to happen?

RANK: Something I have long been prepared for; but I didn't think it would come so soon.

NORA [*catching at his arm*]: What have you discovered? Doctor Rank, you must tell me!

RANK [*sitting down by the stove*]: I am running down hill. There's no help for it.

NORA [*drank a long breath of relief*]: It's you—?

RANK: Who else should it be?—Why lie to one's self? I am the most wretched of all my patients, Mrs. Helmer. In these last days I have been auditing my life-account— bankrupt! Perhaps before a month is over, I shall lie rotting in the churchyard.

NORA: Oh! What an ugly way to talk.

RANK: The thing itself is so confoundedly ugly, you see. But the worst of it is, so many other ugly things have to be gone through first. There is only one last investiga- tion to be made, and when that is over I shall know pretty certainly when the break-up will begin. There's one thing I want to say to you: Helmer's delicate nature shrinks so from all that is horrible: I will not have him in my sick-room—

NORA: But, Doctor Rank—

RANK: I won't have him, I say—not on any account. I shall lock my door against him.—As soon as I am quite certain of the worst, I shall send you my visiting-card with a black cross on it; and then you will know that the final horror has begun.

NORA: Why, you're perfectly unreasonable to-day; and I did so want you to be in a really good humour.

RANK: With death staring me in the face?—And to suffer thus for another's sin! Where's the justice of it? And in one way or another you can trace in every family some such inexorable retribution——

NORA [*stopping her ears*]: Nonsense, nonsense! Now, cheer up!

RANK: Well, after all, the whole thing's only worth laughing at. My poor innocent spine must do penance for my father's wild oats.

NORA [*at table, left*]: I suppose he was too fond of asparagus and Strasbourg pâté, wasn't he?

RANK: Yes; and truffles.

NORA: Yes, truffles, to be sure. And oysters, I believe?

RANK: Yes, oysters; oysters, of course.

NORA: And then all the port and champagne! It's sad that all these good things should attack the spine.

RANK: Especially when the luckless spine attacked never had any good of them.

NORA: Ah, yes, that's the worst of it.

RANK [*looks at her searchingly*]: H'm——

NORA [*a moment later*]: Why did you smile?

RANK: No; it was you that laughed.

NORA: No; it was you that smiled, Doctor Rank.

RANK [*standing up*]: I see you're deeper than I thought.

NORA: I'm in such a crazy mood to-day.

RANK: So it seems.

NORA [*with her hands on his shoulders*]: Dear, dear Doctor Rank, death shall not take you away from Torvald and me.

RANK: Oh, you'll easily get over the loss. The absent are soon forgotten.

NORA [*looks at him anxiously*]: Do you think so?

RANK: People make fresh ties, and then—

NORA: Who make fresh ties?

RANK: You and Helmer will, when I am gone. You yourself are taking time by the forelock, it seems to me. What was that Mrs. Linden doing here yesterday?

NORA: Oh!—you're surely not jealous of poor Christina?

RANK: Yes, I am. She will be my successor in this house. When I am out of the way, this woman will, perhaps—

NORA: Hush! Not so loud! She's in there.

RANK: Today as well? You see!

NORA: Only to put my costume in order—dear me, how unreasonable you are! [*Sits on sofa.*] Now, do be good, Doctor Rank! Tomorrow you shall see how beautifully I shall dance; and then you may fancy that I'm doing it all to please you—and of course Torvald as well. [*Takes various things out of box.*] Doctor Rank, sit down here, and I'll show you something.

RANK [*sitting*]: What is it?

NORA: Look here. Look!

RANK: Silk stockings.

NORA: Flesh-coloured. Aren't they lovely? It's so dark here now; but to-morrow—No, no, no; you must only look at the feet. Oh, well, I suppose you may look at the rest too.

RANK: H'm—

NORA: What are you looking so critical about? Do you think they won't fit me?

RANK: I can't possibly give any competent opinion on that point.

NORA [*looking at him a moment*]:   For shame! [*Hits him lightly on the ear with the stockings.*] Take that. [*Rolls them up again.*]

RANK: And what other wonders am I to see?

NORA: You shan't see anything more; for you don't behave nicely.

[*She hums a little and searches among the things.*]

RANK [*after a short silence*]:   When I sit here gossiping with you, I can't imagine—I simply cannot conceive—what would have become of me if I had never entered this house.

NORA [*smiling*]:   Yes, I think you do feel at home with us.

RANK [*more softly—looking straight before him*]:   And now to have to leave it all—

NORA: Nonsense. You sha'n't leave us.

RANK [*in the same tone*]:   And not to be able to leave behind the slightest token of gratitude; scarcely even a passing regret—nothing but an empty place, that can be filled by the first comer.

NORA: And if I were to ask you for—? No—

RANK: For what?

NORA: For a great proof of your friendship.

RANK: Yes—yes?

NORA: I mean—for a very, very great service—

RANK: Would you really, for once, make me so happy?

NORA: Oh, you don't know what it is.

RANK: Then tell me.

NORA: No, I really can't, Doctor Rank. It's far, far too much—not only a service, but help and advice, besides—

RANK: So much the better. I can't think what you can mean. But go on. Don't you trust me?

NORA: As I trust no one else. I know you are my best and truest friend. So I will tell you. Well, then, Doctor Rank, there is something you must help me to prevent. You know how deeply, how wonderfully Torvald loves me; he wouldn't hesitate a moment to give his very life for my sake.

RANK [*bending towards her*]:   Nora—do you think he is the only one who—?

NORA [*with a slight start*]:   Who—?

RANK: Who would gladly give his life for you?

NORA [*sadly*]:   Oh!

RANK: I have sworn that you shall know it before I—go. I shall never find a better opportunity.—Yes, Nora, now I have told you; and now you know that you can trust me as you can no one else.

NORA [*standing up; simply and calmly*]:   Let me pass, please.

RANK [*makes way for her, but remains sitting*]:   Nora—

NORA [*in the doorway*]:   Ellen, bring the lamp. [*crosses to the stove*] Oh dear, Doctor Rank, that was too bad of you.

RANK [*rising*]: That I have loved you as deeply as—anyone else? Was that too bad of me?

NORA: No, but that you should have told me so. It was so unnecessary—

RANK: What do you mean? Did you know—?

[*Ellen enters with the lamp; sets it on the table and goes out again.*]

RANK: Nora—Mrs. Helmer—I ask you, did you know?

NORA: Oh, how can I tell what I knew or didn't know? I really can't say—How could you be so clumsy, Doctor Rank? It was all so nice!

RANK: Well, at any rate, you know now that I am at your service, body and soul. And now, go on.

NORA [*looking at him*]: Go on—now?

RANK: I beg you to tell me what you want.

NORA: I can tell you nothing now.

RANK: Yes, yes! You mustn't punish me in that way. Let me do for you whatever a man can.

NORA: You can do nothing for me now.—Besides, I really want no help. You shall see it was only my fancy. Yes, it must be so. Of course! [*Sits in the rocking-chair, looks at him and smiles.*] You are a nice person, Doctor Rank! Aren't you ashamed of yourself, now that the lamp is on the table?

RANK: No; not exactly. But perhaps I ought to go—for ever.

NORA: No, indeed you mustn't. Of course you must come and go as you've always done. You know very well that Torvald can't do without you.

RANK: Yes, but you?

NORA: Oh, you know I always like to have you here.

RANK: That is just what led me astray. You are a riddle to me. It has often seemed to me as if you liked being with me almost as much as being with Helmer.

NORA: Yes; don't you see? There are people one loves, and others one likes to talk to.

RANK: Yes—there's something in that.

NORA: When I was a girl, of course I loved papa best. But it always delighted me to steal into the servants' room. In the first place they never lectured me, and in the second it was such fun to hear them talk.

RANK: Ah, I see; then it's their place I have taken?

NORA [*jumps up and hurries towards him*]: Oh, my dear Doctor Rank, I don't mean that. But you understand, with Torvald it's the same as with papa—

[*Ellen enters from the hall.*]

ELLEN: Please, ma'am—[*Whispers to Nora, and gives her a card.*]

NORA [*glancing at card*]: Ah! [*Puts it in her pocket.*]

RANK: Anything wrong?

NORA: No, no, not in the least. It's only—it's my new costume—

RANK: Your costume! Why, it's there.

NORA: Oh, that one, yes. But this is another that—I have ordered it—Torvald mustn't know—

RANK: Aha! So that's the great secret.

NORA: Yes, of course. Please go to him; he's in the inner room. Do keep him while I—

RANK: Don't be alarmed; he sha'n't escape.

[*Goes into Helmer's room.*]

NORA [*to Ellen*]:   Is he waiting in the kitchen?

ELLEN: Yes, he came up the back stair—

NORA: Didn't you tell him I was engaged?

ELLEN: Yes, but it was no use.

NORA: He won't go away?

ELLEN: No, ma'am, not until he has spoken to you.

NORA: Then let him come in; but quietly. And, Ellen—say nothing about it; it's a surprise for my husband.

ELLEN: Oh, yes, ma'am, I understand. [*She goes out.*]

NORA: It is coming! The dreadful thing is coming, after all. No, no, no, it can never be; it shall not!

[*She goes to Helmer's door and slips the bolt. Ellen opens the hall door for Krogstad, and shuts it after him. He wears a travelling-coat, high boots, and a fur cap.*]

NORA [*goes towards him*]:   Speak softly; my husband is at home.

KROGSTAD: All right. That's nothing to me.

NORA: What do you want?

KROGSTAD: A little information.

NORA: Be quick, then. What is it?

KROGSTAD: You know I have got my dismissal.

NORA: I couldn't prevent it, Mr. Krogstad. I fought for you to the last, but it was of no use.

KROGSTAD: Does your husband care for you so little? He knows what I can bring upon you, and yet he dares—

NORA: How could you think I should tell him?

KROGSTAD: Well, as a matter of fact, I didn't think it. It wasn't like my friend Torvald Helmer to show so much courage—

NORA: Mr. Krogstad, be good enough to speak respectfully of my husband.

KROGSTAD: Certainly, with all due respect. But since you are so anxious to keep the matter secret, I suppose you are a little clearer than yesterday as to what you have done.

NORA: Clearer than you could ever make me.

KROGSTAD: Yes, such a bad lawyer as I—

NORA: What is it you want?

KROGSTAD: Only to see how you are getting on, Mrs. Helmer. I've been thinking about you all day. Even a mere money-lender, a gutter-journalist, a—in short, a creature like me—has a little bit of what people call feeling.

NORA: Then show it; think of my little children.

KROGSTAD: Did you and your husband think of mine? But enough of that. I only wanted to tell you that you needn't take this matter too seriously. I shall not lodge any information, for the present.

NORA: No, surely not. I knew you wouldn't.

KROGSTAD: The whole thing can be settled quite amicably. Nobody need know. It can remain among us three.

NORA: My husband must never know.

KROGSTAD: How can you prevent it? Can you pay off the balance?

NORA: No, not at once.

KROGSTAD: Or have you any means of raising the money in the next few days?

NORA: None—that I will make use of.

KROGSTAD: And if you had, it would not help you now. If you offered me ever so much money down, you should not get back your I.O.U.

NORA: Tell me what you want to do with it.

KROGSTAD: I only want to keep it—to have it in my possession. No outsider shall hear anything of it. So, if you have any desperate scheme in your head—

NORA: What if I have?

KROGSTAD: If you should think of leaving your husband and children—

NORA: What if I do?

KROGSTAD: Or if you should think of—something worse—

NORA: How do you know that?

KROGSTAD: Put all that out of your head.

NORA: How did you know what I had in my mind?

KROGSTAD: Most of us think of that at first. I thought of it, too; but I hadn't the courage—

NORA [tonelessly]:   Nor I.

KROGSTAD [relieved]:   No, one hasn't. You haven't the courage either, have you?

NORA: I haven't, I haven't.

KROGSTAD: Besides, it would be very foolish.—Just one domestic storm, and it's all over. I have a letter in my pocket for your husband—

NORA: Telling him everything?

KROGSTAD: Sparing you as much as possible.

NORA [quickly]:   He must never read that letter. Tear it up. I will manage to get the money somehow—

KROGSTAD: Pardon me, Mrs. Helmer, but I believe I told you—

NORA: Oh, I'm not talking about the money I owe you. Tell me how much you demand from my husband—I will get it.

KROGSTAD: I demand no money from your husband.

NORA: What do you demand then?

KROGSTAD: I will tell you. I want to regain my footing in the world. I want to rise; and your husband shall help me to do it. For the last eighteen months my record has been spotless; I have been in bitter need all the time; but I was content to fight my way up, step by step. Now, I've been thrust down again, and I will not be satisfied with merely being reinstated as a matter of grace. I want to rise, I tell you. I must get into the Bank again, in a higher position than before. Your husband shall create a place on purpose for me—

NORA: He will never do that!

KROGSTAD: He will do it; I know him—he won't dare to show fight! And when he and I are together there, you shall soon see! Before a year is out I shall be the manager's right hand. It won't be Torvald Helmer, but Nils Krogstad, that manages the Joint Stock Bank.

NORA: That shall never be.

KROGSTAD: Perhaps you will—?

NORA: Now I have the courage for it.

KROGSTAD: Oh, you don't frighten me! A sensitive, petted creature like you——

NORA: You shall see, you shall see!

KROGSTAD: Under the ice, perhaps? Down into the cold, black water? And next spring to come up again, ugly, hairless, unrecognisable—

NORA: You can't terrify me.

KROGSTAD: Nor you me. People don't do that sort of thing, Mrs. Helmer. And, after all, what would be the use of it? I have your husband in my pocket, all the same.

NORA: Afterwards? When I am no longer—?

KROGSTAD: You forget, your reputation remains in my hands! [*Nora stands speechless and looks at him.*] Well, now you are prepared. Do nothing foolish. As soon as Helmer has received my letter, I shall expect to hear from him. And remember that it is your husband himself who has forced me back again into such paths. That I will never forgive him. Good-bye, Mrs. Helmer.

[*Goes out through the hall. Nora hurries to the door, opens it a little, and listens.*]

NORA: He's going. He's not putting the letter into the box. No, no, it would be impossible! [*Opens the door further and further.*] What's that. He's standing still; not going down stairs. Has he changed his mind? Is he—? [*A letter falls into the box. Krogstad's footsteps are heard gradually receding down the stair. Nora utters a suppressed shriek, and rushes forward towards the sofa-table; pause.*] In the letter-box! [*Slips shrinkingly up to the hall door.*] There it lies.—Torvald, Torvald—now we are lost!

[*Mrs. Linden enters from the left with the costume.*]

MRS. LINDEN: There, I think it's all right now. Shall we just try it on?

NORA [*hoarsely and softly*]: Christina, come here.

MRS. LINDEN [*throws down the dress on the sofa*]: What's the matter? You look quite distracted.

NORA: Come here. Do you see that letter? There, see—through the glass of the letter-box.

MRS. LINDEN: Yes, yes, I see it.

NORA: That latter is from Krogstad—

MRS. LINDEN: Nora—it was Krogstad who lent you the money?

NORA: Yes; and now Torvald will know everything.

MRS. LINDEN: Believe me, Nora, it's the best thing for both of you.

NORA: You don't know all yet. I have forged a name——

MRS. LINDEN: Good heavens!

NORA: Now, listen to me, Christina; you shall bear me witness—

MRS. LINDEN: How "witness"? What am I to—?

NORA: If I should go out of my mind—it might easily happen—

MRS. LINDEN: Nora!

NORA: Or if anything else should happen to me—so that I couldn't be here—!

MRS. LINDEN: Nora, Nora, you're quite beside yourself!

NORA: In case any one wanted to take it all upon himself—the whole blame—you understand—

MRS. LINDEN: Yes, yes; but how can you think—?

NORA: You shall bear witness that it's not true, Christina. I'm not out of my mind at all; I know quite well what I'm saying; and I tell you nobody else knew anything about it; I did the whole thing, I myself. Remember that.

MRS. LINDEN: I shall remember. But I don't understand what you mean—

NORA: Oh, how should you? It's the miracle coming to pass.

MRS. LINDEN: The miracle?

NORA: Yes, the miracle. But it's so terrible, Christina; it mustn't happen for all the world.

MRS. LINDEN: I shall go straight to Krogstad and talk to him.

NORA: Don't; he'll do you some harm.

MRS. LINDEN: Once he would have done anything for me.

NORA: He?

MRS. LINDEN: Where does he live?

NORA: Oh, how can I tell—? Yes—[*Feels in her pocket.*] Here's his card. But the letter, the letter—!

HELMER [*knocking outside*]:   Nora!

NORA [*shrieks in terror*]:   Oh, what is it? What do you want?

HELMER: Well, well, don't be frightened. We're not coming in; you've bolted the door. Are you trying on your dress?

NORA: Yes, yes, I'm trying it on. It suits me so well, Torvald.

MRS. LINDEN [*who has read the card*]:   Why, he lives close by here.

NORA: Yes, but it's no use now. We are lost. The letter is there in the box.

MRS. LINDEN: And your husband has the key?

NORA: Always.

MRS. LINDEN: Krogstad must demand his letter back, unread. He must find some pretext—

NORA: But this is the very time when Torvald generally—

MRS. LINDEN: Prevent him. Keep him occupied. I shall come back as quickly as I can.

[*She goes out hastily by the hall door.*]

NORA [*opens Helmer's door and peeps in*]:   Torvald!

HELMER: Well, may one come into one's own room again at last? Come, Rank, we'll have a look—[*in the doorway*] But how's this?

NORA: What, Torvald dear?

HELMER: Rank led me to expect a grand transformation.

RANK [*in the doorway*]:   So I understood. I suppose I was mistaken.

NORA: No, no one shall see me in my glory till tomorrow evening.

HELMER: Why, Nora dear, you look so tired. Have you been practising too hard?

NORA: No, I haven't practised at all yet.

HELMER: But you'll have to—

NORA: Oh, yes, I must, I must! But, Torvald, I can't get on at all without your help. I've forgotten everything.

HELMER: Oh, we shall soon freshen it up again.

NORA: Yes, do help me, Torvald. You must promise me—Oh, I'm so nervous about it. Before so many people—This evening you must give yourself up entirely to me. You mustn't do a stroke of work; you mustn't even touch a pen. Do promise, Torvald dear!

HELMER: I promise. All this evening I shall be your slave. Little helpless thing—! But, by-the-bye, I must just—[*Going to hall door.*]

NORA: What do you want there?

HELMER: Only to see if there are any letters.

NORA: No, no, don't do that, Torvald.

HELMER: Why not?

NORA: Torvald, I beg you not to. There are none there.

HELMER: Let me just see. [*Is going.*]

[*Nora, at the piano, plays the first bars of the tarantella.*]

HELMER [*at the door, stops*]:   Aha!

NORA: I can't dance to-morrow if I don't rehearse with you first.

HELMER [*going to her*]:   Are you really so nervous, dear Nora?

NORA: Yes, dreadfully! Let me rehearse at once. We have time before dinner. Oh, do sit down and play for me, Torvald dear; direct me and put me right, as you used to do.

HELMER: With all the pleasure in life, since you wish it.

[*Sits at piano. Nora snatches the tambourine out of the box, and hurriedly drapes herself in a long parti-coloured shawl; then, with a bound, stands in the middle of the floor.*]

NORA: Now play for me! Now I'll dance!

[*Helmer plays and Nora dances. Rank stands at the piano behind Helmer and looks on.*]

HELMER [*playing*]:   Slower! Slower!

NORA: Can't do it slower!

HELMER: Not so violently, Nora.

NORA: I must! I must!

HELMER [*stops*]:   No, no, Nora—that will never do.

NORA [*laughs and swings her tambourine*]:   Didn't I tell you so!

RANK: Let me play for her.

HELMER [*rising*]:   Yes, do—then I can direct her better.

[*Rank sits down to the piano and plays; Nora dances more and more wildly. Helmer stands by the stove and addresses frequent corrections to her; she seems not to hear. Her hair breaks loose, and falls over her shoulders. She does not notice it, but goes on dancing. Mrs. Linden enters and stands spellbound in the doorway.*]

MRS. LINDEN: Ah—!

NORA [*dancing*]:   We're having such fun here, Christina!

HELMER: Why, Nora, dear, you're dancing as if it were a matter of life and death.

NORA: So it is.

HELMER: Rank, stop! This is the merest madness, Stop, I say!

[*Rank stops playing, and Nora comes to a sudden standstill.*]

HELMER [*going towards her*]:   I couldn't have believed it. You've positively forgotten all I taught you.

NORA [*throws the tambourine away*]:   You see for yourself.

HELMER: You really do want teaching.

NORA: Yes, you see how much I need it. You must practise with me up to the last moment. Will you promise me, Torvald?

HELMER: Certainly, certainly.

NORA: Neither today nor tomorrow must you think of anything but me. You mustn't open a single letter—mustn't look at the letter-box.

HELMER: Ah, you're still afraid of that man—

NORA: Oh, yes, yes, I am.

HELMER: Nora, I can see it in your face—there's a letter from him in the box.

NORA: I don't know, I believe so. But you're not to read anything now; nothing ugly must come between us until all is over.

RANK [*softly, to Helmer*]: You mustn't contradict her.

HELMER [*putting his arm around her*]: The child shall have her own way. But to-morrow night, when the dance is over—

NORA: Then you shall be free.

[*Ellen appears in the doorway, right.*]

ELLEN: Dinner is on the table, ma'am.

NORA: We'll have some champagne, Ellen.

ELLEN: Yes, ma'am.

[*Goes out.*]

HELMER: Dear me! Quite a banquet.

NORA: Yes, and we'll keep it up till morning [*Calling out.*] And macaroons, Ellen—plenty—just this once.

HELMER [*seizing her hand.*]: Come, come, don't let us have this wild excitement! Be my own little lark again.

NORA: Oh yes, I will. But now go into the dining-room; and you, too, Doctor Rank. Christina, you must help me to do up my hair.

RANK [*softly, as they go*]: There's nothing in the wind? Nothing—I mean—?

HELMER: Oh no, nothing of the kind. It's merely this babyish anxiety I was telling you about.

[*They go out to the right.*]

NORA: Well?

MRS. LINDEN: He's gone out of town.

NORA: I saw it in your face.

MRS. LINDEN: He comes back tomorrow evening. I left a note for him.

NORA: You shouldn't have done that. Things must take their course. After all, there's something glorious in waiting for the miracle.

MRS. LINDEN: What is it you're waiting for?

NORA: Oh, you can't understand. Go to them in the dining-room; I shall come in a moment.

[*Mrs. Linden goes into the dining-room. Nora stands for a moment as though collecting her thoughts; then looks at her watch.*]

NORA: Five. Seven hours till midnight. Then twenty-four hours till the next midnight. Then the tarantella will be over. Twenty-four and seven? Thirty-one hours to live.

[*Helmer appears at the door, right.*]

HELMER: What has become of my little lark?

NORA [*runs to him with open arms*]: Here she is!

Act 3

The same room. The table, with the chairs around it, in the middle. A lighted lamp on the table. The door to the hall stands open. Dance music is heard from the floor above.

Mrs. Linden sits by the table and absently turns the pages of a book. She tries to read, but seems unable to fix her attention; she frequently listens and looks anxiously towards the hall door.

MRS. LINDEN [*looks at her watch*]:   Not here yet; and the time is nearly up. If only he hasn't—[*listens again*] Ah, there he is. [*She goes into the hall and cautiously opens the outer door; soft footsteps are heard on the stairs; she whispers.*] Come in; there is no one here.

KROGSTAD [*in the doorway*]:   I found a note from you at my house. What does it mean?

MRS. LINDEN: I must speak to you.

KROGSTAD: Indeed? And in this house?

MRS. LINDEN: I could not see you at my rooms. They have no separate entrance. Come in; we are quite alone. The servants are asleep, and the Helmers are at the ball upstairs.

KROGSTAD [*coming into the room*]:   Ah! So the Helmers are dancing this evening? Really?

MRS. LINDEN: Yes. Why not?

KROGSTAD: Quite right. Why not?

MRS. LINDEN: And now let us talk a little.

KROGSTAD: Have we two anything to say to each other?

MRS. LINDEN: A great deal.

KROGSTAD: I should not have thought so.

MRS. LINDEN: Because you have never really understood me.

KROGSTAD: What was there to understand? The most natural thing in the world—a heartless woman throws a man over when a better match offers.

MRS. LINDEN: Do you really think me so heartless? Do you think I broke with you lightly?

KROGSTAD: Did you not?

MRS. LINDEN: Do you really think so?

KROGSTAD: If not, why did you write me that letter?

MRS. LINDEN: Was it not best? Since I had to break with you, was it not right that I should try to put an end to all that you felt for me?

KROGSTAD [*clenching his hands together*]:   So that was it? And all this—for the sake of money!

MRS. LINDEN: You ought not to forget that I had a helpless mother and two little brothers. We could not wait for you, Nils, as your prospects then stood.

KROGSTAD: Perhaps not; but you had no right to cast me off for the sake of others, whoever the others might be.

MRS. LINDEN: I don't know. I have often asked myself whether I had the right.

KROGSTAD [*more softly*]:   When I had lost you, I seemed to have no firm ground left under my feet. Look at me now. I am a shipwrecked man clinging to a spar.

MRS. LINDEN: Rescue may be at hand.

KROGSTAD: It was at hand; but then you came and stood in the way.

MRS. LINDEN: Without my knowledge, Nils. I did not know till today that it was you I was to replace in the Bank.

KROGSTAD: Well, I take your word for it. But now that you do know, do you mean to give way?

MRS. LINDEN: No, for that would not help you in the least.

KROGSTAD: Oh, help, help—! I should do it whether or no.

MRS. LINDEN: I have learnt prudence. Life and bitter necessity have schooled me.

KROGSTAD: And life has taught me not to trust fine speeches.

MRS. LINDEN: Then life has taught you a very sensible thing. But deeds you will trust?

KROGSTAD: What do you mean?

MRS. LINDEN: You said you were a shipwrecked man, clinging to a spar.

KROGSTAD: I have good reason to say so.

MRS. LINDEN: I too am shipwrecked, and clinging to a spar. I have no one to mourn
    for, no one to care for.

KROGSTAD: You made your own choice.

MRS. LINDEN: No choice was left me.

KROGSTAD: Well, what then?

MRS. LINDEN: Nils, how if we two shipwrecked people could join hands?

KROGSTAD: What!

MRS. LINDEN: Two on a raft have a better chance than if each clings to a separate spar.

KROGSTAD: Christina!

MRS. LINDEN: What do you think brought me to town?

KROGSTAD: Had you any thought of me?

MRS. LINDEN: I must have work or I can't bear to live. All my life, as long as I can
    remember, I have worked; work has been my one great joy. Now I stand
    quite alone in the world, aimless and forlorn. There is no happiness in work-
    ing for one self. Nils, give me somebody and something to work for.

KROGSTAD: I cannot believe in all this. It is simply a woman's romantic craving for
    self-sacrifice.

MRS. LINDEN: Have you ever found me romantic?

KROGSTAD: Would you really—? Tell me: do you know all my past?

MRS. LINDEN: Yes.

KROGSTAD: And do you know what people say of me?

MRS. LINDEN: Did you not say just now that with me you could have been another man?

KROGSTAD: I am sure of it.

MRS. LINDEN: Is it too late?

KROGSTAD: Christina, do you know what you are doing? Yes, you do; I see it in
    your face. Have you the courage then—?

MRS. LINDEN: I need some one to be a mother to, and your children need a mother.
    You need me, and I—I need you. Nils, I believe in your better self. With you
    I fear nothing.

KROGSTAD [seizing her hands]:   Thank you—thank you, Christina. Now I shall
    make others see me as you do.—Ah, I forgot—

MRS. LINDEN [listening]:   Hush! The tarantella! Go! go!

KROGSTAD: Why? What is it?

MRS. LINDEN: Don't you hear the dancing overhead? As soon as that is over they
    will be here.

KROGSTAD: Oh yes, I shall go. Nothing will come of this, after all. Of course, you
    don't know the step I have taken against the Helmers.

MRS. LINDEN: Yes, Nils, I do know.

KROGSTAD: And yet you have the courage to—?

MRS. LINDEN: I know to what lengths despair can drive a man.

KROGSTAD: Oh, if I could only undo it!

MRS. LINDEN: You could. Your letter is still in the box.

KROGSTAD: Are you sure?

MRS. LINDEN: Yes; but—

KROGSTAD [looking to her searchingly]:   Is that what it all means? You want to save
    your friend at any price. Say it out—is that your idea?

MRS. LINDEN: Nils, a woman who has once sold herself for the sake of others, does not do so again.

KROGSTAD: I shall demand my letter back again.

MRS. LINDEN: No, no.

KROGSTAD: Yes, of course. I shall wait till Helmer comes; I shall tell him to give it back to me—that it's only about my dismissal—that I don't want it read—

MRS. LINDEN: No, Nils, you must not recall the letter.

KROGSTAD: But tell me, wasn't that just why you got me to come here?

MRS. LINDEN: Yes, in my first alarm. But a day has passed since then, and in that day I have seen incredible things in this house. Helmer must know everything; there must be an end to this unhappy secret. These two must come to a full understanding. They must have done with all these shifts and subterfuges.

KROGSTAD: Very well, if you like to risk it. But one thing I can do, and at once—

MRS. LINDEN [*listening*]:   Make haste! Go, go! The dance is over; we're not safe another moment.

KROGSTAD: I shall wait for you in the street.

MRS. LINDEN: Yes, do; you must see me home.

KROGSTAD: I never was so happy in all my life!

[*Krogstad goes out by the outer door. The door between the room and the hall remains open.*]

MRS. LINDEN [*arranging the room and getting her outdoor things together*]:   What a change! What a change! To have some one to work for, to live for; a home to make happy! Well, it shall not be my fault if I fail.—I wish they would come.—[*Listens.*] Ah, here they are! I must get my things on.

[*Takes bonnet and cloak. Helmer's and Nora's voices are heard outside, a key is turned in the lock, and Helmer drags Nora almost by force into the hall. She wears the Italian costume with a large black shawl over it. He is in evening dress and wears a black domino,[3] open.*]

NORA [*struggling with him in the doorway*]:   No, no, no! I won't go in! I want to go upstairs again; I don't want to leave so early!

HELMER: But, my dearest girl—!

NORA: Oh, please, please, Torvald, I beseech you—only one hour more!

HELMER: Not one minute more, Nora dear; you know what we agreed. Come, come in; you're catching cold here.

[*He leads her gently into the room in spite of her resistance.*]

MRS. LINDEN: Good evening.

NORA: Christina!

HELMER: What, Mrs. Linden! You here so late?

MRS. LINDEN: Yes, I ought to apologise. I did so want to see Nora in her costume.

NORA: Have you been sitting here waiting for me?

MRS. LINDEN: Yes; unfortunately, I came too late. You had gone upstairs already, and I felt I couldn't go away without seeing you.

HELMER [*taking Nora's shawl off*]:   Well, then, just look at her! I assure you she's worth it. Isn't she lovely, Mrs. Linden?

---

3. A hooded robe with a mask for the eyes.

MRS. LINDEN: Yes, I must say—

HELMER: Isn't she exquisite? Every one said so. But she's dreadfully obstinate, dear little creature. What's to be done with her? Just think, I had almost to force her away.

NORA: Oh, Torvald, you'll be sorry some day that you didn't let me stay, if only for one half-hour more.

HELMER: There! You hear her, Mrs. Linden? She dances her tarantella with wild applause, and well she deserved it, I must say—though there was, perhaps, a little too much nature in her rendering of the idea—more than was, strictly speaking, artistic. But never mind—the point is, she made a great success, a tremendous success. Was I to let her remain after that— to weaken the impression? Not if I know it. I took my sweet little Capri girl—my capricious little Capri girl, I might say— under my arm; a rapid turn round the room, a curtsey to all sides, and—as they say in novels— the lovely apparition vanished! An exit should always be effective, Mrs. Linden; but I can't get Nora to see it. By Jove! it's warm here. [*Throws his domino on a chair and opens the door to his room.*] What! No light there? Oh, of course. Excuse me—

[*Goes in and lights candles.*]

NORA [*whispers breathlessly*]:   Well?

MRS. LINDEN [*softly*]:   I've spoken to him.

NORA: And—?

MRS. LINDEN: Nora—you must tell your husband everything—

NORA [*tonelessly*]:   I knew it!

MRS. LINDEN: You have nothing to fear from Krogstad; but you must speak out.

NORA: I shall not speak!

MRS. LINDEN: Then the letter will.

NORA: Thank you, Christina. Now I know what I have to do. Hush—!

HELMER [*coming back*]:   Well, Mrs. Linden, have you admired her?

MRS. LINDEN: Yes; and now I must say good-night.

HELMER: What, already? Does this knitting belong to you?

MRS. LINDEN [*takes it*]:   Yes, thanks; I was nearly forgetting it.

HELMER: Then you do knit?

MRS. LINDEN: Yes.

HELMER: Do you know, you ought to embroider instead?

MRS. LINDEN: Indeed! Why?

HELMER: Because it's so much prettier. Look now! You hold the embroidery in the left hand, so, and then work the needle with the right hand, in a long, graceful curve—don't you?

MRS. LINDEN: Yes, I suppose so.

HELMER: But knitting is always ugly. Just look—your arms close to your sides, and the needles going up and down—there's something Chinese about it.—They really gave us splendid champagne tonight.

MRS. LINDEN: Well, good-night, Nora, and don't be obstinate any more.

HELMER: Well said, Mrs. Linden!

MRS. LINDEN: Good-night, Mr. Helmer.

HELMER [*accompanying her to the door*]:   Good-night, good-night; I hope you'll get safely home. I should be glad to—but you have such a short way to go.

Good-night, good-night. [*She goes; Helmer shuts the door after her and comes forward again.*] At last we've got rid of her; she's a terrible bore.

NORA: Aren't you very tired, Torvald?

HELMER: No, not in the least.

NORA: Nor sleepy?

HELMER: Not a bit. I feel particularly lively. But you? You do look tired and sleepy.

NORA: Yes, very tired. I shall soon sleep now.

HELMER: There, you see. I was right, after all, not to let you stay longer.

NORA: Oh, everything you do is right.

HELMER [*kissing her forehead*]: Now my lark is speaking like a reasonable being. Did you notice how jolly Rank was this evening?

NORA: Indeed? Was he? I had no chance of speaking to him.

HELMER: Nor I, much; but I haven't seen him in such good spirits for a long time. [*Looks at Nora a little, then comes nearer her.*] It's splendid to be back in our own home, to be quite alone together!—Oh, you enchanting creature!

NORA: Don't look at me in that way, Torvald.

HELMER: I am not to look at my dearest treasure?—at all the loveliness that is mine, mine only, wholly and entirely mine?

NORA [*goes to the other side of the table*]: You mustn't say these things to me this evening.

HELMER [*following*]: I see you have the tarantella still in your blood—and that makes you all the more enticing. Listen! the other people are going now. [*More softly.*] Nora—soon the whole house will be still.

NORA: Yes, I hope so.

HELMER: Yes, don't you, Nora darling? When we are among strangers, do you know why I speak so little to you, and keep so far away, and only steal a glance at you now and then—do you know why I do it? Because I am fancying that we love each other in secret, that I am secretly betrothed to you, and that no one dreams that there is anything between us.

NORA: Yes, yes, yes. I know all your thoughts are with me.

HELMER: And then, when the time comes to go, and I put the shawl about your smooth, soft shoulders, and this glorious neck of yours, I imagine you are my bride, that our marriage is just over, that I am bringing you for the first time to my home—that I am alone with you for the first time—quite alone with you, in your trembling loveliness! All this evening I have been longing for you, and you only. When I watched you swaying and whirling in the tarantella—my blood boiled—I could endure it no longer; and that's why I made you come home with me so early—

NORA: Go now, Torvald! Go away from me. I won't have all this.

HELMER: What do you mean? Ah, I see you're teasing me, little Nora! Won't—won't! Am I not your husband—?

[*A knock at the outer door.*]

NORA [*starts*]: Did you hear—?

HELMER [*going towards the hall*]: Who's there?

RANK [*outside*]: It is I; may I come in for a moment?

HELMER [*in a low tone, annoyed*]: Oh! what can he want just now? [*Aloud.*] Wait a moment. [*Opens door.*] Come, it's nice of you to look in.

RANK: I thought I heard your voice, and that put it into my head. [*Looks round.*] Ah, this dear old place! How cosy you two are here!

HELMER: You seemed to find it pleasant enough upstairs, too.
RANK: Exceedingly. Why not? Why shouldn't one take one's share of everything in this world? All one can, at least, and as long as one can. The wine was splendid—
HELMER: Especially the champagne.
RANK: Did you notice it? It's incredible the quantity I contrived to get down.
NORA: Torvald drank plenty of champagne, too.
RANK: Did he?
NORA: Yes, and it always puts him in such spirits.
RANK: Well, why shouldn't one have a jolly evening after a well-spent day?
HELMER: Well-spent! Well, I haven't much to boast of in that respect.
RANK [*slapping him on the shoulder*]:   But I have, don't you see?
NORA: I suppose you have been engaged in a scientific investigation, Doctor Rank?
RANK: Quite right.
HELMER: Bless me! Little Nora talking about scientific investigations!
NORA: Am I to congratulate you on the result?
RANK: By all means.
NORA: It was good then?
RANK: The best possible, both for doctor and patient—certainty.
NORA [*quickly and searchingly*]:   Certainty?
RANK: Absolute certainty. Wasn't I right to enjoy myself after that?
NORA: Yes, quite right, Doctor Rank.
HELMER: And so say I, provided you don't have to pay for it tomorrow.
RANK: Well, in this life nothing is to be had for nothing.
NORA: Doctor Rank—I'm sure you are very fond of masquerades?
RANK: Yes, when there are plenty of amusing disguises—
NORA: Tell me, what shall we two be at our next masquerade?
HELMER: Little featherbrain! Thinking of your next already!
RANK: We two? I'll tell you. You must go as a good fairy.
HELMER: Ah, but what costume would indicate that?
RANK: She has simply to wear her everyday dress.
HELMER: Capital! But don't you know what you will be yourself?
RANK: Yes, my dear friend, I am perfectly clear upon that point.
HELMER: Well?
RANK: At the next masquerade I shall be invisible.
HELMER: What a comical idea!
RANK: There's a big black hat—haven't you heard of the invisible hat? It comes down all over you, and then no one can see you.
HELMER [*with a suppressed smile*]:   No, you're right there.
RANK: But I'm quite forgetting what I came for, Helmer, give me a cigar—one of the dark Havanas.
HELMER: With the greatest pleasure. [*Hands cigar-case.*]
RANK [*takes one and cuts the end off*]:   Thank you.
NORA [*striking a wax match*]:   Let me give you a light.
RANK: A thousand thanks.

[*She holds the match. He lights his cigar at it.*]

RANK: And now, good-bye!
HELMER: Good-bye, good-bye, my dear fellow.
NORA: Sleep well, Doctor Rank.

RANK: Thanks for the wish.

NORA: Wish me the same.

RANK: You? Very well, since you ask me—Sleep well. And thanks for the light.

[*He nods to them both and goes out.*]

HELMER [*in an undertone*]:   He's been drinking a good deal.

NORA [*absently*]:   I daresay. [*Helmer takes his bunch of keys from his pocket and goes into the hall.*] Torvald, what are you doing there?

HELMER: I must empty the letter-box; it's quite full; there will be no room for the newspapers tomorrow morning.

NORA: Are you going to work tonight?

HELMER: You know very well I am not.—Why, how is this? Some one has been at the lock.

NORA: The lock—?

HELMER: I'm sure of it. What does it mean? I can't think that the servants—? Here's a broken hair-pin. Nora, it's one of yours.

NORA [*quickly*]:   It must have been the children—

HELMER: Then you must break them of such tricks.—There! At last I've got it open. [*Takes contents out and calls into the kitchen.*] Ellen!—Ellen, just put the hall door lamp out.

[*He returns with letters in his hand, and shuts the inner door.*]

HELMER: Just see how they've accumulated. [*Turning them over.*] Why, what's this?

NORA [*at the window*]:   The letter! Oh no, no, Torvald!

HELMER: Two visiting-cards—from Rank.

NORA: From Doctor Rank?

HELMER [*looking at them*]:   Doctor Rank. They were on the top. He must just have put them in.

NORA: Is there anything on them?

HELMER: There's a black cross over the name. Look at it. What an unpleasant idea! It looks just as if he were announcing his own death.

NORA: So he is.

HELMER: What! Do you know anything? Has he told you anything?

NORA: Yes. These cards mean that he has taken his last leave of us. He is going to shut himself up and die.

HELMER: Poor fellow! Of course. I knew we couldn't hope to keep him long. But so soon—! And to go and creep into his lair like a wounded animal—

NORA: When we must go, it is best to go silently. Don't you think so, Torvald?

HELMER [*walking up and down*]:   He had so grown into our lives, I can't realise that he is gone. He and his sufferings and his loneliness formed a sort of cloudy background to the sunshine of our happiness.—Well, perhaps it's best as it is—at any rate for him. [*Stands still.*] And perhaps for us, too, Nora. Now we two are thrown entirely upon each other. [*Takes her in his arms.*] My darling wife! I feel as if I could never hold you close enough. Do you know, Nora, I often wish some danger might threaten you, that I might risk body and soul, and everything, everything, for your dear sake.

NORA [*tears herself from him and says firmly*]:   Now you shall read your letters, Torvald.

HELMER: No, no; not tonight. I want to be with you, my sweet wife.

NORA: With the thought of your dying friend—?

HELMER: You are right. This has shaken us both. Unloveliness has come between us—thoughts of death and decay. We must seek to cast them off. Till then— we will remain apart.

NORA [*her arms round his neck*]:   Torvald! Good-night! good-night!

HELMER [*kissing her forehead*]:   Good-night, my little song-bird. Sleep well, Nora. Now I shall go and read my letters.

[*He goes with the letters in his hand into his room and shuts the door.*]

NORA [*with wild eyes, gropes about her, seizes Helmer's domino, throws it round her, and whispers quickly, hoarsely, and brokenly*]:   Never to see him again. Never, never, never. [*Throws her shawl over her head.*] Never to see the children again. Never, never.—Oh that black, icy water! Oh that bottomless—! If it were only over! Now he has it; he's reading it. Oh, no, no, no, not yet. Torvald, good-bye—! Good-bye, my little ones—!

[*She is rushing out by the hall; at the same moment Helmer flings his door open, and stands there with an open letter in his hand*]

HELMER: Nora!

NORA [*shrieks*]:   Ah—!

HELMER: What is this? Do you know what is in this letter?

NORA: Yes, I know. Let me go! Let me pass!

HELMER [*holds her back*]:   Where do you want to go?

NORA [*tries to break away from him*]:   You shall not save me, Torvald.

HELMER [*falling back*]:   True! Is what he writes true? No, no, it is impossible that this can be true.

NORA: It is true. I have loved you beyond all else in the world.

HELMER: Pshaw—no silly evasions!

NORA [*a step nearer him*]:   Torvald—!

HELMER: Wretched woman—what have you done?

NORA: Let me go—you shall not save me! You shall not take my guilt upon yourself!

HELMER: I don't want any melodramatic airs. [*Locks the outer door.*] Here you shall stay and give an account of yourself. Do you understand what you have done? Answer! Do you understand it?

NORA [*looks at him fixedly, and says with a stiffening expression*]:   Yes; now I begin fully to understand it.

HELMER [*walking up and down*]:   Oh! what an awful awakening! During all these eight years—she who was my pride and my joy—a hypocrite, a liar—worse, worse—a criminal. Oh, the unfathomable hideousness of it all! Ugh! Ugh!

[*Nora says nothing, and continues to look fixedly at him.*]

HELMER: I ought to have known how it would be. I ought to have foreseen it. All your father's want of principle—be silent!—all your father's want of principle you have inherited—no religion, no morality, no sense of duty. How I am punished for screening him! I did it for your sake; and you reward me like this.

NORA: Yes—like this.

HELMER: You have destroyed my whole happiness. You have ruined my future. Oh, it's frightful to think of! I am in the power of a scoundrel; he can do whatever he pleases with me, demand whatever he chooses; he can domineer over me as much as he likes, and I must submit. And all this disaster and ruin is brought upon me by an unprincipled woman!

NORA: When I am out of the world, you will be free.

HELMER: Oh, no fine phrases. Your father, too, was always ready with them. What good would it do me, if you were "out of the world," as you say? No good whatever! He can publish the story all the same; I might even be suspected of collusion. People will think I was at the bottom of it all and egged you on. And for all this I have you to thank—you whom I have done nothing but pet and spoil during our whole married life. Do you understand now what you have done to me?

NORA [*with cold calmness*]:   Yes.

HELMER: The thing is so incredible, I can't grasp it. But we must come to an understanding. Take that shawl off. Take it off, I say! I must try to pacify him in one way or another—the matter must be hushed up, cost what it may.—As for you and me, we must make no outward change in our way of life—no outward change, you understand. Of course, you will continue to live here. But the children cannot be left in your care. I dare not trust them to you.—Oh, to have to say this to one I have loved so tenderly—whom I still—! But that must be a thing of the past. Henceforward there can be no question of happiness, but merely of saving the ruins, the shreds, the show—[*A ring; Helmer starts.*] What's that? So late! Can it be the worst? Can he—? Hide yourself, Nora; say you are ill.

[*Nora stands motionless. Helmer goes to the door and opens it.*]

ELLEN [*half dressed, in the hall*]:   Here is a letter for you, ma'am.

HELMER: Give it to me. [*Seizes the letter and shuts the door.*] Yes, from him. You shall not have it. I shall read it.

NORA: Read it!

HELMER [*by the lamp*]:   I have hardly the courage to. We may both be lost, both you and I. Ah! I must know. [*Hastily tears the letter open; reads a few lines, looks at an enclosure; with a cry of joy.*] Nora!

[*Nora looks inquiringly at him.*]

HELMER: Nora!—Oh! I must read it again.—Yes, yes, it is so. I am saved! Nora, I am saved!

NORA: And I?

HELMER: You too, of course; we are both saved, both of us. Look here—he sends you back your promissory note. He writes that he regrets and apologises that a happy turn in his life—Oh, what matter what he writes. We are saved, Nora! No one can harm you. Oh, Nora, Nora—; but first to get rid of this hateful thing. I'll just see—[*Glances at the I.O.U.*] No, I will not look at it; the whole thing shall be nothing but a dream to me. [*Tears the I.O.U. and both letters in pieces. Throws them into the fire and watches them burn.*] There! it's gone!—He said that ever since Christmas Eve—Oh, Nora, they must have been three terrible days for you!

NORA: I have fought a hard fight for the last three days.

HELMER: And in your agony you saw no other outlet but—No; we won't think of that horror. We will only rejoice and repeat—it's over, all over! Don't you hear, Nora? You don't seem able to grasp it. Yes, it's over. What is this set look on your face? Oh, my poor Nora, I understand you cannot believe that I have forgiven you. But I have, Nora; I swear it. I have forgiven everything. I know that what you did was all for love of me.

NORA: That is true.

HELMER: You loved me as a wife should love her husband. It was only the means that, in your inexperience, you misjudged. But do you think I love you the less because you cannot do without guidance? No, no. Only lean on me; I will counsel you, and guide you. I should be no true man if this very womanly helplessness did not make you doubly dear in my eyes. You mustn't dwell upon the hard things I said in my first moment of terror, when the world seemed to be tumbling about my ears. I have forgiven you, Nora—I swear I have forgiven you.

NORA: I thank you for your forgiveness.

[Goes out, to the right.]

HELMER: No, stay—! [Looking through the doorway.] What are you going to do?

NORA [inside]:   To take off my masquerade dress.

HELMER [in the doorway]:   Yes, do, dear. Try to calm down, and recover your balance, my scared little song-bird. You may rest secure. I have broad wings to shield you. [Walking up and down near the door.] Oh, how lovely—how cosy our home is, Nora! Here you are safe; here I can shelter you like a hunted dove whom I have saved from the claws of the hawk. I shall soon bring your poor beating heart to rest; believe me, Nora, very soon. Tomorrow all this will seem quite different—everything will be as before. I shall not need to tell you again that I forgive you; you will feel for yourself that it is true. How could you think I could find it in my heart to drive you away, or even so much as to reproach you? Oh, you don't know a true man's heart, Nora. There is something indescribably sweet and soothing to a man in having forgiven his wife—honestly forgiven her, from the bottom of his heart. She becomes his property in a double sense. She is as though born again; she has become, so to speak, at once his wife and his child. That is what you shall henceforth be to me, my bewildered, helpless darling. Don't be troubled about anything, Nora; only open your heart to me, and I will be both will and conscience to you. [Nora enters in everyday dress.] Why, what's this? Not gone to bed? You have changed your dress?

NORA: Yes, Torvald; now I have changed my dress.

HELMER: But why now, so late—?

NORA: I shall not sleep to-night.

HELMER: But, Nora dear—

NORA [looking at her watch]:   It's not so late yet. Sit down, Torvald; you and I have much to say to each other. [She sits at one side of the table.]

HELMER: Nora—what does this mean? Your cold, set face—

NORA: Sit down. It will take some time. I have much to talk over with you.

[Helmer sits at the other side of the table.]

HELMER: You alarm me, Nora. I don't understand you.

NORA: No, that is just it. You don't understand me; and I have never understood you—till tonight. No, don't interrupt. Only listen to what I say.—We must come to a final settlement, Torvald.

HELMER: How do you mean?

NORA [after a short silence]:   Does not one thing strike you as we sit here?

HELMER: What should strike me?

NORA: We have been married eight years. Does it not strike you that this is the first time we two, you and I, man and wife, have talked together seriously?

HELMER: Seriously! What do you call seriously?

NORA: During eight whole years, and more—ever since the day we first met—we have never exchanged one serious word about serious things.

HELMER: Was I always to trouble you with the cares you could not help me to bear?

NORA: I am not talking of cares. I say that we have never yet set ourselves seriously to get to the bottom of anything.

HELMER: Why, my dearest Nora, what have you to do with serious things?

NORA: There we have it! You have never understood me.—I have had great injustice done me, Torvald; first by father, and then by you.

HELMER: What! By your father and me?—By us, who have loved you more than all the world?

NORA [*shaking her head*]:   You have never loved me. You only thought it amusing to be in love with me.

HELMER: Why, Nora, what a thing to say!

NORA: Yes, it is so, Torvald. While I was at home with father, he used to tell me all his opinions, and I held the same opinions. If I had others, I said nothing about them, because he wouldn't have liked it. He used to call me his doll-child, and played with me as I played with my dolls. Then I came to live in your house—

HELMER: What an expression to use about our marriage!

NORA [*undisturbed*]:   I mean I passed from father's hands into yours. You arranged everything according to your taste; and I got the same tastes as you; or I pretended to—I don't know which—both ways, perhaps; sometimes one and sometimes the other. When I look back on it now, I seem to have been living here like a beggar, from hand to mouth. I lived by performing tricks for you, Torvald. But you would have it so. You and father have done me a great wrong. It is your fault that my life has come to nothing.

HELMER: Why, Nora, how unreasonable and ungrateful you are! Have you not been happy here?

NORA: No, never. I thought I was; but I never was.

HELMER: Not—not happy!

NORA: No; only merry. And you have always been so kind to me. But our house has been nothing but a play-room. Here I have been your doll-wife, just as at home I used to be papa's doll-child. And the children, in their turn, have been my dolls. I thought it fun when you played with me, just as the children did when I played with them. That has been our marriage, Torvald.

HELMER: There is some truth in what you say, exaggerated and overstrained though it be. But henceforth it shall be different. Play-time is over; now comes the time for education.

NORA: Whose education? Mine, or the children's?

HELMER: Both, my dear Nora.

NORA: Oh, Torvald, you are not the man to teach me to be a fit wife for you.

HELMER: And you can say that?

NORA: And I—how have I prepared myself to educate the children?

HELMER: Nora!

NORA: Did you not say yourself, a few minutes ago, you dared not trust them to me?

HELMER: In the excitement of the moment! Why should you dwell upon that?

NORA: No—you were perfectly right. That problem is beyond me. There is another to be solved first—I must try to educate myself. You are not the man to help me in that. I must set about it alone. And that is why I am leaving you.

HELMER [*jumping up*]:   What—do you mean to say—?

NORA: I must stand quite alone if I am ever to know myself and my surroundings; so I cannot stay with you.

HELMER: Nora! Nora!

NORA: I am going at once. I daresay Christina will take me in for tonight—

HELMER: You are mad! I shall not allow it! I forbid it!

NORA: It is of no use your forbidding me anything now. I shall take with me what belongs to me. From you I will accept nothing, either now or afterwards.

HELMER: What madness this is!

NORA: Tomorrow I shall go home—I mean to what was my home. It will be easier for me to find some opening there.

HELMER: Oh, in your blind inexperience—

NORA: I must try to gain experience, Torvald.

HELMER: To forsake your home, your husband, and your children! And you don't consider what the world will say.

NORA: I can pay no heed to that. I only know that I must do it.

HELMER: This is monstrous! Can you forsake your holiest duties in this way?

NORA: What do you consider my holiest duties?

HELMER: Do I need to tell you that? Your duties to your husband and your children.

NORA: I have other duties equally sacred.

HELMER: Impossible! What duties do you mean?

NORA: My duties towards myself.

HELMER: Before all else you are a wife and a mother.

NORA: That I no longer believe. I believe that before all else I am a human being, just as much as you are—or at least that I should try to become one. I know that most people agree with you, Torvald, and that they say so in books. But henceforth I can't be satisfied with what most people say, and what is in books. I must think things out for myself, and try to get clear about them.

HELMER: Are you not clear about your place in your own home? Have you not an infallible guide in questions like these? Have you not religion?

NORA: Oh, Torvald, I don't really know what religion is.

HELMER: What do you mean?

NORA: I know nothing but what Pastor Hansen told me when I was confirmed. He explained that religion was this and that. When I get away from all this and stand alone, I will look into that matter too. I will see whether what he taught me is right, or, at any rate, whether it is right for me.

HELMER: Oh, this is unheard of! And from so young a woman! But if religion cannot keep you right, let me appeal to your conscience—for I suppose you have some moral feeling? Or, answer me: perhaps you have none?

NORA: Well, Torvald, it's not easy to say. I really don't know—I am all at sea about these things. I only know that I think quite differently from you about them. I hear, too, that the laws are different from what I thought; but I can't believe that they can be right. It appears that a woman has no right to spare her dying father, or to save her husband's life! I don't believe that.

HELMER: You talk like a child. You don't understand the society in which you live.

NORA: No, I do not. But now I shall try to learn. I must make up my mind which is right—society or I.

HELMER: Nora, you are ill; you are feverish; I almost think you are out of your senses.

NORA: I have never felt so much clearness and certainty as tonight.

HELMER: You are clear and certain enough to forsake husband and children?

NORA: Yes, I am.

HELMER: Then there is only one explanation possible.

NORA: What is that?

HELMER: You no longer love me.

NORA: No; that is just it.

HELMER: Nora!—Can you say so!

NORA: Oh, I'm so sorry, Torvald; for you've always been so kind to me. But I can't help it. I do not love you any longer.

HELMER [*mastering himself with difficulty*]:   Are you clear and certain on this point too?

NORA: Yes, quite. That is why I will not stay here any longer.

HELMER: And can you also make clear to me how I have forfeited your love?

NORA: Yes, I can. It was this evening, when the miracle did not happen; for then I saw you were not the man I had imagined.

HELMER: Explain yourself more clearly; I don't understand.

NORA: I have waited so patiently all these eight years; for of course, I saw clearly enough that miracles don't happen every day. When this crushing blow threatened me, I said to myself so confidently, "Now comes the miracle!" When Krogstad's letter lay in the box, it never for a moment occurred to me that you would think of submitting to that man's conditions. I was convinced that you would say to him, "Make it known to all the world"; and that then—

HELMER: Well? When I had given my own wife's name up to disgrace and shame—?

NORA: Then I firmly believed that you would come forward, take everything upon yourself, and say, "I am the guilty one."

HELMER: Nora—!

NORA: You mean I would never have accepted such a sacrifice? No, certainly not. But what would my assertions have been worth in opposition to yours?— That was the miracle that I hoped for and dreaded. And it was to hinder that that I wanted to die.

HELMER: I would gladly work for you day and night, Nora—bear sorrow and want for your sake. But no man sacrifices his honour, even for one he loves.

NORA: Millions of women have done so.

HELMER: Oh, you think and talk like a silly child.

NORA: Very likely. But you neither think nor talk like the man I can share my life with. When your terror was over—not for what threatened me, but for yourself—when there was nothing more to fear—then it seemed to you as though nothing had happened. I was your lark again, your doll, just as before—whom you would take twice as much care of in future, because she was so weak and fragile. [*Stands up.*] Torvald—in that moment it burst upon me that I had been living here these eight years with a strange man, and had borne him three children.—Oh, I can't bear to think of it! I could tear myself to pieces!

HELMER [*sadly*]:   I see it, I see it; an abyss has opened between us.—But, Nora, can it never be filled up?

NORA: As I now am, I am no wife for you.

HELMER: I have strength to become another man.

NORA: Perhaps—when your doll is taken away from you.

HELMER: To part—to part from you! No, Nora, no; I can't grasp the thought.

NORA [*going out, right*]: All the more reason why it has to be. [*She reenters with her coat and a traveling-bag, which she puts on a chair by the table.*]

HELMER: Nora, Nora, not now! Wait until tomorrow.

NORA: I can't spend the night in a strange man's room.

HELMER: But couldn't we live here like brother and sister—

NORA: You know very well how long that would last. [*Throws her shawl over her shoulders.*] Good-bye, Torvald. I won't look in on the children. I know they're in better hands than mine. The way I am now, I'm no use to them.

HELMER: But someday, Nora—someday—?

NORA: How can I tell? I haven't the least idea what'll become of me.

HELMER: But you're my wife, now and wherever you go.

NORA: Listen, Torvald—when a wife deserts her husband's house, as I am doing, I have heard that in the eyes of the law he is free from all duties toward her. At any rate, I release you from all duties. You must not feel yourself bound, any more than I shall. There must be perfect freedom on both sides. There, I give you back your ring. Give me mine.

HELMER: That too?

NORA: That too.

HELMER: Here it is.

NORA: Very well. Now it is all over. I lay the keys here. The servants know about everything in the house—better than I do. Tomorrow, when I have started, Christina will come to pack up the things I brought with me from home. I will have them sent after me.

HELMER: All over! All over! Nora, will you never think of me again?

NORA: Oh, I shall often think of you, and the children, and this house.

HELMER: May I write to you, Nora?

NORA: No—never. You must not.

HELMER: But I must send you—

NORA: Nothing, nothing.

HELMER: I must help you if you need it.

NORA: No, I say. I take nothing from strangers.

HELMER: Nora—can I never be more than a stranger to you?

NORA [*taking her traveling-bag*]: Oh, Torvald, then the miracle of miracles would have to happen—

HELMER: What is the miracle of miracles?

NORA: Both of us would have to change so that—Oh, Torvald, I no longer believe in miracles.

HELMER: But I will believe. Tell me! We must so change that—?

NORA: That communion between us shall be a marriage. Good-bye. [*She goes out by the hall door.*]

HELMER [*sinks into a chair by the door with his face in his hands*]: Nora! Nora! [*He looks around and rises.*] Empty. She is gone. [*A hope springs up in him.*] Ah! The miracle of miracles—?!

[*From below is heard the reverberation of a heavy door closing.*]

THE END

"All I wanted was to say honestly to people: 'Have a look at yourselves and see how bad and dreary your lives are!' The important thing is that people should realize that, for when they do, they will most certainly create another and better life for themselves. I will not live to see it, but I know that it will be quite different, quite unlike our present life. And so long as this different life does not exist, I shall go on saying to people again and again: 'Please, understand that your life is bad and dreary!'"

A doctor whose own life was weighed down and then cut short at the age of forty-four by tuberculosis, Chekhov was by all accounts anything but dreary himself. Born in southern Russia, son of a merchant and grandson of a freed serf, Chekhov came to Moscow in 1879 to study medicine, receiving his degree in 1884. A lover of games, banter, comic nicknames, vaudeville, and French farce, he began to write jokes and comic sketches for journals to help support himself and his family while he was in school. In time, he wrote a number of hilarious one-act plays for the Moscow stage and hundreds of comic stories. The longer plays that made him famous, masterpieces of the world theater like *The Seagull* (1897), *Uncle Vanya* (1899), *The Three Sisters* (1901), and *The Cherry Orchard* (1904), are often described as tragedies, but Chekhov quarreled with the tragic style in which they were staged by the great director Constantin Stanislavsky, insisting that they were really comedies. The plots alone can't decide this question; as Virginia Woolf once remarked, Chekhov's endings seem "as if a tune had stopped short without the expected chords to close it." Everything depends on the perspective.

The perspective that has come to be called "Chekhovian" is usually characterized by understatement and concealed meaning, scenes of autumn and twilight when things are winding down rather than starting up, prematurely aging heroes who hope for very little and don't know what they want, or perhaps don't even really want what they think they want. Overpowering desire is not Chekhov's trademark effect. What matters is less the actions taken and their consequences than how we look at those actions, whether taken or not. In its outlines, "The Lady with the Dog" might be described as a story about the abrupt and awesome power of passionate love. In its sentence-by-sentence texture, however, it seems easily distracted by other, more mundane matters. Something like the threat of ultimate dreariness seems to hang over even the happiest moments. Can love save us from the hopelessness of everyday banality? Or is love too a farce, nothing but more of that banality? It's as if Chekhov wants us to ask but refuses any conclusive answer.

The Lady with the Dog[1]

1

It was said that a new person had appeared on the sea-front: a lady with a little dog. Dmitri Dmitritch Gurov, who had by then been a fortnight at Yalta, and so was fairly at home there, had begun to take an interest in new arrivals. Sitting in Verney's pavilion, he saw, walking on the sea-front, a fair-haired young lady of medium height, wearing a *béret;* a white Pomeranian dog was running behind her.

---

1. Translated by Constance Garnett.

And afterwards he met her in the public gardens and in the square several times a day. She was walking alone, always wearing the same *béret,* and always with the same white dog; no one knew who she was, and every one called her simply "the lady with the dog."

"If she is here alone without a husband or friends, it wouldn't be amiss to make her acquaintance," Gurov reflected.

He was under forty, but he had a daughter already twelve years old, and two sons at school. He had been married young, when he was a student in his second year, and by now his wife seemed half as old again as he. She was a tall, erect woman with dark eyebrows, staid and dignified, and, as she said of herself, intellectual. She read a great deal, used phonetic spelling,[2] called her husband, not Dmitri, but Dimitri, and he secretly considered her unintelligent, narrow, inelegant, was afraid of her, and did not like to be at home. He had begun being unfaithful to her long ago—had been unfaithful to her often, and, probably on that account, almost always spoke ill of women, and when they were talked about in his presence, used to call them "the lower race."

It seemed to him that he had been so schooled by bitter experience that he might call them what he liked, and yet he could not get on for two days together without "the lower race." In the society of men he was bored and not himself, with them he was cold and uncommunicative; but when he was in the company of women he felt free, and knew what to say to them and how to behave; and he was at ease with them even when he was silent. In his appearance, in his character, in his whole nature, there was something attractive and elusive which allured women and disposed them in his favour; he knew that, and some force seemed to draw him, too, to them.

Experience often repeated, truly bitter experience, had taught him long ago that with decent people, especially Moscow people—always slow to move and irresolute—every intimacy, which at first so agreeably diversifies life and appears a light and charming adventure, inevitably grows into a regular problem of extreme intricacy, and in the long run the situation becomes unbearable. But at every fresh meeting with an interesting woman this experience seemed to slip out of his memory, and he was eager for life, and everything seemed simple and amusing.

One evening he was dining in the gardens, and the lady in the *béret* came up slowly to take the next table. Her expression, her gait, her dress, and the way she did her hair told him that she was a lady, that she was married, that she was in Yalta for the first time and alone, and that she was dull there. . . . The stories told of the immorality in such places as Yalta are to a great extent untrue; he despised them, and knew that such stories were for the most part made up by persons who would themselves have been glad to sin if they had been able; but when the lady sat down at the next table three paces from him, he remembered these tales of easy conquests, of trips to the mountains, and the tempting thought of a swift, fleeting love affair, a romance with an unknown woman, whose name he did not know, suddenly took possession of him.

He beckoned coaxingly to the Pomeranian, and when the dog came up to him he shook his finger at it. The Pomeranian growled: Gurov shook his finger at it again.

The lady looked at him and at once dropped her eyes.

2. Literally, "omitted the 'hard sign,'" a characteristic of a progressive intellectual (this anticipated the reform of the Russian alphabet).

"He doesn't bite," she said, and blushed.

"May I give him a bone?" he asked; and when she nodded he asked courteously, "Have you been long in Yalta?"

"Five days."

"And I have already dragged out a fortnight here."

There was a brief silence.

"Time goes fast, and yet it is so dull here!" she said, not looking at him.

"That's only the fashion to say it is dull here. A provincial will live in Belyov or Zhidra and not be dull, and when he comes here it's 'Oh, the dulness! Oh, the dust!' One would think he came from Grenada."

She laughed. Then both continued eating in silence, like strangers, but after dinner they walked side by side; and there sprang up between them the light jesting conversation of people who are free and satisfied, to whom it does not matter where they go or what they talk about. They walked and talked of the strange light on the sea: the water was of a soft warm lilac hue, and there was a golden streak from the moon upon it. They talked of how sultry it was after a hot day. Gurov told her that he came from Moscow, that he had taken his degree in Arts, but had a post in a bank; that he had trained as an opera-singer, but had given it up, that he owned two houses in Moscow.... And from her he learnt that she had grown up in Petersburg, but had lived in S—— since her marriage two years before, that she was staying another month in Yalta, and that her husband, who needed a holiday too, might perhaps come and fetch her. She was not sure whether her husband had a post in a Crown Department or under the Provincial Council—and was amused by her own ignorance. And Gurov learnt, too, that she was called Anna Sergeyevna.

Afterwards he thought about her in his room at the hotel—thought she would certainly meet him next day; it would be sure to happen. As he got into bed he thought how lately she had been a girl at school, doing lessons like his own daughter; he recalled the diffidence, the angularity, that was still manifest in her laugh and her manner of talking with a stranger. This must have been the first time in her life she had been alone in surroundings in which she was followed, looked at, and spoken to merely from a secret motive which she could hardly fail to guess. He recalled her slender, delicate neck, her lovely grey eyes.

"There's something pathetic about her, anyway," he thought, and fell asleep.

2

A week had passed since they had made acquaintance. It was a holiday. It was sultry indoors, while in the street the wind whirled the dust round and round, and blew people's hats off. It was a thirsty day, and Gurov often went into the pavilion, and pressed Anna Sergeyevna to have syrup and water or an ice. One did not know what to do with oneself.

In the evening when the wind had dropped a little, they went out on the groyne[3] to see the steamer come in. There were a great many people walking about the harbour; they had gathered to welcome some one, bringing bouquets. And two peculiarities of a well-dressed Yalta crowd were very conspicuous: the elderly ladies were dressed like young ones, and there were great numbers of generals.

Owing to the roughness of the sea, the steamer arrived late, after the sun had set, and it was a long time turning about before it reached the groyne. Anna Sergeyevna

---

3. Pier.

looked through her lorgnette at the steamer and the passengers as though looking for acquaintances, and when she turned to Gurov her eyes were shining. She talked a great deal and asked disconnected questions, forgetting next moment what she had asked; then she dropped her lorgnette in the crush.

The festive crowd began to disperse; it was too dark to see people's faces. The wind had completely dropped, but Gurov and Anna Sergeyevna still stood as though waiting to see some one else come from the steamer. Anna Sergeyevna was silent now, and sniffed the flowers without looking at Gurov.

"The weather is better this evening," he said. "Where shall we go now? Shall we drive somewhere?"

She made no answer.

Then he looked at her intently, and all at once put his arm round her and kissed her on the lips, and breathed in the moisture and the fragrance of the flowers; and he immediately looked round him, anxiously wondering whether any one had seen them.

"Let us go to your hotel," he said softly. And both walked quickly.

The room was close and smelt of the scent she had bought at the Japanese shop. Gurov looked at her and thought: "What different people one meets in the world!" From the past he preserved memories of careless, good-natured women, who loved cheerfully and were grateful to him for the happiness he gave them, however brief it might be; and of women like his wife who loved without any genuine feeling, with superfluous phrases, affectedly, hysterically, with an expression that suggested that it was not love nor passion, but something more significant; and of two or three others, very beautiful, cold women, on whose faces he had caught a glimpse of a rapacious expression—an obstinate desire to snatch from life more than it could give, and these were capricious, unreflecting, domineering, unintelligent women not in their first youth, and when Gurov grew cold to them their beauty excited his hatred, and the lace on their linen seemed to him like scales.

But in this case there was still the diffidence, the angularity of inexperienced youth, an awkward feeling; and there was a sense of consternation as though some one had suddenly knocked at the door. The attitude of Anna Sergeyevna—"the lady with the dog"—to what had happened was somehow peculiar, very grave, as though it were her fall—so it seemed, and it was strange and inappropriate. Her face dropped and faded, and on both sides of it her long hair hung down mournfully; she mused in a dejected attitude like "the woman who was a sinner" in an old-fashioned picture.

"It's wrong," she said. "You will be the first to despise me now."

There was a water-melon on the table. Gurov cut himself a slice and began eating it without haste. There followed at least half an hour of silence.

Anna Sergeyevna was touching; there was about her the purity of a good, simple woman who had seen little of life. The solitary candle burning on the table threw a faint light on her face, yet it was clear that she was very unhappy.

"How could I despise you?" asked Gurov. "You don't know what you are saying."

"God forgive me," she said, and her eyes filled with tears. "It's awful."

"You seem to feel you need to be forgiven."

"Forgiven? No. I am a bad, low woman; I despise myself and don't attempt to justify myself. It's not my husband but myself I have deceived. And not only just now; I have been deceiving myself for a long time. My husband may be a good, honest man, but he is a flunkey! I don't know what he does there, what his work is, but I know he is a flunkey! I was twenty when I was married to him. I have been tormented by curiosity; I wanted something better. 'There must be a different sort of life,' I said to myself. I wanted to live! To live, to live!...I was fired by curiosity...you don't understand it, but, I swear to God, I could not control myself; something happened to me: I could not be restrained. I told my husband I was ill, and came here....And here I have been walking about as though I were dazed, like a mad creature;...and now I have become a vulgar, contemptible woman whom any one may despise."

Gurov felt bored already, listening to her. He was irritated by the naive tone, by this remorse, so unexpected and inopportune; but for the tears in her eyes, he might have thought she was jesting or playing a part.

"I don't understand," he said softly. "What is it you want?"

She hid her face on his breast and pressed close to him.

"Believe me, believe me, I beseech you..." she said. "I love a pure, honest life, and sin is loathsome to me. I don't know what I am doing. Simple people say: 'The Evil One has beguiled me.' And I may say of myself now that the Evil One has beguiled me."

"Hush, hush!..." he muttered.

He looked at her fixed, scared eyes, kissed her, talked softly and affectionately, and by degrees she was comforted, and her gaiety returned; they both began laughing.

Afterwards when they went out there was not a soul on the sea-front. The town with its cypresses had quite a deathlike air, but the sea still broke noisily on the shore; a single barge was rocking on the waves, and a lantern was blinking sleepily on it.

They found a cab and drove to Oreanda.

"I found out your surname in the hall just now: it was written on the board—Von Diderits," said Gurov. "Is your husband a German?"

"No; I believe his grandfather was a German, but he is an Orthodox Russian himself."

At Oreanda they sat on a seat not far from the church, looked down at the sea, and were silent. Yalta was hardly visible through the morning mist; white clouds stood motionless on the mountain-tops. The leaves did not stir on the trees, grasshoppers chirruped, and the monotonous hollow sound of the sea rising up from below, spoke of the peace, of the eternal sleep awaiting us. So it must have sounded when there was no Yalta, no Oreanda here; so it sounds now, and it will sound as indifferently and monotonously when we are all no more. And in this constancy, in this complete indifference to the life and death of each of us, there lies hid, perhaps, a pledge of our eternal salvation, of the unceasing movement of life upon earth, of unceasing progress towards perfection. Sitting beside a young woman who in the dawn seemed so lovely, soothed and spellbound in these magical surroundings—the sea, mountains, clouds, the open sky—Gurov thought how in reality everything is beautiful in this world when one reflects: everything except what we think or do ourselves when we forget our human dignity and the higher aims of our existence.

A man walked up to them—probably a keeper—looked at them and walked away. And this detail seemed mysterious and beautiful, too. They saw a steamer come from Theodosia, with its lights out in the glow of dawn.

"There is dew on the grass," said Anna Sergeyevna, after a silence.

"Yes. It's time to go home."

They went back to the town.

Then they met every day at twelve o'clock on the sea-front, lunched and dined together, went for walks, admired the sea. She complained that she slept badly, that her heart throbbed violently; asked the same questions, troubled now by jealousy and now by the fear that he did not respect her sufficiently. And often in the square or gardens, when there was no one near them, he suddenly drew her to him and kissed her passionately. Complete idleness, these kisses in broad daylight while he looked round in dread of some one's seeing them, the heat, the smell of the sea, and the continual passing to and fro before him of idle, well-dressed, well-fed people, made a new man of him; he told Anna Sergeyevna how beautiful she was, how fascinating. He was impatiently passionate, he would not move a step away from her, while she was often pensive and continually urged him to confess that he did not respect her, did not love her in the least, and thought of her as nothing but a common woman. Rather late almost every evening they drove somewhere out of town, to Oreanda or to the waterfall; and the expedition was always a success, the scenery invariably impressed them as grand and beautiful.

They were expecting her husband to come, but a letter came from him, saying that there was something wrong with his eyes, and he entreated his wife to come home as quickly as possible. Anna Sergeyevna made haste to go.

"It's a good thing I am going away," she said to Gurov. "It's the finger of destiny!"

She went by coach and he went with her. They were driving the whole day. When she had got into a compartment of the express, and when the second bell had rung, she said:

"Let me look at you once more...look at you once again. That's right."

She did not shed tears, but was so sad that she seemed ill, and her face was quivering.

"I shall remember you...think of you," she said. "God be with you; be happy. Don't remember evil against me. We are parting forever—it must be so, for we ought never to have met. Well, God be with you."

The train moved off rapidly, its lights soon vanished from sight, and a minute later there was no sound of it, as though everything had conspired together to end as quickly as possible that sweet delirium, that madness. Left alone on the platform, and gazing into the dark distance, Gurov listened to the chirrup of the grasshoppers and the hum of the telegraph wires, feeling as though he had only just waked up. And he thought, musing, that there had been another episode or adventure in his life, and it, too, was at an end, and nothing was left of it but a memory....He was moved, sad, and conscious of a slight remorse. This young woman whom he would never meet again had not been happy with him; he was genuinely warm and affectionate with her, but yet in his manner, his tone, and his caresses there had been a shade of light irony, the coarse condescension of a happy man who was, besides, almost twice her age. All the time she had called him kind, exceptional, lofty; obviously he had seemed to her different from what he really was, so he had unintentionally deceived her....

Here at the station was already a scent of autumn; it was a cold evening.

"It's time for me to go north," thought Gurov as he left the platform. "High time!"

3

At home in Moscow everything was in its winter routine; the stoves were heated, and in the morning it was still dark when the children were having breakfast and getting ready for school, and the nurse would light the lamp for a short time. The frosts had begun already. When the first snow has fallen, on the first day of sledge-driving it is pleasant to see the white earth, the white roofs, to draw soft, delicious breath, and the season brings back the days of one's youth. The old limes and birches, white with hoarfrost, have a good-natured expression; they are nearer to one's heart than cypresses and palms, and near them one doesn't want to be thinking of the sea and the mountains.

Gurov was Moscow born; he arrived in Moscow on a fine frosty day, and when he put on his fur coat and warm gloves, and walked along Petrovka, and when on Saturday evening he heard the ringing of the bells, his recent trip and the places he had seen lost all charm for him. Little by little he became absorbed in Moscow life, greedily read three newspapers a day, and declared he did not read the Moscow papers on principle! He already felt a longing to go to restaurants, clubs, dinner-parties, anniversary celebrations, and he felt flattered at entertaining distinguished lawyers and artists, and at playing cards with a professor at the doctors' club. He could already eat a whole plateful of salt fish and cabbage....

In another month, he fancied, the image of Anna Sergeyevna would be shrouded in a mist in his memory, and only from time to time would visit him in his dreams with a touching smile as others did. But more than a month passed, real winter had come, and everything was still clear in his memory as though he had parted with Anna Sergeyevna only the day before. And his memories glowed more and more vividly. When in the evening stillness he heard from his study the voices of his children, preparing their lessons, or when he listened to a song or the organ at the restaurant, or the storm howled in the chimney, suddenly everything would rise up in his memory: what had happened on the groyne, and the early morning with the mist on the mountains, and the steamer coming from Theodosia, and the kisses. He would pace a long time about his room, remembering it all and smiling; then his memories passed into dreams, and in his fancy the past was mingled with what was to come. Anna Sergeyevna did not visit him in dreams, but followed him about everywhere like a shadow and haunted him. When he shut his eyes he saw her as though she were living before him, and she seemed to him lovelier, younger, tenderer than she was; and he imagined himself finer than he had been in Yalta. In the evenings she peeped out at him from the bookcase, from the fireplace, from the corner—he heard her breathing, the caressing rustle of her dress. In the street he watched the women, looking for some one like her.

He was tormented by an intense desire to confide his memories to some one. But in his home it was impossible to talk of his love, and he had no one outside; he could not talk to his tenants nor to any one at the bank. And what had he to talk of? Had he been in love, then? Had there been anything beautiful, poetical, or edifying or simply interesting in his relations with Anna Sergeyevna? And there was nothing for him but to talk vaguely of love, of woman, and no one guessed what it meant; only his wife twitched her black eyebrows, and said: "The part of a lady-killer does not suit you at all, Dimitri."

One evening, coming out of the doctors' club with an official with whom he had been playing cards, he could not resist saying:

"If only you knew what a fascinating woman I made the acquaintance of in Yalta!"

The official got into his sledge and was driving away, but turned suddenly and shouted:

"Dmitri Dmitritch!"

"What?"

"You were right this evening: the sturgeon was a bit too strong!"

These words, so ordinary, for some reason moved Gurov to indignation, and struck him as degrading and unclean. What savage manners, what people! What senseless nights, what uninteresting, uneventful days! The rage for card-playing, the gluttony, the drunkenness, the continual talk always about the same thing. Useless pursuits and conversations always about the same things absorb the better part of one's time, the better part of one's strength, and in the end there is left a life grovelling and curtailed, worthless and trivial, and there is no escaping or getting away from it—just as though one were in a madhouse or a prison.

Gurov did not sleep all night, and was filled with indignation. And he had a headache all next day. And the next night he slept badly; he sat up in bed, thinking, or paced up and down his room. He was sick of his children, sick of the bank; he had no desire to go anywhere or to talk of anything.

In the holidays in December he prepared for a journey, and told his wife he was going to Petersburg to do something in the interests of a young friend—and he set off for S——. What for? He did not very well know himself. He wanted to see Anna Sergeyevna and to talk with her—to arrange a meeting, if possible.

He reached S—— in the morning, and took the best room at the hotel, in which the floor was covered with grey army cloth, and on the table was an inkstand, grey with dust and adorned with a figure on horseback, with its hat in its hand and its head broken off. The hotel porter gave him the necessary information; Von Diderits lived in a house of his own in Old Gontcharny Street—it was not far from the hotel: he was rich and lived in good style, and had his own horses; every one in the town knew him. The porter pronounced the name "Dridirits."

Gurov went without haste to Old Gontcharny Street and found the house. Just opposite the house stretched a long grey fence adorned with nails.

"One would run away from a fence like that," thought Gurov, looking from the fence to the windows of the house and back again.

He considered: to-day was a holiday, and the husband would probably be at home. And in any case it would be tactless to go into the house and upset her. If he were to send her a note it might fall into her husband's hands, and then it might ruin everything. The best thing was to trust to chance. And he kept walking up and down the street by the fence, waiting for the chance. He saw a beggar go in at the gate and dogs fly at him; then an hour later he heard a piano, and the sounds were faint and indistinct. Probably it was Anna Sergeyevna playing. The front door suddenly opened, and an old woman came out, followed by the familiar white Pomeranian. Gurov was on the point of calling to the dog, but his heart began beating violently, and in his excitement he could not remember the dog's name.

He walked up and down, and loathed the grey fence more and more, and by now he thought irritably that Anna Sergeyevna had forgotten him, and was perhaps already amusing herself with some one else, and that that was very natural in a young woman who had nothing to look at from morning till night but that confounded fence. He went back to his hotel room and sat for a long while on the sofa, not knowing what to do, then he had dinner and a long nap.

"How stupid and worrying it is!" he thought when he woke and looked at the dark windows: it was already evening. "Here I've had a good sleep for some reason. What shall I do in the night?"

He sat on the bed, which was covered by a cheap grey blanket, such as one sees in hospitals, and he taunted himself in his vexation:

"So much for the lady with the dog . . . so much for the adventure. . . . You're in a nice fix. . . ."

That morning at the station a poster in large letters had caught his eye. "The Geisha"[4] was to be performed for the first time. He thought of this and went to the theatre.

---

4. An 1896 operetta by the Englishman Sidney Jones.

"It's quite possible she may go to the first performance," he thought.

The theatre was full. As in all provincial theatres, there was a fog above the chandelier, the gallery was noisy and restless; in the front row the local dandies were standing up before the beginning of the performance, with their hands behind them; in the Governor's box the Governor's daughter, wearing a boa, was sitting in the front seat, while the Governor himself lurked modestly behind the curtain with only his hands visible; the orchestra was a long time tuning up; the stage curtain swayed. All the time the audience were coming in and taking their seats Gurov looked at them eagerly.

Anna Sergeyevna, too, came in. She sat down in the third row, and when Gurov looked at her his heart contracted, and he understood clearly that for him there was in the whole world no creature so near, so precious, and so important to him; she, this little woman, in no way remarkable, lost in a provincial crowd, with a vulgar lorgnette[5] in her hand, filled his whole life now, was his sorrow and his joy, the one happiness that he now desired for himself, and to the sounds of the inferior orchestra, of the wretched provincial violins, he thought how lovely she was. He thought and dreamed.

A young man with small side-whiskers, tall and stooping, came in with Anna Sergeyevna and sat down beside her; he bent his head at every step and seemed to be continually bowing. Most likely this was the husband whom at Yalta, in a rush of bitter feeling, she had called a flunkey. And there really was in his long figure, his side-whiskers, and the small bald patch on his head, something of the flunkey's obsequiousness; his smile was sugary, and in his buttonhole there was some badge of distinction like the number on a waiter.

During the first interval the husband went away to smoke; she remained alone in her stall. Gurov, who was sitting in the stalls, too, went up to her and said in a trembling voice, with a forced smile:

"Good-evening."

She glanced at him and turned pale, then glanced again with horror, unable to believe her eyes, and tightly gripped the fan and the lorgnette in her hands, evidently struggling with herself not to faint. Both were silent. She was sitting, he was standing, frightened by her confusion and not venturing to sit down beside her. The violins and the flute began tuning up. He felt suddenly frightened; it seemed as though all the people in the boxes were looking at them. She got up and went quickly to the door; he followed her, and both walked senselessly along passages, and up and down stairs, and figures in legal, scholastic, and civil service uniforms, all wearing badges, flitted before their eyes. They caught glimpses of ladies, of fur coats hanging on pegs; the draughts blew on them, bringing a smell of stale tobacco. And Gurov, whose heart was beating violently, thought:

"Oh, heavens! Why are these people here and this orchestra!..."

And at that instant he recalled how when he had seen Anna Sergeyevna off at the station he had thought that everything was over and they would never meet again. But how far they were still from the end!

On the narrow, gloomy staircase over which was written, "To the Amphitheatre," she stopped.

"How you have frightened me!" she said, breathing hard, still pale and overwhelmed. "Oh, how you have frightened me! I am half dead. Why have you come? Why?"

5. A pair of eyeglasses with a short handle.

"But do understand, Anna, do understand..." he said hastily in a low voice. "I entreat you to understand..."

She looked at him with dread, with entreaty, with love; she looked at him intently, to keep his features more distinctly in her memory.

"I'm so unhappy," she went on, not heeding him. "I have thought of nothing but you all the time; I live only in the thought of you. And I wanted to forget, to forget you; but why, oh why, have you come?"

On the landing above them two schoolboys were smoking and looking down, but that was nothing to Gurov; he drew Anna Sergeyevna to him, and began kissing her face, her cheeks, and her hands.

"What are you doing, what are you doing!" she cried in horror, pushing him away. "We are mad. Go away to-day; go away at once...I beseech you by all that is sacred, I implore you....There are people coming this way!"

Some one was coming up the stairs.

"You must go away," Anna Sergeyevna went on in a whisper. "Do you hear, Dmitri Dmitritch? I will come and see you in Moscow. I have never been happy; I am miserable now, and I never, never shall be happy, never! Don't make me suffer still more! I swear I'll come to Moscow. But now let us part. My precious, good, dear one, we must part!"

She pressed his hand and began rapidly going downstairs, looking round at him, and from her eyes he could see that she really was unhappy. Gurov stood for a little while, listened, then, when all sound had died away, he found his coat and left the theatre.

4

And Anna Sergeyevna began coming to see him in Moscow. Once in two or three months she left S——, telling her husband that she was going to consult a doctor about an internal complaint—and her husband believed her, and did not believe her. In Moscow she stayed at the Slaviansky Bazaar hotel, and at once sent a man in a red cap to Gurov. Gurov went to see her, and no one in Moscow knew of it.

Once he was going to see her in this way on a winter morning (the messenger had come the evening before when he was out). With him walked his daughter, whom he wanted to take to school: it was on the way. Snow was falling in big wet flakes.

"It's three degrees above freezing-point, and yet it is snowing," said Gurov to his daughter. "The thaw is only on the surface of the earth; there is quite a different temperature at a greater height in the atmosphere."

"And why are there no thunderstorms in the winter, father?"

He explained that, too. He talked, thinking all the while that he was going to see *her,* and no living soul knew of it, and probably never would know. He had two lives: one, open, seen and known by all who cared to know, full of relative truth and of relative falsehood, exactly like the lives of his friends and acquaintances; and another life running its course in secret. And through some strange, perhaps accidental, conjunction of circumstances, everything that was essential, of interest and of value to him, everything in which he was sincere and did not deceive himself, everything that made the kernel of his life, was hidden from other people; and all that was false in him, the sheath in which he hid himself to conceal the truth—such, for instance, as his work in the bank, his discussions at the club, his "lower race," his presence with his wife at anniversary festivities—all that was open. And he judged of others by himself, not believing in what he saw, and always believing that every man had his real, most interesting life under the cover of secrecy and under the cover of night. All personal life rested on secrecy, and possibly it was partly on that account that civilized man was so nervously anxious that personal privacy should be respected.

After leaving his daughter at school, Gurov went on to the Slaviansky Bazaar. He took off his fur coat below, went upstairs, and softly knocked at the door. Anna Sergeyevna, wearing his favourite grey dress, exhausted by the journey and the suspense, had been expecting him since the evening before. She was pale; she looked at him, and did not smile, and he had hardly come in when she fell on his breast. Their kiss was slow and prolonged, as though they had not met for two years.

"Well, how are you getting on there?" he asked. "What news?"

"Wait; I'll tell you directly . . . I can't talk."

She could not speak; she was crying. She turned away from him, and pressed her handkerchief to her eyes.

"Let her have her cry out. I'll sit down and wait," he thought, and he sat down in an arm-chair.

Then he rang and asked for tea to be brought him, and while he drank his tea she remained standing at the window with her back to him. She was crying from emotion, from the miserable consciousness that their life was so hard for them; they could only meet in secret, hiding themselves from people, like thieves! Was not their life shattered?

"Come, do stop!" he said.

It was evident to him that this love of theirs would not soon be over, that he could not see the end of it. Anna Sergeyevna grew more and more attached to him. She adored him, and it was unthinkable to say to her that it was bound to have an end some day; besides, she would not have believed it!

He went up to her and took her by the shoulders to say something affectionate and cheering, and at that moment he saw himself in the looking-glass.

His hair was already beginning to turn grey. And it seemed strange to him that he had grown so much older, so much plainer during the last few years. The shoulders on which his hands rested were warm and quivering. He felt compassion for this life, still so warm and lovely, but probably already not far from beginning to fade and wither like his own. Why did she love him so much? He always seemed to women different from what he was, and they loved in him not himself, but the man created by their imagination, whom they had been eagerly seeking all their lives; and afterwards, when they noticed their mistake, they loved him all the same. And not one of them had been happy with him. Time passed, he had made their acquaintance, got on with them, parted, but he had never once loved; it was anything you like, but not love.

And only now when his head was grey he had fallen properly, really in love—for the first time in his life.

Anna Sergeyevna and he loved each other like people very close and akin, like husband and wife, like tender friends; it seemed to them that fate itself had meant them for one another, and they could not understand why he had a wife and she a husband; and it was as though they were a pair of birds of passage, caught and forced to live in different cages. They forgave each other for what they were ashamed of in their past, they forgave everything in the present, and felt that this love of theirs had changed them both.

In moments of depression in the past he had comforted himself with any arguments that came into his mind, but now he no longer cared for arguments; he felt profound compassion, he wanted to be sincere and tender....

"Don't cry, my darling," he said "You've had your cry; that's enough...Let us talk now, let us think of some plan."

Then they spent a long while taking counsel together, talked of how to avoid the necessity for secrecy, for deception, for living in different towns and not seeing each other for long at a time. How could they be free from this intolerable bondage?

"How? How?" he asked, clutching his head. "How?"

And it seemed as though in a little while the solution would be found, and then a new and splendid life would begin; and it was clear to both of them that they had still a long, long road before them, and that the most complicated and difficult part of it was only just beginning.

RABINDRANATH TAGORE ■ (1861–1941)

In the course of a long and immensely distinguished life, the Bengali writer Rabindranath Tagore was a leading figure in the Indian nationalist movement, an antagonist and intimate of Gandhi, the composer of India's national anthem along with many other popular songs, an educational reformer, and winner of the Nobel Prize for Literature. Born in Calcutta three years after Britain took over the government of India, he died six years before national independence in 1947. It is difficult to describe his life and achievements without linking them at every point with the emergence of modern India.

Tagore's father, the son of one of India's richest men, was a noted religious thinker, and Tagore was encouraged to begin publishing at the age of nineteen in a journal run by his family. The foremost Bengali writer of the day, Bankim Chandra Chatterji (1838–1894), acclaimed his youthful poems. He benefited as well from the example of the Bengali reformer Ram Mohan Roy (1772–1833), who offered an early synthesis of European enlightenment with brilliantly reinterpreted Hindu tradition. Roy helped inspire Tagore's lifelong struggle to eliminate prejudice against women, foreigners, and non-Hindus. The Bengali poems of *Gitanjali* (translated into English in 1912) captured the imagination of W. B. Yeats, Ezra Pound, André Gide, and then the Nobel Prize committee, which gave Tagore its prize for literature in 1913. He was knighted in 1915. Tagore's lectures against the dangers of militaristic nationalism, delivered in the midst of World War I, gave grave offense to many British readers, as did his decision to return his knighthood in protest against the Amritsar massacre by the British army in 1919. Still, his international celebrity continued to grow.

An early leader in the movement for India's national liberation, Tagore was the first to call Gandhi "Mahatma," or "Great Soul." No less generous to one who frequently disagreed with him, Gandhi spoke of Tagore as the "Great Sentinel." Repelled by the violence and coercion spawned by Gandhi's Swaraj or self-rule campaign, Tagore withdrew from it in 1921. This withdrawal is the background to his best-known novel, *The Home and the World,* in which a cosmopolitan landowner and his nationalist rival struggle for the affections of the landowner's wife. To some, Tagore's stubborn faith in the unity of mankind has seemed idealistic. To others his life remains a practical inspiration.

PRONUNCIATION:

Rabindranath Tagore: rah-BIN-dra-nath tah-GORE

The Conclusion[1]

1

Apurba Krishna had just passed his BA examination in Calcutta and was returning to his village. On the way his boat had to cross a small river. Later in the year, after the close of the rainy season, it would have been almost dry. Now at the end of Shraban, the monsoon month, it had reached the edge of the village and was lapping at the ruins of the bamboo grove. But after days and days of heavy rain, the sun shone in a cloudless sky.

Apurba's thoughts as he sat in the boat were brimming too. Had we access to the pictures in his young mind we would have seen them dancing like the sun's rays on the wind-ruffled water.

The boat drew up at the usual ghat.[2] From the riverbank Apurba could see the tiled roof of his house through a gap in the trees. No one there knew of his arrival, and so no one had come to meet him. The boatman offered a hand with the luggage, but Apurba refused it and stepped gaily ashore. His feet touched the mud of the ghat, and he fell over, luggage and all. At that instant a melodious peal of high-pitched laughter came from somewhere and startled the birds in a nearby peepul tree.

Extremely embarrassed, Apurba quickly recovered his balance and looked about him. On top of a pile of bricks in course of being unloaded for the local money-lender, a girl sat doubled up with giggles. Apurba recognized her as Mrinmayi, daughter of their recently arrived neighbours. He knew they had previously lived by a big river some distance away, but when the river had swallowed their land they had settled in the village two or three years ago.

Apurba knew much about this girl's reputation. The men of the village referred to her affectionately as Pagli—"Madcap"—but their wives were in a constant state of alarm at her wayward behaviour. All her playmates were boys, and she had vast scorn for girls her own age. In the ranks of biddable children she was regarded as a scourge.

Being her father's favourite made her all the more unruly. Her mother never stopped grumbling about it to her friends. Yet because the father loved Mrinmayi, her tears would have hurt him deeply if he had been at home. That fact, and natural deference to her absent husband, kept the mother from imposing too strict a discipline.

Mrinmayi was dark complexioned with wavy hair that straggled over her shoulders. Her expression was boyish. Her enormous black eyes held no shame or fear, and not the slightest coyness. She was tall, well built, healthy, strong—but of an age people found hard to estimate; otherwise they would have criticized her parents because she was still unmarried. If the boat of some distant zamindar[3] arrived at the ghat, the villagers became impressively alert. As if at a signal, the women pulled their veils down to the tips of their noses, thus concealing their faces like curtains on a stage. But Mrinmayi would arrive holding a naked child to her chest, her unbound hair hanging free. She would stand like a young doe gazing inquisitively in a land where there was neither hunter nor danger. Eventually she would return to her boy playmates and give them elaborate descriptions of the new arrival's manners and mores.

Our Apurba had set eyes on this untamed creature several times during holidays at home, and had occasionally thought of her in a casual way, and sometimes in a not-so-casual way. In the course of life one sees a great many faces, but only a few

594

1. Translated by Krishna Dutta and Andrew Robinson.
2. Broad riverside stairway.
3. Tax collector.

become fixed in the mind, not for their external appeal but for some other quality—a transparency perhaps. Most faces do not give away much of the personality; but the transparent face—the face in a thousand—clearly reveals the mystery behind it and immediately impresses itself on the mind. Mrinmayi's face was one of these. Her eyes held all the wilful femininity of a nimble, unfettered fawn. It was a face that, once seen, was not easy to forget.

Of course its melodious laughter, however charming it might have been to others, sounded rather painful to the unlucky Apurba. Hastily handing the suitcase to the boatman, he set off red-faced towards home.

And so the scene was beautifully set, with the riverbank, the shady trees, the bird-song, the morning sun, the joy of being twenty—no need to mention a pile of bricks: but as for the person sitting on top of them, she bestowed grace even on that dull and solid heap. How cruel of fate to have turned poetry into farce at the first entrance of the first act.

2

The peal of laughter from that pile was still echoing in Apurba's ears when he picked up his mud-smeared case and chadar,[4] took the path beneath the trees, and arrived at his house. His widowed mother was ecstatic at his unexpected arrival. She sent out at once for rice pudding, curds and *rui* fish and caused a bit of a flurry in the neighbourhood. Once the meal was over she introduced the subject of marriage. Apurba had expected it. He had already received many proposals, and in keeping with the slogan of the day had obstinately insisted "BA pass before bride." But now he was a BA, and his mother had been expectant for so long that he knew further excuses would be useless. He said, "Very well, first let me see the girl. Then I'll decide."

His mother said, "I've seen her. You needn't give it a thought."

Apurba was quite prepared to give it a thought himself and said, "Bride must be seen before marriage." His mother thought she had never heard anything so outrageous, but she consented.

That night, after Apurba had put out the lamp and lain down to sleep in his solitary bed, he caught a sound from beyond the patter of midnight rain and the stillness of the village, the sound of sweet high-pitched laughter. His morning downfall bothered him very much, and he pondered how to rectify the impression he had created. The girl doesn't know that I, Apurba Krishna, am an erudite fellow, he thought, who has spent long periods in Calcutta—not a village bumpkin to be dismissed with a laugh because of a trifling slip in some mud.

The next day Apurba had to inspect the potential bride. She was not far away; the family lived in a neighbouring village. He dressed with some care. Discarding his usual dhoti and chadar, he wore a long silk *chapkan,* a puggree[5] on his head, and his best varnished shoes, and set out at dawn with a silk umbrella in his hand.

The instant he entered the prospective father-in-law's house, he was received with pomp and circumstance. In due time a trembling creature, painted and polished, tinsel round the bun in her hair, and wrapped in a fine colourful sari, was produced before him. She was led silently to a corner, where she remained with her head bent almost to her knees and an elderly maidservant at her back to give her courage. Her

4. Long shawl.
5. Turban.

small brother Rakhal now concentrated his total attention upon this latest intruder into the family and scrutinized its puggree, gold watch-chain and newly sprouted beard. After stroking this last a few times, Apurba finally asked with a solemn air, "What have you read?" The dumb-founded ornamented bundle made no response. After a few more questions and some encouraging prods in the ribs from the maid, the girl blurted out in a faint voice, "*Charupath*-Volume-Two-Grammar-Volume-One-Descriptive-Geography-Arithmetic-History-of-India." Simultaneously there came a sudden series of repeated thuds outside the room, and a moment later Mrinmayi raced breathlessly into the room with her hair flying. Without so much as a glance at Apurba Krishna, she grabbed the brother of the bride-to-be by the hand and began to pull him out of the room. But Rakhal refused to cooperate, so absorbing was the situation indoors. The maid did her best to retrieve this by berating Mrinmayi as sharply as propriety permitted. Apurba Krishna meanwhile preserved his own dignity as best he could by sitting bolt upright in his lofty turban and fiddling with the watch-chain across his stomach. When Mrinmayi finally grasped that she could not distract Rakhal, she slapped him loudly on the back, whipped the veil off the girl's head, and dashed out like a whirlwind. The maid growled in fury, and Rakhal tittered at the sudden sight of his sister minus her precious veil. The slap on the back he did not object to at all, for such exchanges often took place between them. Mrinmayi's hair, for instance, once hung halfway down her back, rather than to her shoulders. One day Rakhal had sneaked up behind her and snipped off a handful with a pair of scissors. She had grabbed the scissors from him in anger and finished the job with a few slashes. Waves of hair had fallen to the ground and lain there like clusters of black grapes. This was the system of discipline between them.

The inspection session fell silent and did not endure much longer. Somehow the girl uncurled herself, regained a perpendicular position and returned to the inner rooms escorted by the old maid. Apurba, still stroking his sparse moustache, rose as solemnly as possible and prepared to depart. But when he reached the door he saw that his new pair of varnished shoes had vanished, and no one could find them. Everyone in the house was frightfully put out and hurled endless reproaches in the direction of the culprit. Eventually a desperate Apurba borrowed an old, torn and flapping pair of slippers belonging to the master of the house. With this additional touch to his fancy *chapkan* and puggree, he very gingerly set out along the village path.

By the edge of a pond, at a deserted point on the path, the high-pitched laughter caught him again. It was as if some fun-loving nymph in the forest had seen the slippers and could not suppress her giggles. While Apurba stood hesitating, she emerged brazenly, placed his new pair of shoes on the path, and was about to take to her heels when Apurba managed to grab both her hands and capture her.

Twisting and turning, Mrinmayi tried to free herself but could not. A stray sunbeam slanted through the trees on to her full, mischievous face. Like a curious traveller stooping to see the sunlit bed of a moving stream through clear water, Apurba gravely gazed on Mrinmayi's upturned face with its sparkling eyes, very gradually loosened his grip on his prisoner, and released her. If he had struck her in anger Mrinmayi would not have been at all surprised, but this gentle sentence of punishment in this empty glade quite baffled her.

The whole sky seemed to ring with laughter like the sound of celestial ankle bells. Lost in thought Apurba Krishna plodded home.

3

All day Apurba made up excuses for not joining his mother in the inner rooms. He had an invitation elsewhere; he ate there. The fact is—though it may be hard to swallow—that even someone as erudite, serious minded and original as Apurba was remarkably eager to regain his lost dignity in the eyes of this simple village girl. What did it matter if she had momentarily reduced him to a laughing-stock, then ignored him in favour of some ignoramus named Rakhal? Must he prove to her that he reviewed books for a magazine called *Visvadip* and carried in his suitcase cologne, shoes, Rubini's camphor, coloured letter paper, and a book on how to play the harmonium, not to mention a notebook awaiting future publication like the dawn in the womb of night? Nevertheless, whatever common sense might say, Mr Apurba Krishna Ray was definitely unprepared to admit defeat at the hands of this flighty rustic girl.

When he appeared in the inner rooms that evening, his mother asked, "Well Apu, you saw the girl. Do you approve?"

Somewhat awkwardly Apurba replied, "I saw the girl, Mother, and there was one I liked."

Astounded, his mother said, "You saw *girls?*"

Then, after much shilly-shallying, he revealed that he had selected Mrinmayi, daughter of their neighbour. What a choice after so much education and study!

At first Apurba was considerably abashed, but he was no longer so when his mother began to object vehemently. He sat there insisting doggedly that he would marry no one but Mrinmayi. The more he thought of the dolled-up kind of girl, the more repulsive became the idea of marrying one.

Battle was joined between them, in the form of tiffs, sulks, fasts and sleepless nights, and after two or three days Apurba was victorious. His mother managed to convince herself that Mrinmayi was still immature, that her own mother had been unable to bring her up properly, but that if taken in hand after marriage Mrinmayi's nature would change. Gradually, she came to believe that the girl had a pretty face. It was when she thought of the girl's cropped hair that her heart filled with despair. Yet even that, she hoped, if tied up firmly and thoroughly soaked in oil, might in time respond to treatment.

To the village people Apurba's choice of bride quickly became labelled *apurba*—original. Many of them rather liked "Pagli Mrinmayi," but not, it had to be said, as a possible daughter-in-law.

Her father, Ishan Majumdar, was informed. He was a clerk in a steamship company, responsible for the correct loading and unloading of goods and the sale of tickets from a decrepit tin-roofed hut at a distant riverside station. When he heard the news, he shed tears of sorrow and joy, mingled in proportions unknown. He petitioned his boss, a head-office sahib, for leave of absence to attend his daughter's wedding. The sahib considered this insufficient grounds and turned down the request. Then, expecting a week's holiday at Puja time, Ishan wrote home to postpone the wedding. But Apurba's mother said, "The auspicious days fall in the present month, the wedding cannot be put off." Twice rejected, the distressed father protested no more and went back to weighing goods and selling tickets.

Whereupon Mrinmayi's mother and all the older women of the village assembled and began to instruct Mrinmayi day and night in her future duties. Their stern prohibitions against playfulness and frolicking around, loud laughter, gossip with boys, and eating when hungry succeeded in making marriage sound like a nightmare. An alarmed Mrinmayi thought she had been sentenced to life imprisonment with hanging at the end of it. Like an unbroken pony she stiffened her neck, reared back, and said, "I'm not going to get married."

4

Nevertheless, she did.

Then her lessons began. Overnight, Mrinmayi's world contracted to the confines of her mother-in-law's inner rooms. Her mother-in-law began the task of correcting her. Assuming a minatory expression, she said, "Look, dear, you are not a little girl any longer. We don't tolerate disgraceful manners in our house." Mrinmayi did not grasp what she meant. If my manners are not tolerated here, I'd better go elsewhere, she thought. That afternoon she went missing. A thorough search was launched. Finally the traitor Rakhal led them to her secret hideout, the abandoned old chariot of the village deity Radha Kanta under a banyan tree. It is easy to imagine how the mother-in-law and willing well-wishers set upon the girl.

That night the clouds gathered and rain began with a pattering sound. Apurba Krishna edged a little closer to Mrinmayi as she lay in bed and whispered in her ear, "Mrinmayi, don't you love me?"

"No!" she said violently, "I will never ever love you!" And then she unleashed all her rage and humiliation on Apurba's head like a thunderbolt.

In a wounded voice he said, "Why, what have I done?"

"Why did you marry me?"

A satisfactory counter to this accusation was tricky. But then and there Apurba decided he must win her over.

The next day the mother-in-law saw all the signs of rebellion and locked Mrinmayi in. At first and for some time she fluttered about the room like a newly captured bird. When she could not escape she shredded the bedsheets with her teeth in futile anger and then, lying prone on the floor, pined for her father and wept.

In time someone slowly came and sat beside her. Affectionately he tried to lift her hair off the floor and away from her face. Mrinmayi shook her head vigorously and threw off the hand. Then Apurba bent down to her and said softly, "I've opened the door. Come, let's get away to the back garden." But Mrinmayi's head shook vehemently and said, "No." Apurba tried to lift her chin and said, "Just look who's here." Rakhal, bewildered at seeing Mrinmayi prostrate on the floor, stood at the door. Without looking up she pushed away Apurba's hand. "Rakhal's come to play with you. Won't you go with him?" In a voice loud with irritation she repeated "No!" Rakhal realized he had chosen the wrong moment and fled with a sigh of relief. Apurba sat on in silence. Mrinmayi wept and wept, until she exhausted herself and fell asleep. Apurba tiptoed out and fastened the door behind him.

The next day she received a letter from her father. He grieved over his inability to attend his darling's marriage, and he sent the newly-weds his heartfelt blessings. Mrinmayi went to her mother-in-law and said, "I want to go to my father." The astonished woman exploded at this outlandish request. "Who knows where her father lives, and she wants to go to him! A fantastic notion!" Mrinmayi went away without replying. She went to her room, bolted the door, and in utter hopelessness began to pray to her father as if to God: "Father, come and take me away. I have no one here. I'll die if I stay here."

In the dead of night, while her husband slept, Mrinmayi very carefully opened the door and left the house. Clouds passed over now and then, but the paths were plain in the moonlight. How to choose one leading to her father was beyond her. She assumed that if she followed the route of the mail runner it would take her to any address in the world. She set off on this familiar path. After walking quite a way she grew weary, and night was nearly over. As a few birds uncertain of the time began to give tentative chirps, she found herself on a riverbank in a place like a large market. She paused to think, and then recognized the "jham jham' sound of the mail runner's ankle bells. Then he himself appeared, out of breath, with the mail bag on his shoulder. Mrinmayi rushed up to him and begged, "I want to go to my father at Kushiganj. Will you take me?"

"I don't know where Kushiganj is." With barely a pause for breath he roused the boatman on the mail boat tied up at the ghat, and the boat cast off. He was not allowed to take time to answer questions.

By and by the market awoke. Mrinmayi went down to the ghat and called to another boatman, "Will you take me to Kushiganj?" Before he could reply, someone in the next boat called out, "So it's you, Minu Ma? What are you doing here?" Bursting with impatience she called back, "Banamali, I'm going to my father at Kushiganj. Can you take me in your boat?" Banamali was a boatman from their village and knew this wilful girl very well. "You're going to your father? That's good. Come on, I'll take you." Mrinmayi jumped in.

The boatman cast off. The clouds descended and a torrential downpour began. The boat tossed in a current swollen with the rains of the month of Bhadra. Mrinmayi was overwhelmed with fatigue. She spread the loose end of her sari, lay down, and went tamely to sleep, rocked by the river like a baby in mother nature's arms.

She awoke in her bed in her married home. Seeing her eyes open the maid began to scold. This brought the mother-in-law and a stream of harsh words. Mrinmayi, wide-eyed, stared at her. But when she made a dig at Mrinmayi's father's bad training, Mrinmayi got up, went to the next room, and bolted the door.

Apurba forsook his usual timidity, went to his mother and said, "What harm is there in sending her to her father for a few days?"

His mother turned on him: "She's bewitched!" and then she took up an old theme: with so many girls to choose from, why had he brought home this bone-burning good-for-nothing?

5

All day the downpour continued, and the atmosphere indoors was equally foul. That night, in the early hours, Apurba woke Mrinmayi and said, "Do you want to go to your father?" Suddenly alert, she clutched his hand and said simply, "Yes!" Apurba whispered, "Come then. We'll escape very quietly. I've arranged a boat."

Mrinmayi looked at her husband with profound gratitude. She got up quickly, dressed, and prepared to leave. Apurba left a note to allay his mother's anxiety, and the two of them stepped out. In the dark, without a soul or a sound nearby, she first put her hand in her husband's of her own free will; the tingle of her excitement thrilled his every nerve.

The boat moved out into the night. In spite of her ecstasy Mrinmayi fell asleep almost at once. The next day, what freedom what delight! On both banks were so many villages, markets, fields of grain, forests, other boats passing back and forth. Soon she was plying her husband with a thousand questions about the tiniest and most trivial of sights. What is in that boat? Where have those people come from? What is the name of this place? Questions whose answers could not be found in any of Apurba's college books or extracted from his Calcutta experience. His friends there would have been embarrassed to know that he answered every one of them and that most of his replies did not tally with the truth. He asserted, for instance, that a boat carrying sesame carried linseed, and he called a magistrate's court a zamindar's warehouse and confused the town of Panchberia with that of Rainagar. His wrong replies did not impede in the slightest the satisfaction in the heart of his trustful questioner.

The following evening they reached Kushiganj. In a tin-roofed hut half lit by an oily old lantern Ishan Chandra sat bare-chested on a stool, bent over a huge leather-bound account book resting on a small desk. The newly-weds entered and Mrinmayi said, "Father!" in a tone of voice quite alien to that room. Ishan wept. He could not think what to say or what to do. His daughter and son-in-law were standing in his hut like the princess and prince of an empire, and all he could offer them for thrones were some bales of jute. He was absolutely disoriented. And what about food? As a poor clerk he cooked his own dal[6] and rice—but this was a joyous occasion. Mrinmayi said, "Father, today we'll all cook." Apurba agreed with alacrity.

The room was without space, servants and food, but joy sprang in abundance from the constricted circumstances of poverty, as a fountain gushes with increased force from a tiny aperture.

Three days went by. Twice the river steamer appeared on schedule with many passengers and much hubbub; but by evening the riverbank had emptied, and then the three of them were at liberty once more. They cooked together, making mistakes, and ended up with meals not quite what they had intended, which Mrinmayi, now the devoted wife, served to son-in-law and father-in-law, while they teased her about a thousand shortcomings in her household arrangements and she jingled her bangles in pretended pique. At last Apurba said they really had to leave. Though Mrinmayi pleaded with him for a few more days, her father said, "Better not."

On the last day he hugged his daughter, stroked her head, and said in a choked voice, "Darling, you must be a Lakshmi[7] to brighten your husband's home. Let no one find fault with my Minu." A sobbing Mrinmayi bade farewell and departed with her husband. Ishan turned and went back to his hut, now twice as cramped and cheerless, and resumed weighing goods, day after day, month after month.

6

When this guilty couple returned home, Apurba's mother wore a long face and said nothing. She blamed no one, and they did not try to exonerate themselves. Unspoken reproof and reproach sat sternly upon the house like a stone. At last the atmosphere became unbearable, and Apurba said, "Mother, college has opened, and I had better return to start my law degree."

His mother said indifferently, "What will you do with your wife?"

"She'll stay here."

"No son, it won't work. You must take her with you." She did not employ the usual affectionate form of address.

Apurba in a mortified tone said, "All right." He began to prepare. On the night before his departure he came to bed and found Mrinmayi in tears. Sorrowfully he asked, "I suppose you don't want to go with me to Calcutta?"

"No."

6. Lentils.
7. Celestial maiden.

"Don't you love me?" There was no answer. Sometimes an answer comes easily, but other times the psychology of it is so complex that a shy girl can only keep silent. Apurba asked, "Will you mind leaving Rakhal?"

"Yes," said Mrinmayi without hesitation.

A pang of jealousy as piercing as the point of a needle passed through this Bachelor of Arts at the thought of the boy Rakhal. He said, "I won't be able to return for a long time."

No reply.

"I think it could even be two years or more."

"When you return, bring a Rogers three-bladed knife for Rakhal," Mrinmayi ordered.

Apurba, who had been reclining against a bolster, rose a little at this and said, "So you really do want to stay here."

"Yes, I'll go and stay with my mother."

Apurba sighed and said, "All right, that's that. I won't come back until you write me a letter. Does that make you very happy?"

Mrinmayi felt that this question did not require a reply and dropped off to sleep. But Apurba did not sleep. He propped himself up with a pillow and remained alert.

Late at night the moon rose, and moonlight fell across the bed. Apurba looked at Mrinmayi and thought he saw a fairy princess put to sleep by the touch of a silver wand. If he could only find a wand of gold he could awaken her and exchange a garland of love. But he knew that such a wand would only bring him heartache instead of happiness, while the silver wand had turned her into a blissfully sleeping beauty.

At dawn he woke her and said, "Mrinmayi, it's time for me to go. Let me take you to your mother's house." She got out of bed and stood there, and Apurba took her hands. "I want you to grant me a wish. I have helped you many times. Now that I am going will you give me a reward?"

Mrinmayi was puzzled. "What?"

"Give me one loving kiss."

Apurba's ridiculous request and earnest voice made Mrinmayi burst into laughter. Then she pulled a long face and prepared to kiss him. She came close and could not, giggled and began to laugh again. Twice she tried, and at last gave up, muffling her hilarity with her sari. Apurba pulled her ears as a punishment but made a stern vow: he must not lower his dignity by snatching his reward by force. It must come spontaneously, as a sacred offering—or not at all.

Mrinmayi laughed no more. They set out together for her mother's house in the hush of early morning. When he returned he said to his own mother, "I thought it over and decided to take her to her mother. Having a wife with me in Calcutta would restrict my studies. She'd have no company there. You don't seem to want her here, so I left her with her own mother." In deep resentment, mother and son parted.

7

In her mother's house Mrinmayi found that she could not settle to anything. The entire house seemed to have altered. Time dragged. What to do, where to go, whom to see, she could not decide. It was as if the house and the village had been obliterated by a total eclipse of the sun at midday. And another thing: the desire to go to Calcutta that overwhelmed her now—where had that been last night? Only a day ago, she had had no conception that the life she loved could completely lose its savour. Today, like a mature leaf ready to detach itself from a tree, she effortlessly rejected her former existence.

There is a tale told of a swordsmith so skilled he could make a weapon keen enough to slice a man in two without his feeling a thing; only when he moved would the two parts divide. Mrinmayi was unaware when the Creator's sword severed her childhood from her youth. She looked around her, astonished and bruised, and saw herself anew. Her bedroom in her old home was no longer familiar. The girl who had lived there had disappeared. Now all her memorable moments gathered around another house, another room, another bed.

No one saw Mrinmayi out of doors any more. No one heard her peals of laughter. Rakhal was afraid even to look at her. Games together were out of the question. She said to her mother, "Take me back to my mother-in-law's house."

There Apurba's mother had been grieving, remembering her son's face at farewell. She agonized over his going away angry and leaving his wife with her own mother. Then the mournful Mrinmayi, veiled with due respect, came to touch her mother-in-law's feet. No wonder the old woman wept, embraced the younger, and in a moment was reconciled. Then the mother-in-law looked into the newly married girl's face and was amazed. The Mrinmayi she had known was no more. Could ordinary beings be so transformed? Such an enormous change would require enormous strength. The mother-in-law had intended to correct Mrinmayi's faults one by one, but an invisible Rectifier had taken charge of her and in one fell swoop had moulded her anew. Now Mrinmayi could understand her mother-in-law, and her mother-in-law Mrinmayi. They intertwined as one household like the branches and twigs of a tree.

A profound sense of womanhood filled every fibre of Mrinmayi and made her feel as tender as heartache. Tears of contrition welled up in her like the inky-black rain-clouds that herald the monsoon. They cast deep shadows beneath her eyelashes. She kept thinking to herself: I didn't know my own mind. You could see that. So why didn't you make it up for me? Why didn't you punish me? I didn't want to go to Calcutta with you and behaved like a witch. Why didn't you make me go? You shouldn't have taken any notice of me and my obstinacy.

She thought of that morning when Apurba had captured her on the lonely road by the pond, had said nothing, only looked at her. She saw the path, the spot beneath the trees, the morning sunbeams, the expression in his eyes and all of a sudden she sensed their full meaning. The half-kiss she had given him before he went away now tormented her like a thirsty bird in the desert darting forward and hesitating before a mirage. Over and over again she thought: I wish I'd done that then, I wish I'd said that, if only it had been like that!

Apurba was similarly despairing. He was telling himself: Mrinmayi has never seen my best self. While Mrinmayi was asking herself: what must he think of me? What must he take me for? A difficult, thoughtless, silly girl, not a mature woman capable of returning his love from an unquenchable heart. She felt sick with shame and remorse and began to repay all her debts to Apurba with kisses and caresses on his pillow.

When he had gone away he had said, "If you don't write, I won't come home." When she remembered that, she shut the door and began a letter on the gold-bordered coloured paper that he had given her. Very carefully she drew some lines and then, after smudging her fingers, without bothering to address her husband with a formal salutation she wrote: "Why don't you write to me? How are you?" and "You come home." What more could she say? Everything worth saying had surely been said, but not perhaps with quite the flair for expression to which humans are accustomed. Mrinmayi understood that and racked her brain for ways to put some new words together. "Now write me a letter, and write how you are and come home, mother is well, Bishu and Puti are well, yesterday our black cow had a calf." With this she ended the letter. She put it in an envelope and in drops of love inscribed each letter: Shrijukta Babu Apurba Krishna Ray. But even so much love could not make the lines straight, the letters neatly formed, the spelling faultless. And on an envelope, besides the name, something else is required. This Mrinmayi did not know. To keep the letter private she gave it to a trusted maid for posting. Needless to say, nothing came of it. Apurba did not come home.

8

His mother knew he had a holiday, yet Apurba had not returned. She and Mrinmayi assumed that he was still angry, and when Mrinmayi thought of her letter she was overcome with shame. It had conveyed nothing she really wanted to say, and Apurba would think her even more immature and even less worthy of his efforts. She was transfixed with anxiety. Again and again she asked the maid, "That letter, did you post it?" A thousand times the maid reassured her, "Yes, I dropped it into the box myself. The master should have got it days ago."

A day eventually came when Apurba's mother called Mrinmayi and told her, "Daughter, Apu has been gone a long time, so I am thinking of going to Calcutta to see him. Will you come?" Mrinmayi nodded in agreement, went to her room, shut the door, fell on the bed, embraced the pillow and shook with silent laughter. Then all her pent-up emotion spilled out and she became serious, gloomy and apprehensive. Finally she started to cry.

With no prior warning these two repentant women set out for Calcutta to plead with Apurba for absolution. There they stayed at the home of his married sister.

That evening Apurba, who had given up hope of a letter from Mrinmayi, broke his vow and sat down to write to her. No words came. He groped for one to convey mingled love and hurt. Not finding it, he became contemptuous of his mother tongue. Just then a note arrived from his brother-in-law: "Mother is here. Come at once and have your meal with us. All is well." In spite of this assurance, Apurba went along in a mood of gloomy apprehension. As he entered his sister's house he promptly asked, "Mother, is everything all right?"

"Everything is perfectly all right. You didn't come home for the holiday, so I have come to fetch you."

"You needn't have troubled," Apurba said. "You know I have to prepare for the law exams..." And so on.

When it was time to eat his sister asked, "*Dada*, why isn't your wife with you?"

"My studies, you know..." her brother said solemnly.

His brother-in-law laughed. "All these feeble excuses! You were afraid of us."

The sister said, "You look ferocious enough to frighten any young person."

The banter continued, but Apurba remained downcast. Nothing made him feel happier. All he could think was that since his mother had come, Mrinmayi could easily have come too if she had wished. Perhaps his mother had tried but been turned down. It was hardly something he felt he could question her about: one must simply accept that all human intercourse, in fact all creation, was a maze of deception and error.

After the meal a blustery wind arose and heavy rain came down. Apurba's sister proposed, "*Dada*, do stay with us tonight."

"No, I must get back. I have to work."

"What can you achieve at this hour?" asked his brother-in-law. "Stay. You're not obliged to anyone. Why worry?"

After more urging Apurba acquiesced. His sister said, "*Dada*, you look tired. Don't stay up. Go to bed." That was Apurba's wish as well. He wanted to be alone in bed in the dark and away from all this chatter. At the bedroom door he saw that the room was dark. His sister said, "That wind has blown out your lamp. Shall I bring another?"

"No need. I sleep without a lamp." His sister left.

Apurba began to feel his way towards the bed. He was about to climb into it when with a sudden sound of bangles, a soft arm took him in its embrace, and a pair of lips like a flowering bud smothered him with a flood of passionate kisses that left no space to express surprise. He was startled only for a moment. Then he knew that the half-kiss interrupted by fits of laughter was at long last being concluded among uninhibited tears.

The Twentieth Century

Umberto Boccioni's *Unique Forms of Continuity in Space*, 1913, is the Futurist Manifesto in Bronze. More than the suggested human form that is contained in the aerodynamic wrappings, Boccioni is praising technology and speed. His sculpture evokes the declaration of the Manifesto that "the roaring automobile is more beautiful than the Winged Victory" (the *Nike of Samothrace*). By the middle of the twentieth century, automobile design would indeed take on the winged fenders of Boccioni's sculpture. One year after the 1909 Futurist Manifesto of Marinetti, Boccioni was one of the signers of a Futurist painting manifesto, and author of "Manifesto of Futurist Sculpture" (1912).

HUMAN HISTORY IS PRINCIPALLY A RECORD OF STRIFE. Few centuries in the history of humanity, though, can rival the magnitude, efficiency, and lethal intensity of the twentieth century's conflicts. No single decade, and few individual years in the course of the century, were free of war, revolutions, uprisings, or military and civil confrontation. The most advanced century in terms of its technological and scientific know-how was also marked by deadly results: two world wars, with a combined human death toll of over ninety million; numerous revolutions, at least a handful of which changed the course of history beyond their particular contexts—the Mexican Revolution of 1910, the Russian Revolution of 1917, the Chinese Revolutions between 1924 and 1949, the Cuban Revolution of 1959; wars of emancipation from colonial regimes that culminated in as many as seventeen new nation-states in a single year (1960) in Africa alone; the use of the deadliest weapon ever devised and deployed by humankind—the atomic bombs dropped on Hiroshima and Nagasaki in August 1945 by the United States; and then a so-called "Cold War" under the constant threat of worldwide nuclear conflagration for more than half of the twentieth century, during which 149 localized proxy wars on behalf of the rival ideologies of the superpowers killed more than twenty-three million people. By the end of the century, no part of the earth and no culture in it remained untouched by some external political and military force, cultural influence, or economic intrusion.

The Art of Strife

Like any art form, literature is neither immune to historical conflict nor is it simply symptomatic or reflective of strife that surrounds it. Art itself serves as instrument and as occasion for engagement, contestation, and struggle. And these struggles intensified in the early twentieth century with the eclipse of nineteenth-century ideals of historical progress and rational explanations of motives and wants. The twentieth century upended that orderliness and rationality in its pursuit of the underside of things and the far side of reason. Surface reality no longer sufficed. Twentieth-century art and science were bent on divulging reality's hidden faces, its surrealist para-realities. And while the nineteenth century may have privileged the role of the individual writer and originality of genius in the creation of science, art, and literature, in the twentieth century the cult of novelty and individuality placed a premium on disruption. Thus, the order of continuity was first subjected to the disorder of rupture, breakage, destruction, and eradication before a new generation of artists or writers, or a new school or mode of art, could feel that they had attained cultural legitimacy. The literature that ushered in and succeeded the conflagration of the Great War of 1914–1918 (it would be dubbed the First World War only in retrospect) would always be marked by an obsessive concern for the underside of reason and the darker side of human ingenuity. All subsequent literature to the end of the century would carry the signs of this ambivalence and equivocation, to the point where such ambiguity came to be prized as the mark of accomplished literature.

The language of war becomes also the language of artistic and aesthetic advancement and self-affirmation. The eruption of twentieth-century modernity becomes synonymous with the self-designation of "avant-garde," a military term for

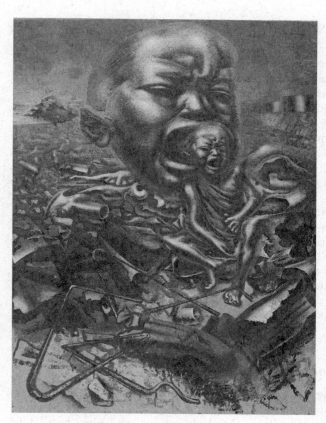

David Alfaro Siqueiros, *Echo of a Scream*, 1937.

the front-line deployment of shock troops. And the self-announcement of a literary movement's arrival invariably is through the shrill proclamation of a "manifesto," or some other form of self-assertive declaration whose shock value spells more an interruption of one's antecedents than an affirmation of one's own program. "Revolution" loses its dictionary sense of returning, or turning over again, in favor of overturning and overthrow of what must be succeeded by the self-contradictory novelty of repetition, often couched in a descriptive language that revels in self-contradiction. Hence, paradoxical assertions like the "the tradition of the new" would be proclaimed by more than one poet and by even a greater number of historians and critics of art and literature. If rational evolution was the progressive cause of eighteenth-century enlightenment and of the science of the nineteenth century, then interruptive revolution was the explanatory method of twentieth-century scientific and artistic processes, especially so in the art of literature.

Modernity, Modernism, Modernization

Modulation and conformity, then, are not attributes one could associate with the twentieth century. Rather, the century elevated modernism, modernization, and modernity to a privileged status as the ultimate mode to which all human activity was destined to advance. Failure to achieve this mode of modes in art, literature, technology, science, or governance pegged a culture as underdeveloped, the opposite of progressive, or, at best, euphemistically designated as in the process of developing. Often judged by criteria of outwardly measurable material achievement, modernity came to be synonymous with the value of what made such material progress possible—namely, modernization.

Modernization moved with and beyond modernism in the arts to designate advancements in technology and industry, especially the scientific harnessing, ordering, and exploitation of natural resources and native populations, with "natural" being rooted in the same etymology as "native." The legacy of late nineteenth-century colonization in Africa and Asia, along with re-colonization in Latin America, neatly divided the world between the civilizing modern colonialist and the premodern native, who depended on the colonist for entry into the course of modern human history. Modernism in the arts was most often in tune with this newly global world order, thus consolidating the division between the modern and the modernizing, the developed and the developing, the arrived and the aspiring but not-yet-accomplished.

Decolonization/Recolonization

The emancipatory movements of decolonization starting at the mid-twentieth century aggravated the contest between the principal ideologies of the century—namely, the Marxist East and the capitalist West. The newly independent nations became the testing ground—and often the battleground—of the two systems competing to bring about the salvation of those new nations in the annals of history. Both systems put forth internationalist conceptions of culture. In the Marxist system, the world was viewed as a transnational culture without frontiers, a world order in which humanity would transcend local divisions and produce a world literature infinitely more meaningful than the bourgeois and parochial. The triumphant capitalist system, for its part, deemed its own cultural paradigm as the point of reference and standard for all world culture, with free capital moving unimpeded in a world without economic borders. In both ideologies, literature was valued in proportion to its universal appeal and its capacity to project the local and the particular onto the world stage and the higher order of humanity's shared cultural heritage.

In the nineteenth century, literature had been closely identified with the project of nation-building. During the twentieth century, as part of the process of decolonization, national literature as such became a subject of debate, as did the language in which literatures would be written and read, since geography, language, culture, and nation did not necessarily coincide as they were arrayed by colonial powers. And when nation, religion, race, ethnicity, and geography would be forcefully constructed as overlapping—secular and scientific history notwithstanding—colonialism and occupation would overflow from the twentieth into the twenty-first century in territorial and cultural struggles from southern Mexico to East Timor in Indonesia to Palestine and Israel.

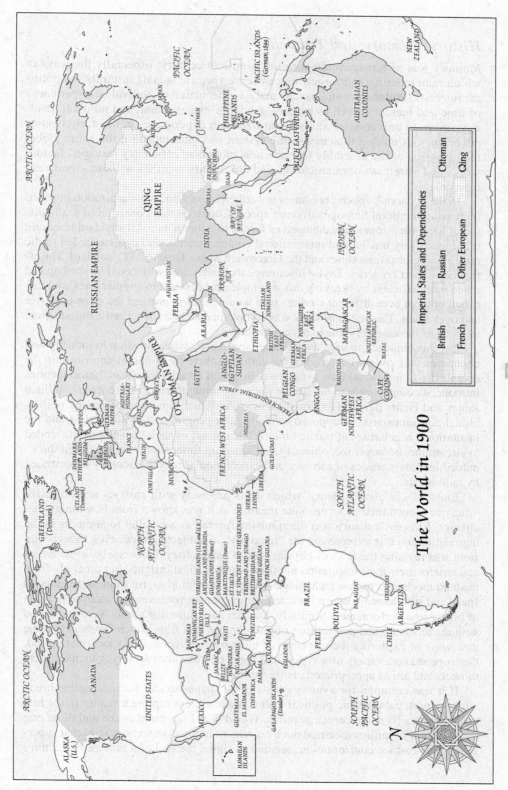

The World in 1900

History, Memory, and Trauma

Memory was of intense interest to the twentieth century, especially the ways in which remembering and forgetting can serve specific social, cultural, and political interests. Philosophy and psychoanalysis speculated on individual experiences of time and memory, even as technology, labor management, and political ideology strove to universalize and standardize such experiences in the early twentieth century. A unified time measuring system was introduced for the entire globe; the invention of the assembly line and new models of efficiency reshaped factory work; and wireless communication tied continents together without significant time delay.

In the economic sphere, pressures toward efficiency and standardization imposed increasing temporal homogeneity and speed. Countries that consisted of many different local time zones saw themselves forced to adopt a national standard to ensure reliable railway traffic, and international communication and commerce led to the creation of global time zones and the Greenwich Mean Time (GMT) standard. The efficiency expert Frederick Taylor discovered that industrial work could be sped up and made more efficient by breaking down complex processes into simpler ones, and distributing them over different workers who would perform one and the same task over and over again. This mode of work was complemented by Henry Ford's introduction, in 1913, of the assembly line in his car factory.

But this tendency toward ever-greater speed and standardization in industry and commerce was counterbalanced in the cultural sphere by in-depth inquiries into the complexity of individual time experience. Sigmund Freud's psychoanalytical theories introduced complexity into the simple notion of remembering. Philosophers William James and Henri Bergson explored the ways in which time is experienced in individual consciousness, as opposed to the regular progression of clock time and the institutional regularities of public time. While one set of social developments tended to streamline, homogenize, objectify and speed up time, another emphasized the irreducible idiosyncrasies of memory and expectation as they are actually experienced by individuals.

Einstein's relativity theory, which deals precisely with abstract and objective time, questioned time as an absolute measure as it was known from Newtonian mechanics. Einstein's theory was often misinterpreted as a parallel to attempts in the humanities and arts to represent the "relativity" of subjective time, even though Einstein was revising the laws of physics, not of psychology. Conversely, some artists and writers drew their inspiration not from psychological insights, but precisely from the hard mechanics of new technologies. The Italian Futurists, for example, exulted in speed and simultaneity, which became their inspiration for inventing innovative types of poetry and performance. Similarly, Dadaist and Surrealist artists were fascinated with the technological possibilities of photography and film, which for them became new ways of exploring the workings of memory and vision. The modernist period, then, opened up a variety of ways of thinking about time and memory, which different thinkers and artists appropriated in diverse ways.

If it was common for avant-gardists of all stripes to call for a complete break with the past, cataclysmic political events made violent rupture a reality in the historical arena. To many contemporaries, World War I appeared as the end of an era: the slaughter of millions, carried out by means of innovative technologies that superseded face-to-face confrontation, seemed to signal the end of a nineteenth-century vision of "civilized" human society. Many of the violent political upheavals of the time echoed the rhetorical proclamations of a historical ground zero: the Mexican Revolution, the Russian Revolution, and the rising fascist movements of Italy, Germany, and Japan, in their own ways, all aimed to wipe clean the slate of historical time and start the future anew. That such complete historical breaks were impossible in practice soon became obvious to those who lived under the new regimes, though the political structures often persisted long after the utopian impulse had vanished.

After World War II, as the rhetoric of historical rupture shifted to those nations that aimed to break away from colonial rule, literature became an important means of working through the history of colonialism and recuperating indigenous myths and memories. In the industrialized world, in the meantime, enormous technological innovations generated new waves of accelerated socioeconomic cycles that spread commercial models into art, information technologies, and scientific knowledge. Since commercialism in combination with new media such as television and the computer seemed to direct people's thinking mostly toward the present, some observers worried that historical thinking might become impossible in the nanosecond culture of the late twentieth century.

History, however, never ceased to be a central cultural concern, as communities and nations around the globe sought to come to terms with legacies of violence, oppression, and discrimination, and they attempted to develop forms of historical discourse that would incorporate a plurality of voices. In Western Europe and the United States, the Holocaust became the main paradigm in debates over how to write and rewrite history, especially as eyewitness testimony progressively succumbed to time's passage. In Spain and Latin America, memories of brutal dictatorial regimes, censorship, death squads, torture, and "disappeared" prisoners came into focus. In Eastern Europe and across the former Soviet Union, the collapse of communist and socialist governments raised a myriad of questions on how to deal with a historical legacy whose relevance to the present was suddenly uncertain. Questions of collaboration and resistance, of historical continuity and rupture emerged in this context in very different guises than in the West.

In countries such as Australia founded as settler colonies, violent controversies erupted over the history of white dominance and discrimination against aboriginals. Histories of racial oppression also occupied center stage in the United States. The South African Truth and Reconciliation Commission, a forum for working through the atrocities committed under white apartheid rule, was one of the most visible manifestations of similar concerns in much of what was formerly called the "Third World." In all of these struggles over what and how to remember historically, literary texts played a crucial role in articulating the perspective of those whose viewpoint had long been ignored, and for preserving the memories of communities that no longer exist.

In such contexts, the psychological notion of "trauma" has helped communities cope with the memory of painful and violent events. Literary texts, with their dual ability to make remote events come close to the reader and yet to preserve a sense of distance through their fictionalization, proved to be one way in which such traumatic histories could be worked through. But recent literature that focuses on the recuperation of history by no means always aims at its darker sides. Quite often, its purpose is simply to draw the readers' attention to individuals and communities that

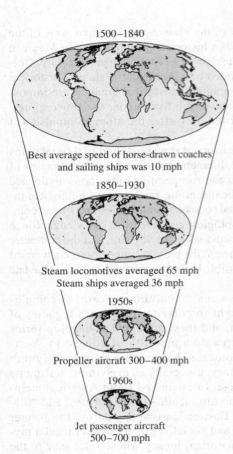

1500–1840

Best average speed of horse-drawn coaches
and sailing ships was 10 mph

1850–1930

Steam locomotives averaged 65 mph
Steam ships averaged 36 mph

1950s

Propeller aircraft 300–400 mph

1960s

Jet passenger aircraft
500–700 mph

Global shrinkage: the effect of changing transport
technologies on "real" distance.

never occupied center stage in world history, but that nevertheless deserve to be remembered as part of a much more abundantly varied cultural legacy than textbook versions of history can convey. In the midst of what some call the "information glut" of the late twentieth and early twenty-first centuries, literature has remained a vital medium for embodying the memories, both individual and collective, that make for a rich and long-range sense of history, even in an era sometimes called posthistorical.

Cultures in Motion: Migration, Travel, and Displacement

In 1990, the anthropologist James Clifford called on ethnographers to shift their focus of study from traditional villages, conceived of as self-contained spatial and cultural entities, to the ways in which cultures traverse space. It was an apt moment for such a call, at the end of a century of unprecedented population movements around the planet. From millions of people displaced by war or political oppression and migrant workers in search of a livelihood to the millions of leisure travelers who seasonally moved between countries and continents, the 1900s were a century on the move.

Political upheaval was a major force behind the uprooting of large numbers of people throughout the century. The military conflicts and geopolitical restructuring of Europe in World War II created nearly a million displaced persons. In the decades since then, the flood of refugees has never stopped: hundreds of thousands fled from communist oppression in Eastern Europe and from colonial violence in northern Africa. Palestinians were dislocated by the creation of Israel in 1948 and the war of 1967, even as the establishment of the state of Israel created a haven for Jews who had been persecuted both in fascist Western Europe and communist Eastern Europe. "Boat people" took to the oceans to escape from political oppression and reprisals in Vietnam, Cuba, and Haiti. Millions of Afghans fled from the Soviet occupation in the 1980s, and over two million people were displaced in Central America during the civil wars of the same decade. Ethnic conflicts and civil wars in sub-Saharan Africa generated an unending stream of internally displaced people and cross-border refugees. The 1990s brought eerie reminiscences of World War II with televised footage of populations on the run in Kosovo. These millions of refugees carried their cultural legacies with them and often recreated them far away from home as "diaspora" cultures, sometimes triggering significant cultural changes in their host environments.

But such diaspora cultures weren't created only by adverse political circumstances. The search for better educational or economic opportunities has likewise taken populations around the globe. Sometimes, these populations followed the routes established by colonialism, migrating from the former colonies to the colonist metropolis, as in the case of Arab minorities in France and Indian and Caribbean emigrants to Britain. The arts in general, and literature in particular, reflected this multiplication of cultural identities in an abundance of themes, genres, and styles that can no longer be attributed to a single national tradition.

But if literature has been greatly enhanced and expanded by what were originally circumstances of dire human necessity, it has also benefited from those travelers who opted to seek different cultural settings. Throughout the twentieth century, artists and writers traveled in unprecedented numbers—sometimes temporarily, sometimes permanently—to places that they thought would better suit their imaginations. American poets and novelists traveled to London and Paris in the 1910s and 1920s, drawn by burgeoning avant-garde movements. In the 1950s and 1960s, they journeyed to India and Japan in search of innovative and perhaps more authentic forms of spiritual inspiration and literary expression. Latin American writers from the 1930s to the 1960s were drawn to Paris, by choice or by political necessity, bridging European literary aesthetics with those of their home countries. Such migrations increased as international communication and transportation became more easily accessible in the second half of the century, and cultural identities became likewise more dispersed. At the same time, a burgeoning global literary market has made international literature more available even to readers and writers who are not willing or able to engage in long-distance travel. James Joyce's *Ulysses*—judged obscene in Ireland and England—was first published in Paris, and the Latin American "boom" novels of the 1960s and 1970s were mostly published in Spain and avidly read by both European and Latin American audiences. Today, Hindi film romances are wildly successful across the Arab world, Brazilian soap operas are viewed by millions in Europe, and the novels of a writer like Salman Rushdie are read around the world.

The heady excitement of global culture traffic, though, should not obscure the fact that many writers' work remains hampered by the difficulties of translation into book markets that are mostly economically driven. When Chinese novelist and playwright Gao Xinjiang was awarded the Nobel Prize in Literature in 2000, booksellers in Europe and the United States went scrambling in search of translations to offer their readers, since his work had not been given much attention by the international book market. By the same token, the celebration of cosmopolitan writers who live in one place, publish their work in another, and are read in several dozen countries should not let us forget that for many writers throughout the twentieth century international migration was a sad necessity rather than a choice. Writers in exile have left their mark on the course of literary history, and exile remained no less a reality for twentieth-century writers.

Science, Technology, and Progress

Few forces have transformed societies around the globe as much as science and technology in the twentieth century. For many, the increasing dependence on science and technology is intimately associated with the notion of progress in material, social, and intellectual terms, just as it was at the beginnings of the Industrial Revolution and throughout much of the nineteenth century. But while the twentieth century gave rise to an unprecedented number of scientific insights and technological innovations, science and technology also came to be questioned with a new intensity, both in terms of their intrinsic nature and in terms of their effects on human societies. This uneasy dependence on science and technology has significant consequences for many dimensions of cultural life, and particularly for literature. In the new millennium, literary creativity is redefining itself both in relation to new media that don't rely on printed text, and in relation to techno-scientific kinds of knowledge and imagination that were conventionally considered the antithesis of literary invention.

Science and technology themselves were transformed by numerous changes in theory and practice over the course of the twentieth century. For the cultural imagination, three changes have held particular significance: the shift in public scientific interest from physics in the early twentieth century to biology, the emergence of new media of communication, and the fusion of information and communication technology that took place during the "digital revolution" in the last quarter of the century. Developments in physical theory between the turn of the century and World War II profoundly changed not only the discipline itself, but exerted an almost magical attraction for the educated public as well as for artists and writers. The public imagination was engaged by concepts such as "relativity theory," "quantum mechanics," or the "uncertainty principle," even though their exact meaning and mathematical bases were often poorly understood. Such concepts led people to wonder what it might mean to live in a world ruled not by certain "laws of nature" but by statistical probabilities, where time and space were no longer the self-evident and self-identical foundations of experience that they had appeared to be.

Physics continued to hold public interest in the aftermath of World War II, as the invention of the atomic bomb and the civilian production of nuclear energy demonstrated its enormous power. But its unprecedented destructiveness in the attacks on Hiroshima and Nagasaki, as well as the long-term dangers associated with nuclear power plants, also aroused skepticism as to the desirability of such "progress," and led to public opposition that reached its peak in the student unrest of the 1960s. In the meantime, however, biology began to attract public attention with the widely publicized discovery of DNA in the 1950s, which promised a completely new understanding of life and reproduction. By the 1990s, public concerns had begun to focus on genetically modified foods and the implications of genetic cloning in some species, including humans. If radioactivity had long become associated with gothic images of deformed or oversized bodies, such images now shifted to the realm of biotechnology. The possibility of artificially created humans in particular called up echoes of literary and cultural motifs with deep roots in history, from Ovid's Pygmalion and the Jewish legend of the Golem to Mary Shelley's *Frankenstein* and the androids, replicants, and cyborgs of much twentieth-century science fiction. As so often in the history of technology, important innovations were accompanied by utopian hopes as well as fears of disaster that represent the latest technologies through age-old cultural templates.

Along with fundamental changes in scientific theory, a whole array of technological inventions transformed twentieth-century societies, from the mass production of automobiles to the invention of plastics, the vacuum tube, and the contraceptive pill. But it was the emergence of new media that proved particularly momentous for the cultural imagination in general and literary production in particular. The invention of the telephone, radio, film, television, the long-playing record, and finally the computer and the World Wide Web all contributed to change the ways in which we imagine space and time. Along with new transportation technologies, the media contributed to shortening distances across the globe and to speeding up the pace at which goods and services could be exchanged. Each new medium also subtly altered the ways in which already existing media functioned. If families in the 1930s would gather around the radio, they would assemble in front of the TV in the 1970s and may now disperse to use an ever-increasing variety of electronic devices conveying stories, images, and games of many sorts. But older media are for the most part not extinguished by the arrival of new ones. In fact, more literary texts are produced and distributed at the turn of the third millennium than ever before. Nevertheless, the social role of literature has changed, since in many literate societies it no longer stands alone as the crucial conveyor of cultural and human values.

New media also open up new possibilities for literary creation broadly understood, as the digital revolution in particular has demonstrated. The invention of computers—especially of the personal computer—and the rise of the Internet have become the latest icons of techno-scientific progress. These have given rise to utopian hopes for a better connected, better informed, more democratic, and more tolerant world society, not unlike the hopes expressed when the radio was invented. While concerns about privacy, surveillance, and commercialism have somewhat dampened the excitement that accompanied the burgeoning of computer culture in the late 1980s and early 1990s, the computer continues to attract those who think of technological innovation as a means for improved human futures. More subtly, the personal computer and the Internet seem to put in question the very meaning of the word "technology" as it was understood in the modern age, when it was mostly associated in the popular imagination with machines and heavy industry. Computers, which increase in power and connectivity even as they shrink in size and communicate by more and more invisible means, seem to defy conventional notions of the "machine," and appear better described by the metaphor of a new "environment." This new medium with its ability to merge text, image, sound, and touch is already beginning to reshape possibilities for story-telling, lyrical expression, and theatrical performance.

At the same time, starting in the 1960s, skepticism toward technology acquired even deeper resonance with the increasingly wide-spread perception that science and technology were contributing to the rapid despoliation of the natural environment. The environmental movement pointed out that technology-based lifestyles were increasingly leading to the destruction of habitats; the extinction of species, the pollution of air, water, and soil; and the rapid consumption of nonrenewable resources. In the former Communist bloc, such perceptions were compounded by the realization that even regimes that explicitly claimed to be acting on behalf of the common people wreaked havoc on nature. In the so-called Third World, environmentalist concerns form an explosive mix with resistance to the economic domination of Western chemical, pharmaceutical, and energy corporations. In all of these contexts, the notion that science and technology are associated with progress in any but the most superficial and material sense has come under intense scrutiny. While such views hardly constitute a majority view in any society, they have given rise to a generalized cultural unease and an ambivalence toward unchecked techno-scientific progress.

In the Romantic period, literature played an important part in formulating concerns over the Enlightenment emphasis on the rational faculties of humans, and over the ways in which science and technology were affecting human minds, bodies, and communities. To this day, literature has often been defined as the medium that best embodies the intuitive and affective faculties that science and technology seem to leave out of consideration. Yet the encounter between literature, science, and technology is a good deal more complicated today than it was at the turn of the nineteenth century. Much of "world literature" did not evolve out of the Western Romantic tradition and defines its relation to techno-scientific modernization quite differently. Even within the Western tradition, resistance to technological dehumanization competes with literary enthusiasm for technology. Literature is in the process of redefining itself in an altered media landscape that sometimes limits the reach of literary expression and sometimes opens up new venues for it. Science, technology, media, and our ambivalence toward them make up part of the force field that shapes literary creation in the third millennium.

YEAR	THE WORLD	LITERATURE
1890		
		1899, 1902 Joseph Conrad, *Heart of Darkness*
1900		
	1900 Boxer Rebellion: nationalist forces rebel in China; suppressed by an international force	
	1901 Queen Victoria dies. Edward VII becomes king (to 1910)	1901 Thomas Mann, *Buddenbrooks*
	1904 Belgian commission investigates atrocities in Congo	1904 Alfred Jarry, *Ubu the King*
	1904–1905 Russo-Japanese War over rivalry in Korea and Manchuria, won by Japan	
	1906 Persian Shah Nasir ud-Din grants constitution	1907 August Strindberg, *The Ghost Sonata* 1907 Premchand publishes first volume of stories, banned by the British as subversive
	1908–1913 Kamal Ataturk leads revolution establishing modernizing government in Turkey	1909 F. I. Marinetti, *Futurist Manifesto*
1910		
	1911–1912 Manchu dynasty overthrown in China; Sun Yat-sen elected president of Republic of China	1911–1923 Rainer Maria Rilke, *Duino Elegies* 1913 Rabindranath Tagore awarded Nobel Prize in Literature
	1913 War in Balkans over Serbian claims to Macedonia	1913–1927 Marcel Proust, *A la recherche du temps perdu*
	1914–1918 World War I	1914 James Joyce, *Dubliners* 1915 Rupert Brooke, *1914 and Other Poems* 1915 Virginia Woolf, *The Voyage Out* 1916 Franz Kafka, *The Metamorphosis*
	1917–1922 Russian Revolution leads to establishment of Soviet Union	1916 W. B. Yeats, *Easter 1916* and other poems on the Irish Rebellion 1918 Lu Xun, "A Madman's Diary" 1918 Tristan Tzara, *Dada Manifesto*
	1919 League of Nations formed 1919 Mahatma Gandhi begins campaign of nonviolent resistance against British rule in India 1919–1922 Irish rebellion leads to formation of independent Republic of Ireland, with Northern Ireland remaining British	1919–1931 Vicente Huidobro, *Altazor*
1920		
	1922 Fascist leader Benito Mussolini becomes Italian prime minister	1922 César Vallejo, *Trilce* 1922 James Joyce, *Ulysses*
	1922 Egypt achieves independence from Britain	1922 T. S. Eliot, *The Waste Land* 1922 Osip Mandelstam, *Tristia*
	1924 Vladimir Lenin dies; Joseph Stalin becomes Soviet leader	1924 André Breton, *First Surrealist Manifesto* 1925 Virginia Woolf, *Mrs Dalloway*
	1927 Charles Lindbergh completes first solo flight across the Atlantic	1928 Mário de Andrade, *Macunaíma: The Hero Without Any Character*
	1929–mid-1930s Wall Street stock market crashes; worldwide depression follows 1929 First airplane flight over South Pole	1929 William Faulkner, *The Sound and the Fury*

continued

YEAR	THE WORLD	LITERATURE
1930		
	1933 Adolf Hitler becomes chancellor of Germany; Nazi party wins elections	
	1935–1949 Mao Zedong's Communist Party gains ascendancy in China	
	1936–1939 Spanish Civil War, won by fascist General Francisco Franco against the constitutional government	1938 Jean-Paul Sartre, *Nausea* 1939–1941 Bertolt Brecht, *Mother Courage and Her Children* 1939, 1954 Aimé Césaire, *Notebook of a Return to the Native Land*
	1936 Italy takes over Ethiopia	
	1939–1945 World War II	
1940		
	1940 Germany, Japan, and Italy form Axis alliance	1940 Richard Wright, *Native Son* 1940 Federico García Lorca, *Poet in New York* 1942 Albert Camus, *The Stranger* 1943 T. S. Eliot, *Four Quartets*
	1945 United States drops atomic bombs on Hiroshima and Nagasaki	1944 Jorge Luis Borges, *Fictions*
	1945 United Nations established	
	1947 India achieves independence from England; Pakistan splits off as separate country	1947 Thomas Mann, *Doktor Faustus*
	1947–1948 Partition of Palestine, creating State of Israel	1948 Léopold Sédar Senghor, *Anthologie de la nouvelle poésie nègre et malgache*
	1948–1949 Soviets blockade West Berlin. U.S. and Western European nations form NATO to oppose Soviet expansion	1948 T. S. Eliot awarded Nobel Prize in Literature
	1949 Apartheid established as South African government policy	1949 George Orwell, *1984* 1949 Bertolt Brecht founds Berliner Ensemble in East Berlin
1950		
	1950–1953 Korean War, resulting in standoff between North and South Korea	
	1951 Chemist Carl Djerassi invents the birth control pill	1952, 1957 Samuel Beckett, *Waiting for Godot* and *Endgame*
	1953 Stalin dies	
	1953 Watson and Crick discover DNA	
	1954–1962 Algerian War of Independence from France	1955 Vladimir Nabokov, *Lolita* 1955 Juan Rulfo, *Pedro Páramo*
	1956 Suez Crisis; Egypt defeats French and English efforts to maintain control of Suez Canal	1956–1957 Naguib Mahfouz, *Cairo Trilogy*
	1956 Hungary's attempt to withdraw from the Warsaw Pact is ended through Soviet military intervention	
	1957 European Economic Community founded, creates the beginnings of a common market in Western Europe	1957 Boris Pasternak, *Doctor Zhivago* 1958 Primo Levi, *Survival in Auschwitz* 1958 Chinua Achebe, *Things Fall Apart* 1959 Günter Grass, *The Tin Drum*
	1959 Fidel Castro overthrows Fulgencio Batista and ascends to power in Cuba	

YEAR	THE WORLD	LITERATURE
1960		
	1960 Seventeen African colonies achieve independence from Europe	1960 Clarice Lispector, *Family Ties*
	1960 Senghor becomes president of Senegal (through 1980)	
	1961 Russian Yuri Gagarin becomes first person in space	1961 Joseph Heller, *Catch-22*
	1961 Berlin Wall built, dividing East and West Berlin	1961 V. S. Naipaul, *A House for Mr. Biswas*
	1962 Cuban missile crisis leads to the brink of nuclear confrontation between the United States and USSR	1962 Derek Walcott, *In a Green Night*
	1962 Publication of Rachel Carson's *Silent Spring;* beginnings of the environmentalist movement	
	1963 U.S. President John F. Kennedy is assassinated	1963 Anna Akhmatova, *Requiem*
	1965–1975 Vietnam War, won by Soviet-supported North against U.S.-supported South	1963 Alain Robbe-Grillet, *Towards a New Novel*
		1963 Julio Cortázar, *Hopscotch*
	1967 Six-day War between Israel and Arab neighbors	1967 Gabriel García Márquez, *One Hundred Years of Solitude*
	1968 Martin Luther King Jr. and Robert Kennedy are assassinated	
	1968 Soviet Union crushes the "Prague Spring" reformist movement	
	1968 Leftist student revolts in Paris, Berlin, and Mexico City; Tet offensive in Vietnam	
	1969 Civil unrest in Ireland leads to the intervention of British troops	1969 Samuel Beckett awarded Nobel Prize in Literature
	1969 American astronauts land on the moon	
1970		
		1972 Italo Calvino, *Invisible Cities*
	1973 Socialist government of Chilean president Salvador Allende overthrown through military coup backed by U.S.	1973 Thomas Pynchon, *Gravity's Rainbow*
	1974 Personal computers begin to be marketed	1974 Emile Habiby, *The Secret Life of Saeed the Pessoptimist*
	1974–1990 Military dictatorship of Augusto Pinochet in Chile	
	1975 General Franco dies; constitutional monarchy established in Spain	1975 Wole Soyinka, *Death and the King's Horseman*
	1976 Mao Zedong dies in China	
	1978 The first "test-tube baby," Louise Brown, born in Britain	
	1979 Nicaraguan dictator Anastasio Somoza Debayle overthrown by Sandinistas	1979 Nadine Gordimer, *Burger's Daughter*
		1979 Mariama Bâ, *So Long a Letter*
	1979 Shah of Iran deposed	

continued

YEAR	THE WORLD	LITERATURE
1980		1980 Mahasweta Devi, *Breast-Giver*
		1981 Salman Rushdie, *Midnight's Children*
		1981 Leslie Marmon Silko, *The Storyteller*
	1984 Bishop Desmond Tutu of South Africa awarded Nobel Peace Prize	1982 Isabel Allende, *The House of the Spirits*
	1986 Philippine dictator Ferdinand Marcos overthrown	1986 Ngugi wa Thiong'o, *Decolonizing the Mind*
	1989 Iran's Ayatollah Khomenei issues a decree of death against Salman Rushdie for *Satanic Verses*	1988 Toni Morrison, *Beloved*
	1989 Eastern European nations begin to break free from Soviet bloc	
	1989 Fall of Berlin Wall; pro-democracy demonstration in Tiananmen Square, Beijing, ends in students' deaths	
1990	1990 East Germany and West Germany reunified	1990 Derek Walcott, *Omeros*
	1990 Iraq invades Kuwait, is repelled by U.S.-led coalition	
	1991 Breakup of Soviet Union	1991 Nadine Gordimer awarded Nobel Prize in Literature
	1992 Earth Summit convened in Rio de Janeiro to discuss global environment	1992 Derek Walcott awarded Nobel Prize in Literature
	1992 Signing of Maastricht Treaty creates European Union	
	1993 World Wide Web becomes accessible to broad public	
	1994 Civil War in Rwanda between Hutu and Tutsi; a half-million casualties	1994 Salman Rushdie, *East, West*
	1994 Nelson Mandela elected first black president of South Africa	
	1996 Cloning of the sheep Dolly	1995 José Saramago, *Blindness*
	1997 British rule ends in Hong Kong, which becomes part of China	
	1999 Adoption of the Euro as common currency by the European Union	1999 Carlos Fuentes, *The Years with Laura Díaz*
2000		2000 Nobel Prize in Literature awarded to Gao Xingjian, first Chinese recipient

One of the greatest English-language novelists, Joseph Conrad didn't seriously begin to learn English until the age of twenty-one. He was already embarked on decades of world travel that would shape his fiction once he finally decided, in 1894, to become a full-time writer. By then, he had long lived in exile from his native Poland—a country no longer even present on the map at that time, carved up between Russia and the Austro-Hungarian empire. Born Josef Teodor Konrad Korzeniowski, he was the son of a noble-born Polish poet and patriot, Apollo, whose ardent nationalism led to his arrest by the Russian government in 1861. The four-year-old Josef and his mother Eva followed Apollo into exile in a bleak village in northern Russia. Ill with tuberculosis, Eva died there in 1865; Apollo also became ill, and was allowed to return to Cracow, where he died in 1869 when Josef was twelve. Josef was raised thereafter by his cultured, cosmopolitan uncle Tadeusz Bobrowski, but he was bored and restless in school in Cracow, and so his uncle eventually sent him to Switzerland with a private tutor. Before long, the tutor had resigned, and instead of returning to Cracow, the sixteen-year-old Josef slipped away to Marseilles and joined the French merchant navy.

He spent the following twenty years as a sailor and eventually as a merchant ship captain, working first for the French merchant marine and then for British companies. His ships took him around the world, to the eastern Mediterranean, Indonesia, China, Thailand, the Philippines, South America, the West Indies, and Africa, giving him the opportunity to see first-hand the unsettling effects of the rising tide of European imperial expansion. At one point he supplemented his observations with active involvement in political conflict: In 1878 he and several friends bought a ship to smuggle guns into Spain on behalf of a claimant to the throne. This effort collapsed, and Conrad was wounded not long after, either in a duel (as he claimed) or else (as his uncle believed) in a suicide attempt. Heavily in debt, he left France and switched into the British merchant marine, where he served for the next sixteen years.

Based in London in 1889 for several months between ships, he began to write *Almayer's Folly,* a novel closely based on some of his South Seas experiences, but in 1890 he interrupted this project to fulfill a childhood dream of sailing up the Congo River. Using an aunt's influence, he went to Brussels and gained an appointment to pilot an aging steamboat upriver—the basis for his most famous novella, *Heart of Darkness* (serialized in 1899, published in book form in 1902). The Congo at the time was controlled by a private corporation set up by King Leopold II of Belgium for personal profit. The king's company was being promoted as a perfect marriage of the noble work of civilization and the profits of free enterprise.

A diary Conrad kept during his journey shows his experience of a much grimmer reality. His work included transporting a sick agent of the Belgian Company downriver; his charge, Georges Klein, died en route. Conrad's encounter with Klein ("Little," in German) provided the germ of the plot of his novella, whose protagonist Marlow journeys upriver to encounter the mysterious, threatening, eloquent company agent Mister Kurtz. Conrad returned to England after four months in the Congo, beset with fever and with a deepening tragic sense of the imperial enterprise and of life overall. "Before the Congo," he later wrote, "I was a mere animal." He became active in the efforts led by the Irish diplomat Roger Casement to expose the cruelty of imperial practices in the Congo, and in his fiction he explored the fatal slippage of idealism into corruption, in language and practice alike.

In 1894 Conrad's life changed in decisive ways. His uncle Bobrowski died, and Conrad decided to settle permanently in England; he Anglicized his name as "Joseph Conrad,"

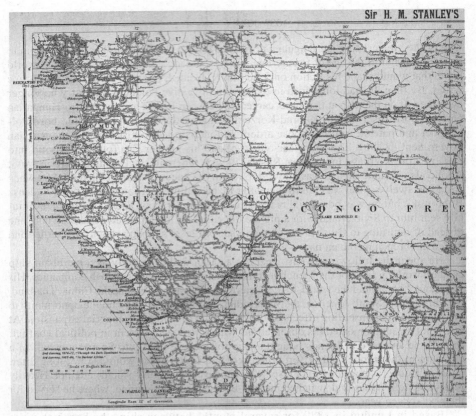

Sir H. M. Stanley's Three African Journeys, c. 1895; detail. When Conrad's Marlow dreamed of voyaging "into the yellow" of the empty spaces on African maps (page 622), he would have been looking at a map like this one. The Congo Free State is shown in yellow on the map, with red, green and blue lines tracing Stanley's travels in the 1870s and 1880s across east and central Africa and up and down the Congo River, as he explored the borders of King Leopold's African domain.

and later married an Englishwoman, Jessie George. He also took a temporary break, which proved to be permanent, from sailing, and completed *Almayer's Folly,* which soon found a publisher. Determined to make a living as a writer, he began a second novel while the first was still in press, and was soon able to establish friendships with some of England's leading writers, including such figures as Bernard Shaw and H. G. Wells. His English friends regarded him with some bemusement as a master of English prose and yet an exotic foreigner; Wells described Conrad driving a carriage rapidly along a country lane, urging his horses on with imperious commands in Polish. General readers were slow to recognize the excellence of his fiction, and such major early works as *Lord Jim, Nostromo,* and *The Secret Agent* sold poorly. As late as 1910 Conrad still considered returning to sea. Gradually, though, he reached a wider public with his tales of the sea and of imperial and political intrigue, becoming a best-selling writer with his novels *Chance* (1910) and *Victory* (1915). World War I only deepened his pessimism about modern life, but he continued to pursue his artistic vocation with undiminished intensity.

In his preface to his early novella *The Nigger of the "Narcissus"* (1897), Conrad issued a personal manifesto for the critical responsibility of the artist, who must seek the truth of life by descending "within himself, and in that lonely region of stress and strife, if he be deserving and fortunate, he finds the terms of his appeal . . . to snatch in a moment of courage, from the remorseless rush of time, a passing phase of life." Conrad insists that this lonely descent into self is not a matter of aesthetic withdrawal but instead should be the basis for "the solidarity . . . which binds men to each other and all mankind to the visible world." That solidarity, however, and even the visibility of the world itself, are severely tested in *Heart of Darkness*. Like many of Conrad's works, it presents a world of shifting uncertainties of vision, understanding, and moral choice. From its multiple framing of stories inside stories to its uncanny portrayal of the African landscape and the Congolese and the displaced Europeans who people it, Conrad's narrative has provoked widely varying responses. Many critics, including the postcolonial critic Edward Said, have seen the novella as a pivotal exposure of the hollowness of imperial rhetoric and the viciousness of imperial practice; others, such as the Nigerian novelist Chinua Achebe, have argued that Conrad's heartfelt imperial critique nonetheless coexists with a stereotyped presentation of African racial primitivism. For other readers, the political dimensions of the story take a secondary place to the interior journey of the story's principal narrator, Charlie Marlow, for whom the African landscape may become a kind of projection of his own hallucinatory loss of psychic moorings.

Heart of Darkness has been one of the most influential narratives of the twentieth century. Chinua Achebe's own great novel *Things Fall Apart* is in part a response to Conrad, as Achebe gives a directly African perspective on the European imperial presence. The Nobel Prize–winning travel writer and novelist V. S. Naipaul has often expressed his indebtedness to Conrad's writing. A notable reuse of Conrad's novella can be found in Francis Ford Coppola's 1979 film *Apocalypse Now,* which cast Marlon Brando in the role of Kurtz and set the story in the midst of the Vietnam War. The novella's haunting blend of stark realities and multiplying uncertainties continues to unsettle and captivate readers today. As Marlow tells his tale to a group of friends aboard a pleasure yacht in the Thames River, his Congo—or King Leopold's Congo—oscillates between an image of all that is uncivilized, or the secret essence of civilization itself.

Heart of Darkness

1

The *Nellie,* a cruising yawl,[1] swung to her anchor without a flutter of the sails, and was at rest. The flood had made, the wind was nearly calm, and being bound down the river, the only thing for it was to come to and wait for the turn of the tide.

The sea-reach of the Thames stretched before us like the beginning of an interminable waterway. In the offing the sea and the sky were welded together without a joint, and in the luminous space the tanned sails of the barges drifting up with the tide seemed to stand still in red clusters of canvas sharply peaked, with gleams of varnished sprits. A haze rested on the low shores that ran out to sea in vanishing flatness. The air was dark above Gravesend, and farther back still seemed condensed into a mournful gloom, brooding motionless over the biggest, and the greatest, town on earth.[2]

---

1. A two-masted ship.
2. London. Gravesend is the last major town on the Thames estuary, from which the river joins the North Sea.

The Director of Companies was our captain and our host. We four affectionately watched his back as he stood in the bows looking to seaward. On the whole river there was nothing that looked half so nautical. He resembled a pilot, which to a seaman is trustworthiness personified. It was difficult to realise his work was not out there in the luminous estuary, but behind him, within the brooding gloom.

Between us there was, as I have already said somewhere, the bond of the sea. Besides holding our hearts together through long periods of separation, it had the effect of making us tolerant of each other's yarns—and even convictions. The Lawyer—the best of old fellows—had, because of his many years and many virtues, the only cushion on deck, and was lying on the only rug. The Accountant had brought out already a box of dominoes, and was toying architecturally with the bones. Marlow sat cross-legged right aft, leaning against the mizzen-mast.[3] He had sunken cheeks, a yellow complexion, a straight back, an ascetic aspect, and, with his arms dropped, the palms of hands outwards, resembled an idol. The Director, satisfied the anchor had good hold, made his way aft and sat down amongst us. We exchanged a few words lazily. Afterwards there was silence on board the yacht. For some reason or other we did not begin that game of dominoes. We felt meditative, and fit for nothing but placid staring. The day was ending in a serenity of still and exquisite brilliance. The water shone pacifically; the sky, without a speck, was a benign immensity of unstained light; the very mist on the Essex marshes was like a gauzy and radiant fabric, hung from the wooded rises inland, and draping the low shores in diaphanous folds. Only the gloom to the west, brooding over the upper reaches, became more sombre every minute, as if angered by the approach of the sun.

And at last, in its curved and imperceptible fall, the sun sank low, and from glowing white changed to a dull red without rays and without heat, as if about to go out suddenly, stricken to death by the touch of that gloom brooding over a crowd of men.

Forthwith a change came over the waters, and the serenity became less brilliant but more profound. The old river in its broad reach rested unruffled at the decline of day, after ages of good service done to the race that peopled its banks, spread out in the tranquil dignity of a waterway leading to the uttermost ends of the earth. We looked at the venerable stream not in the vivid flush of a short day that comes and departs for ever, but in the august light of abiding memories. And indeed nothing is easier for a man who has, as the phrase goes, "followed the sea" with reverence and affection, than to evoke the great spirit of the past upon the lower reaches of the Thames. The tidal current runs to and fro in its unceasing service, crowded with memories of men and ships it has borne to the rest of home or to the battles of the sea. It had known and served all the men of whom the nation is proud, from Sir Francis Drake to Sir John Franklin, knights all, titled and untitled—the great knights-errant of the sea.[4] It had borne all the ships whose names are like jewels flashing in the night of time, from the *Golden Hind* returning with her round flanks full of treasure, to be visited by the Queen's Highness and thus pass out of the gigantic tale, to the *Erebus* and *Terror,* bound on other conquests—and that never returned. It had known the ships and the men. They had sailed from Deptford, from Greenwich, from Erith—the adventurers and the settlers; kings' ships and the ships of men on 'Change; captains,

---

3. A secondary mast at the stern of the ship.

4. Sir Francis Drake (1540–1596) was captain of the *Golden Hind* in the service of Queen Elizabeth I; his reputation came from the successful raids he mounted against Spanish ships returning laden with gold from the New World (South America). In 1845 Sir John Franklin led an expedition in the *Erebus* and *Terror* in search of the Northwest Passage (to the Pacific); all perished.

admirals, the dark "interlopers" of the Eastern trade, and the commissioned "generals" of East India fleets.[5] Hunters for gold or pursuers of fame, they all had gone out on that stream, bearing the sword, and often the torch, messengers of the might within the land, bearers of a spark from the sacred fire. What greatness had not floated on the ebb of that river into the mystery of an unknown earth! . . . The dreams of men, the seed of commonwealths, the germs of empires.

The sun set; the dusk fell on the stream, and lights began to appear along the shore. The Chapman lighthouse, a three-legged thing erect on a mudflat, shone strongly. Lights of ships moved in the fairway—a great stir of lights going up and going down. And farther west on the upper reaches the place of the monstrous town was still marked ominously on the sky, a brooding gloom in sunshine, a lurid glare under the stars.

"And this also," said Marlow suddenly, "has been one of the dark places of the earth."

He was the only man of us who still "followed the sea." The worst that could be said of him was that he did not represent his class. He was a seaman, but he was a wanderer too, while most seamen lead, if one may so express it, a sedentary life. Their minds are of the stay-at-home order, and their home is always with them—the ship; and so is their country—the sea. One ship is very much like another, and the sea is always the same. In the immutability of their surroundings the foreign shores, the foreign faces, the changing immensity of life, glide past, veiled not by a sense of mystery but by a slightly disdainful ignorance; for there is nothing mysterious to a seaman unless it be the sea itself, which is the mistress of his existence and as inscrutable as Destiny. For the rest, after his hours of work, a casual stroll or a casual spree on shore suffices to unfold for him the secret of a whole continent, and generally he finds the secret not worth knowing. The yarns of seamen have a direct simplicity, the whole meaning of which lies within the shell of a cracked nut. But Marlow was not typical (if his propensity to spin yarns be excepted), and to him the meaning of an episode was not inside like a kernel but outside, enveloping the tale which brought it out only as a glow brings out a haze, in the likeness of one of these misty halos that sometimes are made visible by the spectral illumination of moonshine.

His remark did not seem at all surprising. It was just like Marlow. It was accepted in silence. No one took the trouble to grunt even; and presently he said, very slow,—

"I was thinking of very old times, when the Romans first came here, nineteen hundred years ago[6]—the other day. . . . Light came out of this river since—you say Knights? Yes; but it is like a running blaze on a plain, like a flash of lightning in the clouds. We live in the flicker—may it last as long as the old earth keeps rolling! But darkness was here yesterday. Imagine the feelings of a commander of a fine— what d'ye call 'em?—trireme in the Mediterranean, ordered suddenly to the north; run overland across the Gauls in a hurry;[7] put in charge of one of these craft the legionaries,—a wonderful lot of handy men they must have been too—used to build, apparently by the hundred, in a month or two, if we may believe what we read. Imagine him here—the very end of the world, a sea the colour of lead, a sky the colour

5. Deptford, Greenwich, and Erith lie on the Thames between London and Gravesend; "men on 'Change" are brokers on the Stock Exchange; the East India Company, a commercial and trading concern, became *de facto* ruler of large tracts of India in the 18th and 19th centuries.

6. A Roman force under Julius Caesar landed in Britain in 55 B.C.E., but it was not until 43 C.E. that the Emperor Claudius decided to conquer the island.

7. A trireme is an ancient warship, propelled by oarsmen; the Gauls were the pre-Roman tribes who occupied present-day France; they were subdued by Julius Caesar between 58–50 B.C.E.

of smoke, a kind of ship about as rigid as a concertina—and going up this river with stores, or orders, or what you like. Sandbanks, marshes, forests, savages,—precious little to eat fit for a civilised man, nothing but Thames water to drink. No Falernian wine here, no going ashore. Here and there a military camp lost in a wilderness, like a needle in a bundle of hay—cold, fog, tempests, disease, exile, and death,—death skulking in the air, in the water, in the bush. They must have been dying like flies here. Oh yes—he did it. Did it very well, too, no doubt, and without thinking much about it either, except afterwards to brag of what he had gone through in his time, perhaps. They were men enough to face the darkness. And perhaps he was cheered by keeping his eye on a chance of promotion to the fleet at Ravenna by-and-by, if he had good friends in Rome and survived the awful climate. Or think of a decent young citizen in a toga—perhaps too much dice, you know—coming out here in the train of some prefect, or tax-gatherer, or trader even, to mend his fortunes. Land in a swamp, march through the woods, and in some inland post feel the savagery, the utter savagery, had closed round him,—all that mysterious life of the wilderness that stirs in the forest, in the jungles, in the hearts of wild men. There's no initiation either into such mysteries. He has to live in the midst of the incomprehensible, which is also de-testable. And it has a fascination, too, that goes to work upon him. The fascination of the abomination—you know. Imagine the growing regrets, the longing to escape, the powerless disgust, the surrender, the hate."

He paused.

"Mind," he began again, lifting one arm from the elbow, the palm of the hand out-wards, so that, with his legs folded before him, he had the pose of a Buddha preach-ing in European clothes and without a lotus-flower—"Mind, none of us would feel exactly like this. What saves us is efficiency—the devotion to efficiency. But these chaps were not much account, really. They were no colonists; their administration was merely a squeeze, and nothing more, I suspect. They were conquerors, and for that you want only brute force—nothing to boast of, when you have it, since your strength is just an accident arising from the weakness of others. They grabbed what they could get for the sake of what was to be got. It was just robbery with violence, aggravated murder on a great scale, and men going at it blind—as is very proper for those who tackle a darkness. The conquest of the earth, which mostly means the tak-ing it away from those who have a different complexion or slightly flatter noses than ourselves, is not a pretty thing when you look into it too much. What redeems it is the idea only. An idea at the back of it; not a sentimental pretence but an idea; and an un-selfish belief in the idea—something you can set up, and bow down before, and offer a sacrifice to. . . ."

He broke off. Flames glided in the river, small green flames, red flames, white flames, pursuing, overtaking, joining, crossing each other—then separating slowly or hastily. The traffic of the great city went on in the deepening night upon the sleep-less river. We looked on, waiting patiently—there was nothing else to do till the end of the flood; but it was only after a long silence, when he said, in a hesitating voice, "I suppose you fellows remember I did once turn fresh-water sailor for a bit," that we knew we were fated, before the ebb began to run, to hear about one of Marlow's inconclusive experiences.

"I don't want to bother you much with what happened to me personally," he be-gan, showing in this remark the weakness of many tellers of tales who seem so often unaware of what their audience would best like to hear; "yet to understand the effect of it on me you ought to know how I got out there, what I saw, how I went up that river to the place where I first met the poor chap. It was the farthest point of navigation and the culminating point of my experience. It seemed somehow to throw a kind of light on everything about me—and into my thoughts. It was sombre enough too— and pitiful—not extraordinary in any way—not very clear either. No, not very clear. And yet it seemed to throw a kind of light.

"I had then, as you remember, just returned to London after a lot of Indian Ocean, Pacific, China Seas—a regular dose of the East—six years or so, and I was loafing about, hindering you fellows in your work and invading your homes, just as though I had got a heavenly mission to civilise you. It was very fine for a time, but after a bit I did get tired of resting. Then I began to look for a ship—I should think the hardest work on earth. But the ships wouldn't even look at me. And I got tired of that game too.

"Now when I was a little chap I had a passion for maps. I would look for hours at South America, or Africa, or Australia, and lose myself in all the glories of exploration. At that time there were many blank spaces on the earth, and when I saw one that looked particularly inviting on a map (but they all look that) I would put my finger on it and say, When I grow up I will go there. The North Pole was one of these places, I remember. Well, I haven't been there yet, and shall not try now. The glamour's off. Other places were scattered about the Equator, and in every sort of latitude all over the two hemispheres. I have been in some of them, and . . . well, we won't talk about that. But there was one yet—the biggest, the most blank, so to speak—that I had a hankering after.

"True, by this time it was not a blank space any more. It had got filled since my boyhood with rivers and lakes and names. It had ceased to be a blank space of delightful mystery—a white patch for a boy to dream gloriously over. It had become a place of darkness. But there was in it one river especially, a mighty big river, that you could see on the map, resembling an immense snake uncoiled, with its head in the sea, its body at rest curving afar over a vast country, and its tail lost in the depths of the land. And as I looked at the map of it in a shop-window, it fascinated me as a snake would a bird—a silly little bird. Then I remembered there was a big concern, a Company for trade on that river. Dash it all! I thought to myself, they can't trade without using some kind of craft on that lot of fresh water—steamboats! Why shouldn't I try to get charge of one. I went on along Fleet Street, but could not shake off the idea. The snake had charmed me.

"You understand it was a Continental concern, that Trading Society; but I have a lot of relations living on the Continent, because it's cheap and not so nasty as it looks, they say.

"I am sorry to own I began to worry them. This was already a fresh departure for me. I was not used to get things that way, you know. I always went my own road and on my own legs where I had a mind to go. I wouldn't have believed it of myself; but, then—you see—I felt somehow I must get there by hook or by crook. So I worried them. The men said 'My dear fellow,' and did nothing. Then—would you believe it?—I tried the women. I, Charlie Marlow, set the women to work—to get a job. Heavens! Well, you see, the notion drove me. I had an aunt, a dear enthusiastic soul. She wrote: 'It will be delightful. I am ready to do anything, anything for you. It is a glorious idea. I know the wife of a very high personage in the Administration, and also a man who has lots of influence with,' &c., &c. She was determined to make no end of fuss to get me appointed skipper of a river steamboat, if such was my fancy.

"I got my appointment—of course; and I got it very quick. It appears the Company had received news that one of their captains had been killed in a scuffle with the natives. This was my chance, and it made me the more anxious to go. It was only months and months afterwards, when I made the attempt to recover what was left of the body, that I heard the original quarrel arose from a misunderstanding about some hens. Yes, two black hens. Fresleven—that was the fellow's name, a Dane—thought himself wronged somehow in the bargain, so he went ashore and started to hammer the chief of the village with a stick. Oh, it didn't surprise me in the least to hear this, and at the same time to be told that Fresleven was the gentlest, quietest creature that ever walked on two legs. No doubt he was; but he had been a couple of years already out there engaged in the noble cause, you know, and he probably felt the need at last of asserting his self-respect in some way. Therefore he whacked the old nigger mercilessly, while a big crowd of his people watched him, thunderstruck, till some man,—I was told the chief's son,—in desperation at hearing the old chap yell, made a tentative jab with a spear at the white man—and of course it went quite easy between the shoulder-blades. Then the whole population cleared into the forest, expecting all kinds of calamities to happen, while, on the other hand, the steamer Fresleven commanded left also in a bad panic, in charge of the engineer, I believe. Afterwards nobody seemed to trouble much about Fresleven's remains, till I got out and stepped into his shoes. I couldn't let it rest, though; but when an opportunity offered at last to meet my predecessor, the grass growing through his ribs was tall enough to hide his bones. They were all there. The supernatural being had not been touched after he fell. And the village was deserted, the huts gaped black, rotting, all askew within the fallen enclosures. A calamity had come to it, sure enough. The people had vanished. Mad terror had scattered them, men, women, and children, through the bush, and they had never returned. What became of the hens I don't know either. I should think the cause of progress got them, anyhow. However, through this glorious affair I got my appointment, before I had fairly begun to hope for it.

"I flew around like mad to get ready, and before forty-eight hours I was crossing the Channel to show myself to my employers, and sign the contract. In a very few hours I arrived in a city that always makes me think of a whited sepulchre.[8] Prejudice no doubt. I had no difficulty in finding the Company's offices. It was the biggest thing in the town, and everybody I met was full of it. They were going to run an oversea empire, and make no end of coin by trade.

"A narrow and deserted street in deep shadow, high houses, innumerable windows with venetian blinds, a dead silence, grass sprouting between the stones, imposing carriage archways right and left, immense double doors standing ponderously ajar. I slipped through one of these cracks, went up a swept and ungarnished staircase, as arid as a desert, and opened the first door I came to. Two women, one fat and the other slim, sat on straw-bottomed chairs, knitting black wool. The slim one got up and walked straight at me—still knitting with downcast eyes—and only just as I began to think of getting out of her way, as you would for a somnambulist, stood still, and looked up. Her dress was as plain as an umbrella-cover, and she turned round without a word and preceded me into a waiting-room. I gave my name, and looked about. Deal table in the middle, plain chairs all round the walls, on one end a large shining map, marked with all the colours of a rainbow. There was a vast amount of red—good

8. Brussels was the headquarters of the Société Anonyme Belge pour le Commerce du Haut-Congo (Belgian Corporation for Trade in the Upper Congo), with which Conrad obtained his post through the influence of his aunt, Marguerite Poradowska.

to see at any time, because one knows that some real work is done in there, a deuce of a lot of blue, a little green, smears of orange, and, on the East Coast, a purple patch, to show where the jolly pioneers of progress drink the jolly lager-beer.[9] However, I wasn't going into any of these. I was going into the yellow. Dead in the centre. And the river was there—fascinating—deadly—like a snake. Ough! A door opened, a white-haired secretarial head, but wearing a compassionate expression, appeared, and a skinny forefinger beckoned me into the sanctuary. Its light was dim, and a heavy writing-desk squatted in the middle. From behind that structure came out an impression of pale plumpness in a frock-coat. The great man himself. He was five feet six, I should judge, and had his grip on the handle-end of ever so many millions. He shook hands, I fancy, murmured vaguely, was satisfied with my French. *Bon voyage.*

"In about forty-five seconds I found myself again in the waiting-room with the compassionate secretary, who, full of desolation and sympathy, made me sign some document. I believe I undertook amongst other things not to disclose any trade secrets. Well, I am not going to.

"I began to feel slightly uneasy. You know I am not used to such ceremonies, and there was something ominous in the atmosphere. It was just as though I had been let into some conspiracy—I don't know—something not quite right; and I was glad to get out. In the outer room the two women knitted black wool feverishly. People were arriving, and the younger one was walking back and forth introducing them. The old one sat on her chair. Her flat cloth slippers were propped up on a foot-warmer, and a cat reposed on her lap. She wore a starched white affair on her head, had a wart on one cheek, and silver-rimmed spectacles hung on the tip of her nose. She glanced at me above the glasses. The swift and indifferent placidity of that look troubled me. Two youths with foolish and cheery countenances were being piloted over, and she threw at them the same quick glance of unconcerned wisdom. She seemed to know all about them and about me too. An eerie feeling came over me. She seemed uncanny and fateful. Often far away there I thought of these two, guarding the door of Darkness, knitting black wool as for a warm pall, one introducing, introducing continuously to the unknown, the other scrutinising the cheery and foolish faces with unconcerned old eyes. *Ave!* Old knitter of black wool. *Morituri te salutant.*[1] Not many of those she looked at ever saw her again—not half, by a long way.

"There was yet a visit to the doctor. 'A simple formality,' assured me the secretary, with an air of taking an immense part in all my sorrows. Accordingly a young chap wearing his hat over the left eyebrow, some clerk I suppose,—there must have been clerks in the business, though the house was as still as a house in a city of the dead,—came from somewhere upstairs, and led me forth. He was shabby and careless, with ink-stains on the sleeves of his jacket, and his cravat was large and billowy, under a chin shaped like the toe of an old boot. It was a little too early for the doctor, so I proposed a drink, and thereupon he developed a vein of joviality. As we sat over our vermouths he glorified the Company's business, and by-and-by I expressed casually my surprise at him not going out there. He became very cool and collected all at once. 'I am not such a fool as I look, quoth Plato to his disciples,' he said sententiously, emptied his glass with great resolution, and we rose.

---

9. British territories were traditionally marked in red on colonial maps; lager was originally a continental beer, not much drunk in England.

1. Hail! . . . Those who are about to die salute you!—traditional cry of Roman gladiators.

"The old doctor felt my pulse, evidently thinking of something else the while. 'Good, good for there,' he mumbled, and then with a certain eagerness asked me whether I would let him measure my head. Rather surprised, I said Yes, when he produced a thing like calipers and got the dimensions back and front and every way, taking notes carefully. He was an unshaven little man in a threadbare coat like a gaberdine, with his feet in slippers, and I thought him a harmless fool. 'I always ask leave, in the interests of science, to measure the crania of those going out there,' he said. 'And when they come back too?' I asked. 'Oh, I never see them,' he remarked; 'and moreover, the changes take place inside, you know.' He smiled, as if at some quiet joke. 'So you are going out there. Famous. Interesting too.' He gave me a searching glance, and made another note. 'Ever any madness in your family?' he asked, in a matter-of-fact tone. I felt very annoyed. 'Is that question in the interests of science too?' 'It would be,' he said, without taking notice of my irritation, 'interesting for science to watch the mental changes of individuals, on the spot, but . . .' 'Are you an alienist?'[2] I interrupted. 'Every doctor should be—a little,' answered that original, imperturbably. 'I have a little theory which you Messieurs who go out there must help me to prove. This is my share in the advantages my country shall reap from the possession of such a magnificent dependency. The mere wealth I leave to others. Pardon my questions, but you are the first Englishman coming under my observation . . .' I hastened to assure him I was not in the least typical. 'If I were,' said I, 'I wouldn't be talking like this with you.' 'What you say is rather profound, and probably erroneous,' he said, with a laugh. 'Avoid irritation more than exposure to the sun. Adieu. How do you English say, eh? Good-bye. Ah! Good-bye. Adieu. In the tropics one must before everything keep calm.' . . . He lifted a warning forefinger. . . . '*Du calme, du calme. Adieu.*'

"One thing more remained to do—say good-bye to my excellent aunt. I found her triumphant. I had a cup of tea—the last decent cup of tea for many days—and in a room that most soothingly looked just as you would expect a lady's drawing-room to look, we had a long quiet chat by the fireside. In the course of these confidences it became quite plain to me I had been represented to the wife of the high dignitary, and goodness knows to how many more people besides, as an exceptional and gifted creature—a piece of good fortune for the Company—a man you don't get hold of every day. Good heavens! and I was going to take charge of a twopenny-half-penny river-steamboat with a penny whistle attached! It appeared, however, I was also one of the Workers, with a capital—you know. Something like an emissary of light, something like a lower sort of apostle. There had been a lot of such rot let loose in print and talk just about that time, and the excellent woman, living right in the rush of all that humbug, got carried off her feet. She talked about 'weaning those ignorant millions from their horrid ways,' till, upon my word, she made me quite uncomfortable. I ventured to hint that the Company was run for profit.

"'You forget, dear Charlie, that the labourer is worthy of his hire,'[3] she said, brightly. It's queer how out of touch with truth women are. They live in a world of their own, and there had never been anything like it, and never can be. It is too beautiful altogether, and if they were to set it up it would go to pieces before the first sunset. Some confounded fact we men have been living contentedly with ever since the day of creation would start up and knock the whole thing over.

---

2. A psychologist.
3. 1 Timothy 5:18.

"After this I got embraced, told to wear flannel, be sure to write often, and so on—and I left. In the street—I don't know why—a queer feeling came to me that I was an impostor. Odd thing that I, who used to clear out for any part of the world at twenty-four hours' notice, with less thought than most men give to the crossing of a street, had a moment—I won't say of hesitation, but of startled pause, before this commonplace affair. The best way I can explain it to you is by saying that, for a second or two, I felt as though, instead of going to the centre of a continent, I were about to set off for the centre of the earth.

"I left in a French steamer, and she called in every blamed port they have out there, for, as far as I could see, the sole purpose of landing soldiers and custom-house officers. I watched the coast. Watching a coast as it slips by the ship is like thinking about an enigma. There it is before you—smiling, frowning, inviting, grand, mean, insipid, or savage, and always mute with an air of whispering, Come and find out. This one was almost featureless, as if still in the making, with an aspect of monotonous grimness. The edge of a colossal jungle, so dark-green as to be almost black, fringed with white surf, ran straight, like a ruled line, far, far away along a blue sea whose glitter was blurred by a creeping mist. The sun was fierce, the land seemed to glisten and drip with steam. Here and there greyish-whitish specks showed up, clustered inside the white surf, with a flag flying above them perhaps—settlements some centuries old, and still no bigger than pin-heads on the untouched expanse of their background. We pounded along, stopped, landed soldiers; went on, landed custom-house clerks to levy toll in what looked like a Godforsaken wilderness, with a tin shed and a flag-pole lost in it; landed more soldiers—to take care of the custom-house clerks, presumably. Some, I heard, got drowned in the surf; but whether they did or not, nobody seemed particularly to care. They were just flung out there, and on we went. Every day the coast looked the same, as though we had not moved; but we passed various places—trading places—with names like Gran' Bassam, Little Popo,[4] names that seemed to belong to some sordid farce acted in front of a sinister backcloth. The idleness of a passenger, my isolation amongst all these men with whom I had no point of contact, the oily and languid sea, the uniform sombreness of the coast, seemed to keep me away from the truth of things, within the toil of a mournful and senseless delusion. The voice of the surf heard now and then was a positive pleasure, like the speech of a brother. It was something natural, that had its reason, that had a meaning. Now and then a boat from the shore gave one a momentary contact with reality. It was paddled by black fellows. You could see from afar the white of their eyeballs glistening. They shouted, sang; their bodies streamed with perspiration; they had faces like grotesque masks—these chaps; but they had bone, muscle, a wild vitality, an intense energy of movement, that was as natural and true as the surf along their coast. They wanted no excuse for being there. They were a great comfort to look at. For a time I would feel I belonged still to a world of straightforward facts; but the feeling would not last long. Something would turn up to scare it away. Once, I remember, we came upon a man-of-war anchored off the coast. There wasn't even a shed there, and she was shelling the bush. It appears the French had one of their wars going on thereabouts. Her ensign dropped limp like a rag; the muzzles of the long eight-inch guns stuck out all over the low hull; the greasy, slimy swell swung her up lazily and let her down, swaying her thin masts. In the empty immensity of earth, sky, and water, there she was, incomprehensible,

4. Grand Bassam and Grand Popo are the names of ports where Conrad's ship called on its way to the Congo.

firing into a continent. Pop, would go one of the eight-inch guns; a small flame would dart and vanish, a little white smoke would disappear, a tiny projectile would give a feeble screech—and nothing happened. Nothing could happen. There was a touch of insanity in the proceeding, a sense of lugubrious drollery in the sight; and it was not dissipated by somebody on board assuring me earnestly there was a camp of natives—he called them enemies!—hidden out of sight somewhere.

"We gave her letters (I heard the men in that lonely ship were dying of fever at the rate of three a day) and went on. We called at some more places with farcical names, where the merry dance of death and trade goes on in a still and earthy atmosphere as of an overheated catacomb;[5] all along the formless coast bordered by dangerous surf, as if Nature herself had tried to ward off intruders; in and out of rivers, streams of death in life, whose banks were rotting into mud, whose waters, thickened into slime, invaded the contorted mangroves, that seemed to writhe at us in the extremity of an impotent despair. Nowhere did we stop long enough to get a particularised impression, but the general sense of vague and oppressive wonder grew upon me. It was like a weary pilgrimage amongst hints for nightmares.

"It was upward of thirty days before I saw the mouth of the big river. We anchored off the seat of the government. But my work would not begin till some two hundred miles farther on. So as soon as I could I made a start for a place thirty miles higher up.

"I had my passage on a little sea-going steamer. Her captain was a Swede, and knowing me for a seaman, invited me on the bridge. He was a young man, lean, fair, and morose, with lanky hair and a shuffling gait. As we left the miserable little wharf, he tossed his head contemptuously at the shore. 'Been living there?' he asked. I said, 'Yes.' 'Fine lot these government chaps—are they not?' he went on, speaking English with great precision and considerable bitterness. 'It is funny what some people will do for a few francs a month. I wonder what becomes of that kind when it goes up country?' I said to him I expected to see that soon. 'So-o-o!' he exclaimed. He shuffled athwart, keeping one eye ahead vigilantly. 'Don't be too sure,' he continued. 'The other day I took up a man who hanged himself on the road. He was a Swede, too.' 'Hanged himself! Why, in God's name?' I cried. He kept on looking out watchfully. 'Who knows? The sun too much for him, or the country perhaps.'

"At last we opened a reach. A rocky cliff appeared, mounds of turned-up earth by the shore, houses on a hill, others, with iron roofs, amongst a waste of excavations, or hanging to the declivity. A continuous noise of the rapids above hovered over this scene of inhabited devastation. A lot of people, mostly black and naked, moved about like ants. A jetty projected into the river. A blinding sunlight drowned all this at times in a sudden recrudescence of glare. 'There's your Company's station,' said the Swede, pointing to three wooden barrack-like structures on the rocky slope. 'I will send your things up. Four boxes did you say? So. Farewell.'

"I came upon a boiler wallowing in the grass, then found a path leading up the hill. It turned aside for the boulders, and also for an undersized railway-truck lying there on its back with its wheels in the air. One was off. The thing looked as dead as the carcass of some animal. I came upon more pieces of decaying machinery, a stack of rusty rails. To the left a clump of trees made a shady spot, where dark things

---

5. In a letter in May 1890 Conrad wrote: "What makes me rather uneasy is the information that 60 per cent. of our Company's employés return to Europe before they have completed even six months' service. Fever and dysentery! There are others who are sent home in a hurry at the end of a year, so that they shouldn't die in the Congo." According to a 1907 report, 150 out of every 2,000 native Congolese laborers died each month while in company employ; "All along the [railroad] track one would see corpses."

seemed to stir feebly. I blinked, the path was steep. A horn tooted to the right, and I saw the black people run. A heavy and dull detonation shook the ground, a puff of smoke came out of the cliff, and that was all. No change appeared on the face of the rock. They were building a railway. The cliff was not in the way or anything; but this objectless blasting was all the work going on.

"A slight clinking behind me made me turn my head. Six black men advanced in a file, toiling up the path. They walked erect and slow, balancing small baskets full of earth on their heads, and the clink kept time with their footsteps. Black rags were wound round their loins, and the short ends behind wagged to and fro like tails. I could see every rib, the joints of their limbs were like knots in a rope; each had an iron collar on his neck, and all were connected together with a chain whose bights swung between them, rhythmically clinking. Another report from the cliff made me think suddenly of that ship of war I had seen firing into a continent. It was the same kind of ominous voice; but these men could by no stretch of imagination be called enemies. They were called criminals, and the outraged law, like the bursting shells, had come to them, an insoluble mystery from over the sea. All their meagre breasts panted together, the violently dilated nostrils quivered, the eyes stared stonily up-hill. They passed me within six inches, without a glance, with that complete, deathlike indifference of unhappy savages. Behind this raw matter one of the reclaimed, the product of the new forces at work, strolled despondently, carrying a rifle by its middle. He had a uniform jacket with one button off, and seeing a white man on the path, hoisted his weapon to his shoulder with alacrity. This was simple prudence, white men being so much alike at a distance that he could not tell who I might be. He was speedily reassured, and with a large, white, rascally grin, and a glance at his charge, seemed to take me into partnership in his exalted trust. After all, I also was a part of the great cause of these high and just proceedings.

"Instead of going up, I turned and descended to the left. My idea was to let that chain-gang get out of sight before I climbed the hill. You know I am not particularly tender; I've had to strike and to fend off. I've had to resist and to attack sometimes—that's only one way of resisting—without counting the exact cost, according to the demands of such sort of life as I had blundered into. I've seen the devil of violence, and the devil of greed, and the devil of hot desire; but, by all the stars! these were strong, lusty, red-eyed devils, that swayed and drove men—men, I tell you. But as I stood on this hillside, I foresaw that in the blinding sunshine of that land I would become acquainted with a flabby, pretending, weak-eyed devil of a rapacious and pitiless folly. How insidious he could be, too, I was only to find out several months later and a thousand miles farther. For a moment I stood appalled, as though by a warning. Finally I descended the hill, obliquely, towards the trees I had seen.

"I avoided a vast artificial hole somebody had been digging on the slope, the purpose of which I found it impossible to divine. It wasn't a quarry or a sandpit, anyhow. It was just a hole. It might have been connected with the philanthropic desire of giving the criminals something to do. I don't know. Then I nearly fell into a very narrow ravine, almost no more than a scar in the hillside. I discovered that a lot of imported drainage-pipes for the settlement had been tumbled in there. There wasn't one that was not broken. It was a wanton smash-up. At last I got under the trees. My purpose was to stroll into the shade for a moment; but no sooner within than it seemed to me I had stepped into the gloomy circle of some Inferno. The rapids were near, and an uninterrupted, uniform, headlong, rushing noise filled the mournful stillness of the grove, where not a breath stirred, not a leaf moved, with a mysterious sound—as though the tearing pace of the launched earth had suddenly become audible.

"Black shapes crouched, lay, sat between the trees, leaning against the trunks, clinging to the earth, half coming out, half effaced within the dim light, in all the attitudes of pain, abandonment, and despair. Another mine on the cliff went off, followed by a slight shudder of the soil under my feet. The work was going on. The work! And this was the place where some of the helpers had withdrawn to die.

"They were dying slowly—it was very clear. They were not enemies, they were not criminals, they were nothing earthly now,—nothing but black shadows of disease and starvation, lying confusedly in the greenish gloom. Brought from all the recesses of the coast in all the legality of time contracts, lost in uncongenial surroundings, fed on unfamiliar food, they sickened, became inefficient, and were then allowed to crawl away and rest. These moribund shapes were free as air—and nearly as thin. I began to distinguish the gleam of eyes under the trees. Then, glancing down, I saw a face near my hand. The black bones reclined at full length with one shoulder against the tree, and slowly the eyelids rose and the sunken eyes looked up at me, enormous and vacant, a kind of blind, white flicker in the depths of the orbs, which died out slowly. The man seemed young—almost a boy—but you know with them it's hard to tell. I found nothing else to do but to offer him one of my good Swede's ship's biscuits I had in my pocket. The fingers closed slowly on it and held—there was no other movement and no other glance. He had tied a bit of white worsted round his neck— Why? Where did he get it? Was it a badge—an ornament—a charm—a propitiatory act? Was there any idea at all connected with it? It looked startling round his black neck, this bit of white thread from beyond the seas.

"Near the same tree two more bundles of acute angles sat with their legs drawn up. One, with his chin propped on his knees, stared at nothing, in an intolerable and appalling manner: his brother phantom rested its forehead, as if overcome with a great weariness; and all about others were scattered in every pose of contorted collapse, as in some picture of a massacre or a pestilence. While I stood horror-struck, one of these creatures rose to his hands and knees, and went off on all-fours towards the river to drink. He lapped out of his hand, then sat up in the sunlight, crossing his shins in front of him, and after a time let his woolly head fall on his breastbone.

"I didn't want any more loitering in the shade, and I made haste towards the station. When near the buildings I met a white man, in such an unexpected elegance of get-up that in the first moment I took him for a sort of vision. I saw a high starched collar, white cuffs, a light alpaca jacket, snowy trousers, a clear silk necktie, and varnished boots. No hat. Hair parted, brushed, oiled, under a green-lined parasol held in a big white hand. He was amazing, and had a penholder behind his ear.

"I shook hands with this miracle, and I learned he was the Company's chief accountant, and that all the book-keeping was done at this station. He had come out for a moment, he said, 'to get a breath of fresh air.' The expression sounded wonderfully odd, with its suggestion of sedentary desk-life. I wouldn't have mentioned the fellow to you at all, only it was from his lips that I first heard the name of the man who is so indissolubly connected with the memories of that time. Moreover, I respected the fellow. Yes; I respected his collars, his vast cuffs, his brushed hair. His appearance was certainly that of a hairdresser's dummy; but in the great demoralisation of the land he kept up his appearance. That's backbone. His starched collars and got-up shirt-fronts were achievements of character. He had been out nearly three years; and, later on, I could not help asking him how he managed to sport such linen. He had just the faintest blush, and said modestly, 'I've been teaching one of the native women about the station. It was difficult. She had a distaste for the work.' Thus this man had verily accomplished something. And he was devoted to his books, which were in apple-pie order.

"Everything else in the station was in a muddle,—heads, things, buildings. Strings of dusty niggers with splay feet arrived and departed; a stream of manufactured goods, rubbishy cottons, beads, and brass-wire set into the depths of darkness, and in return came a precious trickle of ivory.

"I had to wait in the station for ten days—an eternity. I lived in a hut in the yard, but to be out of the chaos I would sometimes get into the accountant's office. It was built of horizontal planks, and so badly put together that, as he bent over his high desk, he was barred from neck to heels with narrow strips of sunlight. There was no need to open the big shutter to see. It was hot there too; big flies buzzed fiendishly, and did not sting, but stabbed. I sat generally on the floor, while, of faultless appearance (and even slightly scented), perching on a high stool, he wrote, he wrote. Sometimes he stood up for exercise. When a truckle-bed with a sick man (some invalided agent from up-country) was put in there, he exhibited a gentle annoyance. 'The groans of this sick person,' he said, 'distract my attention. And without that it is extremely difficult to guard against clerical errors in this climate.'

"One day he remarked, without lifting his head, 'In the interior you will no doubt meet Mr Kurtz.' On my asking who Mr Kurtz was, he said he was a first-class agent; and seeing my disappointment at this information, he added slowly, laying down his pen, 'He is a very remarkable person.' Further questions elicited from him that Mr Kurtz was at present in charge of a trading-post, a very important one, in the true ivory-country, at 'the very bottom of there. Sends in as much ivory as all the others put together . . .' He began to write again. The sick man was too ill to groan. The flies buzzed in a great peace.

"Suddenly there was a growing murmur of voices and a great tramping of feet. A caravan had come in. A violent babble of uncouth sounds burst out on the other side of the planks. All the carriers were speaking together, and in the midst of the uproar the lamentable voice of the chief agent was heard 'giving it up' tearfully for the twentieth time that day. . . . He rose slowly. 'What a frightful row,' he said. He crossed the room gently to look at the sick man, and returning, said to me, 'He does not hear.' 'What! Dead?' I asked, startled. 'No, not yet,' he answered, with great composure. Then, alluding with a toss of the head to the tumult in the station-yard, 'When one has got to make correct entries, one comes to hate those savages—hate them to the death.' He remained thoughtful for a moment. 'When you see Mr Kurtz,' he went on, 'tell him from me that everything here'—he glanced at the desk—'is very satisfactory. I don't like to write to him—with those messengers of ours you never know who may get hold of your letter—at that Central Station.' He stared at me for a moment with his mild, bulging eyes. 'Oh, he will go far, very far,' he began again. 'He will be a somebody in the Administration before long. They, above—the Council in Europe, you know—mean him to be.'

"He turned to his work. The noise outside had ceased, and presently in going out I stopped at the door. In the steady buzz of flies the homeward-bound agent was lying flushed and insensible; the other, bent over his books, was making correct entries of perfectly correct transactions; and fifty feet below the doorstep I could see the still tree-tops of the grove of death.

"Next day I left that station at last, with a caravan of sixty men, for a two-hundred-mile tramp.

"No use telling you much about that. Paths, paths, everywhere; a stamped-in network of paths spreading over the empty land, through long grass, through burnt grass, through thickets, down and up chilly ravines, up and down stony hills ablaze with heat; and a solitude, a solitude, nobody, not a hut. The population had cleared out a long time ago. Well, if a lot of mysterious niggers armed with all kinds of fearful weapons suddenly took to travelling on the road between Deal[6] and Gravesend, catching the yokels right and left to carry heavy loads for them, I fancy every farm and cottage thereabouts would get empty very soon. Only here the dwellings were gone too. Still, I passed through several abandoned villages. There's something pathetically childish in the ruins of grass walls. Day after day, with the stamp and shuffle of sixty pair of bare feet behind me, each pair under a 60-lb. load. Camp, cook, sleep, strike camp, march. Now and then a carrier dead in harness, at rest in the long grass near the path, with an empty water-gourd and his long staff lying by his side. A great silence around and above. Perhaps on some quiet night the tremor of far-off drums, sinking, swelling, a tremor vast, faint; a sound weird, appealing, suggestive, and wild—and perhaps with as profound a meaning as the sound of bells in a Christian country. Once a white man in an unbuttoned uniform, camping on the path with an armed escort of lank Zanzibaris,[7] very hospitable and festive—not to say drunk. Was looking after the upkeep of the road, he declared. Can't say I saw any road or any upkeep, unless the body of a middle-aged negro, with a bullet-hole in the forehead, upon which I absolutely stumbled three miles farther on, may be considered as a permanent improvement. I had a white companion too, not a bad chap, but rather too fleshy and with the exasperating habit of fainting on the hot hillsides, miles away from the least bit of shade and water. Annoying, you know, to hold your own coat like a parasol over a man's head while he is coming-to. I couldn't help asking him once what he meant by coming there at all. 'To make money, of course. What do you think?' he said, scornfully. Then he got fever, and had to be carried in a hammock slung under a pole. As he weighed sixteen stone I had no end of rows with the carriers. They jibbed, ran away, sneaked off with their loads in the night—quite a mutiny. So, one evening, I made a speech in English with gestures, not one of which was lost to the sixty pairs of eyes before me, and the next morning I started the hammock off in front all right. An hour afterwards I came upon the whole concern wrecked in a bush—man, hammock, groans, blankets, horrors. The heavy pole had skinned his poor nose. He was very anxious for me to kill somebody, but there wasn't the shadow of a carrier near. I remembered the old doctor,—'It would be interesting for science to watch the mental changes of individuals, on the spot.' I felt I was becoming scientifically interesting. However, all that is to no purpose. On the fifteenth day I came in sight of the big river again, and hobbled into the Central Station. It was on a back water surrounded by scrub and forest, with a pretty border of smelly mud on one side, and on the three others enclosed by a crazy fence of rushes. A neglected gap was all the gate it had, and the first glance at the place was enough to let you see the flabby devil was running that show. White men with long staves in their hands appeared languidly from amongst the buildings, strolling up to take a look at me, and then retired out of sight somewhere. One of them, a stout, excitable chap with black moustaches, informed me with great volubility and many digressions, as soon as I told him who I was, that my steamer was at the bottom of the river. I was thunderstruck. What, how, why? Oh, it

---

6. An English port.

7. Africans from Zanzibar, in East Africa; they were widely used as mercenaries.

was 'all right.' The 'manager himself' was there. All quite correct. 'Everybody had behaved splendidly! splendidly!'—'You must,' he said in agitation, 'go and see the general manager at once. He is waiting!'

"I did not see the real significance of that wreck at once. I fancy I see it now, but I am not sure—not at all. Certainly the affair was too stupid—when I think of it—to be altogether natural. Still. . . . But at the moment it presented itself simply as a confounded nuisance. The steamer was sunk. They had started two days before in a sudden hurry up the river with the manager on board, in charge of some volunteer skipper, and before they had been out three hours they tore the bottom out of her on stones, and she sank near the south bank. I asked myself what I was to do there, now my boat was lost. As a matter of fact, I had plenty to do in fishing my command out of the river. I had to set about it the very next day. That, and the repairs when I brought the pieces to the station, took some months.

"My first interview with the manager was curious. He did not ask me to sit down after my twenty-mile walk that morning. He was commonplace in complexion, in feature, in manners, and in voice. He was of middle size and of ordinary build. His eyes, of the usual blue, were perhaps remarkably cold, and he certainly could make his glance fall on one as trenchant and heavy as an axe. But even at these times the rest of his person seemed to disclaim the intention. Otherwise there was only an indefinable, faint expression of his lips, something stealthy—a smile—not a smile—I remember it, but I can't explain. It was unconscious, this smile was, though just after he had said something it got intensified for an instant. It came at the end of his speeches like a seal applied on the words to make the meaning of the commonest phrase appear absolutely inscrutable. He was a common trader, from his youth up employed in these parts—nothing more. He was obeyed, yet he inspired neither love nor fear, nor even respect. He inspired uneasiness. That was it! Uneasiness. Not a definite mistrust—just uneasiness—nothing more. You have no idea how effective such a . . . a . . . faculty can be. He had no genius for organising, for initiative, or for order even. That was evident in such things as the deplorable state of the station. He had no learning, and no intelligence. His position had come to him—why? Perhaps because he was never ill . . . He had served three terms of three years out there . . . Because triumphant health in the general rout of constitutions is a kind of power in itself. When he went home on leave he rioted on a large scale—pompously. Jack ashore—with a difference—in externals only. This one could gather from his casual talk. He originated nothing, he could keep the routine going—that's all. But he was great. He was great by this little thing that it was impossible to tell what could control such a man. He never gave that secret away. Perhaps there was nothing within him. Such a suspicion made one pause—for out there there were no external checks. Once when various tropical diseases had laid low almost every 'agent' in the station, he was heard to say, 'Men who come out here should have no entrails.' He sealed the utterance with that smile of his, as though it had been a door opening into a darkness he had in his keeping. You fancied you had seen things—but the seal was on. When annoyed at meal-times by the constant quarrels of the white men about precedence, he ordered an immense round table to be made, for which a special house had to be built. This was the station's mess-room. Where he sat was the first place—the rest were nowhere. One felt this to be his unalterable conviction. He was neither civil nor uncivil. He was quiet. He allowed his 'boy'—an overfed young negro from the coast—to treat the white men, under his very eyes, with provoking insolence.

"He began to speak as soon as he saw me. I had been very long on the road. He could not wait. Had to start without me. The up-river stations had to be relieved. There had been so many delays already that he did not know who was dead and who was alive, and how they got on—and so on, and so on. He paid no attention to my explanations, and, playing with a stick of sealing-wax, repeated several times that the situation was 'very grave, very grave.' There were rumours that a very important station was in jeopardy, and its chief, Mr Kurtz, was ill. Hoped it was not true. Mr Kurtz was . . . I felt weary and irritable. Hang Kurtz, I thought. I interrupted him by saying I had heard of Mr Kurtz on the coast. 'Ah! So they talk of him down there,' he murmured to himself. Then he began again, assuring me Mr Kurtz was the best agent he had, an exceptional man, of the greatest importance to the Company; therefore I could understand his anxiety. He was, he said, 'very, very uneasy.' Certainly he fidgeted on his chair a good deal, exclaimed, 'Ah, Mr Kurtz!' broke the stick of sealing-wax and seemed dumbfounded by the accident. Next thing he wanted to know 'how long it would take to' . . . I interrupted him again. Being hungry, you know, and kept on my feet too, I was getting savage. 'How can I tell?' I said. 'I haven't even seen the wreck yet—some months, no doubt.' All this talk seemed to me so futile. 'Some months,' he said. 'Well, let us say three months before we can make a start. Yes. That ought to do the affair.' I flung out of his hut (he lived all alone in a clay hut with a sort of verandah) muttering to myself my opinion of him. He was a chattering idiot. Afterwards I took it back when it was borne in upon me startlingly with what extreme nicety he had estimated the time requisite for the 'affair.'

"I went to work the next day, turning, so to speak, my back on that station. In that way only it seemed to me I could keep my hold on the redeeming facts of life. Still, one must look about sometimes; and then I saw this station, these men strolling aimlessly about in the sunshine of the yard. I asked myself sometimes what it all meant. They wandered here and there with their absurd long staves in their hands, like a lot of faithless pilgrims bewitched inside a rotten fence. The word 'ivory' rang in the air, was whispered, was sighed. You would think they were praying to it. A taint of imbecile rapacity blew through it all, like a whiff from some corpse. By Jove! I've never seen anything so unreal in my life. And outside, the silent wilderness surrounding this cleared speck on the earth struck me as something great and invincible, like evil or truth, waiting patiently for the passing away of this fantastic invasion.

"Oh, those months! Well, never mind. Various things happened. One evening a grass shed full of calico, cotton prints, beads, and I don't know what else, burst into a blaze so suddenly that you would have thought the earth had opened to let an avenging fire consume all that trash. I was smoking my pipe quietly by my dismantled steamer, and saw them all cutting capers in the light, with their arms lifted high, when the stout man with moustaches came tearing down to the river, a tin pail in his hand, assured me that everybody was 'behaving splendidly, splendidly,' dipped about a quart of water and tore back again. I noticed there was a hole in the bottom of his pail.

"I strolled up. There was no hurry. You see the thing had gone off like a box of matches. It had been hopeless from the very first. The flame had leaped high, driven everybody back, lighted up everything—and collapsed. The shed was already a heap of embers glowing fiercely. A nigger was being beaten near by. They said he had caused the fire in some way; be that as it may, he was screeching most horribly. I saw him, later on, for several days, sitting in a bit of shade looking very sick and trying to recover himself: afterwards he arose and went out—and the wilderness without a sound took him into its bosom again. As I approached the glow from the dark

I found myself at the back of two men, talking. I heard the name of Kurtz pronounced, then the words, 'take advantage of this unfortunate accident.' One of the men was the manager. I wished him a good evening. 'Did you ever see anything like it—eh? it is incredible,' he said, and walked off. The other man remained. He was a first-class agent, young, gentlemanly, a bit reserved, with a forked little beard and a hooked nose. He was stand-offish with the other agents, and they on their side said he was the manager's spy upon them. As to me, I had hardly ever spoken to him before. We got into talk, and by-and-by we strolled away from the hissing ruins. Then he asked me to his room, which was in the main building of the station. He struck a match, and I perceived that this young aristocrat had not only a silver-mounted dressing-case but also a whole candle all to himself. Just at that time the manager was the only man sup-posed to have any right to candles. Native mats covered the clay walls; a collection of spears, assegais,[8] shields, knives was hung up in trophies. The business intrusted to this fellow was the making of bricks—so I had been informed; but there wasn't a fragment of a brick anywhere in the station, and he had been there more than a year—waiting. It seems he could not make bricks without something, I don't know what—straw maybe. Anyway, it could not be found there, and as it was not likely to be sent from Europe, it did not appear clear to me what he was waiting for. An act of special creation perhaps. However, they were all waiting—all the sixteen or twenty pilgrims of them—for something; and upon my word it did not seem an uncongenial occupation, from the way they took it, though the only thing that ever came to them was disease—as far as I could see. They beguiled the time by backbiting and intrigu-ing against each other in a foolish kind of way. There was an air of plotting about that station, but nothing came of it, of course. It was as unreal as everything else—as the philanthropic pretence of the whole concern, as their talk, as their government, as their show of work. The only real feeling was a desire to get appointed to a trading-post where ivory was to be had, so that they could earn percentages. They intrigued and slandered and hated each other only on that account,—but as to effectually lifting a little finger—oh, no. By heavens! there is something after all in the world allowing one man to steal a horse while another must not look at a halter. Steal a horse straight out. Very well. He has done it. Perhaps he can ride. But there is a way of looking at a halter that would provoke the most charitable of saints into a kick.

"I had no idea why he wanted to be sociable, but as we chatted in there it suddenly occurred to me the fellow was trying to get at something—in fact, pumping me. He alluded constantly to Europe, to the people I was supposed to know there—putting leading questions as to my acquaintances in the sepulchral city, and so on. His little eyes glittered like mica discs—with curiosity,—though he tried to keep up a bit of superciliousness. At first I was astonished, but very soon I became awfully curious to see what he would find out from me. I couldn't possibly imagine what I had in me to make it worth his while. It was very pretty to see how he baffled himself, for in truth my body was full of chills, and my head had nothing in it but that wretched steamboat business. It was evident he took me for a perfectly shameless prevaricator. At last he got angry, and, to conceal a movement of furious annoyance, he yawned. I rose. Then I noticed a small sketch in oils, on a panel, representing a woman, draped and blind-folded, carrying a lighted torch. The background was sombre—almost black. The movement of the woman was stately, and the effect of the torchlight on the face was sinister.

8. Spears.

"It arrested me, and he stood by civilly, holding a half-pint champagne bottle (medical comforts) with the candle stuck in it. To my question he said Mr Kurtz had painted this—in this very station more than a year ago—while waiting for means to go to his trading-post. 'Tell me, pray,' said I, 'who is this Mr Kurtz?'

"'The chief of the Inner Station,' he answered in a short tone, looking away. 'Much obliged,' I said, laughing. 'And you are the brickmaker of the Central Station. Every one knows that.' He was silent for a while. 'He is a prodigy,' he said at last. 'He is an emissary of pity, and science, and progress, and devil knows what else. We want,' he began to declaim suddenly, 'for the guidance of the cause intrusted to us by Europe, so to speak, higher intelligence, wide sympathies, a singleness of purpose.' 'Who says that?' I asked. 'Lots of them,' he replied. 'Some even write that; and so *he* comes here, a special being, as you ought to know.' 'Why ought I to know?' I interrupted, really surprised. He paid no attention. 'Yes. To-day he is chief of the best station, next year he will be assistant-manager, two years more and . . . but I daresay you know what he will be in two years' time. You are of the new gang—the gang of virtue. The same people who sent him specially also recommended you. Oh, don't say no. I've my own eyes to trust.' Light dawned upon me. My dear aunt's influential acquaintances were producing an unexpected effect upon that young man. I nearly burst into a laugh. 'Do you read the Company's confidential correspondence?' I asked. He hadn't a word to say. It was great fun. 'When Mr Kurtz,' I continued severely, 'is General Manager, you won't have the opportunity.'

"He blew the candle out suddenly, and we went outside. The moon had risen. Black figures strolled about listlessly, pouring water on the glow, whence proceeded a sound of hissing; steam ascended in the moonlight; the beaten nigger groaned somewhere. 'What a row the brute makes!' said the indefatigable man with the moustaches, appearing near us. 'Serve him right. Transgression—punishment—bang! Pitiless, pitiless. That's the only way. This will prevent all conflagrations for the future. I was just telling the manager . . .' He noticed my companion, and became crestfallen all at once. 'Not in bed yet,' he said, with a kind of servile heartiness; 'it's so natural. Ha! Danger—agitation.' He vanished. I went on to the river-side, and the other followed me. I heard a scathing murmur at my ear, 'Heap of muffs—go to.' The pilgrims could be seen in knots gesticulating, discussing. Several had still their staves in their hands. I verily believe they took these sticks to bed with them. Beyond the fence the forest stood up spectrally in the moonlight, and through the dim stir, through the faint sounds of that lamentable courtyard, the silence of the land went home to one's very heart,—its mystery, its greatness, the amazing reality of its concealed life. The hurt nigger moaned feebly somewhere near by, and then fetched a deep sigh that made me mend my pace away from there. I felt a hand introducing itself under my arm. 'My dear sir,' said the fellow, 'I don't want to be misunderstood, and especially by you, who will see Mr Kurtz long before I can have that pleasure. I wouldn't like him to get a false idea of my disposition. . . .'

"I let him run on, this papier-mâché Mephistopheles, and it seemed to me that if I tried I could poke my forefinger through him, and would find nothing inside but a little loose dirt, maybe. He, don't you see, had been planning to be assistant-manager by-and-by under the present man, and I could see that the coming of that Kurtz had upset them both not a little. He talked precipitately, and I did not try to stop him. I had my shoulders against the wreck of my steamer, hauled up on the slope like a carcass of some big river animal. The smell of mud, of primeval mud, by Jove! was in my nostrils, the high stillness of primeval forest was before my eyes; there were shiny patches on the black creek. The moon had spread over everything a thin layer of silver—over the rank grass, over the mud, upon the wall of matted vegetation standing higher than the wall of a temple, over the great river I could see through a sombre gap glittering, glittering, as it flowed broadly by without a murmur. All this was great, expectant, mute, while the man jabbered about himself. I wondered whether the stillness on the face of the immensity looking at us two were meant as an appeal or as a menace. What were we who had strayed in here? Could we handle that dumb thing, or would it handle us? I felt how big, how confoundedly big, was that thing that couldn't talk, and perhaps was deaf as well. What was in there? I could see a little ivory coming out from there, and I had heard Mr Kurtz was in there. I had heard enough about it too—God knows! Yet somehow it didn't bring any image with it—no more than if I had been told an angel or a fiend was in there. I believed it in the same way one of you might believe there are inhabitants in the planet Mars. I knew once a Scotch sailmaker who was certain, dead sure, there were people in Mars. If you asked him for some idea how they looked and behaved, he would get shy and mutter something about 'walking on all-fours.' If you as much as smiled, he would—though a man of sixty—offer to fight you. I would not have gone so far as to fight for Kurtz, but I went for him near enough to a lie. You know I hate, detest, and can't bear a lie, not because I am straighter than the rest of us, but simply because it appals me. There is a taint of death, a flavour of mortality in lies,—which is exactly what I hate and detest in the world—what I want to forget. It makes me miserable and sick, like biting something rotten would do. Temperament, I suppose. Well, I went near enough to it by letting the young fool there believe anything he liked to imagine as to my influence in Europe. I became in an instant as much of a pretence as the rest of the bewitched pilgrims. This simply because I had a notion it somehow would be of help to that Kurtz whom at the time I did not see—you understand. He was just a word for me. I did not see the man in the name any more than you do. Do you see him? Do you see the story? Do you see anything? It seems to me I am trying to tell you a dream—making a vain attempt, because no relation of a dream can convey the dream-sensation, that commingling of absurdity, surprise, and bewilderment in a tremor of struggling revolt, that notion of being captured by the incredible which is of the very essence of dreams. . . ."

He was silent for a while.

". . . No, it is impossible; it is impossible to convey the life-sensation of any given epoch of one's existence,—that which makes its truth, its meaning—its subtle and penetrating essence. It is impossible. We live, as we dream—alone. . . ."

He paused again as if reflecting, then added—

"Of course in this you fellows see more than I could then. You see me, whom you know. . . ."

It had become so pitch dark that we listeners could hardly see one another. For a long time already he, sitting apart, had been no more to us than a voice. There was not a word from anybody. The others might have been asleep, but I was awake. I listened, I listened on the watch for the sentence, for the word, that would give me the clue to the faint uneasiness inspired by this narrative that seemed to shape itself without human lips in the heavy night-air of the river.

". . .Yes—I let him run on," Marlow began again, "and think what he pleased about the powers that were behind me. I did! And there was nothing behind me! There was nothing but that wretched, old, mangled steamboat I was leaning against, while he talked fluently about 'the necessity for every man to get on.' 'And when one comes out here, you conceive, it is not to gaze at the moon.' Mr Kurtz was a 'universal genius,' but even a genius would find it easier to work with 'adequate tools—intelligent men.' He did not make bricks—why, there was a physical impossibility in the way—as I was well aware; and if he did secretarial work for the manager, it was because 'no sensible man rejects wantonly the confidence of his superiors.' Did I see it? I saw it. What more did I want? What I really wanted was rivets, by heaven! Rivets. To get on with the work—to stop the hole. Rivets I wanted. There were cases of them down at the coast—cases—piled up—burst—split! You kicked a loose rivet at every second step in that station yard on the hillside. Rivets had rolled into the grove of death. You could fill your pockets with rivets for the trouble of stooping down—and there wasn't one rivet to be found where it was wanted. We had plates that would do, but nothing to fasten them with. And every week the messenger, a lone negro, letter-bag on shoulder and staff in hand, left our station for the coast. And several times a week a coast caravan came in with trade goods,—ghastly glazed calico that made you shudder only to look at it, glass beads value about a penny a quart, confounded spotted cotton handkerchiefs. And no rivets. Three carriers could have brought all that was wanted to set that steamboat afloat.

"He was becoming confidential now, but I fancy my unresponsive attitude must have exasperated him at last, for he judged it necessary to inform me he feared neither God nor devil, let alone any mere man. I said I could see that very well, but what I wanted was a certain quantity of rivets—and rivets were what really Mr Kurtz wanted, if he had only known it. Now letters went to the coast every week. . . . 'My dear sir,' he cried, 'I write from dictation.' I demanded rivets. There was a way—for an intelligent man. He changed his manner; became very cold, and suddenly began to talk about a hippopotamus; wondered whether sleeping on board the steamer (I stuck to my salvage night and day) I wasn't disturbed. There was an old hippo that had the bad habit of getting out on the bank and roaming at night over the station grounds. The pilgrims used to turn out in a body and empty every rifle they could lay hands on at him. Some even had sat up o' nights for him. All this energy was wasted, though. 'That animal has a charmed life,' he said; 'but you can say this only of brutes in this country. No man—you apprehend me?—no man here bears a charmed life.' He stood there for a moment in the moonlight with his delicate hooked nose set a little askew, and his mica eyes glittering without a wink, then, with a curt Good night, he strode off. I could see he was disturbed and considerably puzzled, which made me feel more hopeful than I had been for days. It was a great comfort to turn from that chap to my influential friend, the battered, twisted, ruined, tin-pot steamboat. I clambered on board. She rang under my feet like an empty Huntley & Palmer[9] biscuit-tin kicked along a gutter; she was nothing so solid in make, and rather less pretty in shape, but I had expended enough hard work on her to make me love her. No influential friend would have served me better. She had given me a chance to come out a bit—to find out what I could do. No, I don't like work. I had rather laze about and think of all the fine things that can be done. I don't like work—no man does—but I like what is in the work,—the chance to find yourself. Your own reality—for yourself, not for others—what no other man can ever know. They can only see the mere show, and never can tell what it really means.

"I was not surprised to see somebody sitting aft, on the deck, with his legs dangling over the mud. You see I rather chummed with the few mechanics there were

9. A brand of English cookies.

in that station, whom the other pilgrims naturally despised—on account of their imperfect manners, I suppose. This was the foreman—a boiler-maker by trade—a good worker. He was a lank, bony, yellow-faced man, with big intense eyes. His aspect was worried, and his head was as bald as the palm of my hand; but his hair in falling seemed to have stuck to his chin, and had prospered in the new locality, for his beard hung down to his waist. He was a widower with six young children (he had left them in charge of a sister of his to come out there), and the passion of his life was pigeon-flying. He was an enthusiast and a connoisseur. He would rave about pigeons. After work hours he used sometimes to come over from his hut for a talk about his children and his pigeons; at work, when he had to crawl in the mud under the bottom of the steamboat, he would tie up that beard of his in a kind of white serviette[1] he brought for the purpose. It had loops to go over his ears. In the evening he could be seen squatted on the bank rinsing that wrapper in the creek with great care, then spreading it solemnly on a bush to dry.

"I slapped him on the back and shouted 'We shall have rivets!' He scrambled to his feet exclaiming 'No! Rivets!' as though he couldn't believe his ears. Then in a low voice, 'You . . . eh?' I don't know why we behaved like lunatics. I put my finger to the side of my nose and nodded mysteriously. 'Good for you!' he cried, snapped his fingers above his head, lifting one foot. I tried a jig. We capered on the iron deck. A frightful clatter came out of that hulk, and the virgin forest on the other bank of the creek sent it back in a thundering roll upon the sleeping station. It must have made some of the pilgrims sit up in their hovels. A dark figure obscured the lighted doorway of the manager's hut, vanished, then, a second or so after, the doorway itself vanished too. We stopped, and the silence driven away by the stamping of our feet flowed back again from the recesses of the land. The great wall of vegetation, an exuberant and entangled mass of trunks, branches, leaves, boughs, festoons, motionless in the moonlight, was like a rioting invasion of soundless life, a rolling wave of plants, piled up, crested, ready to topple over the creek, to sweep every little man of us out of his little existence. And it moved not. A deadened burst of mighty splashes and snorts reached us from afar, as though an ichthyosaurus had been taking a bath of glitter in the great river. 'After all,' said the boiler-maker in a reasonable tone, 'why shouldn't we get the rivets?' Why not, indeed! I did not know of any reason why we shouldn't. 'They'll come in three weeks,' I said, confidently.

"But they didn't. Instead of rivets there came an invasion, an infliction, a visitation. It came in sections during the next three weeks, each section headed by a donkey carrying a white man in new clothes and tan shoes, bowing from that elevation right and left to the impressed pilgrims. A quarrelsome band of footsore sulky niggers trod on the heels of the donkey; a lot of tents, camp-stools, tin boxes, white cases, brown bales would be shot down in the courtyard, and the air of mystery would deepen a little over the muddle of the station. Five such instalments came, with their absurd air of disorderly flight with the loot of innumerable outfit shops and provision stores, that, one would think, they were lugging, after a raid, into the wilderness for equitable division. It was an inextricable mess of things decent in themselves but that human folly made look like the spoils of thieving.

"This devoted band called itself the Eldorado Exploring Expedition,[2] and I believe they were sworn to secrecy. Their talk, however, was the talk of sordid

1. Napkin.
2. Eldorado, legendary land of gold in South America and the object of many fruitless 16th-century Spanish expeditions.

buccaneers: it was reckless without hardihood, greedy without audacity, and cruel without courage; there was not an atom of foresight or of serious intention in the whole batch of them, and they did not seem aware these things are wanted for the work of the world. To tear treasure out of the bowels of the land was their desire, with no more moral purpose at the back of it than there is in burglars breaking into a safe. Who paid the expenses of the noble enterprise I don't know; but the uncle of our manager was leader of that lot.

"In exterior he resembled a butcher in a poor neighbourhood, and his eyes had a look of sleepy cunning. He carried his fat paunch with ostentation on his short legs, and during the time his gang infested the station spoke to no one but his nephew. You could see these two roaming about all day long with their heads close together in an everlasting confab.

"I had given up worrying myself about the rivets. One's capacity for that kind of folly is more limited than you would suppose. I said Hang!—and let things slide. I had plenty of time for meditation, and now and then I would give some thought to Kurtz. I wasn't very interested in him. No. Still, I was curious to see whether this man, who had come out equipped with moral ideas of some sort, would climb to the top after all, and how he would set about his work when there."

2

"One evening as I was lying flat on the deck of my steamboat, I heard voices approaching—and there were the nephew and the uncle strolling along the bank. I laid my head on my arm again, and had nearly lost myself in a doze, when somebody said in my ear, as it were: 'I am as harmless as a little child, but I don't like to be dictated to. Am I the manager—or am I not? I was ordered to send him there. It's incredible.' . . . I became aware that the two were standing on the shore alongside the forepart of the steamboat, just below my head. I did not move; it did not occur to me to move: I was sleepy. 'It *is* unpleasant,' grunted the uncle. 'He has asked the Administration to be sent there,' said the other, 'with the idea of showing what he could do; and I was instructed accordingly. Look at the influence that man must have. Is it not frightful?' They both agreed it was frightful, then made several bizarre remarks: 'Make rain and fine weather—one man—the Council—by the nose'—bits of absurd sentences that got the better of my drowsiness, so that I had pretty near the whole of my wits about me when the uncle said, 'The climate may do away with this difficulty for you. Is he alone there?' 'Yes,' answered the manager; 'he sent his assistant down the river with a note to me in these terms: "Clear this poor devil out of the country, and don't bother sending more of that sort. I had rather be alone than have the kind of men you can dispose of with me." It was more than a year ago. Can you imagine such impudence?' 'Anything since then?' asked the other, hoarsely. 'Ivory,' jerked the nephew; 'lots of it—prime sort—lots—most annoying, from him.' 'And with that?' questioned the heavy rumble. 'Invoice,' was the reply fired out, so to speak. Then silence. They had been talking about Kurtz.

"I was broad awake by this time, but, lying perfectly at ease, remained still, having no inducement to change my position. 'How did that ivory come all this way?' growled the elder man, who seemed very vexed. The other explained that it had come with a fleet of canoes in charge of an English half-caste clerk Kurtz had with him; that Kurtz had apparently intended to return himself, the station being by that time bare of goods and stores, but after coming three hundred miles, had suddenly decided to go back, which he started to do alone in a small dug-out with four paddlers, leaving the half-caste to continue down the river with the ivory. The two fellows there seemed astounded at anybody attempting such a thing. They were at a loss for an adequate motive. As to me, I seemed to see Kurtz for the first time. It was a distinct glimpse: the dug-out, four paddling savages, and the lone white man turning his back suddenly on the headquarters, on relief, on thoughts of home—perhaps; setting his face towards the depths of the wilderness, towards his empty and desolate station. I did not know the motive. Perhaps he was just simply a fine fellow who stuck to his work for its own sake. His name, you understand, had not been pronounced once. He was 'that man.' The half-caste, who, as far as I could see, had conducted a difficult trip with great prudence and pluck, was invariably alluded to as 'that scoundrel.' The 'scoundrel' had reported that the 'man' had been very ill—had recovered imperfectly. . . . The two below me moved away then a few paces, and strolled back and forth at some little distance. I heard: 'Military post—doctor—two hundred miles—quite alone now—unavoidable delays—nine months—no news—strange rumours.' They approached again, just as the manager was saying, 'No one, as far as I know, unless a species of wandering trader—a pestilential fellow, snapping ivory from the natives.' Who was it they were talking about now? I gathered in snatches that this was some man supposed to be in Kurtz's district, and of whom the manager did not approve. 'We will not be free from unfair competition till one of these fellows is hanged for an example,' he said. 'Certainly,' grunted the other; 'get him hanged! Why not? Anything—anything can be done in this country. That's what I say; nobody here, you understand, *here,* can endanger your position. And why? You stand the climate—you outlast them all. The danger is in Europe; but there before I left I took care to—' They moved off and whispered, then their voices rose again. 'The extraordinary series of delays is not my fault. I did my possible.' The fat man sighed, 'Very sad.' 'And the pestiferous absurdity of his talk,' continued the other; 'he bothered me enough when he was here. "Each station should be like a beacon on the road towards better things, a centre for trade of course, but also for humanising, improving, instructing." Conceive you—that ass! And he wants to be manager! No, it's—' Here he got choked by excessive indignation, and I lifted my head the least bit. I was surprised to see how near they were—right under me. I could have spat upon their hats. They were looking on the ground, absorbed in thought. The manager was switching his leg with a slender twig: his sagacious relative lifted his head. 'You have been well since you came out this time?' he asked. The other gave a start. 'Who? I? Oh! Like a charm—like a charm. But the rest—oh, my goodness! All sick. They die so quick, too, that I haven't the time to send them out of the country—it's incredible!' 'H'm. Just so,' grunted the uncle. 'Ah! my boy, trust to this—I say, trust to this.' I saw him extend his short flipper of an arm for a gesture that took in the forest, the creek, the mud, the river,—seemed to beckon with a dishonouring flourish before the sunlit face of the land a treacherous appeal to the lurking death, to the hidden evil, to the profound darkness of its heart. It was so startling that I leaped to my feet and looked back at the edge of the forest, as though I had expected an answer of some sort to that black display of confidence. You know the foolish notions that come to one sometimes. The high stillness confronted these two figures with its ominous patience, waiting for the passing away of a fantastic invasion.

"They swore aloud together—out of sheer fright, I believe—then, pretending not to know anything of my existence, turned back to the station. The sun was low; and leaning forward side by side, they seemed to be tugging painfully uphill their two ridiculous shadows of unequal length, that trailed behind them slowly over the tall grass without bending a single blade.

"In a few days the Eldorado Expedition went into the patient wilderness, that closed upon it as the sea closes over a diver. Long afterwards the news came that all the donkeys were dead. I know nothing as to the fate of the less valuable animals. They, no doubt, like the rest of us, found what they deserved. I did not inquire. I was then rather excited at the prospect of meeting Kurtz very soon. When I say very soon I mean it comparatively. It was just two months from the day we left the creek when we came to the bank below Kurtz's station.

"Going up that river was like travelling back to the earliest beginnings of the world, when vegetation rioted on the earth and the big trees were kings. An empty stream, a great silence, an impenetrable forest. The air was warm, thick, heavy, sluggish. There was no joy in the brilliance of sunshine. The long stretches of the waterway ran on, deserted, into the gloom of overshadowed distances. On silvery sandbanks hippos and alligators sunned themselves side by side. The broadening waters flowed through a mob of wooded islands; you lost your way on that river as you would in a desert, and butted all day long against shoals, trying to find the channel, till you thought yourself bewitched and cut off for ever from everything you had known once—somewhere—far away—in another existence perhaps. There were moments when one's past came back to one, as it will sometimes when you have not a moment to spare to yourself; but it came in the shape of an unrestful and noisy dream, remembered with wonder amongst the overwhelming realities of this strange world of plants, and water, and silence. And this stillness of life did not in the least resemble a peace. It was the stillness of an implacable force brooding over an inscrutable intention. It looked at you with a vengeful aspect. I got used to it afterwards; I did not see it any more; I had no time. I had to keep guessing at the channel; I had to discern, mostly by inspiration, the signs of hidden banks; I watched for sunken stones; I was learning to clap my teeth smartly before my heart flew out, when I shaved by a fluke some infernal sly old snag that would have ripped the life out of the tin-pot steamboat and drowned all the pilgrims; I had to keep a look-out for the signs of dead wood we could cut up in the night for next day's steaming. When you have to attend to things of that sort, to the mere incidents of the surface, the reality—the reality, I tell you—fades. The inner truth is hidden—luckily, luckily. But I felt it all the same; I felt often its mysterious stillness watching me at my monkey tricks, just as it watches you fellows performing on your respective tight-ropes for—what is it? half-a-crown a tumble—"

"Try to be civil, Marlow," growled a voice, and I knew there was at least one listener awake besides myself.

"I beg your pardon. I forgot the heartache which makes up the rest of the price. And indeed what does the price matter, if the trick be well done? You do your tricks very well. And I didn't do badly either, since I managed not to sink that steamboat on my first trip. It's a wonder to me yet. Imagine a blindfolded man set to drive a van over a bad road. I sweated and shivered over that business considerably, I can tell you. After all, for a seaman, to scrape the bottom of the thing that's supposed to float all the time under his care is the unpardonable sin. No one may know of it, but you never forget the thump—eh? A blow on the very heart. You remember it, you dream of it, you wake up at night and think of it—years after—and go hot and cold all over. I don't pretend to say that steamboat floated all the time. More than once she had to wade for a bit, with twenty cannibals splashing around and pushing. We had enlisted some of these chaps on the way for a crew. Fine fellows—cannibals—in their place. They were men one could work with, and I am grateful to them. And, after all, they did not eat each other before my face: they had brought along a provision of hippo-meat which went rotten, and made the mystery of the wilderness stink in my nostrils. Phoo! I can sniff it now. I had the manager on board and three or four pilgrims with their staves—all complete. Sometimes we came upon a station close by the bank, clinging to the skirts of the unknown, and the white men rushing out of a tumble-down hovel, with great gestures of joy and surprise and welcome, seemed very strange,—had the appearance of being held there captive by a spell. The word 'ivory' would ring in the air for a while—and on we went again into the silence, along empty reaches, round the still bends, between the high walls of our winding way, reverberating in hollow claps the ponderous beat of the stern-wheel. Trees, trees, millions of trees, massive, immense, running up high; and at their foot, hugging the bank against the stream, crept the little begrimed steamboat, like a sluggish beetle crawling on the floor of a lofty portico. It made you feel very small, very lost, and yet it was not altogether depressing that feeling. After all, if you were small, the grimy beetle crawled on—which was just what you wanted it to do. Where the pilgrims imagined it crawled to I don't know. To some place where they expected to get something, I bet! For me it crawled towards Kurtz—exclusively; but when the steam-pipes started leaking we crawled very slow. The reaches opened before us and closed behind, as if the forest had stepped leisurely across the water to bar the way for our return. We penetrated deeper and deeper into the heart of darkness. It was very quiet there. At night sometimes the roll of drums behind the curtain of trees would run up the river and remain sustained faintly, as if hovering in the air high over our heads, till the first break of day. Whether it meant war, peace, or prayer we could not tell. The dawns were heralded by the descent of a chill stillness; the woodcutters slept, their fires burned low; the snapping of a twig would make you start. We were wanderers on a prehistoric earth, on an earth that wore the aspect of an unknown planet. We could have fancied ourselves the first of men taking possession of an accursed inheritance, to be subdued at the cost of profound anguish and of excessive toil. But suddenly, as we struggled round a bend, there would be a glimpse of rush walls, of peaked grass-roofs, a burst of yells, a whirl of black limbs, a mass of hands clapping, of feet stamping, of bodies swaying, of eyes rolling, under the droop of heavy and motionless foliage. The steamer toiled along slowly on the edge of a black and incomprehensible frenzy. The prehistoric man was cursing us, praying to us, welcoming us—who could tell? We were cut off from the comprehension of our surroundings; we glided past like phantoms, wondering and secretly appalled, as sane men would be before an enthusiastic outbreak in a madhouse. We could not understand, because we were too far and could not remember, because we were travelling in the night of first ages, of those ages that are gone, leaving hardly a sign—and no memories.

"The earth seemed unearthly. We are accustomed to look upon the shackled form of a conquered monster, but there—there you could look at a thing monstrous and free. It was unearthly, and the men were—No, they were not inhuman. Well, you know, that was the worst of it—this suspicion of their not being inhuman. It would come slowly to one. They howled, and leaped, and spun, and made horrid faces; but what thrilled you was just the thought of their humanity—like yours—the thought of your remote kinship with this wild and passionate uproar. Ugly. Yes, it was ugly enough; but if you were man enough you would admit to yourself that there was in you just the faintest trace of a response to the terrible frankness of that noise, a dim suspicion of there being a meaning in it which you—you so remote from the night of first ages—could comprehend. And why not? The mind of man is capable of anything—because everything is in it, all the past as well as all the future. What was there after all? Joy, fear, sorrow, devotion, valour, rage—who can tell?—but truth—truth stripped of its cloak of time. Let the fool gape and shudder—the man knows, and can look on without a wink. But he must at least be as much of a man as these on the shore. He must meet that truth with his own true stuff—with his own inborn strength. Principles? Principles won't do. Acquisitions, clothes, pretty rags—rags that would fly off at the first good shake. No; you want a deliberate belief. An appeal to me in this fiendish row—is there? Very well; I hear; I admit, but I have a voice too, and for good or evil mine is the speech that cannot be silenced. Of course, a fool, what with sheer fright and fine sentiments, is always safe. Who's that grunting? You wonder I didn't go ashore for a howl and a dance? Well, no—I didn't. Fine sentiments, you say? Fine sentiments be hanged! I had no time. I had to mess about with white-lead and strips of woollen blanket helping to put bandages on those leaky steam-pipes—I tell you. I had to watch the steering, and circumvent those snags, and get the tin-pot along by hook or by crook. There was surface-truth enough in these things to save a wiser man. And between whiles I had to look after the savage who was fireman. He was an improved specimen; he could fire up a vertical boiler. He was there below me, and, upon my word, to look at him was as edifying as seeing a dog in a parody of breeches and a feather hat, walking on his hind-legs. A few months of training had done for that really fine chap. He squinted at the steam-gauge and at the water-gauge with an evident effort of intrepidity—and he had filed teeth too, the poor devil, and the wool of his pate shaved into queer patterns, and three ornamental scars on each of his cheeks. He ought to have been clapping his hands and stamping his feet on the bank, instead of which he was hard at work, a thrall to strange witchcraft, full of improving knowledge. He was useful because he had been instructed; and what he knew was this—that should the water in that transparent thing disappear, the evil spirit inside the boiler would get angry through the greatness of his thirst, and take a terrible vengeance. So he sweated and fired up and watched the glass fearfully (with an impromptu charm, made of rags, tied to his arm, and a piece of polished bone, as big as a watch, stuck flatways through his lower lip), while the wooded banks slipped past us slowly, the short noise was left behind, the interminable miles of silence—and we crept on, towards Kurtz. But the snags were thick, the water was treacherous and shallow, the boiler seemed indeed to have a sulky devil in it, and thus neither that fireman nor I had any time to peer into our creepy thoughts.

"Some fifty miles below the Inner Station we came upon a hut of reeds, an inclined and melancholy pole, with the unrecognisable tatters of what had been a flag of some sort flying from it, and a neatly stacked wood-pile. This was unexpected. We came to the bank, and on the stack of firewood found a flat piece of board with some faded pencil-writing on it. When deciphered it said: 'Wood for you. Hurry up. Approach cautiously.' There was a signature, but it was illegible—not Kurtz—a much longer word. Hurry up. Where? Up the river? 'Approach cautiously.' We had not done so. But the warning could not have been meant for the place where it could be only found after approach. Something was wrong above. But what—and how much? That was the question. We commented adversely upon the imbecility of that telegraphic style. The bush around said nothing, and would not let us look very far, either. A torn curtain of red twill hung in the doorway of the hut, and flapped sadly in our faces. The dwelling was dismantled; but we could see a white man had lived there not very long ago. There remained a rude table—a plank on two posts; a heap of rubbish reposed in a dark corner, and by the door I picked up a book. It had lost its covers, and the pages had been thumbed into a state of extremely dirty softness; but the back had been lovingly stitched afresh with white cotton thread, which looked clean yet. It was an extraordinary find. Its title was, 'An Inquiry into some Points of Seamanship,' by a man Tower, Towson—some such name—Master in his Majesty's Navy. The matter looked dreary reading enough, with illustrative diagrams and repulsive tables of figures, and the copy was sixty years old. I handled this amazing antiquity with the greatest possible tenderness, lest it should dissolve in my hands. Within, Towson or Towser was inquiring earnestly into the breaking strain of ships' chains and tackle, and other such matters. Not a very enthralling book; but at the first glance you could see there a singleness of intention, an honest concern for the right way of going to work, which made these humble pages, thought out so many years ago, luminous with another than a professional light. The simple old sailor, with his talk of chains and purchases, made me forget the jungle and the pilgrims in a delicious sensation of having come upon something unmistakably real. Such a book being there was wonderful enough; but still more astounding were the notes pencilled in the margin, and plainly referring to the text. I couldn't believe my eyes! They were in cipher! Yes, it looked like cipher. Fancy a man lugging with him a book of that description into this nowhere and studying it—and making notes—in cipher at that! It was an extravagant mystery.

"I had been dimly aware for some time of a worrying noise, and when I lifted my eyes I saw the wood-pile was gone, and the manager, aided by all the pilgrims, was shouting at me from the river-side. I slipped the book into my pocket. I assure you to leave off reading was like tearing myself away from the shelter of an old and solid friendship.

"I started the lame engine ahead. 'It must be this miserable trader—this intruder,' exclaimed the manager, looking back malevolently at the place we had left. 'He must be English,' I said. 'It will not save him from getting into trouble if he is not careful,' muttered the manager darkly. I observed with assumed innocence that no man was safe from trouble in this world.

"The current was more rapid now, the steamer seemed at her last gasp, the stern-wheel flopped languidly, and I caught myself listening on tiptoe for the next beat of the float, for in sober truth I expected the wretched thing to give up every moment. It was like watching the last flickers of a life. But still we crawled. Sometimes I would pick out a tree a little way ahead to measure our progress towards Kurtz by, but I lost it invariably before we got abreast. To keep the eyes so long on one thing was too much for human patience. The manager displayed a beautiful resignation. I fretted and fumed and took to arguing with myself whether or no I would talk openly with Kurtz; but before I could come to any conclusion it occurred to me that my speech or my silence, indeed any action of mine, would be a mere futility. What did it matter what any one knew or ignored? What did it matter who was manager? One gets sometimes such a flash of insight. The essentials of this affair lay deep under the surface, beyond my reach, and beyond my power of meddling.

"Towards the evening of the second day we judged ourselves about eight miles from Kurtz's station. I wanted to push on; but the manager looked grave, and told me the navigation up there was so dangerous that it would be advisable, the sun being very low already, to wait where we were till next morning. Moreover, he pointed out that if the warning to approach cautiously were to be followed, we must approach in daylight—not at dusk, or in the dark. This was sensible enough. Eight miles meant nearly three hours' steaming for us, and I could also see suspicious ripples at the upper end of the reach. Nevertheless, I was annoyed beyond expression at the delay, and most unreasonably too, since one night more could not matter much after so many months. As we had plenty of wood, and caution was the word, I brought up in the middle of the stream. The reach was narrow, straight, with high sides like a railway cutting. The dusk came gliding into it long before the sun had set. The current ran smooth and swift, but a dumb immobility sat on the banks. The living trees, lashed together by the creepers and every living bush of the undergrowth, might have been changed into stone, even to the slenderest twig, to the lightest leaf. It was not sleep—it seemed unnatural, like a state of trance. Not the faintest sound of any kind could be heard. You looked on amazed, and began to suspect yourself of being deaf—then the night came suddenly, and struck you blind as well. About three in the morning some large fish leaped, and the loud splash made me jump as though a gun had been fired. When the sun rose there was a white fog, very warm and clammy, and more blinding than the night. It did not shift or drive; it was just there, standing all round you like something solid. At eight or nine, perhaps, it lifted as a shutter lifts. We had a glimpse of the towering multitude of trees, of the immense matted jungle, with the blazing little ball of the sun hanging over it—all perfectly still—and then the white shutter came down again, smoothly, as if sliding in greased grooves. I ordered the chain, which we had begun to heave in, to be paid out again. Before it stopped running with a muffled rattle, a cry, a very loud cry, as of infinite desolation, soared slowly in the opaque air. It ceased. A complaining clamour, modulated in savage discords, filled our ears. The sheer unexpectedness of it made my hair stir under my cap. I don't know how it struck the others: to me it seemed as though the mist itself had screamed, so suddenly, and apparently from all sides at once, did this tumultuous and mournful uproar arise. It culminated in a hurried outbreak of almost intolerably excessive shrieking, which stopped short, leaving us stiffened in a variety of silly attitudes, and obstinately listening to the nearly as appalling and excessive silence. 'Good God! What is the meaning—?' stammered at my elbow one of the pilgrims,—a little fat man, with sandy hair and red whiskers, who wore side-spring boots, and pink pyjamas tucked into his socks. Two others remained open-mouthed a whole minute, then dashed into the little cabin, to rush out incontinently and stand darting scared glances, with Winchesters at 'ready' in their hands. What we could see was just the steamer we were on, her outlines blurred as though she had been on the point of dissolving, and a misty strip of water, perhaps two feet broad, around her—and that was all. The rest of the world was nowhere, as far as our eyes and ears were concerned. Just nowhere. Gone, disappeared; swept off without leaving a whisper or a shadow behind.

"I went forward, and ordered the chain to be hauled in short, so as to be ready to trip the anchor and move the steamboat at once if necessary. 'Will they attack?' whispered an awed voice. 'We will all be butchered in this fog,' murmured another. The faces twitched with the strain, the hands trembled slightly, the eyes forgot to wink. It was very curious to see the contrast of expressions of the white men and of the black fellows of our crew, who were as much strangers to that part of the river as we, though their homes were only eight hundred miles away. The whites, of course greatly discomposed, had besides a curious look of being painfully shocked by such an outrageous row. The others had an alert, naturally interested expression; but their faces were essentially quiet, even those of the one or two who grinned as they hauled at the chain. Several exchanged short, grunting phrases, which seemed to settle the matter to their satisfaction. Their headman, a young, broad-chested black, severely draped in dark-blue fringed cloths, with fierce nostrils and his hair all done up artfully in oily ringlets, stood near me. 'Aha!' I said, just for good fellowship's sake. 'Catch

'im,' he snapped, with a bloodshot widening of his eyes and a flash of sharp teeth—
'catch 'im. Give 'im to us.' 'To you, eh?' I asked; 'what would you do with them?'
'Eat 'im!' he said, curtly, and, leaning his elbow on the rail, looked out into the fog in
a dignified and profoundly pensive attitude. I would no doubt have been properly horrified, had it not occurred to me that he and his chaps must be very hungry: that they
must have been growing increasingly hungry for at least this month past. They had
been engaged for six months (I don't think a single one of them had any clear idea of
time, as we at the end of countless ages have. They still belonged to the beginnings of
time—had no inherited experience to teach them, as it were), and of course, as long as
there was a piece of paper written over in accordance with some farcical law or other
made down the river, it didn't enter anybody's head to trouble how they would live.
Certainly they had brought with them some rotten hippo-meat, which couldn't have
lasted very long, anyway, even if the pilgrims hadn't, in the midst of a shocking hul-
labaloo, thrown a considerable quantity of it overboard. It looked like a high-handed
proceeding; but it was really a case of legitimate self-defence. You can't breathe dead
hippo waking, sleeping, and eating, and at the same time keep your precarious grip on
existence. Besides that, they had given them every week three pieces of brass wire,
each about nine inches long; and the theory was they were to buy their provisions
with that currency in river-side villages. You can see how *that* worked. There were either no villages, or the people were hostile, or the director, who like the rest of us fed
out of tins, with an occasional old he-goat thrown in, didn't want to stop the steamer
for some more or less recondite reason. So, unless they swallowed the wire itself, or
made loops of it to snare the fishes with, I don't see what good their extravagant salary could be to them. I must say it was paid with a regularity worthy of a large and
honourable trading company. For the rest, the only thing to eat—though it didn't look
eatable in the least—I saw in their possession was a few lumps of some stuff like half-
cooked dough, of a dirty lavender colour, they kept wrapped in leaves, and now and
then swallowed a piece of, but so small that it seemed done more for the looks of the
thing than for any serious purpose of sustenance. Why in the name of all the gnawing devils of hunger they didn't go for us—they were thirty to five—and have a good
tuck-in for once, amazes me now when I think of it. They were big powerful men,
with not much capacity to weigh the consequences, with courage, with strength, even
yet, though their skins were no longer glossy and their muscles no longer hard. And
I saw that something restraining, one of those human secrets that baffle probability,
had come into play there. I looked at them with a swift quickening of interest—not
because it occurred to me I might be eaten by them before very long, though I own to
you that just then I perceived—in a new light, as it were—how unwholesome the pilgrims looked, and I hoped, yes, I positively hoped, that my aspect was not so—what
shall I say?—so—unappetising: a touch of fantastic vanity which fitted well with the
dream-sensation that pervaded all my days at that time. Perhaps I had a little fever
too. One can't live with one's finger everlastingly on one's pulse. I had often 'a little
fever,' or a little touch of other things—the playful paw-strokes of the wilderness, the
preliminary trifling before the more serious onslaught which came in due course. Yes;
I looked at them as you would on any human being, with a curiosity of their impulses,
motives, capacities, weaknesses, when brought to the test of an inexorable physical
necessity. Restraint! What possible restraint? Was it superstition, disgust, patience,
fear—or some kind of primitive honour? No fear can stand up to hunger, no patience
can wear it out, disgust simply does not exist where hunger is; and as to superstition, beliefs, and what you may call principles, they are less than chaff in a breeze.

Don't you know the devilry of lingering starvation, its exasperating torment, its black thoughts, its sombre and brooding ferocity? Well, I do. It takes a man all his inborn strength to fight hunger properly. It's really easier to face bereavement, dishonour, and the perdition of one's soul—than this kind of prolonged hunger. Sad, but true. And these chaps too had no earthly reason for any kind of scruple. Restraint! I would just as soon have expected restraint from a hyena prowling amongst the corpses of a battlefield. But there was the fact facing me—the fact dazzling, to be seen, like the foam on the depths of the sea, like a ripple on an unfathomable enigma, a mystery greater—when I thought of it—than the curious, inexplicable note of desperate grief in this savage clamour that had swept by us on the river-bank, behind the blind whiteness of the fog.

"Two pilgrims were quarrelling in hurried whispers as to which bank. 'Left.' 'No, no; how can you? Right, right, of course.' 'It is very serious,' said the manager's voice behind me; 'I would be desolated if anything should happen to Mr Kurtz before we came up.' I looked at him, and had not the slightest doubt he was sincere. He was just the kind of man who would wish to preserve appearances. That was his restraint. But when he muttered something about going on at once, I did not even take the trouble to answer him. I knew, and he knew, that it was impossible. Were we to let go our hold of the bottom, we would be absolutely in the air—in space. We wouldn't be able to tell where we were going to—whether up or down stream, or across—till we fetched against one bank or the other,—and then we wouldn't know at first which it was. Of course I made no move. I had no mind for a smash-up. You couldn't imagine a more deadly place for a shipwreck. Whether drowned at once or not, we were sure to perish speedily in one way or another. 'I authorise you to take all the risks,' he said, after a short silence. 'I refuse to take any,' I said shortly; which was just the answer he expected, though its tone might have surprised him. 'Well, I must defer to your judgment. You are captain,' he said, with marked civility. I turned my shoulder to him in sign of my appreciation, and looked into the fog. How long would it last? It was the most hopeless look-out. The approach to this Kurtz grubbing for ivory in the wretched bush was beset by as many dangers as though he had been an enchanted princess sleeping in a fabulous castle. 'Will they attack, do you think?' asked the manager, in a confidential tone.

"I did not think they would attack, for several obvious reasons. The thick fog was one. If they left the bank in their canoes they would get lost in it, as we would be if we attempted to move. Still, I had also judged the jungle of both banks quite impenetrable—and yet eyes were in it, eyes that had seen us. The river-side bushes were certainly very thick; but the undergrowth behind was evidently penetrable. However, during the short lift I had seen no canoes anywhere in the reach—certainly not abreast of the steamer. But what made the idea of attack inconceivable to me was the nature of the noise—of the cries we had heard. They had not the fierce character boding of immediate hostile intention. Unexpected, wild, and violent as they had been, they had given me an irresistible impression of sorrow. The glimpse of the steamboat had for some reason filled those savages with unrestrained grief. The danger, if any, I expounded, was from our proximity to a great human passion let loose. Even extreme grief may ultimately vent itself in violence—but more generally takes the form of apathy. . . .

"You should have seen the pilgrims stare! They had no heart to grin, or even to revile me; but I believe they thought me gone mad—with fright, maybe. I delivered a regular lecture. My dear boys, it was no good bothering. Keep a look-out? Well, you may guess I watched the fog for the signs of lifting as a cat watches a mouse; but for anything else our eyes were of no more use to us than if we had been buried miles deep in a heap of cotton-wool. It felt like it too—choking, warm, stifling. Besides, all I said, though it sounded extravagant, was absolutely true to fact. What we afterwards alluded to as an attack was really an attempt at repulse. The action was very far from being aggressive—it was not even defensive, in the usual sense: it was undertaken under the stress of desperation, and in its essence was purely protective.

"It developed itself, I should say, two hours after the fog lifted, and its commencement was at a spot, roughly speaking, about a mile and a half below Kurtz's station. We had just floundered and flopped round a bend, when I saw an islet, a mere grassy hummock of bright green, in the middle of the stream. It was the only thing of the kind; but as we opened the reach more, I perceived it was the head of a long sandbank, or rather of a chain of shallow patches stretching down the middle of the river. They were discoloured, just awash, and the whole lot was seen just under the water, exactly as a man's backbone is seen running down the middle of his back under the skin. Now, as far as I did see, I could go to the right or to the left of this. I didn't know either channel, of course. The banks looked pretty well alike, the depth appeared the same; but as I had been informed the station was on the west side, I naturally headed for the western passage.

"No sooner had we fairly entered it than I became aware it was much narrower than I had supposed. To the left of us there was the long uninterrupted shoal, and to the right a high, steep bank heavily overgrown with bushes. Above the bush the trees stood in serried ranks. The twigs overhung the current thickly, and from distance to distance a large limb of some tree projected rigidly over the stream. It was then well on in the afternoon, the face of the forest was gloomy, and a broad strip of shadow had already fallen on the water. In this shadow we steamed up—very slowly, as you may imagine. I sheered her well inshore—the water being deepest near the bank, as the sounding-pole informed me.

"One of my hungry and forbearing friends was sounding in the bows just below me. This steamboat was exactly like a decked scow.[3] On the deck there were two little teak-wood houses, with doors and windows. The boiler was in the fore-end, and the machinery right astern. Over the whole there was a light roof, supported on stanchions. The funnel projected through that roof, and in front of the funnel a small cabin built of light planks served for a pilot-house. It contained a couch, two camp-stools, a loaded Martini-Henry[4] leaning in one corner, a tiny table, and the steering-wheel. It had a wide door in front and a broad shutter at each side. All these were always thrown open, of course. I spent my days perched up there on the extreme fore-end of that roof, before the door. At night I slept, or tried to, on the couch. An athletic black belonging to some coast tribe, and educated by my poor predecessor, was the helmsman. He sported a pair of brass earrings, wore a blue cloth wrapper from the waist to the ankles, and thought all the world of himself. He was the most unstable kind of fool I had ever seen. He steered with no end of a swagger while you were by; but if he lost sight of you, he became instantly the prey of an abject funk, and would let that cripple of a steamboat get the upper hand of him in a minute.

"I was looking down at the sounding-pole, and feeling much annoyed to see at each try a little more of it stick out of that river, when I saw my poleman give up the business suddenly, and stretch himself flat on the deck, without even taking the trouble to haul his pole in. He kept hold on it though, and it trailed in the water. At

3. A flat-bottomed boat.
4. A rifle.

the same time the fireman, whom I could also see below me, sat down abruptly before his furnace and ducked his head. I was amazed. Then I had to look at the river mighty quick, because there was a snag in the fairway. Sticks, little sticks, were flying about—thick: they were whizzing before my nose, dropping below me, striking behind me against my pilot-house. All this time the river, the shore, the woods, were very quiet—perfectly quiet. I could only hear the heavy splashing thump of the stern-wheel and the patter of these things. We cleared the snag clumsily. Arrows, by Jove! We were being shot at! I stepped in quickly to close the shutter on the landside. That fool-helmsman, his hands on the spokes, was lifting his knees high, stamping his feet, champing his mouth, like a reined-in horse. Confound him! And we were staggering within ten feet of the bank. I had to lean right out to swing the heavy shutter, and I saw a face amongst the leaves on the level with my own, looking at me very fierce and steady; and then suddenly, as though a veil had been removed from my eyes, I made out, deep in the tangled gloom, naked breasts, arms, legs, glaring eyes,—the bush was swarming with human limbs in movement, glistening, of bronze colour. The twigs shook, swayed, and rustled, the arrows flew out of them, and then the shutter came to. 'Steer her straight,' I said to the helmsman. He held his head rigid, face forward; but his eyes rolled, he kept on lifting and setting down his feet gently, his mouth foamed a little. 'Keep quiet!' I said in a fury. I might just as well have ordered a tree not to sway in the wind. I darted out. Below me there was a great scuffle of feet on the iron deck; confused exclamations; a voice screamed, 'Can you turn back?' I caught sight of a V-shaped ripple on the water ahead. What? Another snag! A fusillade burst out under my feet. The pilgrims had opened with their Winchesters, and were simply squirting lead into that bush. A deuce of a lot of smoke came up and drove slowly forward. I swore at it. Now I couldn't see the ripple or the snag either. I stood in the doorway, peering, and the arrows came in swarms. They might have been poisoned, but they looked as though they wouldn't kill a cat. The bush began to howl. Our wood-cutters raised a warlike whoop; the report of a rifle just at my back deafened me. I glanced over my shoulder, and the pilot-house was yet full of noise and smoke when I made a dash at the wheel. The fool-nigger had dropped everything, to throw the shutter open and let off that Martini-Henry. He stood before the wide opening, glaring, and I yelled at him to come back, while I straightened the sudden twist out of that steamboat. There was no room to turn even if I had wanted to, the snag was somewhere very near ahead in that confounded smoke, there was no time to lose, so I just crowded her into the bank—right into the bank, where I knew the water was deep.

"We tore slowly along the overhanging bushes in a whirl of broken twigs and flying leaves. The fusillade below stopped short, as I had foreseen it would when the squirts got empty. I threw my head back to a glinting whizz that traversed the pilot-house, in at one shutter-hole and out at the other. Looking past that mad helmsman, who was shaking the empty rifle and yelling at the shore, I saw vague forms of men running bent double, leaping, gliding, distinct, incomplete, evanescent. Something big appeared in the air before the shutter, the rifle went overboard, and the man stepped back swiftly, looked at me over his shoulder in an extraordinary, profound, familiar manner, and fell upon my feet. The side of his head hit the wheel twice, and the end of what appeared a long cane clattered round and knocked over a little camp-stool. It looked as though after wrenching that thing from somebody ashore he had lost his balance in the effort. The thin smoke had blown away, we were clear of the snag, and looking ahead I could see that in another hundred yards or so I would be free to sheer off, away from the bank; but my feet felt so very warm and wet that I had to look down. The man had rolled on his back and stared straight up at me; both his hands clutched that cane. It was the shaft of a spear that, either thrown or lunged through the opening, had caught him in the side just below the ribs; the blade had gone in out of sight, after making a frightful gash; my shoes were full; a pool of blood lay very still, gleaming dark-red under the wheel; his eyes shone with an amazing lustre. The fusillade burst out again. He looked at me anxiously, gripping the spear like something precious, with an air of being afraid I would try to take it away from him. I had to make an effort to free my eyes from his gaze and attend to the steering. With one hand I felt above my head for the line of the steam-whistle, and jerked out screech after screech hurriedly. The tumult of angry and warlike yells was checked instantly, and then from the depths of the woods went out such a tremulous and prolonged wail of mournful fear and utter despair as may be imagined to follow the flight of the last hope from the earth. There was a great commotion in the bush; the shower of arrows stopped, a few dropping shots rang out sharply—then silence, in which the languid beat of the stern-wheel came plainly to my ears. I put the helm hard astarboard at the moment when the pilgrim in pink pyjamas, very hot and agitated, appeared in the doorway. 'The manager sends me—' he began in an official tone, and stopped short. 'Good God!' he said, glaring at the wounded man.

"We two whites stood over him, and his lustrous and inquiring glance enveloped us both. I declare it looked as though he would presently put to us some question in an understandable language; but he died without uttering a sound, without moving a limb, without twitching a muscle. Only in the very last moment, as though in response to some sign we could not see, to some whisper we could not hear, he frowned heavily, and that frown gave to his black death-mask an inconceivably sombre, brooding, and menacing expression. The lustre of inquiring glance faded swiftly into vacant glassiness. 'Can you steer?' I asked the agent eagerly. He looked very dubious; but I made a grab at his arm, and he understood at once I meant him to steer whether or no. To tell you the truth, I was morbidly anxious to change my shoes and socks. 'He is dead,' murmured the fellow, immensely impressed. 'No doubt about it,' said I, tugging like mad at the shoelaces. 'And, by the way, I suppose Mr Kurtz is dead as well by this time.'

"For the moment that was the dominant thought. There was a sense of extreme disappointment, as though I had found out I had been striving after something altogether without a substance. I couldn't have been more disgusted if I had travelled all this way for the sole purpose of talking with Mr Kurtz. Talking with . . . I flung one shoe overboard, and became aware that that was exactly what I had been looking forward to—a talk with Kurtz. I made the strange discovery that I had never imagined him as doing, you know, but as discoursing. I didn't say to myself, 'Now I will never see him,' or 'Now I will never shake him by the hand,' but, 'Now I will never hear him.' The man presented himself as a voice. Not of course that I did not connect him with some sort of action. Hadn't I been told in all the tones of jealousy and admiration that he had collected, bartered, swindled, or stolen more ivory than all the other agents together. That was not the point. The point was in his being a gifted creature, and that of all his gifts the one that stood out pre-eminently, that carried with it a sense of real presence, was his ability to talk, his words—the gift of expression, the bewildering, the illuminating, the most exalted and the most contemptible, the pulsating stream of light, or the deceitful flow from the heart of an impenetrable darkness.

"The other shoe went flying unto the devil-god of that river. I thought, By Jove! it's all over. We are too late; he has vanished—the gift has vanished, by means of some spear, arrow, or club. I will never hear that chap speak after all,—and my sorrow had a startling extravagance of emotion, even such as I had noticed in the howling sorrow of these savages in the bush. I couldn't have felt more of lonely desolation somehow, had I been robbed of a belief or had missed my destiny in life. . . . Why do you sigh in this beastly way, somebody? Absurd? Well, absurd. Good Lord! mustn't a man ever—Here, give me some tobacco." . . .

There was a pause of profound stillness, then a match flared, and Marlow's lean face appeared, worn, hollow, with downward folds and dropped eyelids, with an aspect of concentrated attention; and as he took vigorous draws at his pipe, it seemed to retreat and advance out of the night in the regular flicker of the tiny flame. The match went out.

"Absurd!" he cried. "This is the worst of trying to tell . . . Here you all are, each moored with two good addresses, like a hulk with two anchors, a butcher round one corner, a policeman round another, excellent appetites, and temperature normal—you hear—normal from year's end to year's end. And you say, Absurd! Absurd be— exploded! Absurd! My dear boys, what can you expect from a man who out of sheer nervousness had just flung overboard a pair of new shoes? Now I think of it, it is amazing I did not shed tears. I am, upon the whole, proud of my fortitude. I was cut to the quick at the idea of having lost the inestimable privilege of listening to the gifted Kurtz. Of course I was wrong. The privilege was waiting for me. Oh yes, I heard more than enough. And I was right, too. A voice. He was very little more than a voice. And I heard—him—it—this voice—other voices—all of them were so little more than voices—and the memory of that time itself lingers around me, impalpable, like a dying vibration of one immense jabber, silly, atrocious, sordid, savage, or simply mean, without any kind of sense. Voices, voices—even the girl herself—now—"

He was silent for a long time.

"I laid the ghost of his gifts at last with a lie," he began suddenly. "Girl! What? Did I mention a girl? Oh, she is out of it—completely. They—the women I mean—are out of it—should be out of it. We must help them to stay in that beautiful world of their own, lest ours gets worse. Oh, she had to be out of it. You should have heard the disinterred body of Mr Kurtz saying, 'My Intended.' You would have perceived directly then how completely she was out of it. And the lofty frontal bone of Mr Kurtz! They say the hair goes on growing sometimes, but this—ah—specimen was impressively bald. The wilderness had patted him on the head, and, behold, it was like a ball—an ivory ball; it had caressed him, and—lo!—he had withered; it had taken him, loved him, embraced him, got into his veins, consumed his flesh, and sealed his soul to its own by the inconceivable ceremonies of some devilish initiation. He was its spoiled and pampered favourite. Ivory? I should think so. Heaps of it, stacks of it. The old mud shanty was bursting with it. You would think there was not a single tusk left either above or below the ground in the whole country. 'Mostly fossil,' the manager had remarked disparagingly. It was no more fossil than I am; but they call it fossil when it is dug up. It appears these niggers do bury the tusks sometimes—but evidently they couldn't bury this parcel deep enough to save the gifted Mr Kurtz from his fate. We filled the steamboat with it, and had to pile a lot on the deck. Thus he could see and enjoy as long as he could see, because the appreciation of this favour had remained with him to the last. You should have heard him say, 'My ivory.' Oh yes, I heard him. 'My Intended, my ivory, my station, my river, my—' everything belonged to him. It made me hold my breath in expectation of hearing the wilderness burst into a prodigious peal of laughter that would shake the fixed stars in their places. Everything belonged to him—but that was a trifle. The thing was to know what he belonged to, how many powers of darkness claimed him for their own. That was the reflection that made you creepy all over. It was impossible—it was not good for one either—trying to imagine. He had taken a high seat amongst the devils of the land—I mean literally. You can't understand. How could you?—with solid pavement under your feet, surrounded by kind neighbours ready to cheer you or to fall on you, stepping delicately between the butcher and the policeman, in the holy terror of scandal and gallows and lunatic asylums—how can you imagine what particular region of the first ages a man's untrammelled feet may take him into by the way of solitude— utter solitude without a policeman—by the way of silence—utter silence, where no warning voice of a kind neighbour can be heard whispering of public opinion? These little things make all the great difference. When they are gone you must fall back upon your own innate strength, upon your own capacity for faithfulness. Of course you may be too much of a fool to go wrong—too dull even to know you are being assaulted by the powers of darkness. I take it, no fool ever made a bargain for his soul with the devil: the fool is too much of a fool, or the devil too much of a devil—I don't know which. Or you may be such a thunderingly exalted creature as to be altogether deaf and blind to anything but heavenly sights and sounds. Then the earth for you is only a standing place—and whether to be like this is your loss or your gain I won't pretend to say. But most of us are neither one nor the other. The earth for us is a place to live in, where we must put up with sights, with sounds, with smells too, by Jove!—breathe dead hippo, so to speak, and not be contaminated. And there, don't you see? your strength comes in, the faith in your ability for the digging of unostentatious holes to bury the stuff in—your power of devotion, not to yourself, but to an obscure, back-breaking business. And that's difficult enough. Mind, I am not trying to excuse or even explain—I am trying to account to myself for—for—Mr Kurtz—for the shade of Mr Kurtz. This initiated wraith from the back of Nowhere honoured me with its amazing confidence before it vanished altogether. This was because it could speak English to me. The original Kurtz had been educated partly in England, and—as he was good enough to say himself—his sympa- thies were in the right place. His mother was half-English, his father was half-French. All Europe contributed to the making of Kurtz; and by-and-by I learned that, most ap- propriately, the International Society for the Suppression of Savage Customs had in- trusted him with the making of a report, for its future guidance. And he had written it too. I've seen it. I've read it. It was eloquent, vibrating with eloquence, but too high- strung, I think. Seventeen pages of close writing he had found time for! But this must have been before his—let us say—nerves went wrong, and caused him to preside at certain midnight dances ending with unspeakable rites, which—as far as I reluctantly gathered from what I heard at various times—were offered up to him—do you under- stand?—to Mr Kurtz himself. But it was a beautiful piece of writing. The opening para- graph, however, in the light of later information, strikes me now as ominous. He began with the argument that we whites, from the point of development we had arrived at, 'must necessarily appear to them [savages] in the nature of supernatural beings—we ap- proach them with the might as of a deity,' and so on, and so on. 'By the simple exercise of our will we can exert a power for good practically unbounded,' & c., & c. From that point he soared and took me with him. The peroration was magnificent, though difficult to remember, you know. It gave me the notion of an exotic Immensity ruled by an au- gust Benevolence. It made me tingle with enthusiasm. This was the unbounded power of eloquence—of words—of burning noble words. There were no practical hints to in- terrupt the magic current of phrases, unless a kind of note at the foot of the last page, scrawled evidently much later, in an unsteady hand, may be regarded as the exposition of a method. It was very simple, and at the end of that moving appeal to every altruistic sentiment it blazed at you, luminous and terrifying, like a flash of lightning in a serene sky: 'Exterminate all the brutes!' The curious part was that he had apparently forgotten all about that valuable postscriptum, because, later on, when he in a sense came to himself, he repeatedly entreated me to take good care of 'my pamphlet' (he called it), as it was sure to have in the future a good influence upon his career. I had full information about all these things, and, besides, as it turned out, I was to have the care of his memory. I've done enough for it to give me the indisputable right to lay it, if I choose, for an everlasting rest in the dust-bin of progress, amongst all the sweepings and, figuratively speaking, all the dead cats of civilisation. But then, you see, I can't choose. He won't be forgotten. Whatever he was, he was not common. He had the power to charm or frighten rudimentary souls into an aggravated witch-dance in his honour; he could also fill the small souls of the pilgrims with bitter misgivings: he had one devoted friend at least, and he had conquered one soul in the world that was neither rudimentary nor tainted with self-seeking. No; I can't forget him, though I am not prepared to affirm the fellow was exactly worth the life we lost in getting to him. I missed my late helmsman awfully,—I missed him even while his body was still lying in the pilot-house. Perhaps you will think it passing strange this regret for a savage who was no more account than a grain of sand in a black Sahara. Well, don't you see, he had done something, he had steered; for months I had him at my back—a help—an instrument. It was a kind of partnership. He steered for me—I had to look after him, I worried about his deficiencies, and thus a subtle bond had been created, of which I only became aware when it was suddenly broken. And the intimate profundity of that look he gave me when he received his hurt remains to this day in my memory—like a claim of distant kinship affirmed in a supreme moment.

"Poor fool! If he had only left that shutter alone. He had no restraint, no restraint—just like Kurtz—a tree swayed by the wind. As soon as I had put on a dry pair of slippers, I dragged him out, after first jerking the spear out of his side, which operation I confess I performed with my eyes shut tight. His heels leaped together over the little doorstep; his shoulders were pressed to my breast; I hugged him from behind desperately. Oh! he was heavy, heavy; heavier than any man on earth, I should imagine. Then without more ado I tipped him overboard. The current snatched him as though he had been a wisp of grass, and I saw the body roll over twice before I lost sight of it for ever. All the pilgrims and the manager were then congregated on the awning-deck about the pilot-house, chattering at each other like a flock of excited magpies, and there was a scandalised murmur at my heartless promptitude. What they wanted to keep that body hanging about for I can't guess. Embalm it, maybe. But I had also heard another, and a very ominous, murmur on the deck below. My friends the woodcutters were likewise scandalised, and with a better show of reason—though I admit that the reason itself was quite inadmissible. Oh, quite! I had made up my mind that if my late helmsman was to be eaten, the fishes alone should have him. He had been a very second-rate helmsman while alive, but now he was dead he might have become a first-class temptation, and possibly cause some startling trouble. Besides, I was anxious to take the wheel, the man in pink pyjamas showing himself a hopeless duffer at the business.

"This I did directly the simple funeral was over. We were going half-speed, keeping right in the middle of the stream, and I listened to the talk about me. They had given up Kurtz, they had given up the station; Kurtz was dead, and the station had been burnt—and so on—and so on. The red-haired pilgrim was beside himself with the thought that at least this poor Kurtz had been properly revenged. 'Say! We must have made a glorious slaughter of them in the bush. Eh? What do you think? Say?'

He positively danced, the bloodthirsty little gingery beggar. And he had nearly fainted when he saw the wounded man! I could not help saying, 'You made a glorious lot of smoke, anyhow.' I had seen, from the way the tops of the bushes rustled and flew, that almost all the shots had gone too high. You can't hit anything unless you take aim and fire from the shoulder; but these chaps fired from the hip with their eyes shut. The retreat, I maintained—and I was right—was caused by the screeching of the steam-whistle. Upon this they forgot Kurtz, and began to howl at me with indignant protests.

"The manager stood by the wheel murmuring confidentially about the necessity of getting well away down the river before dark at all events, when I saw in the distance a clearing on the river-side and the outlines of some sort of building. 'What's this?' I asked. He clapped his hands in wonder. 'The station!' he cried. I edged in at once, still going half-speed.

"Through my glasses I saw the slope of a hill interspersed with rare trees and perfectly free from undergrowth. A long decaying building on the summit was half buried in the high grass; the large holes in the peaked roof gaped black from afar; the jungle and the woods made a background. There was no enclosure or fence of any kind; but there had been one apparently, for near the house half-a-dozen slim posts remained in a row, roughly trimmed, and with their upper ends ornamented with round carved balls. The rails, or whatever there had been between, had disappeared. Of course the forest surrounded all that. The river-bank was clear, and on the water-side I saw a white man under a hat like a cart-wheel beckoning persistently with his whole arm. Examining the edge of the forest above and below, I was almost certain I could see movements—human forms gliding here and there. I steamed past prudently, then stopped the engines and let her drift down. The man on the shore began to shout, urging us to land. 'We have been attacked,' screamed the manager. 'I know—I know. It's all right,' yelled back the other, as cheerful as you please. 'Come along. It's all right. I am glad.'

"His aspect reminded me of something I had seen—something funny I had seen somewhere. As I manoeuvred to get alongside, I was asking myself, 'What does this fellow look like?' Suddenly I got it. He looked like a harlequin. His clothes had been made of some stuff that was brown holland[5] probably, but it was covered with patches all over, with bright patches, blue, red, and yellow,—patches on the back, patches on front, patches on elbows, on knees; coloured binding round his jacket, scarlet edging at the bottom of his trousers; and the sunshine made him look extremely gay and wonderfully neat withal, because you could see how beautifully all this patching had been done. A beardless, boyish face, very fair, no features to speak of, nose peeling, little blue eyes, smiles and frowns chasing each other over that open countenance like sunshine and shadow on a wind-swept plain. 'Look out, captain!' he cried; 'there's a snag lodged in here last night.' What! Another snag? I confess I swore shamefully. I had nearly holed my cripple, to finish off that charming trip. The harlequin on the bank turned his little pug nose up to me. 'You English?' he asked, all smiles. 'Are you?' I shouted from the wheel. The smiles vanished, and he shook his head as if sorry for my disappointment. Then he brightened up. 'Never mind!' he cried encouragingly. 'Are we in time?' I asked. 'He is up there,' he replied, with a toss of the head up the hill, and becoming gloomy all of a sudden. His face was like the autumn sky, overcast one moment and bright the next.

5. A smooth linen fabric.

"When the manager, escorted by the pilgrims, all of them armed to the teeth, had gone to the house, this chap came on board. 'I say, I don't like this. These natives are in the bush,' I said. He assured me earnestly it was all right. 'They are simple people,' he added; 'well, I am glad you came. It took me all my time to keep them off.' 'But you said it was all right,' I cried. 'Oh, they meant no harm,' he said; and as I stared he corrected himself, 'Not exactly.' Then vivaciously, 'My faith, your pilot-house wants a clean-up!' In the next breath he advised me to keep enough steam on the boiler to blow the whistle in case of any trouble. 'One good screech will do more for you than all your rifles. They are simple people,' he repeated. He rattled away at such a rate he quite overwhelmed me. He seemed to be trying to make up for lots of silence, and actually hinted, laughing, that such was the case. 'Don't you talk with Mr Kurtz?' I said. 'You don't talk with that man—you listen to him,' he exclaimed with severe exaltation. 'But now—' He waved his arm, and in the twinkling of an eye was in the uttermost depths of despondency. In a moment he came up again with a jump, possessed himself of both my hands, shook them continuously, while he gabbled: 'Brother sailor . . . honour . . . pleasure . . . delight . . . introduce myself . . . Russian . . . son of an arch-priest . . . Government of Tambov[6] . . . What? Tobacco! English tobacco; the excellent English tobacco! Now, that's brotherly. Smoke? Where's a sailor that does not smoke?'

"The pipe soothed him, and gradually I made out he had run away from school, had gone to sea in a Russian ship; ran away again; served some time in English ships; was now reconciled with the arch-priest. He made a point of that. 'But when one is young one must see things, gather experience, ideas; enlarge the mind.' 'Here!' I interrupted. 'You can never tell! Here I have met Mr Kurtz,' he said, youthfully solemn and reproachful. I held my tongue after that. It appears he had persuaded a Dutch trading-house on the coast to fit him out with stores and goods, and had started for the interior with a light heart, and no more idea of what would happen to him than a baby. He had been wandering about that river for nearly two years alone, cut off from everybody and everything. 'I am not so young as I look. I am twenty-five,' he said. 'At first old Van Shuyten would tell me to go to the devil,' he narrated with keen enjoyment; 'but I stuck to him, and talked and talked, till at last he got afraid I would talk the hind-leg off his favorite dog, so he gave me some cheap things and a few guns, and told me he hoped he would never see my face again. Good old Dutchman, Van Shuyten. I sent him one small lot of ivory a year ago, so that he can't call me a little thief when I get back. I hope he got it. And for the rest, I don't care. I had some wood stacked for you. That was my old house. Did you see?'

"I gave him Towson's book. He made as though he would kiss me, but restrained himself. 'The only book I had left, and I thought I had lost it,' he said, looking at it ecstatically. 'So many accidents happen to a man going about alone, you know. Canoes get upset sometimes—and sometimes you've got to clear out so quick when the people get angry.' He thumbed the pages. 'You made notes in Russian?' I asked. He nodded. 'I thought they were written in cipher,' I said. He laughed, then became serious. 'I had lots of trouble to keep these people off,' he said. 'Did they want to kill you?' I asked. 'Oh no!' he cried, and checked himself. 'Why did they attack us?' I pursued. He hesitated, then said shamefacedly, 'They don't want him to go.' 'Don't they?' I said, curiously. He nodded a nod full of mystery and wisdom. 'I tell you,' he cried, 'this man has enlarged my mind.' He opened his arms wide, staring at me with his little blue eyes that were perfectly round."

6. A province of Western Russia.

3

"I looked at him, lost in astonishment. There he was before me, in motley, as though he had absconded from a troupe of mimes, enthusiastic, fabulous. His very existence was improbable, inexplicable, and altogether bewildering. He was an insoluble problem. It was inconceivable how he had existed, how he had succeeded in getting so far, how he had managed to remain—why he did not instantly disappear. 'I went a little farther,' he said, 'then still a little farther—till I had gone so far that I don't know how I'll ever get back. Never mind. Plenty time. I can manage. You take Kurtz away quick—quick—I tell you.' The glamour of youth enveloped his particoloured rags, his destitution, his loneliness, the essential desolation of his futile wanderings. For months—for years—his life hadn't been worth a day's purchase; and there he was gallantly, thoughtlessly alive, to all appearance indestructible solely by the virtue of his few years and of his unreflecting audacity. I was seduced into something like admiration—like envy. Glamour urged him on, glamour kept him unscathed. He surely wanted nothing from the wilderness but space to breathe in and to push on through. His need was to exist, and to move onwards at the greatest possible risk, and with a maximum of privation. If the absolutely pure, uncalculating, unpractical spirit of adventure had ever ruled a human being, it ruled this be-patched youth. I almost envied him the possession of this modest and clear flame. It seemed to have consumed all thought of self so completely, that, even while he was talking to you, you forgot that it was he—the man before your eyes—who had gone through these things. I did not envy him his devotion to Kurtz, though. He had not meditated over it. It came to him, and he accepted it with a sort of eager fatalism. I must say that to me it appeared about the most dangerous thing in every way he had come upon so far.

"They had come together unavoidably, like two ships becalmed near each other, and lay rubbing sides at last. I suppose Kurtz wanted an audience, because on a certain occasion, when encamped in the forest, they had talked all night, or more probably Kurtz had talked. 'We talked of everything,' he said, quite transported at the recollection. 'I forgot there was such a thing as sleep. The night did not seem to last an hour. Everything! Everything! . . . Of love too.' 'Ah, he talked to you of love!' I said, much amused. 'It isn't what you think,' he cried, almost passionately. 'It was in general. He made me see things—things.'

"He threw his arms up. We were on deck at the time, and the headman of my wood-cutters, lounging near by, turned upon him his heavy and glittering eyes. I looked around, and I don't know why, but I assure you that never, never before, did this land, this river, this jungle, the very arch of this blazing sky, appear to me so hopeless and so dark, so impenetrable to human thought, so pitiless to human weakness. 'And, ever since, you have been with him, of course?' I said.

"On the contrary. It appears their intercourse had been very much broken by various causes. He had, as he informed me proudly, managed to nurse Kurtz through two illnesses (he alluded to it as you would to some risky feat), but as a rule Kurtz wandered alone, far in the depths of the forest. 'Very often coming to this station, I had to wait days and days before he would turn up,' he said. 'Ah, it was worth waiting for!— sometimes.' 'What was he doing? exploring or what?' I asked. 'Oh yes, of course'; he had discovered lots of villages, a lake too—he did not know exactly in what direction; it was dangerous to inquire too much—but mostly his expeditions had been for ivory. 'But he had no goods to trade with by that time,' I objected. 'There's a good lot of cartridges left even yet,' he answered, looking away. 'To speak plainly, he raided the country,' I said. He nodded. 'Not alone, surely!' He muttered something about the villages round that lake. 'Kurtz got the tribe to follow him, did he?' I suggested. He fidgeted a little. 'They adored him,' he said. The tone of these words was so extraordinary that I looked at him searchingly. It was curious to see his mingled eagerness and reluctance to speak of Kurtz. The man filled his life, occupied his thoughts, swayed his emotions. 'What can you expect?' he burst out; 'he came to them with thunder and lightning, you know—and they had never seen anything like it—and very terrible. He could be very terrible. You can't judge Mr Kurtz as you would an ordinary man. No, no, no! Now—just to give you an idea—I don't mind telling you, he wanted to shoot me too one day—but I don't judge him.' 'Shoot you!' I cried. 'What for?' 'Well, I had a small lot of ivory the chief of that village near my house gave me. You see I used to shoot game for them. Well, he wanted it, and wouldn't hear reason. He declared he would shoot me unless I gave him the ivory and then cleared out of the country, because he could do so, and had a fancy for it, and there was nothing on earth to prevent him killing whom he jolly well pleased. And it was true too. I gave him the ivory. What did I care! But I didn't clear out. No, no. I couldn't leave him. I had to be careful, of course, till we got friendly again for a time. He had his second illness then. Afterwards I had to keep out of the way; but I didn't mind. He was living for the most part in those villages on the lake. When he came down to the river, sometimes he would take to me, and sometimes it was better for me to be careful. This man suffered too much. He hated all this, and somehow he couldn't get away. When I had a chance I begged him to try and leave while there was time; I offered to go back with him. And he would say yes, and then he would remain; go off on another ivory hunt; disappear for weeks; forget himself amongst these people—forget himself—you know.' 'Why! he's mad,' I said. He protested indignantly. Mr Kurtz couldn't be mad. If I had heard him talk, only two days ago, I wouldn't dare hint at such a thing.... I had taken up my binoculars while we talked, and was looking at the shore, sweeping the limit of the forest at each side and at the back of the house. The consciousness of there being people in that bush, so silent, so quiet—as silent and quiet as the ruined house on the hill—made me uneasy. There was no sign on the face of nature of this amazing tale that was not so much told as suggested to me in desolate exclamations, completed by shrugs, in interrupted phrases, in hints ending in deep sighs. The woods were unmoved, like a mask—heavy, like the closed door of a prison—they looked with their air of hidden knowledge, of patient expectation, of unapproachable silence. The Russian was explaining to me that it was only lately that Mr Kurtz had come down to the river, bringing along with him all the fighting men of that lake tribe. He had been absent for several months—getting himself adored, I suppose—and had come down unexpectedly, with the intention to all appearance of making a raid either across the river or down stream. Evidently the appetite for more ivory had got the better of the—what shall I say?—less material aspirations. However, he had got much worse suddenly. 'I heard he was lying helpless, and so I came up—took my chance,' said the Russian. 'Oh, he is bad, very bad.' I directed my glass to the house. There were no signs of life, but there was the ruined roof, the long mud wall peeping above the grass, with three little square window-holes, no two of the same size; all this brought within reach of my hand, as it were. And then I made a brusque movement, and one of the remaining posts of that vanished fence leaped up in the field of my glass. You remember I told you I had been struck at the distance by certain attempts at ornamentation, rather remarkable in the ruinous aspect of the place. Now I had suddenly a nearer view, and its first result was to make me throw my head back as if before a blow. Then I went carefully from post to post with my glass, and

I saw my mistake. These round knobs were not ornamental but symbolic; they were expressive and puzzling, striking and disturbing—food for thought and also for the vultures if there had been any looking down from the sky; but at all events for such ants as were industrious enough to ascend the pole. They would have been even more impressive, those heads on the stakes, if their faces had not been turned to the house. Only one, the first I had made out, was facing my way. I was not so shocked as you may think. The start back I had given was really nothing but a movement of surprise. I had expected to see a knob of wood there, you know. I returned deliberately to the first I had seen—and there it was, black, dried, sunken, with closed eyelids,—a head that seemed to sleep at the top of that pole, and, with the shrunken dry lips showing a narrow white line of the teeth, was smiling too, smiling continuously at some endless and jocose dream of that eternal slumber.

"I am not disclosing any trade secrets. In fact the manager said afterwards that Mr Kurtz's methods had ruined the district. I have no opinion on that point, but I want you clearly to understand that there was nothing exactly profitable in these heads being there. They only showed that Mr Kurtz lacked restraint in the gratification of his various lusts, that there was something wanting in him—some small matter which, when the pressing need arose, could not be found under his magnificent eloquence. Whether he knew of this deficiency himself I can't say. I think the knowledge came to him at last—only at the very last. But the wilderness had found him out early, and had taken on him a terrible vengeance for the fantastic invasion. I think it had whispered to him things about himself which he did not know, things of which he had no conception till he took counsel with this great solitude—and the whisper had proved irresistibly fascinating. It echoed loudly within him because he was hollow at the core.... I put down the glass, and the head that had appeared near enough to be spoken to seemed at once to have leaped away from me into inaccessible distance.

"The admirer of Mr Kurtz was a bit crestfallen. In a hurried, indistinct voice he began to assure me he had not dared to take these—say, symbols—down. He was not afraid of the natives; they would not stir till Mr Kurtz gave the word. His ascendancy was extraordinary. The camps of these people surrounded the place, and the chiefs came every day to see him. They would crawl.... 'I don't want to know anything of the ceremonies used when approaching Mr Kurtz,' I shouted. Curious, this feeling that came over me that such details would be more intolerable than those heads drying on the stakes under Mr Kurtz's windows. After all, that was only a savage sight, while I seemed at one bound to have been transported into some lightless region of subtle horrors, where pure, uncomplicated savagery was a positive relief, being something that had a right to exist—obviously—in the sunshine. The young man looked at me with surprise. I suppose it did not occur to him Mr Kurtz was no idol of mine. He forgot I hadn't heard any of these splendid monologues on, what was it? on love, justice, conduct of life—or what not. If it had come to crawling before Mr Kurtz, he crawled as much as the veriest savage of them all. I had no idea of the conditions, he said: these heads were the heads of rebels. I shocked him excessively by laughing. Rebels! What would be the next definition I was to hear? There had been enemies, criminals, workers—and these were rebels. Those rebellious heads looked very subdued to me on their sticks. 'You don't know how such a life tries a man like Kurtz,' cried Kurtz's last disciple. 'Well, and you?' I said. 'I! I! I am a simple man. I have no great thoughts. I want nothing from anybody. How can you compare me to...?' His feelings were too much for speech, and suddenly he broke down. 'I don't understand,' he groaned. 'I've been doing my best to keep him alive, and that's enough. I had no hand in all this. I have no abilities. There hasn't been a drop of medicine or a mouthful of invalid food for months here. He was shamefully abandoned. A man like this, with such ideas. Shamefully! Shamefully! I—I—haven't slept for the last ten nights....'

"His voice lost itself in the calm of the evening. The long shadows of the forest had slipped down-hill while we talked, had gone far beyond the ruined hovel, beyond the symbolic row of stakes. All this was in the gloom, while we down there were yet in the sunshine, and the stretch of the river abreast of the clearing glittered in a still and dazzling splendour, with a murky and overshadowed bend above and below. Not a living soul was seen on the shore. The bushes did not rustle.

"Suddenly round the corner of the house a group of men appeared, as though they had come up from the ground. They waded waist-deep in the grass, in a compact body, bearing an improvised stretcher in their midst. Instantly, in the emptiness of the landscape, a cry arose whose shrillness pierced the still air like a sharp arrow flying straight to the very heart of the land; and, as if by enchantment, streams of human beings—of naked human beings—with spears in their hands, with bows, with shields, with wild glances and savage movements, were poured into the clearing by the dark-faced and pensive forest. The bushes shook, the grass swayed for a time, and then everything stood still in attentive immobility.

"'Now, if he does not say the right thing to them we are all done for,' said the Russian at my elbow. The knot of men with the stretcher had stopped too, half-way to the steamer, as if petrified. I saw the man on the stretcher sit up, lank and with an uplifted arm, above the shoulders of the bearers. 'Let us hope that the man who can talk so well of love in general will find some particular reason to spare us this time,' I said. I resented bitterly the absurd danger of our situation, as if to be at the mercy of that atrocious phantom had been a dishonouring necessity. I could not hear a sound, but through my glasses I saw the thin arm extended commandingly, the lower jaw moving, the eyes of that apparition shining darkly far in its bony head that nodded with grotesque jerks. Kurtz—Kurtz—that means 'short' in German—don't it? Well, the name was as true as everything else in his life—and death. He looked at least seven feet long. His covering had fallen off, and his body emerged from it pitiful and appalling as from a winding-sheet. I could see the cage of his ribs all astir, the bones of his arm waving. It was as though an animated image of death carved out of old ivory had been shaking its hand with menaces at a motionless crowd of men made of dark and glittering bronze. I saw him open his mouth wide—it gave him a weirdly voracious aspect, as though he had wanted to swallow all the air, all the earth, all the men before him. A deep voice reached me faintly. He must have been shouting. He fell back suddenly. The stretcher shook as the bearers staggered forward again, and almost at the same time I noticed that the crowd of savages was vanishing without any perceptible movement of retreat, as if the forest that had ejected these beings so suddenly had drawn them in again as the breath is drawn in a long aspiration.

"Some of the pilgrims behind the stretcher carried his arms—two shot-guns, a heavy rifle, and a light revolver-carbine—the thunderbolts of that pitiful Jupiter. The manager bent over him murmuring as he walked beside his head. They laid him down in one of the little cabins—just a room for a bed-place and a camp-stool or two, you know. We had brought his belated correspondence, and a lot of torn envelopes and open letters littered his bed. His hand roamed feebly amongst these papers. I was struck by the fire of his eyes and the composed languor of his expression. It was not so much the exhaustion of disease. He did not seem in pain. This shadow looked satiated and calm, as though for the moment it had had its fill of all the emotions.

"He rustled one of the letters, and looking straight in my face said, 'I am glad.' Somebody had been writing to him about me. These special recommendations were turning up again. The volume of tone he emitted without effort, almost without the trouble of moving his lips, amazed me. A voice! a voice! It was grave, profound, vibrating, while the man did not seem capable of a whisper. However, he had enough strength in him—factitious no doubt—to very nearly make an end of us, as you shall hear directly.

"The manager appeared silently in the doorway; I stepped out at once and he drew the curtain after me. The Russian, eyed curiously by the pilgrims, was staring at the shore. I followed the direction of his glance.

"Dark human shapes could be made out in the distance, flitting indistinctly against the gloomy border of the forest, and near the river two bronze figures, leaning on tall spears, stood in the sunlight under fantastic head-dresses of spotted skins, warlike and still in statuesque repose. And from right to left along the lighted shore moved a wild and gorgeous apparition of a woman.

"She walked with measured steps, draped in striped and fringed cloths, treading the earth proudly, with a slight jingle and flash of barbarous ornaments. She carried her head high; her hair was done in the shape of a helmet; she had brass leggings to the knee, brass wire gauntlets to the elbow, a crimson spot on her tawny cheek, innumerable necklaces of glass beads on her neck; bizarre things, charms, gifts of witchmen, that hung about her, glittered and trembled at every step. She must have had the value of several elephant tusks upon her. She was savage and superb, wild-eyed and magnificent; there was something ominous and stately in her deliberate progress. And in the hush that had fallen suddenly upon the whole sorrowful land, the immense wilderness, the colossal body of the fecund and mysterious life seemed to look at her, pensive, as though it had been looking at the image of its own tenebrous and passionate soul.

"She came abreast of the steamer, stood still, and faced us. Her long shadow fell to the water's edge. Her face had a tragic and fierce aspect of wild sorrow and of dumb pain mingled with the fear of some struggling, half-shaped resolve. She stood looking at us without a stir, and like the wilderness itself, with an air of brooding over an inscrutable purpose. A whole minute passed, and then she made a step forward. There was a low jingle, a glint of yellow metal, a sway of fringed draperies, and she stopped as if her heart had failed her. The young fellow by my side growled. The pilgrims murmured at my back. She looked at us all as if her life had depended upon the unswerving steadiness of her glance. Suddenly she opened her bared arms and threw them up rigid above her head, as though in an uncontrollable desire to touch the sky, and at the same time the swift shadows darted out on the earth, swept around on the river, gathering the steamer in a shadowy embrace. A formidable silence hung over the scene.

"She turned away slowly, walked on, following the bank, and passed into the bushes to the left. Once only her eyes gleamed back at us in the dusk of the thickets before she disappeared.

"'If she had offered to come aboard I really think I would have tried to shoot her,' said the man of patches, nervously. 'I had been risking my life every day for the last fortnight to keep her out of the house. She got in one day and kicked up a row about those miserable rags I picked up in the storeroom to mend my clothes with. I wasn't decent. At least it must have been that, for she talked like a fury to Kurtz for an hour, pointing at me now and then. I don't understand the dialect of this tribe. Luckily for me, I fancy Kurtz felt too ill that day to care, or there would have been mischief. I don't understand. . . . No—it's too much for me. Ah, well, it's all over now.'

"At this moment I heard Kurtz's deep voice behind the curtain, 'Save me!—save the ivory, you mean. Don't tell me. Save *me!* Why, I've had to save you. You are interrupting my plans now. Sick! Sick! Not so sick as you would like to believe. Never mind. I'll carry my ideas out yet—I will return. I'll show you what can be done. You with your little peddling notions—you are interfering with me. I will return. I...'

"The manager came out. He did me the honour to take me under the arm and lead me aside. 'He is very low, very low,' he said. He considered it necessary to sigh, but neglected to be consistently sorrowful. 'We have done all we could for him—haven't we? But there is no disguising the fact, Mr Kurtz has done more harm than good to the Company. He did not see the time was not ripe for vigorous action. Cautiously, cautiously—that's my principle. We must be cautious yet. The district is closed to us for a time. Deplorable! Upon the whole, the trade will suffer. I don't deny there is a remarkable quantity of ivory—mostly fossil. We must save it, at all events—but look how precarious the position is—and why? Because the method is unsound.' 'Do you,' said I, looking at the shore, 'call it "unsound method"?' 'Without doubt,' he exclaimed, hotly. 'Don't you?' ... 'No method at all,' I murmured after a while. 'Exactly,' he exulted. 'I anticipated this. Shows a complete want of judgment. It is my duty to point it out in the proper quarter.' 'Oh,' said I, 'that fellow—what's his name?—the brickmaker, will make a readable report for you.' He appeared confounded for a moment. It seemed to me I had never breathed an atmosphere so vile, and I turned mentally to Kurtz for relief—positively for relief. 'Nevertheless, I think Mr Kurtz is a remarkable man,' I said with emphasis. He started, dropped on me a cold heavy glance, said very quietly, 'He was,' and turned his back on me. My hour of favour was over; I found myself lumped along with Kurtz as a partisan of methods for which the time was not ripe: I was unsound! Ah! but it was something to have at least a choice of nightmares.

"I had turned to the wilderness really, not to Mr Kurtz, who, I was ready to admit, was as good as buried. And for a moment it seemed to me as if I also were buried in a vast grave full of unspeakable secrets. I felt an intolerable weight oppressing my breast, the smell of the damp earth, the unseen presence of victorious corruption, the darkness of an impenetrable night.... The Russian tapped me on the shoulder. I heard him mumbling and stammering something about 'brother seaman—couldn't conceal—knowledge of matters that would affect Mr Kurtz's reputation.' I waited. For him evidently Mr Kurtz was not in his grave; I suspect that for him Mr Kurtz was one of the immortals. 'Well!' said I at last, 'speak out. As it happens, I am Mr Kurtz's friend—in a way.'

"He stated with a good deal of formality that had we not been 'of the same profession,' he would have kept the matter to himself without regard to consequences. He suspected 'there was an active ill-will towards him on the part of these white men that—' 'You are right,' I said, remembering a certain conversation I had overheard. 'The manager thinks you ought to be hanged.' He showed a concern at this intelligence which amused me at first. 'I had better get out of the way quietly,' he said, earnestly. 'I can do no more for Kurtz now, and they would soon find some excuse. What's to stop them? There's a military post three hundred miles from here.' 'Well, upon my word,' said I, 'perhaps you had better go if you have any friends amongst the savages near by.' 'Plenty,' he said. 'They are simple people—and I want nothing, you know.' He stood biting his lip, then: 'I don't want any harm to happen to these whites here, but of course I was thinking of Mr Kurtz's reputation—but you are a brother seaman and—' 'All right,' said I, after a time. 'Mr Kurtz's reputation is safe with me.' I did not know how truly I spoke.

"He informed me, lowering his voice, that it was Kurtz who had ordered the attack to be made on the steamer. 'He hated sometimes the idea of being taken away— and then again ... But I don't understand these matters. I am a simple man. He thought it would scare you away—that you would give it up, thinking him dead. I could not stop him. Oh, I had an awful time of it this last month.' 'Very well,' I said. 'He is all right now.' 'Ye-e-es,' he muttered, not very convinced apparently. 'Thanks,' said I; 'I shall keep my eyes open.' 'But quiet—eh?' he urged, anxiously. 'It would be awful for his reputation if anybody here—' I promised a complete discretion with great gravity. 'I have a canoe and three black fellows waiting not very far. I am off. Could you give me a few Martini-Henry cartridges?' I could, and did, with proper secrecy. He helped himself, with a wink at me, to a handful of my tobacco. 'Between sailors—you know—good English tobacco.' At the door of the pilot-house he turned round—'I say, haven't you a pair of shoes you could spare?' He raised one leg. 'Look.' The soles were tied with knotted strings sandal-wise under his bare feet. I rooted out an old pair, at which he looked with admiration before tucking it under his left arm. One of his pockets (bright red) was bulging with cartridges, from the other (dark blue) peeped 'Towson's Inquiry,' &c., &c. He seemed to think himself excellently well equipped for a renewed encounter with the wilderness. 'Ah! I'll never, never meet such a man again. You ought to have heard him recite poetry—his own too it was, he told me. Poetry!' He rolled his eyes at the recollection of these delights. 'Oh, he enlarged my mind!' 'Good-bye,' said I. He shook hands and vanished in the night. Sometimes I ask myself whether I had ever really seen him—whether it was possible to meet such a phenomenon!...

"When I woke up shortly after midnight his warning came to my mind with its hint of danger that seemed, in the starred darkness, real enough to make me get up for the purpose of having a look round. On the hill a big fire burned, illuminating fitfully a crooked corner of the station-house. One of the agents with a picket of a few of our blacks, armed for the purpose, was keeping guard over the ivory; but deep within the forest, red gleams that wavered, that seemed to sink and rise from the ground amongst confused columnar shapes of intense blackness, showed the exact position of the camp where Mr Kurtz's adorers were keeping their uneasy vigil. The monotonous beating of a big drum filled the air with muffled shocks and a lingering vibration. A steady droning sound of many men chanting each to himself some weird incantation came out from the black, flat wall of the woods as the humming of bees comes out of a hive, and had a strange narcotic effect upon my half-awake senses. I believe I dozed off leaning over the rail, till an abrupt burst of yells, an overwhelming outbreak of a pent-up and mysterious frenzy, woke me up in a bewildered wonder. It was cut short all at once, and the low droning went on with an effect of audible and soothing silence. I glanced casually into the little cabin. A light was burning within, but Mr Kurtz was not there.

"I think I would have raised an outcry if I had believed my eyes. But I didn't believe them at first—the thing seemed so impossible. The fact is, I was completely unnerved by a sheer blank fright, pure abstract terror, unconnected with any distinct shape of physical danger. What made this emotion so overpowering was—how shall I define it?—the moral shock I received, as if something altogether monstrous, intolerable to thought and odious to the soul, had been thrust upon me unexpectedly. This lasted of course the merest fraction of a second, and then the usual sense of commonplace, deadly danger, the possibility of a sudden onslaught and massacre, or something of the kind, which I saw impending, was positively welcome and composing. It pacified me, in fact, so much, that I did not raise an alarm.

"There was an agent buttoned up inside an ulster[7] and sleeping on a chair on deck within three feet of me. The yells had not awakened him; he snored very slightly; I left him to his slumbers and leaped ashore. I did not betray Mr Kurtz—it was ordered

7. Long overcoat.

I should never betray him—it was written I should be loyal to the nightmare of my choice. I was anxious to deal with this shadow by myself alone,—and to this day I don't know why I was so jealous of sharing with any one the peculiar blackness of that experience.

"As soon as I got on the bank I saw a trail—a broad trail through the grass. I remember the exultation with which I said to myself, 'He can't walk—he is crawling on all-fours—I've got him.' The grass was wet with dew. I strode rapidly with clenched fists. I fancy I had some vague notion of falling upon him and giving him a drubbing. I don't know. I had some imbecile thoughts. The knitting old woman with the cat obtruded herself upon my memory as a most improper person to be sitting at the other end of such an affair. I saw a row of pilgrims squirting lead in the air out of Winchesters held to the hip. I thought I would never get back to the steamer, and imagined myself living alone and unarmed in the woods to an advanced age. Such silly things—you know. And I remember I confounded the beat of the drum with the beating of my heart, and was pleased at its calm regularity.

"I kept to the track though—then stopped to listen. The night was very clear: a dark blue space, sparkling with dew and starlight, in which black things stood very still. I thought I could see a kind of motion ahead of me. I was strangely cocksure of everything that night. I actually left the track and ran in a wide semicircle (I verily believe chuckling to myself) so as to get in front of that stir, of that motion I had seen—if indeed I had seen anything. I was circumventing Kurtz as though it had been a boyish game.

"I came upon him, and, if he had not heard me coming, I would have fallen over him too, but he got up in time. He rose, unsteady, long, pale, indistinct, like a vapour exhaled by the earth, and swayed slightly, misty and silent before me; while at my back the fires loomed between the trees, and the murmur of many voices issued from the forest. I had cut him off cleverly; but when actually confronting him I seemed to come to my senses, I saw the danger in its right proportion. It was by no means over yet. Suppose he began to shout? Though he could hardly stand, there was still plenty of vigour in his voice. 'Go away—hide yourself,' he said, in that profound tone. It was very awful. I glanced back. We were within thirty yards from the nearest fire. A black figure stood up, strode on long black legs, waving long black arms, across the glow. It had horns—antelope horns, I think—on its head. Some sorcerer, some witch-man, no doubt: it looked fiend-like enough. 'Do you know what you are doing?' I whispered. 'Perfectly,' he answered, raising his voice for that single word: it sounded to me far off and yet loud, like a hail through a speaking-trumpet. If he makes a row we are lost, I thought to myself. This clearly was not a case for fisticuffs, even apart from the very natural aversion I had to beat that Shadow—this wandering and tormented thing. 'You will be lost,' I said—'utterly lost.' One gets sometimes such a flash of inspiration, you know. I did say the right thing, though indeed he could not have been more irretrievably lost than he was at this very moment, when the foundations of our intimacy were being laid—to endure—to endure—even to the end—even beyond.

"'I had immense plans,' he muttered irresolutely. 'Yes,' said I; 'but if you try to shout I'll smash your head with—' there was not a stick or a stone near. 'I will throttle you for good,' I corrected myself. 'I was on the threshold of great things,' he pleaded, in a voice of longing, with a wistfulness of tone that made my blood run cold. 'And now for this stupid scoundrel—' 'Your success in Europe is assured in any case,' I affirmed, steadily. I did not want to have the throttling of him, you understand—and indeed it would have been very little use for any practical purpose. I tried to break the spell—the heavy, mute spell of the wilderness—that seemed to draw him to its pitiless breast by the awakening of forgotten and brutal instincts, by the memory of gratified and monstrous passions. This alone, I was convinced, had driven him out to the edge of the forest, to the bush, towards the gleam of fires, the throb of drums, the drone of weird incantations; this alone had beguiled his unlawful soul beyond the bounds of permitted aspirations. And, don't you see, the terror of the position was not in being knocked on the head—though I had a very lively sense of that danger too—but in this, that I had to deal with a being to whom I could not appeal in the name of anything high or low. I had, even like the niggers, to invoke him—himself—his own exalted and incredible degradation. There was nothing either above or below him, and I knew it. He had kicked himself loose of the earth. Confound the man! he had kicked the very earth to pieces. He was alone, and I before him did not know whether I stood on the ground or floated in the air. I've been telling you what we said—repeating the phrases we pronounced,—but what's the good? They were common everyday words,—the familiar, vague sounds exchanged on every waking day of life. But what of that? They had behind them, to my mind, the terrific suggestiveness of words heard in dreams, of phrases spoken in nightmares. Soul! If anybody had ever struggled with a soul, I am the man. And I wasn't arguing with a lunatic either. Believe me or not, his intelligence was perfectly clear—concentrated, it is true, upon himself with horrible intensity, yet clear; and therein was my only chance—barring, of course, the killing him there and then, which wasn't so good, on account of unavoidable noise. But his soul was mad. Being alone in the wilderness, it had looked within itself, and, by heavens! I tell you, it had gone mad. I had—for my sins, I suppose—to go through the ordeal of looking into it myself. No eloquence could have been so withering to one's belief in mankind as his final burst of sincerity. He struggled with himself, too. I saw it,—I heard it. I saw the inconceivable mystery of a soul that knew no restraint, no faith, and no fear, yet struggling blindly with itself. I kept my head pretty well; but when I had him at last stretched on the couch, I wiped my forehead, while my legs shook under me as though I had carried half a ton on my back down that hill. And yet I had only supported him, his bony arm clasped round my neck—and he was not much heavier than a child.

"When next day we left at noon, the crowd, of whose presence behind the curtain of trees I had been acutely conscious all the time, flowed out of the woods again, filled the clearing, covered the slope with a mass of naked, breathing, quivering, bronze bodies. I steamed up a bit, then swung down-stream, and two thousand eyes followed the evolutions of the splashing, thumping, fierce river-demon beating the water with its terrible tail and breathing black smoke into the air. In front of the first rank, along the river, three men, plastered with bright red earth from head to foot, strutted to and fro restlessly. When we came abreast again, they faced the river, stamped their feet, nodded their horned heads, swayed their scarlet bodies; they shook towards the fierce river-demon a bunch of black feathers, a mangy skin with a pendent tail—something that looked like a dried gourd; they shouted periodically together strings of amazing words that resembled no sounds of human language; and the deep murmurs of the crowd, interrupted suddenly, were like the responses of some satanic litany.

"We had carried Kurtz into the pilot-house: there was more air there. Lying on the couch, he stared through the open shutter. There was an eddy in the mass of human bodies, and the woman with helmeted head and tawny cheeks rushed out to the very brink of the stream. She put out her hands, shouted something, and all that wild mob took up the shout in a roaring chorus of articulated, rapid, breathless utterance.

"'Do you understand this?' I asked.

"He kept on looking out past me with fiery, longing eyes, with a mingled expression of wistfulness and hate. He made no answer, but I saw a smile, a smile of indefinable meaning, appear on his colourless lips that a moment after twitched convulsively. 'Do I not?' he said slowly, gasping, as if the words had been torn out of him by a supernatural power.

"I pulled the string of the whistle, and I did this because I saw the pilgrims on deck getting out their rifles with an air of anticipating a jolly lark. At the sudden screech there was a movement of abject terror through that wedged mass of bodies. 'Don't! don't! you frighten them away,' cried some one on deck disconsolately. I pulled the string time after time. They broke and ran, they leaped, they crouched, they swerved, they dodged the flying terror of the sound. The three red chaps had fallen flat, face down on the shore, as though they had been shot dead. Only the barbarous and superb woman did not so much as flinch, and stretched tragically her bare arms after us over the sombre and glittering river.

"And then that imbecile crowd down on the deck started their little fun, and I could see nothing more for smoke.

"The brown current ran swiftly out of the heart of darkness, bearing us down towards the sea with twice the speed of our upward progress; and Kurtz's life was running swiftly too, ebbing, ebbing out of his heart into the sea of inexorable time. The manager was very placid, he had no vital anxieties now, he took us both in with a comprehensive and satisfied glance: the 'affair' had come off as well as could be wished. I saw the time approaching when I would be left alone of the party of 'unsound method.' The pilgrims looked upon me with disfavour. I was, so to speak, numbered with the dead. It is strange how I accepted this unforeseen partnership, this choice of nightmares forced upon me in the tenebrous land invaded by these mean and greedy phantoms.

"Kurtz discoursed. A voice! a voice! It rang deep to the very last. It survived his strength to hide in the magnificent folds of eloquence the barren darkness of his heart. Oh, he struggled! he struggled! The wastes of his weary brain were haunted by shadowy images now—images of wealth and fame revolving obsequiously round his unextinguishable gift of noble and lofty expression. My Intended, my station, my career, my ideas—these were the subjects for the occasional utterances of elevated sentiments. The shade of the original Kurtz frequented the bedside of the hollow sham, whose fate it was to be buried presently in the mould of primeval earth. But both the diabolic love and the unearthly hate of the mysteries it had penetrated fought for the possession of that soul satiated with primitive emotions, avid of lying fame, of sham distinction, of all the appearances of success and power.

"Sometimes he was contemptibly childish. He desired to have kings meet him at railway-stations on his return from some ghastly Nowhere, where he intended to accomplish great things. 'You show them you have in you something that is really profitable, and then there will be no limits to the recognition of your ability,' he would say. 'Of course you must take care of the motives—right motives—always.' The long reaches that were like one and the same reach, monotonous bends that were exactly alike, slipped past the steamer with their multitude of secular[8] trees looking patiently after this grimy fragment of another world, the forerunner of change, of conquest, of trade, of massacres, of blessings. I looked ahead—piloting. 'Close the shutter,' said Kurtz suddenly one day; 'I can't bear to look at this.' I did so. There was a silence. 'Oh, but I will wring your heart yet!' he cried at the invisible wilderness.

"We broke down—as I had expected—and had to lie up for repairs at the head of an island. This delay was the first thing that shook Kurtz's confidence. One morning he gave me a packet of papers and a photograph,—the lot tied together with a shoe-string. 'Keep this for me,' he said. 'This noxious fool' (meaning the manager) 'is capable of prying into my boxes when I am not looking.' In the afternoon I saw him. He was lying on his back with closed eyes, and I withdrew quietly, but I heard him mutter, 'Live rightly, die, die . . .' I listened. There was nothing more. Was he rehearsing some speech in his sleep, or was it a fragment of a phrase from some newspaper article? He had been writing for the papers and meant to do so again, 'for the furthering of my ideas. It's a duty.'

"His was an impenetrable darkness. I looked at him as you peer down at a man who is lying at the bottom of a precipice where the sun never shines. But I had not much time to give him, because I was helping the engine-driver to take to pieces the leaky cylinders, to straighten a bent connecting-rod, and in other such matters. I lived in an infernal mess of rust, filings, nuts, bolts, spanners, hammers, ratchet-drills—things I abominate, because I don't get on with them. I tended the little forge we fortunately had aboard; I toiled wearily in a wretched scrap-heap—unless I had the shakes too bad to stand.

"One evening coming in with a candle I was startled to hear him say a little tremulously, 'I am lying here in the dark waiting for death.' The light was within a foot of his eyes. I forced myself to murmur, 'Oh, nonsense!' and stood over him as if transfixed.

"Anything approaching the change that came over his features I have never seen before, and hope never to see again. Oh, I wasn't touched. I was fascinated. It was as though a veil had been rent. I saw on that ivory face the expression of sombre pride, of ruthless power, of craven terror—of an intense and hopeless despair. Did he live his life again in every detail of desire, temptation, and surrender during that supreme moment of complete knowledge? He cried in a whisper at some image, at some vision,—he cried out twice, a cry that was no more than a breath—

"'The horror! The horror!'

"I blew the candle out and left the cabin. The pilgrims were dining in the mess-room, and I took my place opposite the manager, who lifted his eyes to give me a questioning glance, which I successfully ignored. He leaned back, serene, with that peculiar smile of his sealing the unexpressed depths of his meanness. A continuous shower of small flies streamed upon the lamp, upon the cloth, upon our hands and faces. Suddenly the manager's boy put his insolent black head in the doorway, and said in a tone of scathing contempt—

"'Mistah Kurtz—he dead.'

"All the pilgrims rushed out to see. I remained, and went on with my dinner. I believe I was considered brutally callous. However, I did not eat much. There was a lamp in there—light, don't you know—and outside it was so beastly, beastly dark. I went no more near the remarkable man who had pronounced a judgment upon the adventures of his soul on this earth. The voice was gone. What else had been there? But I am of course aware that next day the pilgrims buried something in a muddy hole.

"And then they very nearly buried me.

"However, as you see, I did not go to join Kurtz there and then. I did not. I remained to dream the nightmare out to the end, and to show my loyalty to Kurtz once more. Destiny. My destiny! Droll thing life is—that mysterious arrangement of merciless logic for a futile purpose. The most you can hope from it is some knowledge of yourself—that comes too late—a crop of unextinguishable regrets. I have wrestled with death. It is the most unexciting contest you can imagine. It takes place in an impalpable greyness, with nothing underfoot, with nothing around, without spectators, without clamour, without glory, without the great desire of victory, without the great fear of defeat, in a sickly atmosphere of tepid scepticism, without much belief in your own right, and still less in that of your adversary. If such is the form of ultimate wisdom, then life is a greater riddle than some of us think it to be. I was within a hair's-breadth of the last opportunity for pronouncement, and I found with humiliation that probably I would have nothing to say. This is the reason why I affirm that Kurtz was a remarkable man. He had something to say. He said it. Since I had peeped over the edge myself, I understand better the meaning of his stare, that could not see the flame of the candle, but was wide enough to embrace the whole universe, piercing enough to penetrate all the hearts that beat in the darkness. He had summed up—he had judged. 'The horror!' He was a remarkable man. After all, this was the expression of some sort of belief; it had candour, it had conviction, it had a vibrating note of revolt in its whisper, it had the appalling face of a glimpsed truth—the strange commingling of desire and hate. And it is not my own extremity I remember best—a vision of greyness without form filled with physical pain, and a careless contempt for the evanescence of all things—even of this pain itself. No! It is his extremity that I seem to have lived through. True, he had made that last stride, he had stepped over the edge, while I had been permitted to draw back my hesitating foot. And perhaps in this is the whole difference; perhaps all the wisdom, and all truth, and all sincerity, are just compressed into that inappreciable moment of time in which we step over the threshold of the invisible. Perhaps! I like to think my summing-up would not have been a word of careless contempt. Better his cry—much better. It was an affirmation, a moral victory paid for by innumerable defeats, by abominable terrors, by abominable satisfactions. But it was a victory! That is why I have remained loyal to Kurtz to the last, and even beyond, when a long time after I heard once more, not his own voice, but the echo of his magnificent eloquence thrown to me from a soul as translucently pure as a cliff of crystal.

"No, they did not bury me, though there is a period of time which I remember mistily, with a shuddering wonder, like a passage through some inconceivable world that had no hope in it and no desire. I found myself back in the sepulchral city resenting the sight of people hurrying through the streets to filch a little money from each other, to devour their infamous cookery, to gulp their unwholesome beer, to dream their insignificant and silly dreams. They trespassed upon my thoughts. They were intruders whose knowledge of life was to me an irritating pretence, because I felt so sure they could not possibly know the things I knew. Their bearing, which was simply the bearing of commonplace individuals going about their business in the assurance of perfect safety, was offensive to me like the outrageous flauntings of folly in the face of a danger it is unable to comprehend. I had no particular desire to enlighten them, but I had some difficulty in restraining myself from laughing in their faces, so full of stupid importance. I daresay I was not very well at that time. I tottered about the streets—there were various affairs to settle—grinning bitterly at perfectly respectable persons. I admit my behaviour was inexcusable, but then my temperature was seldom normal in these days. My dear aunt's endeavours to 'nurse up my strength' seemed altogether beside the mark. It was not my strength that wanted nursing, it was my imagination that wanted soothing. I kept the bundle of papers given me by Kurtz, not knowing exactly what to do with it. His mother had died lately, watched over, as I was told, by his Intended. A clean-shaved man, with an official manner and wearing gold-rimmed spectacles, called on me one day and made inquiries, at first circuitous, afterwards suavely pressing, about what he was pleased to denominate certain 'documents.' I was not surprised, because I had had two rows with the manager on the subject out there. I had refused to give up the smallest scrap out of that package, and I took the same attitude with the spectacled man. He became darkly menacing at last, and with much heat argued that the Company had the right to every bit of information about its 'territories.' And, said he, 'Mr Kurtz's knowledge of unexplored regions must have been necessarily extensive and peculiar—owing to his great

abilities and to the deplorable circumstances in which he had been placed: therefore—'
I assured him Mr Kurtz's knowledge, however extensive, did not bear upon the problems of commerce or administration. He invoked then the name of science. 'It would be
an incalculable loss if,' &c., &c. I offered him the report on the 'Suppression of Savage
Customs,' with the postscriptum torn off. He took it up eagerly, but ended by sniffing
at it with an air of contempt. 'This is not what we had a right to expect,' he remarked.
'Expect nothing else,' I said. 'There are only private letters.' He withdrew upon some
threat of legal proceedings, and I saw him no more; but another fellow, calling himself
Kurtz's cousin, appeared two days later, and was anxious to hear all the details about
his dear relative's last moments. Incidentally he gave me to understand that Kurtz had
been essentially a great musician. 'There was the making of an immense success,' said
the man, who was an organist, I believe, with lank grey hair flowing over a greasy
coat-collar. I had no reason to doubt his statement; and to this day I am unable to say
what was Kurtz's profession, whether he ever had any—which was the greatest of his
talents. I had taken him for a painter who wrote for the papers, or else for a journalist
who could paint—but even the cousin (who took snuff during the interview) could not
tell me what he had been—exactly. He was a universal genius—on that point I agreed
with the old chap, who thereupon blew his nose noisily into a large cotton handkerchief and withdrew in senile agitation, bearing off some family letters and memoranda
without importance. Ultimately a journalist anxious to know something of the fate of
his 'dear colleague' turned up. This visitor informed me Kurtz's proper sphere ought
to have been politics 'on the popular side.' He had furry straight eyebrows, bristly hair
cropped short, an eye-glass on a broad ribbon, and, becoming expansive, confessed his
opinion that Kurtz really couldn't write a bit—'but heavens! how that man could talk!
He electrified large meetings. He had faith—don't you see?—he had the faith. He could
get himself to believe anything—anything. He would have been a splendid leader of
an extreme party.' 'What party?' I asked. 'Any party,' answered the other. 'He was
an—an—extremist.' Did I not think so? I assented. Did I know, he asked, with a sudden
flash of curiosity, 'what it was that had induced him to go out there?' 'Yes,' said I, and
forthwith handed him the famous Report for publication, if he thought fit. He glanced
through it hurriedly, mumbling all the time, judged 'it would do,' and took himself off
with this plunder.

   "Thus I was left at last with a slim packet of letters and the girl's portrait. She
struck me as beautiful—I mean she had a beautiful expression. I know that the sunlight can be made to lie too, yet one felt that no manipulation of light and pose could
have conveyed the delicate shade of truthfulness upon those features. She seemed
ready to listen without mental reservation, without suspicion, without a thought for
herself. I concluded I would go and give her back her portrait and those letters myself. Curiosity? Yes; and also some other feeling perhaps. All that had been Kurtz's
had passed out of my hands: his soul, his body, his station, his plans, his ivory, his
career. There remained only his memory and his Intended—and I wanted to give that
up too to the past, in a way,—to surrender personally all that remained of him with
me to that oblivion which is the last word of our common fate. I don't defend myself.
I had no clear perception of what it was I really wanted. Perhaps it was an impulse of
unconscious loyalty, or the fulfilment of one of those ironic necessities that lurk in
the facts of human existence. I don't know. I can't tell. But I went.

   "I thought his memory was like the other memories of the dead that accumulate
in every man's life,—a vague impress on the brain of shadows that had fallen on it
in their swift and final passage; but before the high and ponderous door, between the

tall houses of a street as still and decorous as a well-kept alley in a cemetery, I had a vision of him on the stretcher, opening his mouth voraciously, as if to devour all the earth with all its mankind. He lived then before me; he lived as much as he had ever lived—a shadow insatiable of splendid appearances, of frightful realities; a shadow darker than the shadow of the night, and draped nobly in the folds of a gorgeous eloquence. The vision seemed to enter the house with me—the stretcher, the phantom-bearers, the wild crowd of obedient worshippers, the gloom of the forests, the glitter of the reach between the murky bends, the beat of the drum, regular and muffled like the beating of a heart—the heart of a conquering darkness. It was a moment of triumph for the wilderness, an invading and vengeful rush which, it seemed to me, I would have to keep back alone for the salvation of another soul. And the memory of what I had heard him say afar there, with the horned shapes stirring at my back, in the glow of fires, within the patient woods, those broken phrases came back to me, were heard again in their ominous and terrifying simplicity. I remembered his abject pleading, his abject threats, the colossal scale of his vile desires, the meanness, the torment, the tempestuous anguish of his soul. And later on I seemed to see his collected languid manner, when he said one day, 'This lot of ivory now is really mine. The Company did not pay for it. I collected it myself at a very great personal risk. I am afraid they will try to claim it as theirs though. H'm. It is a difficult case. What do you think I ought to do—resist? Eh? I want no more than justice.' ... He wanted no more than justice—no more than justice. I rang the bell before a mahogany door on the first floor, and while I waited he seemed to stare at me out of the glassy panel—stare with that wide and immense stare embracing, condemning, loathing all the universe. I seemed to hear the whispered cry, 'The horror! The horror!'

"The dusk was falling. I had to wait in a lofty drawing-room with three long windows from floor to ceiling that were like three luminous and bedraped columns. The bent gilt legs and backs of the furniture shone in indistinct curves. The tall marble fireplace had a cold and monumental whiteness. A grand piano stood massively in a corner, with dark gleams on the flat surfaces like a sombre and polished sarcophagus. A high door opened—closed. I rose.

"She came forward, all in black, with a pale head, floating towards me in the dusk. She was in mourning. It was more than a year since his death, more than a year since the news came; she seemed as though she would remember and mourn for ever. She took both my hands in hers and murmured, 'I had heard you were coming.' I noticed she was not very young—I mean not girlish. She had a mature capacity for fidelity, for belief, for suffering. The room seemed to have grown darker, as if all the sad light of the cloudy evening had taken refuge on her forehead. This fair hair, this pale visage, this pure brow, seemed surrounded by an ashy halo from which the dark eyes looked out at me. Their glance was guileless, profound, confident, and trustful. She carried her sorrowful head as though she were proud of that sorrow, as though she would say, I—I alone know how to mourn for him as he deserves. But while we were still shaking hands, such a look of awful desolation came upon her face that I perceived she was one of those creatures that are not the playthings of Time. For her he had died only yesterday. And, by Jove! the impression was so powerful that for me too he seemed to have died only yesterday—nay, this very minute. I saw her and him in the same instant of time—his death and her sorrow—I saw her sorrow in the very moment of his death. Do you understand? I saw them together—I heard them together. She had said, with a deep catch of the breath, 'I have survived'; while my strained ears seemed to hear distinctly, mingled with her tone of despairing regret, the summing-up whisper of his eternal condemnation. I asked myself what I was doing there, with a sensation of panic in my heart as though I had blundered into a place of cruel and absurd mysteries not fit for a human being to behold. She motioned me to a chair. We sat down. I laid the packet gently on the little table, and she put her hand over it.... 'You knew him well,' she murmured, after a moment of mourning silence.

"'Intimacy grows quickly out there,' I said. 'I knew him as well as it is possible for one man to know another.'

"'And you admired him,' she said. 'It was impossible to know him and not to admire him. Was it?'

"'He was a remarkable man,' I said, unsteadily. Then before the appealing fixity of her gaze, that seemed to watch for more words on my lips, I went on, 'It was impossible not to—'

"'Love him,' she finished eagerly, silencing me into an appalled dumbness. 'How true! how true! But when you think that no one knew him so well as I! I had all his noble confidence. I knew him best.'

"'You knew him best,' I repeated. And perhaps she did. But with every word spoken the room was growing darker, and only her forehead, smooth and white, remained illumined by the unextinguishable light of belief and love.

"'You were his friend,' she went on. 'His friend,' she repeated, a little louder. 'You must have been, if he had given you this, and sent you to me. I feel I can speak to you—and oh! I must speak. I want you—you who have heard his last words—to know I have been worthy of him.... It is pride.... Yes! I am proud to know I understood him better than any one on earth—he told me so himself. And since his mother died I have had no one—no one—to—to—'

"I listened. The darkness deepened. I was not even sure whether he had given me the right bundle. I rather suspect he wanted me to take care of another batch of his papers which, after his death, I saw the manager examining under the lamp. And the girl talked, easing her pain in the certitude of my sympathy; she talked as thirsty men drink. I had heard that her engagement with Kurtz had been disapproved by her people. He wasn't rich enough or something. And indeed I don't know whether he had not been a pauper all his life. He had given me some reason to infer that it was his impatience of comparative poverty that drove him out there.

"'... Who was not his friend who had heard him speak once?' she was saying. 'He drew men towards him by what was best in them.' She looked at me with intensity. 'It is the gift of the great,' she went on, and the sound of her low voice seemed to have the accompaniment of all the other sounds, full of mystery, desolation, and sorrow, I had ever heard—the ripple of the river, the soughing of the trees swayed by the wind, the murmurs of wild crowds, the faint ring of incomprehensible words cried from afar, the whisper of a voice speaking from beyond the threshold of an eternal darkness. 'But you have heard him! You know!' she cried.

"'Yes, I know,' I said with something like despair in my heart, but bowing my head before the faith that was in her, before that great and saving illusion that shone with an unearthly glow in the darkness, in the triumphant darkness from which I could not have defended her—from which I could not even defend myself.

"'What a loss to me—to us!'—she corrected herself with beautiful generosity; then added in a murmur, 'To the world.' By the last gleams of twilight I could see the glitter of her eyes, full of tears—of tears that would not fall.

"'I have been very happy—very fortunate—very proud,' she went on. 'Too fortunate. Too happy for a little while. And now I am unhappy for—for life.'

"She stood up; her fair hair seemed to catch all the remaining light in a glimmer of gold. I rose too.

"'And of all this,' she went on, mournfully, 'of all his promise, and of all his greatness, of his generous mind, of his noble heart, nothing remains—nothing but a memory. You and I—'

"'We shall always remember him,' I said, hastily.

"'No!' she cried. 'It is impossible that all this should be lost—that such a life should be sacrificed to leave nothing—but sorrow. You know what vast plans he had. I knew of them too—I could not perhaps understand,—but others knew of them. Something must remain. His words, at least, have not died.'

"'His words will remain,' I said.

"'And his example,' she whispered to herself. 'Men looked up to him,—his goodness shone in every act. His example—'

"'True,' I said; 'his example too. Yes, his example. I forgot that.'

"'But I do not. I cannot—I cannot believe—not yet. I cannot believe that I shall never see him again, that nobody will see him again, never, never, never.'

"She put out her arms as if after a retreating figure, stretching them black and with clasped pale hands across the fading and narrow sheen of the window. Never see him! I saw him clearly enough then. I shall see this eloquent phantom as long as I live, and I shall see her too, a tragic and familiar Shade, resembling in this gesture another one, tragic also, and bedecked with powerless charms, stretching bare brown arms over the glitter of the infernal stream, the stream of darkness. She said suddenly very low, 'He died as he lived.'

"'His end,' said I, with dull anger stirring in me, 'was in every way worthy of his life.'

"'And I was not with him,' she murmured. My anger subsided before a feeling of infinite pity.

"'Everything that could be done—' I mumbled.

"'Ah, but I believed in him more than any one on earth—more than his own mother, more than—himself. He needed me! Me! I would have treasured every sigh, every word, every sign, every glance.'

"I felt like a chill grip on my chest. 'Don't,' I said, in a muffled voice.

"'Forgive me. I—I—have mourned so long in silence—in silence. . . . You were with him—to the last? I think of his loneliness. Nobody near to understand him as I would have understood. Perhaps no one to hear. . . .'

"'To the very end,' I said, shakily. 'I heard his very last words. . . .' I stopped in a fright.

"'Repeat them,' she said in a heart-broken tone. 'I want—I want—something—something—to—to live with.'

"I was on the point of crying at her, 'Don't you hear them?' The dusk was repeating them in a persistent whisper all around us, in a whisper that seemed to swell menacingly like the first whisper of a rising wind. 'The horror! the horror!'

"'His last word—to live with,' she murmured. 'Don't you understand I loved him—I loved him—I loved him!'

"I pulled myself together and spoke slowly.

"'The last word he pronounced was—your name.'

"I heard a light sigh, and then my heart stood still, stopped dead short by an exulting and terrible cry, by the cry of inconceivable triumph and of unspeakable pain. 'I knew it—I was sure!' . . . She knew. She was sure. I heard her weeping; she had hidden her face in her hands. It seemed to me that the house would collapse before I could escape, that the heavens would fall upon my head. But nothing happened. The heavens do not fall for such a trifle. Would they have fallen, I wonder, if I had rendered Kurtz that justice which was his due? Hadn't he said he wanted only justice? But I couldn't. I could not tell her. It would have been too dark—too dark altogether. . . ."

Marlow ceased, and sat apart, indistinct and silent, in the pose of a meditating Buddha. Nobody moved for a time. "We have lost the first of the ebb," said the Director, suddenly. I raised my head. The offing was barred by a black bank of clouds, and the tranquil waterway leading to the uttermost ends of the earth flowed sombre under an overcast sky—seemed to lead into the heart of an immense darkness.

LU XUN ■ (1881–1936)

Widely considered the finest Chinese writer of his generation, Lu Xun (the pen name of Zhou Shuren) was born in 1881 to a family of scholar-officials on China's southeast coast. He received the classical education expected of someone with his pedigree, but a scandal during his youth sent his grandfather to prison and the family fortunes went into decline. Lu Xun studied in a school whose focus on science and technology was designed to "strengthen" a new generation of Chinese for the new century. He then received a government scholarship to continue his studies in Japan, where modern Western influences had already taken root. Blaming the death of his father some years before on the failed methods of traditional Chinese quacks, he entered medical school, choosing to study Western medicine. But he was shocked by photographs revealing the abject helplessness of even healthy Chinese before foreign armies fighting on their territory during the Russo-Japanese War of 1904–1905, and he decided that China's real diseases were of the spirit rather than the body. That realization, perhaps coupled with a rather undistinguished record in medical school, led him to embark on a literary career in hopes of effecting a spiritual transformation of the nation.

Lu Xun's publishing projects in Japan didn't elicit the hoped-for response, however, and in 1909 he returned disheartened to China, where he spent the next sixteen years teaching and working in the Ministry of Education. A friend introduced him to the New Culture Movement, which aimed to reform both literature and society by revolutionizing the language of writing itself, and urged Lu Xun to contribute something to the effort in 1917. His initial reaction, recorded in his preface to *A Call to Arms,* was one of apparent futility. But the following year his first short story, "A Madman's Diary," launched one of the movement's most trenchant critiques.

Over the next eight years Lu Xun wrote some two dozen stories, which were published in two volumes, *A Call to Arms* (1923) and *Wandering* (1926). In these works he wrestles with a number of recurring themes centering on the dilemmas and contradictions facing intellectuals committed to a thoroughgoing transformation of the culture. Recognizing the failings and abuses of traditional Chinese thought and practices, he was both unwilling to abandon them wholesale and skeptical of the ability of sweeping utopian reforms to effect real positive change. He was haunted as well by doubts about whether writing could in fact grasp and convey real knowledge, and about whether intellectuals in general could truly communicate with the common people, in whose interests they were presumably working. By 1926 these questions finally led him to abandon fiction writing altogether. Forced to flee Peking following a purge by the Nationalist government of Communists and Communist sympathizers, he turned to the more pointed essay form and to Marxist activism as a means of gaining a less ambiguous leverage over reality. His relations with leftist colleagues remained fraught, however, and he never joined the party, yet he continued writing and left behind a substantial body of work—from essays, poetry, short stories, translations, and works on premodern literature to collections of woodcuts.

PRONUNCIATIONS:

Li Shizhen: LEE SHEE-jen
Lu Xun: LOU SHOON
Zhao: ja'o

A Madman's Diary[1]

Two brothers, whose names I need not mention here, were both good friends of mine in high school; but after a separation of many years we gradually lost touch. Some time ago I happened to hear that one of them was seriously ill, and since I was going back to my old home I broke my journey to call on them. I saw only one, however, who told me that the invalid was his younger brother.

"I appreciate your coming such a long way to see us," he said, "but my brother recovered some time ago and has gone elsewhere to take up an official post." Then, laughing, he produced two volumes of his brother's diary, saying that from these the nature of his past illness could be seen and there was no harm in showing them to an old friend. I took the diary away, read it through, and found that he had suffered from a form of persecution complex. The writing was most confused and incoherent, and he had made many wild statements; moreover he had omitted to give any dates, so that only by the colour of the ink and the differences in the writing could one tell that it was not all written at one time. Certain sections, however, were not altogether disconnected, and I have copied out a part to serve as a subject for medical research. I have not altered a single illogicality in the diary and have changed only the names, even though the people referred to are all country folk, unknown to the world and of no consequence. As for the title, it was chosen by the diarist himself after his recovery, and I did not change it.

I

Tonight the moon is very bright.

I have not seen it for over thirty years, so today when I saw it I felt in unusually high spirits. I begin to realize that during the past thirty-odd years I have been in the dark; but now I must be extremely careful. Otherwise why should the Zhaos' dog have looked at me twice?

I have reason for my fear.

II

Tonight there is no moon at all, I know that this is a bad omen. This morning when I went out cautiously, Mr. Zhao had a strange look in his eyes, as if he were afraid of me, as if he wanted to murder me. There were seven or eight others who discussed me in a whisper. And they were afraid of my seeing them. So, indeed, were all the people I passed. The fiercest among them grinned at me; whereupon I shivered from head to foot, knowing that their preparations were complete.

I was not afraid, however, but continued on my way. A group of children in front were also discussing me, and the look in their eyes was just like that in Mr. Zhao's while their faces too were ghastly pale. I wondered what grudge these children could have against me to make them behave like this. I could not help calling out, "Tell me!" But then they ran away.

1. Translated by Yang Xianyi and Gladys Yang.

I wonder what grudge Mr. Zhao has against me, what grudge the people on the road have against me. I can think of nothing except that twenty years ago I trod on Mr. Gu Jiu's[2] old ledgers, and Mr. Gu was most displeased. Although Mr. Zhao does not know him, he must have heard talk of this and decided to avenge him, thus he is conspiring against me with the people on the road. But then what of the children? At that time they were not yet born, so why should they eye me so strangely today, as if they were afraid of me, as if they wanted to murder me? This really frightens me, it is so bewildering and upsetting.

I know. They must have learned this from their parents!

I can't sleep at night. Everything requires careful consideration if one is to understand it.

Those people, some of whom have been pilloried by the magistrate, slapped in the face by the local gentry, had their wives taken away by bailiffs or their parents driven to suicide by creditors, never looked as frightened and as fierce then as they did yesterday.

The most extraordinary thing was that woman on the street yesterday who was spanking her son. "Little devil!" she cried. "I'm so angry I could eat you!" Yet all the time it was me she was looking at. I gave a start, unable to hide my alarm. Then all those long-toothed people with livid faces began to hoot with laughter. Old Chen hurried forward and dragged me home.

He dragged me home. The folk at home all pretended not to know me; they had the same look in their eyes as all the others. When I went into the study, they locked me in as if cooping up a chicken or a duck. This incident left me even more bewildered.

A few days ago a tenant of ours from Wolf Cub Village came to report the failure of the crops and told my elder brother that a notorious character in their village had been beaten to death; then some people had taken out his heart and liver, fried them in oil, and eaten them as a means of increasing their courage. When I interrupted, the tenant and my brother both stared at me. Only today have I realized that they had exactly the same look in their eyes as those people outside.

Just to think of it sets me shivering from the crown of my head to the soles of my feet.

They eat human beings, so they may eat me.

I see that the woman's "eat you," the laughter of those long-toothed people with livid faces, and the tenant's story the other day are obviously secret signs. I realize all the poison in their speech, all the daggers in their laughter. Their teeth are white and glistening: they use these teeth to eat men.

Evidently, although I am not a bad man, ever since I trod on Mr. Gu's ledgers it has been touch-and-go with me. They seem to have secrets which I cannot guess, and once they are angry they will call anyone a bad character. I remember when my elder brother taught me to write compositions, no matter how good a man was, if I produced arguments to the contrary he would mark that passage to show his approval; while if I excused evildoers he would say, "Good for you, that shows originality." How can I possibly guess their secret thoughts—especially when they are ready to eat people?

Everything requires careful consideration if one is to understand it. In ancient times, as I recollect, people often ate human beings, but I am rather hazy about it. I tried to look this up, but my history has no chronology and scrawled all over each page are the words: "Confucian Virtue and Morality." Since I could not sleep any-way, I read intently half the night until I began to see words between the lines. The whole book was filled with the two words—"Eat people."

All these words written in the book, all the words spoken by our tenant, eye me quizzically with an enigmatic smile.

I too am a man, and they want to eat me!

IV

In the morning I sat quietly for some time. Old Chen brought in lunch: one bowl of vegetables, one bowl of steamed fish. The eyes of the fish were white and hard, and its mouth was open just like those people who want to eat human beings. After a few mouthfuls I could not tell whether the slippery morsels were fish or human flesh, so I brought it all up.

I said, "Old Chen, tell my brother that I feel quite suffocated and want to have a stroll in the garden." Old Chen said nothing but went out, and presently he came back and opened the gate.

I did not move, but watched to see how they would treat me, feeling certain that they would not let me go. Sure enough! My elder brother came slowly out, leading an old man. There was a murderous gleam in his eyes, and fearing that I would see it he lowered his head, stealing side-glances at me from behind his glasses.

"You seem very well today," said my brother.

"Yes," said I.

"I have invited Mr. Ho here today to examine you."

"All right," I replied. Actually I knew quite well that this old man was the ex-ecutioner in disguise! Feeling my pulse was simply a pretext for him to see how fat I was; for this would entitle him to a share of my flesh. Still I was not afraid. Although I do not eat men my courage is greater than theirs. I held out my two fists to see what he would do. The old man sat down, closed his eyes, fumbled for some time, remained motionless for a while; then opened his shifty eyes and said, "Don't let your imagination run away with you. Rest quietly for a few days, and you will be better."

Don't let your imagination run away with you! Rest quietly for a few days! By fattening me of course they'll have more to eat. But what good will it do me? How can it be "better"? The whole lot of them wanting to eat people yet stealthily trying to keep up appearances, not daring to do it outright, was really enough to make me die of laughter. I couldn't help it, I nearly split my sides, I was so amused. I knew that this laughter voiced courage and integrity. Both the old man and my brother turned pale, awed by my courage and integrity.

But my courage just makes them all the more eager to eat me, to acquire some of my courage for themselves. The old man went out of the gate, but before he had gone far he said to my brother in a low voice, "To be eaten at once!" My brother nodded. So you are in it too! This stupendous discovery, though it came as a shock, is no more than I might expect: the accomplice in eating me is my elder brother!

The eater of human flesh is my elder brother!

I am the younger brother of an eater of human flesh!

I, who will be eaten by others, am the younger brother of an eater of human flesh!

V

These few days I have been thinking again: suppose that old man were not an executioner in disguise, but a real doctor; he would be nonetheless an eater of human flesh. That book on herbs by his predecessor Li Shizhen[3] states explicitly that men's flesh can be boiled and eaten; how then can he still deny that he eats men?

As for my elder brother, I have also good reason to suspect him. When he was teaching me, he told me himself, "People exchange their sons to eat."[4] And once in discussing a bad man he said that not only did the fellow deserve to be killed, he should "have his flesh eaten and his hide slept on." I was still young at the time, and for quite a while my heart beat faster. That story our tenant from Wolf Cub Village told the other day about eating a man's heart and liver didn't surprise him at all—he kept nodding his head. He is evidently just as cruel as before. Since it is possible to "exchange sons to eat," then anything can be exchanged, anyone can be eaten. In the past I simply listened to his explanations and let it go at that; now I know that when he gave me these explanations, not only was there human fat at the corner of his lips, but his whole heart was set on eating men.

VI

Pitch dark. I don't know whether it is day or night. The Zhaos' dog has started barking again.

The fierceness of a lion, the timidity of a rabbit, the craftiness of a fox. . . .

VII

I know their way: they are not prepared to kill outright, nor would they dare, for fear of the consequences. Instead they have banded together and set traps everywhere, to force me to kill myself. The behaviour of the men and women in the street a few days ago and my elder brother's attitude these last few days make it quite obvious. What they like best is for a man to take off his belt and hang himself from a beam; for then they can enjoy their hearts' desire without being blamed for murder. Naturally that delights them and sets them roaring with laughter. On the other hand, if a man is frightened or worried to death, though that makes him rather thin, they still nod in approval.

They only eat dead flesh! I remember reading somewhere of a hideous beast with an ugly look in its eye called "hyena," which often eats dead flesh. Even the largest bones it crunches into fragments and swallows; the mere thought of this makes your hair stand on end. Hyenas are related to wolves, wolves belong to the canine species. The other day the Zhaos' dog eyed me several times: it is obviously in the plot too as their accomplice. The old man's eyes were cast down, but that did not deceive me.

The most deplorable is my elder brother. He's a man too, so why isn't he afraid, why is he plotting with others to eat me? Does force of habit blind a man to what's wrong? Or is he so heartless that he will knowingly commit a crime?

In cursing man-eaters, I shall start with my brother. In dissuading man-eaters, I shall start with him too.

3. Famous pharmacologist (1518–93). His *Compendium of Materia Medica* doesn't say that human flesh could be used as a medicine.

4. From a commentary on the canonical chronicle *Spring and Autumn Annals*, which describes the desperate conditions of a besieged population in 488 B.C.E.

Actually such arguments should have convinced them long ago. . . .

Suddenly someone came in. He was only about twenty years old and I did not see his features very clearly. His face was wreathed in smiles, but when he nodded to me his smile didn't seem genuine. I asked him, "Is it right to eat human beings?"

Still smiling, he replied, "When there is no famine how can one eat human beings?"

I realized at once he was one of them; but still I summoned up courage to repeat my question:

"Is it right?"

"What makes you ask such a thing? You really are . . . fond of a joke. . . . It is very fine today."

"It is fine, and the moon is very bright. But I want to ask you: Is it right?"

He looked disconcerted and muttered, "No. . . ."

"No? Then why do they still do it?"

"What are you talking about?"

"What am I talking about? They are eating men now in Wolf Cub Village, and you can see it written all over the books, in fresh red ink."

His expression changed. He grew ghastly pale. "It may be so," he said staring at me. "That's the way it's always been. . . ."

"Does that make it right?"

"I refuse to discuss it with you. Anyway, you shouldn't talk about it. It's wrong for anyone to talk about it."

I leaped up and opened my eyes wide, but the man had vanished. I was soaked with sweat. He was much younger than my elder brother, but even so he was in it. He must have been taught by his parents. And I am afraid he has already taught his son; that is why even the children look at me so fiercely.

IX

Wanting to eat men, at the same time afraid of being eaten themselves, they all eye each other with the deepest suspicion.

How comfortable life would be for them if they could rid themselves of such obsessions and go to work, walk, eat and sleep at ease. They have only this one step to take. Yet fathers and sons, husbands and wives, brothers, friends, teachers and students, sworn enemies and even strangers, have all joined in this conspiracy, discouraging and preventing each other from taking this step.

X

Early this morning I went to find my elder brother. He was standing outside the hall door looking at the sky when I walked up behind him, standing between him and the door, and addressed him with exceptional poise and politeness:

"Brother, I have something to say to you."

"Go ahead then." He turned quickly towards me, nodding.

"It's nothing much, but I find it hard to say. Brother, probably all primitive people ate a little human flesh to begin with. Later, because their views altered some of them stopped and tried so hard to do what was right that they changed into men, into real men. But some are still eating people—just like reptiles. Some have changed into fish, birds, monkeys, and finally men; but those who make no effort to do what's right are still reptiles. When those who eat men compare themselves with those who don't, how ashamed they must be. Probably much more ashamed than the reptiles are before monkeys.

"In ancient times Yi Ya boiled his son for Jie and Zhou to eat; that is the old story.[5] But actually since the creation of heaven and earth by Pan Gu[6] men have been eating each other, from the time of Yi Ya's son to the time of Xu Xilin,[7] and from the time of Xu Xilin down to the man caught in Wolf Cub Village. Last year they executed a criminal in the city, and a consumptive soaked a piece of bread in his blood and sucked it.

"They want to eat me, and of course you can do nothing about it single-handed; but why must you join them? As man-eaters they are capable of anything. If they eat me, they can eat you as well; members of the same group can still eat each other. But if you will just change your ways, change right away, then everyone will have peace. Although this has been going on since time immemorial, today we could make a special effort to do what is right, and say this can't be done! I'm sure you can say that, Brother. The other day when the tenant wanted the rent reduced, you said it couldn't be done."

At first he only smiled cynically, then a murderous gleam came into his eyes, and when I spoke of their secret he turned pale. Outside the gate quite a crowd had gathered, among them Mr. Zhao and his dog, all craning their necks to peer in. I could not see all their faces, some of them seemed to be masked; others were the old lot, long-toothed with livid faces, concealing their laughter. I knew they were one gang, all eaters of human flesh. But I also knew that they did not all think alike by any means. Some of them thought that since it had always been so, men should be eaten. Others knew they shouldn't eat men but still wanted to, and were afraid people might discover their secret; so although what I said made them angry they still smiled their cynical, tight-lipped smiles.

Suddenly my brother's face darkened.

"Clear off, the whole lot of you!" he roared. "What's the point of looking at a madman?"

Then I realized part of their cunning. They would never be willing to change their stand, and their plans were all laid: they had labelled me a madman. In future when I was eaten, not only would there be no trouble but people would probably be grateful to them. When our tenant spoke of the villagers eating a bad character, it was exactly the same device. This is their old trick.

Old Chen came in too in a towering temper. But they could not stop my mouth, I had to warn those people:

"You should change, change from the bottom of your hearts. You must realize that there will be no place for man-eaters in the world in future.

"If you don't change, you may all be eaten by each other. However many of you there are, you will be wiped out by the real men, just as wolves are killed by hunters— just like reptiles!"

Old Chen drove everybody away. My brother had disappeared. Old Chen advised me to go back to my room. It was pitch dark in there. The beams and rafters shook above my head. After shaking for a while they grew bigger and bigger. They piled on top of me.

5. Yi Ya, a favorite of Duke Huan of Qi in the seventh century B.C.E., was a good cook and sycophant. When the duke remarked that he had never tasted the flesh of children, Yi Ya cooked his own son for him to eat. Jie and Zhou were kings of earlier periods.

6. A mythological figure from whom, according to one legend, the entire universe derives.

7. A revolutionary executed in 1907 for assassinating a Qing official. His heart and liver were eaten.

The weight was so great, I couldn't move. They meant that I should die. However, knowing that the weight was false I struggled out, dripping with sweat. But I had to warn them:

"You must change at once, change from the bottom of your hearts! You must know that there'll be no place for man-eaters in future. . . ."

XI

The sun has stopped shining, the door is never opened. Just two meals day after day.

Picking up my chopsticks, I thought of my elder brother. I know now how my little sister died: it was all through him. My sister was only five at the time. I can still remember how sweet she looked, poor thing. Mother wept as if she would never stop, but he begged her not to cry, probably because he had eaten our sister himself and so this weeping made him rather ashamed. If he had any sense of shame. . . .

My sister was eaten by my brother, but I don't know whether Mother realized it or not.

I think Mother must have known, but when she wept she didn't say so outright, probably because she also thought it proper. I remember when I was four or five, sitting in the cool of the hall, my brother told me that if a man's parents were ill he should cut off a piece of his flesh and boil it for them, if he wanted to be considered a good son;[8] and Mother didn't contradict him. If one piece could be eaten, obviously so could the whole. And yet just to think of the weeping then still makes my heart bleed; that is the extraordinary thing about it!

XII

I can't bear to think of it.

It has only just dawned on me that all these years I have been living in a place where for four thousand years human flesh has been eaten. My brother had just taken over the charge of the house when our sister died, and he may well have used her flesh in our food, making us eat it unwittingly.

I may have eaten several pieces of my sister's flesh unwittingly, and now it is my turn. . . .

How can a man like myself, after four thousand years of man-eating history— even though I knew nothing about it at first—ever hope to face real men?

XIII

Perhaps there are still children who haven't eaten men?

Save the children. . . .

JAMES JOYCE ■ (1882–1941)

One of the greatest figures in European modernism, James Joyce emigrated from his native Ireland at the age of twenty-two, and spent his adult life in Italy, Switzerland, and France; yet this most cosmopolitan of writers continued to ground his fiction in the experiences of his

---

8. Traditional doctrines instructed children to cut off their flesh to feed their parents, if necessary.

early years in provincial Dublin. He had been born in a Dublin suburb, the eldest of "sixteen or seventeen children," as his father later hazily recalled, only ten of whom survived infancy. His father, John, worked for the Irish nationalist movement headed by Charles Stewart Parnell in the 1880s, until Parnell's influence collapsed after he was named as an adulterer in a divorce suit in 1889. The Irish Catholic hierarchy turned against him, as did many political supporters, and a broken Parnell died in 1891, an event that prompted the nine-year-old Joyce to compose his first published poem, "Et Tu, Healy?" John Joyce lost his political appointment as a tax collector (problems with alcohol and borrowings from his own tax receipts compounded his political difficulties), and the family moved frequently in the ensuing years, to a series of increasingly rundown lodgings.

Joyce spent his adolescence in the 1890s hoping to get away from what he saw as Dublin's spiritual, political, and intellectual paralysis. A prize-winning student at a Catholic boys' school—where for a time he considered entering the priesthood—Joyce won a scholarship to study at the Jesuit-run University College, Dublin, where he pursued his wide, eclectic reading in ancient and modern authors. By the age of eighteen, he had taught himself Dano-Norwegian in order to read the works of Henrik Ibsen in the original. That year, he published an article on Ibsen in the *Fortnightly Review*, an important London journal. A few months later, he learned that Ibsen had admired the article, and Joyce wrote his hero a glowing letter in Norwegian—never answered—congratulating the aging author on his work and indicating his intention to carry on Ibsen's struggle against social and artistic conventions.

Joyce always had an ambiguous relation to his Irish literary contemporaries. In 1901 he published "The Day of the Rabblement," an essay criticizing as provincial the Irish Literary Theatre recently started by W. B. Yeats and others to promote a revival of Irish culture. Yet in the following years, he sought out Yeats and the other leading literary figures of Dublin, hoping to establish himself as a writer and reviewer. Funds were a constant concern, and an attempt to study medicine in Paris was cut short both by lack of money and by the slow death by cancer of his mother in 1903. Joyce returned home for her final illness, and abandoned his projected medical career; after a desultory year of teaching and writing, he left permanently for the Continent, where he taught for several years in a Berlitz school in Trieste. He was accompanied by Nora Barnacle, whom he had met on 16 June 1904—a day he would immortalize as "Bloomsday," the day on which his great novel *Ulysses* is set. While in Trieste, he completed *Dubliners*, a series of short stories he had begun at the suggestion of a friend who had offered him £1 each for some simple stories for a newspaper called the *Irish Homestead*. He also began an autobiographical novel, first entitled *Stephen Hero* and then rewritten as *A Portrait of the Artist as a Young Man*.

Joyce had great difficulty getting both works published. He insisted on recording the actual language Dubliners used, including vulgarities and even occasional obscenities, and he included real people—often unflatteringly portrayed—along with his fictional characters. Dublin publishers hesitated to take his work, fearing both libel and obscenity charges, and though Joyce had impressed the Irish literary establishment with his talent (as well as his arrogance), he had no obvious group of supporters. At once anti-British and antinationalist, fiercely independent yet expecting others to support him, Joyce was hard to place. This difficulty only increased as time went on, as he continually reinvented himself throughout his career. As soon as one phase of his work finally found a publisher and a small group of fervent admirers, Joyce would abandon the kind of writing they had come to admire and would make new demands on his readers' creativity, intelligence, and sheer patience.

Dubliners was published in 1914, while *Portrait* was being serialized in a magazine of experimental writing run by Harriet Weaver, who became a longtime supporter of Joyce and his work. *Portrait* was published in book form in 1916—in the United States; no Irish or English publisher having been willing to take it. By that point, Joyce was deeply engaged in what was to become one of the most influential novels of the twentieth century—*Ulysses*, the story of several intertwined lives in Dublin on 16 June 1904, centering on the adventures of Leopold Bloom, advertising salesman, and his unfaithful wife Molly. *Ulysses* has direct links with Joyce's previous fiction, including the presence of its third lead character, Stephen Dedalus, the autobiographical hero of *Portrait*. Yet as he worked on his big new novel Joyce rapidly began to move beyond the symbolically charged realism that had characterized his earlier fiction. Like its predecessors, *Ulysses* is filled with realistic detail about Dublin life, but over the course of the book these details are increasingly caught up in an exploding universe of literary styles and cultural references—from an extended parallel with Homer's *Odyssey* to parodies of the entire history of English prose style, experiments in musical writing, and even a chapter in drama form. Arcane references to medieval scholastic philosophy intertwine with parodies of contemporary advertising language, and whole chains of reference to Dante, Shakespeare, and Mozart are developed amid visits to outhouses and brothels. Reading *Ulysses* after it was eventually published in 1922 in Paris—once again, no English or Irish publisher having been found willing to take it—a bemused Virginia Woolf was impressed by its virtuosity and ambition, but couldn't help feeling she was watching "an undergraduate scratching his pimples." T. S. Eliot, on the other hand, wrote an essay called "*Ulysses,* Order, and Myth," in which he praised the novel as one of the great achievements of modern literature, asserting that Joyce had succeeded in "giving a shape and a significance to the immense panorama of futility and anarchy which is contemporary history."

Joyce by this time was living in Paris, together with Nora—they would only formally marry late in life—and their two children. His great novel gradually came to find readers, including in the United States, where it was initially banned as obscene, until a landmark decision by a judge determined in 1928 that the book's obscenities served compelling artistic purposes. By then, Joyce was working on a yet more baffling work, *Finnegans Wake,* which would occupy him for seventeen years, until shortly before his death in 1941. An extraordinary kaleidoscope of styles and languages, the book is a riot of stories, rumors, and hearsay surrounding a series of comically embarrassing moments in the life of a hero of many names but constant initials, H.C.E.; his wife, Anna Livia Plurabelle; and their quarreling sons and daughter. At the same time, it is a compendium of Irish and world history, politics, and culture, a veritable "chaosmos of Alle," as it calls itself. Even this phantasmagoric book, though, remains set in Dublin, and it displays Joyce's abiding interest in intersections of sexual, textual, and political misfortunes, as H.C.E. loses a local election after seducing some girls, or being seduced by them, or exposing himself in Dublin's Phoenix Park, whereupon Anna Livia writes a long letter, her "mamafesta," in his defense.

When he received the commission to write some "simple stories" for the *Irish Homestead* in 1904, Joyce was already engaged in composing a series of short prose experiments that he called "epiphanies"—sketches of seemingly ordinary scenes in which the hidden truth about a person or situation is suddenly brought to the surface, often for the lead character to contemplate, sometimes only for the reader to perceive. Set on January 6, the Feast of the Epiphany, "The Dead" was written in 1907, two years after he had completed the rest of the book. This last and longest of the stories in *Dubliners* shows how its hero's world turns upside down over the course of a single evening, as Gabriel Conroy has a series of unsettling encounters with a servant, a nationalist friend, and his own wife. She reveals a past (based on actual experiences of Nora Barnacle) previously unknown to Gabriel, and dramatically different from the ordinary pleasures of food, drink, and hospitality that the story luminously evokes. As often happens in the stories and novels of Virginia Woolf, memory invades the present, breeding uncertainties that can be compared to those explored in Akutagawa Ryunosuke's modernist mystery stories as well. Like the tales that Premchand was beginning to write during the same period, the stories of *Dubliners* use close, understated observation of everyday objects and events to unfold abiding mysteries of loyalty and betrayal, rivalry and love.

from Dubliners

The Dead

Lily, the caretaker's daughter, was literally run off her feet. Hardly had she brought one gentleman into the little pantry behind the office on the ground floor and helped him off with his overcoat than the wheezy hall-door bell clanged again and she had to scamper along the bare hallway to let in another guest. It was well for her she had not to attend to the ladies also. But Miss Kate and Miss Julia had thought of that and had converted the bathroom upstairs into a ladies' dressing-room. Miss Kate and Miss Julia were there, gossiping and laughing and fussing, walking after each other to the head of the stairs, peering down over the banisters and calling down to Lily to ask her who had come.

It was always a great affair, the Misses Morkan's annual dance. Everybody who knew them came to it, members of the family, old friends of the family, the members of Julia's choir, any of Kate's pupils that were grown up enough and even some of Mary Jane's pupils too. Never once had it fallen flat. For years and years it had gone off in splendid style as long as anyone could remember; ever since Kate and Julia, after the death of their brother Pat, had left the house in Stoney Batter[1] and taken Mary Jane, their only niece, to live with them in the dark gaunt house on Usher's Island,[2] the upper part of which they had rented from Mr Fulham, the cornfactor on the ground floor. That was a good thirty years ago if it was a day. Mary Jane, who was then a little girl in short clothes, was now the main prop of the household for she had the organ in Haddington Road.[3] She had been through the Academy[4] and gave a pupils' concert every year in the upper room of the Antient Concert Rooms. Many of her pupils belonged to better-class families on the Kingstown and Dalkey line.[5] Old as they were, her aunts also did their share. Julia, though she was quite grey, was still the leading soprano in Adam and Eve's,[6] and Kate, being too feeble to go about much, gave music lessons to beginners on the old square piano in the back room. Lily, the caretaker's daughter, did housemaid's work for them. Though their life was modest they believed in eating well; the best of everything: diamond-bone sirloins, three-shilling tea and the best bottled stout.[7] But Lily seldom made a mistake in the orders so that she got on well with her three mistresses. They were fussy, that was all. But the only thing they would not stand was back answers.

Of course they had good reason to be fussy on such a night. And then it was long after ten o'clock and yet there was no sign of Gabriel and his wife. Besides they were dreadfully afraid that Freddy Malins might turn up screwed.[8] They would not wish for worlds that any of Mary Jane's pupils should see him under the influence; and when he was like that it was sometimes very hard to manage him. Freddy Malins always came late but they wondered what could be keeping Gabriel: and that was what brought them every two minutes to the banisters to ask Lily had Gabriel or Freddy come.

—O, Mr Conroy, said Lily to Gabriel when she opened the door for him, Miss Kate and Miss Julia thought you were never coming. Good-night, Mrs Conroy.

---

1. A district in northwest Dublin.
2. Two adjoining quays on the south side of the river Liffey.
3. Played the organ in a church on the Haddington Road.
4. Royal Academy of Music.
5. The train line connecting Dublin to the affluent suburbs south of the city.
6. A Dublin church.
7. An extra-strength ale.
8. Drunk.

—I'll engage[9] they did, said Gabriel, but they forget that my wife here takes three mortal hours to dress herself.

He stood on the mat, scraping the snow from his goloshes, while Lily led his wife to the foot of the stairs and called out:

—Miss Kate, here's Mrs Conroy.

Kate and Julia came toddling down the dark stairs at once. Both of them kissed Gabriel's wife, said she must be perished alive and asked was Gabriel with her.

—Here I am as right as the mail, Aunt Kate! Go on up. I'll follow, called out Gabriel from the dark.

He continued scraping his feet vigorously while the three women went upstairs, laughing, to the ladies' dressing-room. A light fringe of snow lay like a cape on the shoulders of his overcoat and like toecaps on the toes of his goloshes; and, as the buttons of his overcoat slipped with a squeaking noise through the snow-stiffened frieze, a cold fragrant air from out-of-doors escaped from crevices and folds.

—Is it snowing again, Mr Conroy? asked Lily.

She had preceded him into the pantry to help him off with his overcoat. Gabriel smiled at the three syllables she had given his surname and glanced at her. She was a slim, growing girl, pale in complexion and with hay-coloured hair. The gas in the pantry made her look still paler. Gabriel had known her when she was a child and used to sit on the lowest step nursing a rag doll.

—Yes, Lily, he answered, and I think we're in for a night of it.

He looked up at the pantry ceiling, which was shaking with the stamping and shuffling of feet on the floor above, listened for a moment to the piano and then glanced at the girl, who was folding his overcoat carefully at the end of a shelf.

—Tell me, Lily, he said in a friendly tone, do you still go to school?

—O no, sir, she answered. I'm done schooling this year and more.

—O, then, said Gabriel gaily, I suppose we'll be going to your wedding one of these fine days with your young man, eh?

The girl glanced back at him over her shoulder and said with great bitterness:

—The men that is now is only all palaver[1] and what they can get out of you.

Gabriel coloured as if he felt he had made a mistake and, without looking at her, kicked off his goloshes and flicked actively with his muffler at his patent-leather shoes.

He was a stout tallish young man. The high colour of his cheeks pushed upwards even to his forehead where it scattered itself in a few formless patches of pale red; and on his hairless face there scintillated restlessly the polished lenses and the bright gilt rims of the glasses which screened his delicate and restless eyes. His glossy black hair was parted in the middle and brushed in a long curve behind his ears where it curled slightly beneath the groove left by his hat.

When he had flicked lustre into his shoes he stood up and pulled his waistcoat down more tightly on his plump body. Then he took a coin rapidly from his pocket.

—O Lily, he said, thrusting it into her hands, it's Christmas-time, isn't it? Just . . . here's a little. . . .

He walked rapidly towards the door.

—O no, sir! cried the girl, following him. Really, sir, I wouldn't take it.

—Christmas-time! Christmas-time! said Gabriel, almost trotting to the stairs and waving his hand to her in deprecation.

JAMES JOYCE

9. Wager.
1. Empty talk.

The girl, seeing that he had gained the stairs, called out after him:

—Well, thank you, sir.

He waited outside the drawing-room door until the waltz should finish, listening to the skirts that swept against it and to the shuffling of feet. He was still discomposed by the girl's bitter and sudden retort. It had cast a gloom over him which he tried to dispel by arranging his cuffs and the bows of his tie. Then he took from his waistcoat pocket a little paper and glanced at the headings he had made for his speech. He was undecided about the lines from Robert Browning for he feared they would be above the heads of his hearers. Some quotation that they could recognise from Shakespeare or from the Melodies[2] would be better. The indelicate clacking of the men's heels and the shuffling of their soles reminded him that their grade of culture differed from his. He would only make himself ridiculous by quoting poetry to them which they could not understand. They would think that he was airing his superior education. He would fail with them just as he had failed with the girl in the pantry. He had taken up a wrong tone. His whole speech was a mistake from first to last, an utter failure.

Just then his aunts and his wife came out of the ladies' dressing-room. His aunts were two small plainly dressed old women. Aunt Julia was an inch or so taller. Her hair, drawn low over the tops of her ears, was grey; and grey also, with darker shadows, was her large flaccid face. Though she was stout in build and stood erect her slow eyes and parted lips gave her the appearance of a woman who did not know where she was or where she was going. Aunt Kate was more vivacious. Her face, healthier than her sister's, was all puckers and creases, like a shrivelled red apple, and her hair, braided in the same old-fashioned way, had not lost its ripe nut colour.

They both kissed Gabriel frankly. He was their favourite nephew, the son of their dead elder sister, Ellen, who had married T.J. Conroy of the Port and Docks.

—Gretta tells me you're not going to take a cab back to Monkstown[3] to-night, Gabriel, said Aunt Kate.

—No, said Gabriel, turning to his wife, we had quite enough of that last year, hadn't we. Don't you remember, Aunt Kate, what a cold Gretta got out of it? Cab windows rattling all the way, and the east wind blowing in after we passed Merrion. Very jolly it was. Gretta caught a dreadful cold.

Aunt Kate frowned severely and nodded her head at every word.

—Quite right, Gabriel, quite right, she said. You can't be too careful.

—But as for Gretta there, said Gabriel, she'd walk home in the snow if she were let.

Mrs Conroy laughed.

—Don't mind him, Aunt Kate, she said. He's really an awful bother, what with green shades for Tom's eyes at night and making him do the dumb-bells, and forcing Eva to eat the stirabout.[4] The poor child! And she simply hates the sight of it! . . . O, but you'll never guess what he makes me wear now!

She broke out into a peal of laughter and glanced at her husband, whose admiring and happy eyes had been wandering from her dress to her face and hair. The two aunts laughed heartily too, for Gabriel's solicitude was a standing joke with them.

—Goloshes! said Mrs Conroy. That's the latest. Whenever it's wet underfoot I must put on my goloshes. Tonight even he wanted me to put them on, but I wouldn't. The next thing he'll buy me will be a diving suit.

---

2. Thomas Moore's *Irish Melodies,* a perennial favorite volume of poetry.

3. An elegant suburb south of Dublin.

4. Porridge.

Gabriel laughed nervously and patted his tie reassuringly while Aunt Kate nearly doubled herself, so heartily did she enjoy the joke. The smile soon faded from Aunt Julia's face and her mirthless eyes were directed towards her nephew's face. After a pause she asked:

—And what are goloshes, Gabriel?

—Goloshes, Julia! exclaimed her sister. Goodness me, don't you know what goloshes are? You wear them over your . . . over your boots, Gretta, isn't it?

—Yes, said Mrs Conroy. Guttapercha[5] things. We both have a pair now. Gabriel says everyone wears them on the continent.

—O, on the continent, murmured Aunt Julia, nodding her head slowly.

Gabriel knitted his brows and said, as if he were slightly angered:

—It's nothing very wonderful but Gretta thinks it very funny because she says the word reminds her of Christy Minstrels.[6]

—But tell me, Gabriel, said Aunt Kate, with brisk tact. Of course, you've seen about the room. Gretta was saying . . .

—O, the room is all right, replied Gabriel. I've taken one in the Gresham.[7]

—To be sure, said Aunt Kate, by far the best thing to do. And the children, Gretta, you're not anxious about them?

—O, for one night, said Mrs Conroy. Besides, Bessie will look after them.

—To be sure, said Aunt Kate again. What a comfort it is to have a girl like that, one you can depend on! There's that Lily, I'm sure I don't know what has come over her lately. She's not the girl she was at all.

Gabriel was about to ask his aunt some questions on this point but she broke off suddenly to gaze after her sister who had wandered down the stairs and was craning her neck over the banisters.

—Now, I ask you, she said, almost testily, where is Julia going? Julia! Julia! Where are you going?

Julia, who had gone halfway down one flight, came back and announced blandly:

—Here's Freddy.

At the same moment a clapping of hands and a final flourish of the pianist told that the waltz had ended. The drawing-room door was opened from within and some couples came out. Aunt Kate drew Gabriel aside hurriedly and whispered into his ear:

—Slip down, Gabriel, like a good fellow and see if he's all right, and don't let him up if he's screwed. I'm sure he's screwed. I'm sure he is.

Gabriel went to the stairs and listened over the banisters. He could hear two persons talking in the pantry. Then he recognised Freddy Malins' laugh. He went down the stairs noisily.

—It's such a relief, said Aunt Kate to Mrs Conroy, that Gabriel is here. I always feel easier in my mind when he's here. . . . Julia, there's Miss Daly and Miss Power will take some refreshment. Thanks for your beautiful waltz, Miss Daly. It made lovely time.

A tall wizen-faced man, with a stiff grizzled moustache and swarthy skin, who was passing out with his partner said:

—And may we have some refreshment, too, Miss Morkan?

—Julia, said Aunt Kate summarily, and here's Mr Browne and Miss Furlong. Take them in, Julia, with Miss Daly and Miss Power.

5. Rubberized fabric.
6. A 19th-century blackface minstrel show.
7. The most elegant hotel in Dublin.

—I'm the man for the ladies, said Mr Browne, pursing his lips until his moustache bristled and smiling in all his wrinkles. You know, Miss Morkan, the reason they are so fond of me is—

He did not finish his sentence, but, seeing that Aunt Kate was out of earshot, at once led the three young ladies into the back room. The middle of the room was occupied by two square tables placed end to end, and on these Aunt Julia and the caretaker were straightening and smoothing a large cloth. On the sideboard were arrayed dishes and plates, and glasses and bundles of knives and forks and spoons. The top of the closed square piano served also as a sideboard for viands[8] and sweets. At a smaller sideboard in one corner two young men were standing, drinking hop-bitters.[9]

Mr Browne led his charges thither and invited them all, in jest, to some ladies' punch, hot, strong and sweet. As they said they never took anything strong he opened three bottles of lemonade for them. Then he asked one of the young men to move aside, and, taking hold of the decanter, filled out for himself a goodly measure of whisky. The young men eyed him respectfully while he took a trial sip.

—God help me, he said, smiling, it's the doctor's orders.

His wizened face broke into a broader smile, and the three young ladies laughed in musical echo to his pleasantry, swaying their bodies to and fro, with nervous jerks of their shoulders. The boldest said:

—O, now, Mr Browne, I'm sure the doctor never ordered anything of the kind.

Mr Browne took another sip of his whisky and said, with sidling mimicry:

—Well, you see, I'm like the famous Mrs Cassidy, who is reported to have said: *Now, Mary Grimes, if I don't take it, make me take it, for I feel I want it.*

His hot face had leaned forward a little too confidentially and he had assumed a very low Dublin accent so that the young ladies, with one instinct, received his speech in silence. Miss Furlong, who was one of Mary Jane's pupils, asked Miss Daly what was the name of the pretty waltz she had played; and Mr Browne, seeing that he was ignored, turned promptly to the two young men who were more appreciative.

A red-faced young woman, dressed in pansy, came into the room, excitedly clapping her hands and crying:

—Quadrilles![1] Quadrilles!

Close on her heels came Aunt Kate, crying:

—Two gentlemen and three ladies, Mary Jane!

—O, here's Mr Bergin and Mr Kerrigan, said Mary Jane. Mr Kerrigan, will you take Miss Power? Miss Furlong, may I get you a partner, Mr Bergin. O, that'll just do now.

—Three ladies, Mary Jane, said Aunt Kate.

The two young gentlemen asked the ladies if they might have the pleasure, and Mary Jane turned to Miss Daly.

—O, Miss Daly, you're really awfully good, after playing for the last two dances, but really we're so short of ladies to-night.

—I don't mind in the least, Miss Morkan.

—But I've a nice partner for you, Mr Bartell D'Arcy, the tenor. I'll get him to sing later on. All Dublin is raving about him.

—Lovely voice, lovely voice! said Aunt Kate.

8. Meats.
9. Dry ale.
1. A French square dance.

As the piano had twice begun the prelude to the first figure Mary Jane led her recruits quickly from the room. They had hardly gone when Aunt Julia wandered slowly into the room, looking behind her at something.

—What is the matter, Julia? asked Aunt Kate anxiously. Who is it?

Julia, who was carrying in a column of table-napkins, turned to her sister and said, simply, as if the question had surprised her:

—It's only Freddy, Kate, and Gabriel with him.

In fact right behind her Gabriel could be seen piloting Freddy Malins across the landing. The latter, a young man of about forty, was of Gabriel's size and build, with very round shoulders. His face was fleshy and pallid, touched with colour only at the thick hanging lobes of his ears and at the wide wings of his nose. He had coarse features, a blunt nose, a convex and receding brow, tumid and protruded lips. His heavy-lidded eyes and the disorder of his scanty hair made him look sleepy. He was laughing heartily in a high key at a story which he had been telling Gabriel on the stairs and at the same time rubbing the knuckles of his left fist backwards and forwards into his left eye.

—Good-evening, Freddy, said Aunt Julia.

Freddy Malins bade the Misses Morkan good-evening in what seemed an offhand fashion by reason of the habitual catch in his voice and then, seeing that Mr Browne was grinning at him from the sideboard, crossed the room on rather shaky legs and began to repeat in an undertone the story he had just told to Gabriel.

—He's not so bad, is he? said Aunt Kate to Gabriel.

Gabriel's brows were dark but he raised them quickly and answered:

—O no, hardly noticeable.

—Now, isn't he a terrible fellow! she said. And his poor mother made him take the pledge on New Year's Eve. But come on, Gabriel, into the drawing-room.

Before leaving the room with Gabriel she signalled to Mr Browne by frowning and shaking her forefinger in warning to and fro. Mr Browne nodded in answer and, when she had gone, said to Freddy Malins:

—Now, then, Teddy, I'm going to fill you out a good glass of lemonade just to buck you up.

Freddy Malins, who was nearing the climax of his story, waved the offer aside impatiently but Mr Browne, having first called Freddy Malins' attention to a disarray in his dress, filled out and handed him a full glass of lemonade. Freddy Malins' left hand accepted the glass mechanically, his right hand being engaged in the mechanical readjustment of his dress. Mr Browne, whose face was once more wrinkling with mirth, poured out for himself a glass of whisky while Freddy Malins exploded, before he had well reached the climax of his story, in a kink of high-pitched bronchitic laughter and, setting down his untasted and overflowing glass, began to rub the knuckles of his left fist backwards and forwards into his left eye, repeating words of his last phrase as well as his fit of laughter would allow him.

Gabriel could not listen while Mary Jane was playing her Academy piece, full of runs and difficult passages, to the hushed drawing-room. He liked music but the piece she was playing had no melody for him and he doubted whether it had any melody for the other listeners, though they had begged Mary Jane to play something. Four young men, who had come from the refreshment-room to stand in the doorway at the sound of the piano, had gone away quietly in couples after a few minutes. The only persons who seemed to follow the music were Mary Jane herself, her hands racing along the key-board or lifted from it at the pauses like those of a priestess in momentary imprecation, and Aunt Kate standing at her elbow to turn the page.

Gabriel's eyes, irritated by the floor, which glittered with beeswax under the heavy chandelier, wandered to the wall above the piano. A picture of the balcony scene in *Romeo and Juliet* hung there and beside it was a picture of the two murdered princes[2] in the Tower which Aunt Julia had worked in red, blue and brown wools when she was a girl. Probably in the school they had gone to as girls that kind of work had been taught, for one year his mother had worked for him as a birthday present a waistcoat of purple tabinet,[3] with little foxes' heads upon it, lined with brown satin and having round mulberry buttons. It was strange that his mother had had no musical talent though Aunt Kate used to call her the brains carrier of the Morkan family. Both she and Julia had always seemed a little proud of their serious and matronly sister. Her photograph stood before the pierglass.[4] She held an open book on her knees and was pointing out something in it to Constantine who, dressed in a man-o'-war suit, lay at her feet. It was she who had chosen the names for her sons for she was very sensible of the dignity of family life. Thanks to her, Constantine was now senior curate in Balbriggan[5] and, thanks to her, Gabriel himself had taken his degree in the Royal University.[6] A shadow passed over his face as he remembered her sullen opposition to his marriage. Some slighting phrases she had used still rankled in his memory; she had once spoken of Gretta as being country cute and that was not true of Gretta at all. It was Gretta who had nursed her during all her last long illness in their house at Monkstown.

He knew that Mary Jane must be near the end of her piece for she was playing again the opening melody with runs of scales after every bar and while he waited for the end the resentment died down in his heart. The piece ended with a trill of octaves in the treble and a final deep octave in the bass. Great applause greeted Mary Jane as, blushing and rolling up her music nervously, she escaped from the room. The most vigorous clapping came from the four young men in the doorway who had gone away to the refreshment-room at the beginning of the piece but had come back when the piano had stopped.

Lancers[7] were arranged. Gabriel found himself partnered with Miss Ivors. She was a frank-mannered talkative young lady, with a freckled face and prominent brown eyes. She did not wear a low-cut bodice and the large brooch which was fixed in the front of her collar bore on it an Irish device.

When they had taken their places she said abruptly:

—I have a crow to pluck with you.

—With me? said Gabriel.

She nodded her head gravely.

—What is it? asked Gabriel, smiling at her solemn manner.

—Who is G. C.? answered Miss Ivors, turning her eyes upon him.

Gabriel coloured and was about to knit his brows, as if he did not understand, when she said bluntly:

—O, innocent Amy! I have found out that you write for *The Daily Express.*[8] Now, aren't you ashamed of yourself?

2. The young sons of Edward IV, murdered in the Tower of London by order of their uncle, Edward III.
3. Silk and wool fabric.
4. A large high mirror.
5. A seaport southeast of Dublin.
6. The Royal University of Ireland, established in 1882.
7. A type of quadrille for 8 or 16 people.
8. A conservative paper opposed to the struggle for Irish independence.

—Why should I be ashamed of myself? asked Gabriel, blinking his eyes and trying to smile.

—Well, I'm ashamed of you, said Miss Ivors frankly. To say you'd write for a rag like that. I didn't think you were a West Briton.[9]

A look of perplexity appeared on Gabriel's face. It was true that he wrote a literary column every Wednesday in *The Daily Express,* for which he was paid fifteen shillings. But that did not make him a West Briton surely. The books he received for review were almost more welcome than the paltry cheque. He loved to feel the covers and turn over the pages of newly printed books. Nearly every day when his teaching in the college was ended he used to wander down the quays to the second-hand booksellers, to Hickey's on Bachelor's Walk, to Webb's or Massey's on Aston's Quay, or to O'Clohissey's in the by-street. He did not know how to meet her charge. He wanted to say that literature was above politics. But they were friends of many years' standing and their careers had been parallel, first at the University and then as teachers: he could not risk a grandiose phrase with her. He continued blinking his eyes and trying to smile and murmured lamely that he saw nothing political in writing reviews of books.

When their turn to cross had come he was still perplexed and inattentive. Miss Ivors promptly took his hand in a warm grasp and said in a soft friendly tone:

—Of course, I was only joking. Come, we cross now.

When they were together again she spoke of the University question[1] and Gabriel felt more at ease. A friend of hers had shown her his review of Browning's poems. That was how she had found out the secret: but she liked the review immensely. Then she said suddenly:

—O, Mr Conroy, will you come for an excursion to the Aran Isles[2] this summer? We're going to stay there a whole month. It will be splendid out in the Atlantic. You ought to come. Mr Clancy is coming, and Mr Kilkelly and Kathleen Kearney. It would be splendid for Gretta too if she'd come. She's from Connacht,[3] isn't she?

—Her people are, said Gabriel shortly.

—But you will come, won't you? said Miss Ivors, laying her warm hand eagerly on his arm.

—The fact is, said Gabriel, I have already arranged to go—

—Go where? asked Miss Ivors.

—Well, you know, every year I go for a cycling tour with some fellows and so—

—But where? asked Miss Ivors.

—Well, we usually go to France or Belgium or perhaps Germany, said Gabriel awkwardly.

—And why do you go to France and Belgium, said Miss Ivors, instead of visiting your own land?

—Well, said Gabriel, it's partly to keep in touch with the languages and partly for a change.

—And haven't you your own language to keep in touch with—Irish? asked Miss Ivors.

—Well, said Gabriel, if it comes to that, you know, Irish is not my language.

9. Disparaging term for people wishing to identify Ireland as British.
1. Ireland's oldest most and prestigious university, Trinity College, was open only to Protestants; the "University question" involved, in part, the provision of quality university education to Catholics.
2. Islands off the west coast of Ireland where the people still retained their traditional culture and spoke Irish.
3. A province on the west coast of Ireland.

Their neighbours had turned to listen to the cross-examination. Gabriel glanced right and left nervously and tried to keep his good humour under the ordeal which was making a blush invade his forehead.

—And haven't you your own land to visit, continued Miss Ivors, that you know nothing of, your own people, and your own country?

—O, to tell you the truth, retorted Gabriel suddenly, I'm sick of my own country, sick of it!

—Why? asked Miss Ivors.

Gabriel did not answer for his retort had heated him.

—Why? repeated Miss Ivors.

They had to go visiting together and, as he had not answered her, Miss Ivors said warmly:

—Of course, you've no answer.

Gabriel tried to cover his agitation by taking part in the dance with great energy. He avoided her eyes for he had seen a sour expression on her face. But when they met in the long chain he was surprised to feel his hand firmly pressed. She looked at him from under her brows for a moment quizzically until he smiled. Then, just as the chain was about to start again, she stood on tiptoe and whispered into his ear:

—West Briton!

When the lancers were over Gabriel went away to a remote corner of the room where Freddy Malins' mother was sitting. She was a stout feeble old woman with white hair. Her voice had a catch in it like her son's and she stuttered slightly. She had been told that Freddy had come and that he was nearly all right. Gabriel asked her whether she had had a good crossing. She lived with her married daughter in Glasgow and came to Dublin on a visit once a year. She answered placidly that she had had a beautiful crossing and that the captain had been most attentive to her. She spoke also of the beautiful house her daughter kept in Glasgow, and of all the nice friends they had there. While her tongue rambled on Gabriel tried to banish from his mind all memory of the unpleasant incident with Miss Ivors. Of course the girl or woman, or whatever she was, was an enthusiast but there was a time for all things. Perhaps he ought not to have answered her like that. But she had no right to call him a West Briton before people, even in joke. She had tried to make him ridiculous before people, heckling him and staring at him with her rabbit's eyes.

He saw his wife making her way towards him through the waltzing couples. When she reached him she said into his ear:

—Gabriel, Aunt Kate wants to know won't you carve the goose as usual. Miss Daly will carve the ham and I'll do the pudding.

—All right, said Gabriel.

—She's sending in the younger ones first as soon as this waltz is over so that we'll have the table to ourselves.

—Were you dancing? asked Gabriel.

—Of course I was. Didn't you see me? What words had you with Molly Ivors?

—No words. Why? Did she say so?

—Something like that. I'm trying to get that Mr D'Arcy to sing. He's full of conceit, I think.

—There were no words, said Gabriel moodily, only she wanted me to go for a trip to the west of Ireland and I said I wouldn't.

His wife clasped her hands excitedly and gave a little jump.

—O, do go, Gabriel, she cried. I'd love to see Galway again.

—You can go if you like, said Gabriel coldly.

She looked at him for a moment, then turned to Mrs Malins and said:

—There's a nice husband for you, Mrs Malins.

While she was threading her way back across the room Mrs Malins, without adverting to the interruption, went on to tell Gabriel what beautiful places there were in Scotland and beautiful scenery. Her son-in-law brought them every year to the lakes and they used to go fishing. Her son-in-law was a splendid fisher. One day he caught a fish, a beautiful big big fish, and the man in the hotel boiled it for their dinner.

Gabriel hardly heard what she said. Now that supper was coming near he began to think again about his speech and about the quotation. When he saw Freddy Malins coming across the room to visit his mother Gabriel left the chair free for him and retired into the embrasure of the window. The room had already cleared and from the back room came the clatter of plates and knives. Those who still remained in the drawing-room seemed tired of dancing and were conversing quietly in little groups. Gabriel's warm trembling fingers tapped the cold pane of the window. How cool it must be outside! How pleasant it would be to walk out alone, first along by the river and then through the park! The snow would be lying on the branches of the trees and forming a bright cap on the top of the Wellington Monument.[4] How much more pleasant it would be there than at the supper-table!

He ran over the headings of his speech: Irish hospitality, sad memories, the Three Graces, Paris, the quotation from Browning. He repeated to himself a phrase he had written in his review: *One feels that one is listening to a thought-tormented music.* Miss Ivors had praised the review. Was she sincere? Had she really any life of her own behind all her propagandism? There had never been any ill-feeling between them until that night. It unnerved him to think that she would be at the supper-table, looking up at him while he spoke with her critical quizzing eyes. Perhaps she would not be sorry to see him fail in his speech. An idea came into his mind and gave him courage. He would say, alluding to Aunt Kate and Aunt Julia: *Ladies and Gentlemen, the generation which is now on the wane among us may have had its faults but for my part I think it had certain qualities of hospitality, of humour, of humanity, which the new and very serious and hypereducated generation that is growing up around us seems to me to lack.* Very good: that was one for Miss Ivors. What did he care that his aunts were only two ignorant old women?

A murmur in the room attracted his attention. Mr Browne was advancing from the door, gallantly escorting Aunt Julia, who leaned upon his arm, smiling and hanging her head. An irregular musketry of applause escorted her also as far as the piano and then, as Mary Jane seated herself on the stool, and Aunt Julia, no longer smiling, half turned so as to pitch her voice fairly into the room, gradually ceased. Gabriel recognised the prelude. It was that of an old song of Aunt Julia's—*Arrayed for the Bridal.*[5] Her voice, strong and clear in tone, attacked with great spirit the runs which embellish the air and though she sang very rapidly she did not miss even the smallest of the grace notes. To follow the voice, without looking at the singer's face, was to feel and share the excitement of swift and secure flight. Gabriel applauded loudly with all the others at the close of the song and loud applause was borne in from the invisible supper-table. It sounded so genuine that a little colour struggled into Aunt Julia's face

---

4. A monument to the Duke of Wellington, an Irish-born English military hero, located in Phoenix Park, Dublin's major public park.

5. A popular but challenging song set to music from Bellini's opera *I Puritani* (1835).

as she bent to replace in the music-stand the old leather-bound song-book that had her initials on the cover. Freddy Malins, who had listened with his head perched sideways to hear her better, was still applauding when everyone else had ceased and talking animatedly to his mother who nodded her head gravely and slowly in acquiescence. At last, when he could clap no more, he stood up suddenly and hurried across the room to Aunt Julia whose hand he seized and held in both his hands, shaking it when words failed him or the catch in his voice proved too much for him.

—I was just telling my mother, he said, I never heard you sing so well, never. No, I never heard your voice so good as it is to-night. Now! Would you believe that now? That's the truth. Upon my word and honour that's the truth. I never heard your voice sound so fresh and so . . . so clear and fresh, never.

Aunt Julia smiled broadly and murmured something about compliments as she released her hand from his grasp. Mr Browne extended his open hand towards her and said to those who were near him in the manner of a showman introducing a prodigy to an audience:

—Miss Julia Morkan, my latest discovery!

He was laughing very heartily at this himself when Freddy Malins turned to him and said:

—Well, Browne, if you're serious you might make a worse discovery. All I can say is I never heard her sing half so well as long as I am coming here. And that's the honest truth.

—Neither did I, said Mr. Browne. I think her voice has greatly improved.

Aunt Julia shrugged her shoulders and said with meek pride:

—Thirty years ago I hadn't a bad voice as voices go.

—I often told Julia, said Aunt Kate emphatically, that she was simply thrown away in that choir. But she never would be said by me.

She turned as if to appeal to the good sense of the others against a refractory child while Aunt Julia gazed in front of her, a vague smile of reminiscence playing on her face.

—No, continued Aunt Kate, she wouldn't be said or led by anyone, slaving there in that choir night and day, night and day. Six o'clock on Christmas morning! And all for what?

—Well, isn't it for the honour of God, Aunt Kate? asked Mary Jane, twisting round on the piano-stool and smiling.

Aunt Kate turned fiercely on her niece and said:

—I know all about the honour of God, Mary Jane, but I think it's not at all honourable for the pope to turn out the women out of the choirs that have slaved there all their lives and put little whipper-snappers of boys over their heads.[6] I suppose it is for the good of the Church if the pope does it. But it's not just, Mary Jane, and it's not right.

She had worked herself into a passion and would have continued in defence of her sister for it was a sore subject with her but Mary Jane, seeing that all the dancers had come back, intervened pacifically:

—Now, Aunt Kate, you're giving scandal to Mr Browne who is of the other persuasion.

Aunt Kate turned to Mr Browne, who was grinning at this allusion to his religion, and said hastily:

6. In 1903 the Pope had ordered all Catholic churches to start using all-male choirs.

—O, I don't question the pope's being right. I'm only a stupid old woman and I wouldn't presume to do such a thing. But there's such a thing as common everyday politeness and gratitude. And if I were in Julia's place I'd tell that Father Healy straight up to his face . . .

—And besides, Aunt Kate, said Mary Jane, we really are all hungry and when we are hungry we are all very quarrelsome.

—And when we are thirsty we are also quarrelsome, added Mr Browne.

—So that we had better go to supper, said Mary Jane, and finish the discussion afterwards.

On the landing outside the drawing-room Gabriel found his wife and Mary Jane trying to persuade Miss Ivors to stay for supper. But Miss Ivors, who had put on her hat and was buttoning her cloak, would not stay. She did not feel in the least hungry and she had already overstayed her time.

—But only for ten minutes, Molly, said Mrs Conroy. That won't delay you.

—To take a pick itself, said Mary Jane, after all your dancing.

—I really couldn't, said Miss Ivors.

—I am afraid you didn't enjoy yourself at all, said Mary Jane hopelessly.

—Ever so much, I assure you, said Miss Ivors, but you really must let me run off now.

—But how can you get home? asked Mrs Conroy.

—O, it's only two steps up the quay.

Gabriel hesitated a moment and said:

—If you will allow me, Miss Ivors, I'll see you home if you really are obliged to go.

But Miss Ivors broke away from them.

—I won't hear of it, she cried. For goodness sake go in to your suppers and don't mind me. I'm quite well able to take care of myself.

—Well, you're the comical girl, Molly, said Mrs Conroy frankly.

—*Beannacht libh,*[7] cried Miss Ivors, with a laugh, as she ran down the staircase.

Mary Jane gazed after her, a moody puzzled expression on her face, while Mrs Conroy leaned over the banisters to listen for the hall-door. Gabriel asked himself was he the cause of her abrupt departure. But she did not seem to be in ill humour: she had gone away laughing. He stared blankly down the staircase.

At that moment Aunt Kate came toddling out of the supper-room, almost wringing her hands in despair.

—Where is Gabriel? she cried. Where on earth is Gabriel? There's everyone waiting in there, stage to let, and nobody to carve the goose!

—Here I am, Aunt Kate! cried Gabriel, with sudden animation, ready to carve a flock of geese, if necessary.

A fat brown goose lay at one end of the table and at the other end, on a bed of creased paper strewn with sprigs of parsley, lay a great ham, stripped of its outer skin and peppered over with crust crumbs, a neat paper frill round its shin and beside this was a round of spiced beef. Between these rival ends ran parallel lines of side-dishes: two little minsters of jelly, red and yellow; a shallow dish full of blocks of blancmange and red jam, a large green leaf-shaped dish with a stalk-shaped handle, on which lay bunches of purple raisins and peeled almonds, a companion dish on which lay a solid rectangle of Smyrna figs, a dish of custard topped with grated nutmeg, a small bowl full of chocolates and sweets wrapped in gold and silver papers

7. Farewell (Irish).

and a glass vase in which stood some tall celery stalks. In the centre of the table there stood, as sentries to a fruit-stand which upheld a pyramid of oranges and American apples, two squat old-fashioned decanters of cut glass, one containing port and the other dark sherry. On the closed square piano a pudding in a huge yellow dish lay in waiting and behind it were three squads of bottles of stout and ale and minerals, drawn up according to the colours of their uniforms, the first two black, with brown and red labels, the third and smallest squad white, with transverse green sashes.

Gabriel took his seat boldly at the head of the table and, having looked to the edge of the carver, plunged his fork firmly into the goose. He felt quite at ease now for he was an expert carver and liked nothing better than to find himself at the head of a well-laden table.

—Miss Furlong, what shall I send you? he asked. A wing or a slice of the breast?

—Just a small slice of the breast.

—Miss Higgins, what for you?

—O, anything at all, Mr Conroy.

While Gabriel and Miss Daly exchanged plates of goose and plates of ham and spiced beef Lily went from guest to guest with a dish of hot floury potatoes wrapped in a white napkin. This was Mary Jane's idea and she had also suggested apple sauce for the goose but Aunt Kate had said that plain roast goose without apple sauce had always been good enough for her and she hoped she might never eat worse. Mary Jane waited on her pupils and saw that they got the best slices and Aunt Kate and Aunt Julia opened and carried across from the piano bottles of stout and ale for the gentlemen and bottles of minerals for the ladies. There was a great deal of confusion and laughter and noise, the noise of orders and counter-orders, of knives and forks, of corks and glass-stoppers. Gabriel began to carve second helpings as soon as he had finished the first round without serving himself. Everyone protested loudly so that he compromised by taking a long draught of stout for he had found the carving hot work. Mary Jane settled down quietly to her supper but Aunt Kate and Aunt Julia were still toddling round the table, walking on each other's heels, getting in each other's way and giving each other unheeded orders. Mr Browne begged of them to sit down and eat their suppers and so did Gabriel but they said there was time enough so that, at last, Freddy Malins stood up and, capturing Aunt Kate, plumped her down on her chair amid general laughter.

When everyone had been well served Gabriel said, smiling:

—Now, if anyone wants a little more of what vulgar people call stuffing let him or her speak.

A chorus of voices invited him to begin his own supper and Lily came forward with three potatoes which she had reserved for him.

—Very well, said Gabriel amiably, as he took another preparatory draught, kindly forget my existence, ladies and gentlemen, for a few minutes.

He set to his supper and took no part in the conversation with which the table covered Lily's removal of the plates. The subject of talk was the opera company which was then at the Theatre Royal. Mr Bartell D'Arcy, the tenor, a dark-complexioned young man with a smart moustache, praised very highly the leading contralto of the company but Miss Furlong thought she had a rather vulgar style of production. Freddy Malins said there was a negro chieftain singing in the second part of the Gaiety pantomime who had one of the finest tenor voices he had ever heard.

—Have you heard him? he asked Mr Bartell D'Arcy across the table.

—No, answered Mr Bartell D'Arcy carelessly.

—Because, Freddy Malins explained, now I'd be curious to hear your opinion of him. I think he has a grand voice.

—It takes Teddy to find out the really good things, said Mr Browne familiarly to the table.

—And why couldn't he have a voice too? asked Freddy Malins sharply. Is it because he's only a black?

Nobody answered this question and Mary Jane led the table back to the legitimate opera. One of her pupils had given her a pass for *Mignon*. Of course it was very fine, she said, but it made her think of poor Georgina Burns. Mr Browne could go back farther still, to the old Italian companies that used to come to Dublin—Tietjens, Ilma de Murzka, Campanini, the great Trebelli, Giuglini, Ravelli, Aramburo.[8] Those were the days, he said, when there was something like singing to be heard in Dublin. He told too of how the top gallery of the old Royal used to be packed night after night, of how one night an Italian tenor had sung five encores to *Let Me Like a Soldier Fall*, introducing a high C every time, and of how the gallery boys would sometimes in their enthusiasm unyoke the horses from the carriage of some great *prima donna* and pull her themselves through the streets to her hotel. Why did they never play the grand old operas now, he asked, *Dinorah, Lucrezia Borgia?* Because they could not get the voices to sing them: that was why.

—O, well, said Mr Bartell D'Arcy, I presume there are as good singers to-day as there were then.

—Where are they? asked Mr Browne defiantly.

—In London, Paris, Milan, said Mr Bartell D'Arcy warmly. I suppose Caruso,[9] for example, is quite as good, if not better than any of the men you have mentioned.

—Maybe so, said Mr Browne. But I may tell you I doubt it strongly.

—O, I'd give anything to hear Caruso sing, said Mary Jane.

—For me, said Aunt Kate, who had been picking a bone, there was only one tenor. To please me, I mean. But I suppose none of you ever heard of him.

—Who was he, Miss Morkan? asked Mr Bartell D'Arcy politely.

—His name, said Aunt Kate, was Parkinson. I heard him when he was in his prime and I think he had then the purest tenor voice that was ever put into a man's throat.

—Strange, said Mr Bartell D'Arcy. I never even heard of him.

—Yes, yes, Miss Morkan is right, said Mr Browne. I remember hearing of old Parkinson but he's too far back for me.

—A beautiful pure sweet mellow English tenor, said Aunt Kate with enthusiasm.

Gabriel having finished, the huge pudding was transferred to the table. The clatter of forks and spoons began again. Gabriel's wife served out spoonfuls of the pudding and passed the plates down the table. Midway down they were held up by Mary Jane, who replenished them with raspberry or orange jelly or with blancmange and jam. The pudding was of Aunt Julia's making and she received praises for it from all quarters. She herself said that it was not quite brown enough.

—Well, I hope, Miss Morkan, said Mr Browne, that I'm brown enough for you because, you know, I'm all brown.

All the gentlemen, except Gabriel, ate some of the pudding out of compliment to Aunt Julia. As Gabriel never ate sweets the celery had been left for him. Freddy Malins also took a stalk of celery and ate it with his pudding. He had been told that

8. Famous 19th-century opera singers.
9. Enrico Caruso (1874–1921), a famous tenor.

celery was a capital thing for the blood and he was just then under doctor's care. Mrs Malins, who had been silent all through the supper, said that her son was going down to Mount Melleray[1] in a week or so. The table then spoke to Mount Melleray, how bracing the air was down there, how hospitable the monks were and how they never asked for a penny-piece from their guests.

—And do you mean to say, asked Mr Browne incredulously, that a chap can go down there and put up there as if it were a hotel and live on the fat of the land and then come away without paying a farthing?

—O, most people give some donation to the monastery when they leave, said Mary Jane.

—I wish we had an institution like that in our Church, said Mr Browne candidly.

He was astonished to hear that the monks never spoke, got up at two in the morning and slept in their coffins. He asked what they did it for.

—That's the rule of the order, said Aunt Kate firmly.

—Yes, but why? asked Mr Browne.

Aunt Kate repeated that it was the rule, that was all. Mr Browne still seemed not to understand. Freddy Malins explained to him, as best he could, that the monks were trying to make up for the sins committed by all the sinners in the outside world. The explanation was not very clear for Mr Browne grinned and said:

—I like that idea very much but wouldn't a comfortable spring bed do them as well as a coffin?

—The coffin, said Mary Jane, is to remind them of their last end.

As the subject had grown lugubrious it was buried in a silence of the table during which Mrs Malins could be heard saying to her neighbour in an indistinct undertone:

—They are very good men, the monks, very pious men.

The raisins and almonds and figs and apples and oranges and chocolates and sweets were now passed about the table and Aunt Julia invited all the guests to have either port or sherry. At first Mr Bartell D'Arcy refused to take either but one of his neighbours nudged him and whispered something to him upon which he allowed his glass to be filled. Gradually as the last glasses were being filled the conversation ceased. A pause followed, broken only by the noise of the wine and by unsettlings of chairs. The Misses Morkan, all three, looked down at the tablecloth. Someone coughed once or twice and then a few gentlemen patted the table gently as a signal for silence. The silence came and Gabriel pushed back his chair and stood up.

The patting at once grew louder in encouragement and then ceased altogether. Gabriel leaned his ten trembling fingers on the tablecloth and smiled nervously at the company. Meeting a row of upturned faces he raised his eyes to the chandelier. The piano was playing a waltz tune and he could hear the skirts sweeping against the drawing-room door. People, perhaps, were standing in the snow on the quay outside, gazing up at the lighted windows and listening to the waltz music. The air was pure there. In the distance lay the park where the trees were weighted with snow. The Wellington Monument wore a gleaming cap of snow that flashed westward over the white field of Fifteen Acres.[2]

He began:

—Ladies and Gentlemen.

1. A monastery in southern Ireland, specializing in the treatment of alcoholics.
2. A section of Phoenix Park.

—It has fallen to my lot this evening, as in years past, to perform a very pleasing task but a task for which I am afraid my poor powers as a speaker are all too inadequate.

—No, no! said Mr Browne.

—But, however that may be, I can only ask you tonight to take the will for the deed and to lend me your attention for a few moments while I endeavour to express to you in words what my feelings are on this occasion.

—Ladies and Gentlemen. It is not the first time that we have gathered together under this hospitable roof, around this hospitable board. It is not the first time that we have been the recipients—or perhaps, I had better say, the victims—of the hospitality of certain good ladies.

He made a circle in the air with his arm and paused. Everyone laughed or smiled at Aunt Kate and Aunt Julia and Mary Jane who all turned crimson with pleasure. Gabriel went on more boldly:

—I feel more strongly with every recurring year that our country has no tradition which does it so much honour and which it should guard so jealously as that of its hospitality. It is a tradition that is unique as far as my experience goes (and I have visited not a few places abroad) among the modern nations. Some would say, perhaps, that with us it is rather a failing than anything to be boasted of. But granted even that, it is, to my mind, a princely failing, and one that I trust will long be cultivated among us. Of one thing, at least, I am sure. As long as this one roof shelters the good ladies aforesaid—and I wish from my heart it may do so for many and many a long year to come—the tradition of genuine warm-hearted courteous Irish hospitality, which our forefathers have handed down to us and which we in turn must hand down to our descendants, is still alive among us.

A hearty murmur of assent ran round the table. It shot through Gabriel's mind that Miss Ivors was not there and that she had gone away discourteously: and he said with confidence in himself:

—Ladies and Gentlemen.

—A new generation is growing up in our midst, a generation actuated by new ideas and new principles. It is serious and enthusiastic for these new ideas and its enthusiasm, even when it is misdirected, is, I believe, in the main sincere. But we are living in a sceptical and, if I may use the phrase, a thought-tormented age: and sometimes I fear that this new generation, educated or hypereducated as it is, will lack those qualities of humanity, of hospitality, of kindly humour which belonged to an older day. Listening to-night to the names of all those great singers of the past it seemed to me, I must confess, that we were living in a less spacious age. Those days might, without exaggeration, be called spacious days: and if they are gone beyond recall let us hope, at least, that in gatherings such as this we shall still speak of them with pride and affection, still cherish in our hearts the memory of those dead and gone great ones whose fame the world will not willingly let die.

—Hear, hear! said Mr Browne loudly.

—But yet, continued Gabriel, his voice falling into a softer inflection, there are always in gatherings such as this sadder thoughts that will recur to our minds: thoughts of the past, of youth, of changes, of absent faces that we miss here to-night. Our path through life is strewn with many such sad memories: and were we to brood upon them always we could not find the heart to go on bravely with our work among the living. We have all of us living duties and living affections which claim, and rightly claim, our strenuous endeavours.

—Therefore, I will not linger on the past. I will not let any gloomy moralising intrude upon us here to-night. Here we are gathered together for a brief moment from the bustle and rush of our everyday routine. We are met here as friends, in the spirit of goodfellowship, as colleagues, also to a certain extent, in the true spirit of *camaraderie,* and as the guests of—what shall I call them?—the Three Graces[3] of the Dublin musical world.

The table burst into applause and laughter at this sally. Aunt Julia vainly asked each of her neighbors in turn to tell her what Gabriel had said.

—He says we are the Three Graces, Aunt Julia, said Mary Jane.

Aunt Julia did not understand but she looked up, smiling, at Gabriel, who continued in the same vein:

—Ladies and Gentlemen.

—I will not attempt to play to-night the part that Paris[4] played on another occasion. I will not attempt to choose between them. The task would be an invidious one and one beyond my poor powers. For when I view them in turn, whether it be our chief hostess herself, whose good heart, whose too good heart, has become a byword with all who know her, or her sister, who seems to be gifted with perennial youth and whose singing must have been a surprise and a revelation to us all to-night, or, last but not least, when I consider our youngest hostess, talented, cheerful, hard-working and the best of nieces, I confess, Ladies and Gentlemen, that I do not know to which of them I should award the prize.

Gabriel glanced down at his aunts and, seeing the large smile on Aunt Julia's face and the tears which had risen to Aunt Kate's eyes, hastened to his close. He raised his glass of port gallantly, while every member of the company fingered a glass expectantly, and said loudly:

—Let us toast them all three together. Let us drink to their health, wealth, long life, happiness and prosperity and may they long continue to hold the proud and selfwon position which they hold in their profession and the position of honour and affection which they hold in our hearts.

All the guests stood up, glass in hand, and, turning towards the three seated ladies, sang in unison, with Mr Browne as leader:

> *For they are jolly gay fellows,*
> *For they are jolly gay fellows,*
> *For they are jolly gay fellows,*
> *Which nobody can deny.*

Aunt Kate was making frank use of her handkerchief and even Aunt Julia seemed moved. Freddy Malins beat time with his pudding-fork and the singers turned towards one another, as if in melodious conference, while they sang, with emphasis:

> *Unless he tells a lie,*
> *Unless he tells a lie,*

Then, turning once more towards their hostesses, they sang:

> *For they are jolly gay fellows,*
> *For they are jolly gay fellows,*
> *For they are jolly gay fellows,*
> *Which nobody can deny.*

3. Companions to the Muses in Greek mythology.
4. Paris was the judge of a divine beauty contest in which Hera, Athena, and Aphrodite competed; his selection of Aphrodite was, indirectly, the cause of the Trojan War.

The acclamation which followed was taken up beyond the door of the supper-room by many of the other guests and renewed time after time, Freddy Malins acting as officer with his fork on high.

The piercing morning air came into the hall where they were standing so that Aunt Kate said:

—Close the door, somebody. Mrs Malins will get her death of cold.

—Browne is out there, Aunt Kate, said Mary Jane.

—Browne is everywhere, said Aunt Kate, lowering her voice.

Mary Jane laughed at her tone.

—Really, she said archly, he is very attentive.

—He has been laid on here like the gas, said Aunt Kate in the same tone, all during the Christmas.

She laughed herself this time good-humouredly and then added quickly:

—But tell him to come in, Mary Jane, and close the door. I hope to goodness he didn't hear me.

At that moment the hall-door was opened and Mr Browne came in from the door-step, laughing as if his heart would break. He was dressed in a long green overcoat with mock astrakhan cuffs and collar and wore on his head an oval fur cap. He pointed down the snow-covered quay from where the sound of shrill prolonged whistling was borne in.

—Teddy will have all the cabs in Dublin out, he said.

Gabriel advanced from the little pantry behind the office, struggling into his overcoat and looking round the hall, said:

—Gretta not down yet?

—She's getting on her things, Gabriel, said Aunt Kate.

—Who's playing up there? asked Gabriel.

—Nobody. They're all gone.

—O no, Aunt Kate, said Mary Jane. Bartell D'Arcy and Miss O'Callaghan aren't gone yet.

—Someone is strumming at the piano, anyhow, said Gabriel.

Mary Jane glanced at Gabriel and Mr Browne and said with a shiver:

—It makes me feel cold to look at you two gentlemen muffled up like that. I wouldn't like to face your journey home at this hour.

—I'd like nothing better this minute, said Mr Browne stoutly, than a rattling fine walk in the country or a fast drive with a good spanking goer between the shafts.

—We used to have a very good horse and trap at home, said Aunt Julia sadly.

—The never-to-be-forgotten Johnny, said Mary Jane, laughing.

Aunt Kate and Gabriel laughed too.

—Why, what was wonderful about Johnny? asked Mr Browne.

—The late lamented Patrick Morkan, our grandfather, that is, explained Gabriel, commonly known in his later years as the old gentleman, was a glue-boiler.

—O, now, Gabriel, said Aunt Kate, laughing, he had a starch mill.

—Well, glue or starch, said Gabriel, the old gentleman had a horse by the name of Johnny. And Johnny used to work in the old gentleman's mill, walking round and round in order to drive the mill. That was all very well; but now comes the tragic part about Johnny. One fine day the old gentleman thought he'd like to drive out with the quality to a military review in the park.

—The Lord have mercy on his soul, said Aunt Kate compassionately.

—Amen, said Gabriel. So the old gentleman, as I said, harnessed Johnny and put on his very best tall hat and his very best stock collar and drove out in grand style from his ancestral mansion somewhere near Back Lane, I think.

Everyone laughed, even Mrs Malins, at Gabriel's manner and Aunt Kate said:

—O now, Gabriel, he didn't live in Back Lane, really. Only the mill was there.

—Out from the mansion of his forefathers, continued Gabriel, he drove with Johnny. And everything went on beautifully until Johnny came in sight of King Billy's statue:[5] and whether he fell in love with the horse King Billy sits on or whether he thought he was back again in the mill, anyhow he began to walk round the statue.

Gabriel paced in a circle round the hall in his goloshes amid the laughter of the others.

—Round and round he went, said Gabriel, and the old gentleman, who was a very pompous old gentleman, was highly indignant. *Go on, sir! What do you mean, sir? Johnny! Johnny! Most extraordinary conduct! Can't understand the horse!*

The peals of laughter which followed Gabriel's imitation of the incident were interrupted by a resounding knock at the hall-door. Mary Jane ran to open it and let in Freddy Malins. Freddy Malins, with his hat well back on his head and his shoulders humped with cold, was puffing and steaming after his exertions.

—I could only get one cab, he said.

—O, we'll find another along the quay, said Gabriel.

—Yes, said Aunt Kate. Better not keep Mrs Malins standing in the draught.

Mrs Malins was helped down the front steps by her son and Mr Browne and, after many manoeuvres, hoisted into the cab. Freddy Malins clambered in after her and spent a long time settling her on the seat, Mr Browne helping him with advice. At last she was settled comfortably and Freddy Malins invited Mr Browne into the cab. There was a good deal of confused talk, and then Mr Browne got into the cab. The cabman settled his rug over his knees, and bent down for the address. The confusion grew greater and the cabman was directed differently by Freddy Malins and Mr Browne, each of whom had his head out through a window of the cab. The difficulty was to know where to drop Mr Browne along the route and Aunt Kate, Aunt Julia and Mary Jane helped the discussion from the doorstep with cross-directions and contradictions and abundance of laughter. As for Freddy Malins he was speechless with laughter. He popped his head in and out of the window every moment, to the great danger of his hat, and told his mother how the discussion was progressing till at last Mr Browne shouted to the bewildered cabman above the din of everybody's laughter:

—Do you know Trinity College?

—Yes, sir, said the cabman.

—Well, drive bang up against Trinity College gates, said Mr Browne, and then we'll tell you where to go. You understand now?

—Yes, sir, said the cabman.

—Make like a bird for Trinity College.

—Right, sir, cried the cabman.

5. A statue of William of Orange, who defeated the Irish Catholic forces in the Battle of the Boyne in 1690, which stood in College Green in front of Trinity College in the heart of Dublin. It was seen as a symbol of British imperial oppression.

The horse was whipped up and the cab rattled off along the quay amid a chorus of laughter and adieus.

Gabriel had not gone to the door with the others. He was in a dark part of the hall gazing up the staircase. A woman was standing near the top of the first flight, in the shadow also. He could not see her face but he could see the terracotta and salmonpink panels of her skirt which the shadow made appear black and white. It was his wife. She was leaning on the banisters, listening to something. Gabriel was surprised at her stillness and strained his ear to listen also. But he could hear little save the noise of laughter and dispute on the front steps, a few chords struck on the piano and a few notes of a man's voice singing.

He stood still in the gloom of the hall, trying to catch the air that the voice was singing and gazing up at his wife. There was grace and mystery in her attitude as if she were a symbol of something. He asked himself what is a woman standing on the stairs in the shadow, listening to distant music, a symbol of. If he were a painter he would paint her in that attitude. Her blue felt hat would show off the bronze of her hair against the darkness and the dark panels of her skirt would show off the light ones. *Distant Music* he would call the picture if he were a painter.

The hall-door was closed; and Aunt Kate, Aunt Julia and Mary Jane came down the hall, still laughing.

—Well, isn't Freddy terrible? said Mary Jane. He's really terrible.

Gabriel said nothing but pointed up the stairs towards where his wife was standing. Now that the hall-door was closed the voice and the piano could be heard more clearly. Gabriel held up his hand for them to be silent. The song seemed to be in the old Irish tonality and the singer seemed uncertain both of his words and of his voice. The voice, made plaintive by distance and by the singer's hoarseness, faintly illuminated the cadence of the air with words expressing grief:

> *O, the rain falls on my heavy locks*
> *And the dew wets my skin,*
> *My babe lies cold . . .*[6]

—O, exclaimed Mary Jane. It's Bartell D'Arcy singing and he wouldn't sing all the night. O, I'll get him to sing a song before he goes.

—O do, Mary Jane, said Aunt Kate.

Mary Jane brushed past the others and ran to the staircase but before she reached it the singing stopped and the piano was closed abruptly.

—O, what a pity! she cried. Is he coming down, Gretta?

Gabriel heard his wife answer yes and saw her come down towards them. A few steps behind her were Mr Bartell D'Arcy and Miss O'Callaghan.

—O, Mr D'Arcy, cried Mary Jane, it's downright mean of you to break off like that when we were all in raptures listening to you.

—I have been at him all the evening, said Miss O'Callaghan, and Mrs Conroy too and he told us he had a dreadful cold and couldn't sing.

—O, Mr D'Arcy, said Aunt Kate, now that was a great fib to tell.

—Can't you see that I'm as hoarse as a crow? said Mr D'Arcy roughly.

He went into the pantry hastily and put on his overcoat. The others, taken aback by his rude speech, could find nothing to say. Aunt Kate wrinkled her brows and

---

6. From a traditional ballad, *The Lass of Aughrim*, about a peasant girl seduced by a nobleman. She brings their baby to the castle door, only to be turned away; she and her child then die by drowning.

made signs to the others to drop the subject. Mr D'Arcy stood swathing his neck carefully and frowning.

—It's the weather, said Aunt Julia, after a pause.

—Yes, everybody has colds, said Aunt Kate readily, everybody.

—They say, said Mary Jane, we haven't had snow like it for thirty years; and I read this morning in the newspapers that the snow is general all over Ireland.

—I love the look of snow, said Aunt Julia sadly.

—So do I, said Miss O'Callaghan. I think Christmas is never really Christmas unless we have the snow on the ground.

—But poor Mr D'Arcy doesn't like the snow, said Aunt Kate, smiling.

Mr D'Arcy came from the pantry, full swathed and buttoned, and in a repentant tone told them the history of his cold. Everyone gave him advice and said it was a great pity and urged him to be very careful of his throat in the night air. Gabriel watched his wife who did not join in the conversation. She was standing right under the dusty fanlight and the flame of the gas lit up the rich bronze of her hair which he had seen her drying at the fire a few days before. She was in the same attitude and seemed unaware of the talk about her. At last she turned towards them and Gabriel saw that there was colour on her cheeks and that her eyes were shining. A sudden tide of joy went leaping out of his heart.

—Mr D'Arcy, she said, what is the name of that song you were singing?

—It's called *The Lass of Aughrim,* said Mr D'Arcy, but I couldn't remember it properly. Why? Do you know it?

—*The Lass of Aughrim,* she repeated. I couldn't think of the name.

—It's a very nice air, said Mary Jane. I'm sorry you were not in voice to-night.

—Now, Mary Jane, said Aunt Kate, don't annoy Mr D'Arcy. I won't have him annoyed.

Seeing that all were ready to start she shepherded them to the door where good-night was said:

—Well, good-night, Aunt Kate, and thanks for the pleasant evening.

—Good-night, Gabriel. Good-night, Gretta!

—Good-night, Aunt Kate, and thanks ever so much. Good-night, Aunt Julia.

—O, good-night, Gretta, I didn't see you.

—Good-night, Mr D'Arcy. Good-night, Miss O'Callaghan.

—Good-night, Miss Morkan.

—Good-night, again.

—Good-night, all. Safe home.

—Good-night. Good-night.

The morning was still dark. A dull yellow light brooded over the houses and the river; and the sky seemed to be descending. It was slushy underfoot; and only streaks and patches of snow lay on the roofs, on the parapets of the quay and on the area railings. The lamps were still burning redly in the murky air and, across the river, the palace of the Four Courts[7] stood out menacingly against the heavy sky.

She was walking on before him with Mr Bartell D'Arcy, her shoes in a brown parcel tucked under one arm and her hands holding her skirt up from the slush. She had no longer any grace of attitude but Gabriel's eyes were still bright with happiness. The blood went bounding along his veins; and the thoughts went rioting through his brain, proud, joyful, tender, valorous.

7. The Irish law courts.

She was walking on before him so lightly and so erect that he longed to run after her noiselessly, catch her by the shoulders and say something foolish and affectionate into her ear. She seemed to him so frail that he longed to defend her against something and then to be alone with her. Moments of their secret life together burst like stars upon his memory. A heliotrope envelope was lying beside his breakfast-cup and he was caressing it with his hand. Birds were twittering in the ivy and the sunny web of the curtain was shimmering along the floor: he could not eat for happiness. They were standing on the crowded platform and he was placing a ticket inside the warm palm of her glove. He was standing with her in the cold, looking in through a grated window at a man making bottles in a roaring furnace. It was very cold. Her face, fragrant in the cold air, was quite close to his; and suddenly she called out to the man at the furnace:

—Is the fire hot, sir?

But the man could not hear her with the noise of the furnace. It was just as well. He might have answered rudely.

A wave of yet more tender joy escaped from his heart and went coursing in warm flood along his arteries. Like the tender fires of stars moments of their life together, that no one knew of or would ever know of, broke upon and illumined his memory. He longed to recall to her those moments, to make her forget the years of their dull existence together and remember only their moments of ecstasy. For the years, he felt, had not quenched his soul or hers. Their children, his writing, her household cares had not quenched all their souls' tender fire. In one letter that he had written to her then he had said: *Why is it that words like these seem to me so dull and cold? Is it because there is no word tender enough to be your name?*

Like distant music these words that he had written years before were borne towards him from the past. He longed to be alone with her. When the others had gone away, when he and she were in their room in the hotel, then they would be alone together. He would call her softly:

—Gretta!

Perhaps she would not hear at once: she would be undressing. Then something in his voice would strike her. She would turn and look at him. . . .

At the corner of Winetavern Street they met a cab. He was glad of its rattling noise as it saved him from conversation. She was looking out of the window and seemed tired. The others spoke only a few words, pointing out some building or street. The horse galloped along wearily under the murky morning sky, dragging his old rattling box after his heels, and Gabriel was again in a cab with her, galloping to catch the boat, galloping to their honeymoon.

As the cab drove across O'Connell Bridge Miss O'Callaghan said:

—They say you never cross O'Connell Bridge without seeing a white horse.

—I see a white man this time, said Gabriel.

—Where? asked Mr Bartell D'Arcy.

Gabriel pointed to the statue, on which lay patches of snow.[8] Then he nodded familiarly to it and waved his hand.

—Good-night, Dan, he said gaily.

When the cab drew up before the hotel Gabriel jumped out and, in spite of Mr Bartell D'Arcy's protest, paid the driver. He gave the man a shilling over his fare. The man saluted and said:

8. A statue of Daniel O'Connell, 19th-century nationalist leader.

—A prosperous New Year to you, sir.

—The same to you, said Gabriel cordially.

She leaned for a moment on his arm in getting out of the cab and while standing at the curbstone, bidding the others good-night. She leaned lightly on his arm, as lightly as when she had danced with him a few hours before. He had felt proud and happy then, happy that she was his, proud of her grace and wifely carriage. But now, after the kindling again of so many memories, the first touch of her body, musical and strange and perfumed, sent through him a keen pang of lust. Under cover of her silence he pressed her arm closely to his side; and, as they stood at the hotel door, he felt that they had escaped from their lives and duties, escaped from home and friends and run away together with wild and radiant hearts to a new adventure.

An old man was dozing in a great hooded chair in the hall. He lit a candle in the office and went before them to the stairs. They followed him in silence, their feet falling in soft thuds on the thickly carpeted stairs. She mounted the stairs behind the porter, her head bowed in the ascent, her frail shoulders curved as with a burden, her skirt girt tightly about her. He could have flung his arms about her hips and held her still for his arms were trembling with desire to seize her and only the stress of his nails against the palms of his hands held the wild impulse of his body in check. The porter halted on the stairs to settle his guttering candle. They halted too on the steps below him. In the silence Gabriel could hear the falling of the molten wax into the tray and the thumping of his own heart against his ribs.

The porter led them along a corridor and opened a door. Then he set his unstable candle down on a toilet-table and asked at what hour they were to be called in the morning.

—Eight, said Gabriel.

The porter pointed to the tap of the electric-light and began a muttered apology but Gabriel cut him short.

—We don't want any light. We have light enough from the street. And I say, he added, pointing to the candle, you might remove that handsome article, like a good man.

The porter took up his candle again, but slowly for he was surprised by such a novel idea. Then he mumbled good-night and went out. Gabriel shot the lock to.

A ghostly light from the street lamp lay in a long shaft from one window to the door. Gabriel threw his overcoat and hat on a couch and crossed the room towards the window. He looked down into the street in order that his emotion might calm a little. Then he turned and leaned against a chest of drawers with his back to the light. She had taken off her hat and cloak and was standing before a large swinging mirror, unhooking her waist. Gabriel paused for a few moments, watching her, and then said:

—Gretta!

She turned away from the mirror slowly and walked along the shaft of light towards him. Her face looked so serious and weary that the words would not pass Gabriel's lips. No, it was not the moment yet.

—You looked tired, he said.

—I am a little, she answered.

—You don't feel ill or weak?

—No, tired: that's all.

She went on to the window and stood there, looking out. Gabriel waited again and then, fearing that diffidence was about to conquer him, he said abruptly:

—By the way, Gretta!

—What is it?

—You know that poor fellow Malins? he said quickly.

—Yes. What about him?

—Well, poor fellow, he's a decent sort of chap after all, continued Gabriel in a false voice. He gave me back that sovereign I lent him and I didn't expect it really. It's a pity he wouldn't keep away from that Browne, because he's not a bad fellow at heart.

He was trembling now with annoyance. Why did she seem so abstracted? He did not know how he could begin. Was she annoyed, too, about something? If she would only turn to him or come to him of her own accord! To take her as she was would be brutal. No, he must see some ardour in her eyes first. He longed to be master of her strange mood.

—When did you lend him the pound? she asked, after a pause.

Gabriel strove to restrain himself from breaking out into brutal language about the sottish Malins and his pound. He longed to cry to her from his soul, to crush her body against his, to overmaster her. But he said:

—O, at Christmas, when he opened that little Christmas-card shop in Henry Street.

He was in such a fever of rage and desire that he did not hear her come from the window. She stood before him for an instant, looking at him strangely. Then, suddenly raising herself on tiptoe and resting her hands lightly on his shoulders, she kissed him.

—You are a very generous person, Gabriel, she said.

Gabriel, trembling with delight at her sudden kiss and at the quaintness of her phrase, put his hands on her hair and began smoothing it back, scarcely touching it with his fingers. The washing had made it fine and brilliant. His heart was brimming over with happiness. Just when he was wishing for it she had come to him of her own accord. Perhaps her thoughts had been running with his. Perhaps she had felt the impetuous desire that was in him and then the yielding mood had come upon her. Now that she had fallen to him so easily he wondered why he had been so diffident.

He stood, holding her head between his hands. Then, slipping one arm swiftly about her body and drawing her towards him, he said softly:

—Gretta dear, what are you thinking about?

She did not answer nor yield wholly to his arm. He said again, softly:

—Tell me what it is, Gretta. I think I know what is the matter. Do I know?

She did not answer at once. Then she said in an outburst of tears:

—O, I am thinking about that song, *The Lass of Aughrim.*

She broke loose from him and ran to the bed and, throwing her arms across the bed-rail, hid her face. Gabriel stood stock-still for a moment in astonishment and then followed her. As he passed in the way of the cheval-glass he caught sight of himself in full length, his broad, well-filled shirt-front, the face whose expression always puzzled him when he saw it in a mirror and his glimmering gilt-rimmed eyeglasses. He halted a few paces from her and said:

—What about the song? Why does that make you cry?

She raised her head from her arms and dried her eyes with the back of her hand like a child. A kinder note than he had intended went into his voice.

—Why, Gretta? he asked.

—I am thinking about a person long ago who used to sing that song.

—And who was the person long ago? asked Gabriel, smiling.

—It was a person I used to know in Galway when I was living with my grandmother, she said.

The smile passed away from Gabriel's face. A dull anger began to gather again at the back of his mind and the dull fires of his lust began to glow angrily in his veins.

—Someone you were in love with? he asked ironically.

—It was a young boy I used to know, she answered, named Michael Furey. He used to sing that song, *The Lass of Aughrim.* He was very delicate.

Gabriel was silent. He did not wish her to think that he was interested in this delicate boy.

—I can see him so plainly, she said after a moment. Such eyes as he had: big dark eyes! And such an expression in them—an expression!

—O then, you were in love with him? said Gabriel.

—I used to go out walking with him, she said, when I was in Galway.

A thought flew across Gabriel's mind.

—Perhaps that was why you wanted to go to Galway with that Ivors girl? he said coldly.

She looked at him and asked in surprise:

—What for?

Her eyes made Gabriel feel awkward. He shrugged his shoulders and said:

—How do I know? To see him perhaps.

She looked away from him along the shaft of light towards the window in silence.

—He is dead, she said at length. He died when he was only seventeen. Isn't it a terrible thing to die so young as that?

—What was he? asked Gabriel, still ironically.

—He was in the gasworks, she said.

Gabriel felt humiliated by the failure of his irony and by the evocation of this figure from the dead, a boy in the gasworks. While he had been full of memories of their secret life together, full of tenderness and joy and desire, she had been comparing him in her mind with another. A shameful consciousness of his own person assailed him. He saw himself as a ludicrous figure, acting as a pennyboy[9] for his aunts, a nervous well-meaning sentimentalist, orating to vulgarians and idealising his own clownish lusts, the pitiable fatuous fellow he had caught a glimpse of in the mirror. Instinctively he turned his back more to the light lest she might see the shame that burned upon his forehead.

He tried to keep up his tone of cold interrogation but his voice when he spoke was humble and indifferent.

—I suppose you were in love with this Michael Furey, Gretta, he said.

—I was great with him at that time, she said.

Her voice was veiled and sad. Gabriel, feeling now how vain it would be to try to lead her whither he had purposed, caressed one of her hands and said, also sadly:

—And what did he die of so young, Gretta? Consumption, was it?

—I think he died for me, she answered.[1]

A vague terror seized Gabriel at this answer as if, at that hour when he had hoped to triumph, some impalpable and vindictive being was coming against him, gathering forces against him in its vague world. But he shook himself free of it with an effort of reason and continued to caress her hand. He did not question her again for he felt that she would tell him of herself. Her hand was warm and moist: it did not respond to his

9. Errand boy.

1. Gretta here echoes the words of Yeats's Cathleen ní Houlihan: "Singing I am about a man I knew one time, yellow-haired Donough that was hanged in Galway. . . . He died for love of me: many a man has died for love of me." The play was first performed in Dublin on 2 April 1902.

touch but he continued to caress it just as he had caressed her first letter to him that spring morning.

—It was in the winter, she said, about the beginning of the winter when I was going to leave my grandmother's and come up here to the convent. And he was ill at the time in his lodgings in Galway and wouldn't be let out and his people in Oughterard[2] were written to. He was in decline, they said, or something like that. I never knew rightly.

She paused for a moment and sighed.

—Poor fellow, she said. He was very fond of me and he was such a gentle boy. We used to go out together, walking, you know, Gabriel, like the way they do in the country. He was going to study singing only for his health. He had a very good voice, poor Michael Furey.

—Well; and then? asked Gabriel.

—And then when it came to the time for me to leave Galway and come up to the convent he was much worse and I wouldn't be let see him so I wrote a letter saying I was going up to Dublin and would be back in the summer and hoping he would be better then.

She paused for a moment to get her voice under control and then went on:

—Then the night before I left I was in my grandmother's house in Nuns' Island, packing up, and I heard gravel thrown up against the window. The window was so wet I couldn't see so I ran downstairs as I was and slipped out the back into the garden and there was the poor fellow at the end of the garden, shivering.

—And did you not tell him to go back? asked Gabriel.

—I implored him to go home at once and told him he would get his death in the rain. But he said he did not want to live. I can see his eyes as well as well! He was standing at the end of the wall where there was a tree.

—And did he go home? asked Gabriel.

—Yes, he went home. And when I was only a week in the convent he died and he was buried in Oughterard where his people came from. O, the day I heard that, that he was dead!

She stopped, choking with sobs, and, overcome by emotion, flung herself face downward on the bed, sobbing in the quilt. Gabriel held her hand for a moment longer, irresolutely, and then, shy of intruding on her grief, let it fall gently and walked quietly to the window.

She was fast asleep.

Gabriel, leaning on his elbow, looked for a few moments unresentfully on her tangled hair and half-open mouth, listening to her deep-drawn breath. So she had had that romance in her life: a man had died for her sake. It hardly pained him now to think how poor a part he, her husband, had played in her life. He watched her while she slept as though he and she had never lived together as man and wife. His curious eyes rested long upon her face and on her hair: and, as he thought of what she must have been then, in that time of her first girlish beauty, a strange friendly pity for her entered his soul. He did not like to say even to himself that her face was no longer beautiful but he knew that it was no longer the face for which Michael Furey had braved death.

Perhaps she had not told him all the story. His eyes moved to the chair over which she had thrown some of her clothes. A petticoat string dangled to the floor. One boot stood upright, its limp upper fallen down: the fellow of it lay upon its side.

2. A small village in western Ireland.

He wondered at his riot of emotions of an hour before. From what had it proceeded? From his aunt's supper, from his own foolish speech, from the wine and dancing, the merry-making when saying good-night in the hall, the pleasure of the walk along the river in the snow. Poor Aunt Julia! She, too, would soon be a shade with the shade of Patrick Morkan and his horse. He had caught that haggard look upon her face for a moment when she was singing *Arrayed for the Bridal.* Soon, perhaps, he would be sitting in that same drawing-room, dressed in black, his silk hat on his knees. The blinds would be drawn down and Aunt Kate would be sitting beside him, crying and blowing her nose and telling him how Julia had died. He would cast about in his mind for some words that might console her, and would find only lame and useless ones. Yes, yes: that would happen very soon.

The air of the room chilled his shoulders. He stretched himself cautiously along under the sheets and lay down beside his wife. One by one they were all becoming shades. Better pass boldly into that other world, in the full glory of some passion, than fade and wither dismally with age. He thought of how she who lay beside him had locked in her heart for so many years that image of her lover's eyes when he had told her that he did not wish to live.

Generous tears filled Gabriel's eyes. He had never felt like that himself towards any woman but he knew that such a feeling must be love. The tears gathered more thickly in his eyes and in the partial darkness he imagined he saw the form of a young man standing under a dripping tree. Other forms were near. His soul had approached that region where dwell the vast hosts of the dead. He was conscious of, but could not apprehend, their wayward and flickering existence. His own identity was fading out into a grey impalpable world: the solid world itself which these dead had one time reared and lived in was dissolving and dwindling.

A few light taps upon the pane made him turn to the window. It had begun to snow again. He watched sleepily the flakes, silver and dark, falling obliquely against the lamplight. The time had come for him to set out on his journey westward. Yes, the newspapers were right: snow was general all over Ireland. It was falling on every part of the dark central plain, on the treeless hills, falling softly upon the Bog of Allen and, farther westward, softly falling into the dark mutinous Shannon waves.[3] It was falling, too, upon every part of the lonely churchyard on the hill where Michael Furey lay buried. It lay thickly drifted on the crooked crosses and headstones, on the spears of the little gate, on the barren thorns. His soul swooned slowly as he heard the snow falling faintly through the universe and faintly falling, like the descent of their last end, upon all the living and the dead.

VIRGINIA WOOLF ▪ (1882–1941)

"On or about December, 1910," Virginia Woolf once wrote in an essay on fiction, "human character changed." That month saw the opening of a major exhibit of post-Impressionist art in London, and it is characteristic of Woolf to consider that art has the power to change human nature itself. A proper Victorian by upbringing and an avant-garde artist by vocation, Virginia Woolf was deeply interested in the ways human nature was changing in her times, both through artistic revolutions and through the social upheavals that culminated in

---

3. Where Ireland's longest river, the Shannon, empties into the sea.

World War I and its aftermath. By 1910 her own life had changed in many ways from the life she had experienced in her childhood as the young Adeline Virginia Stephen, daughter of the prosperous editor and aspiring philosopher Sir Leslie Stephen, editor of the massive *Dictionary of National Biography*. Her mother, Julia—artistic in temperament, and a famous beauty often sketched by Pre-Raphaelite artist friends—died in 1895, when Virginia was thirteen. A mental breakdown, the first of what became Woolf's recurrent bouts of mental instability, quickly followed. Two years later, her half-sister Stella died in childbirth, and within another two years her brother Thoby died of typhoid.

Having grown up an intensely literary child in a pervasively literary and artistic household, the young Virginia Stephen was nevertheless kept away from the public routes to education offered to her brothers, who attended prestigious private schools and went on to Oxford. Like most upper-class British women of her generation, Woolf and her sisters were educated at home, and never went to college. Woolf read voraciously, and her independence of mind and habits fostered her later freedom to experiment, yet she remained keenly aware of her exclusion from the wealth of resources offered by Oxford and Cambridge. Her path-breaking essay *A Room of One's Own* (1928), on the intellectual and material conditions needed for women to write fiction, opens with a scene in which an angelic beadle prohibits her from entering an Edenlike university library. All her life, Woolf was to be a full member of upper-class British society and yet also in important ways an outsider to it: as a pacifist as World War II approached; as an entirely committed writer when women were supposed to devote most of their attention to husband and children; as someone romantically drawn to women as well as to men, notably to her intimate friend Vita Sackville-West, to whom she dedicated her 1928 novel *Orlando,* whose hero changes sex and becomes a heroine part way into the book.

Following her father's death in 1904, Virginia began to publish her work. Together with her surviving brother Adrian and her artist sister Vanessa, she set up house in Bloomsbury Square in London, forming the center for a loose group of free-thinking artists, writers, and other intellectuals. In 1912 she married Leonard Woolf, himself an outsider as a socialist, an anti-imperialist, and a Jew in the often genially anti-Semitic culture of Edwardian England. The Woolfs founded the Hogarth Press, which published their own books and those of many others, including work by their friends T. S. Eliot, E. M. Forster, and Katherine Mansfield, together with the first English translations of the works of Sigmund Freud.

Once she began publishing, Woolf was extraordinarily productive, creating a wide variety of work. She explored the finest nuances of consciousness and perception in her major novels, starting with *The Voyage Out* (1915). Her work became increasingly experimental as time went on; along with James Joyce she became a pioneering practitioner of the technique of "interior monologue," following the twists and turns of an individual's consciousness from within, most notably in her great novels *Mrs Dalloway* (1925) and *To the Lighthouse* (1927)—a loving, ironic recreation of her parents in the form of the charming, self-centered philosopher Mr. Ramsay and his magnetic, manipulative wife Mrs. Ramsay, who humors her husband and shelters her brood of eight children until her sudden, untimely death. Later Woolf experimented with a shifting, polyphonic multiplicity of voices in *The Waves* (1931) and used a fragmented, drama-based style for her last novel, *Between the Acts* (1941). The pressures for war were building as she was completing this novel, and Woolf grew increasingly depressed. She and Leonard anticipated that the Nazis would soon invade England; they expected that certainly Leonard—and probably Woolf herself, as well as many of their friends—would be killed if the invasion were to succeed. Fearing the onset of a new mental breakdown, Woolf drowned herself in a river near her country home in March of 1941.

By then she had produced not only a major body of fiction but also several volumes of sparkling essays and reviews for "the common reader," whom she hoped to reach even in her most experimental work. She also wrote voluminous diaries and masses of letters (several volumes have been published both of the diaries and of the letters). Together, these works show a life in which conversation, reflection, and writing were constant means of self-understanding and of engagement with the wider world.

The blending of social framing and psychological insight is fully evident in the two stories given here, two of her most compelling short fictions. Like the "epiphanies" of James Joyce, these stories center on an ordinary yet suddenly revelatory moment. "The Lady in the Looking-Glass: A Reflection" (1929) takes vision itself as its theme. The lady of the title is absent for most of the story; an invisible narrator builds a world around her absence by examining what can be seen, or inferred, in the mirror above her mantelpiece. Literature has long been described as "holding a mirror up to nature," though by Woolf's time writers were often revising this image to express less direct sorts of mirroring. In the 1890s, Oscar Wilde had described his art as a *cracked* looking-glass, while in *Ulysses,* Joyce went Wilde one better by having Stephen Dedalus describe Irish art as the cracked mirror "of a servant." Woolf's mirror in turn conceals as well as reveals, and the final appearance of the lady in the looking-glass yields a very different epiphany than we have been led to expect.

For Woolf, as for contemporaries of hers from Joseph Conrad in England to Akutagawa Ryunosuke in Japan, truth can't be reflected directly but must be perceived in fragments, by indirection. Seen rightly, even the smallest image or incident can reveal multiple facets and possibilities, as in "Mrs Dalloway in Bond Street" (1923), in which a woman simply goes out to buy a pair of gloves. This story was the germ of what was to become the novel *Mrs Dalloway.* As she was expanding this story, Woolf clearly had it in mind when writing an essay in 1925 on "Modern Fiction." "Examine for a moment an ordinary mind on an ordinary day," she says:

> The mind receives a myriad impressions—trivial, fantastic, evanescent, or engraved with the sharpness of steel. From all sides they come, an incessant shower of innumerable atom; and, as they fall, as they shape themselves into the life of Monday or Tuesday, the accent falls differently from of old; the moment of importance came not here but there; so that, if a writer were a free man and not a slave, if he could write what he chose, not what he must, if he could base his work upon his own feeling and not upon convention, there would be no plot, no comedy, no tragedy, no love interest or catastrophe in the accepted style, and perhaps not a single button sewn on as the Bond Street tailors would have it.

Mrs Dalloway in Bond Street

Mrs Dalloway said she would buy the gloves herself. Big Ben was striking as she stepped out into the street. It was eleven o'clock and the unused hour was fresh as if issued to children on a beach. But there was something solemn in the deliberate swing of the repeated strokes; something stirring in the murmur of wheels and the shuffle of footsteps.

No doubt they were not all bound on errands of happiness. There is much more to be said about us than that we walk the streets of Westminster.[1] Big Ben too is nothing but steel rods consumed by rust were it not for the care of H.M's Office of Works. Only for Mrs Dalloway the moment was complete; for Mrs Dalloway June was fresh. A happy childhood—and it was not to his daughters only that Justin Parry had seemed a fine fellow (weak of course on the Bench); flowers at evening, smoke rising; the caw of rooks falling from ever so high, down down through the October

---

1. District of central London, including the Houses of Parliament (with their famous clock tower "Big Ben"); it is also a fashionable residential area.

air—there is nothing to take the place of childhood. A leaf of mint brings it back: or a cup with a blue ring.

Poor little wretches, she sighed, and pressed forward. Oh, right under the horses' noses, you little demon! and there she was left on the kerb stretching her hand out, while Jimmy Dawes grinned on the further side.

A charming woman, posed, eager, strangely white-haired for her pink cheeks, so Scope Purvis, C.B., saw her as he hurried to his office. She stiffened a little, waiting for Durtnall's van to pass. Big Ben struck the tenth; struck the eleventh stroke. The leaden circles dissolved in the air. Pride held her erect, inheriting, handing on, acquainted with discipline and with suffering. How people suffered, how they suffered, she thought, thinking of Mrs Foxcroft at the Embassy last night decked with jewels, eating her heart out, because that nice boy was dead, and now the old Manor House (Durtnall's van passed) must go to a cousin.

"Good morning to you," said Hugh Whitbread raising his hat rather extravagantly by the china shop, for they had known each other as children. "Where are you off to?"

"I love walking in London," said Mrs Dalloway. "Really it's better than walking in the country!"

"We've just come up," said Hugh Whitbread. "Unfortunately to see doctors."

"Milly?" said Mrs Dalloway, instantly compassionate.

"Out of sorts," said Hugh Whitbread. "That sort of thing. Dick all right?"

"First rate!" said Clarissa.

Of course, she thought, walking on, Milly is about my age—fifty—fifty-two. So it is probably *that*. Hugh's manner had said so, said it perfectly—dear old Hugh, thought Mrs Dalloway, remembering with amusement, with gratitude, with emotion, how shy, like a brother—one would rather die than speak to one's brother—Hugh had always been, when he was at Oxford, and came over, and perhaps one of them (drat the thing!) couldn't ride. How then could women sit in Parliament? How could they do things with men? For there is this extraordinarily deep instinct, something inside one; you can't get over it; it's no use trying; and men like Hugh respect it without our saying it, which is what one loves, thought Clarissa, in dear old Hugh.

She had passed through the Admiralty Arch and saw at the end of the empty road with its thin trees Victoria's white mound, Victoria's billowing motherliness, amplitude and homeliness, always ridiculous, yet how sublime thought Mrs Dalloway, remembering Kensington Gardens and the old lady in horn spectacles and being told by Nanny to stop dead still and bow to the Queen. The flag flew above the Palace. The King and Queen were back then. Dick had met her at lunch the other day—a thoroughly nice woman. It matters so much to the poor, thought Clarissa, and to the soldiers. A man in bronze stood heroically on a pedestal with a gun on her left hand side—the South African war. It matters, thought Mrs Dalloway walking towards Buckingham Palace. There it stood four-square, in the broad sunshine, uncompromising, plain. But it was character she thought; something inborn in the race; what Indians respected. The Queen went to hospitals, opened bazaars—the Queen of England, thought Clarissa, looking at the Palace. Already at this hour a motor car passed out at the gates; soldiers saluted; the gates were shut. And Clarissa, crossing the road, entered the Park, holding herself upright.

June had drawn out every leaf on the trees. The mothers of Westminster with mottled breasts gave suck to their young. Quite respectable girls lay stretched on the grass. An elderly man, stooping very stiffly, picked up a crumpled paper, spread it out flat and flung it away. How horrible! Last night at the Embassy Sir Dighton had said, "If I want a fellow to hold my horse, I have only to put up my hand." But the religious question is far more serious than the economic, Sir Dighton had said, which she thought extraordinarily interesting, from a man like Sir Dighton. "Oh, the country will never know what it has lost," he had said, talking, of his own accord, about dear Jack Stewart.

She mounted the little hill lightly. The air stirred with energy. Messages were passing from the Fleet to the Admiralty. Piccadilly and Arlington Street and the Mall seemed to chafe the very air in the Park and lift its leaves hotly, brilliantly, upon waves of that divine vitality which Clarissa loved. To ride; to dance; she had adored all that. Or going on long walks in the country, talking, about books, what to do with one's life, for young people were amazingly priggish—oh, the things one had said! But one had conviction. Middle age is the devil. People like Jack'll never know that, she thought; for he never once thought of death, never, they said, knew he was dying. And now can never mourn—how did it go?—a head grown grey. . . . From the contagion of the world's slow stain. . . . Have drunk their cup a round or two before. . . . From the contagion of the world's slow stain![2] She held herself upright.

But how Jack would have shouted! Quoting Shelley, in Piccadilly! "You want a pin," he would have said. He hated frumps. "My God Clarissa! My God Clarissa!"— she could hear him now at the Devonshire House party, about poor Sylvia Hunt in her amber necklace and that dowdy old silk. Clarissa held herself upright for she had spoken aloud and now she was in Piccadilly, passing the house with the slender green columns, and the balconies; passing club windows full of newspapers; passing old Lady Burdett Coutt's house where the glazed white parrot used to hang; and Devonshire House, without its gilt leopards; and Claridge's, where she must remember Dick wanted her to leave a card on Mrs Jepson or she would be gone. Rich Americans can be very charming. There was St James's Palace; like a child's game with bricks; and now—she had passed Bond Street—she was by Hatchard's book shop. The stream was endless—endless—endless. Lords, Ascot, Hurlingham[3]—what was it? What a duck, she thought, looking at the frontispiece of some book of memoirs spread wide in the bow window, Sir Joshua perhaps or Romney; arch, bright, demure; the sort of girl—like her own Elizabeth—the only *real* sort of girl. And there was that absurd book, *Soapy Sponge,* which Jum used to quote by the yard; and Shakespeare's Sonnets. She knew them by heart. Phil and she had argued all day about the Dark Lady, and Dick had said straight out at dinner that night that he had never heard of her. Really, she had married him for that! He had never read Shakespeare! There must be some little cheap book she could buy for Milly—*Cranford*[4] of course! Was there ever anything so enchanting as the cow in petticoats? If only people had that sort of humour, that sort of self-respect now, thought Clarissa, for she remembered the broad pages; the sentences ending; the characters—how one talked about them as if they were real. For all the great things one must go to the past, she thought. From the contagion of the world's slow stain. . . . Fear no more the heat o' the sun. . . . And now can never mourn, can never mourn, she repeated, her eyes straying over the window; for it ran in her head; the test of great poetry; the moderns had never written anything one wanted to read about death, she thought; and turned.

2. From *Adonais* (stanza 40), Percy Shelley's elegy on the early death of Keats.
3. Locations of fashionable sporting events (cricket, horse racing, and polo).
4. Popular novel by Elizabeth Gaskell (1810–1865).

Omnibuses joined motor cars; motor cars vans; vans taxicabs; taxicabs motor cars—here was an open motor car with a girl, alone. Up till four, her feet tingling, I know, thought Clarissa, for the girl looked washed out, half asleep, in the corner of the car after the dance. And another car came; and another. No! No! No! Clarissa smiled good-naturedly. The fat lady had taken every sort of trouble, but diamonds! orchids! at this hour of the morning! No! No! No! The excellent policeman would, when the time came, hold up his hand. Another motor car passed. How utterly unattractive! Why should a girl of that age paint black round her eyes? And a young man with a girl, at this hour, when the country—The admirable policeman raised his hand and Clarissa acknowledging his sway, taking her time, crossed, walked towards Bond Street; saw the narrow crooked street, the yellow banners; the thick notched telegraph wires stretched across the sky.

A hundred years ago her great-great-grandfather, Seymour Parry, who ran away with Conway's daughter, had walked down Bond Street. Down Bond Street the Parrys had walked for a hundred years, and might have met the Dalloways (Leighs on the mother's side) going up. Her father got his clothes from Hill's. There was a roll of cloth in the window, and here just one jar on a black table, incredibly expensive; like the thick pink salmon on the ice block at the fishmonger's. The jewels were exquisite—pink and orange stars, paste, Spanish, she thought, and chains of old gold; starry buckles, little brooches which had been worn on sea-green satin by ladies with high head-dresses. But no looking! One must economise. She must go on past the picture dealer's where one of the odd French pictures hung, as if people had thrown confetti—pink and blue—for a joke. If you had lived with pictures (and it's the same with books and music) thought Clarissa, passing the Aeolian Hall, you can't be taken in by a joke.

The river of Bond Street was clogged. There, like a queen at a tournament, raised, regal, was Lady Bexborough. She sat in her carriage, upright, alone, looking through her glasses. The white glove was loose at her wrist. She was in black, quite shabby, yet, thought Clarissa, how extraordinarily it tells, breeding, self-respect, never saying a word too much or letting people gossip; an astonishing friend; no one can pick a hole in her after all these years, and now, there she is, thought Clarissa, passing the Countess who waited powdered, perfectly still, and Clarissa would have given anything to be like that, the mistress of Clarefield, talking politics, like a man. But she never goes anywhere, thought Clarissa, and it's quite useless to ask her, and the carriage went on and Lady Bexborough was borne past like a queen at a tournament, though she had nothing to live for and the old man is failing and they say she is sick of it all, thought Clarissa and the tears actually rose to her eyes as she entered the shop.

"Good morning," said Clarissa in her charming voice. "Gloves," she said with her exquisite friendliness and putting her bag on the counter began, very slowly, to undo the buttons. "White gloves," she said. "Above the elbow," and she looked straight into the shopwoman's face—but this was not the girl she remembered? She looked quite old. "These really don't fit," said Clarissa. The shop-girl looked at them. "Madame wears bracelets?" Clarissa spread out her fingers. "Perhaps it's my rings," And the girl took the grey gloves with her to the end of the counter.

Yes, thought Clarissa, it's the girl I remember, she's twenty years older. . . . There was only one other customer, sitting sideways at the counter, her elbow poised, her bare hand drooping vacant; like a figure on a Japanese fan, thought Clarissa, too vacant perhaps, yet some men would adore her. The lady shook her head sadly. Again the gloves were too large. She turned round the glass. "Above the wrist," she re-proached the grey-headed woman, who looked and agreed.

They waited; a clock ticked; Bond Street hummed, dulled, distant; the woman went away holding gloves. "Above the wrist," said the lady, mournfully, raising her voice. And she would have to order chairs, ices, flowers, and cloak-room tickets, thought Clarissa. The people she didn't want would come; the others wouldn't. She would stand by the door. They sold stockings—silk stockings. A lady is known by her gloves and her shoes, old Uncle William used to say. And through the hanging silk stockings, quivering silver she looked at the lady, sloping shouldered, her hand drooping, her bag slipping, her eyes vacantly on the floor. It would be intolerable if dowdy women came to her party! Would one have liked Keats if he had worn red socks? Oh, at last—she drew into the counter and it flashed into her mind:

"Do you remember before the war you had gloves with pearl buttons?"

"French gloves, Madame?"

"Yes, they were French," said Clarissa. The other lady rose very sadly and took her bag, and looked at the gloves on the counter. But they were all too large—always too large at the wrist.

"With pearl buttons," said the shop-girl, who looked ever so much older. She split the lengths of tissue paper apart on the counter. With pearl buttons, thought Clarissa, perfectly simple—how French!

"Madame's hands are so slender," said the shop-girl, drawing the glove firmly, smoothly, down over her rings. And Clarissa looked at her arm in the looking-glass. The glove hardly came to the elbow. Were there others half an inch longer? Still it seemed tiresome to bother her—perhaps the one day in the month, thought Clarissa, when it's an agony to stand. "Oh, don't bother," she said. But the gloves were brought.

"Don't you get fearfully tired," she said in her charming voice, "standing? When d'you get your holiday?"

"In September, Madame, when we're not so busy."

When we're in the country thought Clarissa. Or shooting. She has a fortnight at Brighton. In some stuffy lodging. The landlady takes the sugar. Nothing would be easier than to send her to Mrs Lumley's right in the country (and it was on the tip of her tongue). But then she remembered how on their honeymoon Dick had shown her the folly of giving impulsively. It was much more important, he said, to get trade with China. Of course he was right. And she could feel the girl wouldn't like to be given things. There she was in her place. So was Dick. Selling gloves was her job. She had her own sorrows quite separate, "and now can never mourn, can never mourn," the words ran in her head, "From the contagion of the world's slow stain," thought Clarissa holding her arm stiff, for there are moments when it seems utterly futile (the glove was drawn off leaving her arm flecked with powder)—simply one doesn't believe, thought Clarissa, any more in God.

The traffic suddenly roared; the silk stockings brightened. A customer came in.

"White gloves," she said, with some ring in her voice that Clarissa remembered.

It used, thought Clarissa, to be so simple. Down, down through the air came the caw of the rooks. When Sylvia died, hundreds of years ago, the yew hedges looked so lovely with the diamond webs in the mist before early church. But if Dick were to die to-morrow? As for believing in God—no, she would let the children choose, but for herself, like Lady Bexborough, who opened the bazaar, they say, with the telegram in her hand—Roden, her favourite, killed—she would go on. But why, if one doesn't believe? For the sake of others, she thought taking the glove in her hand. The girl would be much more unhappy if she didn't believe.

"Thirty shillings," said the shop-woman. "No, pardon me Madame, thirty-five. The French gloves are more."

For one doesn't live for oneself, thought Clarissa.

And then the other customer took a glove, tugged it, and it split.

"There!" she exclaimed.

"A fault of the skin," said the grey-headed woman hurriedly. "Sometimes a drop of acid in tanning. Try this pair, Madame."

"But it's an awful swindle to ask two pound ten!"

Clarissa looked at the lady; the lady looked at Clarissa.

"Gloves have never been quite so reliable since the war," said the shop-girl, apologising, to Clarissa.

But where had she seen the other lady?—elderly, with a frill under her chin; wearing a black ribbon for gold eyeglasses; sensual, clever, like a Sargent drawing. How one can tell from a voice when people are in the habit, thought Clarissa, of making other people— "It's a shade too tight," she said—obey. The shop-woman went off again. Clarissa was left waiting. Fear no more she repeated, playing her finger on the counter. Fear no more the heat o' the sun. Fear no more she repeated. There were little brown spots on her arm. And the girl crawled like a snail. Thou thy worldly task hast done. Thousands of young men had died that things might go on. At last! Half an inch above the elbow; pearl buttons; five and a quarter. My dear slowcoach, thought Clarissa, do you think I can sit here the whole morning? Now you'll take twenty-five minutes to bring me my change!

There was a violent explosion in the street outside. The shop-women cowered behind the counters. But Clarissa, sitting very upright, smiled at the other lady. "Miss Anstruther!" she exclaimed.

The Lady in the Looking-Glass: A Reflection

People should not leave looking-glasses hanging in their rooms any more than they should leave open cheque books or letters confessing some hideous crime. One could not help looking, that summer afternoon, in the long glass that hung outside in the hall. Chance had so arranged it. From the depths of the sofa in the drawing-room one could see reflected in the Italian glass not only the marble-topped table opposite, but a stretch of the garden beyond. One could see a long grass path leading between banks of tall flowers until, slicing off an angle, the gold rim cut it off.

The house was empty, and one felt, since one was the only person in the drawing-room, like one of those naturalists who, covered with grass and leaves, lie watching the shyest animals—badgers, otters, kingfishers—moving about freely, themselves unseen. The room that afternoon was full of such shy creatures, lights and shadows, curtains blowing, petals falling—things that never happen, so it seems, if someone is looking. The quiet old country room with its rugs and stone chimney pieces, its sunken bookcases and red and gold lacquer cabinets, was full of such nocturnal creatures. They came pirouetting across the floor, stepping delicately with high-lifted feet and spread tails and pecking allusive beaks as if they had been cranes or flocks of elegant flamingoes whose pink was faded, or peacocks whose trains were veined with silver. And there were obscure flushes and darkenings too, as if a cuttlefish had suddenly suffused the air with purple; and the room had its passions and rages and envies and sorrows coming over it and clouding it, like a human being. Nothing stayed the same for two seconds together.

But, outside, the looking-glass reflected the hall table, the sunflowers, the garden path so accurately and so fixedly that they seemed held there in their reality unescapably. It was a strange contrast—all changing here, all stillness there. One could not help looking from one to the other. Meanwhile, since all the doors and windows were open in the heat, there was a perpetual sighing and ceasing sound, the voice of the transient and the perishing, it seemed, coming and going like human breath, while in the looking-glass things had ceased to breathe and lay still in the trance of immortality.

Half an hour ago the mistress of the house, Isabella Tyson, had gone down the grass path in her thin summer dress, carrying a basket, and had vanished, sliced off by the gilt rim of the looking-glass. She had gone presumably into the lower garden to pick flowers; or as it seemed more natural to suppose, to pick something light and fantastic and leafy and trailing, traveller's joy, or one of those elegant sprays of convolvulus that twine round ugly walls and burst here and there into white and violet blossoms. She suggested the fantastic and the tremulous convolvulus rather than the upright aster, the starched zinnia, or her own burning roses alight like lamps on the straight posts of their rose trees. The comparison showed how very little, after all these years, one knew about her; for it is impossible that any woman of flesh and blood of fifty-five or sixty should be really a wreath or a tendril. Such comparisons are worse than idle and superficial—they are cruel even, for they come like the convolvulus itself trembling between one's eyes and the truth. There must be truth; there must be a wall. Yet it was strange that after knowing her all these years one could not say what the truth about Isabella was; one still made up phrases like this about convolvulus and traveller's joy. As for facts, it was a fact that she was a spinster; that she was rich; that she had bought this house and collected with her own hands—often in the most obscure corners of the world and at great risk from poisonous stings and Oriental diseases—the rugs, the chairs, the cabinets which now lived their nocturnal life before one's eyes. Sometimes it seemed as if they knew more about her than we, who sat on them, wrote at them, and trod on them so carefully, were allowed to know. In each of these cabinets were many little drawers, and each almost certainly held letters, tied with bows of ribbon, sprinkled with sticks of lavender or rose leaves. For it was another fact—if facts were what one wanted—that Isabella had known many people, had had many friends; and thus if one had the audacity to open a drawer and read her letters, one would find the traces of many agitations, of appointments to meet, of upbraidings for not having met, long letters of intimacy and affection, violent letters of jealousy and reproach, terrible final words of parting—for all those interviews and assignations had led to nothing—that is, she had never married, and yet, judging from the mask-like indifference of her face, she had gone through twenty times more of passion and experience than those whose loves are trumpeted forth for all the world to hear. Under the stress of thinking about Isabella, her room became more shadowy and symbolic; the corners seemed darker, the legs of chairs and tables more spindly and hieroglyphic.

Suddenly these reflections were ended violently and yet without a sound. A large black form loomed into the looking-glass; blotted out everything, strewed the table with a packet of marble tablets veined with pink and grey, and was gone. But the picture was entirely altered. For the moment it was unrecognisable and irrational and entirely out of focus. One could not relate these tablets to any human purpose. And then by degrees some logical process set to work on them and began ordering and arranging them and bringing them into the fold of common experience. One realised at last that they were merely letters. The man had brought the post.

There they lay on the marble-topped table, all dripping with light and colour at first and crude and unabsorbed. And then it was strange to see how they were drawn in and arranged and composed and made part of the picture and granted that stillness and immortality which the looking-glass conferred. They lay there invested with a new reality and significance and with a greater heaviness, too, as if it would have needed a chisel to dislodge them from the table. And, whether it was fancy or not, they seemed to have become not merely a handful of casual letters but to be tablets graven with eternal truth—if one could read them, one would know everything there was to be known about Isabella, yes, and about life, too. The pages inside those marble-looking envelopes must be cut deep and scored thick with meaning. Isabella would come in, and take them, one by one, very slowly, and open them, and read them carefully word by word, and then with a profound sigh of comprehension, as if she had seen to the bottom of everything, she would tear the envelopes to little bits and tie the letters together and lock the cabinet drawer in her determination to conceal what she did not wish to be known.

The thought served as a challenge. Isabella did not wish to be known—but she should no longer escape. It was absurd, it was monstrous. If she concealed so much and knew so much one must prize her open with the first tool that came to hand—the imagination. One must fix one's mind upon her at that very moment. One must fasten her down there. One must refuse to be put off any longer with sayings and doings such as the moment brought forth—with dinners and visits and polite conversations. One must put oneself in her shoes. If one took the phrase literally, it was easy to see the shoes in which she stood, down in the lower garden, at this moment. They were very narrow and long and fashionable—they were made of the softest and most flexible leather. Like everything she wore, they were exquisite. And she would be standing under the high hedge in the lower part of the garden, raising the scissors that were tied to her waist to cut some dead flower, some overgrown branch. The sun would beat down on her face, into her eyes; but no, at the critical moment a veil of cloud covered the sun, making the expression of her eyes doubtful—was it mocking or tender, brilliant or dull? One could only see the indeterminate outline of her rather faded, fine face looking at the sky. She was thinking, perhaps, that she must order a new net for the strawberries; that she must send flowers to Johnson's widow; that it was time she drove over to see the Hippesleys in their new house. Those were the things she talked about at dinner certainly. But one was tired of the things that she talked about at dinner. It was her profounder state of being that one wanted to catch and turn to words, the state that is to the mind what breathing is to the body, what one calls happiness or unhappiness. At the mention of those words it became obvious, surely, that she must be happy. She was rich; she was distinguished; she had many friends; she travelled—she bought rugs in Turkey and blue pots in Persia. Avenues of pleasure radiated this way and that from where she stood with her scissors raised to cut the trembling branches while the lacy clouds veiled her face.

Here with a quick movement of her scissors she snipped the spray of traveller's joy and it fell to the ground. As it fell, surely some light came in too, surely one could penetrate a little farther into her being. Her mind then was filled with tenderness and regret. . . . To cut an overgrown branch saddened her because it had once lived, and life was dear to her. Yes, and at the same time the fall of the branch would suggest to her how she must die herself and all the futility and evanescence of things. And then again quickly catching this thought up, with her instant good sense, she thought life had treated her well; even if fall she must, it was to lie on the earth and moulder sweetly into the roots of violets. So she stood thinking. Without making any thought precise—for she was one of those reticent people whose minds hold their thoughts enmeshed in clouds of silence—she was filled with thoughts. Her mind was like her room, in which lights advanced and retreated, came pirouetting and stepping delicately, spread their tails, pecked their way; and then her whole being was suffused, like the room again, with a cloud of some profound knowledge, some unspoken regret, and then she was full of locked drawers, stuffed with letters, like her cabinets. To talk of "prizing her open" as if she were an oyster, to use any but the finest and subtlest and most pliable tools upon her was impious and absurd. One must imagine—here was she in the looking-glass. It made one start.

She was so far off at first that one could not see her clearly. She came lingering and pausing, here straightening a rose, there lifting a pink to smell it, but she never stopped; and all the time she became larger and larger in the looking-glass, more and more completely the person into whose mind one had been trying to penetrate. One verified her by degrees—fitted the qualities one had discovered into this visible body. There were her grey-green dress, and her long shoes, her basket, and something sparkling at her throat. She came so gradually that she did not seem to derange the pattern in the glass, but only to bring in some new element which gently moved and altered the other objects as if asking them, courteously, to make room for her. And the letters and the table and the grass walk and the sunflowers which had been waiting in the looking-glass separated and opened out so that she might be received among them. At last there she was, in the hall. She stopped dead. She stood by the table. She stood perfectly still. At once the looking-glass began to pour over her a light that seemed to fix her; that seemed like some acid to bite off the unessential and superficial and to leave only the truth. It was an enthralling spectacle. Everything dropped from her—clouds, dress, basket, diamond—all that one had called the creeper and convolvulus. Here was the hard wall beneath. Here was the woman herself. She stood naked in that pitiless light. And, there was nothing. Isabella was perfectly empty. She had no thoughts. She had no friends. She cared for nobody. As for her letters, they were all bills. Look, as she stood there, old and angular, veined and lined, with her high nose and her wrinkled neck, she did not even trouble to open them.

People should not leave looking-glasses hanging in their rooms.

AKUTAGAWA RYUNOSUKE ■ (1892–1927)

In a life framed by melancholy and early death, Akutagawa Ryunosuke—whose name is given in the usual order, with the family name preceding the given name—became a prolific and pathbreaking short-story writer and essayist. Nine months after his birth in Tokyo, his mother went insane and died; his father, a struggling tradesman, couldn't hold his family together, and sent his son to be raised by an uncle, whose surname—Akutagawa—the boy later adopted as a substitute family name. A brilliant student, Akutagawa founded a literary magazine with two friends while still a student at Tokyo Imperial University, where he studied English, writing a senior thesis on the Victorian poet, painter, and socialist William Morris. At the same time, increasingly unhappy with the rhetoric of progress and the cultural compromises of modern Japan, Akutagawa pursued studies in classical Japanese and Chinese literature.

His early interests are seen in his influential story "Rashōmon" ("The Rashō Gate"), which he published in a university magazine in 1915. Set at a major gateway into the medieval capital of Kyoto, this stark, uncanny tale depicts a period of social collapse at the close of the brilliant cultural flowering of the Heian period (794–1184) when such foundational works of Japanese prose as *The Tale of Genji* and *Tales of the Heike* had been written. In Akutagawa's story, questions of right and wrong, survival and sacrilege develop in a strange confrontation between two desperate commoners. Akutagawa relates this tale without comment, setting up dizzying shifts in perspective on the events as they unfold.

After graduation from college, Akutagawa married, began a family, and wrote incessantly, producing more than 150 stories in a decade. He carried his interest in multiple perspectives still further in "In a Grove" (1922), a short story that takes the form of testimonies given to a magistrate in a murder case, culminating in the confessions of three characters—one of them a ghost, speaking through a medium—all of whom claim to have been the murderer. "Rashōmon" and "In a Grove" achieved international fame after the film director Kurosawa Akira combined them to create *Rashomon* (1950), a brilliant exploration of ambiguities of perception, evidence, and character. Kurosawa's *Rashomon* was the first Japanese film to win major prizes abroad, and brought international attention to the thriving postwar Japanese film industry.

Akutagawa didn't live to see his stories receive this new level of attention. Depressed and in deteriorating health, he committed suicide by taking an overdose of sleeping pills in 1927, at the age of thirty-five. He explained this decision with a chill calm in his suicide note, "A Note Forwarded to a Certain Old Friend"—the friend's anonymity increasing the sense of Akutagawa's isolation. Yet his readers recognized Akutagawa as a brilliant innovator, someone who could combine close naturalistic observation with uncanny hints of mystery and psychological complexity. Akutagawa's use of multiple, conflicting perspectives preceded comparable experiments in modernist narratives—from Virginia Woolf's *The Waves* (1931) to William Faulkner's *Absalom, Absalom!* (1936). In his highly individual synthesis of Japanese and Western literary modes, Akutagawa is a major product of the turn-of-the-century, post-Meiji Japanese culture from which he felt so deeply estranged.

PRONUNCIATIONS:

Akutagawa Ryonosuke: ah-koo-tah-GAW-wah rie-YOU-noh-SUE-kay
Kurosawa Akira: koo-row-SAH-wah ah-KEY-rah
Kanazawa no Takehiro: kah-nah-ZAH-wah noh tah-ka-HE-row
Tajomaru: tah-joe-MAH-rue

Rashōmon[1]

It was a chilly evening. A servant of a samurai stood under the Rashōmon, waiting for a break in the rain.

No one else was under the wide gate. On the thick column, its crimson lacquer rubbed off here and there, perched a cricket. Since the Rashōmon stands on Sujaku Avenue, a few other people at least, in sedge hat or nobleman's headgear, might have been expected to be waiting there for a break in the rain storm. But no one was near except this man.

For the past few years the city of Kyōto had been visited by a series of calamities, earthquakes, whirlwinds, and fires, and Kyōto had been greatly devastated. Old chronicles say that broken pieces of Buddhist images and other Buddhist objects, with their lacquer, gold, or silver leaf worn off, were heaped up on roadsides to be sold as firewood. Such being the state of affairs in Kyōto, the repair of the Rashōmon was out of the question. Taking advantage of the devastation, foxes and other wild animals made their dens in the ruins of the gate, and thieves and robbers found a home there

---

1. Translated by T. Kojima.

too. Eventually it became customary to bring unclaimed corpses to this gate and abandon them. After dark it was so ghostly that no one dared approach.

Flocks of crows flew in from somewhere. During the daytime these cawing birds circled round the ridgepole of the gate. When the sky overhead turned red in the afterlight of the departed sun, they looked like so many grains of sesame flung across the gate. But on that day not a crow was to be seen, perhaps because of the lateness of the hour. Here and there the stone steps, beginning to crumble, and with rank grass growing in their crevices, were dotted with the white droppings of crows. The servant, in a worn blue kimono, sat on the seventh and highest step, vacantly watching the rain. His attention was drawn to a large pimple irritating his right cheek.

As has been said, the servant was waiting for a break in the rain. But he had no particular idea of what to do after the rain stopped. Ordinarily, of course, he would have returned to his master's house, but he had been discharged just before. The prosperity of the city of Kyōto had been rapidly declining, and he had been dismissed by his master, whom he had served many years, because of the effects of this decline. Thus, confined by the rain, he was at a loss to know where to go. And the weather had not a little to do with his depressed mood. The rain seemed unlikely to stop. He was lost in thoughts of how to make his living tomorrow, helpless incoherent thoughts protesting an inexorable fate. Aimlessly he had been listening to the pattering of the rain on the Sujaku Avenue.

The rain, enveloping the Rashōmon, gathered strength and came down with a pelting sound that could be heard far away. Looking up, he saw a fat black cloud impale itself on the tips of the tiles jutting out from the roof of the gate.

He had little choice of means, whether fair or foul, because of his helpless circumstances. If he chose honest means, he would undoubtedly starve to death beside the wall or in the Sujaku gutter. He would be brought to this gate and thrown away like a stray dog. If he decided to steal. . . His mind, after making the same detour time and again, came finally to the conclusion that he would be a thief.

But doubts returned many times. Though determined that he had no choice, he was still unable to muster enough courage to justify the conclusion that he must become a thief.

After a loud fit of sneezing he got up slowly. The evening chill of Kyōto made him long for the warmth of a brazier. The wind in the evening dusk howled through the columns of the gate. The cricket which had been perched on the crimson-lacquered column was already gone.

Ducking his neck, he looked around the gate, and drew up the shoulders of the blue kimono which he wore over his thin underwear. He decided to spend the night there, if he could find a secluded corner sheltered from wind and rain. He found a broad lacquered stairway leading to the tower over the gate. No one would be there, except the dead, if there were any. So, taking care that the sword at his side did not slip out of the scabbard, he set foot on the lowest step of the stairs.

A few seconds later, halfway up the stairs, he saw a movement above. Holding his breath and huddling cat-like in the middle of the broad stairs leading to the tower, he watched and waited. A light coming from the upper part of the tower shone faintly upon his right cheek. It was the cheek with the red, festering pimple visible under his stubbly whiskers. He had expected only dead people inside the tower, but he had only gone up a few steps before he noticed a fire above, about which someone was moving. He saw a dull, yellow, flickering light which made the cobwebs hanging from the ceiling glow in a ghostly way. What sort of person would be making a light in the Rashōmon . . . and in a storm? The unknown, the evil terrified him.

As quietly as a lizard, the servant crept up to the top of the steep stairs. Crouching on all fours, and stretching his neck as far as possible, he timidly peeped into the tower.

As rumor had said, he found several corpses strewn carelessly about the floor. Since the glow of the light was feeble, he could not count the number. He could only see that some were naked and others clothed. Some of them were women, and all were lolling on the floor with their mouths open or their arms outstretched showing no more signs of life than so many clay dolls. One would doubt that they had ever been alive, so eternally silent they were. Their shoulders, breasts, and torsos stood out in the dim light; other parts vanished in shadow. The offensive smell of these decomposed corpses brought his hand to his nose.

The next moment his hand dropped and he stared. He caught sight of a ghoulish form bent over a corpse. It seemed to be an old woman, gaunt, gray-haired, and nunnish in appearance. With a pine torch in her right hand, she was peeping into the face of a corpse which had long black hair.

Seized more with horror than curiosity, he even forgot to breathe for a time. He felt the hair of his head and body stand on end. As he watched, terrified, she wedged the torch between two floor boards and, laying hands on the head of the corpse, began to pull out the long hairs one by one, as a monkey kills the lice of her young. The hair came out smoothly with the movement of her hands.

As the hair came out, fear faded from his heart, and his hatred toward the old woman mounted. It grew beyond hatred, becoming a consuming antipathy against all evil. At this instant if anyone had brought up the question of whether he would starve to death or become a thief—the question which had occurred to him a little while ago—he would not have hesitated to choose death. His hatred toward evil flared up like the piece of pine wood which the old woman had stuck in the floor.

He did not know why she pulled out the hair of the dead. Accordingly, he did not know whether her case was to be put down as good or bad. But in his eyes, pulling out the hair of the dead in the Rashōmon on this stormy night was an unpardonable crime. Of course it never entered his mind that a little while ago he had thought of becoming a thief.

Then, summoning strength into his legs, he rose from the stairs and strode, hand on sword, right in front of the old creature. The hag turned, terror in her eyes, and sprang up from the floor, trembling. For a small moment she paused, poised there, then lunged for the stairs with a shriek.

"Wretch! Where are you going?" he shouted, barring the way of the trembling hag who tried to scurry past him. Still she attempted to claw her way by. He pushed her back to prevent her . . . they struggled, fell among the corpses, and grappled there. The issue was never in doubt. In a moment he had her by the arm, twisted it, and forced her down to the floor. Her arms were all skin and bones, and there was no more flesh on them than on the shanks of a chicken. No sooner was she on the floor than he drew his sword and thrust the silver-white blade before her very nose. She was silent. She trembled as if in a fit, and her eyes were open so wide that they were almost out of their sockets, and her breath come in hoarse gasps. The life of this wretch was his now. This thought cooled his boiling anger and brought a calm pride and satisfaction. He looked down at her, and said in a somewhat calmer voice:

"Look here, I'm not an officer of the High Police Commissioner. I'm a stranger who happened to pass by this gate. I won't bind you or do anything against you, but you must tell me what you're doing up here."

Then the old woman opened her eyes still wider, and gazed at his face intently with the sharp red eyes of a bird of prey. She moved her lips, which were wrinkled into her nose, as though she were chewing something. Her pointed Adam's apple moved in her thin throat. Then a panting sound like the cawing of a crow came from her throat:

"I pull the hair . . . I pull out the hair . . . to make a wig."

Her answer banished all unknown from their encounter and brought disappointment. Suddenly she was only a trembling old woman there at his feet. A ghoul no longer: only a hag who makes wigs from the hair of the dead—to sell, for scraps of food. A cold contempt seized him. Fear left his heart, and his former hatred entered. These feelings must have been sensed by the other. The old creature, still clutching the hair she had pulled off the corpse, mumbled out these words in her harsh broken voice:

"Indeed, making wigs out of the hair of the dead may seem a great evil to you, but these that are here deserve no better. This woman, whose beautiful black hair I was pulling, used to sell cut and dried snake flesh at the guard barracks, saying that it was dried fish. If she hadn't died of the plague, she'd be selling it now. The guards liked to buy from her, and used to say her fish was tasty. What she did couldn't be wrong, because if she hadn't, she would have starved to death. There was no other choice. If she knew I had to do this in order to live, she probably wouldn't care."

He sheathed his sword, and, with his left hand on its hilt, he listened to her meditatively. His right hand touched the big pimple on his cheek. As he listened, a certain courage was born in his heart—the courage which he had not had when he sat under the gate a little while ago. A strange power was driving him in the opposite direction of the courage which he had had when he seized the old woman. No longer did he wonder whether he should starve to death or become a thief. Starvation was so far from his mind that it was the last thing that would have entered it.

"Are you sure?" he asked in a mocking tone, when she finished talking. He took his right hand from his pimple, and, bending forward, seized her by the neck and said sharply:

"Then it's right if I rob you. I'd starve if I didn't."

He tore her clothes from her body and kicked her roughly down on the corpses as she struggled and tried to clutch his leg. Five steps, and he was at the top of the stairs. The yellow clothes he had wrested off were under his arm, and in a twinkling he had rushed down the steep stairs into the abyss of night. The thunder of his descending steps pounded in the hollow tower, and then it was quiet.

Shortly after that the hag raised up her body from the corpses. Grumbling and groaning, she crawled to the top stair by the still flickering torchlight, and through the gray hair which hung over her face, she peered down to the last stair in the torch light.

Beyond this was only darkness . . . unknowing and unknown.

In a Grove[1]

The Story of a Woodcutter Questioned by the Grand Magistrate

Yes, it's just as you say. I was the one who found the body. Like always, I went deep into the mountains this morning to cut cedars. I found the body in a grove hidden in the shadows of the mountain. Where was it? Four or five hundred yards off the Yamashina station road.[2] It's a deserted grove where small cedars grow among the bamboo.

1. Translated by Seiji M. Lippit.
2. A road leading out of Kyoto through deserted countryside.

The body lay face up and was clothed in a light-blue hunting robe with a courtier's hat from the capital. The wound was caused by just a single sword stroke— but it was to his chest, and so the bamboo leaves around him were stained with dark blood. No, he was no longer bleeding. The wound seemed to be dry already. What's more, a huge horsefly was clinging to the wound as if it didn't even hear my footsteps.

Did I see a long sword? No, there was nothing. There was only a piece of rope at the foot of a nearby cedar. And then—yes, there was also a comb in addition to the rope. These were the only two items near the corpse. But the grass and bamboo leaves were completely trampled, so the man must have struggled painfully before being killed. Was there no horse? There's no chance a horse could enter there. A thicket separates it from the road where horses pass.

The Story of a Travelling Priest Questioned by the Grand Magistrate

I believe I met the deceased man yesterday. It was—let me see—about noon yesterday. The location was on the road from Sekiyama to Yamashina. He was leading a woman on a horse toward the barrier. She was wearing a cloth covering over her head, so I never saw her face. The only thing that I saw was the color of the cloth—I believe it was a dark red and blue pattern. The horse was reddish dapple-gray, with its mane cropped close. Its height? I think it must have been more than four feet. But of course as a priest I know little of these matters. The man carried a bow along with the sword he had at his side. I still remember the twenty or so arrows stuck in his black-lacquered quiver.

I never dreamed he would end up like this. Truly, human life is as ephemeral as dew and as brief as lightning. Ah, what a terrible, sad fate!

The Story of a Police Official Questioned by the Grand Magistrate

The man I captured? He is most certainly Tajomaru, the notorious bandit. Of course, when I caught him he'd fallen from his horse and was moaning in pain on the stone bridge at Awataguchi. The time? It was last night, soon after the first watch of the evening. When I nearly captured him the time before, he was also carrying this long sword and wearing this dark blue hunting robe. Yet this time, as you see, he also had a bow. Is that so? The dead man was also carrying one—well then, the murderer must be none other than Tajomaru. The leather-covered bow with black-lacquer quiver, the seventeen arrows with hawk-feather quills—these must have belonged to the man. Yes. Just as you say, the horse is a reddish dapple-gray with a short-cropped mane. It must have been an act of providence he was thrown by that animal. It was standing just beyond the bridge dragging its long halter and eating grass by the roadside.

Of all the bandits lurking about the capital, this Tajomaru is especially known to target women. It's rumored he was behind the murder of a woman and a young girl in the mountains behind the Pindola at the Toribe temple last autumn. If he did kill the man, there's no telling what he may have done with the woman on the gray horse. It's not my place to say so, but won't you investigate this matter as well?

The Story of an Old Woman Questioned by the Grand Magistrate

Yes, this dead man is my daughter's husband. But he's not from the capital. He's a samurai from the province of Wakasa. His name was Kanazawa no Takehiro, and he was twenty-six years of age. No, he had a gentle nature, so he wouldn't have had any enemies.

728

My daughter? Her name is Masago and she's nineteen years old. She's strong-willed like a man, so she's never known any man other than Takehiro. Her face is small and oval-shaped, slightly dark with a birthmark under her left eye.

Takehiro left for Wakasa yesterday with my daughter. What a terrible fate to end up like this! But what has happened to my daughter? I'm resigned to my son-in-law's fate, but I'm still worried about her. Please—my only request is that you find my daughter, even if you have to bend every blade of grass. How I hate that thief Tajomaru! If he killed not only my son-in-law but my daughter too.... (Her voice trails off into sobbing.)

Tajomaru's Confession

Yes, I killed the man—but not the woman. Then where is she? That I don't know. Wait a moment! No matter how much you torture me, I can't tell you what I don't know. And now that you've caught me I have no intention of hiding anything like a coward.

It was yesterday, just past noon, when I saw the man and woman. A slight breeze happened to lift the woman's veil, and I caught a glimpse of her face. One brief look—and the next moment it was hidden again. Maybe it was because I only caught a glimpse, but the woman's face seemed to me like a Boddhisatva's.[3] In that one instant, I decided to make her mine, even if it meant killing the man.

Killing a man is not as difficult as you may think. If I wanted to have the woman, I had to kill him. Of course, when I kill a man I use the sword at my side, but you—you don't use swords, you kill with power and money. Sometimes, you even kill with words that sound like they're full of kindness. There may be no blood, and the man may still breathe, but you've killed him all the same. When you think about it, it's not so easy to tell who is guiltier, you or I. (An ironic smile.)

Still, I would've been happy to have her without killing the man. In fact, I decided to take the woman without killing him, if I could. But that was impossible in the middle of the Yamashina station road. So I hatched a plan to lure them into the mountains.

It was a simple plan. I fell in with them and told them a story—that I'd discovered an old tomb up in the mountains filled with swords and mirrors and that I'd buried them in a grove in the shadow of the mountains unknown to anyone. If I could only find someone to take them, I'd be willing to sell them off cheaply. As I spoke the man grew more and more interested in my story. And then—well, greed is a terrifying thing. In half an instant the two of them were following me with their horse up the mountain path.

When we came to the grove, I said the treasure was buried inside and told them to come have a look. The man was consumed with desire, so of course he agreed. But the woman stayed on her horse and said she would wait. It was only natural after seeing that thick grove. In fact, this fell into my plan perfectly, so I left her alone and entered the grove with the man.

For a while the grove is just bamboo. But some fifty meters in, there's a stand of cedars that opens up a bit. There was no better place to carry out my scheme. Pushing my way through the trees, I uttered a believable enough lie, that the treasure was buried by the cedars. When the man heard these words he rushed forward towards the trees. As the bamboo thinned out we came to the place where the cedars grow. But as

---

3. A Buddhist saint or enlightened being, especially one who remains in the world to help those who suffer.

soon as we had reached this place I pinned him to the ground. He had a long sword by his side and seemed strong enough, but caught by surprise like that there was nothing he could do. Soon enough he was bound to the trunk of a nearby cedar. The rope? A rope is indispensable for a thief like me, since you never know when you might have to scale a wall. I had it by my side. I stuffed bamboo leaves into his mouth so he wouldn't cry out, and it was all over.

After dealing with the man I returned to the woman and told her he'd suddenly fallen ill, that she'd better come have a look. There's no need to tell you I was on the mark once more! The woman took off her sedge hat and I led her by the hand into the grove. When we came to the clearing, she saw the man tied to the base of a tree. One look and she quickly drew a dagger from her sleeve. I've never seen such a strong-willed woman. If I'd let my guard down for an instant, she would've stabbed me in the side. Even dodging her blade as she swung wildly at me I could've been injured. But I'm Tajomaru, after all, so I took the dagger from her without even drawing my own sword. Strong as she was, she was helpless without a weapon. At last, just as I had planned, I was able to take her without killing the man.

Yes—without killing him. I had no desire to take his life on top of it all. I left the woman sobbing on the ground behind me and was about to run from the grove when she grabbed onto my arm as if she'd gone mad. And when I listened to her words through her sobbing, I found she was saying: one of you must die, either you or my husband. It's worse than death, she said, to be shamed like this before two men. She even said through her tears that she would follow whomever was left alive. Then I was seized with a brutal urge to kill the man. (A dark excitement.)

When you hear this, you must think I'm more cruel than you are. But that's because you didn't see her face just then. Because you didn't see her eyes at that moment, lit up like fire. When I looked into her eyes I felt a desire to make her my wife, even if it meant being struck down by lightning. To make her my wife—this was the only thought in my mind. It was not just a question of mere lust, as you may think. If it were only lust, I would've kicked her down and run away. Then the man would've been spared from staining my blade with his blood. Yet as I stared into the woman's face in that shadowy grove, I knew I couldn't leave there without killing him.

But even though I'd decided to take his life, I refused to kill him like a coward. I cut his bonds and told him to take up his sword. (The rope you found at the root of the tree was the one I threw down just then.) The man was pale as he drew his sword. Without a word he jumped at me savagely. There's no need to tell you the outcome of the duel. My blade found his chest on the twenty-third stroke. On the twenty-third stroke—make sure you take note of it! I'm still impressed by the fact. No one else has ever crossed swords with me twenty times. (Energetic laughter.)

As soon as he fell, I threw down my bloody sword and turned back to the woman. But then—yes, she was nowhere to be found. I searched the stand of cedars, but there was no trace of her left among the fallen bamboo leaves. I tried to listen for her, but all I could hear was the death-rattle in the man's throat.

Maybe she ran from the grove to call for help when our sword-fight began. When that thought crossed my mind. I knew my own life was in danger, so I grabbed the man's sword and his bow and arrows, and ran back to the mountain path. I found the woman's horse there grazing quietly on the grass. It's a waste of time to describe what happened next. But before I entered the capital I got rid of the man's sword. That's the end of my confession. All along I knew I would hang from the gallows one day, so go ahead and do your worst. (A defiant attitude.)

The Confession of the Woman Who Came to Kiyomizu Temple[4]

After the man wearing the dark blue robe raped me, he looked at my husband bound to the tree and laughed mockingly. How mortified my husband must have felt! No matter how hard he struggled, the cord binding him only bit deeper into his body. Without even thinking, I stumbled over to his side. No, I tried to run over to him when the man kicked me down to the ground. It was just then. In my husband's eyes, I saw an indescribable light. Even now when I recall his eyes I can't help but tremble. Even though he could not speak, he said everything in his heart with that one look. It was not a look of anger or even sadness, but one of icy contempt. It was that look, rather than the man's kick, that made me cry out and finally lose consciousness.

When I awoke the man in the dark blue robe had left. Only my husband remained, still tied to the base of the cedar. Finally I raised myself from the bamboo leaves and looked into his eyes once again. Yet the expression in his eyes had not changed. They still had the same cold look of contempt tinged with hatred. Shame, despair, anger— I don't know how to describe my feelings at that moment. I stood up trembling and approached his side.

"Now that things have come to this, I cannot stay with you any longer. I am resigned to die. Yet—yet I ask you to die as well. You have witnessed my shame. I cannot leave you alive by yourself this way."

It took all of my strength to say this. Yet still my husband looked at me with disdain. I clutched my breast, which felt as if it were torn asunder, and looked for his long sword. But the thief must have taken it, for the sword and even the bow and arrows were nowhere to be seen in the grove. Yet fortunately my dagger at least was on the ground by my feet. I raised the dagger and then spoke once again to my husband.

"Then I ask you to give your life to me. I will follow soon after."

When he heard these words he finally moved his lips. Of course his mouth was filled with bamboo leaves, so no sound emerged. But when I saw his face, I understood what he was trying to say. Still eyeing me with contempt he had said simply, "Kill me." Then, as if in a dream, I stabbed my husband's chest through his silk robe.

I must have fainted once more. When I was able to look about at last, my husband, still bound, was long dead. The western sun cast a single beam of light on his pale face through the bamboo and cedar trees. Stifling my tears, I unbound his body and cast the rope aside. And then—and then what happened to me? I have no strength left to speak of it. In any case I didn't have the strength to take my own life. I pressed the dagger to my neck, threw myself into the lake at the foot of the mountains, and tried every other way. Living on like this without even the strength to die brings me only shame. (A sad smile.) Even the merciful Kannon[5] must have forsaken such an unfortunate woman as I. After killing my husband, being raped by the thief, what is left for me? What am I to do . . . ? (Suddenly, fierce sobbing.)

The Story of the Ghost Told by a Medium

After raping my wife, the thief sat by her side on the ground, consoling her in various ways. Of course I couldn't speak. My body was bound to the base of the tree. Yet the whole time I tried to make eye contact with my wife. Don't believe anything this man says, no matter what he says don't trust him—I tried to communicate such

---

4. A large temple complex in the wooded hills outside of Kyoto.
5. Bodhisattva of compassion and mercy, often prayed to in Japan for aid in childbirth.

thoughts to her. But my wife sat there vacantly among the fallen leaves and stared quietly into her lap. Did it not appear to me as if she were listening to the thief? I struggled with feelings of jealousy. Yet the thief moved skillfully from one argument to another. Now that your body has been violated, things will not go well between you and your husband. Why not leave him and be my wife instead? It was only because of your beauty that I did such a thing. These were the brazen things he said in the end.

After listening to him my wife raised her head as though spellbound. I have never seen her as beautiful as she was at that moment. Yet what did this beautiful wife of mine say to the thief as I sat bound in front of her? Even as I wander in the darkness, every time I recall my wife's words I burn with anger. In a clear voice she said, "Then take me with you anywhere." (A long silence.)

That was not the extent of my wife's sin. If it were, I would not suffer as I do in the abyss. She grasped the thief's hand as though in a dream and was about to leave the grove, when suddenly the color drained from her face and she pointed to me as I sat bound to the cedar. "Kill that man! As long as he is alive I cannot be with you." As though she had gone mad, my wife screamed these words over and over again. "Kill that man!" Even now, like some tempest these words threaten to blast me into the far-away darkness. Have such hateful words ever been uttered by human mouth? Have human ears ever heard such cursed words? Have ever . . . (Suddenly, scattered mocking laughter.) Even the thief paled when he heard those words. "Kill that man!" my wife screamed as she clung to his arm. He stared at her and did not say whether he would kill me. Suddenly, he kicked her down onto the fallen bamboo leaves. (Once more, scattered mocking laughter.) The thief quietly folded his arms and looked at me. "What do you want me to do with this woman? Kill her or spare her? Just nod in response. Shall I kill her?" For these words, I can almost forgive the thief his crimes. (Again, a long silence.)

While I hesitated my wife screamed and ran off into the thicket. The thief sprang after her, but he was unable to grasp even her sleeve. I stared at the scene before me as if it were some kind of phantasm.

After my wife had run off the thief picked up the long sword and my bow and arrows, and he cut the rope binding me in a single spot. "Now my own life's in danger." I remember him muttering these words as he left the grove. Afterwards all was still. No, there still lingered the sound of someone crying. I listened carefully as I undid my bonds. Then I realized the sobbing voice was my own. (For the third time, a long silence.)

At last I raised my spent body from the base of the cedar. My wife's fallen dagger glinted on the ground before me. I took it in my hand and stabbed myself once in the chest. I could feel something raw coming up into my mouth. Yet there was no pain. Only, as my chest grew colder the surrounding world grew ever more still. Ah, what stillness! Not even a bird in the sky above this grove in the shadows of the mountains. Only a lonely shaft of sunlight behind the cedars and bamboo. The shaft of sunlight—even that gradually dimmed. Then even the cedars and bamboo were no longer visible. As I lay there, I was enveloped in deep stillness.

Then, someone approached me with stealthy footsteps. I tried to look over. But by then the darkness had pressed in all around me. The hand of someone—someone I couldn't see—quietly drew the dagger from my chest. At the same time blood surged into my mouth once more. And I sank forever into the blackness of the abyss. . . .

Thomas Stearns Eliot, an American-born poet and playwright who became a British citizen, is one of the towering presences in modern literature. After its publication in 1922, his poem *The Waste Land* achieved international fame as one of the most poignant expressions of the alienation and despair of the modern age. Also revolutionary in the fragmentation of its lyrical form, *The Waste Land* is stitched together from textual fragments that echo a wide range of literary traditions from Sanskrit to Dante and that connect to each other by means of underlying mythological themes. Along with Eliot's poetic and dramatic work, his criticism equally accounts for his extraordinary stature in modernist literature. In hundreds of essays and reviews, Eliot revisited and partly redefined the British literary canon, setting out principles of literary criticism that were to become foundational for the New Criticism that dominated British and American universities from the early 1930s to the late 1950s. Forty years of work as an editor with the publisher Faber and Faber equally contributed to shaping the literary scene. While he was considered a revolutionary poet in the 1910s and 1920s, the combined weight of Eliot's poetry and criticism turned him into a prime representative of the literary establishment by the 1940s, a figure against whose influence a younger generation of poets rose up to rebel: His winning the Nobel Prize in Literature in 1948 sealed the conversion of one of the foremost innovators of modern poetry into the figurehead of a new literary standard.

Born in Saint Louis, Missouri, Eliot was descended from old New England stock; his family tree included three American presidents. Eliot's grandfather moved to Saint Louis where he established the city's first Unitarian church and later founded Washington University. Eliot returned east for college; he graduated from Harvard in 1909, and completed most of a PhD in philosophy before moving to England in 1916. There he found work as a bank clerk and began to establish himself as a leading young poet together with his friend and ally Ezra Pound.

But it wasn't only Eliot's steadily growing reputation as a poet and critic that changed his status as a writer. His own worldview underwent a radical change only five years after the publication of *The Waste Land:* In 1927, Eliot converted to the Anglican church and only a few months later was naturalized as a British citizen. His literary mode of expression changed in similarly fundamental ways, moving away from the fragmentation, meaninglessness, and isolation portrayed in his earlier works to a much more centered and religious outlook. His greatest achievement in this later mode is a set of four poems called *Four Quartets* (1943); there is considerable debate among critics as to whether this work or the earlier *Waste Land* qualifies as his best poetry, and which one expresses the essence of modernist lyric more successfully.

"The Love Song of J. Alfred Prufrock" belongs to Eliot's earliest work, and it is in fact the poem that first made him visible on London's literary scene. Written between 1910 and 1911 and first published in the magazines *Poetry* and *Catholic Anthology* in 1915 with the help of fellow poet Ezra Pound, "Prufrock" addresses a middle-aged man's anxiety over the passing of time and his own aging; but this specific unease is associated in the poem with more diffuse fears over what the meaning of human existence might be and how it could be found or expressed in a society that exhausts itself in empty social rituals and linguistic clichés. Far from offering an alternative to these oppressive social conventions, however, Prufrock's own voice sounds hollow and uncertain. In counterpoint to nineteenth-century poet Robert Browning's dramatic monologues, on whose model Eliot draws in the poem, Prufrock is as fragmented and empty as the society that surrounds him; his condition prefigures the broader panorama of stagnation and estrangement Eliot was to portray in *The Waste Land*.

The Love Song of J. Alfred Prufrock

S'io credessi che mia risposta fosse
a persona che mai tornasse al mondo,
questa fiamma staria senza più scosse.
Ma per ciò che giammai di questo fondo
non tornò vivo alcun, s'i'odo il vero,
senza tema d'infamia ti rispondo.[1]

Let us go then, you and I,
When the evening is spread out against the sky
Like a patient etherised upon a table;
Let us go, through certain half-deserted streets,
5 The muttering retreats
Of restless nights in one-night cheap hotels
And sawdust restaurants with oyster-shells:
Streets that follow like a tedious argument
Of insidious intent
10 To lead you to an overwhelming question . . .
Oh, do not ask, "What is it?"
Let us go and make our visit.

In the room the women come and go
Talking of Michelangelo.

15 The yellow fog that rubs its back upon the window-panes,
The yellow smoke that rubs its muzzle on the window-panes,
Licked its tongue into the corners of the evening,
Lingered upon the pools that stand in drains,
Let fall upon its back the soot that falls from chimneys,
20 Slipped by the terrace, made a sudden leap,
And seeing that it was a soft October night,
Curled once about the house, and fell asleep.
And indeed there will be time
For the yellow smoke that slides along the street
25 Rubbing its back upon the window-panes;
There will be time, there will be time
To prepare a face to meet the faces that you meet;
There will be time to murder and create,
And time for all the works and days of hands
30 That lift and drop a question on your plate;
Time for you and time for me,
And time yet for a hundred indecisions,
And for a hundred visions and revisions,
Before the taking of a toast and tea.

35 In the room the women come and go
Talking of Michelangelo.

---

1. From Dante's *Inferno* (27.61–66). Dante asks one of the damned souls for its name, and it replies: "If I thought my answer were for one who could return to the world, I would not reply, but as none ever did return alive from this depth, without fear of infamy I answer thee."

And indeed there will be time
To wonder, "Do I dare?" and, "Do I dare?"
Time to turn back and descend the stair,
40 With a bald spot in the middle of my hair—
(They will say: "How his hair is growing thin!")
My morning coat, my collar mounting firmly to the chin,
My necktie rich and modest, but asserted by a simple pin—
(They will say: "But how his arms and legs are thin!")
45 Do I dare
Disturb the universe?
In a minute there is time
For decisions and revisions which a minute will reverse.

For I have known them all already, known them all—
50 Have known the evenings, mornings, afternoons,
I have measured out my life with coffee spoons;
I know the voices dying with a dying fall
Beneath the music from a farther room.
        So how should I presume?

55 And I have known the eyes already, known them all—
The eyes that fix you in a formulated phrase,
And when I am formulated, sprawling on a pin,
When I am pinned and wriggling on the wall,
Then how should I begin
60 To spit out all the butt-ends of my days and ways?
        And how should I presume?

And I have known the arms already, known them all—
Arms that are braceleted and white and bare
(But in the lamplight, downed with light brown hair!)
65 Is it perfume from a dress
That makes me so digress?
Arms that lie along a table, or wrap about a shawl.
        And should I then presume?

And how should I begin?

                    . . .

70 Shall I say, I have gone at dusk through narrow streets
And watched the smoke that rises from the pipes
Of lonely men in shirt-sleeves, leaning out of windows?...

I should have been a pair of ragged claws
Scuttling across the floors of silent seas.

                    . . .

75 And the afternoon, the evening, sleeps so peacefully!
Smoothed by long fingers,
Asleep...tired...or it malingers,

Stretched on the floor, here beside you and me.
Should I, after tea and cakes and ices,
80   Have the strength to force the moment to its crisis?
But though I have wept and fasted, wept and prayed,
Though I have seen my head (grown slightly bald) brought in upon a platter,[2]
I am no prophet—and here's no great matter;
I have seen the moment of my greatness flicker,
85   And I have seen the eternal Footman hold my coat, and snicker,
And in short, I was afraid.

And would it have been worth it, after all,
After the cups, the marmalade, the tea,
Among the porcelain, among some talk of you and me,
90   Would it have been worth while,
To have bitten off the matter with a smile,
To have squeezed the universe into a ball
To roll it towards some overwhelming question,
To say: "I am Lazarus, come from the dead,
95   Come back to tell you all, I shall tell you all"[3]—
If one, settling a pillow by her head,
    Should say: "That is not what I meant at all.
    That is not it, at all."

And would it have been worth it, after all,
100   Would it have been worth while,
After the sunsets and the dooryards and the sprinkled streets,
After the novels, after the teacups, after the skirts that trail along the floor—
And this, and so much more?—
It is impossible to say just what I mean!
105   But as if a magic lantern[4] threw the nerves in patterns on a screen:
Would it have been worth while
If one, settling a pillow or throwing off a shawl,
And turning toward the window, should say:
    "That is not it at all,
110   That is not what I meant, at all."
           . . .

No! I am not Prince Hamlet, nor was meant to be;
Am an attendant lord, one that will do
To swell a progress, start a scene or two,
Advise the prince; no doubt, an easy tool,
115   Deferential, glad to be of use,

2. Cf. Matthew 14. John the Baptist was beheaded by Herod and his head was brought to his wife, Herodias, on a platter.
3. Cf. John 11. Jesus raised Lazarus from the grave after he had been dead four days.
4. A device that employs a candle to project images, rather like a slide projector.

Politic, cautious, and meticulous;
Full of high sentence, but a bit obtuse;
At times, indeed, almost ridiculous—

Almost, at times, the Fool.
120 I grow old...I grow old...
I shall wear the bottoms of my trousers rolled.
Shall I part my hair behind? Do I dare to eat a peach?
I shall wear white flannel trousers, and walk upon the beach.
I have heard the mermaids singing, each to each.

125 I do not think that they will sing to me.
I have seen them riding seaward on the waves
Combing the white hair of the waves blown back
When the wind blows the water white and black.

We have lingered in the chambers of the sea
130 By sea-girls wreathed with seaweed red and brown
Till human voices wake us, and we drown.

The Waste Land[1]

"Nam Sibyllam quidem Cumis ego ipse oculis meis vidi in ampulla
pendere, et cum illi pueri dicerent: Σίβυλλα τί θέλεις;
respondebat illa: ἀποθανεῖν θέλω."[2]

*For Ezra Pound
il miglior fabbro.*[3]

I. The Burial of the Dead

April is the cruellest month, breeding
Lilacs out of the dead land, mixing
Memory and desire, stirring
Dull roots with spring rain.
5 Winter kept us warm, covering
Earth in forgetful snow, feeding
A little life with dried tubers.

1. Not only the title, but the plan and a good deal of the incidental symbolism of the poem were suggested by Miss Jessie L. Weston's book on the Grail legend: *From Ritual to Romance* (Cambridge). Indeed, so deeply am I indebted, Miss Weston's book will elucidate the difficulties of the poem much better than my notes can do; and I recommend it (apart from the great interest of the book itself) to any who think such elucidation of the poem worth the trouble. To another work of anthropology I am indebted in general, one which has influenced our generation profoundly; I mean *The Golden Bough;* I have used especially the two volumes *Adonis, Attis, Osiris.* Anyone who is acquainted with these works will immediately recognize in the poem certain references to vegetation ceremonies [Eliot's note]. Sir James Frazer (1854–1941) brought out the 12 volumes of *The Golden Bough,* a vast work of anthropology, comparative mythology and religion, between 1890 and 1915, with a supplement published in 1936.
2. From the *Satyricon* of Petronius (1st century C.E.). "For once I myself saw with my own eyes the Sybil at Cumae hanging in a cage, and when the boys said to her, 'Sybil, what do you want?' she replied, 'I want to die.'" The Sybil was granted anything she wished by Apollo, if only she would be his; she made the mistake of asking for everlasting life, without asking for eternal youth.
3. "The better craftsman." Pound played a crucial role in editing *The Waste Land* before its publication.

Summer surprised us, coming over the Starnbergersee[4]
With a shower of rain; we stopped in the colonnade,
10   And went on in sunlight, into the Hofgarten,[5]
And drank coffee, and talked for an hour.
Bin gar keine Russin, stamm' aus Litauen, echt deutsch.[6]
And when we were children, staying at the arch-duke's,
My cousin's, he took me out on a sled,
15   And I was frightened. He said, Marie,
Marie, hold on tight. And down we went.
In the mountains, there you feel free.
I read, much of the night, and go south in the winter.

What are the roots that clutch, what branches grow
20   Out of this stony rubbish? Son of man,[7]
You cannot say, or guess, for you know only
A heap of broken images, where the sun beats,
And the dead tree gives no shelter, the cricket no relief,[8]
And the dry stone no sound of water. Only
25   There is shadow under this red rock,
(Come in under the shadow of this red rock),
And I will show you something different from either
Your shadow at morning striding behind you
Or your shadow at evening rising to meet you;
30   I will show you fear in a handful of dust.

        Frisch weht der Wind
        Der Heimat zu
        Mein Irisch Kind,
        Wo weilest du?[9]

35   "You gave me hyacinths first a year ago;
They called me the hyacinth girl."
—Yet when we came back, late, from the hyacinth garden,
Your arms full, and your hair wet, I could not
Speak, and my eyes failed, I was neither
40   Living nor dead, and I knew nothing,
Looking into the heart of light, the silence.
Oed' und leer das Meer.[1]

---

4. A lake near Munich.
5. A public park in Munich, with a zoo and cafés.
6. "I'm not a Russian at all; I come from Lithuania, a true German."
7. Cf. Ezekiel 2.7 [Eliot's note]. Ezekiel 2.8 reads: "But thou, son of man, hear what I say unto thee; Be not thou rebellious like that rebellious house: open thy mouth, and eat that I give thee."
8. Cf. Ecclesiastes 12.5 [Eliot's note]. "They shall be afraid of that which is high, and fears shall be in the way, and the almond tree shall flourish, and the grasshopper shall be a burden, and desire shall fail."
9. *V. Tristan and Isolde,* i, verses 5–8 [Eliot's note]. In Wagner's opera, Tristan sings this about Isolde, the woman he is leaving behind as he sails for home: "Fresh blows the wind to the homeland; my Irish child, where are you staying?"
1. Id. iii, verse 24 [Eliot's note]. Tristan is dying and waiting for Isolde to come to him, but a shepherd, whom Tristan has hired to keep watch for her ship, reports only "Desolate and empty the sea."

Madame Sosostris, famous clairvoyante,
Had a bad cold, nevertheless
45   Is known to be the wisest woman in Europe,
With a wicked pack of cards.[2] Here, said she,
Is your card, the drowned Phoenician Sailor,
(Those are pearls that were his eyes.[3] Look!)
Here is Belladonna, the Lady of the Rocks,
50   The lady of situations.
Here is the man with three staves, and here the Wheel,
And here is the one-eyed merchant, and this card,
Which is blank, is something he carries on his back,
Which I am forbidden to see. I do not find
55   The Hanged Man.[4] Fear death by water.
I see crowds of people, walking round in a ring.
Thank you. If you see dear Mrs. Equitone,
Tell her I bring the horoscope myself:
One must be so careful these days.

60   Unreal City,[5]
Under the brown fog of a winter dawn,
A crowd flowed over London Bridge, so many,
I had not thought death had undone so many.[6]
Sighs, short and infrequent, were exhaled,[7]
65   And each man fixed his eyes before his feet.
Flowed up the hill and down King William Street,
To where Saint Mary Woolnoth kept the hours
With a dead sound on the final stroke of nine.[8]
There I saw one I knew, and stopped him, crying: "Stetson!
70   You who were with me in the ships at Mylae![9]
That corpse you planted last year in your garden,
Has it begun to sprout? Will it bloom this year?
Or has the sudden frost disturbed its bed?

---

2. I am not familiar with the exact constitution of the Tarot pack of cards, from which I have obviously departed to suit my own convenience. The Hanged Man, a member of the traditional pack, fits my purpose in two ways: because he is associated in my mind with the Hanged God of Frazer, and because I associated him with the hooded figure in the passage of the disciples to Emmaus in Part V. The Phoenician Sailor and the Merchant appear later; also the "crowds of people," and Death by Water is executed in Part IV. The Man with Three Staves (an authentic member of the Tarot pack) I associate, quite arbitrarily, with the Fisher King Himself [Eliot's note].

3. From Ariel's song, in Shakespeare's *The Tempest:* "Full fathom five thy father lies; / Of his bones are coral made; / Those are pearls that were his eyes: / Nothing of him that doth fade, / But doth suffer a sea-change" (1.2.399–403).

4. The tarot card that depicts a man hanging by one foot from a cross.

5. Cf. Baudelaire: "Fourmillante cité, cité pleine de rêves, / Où le spectre en plein jour raccroche le passant" [Eliot's note]. From *The Flowers of Evil.* "Swarming city, city full of dreams, / where in plain daylight the spectre accosts the passer-by."

6. Cf. *Inferno,* III, 55–57: "si lunga tratta / di gente, ch'io non avrei mai creduto / che morte tanta n'avesse disfatta" [Eliot's note]. "Such an endless train, / Of people, it never would have entered in my head / There were so many men whom death had slain."

7. Cf. *Inferno,* IV, 25–27: "Ouivi, secondo che per ascoltare, / non avea pianto, ma' che di sospiri, / che l'aura eterna facevan tremare" [Eliot's note]. "We heard no loud complaint, no crying there, / No sound of grief except the sound of sighing / Quivering forever through the eternal air."

8. A phenomenon which I have often noticed [Eliot's note].

9. The Battle of Mylae (260 B.C.E.) in the First Punic War.

O keep the Dog far hence, that's friend to men,[1]
75   Or with his nails he'll dig it up again!
    You! hypocrite lecteur!—mon semblable,—mon frère!"[2]

II. A Game of Chess[3]

    The Chair she sat in, like a burnished throne,[4]
    Glowed on the marble, where the glass
    Held up by standards wrought with fruited vines
80   From which a golden Cupidon peeped out
    (Another hid his eyes behind his wing)
    Doubled the flames of sevenbranched candelabra
    Reflecting light upon the table as
    The glitter of her jewels rose to meet it,
85   From satin cases poured in rich profusion.
    In vials of ivory and coloured glass
    Unstoppered, lurked her strange synthetic perfumes,
    Unguent, powdered, or liquid—troubled, confused
    And drowned the sense in odours; stirred by the air
90   That freshened from the window, these ascended
    In fattening the prolonged candle-flames,
    Flung their smoke into the laquearia,[5]
    Stirring the pattern on the coffered ceiling.
    Huge sea-wood fed with copper
95   Burned green and orange, framed by the coloured stone,
    In which sad light a carvèd dolphin swam.
    Above the antique mantel was displayed
    As though a window gave upon the sylvan scene[6]
    The change of Philomel, by the barbarous king[7]
100   So rudely forced; yet there the nightingale[8]
    Filled all the desert with inviolable voice
    And still she cried, and still the world pursues,
    "Jug Jug" to dirty ears.
    And other withered stumps of time

1. Cf. the Dirge in Webster's *White Devil* [Eliot's note].
2. *V.* Baudelaire, Preface to *Fleurs du Mal* [Eliot's note]. "Hypocrite reader—my double—my brother!"
3. Cf. Thomas Middleton's drama *A Game at Chess* (1625), a political satire.
4. Cf. *Antony and Cleopatra*, II. ii. 190 [Eliot's note].
5. "Laquearia. *V. Aeneid*, I.726: "dependent lychni laquearibus aureis / incensi, et noctem flammis funalia vincunt." [Eliot's note]. "Burning lamps hang from the gold-panelled ceiling / And torches dispel the night with their flames"; a *laquearia* is a panelled ceiling. The passage from Virgil's *Aeneid* describes the banquet given by Dido for her lover Aeneas.
6. "Sylvan scene. *V.* Milton, *Paradise Lost*, IV, 140. [Eliot's note]. "And over head up grew / Insuperable height of loftiest shade, / Cedar, and Pine, and Fir, and branching Palm, / A Silvan Scene, and as the ranks ascend / Shade above shade, a woody Theatre / Of stateliest view." The passage describes the Garden of Eden, as seen through Satan's eyes. A sylvan scene is one taking place in a forest.
7. *V.* Ovid, *Metamorphoses*, vi, Philomela [Eliot's note]. Philomela was raped by King Tereus, her sister's husband, and was then changed into a nightingale.
8. Cf. Part III, 1. 204 [Eliot's note].

105 Were told upon the walls; staring forms
Leaned out, leaning, hushing the room enclosed.
Footsteps shuffled on the stair.
Under the firelight, under the brush, her hair
Spread out in fiery points
110 Glowed into words, then would be savagely still.

     "My nerves are bad to-night. Yes, bad. Stay with me.
Speak to me. Why do you never speak. Speak.
     What are you thinking of? What thinking? What?
I never know what you are thinking. Think."

115   I think we are in rats' alley[9]
Where the dead men lost their bones.

"What is that noise?"
              The wind under the door.[1]
"What is that noise now? What is the wind doing?"
120   Nothing again nothing.
                        "Do
"You know nothing? Do you see nothing? Do you remember
Nothing?"
     I remember
125 Those are pearls that were his eyes.
"Are you alive, or not? Is there nothing in your head?"[2]
                           But

O O O O that Shakespeherian Rag[3]—
It's so elegant
130 So intelligent
"What shall I do now? What shall I do?"
"I shall rush out as I am, and walk the street
With my hair down, so. What shall we do tomorrow?
What shall we ever do?"
135   The hot water at ten.
And if it rains, a closed car at four.
And we shall play a game of chess,
Pressing lidless eyes and waiting for a knock upon the door.[4]

When Lil's husband got demobbed,° I said—   *demobilized*
140 I didn't mince my words, I said to her myself,
HURRY UP PLEASE ITS TIME[5]
Now Albert's coming back, make yourself a bit smart.
He'll want to know what you done with that money he gave you
To get yourself some teeth. He did, I was there.

---

9. Cf. Part III, l. 195 [Eliot's note].

1. Cf. Webster: "Is the wind in that door still?" [Eliot's note]. From John Webster's *The Devil's Law Case,* 3.2.162. The doctor asks this question when he discovers that a "murder victim" is still breathing.

2. Cf. Part I, l. 37, 48 [Eliot's note].

3. Quoting an American ragtime song featured in Ziegfield's Follies of 1912.

4. Cf. the game of chess in Middleton's *Women beware Women* [Eliot's note].

5. A British pub-keeper's call for a last round before closing.

145 You have them all out, Lil, and get a nice set,
He said, I swear, I can't bear to look at you.
And no more can't I, I said, and think of poor Albert,
He's been in the army four years, he wants a good time,
And if you don't give it him, there's others will, I said.
150 Oh is there, she said. Something o' that, I said.
Then I'll know who to thank, she said, and give me a straight look.
HURRY UP PLEASE ITS TIME
If you don't like it you can get on with it, I said.
Others can pick and choose if you can't.
155 But if Albert makes off, it won't be for lack of telling.
You ought to be ashamed, I said, to look so antique.
(And her only thirty-one.)
I can't help it, she said, pulling a long face,
It's them pills I took, to bring it off, she said.
160 (She's had five already, and nearly died of young George.)
The chemist[6] said it would be all right, but I've never been the same.
You *are* a proper fool, I said.
Well, if Albert won't leave you alone, there it is, I said,
What you get married for if you don't want children?
165 HURRY UP PLEASE ITS TIME
Well, that Sunday Albert was home, they had a hot gammon,°   ham
And they asked me in to dinner, to get the beauty of it hot—
HURRY UP PLEASE ITS TIME
HURRY UP PLEASE ITS TIME
170 Goonight Bill. Goonight Lou. Goonight May. Goonight.
Ta ta. Goonight. Goonight.
Good night, ladies, good night, sweet ladies, good night, good night.[7]

III. The Fire Sermon

The river's tent is broken; the last fingers of leaf
Clutch and sink into the wet bank. The wind
175 Crosses the brown land, unheard. The nymphs are departed.
Sweet Thames, run softly, till I end my song.[8]
The river bears no empty bottles, sandwich papers,
Silk handkerchiefs, cardboard boxes, cigarette ends
Or other testimony of summer nights. The nymphs are departed.
180 And their friends, the loitering heirs of City directors;
Departed, have left no addresses.
By the waters of Leman[9] I sat down and wept...
Sweet Thames, run softly till I end my song,

6. Pharmacist.

7. Ophelia speaks these words in Shakespeare's *Hamlet,* and they are understood by the King as certain evidence of her insanity: "Good night ladies, good night. Sweet ladies, good night, good night" (4.5.72–73).

8. V. Spenser, *Prothalamion* [Eliot's note]; Spenser's poem (1596) celebrates the double marriage of Lady Elizabeth and Lady Katherine Somerset.

9. Lake Geneva. The line echoes Psalm 137, in which, exiled in Babylon, the Hebrew poets are too full of grief to sing.

Sweet Thames, run softly, for I speak not loud or long.
185   But at my back in a cold blast I hear
      The rattle of the bones, and chuckle spread from ear to ear.

      A rat crept softly through the vegetation
      Dragging its slimy belly on the bank
      While I was fishing in the dull canal
190   On a winter evening round behind the gashouse
      Musing upon the king my brother's wreck
      And on the king my father's death before him.[1]
      White bodies naked on the low damp ground
      And bones cast in a little low dry garret,
195   Rattled by the rat's foot only, year to year.
      But at my back from time to time I hear[2]
      The sound of horns and motors, which shall bring[3]
      Sweeney to Mrs. Porter in the spring.
      O the moon shone bright on Mrs. Porter[4]
200   And on her daughter
      They wash their feet in soda water
      Et O ces voix d'enfants, chantant dans la coupole![5]

      Twit twit twit
      Jug jug jug jug jug jug
205   So rudely forc'd.
      Tereu

      Unreal City
      Under the brown fog of a winter noon
      Mr. Eugenides, the Smyrna[6] merchant
210   Unshaven, with a pocket full of currants
      C.i.f.[7] London: documents at sight,
      Asked me in demotic° French   *vulgar*
      To luncheon at the Cannon Street Hotel[8]
      Followed by a weekend at the Metropole.[9]

215   At the violet hour, when the eyes and back
      Turn upward from the desk, when the human engine waits
      Like a taxi throbbing waiting,

1. Cf. *The Tempest*, I. ii [Eliot's note].

2. Cf. Marvell, *To His Coy Mistress* [Eliot's note]. "But at my back I always hear / Time's wingèd chariot hurrying near."

3. Cf. Day, *Parliament of Bees:* "When of the sudden, listening, you shall hear, / A noise of horns and hunting, which shall bring / Actaeon to Diana in the spring, / Where all shall see her naked skin…" [Eliot's note].

4. I do not know the origin of the ballad from which these are taken: it was reported to me from Sydney, Australia [Eliot's note]. Sung by Australian soldiers in World War I: "O the moon shone bright on Mrs. Porter / And on the daughter / Of Mrs. Porter / They wash their feet in soda water / And so they oughter / To keep them clean."

5. V. Verlaine, *Parsifal* [Eliot's note]. "And O those children's voices singing in the dome." Paul Verlaine's sonnet describes Parsifal, who keeps himself pure in hopes of seeing the holy grail, and has his feet washed before entering the castle.

6. Seaport in western Turkey.

7. The currants were quoted at a price "carriage and insurance free to London"; and the Bill of Lading, etc., were to be handed to the buyer upon payment of the sight draft [Eliot's note].

8. A Hotel in London near the train station used for travel to and from continental Europe.

9. An upscale seaside resort hotel in Brighton.

I Tiresias,[1] though blind, throbbing between two lives,
Old man with wrinkled female breasts, can see
220 At the violet hour, the evening hour that strives
Homeward, and brings the sailor home from sea,[2]
The typist home at teatime, clears her breakfast, lights
Her stove, and lays out food in tins.
Out of the window perilously spread
225 Her drying combinations touched by the sun's last rays,
On the divan are piled (at night her bed)
Stockings, slippers, camisoles, and stays.
I Tiresias, old man with wrinkled dugs
Perceived the scene, and foretold the rest—
230 I too awaited the expected guest.
He, the young man carbuncular,° arrives,   *pimply*
A small house agent's clerk, with one bold stare,
One of the low on whom assurance sits
As a silk hat on a Bradford[3] millionaire.
235 The time is now propitious, as he guesses,
The meal is ended, she is bored and tired,
Endeavours to engage her in caresses
Which still are unreproved, if undesired.
Flushed and decided, he assaults at once;
240 Exploring hands encounter no defence;
His vanity requires no response,
And makes a welcome of indifference.
(And I Tiresias have foresuffered all
Enacted on this same divan or bed;
245 I who have sat by Thebes below the wall
And walked among the lowest of the dead.)

---

1. Tiresias, although a mere spectator and not indeed a "character," is yet the most important personage in the poem, uniting all the rest. Just as the one-eyed merchant, seller of currants, melts into the Phoenician Sailor, and the latter is not wholly distinct from Ferdinand Prince of Naples, so all the women are one woman, and the two sexes meet in Tiresias. What Tiresias *sees*, in fact, is the substance of the poem. The whole passage from Ovid is of great anthropological interest: "...Cum Iunone iocos et 'maior vestra profecto est / Quam, quae contingit maribus,' dixisse, 'voluptas.' / Illa negat; placuit quae sit sententia docti / Quaerere Tiresiae: venus huic erat utraque nota. / Nam duo magnorum viridi coeuntia silva / Corpora serpentum baculi violaverat ictu / Deque viro factus, mirabile, femina septem / Egerat autumnos; octavo rursus eosdem / Vidit et 'est vestrae si tanta potentia plagae,' / Dixit 'ut auctoris sortem in contraria mutet, / Nunc quoque vos feriam!' percussis anguibus isdem / Forma prior rediit genetivaque venit imago. / Arbiter hic igitur sumptus de lite iocosa / Dicta Iovis firmat; gravius Saturnia iusto / Nec pro materia fertur doluisse suique / Iudicis aeterna damnavit lumina nocte, / At pater omnipotens (neque enim licet inrita cuiquam / Facta dei fecisse deo) pro lumine adempto / Scire futura dedit poenamque levavit honore" [Eliot's note]. This passage from Ovid's *Metamorphoses* describes Tiresias's sex change: "[The story goes that once Jove, having drunk a great deal,] jested with Juno. He said, 'Your pleasure in love is really greater than that enjoyed by men.' She denied it; so they decided to seek the opinion of the wise Tiresias, for he knew both aspects of love. For once, with a blow of his staff, he had committed violence on two huge snakes as they copulated in the green forest; and—wonderful to tell—was turned from a man into a woman and thus spent seven years. In the eighth year he saw the same snakes again and said: 'If a blow struck at you is so powerful that it changes the sex of the giver, I will now strike at you again.' With these words he struck the snakes, and his former shape was restored to him and he became as he had been born. So he was appointed arbitrator in the playful quarrel, and supported Jove's statement. It is said that Saturnia [i.e., Juno] was quite disproportionately upset, and condemned the arbitrator to perpetual blindness. But the almighty father (for no god may undo what has been done by another god), in return for the sight that was taken away, gave him the power to know the future and so lightened the penalty paid by the honor."

2. This may not appear as exact as Sappho's lines but I had in mind the "longshore" or "dory" fisherman, who returns at nightfall [Eliot's note]. "Hesperus, thou bringst home all things bright morning scattered: thou bringest the sheep, the goat, the child to the mother."

3. An industrial town in Yorkshire; many of its residents became wealthy during World War I.

Bestows one final patronising kiss,
And gropes his way, finding the stairs unlit ...

She turns and looks a moment in the glass,
250   Hardly aware of her departed lover;
Her brain allows one half-formed thought to pass:
"Well now that's done: and I'm glad it's over."
When lovely woman stoops to folly and[4]
Paces about her room again, alone,
255   She smoothes her hair with automatic hand,
And puts a record on the gramophone.

"This music crept by me upon the waters"[5]
And along the Strand, up Queen Victoria Street.
O City city, I can sometimes hear
260   Beside a public bar in Lower Thames Street,
The pleasant whining of a mandoline
And a clatter and a chatter from within
Where fishmen lounge at noon: where the walls
Of Magnus Martyr[6] hold
265   Inexplicable splendour of Ionian white and gold.

        The river sweats[7]
        Oil and tar
        The barges drift
        With the turning tide
270   Red sails
        Wide
        To leeward, swing on the heavy spar.
        The barges wash
        Drifting logs
275   Down Greenwich reach
        Past the Isle of Dogs.[8]
            Weialala leia
            Wallala leialala

        Elizabeth and Leicester[9]
280   Beating oars

4. *V.* Goldsmith, the song in *The Vicar of Wakefield* [Eliot's note]. Oliver Goldsmith's character Olivia, on returning to the place where she was seduced, sings, "When lovely woman stoops to folly / And finds too late that men betray / What charm can soothe her melancholy, / What art can wash her guilt away? / The only art her guilt to cover, / To hide her shame from every eye, / To give repentance to her lover / And wring his bosom—is to die."

5. *V. The Tempest,* as above [Eliot's note].

6. The interior of St. Magnus Martyr is to my mind one of the finest among Wren's interiors. See *The Proposed Demolition of Nineteen City Churches* (P.S. King & Son, Ltd.) [Eliot's note].

7. The Song of the (three) Thames-daughters begins here. From line 292 to 306 inclusive they speak in turn. *V. Götterdämmerung,* III.I: the Rhine-daughters [Eliot's note]. In Richard Wagner's opera *Twilight of the Gods,* the Rhine maidens, when their gold is stolen, lament that the beauty of the river is gone.

8. Greenwich is a borough on the south bank of the River Thames; the Isle of Dogs is a peninsula in East London formed by a sharp bend in the Thames called Greenwich Reach.

9. *V.* Froude, *Elizabeth,* vol. I, Ch. iv, letter of De Quadra to Philip of Spain: "In the afternoon we were in a barge, watching the games on the river. (The Queen) was alone with Lord Robert and myself on the poop, when they began to talk nonsense, and went so far that Lord Robert at last said, as I was on the spot there was no reason why they should not be married if the queen pleased" [Eliot's note].

The stern was formed
A gilded shell
Red and gold
The brisk swell
285   Rippled both shores
Southwest wind
Carried down stream
The peal of bells
White towers
290   Weialala leia
        Wallala leialala

"Trams and dusty trees.
Highbury bore me. Richmond and Kew[1]
Undid me. By Richmond I raised my knees
295   Supine on the floor of a narrow canoe."

"My feet are at Moorgate,[2] and my heart
Under my feet. After the event
He wept. He promised 'a new start.'
I made no comment. What should I resent?"

300   "On Margate Sands.[3]
I can connect
Nothing with nothing.
The broken fingernails of dirty hands.
My people humble people who expect
305   Nothing."
        la la

To Carthage then I came[4]

Burning burning burning burning[5]
O Lord Thou pluckest me out[6]
310   O Lord Thou pluckest

burning

IV. Death by Water

Phlebas the Phoenician, a fortnight dead,
Forgot the cry of gulls, and the deep sea swell

1. "Cf. *Purgatorio,* V. 133: "Ricorditi di me, che son la Pia; / Siena mi fe', disfecemi Maremma." [Eliot's note].
"Remember me, that I am called Piety; / Sienna made me and Maremma undid me." Highbury, Richmond, and Kew
are suburbs of London near the Thames.

2. A slum in East London.

3. A seaside resort in the Thames estuary.

4. *V.* St. Augustine's *Confessions:* "to Carthage then I came, where a cauldron of unholy loves sang all about mine ears"
[Eliot's note].

5. The complete text of the Buddha's Fire Sermon (which corresponds in importance to the Sermon on the Mount) from
which these words are taken, will be found translated in the late Henry Clarke Warren's *Buddhism in Translation* (Harvard Oriental Series). Mr. Warren was one of the great pioneers of Buddhist studies in the Occident [Eliot's note].

6. From St. Augustine's *Confessions* again. The collocation of these two representatives of eastern and western asceti-
cism, as the culmination of this part of the poem, is not an accident [Eliot's note]. Augustine writes: "I entangle my steps
with these outward beauties, but thou pluckest me out, O Lord, Thou pluckest me out."

And the profit and loss.

A current under sea

315

Picked his bones in whispers. As he rose and fell
He passed the stages of his age and youth
Entering the whirlpool.

Gentile or Jew

320 O you who turn the wheel and look to windward,
Consider Phlebas, who was once handsome and tall as you.

V. What the Thunder Said[7]

After the torchlight red on sweaty faces
After the frosty silence in the gardens
After the agony in stony places
325 The shouting and the crying
Prison and palace and reverberation
Of thunder of spring over distant mountains
He who was living is now dead
We who were living are now dying
330 With a little patience

Here is no water but only rock
Rock and no water and the sandy road
The road winding above among the mountains
Which are mountains of rock without water
335 If there were water we should stop and drink
Amongst the rock one cannot stop or think
Sweat is dry and feet are in the sand
If there were only water amongst the rock
Dead mountain mouth of carious° teeth that cannot spit   *rotting*
340 Here one can neither stand nor lie nor sit
There is not even silence in the mountains
But dry sterile thunder without rain
There is not even solitude in the mountains
But red sullen faces sneer and snarl
345 From doors of mudcracked houses

If there were water

And no rock
If there were rock
And also water
350 And water
A spring
A pool among the rock
If there were the sound of water only
Not the cicada
355 And dry grass singing

---

7. In the first part of Part V three themes are employed: the journey to Emmaus, the approach to the Chapel Perilous (see Miss Weston's book), and the present decay of eastern Europe [Eliot's note].

But sound of water over a rock
Where the hermit-thrush sings in the pine trees
Drip drop drip drop drop drop drop[8]
But there is no water

360   Who is the third who walks always beside you?
When I count, there are only you and I together[9]
But when I look ahead up the white road
There is always another one walking beside you
Gliding wrapt in a brown mantle, hooded
365   I do not know whether a man or a woman
—But who is that on the other side of you?

What is that sound high in the air[1]
Murmur of maternal lamentation
Who are those hooded hordes swarming
370   Over endless plains, stumbling in cracked earth
Ringed by the flat horizon only
What is the city over the mountains
Cracks and reforms and bursts in the violet air
Falling towers
375   Jerusalem Athens Alexandria
Vienna London
Unreal

A woman drew her long black hair out tight
And fiddled whisper music on those strings
380   And bats with baby faces in the violet light
Whistled, and beat their wings
And crawled head downward down a blackened wall
And upside down in air were towers
Tolling reminiscent bells, that kept the hours
385   And voices singing out of empty cisterns and exhausted wells

In this decayed hole among the mountains
In the faint moonlight, the grass is singing
Over the tumbled graves, about the chapel
There is the empty chapel, only the wind's home.

T. S. ELIOT

8. This is *Turdus aonalaschkae pallasii,* the hermit-thrush which I have heard in Quebec County. Chapman says (*Handbook of Birds of Eastern North America*) "it is most at home in secluded woodland and thickety retreats....Its notes are not remarkable for variety or volume, but in purity and sweetness of tone and exquisite modulation they are unequalled." Its "water-dripping song" is justly celebrated [Eliot's note].

9. The following lines were stimulated by the account of one of the Antarctic expeditions (I forget which, but I think one of Shackleton's): it was related that the party of explorers, at the extremity of their strength, had the constant delusion that there was one more member than could actually be counted [Eliot's note]. There seems also to be an echo of the account of Jesus meeting his disciples on the road to Emmaus: "Jesus himself drew near, and went with them. But their eyes were holden that they should not know him" (Luke 24.13–16).

1. Cf. Hermann Hesse, *Blick ins Chaos:* "Schon ist halb Europa, schon ist zumindest der halbe Osten Europas auf dem Wege zum Chaos, fährt betrunken im heiligen Wahn am Abgrund entlang und singt dazu, singt betrunken und hymnisch wie Dmitri Karamasoff sang. Ueber diese Lieder lacht der Bürger beleidigt, der Heilige und Seher hört sie mit Tränen" [Eliot's note]. "Already half of Europe, already at least half of Eastern Europe, on the way to chaos, drives drunk in sacred infatuation along the edge of the precipice, singing drunkenly, as though singing hymns, as Dmitri Karamazov sang. The offended bourgeois laughs at the songs; the saint and the seer hear them with tears."

390   It has no windows, and the door swings,
        Dry bones can harm no one.
        Only a cock stood on the rooftree
        Co co rico co co rico
        In a flash of lightning. Then a damp gust
395   Bringing rain

        Ganga[2] was sunken, and the limp leaves
        Waited for rain, while the black clouds
        Gathered far distant, over Himavant.[3]
        The jungle crouched, humped in silence.
400   Then spoke the thunder
        DA
        Datta: what have we given?[4]
        My friend, blood shaking my heart
        The awful daring of a moment's surrender
405   Which an age of prudence can never retract
        By this, and this only, we have existed
        Which is not to be found in our obituaries
        Or in memories draped by the beneficent spider[5]
        Or under seals broken by the lean solicitor
410   In our empty rooms
        DA
        Dayadhvam: I have heard the key[6]
        Turn in the door once and turn once only
        We think of the key, each in his prison
415   Thinking of the key, each confirms a prison
        Only at nightfall, aethereal rumours
        Revive for a moment a broken Coriolanus[7]
        DA
        Damyata: The boat responded
420   Gaily, to the hand expert with sail and oar
        The sea was calm, your heart would have responded
        Gaily, when invited, beating obedient
        To controlling hands

---

2. The river Ganges.

3. The Himalayas.

4. "Datta, dayadhvam, damyata" (Give, sympathize, control). The fable of the meaning of the Thunder is found in the *Brihadaranyaka—Upanishad*, 5, I. A translation is found in Deussen's *Sechzig Upanishads des Veda*, p. 489 [Eliot's note]. "That very thing is repented even today by the heavenly voice, in the form of thunder, in the form of thunder as 'Da,' 'Da,' 'Da'.... Therefore one should practice these three things: self-control, alms-giving, and compassion."

5. Cf. Webster, *The White Devil* V, vi: "...they'll remarry / Ere the worm pierce your winding-sheet, ere the spider / make a thin curtain for your epitaphs" [Eliot's note].

6. Cf. *Inferno*, XXXIII, 46: "ed io sentii chiavar l'uscio di sotto / all'orrible torre." Also F. H. *Bradley, Appearance and Reality*, p. 346: "My external sensations are no less private to myself than are my thoughts or my feelings. In either case my experience falls within my own circle, a circle closed on the outside; and, with all its elements alike, every sphere is opaque to the others which surround it.... In brief, regarded as an existence which appears in a soul, the whole world for each is peculiar and private to that soul." [Eliot's note]. In the passage from the *Inferno*, Ugolino tells Dante of his imprisonment and starvation until he became so desperate that he ate his children: "And I heard below me the door of the horrible tower being locked."

7. In Shakespeare's play of the same name, Coriolanus is a Roman general who is exiled and later leads the enemy in an attack against the Romans.

I sat upon the shore
425   Fishing, with the arid plain behind me[8]
Shall I at least set my lands in order?
London Bridge is falling down falling down falling down
Poi s'ascose nel foco che gli affina[9]
Quando fiam uti chelidon—O swallow swallow[1]
430   *Le Prince d'Aquitaine à la tour abolie*[2]
These fragments I have shored against my ruins
Why then Ile fit you. Hieronymo's mad againe.[3]
Datta. Dayadhvam. Damyata.
        Shantih   shantih   shantih[4]

FRANZ KAFKA ■ (1883–1924)

Compared to many other modern novelists, Franz Kafka wrote little, and three of his major novels remained incomplete at his death. Yet in spite of its small bulk, his fiction has become one of the most towering achievements of European modernism: Throughout the twentieth century, Kafka's stories deeply influenced writers across different continents and languages, from the Argentinean short-story writer Jorge Luis Borges to the Japanese novelist Abe Kobo and the American cartoon artist Art Spiegelman. Profoundly enigmatic, Kafka's novels and stories resist attempts at defining their meaning conclusively, but it is precisely their indeterminacy that allows readers from very different backgrounds to understand his works as reflecting a part of their own condition. Indeed, in several languages the adjective "kafkaesque" has become part of the common modern vocabulary as a description of situations that are difficult, intricate, alienating, or absurd.

This usage loosely reflects the kind of predicament Kafka's protagonists typically find themselves confronted with. An event occurs that can't really be explained in terms of ordinary experience and commonsense rationality; as they investigate what the meaning of this event might be, Kafka's characters move gradually away from normal life and become more and more deeply entangled with incomprehensible processes and authorities. In the encounter with immensely powerful but impenetrable structures of authority—whether they are familial, civic, legal, or religious—Kafka's characters come to question their own identities and beliefs about the world, but they are unable to formulate more adequate ones. Sometimes the protagonists die without ever having understood what it was that threw their lives off their normal course in the first place. As they find themselves in an environment that is unintelligible at best and hostile at worst, Kafka's characters experience what is often considered one of the quintessentially modern conditions: *alienation*, the estrangement of the individual from normal social bonds and activities.

The reasons for this alienation in Kafka's fictional world have been hotly debated over the decades. Some readers (among them Max Brod, Kafka's friend and literary executor)

---

8. *V.* Weston, *From Ritual to Romance;* chapter on the Fisher King [Eliot's note].

9. *V. Purgatorio* XXVI, 148: "Ara vos prec per aquella valor / que vos condus al som de l'escalina, / sovegna vos a temps de ma dolor." / Poi s'ascose nel foco che gli affina" [Eliot's note]. In this passage, the poet Arnaut Daniel speaks to Dante: "Now I pray you, by the goodness that guides you to the top of this staircase, be mindful in time of my suffering."

1. *V. Pervigilium Veneris.* Cf. Philomela in Parts II and III [Eliot's note]. Philomel asks, "When shall I be a swallow?"

2. *V.* Gerard de Nerval, Sonnet *El Desdichado* [Eliot's note]. "The Prince of Aquitaine in the ruined tower."

3. *V.* Kyd's *Spanish Tragedy* [Eliot's note]. The subtitle of Kyd's play is, "Hieronymo's Mad Againe." His son having been murdered, Hieronymo is asked to compose a court play, to which he responds "Why then Ile fit you"; his son's murder is avenged in the course of the play.

4. Shantih. Repeated as here, a formal ending to an Upanishad. "The Peace which passeth understanding" is a feeble translation of the content of this word [Eliot's note]. The Upanishads are poetic commentaries on the Hindu Scriptures.

have claimed that Kafka's characters exemplify the predicament of a humankind that needs and seeks out religious redemption but is forever cut off from divine mercy or access to salvation. Others emphasize that Kafka's descriptions of impersonal, inefficient, and incomprehensible institutions reflect some aspects of German sociologist Max Weber's famous characterization of modern bureaucracies. In this view, Kafka's characters would illustrate the condition of the typical modern citizen, whose life, in large part, is determined by abstract bureaucratic networks. Yet others have argued that Kafka's stories refer more specifically to the experience of a particular social group, the bourgeois middle class in an advanced capitalist society, and even more specifically to the double alienation implicit in Kafka's own status as a Jew of mixed German and Czech heritage living in Prague in the waning years of the Austro-Hungarian Empire. And finally, it has been suggested that the best way to approach Kafka's stories is through a psychoanalytical perspective that would foreground Kafka's own extremely troubled relation to his father as one of the basic sources of his characters' conflicted encounters with authority.

The reason that it is often difficult to decide which of these and other interpretations might be the most appropriate lies in the fact that many of Kafka's stories have the structure of a *parable*, a story that describes concrete and everyday events in order to illustrate an abstract concept or condition; unlike allegories, parables are usually not self-explanatory but require interpretive comment. Kafka's parables, however, stand on their own, and his brief reflection "On Parables" shows just how ambiguous the relation to the real can remain in this genre. An understanding of Kafka's texts is further complicated by the fact that even at the most literal level of the plot, they don't remain in the realm of ordinary experience in the way biblical parables do. Rather, many of them start out with what appears at first sight to be an everyday situation, which then mutates into nightmarish circumstances that clearly fall outside the realm of commonsense reality. In *The Trial*, Kafka's protagonist is informed by two officials on what seems like an ordinary morning that a lawsuit has been initiated against him, but he is not told what crime he is accused of, and still doesn't know months later when he is sentenced to death. In *The Metamorphosis*, Gregor Samsa wakes up in the morning with every intention of going to work, only to find himself transformed into a beetle lying on its back. Kafka's literary mastery is most obvious in his ability to make such fantastic occurrences appear perfectly real to the reader.

The apparent simplicity of Kafka's style subtly heightens the enigma of his works. Especially compared to other Prague authors writing in German at the same time, his style is strikingly concrete and literal, without any obvious display of metaphor, symbol, or ornate syntax. But precisely in stripping his fiction of the ordinary trappings of "literary" diction, Kafka often pushes language to an extreme where even very simple words become problematic: What, really, is a "trial" or a "judgment"? How are we to imagine the "singing" of the mouse performer in "Josephine the Singer," who hardly seems to make audible sounds at all? Since words like these don't seem to function in Kafka's texts in quite the way they do in ordinary language, readers have always been tempted to give a variety of symbolic meanings to them. But Kafka's own language stubbornly refuses to yield firm evidence of what these meanings might be. This has led some of his successors, such as the French novelist Alain Robbe-Grillet, to claim that, in fact, Kafka's fiction belongs to an entirely different kind of literature that does away with metaphor as the basis of narrative meaning.

Kafka's work consists not only of narrative fiction but also of extensive diaries and letters that he wrote during most of his life; indeed all of his life was accompanied by constant acts of writing. The diaries and letters reveal an intensely introspective mind that steadily scrutinizes itself and others: "Every person is lost in himself beyond hope of rescue, and one's sole consolation in this is to observe other people and the laws governing them and everything," he noted in a 1914 diary entry. Kafka felt and thought deeply about each of his family and friendship relations and often agonized over what he perceived as his own shortfalls in fulfilling others' expectations. But his letters and diaries are not only fascinating psychological documents; they are also quite often accomplished literary texts. The "Letter to His Father," beyond what it might reveal about Kafka's family experience, is a striking example of character construction, and some of the diary entries contain narrative fragments whose quality rivals that of Kafka's fiction. Though they were never meant for literary publication, they convey the sense of a man who lived almost every aspect of his life through writing. "My happiness, my abilities and every possibility of being useful in any way have always been in the literary field," he wrote in his diary in 1911.

The world that is reflected in Kafka's fiction as well as in his letters and diaries is that of Prague at the turn of the twentieth century, where Kafka was born in 1883 as the first child of Hermann Kafka, who came from a Czech-Jewish family, and his mother, Julie, who was German-Jewish. At the time, Prague formed part of the Empire of Austria-Hungary and was home to three different groups: the Czech majority and significant minorities of Jews and Germans. Jews occupied a somewhat ambiguous position between the Czech majority and the ruling German elite; Prague Jews had for a long time deeply identified with German culture, and it was not unusual for Jewish children to be sent to German-language schools. Kafka attended such a school in Prague from 1893 to 1901. In November 1901 he entered Prague's German University and studied law, graduating in June 1906. After the mandatory first year of unpaid practical experience in law, he started working for a private insurance company, Assicurazioni Generali, but he disliked the working atmosphere and long hours so much that less than a year later, he moved to the Workers' Accident Insurance Institute, for which he continued to work until shortly before his death in 1924.

Kafka's youth was overshadowed by personal, professional, and medical troubles. Some of the most important and intimate relationships in his life were also the most complex and conflicted. He had an intensely ambivalent relationship with his father, who first ran a small business selling women's clothing and later ran an asbestos factory in which his son sometimes helped out. Kafka's ambivalence emerges clearly in the "Letter to His Father," written in 1919 but never actually sent. According to this letter, the father's professional success, self-assurance, and willingness to ignore others' desires stood in stark contrast with the son's self-doubt and uncertainty regarding his success as a writer as well as in his relationships with women. This conflict led Kafka to a mixture of admiration and repulsion and to simultaneous desires to please his father and rebel against him, which precluded any effective communication or deep understanding. Kafka's relationship with his fiancée, Felice Bauer, was similarly troubled: in their five-year relationship between 1912 and 1917, the couple were twice engaged, but both times Kafka broke the engagement in intense self-doubt over his own inability to sustain a marriage and to reconcile it with his devotion to literature.

Kafka's professional life proved no less conflicted. He often agonized over the obligation to earn a living through legal work that he experienced as tedious and burdensome instead of devoting himself to the work that he considered to be his real vocation, writing. His attempt to carve out time to write outside of a long workday frequently led to sleepless nights and ill health during his time at Assicurazioni Generali, and he moved to the Workers' Accident Insurance Institute partly for the more moderate hours required there. Nevertheless, his life remained divided between tedious work that was financially necessary and the work he passionately cared about but was unable to live from. Illness was a constant presence in Kafka's life, starting in his childhood, but it gradually became a more and more serious threat to both his work and his life. From about 1912 on, he complained of insomnia and severe headaches, and symptoms of tuberculosis manifested themselves in 1917. In 1920 and 1921 he was forced to spend several months at a sanatorium. Only a few months before his death in March 1924, he wrote his haunting story "Josephine the Singer," which celebrates the profound significance of artistic creation, only to deny its social relevance. Perhaps not coincidentally, Kafka instructed his friend Max Brod shortly before his death to destroy all his literary works; Brod ignored this instruction and preserved Kafka's unpublished texts for posterity. Kafka died on 3 June 1924, from laryngeal tuberculosis, just a month short of his forty-first birthday.

The Metamorphosis[1]

1

When Gregor Samsa woke up one morning from unsettling dreams, he found himself changed in his bed into a monstrous vermin. He was lying on his back as hard as armor plate, and when he lifted his head a little, he saw his vaulted brown belly, sectioned by arch-shaped ribs, to whose dome the cover, about to slide off completely, could barely cling. His many legs, pitifully thin compared with the size of the rest of him, were waving helplessly before his eyes.

"What's happened to me?" he thought. It was no dream. His room, a regular human room, only a little on the small side, lay quiet between the four familiar walls. Over the table, on which an unpacked line of fabric samples was all spread out— Samsa was a traveling salesman—hung the picture which he had recently cut out of a glossy magazine and lodged in a pretty gilt frame. It showed a lady done up in a fur hat and a fur boa,[2] sitting upright and raising up against the viewer a heavy fur muff in which her whole forearm had disappeared.

Gregor's eyes then turned to the window, and the overcast weather—he could hear raindrops hitting against the metal window ledge—completely depressed him. "How about going back to sleep for a few minutes and forgetting all this nonsense," he thought, but that was completely impracticable, since he was used to sleeping on his right side and in his present state could not get into that position. No matter how hard he threw himself onto his right side, he always rocked onto his back again. He must have tried it a hundred times, closing his eyes so as not to have to see his squirming legs, and stopped only when he began to feel a slight, dull pain in his side, which he had never felt before.

"Oh God," he thought, "what a grueling job I've picked! Day in, day out—on the road. The upset of doing business is much worse than the actual business in the home office, and, besides, I've got the torture of traveling, worrying about changing trains, eating miserable food at all hours, constantly seeing new faces, no relationships that last or get more intimate. To the devil with it all!" He felt a slight itching up on top of his belly; shoved himself slowly on his back closer to the bedpost, so as to be able to lift his head better; found the itchy spot, studded with small white dots which he had no idea what to make of; and wanted to touch the spot with one of his legs but immediately pulled it back, for the contact sent a cold shiver through him.

He slid back again into his original position. "This getting up so early," he thought, "makes anyone a complete idiot. Human beings have to have their sleep. Other traveling salesmen live like harem women. For instance, when I go back to the hotel before lunch to write up the business I've done, these gentlemen are just having breakfast. That's all I'd have to try with my boss; I'd be fired on the spot. Anyway, who knows if that wouldn't be a very good thing for me. If I didn't hold back for my parents' sake, I would have quit long ago, I would have marched up to the boss and spoken my piece from the bottom of my heart. He would have fallen off the desk! It is funny, too, the way he sits on the desk and talks down from the heights to the employees, especially

1. Translated by Stanley Corngold.
2. A long, thin scarf made of feathers or fur that women wear around their necks or shoulders.

when they have to come right up close on account of the boss's being hard of hearing. Well, I haven't given up hope completely; once I've gotten the money together to pay off my parents' debt to him—that will probably take another five or six years—I'm going to do it without fail. Then I'm going to make the big break. But for the time being I'd better get up, since my train leaves at five."

And he looked over at the alarm clock, which was ticking on the chest of drawers. "God Almighty!" he thought. It was six-thirty, the hands were quietly moving forward, it was actually past the half-hour, it was already nearly a quarter to. Could it be that the alarm hadn't gone off? You could see from the bed that it was set correctly for four o'clock; it certainly had gone off, too. Yes, but was it possible to sleep quietly through a ringing that made the furniture shake? Well, he certainly hadn't slept quietly, but probably all the more soundly for that. But what should he do now? The next train left at seven o'clock; to make it he would have to hurry like a madman, and the line of samples wasn't packed yet, and he himself didn't feel especially fresh and ready to march around. And even if he did make the train, he could not avoid getting it from the boss, because the messenger boy had been waiting at the five-o'clock train and would have long ago reported his not showing up. He was a tool of the boss, without brains or backbone. What if he were to say he was sick? But that would be extremely embarrassing and suspicious because during his five years with the firm Gregor had not been sick even once. The boss would be sure to come with the health-insurance doctor, blame his parents for their lazy son, and cut off all excuses by quoting the health-insurance doctor, for whom the world consisted of people who were completely healthy but afraid to work. And, besides, in this case would he be so very wrong? In fact, Gregor felt fine, with the exception of his drowsiness, which was really unnecessary after sleeping so late, and he even had a ravenous appetite.

Just as he was thinking all this over at top speed, without being able to decide to get out of bed—the alarm clock had just struck a quarter to seven—he heard a cautious knocking at the door next to the head of his bed. "Gregor," someone called—it was his mother—"it's a quarter to seven. Didn't you want to catch the train?" What a soft voice! Gregor was shocked to hear his own voice answering, unmistakably his own voice, true, but in which, as if from below, an insistent distressed chirping intruded, which left the clarity of his words intact only for a moment really, before so badly garbling them as they carried that no one could be sure if he had heard right. Gregor had wanted to answer in detail and to explain everything, but given the circumstances, confined himself to saying, "Yes, yes, thanks, Mother, I'm just getting up." The wooden door must have prevented the change in Gregor's voice from being noticed outside, because his mother was satisfied with this explanation and shuffled off. But their little exchange had made the rest of the family aware that, contrary to expectations, Gregor was still in the house, and already his father was knocking on one of the side doors, feebly but with his fist. "Gregor, Gregor," he called, "what's going on?" And after a little while he called again in a deeper, warning voice, "Gregor! Gregor!" At the other side door, however, his sister moaned gently, "Gregor? Is something the matter with you? Do you want anything?" Toward both sides Gregor answered: "I'm all ready," and made an effort, by meticulous pronunciation and by inserting long pauses between individual words, to eliminate everything from his voice that might betray him. His father went back to his breakfast, but his sister whispered, "Gregor, open up, I'm pleading with you." But Gregor had absolutely no intention of opening the door and complimented himself instead on the precaution he had adopted from his business trips, of locking all the doors during the night even at home.

First of all he wanted to get up quietly, without any excitement; get dressed; and, the main thing, have breakfast, and only then think about what to do next, for he saw clearly that in bed he would never think things through to a rational conclusion. He remembered how even in the past he had often felt some kind of slight pain, possibly caused by lying in an uncomfortable position, which, when he got up, turned out to be purely imaginary, and he was eager to see how today's fantasy would gradually fade away. That the change in his voice was nothing more than the first sign of a bad cold, an occupational ailment of the traveling salesman, he had no doubt in the least.

It was very easy to throw off the cover; all he had to do was puff himself up a little, and it fell off by itself. But after this, things got difficult, especially since he was so unusually broad. He would have needed hands and arms to lift himself up, but instead of that he had only his numerous little legs, which were in every different kind of perpetual motion and which, besides, he could not control. If he wanted to bend one, the first thing that happened was that it stretched itself out; and if he finally succeeded in getting this leg to do what he wanted, all the others in the meantime, as if set free, began to work in the most intensely painful agitation. "Just don't stay in bed being useless," Gregor said to himself.

First he tried to get out of bed with the lower part of his body, but this lower part—which by the way he had not seen yet and which he could not form a clear picture of—proved too difficult to budge; it was taking so long; and when finally, almost out of his mind, he lunged forward with all his force, without caring, he had picked the wrong direction and slammed himself violently against the lower bedpost, and the searing pain he felt taught him that exactly the lower part of his body was, for the moment anyway, the most sensitive.

He therefore tried to get the upper part of his body out of bed first and warily turned his head toward the edge of the bed. This worked easily, and in spite of its width and weight, the mass of his body finally followed, slowly, the movement of his head. But when at last he stuck his head over the edge of the bed into the air, he got too scared to continue any further, since if he finally let himself fall in this position, it would be a miracle if he didn't injure his head. And just now he had better not for the life of him lose consciousness; he would rather stay in bed.

But when, once again, after the same exertion, he lay in his original position, sighing, and again watched his little legs struggling, if possible more fiercely, with each other and saw no way of bringing peace and order into this mindless motion, he again told himself that it was impossible for him to stay in bed and that the most rational thing was to make any sacrifice for even the smallest hope of freeing himself from the bed. But at the same time he did not forget to remind himself occasionally that thinking things over calmly—indeed, as calmly as possible—was much better than jumping to desperate decisions. At such moments he fixed his eyes as sharply as possible on the window, but unfortunately there was little confidence and cheer to be gotten from the view of the morning fog, which shrouded even the other side of the narrow street. "Seven o'clock already," he said to himself as the alarm clock struck again, "seven o'clock already and still such a fog." And for a little while he lay quietly, breathing shallowly, as if expecting, perhaps, from the complete silence the return of things to the way they really and naturally were.

But then he said to himself, "Before it strikes a quarter past seven, I must be completely out of bed without fail. Anyway, by that time someone from the firm will be here to find out where I am, since the office opens before seven." And now he started rocking the complete length of his body out of the bed with a smooth rhythm. If he let himself topple out of bed in this way, his head, which on falling he planned to lift up sharply, would presumably remain unharmed. His back seemed to be hard; nothing was likely to happen to it when it fell onto the carpet. His biggest misgiving came from his concern about the loud crash that was bound to occur and would probably create, if not terror, at least anxiety behind all the doors. But that would have to be risked.

When Gregor's body already projected halfway out of bed—the new method was more of a game than a struggle, he only had to keep on rocking and jerking himself along—he thought how simple everything would be if he could get some help. Two strong persons—he thought of his father and the maid—would have been completely sufficient; they would only have had to shove their arms under his arched back, in this way scoop him off the bed, bend down with their burden, and then just be careful and patient while he managed to swing himself down onto the floor, where his little legs would hopefully acquire some purpose. Well, leaving out the fact that the doors were locked, should he really call for help? In spite of all his miseries, he could not repress a smile at this thought.

He was already so far along that when he rocked more strongly he could hardly keep his balance, and very soon he would have to commit himself, because in five minutes it would be a quarter past seven—when the doorbell rang. "It's someone from the firm," he said to himself and almost froze, while his little legs only danced more quickly. For a moment everything remained quiet. "They're not going to answer," Gregor said to himself, captivated by some senseless hope. But then, of course, the maid went to the door as usual with her firm stride and opened up. Gregor only had to hear the visitor's first word of greeting to know who it was—the office manager himself. Why was only Gregor condemned to work for a firm where at the slightest omission they immediately suspected the worst? Were all employees louts without exception, wasn't there a single loyal, dedicated worker among them who, when he had not fully utilized a few hours of the morning for the firm, was driven half-mad by pangs of conscience and was actually unable to get out of bed? Really, wouldn't it have been enough to send one of the apprentices to find out—if this prying were absolutely necessary—did the manager himself have to come, and did the whole innocent family have to be shown in this way that the investigation of this suspicious affair could be entrusted only to the intellect of the manager? And more as a result of the excitement produced in Gregor by these thoughts than as a result of any real decision, he swung himself out of bed with all his might. There was a loud thump, but it was not a real crash. The fall was broken a little by the carpet, and Gregor's back was more elastic than he had thought, which explained the not very noticeable muffled sound. Only he had not held his head carefully enough and hit it; he turned it and rubbed it on the carpet in anger and pain.

"Something fell in there," said the manager in the room on the left. Gregor tried to imagine whether something like what had happened to him today could one day happen even to the manager; you really had to grant the possibility. But as if in rude reply to this question, the manager took a few decisive steps in the next room and made his patent leather boots creak. From the room on the right his sister whispered, to inform Gregor, "Gregor, the manager is here." "I know," Gregor said to himself; but he did not dare raise his voice enough for his sister to hear.

"Gregor," his father now said from the room on the left, "the manager has come and wants to be informed why you didn't catch the early train. We don't know what we should say to him. Besides, he wants to speak to you personally. So please open the door. He will certainly be so kind as to excuse the disorder of the room." "Good morning, Mr. Samsa," the manager called in a friendly voice. "There's something the matter with him," his mother said to the manager while his father was still at the door, talking. "Believe me, sir, there's something the matter with him. Otherwise how would Gregor have missed a train? That boy has nothing on his mind but the business. It's almost begun to rile me that he never goes out nights. He's been back in the city for eight days now, but every night he's been home. He sits there with us at the table, quietly reading the paper or studying timetables. It's already a distraction for him when he's busy working with his fretsaw.[3] For instance, in the span of two or three evenings he carved a little frame. You'll be amazed how pretty it is; it's hanging inside his room. You'll see it right away when Gregor opens the door. You know, I'm glad that you've come, sir. We would never have gotten Gregor to open the door by ourselves; he's so stubborn. And there's certainly something wrong with him, even though he said this morning there wasn't." "I'm coming right away," said Gregor slowly and deliberately, not moving in order not to miss a word of the conversation. "I haven't any other explanation myself," said the manager. "I hope it's nothing serious. On the other hand, I must say that we businessmen—fortunately or unfortunately, whichever you prefer—very often simply have to overcome a slight indisposition for business reasons." "So can the manager come in now?" asked his father, impatient, and knocked on the door again. "No," said Gregor. In the room on the left there was an embarrassing silence; in the room on the right his sister began to sob.

Why didn't his sister go in to the others? She had probably just got out of bed and not even started to get dressed. Then what was she crying about? Because he didn't get up and didn't let the manager in, because he was in danger of losing his job, and because then the boss would start hounding his parents about the old debts? For the time being, certainly, her worries were unnecessary. Gregor was still here and hadn't the slightest intention of letting the family down. True, at the moment he was lying on the carpet, and no one knowing his condition could seriously have expected him to let the manager in. But just because of this slight discourtesy, for which an appropriate excuse would easily be found later on, Gregor could not simply be dismissed. And to Gregor it seemed much more sensible to leave him alone now than to bother him with crying and persuasion. But it was just the uncertainty that was tormenting the others and excused their behavior.

"Mr. Samsa," the manager now called, raising his voice, "what's the matter? You barricade yourself in your room, answer only 'yes' and 'no,' cause your parents serious, unnecessary worry, and you neglect—I mention this only in passing—your duties to the firm in a really shocking manner. I am speaking here in the name of your parents and of your employer and ask you in all seriousness for an immediate, clear explanation. I'm amazed, amazed. I thought I knew you to be a quiet, reasonable person, and now you suddenly seem to want to start strutting about, flaunting strange whims. The head of the firm did suggest to me this morning a possible explanation for your tardiness—it concerned the cash payments recently entrusted to you—but really, I practically gave my word of honor that this explanation could not be right. But now, seeing your incomprehensible obstinacy, I am about to lose even the slightest desire to stick up for you in any way at all. And your job is not the most secure. Originally I intended to tell you all this in private, but since you make me waste my time here for nothing, I don't see why your parents shouldn't hear too. Your performance of late has been very unsatisfactory; I know it is not the best season for doing business,

---

3. A small fine-toothed saw that is used to cut creative, decorative patterns in wood.

we all recognize that; but a season for not doing any business, there is no such thing, Mr. Samsa, such a thing cannot be tolerated."

"But, sir," cried Gregor, beside himself, in his excitement forgetting everything else, "I'm just opening up, in a minute. A slight indisposition, a dizzy spell, prevented me from getting up. I'm still in bed. But I already feel fine again. I'm just getting out of bed. Just be patient for a minute! I'm not as well as I thought yet. But really I'm fine. How something like this could just take a person by surprise! Only last night I was fine, my parents can tell you, or wait, last night I already had a slight premonition. They must have been able to tell by looking at me. Why didn't I report it to the office! But you always think that you'll get over a sickness without staying home. Sir! Spare my parents! There's no basis for any of the accusations that you're making against me now; no one has ever said a word to me about them. Perhaps you haven't seen the last orders I sent in. Anyway, I'm still going on the road with the eight o'clock train; these few hours of rest have done me good. Don't let me keep you, sir. I'll be at the office myself right away, and be so kind as to tell them this, and give my respects to the head of the firm."

And while Gregor hastily blurted all this out, hardly knowing what he was saying, he had easily approached the chest of drawers, probably as a result of the practice he had already gotten in bed, and now he tried to raise himself up against it. He actually intended to open the door, actually present himself and speak to the manager; he was eager to find out what the others, who were now so anxious to see him, would say at the sight of him. If they were shocked, then Gregor had no further responsibility and could be calm. But if they took everything calmly, then he, too, had no reason to get excited and could, if he hurried, actually be at the station by eight o'clock. At first he slid off the polished chest of drawers a few times, but at last, giving himself a final push, he stood upright; he no longer paid any attention to the pains in his abdomen, no matter how much they were burning. Now he let himself fall against the back of a nearby chair, clinging to its slats with his little legs. But by doing this he had gotten control of himself and fell silent, since he could now listen to what the manager was saying.

"Did you understand a word?" the manager was asking his parents. "He isn't trying to make fools of us, is he?" "My God," cried his mother, already in tears, "maybe he's seriously ill, and here we are, torturing him. Grete! Grete!" she then cried. "Mother?" called his sister from the other side. They communicated by way of Gregor's room. "Go to the doctor's immediately. Gregor is sick. Hurry, get the doctor. Did you just hear Gregor talking?" "That was the voice of an animal," said the manager, in a tone conspicuously soft compared with the mother's yelling. "Anna! Anna!" the father called through the foyer into the kitchen, clapping his hands, "get a locksmith right away!" And already the two girls were running with rustling skirts through the foyer—how could his sister have gotten dressed so quickly?—and tearing open the door to the apartment. The door could not be heard slamming; they had probably left it open, as is the custom in homes where a great misfortune has occurred.[4]

But Gregor had become much calmer. It was true that they no longer understood his words, though they had seemed clear enough to him, clearer than before, probably because his ear had grown accustomed to them. But still, the others now believed that there was something the matter with him and were ready to help him. The assurance

---

4. Kafka is referring to a common popular belief that opening a house's doors and windows after a stroke of ill fortune, especially a death, will help to clear bad influences and spirits from the residence.

and confidence with which the first measures had been taken did him good. He felt integrated into human society once again and hoped for marvelous, amazing feats from both the doctor and the locksmith, without really distinguishing sharply between them. In order to make his voice as clear as possible for the crucial discussions that were approaching, he cleared his throat a little—taking pains, of course, to do so in a very muffled manner, since this noise, too, might sound different from human coughing, a thing he no longer trusted himself to decide. In the next room, meanwhile, everything had become completely still. Perhaps his parents were sitting at the table with the manager, whispering; perhaps they were all leaning against the door and listening.

Gregor slowly lugged himself toward the door, pushing the chair in front of him, then let go of it, threw himself against the door, held himself upright against it—the pads on the bottom of his little legs exuded a little sticky substance—and for a moment rested there from the exertion. But then he got started turning the key in the lock with his mouth. Unfortunately it seemed that he had no real teeth—what was he supposed to grip the key with?—but in compensation his jaws, of course, were very strong; with their help he actually got the key moving and paid no attention to the fact that he was undoubtedly hurting himself in some way, for a brown liquid came out of his mouth, flowed over the key, and dripped onto the floor. "Listen," said the manager in the next room, "he's turning the key." This was great encouragement to Gregor; but everyone should have cheered him on, his father and mother too. "Go, Gregor," they should have called, "keep going, at that lock, harder, harder!" And in the delusion that they were all following his efforts with suspense, he clamped his jaws madly on the key with all the strength he could muster. Depending on the progress of the key, he danced around the lock; holding himself upright only by his mouth, he clung to the key, as the situation demanded, or pressed it down again with the whole weight of his body. The clearer click of the lock as it finally snapped back literally woke Gregor up. With a sigh of relief he said to himself, "So I didn't need the locksmith after all," and laid his head down on the handle in order to open wide one wing of the double doors.

Since he had to use this method of opening the door, it was really opened very wide while he himself was still invisible. He first had to edge slowly around the one wing of the door, and do so very carefully if he was not to fall flat on his back just before entering. He was still busy with this difficult maneuver and had no time to pay attention to anything else when he heard the manager burst out with a loud "Oh!"—it sounded like a rush of wind—and now he could see him, standing closest to the door, his hand pressed over his open mouth, slowly backing away, as if repulsed by an invisible, unrelenting force. His mother—in spite of the manager's presence she stood with her hair still unbraided from the night, sticking out in all directions—first looked at his father with her hands clasped, then took two steps toward Gregor, and sank down in the midst of her skirts spreading out around her, her face completely hidden on her breast. With a hostile expression his father clenched his fist, as if to drive Gregor back into his room, then looked uncertainly around the living room, shielded his eyes with his hands, and sobbed with heaves of his powerful chest.

Now Gregor did not enter the room after all but leaned against the inside of the firmly bolted wing of the door, so that only half his body was visible and his head above it, cocked to one side and peeping out at the others. In the meantime it had grown much lighter; across the street one could see clearly a section of the endless, grayish-black building opposite—it was a hospital—with its regular windows starkly piercing the façade; the rain was still coming down, but only in large, separately visible drops that were also pelting the ground literally one at a time. The breakfast dishes were laid out lavishly on the table, since for his father breakfast was the most important meal of the day, which he would prolong for hours while reading various newspapers. On the wall directly opposite hung a photograph of Gregor from his army days, in a lieutenant's uniform, his hand on his sword, a carefree smile on his lips, demanding respect for his bearing and his rank. The door to the foyer was open, and since the front door was open too, it was possible to see out onto the landing and the top of the stairs going down.

"Well," said Gregor—and he was thoroughly aware of being the only one who had kept calm—"I'll get dressed right away, pack up my samples, and go. Will you, will you please let me go? Now, sir, you see, I'm not stubborn and I'm willing to work; traveling is a hardship, but without it I couldn't live. Where are you going, sir? To the office? Yes? Will you give an honest report of everything? A man might find for a moment that he was unable to work, but that's exactly the right time to remember his past accomplishments and to consider that later on, when the obstacle has been removed, he's bound to work all the harder and more efficiently. I'm under so many obligations to the head of the firm, as you know very well. Besides, I also have my parents and my sister to worry about. I'm in a tight spot, but I'll also work my way out again. Don't make things harder for me than they already are. Stick up for me in the office, please. Traveling salesmen aren't well liked there, I know. People think they make a fortune leading the gay life. No one has any particular reason to rectify this prejudice. But you, sir, you have a better perspective on things than the rest of the office, an even better perspective, just between the two of us, than the head of the firm himself, who in his capacity as owner easily lets his judgment be swayed against an employee. And you also know very well that the traveling salesman, who is out of the office practically the whole year round, can so easily become the victim of gossip, coincidences, and unfounded accusations, against which he's completely unable to defend himself, since in most cases he knows nothing at all about them except when he returns exhausted from a trip, and back home gets to suffer on his own person the grim consequences, which can no longer be traced back to their causes. Sir, don't go away without a word to tell me you think I'm at least partly right!"

But at Gregor's first words the manager had already turned away and with curled lips looked back at Gregor only over his twitching shoulder. And during Gregor's speech he did not stand still for a minute but, without letting Gregor out of his sight, backed toward the door, yet very gradually, as if there were some secret prohibition against leaving the room. He was already in the foyer, and from the sudden movement with which he took his last step from the living room, one might have thought he had just burned the sole of his foot. In the foyer, however, he stretched his right hand far out toward the staircase, as if nothing less than an unearthly deliverance were awaiting him there.

Gregor realized that he must on no account let the manager go away in this mood if his position in the firm were not to be jeopardized in the extreme. His parents did not understand this too well; in the course of the years they had formed the conviction that Gregor was set for life in this firm; and furthermore, they were so preoccupied with their immediate troubles that they had lost all consideration for the future. But Gregor had this forethought. The manager must be detained, calmed down, convinced, and finally won over; Gregor's and the family's future depended on it! If only his sister had been there! She was perceptive; she had already begun to cry when Gregor was still lying calmly on his back. And certainly the manager, this ladies' man, would have listened to her; she would have shut the front door and in the foyer talked him out of his scare. But his sister was not there; Gregor had to handle the situation himself. And without stopping to realize that he had no idea what his new faculties of movement were, and without stopping to realize either that his speech had possibly—indeed, probably—not been understood again, he let go of the wing of the door; he shoved himself through the opening, intending to go to the manager, who was already on the landing, ridiculously holding onto the banisters with both hands; but groping for support, Gregor immediately fell down with a little cry onto his numerous little legs. This had hardly happened when for the first time that morning he had a feeling of physical well-being; his little legs were on firm ground; they obeyed him completely, as he noted to his joy; they even strained to carry him away wherever he wanted to go; and he already believed that final recovery from all his sufferings was imminent. But at that very moment, as he lay on the floor rocking with repressed motion, not far from his mother and just opposite her, she, who had seemed so completely self-absorbed, all at once jumped up, her arms stretched wide, her fingers spread, and cried, "Help, for God's sake, help!" held her head bent as if to see Gregor better, but inconsistently darted madly backward instead; had forgotten that the table laden with the breakfast dishes stood behind her; sat down on it hastily, as if her thoughts were elsewhere, when she reached it; and did not seem to notice at all that near her the big coffeepot had been knocked over and coffee was pouring in a steady stream onto the rug.

"Mother, Mother," said Gregor softly and looked up at her. For a minute the manager had completely slipped his mind; on the other hand at the sight of the spilling coffee he could not resist snapping his jaws several times in the air. At this his mother screamed once more, fled from the table, and fell into the arms of his father, who came rushing up to her. But Gregor had no time now for his parents; the manager was already on the stairs; with his chin on the banister, he was taking a last look back. Gregor was off to a running start, to be as sure as possible of catching up with him; the manager must have suspected something like this, for he leaped down several steps and disappeared; but still he shouted "Agh," and the sound carried through the whole staircase. Unfortunately the manager's flight now seemed to confuse his father completely, who had been relatively calm until now, for instead of running after the manager himself, or at least not hindering Gregor in his pursuit, he seized in his right hand the manager's cane, which had been left behind on a chair with his hat and overcoat, picked up in his left hand a heavy newspaper from the table, and stamping his feet, started brandishing the cane and the newspaper to drive Gregor back into his room. No plea of Gregor's helped, no plea was even understood; however humbly he might turn his head, his father merely stamped his feet more forcefully. Across the room his mother had thrown open a window in spite of the cool weather, and leaning out, she buried her face, far outside the window, in her hands. Between the alley and the staircase a strong draft was created, the window curtains blew in, the newspapers on the table rustled, single sheets fluttered across the floor. Pitilessly his father came on, hissing like a wild man. Now Gregor had not had any practice at all walking in reverse, it was really very slow going. If Gregor had only been allowed to turn around, he could have gotten into his room right away, but he was afraid to make his father impatient by this time-consuming gyration, and at any minute the cane in his father's hand threatened to come down on his back or his head with a deadly blow. Finally, however, Gregor had no choice, for he noticed with horror that in reverse he could not even keep going in one direction; and so, incessantly throwing uneasy side-glances at his father, he began to turn around as quickly as possible, in reality turning only very slowly. Perhaps his father realized his good intentions, for he did not interfere with him; instead, he even now and then directed the maneuver from afar with the tip of his cane. If only his father did not keep making this intolerable hissing sound! It made Gregor lose his head completely. He had almost finished the turn when—his mind continually on this hissing—he made a mistake and even started turning back around to his original position. But when he had at last successfully managed to get his head in front of the opened door, it turned out that his body was too broad to get through as it was. Of course in his father's present state of mind it did not even remotely occur to him to open the other wing of the door in order to give Gregor enough room to pass through. He had only the fixed idea that Gregor must return to his room as quickly as possible. He would never have allowed the complicated preliminaries Gregor needed to go through in order to stand up on one end and perhaps in this way fit through the door. Instead he drove Gregor on, as if there were no obstacle, with exceptional loudness; the voice behind Gregor did not sound like that of only a single father; now this was really no joke anymore, and Gregor forced himself—come what may—into the doorway. One side of his body rose up, he lay lop-sided in the opening, one of his flanks was scraped raw, ugly blotches marred the white door, soon he got stuck and could not have budged any more by himself, his little legs on one side dangled tremblingly in midair, those on the other were painfully crushed against the floor—when from behind his father gave him a hard shove, which was truly his salvation, and bleeding profusely, he flew far into his room. The door was slammed shut with the cane, then at last everything was quiet.

2

It was already dusk when Gregor awoke from his deep, comalike sleep. Even if he had not been disturbed, he would certainly not have woken up much later, for he felt that he had rested and slept long enough, but it seemed to him that a hurried step and a cautious shutting of the door leading to the foyer had awakened him. The light of the electric street-lamps lay in pallid streaks on the ceiling and on the upper parts of the furniture, but underneath, where Gregor was, it was dark. Groping clumsily with his antennae, which he was only now beginning to appreciate, he slowly dragged himself toward the door to see what had been happening there. His left side felt like one single long, unpleasantly tautening scar, and he actually had to limp on his two rows of legs. Besides, one little leg had been seriously injured in the course of the morning's events—it was almost a miracle that only one had been injured—and dragged along lifelessly.

Only after he got to the door did he notice what had really attracted him—the smell of something to eat. For there stood a bowl filled with fresh milk, in which small slices of white bread were floating. He could almost have laughed for joy, since he was even hungrier than he had been in the morning, and he immediately dipped his head into the milk, almost to over his eyes. But he soon drew it back again in disappointment; not only because he had difficulty eating on account of the soreness in his left side—and he could eat only if his whole panting body cooperated—but because he didn't like the milk at all, although it used to be his favorite drink, and that was certainly why his sister had put it in the room; in fact, he turned away from the bowl almost with repulsion and crawled back to the middle of the room.

In the living room, as Gregor saw through the crack in the door, the gas had been lit, but while at this hour of the day his father was in the habit of reading the afternoon newspaper in a loud voice to his mother and sometimes to his sister too, now there wasn't a sound. Well, perhaps this custom of reading aloud, which his sister was always telling him and writing him about, had recently been discontinued altogether. But in all the other rooms too it was just as still, although the apartment certainly was not empty. "What a quiet life the family has been leading," Gregor said to himself, and while he stared rigidly in front of him into the darkness, he felt very proud that he had been able to provide such a life in so nice an apartment for his parents and his sister. But what now if all the peace, the comfort, the contentment were to come to a horrible end? In order not to get involved in such thoughts, Gregor decided to keep moving, and he crawled up and down the room.

During the long evening, first one of the side doors and then the other was opened a small crack and quickly shut again; someone had probably had the urge to come in and then had had second thoughts. Gregor now settled into position right by the living-room door, determined somehow to get the hesitating visitor to come in, or at least to find out who it might be; but the door was not opened again, and Gregor waited in vain. In the morning, when the doors had been locked, everyone had wanted to come in; now that he had opened one of the doors and the others had evidently been opened during the day, no one came in, and now the keys were even inserted on the outside.

It was late at night when the light finally went out in the living room, and now it was easy for Gregor to tell that his parents and his sister had stayed up so long, since, as he could distinctly hear, all three were now retiring on tiptoe. Certainly no one would come in to Gregor until the morning; and so he had ample time to consider undisturbed how best to rearrange his life. But the empty high-ceilinged room in which he was forced to lie flat on the floor made him nervous, without his being able to tell why—since it was, after all, the room in which he had lived for the past five years— and turning half unconsciously and not without a slight feeling of shame, he scuttled under the couch where, although his back was a little crushed and he could not raise his head any more, he immediately felt very comfortable and was only sorry that his body was too wide to go completely under the couch.

There he stayed the whole night, which he spent partly in a sleepy trance, from which hunger pangs kept waking him with a start, partly in worries and vague hopes, all of which, however, led to the conclusion that for the time being he would have to lie low and, by being patient and showing his family every possible consideration, help them bear the inconvenience which he simply had to cause them in his present condition.

Early in the morning—it was still almost night—Gregor had the opportunity of testing the strength of the resolutions he had just made, for his sister, almost fully dressed, opened the door from the foyer and looked in eagerly. She did not see him right away, but when she caught sight of him under the couch—God, he had to be somewhere, he couldn't just fly away—she became so frightened that she lost control of herself and slammed the door shut again. But, as if she felt sorry for her behavior, she immediately opened the door again and came in on tiptoe, as if she were visiting someone seriously ill or perhaps even a stranger. Gregor had pushed his head forward just to the edge of the couch and was watching her. Would she notice that he had left the milk standing, and not because he hadn't been hungry, and would she bring in a dish of something he'd like better? If she were not going to do it of her own free will, he would rather starve than call it to her attention, although, really, he felt an enormous urge to shoot out from under the couch, throw himself at his sister's feet, and beg her for something good to eat. But his sister noticed at once, to her astonishment, that the bowl was still full, only a little milk was spilled around it; she picked it up immediately—not with her bare hands, of course, but with a rag—and carried it out. Gregor was extremely curious to know what she would bring him instead, and he racked his brains on the subject. But he would never have been able to guess what his sister, in the goodness of her heart, actually did. To find out his likes and dislikes, she brought him a wide assortment of things, all spread out on an old newspapers: old, half-rotten vegetables; bones left over from the evening meal, caked with congealed white sauce; some raisins and almonds; a piece of cheese, which two days before Gregor had declared inedible; a plain slice of bread, a slice of bread and butter, and one with butter and salt. In addition to all this she put down some water in the bowl apparently permanently earmarked for Gregor's use. And out of a sense of delicacy, since she knew that Gregor would not eat in front of her, she left hurriedly and even turned the key, just so that Gregor should know that he might make himself as comfortable as he wanted. Gregor's legs began whirring now that he was going to eat. Besides, his bruises must have completely healed, since he no longer felt any handicap, and marveling at this he thought how, over a month ago, he had cut his finger very slightly with a knife and how this wound was still hurting him only the day before yesterday. "Have I become less sensitive?" he thought, already sucking greedily at the cheese, which had immediately and forcibly attracted him ahead of all the other dishes. One right after the other, and with eyes streaming with tears of contentment, he devoured the cheese, the vegetables, and the sauce; the fresh foods, on the other hand, he did not care for; he couldn't even stand their smell and even dragged the things he wanted to eat a bit farther away. He had finished with everything long since and was just lying lazily at the same spot when his sister slowly turned the key as a sign for him to withdraw. That immediately startled him, although he was almost asleep, and he scuttled under the couch again. But it took great self-control for him to stay under the couch even for the short time his sister was in the room, since his body had become a little bloated from the heavy meal, and in his cramped position he could hardly breathe. In between slight attacks of suffocation he watched with bulging eyes as his unsuspecting sister took a broom and swept up, not only his leavings, but even the foods which Gregor had left completely untouched—as if they too were no longer usable—and dumping everything hastily into a pail, which she covered with a wooden lid, she carried everything out. She had hardly turned her back when Gregor came out from under the couch, stretching and puffing himself up.

This, then, was the way Gregor was fed each day, once in the morning, when his parents and the maid were still asleep, and a second time in the afternoon after everyone had had dinner, for then his parents took a short nap again, and the maid could be sent out by his sister on some errand. Certainly they did not want him to starve either, but perhaps they would not have been able to stand knowing any more about his meals than from hearsay, or perhaps his sister wanted to spare them even what was possibly only a minor torment, for really, they were suffering enough as it was.

Gregor could not find out what excuses had been made to get rid of the doctor and the locksmith on that first morning, for since the others could not understand what he said, it did not occur to any of them, not even to his sister, that he could understand what they said, and so he had to be satisfied, when his sister was in the room, with only occasionally hearing her sighs and appeals to the saints. It was only later, when she had begun to get used to everything—there could never, of course, be any question of a complete adjustment—that Gregor sometimes caught a remark which was meant to be friendly or could be interpreted as such. "Oh, he liked what he had today," she would say when Gregor had tucked away a good helping, and in the opposite case, which gradually occurred more and more frequently, she used to say, almost sadly, "He's left everything again."

But if Gregor could not get any news directly, he overheard a great deal from the neighboring rooms, and as soon as he heard voices, he would immediately run to the door concerned and press his whole body against it. Especially in the early days, there was no conversation that was not somehow about him, if only implicitly. For two whole days there were family consultations at every mealtime about how they should cope; this was also the topic of discussion between meals, for at least two members of the family were always at home, since no one probably wanted to stay home alone and it was impossible to leave the apartment completely empty. Besides, on the very first day the maid—it was not completely clear what and how much she knew of what had happened—had begged his mother on bended knees to dismiss her immediately; and when she said goodbye a quarter of an hour later, she thanked them in tears for the dismissal, as if for the greatest favor that had ever been done to her in this house, and made a solemn vow, without anyone asking her for it, not to give anything away to anyone.

Now his sister, working with her mother, had to do the cooking too; of course that did not cause her much trouble, since they hardly ate anything. Gregor was always hearing one of them pleading in vain with one of the others to eat and getting no answer except, "Thanks, I've had enough," or something similar. They did not seem to drink anything either. His sister often asked her father if he wanted any beer and gladly offered to go out for it herself; and when he did not answer, she said, in order to remove any hesitation on his part, that she could also send the janitor's wife to get it, but then his father finally answered with a definite "No," and that was the end of that.

In the course of the very first day his father explained the family's financial situation and prospects to both the mother and the sister. From time to time he got up from the table to get some kind of receipt or notebook out of the little strongbox he had rescued from the collapse of his business five years before. Gregor heard him open the complicated lock and secure it again after taking out what he had been looking for. These explanations by his father were to some extent the first pleasant news Gregor had heard since his imprisonment. He had always believed that his father had not been able to save a penny from the business, at least his father had never told him anything to the contrary, and Gregor, for his part, had never asked him any questions. In those days Gregor's sole concern had been to do everything in his power to make the family forget as quickly as possible the business disaster which had plunged everyone into a state of total despair. And so he had begun to work with special ardor and had risen almost overnight from stock clerk to traveling salesman, which of course had opened up very different moneymaking possibilities, and in no time his successes on the job were transformed, by means of commissions, into hard cash that could be plunked down on the table at home in front of his astonished and delighted family. Those had been wonderful times, and they had never returned, at least not with the same glory, although later on Gregor earned enough money to meet the expenses of the entire family and actually did so. They had just gotten used to it, the family as well as Gregor, the money was received with thanks and given with pleasure, but no special feeling of warmth went with it anymore. Only his sister had remained close to Gregor, and it was his secret plan that she, who, unlike him, loved music and could play the violin movingly, should be sent next year to the Conservatory, regardless of the great expense involved, which could surely be made up for in some other way.

Often during Gregor's short stays in the city, the Conservatory would come up in his conversations with his sister, but always merely as a beautiful dream which was not supposed to come true, and his parents were not happy to hear even these innocent allusions; but Gregor had very concrete ideas on the subject and he intended solemnly to announce his plan on Christmas Eve.

Thoughts like these, completely useless in his present state, went through his head as he stood glued to the door, listening. Sometimes out of general exhaustion he could not listen anymore and let his head bump carelessly against the door, but immediately pulled it back again, for even the slight noise he made by doing this had been heard in the next room and made them all lapse into silence. "What's he carrying on about in there now?" said his father after a while, obviously turning toward the door, and only then would the interrupted conversation gradually be resumed.

Gregor now learned in a thorough way—for his father was in the habit of often re-peating himself in his explanations, partly because he himself had not dealt with these matters for a long time, partly, too, because his mother did not understand everything the first time around—that in spite of all their misfortunes a bit of capital, a very little bit, certainly, was still intact from the old days, which in the meantime had increased a little through the untouched interest. But besides that, the money Gregor had brought home every month—he had kept only a few dollars for himself—had never been com-pletely used up and had accumulated into a tidy principal. Behind his door Gregor nodded emphatically, delighted at this unexpected foresight and thrift. Of course he actually could have paid off more of his father's debt to the boss with this extra money, and the day on which he could have gotten rid of his job would have been much closer, but now things were undoubtedly better the way his father had arranged them.

Now this money was by no means enough to let the family live off the interest; the principal was perhaps enough to support the family for one year, or at the most two, but that was all there was. So it was just a sum that really should not be touched and that had to be put away for a rainy day; but the money to live on would have to be earned. Now his father was still healthy, certainly, but he was an old man who had not worked for the past five years and who in any case could not be expected to undertake too much; during these five years, which were the first vacation of his hard-working yet unsuccessful life, he had gained a lot of weight and as a result had become fairly sluggish. And was his old mother now supposed to go out and earn money, when she suffered from asthma, when a walk through the apartment was already an ordeal for her, and when she spent every other day lying on the sofa under the open window, gasping for breath? And was his sister now supposed to work—who for all her sev-enteen years was still a child and whom it would be such a pity to deprive of the life she had led until now, which had consisted of wearing pretty clothes, sleeping late, helping in the house, enjoying a few modest amusements, and above all playing the violin? At first, whenever the conversation turned to the necessity of earning money, Gregor would let go of the door and throw himself down on the cool leather sofa which stood beside it, for he felt hot with shame and grief.

Often he lay there the whole long night through, not sleeping a wink and only scrabbling on the leather for hours on end. Or, not balking at the huge effort of push-ing an armchair to the window, he would crawl up to the window sill and, propped up in the chair, lean against the window, evidently in some sort of remembrance of the feeling of freedom he used to have from looking out the window. For, in fact, from day to day he saw things even a short distance away less and less distinctly; the hospital opposite, which he used to curse because he saw so much of it, was now completely beyond his range of vision, and if he had not been positive that he was living in Charlotte Street—a quiet but still very much a city street—he might have believed that he was looking out of his window into a desert where the gray sky and the gray earth were indistinguishably fused. It took his observant sister only twice to notice that his armchair was standing by the window for her to push the chair back to the same place by the window each time she had finished cleaning the room, and from then on she even left the inside casement of the window open.

If Gregor had only been able to speak to his sister and thank her for everything she had to do for him, he could have accepted her services more easily; as it was, they caused him pain. Of course his sister tried to ease the embarrassment of the whole situation as much as possible, and as time went on, she naturally managed it better and better, but in time Gregor, too, saw things much more clearly. Even the way she came in was terrible for him. Hardly had she entered the room than she would run straight to the window without taking time to close the door—though she was usually so careful to spare everyone the sight of Gregor's room—then tear open the casements with eager hands, almost as if she were suffocating, and remain for a little while at the window even in the coldest weather, breathing deeply. With this racing and crashing she frightened Gregor twice a day; the whole time he cowered under the couch, and yet he knew very well that she would certainly have spared him this if only she had found it possible to stand being in a room with him with the window closed.

One time—it must have been a month since Gregor's metamorphosis, and there was certainly no particular reason any more for his sister to be astonished at Gregor's appearance—she came a little earlier than usual and caught Gregor still looking out the window, immobile and so in an excellent position to be terrifying. It would not have surprised Gregor if she had not come in, because his position prevented her from immediately opening the window, but not only did she not come in, she even sprang back and locked the door; a stranger might easily have thought that Gregor had been lying in wait for her, wanting to bite her. Of course Gregor immediately hid under the couch, but he had to wait until noon before his sister came again, and she seemed much more uneasy than usual. He realized from this that the sight of him was still repulsive to her and was bound to remain repulsive to her in the future, and that she probably had to overcome a lot of resistance not to run away at the sight of even the small part of his body that jutted out from under the couch. So, to spare her even this sight, one day he carried the sheet on his back to the couch—the job took four hours—and arranged it in such a way that he was now completely covered up and his sister could not see him even when she stooped. If she had considered this sheet unnecessary, then of course she could have removed it, for it was clear enough that it could not be for his own pleasure that Gregor shut himself off altogether, but she left the sheet the way it was, and Gregor thought that he had even caught a grateful look when one time he cautiously lifted the sheet a little with his head in order to see how his sister was taking the new arrangement.

During the first two weeks, his parents could not bring themselves to come in to him, and often he heard them say how much they appreciated his sister's work, whereas until now they had frequently been annoyed with her because she had struck them as being a little useless. But now both of them, his father and his mother, often waited outside Gregor's room while his sister straightened it up, and as soon as she came out she had to tell them in great detail how the room looked, what Gregor had eaten, how he had behaved this time, and whether he had perhaps shown a little improvement. His mother, incidentally, began relatively soon to want to visit Gregor, but his father and his sister at first held her back with reasonable arguments to which

Gregor listened very attentively and of which he whole-heartedly approved. But later she had to be restrained by force, and then when she cried out, "Let me go to Gregor, he is my unfortunate boy! Don't you understand that I have to go to him?" Gregor thought that it might be a good idea after all if his mother did come in, not every day of course, but perhaps once a week; she could still do everything much better than his sister, who, for all her courage, was still only a child and in the final analysis had perhaps taken on such a difficult assignment only out of childish flightiness.

Gregor's desire to see his mother was soon fulfilled. During the day Gregor did not want to show himself at the window, if only out of consideration for his parents, but he couldn't crawl very far on his few square yards of floor space, either; he could hardly put up with just lying still even at night; eating soon stopped giving him the slightest pleasure, so, as a distraction, he adopted the habit of crawling criss-cross over the walls and the ceiling. He especially liked hanging from the ceiling; it was completely different from lying on the floor; one could breathe more freely; a faint swinging sensation went through the body; and in the almost happy absent-mindedness which Gregor felt up there, it could happen to his own surprise that he let go and plopped onto the floor. But now, of course, he had much better control of his body than before and did not hurt himself even from such a big drop. His sister immediately noticed the new entertainment Gregor had discovered for himself—after all, he left behind traces of his sticky substance wherever he crawled—and so she got it into her head to make it possible for Gregor to crawl on an altogether wider scale by taking out the furniture which stood in his way—mainly the chest of drawers and the desk. But she was not able to do this by herself; she did not dare ask her father for help; the maid would certainly not have helped her, for although this girl, who was about sixteen, was bravely sticking it out after the previous cook had left, she had asked for the favor of locking herself in the kitchen at all times and of only opening the door on special request. So there was nothing left for his sister to do except to get her mother one day when her father was out. And his mother did come, with exclamations of excited joy, but she grew silent at the door of Gregor's room. First his sister looked to see, of course, that everything in the room was in order; only then did she let her mother come in. Hurrying as fast as he could, Gregor had pulled the sheet down lower still and pleated it more tightly—it really looked just like a sheet accidentally thrown over the couch. This time Gregor also refrained from spying from under the sheet; he renounced seeing his mother for the time being and was simply happy that she had come after all. "Come on, you can't see him," his sister said, evidently leading her mother in by the hand. Now Gregor could hear the two frail women moving the old chest of drawers—heavy for anyone—from its place and his sister insisting on doing the harder part of the job herself, ignoring the warnings of her mother, who was afraid that she would overexert herself. It went on for a long time. After struggling for a good quarter of an hour, his mother said that they had better leave the chest where it was, because, in the first place, it was too heavy, they would not finish before his father came, and with the chest in the middle of the room, Gregor would be completely barricaded; and, in the second place, it was not at all certain that they were doing Gregor a favor by removing his furniture. To her the opposite seemed to be the case; the sight of the bare wall was heart-breaking; and why shouldn't Gregor also have the same feeling, since he had been used to his furniture for so long and would feel abandoned in the empty room. "And doesn't it look," his mother concluded very softly—in fact she had been almost whispering the whole time, as if she wanted to avoid letting Gregor, whose exact whereabouts she did not know, hear even the sound of her voice, for she was convinced that he did not understand the words—"and doesn't it look as if by removing his furniture we were showing him that we have given up all hope of his getting better and are leaving him to his own devices without any consideration? I think the best thing would be to try to keep the room exactly the way it was before, so that when Gregor comes back to us again, he'll find everything unchanged and can forget all the more easily what's happened in the meantime."

When he heard his mother's words, Gregor realized that the monotony of family life, combined with the fact that not a soul had addressed a word directly to him, must have addled his brain in the course of the past two months, for he could not explain to himself in any other way how in all seriousness he could have been anxious to have his room cleared out. Had he really wanted to have his warm room, comfortably fitted with furniture that had always been in the family, changed into a cave, in which, of course, he would be able to crawl around unhampered in all directions but at the cost of simultaneously, rapidly, and totally forgetting his human past? Even now he had been on the verge of forgetting, and only his mother's voice, which he had not heard for so long, had shaken him up. Nothing should be removed; everything had to stay; he could not do without the beneficial influence of the furniture on his state of mind; and if the furniture prevented him from carrying on this senseless crawling around, then that was no loss but rather a great advantage.

But his sister unfortunately had a different opinion; she had become accustomed, certainly not entirely without justification, to adopt with her parents the role of the particularly well-qualified expert whenever Gregor's affairs were being discussed; and so her mother's advice was now sufficient reason for her to insist, not only on the removal of the chest of drawers and the desk, which was all she had been planning at first, but also on the removal of all the furniture with the exception of the indispensable couch. Of course it was not only childish defiance and the self-confidence she had recently acquired so unexpectedly and at such a cost that led her to make this demand; she had in fact noticed that Gregor needed plenty of room to crawl around in; and on the other hand, as best she could tell, he never used the furniture at all. Perhaps, however, the romantic enthusiasm of girls her age, which seeks to indulge itself at every opportunity, played a part, by tempting her to make Gregor's situation even more terrifying in order that she might do even more for him. Into a room in which Gregor ruled the bare walls all alone, no human being beside Grete was ever likely to set foot.

And so she did not let herself be swerved from her decision by her mother, who, besides, from the sheer anxiety of being in Gregor's room, seemed unsure of herself, soon grew silent, and helped her daughter as best she could to get the chest of drawers out of the room. Well, in a pinch Gregor could do without the chest, but the desk had to stay. And hardly had the women left the room with the chest, squeezing against it and groaning, than Gregor stuck his head out from under the couch to see how he could feel his way into the situation as considerately as possible. But unfortunately it had to be his mother who came back first, while in the next room Grete was clasping the chest and rocking it back and forth by herself, without of course budging it from the spot. His mother, however, was not used to the sight of Gregor, he could have made her ill, and so Gregor, frightened, scuttled in reverse to the far end of the couch but could not stop the sheet from shifting a little at the front. That was enough to put his mother on the alert. She stopped, stood still for a moment, and then went back to Grete.

Although Gregor told himself over and over again that nothing special was happening, only a few pieces of furniture were being moved, he soon had to admit that this coming and going of the women, their little calls to each other, the scraping of the furniture along the floor had the effect on him of a great turmoil swelling on all sides, and as much as he tucked in his head and his legs and shrank until his belly touched the floor, he was forced to admit that he would not be able to stand it much longer. They were clearing out his room; depriving him of everything that he loved; they had already carried away the chest of drawers, in which he kept the fretsaw and other tools; were now budging the desk firmly embedded in the floor, the desk he had done his homework on when he was a student at business college, in high school, yes, even in public school—now he really had no more time to examine the good intentions of the two women, whose existence, besides, he had almost forgotten, for they were so exhausted that they were working in silence, and one could hear only the heavy shuffling of their feet.

And so he broke out—the women were just leaning against the desk in the next room to catch their breath for a minute—changed his course four times, he really didn't know what to salvage first, then he saw hanging conspicuously on the wall, which was otherwise bare already, the picture of the lady all dressed in furs, hurriedly crawled up on it and pressed himself against the glass, which gave a good surface to stick to and soothed his hot belly. At least no one would take away this picture, while Gregor completely covered it up. He turned his head toward the living-room door to watch the women when they returned.

They had not given themselves much of a rest and were already coming back; Grete had put her arm around her mother and was practically carrying her. "So what should we take now?" said Grete and looked around. At that her eyes met Gregor's as he clung to the wall. Probably only because of her mother's presence she kept her self-control, bent her head down to her mother to keep her from looking around, and said, though in a quavering and thoughtless voice: "Come, we'd better go back into the living room for a minute." Grete's intent was clear to Gregor, she wanted to bring his mother into safety and then chase him down from the wall. Well, just let her try! He squatted on his picture and would not give it up. He would rather fly in Grete's face.

But Grete's words had now made her mother really anxious; she stepped to one side, caught sight of the gigantic brown blotch on the flowered wallpaper, and before it really dawned on her that what she saw was Gregor, cried in a hoarse, bawling voice: "Oh, God, Oh, God!"; and as if giving up completely, she fell with outstretched arms across the couch and did not stir. "You, Gregor!" cried his sister with raised fist and piercing eyes. These were the first words she had addressed directly to him since his metamorphosis. She ran into the next room to get some kind of spirits to revive her mother; Gregor wanted to help too—there was time to rescue the picture—but he was stuck to the glass and had to tear himself loose by force; then he too ran into the next room, as if he could give his sister some sort of advice, as in the old days; but then had to stand behind her doing nothing while she rummaged among various little bottles; moreover, when she turned around she was startled, a bottle fell on the floor and broke, a splinter of glass wounded Gregor in the face, some kind of corrosive medicine flowed around him; now without waiting any longer, Grete grabbed as many little bottles as she could carry and ran with them inside to her mother; she slammed the door behind her with her foot. Now Gregor was cut off from his mother, who was perhaps near death through his fault; he could not dare open the door if he did not want to chase away his sister, who had to stay with his mother; now there was nothing for him to do except wait; and tormented by self-reproaches and worry, he began to crawl, crawled over everything, walls, furniture and ceiling, and finally in desperation, as the whole room was beginning to spin, fell down onto the middle of the big table.

A short time passed; Gregor lay there prostrate; all around, things were quiet, perhaps that was a good sign. Then the doorbell rang. The maid, of course, was locked up in her kitchen and so Grete had to answer the door. His father had come home. "What's happened?" were his first words; Grete's appearance must have told him everything. Grete answered in a muffled voice, her face was obviously pressed against her father's chest: "Mother fainted, but she's better now. Gregor's broken out." "I knew it," his father said. "I kept telling you, but you women don't want to listen." It was clear to Gregor that his father had put the worst interpretation on Grete's all-too-brief announcement and assumed that Gregor was guilty of some outrage. Therefore Gregor now had to try to calm his father down, since he had neither the time nor the ability to enlighten him. And so he fled to the door of his room and pressed himself against it for his father to see, as soon as he came into the foyer, that Gregor had the best intentions of returning to his room immediately and that it was not necessary to drive him back; if only the door were opened for him, he would disappear at once.

But his father was in no mood to notice such subtleties; "Ah!" he cried as he entered, in a tone that sounded as if he were at once furious and glad. Gregor turned his head away from the door and lifted it toward his father. He had not really imagined his father looking like this, as he stood in front of him now; admittedly Gregor had been too absorbed recently in his newfangled crawling to bother as much as before about events in the rest of the house and should really have been prepared to find some changes. And yet, and yet—was this still his father? Was this the same man who in the old days used to lie wearily buried in bed when Gregor left on a business trip; who greeted him on his return in the evening, sitting in his bathrobe in the armchair, who actually had difficulty getting to his feet but as a sign of joy only lifted up his arms; and who, on the rare occasions when the whole family went out for a walk, on a few Sundays in June and on the major holidays, used to shuffle along with great effort between Gregor and his mother, who were slow walkers themselves, always a little more slowly than they, wrapped in his old overcoat, always carefully planting down his crutch-handled cane, and, when he wanted to say something, nearly always stood still and assembled his escort around him? Now, however, he was holding himself very erect, dressed in a tight-fitting blue uniform with gold buttons, the kind worn by messengers at banking concerns; above the high stiff collar of the jacket his heavy chin protruded; under his bushy eyebrows his black eyes darted bright, piercing glances; his usually rumpled white hair was combed flat, with a scrupulously exact, gleaming part. He threw his cap—which was adorned with a gold monogram, probably that of a bank—in an arc across the entire room onto the couch, and with the tails of his long uniform jacket slapped back, his hands in his pants pockets, went for Gregor with a sullen look on his face. He probably did not know himself what he had in mind; still he lifted his feet unusually high off the floor, and Gregor staggered at the gigantic size of the soles of his boots. But he did not linger over this, he had known right from the first day of his new life that his father considered only the strictest treatment called for in dealing with him. And so he ran ahead of his father, stopped when his father stood still, and scooted ahead again when his father made even the slightest movement. In this way they made more than one tour of the room, without anything decisive happening; in fact the whole movement did not even have the appearance of a chase because of its slow tempo. So Gregor kept to the floor for the time being, especially since he was afraid that his father might interpret a flight onto the walls or the ceiling as a piece of particular nastiness. Of course Gregor had to admit that he would not be able to keep up even this running for long, for whenever his father took one step, Gregor had to execute countless movements. He was already beginning to feel winded, just as in the old days he had not had very reliable lungs. As he now staggered around, hardly keeping his eyes open in order to gather all his strength for the running; in his obtuseness not thinking of any escape other than by running; and having almost forgotten that the walls were at his disposal, though here of course they were blocked up with elaborately carved furniture full of notches and points—at that moment a lightly flung object hit the floor right near him and rolled in front of him. It was an apple; a second one came flying right after it; Gregor stopped dead with fear; further running was useless, for his father was determined to bombard him. He had filled his pockets from the fruit bowl on the buffet and was now pitching one apple after another, for the time being without taking good aim. These little red apples rolled around on the floor as if electrified, clicking into each another. One apple, thrown weakly, grazed Gregor's back and slid off harmlessly. But the very next one that came flying after it literally forced its way into Gregor's back; Gregor tried to drag himself away, as if the startling, unbelievable pain might disappear with a change of place; but he felt nailed to the spot and stretched out his body in a complete confusion of all his senses. With his last glance he saw the door of his room burst open as his mother rushed out ahead of his screaming sister, in her chemise, for his sister had partly undressed her while she was unconscious in order to let her breathe more freely; saw his mother run up to his father and on the way her unfastened petticoats slide to the floor one by one; and saw as, stumbling over the skirts, she forced herself onto his father, and embracing him, in complete union with him—but now Gregor's sight went dim—her hands clasping his father's neck, begged for Gregor's life.

3

Gregor's serious wound, from which he suffered for over a month—the apple remained imbedded in his flesh as a visible souvenir since no one dared to remove it—seemed to have reminded even his father that Gregor was a member of the family, in spite of his present pathetic and repulsive shape, who could not be treated as an enemy; that, on the contrary, it was the commandment of family duty to swallow their disgust and endure him, endure him and nothing more.

And now, although Gregor had lost some of his mobility probably for good because of his wound, and although for the time being he needed long, long minutes to get across his room, like an old war veteran—crawling above ground was out of the question—for this deterioration of his situation he was granted compensation which in his view was entirely satisfactory: every day around dusk the living-room door—which he was in the habit of watching closely for an hour or two beforehand—was opened, so that, lying in the darkness of his room, invisible from the living room, he could see the whole family sitting at the table under the lamp and could listen to their conversation, as it were with general permission; and so it was completely different from before.

Of course these were no longer the animated conversations of the old days, which Gregor used to remember with a certain nostalgia in small hotel rooms when he'd had to throw himself wearily into the damp bedding. Now things were mostly very quiet. Soon after supper his father would fall asleep in his armchair; his mother and sister would caution each other to be quiet; his mother, bent low under the light, sewed delicate lingerie for a clothing store; his sister, who had taken a job as a sales-girl, was learning shorthand and French in the evenings in order to attain a better position some time in the future. Sometimes his father woke up, and as if he had absolutely no idea that he had been asleep, said to his mother, "Look how long you're sewing again today!" and went right back to sleep, while mother and sister smiled wearily at each other.

With a kind of perverse obstinacy his father refused to take off his official uniform even in the house; and while his robe hung uselessly on the clothes hook, his father dozed, completely dressed, in his chair, as if he were always ready for duty and were waiting even here for the voice of his superior. As a result his uniform, which had not been new to start with, began to get dirty in spite of all the mother's and sister's care, and Gregor would often stare all evening long at this garment, covered with stains and gleaming with its constantly polished gold buttons, in which the old man slept most uncomfortably and yet peacefully.

As soon as the clock struck ten, his mother tried to awaken his father with soft encouraging words and then persuade him to go to bed, for this was no place to sleep properly, and his father badly needed his sleep, since he had to be at work at six o'clock. But with the obstinacy that had possessed him ever since he had become a messenger, he always insisted on staying at the table a little longer, although he invariably fell asleep and then could be persuaded only with the greatest effort to exchange his armchair for bed. However much mother and sister might pounce on him with little admonitions, he would slowly shake his head for a quarter of an hour at a time, keeping his eyes closed, and would not get up. Gregor's mother plucked him by the sleeves, whispered blandishments into his ear, his sister dropped her homework in order to help her mother, but all this was of no use. He only sank deeper into his armchair. Not until the women lifted him up under his arms did he open his eyes, look alternately at mother and sister, and usually say, "What a life. So this is the peace of my old age." And leaning on the two women, he would get up laboriously, as if he were the greatest weight on himself, and let the women lead him to the door, where, shrugging them off, he would proceed independently, while Gregor's mother threw down her sewing, and his sister her pen, as quickly as possible so as to run after his father and be of further assistance.

Who in this overworked and exhausted family had time to worry about Gregor any more than was absolutely necessary? The household was stinted more and more; now the maid was let go after all; a gigantic bony cleaning woman with white hair fluttering about her head came mornings and evenings to do the heaviest work; his mother took care of everything else, along with all her sewing. It even happened that various pieces of family jewelry, which in the old days his mother and sister had been overjoyed to wear at parties and celebrations, were sold, as Gregor found out one evening from the general discussion of the prices they had fetched. But the biggest complaint was always that they could not give up the apartment, which was much too big for their present needs, since no one could figure out how Gregor was supposed to be moved. But Gregor understood easily that it was not only consideration for him which prevented their moving, for he could easily have been transported in a suitable crate with a few air holes; what mainly prevented the family from moving was their complete hopelessness and the thought that they had been struck by a misfortune as none of their relatives and acquaintances had ever been hit. What the world demands of poor people they did to the utmost of their ability; his father brought breakfast for the minor officials at the bank, his mother sacrificed herself to the underwear of strangers, his sister ran back and forth behind the counter at the request of the customers; but for anything more than this they did not have the strength. And the wound in Gregor's back began to hurt anew when mother and sister, after getting his father to bed, now came back, dropped their work, pulled their chairs close to each other and sat cheek to cheek; when his mother, pointing to Gregor's room, said, "Close that door, Grete"; and when Gregor was back in darkness, while in the other room the women mingled their tears or stared dry-eyed at the table.

Gregor spent the days and nights almost entirely without sleep. Sometimes he thought that the next time the door opened he would take charge of the family's affairs again, just as he had done in the old days; after this long while there again appeared in his thoughts the boss and the manager, the salesmen and the trainees, the handyman who was so dense, two or three friends from other firms, a chambermaid in a provincial hotel—a happy fleeting memory—a cashier in a millinery store, whom he had courted earnestly but too slowly—they all appeared, intermingled with strangers or people he had already forgotten; but instead of helping him and his family, they were all inaccessible, and he was glad when they faded away. At other times he was in no mood to worry about his family, he was completely filled with rage at his miserable treatment, and although he could not imagine anything that would pique his appetite, he still made plans for getting into the pantry to take what was coming to him, even if he wasn't hungry. No longer considering what she could do to give Gregor a special treat, his sister, before running to business every morning and afternoon, hurriedly shoved any old food into Gregor's room with her foot; and in the evening, regardless of whether the food had only been toyed with or—the most usual case— had been left completely untouched, she swept it out with a swish of the broom. The cleaning up of Gregor's room, which she now always did in the evenings, could not be done more hastily. Streaks of dirt ran along the walls, fluffs of dust and filth lay here and there on the floor. At first, whenever his sister came in, Gregor would place himself in those corners which were particularly offending, meaning by his position in a sense to reproach her. But he could probably have stayed there for weeks without his sister's showing any improvement; she must have seen the dirt as clearly as he did, but she had just decided to leave it. At the same time she made sure—with an irritableness that was completely new to her and which had in fact infected the whole family—that the cleaning of Gregor's room remain her province. One time his mother had submitted Gregor's room to a major housecleaning, which she managed only after employing a couple of pails of water—all this dampness, of course, irritated Gregor too and he lay prostrate, sour and immobile, on the couch—but his mother's punishment was not long in coming. For hardly had his sister noticed the difference in Gregor's room that evening than, deeply insulted, she ran into the living room and, in spite of her mother's imploringly uplifted hands, burst out in a fit of crying, which his parents—his father had naturally been startled out of his armchair—at first watched in helpless amazement; until they too got going; turning to the right, his father blamed his mother for not letting his sister clean Gregor's room; but turning to the left, he screamed at his sister that she would never again be allowed to clean Gregor's room; while his mother tried to drag his father, who was out of his mind with excitement, into the bedroom; his sister, shaken with sobs, hammered the table with her small fists; and Gregor hissed loudly with rage because it did not occur to any of them to close the door and spare him such a scene and a row.

But even if his sister, exhausted from her work at the store, had gotten fed up with taking care of Gregor as she used to, it was not necessary at all for his mother to take her place and still Gregor did not have to be neglected. For now the cleaning woman was there. This old widow, who thanks to her strong bony frame had probably survived the worst in a long life, was not really repelled by Gregor. Without being in the least inquisitive, she had once accidentally opened the door of Gregor's room, and at the sight of Gregor—who, completely taken by surprise, began to race back and forth although no one was chasing him—she had remained standing, with her hands folded on her stomach, marveling. From that time on she never failed to open the door a crack every morning and every evening and peek in hurriedly at Gregor. In the beginning she also used to call him over to her with words she probably considered friendly, like, "Come over here for a minute, you old dung beetle!" or "Look at that old dung beetle!" To forms of address like these Gregor would not respond but remained immobile where he was, as if the door had not been opened. If only they had given this cleaning woman orders to clean up his room every day, instead of letting her disturb him uselessly whenever the mood took her. Once, early in the morning— heavy rain, perhaps already a sign of approaching spring, was beating on the window panes—Gregor was so exasperated when the cleaning woman started in again with her phrases that he turned on her, of course slowly and decrepitly, as if to attack. But the cleaning woman, instead of getting frightened, simply lifted up high a chair near the door, and as she stood there with her mouth wide open, her intention was clearly to shut her mouth only when the chair in her hand came crashing down on Gregor's back. "So, is that all there is?" she asked when Gregor turned around again, and she quietly put the chair back in the corner.

Gregor now hardly ate anything anymore. Only when he accidentally passed the food laid out for him would he take a bite into his mouth just for fun, hold it in for hours, and then mostly spit it out again. At first he thought that his grief at the state of his room kept him off food, but it was the very changes in his room to which he quickly became adjusted. His family had gotten into the habit of putting in this room things for which they could not find any other place, and now there were plenty of these, since one of the rooms in the apartment had been rented to three boarders. These serious gentlemen—all three had long beards, as Gregor was able to register once through a crack in the door—were obsessed with neatness, not only in their room, but since they had, after all, moved in here, throughout the entire household and especially in the kitchen. They could not stand useless, let alone dirty junk. Besides, they had brought along most of their own household goods. For this reason many things had become superfluous, and though they certainly weren't salable, on the other hand they could not just be thrown out. All these things migrated into Gregor's room. Likewise the ash can and the garbage can from the kitchen. Whatever was not being used at the moment was just flung into Gregor's room by the cleaning woman, who was always in a big hurry; fortunately Gregor generally saw only the object involved and the hand that held it. Maybe the cleaning woman intended to reclaim the things as soon as she had a chance or else to throw out everything together in one fell swoop, but in fact they would have remained lying wherever they had been thrown in the first place if Gregor had not squeezed through the junk and set it in motion, at first from necessity, because otherwise there would have been no room to crawl in, but later with growing pleasure, although after such excursions, tired to death and sad, he did not budge again for hours.

Since the roomers sometimes also had their supper at home in the common living room, the living-room door remained closed on certain evenings, but Gregor found it very easy to give up the open door, for on many evenings when it was opened he had not taken advantage of it, but instead, without the family's noticing, had lain in the darkest corner of his room. But once the cleaning woman had left the living-room door slightly open, and it also remained opened a little when the roomers came in in the evening and the lamp was lit. They sat down at the head of the table where in the old days his father, his mother, and Gregor had eaten, unfolded their napkins, and picked up their knives and forks. At once his mother appeared in the doorway with a platter of meat, and just behind her came his sister with a platter piled high with potatoes. A thick vapor steamed up from the food. The roomers bent over the platters set in front of them as if to examine them before eating, and in fact the one who sat in the middle, and who seemed to be regarded by the other two as an authority, cut into a piece of meat while it was still on the platter, evidently to find out whether it was tender enough or whether it should perhaps be sent back to the kitchen. He was satisfied, and mother and sister, who had been watching anxiously, sighed with relief and began to smile.

The family itself ate in the kitchen. Nevertheless, before going into the kitchen, his father came into this room and, bowing once, cap in hand, made a turn around the table. The roomers rose as one man and mumbled something into their beards. When they were alone again, they ate in almost complete silence. It seemed strange to Gregor that among all the different noises of eating he kept picking up the sound of their chewing teeth, as if this were a sign to Gregor that you needed teeth to eat with and that even with the best make of toothless jaws you couldn't do a thing. "I'm hungry enough," Gregor said to himself, full of grief, "but not for these things. Look how these roomers are gorging themselves, and I'm dying!"

On this same evening—Gregor could not remember having heard the violin during the whole time—the sound of violin playing came from the kitchen. The roomers had already finished their evening meal, the one in the middle had taken out a newspaper, given each of the two others a page, and now, leaning back, they read and smoked. When the violin began to play, they became attentive, got up, and went on tiptoe to the door leading to the foyer, where they stood in a huddle. They must have been heard in the kitchen, for his father called, "Perhaps the playing bothers you, gentlemen? It can be stopped right away." "On the contrary," said the middle roomer. "Wouldn't the young lady like to come in to us and play in here where it's much roomier and more comfortable?" "Oh, certainly," called Gregor's father, as if he were the violinist. The boarders went back into the room and waited. Soon Gregor's father came in with the music stand, his mother with the sheet music, and his sister with the violin. Calmly his sister got everything ready for playing; his parents—who had never rented out rooms before and therefore behaved toward the roomers with excessive politeness—did not even dare sit down on their own chairs; his father leaned against the door, his right hand inserted between two buttons of his uniform coat, which he kept closed; but his mother was offered a chair by one of the roomers, and since she left the chair where the roomer just happened to put it, she sat in a corner to one side.

His sister began to play. Father and mother, from either side, attentively followed the movements of her hands. Attracted by the playing, Gregor had dared to come out a little further and already had his head in the living room. It hardly surprised him that lately he was showing so little consideration for the others; once such consideration had been his greatest pride. And yet he would never have had better reason to keep hidden; for now, because of the dust which lay all over his room and blew around at the slightest movement, he too was completely covered with dust; he dragged around with him on his back and along his sides fluff and hairs and scraps of food; his indifference to everything was much too deep for him to have gotten on his back and scrubbed himself clean against the carpet, as once he had done several times a day. And in spite of his state, he was not ashamed to inch out a little farther on the immaculate living-room floor.

Admittedly no one paid any attention to him. The family was completely absorbed by the violin-playing; the roomers, on the other hand, who at first had stationed themselves, hands in pockets, much too close behind his sister's music stand, so that they could all have followed the score, which certainly must have upset his sister, soon withdrew to the window, talking to each other in an undertone, their heads lowered, where they remained, anxiously watched by his father. It now seemed only too obvious that they were disappointed in their expectation of hearing beautiful or entertaining violin-playing, had had enough of the whole performance, and continued to let their peace be disturbed only out of politeness. Especially the way they all blew the cigar smoke out of their nose and mouth toward the ceiling suggested great nervousness. And yet his sister was playing so beautifully. Her face was inclined to one side, sadly and probingly her eyes followed the lines of music. Gregor crawled forward a little farther, holding his head close to the floor, so that it might be possible to catch her eye. Was he an animal, that music could move him so? He felt as if the way to the unknown nourishment he longed for were coming to light. He was determined to force himself on until he reached his sister, to pluck at her skirt, and to let her know in this way that she should bring her violin into his room, for no one here appreciated her playing the way he would appreciate it. He would never again let her out of his room—at least not for as long as he lived; for once, his nightmarish looks would be of use to him; he would be at all the doors of his room at the same time and hiss and spit at the aggressors; his sister, however, should not be forced to stay with him, but would do so of her own free will; she should sit next to him on the couch, bending her ear down to him, and then he would confide to her that he had had the firm intention of sending her to the Conservatory, and that, if the catastrophe had not intervened, he would have announced this to everyone last Christmas—certainly Christmas had come and gone?—without taking notice of any objections. After this declaration his sister would burst into tears of emotion, and Gregor would raise himself up to her shoulder and kiss her on the neck which, ever since she started going out to work, she kept bare, without a ribbon or collar.

"Mr. Samsa!" the middle roomer called to Gregor's father and without wasting another word pointed his index finger at Gregor, who was slowly moving forward. The violin stopped, the middle roomer smiled first at his friends, shaking his head, and then looked at Gregor again. Rather than driving Gregor out, his father seemed to consider it more urgent to start by soothing the roomers although they were not at all upset, and Gregor seemed to be entertaining them more than the violin-playing. He rushed over to them and tried with outstretched arms to drive them into their room and at the same time with his body to block their view of Gregor. Now they actually did get a little angry—it was not clear whether because of his father's behavior or because of their dawning realization of having had without knowing it such a next door neighbor as Gregor. They demanded explanations from his father; in their turn they raised their arms, plucked excitedly at their beards, and, dragging

THE METAMORPHOSIS

777

their feet, backed off toward their room. In the meantime his sister had overcome the abstracted mood into which she had fallen after her playing had been so suddenly interrupted; and all at once, after holding violin and bow for a while in her slackly hanging hands and continuing to follow the score as if she were still playing, she pulled herself together, laid the instrument on the lap of her mother—who was still sitting in her chair, fighting for breath, her lungs violently heaving—and ran into the next room, which the roomers, under pressure from her father, were nearing more quickly than before. One could see the covers and bolsters on the beds, obeying his sister's practiced hands, fly up and arrange themselves. Before the boarders had reached the room, she had finished turning down the beds and had slipped out. Her father seemed once again to be gripped by his perverse obstinacy to such a degree that he completely forgot any respect still due his tenants. He drove them on and kept on driving until, already at the bedroom door, the middle boarder stamped his foot thunderingly and thus brought him to a standstill. "I herewith declare," he said, raising his hand and casting his eyes around for Gregor's mother and sister too, "that in view of the disgusting conditions prevailing in this apartment and family"—here he spat curtly and decisively on the floor—"I give notice as of now. Of course I won't pay a cent for the days I have been living here, either; on the contrary, I shall consider taking some sort of action against you with claims that—believe me—will be easy to substantiate." He stopped and looked straight in front of him, as if he were expecting something. And in fact his two friends at once chimed in with the words, "We too give notice as of now." Thereupon he grabbed the door knob and slammed the door with a bang.

Gregor's father, his hands groping, staggered to his armchair and collapsed into it; it looked as if he were stretching himself out for his usual evening nap, but the heavy drooping of his head, as if it had lost all support, showed that he was certainly not asleep. All this time Gregor had lain quietly at the spot where the roomers had surprised him. His disappointment at the failure of his plan—but perhaps also the weakness caused by so much fasting—made it impossible for him to move. He was afraid with some certainty that in the very next moment a general debacle would burst over him, and he waited. He was not even startled by the violin as it slipped from under his mother's trembling fingers and fell off her lap with a reverberating clang.

"My dear parents," said his sister and by way of an introduction pounded her hand on the table, "things can't go on like this. Maybe you don't realize it, but I do. I won't pronounce the name of my brother in front of this monster, and so all I say is: we have to try to get rid of it. We've done everything humanly possible to take care of it and to put up with it; I don't think anyone can blame us in the least."

"She's absolutely right," said his father to himself. His mother, who still could not catch her breath, began to cough dully behind her hand, a wild look in her eyes.

His sister rushed over to his mother and held her forehead. His father seemed to have been led by Grete's words to more definite thoughts, had sat up, was playing with the cap of his uniform among the plates which were still lying on the table from the roomers' supper, and from time to time looked at Gregor's motionless form.

"We must try to get rid of it," his sister now said exclusively to her father, since her mother was coughing too hard to hear anything. "It will be the death of you two, I can see it coming. People who already have to work as hard as we do can't put up with this constant torture at home, too. I can't stand it anymore either." And she broke out crying so bitterly that her tears poured down onto her mother's face, which she wiped off with mechanical movements of her hand.

"Child," said her father kindly and with unusual understanding, "but what can we do?"

Gregor's sister only shrugged her shoulders as a sign of the bewildered mood that had now gripped her as she cried, in contrast with her earlier confidence.

"If he could understand us," said her father, half questioning; in the midst of her crying Gregor's sister waved her hand violently as a sign that that was out of the question.

"If he could understand us," his father repeated and by closing his eyes, absorbed his daughter's conviction of the impossibility of the idea, "then maybe we could come to an agreement with him. But the way things are——"

"It has to go," cried his sister. "That's the only answer, Father. You just have to try to get rid of the idea that it's Gregor. Believing it for so long, that is our real misfortune. But how can it be Gregor? If it were Gregor, he would have realized long ago that it isn't possible for human beings to live with such a creature, and he would have gone away of his own free will. Then we wouldn't have a brother, but we'd be able to go on living and honor his memory. But as things are, this animal persecutes us, drives the roomers away, obviously wants to occupy the whole apartment and for us to sleep in the gutter. Look, Father," she suddenly shrieked, "he's starting in again!" And in a fit of terror that was completely incomprehensible to Gregor, his sister abandoned even her mother, literally shoved herself off from her chair, as if she would rather sacrifice her mother than stay near Gregor, and rushed behind her father, who, upset only by her behavior, also stood up and half-lifted his arms in front of her as if to protect her.

But Gregor had absolutely no intention of frightening anyone, let alone his sister. He had only begun to turn around in order to trek back to his room; certainly his movements did look peculiar, since his ailing condition made him help the complicated turning maneuver along with his head, which he lifted up many times and knocked against the floor. He stopped and looked around. His good intention seemed to have been recognized; it had only been a momentary scare. Now they all watched him, silent and sad. His mother lay in her armchair, her legs stretched out and pressed together, her eyes almost closing from exhaustion; his father and his sister sat side by side, his sister had put her arm around her father's neck.

Now maybe they'll let me turn around, Gregor thought and began his labors again. He could not repress his panting from the exertion, and from time to time he had to rest. Otherwise no one harassed him; he was left completely on his own. When he had completed the turn, he immediately began to crawl back in a straight line. He was astonished at the great distance separating him from his room and could not understand at all how, given his weakness, he had covered the same distance a little while ago almost without realizing it. Constantly intent only on rapid crawling, he hardly noticed that not a word, not an exclamation from his family interrupted him. Only when he was already in the doorway did he turn his head—not completely, for he felt his neck stiffening; nevertheless he still saw that behind him nothing had changed except that his sister had gotten up. His last glance ranged over his mother, who was now fast asleep.

He was hardly inside his room when the door was hurriedly slammed shut, firmly bolted, and locked. Gregor was so frightened at the sudden noise behind him that his little legs gave way under him. It was his sister who had been in such a hurry. She had been standing up straight, ready and waiting, then she had leaped forward nimbly, Gregor had not even heard her coming, and she cried "Finally!" to her parents as she turned the key in the lock.

"And now?" Gregor asked himself, looking around in the darkness. He soon made the discovery that he could no longer move at all. It did not surprise him; rather, it seemed unnatural that until now he had actually been able to propel himself on these thin little legs. Otherwise he felt relatively comfortable. He had pains, of course, throughout his whole body, but it seemed to him that they were gradually getting fainter and fainter and would finally go away altogether. The rotten apple in his back and the inflamed area around it, which were completely covered with fluffy dust, already hardly bothered him. He thought back on his family with deep emotion and love. His conviction that he would have to disappear was, if possible, even firmer than his sister's. He remained in this state of empty and peaceful reflection until the tower clock struck three in the morning. He still saw that outside the window everything was beginning to grow light. Then, without his consent, his head sank down to the floor, and from his nostrils streamed his last weak breath.

When early in the morning the cleaning woman came—in sheer energy and impatience she would slam all the doors so hard although she had often been asked not to, that once she arrived, quiet sleep was no longer possible anywhere in the apartment—she did not at first find anything out of the ordinary on paying Gregor her usual short visit. She thought that he was deliberately lying motionless, pretending that his feelings were hurt; she credited him with unlimited intelligence. Because she happened to be holding the long broom, she tried from the doorway to tickle Gregor with it. When this too produced no results, she became annoyed and jabbed Gregor a little, and only when she had shoved him without any resistance to another spot did she begin to take notice. When she quickly became aware of the true state of things, she opened her eyes wide, whistled softly, but did not dawdle; instead, she tore open the door of the bedroom and shouted at the top of her voice into the darkness: "Come and have a look, it's croaked; it's lying there, dead as a doornail!"

The couple Mr. and Mrs. Samsa sat up in their marriage bed and had a struggle overcoming their shock at the cleaning woman before they could finally grasp her message. But then Mr. and Mrs. Samsa hastily scrambled out of bed, each on his side, Mr. Samsa threw the blanket around his shoulders, Mrs. Samsa came out in nothing but her nightgown; dressed this way, they entered Gregor's room. In the meantime the door of the living room had also opened, where Grete had been sleeping since the roomers had moved in; she was fully dressed, as if she had not been asleep at all; and her pale face seemed to confirm this. "Dead?" said Mrs. Samsa and looked inquiringly at the cleaning woman, although she could scrutinize everything for herself and could recognize the truth even without scrunity. "I'll say," said the cleaning woman, and to prove it she pushed Gregor's corpse with her broom a good distance sideways. Mrs. Samsa made a movement as if to hold the broom back but did not do it. "Well," said Mr. Samsa, "now we can thank God!" He crossed himself, and the three women followed his example. Grete, who never took her eyes off the corpse, said, "Just look how thin he was. Of course he didn't eat anything for such a long time. The food came out again just the way it went in." As a matter of fact, Gregor's body was completely flat and dry; this was obvious now for the first time, really, since the body was no longer raised up by his little legs and nothing else distracted the eye.

"Come in with us for a little while, Grete," said Mrs. Samsa with a melancholy smile, and Grete, not without looking back at the corpse, followed her parents into their bedroom. The cleaning woman shut the door and opened the window wide. Although it was early in the morning, there was already some mildness mixed in with the fresh air. After all, it was already the end of March.

The three boarders came out of their room and looked around in astonishment for their breakfast; they had been forgotten. "Where's breakfast?" the middle roomer grumpily asked the cleaning woman. But she put her finger to her lips and then hastily and silently beckoned the boarders to follow her into Gregor's room. They came willingly and then stood, their hands in the pockets of their somewhat shabby jackets, in the now already very bright room, surrounding Gregor's corpse.

At that point the bedroom door opened, and Mr. Samsa appeared in his uniform, his wife on one arm, his daughter on the other. They all looked as if they had been crying; from time to time Grete pressed her face against her father's sleeve.

"Leave my house immediately," said Mr. Samsa and pointed to the door, without letting go of the women. "What do you mean by that?" said the middle roomer, somewhat nonplussed, and smiled with a sugary smile. The two others held their hands behind their back and incessantly rubbed them together, as if in joyful anticipation of a big argument, which could only turn out in their favor. "I mean just what I say," answered Mr. Samsa and with his two companions marched in a straight line toward the roomer. At first the roomer stood still and looked at the floor, as if the thoughts inside his head were fitting themselves together in a new order. "So, we'll go, then," he said and looked up at Mr. Samsa as if, suddenly overcome by a fit of humility, he were asking for further permission even for this decision. Mr. Samsa merely nodded briefly several times, his eyes wide open. Thereupon the roomer actually went immediately into the foyer, taking long strides; his two friends had already been listening for a while, their hands completely still, and now they went hopping right after him, as if afraid that Mr. Samsa might get into the foyer ahead of them and interrupt the contact with their leader. In the foyer all three took their hats from the coatrack, pulled their canes from the umbrella stand, bowed silently, and left the apartment. In a suspicious mood which proved completely unfounded, Mr. Samsa led the two women out onto the landing; leaning over the banister, they watched the three roomers slowly but steadily going down the long flight of stairs, disappearing on each landing at a particular turn of the stairway and a few moments later emerging again; the farther down they got, the more the Samsa family's interest in them wore off, and when a butcher's boy with a carrier on his head came climbing up the stairs with a proud bearing, toward them and then up on past them, Mr. Samsa and the women quickly left the banister and all went back, as if relieved, into their apartment.

They decided to spend this day resting and going for a walk; they not only deserved a break in their work, they absolutely needed one. And so they sat down at the table and wrote three letters of excuse, Mr. Samsa to the management of the bank, Mrs. Samsa to her employer, and Grete to the store owner. While they were writing, the cleaning woman came in to say that she was going, since her morning's work was done. The three letter writers at first simply nodded without looking up, but as the cleaning woman still kept lingering, they looked up, annoyed. "Well?" asked Mr. Samsa. The cleaning woman stood smiling in the doorway, as if she had some great good news to announce to the family but would do so only if she were thoroughly questioned. The little ostrich feather which stood almost upright on her hat and which had irritated Mr. Samsa the whole time she had been with them swayed lightly in all directions. "What do you want?" asked Mrs. Samsa, who inspired the most respect in the cleaning woman. "Well," the cleaning woman answered, and for good-natured laughter could not immediately go on, "look, you don't have to worry about getting rid of the stuff next door. It's already been taken care of." Mrs. Samsa and Grete bent down over their letters, as if to continue writing; Mr. Samsa, who noticed that the cleaning woman was now about to start describing everything in detail, stopped her with a firmly outstretched hand. But since she was not going to be permitted to tell her story, she remembered that she was in a great hurry, cried, obviously insulted, "So long, everyone," whirled around wildly, and left the apartment with a terrible slamming of doors.

"We'll fire her tonight," said Mr. Samsa, but did not get an answer from either his wife or his daughter, for the cleaning woman seemed to have ruined their barely regained peace of mind. They got up, went to the window, and stayed there, holding each other tight. Mr. Samsa turned around in his chair toward them and watched them quietly for a while. Then he called, "Come on now, come over here. Stop brooding over the past. And have a little consideration for me, too." The women obeyed him at once, hurried over to him, fondled him, and quickly finished their letters.

Then all three of them left the apartment together, something they had not done in months, and took the trolley into the open country on the outskirts of the city. The car, in which they were the only passengers, was completely filled with warm sunshine. Leaning back comfortably in their seats, they discussed their prospects for the time to come, and it seemed on closer examination that these weren't bad at all, for all three positions—about which they had never really asked one another in any detail—were exceedingly advantageous and especially promising for the future. The greatest immediate improvement in their situation would come easily, of course, from a change in apartments; they would now take a smaller and cheaper apartment, but one better situated and in every way simpler to manage than the old one, which Gregor had picked for them. While they were talking in this vein, it occurred almost simultaneously to Mr. and Mrs. Samsa, as they watched their daughter getting livelier and livelier, that lately, in spite of all the troubles which had turned her cheeks pale, she had blossomed into a good-looking, shapely girl. Growing quieter and communicating almost unconsciously through glances, they thought that it would soon be time, too, to find her a good husband. And it was like a confirmation of their new dreams and good intentions when at the end of the ride their daughter got up first and stretched her young body.

ANNA AKHMATOVA ■ (1889–1966)

Anna Andreyevna Gorenko ("Akhmatova" was an assumed name) was born near Odessa, Ukraine, the daughter of a naval officer. She lived most of her life in Saint Petersburg (Leningrad) and died in Domodedovo, near Moscow. The ups and downs of her life and poetic career are a telling reflection of the tumultuous history of her time. She started writing poetry at age eleven and published her first books of poems in her early twenties shortly after she joined the Poets' Guild, a group that was to found Russian Acmeism. This was the avant-garde of Russian modernism that sought to turn Russian literature away from the belated romanticism being expressed by the poets who referred to themselves as Symbolists. In 1910, Akhmatova married a fellow Acmeist poet, Nikolai Stepanovich Gumilyov, with whom she traveled to Paris and Western Europe in the course of 1910 and 1911. There she met a number of modernist poets and artists, among them the Italian painter Amadeo Modigliani, who drew several portraits of the fetching Akhmatova. She had a son, Lev, by Gumilyov, whom she divorced in 1918. Gumilyov was arrested and shot as a counterrevolutionary in August 1921. Their son would be arrested, in turn, for the first time in 1935 and in 1949 for the third time. He was finally released from prison in 1956.

Akhmatova's third volume of poetry, *The White Flock,* appeared in 1917 just before the Bolshevik Revolution. She went on to publish two more collections of poems, *Plantain* (1921) and *Anno Domini MCMXXI* (1922), after which her career as published poet was interrupted by political vicissitudes until 1940, when she was permitted to resume publication of her poems. During the siege of Leningrad in World War II, Akhmatova was evacuated from the city. She spent the war years in Tashkent, Uzbekistan. Following the war and her return to Leningrad, she was targeted in August 1946 by the cultural freeze under the Stalinist regime, with a Communist Party henchman referring to her as "half-nun, half-whore." Her cycle of poems on the Stalinist terror, *Requiem,* was begun in 1934 with the first arrest of her son but was only published in Munich in 1963. Akhmatova's succinct poetic rendering of her struggles as a poet began with "The Muse," a poem she wrote in 1924 but that wasn't published until 1940. Here, she identifies the source of her strength and reveals as well her identification with another poet, Dante, whose infernal times would find their afterlife in the posterity of poetic expression dictated by the redemptive voice of the muse. After the fall of Stalin, Akhmatova was rehabilitated, and her status became that of a national poet. In 1962 she met with Robert Frost in Leningrad, and in 1965 she traveled to Oxford University, where she was awarded an honorary doctorate in letters. Akhmatova is considered one of Russia's most important poets, and her work is viewed as a monument to the indomitable spirit of Russia's people in the darkest days of the twentieth century.

PRONUNCIATION:
  Akhmatova: akh-MAH-toh-vah

The Muse[1]

  When at night I await her coming,
  It seems that life hangs by a strand.
  What are honors, what is youth, what is freedom,
  Compared to that dear guest with rustic pipe in hand.
5 And she entered. Drawing aside her shawl
  She gazed attentively at me.
  I said to her: "Was it you who dictated to Dante
  The pages of *The Inferno?*"[2] She replied: "It was I."

I am not with those[1]

  I am not with those who abandoned their land
  To the lacerations of the enemy.
  I am deaf to their coarse flattery,
  I won't give them my songs.

1. Translated by Judith Hemschemeyer.
2. Dante Alighieri (1265–1321), Florentine poet and author of the *Divine Comedy,* of which *The Inferno* is the first part.
1. Translated by Judith Hemschemeyer.

5   But to me the exile is forever pitiful,
    Like a prisoner, like someone ill.
    Dark is your road, wanderer,
    Like wormwood smells the bread of strangers.

    But here, in the blinding smoke of the conflagration
10   Destroying what's left of youth,
    We have not deflected from ourselves
    One single stroke.

    And we know that in the final accounting,
    Each hour will be justified . . .
15   But there is no people on earth more tearless
    More simple and more full of pride.

July 1922
Petersburg

Boris Pasternak[1]

    He who compared himself to a horse's eye,
    squints, looks, sees, recognises,
    and already the puddles shine
    like a fused diamond, the ice pines away.

5   The backwoods rest in a lilac haze,
    platforms, logs, leaves, clouds,
    the engine whistles, the crunch of melon peel,
    a timid hand in a fragrant kid glove.

    There is a ringing, a thundering, a gnashing, the crash of surf,
10   and then suddenly quiet: this means
    he is treading the pine needles, fearful lest
    he should scare awake the light dream-sleep of space.

    This means he is counting the grains
    in the empty ears; this means
15   he has come again from some funeral
    to the cursed, black, Daryal Gorge.[2]

    Moscow languor burns again,
    death's little bells ring in the distance—
    Who has got lost two steps from home,
20   where the snow is waist deep and an end to everything?

    For comparing smoke with Laocoön,[3]
    for singing of the graveyard thistle,

---

1. Translated by Richard McKane. Boris Pasternak (1890–1960) was a Russian poet and translator who was most influential in Russian poetry of the 20th century. Akhmatova wrote this poem in 1936, after Pasternak had run afoul of Stalin's repression of experimental poetry and was not allowed to publish.

2. Located in the central Caucasus Mountains of what was then Soviet Georgia. A historic passage and invasion route between east and west, it appears in Mikhail Lermontov's narrative poem *The Demon* (1829–1841).

3. Ancient sculptural grouping found in Rome in 1506, it depicts the Trojan priest Laocoön, who was strangled with his sons by sea snakes sent by the gods who favored the Greeks in the Trojan War because he tried to warn the Trojans against bringing the wooden horse into the city (Virgil, *Aeneid*, bk. 2).

for filling the earth with a new sound
in a new space of mirrored stanzas,

25   he is rewarded with a form of eternal childhood,
with the bounty and vigilance of the stars,
the whole world was his inheritance
and he shared it with everyone.

Why is this century worse[1]

Why is this century worse than those that have gone before?
In a stupor of sorrow and grief
it located the blackest wound
but somehow couldn't heal it.
5   The earth's sun is still shining in the West
and the roofs of towns sparkle in its rays,
while here death marks houses with crosses
and calls in the crows and the crows fly over.

Requiem[1]

1935–1940

No, not under the vault of alien skies,[2]
And not under the shelter of alien wings—
I was with my people then,
There, where my people, unfortunately, were.

1961

Instead of a Preface

In the terrible years of the Yezhov terror,[3] I spent seventeen months in the prison lines
of Leningrad. Once, someone "recognized" me. Then a woman with bluish lips standing behind me, who of course had never heard me called by name before, woke up
from the stupor to which everyone had succumbed and whispered in my ear (everyone
spoke in whispers there):
    "Can you describe this?"
    And I answered: "Yes, I can."
    Then something that looked like a smile passed over what had once been her face.

April 1, 1957
Leningrad

Dedication

Mountains bow down to this grief,
Mighty rivers cease to flow,

---

1. Translated by Richard McKane.

1. Translated by Judith Hemschemeyer. The poem's verses were written at various times during and after the imprisonment
of her son, Lev Gumilyov, in 1935 and the arrest of her lover Nikolai Punin later that year. Her son was arrested again in
1939 and condemned to a labor camp in Siberia, where he remained until 1941; he was imprisoned again from 1949–1956.

2. Quoting "Message to Siberia," by Alexander Pushkin (1799–1837).

3. A major purge in 1937–1938, led by Nikolai Yezhov, head of Stalin's secret police.

But the prison gates hold firm,
And behind them are the "prisoners' burrows"
5   And mortal woe,
For someone a fresh breeze blows,
For someone the sunset luxuriates—
We wouldn't know, we are those who everywhere
Hear only the rasp of the hateful key
10   And the soldiers' heavy tread.
We rose as if for an early service,
Trudged through the savaged capital
And met there, more lifeless than the dead;
The sun is lower and the Neva[4] mistier,
15   But hope keeps singing from afar.
The verdict...And her tears gush forth,
Already she is cut off from the rest,
As if they painfully wrenched life from her heart,
As if they brutally knocked her flat,
20   But she goes on...Staggering...Alone...
Where now are my chance friends
Of those two diabolical years?
What do they imagine is in Siberia's storms,[5]
What appears to them dimly in the circle of the moon?
25   I am sending my farewell greeting to them.

March 1940

Prologue

That was when the ones who smiled
Were the dead, glad to be at rest.
And like a useless appendage, Leningrad
Swung from its prisons.
30   And when, senseless from torment,
Regiments of convicts marched,
And the short songs of farewell
Were sung by locomotive whistles.
The stars of death stood above us
35   And innocent Russia writhed
Under bloody boots
And under the tires of the Black Marias.[6]

I

They led you away at dawn,
I followed you, like a mourner,

4. The famous river around which St. Petersburg (Leningrad) was built.
5. Wives of male prisoners spared execution were allowed to move to Siberia, to be near their husbands' prison camps.
6. Police vans.

40 In the dark front room the children were crying,
By the icon shelf the candle was dying.
On your lips was the icon's chill.[7]
The deathly sweat on your brow...Unforgettable!—
I will be like the wives of the Streltsy,[8]
45 Howling under the Kremlin towers.

1935

II

Quietly flows the quiet Don,[9]
Yellow moon slips into a home.

He slips in with cap askew,
He sees a shadow, yellow moon.

50 This woman is ill,
This woman is alone,

Husband in the grave,[1] son in prison,
Say a prayer for me.

III

No, it is not I, it is somebody else who is suffering.
55 I would not have been able to bear what happened,
Let them shroud it in black,
And let them carry off the lanterns...
                                          Night.

1940

IV

You should have been shown, you mocker,
Minion of all your friends,
60 Gay little sinner of Tsarskoye Selo[2]
What would happen in your life—
How three-hundredth in line, with a parcel,
You would stand by the Kresty prison,
Your fiery tears
65 Burning through the New Year's ice.
Over there the prison poplar bends,
And there's no sound—and over there how many
Innocent lives are ending now...

7. When he was arrested at their apartment in 1935, Akhmatova's husband had kissed an icon (religious painting) in farewell.
8. Rebellious troops executed by Peter the Great in 1698 as their wives watched.
9. A river flowing into the Black Sea.
1. Akhmatova's first husband, the poet Nikolai Gumilyov, executed in 1921.
2. Town outside Leningrad where Akhmatova grew up, site of the tsars' summer palace and elaborate gardens.

V

For seventeen months I've been crying out,
70   Calling you home.
I flung myself at the hangman's feet,
You are my son and my horror.
Everything is confused forever,
And it's not clear to me
75   Who is a beast now, who is a man,
And how long before the execution.
And there are only dusty flowers,
And the chinking of the censer, and tracks
From somewhere to nowhere.
80   And staring me straight in the eyes,
And threatening impending death,
Is an enormous star.

1939

VI

The light weeks will take flight,
I won't comprehend what happened.
85   Just as the white nights[3]
Stared at you, dear son, in prison
So they are staring again,
With the burning eyes of a hawk,
Talking about your lofty cross,
90   And about death.

1939

VII: The Sentence

And the stone word fell
On my still-living breast.
Never mind, I was ready,
I will manage somehow.

95   Today I have so much to do:
I must kill memory once and for all,
I must turn my soul to stone,
I must learn to live again—

Unless... Summer's ardent rustling
100   Is like a festival outside my window.

---

3. Midsummer nights in which the sun barely sets.

For a long time I've foreseen this
Brilliant day, deserted house.

June 22, 1939[4]
Fountain House

VIII: To Death

You will come in any case—so why not now?
I am waiting for you—I can't stand much more.
105   I've put out the light and opened the door
For you, so simple and miraculous.
So come in any form you please,
Burst in as a gas shell
Or, like a gangster, steal in with a length of pipe,
110   Or poison me with your typhus fumes.
Or be that fairy tale you've dreamed up,
So sickeningly familiar to everyone—
In which I glimpse the top of a pale blue cap[5]
And the house attendant white with fear.
115   Now it doesn't matter anymore. The Yenisey[6] swirls,
The North Star shines.
And the final horror dims
The blue luster of beloved eyes.

August 19, 1939
Fountain House

IX

Now madness half shadows
120   My soul with its wing,
And makes it drunk with fiery wine
And beckons toward the black ravine.

And I've finally realized
That I must give in,
125   Overhearing myself
Raving as if it were somebody else.

And it does not allow me to take
Anything of mine with me.
(No matter how much I plead with it,
130   No matter how much I supplicate):

Not the terrible eyes of my son—
Suffering turned to stone,

---

4. The date her son was sentenced to labor camp in Siberia.
5. Often worn by the secret police.
6. Several prison camps were built along this Siberian river.

Not the day of the terror,
Not the hour I met with him in prison,

135   Not the sweet coolness of his hands,
Not the trembling shadow of the lindens,
Not the far-off, fragile sound—
Of the final words of consolation.

May 4, 1940
Fountain House

X: Crucifixion

> *"Do not weep for Me, Mother,*
> *I am in the grave."*[7]

1

A choir of angels sang the praises of that momentous hour,
140   And the heavens dissolved in fire.
To his Father He said: "Why hast Thou forsaken me!"[8]
And to his Mother: "Oh, do not weep for Me…"

1940
Fountain House

2

Mary Magdalene beat her breast and sobbed,
The beloved disciple turned to stone,
145   But where the silent Mother stood, there
No one glanced and no one would have dared.

1943
Tashkent

Epilogue I

I learned how faces fall,
How terror darts from under eyelids,
How suffering traces lines
150   Of stiff cuneiform on cheeks,
How locks of ashen-blonde or black
Turn silver suddenly,
Smiles fade on submissive lips
And fear trembles in a dry laugh.
155   And I pray not for myself alone,
But for all those who stood there with me
In cruel cold, and in July's heat,
At that blind, red wall.

7. From a Russian Orthodox prayer sung at Easter, in which Jesus comforts his mother, Mary.
8. Jesus's last words on the cross, according to Matthew's gospel (27.46).

Epilogue II

Once more the day of remembrance draws near.[9]
160   I see, I hear, I feel you:

The one they almost had to drag at the end,
And the one who tramps her native land no more,

And the one who, tossing her beautiful head,
Said, "Coming here's like coming home."

165   I'd like to name them all by name,
But the list has been confiscated and is nowhere to be found.

I have woven a wide mantle for them
From their meager, overheard words.

I will remember them always and everywhere,
170   I will never forget them no matter what comes.

And if they gag my exhausted mouth
Through which a hundred million scream,

Then may the people remember me
On the eve of my remembrance day.

175   And if ever in this country
They decide to erect a monument to me,

I consent to that honor
Under these conditions—that it stand

Neither by the sea, where I was born:
180   My last tie with the sea is broken,

Nor in the tsar's garden near the cherished pine stump,
Where an inconsolable shade looks for me,

But here, where I stood for three hundred hours,
And where they never unbolted the doors for me.

185   This, lest in blissful death
I forget the rumbling of the Black Marias,

Forget how that detested door slammed shut
And an old woman howled like a wounded animal.

And may the melting snow stream like tears
190   From my motionless lids of bronze,

And a prison dove coo in the distance,
And the ships of the Neva sail calmly on.

March 1940

---

9. "Remembrance Day" is a Russian Orthodox church service held a year after someone's death.

One of the most cosmopolitan of modern writers, Jorge Luis Borges was born in Buenos Aires, Argentina, and spent his formative years in Geneva, Switzerland, after his family was trapped there during World War I while traveling in Europe. He learned German and French in addition to his native Spanish and English (his maternal ancestry was part English) and graduated from the Collège de Geneve. The family moved back to Buenos Aires following the war, after living for some time in Spain, where Borges came in contact with a number of avant-garde poets and where he published his first poem, "Hymn to the Sea," in the avant-garde journal *Grecia.* Borges's first published work was a translation into Spanish of Oscar Wilde's short story "The Happy Prince" when Borges was barely ten years old. Son of a psychology teacher with an extensive family library, Borges would spend most of his life in libraries, starting with his first job in 1939 as librarian in a municipal library in Buenos Aires. He held that position until the populist coup of the military strongman Juan Domingo Perón in 1946, at which time Borges was "promoted" to inspector of rabbits and poultry in the municipal market. Borges, whose rancor ran deep and proved implacable, never forgave Perón, and his politics, often anachronistic and deliberately provocative, were formed by this experience. Upon the fall of the Peronist regime in 1955, Borges was named Director of the National Library of Argentina, a post he held until his retirement in 1973, when Perón returned from exile to the presidency of Argentina. Genetically prone to blindness, Borges became the third director of his country's National Library to have this disability. As with most ironies, the irony of this was not lost on Borges, and several of his writings deal with this turn of fate.

While Borges began his career as a poet and wrote (or later dictated) poetry all his life, he is better known as a literary critic, essayist, and author of enigmatic short stories. His influence as a prose writer extends worldwide, with his works having been translated into many languages. As a critic, he introduced most of the Anglo-American and European modernists to the reading public of his country through his weekly column that appeared between 1936 and 1939 in a ladies' journal called *El Hogar* (The Home). During this period he was also writing some of his classic tales, which were gathered into a collection in 1941 under the title of *The Garden of the Forking Paths,* whose title story became one of his best known works.

Always fascinated by limit states of reason and rationality, Borges explores the thresholds between fantasy and reality, between the imagination and the materiality of the world. Deeply influenced by Idealist philosophers such as Arthur Schopenhauer and Bishop George Berkeley, whom he often cites, Borges speculates in his poetry and in his prose about the possibility that the world as we imagine it could well be a figment of someone else's imagination that imagines us imagining. In this sense, the authorship of the world is as compelling a problem for Borges as his and other writers' authorship of literary worlds. A self-proclaimed unbeliever, Borges doesn't view this as a religious problem but as a problem of the imagination. He is fascinated by creation, but he is not a creationist. The question of the creator, always with a lowercase "c," is of the same order as the question of a Creator with a capital "C." Very much in the metaphysical tradition of the Idealists and mathematicians, Borges sees creation as the product of an imaginative calculus. And he sees the world as a text—really, as a hypertext—whose myriad links could lead to an infinite number of other texts and other links. "The Garden of Forking Paths" and "The Library of Babel" printed here dramatize this open-ended nature of the world and its analog, writing, in Borges's characteristic fashion.

In this regard, Borges anticipated the possibilities of a "world wide web" much before this phenomenon became a commonplace part of our life. And in poems like "The Web" printed here, he had already speculated on what he refers to as "the fatal web of cause and effect / that no man can foresee, nor any god." There is much irony here, and ironic subterfuge, often self-directed, is everywhere in Borges. Even in his death, which he speculates about in this poem, he trumped fate ironically when he chose to go to Geneva upon realizing that he was dying.

Borges's essays on philosophy and literature are likewise speculative and hypertextual. He considers philosophy and metaphysics as branches of literature—that is, of imaginative creation. As a result, he always finds it more interesting to imagine the question rather than find the solution. And in this respect, he never ceases to be fascinated with the masters of the detective genre, Edgar Allan Poe, G. K. Chesterton, and the friend and mentor Borges inherited from his father in Buenos Aires, Macedonio Fernández, a writer who could never finish a novel because no single solution interested him as much as the problem the work explored. His only finished novel has fifty-nine different possible endings.

In addition to his own tales, Borges coauthored a number of stories with his lifetime friend and collaborator, Bioy Casares, publishing their joint productions in the detective genre under the pseudonym of "Bustos Domecq." Borges's translations include works by such authors as Virginia Woolf, Franz Kafka, and William Faulkner. A perennial candidate for the Nobel Prize, which eluded him, he shared the Prix Formentor with Samuel Beckett in 1961, a turning point in Borges's international recognition and world acclaim as one of the key literary figures of the twentieth century.

PRONUNCIATION:
Jorge Luis Borges: HOAR-hay lou-EES BOHR-hays

The Garden of Forking Paths[1]

For Victoria Ocampo

On page 242 of *The History of the World War,* Liddell Hart tells us that an Allied offensive against the Serre-Montauban line (to be mounted by thirteen British divisions backed by one thousand four hundred artillery pieces) had been planned for July 24, 1916, but had to be put off until the morning of the twenty-ninth. Torrential rains (notes Capt. Liddell Hart) were the cause of that delay—a delay that entailed no great consequences, as it turns out. The statement which follows—dictated, reread, and signed by Dr. Yu Tsun, former professor of English in the *Hochschule*[2] at Tsingtao—throws unexpected light on the case. The two first pages of the statement are missing.

...and I hung up the receiver. Immediately afterward, I recognised the voice that had answered in German. It was that of Capt. Richard Madden. Madden's presence in Viktor Runeberg's flat meant the end of our efforts and (though this seemed to me quite secondary, or *should have seemed*) our lives as well. It meant that Runeberg had been arrested, or murdered.[3] Before the sun set on that day, I would face the same fate. Madden was implacable—or rather, he was obliged to be implacable. An Irishman at the orders of the English, a man accused of a certain lack of zealousness, perhaps even treason,

1. Translated by Andrew Hurley.
2. "College" in German.
3. Here an "Editor's" footnote—by Borges—reads as follows: "A bizarre and despicable supposition. The Prussian spy Hans Rabener, alias Viktor Runeberg, had turned an automatic pistol on his arresting officer, Capt. Richard Madden. Madden, in self-defense, inflicted the wound on Rabener that caused his subsequent death."

how could he fail to embrace and give thanks for this miraculous favour—the discovery, capture, perhaps death, of two agents of the German Empire? I went upstairs to my room; absurdly, I locked the door, and then I threw myself, on my back, onto my narrow iron bed. Outside the window were the usual rooftops and the overcast six o'clock sun. I found it incredible that this day, lacking all omens and premonitions, should be the day of my implacable death. Despite my deceased father, despite my having been a child in a symmetrical garden in Hai Feng—was I, now, about to die? Then I reflected that all things happen to *oneself,* and happen precisely, precisely *now.* Century follows century, yet events occur only *in the present;* countless men in the air, on the land and sea, yet everything that truly happens, happens *to me....* The almost unbearable memory of Madden's horsey face demolished those mental ramblings. In the midst of my hatred and my terror (now I don't mind talking about terror—now that I have foiled Richard Madden, now that my neck hungers for the rope), it occurred to me that that brawling and undoubtedly happy warrior did not suspect that I possessed the Secret—the name of the exact location of the new British artillery park on the Ancre.[4] A bird furrowed the grey sky, and I blindly translated it into an aeroplane, and that aeroplane into many (in the French sky), annihilating the artillery park with vertical bombs. If only my throat, before a bullet crushed it, could cry out that name so that it might be heard in Germany.... But my human voice was so terribly inadequate. How was I to make it reach the Leader's ear—the ear of that sick and hateful man who knew nothing of Runeberg and me save that we were in Staffordshire, and who was vainly awaiting word from us in his arid office in Berlin, poring infinitely through the newspapers? ... *I must flee,* I said aloud. I sat up noiselessly, in needless but perfect silence, as though Madden were already just outside my door. Something—perhaps the mere show of proving that my resources were non-existent—made me go through my pockets. I found what I knew I would find: the American watch, the nickel-plated chain and quadrangular coin, the key ring with the compromising and useless keys to Runeberg's flat, the notebook, a letter I resolved to destroy at once (and never did), the false passport, one crown, two shillings, and a few odd pence, the red-and-blue pencil, the handkerchief, the revolver with its single bullet. Absurdly, I picked it up and hefted it, to give myself courage. I vaguely reflected that a pistol shot can be heard at a considerable distance. In ten minutes, my plan was ripe. The telephone book gave me the name of the only person able to communicate the information: he lived in a suburb of Fenton, less than a half hour away by train.

I am a coward. I can say that, now that I have carried out a plan whose dangerousness and daring no man will deny. I know that it was a terrible thing to do. I did not do it for Germany. What do I care for a barbaric country that has forced me to the ignominy of spying? Furthermore, I know of a man of England—a modest man—who in my view is no less a genius than Goethe.[5] I spoke with him for no more than an hour, but for one hour he was Goethe.... No—I did it because I sensed that the Leader looked down on the people of my race—the countless ancestors whose blood flows through my veins. I wanted to prove to him that a yellow man could save his armies. And I had to escape from Madden. His hands, his voice, could beat upon my door at any moment. I silently dressed, said good-bye to myself in the mirror, made my way downstairs, looked up and down the quiet street, and set off. The train station was not far from my flat, but I thought it better to take a cab. I argued that I ran less chance of being recognised that way; the fact is, I felt I was visible and vulnerable—infinitely

---

4. The River Ancre, France. Borges is also punning on "encre," "ink" in French.

5. Johann Wolfgang Goethe (1749–1832), German poet, novelist, dramatist, and essayist, often identified as Germany's greatest writer.

vulnerable—in the deserted street. I recall that I told the driver to stop a little ways from the main entrance to the station. I got down from the cab with willed and almost painful slowness. I would be going to the village of Ashgrove, but I bought a ticket for a station farther down the line. The train was to leave at eight-fifty, scant minutes away. I had to hurry; the next train would not be until nine-thirty. There was almost no one on the platform. I walked through the cars; I recall a few workmen, a woman dressed in mourning weeds, a young man fervently reading Tacitus' *Annals*,[6] and a cheerful-looking wounded soldier. The train pulled out at last. A man I recognised ran, vainly, out to the end of the platform; it was Capt. Richard Madden. Shattered, trembling, I huddled on the other end of the seat, far from the feared window.

From that shattered state I passed into a state of almost abject cheerfulness. I told myself that my duel had begun, and that in dodging my adversary's thrust—even by forty minutes, even thanks to the slightest smile from fate—the first round had gone to me. I argued that this small win prefigured total victory. I argued that the win was not really even so small, since without the precious hour that the trains had given me, I'd be in gaol, or dead. I argued (no less sophistically) that my cowardly cheerfulness proved that I was a man capable of following this adventure through to its successful end. From that weakness I drew strength that was never to abandon me. I foresee that mankind will resign itself more and more fully every day to more and more horrendous undertakings; soon there will be nothing but warriors and brigands. I give them this piece of advice: *He who is to perform a horrendous act should imagine to himself that it is already done, should impose upon himself a future as irrevocable as the past.* That is what I did, while my eyes—the eyes of a man already dead—registered the flow of that day perhaps to be my last, and the spreading of the night. The train ran sweetly, gently, through woods of ash trees. It stopped virtually in the middle of the countryside. No one called out the name of the station. "Ashgrove?" I asked some boys on the platform. "Ashgrove," they said, nodding. I got off the train.

A lamp illuminated the platform, but the boys' faces remained within the area of shadow. "Are you going to Dr. Stephen Albert's house?" one queried. Without waiting for an answer, another of them said: "The house is a far way, but you'll not get lost if you follow that road there to the left, and turn left at every crossing." I tossed them a coin (my last), went down some stone steps, and started down the solitary road. It ran ever so slightly downhill and was of elemental dirt. Branches tangled overhead, and the low round moon seemed to walk along beside me.

For one instant, I feared that Richard Madden had somehow seen through my desperate plan, but I soon realized that that was impossible. The boy's advice to turn always to the left reminded me that that was the common way of discovering the central lawn of a certain type of maze. I am something of a *connoisseur* of mazes: not for nothing am I the great-grandson of that Ts'ui Pen who was governor of Yunan province and who renounced all temporal power in order to write a novel containing more characters than the *Hung Lu Meng*[7] and construct a labyrinth in which all men would lose their way. Ts'ui Pen devoted thirteen years to those disparate labours, but the hand of a foreigner murdered him and his novel made no sense and no one ever found the labyrinth. It was under English trees that I meditated on that lost labyrinth: I pictured it perfect and inviolate on the secret summit of a mountain; I pictured its

6. Cornelius Tacitus (c. 56–120 C.E.), historian of the Roman Empire. His *Annals* narrate the intrigue, corruption, and terror during the reigns of Tiberius, Claudius, and Nero.
7. Cao Xueqin's novel *Dream of the Red Chamber* (1791), China's elaborate family saga with more than 400 characters.

outlines blurred by rice paddies, or underwater; I pictured it as infinite—a labyrinth not of octagonal pavillions and paths that turn back upon themselves, but of rivers and provinces and kingdoms. . . . I imagined a labyrinth of labyrinths, a maze of mazes, a twisting, turning, ever-widening labyrinth that contained both past and future and somehow implied the stars. Absorbed in those illusory imaginings, I forgot that I was a pursued man; I felt myself, for an indefinite while, the abstract perceiver of the world. The vague, living countryside, the moon, the remains of the day did their work in me; so did the gently downward road, which forestalled all possibility of weariness. The evening was near, yet infinite.

The road dropped and forked as it cut through the now-formless meadows. A keen and vaguely syllabic song, blurred by leaves and distance, came and went on the gentle gusts of breeze. I was struck by the thought that a man may be the enemy of other men, the enemy of other men's other moments, yet not be the enemy of a country— of fireflies, words, gardens, watercourses, zephyrs. It was amidst such thoughts that I came to a high rusty gate. Through the iron bars I made out a drive lined with poplars, and a gazebo of some kind. Suddenly, I realised two things—the first trivial, the second almost incredible: the music I had heard was coming from that gazebo, or pavillion, and the music was Chinese. That was why unconsciously I had fully given myself over to it. I do not recall whether there was a bell or whether I had to clap my hands to make my arrival known.

The sputtering of the music continued, but from the rear of the intimate house, a lantern was making its way toward me—a lantern cross-hatched and sometimes blotted out altogether by the trees, a paper lantern the shape of a drum and the colour of the moon. It was carried by a tall man. I could not see his face because the light blinded me. He opened the gate and slowly spoke to me in my own language.

"I see that the compassionate Hsi P'eng has undertaken to remedy my solitude. You will no doubt wish to see the garden?"

I recognised the name of one of our consuls, but I could only disconcertedly repeat, "The garden?"

"The garden of forking paths."

Something stirred in my memory, and I spoke with incomprehensible assurance.

"The garden of my ancestor Ts'ui Pen."

"Your ancestor? Your illustrious ancestor? Please—come in."

The dew-drenched path meandered like the paths of my childhood. We came to a library of Western and Oriental books. I recognised, bound in yellow silk, several handwritten volumes of the Lost Encyclopedia compiled by the third emperor of the Luminous Dynasty but never printed.[8] The disk on the gramophone revolved near a bronze phoenix. I also recall a vase of *famille rose*[9] and another, earlier by several hundred years, of that blue colour our artificers copied from the potters of ancient Persia. . . .

Stephen Albert, with a smile, regarded me. He was, as I have said, quite tall, with sharp features, grey eyes, and a grey beard. There was something priestlike about him, somehow, but something sailorlike as well; later he told me he had been a missionary in Tientsin "before aspiring to be a Sinologist."

8. The third emperor of the Ming, or "Luminous," Dynasty was Yung-lo, and the Encyclopedia is one he commissioned between 1403 and 1408. Originally 11,000 volumes, only 370 volumes now survive.

9. Eighteenth-century pink enamel pottery.

We sat down, I on a long low divan, he with his back to the window and a tall circular clock. I figured that my pursuer, Richard Madden, could not possibly arrive for at least an hour. My irrevocable decision could wait.

"An amazing life, Ts'ui Pen's," Stephen Albert said. "Governor of the province in which he had been born, a man learned in astronomy, astrology, and the unwearying interpretation of canonical books, a chess player, a renowned poet and calligrapher—he abandoned it all in order to compose a book and a labyrinth. He renounced the pleasures of oppression, justice, the populous marriage bed, banquets, and even erudition in order to sequester himself for thirteen years in the Pavillion of Limpid Solitude. Upon his death, his heirs found nothing but chaotic manuscripts. The family, as you perhaps are aware, were about to deliver them to the fire, but his counsellor—a Taoist or Buddhist monk—insisted upon publishing them."

"To this day," I replied, "we who are descended from Ts'ui Pen execrate that monk. It was senseless to publish those manuscripts. The book is a contradictory jumble of irresolute drafts. I once examined it myself; in the third chapter the hero dies, yet in the fourth he is alive again. As for Ts'ui Pen's other labor, his Labyrinth..."

"Here is the Labyrinth," Albert said, gesturing towards a tall lacquered writing cabinet.

"An ivory labyrinth!" I exclaimed. "A very small sort of labyrinth..."

"A labyrinth of symbols," he corrected me. "An invisible labyrinth of time. I, an English barbarian, have somehow been chosen to unveil the diaphanous mystery. Now, more than a hundred years after the fact, the precise details are irrecoverable, but it is not difficult to surmise what happened, Ts'ui Pen must at one point have remarked, 'I shall retire to write a book,' and at another point, 'I shall retire to construct a labyrinth.' Everyone pictured two projects; it occurred to no one that book and labyrinth were one and the same. The Pavillion of Limpid Solitude was erected in the centre of a garden that was, perhaps, most intricately laid out; that fact might well have suggested a physical labyrinth. Ts'ui Pen died; no one in all the wide lands that had been his could find the labyrinth. The novel's confusion—confusedness, I mean, of course—suggested to me that it was that labyrinth. Two circumstances lent me the final solution of the problem—one, the curious legend that Ts'ui Pen had intended to construct a labyrinth which was truly infinite, and two, a fragment of a letter I discovered."

Albert stood. His back was turned to me for several moments; he opened a drawer in the black-and-gold writing cabinet. He turned back with a paper that had once been crimson but was now pink and delicate and rectangular. It was written in Ts'ui Pen's renowned calligraphy. Eagerly yet uncomprehendingly I read the words that a man of my own lineage had written with painstaking brushstrokes: *I leave to several futures (not to all) my garden of forking paths.* I wordlessly handed the paper back to Albert. He continued:

"Before unearthing this letter, I had wondered how a book could be infinite. The only way I could surmise was that it be a cyclical, or circular, volume, a volume whose last page would be identical to the first, so that one might go on indefinitely. I also recalled that night at the centre of the *1001 Nights,* when the queen Scheherazade (through some magical distractedness on the part of the copyist) begins to retell, verbatim, the story of the 1001 Nights, with the risk of returning once again to the night on which she is telling it—and so on, *ad infinitum.* I also pictured to myself a platonic, hereditary sort of work, passed down from father to son, in which each new individual would add a chapter or with reverent care correct his elders' pages. These imaginings amused and distracted me, but none of them seemed to correspond even remotely to Ts'ui Pen's contradictory chapters. As I was floundering about in the mire of these perplexities, I was sent from Oxford the document you have just examined. I paused, as you may well imagine, at the sentence 'I leave to several futures (not to all) my garden of forking paths.' Almost instantly, I saw it—the garden of forking paths was the chaotic novel; the phrase 'several futures (not all)' suggested to me the image of a forking in *time,* rather than in space. A full rereading of the book confirmed my theory. In all fictions, each time a man meets diverse alternatives, he chooses one and eliminates the others; in the work of the virtually impossible-to-disentangle Ts'ui Pen, the character chooses—simultaneously—all of them. *He creates,* thereby, 'several futures,' several *times,* which themselves proliferate and fork. That is the explanation for the novel's contradictions. Fang, let us say, has a secret; a stranger knocks at his door; Fang decides to kill him. Naturally, there are various possible outcomes—Fang can kill the intruder, the intruder can kill Fang, they can both live, they can both be killed, and so on. In Ts'ui Pen's novel, *all* the outcomes in fact occur; each is the starting point for further bifurcations. Once in a while, the paths of that labyrinth converge: for example, you come to this house, but in one of the possible pasts you are my enemy, in another my friend. If you can bear my incorrigible pronunciation, we shall read a few pages."

His face, in the vivid circle of the lamp, was undoubtedly that of an old man, though with something indomitable and even immortal about it. He read with slow precision two versions of a single epic chapter. In the first, an army marches off to battle through a mountain wilderness; the horror of the rocks and darkness inspires in them a disdain for life, and they go on to an easy victory. In the second, the same army passes through a palace in which a ball is being held; the brilliant battle seems to them a continuation of the *fête,* and they win it easily.

I listened with honourable veneration to those ancient fictions, which were themselves perhaps not as remarkable as the fact that a man of my blood had invented them and a man of a distant empire was restoring them to me on an island in the West in the course of a desperate mission. I recall the final words, repeated in each version like some secret commandment: "Thus the heroes fought, their admirable hearts calm, their swords violent, they themselves resigned to killing and to dying."

From that moment on, I felt all about me and within my obscure body an invisible, intangible pullulation—not that of the divergent, parallel, and finally coalescing armies, but an agitation more inaccessible, more inward than that, yet one those armies somehow prefigured. Albert went on:

"I do not believe that your venerable ancestor played at idle variations. I cannot think it probable that he would sacrifice thirteen years to the infinite performance of a rhetorical exercise. In your country, the novel is a subordinate genre; at that time it was a genre beneath contempt. Ts'ui Pen was a novelist of genius, but he was also a man of letters, and surely would not have considered himself a mere novelist. The testimony of his contemporaries proclaims his metaphysical, mystical leanings—and his life is their fullest confirmation. Philosophical debate consumes a good part of his novel. I know that of all problems, none disturbed him, none gnawed at him like the unfathomable problem of time. How strange, then, that that problem should be the *only* one that does not figure in the pages of his *Garden.* He never even uses the word. How do you explain that wilful omission?"

I proposed several solutions—all unsatisfactory. We discussed them; finally, Stephen Albert said:

"In a riddle whose answer is chess, what is the only word that must not be used?"

I thought for a moment.

"The word 'chess,'" I replied.

"Exactly," Albert said. "*The Garden of Forking Paths* is a huge riddle, or parable, whose subject is time; that secret purpose forbids Ts'ui Pen the merest mention of its name. To *always* omit one word, to employ awkward metaphors and obvious circumlocutions, is perhaps the most emphatic way of calling attention to that word. It is, at any rate, the tortuous path chosen by the devious Ts'ui Pen at each and every one of the turnings of his inexhaustible novel. I have compared hundreds of manuscripts, I have corrected the errors introduced through the negligence of copyists, I have reached a hypothesis for the plan of that chaos, I have reestablished, or believe I've reestablished, its fundamental order—I have translated the entire work; and I know that not once does the word 'time' appear. The explanation is obvious: *The Garden of Forking Paths* is an incomplete, but not false, image of the universe as conceived by Ts'ui Pen. Unlike Newton and Schopenhauer,[1] your ancestor did not believe in a uniform and absolute time; he believed in an infinite series of times, a growing, dizzying web of divergent, convergent, and parallel times. That fabric of times that approach one another, fork, are snipped off, or are simply unknown for centuries, contains *all* possibilities. In most of those times, we do not exist; in some, you exist but I do not; in others, I do and you do not; in others still, we both do. In this one, which the favouring hand of chance has dealt me, you have come to my home; in another, when you come through my garden you find me dead; in another, I say these same words, but I am an error, a ghost."

"In all," I said, not without a tremble, "I am grateful for, and I venerate, your recreation of the garden of Ts'ui Pen."

"Not in all," he whispered with a smile. "Time forks, perpetually, into countless futures. In one of them, I am your enemy."

I felt again that pullulation I have mentioned. I sensed that the dew-drenched garden that surrounded the house was saturated, infinitely, with invisible persons. Those persons were Albert and myself—secret, busily at work, multiform—in other dimensions of time. I raised my eyes and the gossamer nightmare faded. In the yellow-and-black garden there was but a single man—but that man was as mighty as a statue, and that man was coming down the path, and he was Capt. Richard Madden.

"The future is with us," I replied, "but I am your friend. May I look at the letter again?"

Albert rose once again. He stood tall as he opened the drawer of the tall writing cabinet; he turned his back to me for a moment. I had cocked the revolver. With utmost care, I fired. Albert fell without a groan, without a sound, on the instant. I swear that he died instantly—one clap of thunder.

The rest is unreal, insignificant. Madden burst into the room and arrested me. I have been sentenced to hang. I have most abhorrently triumphed: I have communicated to Berlin the secret name of the city to be attacked. Yesterday it was bombed—I read about it in the same newspapers that posed to all of England the enigma of the murder of the eminent Sinologist Stephen Albert by a stranger, Yu Tsun. The Leader solved the riddle. He knew that my problem was how to report (over the deafening noise of the war) the name of the city named Albert, and that the only way I could

---

1. Isaac Newton (1642–1727), English physicist and mathematician who formulated laws of gravity and motion. Arthur Schopenhauer (1788–1860), German philosopher whose Idealist notions of the world as the individual's will and ideas are often cited by Borges.

find was murdering a person of that name. He does not know (no one can know) my endless contrition, and my weariness.

The Library of Babel[1]

By this art you may contemplate the variation of the 23 letters....
Anatomy of Melancholy,[2] pt. 2, sec. 2, mem. 4

The universe (which others call the Library) is composed of an indefinite, perhaps infinite number of hexagonal galleries. In the center of each gallery is a ventilation shaft, bounded by a low railing. From any hexagon one can see the floors above and below— one after another, endlessly. The arrangement of the galleries is always the same: Twenty bookshelves, five to each side, line four of the hexagon's six sides; the height of the bookshelves, floor to ceiling, is hardly greater than the height of a normal librarian. One of the hexagon's free sides opens onto a narrow sort of vestibule, which in turn opens onto another gallery, identical to the first—identical in fact to all. To the left and right of the vestibule are two tiny compartments. One is for sleeping, upright; the other, for satisfying one's physical necessities. Through this space, too, there passes a spiral staircase, which winds upward and downward into the remotest distance. In the vestibule there is a mirror, which faithfully duplicates appearances. Men often infer from this mirror that the Library is not infinite—if it were, what need would there be for that illusory replication? I prefer to dream that burnished surfaces are a figuration and promise of the infinite....Light is provided by certain spherical fruits that bear the name "bulbs." There are two of these bulbs in each hexagon, set crosswise. The light they give is insufficient, and unceasing.

Like all the men of the Library, in my younger days I traveled; I have journeyed in quest of a book, perhaps the catalog of catalogs. Now that my eyes can hardly make out what I myself have written, I am preparing to die, a few leagues from the hexagon where I was born. When I am dead, compassionate hands will throw me over the railing; my tomb will be the unfathomable air, my body will sink for ages, and will decay and dissolve in the wind engendered by my fall, which shall be infinite. I declare that the Library is endless. Idealists argue that the hexagonal rooms are the necessary shape of absolute space, or at least of our *perception* of space. They argue that a triangular or pentagonal chamber is inconceivable. (Mystics claim that their ecstasies reveal to them a circular chamber containing an enormous circular book with a continuous spine that goes completely around the walls. But their testimony is suspect, their words obscure. That cyclical book is God.) Let it suffice for the moment that I repeat the classic dictum: *The Library is a sphere whose exact center is any hexagon and whose circumference is unattainable.*

Each wall of each hexagon is furnished with five bookshelves; each bookshelf holds thirty-two books identical in format; each book contains four hundred ten pages; each page, forty lines; each line, approximately eighty black letters. There are also letters on the front cover of each book; those letters neither indicate nor prefigure what the pages inside will say. I am aware that that lack of correspondence once struck men as mysterious. Before summarizing the solution of the mystery (whose discovery, in spite of its tragic consequences, is perhaps the most important event in all history), I wish to recall a few axioms.

JORGE LUIS BORGES

1. Translated by Andrew Hurley.

2. An ironic treatise published in 1621 by the bibliophile Robert Burton. Burton's private library contained more than 2,000 volumes. The epigraph refers to the Latin alphabet, whose 23 letters and their possible combinations constitute any library.

First: *The Library has existed ab aeternitate.* That truth, whose immediate corollary is the future eternity of the world, no rational mind can doubt. Man, the imperfect librarian, may be the work of chance or of malevolent demiurges; the universe, with its elegant appointments—its bookshelves, its enigmatic books, its indefatigable staircases for the traveler, and its water closets for the seated librarian—can only be the handiwork of a god. In order to grasp the distance that separates the human and the divine, one has only to compare these crude trembling symbols which my fallible hand scrawls on the cover of a book with the organic letters inside—neat, delicate, deep black, and inimitably symmetrical.

Second: *There are twenty-five orthographic symbols.* That discovery enabled mankind, three hundred years ago, to formulate a general theory of the Library and thereby satisfactorily solve the riddle that no conjecture had been able to divine—the formless and chaotic nature of virtually all books. One book, which my father once saw in a hexagon in circuit 15–94, consisted of the letters M C V perversely repeated from the first line to the last. Another (much consulted in this zone) is a mere labyrinth of letters whose penultimate page contains the phrase *O Time thy pyramids.* This much is known: For every rational line or forthright statement there are leagues of senseless cacophony, verbal nonsense, and incoherency. (I know of one semi-barbarous zone whose librarians repudiate the "vain and superstitious habit" of trying to find sense in books, equating such a quest with attempting to find meaning in dreams or in the chaotic lines of the palm of one's hand.... They will acknowledge that the inventors of writing imitated the twenty-five natural symbols, but contend that that adoption was fortuitous, coincidental, and that books in themselves have no meaning. That argument, as we shall see, is not entirely fallacious.)

For many years it was believed that those impenetrable books were in ancient or far-distant languages. It is true that the most ancient peoples, the first librarians, employed a language quite different from the one we speak today; it is true that a few miles to the right, our language devolves into dialect and that ninety floors above, it becomes incomprehensible. All of that, I repeat, is true—but four hundred ten pages of unvarying M C V's cannot belong to any language, however dialectal or primitive it may be. Some have suggested that each letter influences the next, and that the value of M C V on page 71, line 3, is not the value of the same series on another line of another page, but that vague thesis has not met with any great acceptance. Others have mentioned the possibility of codes; that conjecture has been universally accepted, though not in the sense in which its originators formulated it.

Some five hundred years ago, the chief of one of the upper hexagons came across a book as jumbled as all the others, but containing almost two pages of homogeneous lines. He showed his find to a traveling decipherer, who told him that the lines were written in Portuguese; others said it was Yiddish. Within the century experts had determined what the language actually was: a Samoyed-Lithuanian dialect of Guaraní, with inflections from classical Arabic. The content was also determined: the rudiments of combinatory analysis, illustrated with examples of endlessly repeating variations. Those examples allowed a librarian of genius to discover the fundamental law of the Library. This philosopher observed that all books, however different from one another they might be, consist of identical elements: the space, the period, the comma, and the twenty-two letters of the alphabet. He also posited a fact which all travelers have since confirmed: *In all the Library, there are no two identical books.* From those incontrovertible premises, the librarian deduced that the Library is "total"—perfect, complete, and whole—and that its bookshelves contain all possible combinations of the twenty-two orthographic symbols (a number which, though unimaginably vast, is not infinite)—that is, all that is able to be expressed, in every language. *All*—the detailed history of the future, the autobiographies of the archangels, the faithful catalog of the Library, thousands and thousands of false catalogs, the proof of the falsity of those false catalogs, a proof of the falsity of the *true* catalog, the gnostic gospel of Basilides,[3] the commentary upon that gospel, the commentary on the commentary on that gospel, the true story of your death, the translation of every book into every language, the interpolations of every book into all books, the treatise Bede could have written (but did not) on the mythology of the Saxon people, the lost books of Tacitus.[4]

When it was announced that the Library contained all books, the first reaction was unbounded joy. All men felt themselves the possessors of an intact and secret treasure. There was no personal problem, no world problem, whose eloquent solution did not exist—somewhere in some hexagon. The universe was justified; the universe suddenly became congruent with the unlimited width and breadth of humankind's hope. At that period there was much talk of The Vindications—books of *apologiae* and prophecies that would vindicate for all time the actions of every person in the universe and that held wondrous arcana for men's futures. Thousands of greedy individuals abandoned their sweet native hexagons and rushed downstairs, upstairs, spurred by the vain desire to find their Vindication. These pilgrims squabbled in the narrow corridors, muttered dark imprecations, strangled one another on the divine staircases, threw deceiving volumes down ventilation shafts, were themselves hurled to their deaths by men of distant regions. Others went insane. . . . The Vindications do exist (I have seen two of them, which refer to persons in the future, persons perhaps not imaginary), but those who went in quest of them failed to recall that the chance of a man's finding his own Vindication, or some perfidious version of his own, can be calculated to be zero.

At that same period there was also hope that the fundamental mysteries of mankind—the origin of the Library and of time—might be revealed. In all likelihood those profound mysteries can indeed be explained in words; if the language of the philosophers is not sufficient, then the multiform Library must surely have produced the extraordinary language that is required, together with the words and grammar of that language. For four centuries, men have been scouring the hexagons. . . . There are official searchers, the "inquisitors." I have seen them about their tasks: they arrive exhausted at some hexagon, they talk about a staircase that nearly killed them—rungs were missing—they speak with the librarian about galleries and staircases, and, once in a while, they take up the nearest book and leaf through it, searching for disgraceful or dishonorable words. Clearly, no one expects to discover anything.

That unbridled hopefulness was succeeded, naturally enough, by a similarly disproportionate depression. The certainty that some bookshelf in some hexagon contained precious books, yet that those precious books were forever out of reach, was almost unbearable. One blasphemous sect proposed that the searches be discontinued and that all men shuffle letters and symbols until those canonical books, through some improbable stroke of chance, had been constructed. The authorities were forced to issue strict orders. The sect disappeared, but in my childhood I have seen old men who for long periods would hide in the latrines with metal disks and a forbidden dice cup, feebly mimicking the divine disorder.

---

3. Scholar and teacher in 2nd-century C.E. Alexandria, Egypt. His *Exegetica,* a major commentary on the Bible, consisted of 24 books.

4. The Venerable Bede (c. 673–735) was an English historian and Benedictine monk. Cornelius Tacitus (c. 56–120 C.E.), historian of the Roman Empire.

Others, going about it in the opposite way, thought the first thing to do was eliminate all worthless books. They would invade the hexagons, show credentials that were not always false, leaf disgustedly through a volume, and condemn entire walls of books. It is to their hygienic, ascetic rage that we lay the senseless loss of millions of volumes. Their name is execrated today, but those who grieve over the "treasures" destroyed in that frenzy overlook two widely acknowledged facts: One, that the Library is so huge that any reduction by human hands must be infinitesimal. And two, that each book is unique and irreplaceable, but (since the Library is total) there are always several hundred thousand imperfect facsimiles—books that differ by no more than a single letter, or a comma. Despite general opinion, I daresay that the consequences of the depredations committed by the Purifiers have been exaggerated by the horror those same fanatics inspired. They were spurred on by the holy zeal to reach—someday, through unrelenting effort—the books of the Crimson Hexagon—books smaller than natural books, books omnipotent, illustrated, and magical.

We also have knowledge of another superstition from that period: belief in what was termed the Book-Man. On some shelf in some hexagon, it was argued, there must exist a book that is the cipher and perfect compendium *of all other books,* and some librarian must have examined that book; this librarian is analogous to a god. In the language of this zone there are still vestiges of the sect that worshiped that distant librarian. Many have gone in search of Him. For a hundred years, men beat every possible path—and every path in vain. How was one to locate the idolized secret hexagon that sheltered Him? Someone proposed searching by regression: To locate book A, first consult book B, which tells where book A can be found; to locate book B, first consult book C, and so on, to infinity....It is in ventures such as these that I have squandered and spent my years. I cannot think it unlikely that there is such a total book on some shelf in the universe. I pray to the unknown gods that some man—even a single man, tens of centuries ago—has perused and read that book. If the honor and wisdom and joy of such a reading are not to be my own, then let them be for others. Let heaven exist, though my own place be in hell. Let me be tortured and battered and annihilated, but let there be one instant, one creature, wherein thy enormous Library may find its justification.

Infidels claim that the rule in the Library is not "sense," but "non-sense," and that "rationality" (even humble, pure coherence) is an almost miraculous exception. They speak, I know, of "the feverish Library, whose random volumes constantly threaten to transmogrify into others, so that they affirm all things, deny all things, and confound and confuse all things, like some mad and hallucinating deity." Those words, which not only proclaim disorder but exemplify it as well, prove, as all can see, the infidels' deplorable taste and desperate ignorance. For while the Library contains all verbal structures, all the variations allowed by the twenty-five orthographic symbols, it includes not a single absolute piece of nonsense. It would be pointless to observe that the finest volume of all the many hexagons that I myself administer is titled *Combed Thunder,* while another is titled *The Plaster Cramp,* and another, *Axaxaxas mlö.* Those phrases, at first apparently incoherent, are undoubtedly susceptible to cryptographic or allegorical "reading"; that reading, that justification of the words' order and existence, is itself verbal and, *ex hypothesi,* already contained somewhere in the Library. There is no combination of characters one can make—*dhcmrlchtdj,* for example—that the divine Library has not foreseen and that in one or more of its secret tongues does not hide a terrible significance. There is no syllable one can speak that is not filled with tenderness and terror, that is not, in one of those languages, the mighty name of a god. To speak is to commit tautologies. This pointless, verbose epistle already exists in one of the thirty volumes of the five bookshelves in one of the countless hexagons—as does its refutation. (A number *n* of the possible languages employ the same vocabulary; in some of them, the *symbol* "library" possesses the correct definition "everlasting, ubiquitous system of hexagonal galleries," while a library—the thing—is a loaf of bread or a pyramid or something else, and the six words that define it themselves have other definitions. You who read me—are you certain you understand my language?)

Methodical composition distracts me from the present condition of humanity. The certainty that everything has already been written annuls us, or renders us phantasmal. I know districts in which the young people prostrate themselves before books and like savages kiss their pages, though they cannot read a letter. Epidemics, heretical discords, pilgrimages that inevitably degenerate into brigandage have decimated the population. I believe I mentioned the suicides, which are more and more frequent every year. I am perhaps misled by old age and fear, but I suspect that the human species—the *only* species—teeters at the verge of extinction, yet that the Library—enlightened, solitary, infinite, perfectly unmoving, armed with precious volumes, pointless, incorruptible, and secret—will endure.

I have just written the word "infinite." I have not included that adjective out of mere rhetorical habit; I hereby state that it is not illogical to think that the world is infinite. Those who believe it to have limits hypothesize that in some remote place or places the corridors and staircases and hexagons may, inconceivably, end—which is absurd. And yet those who picture the world as unlimited forget that the number of possible books is *not*. I will be bold enough to suggest this solution to the ancient problem: *The Library is unlimited but periodic.* If an eternal traveler should journey in any direction, he would find after untold centuries that the same volumes are repeated in the same disorder—which, repeated, becomes order: the Order. My solitude is cheered by that elegant hope.

Borges and I[1]

It's Borges, the other one, that things happen to. I walk through Buenos Aires and I pause—mechanically now, perhaps—to gaze at the arch of an entryway and its inner door; news of Borges reaches me by mail, or I see his name on a list of academics or in some biographical dictionary. My taste runs to hourglasses, maps, seventeenth-century typefaces, etymologies, the taste of coffee, and the prose of Robert Louis Stevenson;[2] Borges shares those preferences, but in a vain sort of way that turns them into the accoutrements of an actor. It would be an exaggeration to say that our relationship is hostile—I live, I allow myself to live, so that Borges can spin out his literature, and that literature is my justification. I willingly admit that he has written a number of sound pages, but those pages will not save *me*, perhaps because the good in them no longer belongs to any individual, not even to that other man, but rather to language itself, or to tradition. Beyond that, I am doomed—utterly and inevitably—to oblivion, and fleeting moments will be all of me that survives in that other man. Little by little, I have been turning everything over to him, though I know the perverse way he has of distorting and magnifying everything. Spinoza[3] believed that all things wish to go on being what they are—stone wishes eternally to be stone, and tiger, to be tiger. I shall endure in Borges, not in myself (if, indeed, I am anybody at all), but I recognize

---

1. Translated by Andrew Hurley.

2. Scottish author (1850–1894) of adventure tales and stories that explore embodiments of good and evil, often cited by Borges.

3. Dutch philosopher Baruch Spinoza (1632–1677).

myself less in his books than in many others', or in the tedious strumming of a guitar. Years ago I tried to free myself from him, and I moved on from the mythologies of the slums and outskirts of the city to games with time and infinity, but those games belong to Borges now, and I shall have to think up other things. So my life is a point-counterpoint, a kind of fugue, and a falling away—and everything winds up being lost to me, and everything falls into oblivion, or into the hands of the other man.

I am not sure which of us it is that's writing this page.

The Web[1]

Which of my cities will I die in?
Geneva, where revelation came to me
through Virgil and Tacitus, certainly not from Calvin?[2]
Montevideo, where Luis Melian Lafinur,[3]
5   blind and heavy with years, died among the archives
of that impartial history of Uruguay
he never wrote?
Nara, where in a Japanese inn
I slept on the floor and dreamed the terrible
10   image of Buddha I had touched sightlessly
but saw in my dream?
Buenos Aires, where I'm almost a foreigner,
given my many years, or else a habitual target
for autograph hunters?
15   Austin, Texas, where my mother and I
in the autumn of '61 discovered America?
Others will know it too and will forget it.
What language am I doomed to die in?
The Spanish my ancestors used
20   to call for the charge or bid at truco?°   *a card game*
The English of that Bible
my grandmother read from at the desert's edge?
Others will know it too and will forget it.
What time will it be?
25   In the dove-colored twilight when color fades away
or in the twilight of the crow
when night abstracts and simplifies
all visible things, or at an odd moment—
two in the afternoon?
30   Others will know it too and will forget it.
These questions are digressions, not from fear
but from impatient hope,
part of the fatal web of cause and effect
that no man can foresee, nor any god.

---

1. Translated by Alastair Reid.
2. Virgil and Tacitus, classical Rome's greatest poet and histrorian; John Calvin (1509–1564), French Protestant theologian whose sect emphasized strict morality in a sinful world.
3. One of Borges's ancestors.

In Samuel Beckett's play *Endgame,* one of the characters asks anxiously, "We're not beginning to...to...mean something?" Whereupon another character responds, "Mean something! You and I, mean something! [Brief laugh.] Ah that's a good one!" This refusal of conventionally understood meaning—whether biographical, psychological, symbolic, or philosophical—characterizes Beckett's groundbreaking work in drama as well as his significant achievements in fiction. In both genres, Beckett persistently attempts to capture the human condition reduced to its barest essentials: through denuded landscapes or tightly enclosed spaces, sparse objects, handicapped or immobilized bodies, repeated gestures, and characters who have no way of escaping from their constrained existential situations. Sometimes they don't even have a voice of their own, functioning instead as an echo of other, perhaps imaginary voices. Yet their fatigue and boredom with their own suicidal despair are always counteracted by their irrepressible urge to keep on talking, adding yet another sentence to the dialogue, telling yet another story. Typically, such characters go back and forth between the assertion that all is over and that nothing will ever stop: "I can't go on, I'll go on," says the narrator in the very last line of Beckett's novel *The Unnamable* (1953), and the only character in his late play *Not I* (1973) is a disembodied mouth speaking incessantly.

The endeavor to get down to essentials and to subtract, reduce, and condense words is quite visible in the steadily diminishing bulk of Beckett's writing; while his works were never voluminous, in the 1940s he did write several full-length novels. By the 1960s and 1970s, he was publishing pieces whose very titles evoked brevity and inconsequence (such as *Ends and Odds* [1974–1976] or *Fizzles* [1976]), and they did indeed tend to become ever shorter: *Come and Go* (1967) and *Lessness* (1970) reduced their linguistic inventory to just a few dozen words or sentences, and some of his late plays such as *Quad* (1984) or *Acts Without Words I* and *Acts Without Words II* dispensed with language altogether, reducing theater to movement and gesture. Yet over a writing career that spanned four decades, Beckett never did stop writing. Instead, he invented ever-new ways to express the absence of meaning that lies at the core of his aesthetics: he once summarized his project as "the expression that there is nothing to express, nothing with which to express, nothing from which to express, no power to express, no desire to express, together with the obligation to express."

Yet this statement by no means implies that Beckett's works are tedious, bleak, and cheerless to read. On the contrary, many of them are uproariously funny, and some of his plays can be performed either as deadly serious drama or as vaudeville slapstick. A good example of this ambivalence is Beckett's most famous work, *Waiting for Godot,* which was an immediate success at its first performance in Paris in 1953 and established his reputation as a major playwright. Its four characters, Vladimir, Estragon, Lucky, and Pozzo, can be played either as existentialist heroes confronted with the absurdity of human life or as clowns who experience life's lack of meaning as a kind of cosmic comedy. The comedian Bert Lahr, in fact—best known as the Cowardly Lion in *The Wizard of Oz*—performed one of the roles in the play's Broadway debut. Beckett's fiction similarly oscillates between slapstick and bitter irony. A reader may be deeply disturbed at the spectacle of the character Molloy dragging himself through the mud with his crutches or laugh out loud at Molloy's insistence that even in this unlikely position, he never fails to doff his hat to passing ladies. While it isn't inappropriate to refer to Beckett as a pessimist, nihilist, or existentialist, he is also one of the twentieth century's great humorists, and his flair for comedy is what sets him apart from such writers as Franz Kafka, Jean-Paul Sartre, or Albert Camus, who also foreground the absurdity of an existence into which humans find themselves thrown without their consent.

Nor does Beckett's rejection of expression and meaning imply that his texts can't or shouldn't be interpreted. In fact, they challenge us to explore precisely the reasons and strategies through which they elude common procedures of sense making. Quite often, Beckett's texts take up problems of philosophy and language that have a long tradition in Western thought and pursue them to a logical impasse from which there is no conceptual escape. Many readers have noted the influence of French philosopher René Descartes on Beckett's work: Descartes's statement "I think, therefore I am" splits the thinking mind into the one who thinks and the one who observes the thinking, a self-referentiality that is often reflected in the relationship between similar or symbiotic characters in Beckett's fiction and plays. How the workings of human consciousness can be represented in literary language at all is a question that takes on a good deal of urgency in this context, one that was also explored by the Irish novelist James Joyce, whom Beckett met and worked with in Paris. In an early essay on the French novelist Marcel Proust, Beckett discussed the problematic connection between past and present self as they are established in the human mind by memory. His own works foreground this theme through characters who seem able to call up only fragments of their former lives. From Dante Alighieri, who is frequently alluded to, Beckett takes an interest in the various kinds of hell that people's lives can become and that they can create for each other—but without the sense of theological justice that informed Dante's *Inferno*. Frequently, then, what makes it difficult to attribute meaning to Beckett's texts is the fact that they question precisely the tools—rationality, logic, chronology, and transparent language—that we normally use to establish such meaning.

The multiple echoes of earlier writings in Beckett's texts point to a writer with a broad knowledge of varied languages and traditions. Born in a suburb of Dublin in 1906, he grew up in a middle-class, Anglo-Irish, Protestant family. From 1923 to 1927 he attended Trinity College in Dublin, where he studied French and Italian. In 1928 he went to Paris on a fellowship to teach English at the École Normale Supérieure and met his countryman James Joyce during his stay. Two years later, in 1930, he returned to Ireland to become a lecturer of French at Trinity College; he completed his master's degree in December 1931 and shortly afterward resigned from teaching, which he disliked intensely. In the following years, he lived and traveled in England, France, Italy, and Germany and finally settled in Paris in 1937. A year later he met Suzanne Deschevaux-Dumesnil, who became his life companion and, in 1961, his wife; she was an indispensable help in getting his first novel, *Murphy,* published in 1938 after it had been rejected by dozens of publishers.

Since Ireland was a neutral power in World War II, Beckett was able to remain in Paris during the Nazi occupation. But he joined an underground resistance group in 1941 and was forced to flee to Roussillon in the unoccupied south of France when some members of his group were arrested by the Germans in 1942. In Roussillon, he worked as a farm laborer until the end of the war and composed his novel *Watt*. In 1945 he worked for some time as an interpreter for the Irish Red Cross in Normandy. He returned to Paris in the winter of 1945, and was awarded the *Croix de guerre* and the *Médaille de la Résistance* for his participation in the French Resistance. Beckett lived and wrote in Paris for the rest of his life; while his main achievements continued to be in drama and narrative, he also ventured into radio plays, a television play, and a film script. He was awarded the Nobel Prize in Literature in 1969, and at his eightieth birthday he was celebrated as one of the most important writers of the twentieth century. He died in Paris at the age of eighty-three.

The period following World War II was one of the most productive in Beckett's life: In the late 1940s, he switched from English to French as his principal literary medium and wrote his most important narrative work, a trilogy of novels entitled *Molloy, Malone Dies,* and *The Unnamable*, which were published between 1951 and 1953. He also completed *Waiting for Godot,* followed in 1957 by *Endgame,* which portrays a bunkerlike setting where human existences that have run far beyond meaning nevertheless stubbornly refuse to end. With its hints at a cultural landscape devastated perhaps by war, perhaps by holocaust, or maybe just by the sheer absurdity of life, *Endgame* is an even starker, more stripped-down play than *Godot*. Yet as in *Godot,* the moments of bleakest despair give rise to the most sweeping comedy.

Endgame[1]

A Play in One Act

Characters

NAGG	HAMM
NELL	CLOV

Bare interior.

Grey light.

Left and right back, high up, two small windows, curtains drawn. Front right, a door. Hanging near door, its face to wall, a picture. Front left, touching each other, covered with an old sheet, two ashbins. Center, in an armchair on castors, covered with an old sheet, Hamm. Motionless by the door, his eyes fixed on Hamm, Clov. Very red face. Brief tableau.

Clov goes and stands under window left. Stiff, staggering walk. He looks up at window left. He turns and looks at window right. He goes and stands under window right. He looks up at window right. He turns and looks at window left. He goes out, comes back immediately with a small step-ladder, carries it over and sets it down under window left, gets up on it, draws back curtain. He gets down, takes six steps (for example) towards window right, goes back for ladder, carries it over and sets it down under window right, gets up on it, draws back curtain. He gets down, takes three steps towards window left, goes back for ladder, carries it over and sets it down under window left, gets up on it, looks out of window. Brief laugh. He gets down, takes one step towards window right, goes back for ladder, carries it over and sets it down under window right, gets up on it, looks out of window. Brief laugh. He gets down, goes with ladder towards ashbins, halts, turns, carries back ladder and sets it down under window right, goes to ashbins, removes sheet covering them, folds it over his arm. He raises one lid, stoops and looks into bin. Brief laugh. He closes lid. Same with other bin. He goes to Hamm, removes sheet covering him, folds it over his arm. In a dressing-gown, a stiff toque[2] on his head, a large blood-stained handkerchief over his face, a whistle hanging from his neck, a rug over his knees, thick socks on his feet, Hamm seems to be asleep. Clov looks him over. Brief laugh. He goes to door, halts, turns towards auditorium.

CLOV [*fixed gaze, tonelessly*]:   Finished, it's finished, nearly finished, it must be nearly finished. [*Pause.*] Grain upon grain, one by one, and one day, suddenly, there's a heap, a little heap, the impossible heap. [*Pause.*] I can't be punished any more. [*Pause.*] I'll go now to my kitchen, ten feet by ten feet by ten feet, and wait for him to whistle me. [*Pause.*] Nice dimensions, nice proportions, I'll lean on the table, and look at the wall, and wait for him to whistle me.

SAMUEL BECKETT

---

1. Written in French, then translated into English by Beckett himself. Beckett dedicated the play to its first director, Roger Blin.
2. A round brimless hat.

[*He remains a moment motionless, then goes out. He comes back immediately, goes to window right, takes up the ladder and carries it out. Pause. Hamm stirs. He yawns under the handkerchief. He removes the handkerchief from his face. Very red face. Black glasses.*]

HAMM: Me—[*he yawns*]—to play. [*He holds the handkerchief spread out before him.*]

Old stancher! [*He takes off his glasses, wipes his eyes, his face, the glasses, puts them on again, folds the handkerchief and puts it back neatly in the breast-pocket of his dressing-gown. He clears his throat, joins the tips of his fingers.*]

Can there be misery—[*he yawns*]—loftier than mine? No doubt. Formerly. But now? [*Pause.*] My father? [*Pause.*] My mother? [*Pause.*] My ... dog? [*Pause.*] Oh I am willing to believe they suffer as much as such creatures can suffer. But does that mean their sufferings equal mine? No doubt. [*Pause.*] No, all is a—[*he yawns*]—bsolute, [*proudly*] the bigger a man is the fuller he is. [*Pause. Gloomily.*] And the emptier. [*He sniffs.*] Clov! [*Pause.*] No, alone. [*Pause.*] What dreams! Those forests! [*Pause.*] Enough, it's time it ended, in the shelter too. [*Pause.*] And yet I hesitate, I hesitate to ... to end. Yes, there it is, it's time it ended and yet I hesitate to—[*he yawns*]—to end. [*Yawns.*] God, I'm tired, I'd be better off in bed.

[*He whistles. Enter Clov immediately. He halts beside the chair.*]

You pollute the air! [*Pause.*] Get me ready, I'm going to bed.

CLOV: I've just got you up.

HAMM: And what of it?

CLOV: I can't be getting you up and putting you to bed every five minutes, I have things to do. [*Pause.*]

HAMM: Did you ever see my eyes?

CLOV: No.

HAMM: Did you never have the curiosity, while I was sleeping, to take off my glasses and look at my eyes?

CLOV: Pulling back the lids? [*Pause.*] No.

HAMM: One of these days I'll show them to you. [*Pause.*] It seems they've gone all white. [*Pause.*] What time is it?

CLOV: The same as usual.

HAMM [*gesture towards window right*]: Have you looked?

CLOV: Yes.

HAMM: Well?

CLOV: Zero.

HAMM: It'd need to rain.

CLOV: It won't rain. [*Pause.*]

HAMM: Apart from that, how do you feel?

CLOV: I don't complain.

HAMM: You feel normal?

CLOV [*irritably*]: I tell you I don't complain.

HAMM: I feel a little queer. [*Pause.*] Clov!

CLOV: Yes.

HAMM: Have you not had enough?
CLOV: Yes! [*Pause.*] Of what?
HAMM: Of this . . . this . . . thing.
CLOV: I always had. [*Pause.*] Not you?
HAMM [*gloomily*]:   Then there's no reason for it to change.
CLOV: It may end. [*Pause.*] All life long the same questions, the same answers.
HAMM: Get me ready.

[*Clov does not move.*]

Go and get the sheet.

[*Clov does not move.*]

Clov!
CLOV: Yes.
HAMM: I'll give you nothing more to eat.
CLOV: Then we'll die.
HAMM: I'll give you just enough to keep you from dying. You'll be hungry all the time.
CLOV: Then we won't die. [*Pause.*] I'll go and get the sheet.

[*He goes towards the door.*]

HAMM: No!

[*Clov halts.*]

I'll give you one biscuit per day. [Pause.] One and a half. [Pause.] Why do you stay with me?
CLOV: Why do you keep me?
HAMM: There's no one else.
CLOV: There's nowhere else. [*Pause.*]
HAMM: You're leaving me all the same.
CLOV: I'm trying.
HAMM: You don't love me.
CLOV: No.
HAMM: You loved me once.
CLOV: Once!
HAMM: I've made you suffer too much. [*Pause.*] Haven't I?
CLOV: It's not that.
HAMM [*shocked*]:   I haven't made you suffer too much?
CLOV: Yes!
HAMM [*relieved*]:   Ah you gave me a fright! [*Pause. Coldly.*] Forgive me. [*Pause. Louder.*] I said, Forgive me.
CLOV: I heard you. [*Pause.*] Have you bled?
HAMM: Less. [*Pause.*] Is it not time for my pain-killer?
CLOV: No. [*Pause.*]
HAMM: How are your eyes?
CLOV: Bad.
HAMM: How are your legs?
CLOV: Bad.

HAMM: But you can move.

CLOV: Yes.

HAMM [*violently*]:   Then move!

[*Clov goes to back wall, leans against it with his forehead and hands.*]

Where are you?

CLOV: Here.

HAMM: Come back!

[*Clov returns to his place beside the chair.*]

Where are you?

CLOV: Here.

HAMM: Why don't you kill me?

CLOV: I don't know the combination of the cupboard. [*Pause.*]

HAMM: Go and get two bicycle-wheels.

CLOV: There are no more bicycle-wheels.

HAMM: What have you done with your bicycle?

CLOV: I never had a bicycle.

HAMM: The thing is impossible.

CLOV: When there were still bicycles I wept to have one. I crawled at your feet. You told me to go to hell. Now there are none.

HAMM: And your rounds? When you inspected my paupers. Always on foot?

CLOV: Sometimes on horse.

[*The lid of one of the bins lifts and the hands of Nagg appear, gripping the rim. Then his head emerges. Nightcap. Very white face. Nagg yawns, then listens.*]

I'll leave you, I have things to do.

HAMM: In your kitchen?

CLOV: Yes.

HAMM: Outside of here it's death. [*Pause.*] All right, be off.

[*Exit Clov. Pause.*]

We're getting on.

NAGG: Me pap!

HAMM: Accursed progenitor!

NAGG: Me pap!

HAMM: The old folks at home! No decency left! Guzzle, guzzle, that's all they think of.

[*He whistles. Enter Clov. He halts beside the chair.*]

Well! I thought you were leaving me.

CLOV: Oh not just yet, not just yet.

NAGG: Me pap!

HAMM: Give him his pap.

CLOV: There's no more pap.

HAMM [*to Nagg*]:   Do you hear that? There's no more pap. You'll never get any more pap.

NAGG: I want me pap!

HAMM: Give him a biscuit.

[*Exit Clov.*]

Accursed fornicator! How are your stumps?
NAGG: Never mind me stumps.

[*Enter Clov with biscuit.*]

CLOV: I'm back again, with the biscuit.

[*He gives biscuit to Nagg who fingers it, sniffs it.*]

NAGG [*plaintively*]:   What is it?
CLOV: Spratt's medium.
NAGG [*as before*]:   It's hard! I can't!
HAMM: Bottle him!

[*Clov pushes Nagg back into the bin, closes the lid.*]

CLOV [*returning to his place beside the chair*]:   If age but knew!
HAMM: Sit on him!
CLOV: I can't sit.
HAMM: True. And I can't stand.
CLOV: So it is.
HAMM: Every man his speciality. [*Pause.*] No phone calls? [*Pause.*] Don't we laugh?
CLOV [*after reflection*]:   I don't feel like it.
HAMM [*after reflection*]:   Nor I. [*Pause.*] Clov!
CLOV: Yes.
HAMM: Nature has forgotten us.
CLOV: There's no more nature.
HAMM: No more nature! You exaggerate.
CLOV: In the vicinity.
HAMM: But we breathe, we change! We lose our hair, our teeth! Our bloom! Our ideals!
CLOV: Then she hasn't forgotten us.
HAMM: But you say there is none.
CLOV [*sadly*]:   No one that ever lived ever thought so crooked as we.
HAMM: We do what we can.
CLOV: We shouldn't. [*Pause.*]
HAMM: You're a bit of all right, aren't you?
CLOV: A smithereen. [*Pause.*]
HAMM: This is slow work. [*Pause.*] Is it not time for my pain-killer?
CLOV: No. [*Pause.*] I'll leave you, I have things to do.
HAMM: In your kitchen?
CLOV: Yes.
HAMM: What, I'd like to know.
CLOV: I look at the wall.
HAMM: The wall! And what do you see on your wall? Mene, mene?[3] Naked bodies?
CLOV: I see my light dying.

3. A phrase that appears written by a supernatural hand on a wall of the Babylonian king Belshazzar's palace in the book of Daniel. The inscription, "mene, mene, tekel, upharsin," is translated by the prophet Daniel as "God has numbered the days of your kingdom and brought it to an end" (Daniel 5.26); Belshazzar is killed the same night.

HAMM: Your light dying! Listen to that! Well, it can die just as well here, *your* light. Take a look at me and then come back and tell me what you think of *your* light.

[*Pause.*]

CLOV: You shouldn't speak to me like that. [*Pause.*]
HAMM [*coldly*]:   Forgive me. [*Pause. Louder.*] I said, Forgive me.
CLOV: I heard you.

[*The lid of Nagg's bin lifts. His hands appear, gripping the rim. Then his head emerges. In his mouth the biscuit. He listens.*]

HAMM: Did your seeds come up?
CLOV: No.
HAMM: Did you scratch round them to see if they had sprouted?
CLOV: They haven't sprouted.
HAMM: Perhaps it's still too early.
CLOV: If they were going to sprout they would have sprouted. [*Violently.*] They'll never sprout!

[*Pause. Nagg takes biscuit in his hand.*]

HAMM: This is not much fun. [*Pause.*] But that's always the way at the end of the day, isn't it, Clov?
CLOV: Always.
HAMM: It's the end of the day like any other day, isn't it, Clov?
CLOV: Looks like it. [*Pause.*]
HAMM [*anguished*]:   What's happening, what's happening?
CLOV: Something is taking its course. [*Pause.*]
HAMM: All right, be off.

[*He leans back in his chair, remains motionless. Clov does not move, heaves a great groaning sigh. Hamm sits up.*]

I thought I told you to be off.
CLOV: I'm trying.

[*He goes to door, halts.*]

Ever since I was whelped.

[*Exit Clov.*]

HAMM: We're getting on.

[*He leans back in his chair, remains motionless. Nagg knocks on the lid of the other bin. Pause. He knocks harder. The lid lifts and the hands of Nell appear, gripping the rim. Then her head emerges. Lace cap. Very white face.*]

NELL: What is it, my pet? [*Pause.*] Time for love?
NAGG: Were you asleep?
NELL: Oh no!
NAGG: Kiss me.
NELL: We can't.
NAGG: Try.

[*Their heads strain towards each other, fail to meet, fall apart again.*]

NELL: Why this farce, day after day? [*Pause.*]

NAGG: I've lost me tooth.

NELL: When?

NAGG: I had it yesterday.

NELL [*elegiac*]:   Ah yesterday!

   [*They turn painfully towards each other.*]

NAGG: Can you see me?

NELL: Hardly. And you?

NAGG: What?

NELL: Can you see me?

NAGG: Hardly.

NELL: So much the better, so much the better.

NAGG: Don't say that. [*Pause.*] Our sight has failed.

NELL: Yes.

   [*Pause. They turn away from each other.*]

NAGG: Can you hear me?

NELL: Yes. And you?

NAGG: Yes. [*Pause.*] Our hearing hasn't failed.

NELL: Our what?

NAGG: Our hearing.

NELL: No. [*Pause.*] Have you anything else to say to me?

NAGG: Do you remember—

NELL: No.

NAGG: When we crashed on our tandem and lost our shanks.

   [*They laugh heartily.*]

NELL: It was in the Ardennes.

   [*They laugh less heartily.*]

NAGG: On the road to Sedan.[4]

   [*They laugh still less heartily.*]

   Are you cold?

NELL: Yes, perished. And you?

NAGG: [*Pause.*] I'm freezing. [*Pause.*] Do you want to go in?

NELL: Yes.

NAGG: Then go in.

   [*Nell does not move.*]

   Why don't you go in?

NELL: I don't know. [*Pause.*]

NAGG: Has he changed your sawdust?

NELL: It isn't sawdust. [*Pause. Wearily.*] Can you not be a little accurate, Nagg?

NAGG: Your sand then. It's not important.

NELL: It is important. [*Pause.*]

---

4. A town in the Ardennes, a wooded region in northern France.

NAGG: It was sawdust once.

NELL: Once!

NAGG: And now it's sand. [*Pause.*] From the shore. [*Pause. Impatiently.*] Now it's sand he fetches from the shore.

NELL: Now it's sand.

NAGG: Has he changed yours?

NELL: No.

NAGG: Nor mine. [*Pause.*] I won't have it! [*Pause. Holding up the biscuit.*] Do you want a bit?

NELL: No. [*Pause.*] Of what?

NAGG: Biscuit. I've kept you half. [*He looks at the biscuit. Proudly.*] Three quarters. For you. Here. [*He proffers the biscuit.*] No? [*Pause.*] Do you not feel well?

HAMM [*wearily*]: Quiet, quiet, you're keeping me awake. [*Pause.*] Talk softer. [*Pause.*] If I could sleep I might make love. I'd go into the woods. My eyes would see...the sky, the earth. I'd run, run, they wouldn't catch me. [*Pause.*] Nature! [*Pause.*] There's something dripping in my head. [*Pause.*] A heart, a heart in my head. [*Pause.*]

NAGG [*soft*]: Do you hear him? A heart in his head! [*He chuckles cautiously.*]

NELL: One mustn't laugh at those things, Nagg. Why must you always laugh at them?

NAGG: Not so loud!

NELL [*without lowering her voice*]: Nothing is funnier than unhappiness, I grant you that. But—

NAGG [*shocked*]: Oh!

NELL: Yes, yes, it's the most comical thing in the world. And we laugh, we laugh, with a will, in the beginning. But it's always the same thing. Yes, it's like the funny story we have heard too often, we still find it funny, but we don't laugh any more. [*Pause.*] Have you anything else to say to me?

NAGG: No.

NELL: Are you quite sure? [*Pause.*] Then I'll leave you.

NAGG: Do you not want your biscuit? [*Pause.*] I'll keep it for you. [*Pause.*] I thought you were going to leave me.

NELL: I am going to leave you.

NAGG: Could you give me a scratch before you go?

NELL: No. [*Pause.*] Where?

NAGG: In the back.

NELL: No. [*Pause.*] Rub yourself against the rim.

NAGG: It's lower down. In the hollow.

NELL: What hollow?

NAGG: The hollow! [*Pause.*] Could you not? [*Pause.*] Yesterday you scratched me there.

NELL [*elegiac*]: Ah yesterday!

NAGG: Could you not? [*Pause.*] Would you like me to scratch you? [*Pause.*] Are you crying again?

NELL: I was trying. [*Pause.*]

HAMM: Perhaps it's a little vein. [*Pause.*]

NAGG: What was that he said?

NELL: Perhaps it's a little vein.

NAGG: What does that mean? [*Pause.*] That means nothing. [*Pause.*] Will I tell you the story of the tailor?

NELL: No. [*Pause.*] What for?

NAGG: To cheer you up.

NELL: It's not funny.

NAGG: It always made you laugh. [*Pause.*] The first time I thought you'd die.

NELL: It was on Lake Como.[5] [*Pause.*] One April afternoon. [*Pause.*] Can you believe it?

NAGG: What?

NELL: That we once went out rowing on Lake Como. [*Pause.*] One April afternoon.

NAGG: We had got engaged the day before.

NELL: Engaged!

NAGG: You were in such fits that we capsized. By rights we should have been drowned.

NELL: It was because I felt happy.

NAGG [*indignant*]:   It was not, it was not, it was my story and nothing else. Happy! Don't you laugh at it still? Every time I tell it. Happy!

NELL: It was deep, deep. And you could see down to the bottom. So white. So clean.

NAGG: Let me tell it again. [*Raconteur's*[6] *voice.*] An Englishman, needing a pair of striped trousers in a hurry for the New Year festivities, goes to his tailor who takes his measurements.

[*Tailor's voice.*]

"That's the lot, come back in four days, I'll have it ready." Good. Four days later.

[*Tailor's voice.*]

"So sorry, come back in a week, I've made a mess of the seat." Good, that's all right, a neat seat can be very ticklish. A week later.

[*Tailor's voice.*]

"Frightfully sorry, come back in ten days, I've made a hash of the crotch." Good, can't be helped, a snug crotch is always a teaser. Ten days later.

[*Tailor's voice.*]

"Dreadfully sorry, come back in a fortnight, I've made a balls of the fly." Good, at a pinch, a smart fly is a stiff proposition. [*Pause. Normal voice.*] I never told it worse. [*Pause. Gloomy.*] I tell this story worse and worse.

[*Pause. Raconteur's voice.*]

Well, to make it short, the bluebells are blowing and he ballockses the buttonholes.

[*Customer's voice.*]

"God damn you to hell, Sir, no, it's indecent, there are limits! In six days, do you hear me, six days, God made the world. Yes Sir, no less Sir, the WORLD! And you are not bloody well capable of making me a pair of trousers in three months!"

[*Tailor's voice, scandalized.*]

"But my dear Sir, my dear Sir, look—[*disdainful gesture, disgustedly*]—at the world—[*pause*] and look—[*loving gesture, proudly*]—at my TROUSERS!"

---

5. A scenic lake in northern Italy.

6. A talented storyteller.

[*Pause. He looks at Nell who has remained impassive, her eyes unseeing, breaks into a high forced laugh, cuts it short, pokes his head towards Nell, launches his laugh again.*]

HAMM: Silence!

[*Nagg starts, cuts short his laugh.*]

NELL: You could see down to the bottom.

HAMM [*exasperated*]:   Have you not finished? Will you never finish? [*With sudden fury.*] Will this never finish?

[*Nagg disappears into his bin, closes the lid behind him. Nell does not move. Frenziedly.*]

My kingdom for a nightman![7]

[*He whistles. Enter Clov.*]

Clear away this muck! Chuck it in the sea!

[*Clov goes to bins, halts.*]

NELL: So white.
HAMM: What? What's she blathering about?

[*Clov stoops, takes Nell's hand, feels her pulse.*]

NELL [*to Clov*]:   Desert!

[*Clov lets go her hand, pushes her back in the bin, closes the lid.*]

CLOV [*returning to his place beside the chair*]:   She has no pulse.
HAMM: What was she drivelling about?
CLOV: She told me to go away, into the desert.
HAMM: Damn busybody! Is that all?
CLOV: No.
HAMM: What else?
CLOV: I didn't understand.
HAMM: Have you bottled her?
CLOV: Yes.
HAMM: Are they both bottled?
CLOV: Yes.
HAMM: Screw down the lids.

[*Clov goes towards door.*]

Time enough.

[*Clov halts.*]

My anger subsides, I'd like to pee.
CLOV [*with alacrity*]:   I'll go and get the catheter.

[*He goes towards door.*]

7. Someone who empties outhouses. Hamm's phrasing alludes to Richard III's call, "My kingdom for a horse!" in Shakespeare's tragedy *Richard III* 5.4.

HAMM: Time enough.

[*Clov halts.*]

Give me my pain-killer.

CLOV: It's too soon. [*Pause.*] It's too soon on top of your tonic, it wouldn't act.

HAMM: In the morning they brace you up and in the evening they calm you down. Unless it's the other way round. [*Pause.*] That old doctor, he's dead naturally?

CLOV: He wasn't old.

HAMM: But he's dead?

CLOV: Naturally. [*Pause.*] *You* ask *me* that? [*Pause.*]

HAMM: Take me for a little turn.

[*Clov goes behind the chair and pushes it forward.*]

Not too fast!

[*Clov pushes chair.*]

Right round the world!

[*Clov pushes chair.*]

Hug the walls, then back to the center again.

[*Clov pushes chair.*]

I was right in the center, wasn't I?

CLOV [*pushing*]:   Yes.

HAMM: We'd need a proper wheel-chair. With big wheels. Bicycle wheels! [*Pause.*] Are you hugging?

CLOV [*pushing*]:   Yes.

HAMM [*groping for wall*]:   It's a lie! Why do you lie to me?

CLOV [*bearing closer to wall*]:   There! There!

HAMM: Stop!

[*Clov stops chair close to back wall. Hamm lays his hand against wall.*]

Old wall! [*Pause.*] Beyond is the . . . other hell. [*Pause. Violently.*] Closer! Closer! Up against!

CLOV: Take away your hand.

[*Hamm withdraws his hand. Clov rams chair against wall.*]

There!

[*Hamm leans towards wall, applies his ear to it.*]

HAMM: Do you hear?

[*He strikes the wall with his knuckles.*]

Do you hear? Hollow bricks!

[*He strikes again.*]

All that's hollow! [*Pause. He straightens up. Violently.*] That's enough. Back!

CLOV: We haven't done the round.

HAMM: Back to my place!

[*Clov pushes chair back to center.*]

   Is that my place?
CLOV: Yes, that's your place.
HAMM: Am I right in the center?
CLOV: I'll measure it.
HAMM: More or less! More or less!
CLOV [*moving chair slightly*]:   There!
HAMM: I'm more or less in the center?
CLOV: I'd say so.
HAMM: You'd say so! Put me right in the center!
CLOV: I'll go and get the tape.
HAMM: Roughly! Roughly!

[*Clov moves chair slightly.*]

   Bang in the center!
CLOV: There! [*Pause.*]
HAMM: I feel a little too far to the left.

[*Clov moves chair slightly.*]

Now I feel a little too far to the right.

[*Clov moves chair slightly.*]

I feel a little too far forward.

[*Clov moves chair slightly.*]

Now I feel a little too far back.

[*Clov moves chair slightly.*]

Don't stay there [*i.e. behind the chair*], you give me the shivers.

[*Clov returns to his place beside the chair.*]

CLOV: If I could kill him I'd die happy. [*Pause.*]
HAMM: What's the weather like?
CLOV: As usual.
HAMM: Look at the earth.
CLOV: I've looked.
HAMM: With the glass?
CLOV: No need of the glass.
HAMM: Look at it with the glass.
CLOV: I'll go and get the glass

[*Exit Clov.*]

HAMM: No need for the glass!

[*Enter Clov with telescope.*]

CLOV: I'm back again, with the glass.

[*He goes to window right, looks up at it.*]

I need the steps.

HAMM: Why? Have you shrunk?

[*Exit Clov with telescope.*]

I don't like that, I don't like that.

[*Enter Clov with ladder, but without telescope.*]

CLOV: I'm back again, with the steps.

[*He sets down ladder under window right, gets up on it, realizes he has not the telescope, gets down.*]

I need the glass.

[*He goes towards door.*]

HAMM [*violently*]:   But you have the glass!

CLOV [*halting, violently*]:   No, I haven't the glass!

[*Exit Clov.*]

HAMM: This is deadly.

[*Enter Clov with telescope. He goes towards ladder.*]

CLOV: Things are livening up.

[*He gets up on the ladder, raises the telescope, lets it fall.*]

I did it on purpose.

[*He gets down, picks up the telescope, turns it on auditorium.*]

I see...a multitude...in transports...of joy. [*Pause.*] That's what I call a magnifier.

[*He lowers the telescope, turns towards Hamm.*]

Well? Don't we laugh?

HAMM [*after reflection*]:   I don't.

CLOV [*after reflection*]:   Nor I.

[*He gets up on ladder, turns the telescope on the without.*]

Let's see.

[*He looks, moving the telescope.*]

Zero...[*he looks*]...zero...[*he looks*]...and zero.

HAMM: Nothing stirs. All is—

CLOV: Zer—

HAMM [*violently*]:   Wait till you're spoken to! [*Normal voice.*] All is...all is...all is what? [*Violently.*] All is what?

CLOV: What all is? In a word? Is that what you want to know? Just a moment.

[He turns the telescope on the without, looks, lowers the telescope, turns towards Hamm.]

Corpsed. *[Pause.]* Well? Content?

HAMM: Look at the sea.

CLOV: It's the same.

HAMM: Look at the ocean!

[Clov gets down, takes a few steps towards window left, goes back for ladder, carries it over and sets it down under window left, gets up on it, turns the telescope on the without, looks at length. He starts, lowers the telescope, examines it, turns it again on the without.]

CLOV: Never seen anything like that!

HAMM *[anxious]*:   What? A sail? A fin? Smoke?

CLOV *[looking]*:   The light is sunk.

HAMM *[relieved]*:   Pah! We all knew that.

CLOV *[looking]*:   There was a bit left.

HAMM: The base.

CLOV *[looking]*:   Yes.

HAMM: And now?

CLOV *[looking]*:   All gone.

HAMM: No gulls?

CLOV *[looking]*:   Gulls!

HAMM: And the horizon? Nothing on the horizon?

CLOV *[lowering the telescope, turning towards Hamm, exasperated]*:   What in God's name could there be on the horizon? *[Pause.]*

HAMM: The waves, how are the waves?

CLOV: The waves?

[He turns the telescope on the waves.]

Lead.

HAMM: And the sun?

CLOV *[looking]*:   Zero.

HAMM: But it should be sinking. Look again.

CLOV *[looking]*:   Damn the sun.

HAMM: Is it night already then?

CLOV *[looking]*:   No.

HAMM: Then what is it?

CLOV *[looking]*:   Gray.

[Lowering the telescope, turning towards Hamm, louder.]

Gray! *[Pause. Still louder.]* GRRAY! *[Pause. He gets down, approaches Hamm from behind, whispers in his ear.]*

HAMM *[starting]*:   Gray! Did I hear you say gray?

CLOV: Light black. From pole to pole.

HAMM: You exaggerate. *[Pause.]* Don't stay there, you give me the shivers.

[Clov returns to his place beside the chair.]

CLOV: Why this farce, day after day?

HAMM: Routine. One never knows. [*Pause.*] Last night I saw inside my breast. There was a big sore.

CLOV: Pah! You saw your heart.

HAMM: No, it was living. [*Pause. Anguished.*] Clov!

CLOV: Yes.

HAMM: What's happening?

CLOV: Something is taking its course. [*Pause.*]

HAMM: Clov!

CLOV [*impatiently*]:   What is it?

HAMM: We're not beginning to...to...mean something?

CLOV: Mean something! You and I, mean something! [*Brief laugh.*] Ah that's a good one!

HAMM: I wonder. [*Pause.*] Imagine if a rational being came back to earth, wouldn't he be liable to get ideas into his head if he observed us long enough. [*Voice of rational being.*] Ah, good, now I see what it is, yes, now I understand what they're at!

[*Clov starts, drops the telescope and begins to scratch his belly with both hands. Normal voice.*]

And without going so far as that, we ourselves...[*with emotion*]...we ourselves...at certain moments...[*Vehemently.*] To think perhaps it won't all have been for nothing!

CLOV [*anguished, scratching himself*]:   I have a flea!

HAMM: A flea! Are there still fleas?

CLOV: On me there's one. [*Scratching.*] Unless it's a crablouse.

HAMM [*very perturbed*]:   But humanity might start from there all over again! Catch him, for the love of God!

CLOV: I'll go and get the powder.

[*Exit Clov.*]

HAMM: A flea! This is awful! What a day!

[*Enter Clov with a sprinkling-tin.*]

CLOV: I'm back again, with the insecticide.

HAMM: Let him have it!

[*Clov loosens the top of his trousers, pulls it forward and shakes powder into the aperture. He stoops, looks, waits, starts, frenziedly shakes more powder, stoops, looks, waits.*]

CLOV: The bastard!

HAMM: Did you get him?

CLOV: Looks like it.

[*He drops the tin and adjusts his trousers.*]

Unless he's laying doggo.

HAMM: Laying! Lying you mean. Unless he's *lying* doggo.

CLOV: Ah? One says lying? One doesn't say laying?

HAMM: Use your head, can't you. If he was laying we'd be bitched.

CLOV: Ah. [*Pause.*] What about that pee?

SAMUEL BECKETT

HAMM: I'm having it.

CLOV: Ah that's the spirit, that's the spirit! [*Pause.*]

HAMM [*with ardour*]:   Let's go from here, the two of us! South! You can make a raft and the currents will carry us away, far away, to other...mammals!

CLOV: God forbid!

HAMM: Alone, I'll embark alone! Get working on that raft immediately. Tomorrow I'll be gone for ever.

CLOV [*hastening towards door*]:   I'll start straight away.

HAMM: Wait!

[*Clov halts.*]

Will there be sharks, do you think?

CLOV: Sharks? I don't know. If there are there will be.

[*He goes towards door.*]

HAMM: Wait!

[*Clov halts.*]

Is it not yet time for my pain-killer?

CLOV [*violently*]:   No!

[*He goes towards door.*]

HAMM: Wait!

[*Clov halts.*]

How are your eyes?

CLOV: Bad.

HAMM: But you can see.

CLOV: All I want.

HAMM: How are your legs?

CLOV: Bad.

HAMM: But you can walk.

CLOV: I come...and go.

HAMM: In my house. [*Pause. With prophetic relish.*] One day you'll be blind, like me. You'll be sitting there, a speck in the void, in the dark, for ever, like me. [*Pause.*] One day you'll say to yourself, I'm tired, I'll sit down, and you'll go and sit down. Then you'll say, I'm hungry, I'll get up and get something to eat. But you won't get up. You'll say, I shouldn't have sat down, but since I have I'll sit on a little longer, then I'll get up and get something to eat. But you won't get up and you won't get anything to eat. [*Pause.*] You'll look at the wall a while, then you'll say, I'll close my eyes, perhaps have a little sleep, after that I'll feel better, and you'll close them. And when you open them again there'll be no wall any more. [*Pause.*] Infinite emptiness will be all around you, all the resurrected dead of all the ages wouldn't fill it, and there you'll be like a little bit of grit in the middle of the steppe. [*Pause.*] Yes, one day you'll know what it is, you'll be like me, except that you won't have anyone with you, because you won't have had pity on anyone and because there won't be anyone left to have pity on. [*Pause.*]

CLOV: It's not certain. [*Pause.*] And there's one thing you forget.

HAMM: Ah?

CLOV: I can't sit down.

HAMM [*impatiently*]:   Well you'll lie down then, what the hell! Or you'll come to a standstill, simply stop and stand still, the way you are now. One day you'll say, I'm tired, I'll stop. What does the attitude matter? [*Pause.*]

CLOV: So you all want me to leave you.

HAMM: Naturally.

CLOV: Then I'll leave you.

HAMM: You can't leave us.

CLOV: Then I won't leave you. [*Pause.*]

HAMM: Why don't you finish us? [*Pause.*] I'll tell you the combination of the cupboard if you promise to finish me.

CLOV: I couldn't finish you.

HAMM: Then you won't finish me. [*Pause.*]

CLOV: I'll leave you, I have things to do.

HAMM: Do you remember when you came here?

CLOV: No. Too small, you told me.

HAMM: Do you remember your father.

CLOV [*wearily*]:   Same answer. [*Pause.*] You've asked me these questions millions of times.

HAMM: I love the old questions. [*With fervour.*] Ah the old questions, the old answers, there's nothing like them! [*Pause.*] It was I was a father to you.

CLOV: Yes. [*He looks at Hamm fixedly.*] You were that to me.

HAMM: My house a home for you.

CLOV: Yes. [*He looks about him.*] This was that for me.

HAMM [*proudly*]:   But for me, [*gesture towards himself*] no father. But for Hamm, [*gesture towards surroundings*] no home. [*Pause.*]

CLOV: I'll leave you.

HAMM: Did you ever think of one thing?

CLOV: Never.

HAMM: That here we're down in a hole. [*Pause.*] But beyond the hills? Eh? Perhaps it's still green. Eh? [*Pause.*] Flora! Pomona! [*Ecstatically.*] Ceres![8] [*Pause.*] Perhaps you won't need to go very far.

CLOV: I can't go very far. [*Pause.*] I'll leave you.

HAMM: Is my dog ready?

CLOV: He lacks a leg.

HAMM: Is he silky?

CLOV: He's a kind of Pomeranian.

HAMM: Go and get him.

CLOV: He lacks a leg.

HAMM: Go and get him!

   [*Exit Clov.*]

We're getting on.

   [*Enter Clov holding by one of its three legs a black toy dog.*]

CLOV: Your dogs are here.

---

8. Flora, Pomona, and Ceres: the Roman goddesses of flowering plants, fruits, and grains.

[He hands the dog to Hamm who feels it, fondles it.]

HAMM: He's white, isn't he?
CLOV: Nearly.
HAMM: What do you mean, nearly? Is he white or isn't he?
CLOV: He isn't. *[Pause.]*
HAMM: You've forgotten the sex.
CLOV *[vexed]*:   But he isn't finished. The sex goes on at the end. *[Pause.]*
HAMM: You haven't put on his ribbon.
CLOV *[angrily]*:   But he isn't finished, I tell you! First you finish your dog and then you put on his ribbon! *[Pause.]*
HAMM: Can he stand?
CLOV: I don't know.
HAMM: Try.

[He hands the dog to Clov who places it on the ground.]

Well?
CLOV: Wait!

[He squats down and tries to get the dog to stand on its three legs, fails, lets it go. The dog falls on its side.]

HAMM *[impatiently]*:   Well?
CLOV: He's standing.
HAMM *[groping for the dog]*:   Where? Where is he?

[Clov holds up the dog in a standing position.]

CLOV: There.

[He takes Hamm's hand and guides it towards the dog's head.]

HAMM *[his hand on the dog's head]*:   Is he gazing at me?
CLOV: Yes.
HAMM *[proudly]*:   As if he were asking me to take him for a walk?
CLOV: If you like.
HAMM *[as before]*:   Or as if he were begging me for a bone.

[He withdraws his hand.]

Leave him like that, standing there imploring me.

[Clov straightens up. The dog falls on its side.]

CLOV: I'll leave you.
HAMM: Have you had your visions?
CLOV: Less.
HAMM: Is Mother Pegg's light on?
CLOV: Light! How could anyone's light be on?
HAMM: Extinguished!
CLOV: Naturally it's extinguished. If it's not on it's extinguished.
HAMM: No, I mean Mother Pegg.
CLOV: But naturally she's extinguished! *[Pause.]* What's the matter with you today?
HAMM: I'm taking my course. *[Pause.]* Is she buried?

CLOV: Buried! Who would have buried her?

HAMM: You.

CLOV: Me! Haven't I enough to do without burying people?

HAMM: But you'll bury me.

CLOV: No I won't bury you. [*Pause.*]

HAMM: She was bonny once, like a flower of the field. [*With reminiscent leer.*] And a great one for the men!

CLOV: We too were bonny—once. It's a rare thing not to have been bonny—once.

[*Pause.*]

HAMM: Go and get the gaff.[9]

[*Clov goes to door, halts.*]

CLOV: Do this, do that, and I do it. I never refuse. Why?

HAMM: You're not able to.

CLOV: Soon I won't do it any more.

HAMM: You won't be able to any more.

[*Exit Clov.*]

Ah the creatures, the creatures, everything has to be explained to them.

[*Enter Clov with gaff.*]

CLOV: Here's your gaff. Stick it up.

[*He gives the gaff to Hamm who, wielding it like a puntpole, tries to move his chair.*]

HAMM: Did I move?

CLOV: No.

[*Hamm throws down the gaff.*]

HAMM: Go and get the oilcan.

CLOV: What for?

HAMM: To oil the castors.

CLOV: I oiled them yesterday.

HAMM: Yesterday! What does that mean? Yesterday!

CLOV [*violently*]:   That means that bloody awful day, long ago, before this bloody awful day. I use the words you taught me. If they don't mean anything any more, teach me others. Or let me be silent. [*Pause.*]

HAMM: I once knew a madman who thought the end of the world had come. He was a painter—and engraver. I had a great fondness for him. I used to go and see him, in the asylum. I'd take him by the hand and drag him to the window. Look! There! All that rising corn! And there! Look! The sails of the herring fleet! All that loveliness! [*Pause.*] He'd snatch away his hand and go back into his corner. Appalled. All he had seen was ashes. [*Pause.*] He alone had been spared. [*Pause.*] Forgotten. [*Pause.*] It appears the case is...was not so...so unusual.

CLOV: A madman? When was that?

HAMM: Oh way back, way back, you weren't in the land of the living.

CLOV: God be with the days!

9. A fishing pole designed for catching large fish.

[*Pause. Hamm raises his toque.*]

HAMM: I had a great fondness for him.

[*Pause. He puts on his toque again.*]

He was a painter—and engraver.

CLOV: There are so many terrible things.

HAMM: No, no, there are not so many now. [*Pause.*] Clov!

CLOV: Yes.

HAMM: Do you not think this has gone on long enough?

CLOV: Yes! [*Pause.*] What?

HAMM: This...this...thing.

CLOV: I've always thought so. [*Pause.*] You not?

HAMM [*gloomily*]:   Then it's a day like any other day.

CLOV: As long as it lasts. [*Pause.*] All life long the same inanities.

HAMM: I can't leave you.

CLOV: I know. And you can't follow me. [*Pause.*]

HAMM: If you leave me how shall I know?

CLOV [*briskly*]:   Well you simply whistle me and if I don't come running it means
          I've left you. [*Pause.*]

HAMM: You won't come and kiss me goodbye?

CLOV: Oh I shouldn't think so. [*Pause.*]

HAMM: But you might be merely dead in your kitchen.

CLOV: The result would be the same.

HAMM: Yes, but how would I know, if you were merely dead in your kitchen?

CLOV: Well...sooner or later I'd start to stink.

HAMM: You stink already. The whole place stinks of corpses.

CLOV: The whole universe.

HAMM [*angrily*]:   To hell with the universe. [*Pause.*] Think of something.

CLOV: What?

HAMM: An idea, have an idea. [*Angrily.*] A bright idea!

CLOV: Ah good.

[*He starts pacing to and fro, his eyes fixed on the ground, his hands behind his
back. He halts.*]

The pains in my legs! It's unbelievable! Soon I won't be able to think any more.

HAMM: You won't be able to leave me.

[*Clov resumes his pacing.*]

What are you doing?

CLOV: Having an idea.

[*He paces.*]

Ah!

[*He halts.*]

HAMM: What a brain! [*Pause.*] Well?

CLOV: Wait! [*He meditates. Not very convinced.*] Yes...[*Pause. More convinced.*]
          Yes! [*He raises his head.*] I have it! I set the alarm. [*Pause.*]

HAMM: This is perhaps not one of my bright days, but frankly—

CLOV: You whistle me. I don't come. The alarm rings. I'm gone. It doesn't ring. I'm dead. [*Pause.*]

HAMM: Is it working? [*Pause. Impatiently.*] The alarm, is it working?

CLOV: Why wouldn't it be working?

HAMM: Because it's worked too much.

CLOV: But it's hardly worked at all.

HAMM [*angrily*]:   Then because it's worked too little!

CLOV: I'll go and see.

[*Exit Clov. Brief ring of alarm off. Enter Clov with alarm-clock. He holds it against Hamm's ear and releases alarm. They listen to it ringing to the end. Pause.*]

Fit to wake the dead! Did you hear it?

HAMM: Vaguely.

CLOV: The end is terrific!

HAMM: I prefer the middle. [*Pause.*] Is it not time for my pain-killer?

CLOV: No! [*He goes to door, turns.*] I'll leave you.

HAMM: It's time for my story. Do you want to listen to my story?

CLOV: No.

HAMM: Ask my father if he wants to listen to my story.

[*Clov goes to bins, raises the lid of Nagg's, stoops, looks into it. Pause. He straightens up.*]

CLOV: He's asleep.

HAMM: Wake him.

[*Clov stoops, wakes Nagg with the alarm. Unintelligible words. Clov straightens up.*]

CLOV: He doesn't want to listen to your story.

HAMM: I'll give him a bon-bon.

[*Clov stoops. As before.*]

CLOV: He wants a sugar-plum.

HAMM: He'll get a sugar-plum.

[*Clov stoops. As before.*]

CLOV: It's a deal.

[*He goes towards door. Nagg's hands appear, gripping the rim. Then the head emerges. Clov reaches door, turns.*]

Do you believe in the life to come?

HAMM: Mine was always that.

[*Exit Clov.*]

Got him that time!

NAGG: I'm listening.

HAMM: Scoundrel! Why did you engender me?

NAGG: I didn't know.

HAMM: What? What didn't you know?

NAGG: That it'd be you. [*Pause.*] You'll give me a sugar-plum?

HAMM: After the audition.

NAGG: You swear?

HAMM: Yes.

NAGG: On what?

HAMM: My honor. [*Pause. They laugh heartily.*]

NAGG: Two.

HAMM: One.

NAGG: One for me and one for—

HAMM: One! Silence! [*Pause.*] Where was I? [*Pause. Gloomily.*] It's finished, we're finished. [*Pause.*] Nearly finished. [*Pause.*] There'll be no more speech. [*Pause.*] Something dripping in my head, ever since the fontanelles.[1] [*Stifled hilarity of Nagg.*] Splash, splash, always on the same spot. [*Pause.*] Perhaps it's a little vein. [*Pause.*] A little artery. [*Pause. More animated.*] Enough of that, it's story time, where was I? [*Pause. Narrative tone.*] The man came crawling towards me, on his belly. Pale, wonderfully pale and thin, he seemed on the point of—[*Pause. Normal tone.*] No, I've done that bit. [*Pause. Narrative tone.*] I calmly filled my pipe—the meerschaum, lit it with . . . let us say a vesta,[2] drew a few puffs. Aah! [*Pause.*] Well, what is it *you* want? [*Pause.*] It was an extra-ordinarily bitter day, I remember, zero by the thermometer. But considering it was Christmas Eve there was nothing . . . extra-ordinary about that. Seasonable weather, for once in a way. [*Pause.*] Well, what ill wind blows you my way? He raised his face to me, black with mingled dirt and tears. [*Pause. Normal tone.*] That should do it.

[*Narrative tone.*]

No no, don't look at me, don't look at me. He dropped his eyes and mumbled something, apologies I presume. [*Pause.*] I'm a busy man, you know, the final touches, before the festivities, you know what it is. [*Pause. Forcibly.*] Come on now, what is the object of this invasion? [*Pause.*] It was a glorious bright day, I remember, fifty by the heliometer, but already the sun was sinking down into the . . . down among the dead.

[*Normal tone.*]

Nicely put, that.

[*Narrative tone.*]

Come on now, come on, present your petition and let me resume my labors.

[*Pause. Normal tone.*]

There's English for you. Ah well . . .

[*Narrative tone.*]

It was then he took the plunge. It's my little one, he said. Tsstss, a little one, that's bad. My little boy, he said, as if the sex mattered. Where did he come from? He named the hole. A good half-day, on horse. What are you insinuating? That the place is still inhabited? No no, not a soul, except himself and the child—assuming

---

1. Soft gaps between an infant's skull bones.
2. A match.

he existed. Good. I enquired about the situation at Kov, beyond the gulf. Not a sinner. Good. And you expect me to believe you have left your little one back there, all alone, and alive into the bargain? Come now! [*Pause.*] It was a howling wild day, I remember, a hundred by the anenometer.[3] The wind was tearing up the dead pines and sweeping them . . . away.

[*Pause. Normal tone.*]

A bit feeble, that.

[*Narrative tone.*]

Come on, man, speak up, what is it you want from me, I have to put up my holly. [*Pause.*]

Well to make it short it finally transpired that what he wanted from me was . . . bread for his brat? Bread? But I have no bread, it doesn't agree with me. Good. Then perhaps a little corn?

[*Pause. Normal tone.*]

That should do it.

[*Narrative tone.*]

Corn, yes, I have corn, it's true, in my granaries. But use your head. I give you some corn, a pound, a pound and a half, you bring it back to your child and you make him—if he's still alive—a nice pot of porridge, [*Nagg reacts*] a nice pot and a half of porridge, full of nourishment. Good. The colors come back into his little cheeks—perhaps. And then? [*Pause.*] I lost patience. [*Violently.*] Use your head, can't you, use your head, you're on earth, there's no cure for that! [*Pause.*] It was an exceedingly dry day, I remember, zero by the hygrometer. Ideal weather, for my lumbago. [*Pause. Violently.*] But what in God's name do you imagine? That the earth will awake in spring? That the rivers and seas will run with fish again? That there's manna in heaven still for imbeciles like you? [*Pause.*] Gradually I cooled down, sufficiently at least to ask him how long he had taken on the way. Three whole days. Good. In what condition he had left the child. Deep in sleep. [*Forcibly.*] But deep in what sleep, deep in what sleep already? [*Pause.*] Well to make it short I finally offered to take him into my service. He had touched a chord. And then I imagined already that I wasn't much longer for this world. [*He laughs. Pause.*] Well? [*Pause.*] Well? Here if you were careful you might die a nice natural death, in peace and comfort. [*Pause.*] Well? [*Pause.*] In the end he asked me would I consent to take in the child as well—if he were still alive. [*Pause.*] It was the moment I was waiting for. [*Pause.*] Would I consent to take in the child . . . [*Pause.*] I can see him still, down on his knees, his hands flat on the ground, glaring at me with his mad eyes, in defiance of my wishes. [*Pause. Normal tone.*] I'll soon have finished with this story. [*Pause.*] Unless I bring in other characters. [*Pause.*] But where would I find them? [*Pause.*] Where would I look for them? [*Pause. He whistles. Enter Clov.*] Let us pray to God.

NAGG: Me sugar-plum!

CLOV: There's a rat in the kitchen!

---

3. An instrument used to measure wind speed.

HAMM: A rat! Are there still rats?

CLOV: In the kitchen there's one.

HAMM: And you haven't exterminated him?

CLOV: Half. You disturbed us.

HAMM: He can't get away?

CLOV: No.

HAMM: You'll finish him later. Let us pray to God.

CLOV: Again!

NAGG: Me sugar-plum!

HAMM: God first! [*Pause.*] Are you right?

CLOV [*resigned*]:   Off we go.

HAMM [*to Nagg*]:   And you?

NAGG [*clasping his hands, closing his eyes, in a gabble*]:   Our Father which art—

HAMM: Silence! In silence! Where are your manners? [*Pause.*] Off we go. [*Attitudes of prayer. Silence. Abandoning his attitude, discouraged.*] Well?

CLOV [*abandoning his attitude*]:   What a hope! And you?

HAMM: Sweet damn all! [*To Nagg.*] And you?

NAGG: Wait! [*Pause. Abandoning his attitude.*] Nothing doing!

HAMM: The bastard! He doesn't exist!

CLOV: Not yet.

NAGG: Me sugar-plum!

HAMM: There are no more sugar-plums! [*Pause.*]

NAGG: It's natural. After all I'm your father. It's true if it hadn't been me it would have been someone else. But that's no excuse. [*Pause.*] Turkish Delight, for example, which no longer exists, we all know that, there is nothing in the world I love more. And one day I'll ask you for some, in return for a kindness, and you'll promise it to me. One must live with the times. [*Pause.*] Whom did you call when you were a tiny boy, and were frightened, in the dark? Your mother? No. Me. We let you cry. Then we moved you out of earshot, so that we might sleep in peace. [*Pause.*] I was asleep, as happy as a king, and you woke me up to have me listen to you. It wasn't indispensable, you didn't really need to have me listen to you. Besides I didn't listen to you. [*Pause.*] I hope the day will come when you'll really need to have me listen to you, and need to hear my voice, any voice. [*Pause.*] Yes, I hope I'll live till then, to hear you calling me like when you were a tiny boy, and were frightened, in the dark, and I was your only hope. [*Pause. Nagg knocks on lid of Nell's bin. Pause.*] Nell! [*Pause. He knocks louder. Pause. Louder.*] Nell! [*Pause. Nagg sinks back into his bin, closes the lid behind him. Pause.*]

HAMM: Our revels now are ended.[4]

[*He gropes for the dog.*]

The dog's gone.

CLOV: He's not a real dog, he can't go.

HAMM [*groping*]:   He's not there.

CLOV: He's lain down.

HAMM: Give him up to me.

---

4. Quoting the exiled magician Prospero in Shakespeare's *The Tempest* (4.1): "Our revels are now ended. These our actors / As I foretold you, were all spirits, and / Are melted into air, into thin air."

[*Clov picks up the dog and gives it to Hamm. Hamm holds it in his arms. Pause. Hamm throws away the dog.*]

Dirty brute!

[*Clov begins to pick up the objects lying on the ground.*]

What are you doing?

CLOV: Putting things in order. [*He straightens up. Fervently.*] I'm going to clear everything away! [*He starts picking up again.*]

HAMM: Order!

CLOV [*straightening up*]: I love order. It's my dream. A world where all would be silent and still and each thing in its last place, under the last dust. [*He starts picking up again.*]

HAMM [*exasperated*]: What in God's name do you think you are doing?

CLOV [*straightening up*]: I'm doing my best to create a little order.

HAMM: Drop it!

[*Clov drops the objects he has picked up.*]

CLOV: After all, there or elsewhere. [*He goes towards door.*]

HAMM [*irritably*]: What's wrong with your feet?

CLOV: My feet?

HAMM: Tramp! Tramp!

CLOV: I must have put on my boots.

HAMM: Your slippers were hurting you? [*Pause.*]

CLOV: I'll leave you.

HAMM: No!

CLOV: What is there to keep me here?

HAMM: The dialogue. [*Pause.*] I've got on with my story. [*Pause.*] I've got on with it well. [*Pause. Irritably.*] Ask me where I've got to.

CLOV: Oh, by the way, your story?

HAMM [*surprised*]: What story?

CLOV: The one you've been telling yourself all your days.

HAMM: Ah you mean my chronicle?

CLOV: That's the one. [*Pause.*]

HAMM [*angrily*]: Keep going, can't you, keep going!

CLOV: You've got on with it, I hope.

HAMM [*modestly*]: Oh not very far, not very far. [*He sighs.*] There are days like that, one isn't inspired. [*Pause.*] Nothing you can do about it, just wait for it to come. [*Pause.*] No forcing, no forcing, it's fatal. [*Pause.*] I've got on with it a little all the same. [*Pause.*] Technique, you know. [*Pause. Irritably.*] I say I've got on with it a little all the same.

CLOV [*admiringly*]: Well I never! In spite of everything you were able to get on with it!

HAMM [*modestly*]: Oh not very far, you know, not very far, but nevertheless, better than nothing.

CLOV: Better than nothing! Is it possible?

HAMM: I'll tell you how it goes. He comes crawling on his belly—

CLOV: Who?

HAMM: What?

CLOV: Who do you mean, he?

HAMM: Who do I mean! Yet another.

CLOV: Ah him! I wasn't sure.

HAMM: Crawling on his belly, whining for bread for his brat. He's offered a job as gardener. Before—

[*Clov bursts out laughing.*]

What is there so funny about that?

CLOV: A job as gardener!

HAMM: Is that what tickles you?

CLOV: It must be that.

HAMM: It wouldn't be the bread?

CLOV: Or the brat. [*Pause.*]

HAMM: The whole thing is comical, I grant you that. What about having a good guffaw the two of us together?

CLOV [*after reflection*]: I couldn't guffaw again today.

HAMM [*after reflection*]: Nor I. [*Pause.*] I continue then. Before accepting with gratitude he asks if he may have his little boy with him.

CLOV: What age?

HAMM: Oh tiny.

CLOV: He would have climbed the trees.

HAMM: All the little odd jobs.

CLOV: And then he would have grown up.

HAMM: Very likely. [*Pause.*]

CLOV: Keep going, can't you, keep going!

HAMM: That's all. I stopped there. [*Pause.*]

CLOV: Do you see how it goes on.

HAMM: More or less.

CLOV: Will it not soon be the end?

HAMM: I'm afraid it will.

CLOV: Pah! You'll make up another.

HAMM: I don't know. [*Pause.*] I feel rather drained. [*Pause.*] The prolonged creative effort. [*Pause.*] If I could drag myself down to the sea! I'd make a pillow of sand for my head and the tide would come.

CLOV: There's no more tide. [*Pause.*]

HAMM: Go and see is she dead.

[*Clov goes to bins, raises the lid of Nell's, stoops, looks into it. Pause.*]

CLOV: Looks like it.

[*He closes the lid, straightens up. Hamm raises his toque. Pause. He puts it on again.*]

HAMM [*with his hand to his toque*]: And Nagg?

[*Clov raises lid of Nagg's bin, stoops, looks into it. Pause.*]

CLOV: Doesn't look like it. [*He closes the lid, straightens up.*]

HAMM [*letting go his toque*]: What's he doing?

[*Clov raises lid of Nagg's bin, stoops, looks into it. Pause.*]

CLOV: He's crying. [*He closes lid, straightens up.*]

HAMM: Then he's living. [*Pause.*] Did you ever have an instant of happiness?
CLOV: Not to my knowledge. [*Pause.*]
HAMM: Bring me under the window.

[*Clov goes towards chair.*]

I want to feel the light on my face.

[*Clov pushes chair.*]

Do you remember, in the beginning, when you took me for a turn? You used to hold the chair too high. At every step you nearly tipped me out. [*With senile quaver.*] Ah great fun, we had, the two of us, great fun. [*Gloomily.*] And then we got into the way of it.

[*Clov stops the chair under window right.*]

There already? [*Pause. He tilts back his head.*] Is it light?
CLOV: It isn't dark.
HAMM [*angrily*]: I'm asking you is it light.
CLOV: Yes. [*Pause.*]
HAMM: The curtain isn't closed?
CLOV: No.
HAMM: What window is it?
CLOV: The earth.
HAMM: I knew it! [*Angrily.*] But there's no light there! The other!

[*Clov pushes chair towards window left.*]

The earth!

[*Clov stops the chair under window left. Hamm tilts back his head.*]

That's what I call light! [*Pause.*] Feels like a ray of sunshine. [*Pause.*] No?
CLOV: No.
HAMM: It isn't a ray of sunshine I feel on my face?
CLOV: No. [*Pause.*]
HAMM: Am I very white? [*Pause. Angrily.*] I'm asking you am I very white!
CLOV: Not more so than usual. [*Pause.*]
HAMM: Open the window.
CLOV: What for?
HAMM: I want to hear the sea.
CLOV: You wouldn't hear it.
HAMM: Even if you opened the window?
CLOV: No.
HAMM: Then it's not worth while opening it?
CLOV: No.
HAMM [*violently*]: Then open it!

[*Clov gets up on the ladder, opens the window. Pause.*]

Have you opened it?
CLOV: Yes. [*Pause.*]
HAMM: You swear you've opened it?
CLOV: Yes. [*Pause.*]

HAMM: Well…! [*Pause.*] It must be very calm. [*Pause. Violently.*] I'm asking you is it very calm!

CLOV: Yes.

HAMM: It's because there are no more navigators. [*Pause.*] You haven't much conversation all of a sudden. Do you not feel well?

CLOV: I'm cold.

HAMM: What month are we? [*Pause.*] Close the window, we're going back.

[*Clov closes the window, gets down, pushes the chair back to its place, remains standing behind it, head bowed.*]

Don't stay there, you give me the shivers!

[*Clov returns to his place beside the chair.*]

Father! [*Pause. Louder.*] Father! [*Pause.*] Go and see did he hear me.

[*Clov goes to Nagg's bin, raises the lid, stoops. Unintelligible words. Clov straightens up.*]

CLOV: Yes.

HAMM: Both times?

[*Clov stoops. As before.*]

CLOV: Once only.

HAMM: The first time or the second?

[*Clov stoops. As before.*]

CLOV: He doesn't know.

HAMM: It must have been the second.

CLOV: We'll never know.

[*He closes lid.*]

HAMM: Is he still crying?

CLOV: No.

HAMM: The dead go fast. [*Pause.*] What's he doing?

CLOV: Sucking his biscuit.

HAMM: Life goes on.

[*Clov returns to his place beside the chair.*]

Give me a rug, I'm freezing.

CLOV: There are no more rugs. [*Pause.*]

HAMM: Kiss me. [*Pause.*] Will you not kiss me?

CLOV: No.

HAMM: On the forehead.

CLOV: I won't kiss you anywhere. [*Pause.*]

HAMM [*holding out his hand*]:   Give me your hand at least. [*Pause.*] Will you not give me your hand?

CLOV: I won't touch you. [*Pause.*]

HAMM: Give me the dog.

[Clov looks round for the dog.]

No!

CLOV: Do you not want your dog?

HAMM: No.

CLOV: Then I'll leave you.

HAMM *[head bowed, absently]*: That's right.

[Clov goes to door, turns.]

CLOV: If I don't kill that rat he'll die.

HAMM *[as before]*: That's right.

[Exit Clov. Pause.]

Me to play.

[He takes out his handkerchief, unfolds it, holds it spread out before him.]

We're getting on. *[Pause.]* You weep, and weep, for nothing, so as not to laugh, and little by little...you begin to grieve.

[He folds the handkerchief, puts it back in his pocket, raises his head.]

All those I might have helped. *[Pause.]* Helped! *[Pause.]* Saved. *[Pause.]* Saved! *[Pause.]* The place was crawling with them! *[Pause. Violently.]* Use your head, can't you, use your head, you're on earth, there's no cure for that! *[Pause.]* Get out of here and love one another! Lick your neighbor as yourself! *[Pause. Calmer.]* When it wasn't bread they wanted it was crumpets. *[Pause. Violently.]* Out of my sight and back to your petting parties! *[Pause.]* All that, all that! *[Pause.]* Not even a real dog! *[Calmer.]* The end is in the beginning and yet you go on. *[Pause.]* Perhaps I could go on with my story, end it and begin another. *[Pause.]* Perhaps I could throw myself out on the floor.

[He pushes himself painfully off his seat, falls back again.]

Dig my nails into the cracks and drag myself forward with my fingers. *[Pause.]* It will be the end and there I'll be, wondering what can have brought it on and wondering what can have...*[he hesitates]*...why it was so long coming. *[Pause.]* There I'll be, in the old shelter, alone against the silence and...*[he hesitates]*...the stillness. If I can hold my peace, and sit quiet, it will be all over with sound, and motion, all over and done with. *[Pause.]* I'll have called my father and I'll have called my...*[he hesitates]*...my son. And even twice, or three times, in case they shouldn't have heard me, the first time, or the second. *[Pause.]* I'll say to myself, He'll come back. *[Pause.]* And then? *[Pause.]* And then? *[Pause.]* He couldn't, he has gone too far. *[Pause.]* And then? *[Pause. Very agitated.]* All kinds of fantasies! That I'm being watched! A rat! Steps! Breath held and then...*[He breathes out.]* Then babble, babble, words, like the solitary child who turns himself into children, two, three, so as to be together, and whisper together, in the dark. *[Pause.]* Moment upon moment, pattering down, like the millet grains of...*[he hesitates]*...that old Greek, and all life long you wait for that to mount up to a life.[5] [*Pause. He opens his mouth to continue, renounces.*] Ah let's get it over!

[*He whistles. Enter Clov with alarm-clock. He halts beside the chair.*]

What? Neither gone nor dead?

CLOV: In spirit only.

HAMM: Which?

CLOV: Both.

HAMM: Gone from me you'd be dead.

CLOV: And vice versa.

HAMM: Outside of here it's death! [*Pause.*] And the rat?

CLOV: He's got away.

HAMM: He can't go far. [*Pause. Anxious.*] Eh?

CLOV: He doesn't need to go far. [*Pause.*]

HAMM: Is it not time for my pain-killer?

CLOV: Yes.

HAMM: Ah! At last! Give it to me! Quick! [*Pause.*]

CLOV: There's no more pain-killer. [*Pause.*]

HAMM [*appalled*]:   Good...! [*Pause.*] No more pain-killer!

CLOV: No more pain-killer. You'll never get any more pain-killer. [*Pause.*]

HAMM: But the little round box. It was full!

CLOV: Yes. But now it's empty.

[*Pause. Clov starts to move about the room. He is looking for a place to put down the alarm-clock.*]

HAMM [*soft*]:   What'll I do? [*Pause. In a scream.*] What'll I do?

[*Clov sees the picture, takes it down, stands it on the floor with its face to the wall, hangs up the alarm-clock in its place.*]

What are you doing?

CLOV: Winding up.

HAMM: Look at the earth.

CLOV: Again!

HAMM: Since it's calling to you.

CLOV: Is your throat sore? [*Pause.*] Would you like a lozenge? [*Pause.*] No. [*Pause.*] Pity.

[*Clov goes, humming, towards window right, halts before it, looks up at it.*]

HAMM: Don't sing.

CLOV [*turning towards Hamm*]:   One hasn't the right to sing any more?

HAMM: No.

CLOV: Then how can it end?

HAMM: You want it to end?

CLOV: I want to sing.

HAMM: I can't prevent you.

5. Hamm is referring to Zeno of Elea (5th century B.C.E.), who is known for his philosophical paradoxes. One of them is based on the sound a bushel of millet makes when it falls on the floor: since this sound is caused by the grains, each grain must make a sound when striking the ground. This sound, however, can't be heard, so the apparent sound is really an accumulation of silences.

[*Pause. Clov turns towards window right.*]

CLOV: What did I do with that steps? [*He looks around for ladder.*] You didn't see that steps? [*He sees it.*] Ah, about time. [*He goes towards window left.*] Sometimes I wonder if I'm in my right mind. Then it passes over and I'm as lucid as before. [*He gets up on ladder, looks out of window.*] Christ, she's under water! [*He looks.*] How can that be? [*He pokes forward his head, his hand above his eyes.*] It hasn't rained. [*He wipes the pane, looks. Pause.*] Ah what a fool I am! I'm on the wrong side! [*He gets down, takes a few steps towards window right.*] Under water! [*He goes back for ladder.*] What a fool I am! [*He carries ladder towards window right.*] Sometimes I wonder if I'm in my right senses. Then it passes off and I'm as intelligent as ever.

[*He sets down ladder under window right, gets up on it, looks out of window. He turns towards Hamm.*]

Any particular sector you fancy? Or merely the whole thing?

HAMM: Whole thing.

CLOV: The general effect? Just a moment. [*He looks out of window. Pause.*]

HAMM: Clov.

CLOV [*absorbed*]: Mmm.

HAMM: Do you know what it is?

CLOV [*as before*]: Mmm.

HAMM: I was never there. [*Pause.*] Clov!

CLOV [*turning towards Hamm, exasperated*]: What is it?

HAMM: I was never there.

CLOV: Lucky for you. [*He looks out of window.*]

HAMM: Absent, always. It all happened without me. I don't know what's happened. [*Pause.*] Do you know what's happened? [*Pause.*] Clov!

CLOV [*turning towards Hamm, exasperated*]: Do you want me to look at this muck-heap, yes or no?

HAMM: Answer me first.

CLOV: What?

HAMM: Do you know what's happened?

CLOV: When? Where?

HAMM [*violently*]: When! What's happened? Use your head, can't you! What has happened?

CLOV: What for Christ's sake does it matter? [*He looks out of window.*]

HAMM: I don't know. [*Pause. Clov turns towards Hamm.*]

CLOV [*harshly*]: When old Mother Pegg asked you for oil for her lamp and you told her to get out to hell, you knew what was happening then, no? [*Pause.*] You know what she died of, Mother Pegg? Of darkness.

HAMM [*feebly*]: I hadn't any.

CLOV [*as before*]: Yes, you had. [*Pause.*]

HAMM: Have you the glass?

CLOV: No, it's clear enough as it is.

HAMM: Go and get it.

[*Pause. Clov casts up his eyes, brandishes his fists. He loses balance, clutches on to the ladder. He starts to get down, halts.*]

CLOV: There's one thing I'll never understand. [*He gets down.*] Why I always obey you. Can you explain that to me?

HAMM: No. . . . Perhaps it's compassion. [*Pause.*] A kind of great compassion. [*Pause.*] Oh you won't find it easy, you won't find it easy.

[*Pause. Clov begins to move about the room in search of the telescope.*]

CLOV: I'm tired of our goings on, very tired. [*He searches.*] You're not sitting on it?

[*He moves the chair, looks at the place where it stood, resumes his search.*]

HAMM [*anguished*]:   Don't leave me there! [*Angrily Clov restores the chair to its place.*] Am I right in the center?

CLOV: You'd need a microscope to find this—[*He sees the telescope.*] Ah, about time.

[*He picks up the telescope, gets up on the ladder, turns the telescope on the without.*]

HAMM: Give me the dog.

CLOV [*looking*]:   Quiet!

HAMM [*angrily*]:   Give me the dog!

[*Clov drops the telescope, clasps his hands to his head. Pause. He gets down precipitately, looks for the dog, sees it, picks it up, hastens towards Hamm and strikes him violently on the head with the dog.*]

CLOV: There's your dog for you!

[*The dog falls to the ground. Pause.*]

HAMM: He hit me!

CLOV: You drive me mad, I'm mad!

HAMM: If you must hit me, hit me with the axe. [*Pause.*] Or with the gaff, hit me with the gaff. Not with the dog. With the gaff. Or with the axe.

[*Clov picks up the dog and gives it to Hamm who takes it in his arms.*]

CLOV [*imploringly*]:   Let's stop playing!

HAMM: Never! [*Pause.*] Put me in my coffin.

CLOV: There are no more coffins.

HAMM: Then let it end!

[*Clov goes towards ladder.*]

With a bang!

[*Clov gets up on ladder, gets down again, looks for telescope, sees it, picks it up, gets up ladder, raises telescope.*]

Of darkness! And me? Did anyone ever have pity on me?

CLOV [*lowering the telescope, turning towards Hamm*]:   What? [*Pause.*] Is it me you're referring to?

HAMM [*angrily*]:   An aside, ape! Did you never hear an aside before? [*Pause.*] I'm warming up for my last soliloquy.

CLOV: I warn you. I'm going to look at this filth since it's an order. But it's the last time. [*He turns the telescope on the without.*] Let's see. [*He moves the telescope.*] Nothing . . . nothing . . . good . . . good . . . nothing . . . goo—[*He starts, lowers the telescope, examines it, turns it again on the without. Pause.*] Bad luck to it!

HAMM: More complications!

[*Clov gets down.*]

Not an underplot, I trust.

[*Clov moves ladder nearer window, gets up on it, turns telescope on the without.*]

CLOV [*dismayed*]: Looks like a small boy!

HAMM [*sarcastic*]: A small...boy!

CLOV: I'll go and see.

[*He gets down, drops the telescope, goes towards door, turns.*]

I'll take the gaff.

[*He looks for the gaff, sees it, picks it up, hastens towards door.*]

HAMM: No!

[*Clov halts.*]

CLOV: No? A potential procreator?

HAMM: If he exists he'll die there or he'll come here. And if he doesn't...[*Pause.*]

CLOV: You don't believe me? You think I'm inventing? [*Pause.*]

HAMM: It's the end, Clov, we've come to the end. I don't need you any more. [*Pause.*]

CLOV: Lucky for you. [*He goes towards door.*]

HAMM: Leave me the gaff.

[*Clov gives him the gaff, goes towards door, halts, looks at alarm-clock, takes it down, looks round for a better place to put it, goes to bins, puts it on lid of Nagg's bin. Pause.*]

CLOV: I'll leave you. [*He goes towards door.*]

HAMM: Before you go...

[*Clov halts near door.*]

...say something.

CLOV: There is nothing to say.

HAMM: A few words...to ponder...in my heart.

CLOV: Your heart!

HAMM: Yes. [*Pause. Forcibly.*] Yes! [*Pause.*] With the rest, in the end, the shadows, the murmurs, all the trouble, to end up with. [*Pause.*] Clov....He never spoke to me. Then, in the end, before he went, without my having asked him, he spoke to me. He said...

CLOV [*despairingly*]: Ah...!

HAMM: Something...from your heart.

CLOV: My heart!

HAMM: A few words...from your heart. [*Pause.*]

CLOV [*fixed gaze, tonelessly, towards auditorium*]: They said to me, That's love, yes, yes, not a doubt, now you see how—

HAMM: Articulate!

CLOV [*as before*]: How easy it is. They said to me, That's friendship, yes, yes, no question, you've found it. They said to me, Here's the place, stop, raise your head and look at all that beauty. That order! They said to me, Come now, you're not a brute beast, think upon these things and you'll see how all becomes clear. And simple! They said to me, What skilled attention they get, all these dying of their wounds.

HAMM: Enough!

CLOV [*as before*]:   I say to myself—sometimes, Clov, you must learn to suffer better than that if you want them to weary of punishing you—one day. I say to myself—sometimes, Clov, you must be there better than that if you want them to let you go—one day. But I feel too old, and too far, to form new habits. Good, it'll never end, I'll never go. [*Pause.*] Then one day, suddenly, it ends, it changes, I don't understand, it dies, or it's me, I don't understand, that either. I ask the words that remain—sleeping, waking, morning, evening. They have nothing to say. [*Pause.*] I open the door of the cell and go. I am so bowed I only see my feet, if I open my eyes, and between my legs a little trail of black dust. I say to myself that the earth is extinguished, though I never saw it lit. [*Pause.*] It's easy going. [*Pause.*] When I fall I'll weep for happiness. [*Pause. He goes towards door.*]

HAMM: Clov!

[*Clov halts, without turning.*]

Nothing.

[*Clov moves on.*]

Clov!

[*Clov halts, without turning.*]

CLOV: This is what we call making an exit.
HAMM: I'm obliged to you, Clov. For your services.
CLOV [*turning, sharply*]:   Ah pardon, it's I am obliged to you.
HAMM: It's we are obliged to each other.

[*Pause. Clov goes towards door.*]

One thing more.

[*Clov halts.*]

A last favor.

[*Exit Clov.*]

Cover me with the sheet. [*Long pause.*] No? Good. [*Pause.*] Me to play. [*Pause. Wearily.*] Old endgame lost of old, play and lose and have done with losing. [*Pause. More animated.*] Let me see. [*Pause.*] Ah yes!

[*He tries to move the chair, using the gaff as before. Enter Clov, dressed for the road. Panama hat, tweed coat, raincoat over his arm, umbrella, bag. He halts by the door and stands there, impassive and motionless, his eyes fixed on Hamm, till the end. Hamm gives up.*]

Good. [*Pause.*] Discard. [*He throws away the gaff, makes to throw away the dog, thinks better of it.*] Take it easy. [*Pause.*] And now? [*Pause.*] Raise hat. [*He raises his toque.*] Peace to our…arses. [*Pause.*] And put on again. [*He puts on his toque.*] Deuce. [*Pause. He takes off his glasses.*] Wipe. [*He takes out his handkerchief and, without unfolding it, wipes his glasses.*] And put on again. [*He puts on his glasses, puts back the handkerchief in his pocket.*] We're coming. A few more squirms like that and I'll call. [*Pause.*] A little poetry. [*Pause.*] You prayed—[*Pause. He corrects himself.*] You CRIED for night; it comes—[*Pause. He corrects himself.*] It FALLS: now cry in darkness. [*He repeats, chanting.*] You cried for night; it falls: now cry in darkness. [*Pause.*] Nicely put, that. [*Pause.*] And now? [*Pause.*] Moments for nothing, now as always, time was never and time is over, reckoning closed and story ended. [*Pause. Narrative tone.*] If he could have his child with him.... [*Pause.*] It was the moment I was waiting for. [*Pause.*] You don't want to abandon him? You want him to bloom while you are withering? Be there to solace your last million last moments? [*Pause.*] He doesn't realize, all he knows is hunger, and cold, and death to crown it all. But you! You ought to know what the earth is like, nowadays. Oh I put him before his responsibilities! [*Pause. Normal tone.*] Well, there we are, there I am, that's enough. [*He raises the whistle to his lips, hesitates, drops it. Pause.*] Yes, truly! [*He whistles. Pause. Louder. Pause.*] Good. [*Pause.*] Father! [*Pause. Louder.*] Father! [*Pause.*] Good. [*Pause.*] We're coming. [*Pause.*] And to end up with? [*Pause.*] Discard. [*He throws away the dog. He tears the whistle from his neck.*] With my compliments.

[*He throws whistle towards auditorium. Pause. He sniffs. Soft.*]

Clov!

[*Long pause.*]

No? Good.

[*He takes out the handkerchief.*]

Since that's the way we're playing it...

[*He unfolds handkerchief*]

...let's play it that way...

[*He unfolds.*]

...and speak no more about it...

[*He finishes unfolding.*]

...speak no more.

[*He holds handkerchief spread out before him.*]

Old stancher!

[*Pause.*]

You...remain.

[*Pause. He covers his face with handkerchief, lowers his arms to armrests, remains motionless.*]

[*Brief tableau.*]

Curtain

Naguib Mahfouz, the first Arab writer to win the Nobel Prize in Literature (1988), was born in the popular quarter of al-Jammaliyyah in the heart of old Cairo in 1911. His urban upbringing prepared him for the role of the scribe of this teeming metropolis, to which he devoted his life and prodigal work. He inscribes its life, space, and modern history into the hearts of Arab readers and familiarizes them with its ways and norms. His vivid recollections of old Cairo were an everlasting source of inspiration for his work, from his early short stories up to his last novel, *Echoes of an Autobiography,* 1994.

Mahfouz's father was a middle-class civil servant who provided his family with a comfortable life. After a few years in the *kuttab,* the traditional Qur'anic school, Mahfouz completed his primary and secondary education in Cairo and then went to Cairo University, where he studied philosophy. Upon his graduation in 1934, he worked for the university, contemplated postgraduate study, and registered for a doctorate in philosophy, but he soon abandoned this academic endeavor and embarked on a career of literary creativity.

He started publishing articles and short stories soon after his graduation and in 1938 published his first book, *Whispers of Madness,* a collection of short stories. In 1939 he published his first novel, *Absurd Fates.* The two ensuing novels were historical works written as part of a grand plan to relate the history of Egypt from the time of the pharaohs to the present. But his historical setting was merely a textual strategy to root the work in Egypt's glorious history, thus participating in the process of shaping its national identity.

But after writing three novels without making a dent in the vast history of Egypt—he was still in the early Pharaonic period—he turned his attention to the reality of his time. This coincided with World War II, which proved to be an important period in Mahfouz's career because during the turbulent years of the war, he became increasingly aware of the need to avoid historical metaphor and deal directly with the burning social issues of the time. The title of his first realistic novel, *New Cairo,* written in the first year of the war but not appearing until 1943, sums up the project of his realistic novels. They are concerned with the transformation of Cairo both as a city and as a distinct urban culture, juxtaposing the urban space of old and new Cairo as the symbol of the clash of cultural values that affect many of the inhabitants of this teeming Third-World metropolis. The novels of this phase reflect various facets of the trauma of change and its social, human, and political ramifications.

This culminated in the *Cairo Trilogy*—*Palace Walk* (1955), *Palace of Desire* (1956), and *Sugar Street* (1957)—the masterpiece of his Cairene urban chronicles. The *Trilogy* spans half a century of Egypt's quest for national identity and modernization over three different generations. It is the greatest family saga of modern Arabic literature and the work that enshrined middle-class morality and culture. Inspired by John Galsworthy's *Forsyte Saga,* it reflects the cultural and political development of a society in turmoil under the pressures of British occupation and draws a highly detailed map of Egypt's social and political orientations in the first half of the twentieth century. The *Trilogy* ends with the death of the patriarch and the birth of a new child, heralding the end of one era and the beginning of a new one. The prophecy came true, for the completion of the trilogy coincided with Gamal Abdel Nasser's revolution of 1952, which ended the *ancien régime.*

The radical change brought by this revolution led Mahfouz to a long period of contemplation in which he stopped writing for five years. In 1959 he published a major novel, *The Children of Gebalawy,* which was serialized in the newspaper *Al-Ahram.* As soon as its serialization was completed, the Azhar, the major religious authority in Egypt, banned its publication in book form. But in 1966 the book was published in Beirut and was allowed calmly into Cairo until it was banned again when Salman Rushdie's *Satanic Verses* was condemned as blasphemous. Mahfouz's novel didn't satirize Islam as Rushdie's had, but it gave a narrative account of creation and humanity's spiritual and intellectual development through three religions—Judaism, Christianity, and Islam—with humanity reaching the peak of intellectual and spiritual maturity with the age of reason. The final section of the novel posits scientific and rational knowledge as the new creed for humanity, and this enraged the religious establishment. Yet the novel can be read as Mahfouz's contribution to the search for a new direction after Egypt achieved its independence. It was his implicit advice to the new officers to adopt a more liberal and rational attitude toward the complex sociopolitical reality of Egypt, advice that was not heeded.

This provoked Mahfouz to start a series of six novels constituting his output in the 1960s and forming what critics call the period of critical-realism in his development. Since these are highly critical political novels emphasizing the importance of freedom and the dire consequences of its absence from society as a whole, they can be seen as documents of the disappointment of Mahfouz's generation in Nasser's regime or as documents of defiance and glorification of the spirit of rebellion. Mahfouz's repartee and sharp sense of humor endows many of these novels, particularly *Chatter on the Nile* (1966), with a fine criticism that turns the novel into one of the most powerful commentaries on corruption and tyranny.

The realization of the prophecy of doom enshrined in *Miramar* (1967), the last novel of this period, came as a shock nonetheless and led to another period of silence in Mahfouz's career. But instead of turning his attention to writing motion pictures, as he did in the years of silence in the 1950s, he poured his energy into short stories and one-act plays. These works are marked by symbolic, even surrealistic, structures used to portray the complexity and absurdity of the unexpected events that followed the 1967 defeat of Arab forces by Israel and Israel's occupation of the Sinai Peninsula, long part of Egypt. His first novel after four years, *Love in the Rain* (1973), was solely concerned with the impact of this tragic event on the Egyptian psyche. The following novel, *Karnak* (1974), written immediately after the death of Nasser, was a harsh and strongly critical re-evaluation of the police state and its responsibility for the destruction of the spirit of opposition, the younger generation, and the will to fight for the country.

The 1970s and 1980s witnessed a marked increase in Mahfouz's productivity. In these two decades he wrote as many novels as he had written in the preceding forty years of his career, with more than twenty novels and eight collections of short stories. Although many of the novels were quickly written and loosely structured and some of them are closer to movie treatments than fully developed novels, Mahfouz had a strong urge to record a rapidly shifting reality. Among these numerous works, however, three novels stand out as some of the best examples of the modern Arabic novel with their subtle intertextuality and original narrative structure. *The Epic of Harafish* (1977) from which there is a selection included here, is a remarkable achievement that rivals the *Trilogy* in its richness, texture, and complexity. It distills the rich tradition of popular story telling and subjects its textual strategies to the demands of modernistic narrative. *The Arabian Nights and Days* (1982) is an ambitious attempt to inscribe the modern preoccupations of the Arab world into the fantastic world of *The Arabian Nights*. Mahfouz posits the modern novel as a rival to the great classic of Arabic narrative and succeeds in reproducing the magic world of the old classic but with a completely modern slant. The dialogue with classical narrative forms, in these two and other novels of this period, enhances Mahfouz's recent work and provides it with potent appeal to the wider reading public without detracting from its complexity and subtlety.

Mahfouz's major novel of the 1980s, *The Talk of Morning and Evening,* is the most significant Arabic novel of the 1980s, subverting narrative structure in order to portray the fragmentation of Egyptian society under the successive failures of the process of modernization.

The world of Naguib Mahfouz is a vast and extremely rich one that extends from Pharaonic times down to the present day. Although the space of his world is mainly Cairo and predominantly the old quarter in which he spent his childhood, he weaves the urban scene into an elaborate and highly significant metaphor for the whole national condition. On the literary plain, his career spans the whole process of the development of the Arabic novel from the historical to the modernistic and lyrical. He earned the Arabic novel respect and popularity and lived to see it flourish in the work of numerous writers throughout the Arab world.

PRONUNCIATIONS:

Naguib Mahfouz: nah-GEEB mah-FOUZ
Qamar: cah-MAHR
Shahriyar: shah-ri-YAAR
Sanaan al-Gamali: sun-ANN al-ga-maa-LI
Shahrzad: shahr-ZAD
Zaabalawi: zah-bah-LAH-wee

Zaabalawi[1]

Finally I became convinced that I had to find Sheikh Zaabalawi.

The first time I had heard his name had been in a song:

> *Oh what's become of the world, Zaabalawi?*
> *They've turned it upside down and taken away its taste.*

It had been a popular song in my childhood, and one day it had occurred to me to demand of my father, in the way children have of asking endless questions:

"Who is Zaabalawi?"

He had looked at me hesitantly as though doubting my ability to understand the answer. However, he had replied, "May his blessing descend upon you, he's a true saint of God, a remover of worries and troubles. Were it not for him I would have died miserably—"

In the years that followed, I heard my father many a time sing the praises of this good saint and speak of the miracles he performed. The days passed and brought with them many illnesses, for each one of which I was able, without too much trouble and at a cost I could afford, to find a cure, until I became afflicted with that illness for which no one possesses a remedy. When I had tried everything in vain and was overcome by despair, I remembered by chance what I had heard in my childhood: Why, I asked myself, should I not seek out Sheikh Zaabalawi? I recollected my father saying that he had made his acquaintance in Khan Gaafar at the house of Sheikh Qamar, one of those sheikhs who practiced law in the religious courts, and so I took myself off to his house. Wishing to make sure that he was still living there, I made inquiries of a vendor of beans whom I found in the lower part of the house.

"Sheikh Qamar!" he said, looking at me in amazement. "He left the quarter ages ago. They say he's now living in Garden City and has his office in al-Azhar Square."

I looked up the office address in the telephone book and immediately set off to the Chamber of Commerce Building, where it was located. On asking to see Sheikh Qamar, I was ushered into a room just as a beautiful woman with a most intoxicating perfume was leaving it. The man received me with a smile and motioned me toward a fine leather-upholstered chair. Despite the thick soles of my shoes, my feet were conscious of the lushness of the costly carpet. The man wore a lounge suit and was smoking a cigar; his manner of sitting was that of someone well satisfied both with himself and with his worldly possessions. The look of warm welcome he gave me left no doubt in my mind that he thought me a prospective client, and I felt acutely embarrassed at encroaching upon his valuable time.

"Welcome!" he said, prompting me to speak.

---

1. Translated by Denys Johnson-Davies. Zaabalawi is a name of a popular Sufi saint.

"I am the son of your old friend Sheikh Ali al-Tatawi," I answered so as to put an end to my equivocal position.

A certain languor was apparent in the glance he cast at me; the languor was not total in that he had not as yet lost all hope in me.

"God rest his soul," he said. "He was a fine man."

The very pain that had driven me to go there now prevailed upon me to stay.

"He told me," I continued, "of a devout saint named Zaabalawi whom he met at Your Honor's. I am in need of him, sir, if he be still in the land of the living."

The languor became firmly entrenched in his eyes, and it would have come as no surprise if he had shown the door to both me and my father's memory.

"That," he said in the tone of one who has made up his mind to terminate the conversation, "was a very long time ago and I scarcely recall him now."

Rising to my feet so as to put his mind at rest regarding my intention of going, I asked, "Was he really a saint?"

"We used to regard him as a man of miracles."

"And where could I find him today?" I asked, making another move toward the door.

"To the best of my knowledge he was living in the Birgawi Residence in al-Azhar," and he applied himself to some papers on his desk with a resolute movement that indicated he would not open his mouth again. I bowed my head in thanks, apologized several times for disturbing him, and left the office, my head so buzzing with embarrassment that I was oblivious to all sounds around me.

I went to the Birgawi Residence, which was situated in a thickly populated quarter. I found that time had so eaten away at the building that nothing was left of it save an antiquated façade and a courtyard that, despite being supposedly in the charge of a caretaker, was being used as a rubbish dump. A small, insignificant fellow, a mere prologue to a man, was using the covered entrance as a place for the sale of old books on theology and mysticism.

When I asked him about Zaabalawi, he peered at me through narrow, inflamed eyes and said in amazement, "Zaabalawi! Good heavens, what a time ago that was! Certainly he used to live in this house when it was habitable. Many were the times he would sit with me talking of bygone days, and I would be blessed by his holy presence. Where, though, is Zaabalawi today?"

He shrugged his shoulders sorrowfully and soon left me, to attend to an approaching customer. I proceeded to make inquiries of many shopkeepers in the district. While I found that a large number of them had never even heard of Zaabalawi, some, though recalling nostalgically the pleasant times they had spent with him, were ignorant of his present whereabouts, while others openly made fun of him, labeled him a charlatan, and advised me to put myself in the hands of a doctor—as though I had not already done so. I therefore had no alternative but to return disconsolately home.

With the passing of days like motes in the air, my pains grew so severe that I was sure I would not be able to hold out much longer. Once again I fell to wondering about Zaabalawi and clutching at the hope his venerable name stirred within me. Then it occurred to me to seek the help of the local sheikh of the district; in fact, I was surprised I had not thought of this to begin with. His office was in the nature of a small shop, except that it contained a desk and a telephone, and I found him sitting at his desk, wearing a jacket over his striped galabeya. As he did not interrupt his conversation with a man sitting beside him, I stood waiting till the man had gone. The sheikh then looked up at me coldly. I told myself that I should win him over by the usual methods, and it was not long before I had him cheerfully inviting me to sit down.

"I'm in need of Sheikh Zaabalawi," I answered his inquiry as to the purpose of my visit.

He gazed at me with the same astonishment as that shown by those I had previously encountered.

"At least," he said, giving me a smile that revealed his gold teeth, "he is still alive. The devil of it is, though, he has no fixed abode. You might well bump into him as you go out of here, on the other hand you might spend days and months in fruitless searching."

"Even you can't find him!"

"Even I! He's a baffling man, but I thank the Lord that he's still alive!"

He gazed at me intently, and murmured, "It seems your condition is serious."

"Very."

"May God come to your aid! But why don't you go about it systematically?" He spread out a sheet of paper on the desk and drew on it with unexpected speed and skill until he had made a full plan of the district, showing all the various quarters, lanes, alleyways, and squares. He looked at it admiringly and said, "These are dwelling-houses, here is the Quarter of the Perfumers, here the Quarter of the Coppersmiths, the Mouski, the police and fire stations. The drawing is your best guide. Look carefully in the cafés, the places where the dervishes perform their rites,[2] the mosques and prayer-rooms, and the Green Gate,[3] for he may well be concealed among the beggars and be indistinguishable from them. Actually, I myself haven't seen him for years, having been somewhat preoccupied with the cares of the world, and was only brought back by your inquiry to those most exquisite times of my youth."

I gazed at the map in bewilderment. The telephone rang, and he took up the receiver.

"Take it," he told me, generously. "We're at your service."

Folding up the map, I left and wandered off through the quarter, from square to street to alleyway, making inquiries of everyone I felt was familiar with the place. At last the owner of a small establishment for ironing clothes told me, "Go to the calligrapher Hassanein in Umm al-Ghulam—they were friends."

I went to Umm al-Ghulam, where I found old Hassanein working in a deep, narrow shop full of signboards and jars of color. A strange smell, a mixture of glue and perfume, permeated its every corner. Old Hassanein was squatting on a sheepskin rug in front of a board propped against the wall; in the middle of it he had inscribed the world "Allah" in silver lettering. He was engrossed in embellishing the letters with prodigious care. I stood behind him, fearful of disturbing him or breaking the inspiration that flowed to his masterly hand. When my concern at not interrupting him had lasted some time, he suddenly inquired with unaffected gentleness, "Yes?"

Realizing that he was aware of my presence, I introduced myself. "I've been told that Sheikh Zaabalawi is your friend; I'm looking for him," I said.

His hand came to a stop. He scrutinized me in astonishment. "Zaabalawi! God be praised!" he said with a sigh.

"He *is* a friend of yours, isn't he?" I asked eagerly.

___

2. Dervishes are a pious group of people interested primarily in worship. Their rite is a weekly evening concert that is open to the faithful.

3. One of the gates of the Mosque of al-Husain in old Cairo.

"He was, once upon a time. A real man of mystery: he'd visit you so often that people would imagine he was your nearest and dearest, then would disappear as though he'd never existed. Yet saints are not to be blamed."

The spark of hope went out with the suddenness of a lamp snuffed by a power-cut.

"He was so constantly with me," said the man, "that I felt him to be a part of everything I drew. But where is he today?"

"Perhaps he is still alive?"

"He's alive, without a doubt.... He had impeccable taste, and it was due to him that I made my most beautiful drawings."

"God knows," I said, in a voice almost stifled by the dead ashes of hope, "how dire my need for him is, and no one knows better than you of the ailments in respect to which he is sought."

"Yes, yes. May God restore you to health. He is in truth, as is said of him, a man, and more...."

Smiling broadly, he added, "And his face possesses an unforgettable beauty. But where is he?"

Reluctantly I rose to my feet, shook hands, and left. I continued wandering eastward and westward through the quarter, inquiring about Zaabalawi from everyone who, by reason of age or experience, I felt might be likely to help me. Eventually I was informed by a vendor of lupine that he had met him a short while ago at the house of Sheikh Gad, the well-known composer. I went to the musician's house in Tabakshiyya, where I found him in a room tastefully furnished in the old style, its walls redolent with history. He was seated on a divan, his famous lute beside him, concealing within itself the most beautiful melodies of our age, while somewhere from within the house came the sound of pestle and mortar and the clamor of children. I immediately greeted him and introduced myself, and was put at my ease by the unaffected way in which he received me. He did not ask, either in words or gesture, what had brought me, and I did not feel that he even harbored any such curiosity. Amazed at his understanding and kindness, which boded well, I said, "O Sheikh Gad, I am an admirer of yours, having long been enchanted by the renderings of your songs."

"Thank you," he said with a smile.

"Please excuse my disturbing you," I continued timidly, "but I was told that Zaabalawi was your friend, and I am in urgent need of him."

"Zaabalawi!" he said, frowning in concentration. "You need him? God be with you, for who knows, O Zaabalawi, where you are."

"Doesn't he visit you?" I asked eagerly.

"He visited me some time ago. He might well come right now; on the other hand I mightn't see him till death!"

I gave an audible sigh and asked, "What made him like that?"

The musician took up his lute. "Such are saints or they would not be saints," he said, laughing.

"Do those who need him suffer as I do?"

"Such suffering is part of the cure!"

He took up the plectrum and began plucking soft strains from the strings. Lost in thought, I followed his movements. Then, as though addressing myself, I said, "So my visit has been in vain."

He smiled, laying his cheek against the side of the lute. "God forgive you," he said, "for saying such a thing of a visit that has caused me to know you and you me!"

I was much embarrassed and said apologetically, "Please forgive me; my feelings of defeat made me forget my manners."

"Do not give in to defeat. This extraordinary man brings fatigue to all who seek him. It was easy enough with him in the old days, when his place of abode was known. Today, though, the world has changed, and after having enjoyed a position attained only by potentates, he is now pursued by the police on a charge of false pretenses. It is therefore no longer an easy matter to reach him, but have patience and be sure that you will do so."

He raised his head from the lute and skillfully fingered the opening bars of a melody. Then he sang:

> *"I make lavish mention, even though I blame myself, of those I love,*
> *For the stories of the beloved are my wine."*

With a heart that was weary and listless, I followed the beauty of the melody and the singing.

"I composed the music to this poem in a single night," he told me when he had finished. "I remember that it was the eve of the Lesser Bairam. Zaabalawi was my guest for the whole of that night, and the poem was of his choosing. He would sit for a while just where you are, then would get up and play with my children as though he were one of them. Whenever I was overcome by weariness or my inspiration failed me, he would punch me playfully in the chest and joke with me, and I would bubble over with melodies, and thus I continued working till I finished the most beautiful piece I have ever composed."

"Does he know anything about music?"

"He is the epitome of things musical. He has an extremely beautiful speaking voice, and you have only to hear him to want to burst into song and to be inspired to creativity...."

"How was it that he cured those diseases before which men are powerless?"

"That is his secret. Maybe you will learn it when you meet him."

But when would that meeting occur? We relapsed into silence, and the hubbub of children once more filled the room.

Again the sheikh began to sing. He went on repeating the words "and I have a memory of her" in different and beautiful variations until the very walls danced in ecstasy. I expressed my wholehearted admiration, and he gave me a smile of thanks. I then got up and asked permission to leave, and he accompanied me to the front door. As I shook him by the hand, he said, "I hear that nowadays he frequents the house of Hagg Wanas al-Damanhouri. Do you know him?"

I shook my head, though a modicum of renewed hope crept into my heart.

"He is a man of private means," the sheikh told me, "who from time to time visits Cairo, putting up at some hotel or other. Every evening, though, he spends at the Negma Bar[4] in Alfi Street."

I waited for nightfall and went to the Negma Bar. I asked a waiter about Hagg Wanas, and he pointed to a corner that was semisecluded because of its position behind a large pillar with mirrors on all four sides. There I saw a man seated alone at a table with two bottles in front of him, one empty, the other two-thirds empty. There were no snacks or food to be seen,[5] and I was sure that I was in the presence of a hardened

---

4. Mahfouz often links drinking in bars (something that is transgressive in the Muslim culture) to spirituality, and to Sufis.

5. In Arabic culture, it is customary to have snacks with alcoholic drinks.

drinker. He was wearing a loosely flowing silk galabeya and a carefully wound turban; his legs were stretched out toward the base of the pillar, and as he gazed into the mirror in rapt contentment, the sides of his face, rounded and handsome despite the fact that he was approaching old age, were flushed with wine. I approached quietly till I stood but a few feet away from him. He did not turn toward me or give any indication that he was aware of my presence.

"Good evening, Mr. Wanas," I greeted him cordially.

He turned toward me abruptly, as though my voice had roused him from slumber, and glared at me in disapproval. I was about to explain what had brought me when he interrupted in an almost imperative tone of voice that was nonetheless not devoid of an extraordinary gentleness, "First, please sit down, and second, please get drunk!"

I opened my mouth to make my excuses, but, stopping up his ears with his fingers, he said, "Not a word till you do what I say."

I realized I was in the presence of a capricious drunkard and told myself that I should at least humor him a bit. "Would you permit me to ask one question?" I said with a smile, sitting down.

Without removing his hands from his ears he indicated the bottle. "When engaged in a drinking bout like this, I do not allow any conversation between myself and another unless, like me, he is drunk, otherwise all propriety is lost and mutual comprehension is rendered impossible."

I made a sign indicating that I did not drink.

"That's your lookout," he said offhandedly. "And that's my condition!"

He filled me a glass, which I meekly took and drank. No sooner had the wine settled in my stomach than it seemed to ignite. I waited patiently till I had grown used to its ferocity, and said, "It's very strong, and I think the time has come for me to ask you about—"

Once again, however, he put his fingers in his ears. "I shan't listen to you until you're drunk!"

He filled up my glass for the second time. I glanced at it in trepidation; then, overcoming my inherent objection, I drank it down at a gulp. No sooner had the wine come to rest inside me than I lost all willpower. With the third glass, I lost my memory, and with the fourth the future vanished. The world turned round about me, and I forgot why I had gone there. The man leaned toward me attentively, but I saw him—saw everything—as a mere meaningless series of colored planes. I don't know how long it was before my head sank down onto the arm of the chair and I plunged into deep sleep. During it, I had a beautiful dream the like of which I had never experienced. I dreamed that I was in an immense garden surrounded on all sides by luxuriant trees, and the sky was nothing but stars seen between the entwined branches, all enfolded in an atmosphere like that of sunset or a sky overcast with cloud. I was lying on a small hummock of jasmine petals, more of which fell upon me like rain, while the lucent spray of a fountain unceasingly sprinkled the crown of my head and my temples. I was in a state of deep contentedness, of ecstatic serenity. An orchestra of warbling and cooing played in my ear. There was an extraordinary sense of harmony between me and my inner self, and between the two of us and the world, everything being in its rightful place, without discord or distortion. In the whole world there was no single reason for speech or movement, for the universe moved in a rapture of ecstasy. This lasted but a short while. When I opened my eyes, consciousness struck at me like a policeman's fist, and I saw Wanas al-Damanhouri peering at me with concern. Only a few drowsy customers were left in the bar.

"You have slept deeply," said my companion. "You were obviously hungry for sleep."

I rested my heavy head in the palms of my hands. When I took them away in astonishment and looked down at them, I found that they glistened with drops of water.

"My head's wet," I protested.

"Yes, my friend tried to rouse you," he answered quietly.

"Somebody saw me in this state?"

"Don't worry, he is a good man. Have you not heard of Sheikh Zaabalawi?"

"Zaabalawi!" I exclaimed, jumping to my feet.

"Yes," he answered in surprise. "What's wrong?"

"Where is he?"

"I don't know where he is now. He was here and then he left."

I was about to run off in pursuit but found I was more exhausted than I had imagined. Collapsed over the table, I cried out in despair, "My sole reason for coming to you was to meet him! Help me to catch up with him or send someone after him."

The man called a vendor of prawns and asked him to seek out the sheikh and bring him back. Then he turned to me. "I didn't realize you were afflicted. I'm very sorry...."

"You wouldn't let me speak," I said irritably.

"What a pity! He was sitting on this chair beside you the whole time. He was playing with a string of jasmine petals he had around his neck,[6] a gift from one of his admirers, then, taking pity on you, he began to sprinkle some water on your head to bring you around."

"Does he meet you here every night?" I asked, my eyes not leaving the doorway through which the vendor of prawns had left.

"He was with me tonight, last night, and the night before that, but before that I hadn't seen him for a month."

"Perhaps he will come tomorrow," I answered with a sigh.

"Perhaps."

"I am willing to give him any money he wants."

Wanas answered sympathetically, "The strange thing is that he is not open to such temptations, yet he will cure you if you meet him."

"Without charge?"

"Merely on sensing that you love him."

The vendor of prawns returned, having failed in his mission.

I recovered some of my energy and left the bar, albeit unsteadily. At every street corner I called out "Zaabalawi!" in the vague hope that I would be rewarded with an answering shout. The street boys turned contemptuous eyes on me till I sought refuge in the first available taxi.

The following evening I stayed up with Wanas al-Damanhouri till dawn, but the sheikh did not put in an appearance. Wanas informed me that he would be going away to the country and would not be returning to Cairo until he had sold the cotton crop.

I must wait, I told myself; I must train myself to be patient. Let me content myself with having made certain of the existence of Zaabalawi, and even of his affection for me, which encourages me to think that he will be prepared to cure me if a meeting takes place between us.

---

6. In Arabic culture, jasmine is a symbol of purity and innocence.

Sometimes, however, the long delay wearied me. I would become beset by despair and would try to persuade myself to dismiss him from my mind completely. How many weary people in this life know him not or regard him as a mere myth! Why, then, should I torture myself about him in this way?

No sooner, however, did my pains force themselves upon me than I would again begin to think about him, asking myself when I would be fortunate enough to meet him. The fact that I ceased to have any news of Wanas and was told he had gone to live abroad did not deflect me from my purpose; the truth of the matter was that I had become fully convinced that I had to find Zaabalawi.

Yes, I have to find Zaabalawi.

The Arabian Nights and Days[1]

Shahriyar

Following the dawn prayer, with clouds of darkness defying the vigorous thrust of light, the vizier Dandan[2] was called to a meeting with the sultan Shahriyar. Dandan's composure vanished. The heart of a father quaked within him as, putting on his clothes, he mumbled, "Now the outcome will be resolved—your fate, Shahrzad."

He went by the road that led up to the mountain on an old jade, followed by a troop of guards; preceding them was a man bearing a torch, in weather that radiated dew and a gentle chilliness. Three years[3] he had spent between fear and hope, between death and expectation; three years spent in the telling of stories; and, thanks to those stories, Shahrzad's life span had been extended. Yet, like everything, the stories had come to an end, had ended yesterday. So what fate was lying in wait for you, O beloved daughter of mine?

He entered the palace that perched on top of the mountain. The chamberlain led him to a rear balcony that overlooked a vast garden. Shahriyar was sitting in the light shed by a single lamp, bare-headed,[4] his hair luxuriantly black, his eyes gleaming in his long face, his large beard spreading across the top of his chest. Dandan kissed the ground before him, feeling, despite their long association, an inner fear for a man whose history had been filled with harshness, cruelty, and the spilling of innocent blood.

The sultan signaled for the sole lamp to be extinguished. Darkness took over and the specters of the trees giving out a fragrant aroma were cast into semi-obscurity.

"Let there be darkness so that I may observe the effusion of the light," Shahriyar muttered.

Dandan felt a certain optimism.

"May God grant Your Majesty enjoyment of everything that is best in the night and the day."

Silence. Dandan could discern behind his expression neither contentment nor displeasure, until the sultan quietly said, "It is our wish that Shahrzad remain our wife."

Dandan jumped to his feet and bent over the sultan's head, kissing it with a sense of gratitude that brought tears from deep inside him.

"May God support you in your rule forever and ever."

---

1. Translated by Denys Johnson-Davies.

2. In Mahfouz's rendering of *The Arabian Nights,* Dandan is the vizier and the father of Shahrzad in the frame story.

3. "Three years" is the period that Mahfouz assigns to the 1,001 nights of the tales of Shahrzad, during which she manages to abate the brutality of Shahriyar.

4. The Sultan is not wearing his turban, the symbol of power and authority.

"Justice," said the sultan, as though remembering his victims, "possesses disparate methods, among them the sword and among them forgiveness. God has His own wisdom."

"May God direct your steps to His wisdom, Your Majesty."

"Her stories are white magic," he said delightedly. "They open up worlds that invite reflection."

The vizier was suddenly intoxicated with joy.

"She bore me a son and my troubled spirits were put at peace."

"May Your Majesty enjoy happiness both here and in the here-after."

"Happiness!" muttered the sultan sharply.

Dandan felt anxious for some reason. The crowing of the roosters rang out. As though talking to himself, the sultan said, "Existence itself is the most inscrutable thing in existence."

But his tone of perplexity vanished when he exclaimed, "Look. Over there!"

Dandan looked toward the horizon and saw it aglow with hallowed joy.

Shahrzad

Dandan asked permission to see his daughter Shahrzad. A handmaid led him to the rose room with its rose-colored carpet and curtains, and the divans and cushions in shades of red. There he was met by Shahrzad and her sister Dunyazad.

"I am overwhelmed with happiness, thanks be to God, Lord of the Worlds."

Shahrzad sat him down beside her while Dunyazad withdrew to her closet.

"I was saved from a bloody fate by our Lord's mercy," said Shahrzad.

But the man was barely mumbling his thanks as she added bitterly, "May God have mercy on those innocent virgins."

"How wise you are and how courageous!"

"But you know, father," she said in a whisper, "that I am unhappy."

"Be careful, daughter, for thoughts assume concrete forms in palaces and give voice."

"I sacrificed myself," she said sorrowfully, "in order to stem the torrent of blood."

"God has His wisdom," he muttered.

"And the Devil his supporters," she said in a fury.

"He loves you, Shahrzad," he pleaded.

"Arrogance and love do not come together in one heart. He loves himself first and last."

"Love also has its miracles."

"Whenever he approaches me I breathe the smell of blood."

"The sultan is not like the rest of humankind."

"But a crime is a crime. How many virgins has he killed![5] How many pious and God-fearing people has he wiped out! Only hypocrites are left in the kingdom."

"My trust in God has never been shaken," he said sadly.

"As for me, I know that my spiritual station lies in patience, as the great sheikh taught me."

To this Dandan said with a smile, "What an excellent teacher and what an excellent pupil!"

---

5. Before his marriage to Shahrzad, every night the Sultan would marry a new virgin, deflower her, and kill her the following morning.

The Sheikh[6]

Sheikh Abdullah al-Balkhi lived in a simple dwelling in the old quarter. His dreamy gaze was reflected in the hearts of many of his old and more recent students and was deeply engraved in the hearts of his disciples. With him, complete devotion was no more than a prologue, for he was a Sheikh of the Way, having attained a high plane in the spiritual station of love and contentment.

When he had left his place of seclusion for the reception room, Zubeida, his young and only daughter, came to him and said happily, "The city is rejoicing, father."

"Hasn't the doctor Abdul Qadir al-Maheeni arrived yet?" he inquired, not heeding her words.

"Maybe he's on his way, father, but the city is rejoicing because the sultan has consented that Shahrzad should be his wife and he has renounced the shedding of blood."

Nothing dislodges him from his calm, however: the contentment in his heart neither diminishes nor increases. Zubeida is a daughter and a disciple, but she is still at the beginning of the Way. Hearing a knock at the door, she left, saying, "Your friend has come on his usual visit."

The doctor Abdul Qadir al-Maheeni entered. The two of them embraced, then he seated himself on a mattress alongside his friend. As usual the conversation was conducted in the light from a lamp in a small recess.

"You have no doubt heard the good news?" said Abdul Qadir.

"I know what it is my business to know," he said with a smile.

"Voices are lifted in prayer for Shahrzad, showing that it is you who primarily deserve the credit," said the doctor.

"Credit is for the Beloved alone," he said in reproof.

"I too am a believer, yet I follow promises and deductions. Had she not been a pupil of yours as a young girl, Shahrzad would not, despite what you may say, have found stories to divert the sultan from shedding blood."

"My friend, the only trouble with you is that you overdo your submission to the intellect."

"It is the ornament of man."

"It is through intellect that we come to know the limits of the intellect."

"There are believers," said Abdul Qadir, "who are of the opinion that it has no limits."

"I have failed in drawing many to the Way—you at the head of them."

"People are poor creatures, master, and are in need of someone to enlighten them about their lives."

"Many a righteous soul will save a whole people," said the sheikh with confidence.

"Ali al-Salouli is the governor of our quarter—how can the quarter be saved from his corruption?" inquired the doctor, suddenly showing resentment.

"But those who strive are of different ranks," the sheikh said sadly.

"I am a doctor and what is right for the world is what concerns me."

The sheikh patted his hand gently and the doctor smiled and said, "But you are goodness itself and good luck."

"I give thanks to God, for no joy carries me away, no sadness touches me."

---

6. This section is an addition to the original frame story by Mahfouz. In this change he is attributing the success of the woman, Shahrzad, in taming her bloodthirsty husband to a man, her teacher, Abdullah al-Balkhi, a wise sheikh "of the Way"—Sufi mystic philosophy.

"As for me, dear friend, I am sad. Whenever I remember the God-fearing who have been martyred for saying the truth in protest against the shedding of blood and the plundering of property, my sadness increases."

"How strongly are we bound to material things!"

"Noble and God-fearing people have been martyred," bewailed Abdul Qadir. "How sorry I am for you, O my city, which today is controlled solely by hypocrites! Why, master, are only the worst cattle left in the stalls?"[7]

"How numerous are the lovers of vile things!"

Sounds of piping and drumming reached them from the fringes of the quarter and they realized that the people were celebrating the happy news. At this the doctor decided to make his way to the Café of the Emirs.

The Café of the Emirs[8]

The café was centered on the right-hand side of the large commercial street. Square in shape, it had a spacious courtyard, with its entrance opening onto the public way and its windows overlooking neighboring sections of the city. Along its sides were couches for the higher-class customers, while in a circle in the middle were ranged mattresses for the common folk to sit on. A variety of things to drink were served, both hot and cold according to the season; also available were the finest sorts of hashish and electuaries. At night many were the high-class customers to be found there, the likes of Sanaan al-Gamali and his son Fadil, Hamdan Tuneisha and Karam al-Aseel, Sahloul and Ibrahim al-Attar the druggist and his son Hasan, Galil al-Bazzaz the draper, Nur al-Din, and Shamloul the hunchback.

There were also ordinary folk like Ragab the porter and his crony Sindbad, Ugr the barber and his son Aladdin, Ibrahim the water-carrier and Ma'rouf the cobbler. There was general merriment on this happy night, and soon the doctor Abdul Qadir al-Maheeni had joined the group that included Ibrahim al-Attar, Karam al-Aseel the millionaire, and Sahloul the bric-a-brac merchant and furnisher. That night they had recovered from a fear that had held sway over them; every father of a beautiful virgin daughter felt reassured and was promised a sleep free from frightening specters.

"Let us recite the Fatiha over the souls of the victims," several voices rang out.

"Of virgins and God-fearing men."[9]

"Farewell to tears."

"Praise and thanks be to God, Lord of the Worlds."

"And long life to Shahrzad, the pearl of women."

"Thanks to those beautiful stories."

"It is nothing but God's mercy that has descended."

The merriment and conversation continued until the voice of Ragab the porter was heard saying with astonishment, "Are you mad, Sindbad?"

And Ugr, who was keen to put his nose into everything, asked, "What's got into him on this happy night?"

"It seems he's come to hate his work and is tired of the city. He no longer wants to be a porter."

"Does he have ambitions to be in charge of the quarter?"

---

7. A common Egyptian proverb.

8. Mahfouz uses the café as the public space in which much of the democratic interaction between people takes place in many of his works.

9. In Mahfouz's tale, good men as well as virgins are suffering the effects of corruption and tyranny.

"He went to a ship's captain and kept insisting till he agreed to take him on as a servant."

Ibrahim the water-carrier said, "Whoever gives up an assured livelihood on dry land to run away after some vague one on water must be really crazy."

"Water that from earliest times has derived its sustenance from corpses," said Ma'rouf the cobbler.

To which Sindbad said defiantly, "I am fed up with lanes and alleys. I am also fed up with carrying furniture around, with no hope of seeing anything new. Over there is another life: the river joins up with the sea and the sea penetrates deeply into the unknown, and the unknown brings forth islands and mountains, living creatures and angels and devils. It is a magical call that cannot be resisted. I said to myself, 'Try your luck, Sindbad, and throw yourself into the arms of the invisible.'"

Nur al-Din the perfume-seller said, "In movement is a blessing."[1]

"A beautiful salutation from a childhood comrade," said Sindbad.

Ugr the barber demanded sarcastically, "Are you making out that you're upper-class, porter?"

"We sat side by side in the prayer room receiving lessons from our master, Abdul-lah al-Balkhi," said Nur al-Din.

"And, like many others, I contented myself with learning the rudiments of reading and religion," said Sindbad.

"The dry land will not be lessened by your leaving, nor the sea increased," said Ugr.

At this the doctor Abdul Qadir al-Maheeni said to him, "Go in God's protection, but keep your wits about you—it would be good if you were able to record the wonderful sights you come across, for God has ordered us to do so. When are you departing?"

"Tomorrow morning," he muttered. "I leave you in the care of God the Living, the Eternal."

"How sad it is to part from you, Sindbad," said his comrade Ragab the porter.

Sanaan al-Gamali

I

Time gives a special knock inside and wakes him. He directs his gaze toward a window close to the bed and through it sees the city wrapped around in darkness. Sleep has stripped it of all movement and sound as it nestles in a silence replete with cosmic calm.

Separating himself from Umm Saad's[2] warm body, he stepped onto the floor, where his feet sank into the downy texture of the Persian carpet. He stretched out his arm as he groped for where the candlestick stood and bumped into something solid and hard. Startled, he muttered, "What's this?"

A strange voice issued forth, a voice the like of which he had never heard: the voice of neither a human nor an animal. It robbed him of all sensation—it was as though it were sweeping throughout the whole city. The voice spoke angrily, "You trod on my head, you blind creature!"

He fell to the ground in fear. He was a man without the tiniest atom of valor: he excelled at nothing but buying and selling and bargaining.

"You trod on my head, you ignorant fellow," said the voice.

"Who are you?" he said in a quaking voice.

"I am Qumqam."

"Qumqam?"

---

1. An Egyptian proverb.
2. His wife, literally the mother of their son, Saad.

"A genie from among the city's dwellers."[3]

Almost vanishing in terror, he was struck speechless.

"You hurt me and you must be punished."

His tongue was incapable of putting up any defense.

"I heard you yesterday, you hypocrite," Qumqam continued, "and you were saying that death is a debt we have to pay, so what are you doing pissing yourself with fear?"

"Have mercy on me!" he finally pleaded. "I am a family man."

"My punishment will descend only on you."

"Not for a single moment did I think of disturbing you."

"What troublesome creatures you are! You don't stop yearning to enslave us in order to achieve your vile objectives. Have you not satisfied your greed by enslaving the weak among you?"

"I swear to you..."

"I have no faith in a merchant's oath," he interrupted him.

"I ask mercy and plead pardon from you," he said.

"You would make me do that?"

"Your big heart..." he said anxiously.

"Don't try to cheat me as you do your customers."

"Do it for nothing, for the love of God."

"There is no mercy without a price and no pardon without a price."

He glimpsed a sudden ray of hope.

"I'll do as you want," he said fervently.

"Really?"

"With all the strength I possess," he said eagerly.

"Kill Ali al-Salouli," he said with frightening calm.

The joy drowned in an unexpected defeat, like something brought at great risk from across the seas whose worthlessness has become apparent on inspection.

"Ali al-Salouli, the governor of our quarter?" he asked in horror.

"None other."

"But he is a governor and lives in the guarded House of Happiness, while I am nothing but a merchant."

"Then there is no mercy, no pardon," he exclaimed.

"Sir, why don't you kill him yourself?"

"He has brought me under his power with black magic," he said with exasperation, "and he makes use of me in accomplishing purposes that my conscience does not approve of."

"But you are a force surpassing black magic."

"We are nevertheless subject to specific laws. Stop arguing—you must either accept or refuse."

"Have you no other wishes?" said Sanaan urgently. "I have plenty of money, also goods from India and China."

"Don't waste time uselessly, you fool."

In utter despair, he said, "I'm at your disposal."

"Take care not to attempt to trick me."

"I have resigned myself to my fate."[4]

"You will be in my grasp even if you were to take refuge in the mountains of Qaf at the ends of the world."

3. The genies are mentioned in the Qur'an, and therefore the Muslims believe in their existence, and they constitute a significant part of the popular culture. There are, however, bad genies and good ones, and they dwell among the people and are often controlled, through magic, by some of them.

4. Fate is a basic concept in Islamic belief. It is normally preordained, and there is no escape from its dictates.

At that, Sanaan felt a sharp pain in his arm. He let out a scream that tore at his depths.

II

Sanaan opened his eyes to the voice of Umm Saad saying, "What's made you sleep so late?" She lit the candle and he began to look about him in a daze. If it were a dream, why did it fill him more than wakefulness itself? He was so alive that he was terrified. Nevertheless he entertained thoughts of escape, and feelings of grateful calm took control of him. The world was brought back to its proper perspective after total ruin. How wonderful was the sweetness of life after the torture of hellfire!

"I take refuge in God from the accursed Devil," he sighed.

Umm Saad looked at him as she tucked scattered locks of hair inside the kerchief round her head, sleep having affected the beauty of her face with a sallow hue. Intoxicated with the sensation of having made his escape, he said, "Praise be to God, Who has rescued me from grievous trouble."

"May God protect us, O father of Fadil."

"A terrible dream, Umm Saad."

"God willing, all will be well."

She led the way to the bathroom and lit a small lamp in the recess. Following her, he said, "I spent part of my night with a genie."

"How is that, you being the God-fearing man you are?"

"I shall recount it to Sheikh Abdullah al-Balkhi. Go now in peace that I may make my ablutions."

As he was doing so and washing his left forearm, he stopped, trembling all over.

"O my Lord!"

He began looking aghast at the wound, which was like a bite. It was no illusion that he was seeing, for blood had broken through where the fangs had penetrated the flesh.

"It is not possible."

In terror he hurried off toward the kitchen. As she was lighting the oven, Umm Saad asked, "Have you made your ablutions?"

"Look," he said, stretching out his arm.

"What has bitten you?" the woman gasped.

"I don't know."

Overcome by anxiety, she said, "But you slept so well."

"I don't know what happened."

"Had it happened during the day..."

"It didn't happen during the day," he interrupted her.

They exchanged an uneasy look fraught with suppressed thoughts.

"Tell me about the dream," she said with dread.

"I told you it was a genie," he said dejectedly. "It was a dream, though."

Once again they exchanged glances and the pain of anxiety.

"Let it be a secret," said Umm Saad warily.

He understood the secret of her fears that corresponded to his own, for if mention were made of the genie, he did not know what would happen to his reputation as a merchant on the morrow, nor to what the reputation of his daughter Husniya and his son Fadil would be exposed. The dream could bring about total ruin. Also, he was sure of nothing.

"A dream's a dream," said Umm Saad, "and the secret of the wound is known to God alone."

"This is what one must remind oneself," he said in despair.

"The important thing now is for you to have it treated without delay, so go now to your friend Ibrahim the druggist."

How could he arrive at the truth? He was so burdened with anxiety that he was enraged and boiled with anger. He felt his position going from bad to worse. All his feelings were charged with anger and resentment, while his nature deteriorated as though he were being created anew in a form that was at variance with his old deep-rooted gentleness. No longer could he put up with the woman's glances; he began to hate them, to loathe her very thoughts. He felt a desire to destroy everything that existed. Unable to control himself, he pierced her with a glance filled with hatred and resentment, as though it were she who was responsible for his plight. Turning his back on her, he went off.

"This is not the Sanaan of old," she muttered.

He found Fadil and Husniya in the living room in a dim light that spilled out through the holes of the wooden latticework. Their faces were distraught at the way his excited voice had been raised. His anger increased and, very unlike himself, he shouted, "Get out of my sight!"

He closed the door of his room behind him and began examining his arm. Fadil boldly joined him.

"I trust you are all right, father," he said anxiously.

"Leave me alone," he said gruffly.

"Did a dog bite you?"

"Who said so?"

"My mother."

He appreciated her wisdom in saying this and he agreed, but his mood did not improve.

"It's nothing. I'm fine, but leave me on my own."

"You should go to the druggist."

"I don't need anybody to tell me that," he said with annoyance.

Outside, Fadil said to Husniya, "How changed father is!"

III

For the first time in his life, Sanaan al-Gamali left his house without performing his prayers. He went at once to the shop of Ibrahim the druggist, an old friend and neighbor in the commercial street. When the druggist saw his arm, he said in astonishment, "What sort of dog was this! But then there are so many stray dogs…"

He set about making a selection of herbs, saying, "I have a prescription that never fails."

He boiled up the herbs until they deposited a sticky sediment. Having washed the wound with rose water, he covered it with the mixture, spreading it over with a wooden spatula, then bound up the arm with Damascene muslin, muttering, "May it be healed, God willing."

At which, despite himself, Sanaan said, "Or let the Devil do what he may."

Ibrahim the druggist looked quizzically into his friend's flushed face, amazed at how much he had changed.

"Don't allow a trifling wound to affect your gentle nature."

With a melancholy face, Sanaan made off, saying, "Ibrahim, don't trust this world."

How apprehensive he was! It was as though he had been washed in a potion of fiery peppers. The sun was harsh and hot, people's faces were glum.

Fadil had arrived at the shop before him and met him with a beaming smile which only increased his ill humor. He cursed the heat, despite his well-known acceptance of all kinds of weather. He greeted no one and scarcely returned a greeting. He was cheered by neither face nor word. He laughed at no joke and took no warning note at a funeral passing. No comely face brought him pleasure. What had happened? Fadil worked harder in order to intervene as far as possible between his father and the customers. More than one inquired of Fadil in a whisper, "What's up with your father today?"

The young man could only reply, "He's indisposed—may God show you no ill."

IV

It was not long before his condition was made known to the habitués of the Café of the Emirs. He made his way to them with a gloomy countenance and either sat in silence or engaged only in distracted conversation. He no longer made his amusing comments; quickly dispirited, he soon left the café.

"A wild dog bit him," Ibrahim the druggist said.

And Galil the draper commented, "He's utterly lost to us."

While Karam al-Aseel, the man with millions and the face of a monkey, said, "But his business is flourishing."

And the doctor Abdul Qadir al-Maheeni said, "The value of money evaporates when you're ill."

And Ugr the barber, the only one among those sitting on the floor who would sometimes thrust himself into the conversation of the upper-class customers, said philosophically, "What is a man? A bite from a dog or a fly's sting..."

But Fadil shouted at him, "My father's fine. It's only that he's indisposed—he'll be all right by daybreak."

But he went deeper and deeper into a state that became difficult to control. Finally, one night he swallowed a crazy amount of dope and left the café full of energy and ready to brave the unknown. Disliking the idea of going home, he went stumbling around in the dark, driven on by crazed fantasies. He hoped for some action that might dispel his rebellious state of tension and relieve it of its torment. He brought to mind women from his family who were long dead and they appeared before him naked and in poses that were sexually suggestive and seductive, and he regretted not having had his way with a single one of them. He passed by the cul-de-sac of Sheikh Abdullah al-Balkhi and for an instant thought of visiting him and confiding to him what had occurred, but he hurried on. In the light of a lamp hanging down from the top of the door of one of the houses he saw a young girl of ten going her way carrying a large metal bowl. He rushed toward her, blocking her way and inquiring, "Where are you going, little girl?"

"I'm going back to my mother," she replied innocently.

He plunged into the darkness till he could see her no more.

"Come here," he said, "and I'll show you something nice."

He picked her up in his arms and the water from the pickles spilt over his silken garment. He took her under the stairway of the elementary school. The girl was puzzled by his strange tenderness and didn't feel at ease with him.

"My mother's waiting," she said nervously.

But he had stirred her curiosity as much as her fears. His age, which reminded her of her father, induced in her a sort of trust, a trust in which an unknown disquiet was mixed with the anticipation of some extraordinary dream. She let out a wailing scream which tore apart his compassionate excitement and sent terrifying phantoms into his murky imagination. He quickly stifled her mouth with the trembling palm of his hand. A sudden return to his senses was like a slap in the face, as he came back to earth.

"Don't cry. Don't be frightened," he whispered entreatingly.

Despair washed over him until it demolished the pillars on which the earth was supported. Out of total devastation he heard the tread of approaching footsteps. Quickly he grasped the thin neck in hands that were alien to him. Like a rapacious beast whose foot has slipped, he tumbled down into an abyss. He realized that he was finished and noticed that a voice was calling, "Baseema...Baseema, my girl."

In utter despair he said to himself, "It is inevitable."

It became clear that the footsteps were approaching his hiding-place. The light from a lamp showed up dimly. He was driven by a desire to go out carrying the body with him. Then the presence of something heavy overtook his own collapsing presence, the memory of the dream took him by storm. He heard the voice of two days ago inquiring, "Is this what we pledged ourselves to?"

"You are a fact, then, and not a dire dream," he said in surrender.

"You are without doubt mad."

"I agree, but you are the cause."

"I never asked you to do something evil," the voice said angrily.

"There's no time for arguing. Save me, so that I can carry out for you what was agreed."

"This is what I came for, but you don't understand."

He felt himself traveling in a vacuum in an intensely silent world. Then he again heard the voice. "No one will find a trace of you. Open your eyes and you will find that you are standing in front of the door of your house. Enter in peace. I shall be waiting."

V

With a superhuman effort Sanaan took control of himself. Umm Saad did not feel that his condition had deteriorated. Taking refuge behind his eyelids in the darkness, he set about calling to mind what he had done. He was another person, the killer-violator was another person. His soul had begotten wild beings of which he had no experience. Now, divested of his past and having buried all his hopes, he was presenting himself to the unknown. Though he hadn't slept, no movement escaped him to indicate that he had been without sleep. Early in the morning there came the sound of wailing. Umm Saad disappeared for a while, then returned and said, "O mother of Baseema, may God be with you."

"What's happened?" he asked, lowering his gaze.

"What's got into people, father of Fadil? The girl's been raped and murdered under the elementary school stairway. A mere child, O Lord. Under the skin of certain humans lie savage beasts."

He bowed his head until his beard lay disheveled against his chest.

"I take my refuge in God from the accursed Devil," he muttered.

"These beasts know neither God nor Prophet."

The woman burst into tears.

He began to ask himself: Was it the genie? Was it the dope he had swallowed? Or was it Sanaan al-Gamali?

VI

The thoughts of everyone in the quarter were in turmoil. The crime was the sole subject of conversation. Ibrahim the druggist, as he prepared him more medicine, said,

"The wound has not healed, but there is no longer any danger from it." Then, as he bound his arm with muslin, "Have you heard of the crime?"

"I take refuge in God," he said in disgust.

"The criminal's not human. Our sons marry directly they reach puberty."

"He's a madman, there's no doubt of that."

"Or he's one of those vagabonds who haven't got the means to marry. They are milling around the streets like stray dogs."

"Many are saying that."

"What is Ali al-Salouli doing in the seat of government?"

At mention of the name he quaked, remembering the pact he had made, a pact that hung over his head like a sword. "Busy with his own interests," he concurred, "and counting the presents and the bribes."

"The favors he rendered us merchants cannot be denied," said the druggist, "but he should remember that his primary duty is to maintain things as they are for us."

Sanaan went off with the words, "Don't put your trust in the world, Ibrahim."

VII

The governor of the quarter, Ali al-Salouli, knew from his private secretary Buteisha Murgan what was being said about security. He was frightened that the reports would reach the vizier Dandan and that he would pass them on to the sultan, so he called the chief of police, Gamasa al-Bulti, and said to him, "Have you heard what is being said about security during my time in office?"

The chief of police's inner calm had not changed when he had learned about his superior's secrets—and acts of corruption.

"Excuse me, governor," he said, "but I have not been negligent or remiss in sending out spies. However, the villain has left no trace and we haven't found a single witness. I myself have interrogated dozens of vagabonds and beggars, but it's an unfathomable crime, unlike anything that has previously happened."

"What a fool you are! Arrest all the vagabonds and beggars—you're an expert on the effective means of interrogation."[5]

"We haven't the prisons to take them," said Gamasa warily.

"What prisons, fellow? Do you want to impose upon the public treasury the expense of providing them with food?" said the governor in a rage. "Drive them into the open and seek the help of the troops—and bring me the criminal before nightfall."

VIII

The police swooped down on the plots of wasteland and arrested the beggars and vagabonds, then drove them in groups into the open. No complaint and no oath availed, no exception was made of old men. Force was used against them until they prayed fervently for help to God and to His Prophet and the members of his family.

Sanaan al-Gamali followed the news with anxious alarm: he was the guilty one, of this there was no doubt, and yet he was going about free and at large, being treated with esteem. How was it that he had become the very pivot of all this suffering? And someone unknown was lying in wait for him, someone indifferent to all that had occurred, while he was utterly lost, succumbing without condition. As for the old Sanaan, he had died and been obliterated, nothing being left of him but a confused mind that chewed over memories as though they were delusions.

5. A clear euphemism for torture.

He became conscious of a clamor sweeping down the commercial street. It was Ali al-Salouli, governor of the quarter, making his way at the head of a squadron of cavalry, reminding people of the governor's power and vigilance, a challenge to any disorder. As he proceeded he replied to the greetings of the merchants to right and left. This was the man he had undertaken to kill. His heart overflowed with fear and loathing. This was the secret of his torment. It was he who had chosen to liberate the genie from his black magic. It was the genie alone who had done this. His escape was conditional on his doing away with al-Salouli. His eyes became fixed on the dark, well-filled face, pointed beard and stocky body. When he passed in front of the shop of Ibrahim the druggist, the owner hurried up to him and they shook hands warmly. Then, passing before Sanaan's shop, he happened to glance toward it and smiled so that Sanaan had no choice but to cross over and shake him by the hand, at which al-Salouli said to him, "We'll be seeing you soon, God willing."

Sanaan al-Gamali returned to the shop, asking himself what he had meant. Why was he inviting him to a meeting? Why? Was he finding the path made easy for him in a way he had not expected? A shudder passed through him from top to toe. In a daze he repeated his words, "I'll be seeing you soon, God willing."

IX

When he lay down to sleep that night the other presence took control and the voice said mockingly, "You eat, drink, and sleep, and it is for me to exercise patience!"

"It's an onerous assignment. Those with such power as yourself do not realize how onerous," he said miserably.

"But it's easier than killing the little girl."

"What a waste! I had long been thought of as among the best of the good."

"External appearances do not deceive me."

"They were not simply external appearances."

"You have forgotten things that would bring sweat to one's brow with shame."

"Perfection is God's alone,"[6] he said in confusion.

"I also don't deny your good points, and it was for this that I nominated you to be saved."[7]

"If you hadn't forced your way into my life, I wouldn't have got myself involved in this crime."

"Don't lie," he said sharply. "You alone are responsible for your crime."

"I don't understand you."

"I really judged you too favorably."

"If only you'd just left me alone!"

"I'm a believing genie and I told myself, 'This man's goodness exceeds his wickedness. Certainly he has suspicious relations with the chief of police and doesn't hesitate to exploit times of inflation, but he is the most honest of merchants, also he is charitable and undertakes his religious devotions and is merciful to the poor.' Thus I chose you to be saved, to be the saving of the quarter from the head of corruption, and the saving of your sinful self. Yet instead of attaining the visible target, your whole structure collapsed and you committed this repugnant crime."

Sanaan moaned and kept silent, while the voice continued, "The chance is still there."

"And the crime?" he asked helplessly.

6. A well-known Islamic formula.

7. Referring on the one hand to the immediate escape from the situation and on the other to the Sufi concept of salvation through performing good deeds, in this case saving the quarter from the tyranny of its corrupt ruler.

"Life gives opportunities for both reflection and repentance."

"But the man is an impregnable fortress," he said in a voice clinging to a vestige of hope.

"He will invite you to meet him."

"That seems unlikely."

"He will invite you—be sure and be prepared."

Sanaan thought for a while, then inquired, "Will you promise me deliverance?"

"I chose you only for deliverance."

So exhausted was Sanaan that he fell into a deep sleep.

X

He was getting ready to go to the café when Umm Saad said, "There's a messenger from the governor waiting for you in the reception room."

He found the private secretary, Buteisha Murgan, waiting for him with his sparkling eyes and short beard.

"The governor wants to see you."

His heart beat fast. He realized that he was going off to commit the gravest crime in the history of the quarter. Perhaps it worried him that Buteisha Murgan should be acquainted with the circumstances surrounding his visit, but he took reassurance in Qumqam's promise.

"Wait for me," he said, "till I put on my clothes."

"I shall go ahead of you so as not to attract attention."

So the man was bent on keeping the secret nature of the meeting, thus facilitating his task: He began anointing himself with musk, while Umm Saad watched, nursing a sense of unease that had not left her since the night of the dream. She was held by a feeling that she was living with another man and that the old Sanaan had vanished into darkness. Without her noticing, he slipped into his pocket a dagger with a handle of pure silver that he had received as a gift from India.[8]

XI

Ali al-Salouli received him in his summer mansion at the governorate's garden, appearing in a flowing white robe and with his head bare, which lessened the awe his position bestowed. A table stood in front of him on which were assembled long-necked bottles, glasses, and various nuts, dried fruits, and sweets, which gave evidence of conviviality. He seated him on a cushion alongside him and asked Buteisha Murgan to stay on.

"Welcome to you, Master Sanaan, true merchant and noble man."

Sanaan mumbled something, hiding his confusion with a smile.

"It is thanks to you, O deputy of the sultan."

Murgan filled three glasses. Sanaan wondered whether Murgan would stay until the end of the meeting. Maybe it was an opportunity that would not be repeated, so what should he do?

"It's a pleasant summer night," said al-Salouli. "Do you like the summer?"

"I love all seasons."

"You are one of those with whom God is content, and it is by His complete contentment that we start a new and productive life."

Impelled by curiosity, Sanaan said, "I ask God to complete His favor to us."

8. India is associated in the popular imagination with magic and powerful potions, linking the dagger to the genie. This is a clear indication of the scale of torture that took place in the investigation. The reader knows the real perpetrator of the crime, while the narrative tells us of this large number of those innocent who confess under police brutality to a crime they did not commit.

They drank, and became elated and invigorated from the wine.

"We have cleansed our quarter of riffraff for you," al-Salouli continued.

"What firmness and determination!" he said with secret sadness.

"We scarcely hear now of a theft or other crime," said Buteisha Murgan.

"Have you discovered who the culprit is?" asked Sanaan cautiously.

"Those confessing to the crime number over fifty," said al-Salouli, laughing.

Murgan laughed too, but said, "The true culprit is doubtless among them."

"It's Gamasa al-Bulti's problem," said al-Salouli.

"We must also increase the exhortations at the mosques and at religious festivals," said Murgan.

Sanaan was beginning to despair, but then al-Salouli gave a special sign to Murgan, who left the place. Even so, the guards were dispersed throughout the garden and there was no way of escape. But not for an instant was he unmindful of Qumqam's promise.

"Let's close the discussion of crimes and criminals," said al-Salouli, changing his tone of voice.

"May your night be a pleasant one, sir," said Sanaan, smiling.

"The fact is that I invited you for more than one reason."

"I'm at your disposal."

"I would like to marry your daughter," he said confidently.

Sanaan was amazed. He was saddened too about an opportunity that was fated to miscarry before it was born. He nevertheless said, "This is a big honor, the greatest of happiness."

"And I also have a daughter as a gift for your son Fadil."

Chasing away his bewilderment, Sanaan said, "He's a lucky young man."

For a while the other was silent and then continued, "As for the final request, it relates to the public welfare."

There gleamed in Sanaan's eyes an inquiring look, at which the governor said, "The contractor Hamdan Tuneisha is your relative, is he not?"

"Yes, sir."

"The point is that I have made up my mind to construct a road alongside the desert the whole length of the quarter."

"A truly excellent project."

"When will you bring him to me here?" he asked in a meaningful tone.

Feeling how ironic the situation was, he said, "Our appointment will be for tomorrow evening, sir."

Al-Salouli gave him a piercing glance and inquired with a smile, "I wonder whether he will come duly prepared?"

"Just as you envisage," said Sanaan with shrewd subtlety.[9]

Al-Salouli laughed and said jovially, "You're intelligent, Sanaan—and don't forget that we are related!"

Sanaan suddenly feared he would summon Buteisha Murgan, and he said to himself, "It's now or the chance will vanish forever."

The man had facilitated things for him without knowing it by relaxing and stretching out his legs and turning over on his back, his eyes closed. Sanaan was immersed in thoughts about the crime and hurling himself into what destiny still remained to him. Unsheathing the dagger, and aiming it at the heart, he stabbed with a strength drawn from determination, despair, and a final desire to escape. The governor gave a violent shuddering, as though wrestling with some unknown force. His face was convulsed and became crazily glazed. He started to bring his arms together as though

9. Sanaan is playing along with al-Salouli's expection of receiving a generous bribe.

to clutch at the dagger, but he was unable to. His terrified eyes uttered unheard words, then he was forever motionless.

XII

Trembling, Sanaan stared at the dagger, whose blade had disappeared from sight, and at the gushing blood. With difficulty he wrested his eyes away and looked fearfully toward the closed door. The silence was rent by the throbbing in his temples, and for the first time he caught sight of the lamps hanging in the corners. He also noted a wooden lectern decorated with mother-of-pearl on which rested a large copy of the Quran. In all his agonies he pleaded to Qumqam, his genie and his fate. The invisible presence enveloped him and he heard the voice saying with satisfaction, "Well done!" Then, joyfully, "Now Qumqam is freed from the black magic."

"Save me," said Sanaan. "I abhor this place and this scene."

The voice said with sympathetic calm, "My faith prevents me from interfering now that I have taken possession of my free will."

"I don't understand what you're saying," he said in terror.

"Your fault, Sanaan, is that you don't think like a human being."

"O Lord, there is no time for discussion. Do you intend to abandon me to my fate?"

"That is exactly what my duty requires of me."

"How despicable! You have deceived me."

"No, rather I have granted you an opportunity of salvation seldom given to a living soul."

"Did you not interfere in my life and cause me to kill this man?"

"I was eager to free myself from the evil of black magic, so I chose you because of your faith, despite the way you fluctuated between good and evil. I reckoned you were more worthy than anyone else to save your quarter and yourself."

"But you did not make clear your thoughts to me," he said desperately.

"I made them sufficiently clear for one who thinks."

"Underhand double-dealing. Who said I was responsible for the quarter?"

"It is a general trust from which no person is free, but it is especially incumbent upon the likes of you, who are not devoid of good intentions."

"Did you not save me from my plight under the stairway of the elementary school?"

"Indeed it was difficult for me to accept that you should, by reason of my intervention, suffer the worst of endings without hope of atonement or repentance, so I decided to give you a new chance."

"And now I have undertaken what I pledged myself to you to do, so it is your duty to save me."

"Then it is a plot and your role in it is that of the instrument, and worthiness, atonement, repentance, and salvation are put an end to."

He went down on his knees and pleaded, "Have mercy on me. Save me."

"Don't waste your sacrifice on the air."

"It's a black outcome."

"He who does good is not troubled by the consequences."

"I don't want to be a hero!" he cried out in terror.

"Be a hero, Sanaan. That is your destiny," said Qumqam sorrowfully.

The voice began to fade as it said, "May God be with you and I ask Him to forgive both you and me."

Sanaan let out a scream that reached the ears of Buteisha Murgan and the men of the guard outside.

Poet and politician: These are the two main dimensions of Aimé Césaire's career. Born on the island of Martinique in 1913, he became not only an influential statesman and a prominent thinker on issues of colonialism and postcolonialism but also one of the most important modern Caribbean poets. During his education in Paris in the 1930s, he met and became close friends with French Guinean writer Léon Damas and Senegalese writer Léopold Sédar Senghor, with whom he co-founded a student journal, *L'Etudiant noir.* From this collaboration emerged the crucial concept of *négritude,* which became a fundamental category for rethinking the relation between white European and black African and Caribbean culture: broadly speaking, it refers to the self-confident assertion of black identity and the achievements of black culture, challenging the colonialist and racist hierarchies in terms of which African cultures had previously been defined. On the eve of World War II in 1939, Césaire returned to Martinique to become a school teacher. In 1945 he was elected mayor of Martinique's capital, Fort-de-France, and a member of the French National Assembly. While holding these offices, he helped redefine the political status of France's former colonies, most importantly in cosponsoring the law that transformed them into French overseas departments, a status that gave them significant political and economic rights. He viewed the fight against colonialism as a part of the struggle of the international working class, and he was a member of the French Communist Party from 1945 to 1956; in 1958 he helped to found the Parti Progressiste Martiniquais. In 1983, a year after the French government created "regional councils" in the French overseas departments, he became president of the Martinican council. He retired from electoral politics in 1993.

Césaire's political struggle on behalf of France's former colonies went hand in hand with his literary works, in which colonial oppression and liberation figure as prominent topics. In both his poetry and his plays, he exposes the cultural and ideological strategies that subject black people to white domination, and he outlines counterimages of a rebellious, imaginative, and self-confident black culture. One of Césaire's most famous later works was a satirical rewriting of Shakespeare's play *The Tempest* (1969), in which Césaire gives an edgy portrait of Caliban as an oppressed native protesting his colonized condition. At the same time, his relationship with European culture remained profoundly ambivalent, including elements of both admiration and rejection, though he remained a lifelong Francophone poet (a speaker and writer of French). His first long poem, *Notebook of a Return to the Native Land,* first published in 1939 and revised in various editions over fifteen years, has remained his most lasting achievement. In the *Notebook,* Césaire addresses the situation of the Caribbean in particular and colonized black cultures in general, using a series of different voices and perspectives; while it is tempting to identify his own view with only one or two of these voices, his full understanding of what *négritude* means emerges only from seeing the different perspectives in the poem together.

By turns outcry, lament, prophecy, and manifesto, the *Notebook* deploys a wide range of poetic strategies from allusions to the Bible and Shakespeare all the way to the striking metaphoric juxtapositions of surrealist poetry. Césaire uses these resources to evoke visions of Caribbean misery and beauty, the suffering of African slaves on their journey West, and the self-confidence of blacks rising up against their oppressors. Though the overall thrust of the poem isn't difficult to understand, the details are often quite hard to grasp, as they are in the surrealist poetry that influenced Césaire deeply. But this difficulty itself has a political thrust: By writing poetry that even French readers find challenging, Césaire, as the poetic voice of the colonized, thrusts all the weight, complexity, and beauty of French education and the French language back at his oppressors. This, certainly, is a message that no French reader of the poem could miss.

PRONUNCIATIONS:
Aimé Césaire: ay-MAY say-ZAIR
grigri: GREE-gree

Notebook of a Return to the Native Land[1]

At the end of the wee hours...

Beat it, I said to him, you cop, you lousy pig, beat it, I detest the flunkies of order and the cockchafers of hope. Beat it, evil grigri,[2] you bedbug of a petty monk. Then I turned toward paradises lost for him and his kin, calmer than the face of a woman telling lies, and there, rocked by the flux of a never exhausted thought I nourished the wind, I unlaced the monsters and heard rise, from the other side of disaster, a river of turtledoves and savanna clover which I carry forever in my depths height-deep as the twentieth floor of the most arrogant houses and as a guard against the putrefying force of crepuscular surroundings, surveyed night and day by a cursed venereal sun.

At the end of the wee hours burgeoning with frail coves, the hungry Antilles, the Antilles pitted with smallpox, the Antilles dynamited by alcohol, stranded in the mud of this bay, in the dust of this town sinisterly stranded.

At the end of the wee hours, the extreme, deceptive desolate bedsore on the wound of the waters; the martyrs who do not bear witness; the flowers of blood that fade and scatter in the empty wind like the screeches of babbling parrots; an aged life mendaciously smiling, its lips opened by vacated agonies; an aged poverty rotting under the sun, silently; an aged silence bursting with tepid pustules, the awful futility of our raison d'être.[3]

At the end of the wee hours, on this very fragile earth thickness exceeded in a humiliating way by its grandiose future—the volcanoes will explode, the naked water will bear away the ripe sun stains and nothing will be left but a tepid bubbling pecked at by sea birds—the beach of dreams and the insane awakenings.

At the end of the wee hours, this town sprawled-flat toppled from its common sense, inert, winded under its geometric weight of an eternally renewed cross, indocile to its fate, mute, vexed no matter what, incapable of growing with the juice of this earth, self-conscious, clipped, reduced, in breach of fauna and flora.

At the end of the wee hours, this town sprawled-flat...

And in this inert town, this squalling throng so astonishingly detoured from its cry as this town has been from its movement, from its meaning, not even worried, detoured from its true cry, the only cry you would have wanted to hear because you feel it alone belongs to this town; because you feel it lives in it in some deep refuge and pride of this inert town, this throng detoured from its cry of hunger, of poverty, of revolt, of hatred, this throng so strangely chattering and mute.

1. Translated by Clayton Eshleman and Annette Smith.
2. African amulet.
3. Reason for being.

In this inert town, this strange throng which does not pack, does not mix: clever at discovering the point of disencasement,[4] of flight, of dodging. This throng which does not know how to throng, this throng, clearly so perfectly alone under the sun, like a woman one thought completely occupied with her lyric cadence, who abruptly challenges a hypothetical rain and enjoins it not to fall; or like a rapid sign of the cross without perceptive motive; or like the sudden grave animality of a peasant, urinating standing, her legs parted, stiff.

In this inert town, this desolate throng under the sun, not connected with anything that is expressed, asserted, released in broad earth daylight, its own. Neither with Josephine, Empress of the French, dreaming way up there above the nigger scum. Nor with the liberator fixed in his whitewashed stone liberation.[5] Nor with the conquistador. Nor with this contempt, with this freedom, with this audacity.

At the end of the wee hours, this inert town and its beyond of lepers, of consumption, of famines, of fears squatting in the ravines, fears perched in the trees, fears dug in the ground, fears adrift in the sky, piles of fears and their fumaroles of anguish.

At the end of the wee hours, the morne[6] forgotten, forgetful of leaping.

At the end of the wee hours, the morne in restless, docile hooves—its malarial blood routs the sun with its overheated pulse.

At the end of the wee hours, the restrained conflagration of the morne like a sob gagged on the verge of a bloodthirsty burst, in quest of an ignition that slips away and ignores itself.

At the end of the wee hours, the morne crouching before bulimia on the lookout for tuns and mills,[7] slowly vomiting out its human fatigue, the morne solitary and its blood shed, the morne bandaged in shades, the morne and its ditches of fear, the morne and its great hands of wind.

At the end of the wee hours, the famished morne and no one knows better than this bastard morne why the suicide choked with a little help from his hypoglossal[8] jamming his tongue backward to swallow it; why a woman seems to float belly up on the Capot River (her chiaroscuro body submissively organized at the command of her navel) but she is only a bundle of sonorous water.

And neither the teacher in his classroom, nor the priest at catechism will be able to get a word out of this sleepy little nigger, no matter how energetically they drum on his shorn skull, for starvation has quick-sanded his voice into the swamp of hunger (a word-one-single-word and we-will-forget-about-Queen-Blanche-of-Castille,[9] a-word-one-single-word, you-should-see-this-little-savage-who-doesn't-know-any-of-The-Ten-Commandments)

4. Joint where a piece of machinery can be taken apart.
5. French abolitionist Victor Schoelcher (1804–1893), honored with a statue in Martinique's capital.
6. Hill.
7. Casks of rum at the island's sugar mills.
8. Nerve under the tongue.
9. Medieval queen, whose name means "White."

for his voice gets lost in the swamp of hunger,
and there is nothing, really nothing to squeeze out of this little brat,
other than a hunger which can no longer climb to the rigging of his voice
a sluggish flabby hunger,
a hunger buried in the depths of the Hunger of this famished morne.

At the end of the wee hours, the disparate stranding, the exacerbated stench of corruption, the monstrous sodomies of the host and the sacrificing priest, the impassable beakhead frames of prejudice and stupidity, the prostitutions, the hypocrisies, the lubricities, the treasons, the lies, the frauds, the concussions—the panting of a deficient cowardice, the heave-holess enthusiasms of supernumerary sahibs, the greeds, the hysterias, the perversions, the clownings of poverty, the cripplings, the itchings, the hives, the tepid hammocks of degeneracy. Right here the parade of laughable and scrofulous buboes,[1] the forced feedings of very strange microbes, the poisons without known alexins,[2] the sanies of really ancient sores, the unforeseeable fermentations of putrescible species.

At the end of the wee hours, the great motionless night, the stars deader than a caved-in balafo.[3]

the teratical[4] bulb of night, sprouted from our vileness and our renunciations.

And our foolish and crazy stunts to revive the golden splashing of privileged moments, the umbilical cord restored to its ephemeral splendor, the bread, and the wine of complicity, the bread, the wine, the blood of honest weddings.

And this joy of former times making me aware of my present poverty, a bumpy road plunging into a hollow where it scatters a few shacks; an indefatigable road charging at full speed a morne at the top of which it brutally quicksands into a pool of clumsy houses, a road foolishly climbing, recklessly descending, and the carcass of wood, which I call "our house," comically perched on minute cement paws, its coiffure of corrugated iron in the sun like a skin laid out to dry, the main room, the rough floor where the nail heads gleam, the beams of pine and shadow across the ceiling, the spectral straw chairs, the grey lamp light, the glossy flash of cockroaches in a maddening buzz…

At the end of the wee hours, this most essential land restored to my gourmandise,[5] not in diffuse tenderness, but the tormented sensual concentration of the fat tits of the mornes with an occasional palm tree as their hardened sprout, the jerky orgasm of torrents from Trinité to Grand Rivière,[6] the hysterical grandsuck of the sea.

And time passed quickly, very quickly.
After August and mango trees decked out in all their little moons, September begetter of cyclones, October igniter of sugar-cane, November who purrs in the distilleries, there came Christmas.

1. Pus-filled swellings.
2. Antidotes. Sanies: oozings.
3. African instrument.
4. Monstrous.
5. Greedy hunger.
6. Towns in Martinique.

It had come in at first, Christmas did, with a tingling of desires, a thirst for new tenderness, a burgeoning of vague dreams, then with a purple rustle of its great joyous wings it had suddenly flown away, and then its abrupt fall out over the village that made the shack life burst like an overripe pomegranate.

Christmas was not like other holidays. It didn't like to gad about the streets, to dance on public squares, to mount the wooden horses, to use the crowd to pinch women, to hurl fireworks in the faces of the tamarind trees. It had agoraphobia,[7] Christmas did. What it wanted was a whole day of bustling, preparing, a cooking and cleaning spree, endless jitters
about-not-having-enough,
about-running-short,
about-getting-bored,

then at evening an unimposing little church, which would benevolently make room for the laughter, the whispers, the secrets, the love talk, the gossip and the guttural cacophony of a plucky singer and also boisterous pals and shameless hussies and shacks up to their guts in succulent goodies, and not stingy, and twenty people can crowd in, and the street is deserted, and the village turns into a bouquet of singing, and you are cozy in there, and you eat good, and you drink hearty and there are blood sausages, one kind only two fingers wide twined in coils, the other broad and stocky, the mild one tasting of wild thyme, the hot one spiced to an incandescence, and steaming coffee and sugared anise and milk punch, and the liquid sun of rums, and all sorts of good things which drive your taste buds wild or distill them to the point of ecstasy or cocoon them with fragrances, and you laugh, and you sing, and the refrains flare on and on like coco-palms:

ALLELUIA
KYRIE ELEISON...LEISON...LEISON
CHRISTE ELEISON...LEISON...LEISON.

And not only do the mouths sing, but the hands, the feet, the buttocks, the genitals, and your entire being liquefies into sounds, voices, and rhythm.

At the peak of its ascent, joy bursts like a cloud. The songs don't stop, but now anxious and heavy roll through the valleys of fear, the tunnels of anguish and the fires of hell.

And each one starts pulling the nearest devil by his tail, until fear imperceptibly fades in the fine sand lines of dream, and you really live as in a dream, and you drink and you shout and you sing as in a dream, and doze too as in a dream, with rose petal eyelids, and the day comes velvety as a sapodilla tree, and the liquid manure smell of the cacao trees, and the turkeys which shell their red pustules in the sun, and the obsessive bells, and the rain
the bells...the rain...
that tinkle, tinkle, tinkle...

At the end of the wee hours, this town sprawled-flat...

It crawls on its hands without the slightest desire to drill the sky with a stature of protest. The backs of the houses are afraid of the sky truffled with fire, their feet of the

7. Fear of open spaces.

drownings of the soil, they chose to perch shallowly between surprises and treacheries. And yet it advances, the town does. It even grazes every day further out into its tide of tiled corridors, prudish shutters, gluey courtyards, dripping paintwork. And petty hushed-up scandals, petty unvoiced guilts, petty immense hatreds knead the narrow streets into bumps and potholes where the waste-water grins longitudinally through turds...

At the end of the wee hours, life prostrate, you don't know how to dispose of your aborted dreams, the river of life desperately torpid in its bed, neither turgid nor low, hesitant to flow, pitifully empty, the impartial heaviness of boredom distributing shade equally on all things, the air stagnant, unbroken by the brightness of a single bird.

At the end of the wee hours, another little house very bad-smelling in a very narrow street, a minuscule house which harbors in its guts of rotten wood dozens of rats and the turbulence of my six brothers and sisters, a cruel little house whose demands panic the ends of our months and my temperamental father gnawed by one persistent ache, I never knew which one, whom an unexpected sorcery could lull to melancholy tenderness or drive to towering flames of anger; and my mother whose legs pedal, pedal, night and day, for our tireless hunger, I was even awakened at night by these tireless legs which pedal the night and the bitter bite in the soft flesh of the night of a Singer[8] that my mother pedals, pedals for our hunger and day and night.

At the end of the wee hours, beyond my father, my mother, the shack chapped with blisters, like a peach tree afflicted with curl, and the thin roof patched with pieces of gasoline cans, which create swamps of rust in the stinking sordid grey straw pulp, and when the wind whistles, these odds and ends make a noise bizarre, first like the crackling of frying, then like a brand dropped into water the smoke of its twigs flying up. And the bed of boards from which my race arose, my whole entire race from this bed of boards, with its kerosene case paws, as if it had elephantiasis,[9] that bed, and its kidskin, and its dry banana leaves, and its rags, yearning for a mattress, my grandmother's bed. (Above the bed, in a jar full of oil a dim light whose flame dances like a fat cockroach...on the jar in gold letters: MERCI.)[1]
And this rue Paille, this disgrace,

an appendage repulsive as the private parts of the village which extends right and left, along the colonial highway, the grey surge of its shingled roofs. Here there are only straw roofs, spray browned and wind plucked.

Everybody despises rue Paille. It's there that the village youth go astray. It's there especially that the sea pours forth its garbage, its dead cats and its croaked dogs. For the street opens on to the beach, and the beach alone cannot satisfy the sea's foaming rage.

A blight this beach as well, with its piles of rotting muck, its furtive rumps relieving themselves, and the sand is black, funereal, you've never seen a sand so black, and the scum glides over it yelping, and the sea pummels it like a boxer, or rather the sea is a huge dog licking and biting the shins of the beach, biting them so fiercely that it will end up devouring it, the beach and rue Paille along with it.

8. A brand of sewing machine.
9. A disease that causes extreme enlargement of the legs.
1. Thank you (French).

At the end of the wee hours, the wind of long ago—of betrayed trusts, of uncertain evasive duty and that other dawn in Europe—arises…

To go away.
As there are hyena-men and panther-men, I would be a jew-man
a Kaffir-man[2]
a Hindu-man-from-Calcutta
a Harlem-man-who-doesn't-vote

the famine man, the insult-man, the torture man you can grab anytime, beat up, kill—no joke, kill—without having to account to anyone, without having to make excuses to anyone
a jew-man
a pogrom-man
a puppy
a beggar
but *can* one kill Remorse, perfect as the stupefied face of an English lady discovering a Hottentot skull in her soup-tureen?

I would rediscover the secret of great communications and great combustions. I would say storm. I would say river. I would say tornado. I would say leaf. I would say tree. I would be drenched by all rains, moistened by all dews. I would roll like frenetic blood on the slow current of the eye of words turned into mad horses into fresh children into clots into curfew into vestiges of temples into precious stones remote enough to discourage miners. Whoever would not understand me would not understand any better the roaring of a tiger.

And you ghosts rise blue from alchemy from a forest of hunted beasts of twisted machines of a jujube tree of rotten flesh of a basket of oysters of eyes of a network of straps in the beautiful sisal of human skin I would have words vast enough to contain you earth taut earth drunk
earth great vulva raised to the sun
earth great delirium of God's mentula[3]
savage earth arisen from the storerooms of the sea a clump of Cecropia[4] in your mouth earth whose tumultuous face I can only compare to the virgin and mad forest which were it in my power I would show in guise of a face to the undeciphering eyes of men all I would need is a mouthful of jiculi milk[5] to discover in you always as distant as a mirage—a thousand times more native and made golden by a sun that no prism divides—the earth where everything is free and fraternal, my earth.

To go away. My heart was pounding with emphatic generosities. To go away…I would arrive sleek and young in this land of mine and I would say to this land whose

2. South African whites' term of insult for blacks.
3. Penis.
4. A kind of tree native to the tropical regions of the Americas.
5. Césaire's variation on the term for a kind of tree. Jiculi milk is a plant-based poison that is believed not to harm wild creatures.

loam is part of my flesh: "I have wandered for a long time and I am coming back to the deserted hideousness of your sores."

I would go to this land of mine and I would say to it. "Embrace me without fear...And if all I can do is speak, it is for you I shall speak."

And again I would say:

"My mouth shall be the mouth of those calamities that have no mouth, my voice the freedom of those who break down in the solitary confinement of despair."

And on the way I would say to myself:

"And above all, my body as well as my soul, beware of assuming the sterile attitude of a spectator, for life is not a spectacle, a sea of miseries is not a proscenium, a man screaming is not a dancing bear..."

And behold here I am!

Once again this life hobbling before me, what am I saying life, *this death,* this death without sense or piety, this death that so pathetically falls short of greatness, the dazzling pettiness of this death, this death hobbling from pettiness to pettiness; these shovelfuls of petty greeds over the conquistador; these shovelfuls of petty flunkies over the great savage, these shovelfuls of petty souls over the three-souled Carib,[6] and all these deaths futile
absurdities under the splashing of my open conscience
tragic futilities lit up by this single noctiluca[7]
and I alone, sudden stage of these wee hours when the apocalypse of monsters cavorts
then, capsized, hushes
warm election of cinders, of ruins and collapses
—One more thing! only one, but please make it only one: I have no right to measure life by my sooty finger span; to reduce myself to this little ellipsoidal nothing trembling four fingers above the line, I a man, to so overturn creation, that I include myself between latitude and longitude!

> At the end of the wee hours,
> the male thirst and the desire stubborn,
> here I am, severed from the cool oases of brotherhood
> this so modest nothing bristles with hard splinters
> this too safe horizon is startled like a jailer.

Your last triumph, tenacious crow of Treason.

What is mine, these few thousand deathbearers who mill in the calabash of an island and mine too, the archipelago arched with an anguished desire to negate itself, as if from maternal anxiety to protect this impossibly delicate tenuity separating one America from another; and these loins which secrete for Europe the hearty liquor of a Gulf Stream, and one of the two slopes of incandescence between which the Equator tightropewalks toward Europe. And my nonfence island, its brave audacity standing at the stern of this Polynesia, before it, Guadeloupe, split in two down its dorsal line and equal in poverty to us, Haiti where negritude rose for the first time and stated that it believed in its humanity and the funny little tail of Florida where the

6. The Caribs were the native people who inhabited the Antilles before the arrival of the Europeans.
7. An organism that is luminescent in the dark.

strangulation of a nigger is being completed, and Africa gigantically caterpillaring up
to the Hispanic foot of Europe it nakedness where Death scythes widely.

And I say to myself Bordeaux and Nantes and Liverpool and New York and San
Francisco

not an inch of this world devoid of my fingerprint
and my calcaneum[8] on the spines of skyscrapers and my filth in the glitter of
gems!
Who can boast of being better off than I? Virginia.
Tennessee. Georgia. Alabama
monstrous putrefactions of stymied
revolts
marshes of putrid blood
trumpets absurdly muted
land red, sanguineous, consanguineous land.

What is mine also: a little
cell in the Jura,[9]
a little cell, the snow lines it with white bars
the snow is a jailer mounting
guard before a prison

What is mine
a lonely man imprisoned in
whiteness
a lonely man defying the white
screams of white death
(TOUSSAINT, TOUSSAINT L'OUVERTURE)[1]

a man who mesmerizes
the white hawk of white death
a man alone in the sterile
sea of white sand
a coon grown old standing up to
the waters of the sky

Death traces a shining circle
above this man
death stars softly above his head
death breathes, crazed, in the ripened
cane field of his arms
death gallops in the prison like
a white horse
death gleams in the dark like the
eyes of a cat

8. Heel bone.
9. A range of mountains in France.
1. Toussaint l'Ouverture (1743–1803) was originally a slave. He became one of the leaders of uprisings in the 1790s and
the governor of Haiti, but he was arrested by the French shortly afterward; he died imprisoned in the Jura mountains.

death hiccups like water under the Keys
death is a struck bird
death wanes
death flickers
death is a very shy patyura[2]
death expires in a white pool
of silence.
Swellings of night in the four corners
of this dawn
convulsions of congealed death
tenacious fate
screams erect from mute earth
the splendor of this blood will it not burst open?

    At the end of the wee hours this land without a stele,[3] these paths without mem-
ory, these winds without a tablet.
    So what?
    We would tell. Would sing. Would howl.
    Full voice, ample voice, you would be our wealth, our spear pointed.
    Words?
    Ah yes, words!

Reason, I crown you evening wind.
Your name voice of order?
To me the whip's corolla.
Beauty I call you the false claim of the stone.
But ah! my raucous laughter
smuggled in
Ah! my saltpetre treasure!
Because we hate you
and your reason, we claim kinship
with dementia praecox[4] with the flaming madness
of persistent cannibalism

Treasure, let's count:
the madness that remembers
the madness that howls
the madness that sees
the madness that is unleashed
And you know the rest

That 2 and 2 are 5
that the forest miaows
that the tree plucks the maroons[5] from the fire
that the sky strokes its beard
etc. etc....

2. Césaire's variation on the French term for a kind of peccary.
3. A column or upright slab of stone that is inscribed or decorated with images.
4. Schizophrenia (literally, premature dementia).
5. Chestnuts; also slang for "runaway slaves."

Who and what are we?
A most worthy question!

From staring too long at trees I have
become a tree and my long tree
feet have dug in the ground large
venom sacs high cities of bone
from brooding too long on the Congo
I have become a Congo resounding with
forests and rivers
where the whip cracks like a great banner
the banner of a prophet
where the water goes
likouala-likouala
where the angerbolt hurls its greenish
axe forcing the boars of
putrefaction to the lovely wild edge
of the nostrils.

At the end of the wee hours the sun which
hacks and spits up its lungs

At the end of the wee hours
a slow gait of sand
a slow gait of gauze
a slow gait of corn kernels
At the end of the wee hours
a full gallop of pollen
a full gallop of a slow gait of
little girls
a full gallop of hummingbirds
a full gallop of daggers to stave in
the earth's breast

customs angels mounting guard over
prohibitions at the gates of foam

I declare my crimes and that there is nothing
to say in my defense.
Dances. Idols. An apostate.[6] I too
I have assassinated God with my laziness with
my words with my gestures
with my obscene songs

I have worn parrot plumes
musk cat skins
I have exhausted the missionaries' patience
insulted the benefactors of mankind.
Defied Tyre. Defied Sidon.

6. A person who has abandoned his or her faith.

Worshipped the Zambezi.[7]
The extent of my perversity overwhelms me!

But why impenetrable jungle are you still hiding the raw zero of my mendacity and from a self-conscious concern for nobility not celebrating the horrible leap of my Pahouin[8] ugliness?

voum rooh oh
voum rooh oh
to charm the snakes to conjure
the dead
voum rooh oh
to compel the rain to turn back
the tidal waves
voum rooh oh
to keep the shade from moving
voum rooh oh that my own skies
may open

—me on a road, a child, chewing
sugar cane root
—a dragged man on a bloodspattered road
a rope around his neck
—standing in the center of a huge circus,
on my black forehead a crown of daturas[9]
voum rooh
to fly off
higher than quivering higher
than the sorceresses toward other stars
ferocious exultation of forests and
mountains uprooted at the hour
when no one expects it
the islands linked for a thousand years!

voum rooh oh
that the promised times may return
and the bird who knew my name
and the woman who had a thousand names
names of fountain sun and tears
and her hair of minnows
and her steps my climates
and her eyes my seasons
and the days without injury
and the nights without offense
and the stars my confidence
and the wind my accomplice

AIMÉ CÉSAIRE

7. Tyre and Sidon, cities on the coast of Palestine, were important Phoenician centers of commerce and culture in antiquity. The Zambezi is a river in south-central Africa.
8. A group of peoples in West Africa.
9. Plants with large flowers in the shape of a trumpet that have a narcotic or poisonous effect.

But who misleads my voice? who grates
my voice? Stuffing my throat
with a thousand bamboo fangs. A thousand
sea urchin stakes. It is you dirty end
of the world. Dirty end of the wee hours.
It is you dirty hatred. It is you weight
of the insult and a hundred years of whip
lashes. It is you one hundred years of my
patience, one hundred years of my effort
simply to stay alive
rooh oh
we sing of venomous flowers
flaring in fury-filled prairies;
the skies of love cut with bloodclots;
the epileptic mornings; the white blaze
of abyssal sands, the sinking
of flotsam in nights electrified
with feline smells.

What can I do?

One must begin somewhere.

Begin what?

The only thing in the world
worth beginning:
The End of the world of course.

Torte[1]
oh torte of the terrifying autumn
where the new steel and the perennial concrete
grow
torte oh torte
where the air rusts in great sheets
of evil glee
where the sanious water scars the great
solar cheeks
I hate you
one still sees madras rags around the loins
of women rings in their ears
smiles on their lips babies
at their nipples, these for starters:

ENOUGH OF THIS OUTRAGE!

So here is the great challenge and the satanic
compulsion and the insolent
nostalgic drift of April moons,
of green fires, of yellow fevers!

1. Loaf of local bread.

Vainly in the tepidity of your throat
you ripen for the twentieth time the same indigent
solace that we are
mumblers of words

Words? while we handle
quarters of earth, while we wed
delirious continents, while
we force steaming gates,
words, ah yes, words! but
words of fresh blood, words that are
tidal waves and erysipelas[2]
malarias and lava and brush
fires, and blazes of flesh,
and blazes of cities…

Know this:
the only game I play is the millennium
the only game I play is the Great
Fear

Put up with me. I won't put up with you!

Sometimes you see me with a great display of brains
snap up a cloud too red
or a caress of rain, or a prelude
of wind,
don't fool yourself:

I am forcing the vitelline membrane[3] that separates
me from myself,
I am forcing the great waters which girdle me with blood

I and I alone choose
a seat on the last train of the last
surge of the last tidal wave

I and I alone
make contact with the latest
anguish

I and oh, only I
secure the first
drops of virginal milk through a straw!

And now a last boo:
to the sun (not strong enough to inebriate
my very tough head)
to the mealy night with its golden
hatchings of erratic fireflies
to the head of hair trembling at the very

2. Infectious skin disease.
3. Thin membrane around a fertilized egg in the womb.

top of the cliff
where the wind leaps in bursts of salty
cavalries
I clearly read in my pulse that for me
exoticism is no provender

Leaving Europe utterly twisted with screams
the silent currents of despair
leaving timid Europe which
collects and proudly overrates itself
I summon this egotism beautiful
and bold
and my ploughing reminds me of an implacable cutwater.

So much blood in my memory! In my memory are lagoons. They are covered with
        death's-heads.
They are not covered with water lilies.
In my memory are lagoons. No women's loincloths spread out on their shores.
My memory is encircled with blood. My memory has a belt of corpses!
and machine gun fire of rum barrels brilliantly sprinkling
our ignominious revolts, amorous glances swooning from having
swigged too much ferocious freedom

(niggers-are-all-alike, I-tell-you vices-all-the-vices-believe-you-me
nigger-smell, that's-what-makes-cane-grow
remember-the-old-saying:
beat-a-nigger, and you feed him)
among "rocking chairs" contemplating the voluptuousness of quirts[4]
I circle about, an unappeased filly

Or else quite simply as they like to think of us!
Cheerfully obscene, completely nuts about jazz to cover their extreme boredom
I can boogie-woogie, do the Lindy-hop and tap-dance.
And for a special treat the muting of our cries muffled with wah-wah. Wait...
        Everything is as it should be. My good angel grazes the neon. I swallow
        batons. My dignity wallows in puke...

    Sun, Angel Sun, curled Angel of the Sun
        for a leap beyond the sweet and greenish
    treading of the waters of abjection!

    But I approached the wrong sorcerer, on this exorcised earth, cast adrift from its
precious malignant purpose, this voice that cries, little by little hoarse, vainly, vainly
hoarse,
    and there remains only the accumulated droppings of our lies—and they do not
respond.
What madness to dream up a marvelous caper above the baseness!
Oh Yes the Whites are great warriors hosannah to the master and to the nigger-gelder!

---

4. Slave whips.

Victory! Victory, I tell you: the defeated are content!
Joyous stenches and songs of mud!

By a sudden and beneficent inner revolution, I now ignore my repugnant ugliness.

On Midsummer Day, as soon as the first shadows fall on the village of Gros-Morne, hundreds of horse dealers gather on rue "De PROFUNDIS,"[5] a name at least honest enough to announce an onrush from the shoals of Death. And it truly is from Death, from its thousand petty local forms (cravings unsatisfied by Para grass and tipsy bondage to the distilleries) that the astonishing cavalry of impetuous nags surges unfenced toward the great-life. What a galloping! what neighing! what sincere urinating! what prodigious droppings! "A fine horse difficult to mount!"—"A proud mare sensitive to the spur"—"A fearless foal superbly pasterned!"

And the shrewd fellow whose waistcoat displays a proud watch chain, palms off instead of full udders, youthful mettle and genuine contours, either the systematic puffiness from obliging wasps, or the obscene stings from ginger, or the helpful distribution of several gallons of sugared water.

I refuse to pass off my puffiness for authentic glory.
And I laugh at my former childish fantasies.
No, we've never been Amazons of the king of Dahomey, nor princes of Ghana with eight hundred camels, nor wise men in Timbuktu under Askia the Great, nor the architects of Djenne, nor Madhis, nor warriors.[6] We don't feel under our armpit the itch of those who in the old days carried a lance. And since I have sworn to leave nothing out of our history (I who love nothing better than a sheep grazing his own afternoon shadow), I may as well confess that we were at all times pretty mediocre dishwashers, shoeblacks without ambition, at best conscientious sorcerers and the only unquestionable record that we broke was that of endurance under the chicote[7]. . .

And this land screamed for centuries that we are bestial brutes; that the human pulse stops at the gates of the slave compound; that we are walking compost hideously promising tender cane and silky cotton and they would brand us with red-hot irons and we would sleep in our excrement and they would sell us on the town square and an ell of English cloth and salted meat from Ireland cost less than we did, and this land was calm, tranquil, repeating that the spirit of the Lord was in its acts.

We the vomit of slave ships
We the venery of the Calabars[8]
what? Plug up our ears?
We, so drunk on jeers and inhaled fog that we rode the roll to death!
Forgive us fraternal whirlwind!

I hear coming up from the hold the enchained curses, the gasps of the dying, the noise of someone thrown into the sea . . . the baying of a woman in labor . . . the

5. Literally, "from the depths": the beginning of Psalm 129, a psalm sung during Christian liturgy to express the suffering of souls exiled from heaven; it is often used as a prayer for the dead.
6. Dahomey and Ghana are countries in West Africa; Timbuktu and Djenné are cities in Mali, also in West Africa. Djenné was once the capital of the Songhaï Empire, which was ruled by Askia the Great from 1493 to 1529. Madhis were Islamic sovereigns in some parts of Africa, especially in the Sudan.
7. A leather whip.
8. The hunting targets of the Coast of Calabars in West Africa, which was notorious for slave trade.

scrape of fingernails seeking throats…the flouts of the whip…the seethings of vermin amid the weariness…

Nothing could ever lift us toward a noble hopeless adventure.
So be it. So be it.
I am of no nationality recognized by the chancelleries.
I defy the craniometer. Homo sum[9] etc.
Let them serve and betray and die
So be it. So be it. It was written in the shape of their pelvis.

And I, and I,
I was singing the hard fist
You must know the extent of my cowardice. One evening on the streetcar facing me, a nigger.

A nigger big as a pongo[1] trying to make himself small on the streetcar bench. He was trying to leave behind, on this grimy bench, his gigantic legs and his trembling famished boxer hands. And everything had left him, was leaving him. His nose which looked like a drifting peninsula and even his negritude discolored as a result of untiring tawing.[2] And the tawer was Poverty. A big unexpected lop-eared bat whose claw marks in his face had scabbed over into crusty islands. Or rather, it was a tireless worker, Poverty was, working on some hideous cartouche.[3] One could easily see how that industrious and malevolent thumb had kneaded bumps into his brow, bored two bizarre parallel tunnels in his nose, overexaggerated his lips, and in a masterpiece of caricature, planed, polished and varnished the tiniest cutest little ear in all creation.

He was a gangly nigger without rhythm or measure.

A nigger whose eyes rolled a bloodshot weariness.

A shameless nigger and his toes sneered in a rather stinking way at the bottom of the yawning lair of his shoes.

Poverty, without any question, had knocked itself out to finish him off.

It had dug the socket, had painted it with a rouge of dust mixed with rheum.

It had stretched an empty space between the solid hinge of the jaw and bone of an old tarnished cheek. Had planted over it the small shiny stakes of a two- or three-day beard. Had panicked his heart, bent his back.

And the whole thing added up perfectly to a hideous nigger, a grouchy nigger, a melancholy nigger, a slouched nigger, his hands joined in prayer on a knobby stick. A nigger shrouded in an old threadbare coat. A comical and ugly nigger, with some women behind me sneering at him.

> He was COMICAL AND UGLY,
> COMICAL AND UGLY for sure.
> I displayed a big complicitous smile…
> My cowardice rediscovered!

Hail to the three centuries which uphold my civil rights and my minimized blood! My heroism, what a farce!

---

9. "I am human." Craniometers were instruments used to measure the size and shape of heads, thought to indicate crucial differences between "primitive" and "civilized" races.

1. A large ape.

2. Curing into white leather.

3. A carved ornamental tablet.

This town fits me to a t.
And my soul is lying down. Lying down like this town in its refuse and mud.
This town, my face of mud.
For my face I demand the vivid homage of spit!...
So, being what we are, ours the warrior thrust, the triumphant knee, the well-plowed
        plains of the future?
Look, I'd rather admit to uninhibited ravings, my heart in my brain like a drunken
        knee.
My star now, the funereal menfenil.[4]
And on this former dream my cannibalistic cruelties:

(The bullets in the mouth thick saliva
our heart from daily lowness bursts the continents break the fragile bond of
        isthmuses
lands leap in accordance with the fatal division of rivers
and the morne which for centuries kept its scream within itself, it is its turn to draw
        and quarter the silence and this people an ever-rebounding spirit
and our limbs vainly disjointed by the most refined tortures
and life even more impetuously jetting from this compost—unexpected as a soursop
        amidst the decomposition of jack tree fruit!)

On this dream so old in me my cannibalistic cruelties

I was hiding behind a stupid vanity destiny called me I was hiding behind it and sud-
        denly there was a man on the ground, his feeble defenses scattered,
his sacred maxims trampled underfoot, his pedantic rhetoric oozing air through each
        wound.
There is a man on the ground
and his soul is almost naked
and destiny triumphs in watching this soul which defied its metamorphosis in the
        ancestral slough.

I say that this is right.
My back will victoriously exploit the chalaza of fibers.[5]
I will deck my natural obsequiousness with gratitude
And the silver-braided bullshit of the postillion of Havana, lyrical baboon pimp for
        the glamour of slavery, will be more than a match for my enthusiasm.

I say that this is right.
I live for the flattest part of my soul.
For the dullest part of my flesh!

      Tepid dawn of ancestral heat and fear
I now tremble with the collective trembling that our docile blood sings in the
        madrepore.[6]

And these tadpoles hatched in me by my prodigious ancestry!
Those who invented neither powder nor compass
those who could harness neither steam nor electricity

4. A kind of hawk.
5. The flexibility of a whip.
6. A kind of coral.

those who explored neither the seas nor the sky but who know
in its most minute corners the land of suffering
those who have known voyages only through uprootings
those who have been lulled to sleep by so much kneeling
those whom they domesticated and Christianized
those whom they inoculated with degeneracy
tom-toms of empty hands
inane tom-toms of resounding sores
burlesque tom-toms of tabetic treason[7]

       Tepid dawn of ancestral heat and fears
overboard with alien riches
overboard with my genuine falsehoods
But what strange pride suddenly illuminates me!
let the hummingbird come
let the sparrow hawk come
the breach in the horizon
the cynocephalus[8]
let the lotus bearer of the world come
the pearly upheaval of dolphins
cracking the shell of the sea
let a plunge of islands come
let it come from the disappearing of days of dead
flesh in the quicklime of birds of prey
let the ovaries of the water come where the future stirs its testicles
let the wolves come who feed in the untamed openings of the body at the hour when my
      moon and your sun meet at the ecliptic inn

under the reserve of my uvula[9] there is a wallow of boars
under the grey stone of the day there are your eyes which are a shimmering conglomer-
      ate of coccinella[1]
in the glance of disorder there is this swallow of mint and broom which melts always to
      be reborn in the tidal wave of your light
Calm and lull oh my voice the child who does not know that the map of spring is always
      to be drawn again
the tall grass will sway gentle ship of hope for the cattle
the long alcoholic sweep of the swell
the stars with the bezels of their rings never in sight will cut the pipes of the glass organ
      of evening zinnias
coryanthas
will then pour into the rich extremity of my fatigue
and you star please from your luminous foundation draw lemurian being—of man's
      unfathomable sperm the yet undared form
carried like an ore in woman's trembling belly!

---

7. Wasted, weak treason.
8. Species of apes with doglike snouts, such as baboons or mandrills.
9. Tissue at the back of the throat.
1. Beetles.

oh friendly light
oh fresh source of light
those who have invented neither powder nor compass
those who could harness neither steam nor electricity
those who explored neither the seas nor the sky but those
without whom the earth would not be the earth
gibbosity[2] all the more beneficent as the bare earth even more earth
silo where that which is earthiest about earth ferments and ripens
my negritude is not a stone, its deafness hurled against the clamor of the day
my negritude is not a leukoma[3] of dead liquid over the earth's dead eye
my negritude is neither tower nor cathedral
it takes root in the red flesh of the soil
it takes root in the ardent flesh of the sky
it breaks through the opaque prostration with its upright patience

Eia for the royal Cailcedra![4]
Eia for those who have never invented anything
for those who never explored anything
for those who never conquered anything

but yield, captivated, to the essence of all things
ignorant of surfaces but captivated by the motion of all things
indifferent to conquering, but playing the game of the world
truly the eldest sons of the world
porous to all the breathing of the world
fraternal locus for all the breathing of the world
drainless channel for all the water of the world
spark of the sacred fire of the world
flesh of the world's flesh pulsating with the very motion of the world!
      Tepid dawn of ancestral virtues

Blood! Blood! all our blood aroused by the male heart of the sun
those who know about the femininity of the moon's oily body
the reconciled exultation of antelope and star
those whose survival travels in the germination of grass!
Eia perfect circle of the world, enclosed concordance!

Hear the white world
horribly weary from its immense efforts
its stiff joints crack under the hard stars
hear its blue steel rigidity pierce the mystic flesh
its deceptive victories tout its defeats
hear the grandiose alibis of its pitiful stumblings

Pity for our omniscient and naive conquerors!

Eia for grief and its udders of reincarnated tears
for those who have never explored anything
for those who have never conquered anything

2. Bulging.
3. A white scar on the cornea of the eye.
4. An African tree species.

Eia for joy
Eia for love
Eia for grief and its udders of reincarnated tears

and here at the end of these wee hours is my virile prayer that I hear neither the
laughter nor the screams, my eyes fixed on this town which I prophesy, beautiful,

grant me the savage faith of the sorcerer
grant my hands power to mold
grant my soul the sword's temper
I won't flinch. Make my head into a figurehead
and as for me, my heart, do not make me into a father nor a brother,
nor a son, but into the father, the brother, the son,
nor a husband, but the lover of this unique people.

Make me resist any vanity, but espouse its genius as the fist the extended arm!

Make me a steward of its blood
make me trustee of its resentment
make me into a man for the ending
make me into a man for the beginning
make me into a man of meditation
but also make me into a man of germination

make me into the executor of these lofty works
the time has come to gird one's loins like a brave man—

But in doing so, my heart, preserve me from all hatred
do not make me into that man of hatred for whom I feel only hatred
for entrenched as I am in this unique race
you still know my tyrannical love
you know that it is not from hatred of other races
that I demand a digger for this unique race
that what I want
is for universal hunger
for universal thirst

to summon it to generate,
free at last, from its intimate closeness
the succulence of fruit.

And be the tree of our hands!
it turns, for all, the wounds cut
in its trunk
the soil works for all
and toward the branches a headiness of fragrant precipitation!

But before stepping on the shores of future orchards
grant that I deserve those on their belt of sea
grant me my heart while awaiting the earth
grant me on the ocean sterile
but somewhere caressed by the promise of the clew-line[5]
grant me on this diverse ocean

5. Line fastened to the lower corner of a sail.

the obstinacy of the fierce pirogue[6]
and its marine vigor.

See it advance rising and falling on the pulverized wave
see it dance the sacred dance before the greyness of the village
see it trumpet from a vertiginous conch

see the conch gallop up to the uncertainty of the morne

and see twenty times over the paddle
vigorously
plow the water
the pirogue rears under the attack of the swells
deviates for an instant
tries to escape, but the paddle's rough caress turns it,
then it charges, a shudder runs along the wave's spine,
the sea slobbers and rumbles
the pirogue like a sleigh glides onto the sand.

      At the end of these wee hours, my virile prayer:

grant me pirogue muscles on this raging sea
and the irresistible gaiety of the conch of good tidings!
Look, now I am only a man, no degradation, no spit perturbs him, now I am only a
         man who accepts emptied of anger
(nothing left in his heart but immense love, which burns)

I accept...I accept...totally, without reservation...
my race that no ablution of hyssop[7] mixed with lilies could purify
my race pitted with blemishes
my race a ripe grape for drunken feet
my queen of spittle and leprosy
my queen of whips and scrofula
my queen of squasma and chloasma (oh those queens I once loved in the remote gardens of spring against the illumination of all the candles of the chestnut trees!)
I accept. I accept.
and the flogged nigger saying: "Forgive me master"
and the twenty-nine legal blows of the whip
and the four-feet-high cell
and the spiked iron-collar
and the hamstringing of my runaway audacity
and the fleur de lys flowing from the red iron into the fat of my shoulder
and Monsieur VAULTIER MAYENCOURT'S dog house where I barked
six poodle months
and Monsieur BRAFIN
and Monsieur FOURNIOL
and Monsieur de la MAHAUDIERE[8]
and the yaws

---

6. A dug-out canoe with a sail.
7. A plant that is commonly used as medicine, perfume, and condiment.
8. The names and details mentioned here are based on historical accounts of slave treatment.

the mastiff
the suicide
the promiscuity
the bootkin
the shackles
the rack
the cippus
the head screw

Look, am I humble enough? Have I enough calluses on my knees? Muscles on my loins?

Grovel in mud. Brace yourself in the thick of the mud. Carry.

Soil of mud. Horizon of mud. Sky of mud.

Dead of the mud, oh names to thaw in the palm of a feverish breathing!

Siméon Piquine, who never knew his father or mother; unheard of in any town hall and who wandered his whole life—seeking a new name.

Grandvorka—of him I only know that he died, crushed one harvest evening, it was his job, apparently, to throw sand under the wheels of the running locomotive, to help it across bad spots.

Michel who used to write me signing a strange name. Lucky Michel address *Condemned District* and you their living brothers Exélie Vêté Congolo Lemké Boussolongo what healer with his thick lips would suck from the depths of the gaping wound the tenacious secret of venom?

what cautious sorcerer would undo from your ankles the viscous tepidity of mortal rings?

Presences it is not on your back that I will make my peace with the world

Islands scars of the water
Islands evidence of wounds
Islands crumbs
Islands unformed
Islands cheap paper shredded upon the water
Islands stumps skewered side by side on the flaming sword of the Sun
Mulish reason you will not stop me from casting on the waters at the mercy of the
currents of my thirst
your form, deformed islands,
your end, my defiance.

Annulose islands,[9] single beautiful hull
And I caress you with my oceanic hands. And I turn you
around with the tradewinds of my speech. And I lick you with my seaweed
　　　　tongues.
And I sail you unfreebootable!

9. Ring-shaped islands.

O death your mushy marsh!
Shipwreck your hellish debris! I accept!

At the end of the wee hours, lost puddles, wandering scents, beached hurricanes, demasted hulls, old sores, rotted bones, vapors, shackled volcanoes, shallow-rooted dead, bitter cry. I accept!

And my special geography too; the world map made for my own use, not tinted with the arbitrary colors of scholars, but with the geometry of my spilled blood, I accept both the determination of my biology, not a prisoner to a facial angle, to a type of hair, to a well-flattened nose, to a clearly Melanian coloring,[1] and negritude, no longer a cephalic index, or plasma, or soma, but measured by the compass of suffering and the Negro every day more base, more cowardly, more sterile, less profound, more spilled out of himself, more separated from himself, more wily with himself, less immediate to himself,

I accept, I accept it all

and far from the palatial sea that foams beneath the suppurating syzygy[2] of blisters, miraculously lying in the despair of my arms the body of my country, its bones shocked and, in its veins, the blood hesitating like a drop of vegetal milk at the injured point of the bulb . . .

Suddenly now strength and life assail me like a bull and the water of life overwhelms the papilla of the morne, now all the veins and veinlets are bustling with new blood and the enormous breathing lung of cyclones and the fire hoarded in volcanoes and the gigantic seismic pulse which now beats the measure of a living body in my firm conflagration.

And we are standing now, my country and I, hair in the wind, my hand puny in its enormous fist and now the strength is not in us but above us, in a voice that drills the night and the hearing like the penetrance of an apocalyptic wasp. And the voice proclaims that for centuries Europe has force-fed us with lies and bloated us with pestilence,

for it is not true that the work of man is done
that we have no business being on earth
that we parasite the world
that it is enough for us to heel to the world
whereas the work has only begun
and man still must overcome all the interdictions wedged in the recesses of his fervor
and no race has a monopoly on beauty, on intelligence, on strength

and there is room for everyone at the convocation of conquest and we know now that the sun turns around our earth lighting the parcel designated by our will alone and that every star falls from sky to earth at our omnipotent command.

AIMÉ CÉSAIRE

1. Dark-skinned.
2. Configuration in which a planet or star forms a straight line with the sun and the earth.

I now see the meaning of this trial by the sword: my country is the "lance of night" of my Bambara ancestors.[3] It shrivels and its point desperately retreats toward the haft when it is sprinkled with chicken blood and it says that its nature requires the blood of man, his fat, his liver, his heart, not chicken blood.

And I seek for my country not date hearts, but men's hearts which, in order to enter the silver cities through the great trapezoidal gate, beat with warrior blood, and as my eyes sweep my kilometers of paternal earth I number its sores almost joyfully and I pile one on top of the other like rare species, and my total is ever lengthened by unexpected mintings of baseness.

And there are those who will never get over not being made in the likeness of God but of the devil, those who believe that being a nigger is like being a second-class clerk; waiting for a better deal and upward mobility; those who beat the drum of compromise in front of themselves, those who live in their own dungeon pit; those who drape themselves in proud pseudomorphosis; those who say to Europe: "You see, I *can* bow and scrape, like you I pay my respects, in short, I am no different from you; pay no attention to my black skin: the sun did it."

And there is the nigger pimp, the nigger askari,[4] and all the zebras shaking themselves in various ways to get rid of their stripes in a dew of fresh milk. And in the midst of all that I say right on! my grandfather dies, I say right on! the old negritude progressively cadavers itself.

No question about it: he was good nigger. The Whites say he was a good nigger, a really good nigger, massa's good ole darky. I say right on!

He was a good nigger, indeed,
poverty had wounded his chest and back and they had stuffed into his brain that a fatality impossible to trap weighed on him; that he had no control over his own fate; that an evil Lord had for all eternity inscribed Thou Shall Not in his pelvic constitution; that he must be a good nigger; must sincerely believe in his worthlessness, without any perverse curiosity to check out the fatidic[5] hieroglyphs.

He was a very good nigger

and it never occurred to him that he could hoe, burrow, cut anything, anything else really than insipid cane

He was a very good nigger.

And they threw stones at him, bits of scrap iron, broken bottles, but neither these stones, nor this scrap iron, nor these bottles ... O peaceful years of God on this terraqueous[6] clod!

and the whip argued with the bombilation of the flies over the sugary dew of our sores.

---

3. A West African ethnicity.
4. African working as a colonial soldier.
5. Prophetic.
6. Earth-and-water.

I say right on! The old negritude
progressively cadavers itself
the horizon breaks, recoils and expands
and through the shedding of clouds and the flashing of a sign
the slave ship cracks everywhere...Its belly convulses and resounds...The ghastly
tapeworm of its cargo gnaws the fetid guts of the strange suckling of the sea!

And neither the joy of sails filled like a pocket stuffed with doubloons, nor the tricks
played on the dangerous stupidity of the frigates of order prevent it from hearing the
threat of its intestinal rumblings

In vain to ignore them the captain hangs the biggest loudmouth nigger from the main
yard or throws him into the sea, or feeds him to his mastiffs

Reeking of fried onions the nigger scum rediscovers the bitter taste of freedom in its
spilled blood

And the nigger scum is on its feet

the seated nigger scum
unexpectedly standing
standing in the hold
standing in the cabins
standing on the deck
standing in the wind
standing under the sun
standing in the blood
    standing
       and
          free
standing and no longer a poor madwoman in her maritime freedom and destitution
gyrating in perfect drift
and there she is:
most unexpectedly standing
standing in the rigging
standing at the tiller
standing at the compass
standing at the map
standing under the stars
    standing
       and
          free
and the lustral[7] ship fearlessly advances on the crumbling water.

And now our ignominious plops are rotting away!
by the clanking noon sea
by the burgeoning midnight sun

7. Purified.

listen sparrow hawk who holds the keys to the orient
by the disarmed day
by the stony spurt of the rain

listen dogfish that watches over the occident

listen white dog of the north, black serpent of the south that cinches the sky girdle
There still remains one sea to cross
oh still one sea to cross
that I may invent my lungs
that the prince may hold his tongue
that the queen may lay me
still one old man to murder
one madman to deliver
that my soul may shine bark shine
bark bark bark
and the owl my beautiful inquisitive animal angel may hoot.
The master of laughter?
The master of ominous silence?
The master of hope and despair?
The master of laziness? Master of the dance?
    It is I!
and for this reason, Lord,
the frail-necked men
receive and perceive deadly triangular calm[8]

Rally to my side my dances
you bad nigger dances
the carcan-cracker dance
the prison-break dance
the it-is-beautiful-good-and-legitimate-to-be-a-nigger-dance
Rally to my side my dances and let the sun bounce on the racket of my hands

but no the unequal sun is not enough for me
coil, wind, around my new growth
light on my cadenced fingers
to you I surrender my conscience and its fleshy rhythm
to you I surrender the fire in which my weakness smolders
to you I surrender the "chain-gang"
to you the swamps
to you the nontourist of the triangular circuit
devour wind
to you I surrender my abrupt words
devour and encoil yourself
and self-encoiling embrace me with a more ample shudder
embrace me unto furious us
embrace, embrace US

---

8. Referring both to the Holy Trinity and to the triangular trade in slaves between Europe, Africa, and the Americas.

but after having drawn from us blood
drawn by our own blood!
embrace, my purity mingles only with yours
so then embrace
like a field of even filagos[9]
at dusk
our multicolored purities
and bind, bind me without remorse
bind me with your vast arms to the luminous clay
bind my black vibration to the very navel of the world
bind, bind me, bitter brotherhood
then, strangling me with your lasso of stars
rise,
Dove
rise
rise
rise
I follow you who are imprinted on my ancestral white cornea.
rise sky licker
and the great black hole where a moon ago I wanted to drown it is there I will now fish
   the malevolent tongue of the night in its motionless veerition![1]

GABRIEL GARCÍA MÁRQUEZ ▪ (b. 1928)

The publication of Colombian writer Gabriel García Márquez's novel *Cien años de sole-dad* ("One Hundred Years of Solitude") in 1967 changed the course of twentieth-century fiction. Translated into more than thirty languages, it attracted the attention of a world-wide reading public and started what became known as the "boom" period for Latin American literature in the 1970s and after. García Márquez's international importance was confirmed when he was awarded the Nobel Prize in Literature in 1982. One of the characteristic features of García Márquez's novels as well as of other Latin American fiction is "magic realism," a term coined by Cuban novelist Alejo Carpentier in the 1940s: Magical realist fiction blends accounts of ordinary events and historical occurrences with elements of the supernatural and the fantastic but narrates both with the same matter-of-fact tone. It thereby often conveys a very different sense of the boundaries between the real and the unreal, and the physical and spiritual worlds, than European and North American novels. For all that, García Márquez's magic realism still *is* a form of realism—he had worked for many years as a journalist for various Latin American newspapers while also writing fiction and film scripts. His fiction relies on close observation of how people act and communicate in everyday circumstances; his talent in turning such observations into compelling fiction is evident in the novel *Chronicle of a Death Foretold* (1981), which features no obvious "magic realist" elements but describes in minute and suspenseful detail the events leading up to a murder in a small town—a murder everyone except the victim knows will happen. This talent is also obvious in his earlier fiction: The short story "Artificial Roses" (1962) focuses entirely on quite common events and conversations in the life of a young woman and her grandmother, but through the details we catch a glimpse of the deeper relationship between the two women as well as of the girl's disappointment with her lover.

9. A kind of pine tree that grows in the tropics.
1. A noun derived from the verb "to veer": change of direction.

Artificial Roses[1]

Feeling her way in the gloom of dawn, Mina put on the sleeveless dress which the night before she had hung next to the bed, and rummaged in the trunk for the detachable sleeves. Then she looked for them on the nails on the walls, and behind the doors, trying not to make noise so as not to wake her blind grandmother, who was sleeping in the same room. But when she got used to the darkness, she noticed that the grandmother had got up, and she went into the kitchen to ask her for the sleeves.

"They're in the bathroom," the blind woman said. "I washed them yesterday afternoon."

There they were, hanging from a wire with two wooden clothespins. They were still wet. Mina went back into the kitchen and stretched the sleeves out on the stones of the fireplace. In front of her, the blind woman was stirring the coffee, her dead pupils fixed on the stone border of the veranda, where there was a row of flowerpots with medicinal herbs.

"Don't take my things again," said Mina. "These days, you can't count on the sun."

The blind woman moved her face toward the voice.

"I had forgotten that it was the first Friday,"[2] she said.

After testing with a deep breath to see if the coffee was ready, she took the pot off the fire.

"Put a piece of paper underneath, because these stones are dirty," she said.

Mina ran her index finger along the fireplace stones. They were dirty, but with a crust of hardened soot which would not dirty the sleeves if they were not rubbed against the stones.

"If they get dirty you're responsible," she said.

The blind woman had poured herself a cup of coffee. "You're angry," she said, pulling a chair toward the veranda. "It's a sacrilege to take Communion when one is angry." She sat down to drink her coffee in front of the roses in the patio. When the third call for Mass rang, Mina took the sleeves off the fireplace and they were still wet. But she put them on. Father Angel would not give her Communion with a bare-shouldered dress on. She didn't wash her face. She took off the traces of rouge with a towel, picked up the prayer book and shawl in her room, and went into the street. A quarter of an hour later she was back.

"You'll get there after the reading of the gospel," the blind woman said, seated opposite the roses in the patio.

Mina went directly to the toilet. "I can't go to Mass," she said. "The sleeves are wet, and my whole dress is wrinkled." She felt a knowing look follow her.

"First Friday and you're not going to Mass," exclaimed the blind woman.

Back from the toilet, Mina poured herself a cup of coffee and sat down against the whitewashed doorway, next to the blind woman. But she couldn't drink the coffee.

"You're to blame," she murmured, with a dull rancor, feeling that she was drowning in tears.

"You're crying," the blind woman exclaimed.

She put the watering can next to the pots of oregano and went out into the patio, repeating, "You're crying." Mina put her cup on the ground before sitting up.

"I'm crying from anger," she said. And added, as she passed next to her grandmother, "You must go to confession because you made me miss the first-Friday Communion."

1. Translated by J. S. Bernstein.

2. In Roman Catholicism, there is a custom to take Communion on the first Fridays of nine consecutive months with a special devotion to Christ's Sacred Heart. The custom originated in the 17th century and is believed to ensure that those who follow it will not die in sin or without sacraments.

The blind woman remained motionless, waiting for Mina to close the bedroom door. Then she walked to the end of the veranda. She bent over haltingly until she found the untouched cup in one piece on the ground. While she poured the coffee into the earthen pot, she went on:

"God knows I have a clear conscience."

Mina's mother came out of the bedroom.

"Who are you talking to?" she asked.

"To no one," said the blind woman. "I've told you already that I'm going crazy."

Ensconced in her room, Mina unbuttoned her bodice and took out three little keys which she carried on a safety pin. With one of the keys she opened the lower drawer of the armoire and took out a miniature wooden trunk. She opened it with another key. Inside there was a packet of letters written on colored paper, held together by a rubber band. She hid them in her bodice, put the little trunk in its place, and locked the drawer. Then she went to the toilet and threw the letters in.

"I thought you were at church," her mother said when Mina came into the kitchen.

"She couldn't go," the blind woman interrupted. "I forgot that it was first Friday, and I washed the sleeves yesterday afternoon."

"They're still wet," murmured Mina.

"I've had to work hard these days," the blind woman said.

"I have to deliver a hundred and fifty dozen roses for Easter," Mina said.

The sun warmed up early. Before seven Mina set up her artificial-rose shop in the living room: a basket full of petals and wires, a box of crêpe paper, two pairs of scissors, a spool of thread, and a pot of glue. A moment later Trinidad arrived, with a pasteboard box under her arm, and asked her why she hadn't gone to Mass.

"I didn't have any sleeves," said Mina.

"Anyone could have lent some to you," said Trinidad.

She pulled over a chair and sat down next to the basket of petals.

"I was too late," Mina said.

She finished a rose. Then she pulled the basket closer to shirr the petals with the scissors.[3] Trinidad put the pasteboard box on the floor and joined in the work.

Mina looked at the box.

"Did you buy shoes?" she asked.

"They're dead mice," said Trinidad.

Since Trinidad was an expert at shirring petals, Mina spent her time making stems of wire wound with green paper. They worked silently without noticing the sun advance in the living room, which was decorated with idyllic prints and family photographs. When she finished the stems, Mina turned toward Trinidad with a face that seemed to end in something immaterial. Trinidad shirred with admirable neatness, hardly moving the petal tip between her fingers, her legs close together. Mina observed her masculine shoes. Trinidad avoided the look without raising her head, barely drawing her feet backward, and stopped working.

"What's the matter?" she said.

Mina leaned toward her.

"He went away," she said.

Trinidad dropped the scissors in her lap.

"No."

---

3. Pulling the fabric together.

"He went away," Mina repeated.

Trinidad looked at her without blinking. A vertical wrinkle divided her knit brows. "And now?" she asked.

Mina replied in a steady voice.

"Now nothing."

Trinidad said goodbye before ten.

Freed from the weight of her intimacy, Mina stopped her a moment to throw the dead mice into the toilet. The blind woman was pruning the rosebush.

"I'll bet you don't know what I have in this box," Mina said to her as she passed. She shook the mice.

The blind woman began to pay attention. "Shake it again," she said. Mina repeated the movement, but the blind woman could not identify the objects after listening for a third time with her index finger pressed against the lobe of her ear.

"They are the mice which were caught in the church traps last night," said Mina.

When she came back, she passed next to the blind woman without speaking. But the blind woman followed her. When she got to the living room, Mina was alone next to the closed window, finishing the artificial roses.

"Mina," said the blind woman. "If you want to be happy, don't confess with strangers."

Mina looked at her without speaking. The blind woman sat down in the chair in front of her and tried to help with the work. But Mina stopped her.

"You're nervous," said the blind woman.

"Why didn't you go to Mass?" asked the blind woman.

"You know better than anyone."

"If it had been because of the sleeves, you wouldn't have bothered to leave the house," said the blind woman. "Someone was waiting for you on the way who caused you some disappointment."

Mina passed her hands before her grandmother's eyes, as if cleaning an invisible pane of glass.

"You're a witch," she said.

"You went to the toilet twice this morning," the blind woman said. "You never go more than once."

Mina kept making roses.

"Would you dare show me what you are hiding in the drawer of the armoire?" the blind woman asked.

Unhurriedly, Mina stuck the rose in the window frame, took the three little keys out of her bodice, and put them in the blind woman's hand. She herself closed her fingers.

"Go see with your own eyes," she said.

The blind woman examined the little keys with her finger-tips.

"My eyes cannot see down the toilet."

Mina raised her head and then felt a different sensation: she felt that the blind woman knew that she was looking at her.

"Throw yourself down the toilet if what I do is so interesting to you," she said.

The blind woman ignored the interruption.

"You always stay up writing in bed until early morning," she said.

"You yourself turn out the light," Mina said.

"And immediately you turn on the flashlight," the blind woman said. "I can tell that you're writing by your breathing."

Mina made an effort to stay calm. "Fine," she said without raising her head. "And supposing that's the way it is. What's so special about it?"

"Nothing," replied the blind woman. "Only that it made you miss first-Friday Communion."

With both hands Mina picked up the spool of thread, the scissors, and a fistful of unfinished stems and roses. She put it all in the basket and faced the blind woman. "Would you like me to tell you what I went to do in the toilet, then?" she asked. They both were in suspense until Mina replied to her own question:

"I went to take a shit."

The blind woman threw the three little keys into the basket. "It would be a good excuse," she murmured, going into the kitchen. "You would have convinced me if it weren't the first time in your life I've ever heard you swear." Mina's mother was coming along the corridor in the opposite direction, her arms full of bouquets of thorned flowers.

"What's going on?" she asked.

"I'm crazy," said the blind woman. "But apparently you haven't thought of sending me to the madhouse so long as I don't start throwing stones."

DEREK WALCOTT ■ (b. 1930)

Born and raised on the Caribbean island of Saint Lucia, a British colony until 1967, Derek Walcott has both experienced and written about the often-troubled transition from colonial to postcolonial conditions. Imperial colonial trade in human labor had brought some of his ancestors to the island: Both of his grandmothers were descended from slaves. Walcott's heritage, like that of many, was mixed: His father, Warwick Walcott, was of English descent on his father's side, and Walcott has written of the irony that his father should have been named after Warwickshire, Shakespeare's home county.

Walcott's education in colonial Saint Lucia was thoroughly British. "The writers of my generation were natural assimilators," Walcott has written in his introduction to *Dream on Monkey Mountain and Other Plays*. "We knew the literatures of Empires, Greek, Roman, British, through their essential classics; and both the patois of the street and the language of the classroom had the elation of discovery." Walcott won a British government scholarship to a college in Jamaica, where he earned a degree in English in 1953. After several years as a schoolteacher, he won a fellowship to study theater in New York, then moved to Trinidad and founded the Little Carib Theater Workshop. From that time on, he has written plays fusing Caribbean and European elements while also developing skills as a watercolorist and an extraordinary lyric and narrative poet. He has continued to cross physical borders over the years, dividing his time between his home in Trinidad and a teaching post at Boston University.

Walcott's poems create a landscape of historical and personal memory, overlaying empires, centuries, continents, and stages of his own life, most notably in his 1990 verse novel *Omeros,* which rewrites Homer's epics—and James Joyce's *Ulysses*—as a Caribbean story of imperial and romantic conflict and a multiple search for the past. He was awarded the Nobel Prize in Literature two years after its publication. The first two poems given here illustrate two major sides of Walcott's response to colonial and post-colonial conditions. His important early poem "A Far Cry from Africa" (1962) expresses the divisions of history and self that arise from so mixed a heritage, while in "Volcano"

(1976) he pays affectionate, ironic homage to his modernist predecessors Conrad and Joyce—artistic exiles both and prime models for the transmutation of colonial experience into lasting art. These poems are followed by "The Fortunate Traveller," a harrowing account of postcolonial border-crossing, self-seeking charity work, and moral corruption.

A Far Cry from Africa

A wind is ruffling the tawny pelt
Of Africa. Kikuyu,[1] quick as flies,
Batten° upon the bloodstreams of the veldt.°   *fasten / open country*
Corpses are scattered through a paradise.
5 Only the worm, colonel of carrion, cries:
"Waste no compassion on these separate dead!"
Statistics justify and scholars seize
The salients of colonial policy.
What is that to the white child hacked in bed?
10 To savages, expendable as Jews?

Threshed out by beaters, the long rushes break
In a white dust of ibises[2] whose cries
Have wheeled since civilization's dawn
From the parched river or beast-teeming plain.
15 The violence of beast on beast is read
As natural law, but upright man
Seeks his divinity by inflicting pain.
Delirious as these worried beasts, his wars
Dance to the tightened carcass of a drum,
20 While he calls courage still that native dread
Of the white peace contracted by the dead.

Again brutish necessity wipes its hands
Upon the napkin of a dirty cause, again
A waste of our compassion, as with Spain,[3]
25 The gorilla wrestles with the superman.
I who am poisoned with the blood of both,
Where shall I turn, divided to the vein?
I who have cursed
The drunken officer of British rule, how choose
30 Between this Africa and the English tongue I love?
Betray them both, or give back what they give?
How can I face such slaughter and be cool?
How can I turn from Africa and live?

1. Indigenous people of Kenya.
2. Wading birds resembling storks.
3. In 1936–1939, many in the international community supported the constitutional government of Spain against a coup led by fascist General Francisco Franco. Franco's forces won, and he ruled as a dictator until his death in 1975.

Volcano

Joyce was afraid of thunder,
but lions roared at his funeral
from the Zurich zoo.
Was it Zurich or Trieste?[1]
5   No matter. These are legends, as much
As the death of Joyce is a legend,
or the strong rumor that Conrad
is dead, and that *Victory* is ironic.[2]
On the edge of the night-horizon
10   from this beach house on the cliffs
there are now, till dawn,
two glares from the miles-out-
at-sea derricks; they are like
the glow of the cigar
15   and the glow of the volcano
at *Victory*'s end.
One could abandon writing
for the slow-burning signals
of the great, to be, instead,
20   their ideal reader, ruminative,
voracious, making the love of masterpieces
superior to attempting
to repeat or outdo them,
and be the greatest reader in the world.
25   At least it requires awe,
which has been lost to our time;
so many people have seen everything,
so many people can predict,
so many refuse to enter the silence
30   of victory, the indolence
that burns at the core,
so many are no more than
erect ash, like the cigar,
so many take thunder for granted.
35   How common is the lightning,
how lost the leviathans
we no longer look for!
There were giants in those days.
In those days they made good cigars.
40   I must read more carefully.

1. Early in his career James Joyce lived in Trieste, where he began *Ulysses*; he died in Zurich in 1941.
2. *Victory* is a 1915 novel by Joseph Conrad concerning a European man's unsuccessful attempt to flee from the corruption of modern civilization by settling on a deserted island in Malaysia.

The Fortunate Traveller[1]

for Susan Sontag

> And I heard a voice in the midst of the four beasts say,
> A measure of wheat for a penny,
> and three measures of barley for a penny;
> and see thou hurt not the oil and the wine.
>
> *Revelation 6:6*[2]

1

It was in winter. Steeples, spires
congealed like holy candles. Rotting snow
flaked from Europe's ceiling. A compact man,
I crossed the canal in a grey overcoat,
5   on one lapel a crimson buttonhole
for the cold ecstasy of the assassin.
In the square coffin manacled to my wrist:
small countries pleaded through the mesh of graphs,
in treble-spaced, Xeroxed forms to the World Bank
10   on which I had scrawled the one word, MERCY;

I sat on a cold bench
under some skeletal lindens.
Two other gentlemen, black skins gone grey
as their identical, belted overcoats,
15   crossed the white river.
They spoke the stilted French
of their dark river,
whose hooked worm, multiplying its pale sickle,
could thin the harvest of the winter streets.
20   "Then we can depend on you to get us those tractors?"
"I gave my word."
"May my country ask you why you are doing this, sir?"
Silence.
"You know if you betray us, you cannot hide?"
25   A tug. Smoke trailing its dark cry.

At the window in Haiti, I remember
a gecko° pressed against the hotel glass,   *lizard*
with white palms, concentrating head.
With a child's hands. Mercy, monsieur. Mercy.
30   Famine sighs like a scythe
across the field of statistics and the desert
is a moving mouth. In the hold of this earth
10,000,000 shoreless souls are drifting.
Somalia: 765,000, their skeletons will go under the tidal sand.
35   "We'll meet you in Bristol to conclude the agreement?"

---

1. Walcott's title invokes Thomas Nashe's tale *The Unfortunate Traveller* (1594). Susan Sontag (1933–2004) was an American cultural critic and novelist.
2. One of the Four Horsemen of the Apocalypse is decreeing the famine and inflation that accompany wars as the end of the world approaches.

Steeples like tribal lances, through congealing fog
the cries of wounded church bells wrapped in cotton,
grey mist enfolding the conspirator
like a sealed envelope next to its heart.

40 No one will look up now to see the jet
fade like a weevil through a cloud of flour.
One flies first-class, one is so fortunate.
Like a telescope reversed, the traveller's eye
swiftly screws down the individual sorrow
45 to an oval nest of antic numerals,
and the iris, interlocking with this globe,
condenses it to zero, then a cloud.
Beetle-black taxi from Heathrow[3] to my flat.
We are roaches,
50 riddling the state cabinets, entering the dark holes
of power, carapaced in topcoats,
scuttling around columns, signalling for taxis,
with frantic antennae, to other huddles with roaches;
we infect with optimism, and when
55 the cabinets crack, we are the first
to scuttle, radiating separately
back to Geneva, Bonn, Washington, London.

Under the dripping planes of Hampstead Heath,
I read her letter again, watching the drizzle
60 disfigure its pleading like mascara. Margo,
I cannot bear to watch the nations cry.
Then the phone: "We will pay you in Bristol."
Days in fetid bedclothes swallowing cold tea,
the phone stifled by the pillow. The telly
65 a blue storm with soundless snow.
I'd light the gas and see a tiger's tongue.
I was rehearsing the ecstasies of starvation
for what I had to do. *And have not charity.*[4]

I found my pity, desperately researching
70 the origins of history, from reed-built communes
by sacred lakes, turning with the first sprocketed
water-driven wheels. I smelled imagination
among bestial hides by the gleam of fat,
seeking in all races a common ingenuity.
75 I envisaged an Africa flooded with such light
as alchemized the first fields of emmer wheat and barley,
when we savages dyed our pale dead with ochre,
and bordered our temples

DEREK WALCOTT

902

3. London's primary airport.
4. Quoting St. Paul: "Though I speak with the tongues of men and of angels, and have not charity, I am become as sounding brass, or a tinkling cymbal" (1 Corinthians 13:1).

80   with the ceremonial vulva of the conch
in the grey epoch of the obsidian adze.
I sowed the Sahara with rippling cereals,
my charity fertilized these aridities.

What was my field? Late sixteenth century.
My field was a dank acre. A Sussex don,
85   I taught the Jacobean anxieties: *The White Devil.*[5]
Flamineo's torch startles the brooding yews.
The drawn end comes in strides. I loved my Duchess,
the white flame of her soul blown out between
the smoking cypresses. Then I saw children pounce
90   on green meat with a rat's ferocity.

I called them up and took the train to Bristol,
my blood the Severn's[6] dregs and silver.
On Severn's estuary the pieces flash,
Iscariot's salary,[7] patron saint of spies.
95   I thought, who cares how many million starve?
Their rising souls will lighten the world's weight
and level its gull-glittering waterline;
we left at sunset down the estuary.

England recedes. The forked white gull
100   screeches, circling back.
Even the birds are pulled back by their orbit,
even mercy has its magnetic field.
                         Back in the cabin,
I uncap the whisky, the porthole
105   mists with glaucoma. By the time I'm pissed,°   *drunk*
England, England will be
that pale serrated indigo on the sea-line.
"You are so fortunate, you get to see the world—"
Indeed, indeed, sirs, I have seen the world.
110   Spray splashes the portholes and vision blurs.

Leaning on the hot rail, watching the hot sea,
I saw them far off, kneeling on hot sand
in the pious genuflections of the locust,
as Ponce's armoured knees crush Florida
115   to the funereal fragrance of white lilies.

                2

Now I have come to where the phantoms live,
I have no fear of phantoms, but of the real.
The Sabbath benedictions of the islands.
Treble clef of the snail on the scored leaf,

---

5. Revenge tragedy (c. 1612) by John Webster.
6. A river running through Wales and England.
7. For betraying Jesus Christ, Judas Iscariot was paid 30 pieces of silver by the Roman authorities.

120   the Tantum Ergo[8] of black choristers
      soars through the organ pipes of coconuts.
      Across the dirty beach surpliced with lace,
      they pass a brown lagoon behind the priest,
      pale and unshaven in his frayed soutane,°   *black robe*
125   into the concrete church at Canaries;
      as Albert Schweitzer[9] moves to the harmonium
      of morning, and to the pluming chimneys,
      the groundswell lifts *Lebensraum, Lebensraum.*[1]

      Black faces sprinkled with continual dew—
130   dew on the speckled croton,[2] dew
      on the hard leaf of the knotted plum tree,
      dew on the elephant ears of the dasheen.[3]
      Through Kurtz's teeth, white skull in elephant grass,
      the imperial fiction sings. Sunday
135   wrinkles downriver from the Heart of Darkness.
      The heart of darkness is not Africa.
      The heart of darkness is the core of fire
      in the white center of the holocaust.
      The heart of darkness is the rubber claw
140   selecting a scalpel in antiseptic light,
      the hills of children's shoes outside the chimneys,
      the tinkling nickel instruments on the white altar;
      Jacob, in his last card, sent me these verses:
      "Think of a God who doesn't lose His sleep
145   if trees burst into tears or glaciers weep.
      So, aping His indifference, I write now,
      not Anno Domini: After Dachau."[4]

                              3

      The night maid brings a lamp and draws the blinds.
      I stay out on the verandah with the stars.
150   Breakfast congealed to supper on its plate.

      There is no sea as restless as my mind.
      The promontories snore. They snore like whales.
      Cetus, the whale, was Christ.
      The ember dies, the sky smokes like an ash heap.
155   Reeds wash their hands of guilt and the lagoon
      is stained. Louder, since it rained,
      a gauze of sand flies hisses from the marsh.

      Since God is dead,[5] and these are not His stars,
      but man-lit, sulphurous, sanctuary lamps,

8. A hymn sung after the Blessed Sacrament has been exposed in the mass.
9. German physician, missionary, and musician in Africa; winner of the Nobel Peace Prize in 1952.
1. Space to live in; the term is especially associated with Nazi Germany's territorial expansion.
2. A tropical plant.
3. The taro plant of tropical Asia.
4. Site of the notorious Nazi concentration camp.
5. So the German philosopher Friedrich Nietzsche declared in his 1882 text *The Gay Science.*

160   it's in the heart of darkness of this earth
    that backward tribes keep vigil of His Body,
    in deya, lampion,[6] and this bedside lamp.
    Keep the news from their blissful ignorance.
    Like lice, like lice, the hungry of this earth
165   swarm to the tree of life. If those who starve
    like these rain-flies who shed glazed wings in light
    grew from sharp shoulder blades their brittle vans
    and soared towards that tree, how it would seethe—
    ah, Justice! But fires
170   drench them like vermin, quotas
    prevent them, and they remain
    compassionate fodder for the travel book,
    its paragraphs like windows from a train,
    for everywhere that earth shows its rib cage
175   and the moon goggles with the eyes of children,
    we turn away to read. Rimbaud[7] learned that.
       Rimbaud, at dusk,
    idling his wrist in water past temples
    the plumed dates still protect in Roman file,
180   knew that we cared less for one human face
    than for the scrolls in Alexandria's ashes,
    that the bright water could not dye his hand
    any more than poetry. The dhow's[8] silhouette
    moved through the blinding coinage of the river
185   that, endlessly, until we pay one debt,
    shrouds, every night, an ordinary secret.

               4
    The drawn sword comes in strides.
    It stretches for the length of the empty beach;
    the fishermen's huts shut their eyes tight.
190   A frisson° shakes the palm trees.   *excited shiver*
    and sweats on the traveller's tree.
    They've found out my sanctuary. Philippe, last night:
    "It had two gentlemen in the village yesterday, sir,
    asking for you while you was in town.
195   I tell them you was in town. They send to tell you,
    there is no hurry. They will be coming back."

    In loaves of cloud, *and have not charity,*
    the weevil will make a sahara of Kansas,
    the ant shall eat Russia.
200   Their soft teeth shall make, *and have not charity,*
    the harvest's desolation,
    and the brown globe crack like a begging bowl,

---

6. A small oil lamp with tinted glass.

7. Arthur Rimbaud (1854–1891), French poet. After abandoning poetry at the age of 20, he traveled in Egypt and the Sudan, later settling in Ethiopia as a trader and arms dealer.

8. A sailing vessel used by Arabs.

and though you fire oceans of surplus grain,
and have not charity,

205   still, through thin stalks,
the smoking stubble, stalks
grasshopper: third horseman,
the leather-helmed locust.[9]

Chinua Achebe occupies a key position in the history of postcolonial African literature. Until the 1958 publication of his novel *Things Fall Apart,* readers outside Africa encountered Africa in fiction largely through European perspectives. Joseph Conrad's *Heart of Darkness* (page 623) occupied a preeminent position in literature about Africa and its European colonization. Though incisive and critical of the European imperial enterprise in the continent, Conrad's remains a European perspective, and it was Achebe who presented an African reading of Africa to the wider world for the first time in the twentieth century. Some have felt that Achebe's narrative isn't actually African enough. Critics point out that the novel is written in one of the colonists' imperial languages, English, and, starting with the title of the novel (taken from W. B. Yeats), its literary antecedents and narrative strategies are as much European as the story is African. Achebe hasn't shied away from engaging in this discussion among critics and scholars of postcolonialism. As an African author and a Western academic and critic, he clearly is an interested party in more than one sense. As such, he can be seen as a writer who embodies simultaneously the cultures of the colonized and of the colonizer.

It is interesting, and also historically intriguing, that Achebe has viewed himself as an African insider, as attested to by his essay on the 1962 meeting of African intellectuals at Makarere University College in Uganda. That was an occasion for a "declaration of literary independence" by the African writers who gathered there, many of whom would in fact form the first cohort of postcolonial African authors. It would be some years before it came to light that Achebe along with the other African writers at that defining moment were indeed insiders, but they were also in the process of being turned inside out by the circumstances of the very occasion in which they were defining themselves. They would come to learn that their self-defining moment was in fact a move in a larger ideological and neocolonial chess game played by superpowers in the course of the Cold War. Unbeknownst to most of them, they were being gathered under the auspices of the U.S. Central Intelligence Agency through one of the proxy organizations it operated in Paris called the Society for Cultural Freedom.

Like his writing, Achebe himself is the product of an interesting mixture of educational institutions and religious traditions. Born in Ogidi, eastern Nigeria, an Igbo region, Achebe was the fifth of six children. His father was a teacher in an evangelical Protestant school of the Church Missionary Society. He was originally christened "Albert," after Prince Albert, the husband of Queen Victoria. Upon entering the university, he dropped his English name and kept his indigenous Igbo name, "Chinua." His secondary schooling was in Government College in Umuahia, which he entered in 1944. He received his university education at University College of Ibadan, from which he graduated in 1953 with a degree in English, history, and theology. Upon graduation he traveled throughout Africa and to America and then joined the Nigerian Broadcasting Company in 1954. Four years later he published his first novel, *Things Fall Apart,* in which he attempted to portray traditional life before the arrival of the colonizing Europeans. The work became a classic of

---

9. The locust, eater of crops, is here identified with the horseman of the Apocalypse quoted in the poem's epigraph.

African literature with translations into more than fifty languages. In 1960 he published his second novel, *No Longer at Ease,* followed by *Arrow of God* in 1964. These novels depict the clash of traditional Igbo life with colonial and missionary incursions by European powers.

Throughout the 1950s and 1960s Achebe worked in broadcasting, becoming director of External Services in charge of the Voice of Nigeria in 1961. He cofounded a publishing company in 1967 and was then appointed a research fellow at the University of Nigeria. Starting in 1971 he edited the journal *Okike,* which published and promoted new writing in Nigeria. Nigeria was torn by civil wars from 1966 to 1970, which were chiefly between his own Igbo people and the non-Igbo; these conflicts forced Achebe and his family to flee to Lagos, then Nigeria's capital. His collection of poems based on his country's internecine strife won the Commonwealth Poetry Prize in 1972. In the same year Achebe published a collection of short stories, *Girls at War,* and traveled to the United States to teach at the University of Massachusetts in Amherst. He returned to Nigeria in 1976 to continue his engagement in the political life of his country, and in 1983 he published *The Trouble with Nigeria,* a scathing attack on the national corruption among Nigeria's leaders. Yet another military coup, the fifth, two years later became the basis for Achebe's fifth novel, *Anthills of the Savannah* (1987), an indictment of military power and dictatorship. The following year he was partially paralyzed as a result of a

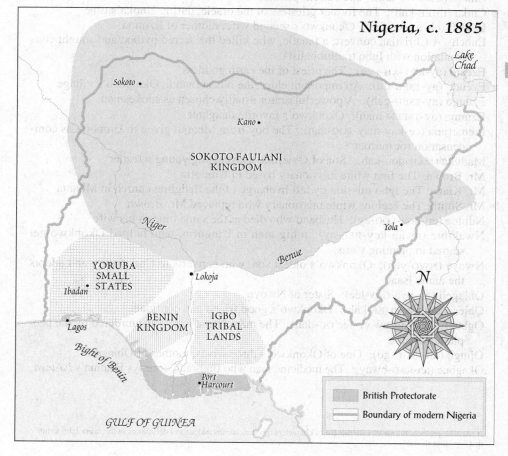

Nigeria, c. 1885

car accident but recovered enough to resume his writing career and to accept a teaching position at Bard College in New York, where he has taught since. *Things Fall Apart* has remained his best known and most influential work. Situated between a complex, traditional world and the European invasion and colonization that ensued, the narrative of *Things Fall Apart* has taken on much greater historical and cultural significance than usually accorded a work of fiction.

PRONUNCIATIONS:

Chinua Achebe: CHIN-ow-ah ah-CHAY-bay
Mbwil Ngal: m'BWEEL n'GAHL
Ngugi wa-Thiong'o: GOU-gie wah-tee-ON-go

Things Fall Apart

Principal Characters in the Novel[1]

Akueke (ah-KWAY-kay): Daughter of Obierika, whose marriage is negotiated

Anene (ah-NAY-nay): Ekwefi's first husband

Chielo (chee-AY-lah): The current priestess of the oracle

Chika (CHEE-kah): The former priestess of the oracle, during Unoka's time

Ekwefi (eh-KWAY-fee): Okonkwo's second wife; mother of Ezinma

Enoch: A Christian convert; a fanatic, who killed the sacred python and sought confrontation with Igbo traditionalists

Ezeani (ay-tsay-AH-nee): The priest of the earth goddess

Ezeudu (ay-TSEU-du): An important elder; the oldest man in Okonkwo's village

Ezeugo (ay-TSEU-gah): A powerful orator usually chosen as spokesman

Ezinma (ay-TSEEN-mah): Okonkwo's favorite daughter

Ikemefuna (ee-kay-may-FOO-nah): The boy from Mbaino given to Umuofia as compensation for murder

Maduka (MAH-dou-kah): Son of Obierika, a promising young wrestler

Mr. Brown: The first white missionary based in Umuofia

Mr. Kiaga: The Igbo missionary left in charge of the fledgling church in Mbanta

Mr. Smith: The zealous white missionary who replaced Mr. Brown

Ndulue (en-dou-LOO-ay): Husband who died at the same time as his wife

Nwakibie (nwah-key-BEE-ay): a big man in Umuofia, who helped Okonkwo get started in planting yams

Nwoye (NWO-yeh): Okonkwo's oldest son, who converts to Christianity and adopts the name Isaac

Obiageli (ah-bya-GAY-lee): Sister of Nwoye

Obierika (ah-byer-EE-kah): Okonkwo's good friend and confidant

Ogbuefi Udo (ag-BWAY-fee OU-dah): The man whose wife was murdered by the people of Mbaino

Ojiugo (ah-JYOU-go): One of Okonkwo's three wives, mother of Obiageli

Okagbue (ah-KAG-bway): The medicine man who finds and destroys Ezinma's *iyi-uwa*

---

1. Achebe prefaces his novel with this list of characters (pronunciations added) and definitions of the many Igbo terms that appear in the text.

Okonkwo (ah-CONK-wah): The main character, a strong, proud man

Okoye (ah-CO-yay): A friend of Okonkwo's father, who tries unsuccessfully to get back the money Unoka had borrowed

Ozoemena (ah-tso-ay-MAY-nah): Wife who dies at the same time as her husband

Uchendu (ou-CHEN-dou): Okonkwo's uncle, the senior man of Mbanta where Okonkwo's family lives in exile

Unoka (ou-NO-kah): Okonkwo's late father, an easygoing, rather lazy person

Glossary of Words and Phrases Used in the Text

(Igbo terms are in italics; *o* indicates "aw" sound as in *awful*.)

Afo: One of the four market days

agadi-nwayi: Old woman

agbala: Woman; also, an insulting term for a man who has taken no title

Agbala: The name of the oracle consulted by the people of Umuofia

Amadiora: The god of thunder and lightning

Ani: The earth goddess

bride-price: Or bridewealth; the gifts transferred from the groom's family to that of the bride, which cement the marriage and legitimize the children

chi: One's personal god, or guardian spirit

Chukwu: The supreme god

cowries: Shells imported from the Indian Ocean, widely used as currency in precolonial Africa

District Commissioner: The British official in charge of a particular African district

efulefu: An empty, worthless man

egwugwu: The masked spirits, representing the ancestral spirits of the village

Eke: One of the four market days

ekwe: A wooden drum

eneke-nti-oba: A kind of bird

eze-agai-nwayi: The teeth of an old woman

foo-foo: Or fufu; pounded yam eaten as part of most meals

harmattan: A cold, dry wind that blows from the North

iba: Fever

Ibo: The older spelling of "Igbo," less commonly used today

Idemili: One of the three most prestigious titles in Igboland

Ifejioku: The god of yams, the men's crop and principal food of the Igbo

Iguedo: Okonkwo's village, one of the nine villages that make up Umuofia

ikenga: A wooden carving that becomes imbued with a man's personal spirit

ilo: The village common, where meetings, ceremonies, and sports competitions take place

inyanga: Showing off; bragging

isa-ifi: A ceremony held to determine faithfulness if a woman had been separated from her fiancé or husband for some time and were then reunited with him

iyi-uwa: A special stone that forms the link between an *ogbanje* and the spirit world. The child would eventually die if the *iyi-uwa* were not discovered and destroyed.

jigida: A string of waist-beads

kite: A bird that appears during the dry season

kola nuts: Offered to guests on special occasions

kotma: "Court man," or court messenger; a corruption of the English term

kwenu: A shout of approval and greeting

maize: Corn

ndichie: The elders, who meet in council and make decisions binding the clan

nna ayi: Our father

nne: Mother

nno: An expression of welcome

nso-ani: Sacrilege

nza: A tiny bird

obi: The living quarters of the head of the family

obodo dike: The land of the brave

ochu: Murder or manslaughter

ogbanje: A changeling; a child who repeatedly dies and returns to its mother to be reborn

Ogbuefi: An honorific used before the name of a man who has taken the *ozo* title

ogene: A kind of gong

ogwu: Supernatural medicine

osu: An outcast; having been dedicated to a god, the *osu* was not allowed to mix with the freeborn, or to marry one of them

Oye: One of the four market days

ozo: One of the titles an important Igbo man could aspire to

palm kernels: The core of the fruit of the oil palm tree, which were cracked to release the oil

palm-oil: Used in cooking and for preparing food, also a major cash crop exported to Europe

palm-wine: A fermented drink prepared from the sap of certain palm trees

plantain: A starchy kind of banana, cooked as food

pottage: A stew

singlets: Men's undershirts

sisal: A kind of cactus plant with fibrous leaves

tufia: A curse or oath

udu: A type of drum made from pottery

uli: A dye used by women for drawing patterns on the skin

umuada: A family gathering of daughters, for which the female kinsfolk return to their village of origin

Umuofia: The clan Okonkwo belonged to, made up of nine villages

umunna: A wide group of kinsmen (the masculine form of *umuada*)

Uri: Part of the betrothal ceremony when the dowry or bridewealth is paid

Things Fall Apart

Turning and turning in the widening gyre
The falcon cannot hear the falconer;
Things fall apart; the centre cannot hold;
Mere anarchy is loosed upon the world.

W. B. Yeats, "The Second Coming"[1]

1. The Irish poet, writing after World War I, refers to Judgment Day and the new age to commence with Christ's second coming as announced in Matthew 24:31–46, a cosmic recommencement that is preceded by apocalyptic calamity and cosmic catastrophe. With the title of his novel, Achebe alludes to the catastrophe in Yeats's poem and refers as well to the undoing of a traditional African order by the calamities of colonization, religious conversion, and imposed political transition from traditional society to a modernized order.

Part 1

Chapter 1

Okonkwo was well known throughout the nine villages and even beyond. His fame rested on solid personal achievements. As a young man of eighteen he had brought honour to his village by throwing Amalinze the Cat. Amalinze was the great wrestler who for seven years was unbeaten, from Umuofia to Mbaino. He was called the Cat because his back would never touch the earth. It was this man that Okonkwo threw in a fight which the old men agreed was one of the fiercest since the founder of their town engaged a spirit of the wild for seven days and seven nights.

The drums beat and the flutes sang and the spectators held their breath. Amalinze was a wily craftsman, but Okonkwo was as slippery as a fish in water. Every nerve and every muscle stood out on their arms, on their backs and their thighs, and one almost heard them stretching to breaking point. In the end Okonkwo threw the Cat.

That was many years ago, twenty years or more, and during this time Okonkwo's fame had grown like a bush-fire in the harmattan. He was tall and huge, and his bushy eyebrows and wide nose gave him a very severe look. He breathed heavily, and it was said that, when he slept, his wives and children in their out-houses could hear him breathe. When he walked, his heels hardly touched the ground and he seemed to walk on springs, as if he was going to pounce on somebody. And he did pounce on people quite often. He had a slight stammer and whenever he was angry and could not get his words out quickly enough, he would use his fists. He had no patience with unsuccessful men. He had had no patience with his father.

Unoka, for that was his father's name, had died ten years ago. In his day he was lazy and improvident and was quite incapable of thinking about tomorrow. If any money came his way, and it seldom did, he immediately bought gourds of palm-wine, called round his neighbours and made merry. He always said that whenever he saw a dead man's mouth he saw the folly of not eating what one had in one's lifetime. Unoka was, of course, a debtor, and he owed every neighbour some money, from a few cowries to quite substantial amounts.

He was tall but very thin and had a slight stoop. He wore a haggard and mournful look except when he was drinking or playing on his flute. He was very good on his flute, and his happiest moments were the two or three moons after the harvest when the village musicians brought down their instruments, hung above the fireplace. Unoka would play with them, his face beaming with blessedness and peace. Sometimes another village would ask Unoka's band and their dancing *egwugwu* to come and stay with them and teach them their tunes. They would go to such hosts for as long as three or four markets, making music and feasting. Unoka loved the good fare and the good fellowship, and he loved this season of the year, when the rains had stopped and the sun rose every morning with dazzling beauty. And it was not too hot either, because the cold and dry harmattan wind was blowing down from the north. Some years the harmattan was very severe and a dense haze hung on the atmosphere. Old men and children would then sit round log fires, warming their bodies. Unoka loved it all, and he loved the first kites that returned with the dry season, and the children who sang songs of welcome to them. He would remember his own childhood, how he had often wandered around looking for a kite sailing leisurely against the blue sky. As soon as he found one he would sing with his whole being, welcoming it back from its long, long journey, and asking it if it had brought home any lengths of cloth.

That was years ago, when he was young. Unoka, the grown-up, was a failure. He was poor and his wife and children had barely enough to eat. People laughed at him because he was a loafer, and they swore never to lend him any more money because he never paid back. But Unoka was such a man that he always succeeded in borrowing more, and piling up his debts.

One day a neighbour called Okoye came in to see him. He was reclining on a mud bed in his hut playing on the flute. He immediately rose and shook hands with Okoye, who then unrolled the goatskin which he carried under his arm, and sat down. Unoka went into an inner room and soon returned with a small wooden disc containing a kola nut, some alligator pepper and a lump of white chalk.

"I have kola," he announced when he sat down, and passed the disc over to his guest.

"Thank you. He who brings kola brings life. But I think you ought to break it," replied Okoye passing back the disc.

"No, it is for you, I think," and they argued like this for a few moments before Unoka accepted the honour of breaking the kola. Okoye, meanwhile, took the lump of chalk, drew some lines on the floor, and then painted his big toe. As he broke the kola, Unoka prayed to their ancestors for life and health, and for protection against their enemies. When they had eaten they talked about many things: about the heavy rains which were drowning the yams, about the next ancestral feast and about the impending war with the village of Mbaino. Unoka was never happy when it came to wars. He was in fact a coward and could not bear the sight of blood. And so he changed the subject and talked about music, and his face beamed. He could hear in his mind's ear the blood-stirring and intricate rhythms of the *ekwe* and the *udu* and the *ogene,* and he could hear his own flute weaving in and out of them, decorating them with a colourful and plaintive tune. The total effect was gay and brisk, but if one picked out the flute as it went up and down and then broke up into short snatches, one saw that there was sorrow and grief there.

Okoye was also a musician. He played on the *ogene.* But he was not a failure like Unoka. He had a large barn full of yams and he had three wives. And now he was going to take the Idemili title, the third highest in the land. It was a very expensive ceremony and he was gathering all his resources together. That was in fact the reason why he had come to see Unoka. He cleared his throat and began:

"Thank you for the kola. You may have heard of the title I intend to take shortly."

Having spoken plainly so far, Okoye said the next half a dozen sentences in proverbs. Among the Ibo the art of conversation is regarded very highly, and proverbs are the palm-oil with which words are eaten. Okoye was a great talker and he spoke for a long time, skirting round the subject and then hitting it finally. In short, he was asking Unoka to return the two hundred cowries he had borrowed from him more than two years before. As soon as Unoka understood what his friend was driving at, he burst out laughing. He laughed loud and long and his voice rang out clear as the *ogene,* and tears stood in his eyes. His visitor was amazed, and sat speechless. At the end, Unoka was able to give an answer between fresh outbursts of mirth.

"Look at that wall," he said, pointing at the far wall of his hut, which was rubbed with red earth so that it shone. "Look at those lines of chalk;" and Okoye saw groups of short perpendicular lines drawn in chalk. There were five groups, and the smallest group had ten lines. Unoka had a sense of the dramatic and so he allowed a pause, in which he took a pinch of snuff and sneezed noisily, and then he continued: "Each group there represents a debt to someone, and each stroke is one hundred cowries. You see, I owe that man a thousand cowries. But he has not come to wake me up in the morning for it. I shall pay you, but not today. Our elders say that the sun will shine on those who stand before it shines on those who kneel under them. I shall pay my big debts first." And he took another pinch of snuff, as if that was paying the big debts first. Okoye rolled his goatskin and departed.

When Unoka died he had taken no title at all and he was heavily in debt. Any wonder then that his son Okonkwo was ashamed of him? Fortunately, among these people a man was judged according to his worth and not according to the worth of his father. Okonkwo was clearly cut out for great things. He was still young but he had won fame as the greatest wrestler in the nine villages. He was a wealthy farmer and had two barns full of yams, and had just married his third wife. To crown it all he had taken two titles and had shown incredible prowess in two inter-tribal wars. And so although Okonkwo was still young, he was already one of the greatest men of his time. Age was respected among his people, but achievement was revered. As the elders said, if a child washed his hands he could eat with kings. Okonkwo had clearly washed his hands and so he ate with kings and elders. And that was how he came to look after the doomed lad who was sacrificed to the village of Umuofia by their neighbours to avoid war and bloodshed. The ill-fated lad was called Ikemefuna.

Chapter 2

Okonkwo had just blown out the palm-oil lamp and stretched himself on his bamboo bed when he heard the *ogene* of the town-crier piercing the still night air. *Gome, gome, gome, gome,* boomed the hollow metal. Then the crier gave his message, and at the end of it beat his instrument again. And this was the message. Every man of Umuofia was asked to gather at the market-place tomorrow morning. Okonkwo wondered what was amiss, for he knew certainly, that something was amiss. He had discerned a clear overtone of tragedy in the crier's voice, and even now he could still hear it as it grew dimmer and dimmer in the distance.

The night was very quiet. It was always quiet except on moonlight nights. Darkness held a vague terror for these people, even the bravest among them. Children were warned not to whistle at night for fear of evil spirits. Dangerous animals became even more sinister and uncanny in the dark. A snake was never called by its name at night, because it would hear. It was called a string. And so on this particular night as the crier's voice was gradually swallowed up in the distance, silence returned to the world, a vibrant silence made more intense by the universal trill of a million million forest insects.

On a moonlight night it would be different. The happy voices of children playing in open fields would then be heard. And perhaps those not so young would be playing in pairs in less open places, and old men and women would remember their youth. As the Ibo say: "When the moon is shining the cripple becomes hungry for a walk."

But this particular night was dark and silent. And in all the nine villages of Umuofia a town-crier with his *ogene* asked every man to be present tomorrow morning. Okonkwo on his bamboo bed tried to figure out the nature of the emergency—war with a neighbouring clan? That seemed the most likely reason, and he was not afraid of war. He was a man of action, a man of war. Unlike his father he could stand the look of blood. In Umuofia's latest war he was the first to bring home a human head. That was his fifth head; and he was not an old man yet. On great occasions such as the funeral of a village celebrity he drank his palm-wine from his first human head.

In the morning the market-place was full. There must have been about ten thousand men there, all talking in low voices. At last Ogbuefi Ezeugo stood up in the midst of them and bellowed four times, "*Umuofia kwenu,*" and on each occasion he faced a different direction and seemed to push the air with a clenched fist. And ten thousand men answered "*Yaa!*" each time. Then there was perfect silence. Ogbuefi Ezeugo was a powerful orator and was always chosen to speak on such occasions. He moved his hand over his white head and stroked his white beard. He then adjusted his cloth, which was passed under his right arm-pit and tied above his left shoulder.

"*Umuofia kwenu,*" he bellowed a fifth time, and the crowd yelled in answer. And then suddenly like one possessed he shot out his left hand and pointed in the direction of Mbaino, and said through gleaming white teeth firmly clenched: "Those sons of wild animals have dared to murder a daughter of Umuofia." He threw his head down and gnashed his teeth, and allowed a murmur of suppressed anger to sweep the crowd. When he began again, the anger on his face was gone and in its place a sort of smile hovered, more terrible and more sinister than the anger. And in a clear unemotional voice he told Umuofia how their daughter had gone to market at Mbaino and had been killed. That woman, said Ezeugo, was the wife of Ogbuefi Udo, and he pointed to a man who sat near him with a bowed head. The crowd then shouted with anger and thirst for blood.

Many others spoke, and at the end it was decided to follow the normal course of action. An ultimatum was immediately dispatched to Mbaino asking them to choose between war on the one hand, and on the other the offer of a young man and a virgin as compensation.

Umuofia was feared by all its neighbours. It was powerful in war and in magic, and its priests and medicine-men were feared in all the surrounding country. Its most potent war-medicine was as old as the clan itself. Nobody knew how old. But on one point there was general agreement—the active principle in that medicine had been an old woman with one leg. In fact, the medicine itself was called *agadi-nwayi,* or old woman. It had its shrine in the centre of Umuofia, in a cleared spot. And if anybody was so foolhardy as to pass by the shrine after dusk he was sure to see the old woman hopping about.

And so the neighbouring clans who naturally knew of these things feared Umuofia, and would not go to war against it without first trying a peaceful settlement. And in fairness to Umuofia it should be recorded that it never went to war unless its case was clear and just and was accepted as such by its Oracle—the Oracle of the Hills and the Caves. And there were indeed occasions when the Oracle had forbidden Umuofia to wage a war. If the clan had disobeyed the Oracle they would surely have been beaten, because their dreaded *agadi-nwayi* would never fight what the Ibo call *a fight of blame.*

But the war that now threatened was a just war. Even the enemy clan knew that. And so when Okonkwo of Umuofia arrived at Mbaino as the proud and imperious emissary of war, he was treated with great honour and respect, and two days later he returned home with a lad of fifteen and a young virgin. The lad's name was Ikeme-funa, whose sad story is still told in Umuofia unto this day.

The elders, or *ndichie,* met to hear a report of Okonkwo's mission. At the end they decided, as everybody knew they would, that the girl should go to Ogbuefi Udo to replace his murdered wife. As for the boy, he belonged to the clan as a whole, and there was no hurry to decide his fate. Okonkwo was, therefore, asked on behalf of the clan to look after him in the interim. And so for three years Ikemefuna lived in Okonkwo's household.

Okonkwo ruled his household with a heavy hand. His wives, especially the youngest, lived in perpetual fear of his fiery temper, and so did his little children. Perhaps down in his heart Okonkwo was not a cruel man. But his whole life was dominated by fear, the fear of failure and of weakness. It was deeper and more intimate than the fear of evil and capricious gods and of magic, the fear of the forest, and the forces of nature, malevolent, red in tooth and claw. Okonkwo's fear was greater than these. It was not external but lay deep within himself. It was the fear of himself, lest he should be found to resemble his father. Even as a little boy he had resented his father's failure and weakness, and even now he still remembered how he had suffered when a playmate had told him that his father was *agbala*. That was how Okonkwo first came to know that *agbala* was not only another name for a woman, it could also mean a man who had taken no title. And so Okonkwo was ruled by one passion—to hate everything that his father Unoka had loved. One of those things was gentleness and another was idleness.

During the planting season Okonkwo worked daily on his farms from cock-crow until the chickens went to roost. He was a very strong man and rarely felt fatigue. But his wives and young children were not as strong, and so they suffered. But they dared not complain openly. Okonkwo's first son, Nwoye, was then twelve years old but was already causing his father great anxiety for his incipient laziness. At any rate, that was how it looked to his father, and he sought to correct him by constant nagging and beating. And so Nwoye was developing into a sad-faced youth.

Okonkwo's prosperity was visible in his household. He had a large compound enclosed by a thick wall of red earth. His own hut, or *obi,* stood immediately behind the only gate in the red walls. Each of his three wives had her own hut, which together formed a half moon behind the *obi.* The barn was built against one end of the red walls, and long stacks of yam stood out prosperously in it. At the opposite end of the compound was a shed for the goats, and each wife built a small attachment to her hut for the hens. Near the barn was a small house, the "medicine house" or shrine where Okonkwo kept the wooden symbols of his personal god and of his ancestral spirits. He worshipped them with sacrifices of kola nut, food and palm-wine, and offered prayers to them on behalf of himself, his three wives and eight children.

So when the daughter of Umuofia was killed in Mbaino, Ikemefuna came into Okonkwo's household. When Okonkwo brought him home that day he called his most senior wife and handed him over to her.

"He belongs to the clan," he told her. "So look after him."

"Is he staying long with us?" she asked.

"Do what you are told, woman," Okonkwo thundered, and stammered. "When did you become one of the *ndichie* of Umuofia?"

And so Nwoye's mother took Ikemefuna to her hut and asked no more questions.

As for the boy himself, he was terribly afraid. He could not understand what was happening to him or what he had done. How could he know that his father had taken a hand in killing a daughter of Umuofia? All he knew was that a few men had arrived at their house, conversing with his father in low tones, and at the end he had been taken out and handed over to a stranger. His mother had wept bitterly, but he had been too surprised to weep. And so the stranger had brought him, and a girl, a long, long way from home, through lonely forest paths. He did not know who the girl was, and he never saw her again.

Chapter 3

Okonkwo did not have the start in life which many young men usually had. He did not inherit a barn from his father. There was no barn to inherit. The story was told in Umuofia of how his father, Unoka, had gone to consult the Oracle of the Hills and the Caves to find out why he always had a miserable harvest.

The Oracle was called Agbala, and people came from far and near to consult it. They came when misfortune dogged their steps or when they had a dispute with their neighbours. They came to discover what the future held for them or to consult the spirits of their departed fathers.

The way into the shrine was a round hole at the side of a hill, just a little bigger than the round opening into a hen-house. Worshippers and those who came to seek knowledge from the god crawled on their belly through the hole and found themselves in a dark, endless space in the presence of Agbala. No one had ever beheld Agbala, except his priestess. But no one who had ever crawled into his awful shrine had come out without the fear of his power. His priestess stood by the sacred fire which she built in the heart of the cave and proclaimed the will of the god. The fire did not burn with a flame. The glowing logs only served to light up vaguely the dark figure of the priestess.

Sometimes a man came to consult the spirit of his dead father or relative. It was said that when such a spirit appeared, the man saw it vaguely in the darkness, but never heard its voice. Some people even said that they had heard the spirits flying and flapping their wings against the roof of the cave.

Many years ago when Okonkwo was still a boy his father, Unoka, had gone to consult Agbala. The priestess in those days was a woman called Chika. She was full of the power of her god, and she was greatly feared. Unoka stood before her and began his story.

"Every year," he said sadly, "before I put any crop in the earth, I sacrifice a cock to Ani, the owner of all land. It is the law of our fathers. I also kill a cock at the shrine of Ifejioku, the god of yams. I clear the bush and set fire to it when it is dry. I sow the yams when the first rain has fallen, and stake them when the young tendrils appear. I weed—"

"Hold your peace!" screamed the priestess, her voice terrible as it echoed through the dark void. "You have offended neither the gods nor your fathers. And when a man is at peace with his gods and his ancestors, his harvest will be good or bad according to the strength of his arm. You, Unoka, are known in all the clan for the weakness of your matchet and your hoe. When your neighbours go out with their axe to cut down virgin forests, you sow your yams on exhausted farms that take no labour to clear. They cross seven rivers to make their farms; you stay at home and offer sacrifices to a reluctant soil. Go home and work like a man."

Unoka was an ill-fated man. He had a bad *chi* or personal god, and evil fortune followed him to the grave, or rather to his death, for he had no grave. He died of the swelling which was an abomination to the earth goddess. When a man was afflicted with swelling in the stomach and the limbs he was not allowed to die in the house. He was carried to the Evil Forest and left there to die. There was a story of a very stubborn man who staggered back to his house and had to be carried again to the forest and tied to a tree. The sickness was an abomination to the earth, and so the victim could not be buried in her bowels. He died and rotted away above the earth, and was not given the first or the second burial. Such was Unoka's fate. When they carried him away, he took with him his flute.

With a father like Unoka, Okonkwo did not have the start in life which many young men had. He neither inherited a barn nor a title, nor even a young wife. But in spite of these disadvantages, he had begun even in his father's lifetime to lay the foundations of a prosperous future. It was slow and painful. But he threw himself into it like one possessed. And indeed he was possessed by the fear of his father's contemptible life and shameful death.

There was a wealthy man in Okonkwo's village who had three huge barns, nine wives and thirty children. His name was Nwakibie and he had taken the highest but one title which a man could take in the clan. It was for this man that Okonkwo worked to earn his first seed yams.

He took a pot of palm-wine and a cock of Nwakibie. Two elderly neighbours were sent for, and Nwakibie's two grown-up sons were also present in his *obi*. He presented a kola nut and an alligator pepper, which was passed round for all to see and then returned to him. He broke it, saying: "We shall all live. We pray for life, children, a good harvest and happiness. You will have what is good for you and I will have what is good for me. Let the kite perch and let the eagle perch too. If one says no to the other, let his wing break."

After the kola nut had been eaten Okonkwo brought his palm-wine from the corner of the hut where it had been placed and stood it in the centre of the group. He addressed Nwakibie, calling him "Our father."

"*Nna ayi,*" he said. "I have brought you this little kola. As our people say, a man who pays respect to the great paves the way for his own greatness. I have come to pay you my respects and also to ask a favour. But let us drink the wine first."

Everybody thanked Okonkwo and the neighbours brought out their drinking horns from the goatskin bags they carried. Nwakibie brought down his own horn, which was fastened to the rafters. The younger of his sons, who was also the youngest man in the group, moved to the centre, raised the pot on his left knee and began to pour out the wine. The first cup went to Okonkwo, who must taste his wine before anyone else. Then the group drank, beginning with the eldest man. When everyone had drunk two or three horns, Nwakibie sent for his wives. Some of them were not at home and only four came in.

"Is Anasi not in?" he asked them. They said she was coming. Anasi was the first wife and the others could not drink before her, and so they stood waiting.

Anasi was a middle-aged woman, tall and strongly built. There was authority in her bearing and she looked every inch the ruler of the womenfolk in a large and prosperous family. She wore the anklet of her husband's titles, which the first wife alone could wear.

She walked up to her husband and accepted the horn from him. She then went down on one knee, drank a little and handed back the horn. She rose, called him by his name and went back to her hut. The other wives drank in the same way, in their proper order, and went away.

The men then continued their drinking and talking. Ogbuefi Idigo was talking about the palm-wine tapper, Obiako, who suddenly gave up his trade.

"There must be something behind it," he said, wiping the foam of wine from his moustache with the back of his left hand. "There must be a reason for it. A toad does not run in the daytime for nothing."

"Some people say the Oracle warned him that he would fall off a palm tree and kill himself," said Akukalia.

"Obiako has always been a strange one," said Nwakibie. "I have heard that many years ago, when his father had not been dead very long, he had gone to consult the Oracle. The Oracle said to him, 'Your dead father wants you to sacrifice a goat to him.' Do you know what he told the Oracle? He said, 'Ask my dead father if he ever had a fowl when he was alive.'" Everybody laughed heartily except Okonkwo, who laughed uneasily because as the saying goes, an old woman is always uneasy when dry bones are mentioned in a proverb. Okonkwo remembered his own father.

At last the young man who was pouring out the wine held up half a horn of the thick, white dregs and said, "What we are eating is finished." "We have seen it," the others replied. "Who will drink the dregs?" he asked. "Whoever has a job in hand," said Idigo, looking at Nwakibie's elder son, Igwelo, with a mischievous twinkle in his eye.

Everybody agreed that Igwelo should drink the dregs. He accepted the half-full horn from his brother and drank it. As Idigo had said, Igwelo had a job in hand because he had married his first wife a month or two before. The thick dregs of palm-wine were supposed to be good for men who were going in to their wives.

After the wine had been drunk Okonkwo laid his difficulties before Nwakibie.

"I have come to you for help," he said. "Perhaps you can already guess what it is. I have cleared a farm but have no yams to sow. I know what it is to ask a man to trust another with his yams, especially these days when young men are afraid of hard work. I am not afraid of work. The lizard that jumped from the high iroko tree to the ground said he would praise himself if no one else did. I began to fend for myself at an age when most people still suck at their mothers' breasts. If you give me some yam seeds I shall not fail you."

Nwakibie cleared his throat. "It pleases me to see a young man like you these days when our youth have gone so soft. Many young men have come to me to ask for yams but I have refused because I knew they would just dump them in the earth and leave them to be choked by weeds. When I say no to them they think I am hardhearted. But it is not so. Eneke the bird says that since men have learnt to shoot without missing, he has learnt to fly without perching. I have learnt to be stingy with my yams. But I can trust you. I know it as I look at you. As our fathers said, you can tell a ripe corn by its look. I shall give you twice four hundred yams. Go ahead and prepare your farm."

Okonkwo thanked him again and again and went home feeling happy. He knew that Nwakibie would not refuse him, but he had not expected he would be so generous. He had not hoped to get more than four hundred seeds. He would now have to make a bigger farm. He hoped to get another four hundred yams from one of his father's friends at Isiuzo.

Share-cropping was a very slow way of building up a barn of one's own. After all the toil one only got a third of the harvest. But for a young man whose father had no yams, there was no other way. And what made it worse in Okonkwo's case was that he had to support his mother and two sisters from his meagre harvest. And supporting his mother also meant supporting his father. She could not be expected to cook and eat while her husband starved. And so at a very early age when he was striving desperately to build a barn through sharecropping Okonkwo was also fending for his father's house. It was like pouring grains of corn into a bag full of holes. His mother and sisters worked hard enough, but they grew women's crops, like coco-yams, beans and cassava. Yam, the king of crops, was a man's crop.

The year that Okonkwo took eight hundred seed-yams from Nwakibie was the worst year in living memory. Nothing happened at its proper time; it was either too early or too late. It seemed as if the world had gone mad. The first rains were late, and, when they came, lasted only a brief moment. The blazing sun returned, more fierce than it had ever been known, and scorched all the green that had appeared with the rains. The earth burned like hot coals and roasted all the yams that had been sown. Like all good farmers, Okonkwo had begun to sow with the first rains. He had sown four hundred seeds when the rains dried up and the heat returned. He watched the sky all day for signs of rain-clouds and lay awake all night. In the morning he went back to his farm and saw the withering tendrils. He had tried to protect them from the smouldering earth by making rings of thick sisal leaves around them. But by the end of the day the sisal rings were burnt dry and grey. He changed them every day, and prayed that the rain might fall in the night. But the drought continued for eight market weeks and the yams were killed.

Some farmers had not planted their yams yet. They were the lazy easy-going ones who always put off clearing their farms as long as they could. This year they were the wise ones. They sympathised with their neighbours with much shaking of the head, but inwardly they were happy for what they took to be their own foresight.

Okonkwo planted what was left of his seed-yams when the rains finally returned. He had one consolation. The yams he had sown before the drought were his own, the harvest of the previous year. He still had the eight hundred from Nwakibie and the four hundred from his father's friend. So he would make a fresh start.

But the year had gone mad. Rain fell as it had never fallen before. For days and nights together it poured down in violent torrents, and washed away the yam heaps. Trees were uprooted and deep gorges appeared everywhere. Then the rain became less violent. But it went on from day to day without a pause. The spell of sunshine which always came in the middle of the wet season did not appear. The yams put on luxuriant green leaves, but every farmer knew that without sunshine the tubers would not grow.

That year the harvest was sad, like a funeral, and many farmers wept as they dug up the miserable and rotting yams. One man tied his cloth to a tree branch and hanged himself.

Okonkwo remembered that tragic year with a cold shiver throughout the rest of his life. It always surprised him when he thought of it later that he did not sink under the load of despair. He knew he was a fierce fighter, but that year had been enough to break the heart of a lion.

"Since I survived that year," he always said, "I shall survive anything." He put it down to his inflexible will.

His father, Unoka, who was then an ailing man, had said to him during that terrible harvest month: "Do not despair. I know you will not despair. You have a manly and a proud heart. A proud heart can survive a general failure because such a failure does not prick its pride. It is more difficult and more bitter when a man fails *alone.*"

Unoka was like that in his last days. His love of talk had grown with age and sickness. It tried Okonkwo's patience beyond words.

Chapter 4

"Looking at a king's mouth," said an old man, "one would think he never sucked at his mother's breast." He was talking about Okonkwo, who had risen so suddenly from great poverty and misfortune to be one of the lords of the clan. The old man bore no ill-will towards Okonkwo. Indeed he respected him for his industry and success. But he was struck, as most people were, by Okonkwo's brusqueness in dealing with less successful men. Only a week ago a man had contradicted him at a kindred meeting which they held to discuss the next ancestral feast. Without looking at the man Okonkwo had said: "This meeting is for men." The man who had contradicted him had no titles. That was why he had called him a woman. Okonkwo knew how to kill a man's spirit.

Everybody at the kindred meeting took sides with Osugo when Okonkwo called him a woman. The oldest man present said sternly that those whose palm-kernels were cracked for them by a benevolent spirit should not forget to be humble. Okonkwo said he was sorry for what he had said, and the meeting continued.

But it was really not true that Okonkwo's palm-kernels had been cracked for him by a benevolent spirit. He had cracked them himself. Anyone who knew his grim struggle against poverty and misfortune could not say he had been lucky. If ever a man deserved his success, that man was Okonkwo. At an early age he had achieved fame as the greatest wrestler in all the land. That was not luck. At the most one could say that his *chi* or personal god was good. But the Ibo people have a proverb that when a man says yes his *chi* says yes also. Okonkwo said yes very strongly; so his *chi* agreed. And not only his *chi* but his clan too, because it judged a man by the work of his hands. That was why Okonkwo had been chosen by the nine villages to carry a message of war to their enemies unless they agreed to give up a young man and a virgin to atone for the murder of Udo's wife. And such was the deep fear that their enemies had for Umuofia that they treated Okonkwo like a king and brought him a virgin who was given to Udo as wife, and the lad Ikemefuna.

The elders of the clan had decided that Ikemefuna should be in Okonkwo's care for a while. But no one thought it would be as long as three years. They seemed to forget all about him as soon as they had taken the decision.

At first Ikemefuna was very much afraid. Once or twice he tried to run away, but he did not know where to begin. He thought of his mother and his three-year-old sister and wept bitterly. Nwoye's mother was very kind to him and treated him as one of her own children. But all he said was: "When shall I go home?" When Okonkwo heard that he would not eat any food he came into the hut with a big stick in his hand and stood over him while he swallowed his yams, trembling. A few moments later he went behind the hut and began to vomit painfully. Nwoye's mother went to him and placed her hands on his chest and on his back. He was ill for three market weeks, and when he recovered he seemed to have overcome his great fear and sadness.

He was by nature a very lively boy and he gradually became popular in Okonkwo's household, especially with the children. Okonkwo's son, Nwoye, who was two years younger, became quite inseparable from him because he seemed to know everything. He could fashion out flutes from bamboo stems and even from the elephant grass. He knew the names of all the birds and could set clever traps for the little bush rodents. And he knew which trees made the strongest bows.

Even Okonkwo himself became very fond of the boy—inwardly of course. Okonkwo never showed any emotion openly, unless it be the emotion of anger. To show affection was a sign of weakness; the only thing worth demonstrating was strength. He therefore treated Ikemefuna as he treated everybody else—with a heavy hand. But there was no doubt that he liked the boy. Sometimes when he went to big village meetings or communal ancestral feasts he allowed Ikemefuna to accompany him, like a son, carrying his stool and his goatskin bag. And, indeed, Ikemefuna called him father.

Ikemefuna came to Umuofia at the end of the carefree season between harvest and planting. In fact he recovered from his illness only a few days before the Week of Peace began. And that was also the year Okonkwo broke the peace, and was punished, as was the custom, by Ezeani, the priest of the earth goddess.

Okonkwo was provoked to justifiable anger by his youngest wife, who went to plait her hair at her friend's house and did not return early enough to cook the afternoon meal. Okonkwo did not know at first that she was not at home. After waiting in vain for the dish he went to her hut to see what she was doing. There was nobody in the hut and the fireplace was cold.

"Where is Ojiugo?" he asked his second wife, who came out of her hut to draw water from the gigantic pot in the shade of a small tree in the middle of the compound.

"She has gone to plait her hair."

Okonkwo bit his lips as anger welled up within him.

"Where are her children? Did she take them?" he asked with unusual coolness and restraint.

"They are here," answered his first wife, Nwoye's mother. Okonkwo bent down and looked into her hut. Ojiugo's children were eating with the children of his first wife.

"Did she ask you to feed them before she went?"

"Yes," lied Nwoye's mother, trying to minimise Ojiugo's thoughtlessness.

Okonkwo knew she was not speaking the truth. He walked back to his *obi* to wait Ojiugo's return. And when she returned he beat her very heavily. In his anger he had forgotten that it was the Week of Peace. His first two wives ran out in great alarm pleading with him that it was the sacred week. But Okonkwo was not the man to stop beating somebody half-way through, not even for fear of a goddess.

Okonkwo's neighbours heard his wife crying and sent their voices over the compound walls to ask what was the matter. Some of them came over to see for themselves. It was unheard of to beat somebody during the sacred week.

Before it was dusk Ezeani, who was the priest of the earth goddess, Ani, called on Okonkwo in his *obi*. Okonkwo brought out kola nut and placed it before the priest.

"Take away your kola nut. I shall not eat in the house of a man who has no respect for our gods and ancestors."

Okonkwo tried to explain to him what his wife had done, but Ezeani seemed to pay no attention. He held a short staff in his hand which he brought down on the floor to emphasize his points.

"Listen to me," he said when Okonkwo had spoken. "You are not a stranger in Umuofia. You know as well as I do that our forefathers ordained that before we plant any crops in the earth we should observe a week in which a man does not say a harsh word to his neighbour. We live in peace with our fellows to honour our great goddess of the earth without whose blessing our crops will not grow. You have committed a great evil." He brought down his staff heavily on the floor. "You wife was at fault, but even if you came into your *obi* and found her lover on top of her, you would still have committed a great evil to beat her." His staff came down again. "The evil you have done can ruin the whole clan. The earth goddess whom you have insulted may refuse to give us her increase, and we shall all perish." His tone now changed from anger to command. "You will bring to the shrine of Ani tomorrow one she-goat, one hen, a length of cloth and a hundred cowries." He rose and left the hut.

Okonkwo did as the priest said. He also took with him a pot of palm-wine. Inwardly, he was repentant. But he was not the man to go about telling his neighbours that he was in error. And so people said he had no respect for the gods of the clan. His enemies said his good fortune had gone to his head. They called him the little bird *nza* who so far forgot himself after a heavy meal that he challenged his *chi*.

No work was done during the Week of Peace. People called on their neighbours and drank palm-wine. This year they talked of nothing else but the *nso-ani* which Okonkwo had committed. It was the first time for many years that a man had broken the sacred peace. Even the oldest men could only remember one or two other occasions somewhere in the dim past.

Ogbuefi Ezeudu, who was the oldest man in the village, was telling two other men who came to visit him that the punishment for breaking the Peace of Ani had become very mild in their clan.

"It has not always been so," he said. "My father told me that he had been told that in the past a man who broke the peace was dragged on the ground through the village until he died. But after a while this custom was stopped because it spoilt the peace which it was meant to preserve."

"Somebody told me yesterday," said one of the younger men, "that in some clans it is an abomination for a man to die during the Week of Peace."

"It is indeed true," said Ogbuefi Ezeudu. "They have that custom in Obodoani. If a man dies at this time he is not buried but cast into the Evil Forest. It is a bad custom which these people observe because they lack understanding. They throw away large numbers of men and women without burial. And what is the result? Their clan is full of the evil spirits of these unburied dead, hungry to do harm to the living."

After the Week of Peace every man and his family began to clear the bush to make new farms. The cut bush was left to dry and fire was then set to it. As the smoke rose into the sky kites appeared from different directions and hovered over the burning field in silent valediction. The rainy season was approaching when they would go away until the dry season returned.

Okonkwo spent the next few days preparing his seed-yams. He looked at each yam carefully to see whether it was good for sowing. Sometimes he decided that a yam was too big to be sown as one seed and he split it deftly along its length with his sharp knife. His eldest son, Nwoye, and Ikemefuna helped him by fetching the yams in long baskets from the barn and in counting the prepared seeds in groups of four hundred. Sometimes Okonkwo gave them a few yams each to prepare. But he always found fault with their effort, and he said so with much threatening.

"Do you think you are cutting up yams for cooking?" he asked Nwoye. "If you split another yam of this size, I shall break your jaw. You think you are still a child. I began to own a farm at your age. And you," he said to Ikemefuna, "do you not grow yams where you come from?"

Inwardly Okonkwo knew that the boys were still too young to understand fully the difficult art of preparing seed-yams. But he thought that one could not begin too early. Yam stood for manliness, and he who could feed his family on yams from one harvest to another was a very great man indeed. Okonkwo wanted his son to be a great farmer and a great man. He would stamp out the disquieting signs of laziness which he thought he already saw in him.

"I will not have a son who cannot hold up his head in the gathering of the clan. I would sooner strangle him with my own hands. And if you stand staring at me like that," he swore, "Amadiora will break your head for you!"

Some days later, when the land had been moistened by two or three heavy rains, Okonkwo and his family went to the farm with baskets of seed-yams, their hoes and matchets, and the planting began. They made single mounds of earth in straight lines all over the field and sowed the yams in them.

Yam, the king of crops, was a very exacting king. For three or four moons it demanded hard work and constant attention from cockcrow till the chickens went back to roost. The young tendrils were protected from earth-heat with rings of sisal leaves. As the rains became heavier the women planted maize, melons and beans between the yam mounds. The yams were then staked, first with little sticks and later with tall and big tree branches. The women weeded the farm three times at definite periods in the life of the yams, neither early nor late.

And now the rains had really come, so heavy and persistent that even the village rain-maker no longer claimed to be able to intervene. He could not stop the rain now, just as he would not attempt to start it in the heart of the dry season, without serious danger to his own health. The personal dynamism required to counter the forces of these extremes of weather would be far too great for the human frame.

And so nature was not interfered with in the middle of the rainy season. Sometimes it poured down in such thick sheets of water that earth and sky seemed merged in one grey wetness. It was then uncertain whether the low rumbling of Amadiora's thunder came from above or below. At such times, in each of the countless thatched huts of Umuofia, children sat around their mother's cooking fire telling stories, or with their father in his *obi* warming themselves from a log fire, roasting and eating maize. It was a brief resting period between the exacting and arduous planting season and the equally exacting but light-hearted month of harvests.

Ikemefuna had begun to feel like a member of Okonkwo's family. He still thought about his mother and his three-year-old sister, and he had moments of sadness and depression. But he and Nwoye had become so deeply attached to each other that such moments became less frequent and less poignant. Ikemefuna had an endless stock of folk tales. Even those which Nwoye knew already were told with a new freshness and the local flavour of a different clan. Nwoye remembered this period very vividly till the end of his life. He even remembered how he had laughed when Ikemefuna told him that the proper name for a corn-cob with only a few scattered grains was *ezeagadi-nwayi,* or the teeth of an old woman. Nwoye's mind had gone immediately to Nwayieke, who lived near the udala tree. She had about three teeth and was always smoking her pipe.

Gradually the rains became lighter and less frequent, and earth and sky once again became separate. The rain fell in thin, slanting showers through sunshine and quiet breeze. Children no longer stayed indoors but ran about singing:

> *"The rain is falling, the sun is shining,*
> *Alone Nnadi is cooking and eating."*

Nwoye always wondered who Nnadi was and why he should live all by himself, cooking and eating. In the end he decided that Nnadi must live in that land of Ikemefuna's favourite story where the ant holds his court in splendour and the sands dance for ever.

Chapter 5

The Feast of the New Yam was approaching and Umuofia was in a festival mood. It was an occasion for giving thanks to Ani, the earth goddess and the source of all fertility. Ani played a greater part in the life of the people than any other deity. She was the ultimate judge of morality and conduct. And what was more, she was in close communion with the departed fathers of the clan whose bodies had been committed to earth.

The Feast of the New Yam was held every year before the harvest began, to honour the earth goddess and the ancestral spirits of the clan. New yams could not be eaten until some had first been offered to these powers. Men and women, young and old, looked forward to the New Yam Festival because it began the season of plenty— the new year. On the last night before the festival, yams of the old year were all disposed of by those who still had them. The new year must begin with tasty, fresh yams and not the shrivelled and fibrous crop of the previous year. All cooking-pots, calabashes and wooden bowls were thoroughly washed, especially the wooden mortar in which yam was pounded. Yam foo-foo and vegetable soup was the chief food in the celebration. So much of it was cooked that, no matter how heavily the family ate or how many friends and relations they invited from neighbouring villages, there was always a huge quantity of food left over at the end of the day. The story was always told of a wealthy man who set before his guests a mount of foo-foo so high that those who sat on one side could not see what was happening on the other, and it was not until late in the evening that one of them saw for the first time his in-law who had arrived during the course of the meal and had fallen to on the opposite side. It was only then that they exchanged greetings and shook hands over what was left of the food.

The New Yam Festival was thus an occasion for joy throughout Umuofia. And every man whose arm was strong, as the Ibo people say, was expected to invite large numbers of guests from far and wide. Okonkwo always asked his wives' relations, and since he now had three wives his guests would make a fairly big crowd.

But somehow Okonkwo could never become as enthusiastic over feasts as most people. He was a good eater and he could drink one or two fairly big gourds of palm-wine. But he was always uncomfortable sitting around for days waiting for a feast or getting over it. He would be very much happier working on his farm.

The festival was now only three days away. Okonkwo's wives had scrubbed the walls and the huts with red earth until they reflected light. They had then drawn patterns on them in white, yellow and dark green. They then set about painting themselves with cam wood and drawing beautiful black patterns on their stomachs and on their backs. The children were also decorated, especially their hair, which was shaved in beautiful patterns. The three women talked excitedly about the relations who had been invited, and the children revelled in the thought of being spoilt by these visitors from mother-land. Ikemefuna was equally excited. The New Yam Festival seemed to him to be a much bigger event here than in his own village, a place which was already becoming remote and vague in his imagination.

And then the storm burst. Okonkwo, who had been walking about aimlessly in his compound in suppressed anger, suddenly found an outlet.

"Who killed this banana tree?" he asked.

A hush fell on the compound immediately.

"Who killed this tree? Or are you all deaf and dumb?"

As a matter of fact the tree was very much alive. Okonkwo's second wife had merely cut a few leaves off it to wrap some food, and she said so. Without further argument Okonkwo gave her a sound beating and left her and her only daughter weeping. Neither of the other wives dared to interfere beyond an occasional and tentative, "It is enough, Okonkwo," pleaded from a reasonable distance.

His anger thus satisfied, Okonkwo decided to go out hunting. He had an old rusty gun made by a clever blacksmith who had come to live in Umuofia long ago. But although Okonkwo was a great man whose prowess was universally acknowledged, he was not a hunter. In fact he had not killed a rat with his gun. And so when he called Ikemefuna to fetch his gun, the wife who had just been beaten murmured something about guns that never shot. Unfortunately for her, Okonkwo heard it and ran madly into his room for the loaded gun, ran out again and aimed at her as she clambered over the dwarf wall of the barn. He pressed the trigger and there was a loud report accompanied by the wail of his wives and children. He threw down the gun and jumped into the barn, and there lay the woman, very much shaken and frightened but quite unhurt. He heaved a heavy sigh and went away with the gun.

In spite of this incident the New Yam Festival was celebrated with great joy in Okonkwo's household. Early that morning as he offered a sacrifice of new yam and palm-oil to his ancestors he asked them to protect him, his children and their mothers in the new year.

As the day wore on his in-laws arrived from three surrounding villages, and each party brought with them a huge pot of palm-wine. And there was eating and drinking till night, when Okonkwo's in-laws began to leave for their homes.

The second day of the new year was the day of the great wrestling match between Okonkwo's village and their neighbours. It was difficult to say which the people enjoyed more—the feasting and fellowship of the first day or the wrestling contest of the second. But there was one woman who had no doubt whatever in her mind. She was Okonkwo's second wife, Ekwefi, whom he nearly shot. There was no festival in all the seasons of the year which gave her as much pleasure as the wrestling match. Many years ago when she was the village beauty Okonkwo had won her heart by throwing the Cat in the greatest contest within living memory. She did not marry him because he was too poor to pay her bride-price. But a few years later she ran away from her husband and came to live with Okonkwo. All this happened many years ago. Now Ekwefi was a woman of forty-five who had suffered a great deal in her time. But her love of wrestling contests was still as strong as it was thirty years ago.

It was not yet noon on the second day of the New Yam Festival. Ekwefi and her only daughter, Ezinma, sat near the fireplace waiting for the water in the pot to boil. The fowl Ekwefi had just killed was in the wooden mortar. The water began to boil, and in one deft movement she lifted the pot from the fire and poured the boiling water on to the fowl. She put back the empty pot on the circular pad in the corner, and looked at her palms, which were black with soot. Ezinma was always surprised that her mother could lift a pot from the fire with her bare hands.

"Ekwefi," she said, "is it true that when people are grown up, fire does not burn them?" Ezinma, unlike most children, called her mother by her name.

"Yes," replied Ekwefi, too busy to argue. Her daughter was only ten years old but she was wiser than her years.

"But Nwoye's mother dropped her pot of hot soup the other day and it broke on the floor."

Ekwefi turned the hen over in the mortar and began to pluck the feathers.

"Ekwefi," said Ezinma, who had joined in plucking the feathers, "my eyelid is twitching."

"It means you are going to cry," said her mother.

"No," Ezinma said, "it is this eyelid, the top one."

"That means you will see something."

"What will I see?" she asked.

"How can I know?" Ekwefi wanted her to work it out herself.

"Oho," said Ezinma at last. "I know what it is—the wrestling match."

At last the hen was plucked clean. Ekwefi tried to pull out the horny beak but it was too hard. She turned round on her low stool and put the beak in the fire for a few moments. She pulled again and it came off.

"Ekwefi!" a voice called from one of the other huts. It was Nwoye's mother, Okonkwo's first wife.

"Is that me?" Ekwefi called back. That was the way people answered calls from outside. They never answered yes for fear it might be an evil spirit calling.

"Will you give Ezinma some fire to bring to me?" Her own children and Ikeme-funa had gone to the stream.

Ekwefi put a few live coals into a piece of broken pot and Ezinma carried it across the clean-swept compound to Nwoye's mother.

"Thank you, Nma," she said. She was peeling new yams, and in a basket beside her were green vegetables and beans.

"Let me make the fire for you," Ezinma offered.

"Thank you, Ezigbo," she said. She often called her Ezigbo, which means "the good one."

Ezinma went outside and brought some sticks from a huge bundle of firewood. She broke them into little pieces across the sole of her foot and began to build a fire, blowing it with her breath.

"You will blow your eyes out," said Nwoye's mother, looking up from the yams she was peeling. "Use the fan." She stood up and pulled out the fan which was fastened into one of the rafters. As soon as she got up, the troublesome nanny-goat, which had been dutifully eating yam peelings, dug her teeth into the real thing, scooped out two mouthfuls and fled from the hut to chew the cud in the goats' shed. Nwoye's mother swore at her and settled down again to her peeling. Ezinma's fire was now sending up thick clouds of smoke. She went on fanning it until it burst into flames. Nwoye's mother thanked her and she went back to her mother's hut.

Just then the distant beating of drums began to reach them. It came from the direction of the *ilo,* the village playground. Every village had its own *ilo* which was as old as the village itself and where all the great ceremonies and dances took place. The drums beat the unmistakable wrestling dance—quick, light and gay, and it came floating on the wind.

Okonkwo cleared his throat and moved his feet to the beat of the drums. It filled him with fire as it had always done from his youth. He trembled with the desire to conquer and subdue. It was like the desire for woman.

"We shall be late for the wrestling," said Ezinma to her mother.

"They will not begin until the sun goes down."

"But they are beating the drums."

"Yes. The drums begin at noon but the wrestling waits until the sun begins to sink. Go and see if your father has brought out yams for the afternoon."

"He has. Nwoye's mother is already cooking."

"Go and bring our own, then. We must cook quickly or we shall be late for the wrestling."

Ezinma ran in the direction of the barn and brought back two yams from the dwarf wall.

Ekwefi peeled the yams quickly. The troublesome nanny-goat sniffed about, eating the peelings. She cut the yams into small pieces and began to prepare a pottage, using some of the chicken.

At that moment they heard someone crying just outside their compound. It was very much like Obiageli, Nwoye's sister.

"Is that not Obiageli weeping?" Ekwefi called across the yard to Nwoye's mother.

"Yes," she replied. "She must have broken her water-pot."

The weeping was now quite close and soon the children filed in, carrying on their heads various sizes of pots suitable to their years. Ikemefuna came first with the biggest pot, closely followed by Nwoye and his two younger brothers. Obiageli brought up the rear, her face streaming with tears. In her hand was the cloth pad on which the pot should have rested on her head.

"What happened?" her mother asked, and Obiageli told her mournful story. Her mother consoled her and promised to buy her another pot.

Nwoye's younger brothers were about to tell their mother the true story of the accident when Ikemefuna looked at them sternly and they held their peace. The fact was that Obiageli had been making *inyanga* with her pot. She had balanced it on her head, folded her arms in front of her and began to sway her waist like a grown-up young lady. When the pot fell down and broke she burst out laughing. She only began to weep when they got near the iroko tree outside their compound.

The drums were still beating, persistent and unchanging. Their sound was no longer a separate thing from the living village. It was like the pulsation of its heart. It throbbed in the air, in the sunshine, and even in the trees, and filled the village with excitement.

Ekwefi ladled her husband's share of the pottage into a bowl and covered it. Ezinma took it to him in his *obi*.

Okonkwo was sitting on a goatskin already eating his first wife's meal. Obiageli, who had brought it from her mother's hut, sat on the floor waiting for him to finish. Ezinma placed her mother's dish before him and sat with Obiageli.

"Sit like a woman!" Okonkwo shouted at her. Ezinma brought her two legs together and stretched them in front of her.

"Father, will you go to see the wrestling?" Ezinma asked after a suitable interval.

"Yes," he answered. "Will you go?"

"Yes." And after a pause she said: "Can I bring your chair for you?"

"No, that is a boy's job." Okonkwo was specially fond of Ezinma. She looked very much like her mother, who was once the village beauty. But his fondness only showed on very rare occasions.

"Obiageli broke her pot today," Ezinma said.

"Yes, she has told me about it," Okonkwo said between mouthfuls.

"Father," said Obiageli, "people should not talk when they are eating or pepper may go down the wrong way."

"That is very true. Do you hear that, Ezinma? You are older than Obiageli but she has more sense."

He uncovered his second wife's dish and began to eat from it. Obiageli took the first dish and returned to her mother's hut. And then Nkechi came in, bringing the third dish. Nkechi was the daughter of Okonkwo's third wife.

In the distance the drums continued to beat.

Chapter 6

The whole village turned out on the *ilo*, men, women and children. They stood round in a huge circle leaving the centre of the playground free. The elders and grandees of the village sat on their own stools brought there by their young sons or slaves. Okonkwo was among them. All others stood except those who came early enough to secure places on the few stands which had been built by placing smooth logs on forked pillars.

The wrestlers were not there yet and the drummers held the field. They too sat just in front of the huge circle of spectators, facing the elders. Behind them was the big and ancient silk-cotton tree which was sacred. Spirits of good children lived in that tree waiting to be born. On ordinary days young women who desired children came to sit under its shade.

There were seven drums and they were arranged according to their sizes in a long wooden basket. Three men beat them with sticks, working feverishly from one drum to another. They were possessed by the spirit of the drums.

The young men who kept order on these occasions dashed about, consulting among themselves and with the leaders of the two wrestling teams, who were still outside the circle, behind the crowd. Once in a while two young men carrying palm fronds ran round the circle and kept the crowd back by beating the ground in front of them or, if they were stubborn, their legs and feet.

At last the two teams danced into the circle and the crowd roared and clapped. The drums rose to a frenzy. The people surged forwards. The young men who kept order flew around, waving their palm fronds. Old men nodded to the beat of the drums and remembered the days when they wrestled to its intoxicating rhythm.

The contest began with boys of fifteen or sixteen. There were only three such boys in each team. They were not the real wrestlers; they merely set the scene. Within a short time the first two bouts were over. But the third created a big sensation even among the elders who did not usually show their excitement so openly. It was as quick as the other two, perhaps even quicker. But very few people had ever seen that kind of wrestling before. As soon as the two boys closed in, one of them did something which no one could describe because it had been as quick as a flash. And the other boy was flat on his back. The crowd roared and clapped and for a while drowned the frenzied drums. Okonkwo sprang to his feet and quickly sat down again. Three young men from the victorious boy's team ran forward, carried him shoulder-high and danced through the cheering crowd. Everybody soon knew who the boy was. His name was Maduka, the son of Obierika.

The drummers stopped for a brief rest before the real matches. Their bodies shone with sweat, and they took up fans and began to fan themselves. They also drank water from small pots and ate kola nuts. They became ordinary human beings again, talking and laughing among themselves and with others who stood near them. The air, which had been stretched taut with excitement, relaxed again. It was as if water had been poured on the tightened skin of a drum. Many people looked around, perhaps for the first time, and saw those who stood or sat next to them.

"I did not know it was you," Ekwefi said to the woman who had stood shoulder to shoulder with her since the beginning of the matches.

"I do not blame you," said the woman. "I have never seen such a large crowd of people. Is it true that Okonkwo nearly killed you with his gun?"

"It is true indeed, my dear friend. I cannot yet find a mouth with which to tell the story."

"Your *chi* is very much awake, my friend. And how is my daughter, Ezinma?"

"She has been very well for some time now. Perhaps she has come to stay."

"I think she has. How old is she now?"

"She is about ten years old."

"I think she will stay. They usually stay if they do not die before the age of six."

"I pray she stays," said Ekwefi with a heavy sigh.

The woman with whom she talked was called Chielo. She was the priestess of Agbala, the Oracle of the Hills and the Caves. In ordinary life Chielo was a widow with two children. She was very friendly with Ekwefi and they shared a common shed in the market. She was particularly fond of Ekwefi's only daughter, Ezinma, whom she called "my daughter." Quite often she bought bean-cakes and gave Ekwefi some to take home to Ezinma. Anyone seeing Chielo in ordinary life would hardly believe she was the same person who prophesied when the spirit of Agbala was upon her.

The drummers took up their sticks again and the air shivered and grew tense like a tightened bow.

The two teams were ranged facing each other across the clear space. A young man from one team danced across the centre to the other side and pointed at whomever he wanted to fight. They danced back to the centre together and then closed in.

There were twelve men on each side and the challenge went from one side to the other. Two judges walked around the wrestlers and when they thought they were equally matched, stopped them. Five matches ended in this way. But the really exciting moments were when a man was thrown. The huge voice of the crowd then rose to the sky and in every direction. It was even heard in the surrounding villages.

The last match was between the leaders of the teams. They were among the best wrestlers in all the nine villages. The crowd wondered who would throw the other this year. Some said Okafo was the better man; others said he was not the equal of Ikezue. Last year neither of them had thrown the other even though the judges had allowed the contest to go on longer than was the custom. They had the same style and one saw the other's plans beforehand. It might happen again this year.

Dusk was already approaching when their contest began. The drums went mad and the crowds also. They surged forward as the two young men danced into the circle. The palm fronds were helpless in keeping them back.

Ikezue held out his right hand. Okafo seized it, and they closed in. It was a fierce contest. Ikezue strove to dig in his right heel behind Okafo so as to pitch him backwards in the clever *ege* style. But the one knew what the other was thinking. The crowd had surrounded and swallowed up the drummers, whose frantic rhythm was no longer a mere disembodied sound but the very heart-beat of the people.

The wrestlers were now almost still in each other's grip. The muscles on their arms and their thighs and on their backs stood out and twitched. It looked like an equal match. The two judges were already moving forward to separate them when Ikezue, now desperate, went down quickly on one knee in an attempt to fling his man backwards over his head. It was a sad miscalculation. Quick as the lightning of Amadiora, Okafo raised his right leg and swung it over his rival's head. The crowd burst into a thunderous roar. Okafo was swept off his feet by his supporters and carried home shoulder-high. They sang his praise and the young women clapped their hands:

> *Who will wrestle for our village?*
> *Okafo will wrestle for our village.*
> *Has he thrown a hundred men?*
> *He has thrown four hundred men.*
> *Has he thrown a hundred Cats?*
> *He has thrown four hundred Cats.*
> *Then send him word to fight for us.*

Chapter 7

For three years Ikemefuna lived in Okonkwo's household and the elders of Umuofia seemed to have forgotten about him. He grew rapidly like a yam tendril in the rainy season, and was full of the sap of life. He had become wholly absorbed into his new family. He was like an elder brother to Nwoye, and from the very first seemed to have kindled a new fire in the younger boy. He made him feel grown-up; and they no longer spent the evenings in mother's hut while she cooked, but now sat with Okonkwo in his *obi*, or watched him as he tapped his palm tree for the evening wine. Nothing pleased Nwoye now more than to be sent for by his mother or another of his father's wives to do one of those difficult and masculine tasks in the home, like splitting wood, or pounding food. On receiving such a message through a younger brother or sister, Nwoye would feign annoyance and grumble aloud about women and their troubles.

Okonkwo was inwardly pleased at his son's development, and he knew it was due to Ikemefuna. He wanted Nwoye to grow into a tough young man capable of ruling his father's household when he was dead and gone to join the ancestors. He wanted him to be a prosperous man, having enough in his barn to feed the ancestors with regular sacrifices. And so he was always happy when he heard him grumbling about women. That showed that in time he would be able to control his women-folk. No matter how prosperous a man was, if he was unable to rule his women and his children (and especially his women) he was not really a man. He was like the man in the song who had ten and one wives and not enough soup for his foo-foo.

So Okonkwo encouraged the boys to sit with him in his *obi*, and he told them stories of the land—masculine stories of violence and bloodshed. Nwoye knew that it was right to be masculine and to be violent, but somehow he still preferred the stories that his mother used to tell, and which she no doubt still told to her younger children—stories of the tortoise and his wily ways, and of the bird *eneke-nti-oba* who challenged the whole world to a wrestling contest and was finally thrown by the cat. He remembered the story she often told of the quarrel between Earth and Sky long ago, and how Sky withheld rain for seven years, until crops withered and the dead could not be buried because the hoes broke on the stony Earth. At last Vulture was sent to plead with Sky, and to soften his heart with a song of the suffering of the sons of men. Whenever Nwoye's mother sang this song he felt carried away to the distant scene in the sky where Vulture, Earth's emissary, sang for mercy. At last Sky was moved to pity, and he gave to Vulture rain wrapped in leaves of coco-yam. But as he flew home his long talon pierced the leaves and the rain fell as it had never fallen before. And so heavily did it rain on Vulture that he did not return to deliver his message but flew to a distant land, from where he had espied a fire. And when he got there he found it was a man making a sacrifice. He warmed himself in the fire and ate the entrails.

That was the kind of story that Nwoye loved. But he now knew that they were for foolish women and children, and he knew that his father wanted him to be a man. And so he feigned that he no longer cared for women's stories. And when he did this he saw that his father was pleased, and no longer rebuked him or beat him. So Nwoye and Ikemefuna would listen to Okonkwo's stories about tribal wars or how, years ago, he had stalked his victim, overpowered him and obtained his first human head. And as he told them of the past they sat in darkness or the dim glow of logs, waiting for the women to finish their cooking. When they finished, each brought her bowl of foo-foo and bowl of soup to her husband. An oil lamp was lit and Okonkwo tasted from each bowl, and then passed two shares to Nwoye and Ikemefuna.

In this way the moons and the seasons passed. And then the locusts came. It had not happened for many a long year. The elders said locusts came once in a generation, reappeared every year for seven years and then disappeared for another lifetime. They went back to their caves in a distant land, where they were guarded by a race of stunted men. And then after another lifetime these men opened the caves again and the locusts came to Umuofia.

They came in the cold harmattan season after the harvests had been gathered, and ate up all the wild grass in the fields.

Okonkwo and the two boys were working on the red outer walls of the compound. This was one of the lighter tasks of the after-harvest season. A new cover of thick palm branches and palm leaves was set on the walls to protect them from the next rainy season. Okonkwo worked on the outside of the wall and the boys worked from within. There were little holes from one side to the other in the upper levels of the wall, and through these Okonkwo passed the rope, or *tie-tie,* to the boys and they passed it round the wooden stays and then back to him; and in this way the cover was strengthened on the wall.

The women had gone to the bush to collect firewood, and the little children to visit their playmates in the neighbouring compounds. The harmattan was in the air and seemed to distil a hazy feeling of sleep on the world. Okonkwo and the boys worked in complete silence, which was only broken when a new palm frond was lifted on to the wall or when a busy hen moved dry leaves about in her ceaseless search for food.

And then quite suddenly a shadow fell on the world, and the sun seemed hidden behind a thick cloud. Okonkwo looked up from his work and wondered if it was going to rain at such an unlikely time of the year. But almost immediately a shout of joy broke out in all directions, and Umuofia, which had dozed in the noon-day haze, broke into life and activity.

"Locusts are descending," was joyfully chanted everywhere, and men, women and children left their work or their play and ran into the open to see the unfamiliar sight. The locusts had not come for many, many years, and only the old people had seen them before.

At first, a fairly small swarm came. They were the harbingers sent to survey the land. And then appeared on the horizon a slowly-moving mass like a boundless sheet of black cloud drifting towards Umuofia. Soon it covered half the sky, and the solid mass was now broken by tiny eyes of light like shining star-dust. It was a tremendous sight, full of power and beauty.

Everyone was now about, talking excitedly and praying that the locusts should camp in Umuofia for the night. For although locusts had not visited Umuofia for many years, everybody knew by instinct that they were very good to eat. And at last the locusts did descend. They settled on every tree and on every blade of grass; they settled on the roofs and covered the bare ground. Mighty tree branches broke away under them, and the whole country became the brown-earth colour of the vast, hungry swarm.

Many people went out with baskets trying to catch them, but the elders counselled patience till nightfall. And they were right. The locusts settled in the bushes for the night and their wings became wet with dew. Then all Umuofia turned out in spite of the cold harmattan, and everyone filled his bags and pots with locusts. The next morning they were roasted in clay pots and then spread in the sun until they became dry and brittle. And for many days this rare food was eaten with solid palm-oil.

Okonkwo sat in his *obi* crunching happily with Ikemefuna and Nwoye, and drinking palm-wine copiously, when Ogbuefi Ezeudu came in. Ezeudu was the oldest man in this quarter of Umuofia. He had been a great and fearless warrior in his time, and was now accorded great respect in all the clan. He refused to join in the meal, and asked Okonkwo to have a word with him outside. And so they walked out together, the old man supporting himself with his stick. When they were out of ear-shot, he said to Okonkwo:

"That boy calls you father. Do not bear a hand in his death." Okonkwo was surprised, and was about to say something when the old man continued:

"Yes, Umuofia has decided to kill him. The Oracle of the Hills and the Caves has pronounced it. They will take him outside Umuofia as is the custom, and kill him there. But I want you to have nothing to do with it. He calls you his father."

The next day a group of elders from all the nine villages of Umuofia came to Okonkwo's house early in the morning, and before they began to speak in low tones Nwoye and Ikemefuna were sent out. They did not stay very long, but when they went away Okonkwo sat still for a very long time supporting his chin in his palms. Later in the day he called Ikemefuna and told him that he was to be taken home the next day. Nwoye overheard it and burst into tears, whereupon his father beat him heavily. As for Ikemefuna, he was at a loss. His own home had gradually become very faint and distant. He still missed his mother and his sister and would be very glad to see them. But somehow he knew he was not going to see them. He remembered once when men had talked in low tones with his father; and it seemed now as if it was happening all over again.

Later, Nwoye went to his mother's hut and told her that Ikemufuna was going home. She immediately dropped the pestle with which she was grinding pepper, folded her arms across her breast and sighed, "Poor child."

The next day, the men returned with a pot of wine. They were all fully dressed as if they were going to a big clan meeting or to pay a visit to a neighbouring village. They passed their cloths under the right arm-pit, and hung their goatskin bags and sheathed matchets over their left shoulders. Okonkwo got ready quickly and the party set out with Ikemefuna carrying the pot of wine. A deathly silence descended on Okonkwo's compound. Even the very little children seemed to know. Throughout that day Nwoye sat in his mother's hut and tears stood in his eyes.

At the beginning of their journey the men of Umuofia talked and laughed about the locusts, about their women, and about some effeminate men who had refused to come with them. But as they drew near to the outskirts of Umuofia silence fell upon them too.

The sun rose slowly to the centre of the sky, and the dry, sandy footway began to throw up the heat that lay buried in it. Some birds chirruped in the forests around. The men trod dry leaves on the sand. All else was silent. Then from the distance came the faint beating of the *ekwe*. It rose and faded with the wind—a peaceful dance from a distant clan.

"It is an *ozo* dance," the men said among themselves. But no one was sure where it was coming from. Some said Ezimili, others Abame or Aninta. They argued for a short while and fell into silence again, and the elusive dance rose and fell with the wind. Somewhere a man was taking one of the titles of his clan, with music and dancing and a great feast.

The footway had now become a narrow line in the heart of the forest. The short trees and sparse undergrowth which surrounded the men's village began to give way to giant trees and climbers which perhaps had stood from the beginning of things, untouched by the axe and the bush-fire. The sun breaking through their leaves and branches threw a pattern of light and shade on the sandy footway.

Ikemefuna heard a whisper close behind him and turned round sharply. The man who had whispered now called out aloud, urging the others to hurry up.

"We still have a long way to go," he said. Then he and another man went before Ikemefuna and set a faster pace.

Thus the men of Umuofia pursued their way, armed with sheathed matchets, and Ikemefuna, carrying a pot of palm-wine on his head, walked in their midst. Although he had felt uneasy at first, he was not afraid now. Okonkwo walked behind him. He could hardly imagine that Okonkwo was not his real father. He had never been fond of his real father, and at the end of three years he had become very distant indeed. But his mother and his three-year-old sister . . . of course she would not be three now, but six. Would he recognize her now? She must have grown quite big. How his mother would weep for joy, and thank Okonkwo for having looked after him so well and for bringing him back. She would want to hear everything that had happened to him in all these years. Could he remember them all? He would tell her about Nwoye and his mother, and about the locusts . . . Then quite suddenly a thought came upon him. His mother might be dead. He tried in vain to force the thought out of his mind. Then he tried to settle the matter the way he used to settle such matters when he was a little boy. He still remembered the song:

> *Eze elina, elina!*
> *Sala*
> *Eze ilikwa ya*
> *Ikwaba akwa oligholi*
> *Ebe Danda nechi eze*
> *Ebe Uzuzu nete egwu*
> *Sala*

He sang it in his mind, and walked to its beat. If the song ended on his right foot, his mother was alive. If it ended on his left, she was dead. No, not dead, but ill. It ended on the right. She was alive and well. He sang the song again, and it ended on the left. But the second time did not count. The first voice gets to Chukwu, or God's house. That was a favourite saying of children. Ikemefuna felt like a child once more. It must be the thought of going home to his mother.

One of the men behind him cleared his throat. Ikemefuna looked back, and the man growled at him to go on and not stand looking back. The way he said it sent cold fear down Ikemefuna's back. His hands trembled vaguely on the black pot he carried. Why had Okonkwo withdrawn to the rear? Ikemefuna felt his legs melting under him. And he was afraid to look back.

As the man who had cleared his throat drew up and raised his matchet, Okonkwo looked away. He heard the blow. The pot fell and broke in the sand. He heard Ikemefuna cry, "My father, they have killed me!" as he ran towards him. Dazed with fear, Okonkwo drew his matchet and cut him down. He was afraid of being thought weak.

As soon as his father walked in, that night, Nwoye knew that Ikemefuna had been killed, and something seemed to give way inside him, like the snapping of a tightened bow. He did not cry. He just hung limp. He had had the same kind of feeling not long ago, during the last harvest season. Every child loved the harvest season. Those who were big enough to carry even a few yams in a tiny basket went with grown-ups to the farm. And if they could not help in digging up the yams, they could gather firewood together for roasting the ones that would be eaten there on the farm. This roasted yam soaked in red palm-oil and eaten in the open farm was sweeter than any meal at home. It was after such a day at the farm during the last harvest that Nwoye had felt for the first time a snapping inside him like the one he now felt. They were returning home with baskets of yams from a distant farm across the stream when they had heard the voice of an infant crying in the thick forest. A sudden hush had fallen on the women, who had been talking, and they had quickened their steps. Nwoye had heard that twins were put in earthenware pots and thrown away in the forest, but he had never yet come across them. A vague chill had descended on him and his head had seemed to swell, like a solitary walker at night who passes an evil spirit on the way. Then something had given way inside him. It descended on him again, this feeling, when his father walked in, that night after killing Ikemefuna.

Chapter 8

Okonkwo did not taste any food for two days after the death of Ikemefuna. He drank palm-wine from morning till night, and his eyes were red and fierce like the eyes of a rat when it was caught by the tail and dashed against the floor. He called his son, Nwoye, to sit with him in his *obi*. But the boy was afraid of him and slipped out of the hut as soon as he noticed him dozing.

He did not sleep at night. He tried not to think about Ikemefuna, but the more he tried the more he thought about him. Once he got up from bed and walked about his compound. But he was so weak that his legs could hardly carry him. He felt like a drunken giant walking with the limbs of a mosquito. Now and then a cold shiver descended on his head and spread down his body.

On the third day he asked his second wife, Ekwefi, to roast some plantains for him. She prepared them the way he liked—with slices of oil-bean and fish.

"You have not eaten for two days," said his daughter Ezinma when she brought the food to him. "So you must finish this." She sat down and stretched her legs in front of her. Okonkwo ate the food absentmindedly. "She should have been a boy," he thought as he looked at his ten-year-old daughter. He passed her a piece of fish.

"Go and bring me some cold water," he said. Ezinma rushed out of the hut, chewing the fish, and soon returned with a bowl of cool water from the earthen pot in her mother's hut.

Okonkwo took the bowl from her and gulped the water down. He ate a few more pieces of plantain and pushed the dish aside.

"Bring me my bag," he asked, and Ezinma brought his goatskin bag from the far end of the hut. He searched in it for his snuff-bottle. It was a deep bag and took almost the whole length of his arm. It contained other things apart from his snuff-bottle. There was a drinking horn in it, and also a drinking gourd, and they knocked against each other as he searched. When he brought out the snuff-bottle he tapped it a few times against his kneecap before taking out some snuff on the palm of his left hand. Then he remembered that he had not taken out his snuff-spoon. He searched his bag again and brought out a small, flat, ivory spoon, with which he carried the brown snuff to his nostrils.

Ezinma took the dish in one hand and the empty water bowl in the other and went back to her mother's hut. "She should have been a boy," Okonkwo said to himself again. His mind went back to Ikemefuna and he shivered. If only he could find some work to do he would be able to forget. But it was the season of rest between the harvest and the next planting season. The only work that men did at this time was covering the walls of their compound with new palm fronds. And Okonkwo had already done that. He had finished it on the very day the locusts came, when he had worked on one side of the wall and Ikemefuna and Nwoye on the other.

"When did you become a shivering old woman," Okonkwo asked himself, "you are known in all the nine villages for your valour in war. How can a man who has killed five men in battle fall to pieces because he has added a boy to their number? Okonkwo, you have become a woman indeed."

He sprang to his feet, hung his goatskin bag on his shoulder and went to visit his friend, Obierika.

Obierika was sitting outside under the shade of an orange tree making thatches from leaves of the raffia-palm. He exchanged greetings with Okonkwo and led the way into his *obi*.

"I was coming over to see you as soon as I finished that thatch," he said, rubbing off the grains of sand that clung to his thighs.

"Is it well?" Okonkwo asked.

"Yes," replied Obierika. "My daughter's suitor is coming today and I hope we will clinch the matter of the bride-price. I want you to be there."

Just then Obierika's son, Maduka, came into the *obi* from outside, greeted Okonkwo and turned towards the compound.

"Come and shake hands with me," Okonkwo said to the lad. "Your wrestling the other day gave me much happiness." The boy smiled, shook hands with Okonkwo and went into the compound.

"He will do great things," Okonkwo said. "If I had a son like him I should be happy. I am worried about Nwoye. A bowl of pounded yams can throw him in a wrestling match. His two younger brothers are more promising. But I can tell you, Obierika, that my children do not resemble me. Where are the young suckers that will grow when the old banana tree dies? If Ezinma had been a boy I would have been happier. She has the right spirit."

"You worry yourself for nothing," said Obierika. "The children are still very young."

"Nwoye is old enough to impregnate a woman. At his age I was already fending for myself. No, my friend, he is not too young. A chick that will grow into a cock can be spotted the very day it hatches. I have done my best to make Nwoye grow into a man, but there is too much of his mother in him."

"Too much of his grandfather," Obierika thought, but he did not say it. The same thought also came to Okonkwo's mind. But he had long learnt how to lay that ghost. Whenever the thought of his father's weakness and failure troubled him he expelled it by thinking about his own strength and success. And so he did now. His mind went to his latest show of manliness.

"I cannot understand why you refused to come with us to kill that boy," he asked Obierika.

"Because I did not want to," Obierika replied sharply. "I had something better to do."

"You sound as if you question the authority and the decision of the Oracle, who said he should die."

"I do not. Why should I? But the Oracle did not ask me to carry out its decision."

"But someone had to do it. If we were all afraid of blood, it would not be done. And what do you think the Oracle would do then?"

"You know very well, Okonkwo, that I am not afraid of blood; and if anyone tells you that I am, he is telling a lie. And let me tell you one thing, my friend. If I were you I would have stayed at home. What you have done will not please the Earth. It is the kind of action for which the goddess wipes out whole families."

"The Earth cannot punish me for obeying her messenger," Okonkwo said. "A child's fingers are not scalded by a piece of hot yam which its mother puts into its palm."

"That is true," Obierika agreed. "But if the Oracle said that my son should be killed I would neither dispute it nor be the one to do it."

They would have gone on arguing had Ofoedu not come in just then. It was clear from his twinkling eyes that he had important news. But it would be impolite to rush him. Obierika offered him a lobe of the kola nut he had broken with Okonkwo. Ofoedu ate slowly and talked about the locusts. When he finished his kola nut he said:

"The things that happen these days are very strange."

"What has happened?" asked Okonkwo.

"Do you know Ogbuefi Ndulue?" Ofoedu asked.

"Ogbuefi Ndulue of Ire village," Okonkwo and Obierika said together.

"He died this morning," said Ofoedu.

"That is not strange. He was the oldest man in Ire," said Obierika.

"You are right," Ofoedu agreed. "But you ought to ask why the drum has not been beaten to tell Umuofia of his death."

"Why?" asked Obierika and Okonkwo together.

"That is the strange part of it. You know his first wife who walks with a stick?"

"Yes. She is called Ozoemena."

"That is so," said Ofoedu. "Ozoemena was, as you know, too old to attend Ndulue during his illness. His younger wives did that. When he died this morning, one of these women went to Ozoemena's hut and told her. She rose from her mat, took her stick and walked over to the *obi*. She knelt on her knees and hands at the threshold and called her husband, who was laid on a mat. 'Ogbuefi Ndulue,' she called, three times, and went back to her hut. When the youngest wife went to call her again to be present at the washing of the body, she found her lying on the mat, dead."

"That is very strange indeed," said Okonkwo. "They will put off Ndulue's funeral until his wife has been buried."

"That is why the drum has not been beaten to tell Umuofia."

"It was always said that Ndulue and Ozoemena had one mind," said Obierika. "I remember when I was a young boy there was a song about them. He could not do anything without telling her."

"I did not know that," said Okonkwo. "I thought he was a strong man in his youth."

"He was indeed," said Ofoedu.

Okonkwo shook his head doubtfully.

"He led Umuofia to war in those days," said Obierika.

Okonkwo was beginning to feel like his old self again. All that he required was something to occupy his mind. If he had killed Ikemefuna during the busy planting season or harvesting it would not have been so bad; his mind would have been centred on his work. Okonkwo was not a man of thought but of action. But in the absence of work, talking was the next best.

Soon after Ofoedu left, Okonkwo took up his goatskin bag to go.

"I must go home to tap my palm trees for the afternoon," he said.

"Who taps your tall trees for you?" asked Obierika.

"Umezulike," replied Okonkwo.

"Sometimes I wish I had not taken the *ozo* title," said Obierika. "It wounds my heart to see these young men killing palm trees in the name of tapping."

"It is so indeed," Okonkwo agreed. "But the law of the land must be obeyed."

"I don't know how we got that law," said Obierika. "In many other clans a man of title is not forbidden to climb the palm tree. Here we say he cannot climb the tall tree but he can tap the short ones standing on the ground. It is like Dimaragana, who would not lend his knife for cutting up dog-meat because the dog was taboo to him, but offered to use his teeth."

"I think it is good that our clan holds the *ozo* title in high esteem," said Okonkwo. "In those other clans you speak of, *ozo* is so low that every beggar takes it."

"I was only speaking in jest," said Obierika. "In Abame and Aninta the title is worth less than two cowries. Every man wears the thread of title on his ankle, and does not lose it even if he steals."

"They have indeed soiled the name of *ozo,*" said Okonkwo as he rose to go.

"It will not be very long now before my in-laws come," said Obierika.

"I shall return very soon," said Okonkwo, looking at the position of the sun.

There were seven men in Obierika's hut when Okonkwo returned. The suitor was a young man of about twenty-five, and with him were his father and uncle. On Obierika's side were his two elder brothers and Maduka, his sixteen-year-old son.

"Ask Akueke's mother to send us some kola nuts," said Obierika to his son. Maduka vanished into the compound like lightning. The conversation at once centred on him, and everybody agreed that he was as sharp as a razor.

"I sometimes think he is too sharp," said Obierika, somewhat indulgently. "He hardly ever walks. He is always in a hurry. If you are sending him on an errand he flies away before he has heard half of the message."

"You were very much like that yourself," said his eldest brother. "As our people say, 'When mother-cow is chewing grass its young ones watch its mouth.' Maduka has been watching your mouth."

As he was speaking the boy returned, followed by Akueke, his half-sister, carrying a wooden dish with three kola nuts and alligator pepper. She gave the dish to her father's eldest brother and then shook hands, very shyly, with her suitor and his relatives. She was about sixteen and just ripe for marriage. Her suitor and his relatives surveyed her young body with expert eyes as if to assure themselves that she was beautiful and ripe.

She wore a coiffure which was done up into a crest in the middle of the head. Cam wood was rubbed lightly into her skin, and all over her body were black patterns drawn with *uli.* She wore a black necklace which hung down in three coils just above her full, succulent breasts. On her arms were red and yellow bangles, and on her waist four or five rows of *jigida,* or waist-beads.

When she had shaken hands, or rather held out her hand to be shaken, she returned to her mother's hut to help with the cooking.

"Remove *your jigida* first," her mother warned as she moved near the fireplace to bring the pestle resting against the wall. "Every day I tell you that *jigida* and fire are not friends. But you will never hear. You grew your ears for decoration, not for hearing. One of these days your *jigida* will catch fire on your waist, and then you will know."

Akueke moved to the other end of the hut and began to remove the waist-beads. It had to be done slowly and carefully, taking each string separately, else it would break and the thousand tiny rings would have to be strung together again. She rubbed each string downwards with her palms until it passed the buttocks and slipped down to the floor around her feet.

The men in the *obi* had already begun to drink the palm-wine which Akueke's suitor had brought. It was a very good wine and powerful, for in spite of the palm fruit hung across the mouth of the pot to restrain the lively liquor, white foam rose and spilled over.

"That wine is the work of a good tapper," said Okonkwo.

The young suitor, whose name was Ibe, smiled broadly and said to his father: "Do you hear that?" He then said to the others: "He will never admit that I am a good tapper."

"He tapped three of my best palm trees to death," said his father, Ukegbu.

"That was about five years ago," said Ibe, who had begun to pour out the wine, "before I learnt how to tap." He filled the first horn and gave it to his father. Then he poured out for the others. Okonkwo brought out his big horn from the goatskin bag, blew into it to remove any dust that might be there, and gave it to Ibe to fill.

As the men drank, they talked about everything except the thing for which they had gathered. It was only after the pot had been emptied that the suitor's father cleared his voice and announced the object of their visit.

Obierika then presented to him a small bundle of short broomsticks. Ukegbu counted them.

"They are thirty?" he asked.

Obierika nodded in agreement.

"We are at last getting somewhere," Ukegbu said, and then turning to his brother and his son he said: "Let us go out and whisper together." The three rose and went outside. When they returned Ukegbu handed the bundle of sticks back to Obierika. He counted them; instead of thirty there were now only fifteen. He passed them over to his eldest brother, Machi, who also counted them and said:

"We had not thought to go below thirty. But as the dog said, 'If I fall down for you and you fall down for me, it is play.' Marriage should be a play and not a fight; so we are falling down again." He then added ten sticks to the fifteen and gave the bundle to Ukegbu.

In this way Akueke's bride-price was finally settled at twenty bags of cowries. It was already dusk when the two parties came to this agreement.

"Go and tell Akueke's mother that we have finished," Obierika said to his son, Maduka. Almost immediately the woman came in with a big bowl of foo-foo. Obierika's second wife followed with a pot of soup, and Maduka brought in a pot of palm-wine.

As the men ate and drank palm-wine they talked about the customs of their neighbours.

"It was only this morning," said Obierika, "that Okonkwo and I were talking about Abame and Aninta, where titled men climb trees and pound foo-foo for their wives."

"All their customs are upside-down. They do not decide bride-price as we do, with sticks. They haggle and bargain as if they were buying a goat or a cow in the market."

"That is very bad," said Obierika's eldest brother. "But what is good in one place is bad in another place. In Umunso they do not bargain at all, not even with broomsticks. The suitor just goes on bringing bags of cowries until his in-laws tell him to stop. It is a bad custom because it always leads to a quarrel."

"The world is large," said Okonkwo. "I have even heard that in some tribes a man's children belong to his wife and her family."

"That cannot be," said Machi. "You might as well say that the woman lies on top of the man when they are making the children."

"It is like the story of white men who, they say, are white like this piece of chalk," said Obierika. He held up a piece of chalk, which every man kept in his *obi* and with which his guests drew lines on the floor before they ate kola nuts. "And these white men, they say, have no toes."[2]

"And have you never seen them?" asked Machi.

"Have you?" asked Obierika.

"One of them passes here frequently," said Machi. "His name is Amadi."

Those who knew Amadi laughed. He was a leper, and the polite name for leprosy was "the white skin."

Chapter 9

For the first time in three nights, Okonkwo slept. He woke up once in the middle of the night and his mind went back to the past three days without making him feel uneasy. He began to wonder why he had felt uneasy at all. It was like a man wondering in broad day-light why a dream had appeared so terrible to him at night. He stretched himself and scratched his thigh where a mosquito had bitten him as he slept. Another one was wailing near his right ear. He slapped the ear and hoped he had killed it. Why do they always go for one's ears? When he was a child his mother had told him a story about it. But it was as silly as all women's stories. Mosquito, she had said, had asked Ear to marry him, whereupon Ear fell on the floor in uncontrollable laughter. "How much longer do you think you will live?" she asked. "You are already a skeleton." Mosquito went away humiliated, and any time he passed her way he told Ear that he was still alive.

Okonkwo turned on his side and went back to sleep. He was roused in the morning by someone banging on his door.

"Who is that?" he growled. He knew it must be Ekwefi. Of his three wives Ekwefi was the only one who would have the audacity to bang on his door.

"Ezinma is dying," came her voice, and all the tragedy and sorrow of her life were packed in those words.

Okonkwo sprang from his bed, pushed back the bolt on his door and ran into Ekwefi's hut.

Ezinma lay shivering on a mat beside a huge fire that her mother had kept burning all night.

"It is *iba*," said Okonkwo as he took his matchet and went into the bush to collect the leaves and grasses and barks of trees that went into making the medicine for *iba*.

Ekwefi knelt beside the sick child, occasionally feeling with her palm the wet, burning forehead.

Ezinma was an only child and the centre of her mother's world. Very often it was Ezinma who had decided what food her mother should prepare. Ekwefi even gave her such delicacies as eggs, which children were rarely allowed to eat because such food tempted them to steal. One day as Ezinma was eating an egg Okonkwo had come in unexpectedly from his hut. He was greatly shocked and swore to beat Ekwefi if she dared to give the child eggs again. But it was impossible to refuse Ezinma anything. After her father's rebuke she developed an even keener appetite for eggs. And she enjoyed above all the secrecy in which she now ate them. Her mother always took her into their bedroom and shut the door.

Ezinma did not call her mother *Nne* like all children. She called her by her name, Ekwefi, as her father and other grown-up people did. The relationship between them

2. Their feet are hidden in shoes.

was not only that of mother and child. There was something in it like the companionship of equals, which was strengthened by such little conspiracies as eating eggs in the bedroom.

Ekwefi had suffered a good deal in her life. She had borne ten children and nine of them had died in infancy, usually before the age of three. As she buried one child after another her sorrow gave way to despair and then to grim resignation. The birth of her children, which should be a woman's crowning glory, became for Ekwefi mere physical agony devoid of promise. The naming ceremony after seven market weeks became an empty ritual. Her deepening despair found expression in the names she gave her children. One of them was a pathetic cry, Onwumbiko—"Death, I implore you." But Death took no notice; Onwumbiko died in his fifteenth month. The next child was a girl, Ozoemena—"May it not happen again." She died in her eleventh month, and two others after her. Ekwefi then became defiant and called her next child Onwuma—"Death may please himself." And he did.

After the death of Ekwefi's second child, Okonkwo had gone to a medicine-man, who was also a diviner of the Afa Oracle, to inquire what was amiss. This man told him that the child was an *ogbanje*, one of those wicked children who, when they died, entered their mother's wombs to be born again.

"When your wife becomes pregnant again," he said, "let her not sleep in her hut. Let her go and stay with her people. In that way she will elude her wicked tormentor and break its evil cycle of birth and death."

Ekwefi did as she was asked. As soon as she became pregnant she went to live with her old mother in another village. It was there that her third child was born and circumcised on the eighth day. She did not return to Okonkwo's compound until three days before the naming ceremony. The child was called Onwumbiko.

Onwumbiko was not given proper burial when he died. Onkonkwo had called in another medicine-man who was famous in the clan for his great knowledge about *ogbanje* children. His name was Okagbue Uyanwa. Okagbue was a very striking figure, tall, with a full beard and a bald head. He was light in complexion and his eyes were red and fiery. He always gnashed his teeth as he listened to those who came to consult him. He asked Okonkwo a few questions about the dead child. All the neighbours and relations who had come to mourn gathered round them.

"On what market-day was it born?" he asked.

"*Oye*," replied Okonkwo.

"And it died this morning?"

Okonkwo said yes, and only then realised for the first time that the child had died on the same market-day as it had been born. The neighbours and relations also saw the coincidence and said among themselves that it was very significant.

"Where do you sleep with your wife, in your *obi* or in her own hut?" asked the medicine-man.

"In her hut."

"In future call her into your *obi*."

The medicine-man then ordered that there should be no mourning for the dead child. He brought out a sharp razor from the goatskin bag slung from his left shoulder and began to mutilate the child. Then he took it away to bury in the Evil Forest, holding it by the ankle and dragging it on the ground behind him. After such treatment it would think twice before coming again, unless it was one of the stubborn ones who returned, carrying the stamp of their mutilation—a missing finger or perhaps a dark line where the medicine-man's razor had cut them.

By the time Onwumbiko died Ekwefi had become a very bitter woman. Her husband's first wife had already had three sons, all strong and healthy. When she had borne her third son in succession, Okonkwo had slaughtered a goat for her, as was the custom. Ekwefi had nothing but good wishes for her. But she had grown so bitter about her own *chi* that she could not rejoice with others over their good fortune. And so, on the day that Nwoye's mother celebrated the birth of her three sons with feasting and music, Ekwefi was the only person in the happy company who went about with a cloud on her brow. Her husband's wife took this for malevolence, as husbands' wives were wont to. How could she know that Ekwefi's bitterness did not flow outwards to others but inwards into her own soul; that she did not blame others for their good fortune but her own evil *chi* who denied her any?

At last Ezinma was born, and although ailing she seemed determined to live. At first Ekwefi accepted her, as she had accepted others—with listless resignation. But when she lived on to her fourth, fifth and sixth years, love returned once more to her mother, and, with love, anxiety. She determined to nurse her child to health, and she put all her being into it. She was rewarded by occasional spells of health during which Ezinma bubbled with energy like fresh palm-wine. At such times she seemed beyond danger. But all of a sudden she would go down again. Everybody knew she was an *ogbanje*. These sudden bouts of sickness and health were typical of her kind. But she had lived so long that perhaps she had decided to stay. Some of them did become tired of their evil rounds of birth and death, or took pity on their mothers, and stayed. Ekwefi believed deep inside her that Ezinma had come to stay. She believed because it was that faith alone that gave her own life any kind of meaning. And this faith had been strengthened when a year or so ago a medicine-man had dug up Ezinma's *iyi-uwa*. Everyone knew then that she would live because her bond with the world of *ogbanje* had been broken. Ekwefi was reassured. But such was her anxiety for her daughter that she could not rid herself completely of her fear. And although she believed that the *iyi-uwa* which had been dug up was genuine, she could not ignore the fact that some really evil children sometimes misled people into digging up a specious one.

But Ezinma's *iyi-uwa* had looked real enough. It was a smooth pebble wrapped in a dirty rag. The man who dug it up was the same Okagbue who was famous in all the clan for his knowledge in these matters. Ezinma had not wanted to co-operate with him at first. But that was only to be expected. No *ogbanje* would yield her secrets easily, and most of them never did because they died too young—before they could be asked questions.

"Where did you bury your *iyi-uwa?*" she asked in return.

"You know where it is. You buried it in the ground somewhere so that you can die and return again to torment your mother."

Ezinma looked at her mother, whose eyes, sad and pleading, were fixed on her.

"Answer the question at once," roared Okonkwo, who stood beside her. All the family were there and some of the neighbours too.

"Leave her to me," the medicine-man told Okonkwo in a cool, confident voice. He turned again to Ezinma. "Where did you bury your *iyi-uwa?*"

"Where they bury children," she replied, and the quiet spectators murmured to themselves.

"Come along then and show me the spot," said the medicine-man.

The crowd set out with Ezinma leading the way and Okagbue following closely behind her. Okonkwo came next and Ekwefi followed him. When she came to the main road, Ezinma turned left as if she was going to the stream.

"But you said it was where they bury children?" asked the medicine-man.

"No," said Ezinma, whose feeling of importance was manifest in her sprightly walk. She sometimes broke into a run and stopped again suddenly. The crowd followed her silently. Women and children returning from the stream with pots of water on their heads wondered what was happening until they saw Okagbue and guessed that it must be something to do with *ogbanje*. And they all knew Ekwefi and her daughter very well.

When she got to the big udala tree Ezinma turned left into the bush, and the crowd followed her. Because of her size she made her way through trees and creepers more quickly than her followers. The bush was alive with the tread of feet on dry leaves and sticks and the moving aside of tree branches. Ezinma went deeper and deeper and the crowd went with her. Then she suddenly turned round and began to walk back to the road. Everybody stood to let her pass and then filed after her.

"If you bring us all this way for nothing I shall beat sense into you," Okonkwo threatened.

"I have told you to let her alone. I know how to deal with them," said Okagbue.

Ezinma led the way back to the road, looked left and right and turned right. And so they arrived home again.

"Where did you bury your *iyi-uwa?*" asked Okagbue when Ezinma finally stopped outside her father's *obi*. Okagbue's voice was unchanged. It was quiet and confident.

"It is near that orange tree," Ezinma said.

"And why did you not say so, you wicked daughter of Akalogoli?" Okonkwo swore furiously. The medicine-man ignored him.

"Come and show me the exact spot," he said quietly to Ezinma.

"It is here," she said when they got to the tree.

"Point at the spot with your finger," said Okagbue.

"It is here," said Ezinma touching the ground with her finger. Okonkwo stood by, rumbling like thunder in the rainy season.

"Bring me a hoe," said Okagbue.

When Ekwefi brought the hoe, he had already put aside his goatskin bag and his big cloth and was in his underwear, a long and thin strip of cloth wound round the waist like a belt and then passed between the legs to be fastened to the belt behind. He immediately set to work digging a pit where Ezinma had indicated. The neighbours sat around watching the pit becoming deeper and deeper. The dark top-soil soon gave way to the bright-red earth with which women scrubbed the floor and walls of huts. Okagbue worked tirelessly and in silence, his back shining with perspiration. Okonkwo stood by the pit. He asked Okagbue to come up and rest while he took a hand. But Okagbue said he was not tired yet.

Ekwefi went into her hut to cook yams. Her husband had brought out more yams than usual because the medicine-man had to be fed. Ezinma went with her and helped in preparing the vegetables.

"There is too much green vegetable," she said.

"Don't you see the pot is full of yams?" Ekwefi asked. "And you know how leaves become smaller after cooking."

"Yes," said Ezinma, "that was why the snake-lizard killed his mother."

"Very true," said Ekwefi.

"He gave his mother seven baskets of vegetables to cook and in the end there were only three. And so he killed her," said Ezinma.

"That is not the end of the story."

"Oho," said Ezinma, "I remember now. He brought another seven baskets and cooked them himself. And there were again only three. So he killed himself too."

Outside the *obi* Okagbue and Okonkwo were digging the pit to find where Ezinma had buried her *iyi-uwa*. Neighbours sat around, watching. The pit was now so deep that they no longer saw the digger. They only saw the red earth he threw up mounting higher and higher. Okonkwo's son, Nwoye, stood near the edge of the pit because he wanted to take in all that happened.

Okagbue had again taken over the digging from Okonkwo. He worked, as usual, in silence. The neigbours and Okonkwo's wives were now talking. The children had lost interest and were playing.

Suddenly Okagbue sprang to the surface with the agility of a leopard.

"It is very near now," he said. "I have felt it."

There was immediate excitement and those who were sitting jumped to their feet.

"Call your wife and child," he said to Okonkwo. But Ekwefi and Ezinma had heard the noise and run out to see what it was.

Okagbue went back into the pit, which was now surrounded by spectators. After a few more hoe-fuls of earth he struck the *iyi-uwa*. He raised it carefully with the hoe and threw it to the surface. Some women ran away in fear when it was thrown. But they soon returned and everyone was gazing at the rag from a reasonable distance. Okagbue emerged and without saying a word or even looking at the spectators he went to his goatskin bag, took out two leaves and began to chew them. When he had swallowed them, he took up the rag with his left hand and began to untie it. And then the smooth, shiny pebble fell out. He picked it up.

"Is this yours?" he asked Ezinma.

"Yes," she replied. All the women shouted with joy because Ekwefi's troubles were at last ended.

All this had happened more than a year ago and Ezinma had not been ill since. And then suddenly she had begun to shiver in the night. Ekwefi brought her to the fireplace, spread her mat on the floor and built a fire. But she had got worse and worse. As she knelt by her, feeling with her palm the wet, burning forehead, she prayed a thousand times. Although her husband's wives were saying that it was nothing more than *iba*, she did not hear them.

Okonkwo returned from the bush carrying on his left shoulder a large bundle of grasses and leaves, roots and barks of medicinal trees and shrubs. He went into Ekwefi's hut, put down his load and sat down.

"Get me a pot," he said, "and leave the child alone."

Ekwefi went to bring the pot and Okonkwo selected the best from his bundle, in their due proportion, and cut them up. He put them in the pot and Ekwefi poured in some water.

"Is that enough?" she asked when she had poured in about half of the water in the bowl.

"A little more...I said a *little*. Are you deaf?" Okonkwo roared at her.

She set the pot on the fire and Okonkwo took up his matchet to return to his *obi*.

"You must watch the pot carefully," he said as he went, "and don't allow it to boil over. If it does its power will be gone." He went away to his hut and Ekwefi began to tend the medicine pot almost as if it was itself a sick child. Her eyes went constantly from Ezinma to the boiling pot and back to Ezinma.

Okonkwo returned when he felt the medicine had cooked long enough. He looked it over and said it was done.

"Bring a low stool for Ezinma," he said, "and a thick mat."

He took down the pot from the fire and placed it in front of the stool. He then roused Ezinma and placed her on the stool, astride the steaming pot. The thick mat was thrown over both. Ezinma struggled to escape from the choking and overpowering steam, but she was held down. She started to cry.

When the mat was at last removed she was drenched in perspiration. Ekwefi mopped her with a piece of cloth and she lay down on a dry mat and was soon asleep.

Chapter 10

Large crowds began to gather on the village *ilo* as soon as the edge had worn off the sun's heat and it was no longer painful on the body. Most communal ceremonies took place at that time of the day, so that even when it was said that a ceremony would begin "after the midday meal" everyone understood that it would begin a long time later, when the sun's heat had softened.

It was clear from the way the crowd stood or sat that the ceremony was for men. There were many women, but they looked on from the fringe like outsiders. The titled men and elders sat on their stools waiting for the trials to begin. In front of them was a row of stools on which nobody sat. There were nine of them. Two little groups of people stood at a respectable distance beyond the stools. They faced the elders. There were three men in one group and three men and one woman in the other. The woman was Mgbafo and the three men with her were her brothers. In the other group were her husband, Uzowulu, and his relatives. Mgbafo and her brothers were as still as statues into whose faces the artist has moulded defiance. Uzowulu and his relatives, on the other hand, were whispering together. It looked like whispering, but they were really talking at the top of their voices. Everybody in the crowd was talking. It was like the market. From a distance the noise was a deep rumble carried by the wind.

An iron gong sounded, setting up a wave of expectation in the crowd. Everyone looked in the direction of the *egwugwu* house. *Gome, gome, gome, gome* went the gong, and a powerful flute blew a high-pitched blast. Then came the voices of the *egwugwu*, gutteral and awesome. The wave struck the women and children and there was a backward stampede. But it was momentary. They were already far enough where they stood and there was room for running away if any of the *egwugwu* should go towards them.

The drum sounded again and the flute blew. The *egwugwu* house was now a pandemonium of quavering voices: *Aru oyim de de de de dei!*[3] filled the air as the spirits of the ancestors, just emerged from the earth, greeted themselves in their esoteric language. The *egwugwu* house into which they emerged faced the forest, away from the crowd, who saw only its back with the many-coloured patterns and drawings done by specially chosen women at regular intervals. These women never saw the inside of the hut. No woman ever did. They scrubbed and painted the outside walls under the supervision of men. If they imagined what was inside, they kept their imagination to themselves. No woman ever asked questions about the most powerful and the most secret cult in the clan.

3. Greetings, body of my friend.

Aru oyim de de de dei! flew around the dark, closed hut like tongues of fire. The ancestral spirits of the clan were abroad. The metal gong beat continuously now and the flute, shrill and powerful, floated on the chaos.

And then the *egwugwu* appeared. The women and children sent up a great shout and took to their heels. It was instinctive. A woman fled as soon as an *egwugwu* came in sight. And when, as on that day, nine of the greatest masked spirits in the clan came out together it was a terrifying spectacle. Even Mgbafo took to her heels and had to be restrained by her brothers.

Each of the nine *egwugwu* represented a village of the clan. Their leader was called Evil Forest. Smoke poured out of his head.

The nine villages of Umuofia had grown out of the nine sons of the first father of the clan. Evil Forest represented the village of Umeru, or the children of Eru, who was the eldest of the nine sons.

" *Umuofia kwenu!*" shouted the leading *egwugwu*, pushing the air with his raffia arms. The elders of the clan replied, *"Yao!"*

"Umuofia kwenu!"

"Yaa!"

"Umuofia kwenu!"

"Yaa!"

Evil Forest then thrust the pointed end of his rattling staff into the earth. And it began to shake and rattle, like something agitating with a metallic life. He took the first of the empty stools and the eight other *egwugwu* began to sit in order of seniority after him.

Okonkwo's wives, and perhaps other women as well, might have noticed that the second *egwugwu* had the springy walk of Okonkwo. And they might also have noticed that Okonkwo was not among the titled men and elders who sat behind the row of *egwugwu*. But if they thought these things they kept them within themselves. The *egwugwu* with the springy walk was one of the dead fathers of the clan. He looked terrible with the smoked raffia body, a huge wooden face painted white except for the round hollow eyes and the charred teeth that were as big as a man's fingers. On his head were two powerful horns.

When all the *egwugwu* had sat down and the sound of the many tiny bells and rattles on their bodies had subsided, Evil Forest addressed the two groups of people facing them.

"Uzowulu's body, I salute you," he said. Spirits always addressed humans as "bodies." Uzowulu bent down and touched the earth with his right hand as a sign of submission.

"Our father, my hand has touched the ground," he said.

"Uzowulu's body, do you know me?" asked the spirit.

"How can I know you, father? You are beyond our knowledge."

Evil Forest then turned to the other group and addressed the eldest of the three brothers.

"The body of Odukwe, I greet you," he said, and Odukwe bent down and touched the earth. The hearing then began.

Uzowulu stepped forward and presented his case.

"That woman standing there is my wife, Mgbafo. I married her with my money and my yams. I do not owe my in-laws anything. I owe them no yams. I owe them no coco-yams. One morning three of them came to my house, beat me up and took my wife and children away. This happened in the rainy season. I have waited in vain for my wife to return. At last I went to my in-laws and said to them, 'You have taken back your sister. I did not send her away. You yourselves took her. The law of the clan is that you should return her bride-price.' But my wife's brother said they had nothing to tell me. So I have brought the matter to the fathers of the clan. My case is finished. I salute you."

"Your words are good," said the leader of the *egwugwu*. "Let us hear Odukwe. His words may also be good."

Odukwe was short and thick-set. He stepped forward, saluted the spirits and began his story.

"My in-law has told you that we went to his house, beat him up and took our sister and her children away. All that is true. He told you that he came to take back her bride-price and we refused to give it him. That is also true. My in-law, Uzowulu, is a beast. My sister lived with him for nine years. During those years no single day passed in the sky without his beating the woman. We have tried to settle their quarrels time without number and on each occasion Uzowulu was guilty—"

"It is a lie!" Uzowulu shouted.

"Two years ago," continued Odukwe, "when she was pregnant, he beat her until she miscarried."

"It is a lie. She miscarried after she had gone to sleep with her lover."

"Uzowulu's body, I salute you," said Evil Forest, silencing him. "What kind of lover sleeps with a pregnant woman?" There was a loud murmur of approbation from the crowd. Odukwe continued:

"Last year when my sister was recovering from an illness, he beat her again so that if the neighbours had not gone in to save her she would have been killed. We heard of it, and did as you have been told. The law of Umuofia is that if a woman runs away from her husband her bride-price is returned. But in this case she ran away to save her life. Her two children belong to Uzowulu. We do not dispute it, but they are too young to leave their mother. If, on the other hand, Uzowulu should recover from his madness and come in the proper way to beg his wife to return she will do so on the understanding that if he ever beats her again we shall cut off his genitals for him."

The crowd roared with laughter. Evil Forest rose to his feet and order was immediately restored. A steady cloud of smoke rose from his head. He sat down again and called two witnesses. They were both Uzowulu's neighbours, and they agreed about the beating. Evil Forest then stood up, pulled out his staff and thrust it into the earth again. He ran a few steps in the direction of the women; they all fled in terror, only to return to their places almost immediately. The nine *egwugwu* then went away to consult together in their house. They were silent for a long time. Then the metal gong sounded and the flute was blown. The *egwugwu* had emerged once again from their underground home. They saluted one another and then reappeared on the *ilo*.

"*Umuofia kwenu!*" roared Evil Forest, facing the elders and grandees of the clan.

"*Yaa!*" replied the thunderous crowd, then silence descended from the sky and swallowed the noise.

Evil Forest began to speak and all the while he spoke everyone was silent. The eight other *egwugwu* were as still as statues.

"We have heard both sides of the case," said Evil Forest. "Our duty is not to blame this man or to praise that, but to settle the dispute." He turned to Uzowulu's group and allowed a short pause.

"Uzowulu's body, do you know me?"

"How can I know you, father? You are beyond our knowledge," Uzowulu replied.

"I am Evil Forest. I kill a man on the day that his life is sweetest to him."

"That is true," replied Uzowulu.

"Go to your in-laws with a pot of wine and beg your wife to return to you. It is not bravery when a man fights with a woman." He turned to Odukwe, and allowed a brief pause.

"Odukwe's body, I greet you," he said.

"My hand is on the ground," replied Odukwe.

"Do you know me?"

"No man can know you," replied Odukwe.

"I am Evil Forest, I am Dry-meat-that-fills-the-mouth, I am Fire-that-burns-without-faggots. If your in-law brings wine to you, let your sister go with him. I salute you." He pulled his staff from the hard earth and thrust it back.

"Umuofia kwenu!" he roared, and the crowd answered.

"I don't know why such a trifle should come before the *egwugwu*," said one elder to another.

"Don't you know what kind of man Uzowulu is? He will not listen to any other decision," replied the other.

As they spoke two other groups of people had replaced the first before the *egwugwu*, and a great land case began.

Chapter 11

The night was impenetrably dark. The moon had been rising later and later every night until now it was seen only at dawn. And whenever the moon forsook evening and rose at cock-crow the nights were as black as charcoal.

Ezinma and her mother sat on a mat on the floor after their supper of yam foo-foo and bitter leaf soup. A palm-oil lamp gave out yellowish light. Without it, it would have been impossible to eat; one could not have known where one's mouth was in the darkness of that night. There was an oil lamp in all four huts on Okonkwo's compound, and each hut seen from the others looked like a soft eye of yellow half-light set in the solid massiveness of night.

The world was silent except for the shrill cry of insects, which was part of the night, and the sound of wooden mortar and pestle as Nwayieke pounded her foo-foo. Nwayieke lived four compounds away, and she was notorious for her late cooking. Every woman in the neighbourhood knew the sound of Nwayieke's mortar and pestle. It was also part of the night.

Okonkwo had eaten from his wives' dishes and was now reclining with his back against the wall. He searched his bag and brought out his snuff-bottle. He turned it on to his left palm, but nothing came out. He hit the bottle against his knee to shake up the tobacco. That was always the trouble with Okeke's snuff. It very quickly went damp, and there was too much saltpetre in it. Okonkwo had not bought snuff from him for a long time. Idigo was the man who knew how to grind good snuff. But he had recently fallen ill.

Low voices, broken now and again by singing, reached Okonkwo from his wives' huts as each woman and her children told folk stories. Ekwefi and her daughter, Ezinma, sat on a mat on the floor. It was Ekwefi's turn to tell a story.

"Once upon a time," she began, "all the birds were invited to a feast in the sky. They were very happy and began to prepare themselves for the great day. They painted their bodies with red cam wood and drew beautiful patterns on them with *uli*.

"Tortoise saw all these preparations and soon discovered what it all meant. Nothing that happened in the world of the animals ever escaped his notice; he was full of

cunning. As soon as he heard of the great feast in the sky his throat began to itch at the very thought. There was a famine in those days and Tortoise had not eaten a good meal for two moons. His body rattled like a piece of dry stick in his empty shell. So he began to plan how he would go to the sky."

"But he had no wings," said Ezinma.

"Be patient," replied her mother. "That is the story. Tortoise had no wings, but he went to the birds and asked to be allowed to go with them.

"'We know you too well,' said the birds when they had heard him. 'You are full of cunning and you are ungrateful. If we allow you to come with us you will soon begin your mischief.'"

"'You do not know me,' said Tortoise. 'I am a changed man. I have learnt that a man who makes trouble for others is also making it for himself.'

"Tortoise had a sweet tongue, and within a short time all the birds agreed that he was a changed man, and they each gave him a feather, with which he made two wings.

"At last the great day came and Tortoise was the first to arrive at the meeting-place. When all the birds had gathered together, they set off in a body. Tortoise was very happy and voluble as he flew among the birds, and he was soon chosen as the man to speak for the party because he was a great orator.

"'There is one important thing which we must not forget,' he said as they flew on their way. 'When people are invited to a great feast like this, they take new names for the occasion. Our hosts in the sky will expect us to honour this age-old custom.'

"None of the birds had heard of this custom but they knew that Tortoise, in spite of his failings in other directions, was a widely-travelled man who knew the customs of different people. And so they each took a new name. When they had all taken, Tortoise also took one. He was to be called *All of you*.

"At last the party arrived in the sky and their hosts were very happy to see them. Tortoise stood up in his many-coloured plumage and thanked them for their invitation. His speech was so eloquent that all the birds were glad they had brought him, and nodded their heads in approval of all he said. Their hosts took him as the king of the birds, especially as he looked somewhat different from the others.

"After kola nuts had been presented and eaten, the people of the sky set before their guests the most delectable dishes Tortoise had ever seen or dreamt of. The soup was brought out hot from the fire and in the very pot in which it had been cooked. It was full of meat and fish. Tortoise began to sniff aloud. There was pounded yam and also yam pottage cooked with palm-oil and fresh fish. There were also pots of palm-wine. When everything had been set before the guests, one of the people of the sky came forward and tasted a little from each pot. He then invited the birds to eat. But Tortoise jumped to his feet and asked: 'For whom have you prepared this feast?'

"'For all of you,' replied the man.

"Tortoise turned to the birds and said: 'You remember that my name is *All of you*. The custom here is to serve the spokesman first and the others later. They will serve you when I have eaten.'

"He began to eat and the birds grumbled angrily. The people of the sky thought it must be their custom to leave all the food for their king. And so Tortoise ate the best part of the food and then drank two pots of palm-wine, so that he was full of food and drink and his body filled out in his shell.

"The birds gathered round to eat what was left and to peck at the bones he had thrown all about the floor. Some of them were too angry to eat. They chose to fly home on an empty stomach. But before they left each took back the feather he had

948

lent to Tortoise. And there he stood in his hard shell full of food and wine but without any wings to fly home. He asked the birds to take a message for his wife, but they all refused. In the end Parrot, who had felt more angry than the others, suddenly changed his mind and agreed to take the message.

"'Tell my wife,' said Tortoise, 'to bring out all the soft things in my house and cover the compound with them so that I can jump down from the sky without very great danger.'

"Parrot promised to deliver the message, and then flew away. But when he reached Tortoise's house he told his wife to bring out all the hard things in the house. And so she brought out her husband's hoes, matchets, spears, guns and even his cannon. Tortoise looked down from the sky and saw his wife bringing things out, but it was too far to see what they were. When all seemed ready he let himself go. He fell and fell and fell until he began to fear that he would never stop falling. And then like the sound of his cannon he crashed on the compound."

"Did he die?" asked Ezinma.

"No," replied Ekwefi. "His shell broke into pieces. But there was a great medicine-man in the neigbourhood. Tortoise's wife sent for him and he gathered all the bits of shell and stuck them together. That is why Tortoise's shell is not smooth."

"There is no song in the story," Ezinma pointed out.

"No," said Ekwefi. "I shall think of another one with a song. But it is your turn now."

"Once upon a time," Ezinma began, "Tortoise and Cat went to wrestle against Yams—no, that is not the beginning. Once upon a time there was a great famine in the land of animals. Everybody was lean except Cat, who was fat and whose body shone as if oil was rubbed on it . . . ."

She broke off because at that very moment a loud and high-pitched voice broke the outer silence of the night. It was Chielo, the priestess of Agbala, prophesying. There was nothing new in that. Once in a while Chielo was possessed by the spirit of her god and she began to prophesy. But tonight she was addressing her prophecy and greetings to Okonkwo, and so everyone in his family listened. The folk stories stopped.

"*Agbala do-o-o-o! Agbala ekeneo-o-o-o,*"[4] came the voice like a sharp knife cutting through the night. "*Okonkwo! Agbala ekene gio-o-o-o! Agbala cholu ifu ada ya Ezinmao-o-o-o!*"[5]

At the mention of Ezinma's name Ekwefi jerked her head sharply like a animal that had sniffed death in the air. Her heart jumped painfully within her.

The priestess had now reached Okonkwo's compound and was talking with him outside his hut. She was saying again and again that Agbala wanted to see his daughter, Ezinma. Okonkwo pleaded with her to come back in the morning because Ezinma was now asleep. But Chielo ignored what he was trying to say and went on shouting that Agbala wanted to see his daughter. Her voice was as clear as metal, and Okonkwo's women and children heard from their huts all that she said. Okonkwo was still pleading that the girl had been ill of late and was asleep. Ekwefi quickly took her to their bedroom and placed her on their high bamboo bed.

The priestess suddenly screamed. "Beware, Okonkwo!" she warned. "Beware of exchanging words with Agbala. Does a man speak when a god speaks? Beware!"

---

4. Agbala greets you. Agbala wants something.
5. Agbala greets you. Agbala wants to see his daughter, Ezinma.

She walked through Okonkwo's hut into the circular compound and went straight towards Ekwefi's hut. Okonkwo came after her.

"Ekwefi," she called, "Agbala greets you. Where is my daughter, Ezinma? Ag-bala wants to see her."

Ekwefi came out from her hut carrying her oil lamp in her left hand. There was a light wind blowing, so she cupped her right hand to shelter the flame. Nwoye's mother, also carrying an oil lamp, emerged from her hut. Her children stood in the darkness outside their hut watching the strange event. Okonkwo's youngest wife also came out and joined the others.

"Where does Agbala want to see her?" Ekwefi asked.

"Where else but in his house in the hills and the caves?" replied the priestess.

"I will come with you, too," Ekwefi said firmly.

"*Tufia-a!*"[6] the priestess cursed, her voice cracking like the angry bark of thunder in the dry season. "How dare you, woman, to go before the mighty Agbala of your own accord? Beware, woman, lest he strike you in his anger. Bring me my daughter."

Ekwefi went into her hut and came out again with Ezinma.

"Come, my daughter," said the priestess. "I shall carry you on my back. A baby on its mother's back does not know that the way is long."

Ezinma began to cry. She was used to Chielo calling her "my daughter." But it was a different Chielo she now saw in the yellow half-light.

"Don't cry, my daughter," said the priestess, "lest Agbala be angry with you."

"Don't cry," said Ekwefi, "she will bring you back very soon. I shall give you some fish to eat." She went into the hut again and brought down the smoke-black basket in which she kept her dried fish and other ingredients for cooking soup. She broke a piece in two and gave it to Ezinma, who clung to her.

"Don't be afraid," said Ekwefi, stroking her head, which was shaved in places, leaving a regular pattern of hair. They went outside again. The priestess bent down on one knee and Ezinma climbed on her back, her left palm closed on her fish and her eyes gleaming with tears.

"*Agbala do-o-o-o! Agbala ekeneo-o-o-o!...*" Chielo began once again to chant greetings to her god. She turned round sharply and walked through Okonkwo's hut, bending very low at the eaves. Ezinma was crying loudly now, calling on her mother. The two voices disappeared into the thick darkness.

A strange and sudden weakness descended on Ekwefi as she stood gazing in the direction of the voices like a hen whose only chick has been carried away by a kite. Ezinma's voice soon faded away and only Chielo was heard moving farther and farther into the distance.

"Why do you stand there as though she had been kidnapped?" asked Okonkwo as he went back to his hut.

"She will bring her back soon," Nwoye's mother said.

But Ekwefi did not hear these consolations. She stood for a while, and then, all of a sudden, made up her mind. She hurried through Okonkwo's hut and went outside.

"Where are you going?" he asked.

"I am following Chielo," she replied and disappeared in the darkness. Okonkwo cleared his throat, and brought out his snuff-bottle from the goatskin bag by his side.

---

6. Spit!

The priestess's voice was already growing faint in the distance. Ekwefi hurried to the main footpath and turned left in the direction of the voice. Her eyes were useless to her in the darkness. But she picked her way easily on the sandy footpath hedged on either side by branches and damp leaves. She began to run, holding her breasts with her hands to stop them flapping noisily against her body. She hit her left foot against an outcropped root, and terror seized her. It was an ill omen. She ran faster. But Chielo's voice was still a long way away. Had she been running too? How could she go so fast with Ezinma on her back? Although the night was cool, Ekwefi was beginning to feel hot from her running. She continually ran into the luxuriant weeds and creepers that walled in the path. Once she tripped up and fell. Only then did she realise, with a start, that Chielo had stopped her chanting. Her heart beat violently and she stood still. Then Chielo's renewed outburst came from only a few paces ahead. But Ekwefi could not see her. She shut her eyes for a while and opened them again in an effort to see. But it was useless. She could not see beyond her nose.

There were no stars in the sky because there was a rain-cloud. Fireflies went about with their tiny green lamps, which only made the darkness more profound. Between Chielo's outbursts the night was alive with the shrill tremor of forest insects woven into the darkness.

"*Agbala do-o-o-o! . . . Agbala ekeneo-o-o-o! . . .* " Ekwefi trudged behind, neither getting too near nor keeping too far back. She thought they must be going towards the sacred cave. Now that she walked slowly she had time to think. What would she do when they got to the cave? She would not dare to enter. She would wait at the mouth, all alone in that fearful place. She thought of all the terrors of the night. She remembered the night, long ago, when she had seen *Ogbuagali-odu,* one of those evil essences loosed upon the world by the potent "medicines" which the tribe had made in the distant past against its enemies but had now forgotten how to control. Ekwefi had been returning from the stream with her mother on a dark night like this when they saw its glow as it flew in their direction. They had thrown their water-pots and lain by the roadside expecting the sinister light to descend on them and kill them. That was the only time Ekwefi ever saw *Ogbuagali-odu.* But although it had happened so long ago, her blood still ran cold whenever she remembered that night.

The priestess's voice came at longer intervals now, but its vigour was undiminished. The air was cool and damp with dew. Ezinma sneezed. Ekwefi muttered, "Life to you." At the same time the priestess also said, "Life to you, my daughter." Ezinma's voice from the darkness warmed her mother's heart. She trudged slowly along.

And then the priestess screamed. "Somebody is walking behind me!" she said. "Whether you are spirit or man, may Agbala shave your head with a blunt razor! May he twist your neck until you see your heels!"

Ekwefi stood rooted to the spot. One mind said to her: "Woman, go home before Agbala does you harm." But she could not. She stood until Chielo had increased the distance between them and she began to follow again. She had already walked so long that she began to feel a slight numbness in the limbs and in the head. Then it occurred to her that they could not have been heading for the cave. They must have by-passed it long ago; they must be going towards Umuachi, the farthest village in the clan. Chielo's voice now came after long intervals.

It seemed to Ekwefi that the night had become a little lighter. The cloud had lifted and a few stars were out. The moon must be preparing to rise, its sullenness over. When the moon rose later in the night, people said it was refusing food, as a sullen husband refuses his wife's food when they have quarrelled.

"Agbala do-o-o-o! Umuachi! Agbala ekene unuo-o-o!" It was just as Ekwefi had thought. The priestess was now saluting the village of Umuachi. It was unbelievable, the distance they had covered. As they emerged into the open village from the narrow forest track the darkness was softened and it became possible to see the vague shape of trees. Ekwefi screwed her eyes up in an effort to see her daughter and the priestess, but whenever she thought she saw their shape it immediately dissolved like a melting lump of darkness. She walked numbly along.

Chielo's voice was now rising continuously, as when she first set out. Ekwefi had a feeling of spacious openness, and she guessed they must be on the village *ilo,* or playground. And she realised too with something like a jerk that Chielo was no longer moving forward. She was, in fact, returning. Ekwefi quickly moved away from her line of retreat. Chielo passed by, and they began to go back the way they had come.

It was a long and weary journey and Ekwefi felt like a sleepwalker most of the way. The moon was definitely rising, and although it had not yet appeared on the sky its light had already melted down the darkness. Ekwefi could now discern the figure of the priestess and her burden. She slowed down her pace so as to increase the distance between them. She was afraid of what might happen if Chielo suddenly turned round and saw her.

She had prayed for the moon to rise. But now she found the half-light of the incipient moon more terrifying than the darkness. The world was now peopled with vague, fantastic figures that dissolved under her steady gaze and then formed again in new shapes. At one stage Ekwefi was so afraid that she nearly called out to Chielo for companionship and human sympathy. What she had seen was the shape of a man climbing a palm tree, his head pointing to the earth and his legs skywards. But at that very moment Chielo's voice rose again in her possessed chanting, and Ekwefi recoiled, because there was no humanity there. It was not the same Chielo who sat with her in the market and sometimes bought bean-cakes for Ezinma, whom she called her daughter. It was a different woman—the priestess of Agbala, the Oracle of the Hills and Caves. Ekwefi trudged along between two fears. The sound of her benumbed steps seemed to come from some other person walking behind her. Her arms were folded across her bare breasts. Dew fell heavily and the air was cold. She could no longer think, not even about the terrors of night. She just jogged along in a half-sleep only waking to full life when Chielo sang.

At last they took a turning and began to head for the caves. From then on, Chielo never ceased in her chanting. She greeted her god in a multitude of names—the owner of the future, the messenger of earth, the god who cut a man down when his life was sweetest to him. Ekwefi was also awakened and her benumbed fears revived.

The moon was now up and she could see Chielo and Ezinma clearly. How a woman could carry a child of that size so easily and for so long was a miracle. But Ekwefi was not thinking about that. Chielo was not a woman that night.

"Agbala do-o-o-o! Agbala ekeneo-o-o! Chi negbu madu ubosi ndu ya nato ya uto daluo-o-o! . . ."[7]

Ekwefi could already see the hills looming in the moonlight. They formed a circular ring with a break at one point through which the foot-track led to the centre of the circle.

As soon as the priestess stepped into this ring of hills her voice was not only doubled in strength but was thrown back on all sides. It was indeed the shrine of a

---

7. Agbala wants! Agbala greets! Spirit who kills one on the day his life is so pleasant he gives thanks!

great god. Ekwefi picked her way carefully and quietly. She was already beginning to doubt the wisdom of her coming. Nothing would happen to Ezinma, she thought. And if anything happened to her could she stop it? She would not dare to enter the underground caves. Her coming was quite useless, she thought.

As these things went through her mind she did not realise how close they were to the cave mouth. And so when the priestess with Ezinma on her back disappeared through a hole hardly big enough to pass a hen, Ekwefi broke into a run as though to stop them. As she stood gazing at the circular darkness which had swallowed them, tears gushed from her eyes, and she swore within her that if she heard Ezinma cry she would rush into the cave to defend her against all the gods in the world. She would die with her.

Having sworn that oath, she sat down on a stony ledge and waited. Her fear had vanished. She could hear the priestess's voice, all its metal taken out of it by the vast emptiness of the cave. She buried her face in her lap and waited.

She did not know how long she waited. It must have been a very long time. Her back was turned on the footpath that led out of the hills. She must have heard a noise behind her and turned round sharply. A man stood there with a matchet in his hand. Ekwefi uttered a scream and sprang to her feet.

"Don't be foolish," said Okonkwo's voice. "I thought you were going into the shrine with Chielo," he mocked.

Ekwefi did not answer. Tears of gratitude filled her eyes. She knew her daughter was safe.

"Go home and sleep," said Okonkwo. "I shall wait here."

"I shall wait too. It is almost dawn. The first cock has crowed."

As they stood there together, Ekwefi's mind went back to the days when they were young. She had married Anene because Okonkwo was too poor then to marry. Two years after her marriage to Anene she could bear it no longer and she ran away to Okonkwo. It had been early in the morning. The moon was shining. She was going to the stream to fetch water. Okonkwo's house was on the way to the stream. She went in and knocked at his door and he came out. Even in those days he was not a man of many words. He just carried her into his bed and in the darkness began to feel around her waist for the loose end of her cloth.

Chapter 12

On the following morning the entire neighbourhood wore a festive air because Okonkwo's friend, Obierika, was celebrating his daughter's *uri*. It was the day on which her suitor (having already paid the greater part of her bride-price) would bring palm-wine not only to her parents and immediate relatives but to the wide and extensive group of kinsmen called *umunna*. Everybody had been invited—men, women and children. But it was really a woman's ceremony and the central figures were the bride and her mother.

As soon as day broke, breakfast was hastily eaten and women and children began to gather at Obierika's compound to help the bride's mother in her difficult but happy task of cooking for a whole village.

Okonkwo's family was astir like any other family in the neighbourhood. Nwoye's mother and Okonkwo's youngest wife were ready to set out for Obierika's compound with all their children. Nwoye's mother carried a basket of coco-yams, a cake of salt and smoked fish which she would present to Obierika's wife. Okonkwo's youngest wife, Ojiugo, also had a basket of plantains and coco-yams and a small pot of palm-oil. Their children carried pots of water.

Ekwefi was tired and sleepy from the exhausting experiences of the previous night. It was not very long since they had returned. The priestess, with Ezinma sleeping on her back, had crawled out of the shrine on her belly like a snake. She had not as much as looked at Okonkwo and Ekwefi or shown any surprise at finding them at the mouth of the cave. She looked straight ahead of her and walked back to the village. Okonkwo and his wife followed at a respectful distance. They thought the priestess might be going to her house, but she went to Okonkwo's compound, passed through his *obi* and into Ekwefi's hut and walked into her bedroom. She placed Ezinma carefully on the bed and went away without saying a word to anybody.

Ezinma was still sleeping when everyone else was astir, and Ekwefi asked Nwoye's mother and Ojiugo to explain to Obierika's wife that she would be late. She had got ready her basket of coco-yams and fish, but she must wait for Ezinma to wake.

"You need some sleep yourself," said Nwoye's mother. "You look very tired."

As they spoke Ezinma emerged from the hut, rubbing her eyes and stretching her spare frame. She saw the other children with their water-pots and remembered that they were going to fetch water for Obierika's wife. She went back to the hut and brought her pot.

"Have you slept enough?" asked her mother.

"Yes," she replied. "Let us go."

"Not before you have had your breakfast," said Ekwefi. And she went into her hut to warm the vegetable soup she had cooked last night.

"We shall be going," said Nwoye's mother. "I will tell Obierika's wife that you are coming later." And so they all went to help Obierika's wife—Nwoye's mother and her four children and Ojiugo with her two.

As they trooped through Okonkwo's *obi* he asked: "Who will prepare my afternoon meal?"

"I shall return to do it," said Ojiugo.

Okonkwo was also feeling tired and sleepy, for although nobody else knew it, he had not slept at all last night. He had felt very anxious but did not show it. When Ekwefi had followed the priestess, he had allowed what he regarded as a reasonable and manly interval to pass and then gone with his matchet to the shrine, where he thought they must be. It was only when he had got there that it had occurred to him that the priestess might have chosen to go round the villages first. Okonkwo had returned home and sat waiting. When he thought he had waited long enough he again returned to the shrine. But the Hills and the Caves were as silent as death. It was only on his fourth trip that he had found Ekwefi, and by then he had become gravely worried.

Obierika's compound was as busy as an ant-hill. Temporary cooking tripods were erected on every available space by bringing together three blocks of sun-dried earth and making a fire in their midst. Cooking pots went up and down the tripods, and foo-foo was pounded in a hundred wooden mortars. Some of the women cooked the yams and the cassava, the others prepared vegetable soup. Young men pounded the foo-foo or split firewood. The children made endless trips to the stream.

Three young men helped Obierika to slaughter the two goats with which the soup was made. They were very fat goats, but the fattest of all was tethered to a peg near the wall of the compound. It was as big as a small cow. Obierika had sent one of his relatives all the way to Umuike to buy that goat. It was the one he would present alive to his in-laws.

"The market of Umuike is a wonderful place," said the young man who had been sent by Obierika to buy the giant goat. "There are so many people on it that if you threw up a grain of sand it would not find a way to fall to earth again."

"It is the result of a great medicine," said Obierika. "The people of Umuike wanted their market to grow and swallow up the markets of their neighbours. So they made a powerful medicine. Every market-day, before the first cock-crow, this medicine stands on the market-ground in the shape of an old woman with a fan. With this magic fan she beckons to the market all the neighbouring clans. She beckons in front of her and behind her, to her right and to her left."

"And so everybody comes," said another man, "honest men and thieves. They can steal your cloth from off your waist in that market."

"Yes," said Obierika. "I warned Nwankwo to keep a sharp eye and a sharp ear. There was once a man who went to sell a goat. He led it on a thick rope which he tied round his wrist. But as he walked through the market he realised that people were pointing at him as they do to a madman. He could not understand it until he looked back and saw that what he led at the end of the tether was not a goat but a heavy log of wood."

"Do you think a thief can do that kind of thing single-handed?" asked Nwankwo.

"No," said Obierika. "They use medicine."

When they had cut the goats' throats and collected the blood in a bowl, they held them over an open fire to burn off the hair, and the smell of burning hair blended with the smell of cooking. Then they washed them and cut them up for the women who prepared the soup.

All this ant-hill activity was going smoothly when a sudden interruption came. It was a cry in the distance: *Oji odu achu iiiji-o-o! (The one that uses its tail to drive flies away!)* Every woman immediately abandoned whatever she was doing and rushed out in the direction of the cry.

"We cannot all rush out like that, leaving what we are cooking to burn in the fire," shouted Chielo, the priestess. "Three or four of us should stay behind."

"It is true," said another woman. "We will allow three or four women to stay behind."

Five women stayed behind to look after the cooking-pots, and all the rest rushed away to see the cow that had been let loose. When they saw it they drove it back to its owner, who at once paid the heavy fine which the village imposed on anyone whose cow was let loose on his neighbours' crops. When the women had exacted the penalty they checked among themselves to see if any woman had failed to come out when the cry had been raised.

"Where is Mgbogo?" asked one of them.

"She is ill in bed," said Mgbogo's next-door neighbour. "She has *iba.*"

"The only other person is Udenkwo," said another woman, "and her child is not twenty-eight days yet."

Those women whom Obierika's wife had not asked to help her with the cooking returned to their homes, and the rest went back, in a body, to Obierika's compound.

"Whose cow is it?" asked the women who had been allowed to stay behind.

"It was my husband's," said Ezelagbo. "One of the young children had opened the gate of the cow-shed."

Early in the afternoon the first two pots of palm-wine arrived from Obierika's in-laws. They were duly presented to the women, who drank a cup or two each, to help them in their cooking. Some of it also went to the bride and her attendant maidens, who were putting the last delicate touches of razor to her coiffure and cam wood on her smooth skin.

When the heat of the sun began to soften, Obierika's son, Maduka, took a long broom and swept the ground in front of his father's *obi*. And as if they had been waiting for that, Obierika's relatives and friends began to arrive, every man with his goatskin bag hung on one shoulder and a rolled goatskin mat under his arm. Some of them were accompanied by their sons bearing carved wooden stools. Okonkwo was one of them. They sat in a half circle and began to talk of many things. It would not be long before the suitors came.

Okonkwo brought out his snuff-bottle and offered it to Ogbuefi Ezenwa, who sat next to him. Ezenwa took it, tapped it on his knee-cap, rubbed his left palm on his body to dry it before tipping a little snuff into it. His actions were deliberate, and he spoke as he performed them.

"I hope our in-laws will bring many pots of wine. Although they come from a village that is known for being close-fisted, they ought to know that Akueke is the bride for a king."

"They dare not bring fewer than thirty pots," said Okonkwo. "I shall tell them my mind if they do."

At that moment Obierika's son, Maduka, led out the giant goat from the inner compound, for his father's relatives to see. They all admired it and said that that was the way things should be done. The goat was then led back to the inner compound.

Very soon after, the in-laws began to arrive. Young men and boys in single file, each carrying a pot of wine, came first. Obierika's relatives counted the pots as they came. Twenty, twenty-five. There was a long break, and the hosts looked at each other as if to say, "I told you." Then more pots came. Thirty, thirty-five, forty, forty-five. The hosts nodded in approval and seemed to say, "Now they are behaving like men." Altogether there were fifty pots of wine. After the pot-bearers came Ibe, the suitor, and the elders of his family. They sat in a half-moon, thus completing a circle with their hosts. The pots of wine stood in their midst. Then the bride, her mother and half a dozen other women and girls emerged from the inner compound, and went round the circle shaking hands with all. The bride's mother led the way, followed by the bride and the other women. The married women wore their best cloths and the girls wore red and black waist-beads and anklets of brass.

When the women retired. Obierika presented kola nuts to his in-laws. His eldest brother broke the first one. "Life to all of us," he said as he broke it. "And let there be friendship between your family and ours."

The crowd answered: *"Ee-e-e!"*

"We are giving you our daughter today. She will be a good wife to you. She will bear you nine sons like the mother of our town."

"Ee-e-e!"

The oldest man in the camp of the visitors replied: "It will be good for you and it will be good for us."

"Ee-e-e!"

"This is not the first time my people have come to marry your daughter. My mother was one of you."

"Ee-e-e!"

"And this will not be the last, because you understand us and we understand you. You are a great family."

"Ee-e-e!"

"Prosperous men and great warriors." He looked in the direction of Okonkwo. "Your daughter will bear us sons like you."

"Ee-e-e!"

The kola was eaten and the drinking of palm-wine began. Groups of four or five men sat round with a pot in their midst. As the evening wore on, food was presented to the guests. There were huge bowls of foo-foo and steaming pots of soup. There were also pots of yam pottage. It was a great feast.

As night fell, burning torches were set on wooden tripods and the young men raised a song. The elders sat in a circle and the singers went round singing each man's praise as they came before him. They had something to say for every man. Some were great farmers, some were orators who spoke for the clan; Okonkwo was the greatest wrestler and warrior alive. When they had gone round the circle they settled down in the centre, and girls came from the inner compound to dance. At first the bride was not among them. But when she finally appeared holding a cock in her right hand, a loud cheer rose from the crowd. All the other dancers made way for her. She presented the cock to the musicians and began to dance. Her brass anklets rattled as she danced and her body gleamed with cam wood in the soft yellow light. The musicians with their wood, clay and metal instruments went from song to song. And they were all gay. They sang the latest song in the village:

> *If I hold her hand*
> *She says, "Don't touch!"*
> *If I hold her foot*
> *She says, "Don't touch!"*
> *But when I hold her waist-beads*
> *She pretends not to know.*

The night was already far spent when the guests rose to go, taking their bride home to spend seven market weeks with her suitor's family. They sang songs as they went, and on their way they paid short courtesy visits to prominent men like Okonkwo, before they finally left for their village. Okonkwo made a present of two cocks to them.

Chapter 13

Go-di-di-go-go-di-go. Di-go-go-di-go. It was the *ekwe* talking to the clan. One of the things every man learned was the language of the hollowed-out instrument. Diim! Diim! Diim! boomed the cannon at intervals.

The first cock had not crowed, and Umuofia was still swallowed up in sleep and silence when the *ekwe* began to talk, and the cannon shattered the silence. Men stirred on their bamboo beds and listened anxiously. Somebody was dead. The cannon seemed to rend the sky. Di-go-go-di-go-di-di-go-go floated in the message-laden night air. The faint and distant wailing of women settled like a sediment of sorrow on the earth. Now and again a full-chested lamentation rose above the wailing when- ever a man came into the place of death. He raised his voice once or twice in manly sorrow and then sat down with the other men listening to the endless wailing of the women and the esoteric language of the *ekwe*. Now and again the cannon boomed. The wailing of the women would not be heard beyond the village, but the *ekwe* car- ried the news to all the nine villages and even beyond. It began by naming the clan: *Umuofia obodo dike* "the land of the brave." *Umuofia obodo dike! Umuofia obodo dike!* It said this over and over again, and as it dwelt on it, anxiety mounted in every heart that heaved on a bamboo bed that night. Then it went nearer and named the village: *Iguedo of the yellow grinding-stone!* It was Okonkwo's village. Again and again Iguedo was called and men waited breathlessly in all the nine villages. At last the man was named and people sighed "E-u-u, Ezeudu is dead." A cold shiver ran down Okonkwo's back as he remembered the last time the old man had visited him. "That boy calls you father," he had said. "Bear no hand in his death."

Ezeudu was a great man, and so all the clan was at his funeral. The ancient drums of death beat, guns and cannon were fired, and men dashed about in frenzy, cutting down every tree or animal they saw, jumping over walls and dancing on the roof. It was a warrior's funeral, and from morning till night warriors came and went in their age-groups. They all wore smoked raffia skirts and their bodies were painted with chalk and charcoal. Now and again an ancestral spirit or *egwugwu* appeared from the underworld, speaking in a tremulous, unearthly voice and completely covered in raffia. Some of them were very violent, and there had been a mad rush for shelter earlier in the day when one appeared with a sharp matchet and was only prevented from doing serious harm by two men who restrained him with the help of a strong rope tied round his waist. Sometimes he turned round and chased those men, and they ran for their lives. But they always returned to the long rope he trailed behind. He sang, in a terrifying voice, that Ekwenzu, or Evil Spirit, had entered his eye.

But the most dreaded of all was yet to come. He was always alone and was shaped like a coffin. A sickly odour hung in the air wherever he went, and flies went with him. Even the greatest medicine-men took shelter when he was near. Many years ago another *egwugwu* had dared to stand his ground before him and had been transfixed to the spot for two days. This one had only one hand and with it carried a basket full of water.

But some of the *egwugwu* were quite harmless. One of them was so old and infirm that he leaned heavily on a stick. He walked unsteadily to the place where the corpse was laid, gazed at it a while and went away again—to the underworld.

The land of the living was not far removed from the domain of the ancestors. There was coming and going between them, especially at festivals and also when an old man died, because an old man was very close to the ancestors. A man's life from birth to death was a series of transition rites which brought him nearer and nearer to his ancestors.

Ezeudu had been the oldest man in the village, and at his death there were only three men in the whole clan who were older, and four or five others in his own age-group. Whenever one of these ancient men appeared in the crowd to dance unsteadily the funeral steps of the tribe, younger men gave way and the tumult subsided.

It was a great funeral, such as befitted a noble warrior. As the evening drew near, the shouting and the firing of guns, the beating of drums and the brandishing and clanging of matchets increased.

Ezeudu had taken three titles in his life. It was a rare achievement. There were only four titles in the clan, and only one or two men in any generation ever achieved the fourth and highest. When they did, they became the lords of the land. Because he had taken titles, Ezeudu was to be buried after dark with only a glowing brand to light the sacred ceremony.

But before this quiet and final rite, the tumult increased tenfold. Drums beat violently and men leaped up and down in a frenzy. Guns were fired on all sides and sparks flew out as matchets clanged together in warriors' salutes. The air was full of dust and the smell of gunpowder. It was then that the one-handed spirit came, carrying a basket full of water. People made way for him on all sides and the noise subsided. Even the smell of gunpowder was swallowed in the sickly smell that now filled the air. He danced a few steps to the funeral drums and then went to see the corpse.

"Ezeudu!" he called in his gutteral voice. "If you had been poor in your last life I would have asked you to be rich when you come again. But you were rich. If you had been a coward, I would have asked you to bring courage. But you were a fearless warrior. If you had died young, I would have asked you to get life. But you lived long. So I shall ask you to come again the way you came before. If your death was the death of nature, go in peace. But if a man caused it, do not allow him a moment's rest." He danced a few more steps and went away.

The drums and the dancing began again and reached fever-heat. Darkness was around the corner, and the burial was near. Guns fired the last salute and the cannon rent the sky. And then from the centre of the delirious fury came a cry of agony and shouts of horror. It was as if a spell had been cast. All was silent. In the centre of the crowd a boy lay in a pool of blood. It was the dead man's sixteen-year-old son, who with his brothers and half-brothers had been dancing the traditional farewell to their father. Okonkwo's gun had exploded and a piece of iron had pierced the boy's heart.

The confusion that followed was without parallel in the tradition of Umuofia. Violent deaths were frequent, but nothing like this had ever happened.

The only course open to Okonkwo was to flee from the clan. It was a crime against the earth goddess to kill a clansman, and a man who committed it must flee from the land. The crime was of two kinds, male and female. Okonkwo had committed the female, because it had been inadvertent. He could return to the clan after seven years.

That night he collected his most valuable belongings into headloads. His wives wept bitterly and their children wept with them without knowing why. Obierika and half a dozen other friends came to help and to console him. They each made nine or ten trips carrying Okonkwo's yams to store in Obierika's barn. And before the cock crowed Okonkwo and his family were fleeing to his motherland. It was a little village called Mbanta, just beyond the borders of Mbaino.

As soon as the day broke, a large crowd of men from Ezeudu's quarter stormed Okonkwo's compound, dressed in garbs of war. They set fire to his houses, demolished his red walls, killed his animals and destroyed his barn. It was the justice of the earth goddess, and they were merely her messengers. They had no hatred in their hearts against Okonkwo. His greatest friend, Obierika, was among them. They were merely cleansing the land which Okonkwo had polluted with the blood of a clansman.

Obierika was a man who thought about things. When the will of the goddess had been done, he sat down in his *obi* and mourned his friend's calamity. Why should a man suffer so greviously for an offence he had committed inadvertently? But although he thought for a long time he found no answer. He was merely led into greater complexities. He remembered his wife's twin children, whom he had thrown away. What crime had they committed? The Earth had decreed that they were an offence on the land and must be destroyed. And if the clan did not exact punishment for an offence against the great goddess, her wrath was loosed on all the land and not just on the offender. As the elders said, if one finger brought oil it soiled the others.

Okonkwo was well received by his mother's kinsmen in Mbanta. The old man who received him was his mother's younger brother, who was now the eldest surviving member of that family. His name was Uchendu, and it was he who had received Okonkwo's mother twenty and ten years before when she had been brought home from Umuofia to be buried with her people. Okonkwo was only a boy then and Uchendu still remembered him crying the traditional farewell: "Mother, mother, mother is going."

That was many years ago. Today Okonkwo was not bringing his mother home to be buried with her people. He was taking his family of three wives and eleven children to seek refuge in his motherland. As soon as Uchendu saw him with his sad and weary company he guessed what had happened, and asked no questions. It was not until the following day that Okonkwo told him the full story. The old man listened silently to the end and then said with some relief: "It is a female *ochu.*" And he arranged the requisite rites and sacrifices.

Okonkwo was given a plot of ground on which to build his compound, and two or three pieces of land on which to farm during the coming planting season. With the help of his mother's kinsmen he built himself an *obi* and three huts for his wives. He then installed his personal god and the symbols of his departed fathers. Each of Uchendu's five sons contributed three hundred seed-yams to enable their cousin to plant a farm, for as soon as the first rain came farming would begin.

At last the rain came. It was sudden and tremendous. For two or three moons the sun had been gathering strength till it seemed to breathe a breath of fire on the earth. All the grass had long been scorched brown, and the sand felt like live coals to the feet. Evergreen trees wore a dusty coat of brown. The birds were silenced in the forests, and the world lay panting under the live, vibrating heat. And then came the clap of thunder. It was an angry, metallic and thirsty clap, unlike the deep and liquid rumbling of the rainy season. A mighty wind arose and filled the air with dust. Palm trees swayed as the wind combed their leaves into flying crests like strange and fantastic coiffure.

When the rain finally came, it was in large, solid drops of frozen water which the people called "the nuts of the water of heaven." They were hard and painful on the body as they fell, yet young people ran about happily picking up the cold nuts and throwing them into their mouths to melt.

The earth quickly came to life and the birds in the forests fluttered around and chirped merrily. A vague scent of life and green vegetation was diffused in the air. As the rain began to fall more soberly and in smaller liquid drops, children sought for shelter, and all were happy, refreshed and thankful.

Okonkwo and his family worked very hard to plant a new farm. But it was like beginning life anew without the vigour and enthusiasm of youth, like learning to become left-handed in old age. Work no longer had for him the pleasure it used to have, and when there was no work to do he sat in a silent half-sleep.

His life had been ruled by a great passion—to become one of the lords of the clan. That had been his life-spring. And he had all but achieved it. Then everything had been broken. He had been cast out of his clan like a fish on to a dry, sandy beach, panting. Clearly his personal god or *chi* was not made for great things. A man could not rise beyond the destiny of his *chi*. The saying of the elders was not true—that if a man said yea his *chi* also affirmed. Here was a man whose *chi* said nay despite his own affirmation.

The old man, Uchendu, saw clearly that Okonkwo had yielded to despair and he was greatly troubled. He would speak to him after the *isa-ifi* ceremony.

The youngest of Uchendu's five sons, Amikwu, was marrying a new wife. The bride-price had been paid and all but the last ceremony had been performed. Amikwu and his people had taken palm-wine to the bride's kinsmen about two moons before Okonkwo's arrival in Mbanta. And so it was time for the final ceremony of confession.

The daughters of the family were all there, some of them having come a long way from their homes in distant villages. Uchendu's eldest daughter had come from Obodo, nearly half a day's journey away. The daughters of Uchendu's brothers were also there. It was a full gathering of *umuada*, in the same way as they would meet if a death occurred in the family. There were twenty-two of them.

They sat in a big circle on the ground and the bride sat in the centre with a hen in her right hand. Uchendu sat by her, holding the ancestral staff of the family. All the other men stood outside the circle, watching. Their wives watched also. It was evening and the sun was setting.

Uchendu's eldest daughter, Njide, asked the questions.

"Remember that if you do not answer truthfully you will suffer or even die at child-birth," she began. "How many men have lain with you since my brother first expressed the desire to marry you?"

"None," she replied simply.

"Answer truthfully," urged the other women.

"None?" asked Njide.

"None," she answered.

"Swear on this staff of my fathers," said Uchendu.

"I swear," said the bride.

Uchendu took the hen from her, slit its throat with a sharp knife and allowed some of the blood to fall on his ancestral staff.

From that day Amikwu took the young bride to his hut and she became his wife. The daughters of the family did not return to their homes immediately but spent two or three days with their kinsmen.

On the second day Uchendu called together his sons and daughters and his nephew, Okonkwo. The men brought their goatskin mats, with which they sat on the floor, and the women sat on a sisal mat spread on a raised bank of earth. Uchendu pulled gently at his grey beard and gnashed his teeth. Then he began to speak, quietly and deliberately, picking his words with great care:

"It is Okonkwo that I primarily wish to speak to," he began. "But I want all of you to note what I am going to say. I am an old man and you are all children. I know more about the world than any of you. If there is any one among you who thinks he knows more let him speak up." He paused, but no one spoke.

"Why is Okonkwo with us today? This is not his clan. We are only his mother's kinsmen. He does not belong here. He is an exile, condemned for seven years to live in a strange land. And so he is bowed with grief. But there is just one question I would like to ask him. Can you tell me, Okonkwo, why it is that one of the commonest names we give our children is Nneka, or 'Mother is Supreme?' We all know that a man is the head of the family and his wives do his bidding. A child belongs to its father and his family and not to its mother and her family. A man belongs to his fatherland and not to his motherland. And yet we say Nneka—'Mother is Supreme.' Why is that?"

There was silence. "I want Okonkwo to answer me," said Uchendu.

"I do not know the answer," Okonkwo replied.

"You do not know the answer? So you see that you are a child. You have many wives and many children—more children than I have. You are a great man in your clan. But you are still a child, *my* child. Listen to me and I shall tell you. But there is one more question I shall ask. Why is it that when a woman dies she is taken home to be buried with her own kinsmen? She is not buried with her husband's kinsmen. Why is that? Your mother was brought home to me and buried with my people. Why was that?"

Okonkwo shook his head.

"He does not know that either," said Uchendu, "and yet he is full of sorrow because he has come to live in his motherland for a few years." He laughed a mirthless laughter, and turned to his sons and daughters. "What about you? Can you answer my question?"

They all shook their heads.

"Then listen to me," he said and cleared his throat. "It's true that a child belongs to its father. But when a father beats his child, it seeks sympathy in its mother's hut. A man belongs to his fatherland when things are good and life is sweet. But when there is sorrow and bitterness he finds refuge in his motherland. Your mother is there to protect you. She is buried there. And that is why we say that mother is supreme. Is it right that you, Okonkwo, should bring your mother a heavy face and refuse to be comforted? Be careful or you may displease the dead. Your duty is to comfort your wives and children and take them back to your fatherland after seven years. But if you allow sorrow to weigh you down and kill you, they will all die in exile." He paused for a long while. "These are now your kinsmen." He waved at his sons and daughters. "You think you are the greatest sufferer in the world. Do you know that men are sometimes banished for life? Do you know that men sometimes lose all their yams and even their children? I had six wives once. I have none now except that young girl who knows not her right from her left. Do you know how many children I have buried—children I begot in my youth and strength? Twenty-two. I did not hang myself, and I am still alive. If you think you are the greatest sufferer in the world ask my daughter, Akeuni, how many twins she has borne and thrown away. Have you not heard the song they sing when a woman dies?

> For whom is it well, for whom is it well?
> There is no one for whom it is well.

"I have no more to say to you."

Chapter 15

It was in the second year of Okonkwo's exile that his friend, Obierika, came to visit him. He brought with him two young men, each of them carrying a heavy bag on his head. Okonkwo helped them put down their loads. It was clear that the bags were full of cowries.

Okonkwo was very happy to receive his friend. His wives and children were very happy too, and so were his cousins and their wives when he sent for them and told them who his guest was.

"You must take him to salute our father," said one of the cousins.

"Yes," replied Okonkwo. "We are going directly." But before they went he whispered something to his first wife. She nodded, and soon the children were chasing one of their cocks.

Uchendu had been told by one of his grandchildren that three strangers had come to Okonkwo's house. He was therefore waiting to receive them. He held out his hands to them when they came into his *obi*, and after they had shaken hands he asked Okonkwo who they were.

"This is Obierika, my great friend. I have already spoken to you about him."

"Yes," said the old man, turning to Obierika. "My son has told me about you, and I am happy you have come to see us. I knew your father, Iweka. He was a great man. He had many friends here and came to see them quite often. Those were good days when a man had friends in distant clans. Your generation does not know that. You stay at home, afraid of your next-door neighbour. Even a man's motherland is strange to him nowadays." He looked at Okonkwo. "I am an old man and I like to talk. That is all I am good for now." He got up painfully, went into an inner room and came back with a kola nut.

"Who are the young men with you?" he asked as he sat down again on his goat-skin. Okonkwo told him.

"Ah," he said. "Welcome, my sons." He presented the kola nut to them, and when they had seen it and thanked him, he broke it and they ate.

"Go into that room," he aid to Okonkwo, pointing with his finger. "You will find a pot of wine there."

Okonkwo brought the wine and they began to drink. It was a day old, and very strong.

"Yes," said Uchendu after a long silence. "People travelled more in those days. There is not a single clan in these parts that I do not know very well. Aninta, Umuazu, Ikeocha, Elumelu, Abame—I know them all."

"Have you heard," asked Obierika, "that Abame is no more?"

"How is that?" asked Uchendu and Okonkwo together.

"Abame has been wiped out," said Obierika. "It is a strange and terrible story. If I had not seen the few survivors with my own eyes and heard their story with my own ears, I would not have believed. Was it not on an Eke day that they fled into Umuofia?" he asked his two companions, and they nodded their heads.

"Three moons ago," said Obierika, "on an Eke market-day a little band of fugitives came into our town. Most of them were sons of our land whose mothers had been buried with us. But there were some too who came because they had friends in our town, and others who could think of nowhere else open to escape. And so they fled into Umuofia with a woeful story." He drank his palm-wine, and Okonkwo filled his horn again. He continued:

"During the last planting season a white man had appeared in their clan."

"An albino," suggested Okonkwo.

"He was not an albino. He was quite different." He sipped his wine. "And he was riding an iron horse.[1] The first people who saw him ran away, but he stood beckoning to them. In the end the fearless ones were near and even touched him. The elders consulted their Oracle and it told them that the strange man would break their clan and spread destruction among them." Obierika again drank a little of his wine. "And so they killed the white man and tied his iron horse to their sacred tree because it looked as if it would run away to call the man's friends. I forgot to tell you another thing which the Oracle said. It said that other white men were on their way. They were locusts, it said, and that first man was their harbinger sent to explore the terrain. And so they killed him."

1. Bicycle.

"What did the white man say before they killed him?" asked Uchendu.

"He said nothing," answered one of Obierika's companions.

"He said something, only they did not understand him," said Obierika. "He seemed to speak through his nose."

"One of the men told me," said Obierika's other companion, "that he repeated over and over again a word that resembled Mbaino. Perhaps he had been going to Mbaino and had lost his way."

"Anyway," resumed Obierika, "they killed him and tied up his iron horse. This was before the planting season began. For a long time nothing happened. The rains had come and yams had been sown. The iron horse was still tied to the sacred silk-cotton tree. And then one morning three white men led by a band of ordinary men like us came to the clan. They saw the iron horse and went away again. Most of the men and women of Abame had gone to their farms. Only a few of them saw these white men and their followers. For many market weeks nothing else happened. They have a big market in Abame on every other Afo day and, as you know, the whole clan gathers there. That was the day it happened. The three white men and a very large number of other men surrounded the market. They must have used a powerful medicine to make themselves invisible until the market was full. And they began to shoot. Everybody was killed, except the old and the sick who were at home and a handful of men and women whose *chi* were wide awake and brought them out of that market." He paused.

"Their clan is now completely empty. Even the sacred fish in their mysterious lake have fled and the lake has turned the colour of blood. A great evil has come upon their land as the Oracle had warned."

There was a long silence. Uchendu ground his teeth audibly. Then he burst out:

"Never kill a man who says nothing. Those men of Abame were fools. What did they know about the man?" He ground his teeth again and told a story to illustrate his point. "Mother Kite once sent her daughter to bring food. She went, and brought back a duckling. 'You have done very well,' said Mother Kite to her daughter, 'but tell me, what did the mother of this duckling say when you swooped and carried its child away?' 'It said nothing,' replied the young kite. 'It just walked away.' 'You must return the duckling,' said the Mother Kite. 'There is something ominous behind the silence.' And so Daughter Kite returned the duckling and took a chick instead. 'What did the mother of this chick do?' asked the old kite. 'It cried and raved and cursed me,' said the young kite. 'Then we can eat the chick,' said her mother. 'There is nothing to fear from someone who shouts.' Those men of Abame were fools."

"They were fools," said Okonkwo after a pause. "They had been warned that danger was ahead. They should have armed themselves with their guns and their matchets even when they went to market."

"They have paid for their foolishness," said Obierika. "But I am greatly afraid. We have heard stories about white men who made the powerful guns and the strong drinks and took slaves away across the seas, but no one thought the stories were true."

"There is no story that is not true," said Uchendu. "The world has no end, and what is good among one people is an abomination with others. We have albinos among us. Do you not think that they came to our clan by mistake, that they have strayed from their ways to a land where everybody is like them?"

Okonkwo's first wife soon finished her cooking and set before their guests a big meal of pounded yams and bitter-leaf soup. Okonkwo's son, Nwoye, brought in a pot of sweet wine tapped from the raffia palm.

"You are a big man now," Obierika said to Nwoye. "Your friend Anene asked me to greet you."

"Is he well?" asked Nwoye.

"We are all well," said Obierika.

Ezinma brought them a bowl of water with which to wash their hands. After that they began to eat and to drink the wine.

"When did you set out from home?" asked Okonkwo.

"We had meant to set out from my house before cock-crow," said Obierika. "But Nweke did not appear until it was quite light. Never make an early morning appointment with a man who has just married a new wife." They all laughed.

"Has Nweke married a wife?" asked Okonkwo.

"He has married Okadigbo's second daughter," said Obierika.

"That is very good," said Okonkwo. "I do not blame you for not hearing the cock crow."

When they had eaten, Obierika pointed at the two heavy bags.

"That is the money from your yams," he said. "I sold the big ones as soon as you left. Later on I sold some of the seed-yams and gave out others to share-croppers. I shall do that every year until you return. But I thought you would need the money now and so I brought it. Who knows what may happen tomorrow? Perhaps green men will come to our clan and shoot us."

"God will not permit it," said Okonkwo. "I do not know how to thank you."

"I can tell you," said Obierika. "Kill one of your sons for me."

"That will not be enough," said Okonkwo.

"Then kill yourself," said Obierika.

"Forgive me," said Okonkwo, smiling. "I shall not talk about thanking you any more."

Chapter 16

When nearly two years later Obierika paid another visit to his friend in exile the circumstances were less happy. The missionaries had come to Umuofia. They had built their church there, won a handful of converts and were already sending evangelists to the surrounding towns and villages. That was a source of great sorrow to the leaders of the clan; but many of them believed that the strange faith and the white man's god would not last. None of his converts was a man whose word was heeded in the assembly of the people. None of them was a man of title. They were mostly the kind of people that were called *efulefu*, worthless, empty men. The imagery of an *efulefu* in the language of the clan was a man who sold his matchet and wore the sheath to battle. Chielo, the priestess of Agbala, called the converts the excrement of the clan, and the new faith was a mad dog that had come to eat it up.

What moved Obierika to visit Okonkwo was the sudden appearance of the latter's son, Nwoye, among the missionaries in Umuofia.

"What are you doing here?" Obierika had asked when after many difficulties the missionaries had allowed him to speak to the boy.

"I am one of them," replied Nwoye.

"How is your father?" Obierika asked, not knowing what else to say.

"I don't know. He is not my father," said Nwoye, unhappily.

And so Obierika went to Mbanta to see his friend. And he found that Okonkwo did not wish to speak about Nwoye. It was only from Nwoye's mother that he heard scraps of the story.

The arrival of the missionaries had caused a considerable stir in the village of Mbanta. There were six of them and one was a white man. Every man and woman came out to see the white man. Stories about these strange men had grown since one of them had been killed in Abame and his iron horse tied to the sacred silk-cotton tree. And so everybody came to see the white man. It was the time of the year when everybody was at home. The harvest was over.

When they had all gathered, the white man began to speak to them. He spoke through an interpreter who was an Ibo man, though his dialect was different and harsh to the ears of Mbanta. Many people laughed at his dialect and the way he used words strangely. Instead of saying "myself" he always said "my buttocks." But he was a man of commanding presence and the clansmen listened to him. He said he was one of them, as they could see from his colour and his language. The other four black men were also their brothers, although one of them did not speak Ibo. The white man was also their brother because they were all sons of God. And he told them about this new God, the Creator of all the world and all the men and women. He told them that they worshipped false gods, gods of wood and stone. A deep murmur went through the crowd when he said this. He told them that the true God lived on high and that all men when they died went before Him for judgment. Evil men and all the heathen who in their blindness bowed to wood and stone were thrown into a fire that burned like palm-oil. But good men who worshipped the true God lived for ever in His happy kingdom. "We have been sent by this great God to ask you to leave your wicked ways and false gods and turn to Him so that you may be saved when you die," he said.

"Your buttocks understand our language," said someone lightheartedly and the crowd laughed.

"What did he say?" the white man asked his interpreter. But before he could answer, another man asked a question: "Where is the white man's horse?" he asked. The Ibo evangelists consulted among themselves and decided that the man probably meant bicycle. They told the white man and he smiled benevolently.

"Tell them," he said, "that I shall bring many iron horses when we have settled down among them. Some of them will even ride the iron horse themselves." This was interpreted to them but very few of them heard. They were talking excitedly among themselves because the white man had said he was going to live among them. They had not thought about that.

At this point an old man said he had a question. "Which is this god of yours," he asked, "the goddess of the earth, the god of the sky, Amadiora of the thunderbolt, or what?"

The interpreter spoke to the white man and he immediately gave his answer. "All the gods you have named are not gods at all. They are gods of deceit who will tell you to kill your fellows and destroy innocent children. There is only one true God and He has made the earth, the sky, you and me and all of us."

"If we leave our gods and follow your god," asked another man, "who will protect us from the anger of our neglected gods and ancestors?"

"Your gods are not alive and cannot do you any harm," replied the white man. "They are pieces of wood and stone."

When this was interpreted to the men of Mbanta they broke into derisive laughter. These men must be mad, they said to themselves. How else could they say that Ani and Amadior were harmless? And Idemili and Ogwugwu too? And some of them began to go away.

Then the missionaries burst into song. It was one of those gay and rollicking tunes of evangelism which had the power of plucking at silent and dusty chords in the heart of an Ibo man. The interpreter explained each verse to the audience, some of whom now stood enthralled. It was a story of brothers who lived in darkness and in fear, ignorant of the love of God. It told of one sheep out on the hills, away from the gates of God and from the tender shepherd's care.

After the singing the interpreter spoke about the Son of God whose name was Jesu Kristi. Okonkwo, who only stayed in the hope that it might come to chasing the men out of the village or whipping them, now said:

"You told us with your own mouth that there was only one god. Now you talk about his son. He must have a wife, then." The crowd agreed.

"I did not say He had a wife," said the interpreter, somewhat lamely.

"Your buttocks said he had a son," said the joker. "So he must have a wife and all of them must have buttocks."

The missionary ignored him and went on to talk about the Holy Trinity. At the end of it Okonkwo was fully convinced that the man was mad. Hs shrugged his shoulders and went away to tap his afternoon palm-wine.

But there was a young lad who had been captivated. His name was Nwoye, Okonkwo's first son. It was not the mad logic of the Trinity that captivated him. He did not understand it. It was the poetry of the new religion, something felt in the marrow. The hymn about brothers who sat in darkness and in fear seemed to answer a vague and persistent question that haunted his young soul——the question of the twins crying in the bush and the question of Ikemefuna who was killed. He felt a relief within as the hymn poured into his parched soul. The words of the hymn were like the drops of frozen rain melting on the dry plate of the panting earth. Nwoye's callow mind was greatly puzzled.

Chapter 17

The missionaries spent their first four or five nights in the market-place, and went into the village in the morning to preach the gospel. They asked who the king of the village was, but the villagers told them that there was no king. "We have men of high title and the chief priests and the elders," they said.

It was not very easy getting the men of high title and the elders together after the excitement of the first day. But the missionaries persevered, and in the end they were received by the rulers of Mbanta. They asked for a plot of land to build their church.

Every clan and village had its "evil forest." In it were buried all those who died of the really evil diseases, like leprosy and smallpox. It was also the dumping ground for the potent fetishes of great medicine-men when they died. An "evil forest" was, therefore, alive with sinister forces and powers of darkness. It was such a forest that the rulers of Mbanta gave to the missionaries. They did not really want them in their clan, and so they made them that offer which nobody in his right senses would accept.

"They want a piece of land to build their shrine," said Uchendu to his peers when they consulted among themselves. "We shall give them a piece of land." He paused, and there was a murmur of surprise and disagreement. "Let us give them a portion of the Evil Forest. They boast about victory over death. Let us give them a real battle-field in which to show their victory." They laughed and agreed, and sent for the missionaries, whom they had asked to leave them for a while so that they might "whisper together." They offered them as much of the Evil Forest as they cared to take. And to their greatest amazement the missionaries thanked them and burst into song.

"They do not understand," said some of the elders. "But they will understand when they go to their plot of land tomorrow morning." And they dispersed.

The next morning the crazy men actually began to clear a part of the forest and to build their house. The inhabitants of Mbanta expected them all to be dead within four days. The first day passed and the second and third and fourth, and none of them died. Everyone was puzzled. And then it became known that the white man's fetish had unbelievable power. It was said that he wore glasses on his eyes so that he could see and talk to evil spirits. Not long after, he won his first three converts.

Although Nwoye had been attracted to the new faith from the very first day, he kept it secret. He dared not go too near the missionaries for fear of his father. But whenever they came to preach in the open market-place or the village playground, Nwoye was there. And he was already beginning to know some of the simple stories they told.

"We have now built a church," said Mr. Kiaga, the interpreter, who was now in charge of the infant congregation. The white man had gone back to Umuofia, where he built his headquarters and from where he paid regular visits to Mr. Kiaga's congregation at Mbanta.

"We have now built a church," said Mr. Kiaga, "and we want you all to come in every seventh day to worship the true God."

On the following Sunday, Nwoye passed and re-passed the little red-earth and thatch building without summoning enough courage to enter. He heard the voice of singing and although it came from a handful of men it was loud and confident. Their church stood on a circular clearing that looked like the open mouth of the Evil Forest. Was it waiting to snap its teeth together? After passing and re-passing by the church, Nwoye returned home.

It was well known among the people of Mbanta that their gods and ancestors were sometimes long-suffering and would deliberately allow a man to go on defying them. But even in such cases they set their limit at seven market weeks or twenty-eight days. Beyond that limit no man was suffered to go. And so excitement mounted in the village as the seventh week approached since the impudent missionaries built their church in the Evil Forest. The villagers were so certain about the doom that awaited these men that one or two converts thought it wise to suspend their allegiance to the new faith.

At last the day came by which all the missionaries should have died. But they were still alive, building a new red-earth and thatch house for their teacher, Mr. Kiaga. That week they won a handful more converts. And for the first time they had a woman. Her name was Nneka, the wife of Amadi, who was a prosperous farmer. She was very heavy with child.

Nneka had had four previous pregnancies and childbirths. But each time she had borne twins, and they had been immediately thrown away. Her husband and his family were already becoming highly critical of such a woman and were not unduly perturbed when they found she had fled to join the Christians. It was a good riddance.

One morning Okonkwo's cousin, Amikwu, was passing by the church on his way from the neighbouring village, when he saw Nwoye among the Christians. He was greatly surprised, and when he got home he went straight to Okonkwo's hut and told him what he had seen. The women began to talk excitedly, but Okonkwo sat unmoved.

It was late afternoon before Nwoye returned. He went into the *obi* and saluted his father, but he did not answer. Nwoye turned round to walk into the inner compound when his father, suddenly overcome with fury, sprang to his feet and gripped him by the neck.

"Where have you been?" he stammered.

Nwoye struggled to free himself from the choking grip.

"Answer me," roared Okonkwo, "before I kill you!" He seized a heavy stick that lay on the dwarf wall and hit him two or three savage blows.

"Answer me!" he roared again. Nwoye stood looking at him and did not say a word. The women were screaming outside, afraid to go in.

"Leave that boy at once!" said a voice in the outer compound. It was Okonkwo's uncle Uchendu. "Are you mad?"

Okonkwo did not answer. But he left hold of Nwoye, who walked away and never returned.

He went back to the church and told Mr. Kiaga that he had decided to go to Umuofia, where the white missionary had set up a school to teach young Christians to read and write.

Mr. Kiaga's joy was very great. "Blessed is he who forsakes his father and his mother for my sake," he intoned. "Those that hear my words are my father and my mother."

Nwoye did not fully understand. But he was happy to leave his father. He would return later to his mother and his brothers and sisters and convert them to the new faith.

As Okonkwo sat in his hut that night, gazing into a log fire, he thought over the matter. A sudden fury rose within him and he felt a strong desire to take up his matchet, go to the church and wipe out the entire vile and miscreant gang. But on further thought he told himself that Nwoye was not worth fighting for. Why, he cried in his heart, should he, Okonkwo, of all people be cursed with such a son? He saw clearly in it the finger of his personal god or *chi*. For how else could he explain his great misfortune and exile and now his despicable son's behaviour? Now that he had time to think of it, his son's crime stood out in stark enormity. To abandon the gods of one's father and go about with a lot of effeminate men clucking like old hens was the very depth of abomination. Suppose when he died all his male children decided to follow Nwoye's steps and abandon their ancestors? Okonkwo felt a cold shudder run through him at the terrible prospect, like the prospect of annihilation. He saw himself and his father crowding round their ancestral shrine waiting in vain for worship and sacrifice and finding nothing but ashes of bygone days, and his children the while praying to the white man's god. If such a thing were ever to happen, he, Okonkwo, would wipe them off the face of the earth.

Okonkwo was popularly called the "Roaring Flame." As he looked into the log fire he recalled the name. He was a flaming fire. How then could he have begotten a son like Nwoye, degenerate and effeminate? Perhaps he was not his son. No! he could not be. His wife had played him false. He would teach her! But Nwoye resembled his grandfather, Unoka, who was Okonkwo's father. He pushed the thought out of his mind. He, Okonkwo, was called a flaming fire. How could he have begotten a woman for a son? At Nwoye's age Okonkwo had already become famous throughout Umuofia for his wrestling and his fearlessness.

He sighed heavily, and as if in sympathy the smouldering log also sighed. And immediately Okonkwo's eyes were opened and he saw the whole matter clearly. Living fire begets cold, impotent ash. He sighed again, deeply.

Chapter 18

The young church in Mbanta had a few crises early in its life. At first the clan had assumed that it would not survive. But it had gone on living and gradually becoming stronger. The clan was worried, but not overmuch. If a gang of *efulefu* decided to live in the Evil Forest it was their own affair. When one came to think of it, the Evil Forest was a fit home for such undesirable people. It was true they were rescuing twins from the bush, but they never brought them into the village. As far as the villagers were concerned, the twins still remained where they had been thrown away. Surely the earth goddess would not visit the sins of the missionaries on the innocent villagers?

But on one occasion the missionaries had tried to overstep the bounds. Three converts had gone into the village and boasted openly that all the gods were dead and impotent and that they were prepared to defy them by burning all their shrines.

"Go and burn your mothers' genitals," said one of the priests. The men were seized and beaten until they streamed with blood. After that nothing happened for a long time between the church and the clan.

But stories were already gaining ground that the white man had not only brought a religion but also a government. It was said that they had built a place of judgement in Umuofia to protect the followers of their religion. It was even said that they had hanged one man who killed a missionary.

Although such stories were now often told they looked like fairy-tales in Mbanta and did not as yet affect the relationship between the new church and the clan. There was no question of killing a missionary here, for Mr. Kiaga, despite his madness, was quite harmless. As for his converts, no one could kill them without having to flee from the clan, for in spite of their worthlessness they still belonged to the clan. And so nobody gave serious thought to the stories about the white man's government or the consequences of killing the Christians. If they became more troublesome than they already were they would simply be driven out of the clan.

And the little church was at that moment too deeply absorbed in its own troubles to annoy the clan. It all began over the question of admitting outcasts.

These outcasts, or *osu*, seeing that the new religion welcomed twins and such abominations, thought that it was possible that they would also be received. And so one Sunday two of them went into the church. There was an immediate stir; but so great was the work the new religion had done among the converts that they did not immediately leave the church when the outcasts came in. Those who found themselves nearest to them merely moved to another seat. It was a miracle. But it only lasted till the end of the service. The whole church raised a protest and were about to drive these people out, when Mr. Kiaga stopped them and began to explain.

"Before God," he said, "there is no slave or free. We are all children of God and we must receive these our brothers."

"You do not understand," said one of the converts. "What will the heathen say of us when they hear that we receive *osu* into our midst? They will laugh."

"Let them laugh," said Mr. Kiaga. "God will laugh at them on the judgment day. Why do the nations rage and the peoples imagine a vain thing? He that sitteth in the heavens shall laugh. The Lord shall have them in derision."

"You do not understand," the convert maintained. "You are our teacher, and you can teach us the things of the new faith. But this is a matter which we know." And he told him what an *osu* was.

He was a person dedicated to a god, a thing set apart—a taboo for ever, and his children after him. He could neither marry nor be married by the free-born. He was in fact an outcast, living in a special area of the village, close to the Great Shrine. Wherever he went he carried with him the mark of his forbidden caste—long, tangled and dirty hair. A razor was taboo to him. An *osu* could not attend an assembly of the free-born, and they, in turn, could not shelter under his roof. He could not take any of the four titles of the clan, and when he died he was buried by his kind in the Evil Forest. How could such a man be a follower of Christ?

"He needs Christ more than you and I," said Mr. Kiaga.

"Then I shall go back to the clan," said the convert. And he went. Mr. Kiaga stood firm, and it was his firmness that saved the young church. The wavering converts drew inspiration and confidence from his unshakable faith. He ordered the outcasts to shave off their long, tangled hair. At first they were afraid they might die.

"Unless you shave off the mark of your heathen belief I will not admit you into the church," said Mr. Kiaga. "You fear that you will die. Why should that be? How are you different from other men who shave their hair? The same God created you and them. But they have cast you out like lepers. It is against the will of God, who has promised everlasting life to all who believe in His holy name. The heathen say you will die if you do this or that, and you are afraid. They also said I would die if I built my church on this ground. Am I dead? They said I would die if I took care of twins. I am still alive. The heathen speak nothing but falsehood. Only the word of our God is true."

The two outcasts shaved off their hair, and soon they were among the strongest adherents of the new faith. And what was more, nearly all the *osu* in Mbanta followed their example. It was in fact one of them who in his zeal brought the church into serious conflict with the clan a year later by killing the sacred python, the emanation of the god of water.

The royal python was the most revered animal in Mbanta and all the surrounding clans. It was addressed as "Our Father," and was allowed to go wherever it chose, even into people's beds. It ate rats in the house and sometimes swallowed hens' eggs. If a clansman killed a royal python accidentally, he made sacrifices of atonement and performed an expensive burial ceremony such as was done for a great man. No punishment was prescribed for a man who killed the python knowingly. Nobody thought that such a thing could ever happen.

Perhaps it never did happen. That was the way the clan at first looked at it. No one had actually seen the man do it. The story had arisen among the Christians themselves.

But, all the same, the rulers and elders of Mbanta assembled to decide on their action. Many of them spoke at great length and in fury. The spirit of war was upon them. Okonkwo, who had begun to play a part in the affairs of his motherland, said that until the abominable gang was chased out of the village with whips there would be no peace.

But there were many others who saw the situation differently, and it was their counsel that prevailed in the end.

"It is not our custom to fight for our gods," said one of them. "Let us not presume to do so now. If a man kills the sacred python in the secrecy of his hut, the matter lies between him and the god. We did not see it. If we put ourselves between the god and his victim we may receive blows intended for the offender. When a man blasphemes what do we do? Do we go and stop his mouth? No. We put our fingers into our ears to stop us hearing. That is a wise action."

"Let us not reason like cowards," said Okonkwo. "If a man comes into my hut and defaecates on the floor, what do I do? Do I shut my eyes? No! I take a stick and break his head. That is what a man does. These people are daily pouring filth over us, and Okeke says we should pretend not to see." Okonkwo made a sound full of disgust. This was a womanly clan, he thought. Such a thing could never happen in his fatherland, Umuofia.

"Okonkwo has spoken the truth," said another man. "We should do something. But let us ostracise these men. We would then not be held accountable for their abominations."

Everybody in the assembly spoke, and in the end it was decided to ostracise the Christians. Okonkwo ground his teeth in disgust.

That night a bell-man went through the length and breadth of Mbanta proclaiming that the adherents of the new faith were thenceforth excluded from the life and privileges of the clan.

The Christians had grown in number and were now a small community of men, women and children, self-assured and confident. Mr. Brown, the white missionary, paid regular visits to them. "When I think that it is only eighteen months since the Seed was first sown among you," he said, "I marvel at what the Lord hath wrought."

It was Wednesday in Holy week and Mr. Kiaga had asked the women to bring red earth and white chalk and water to scrub the church for Easter, and the women had formed themselves into three groups for this purpose. They set out early that morning, some of them with their water-pots to the stream, another group with hoes and baskets to the village red-earth pit, and the others to the chalk quarry.

Mr. Kiaga was praying in the church when he heard the women talking excitedly. He rounded off his prayer and went to see what it was all about. The women had come to the church with empty water-pots. They said that some young men had chased them away from the stream with whips. Soon after, the women who had gone for red earth returned with empty baskets. Some of them had been heavily whipped. The chalk women also returned to tell a similar story.

"What does it all mean?" asked Mr. Kiaga, who was greatly perplexed.

"The village has outlawed us," said one of the women. "The bell-man announced it last night. But it is not our custom to debar anyone from the stream or the quarry."

Another woman said, "They want to ruin us. They will not allow us into the markets. They have said so."

Mr. Kiaga was going to send into the village for his men-converts when he saw them coming on their own. Of course they had all heard the bell-man, but they had never in all their lives heard of women being debarred from the stream.

"Come along," they said to the women. "We will go with you to meet those cowards." Some of them had big sticks and some even matchets.

But Mr. Kiaga restrained them. He wanted first to know why they had been outlawed.

"They say that Okoli killed the sacred python," said one man.

"It is false," said another. "Okoli told me himself that it was false."

Okoli was not there to answer. He had fallen ill on the previous night. Before the day was over he was dead. His death showed that the gods were still able to fight their own battles. The clan saw no reason then for molesting the Christians.

Chapter 19

The last big rains of the year were falling. It was the time for treading red earth with which to build walls. It was not done earlier because the rains were too heavy and would have washed away the heap of trodden earth; and it could not be done later because harvesting would soon set in, and after that the dry season.

972

It was going to be Okonkwo's last harvest in Mbanta. The seven wasted and weary years were at last dragging to a close. Although he had prospered in his motherland Okonkwo knew that he would have prospered even more in Umuofia, in the land of his fathers where men were bold and warlike. In these seven years he would have climbed to the utmost heights. And so he regretted every day of his exile. His mother's kinsmen had been very kind to him, and he was grateful. But that did not alter the facts. He had called the first child born to him in exile Nneka—"Mother is Supreme"—out of politeness to his mother's kinsmen. But two years later when a son was born he called him Nwofia—"Begotten in the Wilderness."

As soon as he entered his last year in exile Okonkwo sent money to Obierika to build him two huts in his old compound where he and his family would live until he built more huts and the outside wall of his compound. He could not ask another man to build his own *obi* for him, nor the walls of his compound. Those things a man built for himself or inherited from his father.

As the last heavy rains of the year began to fall, Obierika sent word that the two huts had been built and Okonkwo began to prepare for his return, after the rains. He would have liked to return earlier and build his compound that year before the rains stopped, but in doing so he would have taken something from the full penalty of seven years. And that could not be. So he waited impatiently for the dry season to come.

It came slowly. The rain became lighter and lighter until it fell in slanting showers. Sometimes the sun shone through the rain and a light breeze blew. It was a gay and airy kind of rain. The rainbow began to appear, and sometimes two rainbows, like a mother and her daughter, the one young and beautiful, and the other an old and faint shadow. The rainbow was called the python of the sky.

Okonkwo called his three wives and told them to get things together for a great feast. "I must thank my mother's kinsmen before I go," he said.

Ekwefi still had some cassava left on her farm from the previous year. Neither of the other wives had. It was not that they had been lazy, but that they had many children to feed. It was therefore understood that Ekwefi would provide cassava for the feast. Nwoye's mother and Ojiugo would provide the other things like smoked fish, palm-oil and pepper for the soup. Okonkwo would take care of meat and yams.

Ekwefi rose early on the following morning and went to her farm with her daughter, Ezinma, and Ojiugo's daughter, Obiageli, to harvest cassava tubers. Each of them carried a long cane basket, a matchet for cutting down the soft cassava stem, and a little hoe for digging out the tuber. Fortunately, a light rain had fallen during the night and the soil would not be very hard.

"It will not take us long to harvest as much as we like," said Ekwefi.

"But the leaves will be wet," said Ezinma. Her basket was balanced on her head, and her arms folded across her breasts. She felt cold. "I dislike cold water dropping on my back. We should have waited for the sun to rise and dry the leaves."

Obiageli called her "Salt" because she said that she disliked water. "Are you afraid you may dissolve?"

The harvesting was easy, as Ekwefi had said. Ezinma shook every tree violently with a long stick before she bent down to cut the stem and dig out the tuber. Sometimes it was not necessary to dig. They just pulled the stump and earth rose, roots snapped below, and the tuber was pulled out.

When they had harvested a sizeable heap they carried it down in two trips to the steam, where every woman had a shallow well for fermenting her cassava.

"It should be ready in four days or even three," said Obiageli. "They are young tubers."

"They are not all that young," said Ekwefi. "I planted the farm nearly two years ago. It is a poor soil and that is why the tubers are so small."

Okonkwo never did things by halves. When his wife Ekwefi protested that two goats were sufficient for the feast he told her that it was not her affair.

"I am calling a feast because I have the wherewithal. I cannot live on the bank of a river and wash my hands with spittle. My mother's people have been good to me and I must show my gratitude."

And so three goats were slaughtered and a number of fowls. It was like a wedding feast. There was foo-foo and yam pottage, egusi[2] soup and bitter-leaf soup and pots and pots of palm-wine.

All the *umunna* were invited to the feast, all the descendants of Okolo, who had lived about two hundred years before. The oldest member of this extensive family was Okonkwo's uncle, Uchendu. The kola nut was given to him to break, and he prayed to the ancestors. He asked them for health and children. "We do not ask for wealth because he that has health and children will also have wealth. We do not pray to have more money but to have more kinsmen. We are better than animals because we have kinsmen. An animal rubs its aching flank against a tree, a man asks his kinsman to scratch him." He prayed especially for Okonkwo and his family. He then broke the kola nut and threw one of the lobes on the ground for the ancestors.

As the broken kola nuts were passed round, Okonkwo's wives and children and those who came to help them with the cooking began to bring out the food. His sons brought out the pots of palm-wine. There was so much food and drink that many kinsmen whistled in surprise. When all was laid out, Okonkwo rose to speak.

"I beg you to accept this little kola," he said. "It is not to pay you back for all you did for me in these seven years. A child cannot pay for its mother's milk. I have only called you together because it is good for kinsmen to meet."

Yam pottage was served first because it was lighter than foo-foo and because yam always came first. Then the foo-foo was served. Some kinsmen ate it with egusi soup and others with bitter-leaf soup. The meat was then shared so that every member of the *umunna* had a portion. Every man rose in order of years and took a share. Even the few kinsmen who had not been able to come had their shares taken out for them in due turn.

As the palm-wine was drunk one of the oldest members of the *umunna* rose to thank Okonkwo:

"If I say that we did not expect such a big feast I will be suggesting that we did not know how open-handed our son, Okonkwo is. We all know him, and we expected a big feast. But it turned out to be even bigger than we expected. Thank you. May all you took out return again tenfold. It is good in these days when the younger generation consider themselves wiser than their sires to see a man doing things in the grand, old way. A man who calls his kinsmen to a feast does not do so to save them from starving. They all have food in their own homes. When we gather together in the moonlit village ground it is not because of the moon. Every man can see it in his own compound. We come together because it is good for kinsmen to do so. You may ask

974

2. Melon seed.

why I am saying all this. I say it because I fear for the younger generation, for you people." He waved his arm where most of the young men sat. "As for me, I have only a short while to live, and so have Uchendu and Unachukwu and Emefo. But I fear for you young people because you do not understand how strong is the bond of kinship. You do not know what it is to speak with one voice. And what is the result? An abominable religion has settled among you. A man can now leave his father and his brothers. He can curse the gods of his fathers and his ancestors, like a hunter's dog that suddenly goes mad and turns on his master. I fear for you; I fear for the clan." He turned again to Okonkwo and said, "Thank you for calling us together."

Part 3
Chapter 20

Seven years was a long time to be away from one's clan. A man's place was not always there, waiting for him. As soon as he left, someone else rose and filled it. The clan was like a lizard; if it lost its tail it soon grew another.

Okonkwo knew these things. He knew that he had lost his place among the nine masked spirits who administered justice in the clan. He had lost the chance to lead his warlike clan against the new religion, which, he was told, had gained ground. He had lost the years in which he might have taken the highest titles in the clan. But some of these losses were not irreparable. He was determined that his return should be marked by his people. He would return with a flourish, and regain the seven wasted years.

Even in his first year in exile he had begun to plan for his return. The first thing he would do would be to rebuild his compound on a more magnificent scale. He would build a bigger barn than he had before and he would build huts for two new wives. Then he would show his wealth by initiating his sons in the *ozo* society. Only the really great men in the clan were able to do this. Okonkwo saw clearly the high esteem in which he would be held, and he saw himself taking the highest title in the land.

As the years of exile passed one by one it seemed to him that his *chi* might now be making amends for the past disaster. His yams grew abundantly, not only in his motherland but also in Umuofia, where his friend gave them out year by year to share-croppers.

Then the tragedy of his first son had occurred. At first it appeared as if it might prove too great for his spirit. But it was a resilient spirit, and in the end Okonkwo overcame his sorrow. He had five other sons and he would bring them up in the way of the clan.

He sent for the five sons and they came and sat in his *obi*. The youngest of them was four years old.

"You have all seen the great abomination of your brother. Now he is no longer my son or your brother. I will only have a son who is a man, who will hold his head up among my people. If any one of you prefers to be a woman, let him follow Nwoye now while I am alive so that I can curse him. If you turn against me when I am dead I will visit you and break your neck."

Okonkwo was very lucky in his daughters. He never stopped regretting that Ez-inma was a girl. Of all his children she alone understood his every mood. A bond of sympathy had grown between them as the years had passed.

Ezinma grew up in her father's exile and became one of the most beautiful girls in Mbanta. She was called Crystal of Beauty, as her mother had been called in her youth. The young ailing girl who had caused her mother so much heartache had been transformed, almost overnight, into a healthy, buoyant maiden. She had, it was true, her moments of depression when she would snap at everybody like an angry dog. These moods descended on her suddenly and for no apparent reason. But they were very rare and short-lived. As long as they lasted, she could bear no other person but her father.

Many young men and prosperous middle-aged men of Mbanta came to marry her. But she refused them all, because her father had called her one evening and said to her: "There are many good and prosperous people here, but I shall be happy if you marry in Umuofia when we return home."

That was all he had said. But Ezinma had seen clearly all the thought and hidden meaning behind the few words. And she had agreed.

"Your half-sister, Obiageli, will not understand me," Okonkwo said. "But you can explain to her."

Although they were almost the same age. Ezinma wielded a strong influence over her half-sister. She explained to her why they should not marry yet, and she agreed also. And so the two of them refused every offer of marriage in Mbanta.

"I wish she were a boy," Okonkwo thought within himself. She understood things so perfectly. Who else among his children could have read his thought so well? With two beautiful grown-up daughters his return to Umuofia would attract considerable attention. His future sons-in-law would be men of authority in the clan. The poor and unknown would not dare to come forth.

Umuofia had indeed changed during the seven years Okonkwo had been in exile. The church had come and led many astray. Not only the low-born and the outcast but sometimes a worthy man had joined it. Such a man was Ogbuefi Ugonna,[1] who had taken two titles, and who like a madman had cut the anklet of his titles and cast it away to join the Christians. The white missionary was very proud of him and he was one of the first men in Umuofia to receive the sacrament of Holy Communion, or Holy Feast as it was called in Ibo. Ogbuefi Ugonna had thought of the Feast in terms of eating and drinking, only more holy than the village variety. He had therefore put his drinking-horn into his goatskin bag for the occasion.

But apart from the church, the white men had also brought a government. They had built a court where the District Commissioner judged cases in ignorance. He had court messengers who brought men to him for trial. Many of these messengers came from Umuru on the bank of the Great River, where the white men first came many years before and where they had built the centre of their religion and trade and government. These court messengers were greatly hated in Umuofia because they were foreigners and also arrogant and high-handed. They were called kotma, and because of their ash-coloured shorts they earned the additional name of Ashy-Buttocks. They guarded the prison, which was full of men who had offended against the white man's law. Some of these prisoners had thrown away their twins and some had molested the Christians. They were beaten in the prison by the kotma and made to work every morning clearing the government compound and fetching wood for the white Commissioner and the court messengers. Some of these prisoners were men of title who should be above such mean occupation. They were grieved by the indignity and mourned for their neglected farms. As they cut grass in the morning the younger men sang in time with the strokes of their matchets:

---

1. Father's honor, literally, "with an eagle feather."

Kotma *of the ash buttocks,*
He is fit to be a slave
The white man has no sense,
He is fit to be a slave

The court messengers did not like to be called Ashy-Buttocks, and they beat the men. But the song spread in Umuofia.

Okonkwo's head was bowed in sadness as Obierika told him these things.

"Perhaps I have been away too long," Okonkwo said, almost to himself. "But I cannot understand these things you tell me. What is it that has happened to our people? Why have they lost the power to fight?"

"Have you not heard how the white man wiped out Abame?" asked Obierika.

"I have heard," said Okonkwo. "But I have also heard that Abame people were weak and foolish. Why did they not fight back? Had they no guns and matchets? We would be cowards to compare ourselves with the men of Abame. Their fathers had never dared to stand before our ancestors. We must fight these men and drive them from the land."

"It is already too late," said Obierika sadly. "Our own men and our sons have joined the ranks of the stranger. They have joined his religion and they help to uphold his government. If we should try to drive out the white men in Umuofia we should find it easy. There are only two of them. But what of our own people who are following their way and have been given power? They would go to Umuru and bring the soldiers, and we would be like Abame." He paused for a long time and then said: "I told you on my last visit to Mbanta how they hanged Aneto."

"What has happened to that piece of land in dispute?" asked Okonkwo.

"The white man's court has decided that it should belong to Nnama's family, who had given much money to the white man's messengers and interpreter."

"Does the white man understand our custom about land?"

"How can he when he does not even speak our tongue? But he says that our customs are bad; and our own brothers who have taken up his religion also say that our customs are bad. How do you think we can fight when our own brothers have turned against us? The white man is very clever. He came quietly and peaceably with his religion. We were amused at his foolishness and allowed him to stay. Now he has won our brothers, and our clan can no longer act like one. He has put a knife on the things that held us together and we have fallen apart."

"How did they get hold of Aneto to hang him?" asked Okonkwo.

"When he killed Oduche in the fight over the land, he fled to Aninta to escape the wrath of the earth. This was about eight days after the fight, because Oduche had not died immediately from his wounds. It was on the seventh day that he died. But everybody knew that he was going to die and Aneto got his belongings together in readiness to flee. But the Christians had told the white man about the accident, and he sent his *kotma* to catch Aneto. He was imprisoned with all the leaders of his family. In the end Oduche died and Aneto was taken to Umuru and hanged. The other people were released, but even now they have not found the mouth with which to tell of their suffering."

The two men sat in silence for a long while afterwards.

Chapter 21

There were many men and women in Umuofia who did not feel as strongly as Okonkwo about the new dispensation. The white man had indeed brought a lunatic religion, but he had also built a trading store and for the first time palm-oil and kernel became things of great price, and much money flowed into Umuofia.

And even in the matter of religion there was a growing feeling that there might be something in it after all, something vaguely akin to method in the overwhelming madness.

This growing feeling was due to Mr. Brown, the white missionary, who was very firm in restraining his flock from provoking the wrath of the clan. One member in particular was very difficult to restrain. His name was Enoch and his father was the priest of the snake cult. The story went around that Enoch had killed and eaten the sacred python, and that his father had cursed him.

Mr. Brown preached against such excess of zeal. Everything was possible, he told his energetic flock, but everything was not expedient. And so Mr. Brown came to be respected even by the clan, because he trod softly on its faith. He made friends with some of the great men of the clan and on one of his frequent visits to the neighbour-ing villages he had been presented with a carved elephant tusk, which was a sign of dignity and rank. One of the great men in that village was called Akunna and he had given one of his sons to be taught the white man's knowledge in Mr. Brown's school.

Whenever Mr. Brown went to that village he spent long hours with Akunna in his *obi* talking through an interpreter about religion. Neither of them succeeded in con-verting the other but they learnt more about their different beliefs.

"You say that there is one supreme God who made heaven and earth," said Akunna on one of Mr. Brown's visits. "We also believe in Him and call Him Chukwu. He made all the world and the other gods."

"There are no other gods," said Mr. Brown. "Chukwu is the only God and all others are false. You carve a piece of wood—like that one" (he pointed at the rafters from which Akunna's carved *Ikenga* hung), "and you call it a god. But it is still a piece of wood."

"Yes," said Akunna. "It is indeed a piece of wood. The tree from which it came was made by Chukwu, as indeed all minor gods were. But He made them for His messengers so that we could approach Him through them. It is like yourself. You are the head of your church."

"No," protested Mr. Brown. "The head of my church is God Himself."

"I know," said Akunna, "but there must be a head in this world among men. Somebody like yourself must be the head here."

"The head of my church in that sense is in England."

"That is exactly what I am saying. The head of your church is in your country. He has sent you here as his messenger. And you have also appointed your own mes-sengers and servants. Or let me take another example, the District Commissioner. He is sent by your king."

"They have a queen," said the interpreter on his own account.

"Your queen sends her messenger, the District Commissioner. He finds that he cannot do the work alone and so he appoints *kotma* to help him. It is the same with God, or Chukwu. He appoints the smaller gods to help Him because His work is too great for one person."

"You should not think of him as a person," said Mr. Brown. "It is because you do so that you imagine He must need helpers. And the worst thing about it is that you give all the worship to the false gods you have created."

"That is not so. We make sacrifices to the little gods, but when they fail and there is no one else to turn to we go to Chukwu. It is right to do so. We approach a great man through his servants. But when his servants fail to help us, then we go to the last source of hope. We appear to pay greater attention to the little gods but that is not so. We worry them more because we are afraid to worry their Master. Our fathers knew that Chukwu was the Overlord and that is why many of them gave their children the name Chukwuka—'Chukwu is Supreme.'"

"You said one interesting thing," said Mr. Brown. "You are afraid of Chukwu. In my religion Chukwu is a loving Father and need not be feared by those who do His will."

"But we must fear Him when we are not doing His will," said Akunna. "And who is to tell His will? It is too great to be known."

In this way Mr. Brown learnt a good deal about the religion of the clan and he came to the conclusion that a frontal attack on it would not succeed. And so he built a school and a little hospital in Umuofia. He went from family to family begging people to send their children to his school. But at first they only sent their slaves or sometimes their lazy children. Mr. Brown begged and argued and prophesied. He said that the leaders of the land in the future would be men and women who had learnt to read and write. If Umuofia failed to send her children to the school, strangers would come from other places to rule them. They could already see that happening in the Native Court, where the D. C. was surrounded by strangers who spoke his tongue. Most of these strangers came from the distant town of Umuru on the bank of the Great River where the white man first went.

In the end Mr. Brown's arguments began to have an effect. More people came to learn in his school, and he encouraged them with gifts of singlets[2] and towels. They were not all young, these people who came to learn. Some of them were thirty years old or more. They worked on their farms in the morning and went to school in the afternoon. And it was not long before the people began to say that the white man's medicine was quick in working. Mr. Brown's school produced quick results. A few months in it were enough to make one a court messenger or even a court clerk. Those who stayed longer became teachers; and from Umuofia labourers went forth into the Lord's vineyard. New churches were established in the surrounding villages and a few schools with them. From the very beginning religion and education went hand in hand.

Mr. Brown's mission grew from strength to strength, and because of its link with the new administration it earned a new social prestige. But Mr. Brown himself was breaking down in health. At first he ignored the warning signs. But in the end he had to leave his flock, sad and broken.

It was in the first rainy season after Okonkwo's return to Umuofia that Mr. Brown left for home. As soon as he had learnt of Okonkwo's return five months earlier, the missionary had immediately paid him a visit. He had just sent Okonkwo's son, Nwoye, who was now called Isaac,[3] to the new training college for teachers in Umuru. And he had hoped that Okonkwo would be happy to hear of it. But Okonkwo had driven him away with the threat that if he came into his compound again, he would be carried out of it.

Okonkwo's return to his native land was not as memorable as he had wished. It was true his two beautiful daughters aroused great interest among suitors and marriage negotiations were soon in progress, but, beyond that, Umuofia did not appear to have taken any special notice of the warrior's return. The clan had undergone such profound change during his exile that it was barely recognizable. The new religion

---

2. T-shirts.
3. Son of Abraham, Genesis 22.

and government and the trading stores were very much in the people's eyes and minds. There were still many who saw these new institutions as evil, but even they talked and thought about little else, and certainly not about Okonkwo's return.

And it was the wrong year too. If Okonkwo had immediately initiated his two sons into the *ozo* society as he had planned he would have caused a stir. But the initiation rite was performed once in three years in Umuofia, and he had to wait for nearly two years for the next round of ceremonies.

Okonkwo was deeply grieved. And it was not just a personal grief. He mourned for the clan, which he saw breaking up and falling apart, and he mourned for the warlike men of Umuofia, who had so unaccountably become soft like women.

Chapter 22

Mr. Brown's successor was the Reverend James Smith, and he was a different kind of man. He condemned openly Mr. Brown's policy of compromise and accommodation. He saw things as black and white. And black was evil. He saw the world as a battlefield in which the children of light were locked in mortal conflict with the sons of darkness. He spoke in his sermons about sheep and goats and about wheat and tares. He believed in slaying the prophets of Baal.

Mr. Smith was greatly distressed by the ignorance which many of his flock showed even in such things as the Trinity and the Sacraments. It only showed that they were seeds sown on a rocky soil. Mr. Brown had thought of nothing but numbers. He should have known that the kingdom of God did not depend on large crowds. Our Lord Himself stressed the importance of fewness. Narrow is the way and few the number. To fill the Lord's holy temple with an idolatrous crowd clamouring for signs was a folly of everlasting consequence. Our Lord used the whip only once in His Life—to drive the crowd away from His church.

Within a few weeks of his arrival in Umuofia Mr. Smith suspended a young woman from the church for pouring new wine into old bottles. This woman had allowed her heathen husband to mutilate her dead child. The child had been declared an *ogbanje*, plaguing its mother by dying and entering her womb to be born again. Four times this child had run its evil round. And so it was mutilated to discourage it from returning.

Mr. Smith was filled with wrath when he heard of this. He disbelieved the story which even some of the most faithful confirmed, the story of really evil children who were not deterred by mutilation, but came back with all the scars. He replied that such stories were spread in the world by the Devil to lead men astray. Those who believed such stories were unworthy of the Lord's table.

There was a saying in Umuofia that as a man danced so the drums were beaten for him. Mr. Smith danced a furious step and so the drums went mad. The over-zealous converts who had smarted under Mr. Brown's restraining hand now flourished in full favour. One of them was Enoch, the son of the snake-priest who was believed to have killed and eaten the sacred python. Enoch's devotion to the new faith had seemed so much greater than Mr. Brown's that the villagers called him The Outsider who wept louder than the bereaved.

Enoch was short and slight of build, and always seemed in great haste. His feet were short and broad, and when he stood or walked his heels came together and his feet opened outwards as if they had quarrelled and meant to go in different directions. Such was the excessive energy bottled up in Enoch's small body that it was always erupting in quarrels and fights. On Sundays he always imagined that the sermon was preached for the benefit of his enemies. And if he happened to sit near one of them he would occasionally turn to give him a meaningful look, as if to say, "I told you so." It was Enoch who touched off the great conflict between church and clan in Umuofia which had been gathering since Mr. Brown left.

It happened during the annual ceremony which was held in honour of the earth deity. At such times the ancestors of the clan who had been committed to Mother Earth at their death emerged again as *egwugwu* through tiny ant-holes.

One of the greatest crimes a man could commit was to unmask an *egwugwu* in public, or to say or do anything which might reduce its immortal prestige in the eyes of the uninitiated. And this was what Enoch did.

The annual worship of the earth goddess fell on a Sunday, and the masked spirits were abroad. The Christian women who had been to church could not therefore go home. Some of their men had gone out to beg the *egwugwu* to retire for a short while for the women to pass. They agreed and were already retiring, when Enoch boasted aloud that they would not dare to touch a Christian. Whereupon they all came back and one of them gave Enoch a good stroke of the cane, which was always carried. Enoch fell on him and tore off his mask. The other *egwugwu* immediately surrounded their desecrated companion, to shield him from the profane gaze of women and children, and led him away. Enoch had killed an ancestral spirit, and Umuofia was thrown into confusion.

That night the Mother of the Spirits walked the length and breadth of the clan, weeping for her murdered son. It was a terrible night. Not even the oldest man in Umuofia had ever heard such a strange and fearful sound, and it was never to be heard again. It seemed as if the very soul of the tribe wept for a great evil that was coming— its own death.

On the next day all the masked *egwugwu* of Umuofia assembled in the market-place. They came from all the quarters of the clan and even from the neighbouring villages. The dreadful Otakagu came from Imo, and Ekwensu, dangling a white cock, arrived from Uli. It was a terrible gathering. The eerie voices of countless spirits, the bells that clattered behind some of them, and the clash of matchets as they ran forwards and backwards and saluted one another, sent tremors of fear into every heart. For the first time in living memory the sacred bullroarer was heard in broad daylight.

From the market-place the furious band made for Enoch's compound. Some of the elders of the clan went with them, wearing heavy protections of charms and amulets. These were men whose arms were strong in *ogwu*, or medicine. As for the ordinary men and women, they listened from the safety of their huts.

The leaders of the Christians had met together at Mr. Smith's parsonage on the previous night. As they deliberated they could hear the Mother of Spirits wailing for her son. The chilling sound affected Mr. Smith, and for the first time he seemed to be afraid.

"What are they planning to do?" he asked. No one knew, because such a thing had never happened before. Mr. Smith would have sent for the District Commissioner and his court messengers, but they had gone on tour on the previous day.

"One thing is clear," said Mr. Smith. "We cannot offer physical resistance to them. Our strength lies in the Lord." They knelt down together and prayed to God for delivery.

"O Lord save Thy people," cried Mr. Smith.

"And bless Thine inheritance," replied the men.

They decided that Enoch should be hidden in the parsonage for a day or two. Enoch himself was greatly disappointed when he heard this, for he had hoped that a holy war was imminent; and there were a few other Christians who thought like him. But wisdom prevailed in the camp of the faithful and many lives were thus saved.

The band of *egwugwu* moved like a furious whirlwind to Enoch's compound and with matchet and fire reduced it to a desolate heap. And from there they made for the church, intoxicated with destruction.

Mr. Smith was in his church when he heard the masked spirits coming. He walked quietly to the door which commanded the approach to the church compound, and stood there. But when the first three or four *egwugwu* appeared on the church compound he nearly bolted. He overcame this impulse and instead of running away he went down the two steps that led up to the church and walked towards the approaching spirits.

They surged forward, and a long stretch of the bamboo fence with which the church compound was surrounded gave way before them. Discordant bells clanged, matchets clashed and the air was full of dust and weird sounds. Mr. Smith heard a sound of footsteps behind him. He turned round and saw Okeke, his interpreter. Okeke had not been on the best of terms with his master since he had strongly condemned Enoch's behaviour at the meeting of the leaders of the church during the night. Okeke had gone as far as to say that Enoch should not be hidden in the parsonage, because he would only draw the wrath of the clan on the pastor. Mr. Smith had rebuked him in very strong language, and had not sought his advice that morning. But now, as he came up and stood by him confronting the angry spirits, Mr. Smith looked at him and smiled. It was a wan smile, but there was deep gratitude there.

For a brief moment the onrush of the *egwugwu* was checked by the unexpected composure of the two men. But it was only a momentary check, like the tense silence between blasts of thunder. The second onrush was greater than the first. It swallowed up the two men. Then an unmistakable voice rose above the tumult and there was immediate silence. Space was made around the two men, and Ajofia began to speak.

Ajofia was the leading *egwugwu* of Umuofia. He was the head and spokesman of the nine ancestors who administered justice in the clan. His voice was unmistakable and so he was able to bring immediate peace to the agitated spirits. He then addressed Mr. Smith, and as he spoke clouds of smoke rose from his head.

"The body of the white man, I salute you," he said, using the language in which immortals spoke to men.

"The body of the white man, do you know me?" he asked.

Mr. Smith looked at his interpreter, but Okeke, who was a native of distant Umuru, was also at a loss.

Ajofia laughed in his gutteral voice. It was like the laugh of rusty metal. "They are strangers," he said, "and they are ignorant. But let that pass." He turned round to his comrades and saluted them, calling them the fathers of Umuofia. He dug his rattling spear into the ground and it shook with metallic life. Then he turned once more to the missionary and his interpreter.

"Tell the white man that we will not do him any harm," he said to the interpreter. "Tell him to go back to his house and leave us alone. We liked his brother who was with us before. He was foolish, but we liked him, and for his sake we shall not harm his brother. But this shrine which he built must be destroyed. We shall no longer allow it in our midst. It has bred untold abominations and we have come to put an end to it." He turned to his comrades, "Fathers of Umuofia, I salute you;" and they replied with one gutteral voice. He turned again to the missionary. "You can stay with us if you like our ways. You can worship your own god. It is good that a man should worship the gods and the spirits of his fathers. Go back to your house so that you may not be hurt. Our anger is great but we have held it down so that we can talk to you."

Mr. Smith said to his interpreter: "Tell them to go away from here. This is the house of God and I will not live to see it desecrated."

Okeke interpreted wisely to the spirits and leaders of Umuofia: "The white man says he is happy you have come to him with your grievances, like friends. He will be happy if you leave the matter in his hands."

"We cannot leave the matter in his hands because he does not understand our customs, just as we do not understand his. We say he is foolish because he does not know our ways, and perhaps he says we are foolish because we do not know his. Let him go away."

Mr. Smith stood his ground. But he could not save his church. When the *egwugwu* went away the red-earth church which Mr. Brown had built was a pile of earth and ashes. And for the moment the spirit of the clan was pacified.

Chapter 23

For the first time in many years Okonkwo had a feeling that was akin to happiness. The times which had altered so unaccountably during his exile seemed to be coming round again. The clan which had turned false on him appeared to be making amends.

He had spoken violently to his clansmen when they had met in the market-place to decide on their action. And they had listened to him with respect. It was like the good old days again, when a warrior was a warrior. Although they had not agreed to kill the missionary or drive away the Christians, they had agreed to do something substantial. And they had done it. Okonkwo was almost happy again.

For two days after the destruction of the church, nothing happened. Every man in Umuofia went about armed with a gun or a matchet. They would not be caught unawares, like the men of Abame.

Then the District Commissioner returned from his tour. Mr. Smith went immediately to him and they had a long discussion. The men of Umuofia did not take any notice of this, and if they did, they thought it was not important. The missionary often went to see his brother white man. There was nothing strange in that.

Three days later the District Commissioner sent his sweet-tongued messenger to the leaders of Umuofia asking them to meet him in his headquarters. That also was not strange. He often asked them to hold such palavers, as he called them. Okonkwo was among the six leaders he invited.

Okonkwo warned the others to be fully armed. "An Umuofia man does not refuse a call," he said. "He may refuse to do what he is asked; he does not refuse to be asked. But the times have changed, and we must be fully prepared."

And so the six men went to see the District Commissioner, armed with their matchets. They did not carry guns, for that would be unseemly. They were led into the courthouse where the District Commissioner sat. He received them politely. They unslung their goatskin bags and their sheathed matchets, put them on the floor, and sat down.

"I have asked you to come," began the Commissioner, "because of what happened during my absence. I have been told a few things but I cannot believe them until I have heard your own side. Let us talk about it like friends and find a way of ensuring that it does not happen again."

Ogbuefi Ekwueme rose to his feet and began to tell the story.

"Wait a minute," said the Commissioner. "I want to bring in my men so that they too can hear your grievances and take warning. Many of them come from distant places and although they speak your tongue they are ignorant of your customs. James! Go and bring in the men." His interpreter left the court-room and soon returned with twelve men. They sat together with the men of Umuofia, and Ogbuefi Ekwueme began again to tell the story of how Enoch murdered an *egwugwu*.

It happened so quickly that the six men did not see it coming. There was only a brief scuffle, too brief even to allow the drawing of a sheathed matchet. The six men were handcuffed and led into the guardroom.

"We shall not do you any harm," said the District Commissioner to them later, "if only you agree to co-operate with us. We have brought a peaceful administration to you and your people so that you may be happy. If any man ill-treats you we shall come to your rescue. But we will not allow you to ill-treat others. We have a court of law where we judge cases and administer justice just as it is done in my own country under a great queen. I have brought you here because you joined together to molest others, to burn people's houses and their place of worship. That must not happen in the dominion of our queen, the most powerful ruler in the world. I have decided that you will pay a fine of two hundred bags of cowries. You will be released as soon as you agree to this and undertake to collect that fine from your people. What do you say to that?"

The six men remained sullen and silent and the Commissioner left them for a while. He told the court messengers, when he left the guardroom, to treat the men with respect because they were the leaders of Umuofia. They said, "Yes, sir," and saluted.

As soon as the District Commissioner left, the head messenger, who was also the prisoners' barber, took down his razor and shaved off all the hair on the men's heads. They were still handcuffed, and they just sat and moped.

"Who is the chief among you?" the court messenger asked in jest. "We see that every pauper wears the anklet of title in Umuofia. Does it cost as much as ten cowries?"

The six men ate nothing throughout that day and the next. They were not even given any water to drink, and they could not go out to urinate or go into the bush when they were pressed. At night the messengers came in to taunt them and to knock their shaven heads together.

Even when the men were left alone they found no words to speak to one another. It was only on the third day, when they could no longer bear the hunger and the insults, that they began to talk about giving in.

"We should have killed the white man if you had listened to me," Okonkwo snarled.

"We could have been in Umuru now waiting to be hanged," someone said to him.

"Who wants to kill the white man?" asked a messenger who had just rushed in. Nobody spoke.

"You are not satisfied with your crime, but you must kill the white man on top of it." He carried a strong stick, and he hit each man a few blows on the head and back. Okonkwo was choked with hate.

As soon as the six men were locked up, court messengers went into Umuofia to tell the people that their leaders would not be released unless they paid a fine of two hundred and fifty bags of cowries.

"Unless you pay the fine immediately," said their headman, "we will take your leaders to Umuru before the big white man, and hang them."

This story spread quickly through the villages, and was added to as it went. Some said that the men had already been taken to Umuru and would be hanged on the following day. Some said that their families would also be hanged. Others said that soldiers were already on their way to shoot the people of Umuofia as they had done in Abame.

It was the time of the full moon. But that night the voice of children was not heard. The village *ilo* where they always gathered for a moon-play was empty. The women of Iguedo did not meet in their secret enclosure to learn a new dance to be displayed later to the village. Young men who were always abroad in the moonlight kept their huts that night. Their manly voices were not heard on the village paths as they went to visit their friends and lovers. Umuofia was like a startled animal with ears erect, sniffing the silent, ominous air and not knowing which way to run.

The silence was broken by the village crier beating his sonorous *ogene*. He called every man in Umuofia, from the Akakanma age-group upwards, to a meeting in the market-place after the morning meal. He went from one end of the village to the other and walked all its breadth. He did not leave out any of the main footpaths.

Okonkwo's compound was like a deserted homestead. It was as if cold water had been poured on it. His family was all there, but everyone spoke in whispers. His daughter Ezinma had broken her twenty-eight day visit to the family of her future husband, and returned home when she heard that her father had been imprisoned, and was going to be hanged. As soon as she got home she went to Obierika to ask what the men of Umuofia were going to do about it. But Obierika had not been home since morning. His wives thought he had gone to a secret meeting. Ezinma was satisfied that something was being done.

On the morning after the village crier's appeal the men of Umuofia met in the market-place and decided to collect without delay two hundred and fifty bags of cowries to appease the white man. They did not know that fifty bags would go to the court messengers, who had increased the fine for that purpose.

Chapter 24

Okonkwo and his fellow prisoners were set free as soon as the fine was paid. The District Commissioner spoke to them again about the great queen, and about peace and good government. But the men did not listen. They just sat and looked at him and at his interpreter. In the end they were given back their bags and sheathed matchets and told to go home. They rose and left the court-house. They neither spoke to anyone nor among themselves.

The court-house, like the church, was built a little way outside the village. The footpath that linked them was a very busy one because it also led to the stream, beyond the court. It was open and sandy. Footpaths were open and sandy in the dry season. But when the rains came the bush grew thick on either side and closed in on the path. It was now dry season.

As they made their way to the village the six men met women and children going to the stream with their waterpots. But the men wore such heavy and fearsome looks that the women and children did not say "*nno*" or "welcome" to them, but edged out of the way to let them pass. In the village little groups of men joined them until they became a sizeable company. They walked silently. As each of the six men got to his compound, he turned in, taking some of the crowd with him. The village was astir in a silent, suppressed way.

Ezinma had prepared some food for her father as soon as news spread that the six men would be released. She took it to him in his *obi*. He ate absent-mindedly. He had no appetite; he only ate to please her. His male relations and friends had gathered in his *obi*, and Obierika was urging him to eat. Nobody else spoke, but they noticed the long stripes on Okonkwo's back where the warder's whip had cut into his flesh.

The village crier was abroad again in the night. He beat his iron gong and announced that another meeting would be held in the morning. Everyone knew that Umuofia was at last going to speak its mind about the things that were happening.

Okonkwo slept very little that night. The bitterness in his heart was now mixed with a kind of child-like excitement. Before he had gone to bed he had brought down his war dress, which he had not touched since his return from exile. He had shaken out his smoked raffia skirt and examined his tall feather head-gear and his shield. They were all satisfactory, he had thought.

As he lay on his bamboo bed he thought about the treatment he had received in the white man's court, and he swore vengeance. If Umuofia decided on war, all would be well. But if they chose to be cowards he would go out and avenge himself. He thought about wars in the past. The noblest, he thought, was the war against Isike. In those days Okudo was still alive. Okudo sang a war song in a way that no other man could. He was not a fighter, but his voice turned every man into a lion.

"Worthy men are no more," Okonkwo sighed as he remembered those days. "Isike will never forget how we slaughtered them in that war. We killed twelve of their men and they killed only two of ours. Before the end of the fourth market week they were suing for peace. Those were days when men were men."

As he thought of these things he heard the sound of the iron gong in the distance. He listened carefully, and could just hear the crier's voice. But it was very faint. He turned on his bed and his back hurt him. He ground his teeth. The crier was drawing nearer and nearer until he passed by Okonkwo's compound.

"The greatest obstacle in Umuofia," Okonkwo thought bitterly, "is that coward, Egonwanne. His sweet tongue can change fire into cold ash. When he speaks he moves our men to impotence. If they had ignored his womanish wisdom five years ago, we would not have come to this." He ground his teeth. "Tomorrow he will tell them that our fathers never fought a 'war of blame.' If they listen to him I shall leave them and plan my own revenge."

The crier's voice had once more become faint, and the distance had taken the harsh edge off his iron gong. Okonkwo turned from one side to the other and derived a kind of pleasure from the pain his back gave him. "Let Egonwanne talk about a 'war of blame' tomorrow and I shall show him my back and head." He ground his teeth.

The market-place began to fill as soon as the sun rose. Obierika was waiting in his *obi* when Okonkwo came along and called him. He hung his goatskin bag and his sheathed matchet on his shoulder and went out to join him. Obierika's hut was close to the road and he saw every man who passed to the market-place. He had exchanged greetings with many who had already passed that morning.

When Okonkwo and Obierika got to the meeting-place there were already so many people that if one threw up a grain of sand it would not find its way to the earth again. And many more people were coming from every quarter of the nine villages. It warmed Okonkwo's heart to see such strength of numbers. But he was looking for one man in particular, the man whose tongue he dreaded and despised so much.

"Can you see him?" he asked Obierika.

"Who?"

"Egonwanne," he said, his eyes roving from one corner of the huge market-place to the other. Most of the men were seated on goatskins on the ground. A few of them sat on wooden stools they had brought with them.

"No," said Obierika, casting his eyes over the crowd. "Yes, there he is, under the silk-cotton tree. Are you afraid he would convince us not to fight?"

"Afraid? I do not care what he does to *you*. I despise him and those who listen to him. I shall fight alone if I choose."

They spoke at the top of their voices because everybody was talking, and it was like the sound of a great market.

"I shall wait till he has spoken," Okonkwo thought. "Then I shall speak."

"But how do you know he will speak against war?" Obierika asked after a while.

"Because I know he is a coward," said Okonkwo. Obierika did not hear the rest of what he said because at that moment somebody touched his shoulder from behind and he turned round to shake hands and exchange greetings with five or six friends. Okonkwo did not turn around even though he knew the voices. He was in no mood to exchange greetings. But one of the men touched him and asked about the people of his compound.

"They are well," he replied without interest.

The first man to speak to Umuofia that morning was Okika, one of the six who had been imprisoned. Okika was a great man and an orator. But he did not have the booming voice which a first speaker must use to establish silence in the assembly of the clan. Onyeka had such a voice; and so he was asked to salute Umuofia before Okika began to speak.

" *Umuofia kwenu!*" he bellowed, raising his left arm and pushing the air with his open hand.

"*Yaa!*" roared Umuofia.

" *Umuofia kwenu!*" he bellowed again, and again and again, facing a new direction each time. And the crowd answered, "*Yaa!*"

There was immediate silence as though cold water had been poured on a roaring flame.

Okika sprang to his feet and also saluted his clansmen four times. Then he began to speak:

"You all know why we are here, when we ought to be building our barns or mending our huts, when we should be putting our compounds in order. My father used to say to me: 'Whenever you see a toad jumping in broad daylight, then know that something is after its life.' When I saw you all pouring into this meeting from all the quarters of our clan so early in the morning, I knew that something was after our life." He paused for a brief moment and then began again:

"All our gods are weeping. Idemili is weeping. Ogwugwu is weeping. Agbala is weeping, and all the others. Our dead fathers are weeping because of the shameful sacrilege they are suffering and the abomination we have all seen with our eyes." He stopped again to steady his trembling voice.

"This is a great gathering. No clan can boast of greater numbers or greater valour. But are we all here? I ask you: Are all the sons of Umuofia with us here?" A deep murmur swept through the crowd.

"They are not," he said. "They have broken the clan and gone their several ways. We who are here this morning have remained true to our fathers, but our brothers have deserted us and joined a stranger to soil their fatherland. If we fight the stranger we shall hit our brothers and perhaps shed the blood of a clansman. But we must do it. Our fathers never dreamt of such a thing, they never killed their brothers. But a white man never came to them. So we must do what our fathers would never have done. Eneke the bird was asked why he was always on the wing and he replied: 'Men have learnt to shoot without missing their mark and I have learnt to fly without perching on a twig.' We must root out this evil. And if our brothers take the side of evil we must root them out too. And we must do it *now*. We must bale this water now that it is only ankle-deep ..."

At this point here was a sudden stir in the crowd and every eye was turned in one direction. There was a sharp bend in the road that led from the market-place to the white man's court, and to the stream beyond it. And so no one had seen the approach of the five court messengers until they had come round the bend, a few paces from the edge of the crowd. Okonkwo was sitting at the edge.

He sprang to his feet as soon as he saw who it was. He confronted the head messenger, trembling with hate, unable to utter a word. The man was fearless and stood his ground, his four men lined up behind him.

In that brief moment the world seemed to stand still, waiting. There was utter silence. The men of Umuofia were merged into the mute backcloth of trees and giant creepers, waiting.

The spell was broken by the head messenger. "Let me pass!" he ordered.

"What do you want here?"

"The white man whose power you know too well has ordered this meeting to stop."

In a flash Okonkwo drew his matchet. The messenger crouched to avoid the blow. It was useless. Okonkwo's matchet descended twice and the man's head lay beside his uniformed body.

The waiting backcloth jumped into tumultuous life and the meeting was stopped. Okonkwo stood looking at the dead man. He knew that Umuofia would not go to war. He knew because they had let the other messengers escape. They had broken into tumult instead of action. He discerned fright in that tumult. He heard voices asking: "Why did he do it?"

He wiped his matchet on the sand and went away.

Chapter 25

When the District Commissioner arrived at Okonkwo's compound at the head of an armed band of soldiers and court messengers he found a small crowd of men sitting wearily in the *obi*. He commanded them to come outside, and they obeyed without a murmur.

"Which among you is called Okonkwo?" he asked through his interpreter.

"He is not here," replied Obierika.

"Where is he?"

"He is not here!"

The Commissioner became angry and red in the face. He warned the men that unless they produced Okonkwo forthwith he would lock them all up. The men murmured among themselves, and Obierika spoke again.

"We can take you where he is, and perhaps your men will help us."

The Commissioner did not understand what Obierika meant when he said, "Perhaps your men will help us." One of the most infuriating habits of these people was their love of superfluous words, he thought.

Obierika with five or six others led the way. The Commissioner and his men followed, their firearms held at the ready. He had warned Obierika that if he and his men played any monkey tricks they would be shot. And so they went.

There was a small bush behind Okonkwo's compound. The only opening into this bush from the compound was a little round hole in the red-earth wall through which fowls went in and out in their endless search for food. The hole would not let a man through. It was to this bush that Obierika led the Commissioner and his men. They skirted round the compound, keeping close to the wall. The only sound they made was with their feet as they crushed dry leaves.

Then they came to the tree from which Okonkwo's body was dangling, and they stopped dead.

"Perhaps your men can help us bring him down and bury him," said Obierika. "We have sent for strangers from another village to do it for us, but they may be a long time coming."

The District Commissioner changed instantaneously. The resolute administrator in him gave way to the student of primitive customs.

"Why can't you take him down yourselves?" he asked.

"It is against our custom," said one of the men. "It is an abomination for a man to take his own life. It is an offence against the Earth, and a man who commits it will not be buried by his clansmen. His body is evil, and only strangers may touch it. That is why we ask your people to bring him down, because you are strangers."

"Will you bury him like any other man?" asked the Commissioner.

"We cannot bury him. Only strangers can. We shall pay your men to do it. When he has been buried we will then do our duty by him. We shall make sacrifices to cleanse the desecrated land."

Obierika, who had been gazing steadily at his friend's dangling body, turned suddenly to the District Commissioner and said ferociously: "That man was one of the greatest men in Umuofia. You drove him to kill himself; and now he will be buried like a dog …" He could not say any more. His voice trembled and choked his words.

"Shut up!" shouted one of the messengers, quite unnecessarily.

"Take down the body," the Commissioner ordered his chief messenger, "and bring it and all these people to court."

"Yes, sah," the messenger said, saluting.

The Commissioner went away, taking three or four of the soldiers with him. In the many years in which he had toiled to bring civilization to different parts of Africa he had learnt a number of things. One of them was that a District Commissioner must never attend to such undignified details as cutting down a dead man from the tree. Such attention would give the natives a poor opinion of him. In the book which he planned to write he would stress that point. As he walked back to the court he thought about that book. Every day brought him some new material. The story of this man who had killed a messenger and hanged himself would make interesting reading. One could almost write a whole chapter on him. Perhaps not a whole chapter but a reasonable paragraph, at any rate. There was so much else to include, and one must be firm in cutting out details. He had already chosen the title of the book, after much thought: *The Pacification of the Primitive Tribes of the Lower Niger*.

SALMAN RUSHDIE ■ (b. 1947)

Born in Bombay on the day India achieved independence from Britain, Salman Rushdie was raised in largely Muslim Pakistan after the subcontinent was divided later that year. He later settled in England and achieved international fame with his 1981 novel *Midnight's Children*, a sprawling, fantasy-filled comedy of Indian history and individual romance, drawing upon both a multitude of Indian tales and the heritage of British novelists from Laurence Sterne to E. M. Forster. *Midnight's Children* won England's prestigious Booker Prize that year and was later judged the best novel of all the winners in the award's first twenty-five years.

Rushdie's fortunes took a very different turn after he published his 1988 novel *Satanic Verses,* which treated the history of Islam with sometimes sardonic irony. The book was taken by many Muslims as a blasphemous affront, and in 1989 Iran's religious and political leader, the Ayatollah Khomeini, issued a *fatwa,* or religious decree, ordering Rushdie's death. Rushdie had to go into hiding, somewhat reluctantly protected by the government of Britain's Margaret Thatcher, whose policies he had satirized as well. Following Khomeini's death, subsequent Iranian leaders have suggested that the decree would not be enforced; Rushdie eventually settled in the United States and resumed making public appearances.

Rushdie has continued to cross borders in his work as well as in his life; the story given here, "Chekov and Zulu," comes from his 1994 collection *East, West*. At first sight, the title may seem to link a classic European writer with an African tribalist, but in fact the names derive from two of the supporting characters in the television and movie series *Star Trek*. The story plays throughout on the overlays and the gaps between visual and verbal media, popular and classical culture, high tech and low humor. Rushdie's unheroic heroes fancy themselves characters aboard the starship *Enterprise,* blasted somehow into a conflict in the Middle Earth of J. R. R. Tolkien. They use this doubled frame of reference to try and make sense of the cultural dislocations and the growing political violence they experience as they move between England and India. Told in a riot of Indian-inflected English and using a wide array of cultural references, Rushdie's story moves from social comedy to a surprising and chilling conclusion.

Chekov and Zulu

1

On 4th November, 1984, Zulu disappeared in Birmingham, and India House sent his old schoolfriend Chekov to Wembley[1] to see the wife.

"Adaabarz, Mrs. Zulu. Permission to enter?"

"Of course come in, Dipty sahib, why such formality?"

"Sorry to disturb you on a Sunday, Mrs. Zulu, but Zulu-tho hasn't been in touch this morning?"

"With me? Since when he contacts me on official trip? Why to hit a telephone call when he is probably enjoying?"

"Whoops, sore point, excuse *me*. Always been the foot-in-it blunderbuss type."

"At least sit, take tea-shee."

---

1. Birmingham is a city in West Midlands, central England; Wembley is a London suburb.

"Fixed the place up damn fine, Mrs. Zulu, wah-wah.[2] Tasteful decor, in spades, I must say. So much cut-glass! That bounder Zulu must be getting too much pay, more than yours truly, clever dog."

"No, how is it possible? Acting Dipty's tankha[3] must be far in excess of Security Chief."

"No suspicion intended, ji.[4] Only to say what a bargain-hunter you must be."

"Some problem but there is, na?"

"Beg pardon?"

"Arré,[5] Jaisingh! Where have you been sleeping? Acting Dipty Sahib is thirsting for his tea. And biscuits and jalebis, can you not keep two things in your head? Jump, now, guest is waiting."

"Truly, Mrs. Zulu, please go to no trouble."

"No trouble is there, Diptyji, only this chap has become lazy since coming from home. Days off, TV in room, even pay in pounds sterling, he expects all. So far we brought him but no gratitude, what to tell you, noth-*thing*."

"Ah, Jaisingh; why not? Excellent jalebi, Mrs. Z. Thanking you."

Assembled on top of the television and on shelf units around it was the missing man's collection of *Star Trek* memorabilia: Captain Kirk and Spock dolls, spaceship models— a Klingon Bird of Prey, a Romulan vessel, a space station, and of course the Starship *Enterprise*. In pride of place were large figurines of two of the series's supporting cast.

"These old Doon School nicknames," Chekov exclaimed heartily. "They stay put like stuck records. Dumpy, Stumpy, Grumpy, Humpy. They take over from our names. As in our case our intrepid cosmonaut aliases."

"I don't like. This 'Mrs. Zulu' I am landed with! It sounds like a blackie."

"Wear the name with pride, begum[6] sahib. We're old comrades-in-arms, your husband and I; since boyhood days, perhaps he was good enough to mention? Intrepid diplonauts. Our umpteen-year mission to explore new worlds and new civilisations. See there, our alter egos standing on your TV, the Asiatic-looking Russky and the Chink. Not the leaders, as you'll appreciate, but the ultimate professional servants. 'Course laid in!' 'Hailing frequencies open!' 'Warp factor three!' What would that strutting Captain have been without his top-level staffers? Likewise with the good ship Hindustan.[7] We are servants also, you see, just like your fierce Jaisingh here. Never more important than in a moment like the present sad crisis, when an even keel must be maintained, jalebis must be served and tea poured, no matter what. We do not lead, but we enable. Without us, no course can be laid, no hailing frequency opened. No factors can be warped."

"Is he in difficulties, then, your Zulu? As if it wasn't bad enough, this terrible time."

On the wall behind the TV was a framed photograph of Indira Gandhi,[8] with a garland hung around it. She had been dead since Wednesday. Pictures of her cremation had been on the TV for hours. The flower-petals, the garish, unbearable flames.

"Hard to believe it. Indiraji! Words fail one. She was our mother. Hai, hai! Cut down in her prime."

---

2. Excellent.

3. Wages.

4. Term of respect added to ends of sentences or words.

5. Exclamation of surprise.

6. High-ranking Muslim woman.

7. Persian name for India.

8. Indian prime minister between 1966–1977 and 1980–1984; assassinated in 1984.

"And on radio-TV, such-such stories are coming about Delhi goings-on. So many killings, Dipty Sahib. So many of our decent Sikh[9] people done to death, as if all were guilty for the crimes of one-two badmash guards."

"The Sikh community has always been thought loyal to the nation," Chekov reflected. "Backbone of the Army, to say nothing of the Delhi taxi service. Super-citizens, one might say, seemingly wedded to the national idea. But such ideas are being questioned now, you must admit; there are those who would point to the comb, bangle, dagger et cetera as signs of the enemy within."

"Who would dare say such a thing about us? Such an evil thing."

"I know. I know. But you take Zulu. The ticklish thing is, he's not on any official business that we know of. He's dropped off the map, begum sahib. AWOL[1] ever since the assassination. No contact for two days plus."

"O God."

"There is a view forming back at HQ that he may have been associated with the gang. Who have in all probability long-established links with the community over here."

"O God."

"Naturally I am fighting strenuously against the proponents of this view. But his absence is damning, you must see. We have no fear of these tinpot Khalistan wallahs.[2] But they have a ruthless streak. And with Zulu's inside knowledge and security background . . . They have threatened further attacks, as you know. As you must know. As some would say you must know all too well."

"O God."

"It is possible," Chekov said, eating his jalebi, "that Zulu has boldly gone where no Indian diplonaut has gone before."

The wife wept. "Even the stupid name you could never get right. It was with S. 'Sulu.' So-so many episodes I have been made to see, you think I don't know? Kirk Spock McCoy Scott Uhura Chekov *Sulu*."

"But Zulu is a better name for what some might allege to be a wild man," Chekov said. "For a suspected savage. For a putative traitor. Thank you for excellent tea."

2

In August, Zulu, a shy, burly giant, had met Chekov off the plane from Delhi. Chekov at thirty-three was a small, slim, dapper man in grey flannels, stiff-collared shirt and a double-breasted navy blue blazer with brass buttons. He had bat's-wing eyebrows and a prominent and pugnacious jaw, so that his cultivated tones and habitual soft-spokenness came as something of a surprise, disarming those who had been led by the eyebrows and chin to expect an altogether more aggressive personality. He was a high flyer, with one small embassy already notched up. The Acting Number Two job in London, while strictly temporary, was his latest plum.

"What-ho, Zools! Years, yaar,[3] years," Chekov said, thumping his palm into the other man's chest. "So," he added, "I see you've become a hairy fairy." The young Zulu had been a modern Sikh in the matter of hair—sporting a fine moustache at eighteen, but beardless, with a haircut instead of long tresses wound tightly under a turban. Now, however, he had reverted to tradition.

---

9. Community in the Punjab whose religion attempts to combine Hinduism and Islam.
1. Absent without leave.
2. Sikh military who call for a separate Sikh state called Khalistan; *wallah* means boy or man.
3. Friend, buddy.

"Hullo, ji," Zulu greeted him cautiously. "So then is it OK to utilise the old modes of address?"

"Utilise away! Wouldn't hear of anything else," Chekov said, handing Zulu his bags and baggage tags. "Spirit of the *Enterprise* and all that jazz."

In his public life the most urbane of men, Chekov when letting his hair down in private enjoyed getting interculturally hot under the collar. Soon after his taking up his new post he sat with Zulu one lunchtime on a bench in Embankment Gardens and jerked his head in the direction of various passers-by.

"Crooks," he said, *sotto voce*.[4]

"Where?" shouted Zulu, leaping athletically to his feet. "Should I pursue?"

Heads turned. Chekov grabbed the hem of Zulu's jacket and pulled him back on to the bench. "Don't be such a hero," he admonished fondly. "I meant all of them, generally; thieves, every last one. God, I love London! Theatre, ballet, opera, restaurants! The Pavilion at Lord's on the Saturday of the Test Match![5] The royal ducks on the royal pond in royal St. James's Park! Decent tailors, a decent mixed grill when you want it, decent magazines to read! I see the remnants of greatness and I don't mind telling you I am impressed. The Athenaeum, Buck House, the lions in Trafalgar Square. *Damn* impressive. I went to a meeting with the junior Minister at the F. & C.O. and realised I was in the old India Office. All that John Company black teak, those tuskers rampant on the old bookcases. Gave me quite a turn. I applaud them for their success: hurrah! But then I look at my own home, and I see that it has been plundered by burglars. I can't deny there is a residue of distress."

"I am sorry to hear of your loss," Zulu said, knitting his brows. "But surely the culpables are not in the vicinity."

"Zulu, Zulu, a figure of speech, my simpleton warrior prince. Their museums are full of our treasures, I meant. Their fortunes and cities, built on the loot they took. So on, so forth. One forgives, of course; that is our national nature. One need not forget."

Zulu pointed at a tramp, sleeping on the next bench in a ragged hat and coat. "Did he steal from us, too?" he asked.

"Never forget," said Chekov, wagging a finger, "that the British working class collaborated for its own gain in the colonial project. Manchester cotton workers, for instance, supported the destruction of our cotton industry. As diplomats we must never draw attention to such facts; but facts, nevertheless, they remain."

"But a beggarman is not in the working class," objected Zulu, reasonably. "Surely this fellow at least is not our oppressor."

"Zulu," Chekov said in exasperation, "don't be so bleddy difficult."

Chekov and Zulu went boating on the Serpentine, and Chekov got back on his hobby-horse. "They have stolen us," he said, reclining boatered and champagned on striped cushions while mighty Zulu rowed. "And now we are stealing ourselves back. It is an Elgin marbles[6] situation."

"You should be more content," said Zulu, shipping oars and gulping cola. "You should be less hungry, less cross. See how much you have! It is enough. Sit back and enjoy. I have less, and it suffices for me. The sun is shining. The colonial period is a closed book."

---

4. Softly.

5. A cricket match played between international all-star teams.

6. A group of sculptures removed from the Acropolis in Athens by Lord Elgin in 1801–1803 and purchased by the British Museum in 1816. Recent opinion polls have suggested that over 90 percent of the British public support the return of the marbles to Greece, though a 1996 resolution in the Parliament was tabled.

"If you don't want that sandwich, hand it over," said Chekov. "With my natural radicalism I should not have been a diplomat. I should have been a terrorist."

"But then we would have been enemies, on opposite sides," protested Zulu, and suddenly there were real tears in his eyes. "Do you care nothing for our friendship? For my responsibilities in life?"

Chekov was abashed. "Quite right, Zools old boy. Too bleddy true. You can't imagine how delighted I was when I learned we would be able to join forces like this in London. Nothing like the friendships of one's boyhood, eh? Nothing in the world can take their place. Now listen, you great lummox, no more of that long face. I won't permit it. Great big chap like you shouldn't look like he's about to blub. Blood brothers, old friend, what do you say? All for one and one for all."

"Blood brothers," said Zulu, smiling a shy smile.

"Onward, then," nodded Chekov, settling back on his cushions. "Impulse power only."

The day Mrs. Gandhi was murdered by her Sikh bodyguards, Zulu and Chekov played squash in a private court in St. John's Wood. In the locker-room after showering, prematurely-greying Chekov still panted heavily with a towel round his softening waist, reluctant to expose his exhaustion-shrivelled purple penis to view; Zulu stood proudly naked, thick-cocked, tossing his fine head of long black hair, caressing and combing it with womanly sensuality, and at last twisting it swiftly into a knot.

"Too good, Zulu yaar. Fataakh! Fataakh! What shots! Too bleddy good for me."

"You desk-pilots, ji. You lose your edge. Once you were ready for anything."

"Yeah, yeah, I'm over the hill. But you were only one year junior."

"I have led a purer life, ji—action, not words."

"You understand we will have to blacken your name," Chekov said softly.

Zulu turned slowly in Charles Atlas pose in front of a full-length mirror.

"It has to look like a maverick stunt. If anything goes wrong, deniability is essential. Even your wife must not suspect the truth."

Spreading his arms and legs, Zulu made his body a giant X, stretching himself to the limit. Then he came to attention. Chekov sounded a little frayed.

"Zools? What do you say?"

"Is the transporter ready?"

"Come on, yaar, don't arse around."

"Respectfully, Mister Chekov, sir, it's my arse. Now then: is the transporter ready?"

"Transporter ready. Aye."

"Then, energise."

Chekov's memorandum, classified top-secret, eyes-only, and addressed to "JTK" (James T. Kirk):

My strong recommendation is that Operation Startrek be aborted. To send a Federation employee of Klingon origin unarmed into a Klingon cell to spy is the crudest form of loyalty test. The operative in question has never shown ideological deviation of any sort and deserves better, even in the present climate of mayhem, hysteria and fear. If he fails to persuade the Klingons of his bona fides he can expect to be treated with extreme prejudice. These are not hostage takers.

The entire undertaking is misconceived. The locally settled Klingon population is not the central problem. Even should we succeed, such intelligence as can be gleaned about more important principals back home will no doubt be of dubious accuracy and limited value. We should advise Star Fleet Headquarters to engage urgently with the grievances and aspirations of the Klingon people. Unless these are dealt with fair and square there cannot be a lasting peace.

The reply from JTK:

Your closeness to the relevant individual excuses what is otherwise an explosively communalist document. It is not for you to define the national interest nor to determine what undercover operations are to be undertaken. It is for you to enable such operations to occur and to provide back-up as and when required to do so. As a personal favour to you and in the name of my long friendship with your eminent Papaji I have destroyed your last without keeping a copy and suggest you do the same. Also destroy this.

Chekov asked Zulu to drive him up to Stratford for a performance of *Coriolanus*.[7]
"How many kiddiwinks by now? Three?"
"Four," said Zulu. "All boys."
"By the grace of God. She must be a good woman."
"I have a full heart," said Zulu, with sudden feeling. "A full house, a full belly, a full bed."
"Lucky so and so," said Chekov. "Always were warm-blooded. I, by contrast, am not. Reptiles, certain species of dinosaur, and me. I am in the wife market, by the way, if you know any suitable candidates. Bachelordom being, after a certain point, an obstacle on the career path."
Zulu was driving strangely. In the slow lane of the motorway, as they approached an exit lane, he accelerated towards a hundred miles an hour. Once the exit was behind them, he slowed. Chekov noticed that he varied his speed and lane constantly. "Doesn't the old rattletrap have cruise control?" he asked. "Because, sport, this kind of performance would not do on the bridge of the flagship of the United Federation of Planets."
"Anti-surveillance," said Zulu. "Dry-cleaning." Chekov, alarmed, looked out of the back window.
"Have we been rumbled, then?"
"Nothing to worry about," grinned Zulu. "Better safe than sorry is all. Always anticipate the worst-case scenario."
Chekov settled back in his seat. "You liked toys and games," he said. Zulu had been a crack rifle shot, the school's champion wrestler, and an expert fencer. "Every Speech Day," Zulu said, "I would sit in the hall and clap, while you went up for all the work prizes. English Prize, History Prize, Latin Prize, Form Prize. Clap, clap, clap, term after term, year after year. But on Sports Day I got my cups. And now also I have my area of expertise."
"Quite a reputation you're building up, if what I hear is anything to go by."
There was a silence. England passed by at speed.
"Do you like Tolkien?" Zulu asked.
"I wouldn't have put you down as a big reader," said Chekov, startled. "No offence."
"J. R. R. Tolkien," said Zulu. "*The Lord of the Rings*."[8]
"Can't say I've read the gentleman. Heard of him, of course. Elves and pixies. Not your sort of thing at all, I'd have thought."

7. Shakespeare's bloodiest tragedy; its themes are civil unrest and revolt.
8. Tolkien's trilogy (1954–1955), written during and just after World War II, concerns a war for control of Middle Earth, in which men, elves, dwarves, and a few British-like hobbits band together to defeat the evil eastern empire of Sauron.

"It is about a war to the finish between Good and Evil," said Zulu intently. "And while this great war is being fought there is one part of the world, the Shire, in which nobody even knows it's going on. The hobbits who live there work and squabble and make merry and they have no fucking clue about the forces that threaten them, and those that save their tiny skins." His face was red with vehemence.

"Meaning me, I suppose," Chekov said.

"I am a soldier in that war," said Zulu. "If you sit in an office you don't have one small idea of what the real world is like. The world of action, ji. The world of deeds, of things that are done and maybe undone too. The world of life and death."

"Only in the worst case," Chekov demurred.

"Do I tell you how to apply your smooth-tongued musca-polish to people's behinds?" stormed Zulu. "Then do not tell me how to ply my trade."

Soldiers going into battle pump themselves up, Chekov knew. This chest-beating was to be expected, it must not be misunderstood. "When will you vamoose?" he quietly asked.

"Chekov ji, you won't see me go."

Stratford approached. "Did you know, ji," Zulu offered, "that the map of Tolkien's Middle-earth fits quite well over central England and Wales? Maybe all fairylands are right here, in our midst."

"You're a deep one, old Zools," said Chekov. "Full of revelations today."

Chekov had a few people over for dinner at his modern-style official residence in a private road in Hampstead: a Very Big Businessman he was wooing, journalists he liked, prominent India-lovers, noted Non-Resident Indians. The policy was business as usual. The dreadful event must not be seen to have derailed the ship of State: whose new captain, Chekov mused, was a former pilot himself. As if a Sulu, a Chekov had been suddenly promoted to the skipper's seat.

Damned difficult doing all this without a lady wife to act as hostess, he grumbled inwardly. The best golden plates with the many-headed lion at the centre, the finest crystal, the menu, the wines. Personnel had been seconded from India House to help him out, but it wasn't the same. The secrets of good evenings, like God, were in the details. Chekov meddled and fretted.

The evening went off well. Over brandy, Chekov even dared to introduce a blacker note. "England has always been a breeding ground for our revolutionists," he said. "What would Pandit Nehru[9] have been without Harrow?[1] Or Gandhiji without his formative experiences here? Even the Pakistan idea was dreamt up by young radicals at college in what we then were asked to think of as the Mother Country. Now that England's status has declined, I suppose it is logical that the quality of the revolutionists she breeds has likewise fallen. The Kashmiris![2] Not a hope in hell. And as for these Khalistan types, let them not think that their evil deed has brought their dream a day closer. On the contrary. On the contrary. We will root them out and smash them to—what's the right word?—to *smithereens*."

To his surprise he had begun speaking loudly and had risen to his feet. He sat down hard and laughed. The moment passed.

"The funny thing about this blasted nickname of mine," he said quickly to his dinner-table neighbour, the septuagenarian Very Big Businessman's improbably

---

9. Jawaharlal Nehru, first prime minister of the Republic of India (1947–1964), father of Indira Gandhi.

1. An exclusive English preparatory school.

2. Residents of Kashmir, a territory in dispute between India and Pakistan since 1947.

young and attractive wife, "is that back then we never saw one episode of the TV series. No TV to see it on, you see. The whole thing was just a legend wafting its way from the US and UK to our lovely hill-station of Dehra Dun.

"After a while we got a couple of cheap paperback novelisations and passed them round as if they were naughty books like *Lady C* or some such. Lots of us tried the names on for size but only two of them stuck; probably because they seemed to go together, and the two of us got on pretty well, even though he was younger. A lovely boy. So just like Laurel and Hardy we were Chekov and Zulu."

"Love and marriage," said the woman.

"Beg pardon?"

"*You* know," she said. "Go together like is it milk and porridge. Or a car and garage, that's right. I love old songs. La-la-la-something-brother, you can't have fun without I think it's your mother."[3]

"Yes, now I do recall," said Chekov.

3

Three months later Zulu telephoned his wife.

"O my God where have you vanished are you dead?"

"Listen please my bivi. Listen carefully my wife, my only love."

"Yes. OK. I am calm. Line is bad, but."

"Call Chekov and say condition red."

"Arré! What is wrong with your condition?"

"Please. Condition red."

"Yes. OK. Red."

"Say the Klingons may be smelling things."

"Clingers-on may be smelly things. Means what?"

"My darling, I beg you."

"I have it all right here only. With this pencil I have written it, both."

"Tell him, get Scotty to lock on to my signal and beam me up at once."

"What rubbish! Even now you can't leave off that stupid game."

"Bivi. It is urgent. *Beam me up.*"

Chekov dropped everything and drove. He went via the dry-cleaners as instructed; he drove round roundabouts twice, jumped red lights, deliberately took a wrong turning, stopped and turned round, made as many right turns as possible to see if anything followed him across the stream of traffic, and, on the motorway, mimicked Zulu's techniques. When he was as certain as he could be that he was clean, he headed for the rendezvous point. "Roll over Len Deighton," he thought, "and tell le Carré the news."[4]

He turned off the motorway and pulled into a lay-by. A man stepped out of the trees, looking newly bathed and smartly dressed, with a sheepish smile on his face. It was Zulu.

Chekov jumped out of the car and embraced his friend, kissing him on both cheeks. Zulu's bristly beard pricked his lips. "I expected you'd have an arm missing, or blood pouring from a gunshot wound, or some black eyes at least," he said. "Instead here you are dressed for the theatre, minus only an opera cloak and cane."

3. She is mangling the lyrics of Sammy Cahn's 1955 song *Love and Marriage:* "Love and marriage, love and marriage / Go together like a horse and carriage / This I tell you brother / You can't have one without the other."

4. Len Deighton and John le Carré are two writers of spy novels. The line refers to the popular song lyric, "Roll over, Beethoven."

"Mission accomplished," said Zulu, patting his breast pocket. "All present and correct."

"Then what was that 'condition red' bakvaas?"

"The worst-case scenario," said Zulu, "does not always materialise."

In the car, Chekov scanned the names, places, dates in Zulu's brown envelope. The information was better than anyone had expected. From this anonymous Midlands lay-by a light was shining on certain remote villages and urban back-alleys in Punjab.[5] There would be a round-up, and, for some big badmashes at least, there would no longer be shadows in which to hide.

He gave a little, impressed whistle.

Zulu in the passenger seat inclined his head. "Better move off now," he said. "Don't tempt fate."

They drove south through Middle-earth.

Not long after they came off the motorway, Zulu said, "By the way, I quit."

Chekov stopped the car. The two towers of Wembley Stadium were visible through a gap in the houses to the left.

"What's this? Did those extremists manage to turn your head or what?"

"Chekov, ji, don't be a fool. Who needs extremists when there are the killings in Delhi? Hundreds, maybe thousands. Sikh men scalped and burned alive in front of their families. Boy-children, too."

"We know this."

"Then, ji, we also know who was behind it."

"There is not a shred of evidence," Chekov repeated the policy line.

"There are eyewitnesses and photographs," said Zulu. "We know this."

"There are those who think," said Chekov slowly, "that after Indiraji the Sikhs deserved what they got."

Zulu stiffened.

"You know me better than that, I hope," said Chekov. "Zulu, for God's sake, come on. All our bleddy lives."

"No Congress workers have been indicted," said Zulu. "In spite of all the evidence of complicity. Therefore, I resign. You should quit, too."

"If you have gone so damn radical," cried Chekov, "why hand over these lists at all? Why go only half the bleddy hog?"

"I am a security wallah," said Zulu, opening the car door. "Terrorists of all sorts are my foes. But not, apparently, in certain circumstances, yours."

"Zulu, get in, damn it," Chekov shouted. "Don't you care for your career? A wife and four kiddiwinks to support. What about your old chums? Are you going to turn your back on me?"

But Zulu was already too far away.

Chekov and Zulu never met again. Zulu settled in Bombay and as the demand for private-sector protection increased in that cash-rich boom-town, so his Zulu Shield and Zulu Spear companies prospered and grew. He had three more children, all of them boys, and remains happily married to this day.

As for Chekov, he never did take a wife. In spite of this supposed handicap, however, he did well in his chosen profession. His rapid rise continued. But one day in May 1991 he was, by chance, a member of the entourage accompanying Mr. Rajiv

---

5. Province divided between India and Pakistan.

Gandhi[6] to the South Indian village of Sriperumbudur, where Rajiv was to address an election rally. Security was lax, intentionally so. In the previous election, Rajivji felt, the demands of security had placed an alienating barrier between himself and the electorate. On this occasion, he decreed, the voters must be allowed to feel close.

After the speeches, the Rajiv group descended from the podium. Chekov, who was just a few feet behind Rajiv, saw a small Tamil[7] woman come forward, smiling. She shook Rajiv's hand and did not let go. Chekov understood what she was smiling about, and the knowledge was so powerful that it stopped time itself.

Because time had stopped, Chekov was able to make a number of private observations. "These Tamil revolutionists are not England-returned," he noted. "So, finally, we have learned to produce the goods at home, and no longer need to import. Bang goes that old dinner-party standby; so to speak." And, less dryly: "The tragedy is not how one dies," he thought. "It is how one has lived."

The scene around him vanished, dissolving in a pool of light, and was replaced by the bridge of the Starship *Enterprise*. All the leading figures were in their appointed places. Zulu sat beside Chekov at the front.

"Shields no longer operative," Zulu was saying. On the main screen, they could see the Klingon Bird of Prey uncloaking, preparing to strike.

"One direct hit and we're done for," cried Dr. McCoy. "For God's sake, Jim, get us out of here!"

"Illogical," said First Officer Spock. "The degradation of our dilithium crystal drive means that warp speed is unavailable. At impulse power only, we would make a poor attempt indeed to flee the Bird of Prey. Our only logical course is unconditional surrender."

"Surrender to a Klingon!" shouted McCoy. "Damn it, you cold-blooded, pointy-eared adding-machine, don't you know how they treat their prisoners?"

"Phaser banks completely depleted," said Zulu. "Offensive capability nil."

"Should I attempt to contact the Klingon captain, sir?" Chekov inquired. "They could fire at any moment."

"Thank you, Mr. Chekov," said Captain Kirk. "I'm afraid that won't be necessary. On this occasion, the worst-case scenario is the one we are obliged to play out. Hold your position. Steady as she goes."

"The Bird of Prey has fired, sir," said Zulu.

Chekov took Zulu's hand and held it firmly, victoriously, as the speeding balls of deadly light approached.

MURAKAMI HARUKI ■ (b. 1949)

The novels and short stories of Murakami Haruki—whose name is here given in the usual Japanese order, with the family name preceding the given name—are enormously popular among young readers in Japan and have won the author numerous literary prizes. Increasingly, his works are also becoming best-sellers around the globe among readers who find themselves attracted to Murakami's mix of reflections on specifically Japanese situations and his abundant references to a popular culture of mostly American origin that is shared by young people today across a wide variety of regions, languages, and nations. Murakami

6. Indian prime minister 1984–1989, assassinated in May 1991, son of Indira Gandhi.

7. A people of South India and Sri Lanka. The government of India had been aiding the Sri Lankan government in suppressing violent protests by Tamil separatists in Sri Lanka.

himself forms part of the generation of Japanese growing up after World War II who first experienced the full impact of this imported pop culture. Born near Kobe, Japan, in 1949, he studied screenwriting and Greek drama in Tokyo from 1968 until the completion of his bachelor's degree in 1975 and witnessed the upheaval of violent student protests first-hand during this time. From 1974 to 1981 he ran a Tokyo jazz bar together with his wife, thereby establishing another conduit between American and Japanese culture. His first novel, *Hear the Wind Sing,* was published in 1979, and since 1981 he has dedicated himself full time to writing.

The insistently, almost aggressively contemporary idiom of Murakami's fiction has sometimes alienated older Japanese readers, who prefer the more timeless topics and formal diction of a Tanizaki Junichiro or Kawabata Yasunari. Murakami captures elements of late-twentieth-century culture in his themes as well as his language; references to recent technology, Western pop music, and brand-name consumer products come up frequently in his texts, as do changing sexual relations, divorce, and alienation from the professional and social worlds. Some of Murakami's novels are quite realistic, such as *Norwegian Wood* (1987), an account of student life in the 1960s (its title is taken from a Beatles' song), or the parts of *The Wind-up Bird Chronicle* (1994), that deal with the violent confrontations between Chinese and Japanese in World War II. But many others combine late-twentieth-century realism, the hard-boiled detective novel (Raymond Chandler being one of Murakami's models), and science fiction: *A Wild Sheep Chase* (1982) and *Hard-Boiled Wonderland and the End of the World* (1985) are good examples of this signature style. The short story "TV People" also belongs to this kind of writing. As is often the case in Murakami's idiosyncratic narrative worlds, it is difficult to know which of the strange incidents the protagonist experiences are part of an objective reality and which ones are figments of his private imagination; neither is it easy to decide just where the boundary between these two realms lies in a world of television and glossy magazines. In this universe that seems part Kafka and part cyberpunk, what is clearly at stake is the protagonist's encounter with television—a medium that has fundamentally transformed late-twentieth-century culture.

TV People[1]

It was Sunday evening when the TV People showed up.

The season, spring. At least, I think it was spring. In any case, it wasn't particularly hot as seasons go, not particularly chilly.

To be honest, the season's not so important. What matters is that it's a Sunday evening.

I don't like Sunday evenings. Or, rather, I don't like everything that goes with them—that Sunday-evening state of affairs. Without fail, come Sunday evening my head starts to ache. In varying intensity each time. Maybe a third to a half of an inch into my temples, the soft flesh throbs—as if invisible threads lead out and someone far off is yanking at the other ends. Not that it hurts so much. It ought to hurt, but strangely, it doesn't—it's like long needles probing anesthetized areas.

And I hear things. Not sounds, but thick slabs of silence being dragged through the dark. *KRZSHAAAL KKRZSHAAAAAL KKKKRMMMS.* Those are the initial indications. First, the aching. Then, a slight distortion of my vision. Tides of confusion wash through, premonitions tugging at memories, memories tugging at premonitions. A finely honed razor moon floats white in the sky, roots of doubt burrow into

---

1. Translated by Ian Wedde and Fawwaz Tuqan.

the earth. People walk extra loud down the hall just to get me. *KRRSPUMK DUWB KRRSPUMK DUWB KRRSPUMK DUWB.*

All the more reason for the TV People to single out Sunday evening as the time to come around. Like melancholy moods, or the secretive, quiet fall of rain, they steal into the gloom of that appointed time.

Let me explain how the TV People look.

The TV People are slightly smaller than you or me. Not obviously smaller— *slightly* smaller. About, say, 20 or 30%. Every part of their bodies is uniformly smaller. So rather than "small," the more terminologically correct expression might be "reduced."

In fact, if you see TV People somewhere, you might not notice at first that they're small. But even if you don't, they'll probably strike you as somehow strange. Unsettling, maybe. You're sure to think something's odd, and then you'll take another look. There's nothing unnatural about them at first glance, but that's what's so unnatural. Their smallness is completely different from that of children and dwarfs. When we see children, we *feel* they're small, but this sense of recognition comes mostly from

Nam June Paik, *Global Encoder*, 1994 (video sculpture, 122 × 84 × 55 inches).

the misproportioned awkwardness of their bodies. They are small, granted, but not uniformly so. The hands are small, but the head is big. Typically, that is. No, the smallness of TV People is something else entirely. TV People look as if they were reduced by photocopy, everything mechanically calibrated. Say their height has been reduced by a factor of 0.7, then their shoulder width is also in 0.7 reduction; ditto (0.7 reduction) for the feet, head, ears, and fingers. Like plastic models, only a little smaller than the real thing.

Or like perspective demos. Figures that look far away even close up. Something out of a trompe-l'oeil painting where the surface warps and buckles. An illusion where the hand fails to touch objects close by, yet brushes what is out of reach.

That's TV People.

That's TV People.

That's TV People.

There were three of them altogether.

They don't knock or ring the doorbell. Don't say hello. They just sneak right in. I don't even hear a footstep. One opens the door, the other two carry in a TV. Not a very big TV. Your ordinary Sony color TV. The door was locked, I think, but I can't be certain. Maybe I forgot to lock it. It really wasn't foremost in my thoughts at the time, so who knows? Still, I think the door was locked.

When they come in, I'm lying on the sofa, gazing up at the ceiling. Nobody at home but me. That afternoon, the wife has gone out with the girls—some close friends from her high-school days—getting together to talk, then eating dinner out. "Can you grab your own supper?" the wife said before leaving. "There's vegetables in the fridge and all sorts of frozen foods. That much you can handle for yourself, can't you? And before the sun goes down, remember to take in the laundry, okay?"

"Sure thing," I said. Doesn't faze me a bit. Rice, right? Laundry, right? Nothing to it. Take care of it, simple as *SLUPPP KRRRTZ!*

"Did you say something, dear?" she asked.

"No, nothing," I said.

All afternoon I take it easy and loll around on the sofa. I have nothing better to do. I read a bit—that new novel by García Márquez[2]—and listen to some music. I have myself a beer. Still, I'm unable to give my mind to any of this. I consider going back to bed, but I can't even pull myself together enough to do that. So I wind up lying on the sofa, staring at the ceiling.

The way my Sunday afternoons go, I end up doing a little bit of various things, none very well. It's a struggle to concentrate on any one thing. This particular day, everything seems to be going right. I think, Today I'll read this book, listen to these records, answer these letters. Today, for sure, I'll clean out my desk drawers, run errands, wash the car for once. But two o'clock rolls around, three o'clock rolls around, gradually dusk comes on, and all my plans are blown. I haven't done a thing; I've been lying around on the sofa the whole day, same as always. The clock ticks in my ears. *TRPP Q SCHAOUS TRPP Q SCHAOUS.* The sound erodes everything around me, little by little, like dripping rain. *TRPP Q SCHAOUS TRPP Q SCHAOUS.* Little by little, Sunday afternoon wears down, shrinking in scale. Just like the TV People themselves.

---

2. Colombian novelist who won the Nobel Prize in Literature in 1982.

The TV people ignore me from the very outset. All three of them have this look that says the likes of me don't exist. They open the door and carry in their TV. The two put the set on the sideboard, the other one plugs it in. There's a mantel clock and a stack of magazines on the sideboard. The clock was a wedding gift, big and heavy—big and heavy as time itself—with a loud sound, too. *TRPP Q SCHAOUS TRPP Q SCHAOUS.* All through the house you can hear it. The TV People move it off the sideboard, down onto the floor. The wife's going to raise hell, I think. She hates it when things get randomly shifted about. If everything isn't in its proper place, she gets really sore. What's worse, with the clock there on the floor, I'm bound to trip over it in the middle of the night. I'm forever getting up to go to the toilet at two in the morning, bleary-eyed and stumbling over something.

Next, the TV People move the magazines to the table. All of them women's magazines. (I hardly ever read magazines; I read books—personally, I wouldn't mind if every last magazine in the world went out of business.) *Elle* and *Marie Claire* and *Home Ideas,* magazines of that ilk. Neatly stacked on the sideboard. The wife doesn't like me touching her magazines—change the order of the stack, and I never hear the end of it—so I don't go near them. Never once flipped through them. But the TV People couldn't care less: They move them right out of the way, they show no concern, they sweep the whole lot off the sideboard, they mix up the order. *Marie Claire* is on top of *Croissant; Home Ideas* is underneath *An-An.* Unforgivable. And worse, they're scattering the bookmarks onto the floor. They've lost her place, pages with important information. I have no idea what information or how important—might have been for work, might have been personal—but whatever, it was important to the wife, and she'll let me know about it. "What's the meaning of this? I go out for a nice time with friends, and when I come back, the house is a shambles!" I can just hear it, line for line. Oh, great, I think, shaking my head.

Everything gets removed from the sideboard to make room for the television. The TV People plug it into a wall socket, then switch it on. Then there is a tinkling noise, and the screen lights up. A moment later, the picture floats into view. They change the channels by remote control. But all the channels are blank—probably, I think, because they haven't connected the set to an antenna. There has to be an antenna outlet somewhere in the apartment. I seem to remember the superintendent telling us where it was when we moved into this condominium. All you had to do was connect it. But I can't remember where it is. We don't own a television, so I've completely forgotten.

Yet somehow the TV People don't seem bothered that they aren't picking up any broadcast. They give no sign of looking for the antenna outlet. Blank screen, no image—makes no difference to them. Having pushed the button and had the power come on, they've completed what they came to do.

The TV is brand-new. It's not in its box, but one look tells you it's new. The instruction manual and guarantee are in a plastic bag taped to the side; the power cable shines, sleek as a freshly caught fish.

All three TV People look at the blank screen from here and there around the room. One of them comes over next to me and verifies that you can see the TV screen from where I'm sitting. The TV is facing straight toward me, at an optimum viewing distance. They seem satisfied. One operation down, says their air of accomplishment. One of the TV People (the one who'd come over next to me) places the remote control on the table.

The TV People speak not a word. Their movements come off in perfect order, hence they don't need to speak. Each of the three executes his prescribed function with maximum efficiency. A professional job. Neat and clean. Their work is done in no time. As an afterthought, one of the TV People picks the clock up from the floor and casts a quick glance around the room to see if there isn't a more appropriate place to put it, but he doesn't find any and sets it back down. *TRPP Q SCHAOUS TRPP Q SCHAOUS.* It goes on ticking weightily on the floor. Our apartment is rather small, and a lot of floor space tends to be taken up with my books and the wife's reference materials. I am bound to trip on that clock. I heave a sigh. No mistake, stub my toes for sure. You can bet on it.

All three TV People wear dark-blue jackets. Of who-knows-what fabric, but slick. Under them, they wear jeans and tennis shoes. Clothes and shoes all proportionately reduced in size. I watch their activities for the longest time, until I start to think maybe it's *my* proportions that are off. Almost as if I were riding backward on a roller coaster, wearing strong prescription glasses. The view is dizzying, the scale all screwed up. I'm thrown off balance, my customary world is no longer absolute. That's the way the TV People make you feel.

Up to the very last, the TV People don't say a word. The three of them check the screen one more time, confirm that there are no problems, then switch it off by remote control. The glow contracts to a point and flickers off with a tinkling noise. The screen returns to its expressionless, gray, natural state. The world outside is getting dark. I hear someone calling out to someone else. Anonymous footsteps pass by down the hall, intentionally loud as ever. *KRRSPUMK DUWB KRRSPUMK DUWB.* A Sunday evening.

The TV People give the room another whirlwind inspection, open the door, and leave. Once again, they pay no attention to me whatsoever. They act as if I don't exist.

From the time the TV People come into the apartment to the moment they leave, I don't budge. Don't say a word. I remain motionless, stretched out on the sofa, surveying the whole operation. I know what you're going to say: That's unnatural. Total strangers—not one but three—walk unannounced right into your apartment, plunk down a TV set, and you just sit there staring at them, dumbfounded. Kind of odd, don't you think?

I know, I know. But for whatever reason, I don't speak up, I simply observe the proceedings. Because they ignore me so totally. And if you were in my position, I imagine you'd do the same. Not to excuse myself, but *you* have people right in front of you denying your very presence like that, then see if you don't doubt whether you actually exist. I look at my hands half expecting to see clear through them. I'm devastated, powerless, in a trance. My body, my mind are vanishing fast. I can't bring myself to move. It's all I can do to watch the three TV People deposit their television in my apartment and leave. I can't open my mouth for fear of what my voice might sound like.

The TV People exit and leave me alone. My sense of reality comes back to me. These hands are once again my hands. It's only then I notice that the dusk has been swallowed by darkness. I turn on the light. Then I close my eyes. Yes, that's a TV set sitting there. Meanwhile, the clock keeps ticking away the minutes. *TRPP Q SCHAOUS TRPP Q SCHAOUS.*

Curiously, the wife makes no mention of the appearance of the television set in the apartment. No reaction at all. Zero. It's as if she doesn't even see it. Creepy. Because, as I said before, she's extremely fussy about the order and arrangement of furniture and other things. If someone dares to move anything in the apartment, even by a hair, she'll jump on it in an instant. That's her ascendancy. She knits her brows, then gets things back the way they were.

Not me. If an issue of *Home Ideas* gets put under an *An-An,* or a ballpoint pen finds its way into the pencil stand, you don't see me go to pieces. I don't even notice. This is her problem; I'd wear myself out living like her. Sometimes she flies into a rage. She tells me she can't abide my carelessness. Yes, I say, and sometimes I can't stand carelessness about universal gravitation and π and $E = mc^2$, either. I mean it. But when I say things like this, she clams up, taking them as a personal insult. I never mean it that way; I just say what I feel.

That night, when she comes home, first thing she does is look around the apartment. I've readied a full explanation—how the TV People came and mixed everything up. It'll be difficult to convince her, but I intend to tell her the whole truth.

She doesn't say a thing, just gives the place the once-over. There's a TV on the sideboard, the magazines are out of order on the table, the mantel clock is on the floor, and the wife doesn't even comment. There's nothing for me to explain.

"You get your own supper okay?" she asks me, undressing.

"No, I didn't eat," I tell her.

"Why not?"

"I wasn't really hungry," I say.

The wife pauses, half-undressed, and thinks this over. She gives me a long look. Should she press the subject or not? The clock breaks up the protracted, ponderous silence. *TRPP Q SCHAOUS TRPP Q SCHAOUS.* I pretend not to hear; I won't let it in my ears. But the sound is simply too heavy, too loud to shut out. She, too, seems to be listening to it. Then she shakes her head and says, "Shall I whip up something quick?"

"Well, maybe," I say. I don't really feel much like eating, but I won't turn down the offer.

The wife changes into around-the-house wear and goes to the kitchen to fix zosui and tamago-yaki[3] while filling me in on her friends. Who'd done what, who'd said what, who'd changed her hairstyle and looked so much younger, who'd broken up with her boyfriend. I know most of her friends, so I pour myself a beer and follow along, inserting attentive uh-huhs at proper intervals. Though, in fact, I hardly hear a thing she says. I'm thinking about the TV People. That, and why she didn't remark on the sudden appearance of the television. No way she couldn't have noticed. Very odd. Weird, even. Something is wrong here. But what to do about it?

The food is ready, so I sit at the dining-room table and eat. Rice, egg, salt plum. When I've finished, the wife clears away the dishes. I have another beer, and she has a beer, too. I glance at the sideboard, and there's the TV set, with the power off, the remote-control unit sitting on the table. I get up from the table, reach for the remote control, and switch it on. The screen glows and I hear it tinkling. Still no picture. Only the same blank tube. I press the button to raise the volume, but all that does is increase the white-noise roar. I watch the snowstorm for twenty, thirty seconds, then switch it off. Light and sound vanish in an instant. Meanwhile, the wife has seated herself on the carpet and is flipping through *Elle,* oblivious of the fact that the TV has just been turned on and off.

---

3. A rice stew cooked with a thick broth and a rolled omelette.

I replace the remote control on the table and sit down on the sofa again, thinking I'll go on reading that long García Márquez novel. I always read after dinner. I might set the book down after thirty minutes, or I might read for two hours, but the thing is to read every day. Today, though, I can't get myself to read more than a page and a half. I can't concentrate; my thoughts keep returning to the TV set. I look up and see it, right in front of me.

I wake at half past two in the morning to find the TV still there. I get out of bed half hoping the thing has disappeared. No such luck. I go to the toilet, then plop down on the sofa and put my feet up on the table. I take the remote control in hand and try turning on the TV. No new developments in that department, either; only a rerun of the same glow and noise. Nothing else. I look at it a while, then switch it off.

I go back to bed and try to sleep. I'm dead tired, but sleep isn't coming. I shut my eyes and I see them. The TV People carrying the TV set, the TV People moving the clock out of the way, the TV People transferring magazines to the table, the TV People plugging the power cable into the wall socket, the TV People checking the screen, the TV People opening the door and silently exiting. They've stayed on in my head. They're in there walking around. I get back out of bed, go to the kitchen, and pour a double brandy into a coffee cup. I down the brandy and head over to the sofa for another session with Márquez. I open the pages, yet somehow the words won't sink in. The writing is opaque.

Very well, then, I throw García Márquez aside and pick up *Elle*. Reading *Elle* from time to time can't hurt anyone. But there isn't anything in *Elle* that catches my fancy. New hairstyles and elegant white silk blouses and eateries that serve good beef stew and what to wear to the opera, articles like that. Do I care? I throw *Elle* aside. Which leaves me the television on the sideboard to look at.

I end up staying awake until dawn, not doing a thing. At six o'clock, I make myself some coffee. I don't have anything else to do, so I go ahead and fix ham sandwiches before the wife gets up.

"You're up awful early," she says drowsily.

"Mmm," I mumble.

After a nearly wordless breakfast, we leave home together and go our separate ways to our respective offices. The wife works at a small publishing house. Edits a natural-food and life-style magazine. "Shiitake Mushrooms Prevent Gout," "The Future of Organic Farming," you know the kind of magazine. Never sells very well, but hardly costs anything to produce; kept afloat by a handful of zealots. Me, I work in the advertising department of an electrical-appliance manufacturer. I dream up ads for toasters and washing machines and microwave ovens.

In my office building, I pass one of the TV People on the stairs. If I'm not mistaken, it's one of the three who brought the TV the day before—probably the one who first opened the door, who didn't actually carry the set. Their singular lack of distinguishing features makes it next to impossible to tell them apart, so I can't swear to it, but I'd say I'm eight to nine out of ten on the mark. He's wearing the same blue jacket he had on the previous day, and he's not carrying anything in his hands. He's merely walking down the stairs. I'm walking up. I dislike elevators, so I generally take the stairs. My office is on the ninth floor, so this is no mean feat. When I'm in a rush, I get all sweaty by the time I reach the top. Even so, getting sweaty has got to be better than taking the elevator, as far as I'm concerned. Everyone jokes about it: doesn't own a TV or a VCR, doesn't take elevators, must be a modern-day Luddite.[4] Maybe a childhood trauma leading to arrested development. Let them think what they like. They're the ones who are screwed up, if you ask me.

In any case, there I am, climbing the stairs as always; I'm the only one on the stairs—almost nobody else uses them—when between the fourth and fifth floors I pass one of the TV People coming down. It happens so suddenly I don't know what to do. Maybe I should say something?

But I don't say anything. I don't know what to say, and he's unapproachable. He leaves no opening; he descends the stairs so functionally, at one set tempo, with such regulated precision. Plus, he utterly ignores my presence, same as the day before. I don't even enter his field of vision. He slips by before I can think what to do. In that instant, the field of gravity warps.

At work, the day is solid with meetings from the morning on. Important meetings on sales campaigns for a new product line. Several employees read reports. Blackboards fill with figures, bar graphs proliferate on computer screens. Heated discussions. I participate, although my contribution to the meetings is not that critical because I'm not directly involved with the project. So between meetings I keep puzzling things over. I voice an opinion only once. Isn't much of an opinion, either—something perfectly obvious to any observer—but I couldn't very well go without saying anything, after all. I may not be terribly ambitious when it comes to work, but so long as I'm receiving a salary I have to demonstrate responsibility. I summarize the various opinions up to that point and even make a joke to lighten the atmosphere. Half covering for my daydreaming about the TV People. Several people laugh. After that one utterance, however, I only pretend to review the materials; I'm thinking about the TV People. If they talk up a name for the new microwave oven, I certainly am not aware of it. My mind is all TV People. What the hell was the meaning of that TV set? And why haul the TV all the way to my apartment in the first place? Why hasn't the wife remarked on its appearance? Why have the TV People made inroads into my company?

The meetings are endless. At noon, there's a short break for lunch. Too short to go out and eat. Instead, everyone gets sandwiches and coffee. The conference room is a haze of cigarette smoke, so I eat at my own desk. While I'm eating, the section chief comes around. To be perfectly frank, I don't like the guy. For no reason I can put my finger on: There's nothing you can fault him on, no single target for attack. He has an air of breeding. Moreover, he's not stupid. He has good taste in neckties, he doesn't wave his own flag or lord it over his inferiors. He even looks out for me, invites me out for the occasional meal. But there's just something about the guy that doesn't sit well with me. Maybe it's his habit of coming into body contact with people he's talking to. Men or women, at some point in the course of the conversation he'll reach out a hand and touch. Not in any suggestive way, mind you. No, his manner is brisk, his bearing perfectly casual. I wouldn't be surprised if some people don't even notice, it's so natural. Still—I don't know why—it does bother me. So whenever I see him, almost instinctively I brace myself. Call it petty, it gets to me.

He leans over, placing a hand on my shoulder. "About your statement at the meeting just now. Very nice," says the section chief warmly. "Very simply put, very pivotal. I was impressed. Points well taken. The whole room buzzed at that statement of yours. The timing was perfect, too. Yessir, you keep 'em coming like that."

4. An opponent of modern technology.

And he glides off. Probably to lunch. I thank him straight out, but the honest truth is I'm taken aback. I mean, I don't remember a thing of what I said at the meeting. Why does the section chief have to come all the way over to my desk to praise me for *that?* There have to be more brilliant examples of *Homo loquens*[5] around here. Strange. I go on eating my lunch, uncomprehending. Then I think about the wife. Wonder what she's up to right now. Out to lunch? Maybe I ought to give her a call, exchange a few words, anything. I dial the first three digits, have second thoughts, hang up. I have no reason to be calling her. My world may be crumbling, out of balance, but is that a reason to ring up her office? What can I say about all this, anyway? Besides, I hate calling her at work. I set down the receiver, let out a sigh, and finish off my coffee. Then I toss the Styrofoam cup into the wastebasket.

At one of the afternoon meetings, I see TV People again. This time, their number has increased by two. Just as on the previous day, they come traipsing across the conference room, carrying a Sony color TV. A model one size bigger. Uh-oh. Sony's the rival camp. If, for whatever reason, any competitor's product gets brought into our offices, there's hell to pay, barring when other manufacturers' products are brought in for test comparisons, of course. But then we take pains to remove the company logo—just to make sure no outside eyes happen upon it. Little do the TV People care: The Sony mark is emblazoned for all to see. They open the door and march right into the conference room, flashing it in our direction. Then they parade the thing around the room, scanning the place for somewhere to set it down, until at last, not finding any location, they carry it backward out the door. The others in the room show no reaction to the TV People. And they can't have missed them. No, they've definitely seen them. And the proof is they even got out of the way, clearing a path for the TV People to carry their television through. Still, that's as far as it went: a reaction no more alarmed than when the nearby coffee shop delivered. They'd made it a ground rule not to acknowledge the presence of the TV People. The others all knew they were there; they just acted as if they weren't.

None of it makes any sense. Does everybody know about the TV People? Am I alone in the dark? Maybe the wife knew about the TV People all along, too. Probably. I'll bet that's why she wasn't surprised by the television and why she didn't mention it. That's the only possible explanation. Yet this confuses me even more. Who or what, then, are the TV People? And why are they always carrying around TV sets?

One colleague leaves his seat to go to the toilet, and I get up to follow. This is a guy who entered the company around the same time I did. We're on good terms. Sometimes we go out for a drink together after work. I don't do that with most people. I'm standing next to him at the urinals. He's the first to complain. "Oh, joy! Looks like we're in for more of the same, straight through to evening. I swear! Meetings, meetings, meetings, going to drag on forever."

"You can say that again," I say. We wash our hands. He compliments me on the morning meeting's statement. I thank him.

"Oh, by the way, those guys who came in with the TV just now..." I launch forth, then cut off.

He doesn't say anything. He turns off the faucet, pulls two paper towels from the dispenser, and wipes his hands. He doesn't even shoot a glance in my direction. How long can he keep drying his hands? Eventually, he crumples up his towels and throws them away. Maybe he didn't hear me. Or maybe he's pretending not to hear. I can't

5. The speaking human (Latin).

tell. But from the sudden strain in the atmosphere, I know enough not to ask. I shut up, wipe my hands, and walk down the corridor to the conference room. The rest of the afternoon's meetings, he avoids my eyes.

When I get home from work, the apartment is dark. Outside, dark clouds have swept in. It's beginning to rain. The apartment smells like rain. Night is coming on. No sign of the wife. I loosen my tie, smooth out the wrinkles, and hang it up. I brush off my suit. I toss my shirt into the washing machine. My hair smells like cigarette smoke, so I take a shower and shave. Story of my life: I go to endless meetings, get smoked to death, then the wife gets on my case about it. The very first thing she did after we were married was make me stop smoking. Four years ago, that was.

Out of the shower, I sit on the sofa with a beer, drying my hair with a towel. The TV People's television is still sitting on the sideboard. I pick up the remote control from the table and push the "on" switch. Again and again I press, but nothing happens. The screen stays dark. I check the plug; it's in the socket, all right. I unplug it, then plug it back in. Still no go. No matter how often I press the "on" switch, the screen does not glow. Just to be sure, I pry open the back cover of the remote-control unit, remove the batteries, and check them with my handy electrical-contact tester. The batteries are fine. At this point, I give up, throw the remote control aside, and slosh down more beer.

Why should it upset me? Supposing the TV did come on, what then? It would glow and crackle with white noise. Who cares, if that's all that'd come on?

I care. Last night it worked. And I haven't laid a finger on it since. Doesn't make sense.

I try the remote control one more time. I press slowly with my finger. But the result is the same. No response whatsoever. The screen is dead. Cold.

Dead cold.

I pull another beer out of the fridge and eat some potato salad from a plastic tub. It's past six o'clock. I read the whole evening paper. If anything, it's more boring than usual. Almost no article worth reading, nothing but inconsequential news items. But I keep reading, for lack of anything better to do. Until I finish the paper. What next? To avoid pursuing that thought any further, I dally over the newspaper. Hmm, how about answering letters? A cousin of mine has sent us a wedding invitation, which I have to turn down. The day of the wedding, the wife and I are going to be off on a trip. To Okinawa.[6] We've been planning it for ages; we're both taking time off from work. We can't very well go changing our plans now. God only knows when we'll get the next chance to spend a long holiday together. And to clinch it all, I'm not even that close to my cousin; haven't seen her in almost ten years. Still, I can't leave replying to the last minute. She has to know how many people are coming, how many settings to plan for the banquet. Oh, forget it. I can't bring myself to write, not now. My heart isn't in it.

I pick up the newspaper again and read the same articles over again. Maybe I ought to start preparing dinner. But the wife might be working late and could come home having eaten. Which would mean wasting one portion. And if I am going to eat alone, I can make do with leftovers; no reason to make something up special. If she hasn't eaten, we can go out and eat together.

Odd, though. Whenever either of us knows he or she is going to be later than six, we always call in. That's the rule. Leave a message on the answering machine if

---

6. One of the islands that make up the nation of Japan.

necessary. That way, the other can coordinate: go ahead and eat alone, or set something out for the late arriver, or hit the sack. The nature of my work sometimes keeps me out late, and she often has meetings, or proofs to dispatch, before coming home. Neither of us has a regular nine-to-five job. When both of us are busy, we can go three days without a word to each other. Those are the breaks—just one of those things that nobody planned. Hence we always keep certain rules, so as not to place unrealistic burdens on each other. If it looks as though we're going to be late, we call in and let the other one know. I sometimes forget, but she, never once.

Still, there's no message on the answering machine.

I toss the newspaper, stretch out on the sofa, and shut my eyes.

I dream about a meeting. I'm standing up, delivering a statement I myself don't understand. I open my mouth and talk. If I don't, I'm a dead man. I have to keep talking. Have to keep coming out with endless blah-blah-blah. Everyone around me is dead. Dead and turned to stone. A roomful of stone statues. A wind is blowing. The windows are all broken; gusts of air are coming in. And the TV People are here. Three of them. Like the first time. They're carrying a Sony color TV. And on the screen are the TV People. I'm running out of words; little by little I can feel my fingertips growing stiffer. Gradually turning to stone.

I open my eyes to find the room aglow. The color of corridors at the Aquarium. The television is on. Outside, everything is dark. The TV screen is flickering in the gloom, static crackling. I sit up on the sofa, and press my temples with my fingertips. The flesh of my fingers is still soft; my mouth tastes like beer. I swallow. I'm dried out; the saliva catches in my throat. As always, the waking world pales after an all-too-real dream. But no, this is real. Nobody's turned to stone. What time is it getting to be? I look for the clock on the floor. *TRPP Q SCHAOUS TRPP Q SCHAOUS.* A little before eight.

Yet, just as in the dream, one of the TV People is on the television screen. The same guy I passed on the stairs to the office. No mistake. The one who first opened the door to the apartment. I'm 100% sure. He stands there—against a bright, fluorescent white background, the tail end of a dream infiltrating my conscious reality—staring at me. I shut, then reopen my eyes, hoping he'll have slipped back to never-never land. But he doesn't disappear. Far from it. He gets bigger. His face fills the whole screen, getting closer and closer.

The next thing I know, he's stepping through the screen. Hands gripping the frame, lifting himself up and over, one foot after the other, like climbing out of a window, leaving a white TV screen glowing behind him.

He rubs his left hand in the palm of his right, slowly acclimating himself to the world outside the television. On and on, reduced right-hand fingers rubbing reduced left-hand fingers, no hurry. He has that all-the-time-in-the-world nonchalance. Like a veteran TV-show host. Then he looks me in the face.

"We're making an airplane," says my TV People visitant. His voice has no perspective to it. A curious, paper-thin voice.

He speaks, and the screen is all machinery. Very professional fade-in. Just like on the news. First, there's an opening shot of a large factory interior, then it cuts to a close-up of the work space, camera center. Two TV People are hard at work on some machine, tightening bolts with wrenches, adjusting gauges. The picture of concentration. The machine, however, is unlike anything I've ever seen: an upright cylinder except that it narrows toward the top, with streamlined protrusions along its surface. Looks more like some kind of gigantic orange juicer than an airplane. No wings, no seats.

"Doesn't look like an airplane," I say. Doesn't sound like my voice, either. Strangely brittle, as if the nutrients had been strained out through a thick filter. Have I grown so old all of a sudden?

"That's probably because we haven't painted it yet," he says. "Tomorrow we'll have it the right color. Then you'll see it's an airplane."

"The color's not the problem. It's the shape. That's not an airplane."

"Well, if it's not an airplane, what is it?" he asks me. If he doesn't know, and I don't know, then what *is* it? "So, that's why it's got to be the color." The TV People rep puts it to me gently. "Paint it the right color, and it'll be an airplane."

I don't feel like arguing. What difference does it make? Orange juicer or airplane—flying orange juicer?—what do I care? Still, where's the wife while all this is happening? Why doesn't she come home? I massage my temples again. The clock ticks on. *TRPP Q SCHAOUS TRPP Q SCHAOUS.* The remote control lies on the table, and next to it the stack of women's magazines. The telephone is silent, the room illuminated by the dim glow of the television.

The two TV People on the screen keep working away. The image is much clearer than before. You can read the numbers on the dials, hear the faint rumble of machinery. *TAABZHRAYBGG TAABZHRAYBGG ARP ARRP TAABZHRAYBGG.* This bass line is punctuated periodically by a sharp, metallic grating. *AREEEENBT AREEEENBT.* And various other noises are interspersed through the remaining aural space; I can't hear anything clearly over them. Still, the two TV People labor on for all they're worth. That, apparently, is the subject of this program. I go on watching the two of them as they work on and on. Their colleague outside the TV set also looks on in silence. At them. At that *thing*—for the life of me, it does not look like an airplane—that insane machine all black and grimy, floating in a field of white light.

The TV People rep speaks up. "Shame about your wife."

I look him in the face. Maybe I didn't hear him right. Staring at him is like peering into the glowing tube itself.

"Shame about your wife," the TV People rep repeats in exactly the same absent tone.

"How's that?" I ask.

"How's that? It's gone too far," says the TV People rep in a voice like a plastic-card hotel key. Flat, uninflected, it slices into me as if it were sliding through a thin slit. "It's gone too far: She's out there."

"It's gone too far: She's out there," I repeat in my head. Very plain, and without reality. I can't grasp the context. Cause has effect by the tail and is about to swallow it whole. I get up and go to the kitchen. I open the refrigerator, take a deep breath, reach for a can of beer, and go back to the sofa. The TV People rep stands in place in front of the television, right elbow resting on the set, and watches me extract the pull-tab. I don't really want to drink beer at this moment; I just need to do something. I drink one sip, but the beer doesn't taste good. I hold the can in my hand dumbly until it becomes so heavy I have to set it down on the table.

Then I think about the TV People rep's revelation, about the wife's failure to materialize. He's saying she's gone. That she isn't coming home. I can't bring myself to believe it's over. Sure, we're not the perfect couple. In four years, we've had our spats; we have our little problems. But we always talk them out. There are things we've resolved and things we haven't. Most of what we couldn't resolve we let ride. Okay, so we have our ups and downs as a couple. I admit it. But is this cause for despair? C'mon, show me a couple who don't have problems. Besides, it's only a little past eight. There must be some reason she can't get to a phone. Any number of possible reasons. For instance . . . I can't think of a single one. I'm hopelessly confused.

I fall back deep into the sofa.

How on earth is that airplane—if it is an airplane—supposed to fly? What propels it? Where are the windows? Which is the front, which is the back?

I'm dead tired. Exhausted. I still have to write that letter, though, to beg off from my cousin's invitation. My work schedule does not afford me the pleasure of attending. Regrettable. Congratulations, all the same.

The two TV People in the television continue building their airplane, oblivious of me. They toil away; they don't stop for anything. They have an infinite amount of work to get through before the machine is complete. No sooner have they finished one operation than they're busy with another. They have no assembly instructions, no plans, but they know precisely what to do and what comes next. The camera ably follows their deft motions. Clear-cut, easy-to-follow camera work. Highly credible, convincing images. No doubt other TV People (Nos. 4 and 5?) are manning the camera and control panel.

Strange as it may sound, the more I watch the flawless form of the TV People as they go about their work, the more the thing starts to look like an airplane. At least, it'd no longer surprise me if it actually flew. What does it matter which is front or back? With all the exacting detail work they're putting in, it *has* to be an airplane. Even if it doesn't appear so—to them, it's an airplane. Just as the little guy said, "If it's not an airplane, then what is it?"

The TV People rep hasn't so much as twitched in all this time. Right elbow still propped up on the TV set, he's watching me. I'm being watched. The TV People factory crew keeps working. Busy, busy, busy. The clock ticks on. *TRPP Q SCHAOUS TRPP Q SCHAOUS*. The room has grown dark, stifling. Someone's footsteps echo down the hall.

Well, it suddenly occurs to me, maybe so. Maybe the wife *is* out there. She's gone somewhere far away. By whatever means of transport, she's gone somewhere far out of my reach. Maybe our relationship has suffered irreversible damage. Maybe it's a total loss. Only I haven't noticed. All sorts of thoughts unravel inside me, then the frayed ends come together again. "Maybe so," I say out loud. My voice echoes, hollow.

"Tomorrow, when we paint it, you'll see better," he resumes. "All it needs is a touch of color to make it an airplane."

I look at the palms of my hands. They have shrunk slightly. Ever so slightly. Power of suggestion? Maybe the light's playing tricks on me. Maybe my sense of perspective has been thrown off. Yet, my palms really do look shriveled. Hey now, wait just a minute! Let me speak. There's something I should say. I must say. I'll dry up and turn to stone if I don't. Like the others.

"The phone will ring soon," the TV People rep says. Then, after a measured pause, he adds, "In another five minutes."

I look at the telephone; I think about the telephone cord. Endless lengths of phone cable linking one telephone to another. Maybe somewhere, at some terminal of that awesome megacircuit, is my wife. Far, far away, out of my reach. I can feel her pulse. Another five minutes, I tell myself. *Which way is front, which way is back?* I stand up and try to say something, but no sooner have I got to my feet than the words slip away.

One of the most worldly of American writers, Gish Jen has devoted her fiction to exploring the question of national identity in a transnational world. As she has remarked, "As soon as you ask yourself the question, 'What does it mean to be Irish-American, Iranian-American, Greek-American,' you are American." Gish Jen was born in Queens, New York, the daughter of Chinese immigrants; as her family's fortunes improved, they moved first to the working-class suburb of Yonkers and then to the wealthy suburb of Scarsdale. Themes of immigration, identity, and the quest for upward mobility are already prominent in her first novel, *Typical American* (1991), which tells of the shifting fortunes of Ralph Chang. After he emigrates from China to New England, Chang and his family try to find themselves as "Chang-kees," gradually discovering the limits of material success but also the new American freedom of fashioning one's own identity. In Jen's second novel, *Mona in the Promised Land* (1996), the Changs move to a Scarsdale-like suburb, where Ralph's daughter Mona experiments with American freedoms by deciding to become Jewish.

Jen has further expanded and complicated her accounts of American life in a globalizing world in her later novels, *The Love Wife* (2004) and then in *World and Town*. This 2009 novel features a retired school teacher, Hattie Kong, comfortably settled in a small New Hampshire town but grieving for the loss of her husband and best friend; her world begins to change when a local church takes in a troubled family of Cambodian refugees. Far from "model minorities," the new Cambodian arrivals are haunted by traumatic memories of their time during the genocidal regime of Pol Pot, and they become entangled with alcohol and gang violence. Hattie imagines her husband telling her, "It's the world come to town. As it will, you know, as it will."

Even as they explore deep themes, Gish Jen's works sparkle with dry wit, often conveyed in multiple voices by different narrators; *The Love Wife* actually employs three typefaces to convey different narrative styles. Jen's keen ear for American dialects, and her sensitivity for nuances of what is said and left unsaid, are beautifully shown in the voice of the Chinese grandmother who narrates the title story of Jen's 1999 story collection *Who's Irish?* Comic in tone but with a melancholy undercurrent, "Who's Irish?" probes the tensions between old and new identities, earlier and later migrations, husbands and wives, parents and children.

Who's Irish?

In China, people say mixed children are supposed to be smart, and definitely my granddaughter Sophie is smart. But Sophie is wild, Sophie is not like my daughter Natalie, or like me. I am work hard my whole life, and fierce besides. My husband always used to say he is afraid of me, and in our restaurant, bus-boys and cooks all afraid of me too. Even the gang members come for protection money, they try to talk to my husband. When I am there, they stay away. If they come by mistake, they pretend they are come to eat. They hide behind the menu, they order a lot of food. They talk about their mothers. Oh, my mother have some arthritis, need to take herbal medicine, they say. Oh, my mother getting old, her hair all white now.

I say, Your mother's hair used to be white, but since she dye it, it become black again. Why don't you go home once in a while and take a look? I tell them, Confucius[1] say a filial son knows what color his mother's hair is.

---

1. The foundational Chinese philosopher and social thinker Confucius (551–479 BCE) is best known for the sayings recorded in his *Analects*.

My daughter is fierce too, she is vice president in the bank now. Her new house is big enough for everybody to have their own room, including me. But Sophie take after Natalie's husband's family, their name is Shea. Irish. I always thought Irish people are like Chinese people, work so hard on the railroad, but now I know why the Chinese beat the Irish. Of course, not all Irish are like the Shea family, of course not. My daughter tell me I should not say Irish this, Irish that.

How do you like it when people say the Chinese this, the Chinese that, she say.

You know, the British call the Irish heathen, just like they call the Chinese, she say.

You think the Opium War[2] was bad, how would you like to live right next door to the British, she say.

And that is that. My daughter have a funny habit when she win an argument, she take a sip of something and look away, so the other person is not embarrassed. So I am not embarrassed. I do not call anybody anything either. I just happen to mention about the Shea family, an interesting fact: four brothers in the family, and not one of them work. The mother, Bess, have a job before she got sick, she was executive secretary in a big company. She is handle everything for a big shot, you would be surprised how complicated her job is, not just type this, type that. Now she is a nice woman with a clean house. But her boys, every one of them is on welfare, or so-called severance pay, or so-called disability pay. Something. They say they cannot find work, this is not the economy of the fifties, but I say, Even the black people doing better these days, some of them live so fancy, you'd be surprised. Why the Shea family have so much trouble? They are white people, they speak English. When I come to this country, I have no money and do not speak English. But my husband and I own our restaurant before he die. Free and clear, no mortgage. Of course, I understand I am just lucky, come from a country where the food is popular all over the world. I understand it is not the Shea family's fault they come from a country where everything is boiled. Still, I say.

She's right, we should broaden our horizons, say one brother, Jim, at Thanksgiving. Forget about the car business. Think about egg rolls.

Pad thai, say another brother, Mike. I'm going to make my fortune in pad thai. It's going to be the new pizza.

I say, You people too picky about what you sell. Selling egg rolls not good enough for you, but at least my husband and I can say, We made it. What can you say? Tell me. What can you say?

Everybody chew their tough turkey.

I especially cannot understand my daughter's husband John, who has no job but cannot take care of Sophie either. Because he is a man, he say, and that's the end of the sentence.

Plain boiled food, plain boiled thinking. Even his name is plain boiled: John. Maybe because I grew up with black bean sauce and hoisin sauce and garlic sauce, I always feel something is missing when my son-in-law talk.

But, okay: so my son-in-law can be man, I am baby-sitter. Six hours a day, same as the old sitter, crazy Amy, who quit. This is not so easy, now that I am sixty-eight, Chinese age almost seventy. Still, I try. In China, daughter take care of mother. Here it is the other way around. Mother help daughter, mother ask, Anything else I can do? Otherwise daughter complain mother is not supportive. I tell daughter, We do not have this word in Chinese, *supportive*. But my daughter too busy to listen, she has to

---

2. Opium War: conflicts, 1839–1842 and 1856–1860, between China and Great Britain, involving the opium trade.

go to meeting, she has to write memo while her husband go to the gym to be a man. My daughter say otherwise he will be depressed. Seems like all his life he has this trouble, depression.

No one wants to hire someone who is depressed, she say. It is important for him to keep his spirits up.

Beautiful wife, beautiful daughter, beautiful house, oven can clean itself automatically. No money left over, because only one income, but lucky enough, got the baby-sitter for free. If John lived in China, he would be very happy. But he is not happy. Even at the gym things go wrong. One day, he pull a muscle. Another day, weight room too crowded. Always something.

Until finally, hooray, he has a job. Then he feel pressure.

I need to concentrate, he say. I need to focus.

He is going to work for insurance company. Salesman job. A paycheck, he say, and at least he will wear clothes instead of gym shorts. My daughter buy him some special candy bars from the health-food store. They say THINK! on them, and are supposed to help John think.

John is a good-looking boy, you have to say that, especially now that he shave so you can see his face.

I am an old man in a young man's game, say John.

I will need a new suit, say John.

This time I am not going to shoot myself in the foot, say John.

Good, I say.

She means to be supportive, my daughter say. Don't start the send her back to China thing, because we can't.

Sophie is three years old American age, but already I see her nice Chinese side swallowed up by her wild Shea side. She looks like mostly Chinese. Beautiful black hair, beautiful black eyes. Nose perfect size, not so flat looks like something fell down, not so large looks like some big deal got stuck in wrong face. Everything just right, only her skin is a brown surprise to John's family. So brown, they say. Even John say it. She never goes in the sun, still she is that color, he say. Brown. They say, Nothing the matter with brown. They are just surprised. So brown. Nattie is not that brown, they say. They say, It seems like Sophie should be a color in between Nattie and John. Seems funny, a girl named Sophie Shea be brown. But she is brown, maybe her name should be Sophie Brown. She never go in the sun, still she is that color, they say. Nothing the matter with brown. They are just surprised.

The Shea family talk is like this sometimes, going around and around like a Christmas-tree train.

Maybe John is not her father, I say one day, to stop the train. And sure enough, train wreck. None of the brothers ever say the word *brown* to me again.

Instead, John's mother, Bess, say, I hope you are not offended.

She say, I did my best on those boys. But raising four boys with no father is no picnic.

You have a beautiful family, I say.

I'm getting old, she say.

You deserve a rest, I say. Too many boys make you old.

I never had a daughter, she say. You have a daughter.

I have a daughter, I say. Chinese people don't think a daughter is so great, but you're right. I have a daughter.

I was never against the marriage, you know, she say. I never thought John was marrying down. I always thought Nattie was just as good as white.

I was never against the marriage either, I say. I just wonder if they look at the whole problem.

Of course you pointed out the problem, you are a mother, she say. And now we both have a granddaughter. A little brown granddaughter, she is so precious to me.

I laugh. A little brown granddaughter, I say. To tell you the truth, I don't know how she came out so brown.

We laugh some more. These days Bess need a walker to walk. She take so many pills, she need two glasses of water to get them all down. Her favorite TV show is about bloopers, and she love her bird feeder. All day long, she can watch that bird feeder, like a cat.

I can't wait for her to grow up, Bess say. I could use some female company.

Too many boys, I say.

Boys are fine, she say. But they do surround you after a while.

You should take a break, come live with us, I say. Lots of girls at our house.

Be careful what you offer, say Bess with a wink. Where I come from, people mean for you to move in when they say a thing like that.

Nothing the matter with Sophie's outside, that's the truth. It is inside that she is like not any Chinese girl I ever see. We go to the park, and this is what she does. She stand up in the stroller. She take off all her clothes and throw them in the fountain.

Sophie! I say. Stop!

But she just laugh like a crazy person. Before I take over as baby-sitter, Sophie has that crazy-person sitter, Amy the guitar player. My daughter thought this Amy very creative—another word we do not talk about in China. In China, we talk about whether we have difficulty or no difficulty. We talk about whether life is bitter or not bitter. In America, all day long, people talk about creative. Never mind that I cannot even look at this Amy, with her shirt so short that her belly button showing. This Amy think Sophie should love her body. So when Sophie take off her diaper, Amy laugh. When Sophie run around naked, Amy say she wouldn't want to wear a diaper either. When Sophie go *shu-shu* in her lap, Amy laugh and say there are no germs in pee. When Sophie take off her shoes, Amy say bare feet is best, even the pediatrician say so. That is why Sophie now walk around with no shoes like a beggar child. Also why Sophie love to take off her clothes.

Turn around! say the boys in the park. Let's see that ass!

Of course, Sophie does not understand. Sophie clap her hands, I am the only one to say, No! This is not a game.

It has nothing to do with John's family, my daughter say. Amy was too permissive, that's all.

But I think if Sophie was not wild inside, she would not take off her shoes and clothes to begin with.

You never take off your clothes when you were little, I say. All my Chinese friends had babies, I never saw one of them act wild like that.

Look, my daughter say. I have a big presentation tomorrow.

John and my daughter agree Sophie is a problem, but they don't know what to do.

You spank her, she'll stop, I say another day.

But they say, Oh no.

In America, parents not supposed to spank the child.

It gives them low self-esteem, my daughter say. And that leads to problems later, as I happen to know.

My daughter never have big presentation the next day when the subject of spanking come up.

I don't want you to touch Sophie, she say. No spanking, period.

Don't tell me what to do, I say.

I'm not telling you what to do, say my daughter. I'm telling you how I feel.

I am not your servant, I say. Don't you dare talk to me like that.

My daughter have another funny habit when she lose an argument. She spread out all her fingers and look at them, as if she like to make sure they are still there.

My daughter is fierce like me, but she and John think it is better to explain to Sophie that clothes are a good idea. This is not so hard in the cold weather. In the warm weather, it is very hard.

Use your words, my daughter say. That's what we tell Sophie. How about if you set a good example.

As if good example mean anything to Sophie. I am so fierce, the gang members who used to come to the restaurant all afraid of me, but Sophie is not afraid.

I say, Sophie, if you take off your clothes, no snack.

I say, Sophie, if you take off your clothes, no lunch.

I say, Sophie, if you take off your clothes, no park.

Pretty soon we are stay home all day, and by the end of six hours she still did not have one thing to eat. You never saw a child stubborn like that.

I'm hungry! she cry when my daughter come home.

What's the matter, doesn't your grandmother feed you? My daughter laugh.

No! Sophie say. She doesn't feed me anything!

My daughter laugh again. Here you go, she say.

She say to John, Sophie must be growing.

Growing like a weed, I say.

Still Sophie take off her clothes, until one day I spank her. Not too hard, but she cry and cry, and when I tell her if she doesn't put her clothes back on I'll spank her again, she put her clothes back on. Then I tell her she is good girl, and give her some food to eat. The next day we go to the park and, like a nice Chinese girl, she does not take off her clothes.

She stop taking off her clothes, I report. Finally!

How did you do it? my daughter ask.

After twenty-eight years experience with you, I guess I learn something, I say.

It must have been a phase, John say, and his voice is suddenly like an expert.

His voice is like an expert about everything these days, now that he carry a leather briefcase, and wear shiny shoes, and can go shopping for a new car. On the company, he say. The company will pay for it, but he will be able to drive it whenever he want.

A free car, he say. How do you like that.

It's good to see you in the saddle again, my daughter say. Some of your family patterns are scary.

At least I don't drink, he say. He say, And I'm not the only one with scary family patterns.

That's for sure, say my daughter.

Everyone is happy. Even I am happy, because there is more trouble with Sophie, but now I think I can help her Chinese side fight against her wild side. I teach her to eat food with fork or spoon or chopsticks, she cannot just grab into the middle of a bowl of noodles. I teach her not to play with garbage cans. Sometimes I spank her, but not too often, and not too hard.

Still, there are problems. Sophie like to climb everything. If there is a railing, she is never next to it. Always she is on top of it. Also, Sophie like to hit the mommies of her friends. She learn this from her playground best friend, Sinbad, who is four. Sinbad wear army clothes every day and like to ambush his mommy. He is the one who dug a big hole under the play structure, a foxhole he call it, all by himself. Very hardworking. Now he wait in the foxhole with a shovel full of wet sand. When his mommy come, he throw it right at her.

Oh, it's all right, his mommy say. You can't get rid of war games, it's part of their imaginative play. All the boys go through it.

Also, he like to kick his mommy, and one day he tell Sophie to kick his mommy too.

I wish this story is not true.

Kick her, kick her! Sinbad say.

Sophie kick her. A little kick, as if she just so happened was swinging her little leg and didn't realize that big mommy leg was in the way. Still I spank Sophie and make Sophie say sorry, and what does the mommy say?

Really, it's all right, she say. It didn't hurt.

After that, Sophie learn she can attack mommies in the playground, and some will say, Stop, but others will say, Oh, she didn't mean it, especially if they realize Sophie will be punished.

This is how, one day, bigger trouble come. The bigger trouble start when Sophie hide in the foxhole with that shovel full of sand. She wait, and when I come look for her, she throw it at me. All over my nice clean clothes.

Did you ever see a Chinese girl act this way?

Sophie! I say. Come out of there, say you're sorry.

But she does not come out. Instead, she laugh. Naaah, naah-na, naaa-naaa, she say.

I am not exaggerate: millions of children in China, not one act like this.

Sophie! I say. Now! Come out now!

But she know she is in big trouble. She know if she come out, what will happen next. So she does not come out. I am sixty-eight, Chinese age almost seventy, how can I crawl under there to catch her? Impossible. So I yell, yell, yell, and what happen? Nothing. A Chinese mother would help, but American mothers, they look at you, they shake their head, they go home. And, of course, a Chinese child would give up, but not Sophie.

I hate you! she yell. I hate you, Meanie!

Meanie is my new name these days.

Long time this goes on, long long time. The foxhole is deep, you cannot see too much, you don't know where is the bottom. You cannot hear too much either. If she does not yell, you cannot even know she is still there or not. After a while, getting cold out, getting dark out. No one left in the playground, only us.

Sophie, I say. How did you become stubborn like this? I am go home without you now.

I try to use a stick, chase her out of there, and once or twice I hit her, but still she does not come out. So finally I leave. I go outside the gate.

Bye-bye! I say. I'm go home now.

But still she does not come out and does not come out. Now it is dinnertime, the sky is black. I think I should maybe go get help, but how can I leave a little girl by herself in the playground? A bad man could come. A rat could come. I go back in to see what is happen to Sophie. What if she have a shovel and is making a tunnel to escape?

Sophie! I say.

No answer.

Sophie!

I don't know if she is alive. I don't know if she is fall asleep down there. If she is crying, I cannot hear her.

So I take the stick and poke.

Sophie! I say. I promise I no hit you. If you come out, I give you a lollipop.

No answer. By now I worried. What to do, what to do, what to do? I poke some more, even harder, so that I am poking and poking when my daughter and John suddenly appear.

What are you doing? What is going on? say my daughter.

Put down that stick! say my daughter.

You are crazy! say my daughter.

John wiggle under the structure, into the foxhole, to rescue Sophie.

She fell asleep, say John the expert. She's okay. That is one big hole.

Now Sophie is crying and crying.

Sophie, my daughter say, hugging her. Are you okay, peanut? Are you okay?

She's just scared, say John.

Are you okay? I say too. I don't know what happen, I say.

She's okay, say John. He is not like my daughter, full of questions. He is full of answers until we get home and can see by the lamplight.

Will you look at her? he yell then. What the hell happened?

Bruises all over her brown skin, and a swollen-up eye.

You are crazy! say my daughter. Look at what you did! You are crazy!

I try very hard, I say.

How could you use a stick? I told you to use your words!

She is hard to handle, I say.

She's three years old! You cannot use a stick! say my daughter.

She is not like any Chinese girl I ever saw, I say.

I brush some sand off my clothes. Sophie's clothes are dirty too, but at least she has her clothes on.

Has she done this before? ask my daughter. Has she hit you before?

She hits me all the time, Sophie say, eating ice cream.

Your family, say John.

Believe me, say my daughter.

A daughter I have, a beautiful daughter. I took care of her when she could not hold her head up. I took care of her before she could argue with me, when she was a little girl with two pigtails, one of them always crooked. I took care of her when we have to escape from China, I took care of her when suddenly we live in a country with cars everywhere, if you are not careful your little girl get run over. When my husband die, I promise him I will keep the family together, even though it was just two of us, hardly a family at all.

But now my daughter take me around to look at apartments. After all, I can cook, I can clean, there's no reason I cannot live by myself, all I need is a telephone. Of course, she is sorry. Sometimes she cry, I am the one to say everything will be okay. She say she have no choice, she doesn't want to end up divorced. I say divorce is terrible, I don't know who invented this terrible idea. Instead of live with a telephone, though, surprise, I come to live with Bess. Imagine that. Bess make an offer and, sure enough, where she come from, people mean for you to move in when they say things like that. A crazy idea, go to live with someone else's family, but she like to have some female company, not like my daughter, who does not believe in company. These days when my daughter visit, she does not bring Sophie. Bess say we should give Nattie time, we will see Sophie again soon. But seems like my daughter have more presentation than ever before, every time she come she have to leave.

I have a family to support, she say, and her voice is heavy, as if soaking wet. I have a young daughter and a depressed husband and no one to turn to.

When she say no one to turn to, she mean me.

These days my beautiful daughter is so tired she can just sit there in a chair and fall asleep. John lost his job again, already, but still they rather hire a baby-sitter than ask me to help, even they can't afford it. Of course, the new baby-sitter is much younger, can run around. I don't know if Sophie these days is wild or not wild. She call me Meanie, but she like to kiss me too, sometimes. I remember that every time I see a child on TV. Sophie like to grab my hair, a fistful in each hand, and then kiss me smack on the nose. I never see any other child kiss that way.

The satellite TV has so many channels, more channels than I can count, including a Chinese channel from the Mainland and a Chinese channel from Taiwan, but most of the time I watch bloopers with Bess. Also, I watch the bird feeder—so many, many kinds of birds come. The Shea sons hang around all the time, asking when will I go home, but Bess tell them, Get lost.

She's a permanent resident, say Bess. She isn't going anywhere.

Then she wink at me, and switch the channel with the remote control.

Of course, I shouldn't say Irish this, Irish that, especially now I am become honorary Irish myself, according to Bess. Me! Who's Irish? I say, and she laugh. All the same, if I could mention one thing about some of the Irish, not all of them of course, I like to mention this: Their talk just stick. I don't know how Bess Shea learn to use her words, but sometimes I hear what she say a long time later. *Permanent resident. Not going anywhere.* Over and over I hear it, the voice of Bess.

GISH JEN

1020

The Seventeenth and Eighteenth Centuries

General Background • Linda Colley, *Britons: Forging the Nation, 1707–1837*, 1992. • Christine Guth, *Art of Edo Japan: The Artist and the City, 1615–1868*, 1996. • John Whitney Hall, ed. *The Cambridge History of Japan*. Vol. 4, *Early Modern Japan*, 1988. • Julie C. Hayes, *Reading the French Enlightenment: System and Subversion*, 1999. • Donald Keene, *World Within Walls: Japanese Literature of the Pre-Modern Era, 1600–1868*, 1976. • Chie Nakane and Shinzaburō Ōishi, eds. *Tokugawa Japan: The Social and Economic Antecedents of Modern Japan*, 1991. • Matsunosuke Nishiyama, *Edo Culture: Daily Life and Diversions in Urban Japan, 1600–1868*, 1997. • Felicity Nussbaum and Laura Brown, eds., *The New Eighteenth Century*, 1987. • James Sambrook, *The Eighteenth Century: The Intellectual and Cultural Context of English Literature, 1700–1789*, 1986. • Conrad Totman, *Early Modern Japan*, 1993. • Steven N. Zwicker, *The Cambridge Companion to English Literature, 1650–1740*, 1998.

The Age of the Enlightenment • John Bender, *Imagining the Penitentiary: Fiction and the Architecture of Mind in Eighteenth-Century England*, 1987. • Linda Colley, *Britons: Forging the Nation, 1707–1837*, 1992. • Robert Darnton, *George Washington's False Teeth: An Unconventional Guide to the Eighteenth Century*, 2003. • Joan DeJean, *Ancients Against Moderns: Culture Wars and the Making of a Fin de Siècle*, 1997. • Catherine Gallagher, *Nobody's Story: The Vanishing Acts of Women Writers in the Marketplace, 1670–1820*, 1994. • Julie C. Hayes, *Reading the French Enlightenment: System and Subversion*, 1999. • David Marshall, *The Surprising Effects of Sympathy: Marivaux, Diderot, Rousseau, and Mary Shelley*, 1988. • Michael McKeon, *The Origins of the English Novel, 1600–1740*, 1987. • Nancy K. Miller, *The Heroine's Text: Readings in the French and English Novel, 1722–1782*, 1980. • Dorothea E. von Mücke, *Virtue and the Veil of Illusion: Generic Innovation and the Pedagogical Project in Eighteenth-Century Literature*, 1991. • Felicity Nussbaum and Laura Brown, eds. *The New Eighteenth Century*, 1987. • William Ray, *Story and History: Narrative Authority and Social Identity in the Eighteenth-Century French and English Novel*, 1990. • James Sambrook, *The Eighteenth Century: The Intellectual and Cultural Context of English Literature, 1700–1789*, 1986. • Londa Schiebinger, *Nature's Body: Gender in the Making of Modern Science*, 1993. • Stuart Sherman, *Telling Time: Clocks, Diaries, and English Diurnal Form, 1660–1785*, 1996. • Julia Simon, *Mass Enlightenment: Critical Studies in Rousseau and Diderot*, 1995. • Aram Vartanian, *Science and Humanism in the French Enlightenment*, 1999. • Anne C. Vila, *Enlightenment and Pathology: Sensibility in the Literature and Medicine of Eighteenth-Century France*, 1998. • Ian Watt, *The Rise of the Novel: Studies in Defoe, Richardson, and Fielding*, 1957. • Steven N. Zwicker, *The Cambridge Companion to English Literature, 1650–1740*, 1998.

CaoXueqin • Cao Xueqin, *The Story of the Stone: A Chinese Novel in Five Volumes*, trans. David Hawkes, 1973–1986. • Louise P. Edwards, *Men and Women in Qing China: Gender in the Red Chamber Dream*, 1994. • Martin Huang, *Desire and Fictional Narrative in Late Imperial China*, 2001. • Martin Huang, *Literati and Self-Re/Presentation: Autobiographical Sensibility in the Eighteenth-Century Chinese Novel*, 1995. • Jeanne Knoerle, *The Dream of the Red Chamber: A Critical Study*, 1972. • Dore Jesse Levy, *Ideal and Actual in the Story of the Stone*, 1999. • Florence and Isabel McHugh, trans. *The Dream of the Red Chamber*, 1958. • Lucien Miller, *Masks of Fiction in Dream of the Red Chamber: Myth, Mimesis and Persona*, 1975. • Andrew H. Plaks, *Archetype and Allegory in the Dream of the Red Chamber*, 1976 • C. C. Wang, trans. *Dream of the Red Chamber*, 1958. • Jing Wang, *The Story of Stone: Intertextuality, Ancient Chinese Stone Lore, and the Stone Symbolism in Dream of the Red Chamber, Water Margin, and The Journey to the West*, 1992. • Chi Xiao, *The Chinese Garden as Lyric Enclave: A Generic Study of "The Story of the Stone,"* 2001. • Xianyi and Gladys Yang, trans. *A Dream of Red Mansions*, 1999. • Anthony C. Yu. *Rereading the Stone: Desire and the Making of Fiction in "Dream of the Red Chamber,"* 2001.

Chikamatsu Mon'zaemon • Barbara Curtis Adachi, *Backstage at Bunraku: A Behind the Scenes Look at Japan's Traditional Puppet Theater*, 1985. • Barbara Curtis Adachi, *The Voices and Hands of Bunraku*, 1978. • C. U. Dunn, *The Early Japanese Puppet Drama*, 1966. • C. Andrew Gerstle, trans. *Chikamatsu: Five Late Plays*, 2001. • C. Andrew Gerstle, *Circles of Fantasy: Convention in the Plays of Chikamatsu*, 1986. • C. Andrew Gerstle, "Hero as Murderer in Chikamatsu," *Monumenta Nipponica*, vol. 51, 1996, 317–356. • C. Andrew Gerstle, "Heroic Honor: Chikamatsu and the Samurai Ideal," *Harvard Journal of Asiatic Studies*, vol. 57, 1997, 307–382. • Donald Keene, *Bunraku: The Art of the Japanese Puppet Theatre*, 1965. • Donald Keene, trans. *Four Major Plays of Chikamatsu*, 1969. • Donald Keene, trans. *Major Plays of Chikamatsu*, 1961. • Adolphe Clarence Scott, *The Puppet Theater of Japan*, 1963. • Donald H. Shively, trans. *The Love Suicides at Amijima*, 1953.

Eliza Haywood • Ros Ballaster, *Seductive Forms: Women's Amatory Fiction from 1684 to 1740*, 1992. • Christine Blouch, "Eliza Haywood and the Romance of Obscurity," *Studies in English Literature*, vol. 31, 1991, 535–552. • Catherine Craft-Fairchild, *Masquerade and Gender: Disguise and Female Identity in Eighteenth-Century Fictions by Women*, 1993. • Eliza Haywood, *Selections from "The Female Spectator,"* ed. Gabrielle M. Firmager, 1993. • Eliza Haywood, *The Plays of Eliza Haywood*, ed. Valerie C. Rudolph, 1983. • Kirsten T. Saxton and Rebecca P. Bocchicchio, eds. *The Passionate Fictions of Eliza Haywood*, 2000. • Mary Anne Schofield, *Eliza Haywood*, 1985. • Eliza Haywood, *The Masquerade Novels of Eliza Haywood*, ed. Mary Anne Schofield, 1986. • Mary Ann Schofield, *Masking and Unmasking the Female Mind: Disguising Romances in Feminine Fiction, 1713–1799*, 1990. • Jane Spencer, *The Rise of the Woman Novelist: From Aphra Behn to Jane Austen*, 1986. • William B. Warner, *Licensing Entertainment: The Elevation of Novel Reading in Britain, 1684–1750*, 1957. • George Frisbie Whicher, *The Life and Romances of Mrs. Eliza Haywood*, 1915.

Matsuo Bashō • Dorothy Britton, trans. *A Haiku Journey: Bashō's "Narrow Road to a Far Province,"* 1980. • Cid Corman and Susumu Kamaike, trans. *Back Roads to Far Towns*, 1968. • Koji Kawamoto, *The Poetics of Japanese Verse: Imagery, Structure, Meter*, 2000. • Donald Keene, "Bashō's Diaries," *Japan Quarterly,*

vol. 32, 1985, 374–383. • Donald Keene, "Bashō's Journey of 1684," *Asia Major*, vol. 7, 1959, 131–144. • Donald Keene, trans. *The Narrow Road to Oku*, 1996. • Helen McCullough, trans. "The Narrow Road of the Interior," in *Classical Japanese Prose: An Anthology*, ed. Helen McCullough, 1990. • Hiroaki Sato, trans. *Bashō's "Narrow Road": Spring and Autumn Passages: Two Works*, 1996. • Haruo Shirane, *Traces of Dreams: Landscape, Cultural Memory, and the Poetry of Bashō*, 1997. • Makoto Ueda, trans. *Bashō and His Interpreters: Selected Hokku with Commentary*, 1992. • Makoto Ueda, *Matsuo Bashō: The Master Haiku Poet*, 1982. • Nobuyuki Yuasa, trans. *Bashō: The Narrow Road to the Deep North and Other Travel Sketches*, 1968.

Jean Baptiste Poquelin (Molière) • Thomas P. Finn, "Dueling Capitalism in Molière: Cornering the Corner Markets," *Papers on French Seventeenth Century Literature* 29 (2002): 23–32. • J. F. Gaines, *Social Structures in Molière's Theater*, 1984. • Lionel Gossman, *Men and Masks: A Study of Molière*, 1963. • N. Gross, *From Gesture to Idea: Esthetics and Ethics in Molière's Comedy*, 1982. • Jacques Guicharnaud, ed. *Molière: A Collection of Critical Essays*, 1964. • Martha M. Houle, "The Marriage Question, or the Querélle des hommes in Rabelais, Molière, and Boileau," *Dalhousie French Studies*, vol. 56, 2001, 46–54. • W. D. Howarth, *Molière: A Playwright and His Audience*, 1984. • Harold C. Knutson, *The Triumph of Wit*, 1988. • Molière, *The Miser and Other Plays*, ed. and trans. David Coward, trans. John Wood, 2000. • L. F. Norman, *The Public Mirror: Molière and the Social Commerce of Depiction*, 1999. • Molière, *The Misanthrope, Tartuffe, and Other Plays*, trans. Maya Slater, 2001. • Martin Turnell, *The Classical Moment: Studies of Corneille, Molière, and Racine*, 1975. • H. Walker, *Molière*, 1990.

François Marie Arouet (Voltaire) • T. Besterman, *Voltaire*, 1969. • William Bottiglia, *Voltaire's Candide: Analysis of a Classic*, 1964. • William Bottiglia, ed. *Voltaire: A Collection of Critical Essays*, 1968. • Maxine G. Cutler, ed. *Voltaire, the Enlightenment, and the Comic Mode: Essays in Honor of Jean Sareil*, 1990. • Diane Fourny, "Literature of Violence or Literature on Violence? The French Enlightenment on Trial," *SubStance: A Review of Theory and Literary Criticism*, vol. 27, 1998, 43–60. • Voltaire, *Candide*, ed. D. Gordon, 1999. • M. Hayden, *Voltaire: A Biography*, 1981. • F. M. Keener, *The Chain of Becoming*, 1983. • Susan Klute,

"The Admirable Cunegonde," *Eighteenth-Century Women: Studies in Their Lives, Work, and Culture,* vol. 2, 2002, 95–107. • Bettina L. Knapp, *Voltaire Revisited,* 2000. • Haydn Mason, *Candide: Optimism Demolished,* 1992. • Voltaire, *Candide and Other Stories,* ed. and trans. Roger Pearson, 1998. • P. E. Richter and Ilona Ricardo, *Voltaire,* 1980. • R. S. Ridgway, *Voltaire and Sensibility,* 1973. • I. O. Wade, *Voltaire and "Candide,"* 1959. • Voltaire, *The Complete Tales of Voltaire,* trans. William Walton, 1990. • D. Williams, *Candide,* 1997. • Voltaire, *Candide and Related Texts,* ed. and trans. David Wooton, 2000.

The Nineteenth Century

General Background • Meyer H. Abrams, *The Mirror and the Lamp: Romantic Theory and the Critical Tradition,* 1953. • Meyer H. Abrams, *Natural Supernaturalism: Tradition and Revolution in Romantic Literature,* 1971. • Nancy Armstrong, *Desire and Domestic Fiction: A Political History of the Novel,* 1987. • Marshall Brown, *The Shape of German Romanticism,* 1979. • J. W. Burrow, *Evolution and Social Theory,* 1970. • Marilyn Butler, *Romantics, Rebels, and Reactionaries: English Literature and Its Background, 1760–1830,* 1981. • Linda Colley, *Britons: Forging the Nation, 1707–1837,* 1992. • Albert Cook, *Thresholds: Studies in the Romantic Experience,* 1985. • Stuart Curran, *Poetic Form and British Romanticism,* 1986. • Sandra M. Gilbert and Susan Gubar, *The Madwoman in the Attic: The Woman Writer and the Nineteenth-Century Imagination,* 1979. • Vesna Goldsworthy, *Inventing Ruritania: The Imperialism of the Imagination* 1998. • Catherine Hall, *Civilising Subjects: Metropole and Colony in the English Imagination 1830–1867,* 2002. • E. J. Hobsbawm, *The Age of Capital, 1848–1875,* 1975. • E. J. Hobsbawm, *The Age of Empire, 1875–1914,* 1987. • Everett Knight, *A Theory of the Classical Novel,* 1970. • Georges Lefebvre, *The Coming of the French Revolution 1789,* trans. R. R. Palmer, 1947. • Jerome J. McGann, *The Romantic Ideology: A Critical Investigation,* 1983. • Ellen Moers, *Literary Women,* 1976. • Franco Moretti, *Atlas of the European Novel, 1800–1900,* 1998. • Karl Polányi, *The Great Transformation: The Political and Economic Origins of Our Time,* 1944. • Charles Rosen, *The Romantic Generation,* 1995. • Kristin Ross, *The Emergence of Social Space: Rimbaud and the Paris Commune,* 1988. • Wolfgang Schivelbusch, *Disenchanted Night: The Industrialization of Light in the Nineteenth Century,* 1983. • Wolfgang Schivelbusch, *The Railway Journey: The Industrialization of Time and Space in the Nineteenth Century,* 1977. • Malini Schueller, *U.S. Orientalisms: Race, Nation, and Gender in Literature 1790–1890,* 1998. • Jean Starobinski, *1789: The Emblems of Reason,* trans. Barbara Bray, 1982. • Alan Trachtenberg, *The Incorporation of America: Culture and Society in the Gilded Age,* 1982. • Gauri Viswanathan, *Masks of Conquest: Literary Study and British Rule in India,* 1989. • Susan J. Wolfson, *Formal Charges: The Shaping of Poetry in British Romanticism,* 1997.

Charles Baudelaire • Robert Baldick, trans., *Pages from the Goncourt Journals,* 1962. • Charles Baudelaire: *Les fleurs du mal: The Complete Text of "The Flowers of Evil,"* Richard Howard, trans., 1982. • Charles Baudelaire: *Selected Writings on Art and Literature,* trans. P. E. Charvet, 1992. • Walter Benjamin, *Charles Baudelaire: A Lyric Poet in the Era of High Capitalism,* trans. Harry Zohn, 1973. • Leo Bersani, *Baudelaire and Freud,* 1977. • Keith Bosley, trans., *Mallarmé: The Poems: A Bilingual Edition.* • David Carrier, *High Art: Charles Baudelaire and the Origins of Modernist Painting,* 1996. • A. E. Carter, *Charles Baudelaire,* 1977. • Carol Clark and Robert Sykes, eds. *Baudelaire in English,* 1997. • T. J. Clark, *The Absolute Bourgeois: Artists and Politics in France, 1848–1851,* 1999. • T. J. Clark, *The Painting of Modern Life: Paris in the Art of Manet and His Followers,* 1999. • Arthur Rimbaud, *Complete Works, Selected Letters,* trans., Wallace Fowlie, 1966. • J. A. Hiddleston, *Baudelaire and the Art of Memory,* 1999. • J. A. Hiddleston, *Baudelaire and Le spleen de Paris,* 1987. • Louise Boe Hyslop, *Charles Baudelaire Revisited,* 1992. • Edward K. Kaplan, *Baudelaire's Prose Poems: The Esthetic, the Ethical, and the Religious in "The Parisian Prowler,"* 1990. • Edward K. Kaplan, trans., *The Parisian Prowler: Le spleen de Paris: petits poèmes en prose,* 1997. • F. W. Leakey, *Baudelaire and Nature,* 1969. • F. W. Leakey, *Baudelaire, Les fleurs du mal,* 1992. • Rosemary Lloyd, *Baudelaire's World,* 2002. • Elissa Marder, *Dead Time: Temporal Disorders in the Wake of Modernity (Baudelaire and Flaubert),* 2001.

• Derek Joseph Mossop *Baudelaire's Tragic Hero: A Study of the Architecture of "Les fleurs du mal,"* 1961. • Henri Peyre, *Baudelaire: A Collection of Critical Essays,* 1962. • Claude Pichois, *Baudelaire,* trans. Graham Robb, 1989. • *Approaches to Teaching Baudelaire's "Flowers of Evil,"* 2000. *Correspondence/Charles Baudelaire,* 2 vols. 1973. • Claude Pichois, ed. Charles Baudelaire *Oeuvres complètes,* 2 vols., 1993. • Laurence M. Porter, *The Crisis of French Symbolism,* 1990. • Georges Poulet, *Exploding Poetry: Baudelaire/Rimbaud,* trans. Francoise Meltzer, 1984. • Sonya Stephens, *Baudelaire's Prose Poems: The Practice and Politics of Irony,* 1999. • William J. Thompson, *Understanding "Les fleurs du mal": Critical Readings,* 1997. • Nathaniel Wing, *The Limits of Narrative: Essays on Baudelaire, Flaubert, Rimbaud, and Mallarmé,* 1986.

Anton Chekhov • Harold Bloom, ed., *Anton Chekhov: Modern Critical Views,* 1999. • John Coope, *Doctor Chekhov: A Study in Literature and Medicine,* 1997. • Vera Gottlieb and Paul Allain, eds., *The Cambridge Companion to Chekhov,* 2000. • Ronald Hingley, *Chekhov: A Biographical and Critical Study,* 1966. • V. B. Kataev, *If Only We Could Know: An Interpretation of Anton Chekhov,* 2002. • Virginia Llewellyn Smith, *Anton Chekhov and "The Lady with the Dog,"* 1973. • Janet Malcolm, *Reading Chekhov: A Critical Journey,* 2001. • Donald Rayfield, *Anton Chekhov: A Life,* 1998. • Donald Rayfield, *Understanding Chekhov,* 1999.

Gustave Flaubert • Julian Barnes, *Flaubert's Parrot,* 1990. • Jonathan Culler, *Flaubert: The Uses of Uncertainty,* 1974. • Peter Eyre, *Chere Maître: The Correspondence of Gustave Flaubert and George Sand,* 2002. • Harry Levin, *The Gates of Horn: A Study of Five French Realists,* 1963. • Herbert Lottman, *Flaubert: A Biography,* 1989. • Franco Moretti, *The Way of the World.* • Laurence Porter, *A Gustave Flaubert Encyclopedia,* 2001. • Francis Steegmuller, *Flaubert in Egypt: A Sensibility on Tour,* 1972. • Richard Terdiman, *Discourse/Counter-Discourse: The Theory and Practice of Symbolic Resistance in Nineteenth-Century France,* 1985. • Geoffrey Wall, *Flaubert: A Life,* 2001.

Ghalib • Aga Shahid Ali, *Call Me Ishmael Tonight: A Book of Ghazals,* 2003. • R. K. Kuldip, *Mirza Ghalib; A Critical Appreciation of Ghalib's Thought and Verse,* 1967. • Daud Rahbar, ed., *Urdu Letters of Mirza Asadu'llah Khan Ghalib,* 1987. • Ralph Russell, Khurshidul Islam, eds., *Ghalib (1787–1869): Life and Letters,* 1994. • Ralph Russell, ed., *Ghalib: The Poet and His Age,* 1972. • Ralph Russell, ed., *The Famous Ghalib,* 2000. • Christopher Shackle, "Classics and the Comparison of Adjacent Literatures: Some Pakistani Perspectives," *Comparative Criticism: An Annual Journal* 21–38 vol. 22, 2000. • Pavan K. Varma, *Ghalib, the Man, the Times,* 1989.

Charlotte Perkins Gilman • Catherine Golden, *The Captive Imagination: A Casebook on "The Yellow Wallpaper,"* 1992. • Joanne Karpinski, ed., *Critical Essays on Charlotte Perkins Gilman,* 1992. • Catherine Golden and Joanna Zangrando, eds., *The Mixed Legacy of Charlotte Perkins Gilman,* 2000. • Jill Rudd and Val Gough, *A Very Different Story: Studies on the Fiction of Charlotte Perkins Gilman,* 1998. • Charlotte Perkins Gilman, *The Living of Charlotte Perkins Gilman: An Autobiography,* 1990. • Ann Lane, *To Herland and Beyond: The Life and Work of Charlotte Perkins Gilman,* 1990.

Johann Wolfgang Goethe • Stuart Atkins, *Goethe's Faust: A Literary Analysis,* 1958. • Marshall Berman, *All That Is Solid Melts into Air: The Experience of Modernity,* 1982. • Nicholas Boyle, *Goethe: The Poet and the Age,* 2 vols., 1991. • Jane K. Brown, *Faust: Theater of the World,* 1992. • Jane K. Brown, *Goethe's Faust: The German Tragedy,* 1986. • Richard Friedenthal, *Goethe: His Life and Times,* 3 vols., 1963. • Ilse Graham, *Goethe: A Portrait of the Artist,* 1977. • Harry G. Haile, *Invitation to Goethe's "Faust,"* 1978. • *Faust,* Cyrus Hamlin, ed., 2001. • Victor Lange, Eric A. Blackall, and Cyrus Hamlin, eds. *Goethe's Collected Works,* 12 vols., 1983–1989. • Franco Moretti, *Modern Epic: The World-System from Goethe to García Marquez,* trans. Quintin Hoare, 1996. • Lesley Sharpe, ed., *The Cambridge Companion to Goethe,* 2002. • Elizabeth M. Wilkinson and Leonard A. Willoughby, *Goethe: Poet and Thinker,* 1962.

Henrik Ibsen • Robert Ferguson, *Ibsen: A New Biography,* 1996. • Michael Goldman, *Ibsen: The Dramaturgy of Fear,* 1999. • C. D. Innes, *A Sourcebook on Naturalist Theater,* 2000. • Charles Lyons, *Critical Essays on Henrik Ibsen,* 1987. • Frederick Marker, *Ibsen's Lively Art,* 1989. • James McFarlane, *The Cambridge Companion to Ibsen,* 1994. • Yvonne Shafer, *Approaches to Teaching Ibsen's "A Doll's House,"* 1985. • George Bernard Shaw, *The*

Quintessence of Ibsenism, 1994. • Joan Templeton "The Doll House Backlash: Criticism, Feminism, and Ibsen," *PMLA,* vol. 104 (1989), pp. 28–40. • Joan Templeton, *Ibsen's Women,* 1997.

Joaquim María Machado de Assis • Piers Armstrong, *Third World Literary Fortunes: Brazilian Culture and Its International Reception,* 1999. • Earl Fitz, *Machado de Assis,* 1989. • Richard Graham, *Machado de Assis: Reflections on a Brazilian Master Writer* 1999. • Jose Raimundo Maia Neto, *Machado de Assis, the Brazilian Pyrrhonian,* 1994 • Maria Luisa Nunes, *The Craft of an Absolute Winner,* 1989. • Roberto Schwartz, *A Master on the Periphery of Capitalism: Machado de Assis,* 2001.

Nguyen Du • Nguyen Du, *Tale of Kieu: A Bilingual Edition of Truyen Kieu,* trans. Huynh Sanh, 1983. www.vietspring.org/literature/kieu.html

Alexander Pushkin • John Bayley, *Pushkin: A Comparative Commentary,* 1971. • J. Douglas Clayton, *Ice and Flame: Pushkin's "Eugene Onegin,"* 1985. • D. S. Mirsky, *Pushkin,* 1926. • Alexander Pushkin, *Eugene Onegin,* trans. Vladimir Nabokov, 4 vols., 1964. • Gary Rosenshield, *Pushkin and the Genres of Madness: The Masterpieces of 1833,* 2003.

Rabindranath Tagore • Ayuiba Abu Sayida, *Modernism and Tagore,* 1995. • Carol A. Breckenridge and Peter van der Veer, eds., *Orientalism and the Postcolonial Predicament: Perspectives on South Asia,* 1993. • K. Chandrasekharan, *Tagore: A Master Spirit,* 1961. • Bhabatosh Chatterjee, *Rabindranath Tagore and Modern Sensibility,* 1996. • Rimi B. Chatterjee, "Canon Without Consensus: Rabindranath Tagore and *The Oxford Book of Bengali Verse," Book History,* vol. 4, 2001. • Shyamal Chattopadhyaya, *Art and the Abyss: Six Essays in Interpretation of Tagore,* 1977. • Krishna Dutta, *Rabindranath Tagore: The Myriad-Minded Man,* 1995. • Krishna Dutta and Andrew Robinson, ed., *Purabi: A Miscellany Memory of Rabindranath Tagore 1941–1991,* 1991. • Rabindranath Tagore: *Selected Letters of Rabindranath Tagore,* Krishna Dutta and Andrew Robinson, eds., 1997. • Rabindranath Tagore: *Rabindranath Tagore: An Anthology,* Krishna Dutta and Andrew Robinson, eds., 1997. • Mahatma Gandhi, *The Mahatma and the Poet: Letters and Debates Between Gandhi and Tagore, 1915–1941,* 1997. • Krishna Kripalani, *Tagore: A Life,* 1971. • Sudhirkumara Nandi, *Art and Aesthetics of Rabindranath Tagore,* 1999. • Ashis Nandy, *The Illegitimacy of Nationalism: Rabindranath Tagore and the Politics of Self,* 1994. • Rabindranath Tagore, *Selected Writings on Literature and Language,* 2001.

Leo Tolstoy • John Bayley, *Leo Tolstoy,* 1997. • Italo Calvino, *Why Read the Classics?* 1999. • Henry Gifford, *Tolstoy,* 1982. • Georg Lukács, *Studies in European Realism,* 1964. • Donna Orwin, ed., *The Cambridge Companion to Tolstoy,* 2002. • William Rowe, *Leo Tolstoy,* 1986. • George Steiner, *Tolstoy or Dostoevsky?* 1996 • Raymond Williams, *Modern Tragedy,* 2001. • A. N. Wilson, *Tolstoy,* 1988.

The Twentieth Century

General Background • Benedict Anderson, *Imagined Communities: Reflections on the Origin and Spread of Nationalism,* 1991. • Michael Bell, *Myth and the Making of Modernity: The Problem of Grounding in Early Twentieth-Century Literature,* 1998. • Hans Bertens, *The Idea of the Postmodern: A History,* 1995. • James Clifford, *The Predicament of Culture: Twentieth-Century Ethnography, Literature, and Art,* 1988. • Fredric Jameson, *Postmodernism, or, The Cultural Logic of Late Capitalism,* 1991. • Brian McHale, *Postmodernist Fiction,* 1993. • Michael North, *The Dialect of Modernism: Race, Language, and Twentieth-Century Literature,* 1994. • Kenneth Richardson, *Twentieth Century Writing: A Reader's Guide to Contemporary Literature,* 1971. • Steven Serafin, *Encyclopedia of World Literature in the 20th Century,* 1999. • Randall Stevenson, *Modernist Fiction: An Introduction,* 1992. • Philip Malcolm Waller Thody, *Twentieth-Century Literature: Critical Issues and Themes,* 1996. • Tzvetan Todorov, *Literature and Its Theorists: A Personal View of Twentieth-Century Criticism,* 1987.

Postcolonial Writing • Fawzia Afzal-Khan, *Cultural Imperialism and the Indo-English Novel: Genre and Ideology in R. K. Narayan, Anita Desai, Kamala Markandaya, and Salman Rushdie,* 1993. • Munir Akash, ed., • *Mahmoud Darwish: The Adam of Two Edens,* 2002. • Bill Ashcroft, Gareth Griffiths, and Helen Tiffin, eds., *The Post-Colonial Studies Reader*, 1995. • Bill Ashcroft, ed., *The Empire Writes Back: Theory and Practice in Post-Colonial Literatures*, 1989. • Mita Banerjee, *Chutneyfication of History: Salman Rushdie, Michael Ondaatje, Bharati Mukherjee and the Postcolonial Debate*, 2002. • Mahmoud Darwish: *Unfortunately, It Was Paradise: Selected Poems*, ed., Munir Akash, 2003. • Frantz Fanon, *Black Skin, White Masks*, 1991. • Frantz Fanon, *The Wretched of the Earth*, 1991. • Nadine Gordimer, *The Essential Gesture: Writing, Politics, and Places*, 1989. • Gareth Griffiths, *African Literatures in English: East and West*, 2000. • Dominic Head, *Nadine Gordimer*, 1994. • Michael C. Hillmann, *Forugh Farrokhzad: A Quarter-Century Later*, 1988. • Michael C. Hillmann, *A Lonely Woman: Forugh Farrokhzad and Her Poetry*, 1987. • Nico Israel, *Outlandish: Writing Between Exile and Diaspora*, 2000. • Bruce Alvin King, ed., *New National and Post-Colonial Literatures: An Introduction*, 1996. • Aneete Mansson, *Passage to a New Wor(l)d: Exile and Restoration in Mahmoud Darwish's Writings*, 2003. • Anne McClintock, Aamir Mufti, Ella Shohat, and Social Text Collective, eds., *Dangerous Liaisons: Gender, Nations, and Postcolonial Perspectives*, 1997. • Albert Memmi, *The Colonizer and the Colonized*, 1991. • Padmini Mongia, *Contemporary Postcolonial Theory: A Reader*, 1996. • Ngugi wa Thiong'o, *Decolonising the Mind: The Politics of Language in African Literature*, 1986. • Lulu Norman, trans., "Mahmoud Darwish on Translating Poetry: The Place of the Universal," *Banipal: Magazine of Modern Arab Literature*, vol. 8, 2000, 25–27. • Edward Said, *Orientalism*, 1979. • Edward Said, *Culture and Imperialism*, 1998. • Barbara Temple-Thurston, *Nadine Gordimer Revisited*, 1999.

Anna Akhmatova • György Dalos, *The Guest from the Future: Anna Akhmatova and Isaiah Berlin*, 1999. • T. Patera, *A Concordance to the Poetry of Anna Akhmatova*, 1995. • Robert Porter, *Seven Soviet Poets*, 2000. • Roberta Reeder, *Anna Akhmatova: Poet and Prophet*, 1995. • David N. Wells, *Anna Akhmatova: Her Poetry*, 1996.

Akutagawa Ryunosuke • David Boyd, "Rashomon: From Akutagawa to Kurosawa," *Literature/Film Quarterly*, vol. 15, 1987, 155–158. • A. A. Gerow, "The Self Seen as Other: Akutagawa and Film," *Literature/Film Quarterly*, vol. 23, 1995, 197–203. • Hendrik van Gorn and Ulla Musarra-Schroeder, eds., *Genres as Repositories of Cultural Memory*, 2000. • Dennis Washburn and Alan Transman, eds., *Studies in Modern Japanese Literature*, 1997. • Valerie Wayne and Cornelia Moore, eds., *Translations/Transformations: Gender and Culture in Film and Literature East and West: Selected Conference Papers*, 1993.

Samuel Beckett • Arthur N. Athanason, *Endgame: The Ashbin Play*, 1993. • Deirdre Bair, *Samuel Beckett: A Biography*, 1978. • Harold Bloom, ed., *Samuel Beckett's "Endgame,"* 1988. • Anthony Cronin, *Samuel Beckett: The Last Modernist*, 1996. • Bell Gale Chevigny, ed., *Twentieth-Century Interpretations of "Endgame": A Collection of Critical Essays*, 1969. • Martin Esslin, *The Theatre of the Absurd*, 2001. • Sean Golden, "Familiars in a Ruinstrewn Land: *Endgame* as Political Allegory," *Contemporary Literature*, vol. 22, 1981, 425–455. • James Knowlson, *Damned to Fame: The Life of Samuel Beckett*, 1996. • Patrick A. McCarthy, ed., *Critical Essays on Samuel Beckett*, 1986. • John Pilling, ed., *The Cambridge Companion to Beckett*, 1994. • Richard Keller Simon, "Dialectical Laughter: A Study of *Endgame*," *Modern Drama*, vol. 25, 1982, 505–513.

Jorge Luis Borges • Lisa Block de Behar, *Borges, the Passion of an Endless Quotation*, 2003. • Gene H. Bell-Villada, *Borges and His Fiction: A Guide to His Mind and Art*, 1999. • Norman Thomas Di Giovanni, *Lesson of the Master: Borges and His Work*, 2003. • Djelal Kadir, *Questing Fictions: Latin America's Family Romance*, 1986. • Martín Lafforgue, *AntiBorges*, 1999. • Selden Rodman and Jorge Luis Borges, *Tongues of Fallen Angels: Conversations with Jorge Luis Borges (and Others)*, 1974. • Florence L. Yudin, *Nightglow: Borges' Poetics of Blindness*, 1997.

Aimé Césaire • A. James Arnold, *Modernism and Négritude: The Poetry and Poetics of Aimé Césaire*, 1981. • Maryse Condé, *Cahier d'un retour au pays natal: Césaire: analyse critique*, 1978. • Gregson Davis, *Aimé Césaire*, 1997. • Lilyan Kesteloot, *Aimé Césaire: L'homme et l'oeuvre*, 1993. • Janis L. Pallister, *Aimé Césaire*, 1991. • Michael Richardson, ed., *Refusal of the Shadow: Surrealism and the Caribbean*, trans. Krzysztof Fijalkowski and Michael Richardson, 1996. • Ronnie Leah Scharfman, *Engagement and the Language of the Subject in the Poetry of Aimé Césaire*, 1987.

Joseph Conrad • John Batchelor, *The Life of Joseph Conrad: A Critical Biography*, 1993. • Ted Billy ed., *Critical Essays on Joseph Conrad*, 1987. • Harold Bloom, ed., *Joseph Conrad's "Heart of*

Darkness," 1987. • Keith Carabine, ed., *Joseph Conrad: Critical Assessments*, 4 vols., 1992. • Ford Madox Ford, *Joseph Conrad: A Personal Remembrance*, 1989. • Christopher L. GoGwilt, *The Invention of the West: Joseph Conrad and the Double-Mapping of Europe and Empire*, 1995. • Nico Israel, *Outlandish: Writing Between Exile and Diaspora*, 2000. • Fredric Jameson, *The Political Unconscious: Narrative as a Socially Symbolic Act*, 1981. • Fredric R. Karl and Laurence Davies, eds., *The Collected Letters of Joseph Conrad*, 1983. • Owen Knowles and Gene Moore, eds., *The Oxford Reader's Companion to Conrad*, 2000. • Martin Ray, ed., *Joseph Conrad: Interviews and Recollections*, 1990. • Edward W. Said, *The World, the Text, and the Critic*, 1966. • Norman Sherry, ed., *Conrad: The Critical Heritage*, 1973. • Ian Watt, *Joseph Conrad: A Critical Biography*, 1979. • Mark A. Wollaeger, *Joseph Conrad and the Fictions of Skepticism*, 1990.

T. S. Eliot • Peter Ackroyd, *T. S. Eliot: A Life*, 1984. • Harold Bloom, ed., *T. S. Eliot's "The Waste Land,"* 1986. • Jewel Spears Brooker and Joseph Bentley, *Reading "The Wasteland": Modernism and the Limits of Interpretation*, 1990. • Valerie Eliot, ed., *"The Waste Land": Fascimile and Transcript of the Original Drafts Including the Annotations of Ezra Pound*, 1971. • Maud Ellman, *The Poetics of Impersonality: T. S. Eliot and Ezra Pound*, 1987. • Nancy K. Gish, *"The Waste Land": A Poem of Memory and Desire*, 1988. • Louis Menand, *Discovering Modernism: T. S. Eliot and His Context*, 1986. • Anthony David Moody, ed., *The Cambridge Companion to T. S. Eliot*, 1994. • Jeffrey M. Perl, *Skepticism and Modern Enmity: Before and After Eliot*, 1989. • John Paul Riquelme, *Harmony of Dissonances: T. S. Eliot, Romanticism and Imagination*, 1990. • Stanley Sultan, *Eliot, Joyce, and Company*, 1987.

Gabriel García Márquez • R. Thomas Berner, *The Literature of Journalism: Text and Context*, 1999. • J. G. Cobo Borda, *Repertorio crítico sobre Gabriel García Márquez*, 1995. • Robin W. Fiddian, *García Márquez*, 1995. • Nelly S. Gonzalez, *Bibliographic Guide to Gabriel García Márquez, 1986–1992*, 1994. • Djelal Kadir, *The Other Writing: Postcolonial Essays in Latin America's Writing Culture*, 1993. • Rubén Pelayo, *Gabriel García Márquez: A Critical Companion*, 2001.

Gish Jen • Gish Jen, *The Love Wife*, 2004. • Gish Jen, *Mona in the Promised Land*, 1996. • Gish Jen, *Typical American*, 1991. • Gish Jen, *Who's Irish?*, 1999. • Gish Jen, *World and Town*, 2010. • Rachel C. Lee, *The Americas of Asian American Literature: Gendered Fictions of Nation and Transnation*, 1999. • Martha Satz, "Writing About the Things that Are Dangerous: A Conversation with Gish Jen" *Southwest Review* 78:1, 132–40. • Weiming Tang, "Translating and Transforming the American Dream," in Julia Kuehn, ed., *China Abroad*, 2009.

James Joyce • Derek Attridge, ed., *The Cambridge Companion to James Joyce*, 1990. • Vincent Cheng, *Joyce, Race and Empire*, 1995. • Kevin J. H. Dettmar, *The Illicit Joyce of Postmodernism: Reading Against the Grain*, 1996. • Richard Ellman, *James Joyce*, 1982. • Herbert S. Gorman, *James Joyce*, 1948. • Clive Hart and David Hayman, eds., *James Joyce's "Ulysses": Critical Essays*, 1974. • Hugh Kenner, *Joyce's Voices*, 1978. • R. B. Kershner, *Joyce, Bakhtin, and Popular Literature: Chronicles of Disorder*, 1989. • Patrick McGee, *Joyce Beyond Marx*, 2001. • Dominic Manganiello, *Joyce's Politics*, 1980. • E. H. Mikhail, *James Joyce: Interviews and Recollections*, 1990. • Margot Norris, *Joyce's Web: The Social Unraveling of Modernism*, 1992. • Marty T. Reynolds, ed., *James Joyce: A Collection of Critical Essays*, 1993. • Fritz Senn, *Joyce's Dislocutions*, 1984. • Joseph Valente, ed., *Quare Joyce*, 1998.

Franz Kafka • Theodor W. Adorno, "Notes on Kafka," in *Prisms*, trans. Samuel and Shierry Weber, 1967. • Harold Bloom, ed., *Franz Kafka's "The Metamorphosis"*, 1988. • Max Brod, *Franz Kafka: A Biography*, 1960. • Stanley Corngold, "Kafka's *The Metamorphosis*: Metamorphosis of the Metaphor," in *Franz Kafka: The Metamorphosis: Translation, Backgrounds and Contexts, Criticism*, trans. and ed. Stanley Corngold, 1996. • Stanley Corngold, *The Commentators' Despair: The Interpretation of Kafka's "Metamorphosis,"* 1971. • Gilles Deleuze and Félix Guattari, *Kafka: Toward a Minor Literature*, trans. Dana Polan, 1986. • Vladimir Nabokov, "Franz Kafka (1883–1924): 'The Metamorphosis (1915),' " in *Lectures on Literature*, ed. Fredson Bowers, 1980. • Johannes Pfeiffer, "The Metamorphosis," trans. Ronald Gray, in *Kafka: A Collection of Critical Essays*, ed. Ronald Gray, 1962. • Heinz Politzer, *Franz Kafka: Parable and Paradox*, 1962. • Allen Thiher, *Franz Kafka: A Study of the Short Fiction*, 1990. • Klaus Wagenbach, *Franz Kafka: Pictures of a Life*, 1984.

Lu Xun • Lee Ou-Fan Lee, ed., *Lu Xun and His Legacy,* 1985. • Kang Liu and Xiaobing Tang, eds., *Politics, Ideology, and Literary Discourse in Modern China: Theoretical Interventions and Cultural Critique,* 1993. • Wolfgang Kubin, ed., *Symbols of Anguish: In Search of Melancholy in China,* 2001. • Hua Meng and Sukehiro Hirakawa, eds., *Images of Westerners in Chinese and Japanese Literature,* 2000. • Barbara Stoler Miller, ed., *Masterworks of Asian Literature in Comparative Perspective: A Guide for Teaching,* 1994.

Naguib Mahfouz • Salih J. Altoma, "Naguib Mahfouz: A Profile," *International Fiction Review;* vol. 17, 1990, 128–132. • Michael Beard and Adnan Haydar, eds., *Naguib Mahfouz: From Regional Fame to Global Recognition,* 1993. • Miriam Cooke, "Naguib Mahfouz, Men, and the Egyptian Underworld," in *Fictions of Masculinity: Crossing Cultures, Crossing Sexualities,* ed. Peter F. Murphy, 1994. • Rasheed El-Enany, *Naguib Mahfouz: The Pursuit of Meaning,* 1993. • Hoda Gindi, ed., *Images of Egypt in Twentieth Century Literature,* 1991. • Haim Gordon, *Naguib Mahfouz's Egypt: Existential Themes in His Writings,* 1990. •John C. Hawley, ed., *The Postcolonial Crescent: Islam's Impact on Contemporary Literature,* 1998. • Trevor Le Gassick, ed., *Critical Perspectives on Naguib Mahfouz,* 1991. • Naguib Mahfouz, *The Nobel Lecture,* trans. Mohammed Salmawy, 1998. • Amin Malak, "The Private and the Universal: The Fiction of Naguib Mahfouz," *Toronto South Asian Review,* vol. 11, 1992, 1–8. • Samia Mehrez, *Egyptian Writers Between History and Fiction: Essays on Naguib Mahfouz, Sonallah Ibrahim, and Gamal al-Ghitani,* 1994. • Matti Moosa, *The Early Novels of Naguib Mahfouz: Images of Modern Egypt,* 1994. • Nedal Al-Mousa, "The Nature and Uses of the Fantastic in the Fictional World of Naguib Mahfouz," *Journal of Arabic Literature,* vol. 23, 1992, 36–48.

Salman Rushdie • M. Keith Booker, ed., *Critical Essays on Salman Rushdie,* 1999. • Timothy Brennan, *Salman Rushdie and the Third World: Myths of the Nation,* 1989. • Roger Y. Clark, *Stranger Gods: Salman Rushdie's Other Worlds,* 2001. • Catherine Cundy, *Salman Rushdie,* 1996. • Damian Grant, *Salman Rushdie,* 1999. • James Harrison, *Salman Rushdie,* 1992. • Sabrina Hassumani, *Salman Rushdie: A Postmodern Reading of His Major Works,* 2002. • Jaina C. Sanga, *Salman Rushdie's Postcolonial Metaphors: Migration, Translation, Hybridity, Blasphemy, and Globalization,* 2001.

Wole Soyinka • A. O. Dasylva, *Understanding Wole Soyinka: Death and the King's Horseman,* 1996. • James Gibbs, ed., *Critical Perspectives on Wole Soyinka,* 1980. • Adewale Maja-Pearce, ed., *Wole Soyinka: An Appraisal,* 1994. • Oyin Ogunba, ed., *Soyinka: A Collection of Critical Essays,* 1994. • Wole Soyinka, *Art, Dialogue, and Outrage: Essays on Literature and Culture,* 1993. • Wole Soyinka, *The Burden of Memory, the Muse of Forgiveness,* 1999. • Wole Soyinka, *Myth, Literature, and the African World,* 1990.

Derek Walcott • Robert D. Hamner, ed., *Critical Perspectives on Derek Walcott,* 1993. • Bruce King, *Derek Walcott: A Caribbean Life,* 2000. • José Luis Martínez-Dueñas Espejo and José María Pérez Fernández, eds., *Approaches to the Poetics of Derek Walcott,* 2001. • Michael Parker and Roger Starkey, eds., *Postcolonial Literatures: Achebe, Ngugi, Desai, Walcott,* 1995. • Rei Terada, *Derek Walcott's Poetry: American Mimicry,* 1992.

Virginia Woolf • Quentin Bell, *Virginia Woolf: A Biography,* 1972. • Alison Booth, *Greatness Engendered: George Eliot and Virginia Woolf,* 1992. • Thomas C. Carmagno, *The Flight of the Mind: Virginia Woolf's Art and Manic-Depressive Illness,* 1992. • Pamela L. Caughie, *Virginia Woolf and the Postmodern Tradition: Literature in Quest and Question of Itself,* 1991. • Margaret Homans, ed., *Virginia Woolf: A Collection of Critical Essays* (*Twentieth Century Views*), 1992. • Mark Hussey, *Virginia Woolf, A to Z: A Comprehensive Reference for Students, Teachers, and Common Readers to Her Work, and Critical Reception,* 1996. • Douglas Mao, *Solid Objects: Modernism and the Test of Production,* 1998. • John Mepham, *Virginia Woolf: A Literary Life,* 1991. • Panthea Reid, *Archives and Art and Affection: A Life of Virginia Woolf,* 1988. • S. P. Rosenbaum, ed., *Virginia Woolf / Women and Fiction: The Manuscript Versions of A Room of One's Own,* 1992. • Sue Roe and Susan Sellers, eds., *The Cambridge Companion to Virginia Woolf,* 2000. • Bonnie Kime Scott, *Refiguring Modernism,* 2 vols., 1995. • Peter Stansky, *On or About December 1910: Early Bloomsbury and Its Intimate World,* 1996. • J. H. Stape, ed., *Virginia Woolf: Interviews and Recollections,* 1995. • Alex Zwerdling, *Virginia Woolf and Real Life,* 1987.

Text Credits

"During meditation my lama's face," "Rock and wind kept tryst," "Beyond death, in the Realm of Hell," and "In this life's short walk" from *Divinity Secularized: An Inquiry into Nature and Form of Songs Ascribed to the Sixth Dali Lama*, translated by Per K. Sorensen, © 1990. Used by permission.

Photo Credits

Page 1: Anonymous drawing of Louis XIV the "Sun King": Snark/Art Resource.

Page 99: Morikawa Kyoritku, *haiga* (haikai sketch): Courtesy of Idemitsu Museum of Arts.

Page 273: *The Pilgrim's Vision*, frontispiece to Mark Twain, *The Innocents Abroad*: Public Domain.

Page 283: Four title pages: *(Top Left)* The Granger Collection; *(Top Right)* Title Page from *Sense and Sensibility* by Jane Austen, 1856. Private Collection; *(Bottom Left)* S.P. Avery Collection. Miriam and Ira D. Wallach Division of Arts, Prints and Photographs. The New York Public Library. Astor, Lenox and Tilden Foundations; *(Bottom Right)* Fair Street Pictures.

Page 317: Rembrandt van Rijn, *The Scholar in His Study*: Museum and Galleries (City Art Gallery) U.K./The Bridgeman Art Library.

Page 605: Umberto Boccioni, *Unique Forms of Continuity in Space*: Digital Image © The Museum of Modern Art/Licensed by Scala/Art Resource, New York.

Page 607: David Alfaro Siqueiros, *Echo of a Scream*: David Alfaro Siqueiros (1896–1974).

Page 612: Global Shrinkage: The Effect of Changing Transport Technologies on "Real" Distance: From *The Future of the Future* by John McHale (New York: Braziller, 1969).

Page 622: *Sir H. M. Stanley's Three African Journeys*: Public Domain.

Page 1001: Nam June Paik, *Global Encoder:* Photo Courtesy Nam June Paik and Carl Solway Gallery, Cincinnati, Ohio. Photo by Chris Gomien and Tom Allison.

pearson penguin packages

Edward Albee
Three Tall Women

Matsuo Bashō
On Love and Barley

Aphra Behn
Oroonoko, the Rover, and Other Works

Miguel de Cervantes
Don Quixote

Denis Diderot
Rameau's Nephew and D'Alembert's Dream

Frederick Douglass
Narrative of the Life of Frederick Douglass

Gustave Flaubert
Madame Bovary

ed. Henry Louis Gates
Classic Slave Narratives
(includes *The Life of Olaudah Equiano; The History of Mary Prince; Narrative of the Life of Frederick Douglass;* and *Incidents in the Life of Slave Girl*)

Johanne Wolfgang von Goethe
Faust

Khaled Hosseini
The Kite Runner

Henrik Ibsen
Four Major Plays: A Doll's House, Wild Duck, Hedda Gabler, Master Builder

Isaac Kramnick
Portable Enlightenment Reader

Thomas Mann
Death in Venice and Other Stories

Jean-Baptiste Molière
The Misanthrope and Other Plays

George Orwell
1984

George Orwell
Animal Farm

Luigi Pirandello
Six Characters in Search of an Author

Mary Shelley
Frankenstein

Jonathan Swift
Gulliver's Travels

Leo Tolstoy
Anna Karenina

Voltaire
Candide, Zadig, and Selected Stories

Virginia Woolf
Jacob's Room